Whitman Encyclopedia of Obsolete Paper Money

Whitman Encyclopedia of Obsolete Paper Money

Notes Issued by United States Banks, 1782–1866

Q. David Bowers

States, districts, and territories covered in this series, in order:

Connecticut, Maine, New Hampshire, Massachusetts, Rhode Island, Vermont, Florida, Georgia, North Carolina, South Carolina, Alabama, Arkansas, Kentucky, Louisiana, Mississippi, Tennessee, Texas, Delaware, District of Columbia, Maryland, Virginia, New Jersey, Pennsylvania, New York, Illinois, Indiana, Michigan, Ohio, Iowa, Kansas, Minnesota, Missouri, Nebraska, Utah, and Wisconsin

Also see volume 1, *An Introduction for Collectors and Historians.*

For news (or announcements) and more information, refer to www.Whitman.com.

Volume 5
New England Region, Part 3
Rhode Island and Vermont

Edited by C. John Ferreri

Whitman
Publishing, LLC
PUBLISHING SINCE 1934
www.whitman.com

WHITMAN ENCYCLOPEDIA OF OBSOLETE PAPER MONEY
NOTES ISSUED BY UNITED STATES BANKS, 1782–1866
VOLUME 5: NEW ENGLAND REGION, PART 3
RHODE ISLAND AND VERMONT

www.whitman.com

© 2015 Whitman Publishing, LLC
3101 Clairmont Road • Suite G • Atlanta, GA 30329

ISBN: 0794843263
Printed in China

CONTENTS

FOREWORD

If asked to explain what an obsolete note is, I often hesitate for a few seconds. After all, how, indeed, could I explain the visual "deliciousness" of hand-engraved intricate images, the intrigue of tracking down the history of a note's signer, or the fun of finding the story behind the issuing bank? What I have learned to say is that these notes are paper relics that tell a story through pictures, place names, and signatures of small communities in days gone by.

I attended my first "Memphis show" (the annual International Paper Money Show) in 1992 and was delighted to see many obsolete notes displayed in dealers' cases. I had already been captivated in my previous seven years at *Coin World* by looking through auction catalogs displaying the notes with scenes of farm fields, blacksmiths, cherubs, and the small, engraved flourishes tucked into corners and wrapped around numerals. Though the businesses and their owners who issued the notes are long gone, the notes help trace the roots of goods and services provided to residents in America's towns and cities.

So it is pure delight to consider the unbelievably massive task Whitman Publishing has taken on to compile the multi-volume series now known as the *Whitman Encyclopedia of Obsolete Paper Money,* authored by Q. David Bowers. These volumes provide a great resource to study paper notes issued from 1782 to 1866, before National Bank and Federal Reserve notes were a reality. Combined, these volumes provide collectors, both seasoned and new, with vital information about notes issued by more than 3,000 state-chartered banks.

Dave Bowers has clearly fallen head over heels for the allure of obsolete notes. His text provides collectors with opportunities to enjoy the designs and history contained in these pieces of paper. After all, he is no stranger to the topic, as he's written much about these charming objects of commerce in his "The Joys of Collecting" columns, published weekly in *Coin World.* He's also given presentations about these notes and written many articles for publication in collector journals, as well as researching and writing several books on the subject.

While the Internet has granted researchers access to much historical information, it still takes determination for a writer to follow up on the leads that can be uncovered. Dave has explored all sources of information—from long-ago books and journals to current-day discussions with advanced collectors—to glean the best and most helpful information available.

The first four volumes of the *Whitman Encyclopedia of Obsolete Paper Money* provide any collector many adventures, whether by armchair, bourse floor, or auction catalog. This volume, focusing on Rhode Island and Vermont obsolete notes and their issuers, showcases the rich paper-money history of those states, rounding out the *Encyclopedia*'s coverage of New England. I look forward to the journeys the next volume takes us on.

Michele Orzano
Sidney, Ohio

CREDITS AND ACKNOWLEDGEMENTS

For global and general credits for the *Whitman Encyclopedia of Obsolete Paper Money,* see volume 1. For volume 5's study of Rhode Island and Vermont, specific credit goes to:

American Bank Note Co.; American Numismatic Association; American Numismatic Society; Irene Axelrod; Georgia Barnhill; Anne E. Bentley; Steve Blum; Wynn Bowers; Karen Bridges; Mark Carter; Ashley Clark; Rich Deming; Thomas Denly; Richard Doty; Roger Durand; C. John Ferreri; Jeffrey M. Feuerman; Roberta French; Bruce Hagen; James A. Haxby; Heritage Auctions; Wayne Homren; Peter Huntoon; Christine Karstedt; Michael Keane; Kevin Lafond; Littleton Coin Co.; Don Munro; Eric P. Newman; Steve Noyes; Gary Parietti; Phillips Library at the Peabody-Essex Museum; Michael Rocco; Neil Shafer; Smithsonian Institution; Stack's Bowers Galleries; David M. Sundman; John and Nancy Wilson.

Valuations editors for volume 5: C. John Ferreri, Bruce Hagen, and Bruce McLean.
Special valuations contributor: Roger Durand.

IMAGE CREDITS

ANS	American Numismatic Society, New York City, New York
BH	Bruce Hagen Collection
BM	Bruce McLean Collection
CC	Caine Collection
CJF	C. John Ferreri Collection
52	52 Collection
HA	Heritage Auction Archives
JF	Jeffrey M. Feuerman Collection
MK	Michael Keane Collection
MR	Michael Rocco Collection
NJW	Nancy and John Wilson Collection
PEM	Peabody-Essex Museum, Salem, Massachusetts
QDB	Q. David Bowers Archives
RMS	R.M. Smythe Collection
SBG	Stack's Bowers Galleries
SI	Smithsonian Institution, National Numismatic Collection
TD	Tom Denly Archives

HOW TO USE THIS BOOK

When considering the purchase or sale of a note, two main considerations are grade and price. Beyond that, there are other aspects that are important in study and set one note apart from another. In certain aspects the study of notes is different from that of coins. Notes that are spurious (not official) can have significant value, as can counterfeits of standard notes. In some instances, a note in Extremely Fine-40 (EF-40) grade can be more valuable than an Uncirculated or unused note.

This guide explains the different aspects of typical bank listings in this book—covering the states of Rhode Island and Vermont. Volume 1 of this series contains a thoroughly detailed study of the entire field of obsolete state bank notes issued from 1782 to 1866, including a glossary of bank-note engravers, information on how currency was designed, printed, and distributed, and much more. If read even casually, volume 1 will set you on your way to becoming an expert. In the meantime, "How to Use This Book" will explain the current listings in the volume at hand.

Types of Notes

There are several classes of collectible notes in this series. Their status affects their collectability and desirability.

Valid Issues

Valid issues are notes that were printed from plates made by skilled engravers and produced by bank-note companies or other authorized sources. In their time, they were paid out at face value by banks. Such bills were often later redeemed for face value and replaced by new issues. If a bank failed and its notes could not be redeemed, today its notes are still considered to be valid issues by collectors. Valid notes form the main focus of collecting obsolete currency.

A valid issue from the North River Banking Co., New York.

Non-Valid Issues

These exist in several categories:

Counterfeit notes: Illegally issued notes from false plates that imitated genuine bills. They are collectible as "fillers" in some instances but generally sell for low prices. They are collectible mainly as curiosities.

Note counterfeited to be passed as an
issue from the Bank of Cumberland, Maine.

Raised notes: It was a common deceptive practice to raise the value of a low-denomination note to a higher one by chemically removing the counters (as they are called) or denomination ornaments and altering them to read as a higher value. Such notes have nominal values as collectibles today.

Original note of the Merchants & Manufacturers Bank.

Raised note.

Altered notes: Notes that were valid or spurious when first printed but then fell into the hands of criminals who altered them. When a bank failed, its notes became worthless and could not be redeemed for face value. There was a market for such, often at 2 percent or 3 percent of face value. Criminals bought them and, by the use of chemicals, removed certain information such as the town, state, and sometimes even the name of the bank. New information was then printed in the blank spaces. As an example, quantities of worthless $10 notes of the Egg Harbor Bank, Egg Harbor, New Jersey, were altered to appear as $10 notes of the active and strong Valley Bank, Hillsborough, New Hampshire. Altered notes are collectible, but their values are considerably less than the genuine.

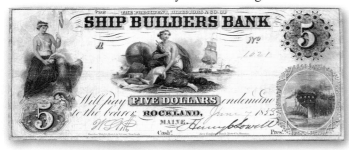

Original note of the Ship Builders Bank.

Altered note.

Spurious Issues

Spurious issues are notes from established engravers and printers that were delivered to banks that never opened their doors or to fraudsters who issued notes bearing the names of banks that never existed. Often these have fascinating stories. These are a basic part of collecting and in many instances are valued for as much as, or higher than, valid issues.

In this text Spurious issues are located in one of two places—under Valid Issues if the bank as a whole never opened or was fraudulently run, but the notes were genuinely printed, or under Non-Valid issues if notes from a genuine bank were taken into the hands of fraudsters and illegally distributed in a similar fashion to other Non-Valid notes such as counterfeits and altered notes.

Spurious note from a non-existent bank in a
non-existent town. Fraudsters intended to alter it
to represent the BOSTON bank of the same name.

Signed and Issued Notes

Banks typically received notes from the printer in sheets, most often a four-subject sheet bearing one to four denominations. Certain features needed to be added once the notes were received. Law cases affirmed that a bill was monetized only after the cashier affixed his signature. It was standard practice in small banks for the cashier to prepare the sheets in advance and then sign them only when the sheets were cut apart and ready to be issued. These features were added to prepare a note for distribution:

Date: Each note needed to bear a year, month, and day of when it was issued. Some notes had printed dates, such as *Jan.y 1st, 1854*, and did not require hand entry. Sometimes these referred to the charter date or were an annual date. It was not unusual for a note to be issued later than the date shown. Accordingly, if a note with a printed date of *Jan.y 1st, 1854*, was signed by cashier John Doe, who was named to that office on May 6, 1856, this was not an extraordinary situation. Many other notes had the number partially printed, such as 18__ or 185_, with the remainder to be inked in.

Partially printed date with the remainder inked in by hand.

Serial number: Serial numbers were usually added by hand in ink. Some notes had the same serial number twice on a note. The combination of the serial number, the date, and the plate letter defines a note as one of a kind.

To cut down on the work involved, serial-number sequences were often started anew when the date changed. This kept the numbers low. Unlike the situation for federal paper money, it is not unusual for an obsolete note to have a serial number below 100. Very few were higher than four digits. Sometimes colored ink was used for serial numbers. Certain notes of larger banks have the serial numbers printed by machine, but these are unusual.

Printed serial number.

President's signature: The primary duty of the president was to conduct meetings of the board of directors and the annual meeting of stockholders. Many directors lived at a distance from the bank and visited it infrequently. Accordingly, it was the custom of the president to sign large quantities of notes far in advance. The president of a small bank usually received a nominal salary, say $100 or $200 per year, or none at all.

Cashier's signature on the left. President's signature on the right.

Cashier's signature: The cashier was the person in charge. Often, for small banks, he was the only employee. It was not unusual for banks in small villages to be kept in the house of the cashier or, if the bank had its own building, for the cashier and his family to live on the premises. Security systems usually consisted only of locks and bolts. The cashier could keep watch at all times, including when the bank was closed.

The cashier was the highest-paid person, often $1,000 per year, more or less. The cashier opened the bank and closed it, kept the books, and took charge of money receipts and payments. Loans were usually arranged with another person on hand, such as one or two directors. Loans were given on "discount days," usually one or two days a week. This made it easier for one or more directors to attend. The discount day schedule was published in local papers. When the cashier affixed his signature to a note, it was officially monetized. That way, if notes were stolen but lacked the signature, the bank could simply declare them to be worthless.

Cashier's signature *D. Holmes.*

Notes in Circulation

Most bills circulated at face value locally or regionally. A $10 bill issued in New Haven, Connecticut, by a sound bank would be received at par with a slight discount for handling in Providence, Boston, or New York City. In Pittsburgh, Richmond, or another distant place, it would be taken in at a discount. Many earned extra profits by selling notes at a discount to brokers or runners who put them into circulation in distant places. The Hillsborough Bank of Amherst, New Hampshire, shipped bundles of notes to Marietta, Ohio, where they were placed into circulation easily. Storekeepers would buy them at a discount. The recipients would spend them, as would others. Hardly anyone went back to New Hampshire to exchange them for coins. Brokers in New York City handled large quantities of discounted notes.

Printed bank-note reporters and counterfeit detectors, as they were called, were published in many forms. These usually told of new counterfeits as well as of banks that had failed or were in financial difficulty. Long lists were presented by state, town, and bank, rating the notes and stating the discount from par at which banks and merchants should be valued.

Grading of Notes

There are no hard and fast rules for grading obsolete currency. Interpretations can vary, sometimes widely. Most old-time dealers and experienced auction houses tend to be more conservative than many who list in Internet sales or who are otherwise not part of the profession. A "Fine" note to one dealer may be another's "Very Fine." Similar to the situation for coins, grading has become looser over the years. A bill bought in the 1960s as Fine will easily be Very Fine today. Years ago, a bill with even a slight trace of a fold or crease was automatically excluded from the Uncirculated category. Today, bills described as such can have these traces, and, perhaps, one without such traces would be given a loftier designation such as Choice Uncirculated or Gem Uncirculated. And so it goes. The methodology is not as consistent or as well developed as is the grading of coins. Two commercial grading services are prominent in grading notes. PCGS Currency, once a part of the Professional Coin Grading Service but now independently owned, and PMG (Paper Money Grading), a division of the Numismatic Guaranty Corporation, have found wide acceptance in the marketplace. As of today they have published no standards, but they seem to more or less follow the guidelines given below.

These categories reflect the author's observations of current grading methods by many dealers and collectors. Beginning in the early 21st century, numbers have been attached to grades by some sellers based on the American Numismatic Association Grading Standards for United States Coins. However, as bills were printed, not minted, the term "Mint State" is not used for paper money.

Grading System
Choice or Gem Uncirculated
Unc-63 and 64 (Choice), Unc-65 (Gem).
A crisp, bright bill with no evidence of creases, folds, or stains. Tom Denly commented in 2004: "I consider centering to be a most important part of grade. For instance, a poorly centered note possibly cut into the design can never be called Gem or even Choice, no matter how nice it otherwise is." Most notes in this category are remainders.

Uncirculated
Unc-60.
A new, never circulated bill, but perhaps with slight evidences of a fold, a crease, or smudges from handling (presumably by bank officers). If part of the margin is trimmed away, this should be mentioned, but often is not. Most notes in this category are remainders.

About Uncirculated
AU-53, 55, and 58.
A bright, attractive note, with some creases, folds, or light discoloration, but with only slight evidences of use in commerce or, in the case of remainders, numismatic or bank handling. If signed and issued for circulation, this is a top-of-the-line grade in great demand.

Extremely Fine
EF-40 and 45.
Bright and attractive but with some slight stains or discoloration, perhaps with a pinhole or two or some small defect. Overall excellent appearance. A bill in this grade saw limited service in circulation.

Very Fine
VF-20 and 30.
This is a widely used grade for a "nice" note, worn but with nice features. Such a bill may be somewhat faded, but the printing and vignettes will be clear and with an attractive overall appearance. There may be an edge chip or two or perhaps a tiny piece off of a corner (but not into the printed part of the note). As most bank tellers and users were right-handed, the right side of a note usually has some discoloration from everyday handling.

Fine
Fine-12.
A note with even more wear, often limp or flimsy from extended use in commerce, but with all printed areas intact and most of them sharply defined. May be stained or discolored in areas.

Very Good
VG-8.
Well circulated, usually with some problems, tears, perhaps a small piece missing from the border, etc. Flimsy and often faded or discolored.

Good
G-4.
Extensively circulated and with evidence of such, including small tears, perhaps edge pieces missing, areas of the printing and vignettes indistinct, and, often, old writing on the face of the note.

Poor, Fair, and About Good
Poor-1, Fair-2, AG-3.
Notes that have been in circulation for a very long time, now with ragged edges or pieces missing and often with significant areas of the note faded or otherwise indiscernible. A filler note. There are quite a few very early bills from the late 18th and early 19th century for which these grades may represent the finest known.

Grade as a Determinant of Value
Remainder notes: Surprise! In the field of bank notes, a well-worn example is often worth more than an Uncirculated bill of the same variety! However, the explanation is simple: most Uncirculated bills are remainders that were never distributed. Most have no officers' signatures. Years after certain banks closed, large quantities of their unissued notes became available. In most instances, a nice Very Fine bill of the same denomination and design, signed and serially numbered, is worth more. Remainder notes of this kind are designated as Unc-Rem. A signed and dated Uncirculated note is designated as Unc-S&D.

An Uncirculated remainder note.

Circulated notes: Among signed and numbered notes, higher-grade examples are more desirable than those in lower levels of preservation. In all instances, an About Uncirculated bill is worth more than an Extremely Fine one, and an EF is worth more than a Very Fine, and on down the line. Among the most desirable of circulated notes are those that are serially numbered, dated, and signed in ink by the cashier and president and which are in a high grade today.

A signed, dated, circulated note.

Cancelled notes: When worn notes were redeemed to be exchanged for others, banks often destroyed them. In many instances, however, they were saved but "canceled" to prevent them from being placed into circulation again. Several small, circular punch holes will either not affect the value of a note or will affect it only slightly, unless uncancelled notes are readily available. Large holes, notches cut out from the border, signatures cut off, and other cancellations that are unattractive are viewed negatively, as are stamped overprints, such as the common WORTHLESS and COUNTERFEIT.

A note cancelled to prevent further circulation.

Proof notes: Proof notes are special printings on special paper or light card stock, are usually found Uncirculated, and can be very valuable, if they are contemporary (made in the 19th century). Modern Proof reprints are worth varying lesser amounts. Beware of scanned or photographic modern copies.

A Proof note, without signatures, printed on special stock.

Proprietary Proofs: Now and then Proprietary Proofs or modern reprints are made of existing genuine notes. These are often given brightly colored tints or overprints and are crisp and clean, but they were never seen during the bank-note–issuing era. Collectors should be aware that these notes are nearly always worth less than genuine notes. For more information, see page 12 of volume 1.

A genuine Northfield Bank note, Northfield, Vermont.

A Proprietary Proof note made from the same plates as the above genuine note. The tint is on a separate plate from the engraving.

Valuation of Notes
Explanation of Values

Values assigned to notes in given grades have been compiled by consulting with dealers and collectors and by studying listed prices and auction results. Unlike coins, which often have values determined by "bid" prices and, for some such as gold, trade on close margins, the valuation of paper currency is much more subjective. In a way, the pricing can be compared to that in the fields of tokens and medals.

Many notes are infrequently traded. This is especially true for rare early issues. Sometimes, years can elapse between offerings. In such instances the values here are "educated guesses." Actual sale results such as an offering at auction may differ widely. For that reason values in this book should be considered as estimates compiled at the time of publication. Although the future is unknown, in past decades the price

trends have been upward. Many notes valued at $100 a decade ago may be valued at $125 to $175 or more now. Few if any valid-issue notes have decreased in value. When contemplating a purchase or sale it is recommended that you check with experts and other sources for current values.

Even for common remainder notes and for certain common circulated bills in a given grade, prices can vary in the same time frame. One note might be priced at $200, another at $175, and a third at $250. It may be worthwhile to say that the same variations are seen in many other collectibles markets—such as Currier & Ives prints, postcards, colonial coins, ancient coins, antique furniture, tokens and medals, and more. The point here is that federal coins of the past 200 years are often quite common, trade frequently, and have bid and ask prices—a situation not comparable to other collectible specialties as mentioned.

To aid in current valuation we recommend subscribing to publications about paper money and checking auction and sale listings, often available on the Internet.

If a long-sought rarity is offered, many if not most experienced dealers and collectors will "reach" for it. A rarity listed for $1,000 may be a good buy for $2,000 if it is the only one to be offered in recent years.

With some experience, you will get a grasp for pricing—just as collectors of tokens, medals, prints, and other things have. What starts as being esoteric will in time become familiar.

Factors Affecting Values

Grade or condition: Among notes that were signed, numbered, dated, and placed into circulation, the higher the grade, the more valuable the note is. Uncirculated notes or remainders can be worth less than a circulated signed note.

Location: Notes of certain states or territories can be worth a premium. Western notes of a given rarity, such as from Utah, Kansas Territory, or Arkansas can be worth more than notes from New York, Pennsylvania, or New Jersey.

Rarity: In a given series, a rare note is worth more a common one.

Demand and popularity: Notes of certain towns and states can be worth more if there are more collectors desiring to buy them. Notes from Florida are more widely collected than are those of Vermont. Accordingly, a note of a given rarity can be worth more if from Florida. Such popularity may change over a period of time. If two or three well-financed buyers each seek to build a collection of a state, there will be great competition for rarities, and prices will be much higher than if this competition were not present. In addition, the publication of a new reference work on a particular state or category can serve to increase the number of people desiring such notes.

Denomination: Within a given rarity, an unusual denomination such as $4, $6, $7, $8, or $9 will be worth more than a $1, $2, $3, $5, $10, or $20 (these being the most often seen). On their own, $3 notes have always attracted a following; once common in circulation, the denomination is considered unusual today. It has not been used since the federal government began issuing notes in quantity in 1861, despite being very popular with state-chartered banks. $50 and $100 notes are scarce for most banks, and with relatively few exceptions, $500 and $1,000 notes are great rarities.

Vignette topic: The illustration or vignette of a note can add value. A Connecticut note showing Iranistan, the palatial home of P.T. Barnum, or "the Battle of the Frogs" is worth more than one showing a train or buildings. Notes showing Santa Claus are extremely popular and often sell for much more than what a comparable-rarity bill of a miscellaneous subject might command.

"Battle of the Frogs."

Santa Claus at upper left.

Proofs: Proof notes printed on special paper and intended as samples or for reference are usually found in Uncirculated preservation and will sell for many multiples of the price of common remainder notes.

Market and economic trends: The general market for obsolete paper money has been quite strong in recent decades. However, it was rather quiet before then. Market strength is based on the number of buyers at a given time and how much money they have to spend.

Imaging of Notes

Given their age and extensive circulation, obsolete bank notes are sometimes found with a high level of wear and tear. Within this encyclopedia, some images have been digitally enhanced to mitigate the effects of rust, water damage, stains, age, circulation wear, color fading, and other environmental stresses. Where necessary, they have been conceptually restored to more closely resemble their original form in an attempt to aid collectors and historians in identifying and analyzing the various issues, vignettes, engravings, and styles of the bank notes.

Printed Features of Note Designs

A typical note includes these printed features:

Name of bank: The name of the bank is usually the most prominently printed figure and can be found either high on the center of the note face or in a position about half way down. New Haven Bank, Derby Bank, Cochituate Bank, Bank of Commerce, Warner Bank, and Butchers and Drovers Bank are

examples. Such titles often reflect the location of the bank, an industry such as farming or manufacturing, a geographical feature such as an ocean or river, or a proper name from history. Among the latter there are banks named Franklin, Washington, Lafayette, and Indian names such as Amoskeag, Oneida, Quinnipiack, and Mohawk. At any given time there was only one bank of a certain name in operation in a given state.

Location of bank: Every note gives the town and state. The town often appears near the bank name or is sometimes tagged on to it, such as the Tradesmens Bank of New Haven. The name of the state often appears away from the town name, perhaps in the field of the note or at a border.

Denomination: This is the face value of a note. The most popular values were $1, $2, $3, $5, and $10 among the lower denominations and were made in the largest quantities. $20, $50, and $100 values were made in smaller quantities. Only a few banks issued $500 or $1,000 notes. There are also fractional notes such as 25¢, 50¢, and 75¢ in existence, issued by banks as part of a series that included higher denominations. The more times a denomination was printed on a note, the harder it was to alter by raising. Many notes have the denomination given dozens of times in micro-letters in addition to larger digits. Odd-value notes such as $1.25, $1.50, $1.75, $4, and $6 to $9 were issued by a few banks.

Scattered small notes denominated in cents were sometimes issued, usually but not always privately, in times of economic distress and are called scrip. Scrip notes were usually made by local printers. They are not studied herein.

Denomination counters: While the denominations of many notes, especially early ones, were lettered or in script, most bills after about 1810 had the value as a number surrounded with an oval, circle, or fancy engraving. These are referred to as counters. Volume 1 gives many examples.

Main vignette: Most notes have a large vignette at the center or to one side extending to the center. These are often scenic in nature—a seated figure, laborers at work, a train and cars, capitols and commercial buildings, figures from mythology, seascapes, and more. After 1820 vignettes became increasingly ornate.

Other vignettes: Most notes also had two or more smaller vignettes. Portraits of people ranging from well-known, such as a national president, to obscure, such as a bank president, were popular. Others show standing or seated figures, people in various activities, etc. Medallion vignettes reproduce medals, cameos, or plaques by means of a medal-ruling machine.

Ornaments and borders: Various geometric figures and engraved ornaments add to the complexity of many notes, as do ornamental borders.

Seals and arms: State arms, seals stating that a note was backed by securities or liens on real estate, etc., were added to many notes.

The state arms of Connecticut can be seen in the upper left corner.

Plate letter: It was common practice to assign a letter such as A, B, or C to the face of a note. A sheet of four notes might include, as an example, $1-$1-$1-$2. The three $1 notes would bear letters A, B, and C, and the $2 note would start again with A.

Engraver's imprint: The name of the bank-note printing company was nearly always stated in the face, usually in tiny letters at the bottom border but sometimes elsewhere. On some occasions ornamental vignettes were signed in micro-letters by engravers.

Place of redemption: While most bank notes could be redeemed over the counter of the banks that issued them, some others gave distant places where they could be redeemed, as at an office in another state, often in New York City. Such notes were frequently of questionable value.

Time of redemption: Most notes could be redeemed on demand, but many had a printed inscription stating that they could be redeemed only at a specified time later than the date on the note—six months, a year, or some other interval. Later-payment bills are called post notes, a term printed on some of them. Confederate States of America notes were redeemable two years after a peace treaty was signed with the United States, which, of course, never happened.

Overprints: Many notes, especially those after the 1820s, have overprints in color. These often give the denomination, such as ONE, FIVE, or TWENTY. Some later notes have grillwork, the denomination in micro-printing, or other features added in panels of color printing. On some the entire face can be overprinted in color.

Backs of notes: With only scattered exceptions, the backs of notes have not been discussed in reference books or auction catalogs. Hence, there are many notes listed in this book that have ornate backs not described.

Security features: Security features to deter counterfeiting or altering are seen on many notes. The most common is the "Canada green" or "Patent Green Tint" used on notes of Rawdon, Wright, Hatch & Edson in 1857 and by the American Bank Note Co. from 1858 onward. This color was said to deter copying by photographic means. Jacob Perkins's Patented Stereotype Steel Plate (PSSP) used micro-lettering to deter counterfeiting.

Other information: Ruled spaces and lettering were provided to indicate where the bank officers should sign and where the serial number should be placed. Various inscriptions, monograms, and other elements were sometimes added.

Listings of Notes

There are various elements to each bank and note in this book. Not every note will have the same or all of these characteristics. For ease of communication, description, and inventory, "Whitman numbers" have been assigned to the various notes.

Town / Town information: The name of and a brief historical sketch of the city or town in which the bank was located.

Bank name: The name of the bank. This is usually the name as imprinted on notes. Often on a note "The" will be the preface. "And" in a bank title is used in bank charters and is used here, as in Farmers and Merchants Bank. However, some notes and many numismatic listings use an ampersand (&) instead. It is numismatic practice to drop punctuation, to use Citizens instead of Citizens', for example. On some notes the name of the town is added to the title, such as the Farmers Bank of River City or the Farmers Bank in River City. Some notes of a given bank have such suffixes and others do not. They are not used here unless they are a main part of the title as boldly printed on a note, such as Smithville Bank of Commerce or Greenville Grocers Bank.

Date of operation: Years of existence, from the bank's charter date until it ceased operations, such as 1851–1865. Sometimes a bank did not begin operations until a year or two after it was chartered.

History: A synopsis of the history of the bank during its note-issuing period. Often much additional information can be found in historical texts or on the Internet and makes an interesting pursuit.

Numismatic commentary: Comments on the bank, the notes' overall availability, and more. In this volume C. John Ferreri was among those who assisted with this content.

Note listing: Divided into sections by Valid Issues (genuine notes from functioning banks), Issues (spurious notes from non-functioning or fraudulent banks), and Non-Valid Issues (notes from genuine banks that were later counterfeited, raised, made spurious by fraudsters, altered, etc.). The sample listing following is from the Richmond Bank, Alton, Rhode Island.

$1 • W-RI-010-001-G010a

CC

Overprint: Red ONE. **Engraver:** Danforth, Wright & Co. **Comments:** H-RI-425-G2a, Durand-2. Similar to W-RI-010-001-G010. Remainder. August 12th, 185_. 1850s.

Rarity: URS-6
VF $400

$1: Denomination of the note shown.

W-RI-010-001-G010a

W: Whitman number. This number is a sortable code unique to each bank and note.

RI: Abbreviation for the state under study.

010: Numerical designation for the Richmond Bank, Alton. Other banks have different numbers.

001: The denomination in dollars.

G010a: G indicates a good or valid note. Other categories are indicated thus: C (counterfeit); R (raised); S (spurious); N (not-attributed); A (altered). 010a is the specific note shown. Notes are listed in a bank-series by increments of 10 in order of denomination—a "porous" system so new discoveries can be added if needed. Terminal letters following the numerical designation, in this example "a," indicate variations of a note: a series of different colored overprints, tints, payees, etc., all on the same design of note. Thus the first type of a note will have no letter, the second an "a," the third a "b," the fourth a "c," and so on as necessary.

CC: Photographic image of an actual note in a collection, museum, or other location. Each photograph shown identifies its original source, when known, by an abbreviation at the upper right-hand corner of the image. A list of these creditors can be found at the front of the volume.

Vignette description: Primarily divided into Left, Center, Bottom center, and Right, these describe what is seen on the face of the note. Other descriptors include Overprint, Tint, Back, Payee, Engraver, and Comments, which includes other details about the note. For notes that are not illustrated, descriptions are given—based on information, when available, from contemporary bank-note reporters, counterfeit detectors, and other listings. Some are partial or may even prove to be inaccurate if an actual note is discovered. PSSP refers to a note of the Patent Stereotype Steel Plate by Jacob Perkins or his successor, the New England Bank Note Co. (see volume 1 for details). Illustrated notes will not have the primary descriptions included.

Rarity and Value: Estimate of the number of notes in existence today and the typical market value of a note at the time of publication. The figure indicates the center of a range. As an example, $400 suggests a range of about $350 to $450. Included as available.

Rarity (URS) Ratings
The Universal Rarity Scale

The Universal Rarity Scale uses a simple geometric progression of numbers by doubling the preceding value for each successive "rank": 1, 2, 4, 8, 16, 32, etc. (see the rightmost of each number pair), with the higher numbers rounded off for simplicity. Introduced in 1993, this has been widely used in various publications since that time. It is not copyrighted.

URS-1 = 1 known, unique
URS-2 = 2 known
URS-3 = 3 or 4
URS-4 = 5 to 8
URS-5 = 9 to 16
URS-6 = 17 to 32
URS-7 = 33 to 64
URS-8 = 65 to 124
URS-9 = 125 to 249
URS-10 = 250 to 499
URS-11 = 500 to 999
URS-12 = 1,000 to 1,999
URS-13 = 2,000 to 3,999
URS-14 = 4,000 to 7,999

Population Estimates

Drawing from authoritative catalogs, input from dealers and collectors, and other sources, rarity estimates have been given for many notes. In the past there have been many instances in which additional examples of previously rare notes have been found or new information has been learned. This will continue to be the case. Accordingly, some notes may become more plentiful than now listed. Many estates and other holdings with notes have not as of yet been examined or surveyed. To paraphrase an old comment, if Jones was not seen at a football game, he still might have been there.

Factors Affecting Present-Day Rarity

Some obsolete notes are very common. Others are so rare that only one or two exist. In some cases, a note may have been described in a bank-note reporter or other early reference, but no physical examples are known to exist. Such notes are assigned a Rarity listing of *None known*. Still others are so intangible that a guess has not been made as to their rarity; these are given a dash (—) as their Rarity listing.

If a bank was well-run and had no difficulties, its notes were usually redeemed at par. Sometimes these were burned—as mandated for banks in the state of Maine. There are many Maine notes that were once in circulation by the thousand but for which few are known today. In other states, notes were burned or were canceled at the option of the directors. In many instances quantities of canceled notes were saved, and later generations of collectors and dealers obtained them.

Many banks failed or otherwise could not redeem their notes. Spurious banks did not redeem any currency. Bills of such banks can be very common today. Quantities of unissued remainder notes, often as original sheets, exist for some banks. With increasing demand, many of the sheets have been cut apart. Notes of certain banks are extremely common as Uncirculated remainders, but signed and issued notes are rare and much more valuable. Original sheets can be collected as a specialty and are listed in this book. However, as they are not convenient to display and as the four notes to a sheet have been worth more individually in the past, most have been cut apart, as noted.

Learning More

Collecting obsolete bank notes can be a fascinating pursuit. Scarce and rare bills can often be obtained for fractions of the cost of comparably rare coins. With modest financial means it is often possible to build a first-class collection of notes from a particular area or with a particular theme.

As you have read to this point, you know that notes can be complex—and to an enthusiast, wonderfully so. Your enjoyment can be enriched by learning more. Whitman Publishing offers three key volumes that are guaranteed to please:

Volume 1 of the *Whitman Encyclopedia of Obsolete Paper Money* series is an in-depth study of obsolete paper money,

how it was conceived, created, and distributed. Chapters go into great detail concerning engravers, vignettes, counterfeiting, and more. It is probably correct to say that if you spend a few evenings with your copy, you will be well on your way to becoming an expert. This book is a companion to the volume you are now holding and has been designed to complement it with much additional information.

Obsolete Paper Money Issued by Banks in the United States 1782–1866, published in 2006, is another essential volume on your way to becoming an expert and smart buyer.

The third book in the Whitman suite is *100 Greatest American Currency Notes*, a "for fun" volume that includes many different types of paper money with many obsolete bills featured.

Bank Note Reporter, issued monthly by Krause Publications, is filled with news and offerings. *Paper Money*, the journal of the Society of Paper Money Collectors, has much valuable information and many research articles.

The Professional Currency Dealers Association (PCDA) has dozens of members and opens the door to buying notes. It is strongly recommended that unless you are aware of special qualifications, you avoid buying notes on the Internet or other non-professional sources without an iron-clad money-back guarantee.

Obsolete notes are meant to be enjoyed. With some study of historical books and newspapers on the Internet or in a library, a single note can be your passport to a lot of ownership pleasure.

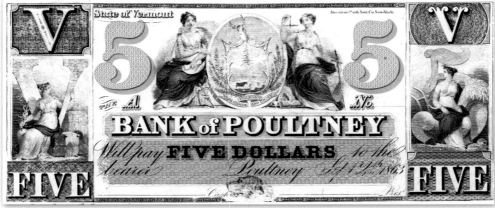

THE OBSOLETE BANK NOTES OF RHODE ISLAND

STATE BANKING IN RHODE ISLAND

The Early Banks

Similar to the coastal states adjacent to it, Rhode Island was early to engage in the banking business. The Providence Bank opened in the thriving port of Providence on October 10, 1791, following an unsuccessful attempt to establish a bank in that city in 1784. Capital was authorized at $400,000. The charter placed no limit on the amount of paper money the bank could issue.

The Bank of Rhode Island was incorporated in Newport in October 1795 with an authorized capital of $100,000, and it opened its doors soon thereafter. This institution remained in business until August 21, 1865, when its business interests were succeeded by the National Bank of Rhode Island.

The Washington Bank was chartered in Westerly in 1800 with the modest authorized capital of $50,000. The charter required that two-thirds of the directors and the president should reside in the same county as the bank. Bills for the bank were made from copper plates engraved by Amos Doolittle of New Haven, Connecticut. These featured the portrait of the recently deceased George Washington and are considered to be the earliest depiction of Washington on a bank note.

The Bank of Bristol was chartered in 1800 and soon opened in the Rhode Island town of the same name. The authorized capital was set at $120,000. The institution began as a holding company for the Bristol Insurance Company, which through political connections held federal deposits in the district.[1] The bank was dissolved in the mid-1860s after decades of profitable operation.

A Notable Fraud

The Farmers Exchange Bank of Gloucester, Rhode Island, was incorporated in February 1804. Andrew Dexter Jr., who operated a currency exchange in Boston, was the organizer. The capital was authorized at $100,000 to be paid in specie in seven installments. Subscriptions were authorized at 2,000 shares worth $50 each. However, very little of the capital was ever paid in, and although the directors each remitted the first installment in gold and silver coins, the same amount was quickly taken back from the bank by each—without giving any security in return. Each director eventually held 103 shares essentially free of charge. Of the bank's 2,000 shares, only 661 were ever paid for in gold and silver, and deducting the loans taken back by the directors, the capital of $100,000 amounted to only $3,081.11 in actual specie!

Dexter called upon bank-note printer Jacob Perkins of Newburyport, Massachusetts, to print and deliver large quantities of notes. Perkins was an accessory in this and certain other frauds (most notably the Hillsborough Bank of Amherst, New Hampshire). Unconcerned with the solidity or reputation of banks, he filled orders as requested. By 1809 the fraud was exposed and widely reported in the newspapers. The bank (such as it was) collapsed, and its bills became worthless. At the time there were no state regulations or oversight regarding currency, and Dexter was never prosecuted. Instead he went to the South, where he engaged in real estate and other businesses. The main avenue leading up to the Alabama State Capitol in Montgomery bears his name.

After the collapse of Dexter's bank in 1809, Rhode Island would be free of bank failures for two decades.

The Early 19th Century

By 1805 there were 13 banks operating in Rhode Island with a declared authorized capital of $1,500,000 combined. A part of this total was illusory and consisted of promissory notes, but only the Farmers Exchange Bank was engaged in outright fraud.

Until 1820 there was no restriction on the issue of notes. In that year the circulation of each bank was limited to the paid-in capital as declared (without audit). Most of the banks, however, were inside this limit before the law was passed. As the banks were unhampered for years in their circulation privileges, possessed extraordinary powers for the collection of their debts, were not compelled to pay a bonus to the state, and were free from taxation, their number multiplied rapidly. The total number of operating banks in 1826 was 44, and their authorized capital was $10,350,000. Although the banks could collect debts from parties to whom they had made loans, there was no way that holders of worthless notes could collect indemnity from bank directors or shareholders should a bank collapse.

The Burrillville Bank, another customer of the Perkins printing factory in Newburyport, failed in 1829 with an unknown number of worthless bills in circulation. The bank declared $49,000 as being the total, but this was probably a false statement. The Farmers and Mechanics Bank of Pawtuxet closed its doors the same year. Its currency remained good, although the stockholders's equity was lost. The Phenix Bank of Providence was formed under the same charter.

Beginning in 1833, charters specified that stockholders would be liable for debts after the bank's assets were exhausted. However, then and at later times, no such recoveries were ever made. In this and other states, bank fraud by creating over-issue of paper money and falsifying documents was not prosecuted in court. On the other hand, someone robbing a bank of $100 was likely to be arrested and put in jail.

An 1836 law provided for a minimum bank capital of $50,000, with half to be paid in specie (silver and gold coins) before business could commence. This was widely ignored as shares continued to be "paid in" with IOUs or promissory notes. The Board of Bank Commissioners was also set up that year. In this aspect Rhode Island was ahead of many other states, as it was the Panic of 1837 that prompted such groups in other parts of the country. The Board was later eliminated, after which time banks sent reports to other officials in the state. In 1857 the Board was reconstituted.

Banks in Rhode Island operated fairly and profitably for the most part, with only scattered failures after the early years. No banks went under because of the Panic of 1837, but most experienced difficulties and suspended specie payments. In Rhode Island, as elsewhere, the vaults of many suspending banks were well-stocked with silver and gold coins during this time. It was the realization that the stocks of specie would soon be depleted if exchange were permitted that prompted most banks to take this action.

The Rhode Island Agricultural Bank, located in Johnston, ceased business in 1843, but currency holders were able to redeem part of the value of the bills. The Pascoag Bank in the district of that name (an area located in Burrillville) stopped issuing bills about this time. Its books remained in a muddled state of affairs for the rest of the decade, and by 1850 it was still not able to make a proper financial report.[2] It survived, however, and in June 1851, perhaps to start afresh with a better reputation, it changed its name to the Granite Bank, which continued into the 1860s.

Among Rhode Island institutions, the Scituate Bank had a particularly convoluted career. Incorporated in 1818, it seems to have operated normally for many years. In 1836, however, an investigation revealed that out-of-state parties had secured control of the bank, stripped it of assets, and released large quantities of essentially worthless bills. As a result, the bank went into liquidation. In 1841 it reopened with a new name: the Hamilton

Bank of Scituate. In the same year a large quantity of new bills was stolen, given forged signatures, and placed into circulation. The bank refused to redeem them, stirring up a big controversy. In the following years the bank teetered on insolvency, and in 1849 an act of the State Legislature forced its closing and liquidation.[3] The perpetrators got off scot-free.

Later Years

The *Illustrated News*, April 23, 1853, printed this, reflective of an action taken when silver coins were absent from circulation, as they had been since 1850:

> Three banks in Rhode Island have issued fractional bills in large quantities. In the present dearth of change, they are found to be a great convenience, and are very generally welcomed wherever they can be obtained. About four weeks since, one bank issued $30,000 in fractional bills, not a dollar of which has yet been presented at the bank for redemption. They are not received at the Suffolk Bank [Boston clearing house].

Curiously, after most of these bills found their way back to the banks in the early summer of 1853, when new silver coins of lower authorized weight again reached circulation, the notes had another use, as reported by the *Boston Traveller*:

> *Fractional paper of Providence, R.I.* The circulation of fractional bills is rapidly diminished in this vicinity, and hundreds of dollars of these bills are being returned through the brokers to those banks that issued them. We understand that the Providence banks are very happy to have these bills returned, as there is a large demand for them in the West, where they are used in paying the laborers on the railroads now being built. One bank has an order for $10,000 worth of these bills, and has employed a number of extra hands to prepare them for circulation. The issue, so far, has proved highly successful and profitable.[4]

Why a railroad worker in the American West (defined at the time as regions west of the Allegheny Mountains) would accept worn fractional bills of distant Rhode Island banks seems curious, but perhaps there is an explanation. Probably, the bills, although having no real value, continued to change hands in commerce in remote areas, to the satisfaction of all. Eventually, they became worthless.

The Peacedale Bank, incorporated in 1853, never opened. Similarly, in 1854 the Island Bank was chartered to be located in the village of East Shoreham on Block Island. It too never went into operation. Other banks arose without opening their doors, such as this group of six chartered by the legislature in early 1856: the Marine, Northern, and Moshassuck banks in Providence; the Greenwich Bank; the Pokanoket Bank in Bristol; and the Washington County Bank in Richmond. Gaining a charter did not always mean that a bank ever operated. As a numismatic aspect, it is always possible that Proof notes ordered in anticipation of opening might be found from time to time.

In 1856 the Bank of the Republic, located in Providence, suspended operation. Cashier Charles M. Howlett, with the advice and consent of the directors, had speculated heavily in the West and sent large quantities of paper money there to be sold at a discount. A large amount of the bank's assets were tied up in drafts on a New York City concern that failed and thus were lost. The state banking commissioners investigated and found that the institution had been incompetently, but not necessarily fraudulently, managed.[5] Again, there were no prosecutions.

From 1857—a panic year—to 1859, the number of banks in Rhode Island dropped from 98 to 90. The Tiverton Bank fell victim to the hard economic times and was revealed to be a fraud owned by speculators who used it to circulate worthless bills. The Farmers Bank of Wickford was a similar phony operation that also failed in 1857. Most surviving banks remained strong after 1859, and in the mid-1860s their shareholders voted to organize national banks which would assume the businesses of state-chartered institutions.

Numismatic Comments

Paper money of Rhode Island is quite varied in appearance, as the use of the historical but numismatically monotonous Patent Stereotype Steel Plate (PSSP) issues were not as prevalent here as in states to the north. Many different institutions issued a wide variety of designs over a long period of years. Today, availability ranges from plentiful for failed institutions—as well as those that redeemed their notes but later made them available to collectors—to very rare. The last category primarily covers issues of the 1850s and early 1860s, when banks that redeemed their currency at face value then destroyed it.

There are many Rhode Island notes with interesting stories. Bills of the fraudulent Farmers Exchange Bank of Gloucester are easily available today and invite owners of such to further investigate the bank's history. A few other phony institutions sprang up from time to time, and their currency can be found easily on the market today. Notes of the Freemens Bank of Bristol featuring an Abner Reed imprint from the 1810s that were issued in the 1860s can be found easily enough and have an interesting story as related in the text.

Proofs and remainders exist for bills of many institutions, mainly for later issues. Nearly all Proofs are from the American Bank Note Co. paper archives and include varieties for which circulating examples are either very rare or altogether unknown. Many of these were auctioned in 1990 by Christie's. Similar to other New England states, Rhode Island notes are perhaps most often collected by gathering available types, ignoring the expensive rarities, and in the process forming a very nice display.

The 1981 book by Roger H. Durand, *Obsolete Notes and Scrip of Rhode Island and the Providence Plantations*, is highly recommended as a source of additional information.

ALTON, RHODE ISLAND

One of the villages within Richmond, Alton is located close to the Pawcatuck River.

See also Richmond, Rhode Island.

Richmond Bank
1856–1866
W-RI-010

History: The Richmond Bank was chartered in May 1856 with an authorized capital of $50,000. By 1857 the figure had doubled. Later, the bank had an address in Alton, a village within Richmond. In 1860 the capital amount was back at the original $50,000. Circulation averaged at $31,000, and specie totaled $1,293.17 in 1857.[6]

In 1865 the bank was located in Hopkinton, and by 1866 the bank had closed its affairs. Its business was succeeded by the First National Bank of Hopkinton, chartered in 1865.

See also listings under Hopkinton, W-RI-460, and Richmond, W-RI-1270.

Numismatic Commentary: One would think that notes of this "village" bank from Alton would be extremely hard to find. However, that does not apply for every denomination. As a class these notes can be classified as scarce, yet the circulated $10 denomination seems to turn up with some regularity. A few uncut sheets bearing the Alton address are known to have survived. As is generally true with most sheets, they continue to be cut apart by collectors and dealers who can realize a greater value from the individual notes.

VALID ISSUES
$1 • W-RI-010-001-G010
SBG

Engraver: Danforth, Wright & Co. ***Comments:*** H-RI-425-G2, Durand-1. Proof. August 12th, 185_. 1850s.
Rarity: URS-3
Proof $1,500

$1 • W-RI-010-001-G010a
CC

Overprint: Red ONE. ***Engraver:*** Danforth, Wright & Co. ***Comments:*** H-RI-425-G2a, Durand-2. Similar to W-RI-010-001-G010. Remainder. August 12th, 185_. 1850s.
Rarity: URS-6
VF $400

$2 • W-RI-010-002-G020

Left: Woman standing, Woman holding up sheaf. *Center:* 2 on die / Two women reclining with shield bearing sheaf and plow. *Right:* 2 on die / Cherubs holding sheaf. *Engraver:* Danforth, Wright & Co. *Comments:* H-RI-425-G4, Durand-7. August 12th, 185_. 1850s.

Rarity: URS-3

Proof $1,800

$2 • W-RI-010-002-G020a

CJF

Overprint: Red TWO. *Engraver:* Danforth, Wright & Co. *Comments:* H-RI-425-G4a, Durand-8. Similar to W-RI-010-002-G020. August 12th, 185_. 1850s.

Rarity: URS-6

VF $400

$3 • W-RI-010-003-G030

Left: 3 / Blacksmith's hand on anvil. *Center:* Two horses flanking state arms surmounted by eagle. *Bottom center:* Legend. *Right:* 3 / Woman seated, Two men standing. *Engraver:* Danforth, Wright & Co. *Comments:* H-RI-425-G6, Durand-13. Aug.t 12th, 185_. 1850s.

Rarity: URS-3

Proof $2,000

$3 • W-RI-010-003-G030a

SBG

Overprint: Red THREE. *Engraver:* Danforth, Wright & Co. *Comments:* H-RI-425-G6a. Similar to W-RI-010-003-G030. Proof. Aug.t 12th, 185_. 1850s.

Rarity: URS-1

Proof $4,000

$5 • W-RI-010-005-G040

Left: 5 on die / FIVE / Ruling machine. *Center:* Three angels holding hands. *Right:* 5 on die / Pledge. *Engraver:* Danforth, Wright & Co. *Comments:* H-RI-425-G8, Durand-15. August 12th, 185_. 1850s.

Rarity: URS-3

Proof $2,000

$5 • W-RI-010-005-G040a

CJF

Overprint: Red 5 / V / 5. *Engraver:* Danforth, Wright & Co. *Comments:* H-RI-425-G8a, Durand-16. Similar to W-RI-010-005-G040. August 12th, 185_. 1850s.

Rarity: URS-3

VF $500

$10 • W-RI-010-010-G050

Left: 10 / Portrait of Henry Clay. *Center:* Three men forging iron. *Right:* 10 / Girl feeding chickens. *Engraver:* Danforth, Wright & Co. *Comments:* H-RI-425-G10, Durand-17a. August 12th, 185_. 1850s.

Rarity: URS-3

Proof $2,500

$10 • W-RI-010-010-G050a

CJF

Overprint: Red TEN / X. *Engraver:* American Bank Note Co. *Comments:* H-RI-425-G10a, Durand-17b. Similar to W-RI-010-010-G050 but with different engraver imprint. August 12th, 185_. 1850s.

Rarity: URS-6

VF $400; Proof $3,000

Uncut Sheets

$1-$1-$2-$5 • W-RI-010-001.001.002.005-US010

Vignette(s): ($1) Man with sledge hammer / Horses drinking from trough / Portrait of Jenny Lind. *($1)* Man with sledge hammer / Horses drinking from trough / Portrait of Jenny Lind. *($2)* Woman standing, Woman kneeling holding up sheaf / Two women reclining with shield bearing sheaf and plow / Helmeted man holding sheaf. *($5)* Three angels holding hands / Ruling machine. *Engraver:* Danforth, Wright & Co. *Comments:* H-RI-425-G2, G2, G4, G8. August 12th, 185_. 1850s.

Rarity: URS-1

Proof $7,500

$1-$1-$2-$5 • W-RI-010-001.001.002.005-US010a

Overprint(s): Red. *Engraver:* Danforth, Wright & Co. *Comments:* H-RI-425-G2a, G2a, G4a, G8a. Similar to W-RI-010-001.001.002.005-US010. August 12th, 185_. 1850s.

Rarity: URS-4

VF $2,500

$3-$10 • W-RI-010-003.010-US020

Vignette(s): *($3)* Blacksmith with hand on anvil / State arms / Legend / Woman seated, Two men standing. *($10)* Portrait of Henry Clay / Three men forging iron / Girl feeding chickens. *Overprint(s):* Red. *Engraver:* Danforth, Wright & Co. *Comments:* H-RI-425-G6a, G10a. Variously dated Aug.t 12th, 185_, August 12th, 185_. 1850s.

Rarity: URS-1

NON-VALID ISSUES

$1 • W-RI-010-001-A010

Left: 1 / Female portrait. *Center:* Overseer on horse and men picking cotton / Indian stalking deer. *Bottom center:* Sleeping dog. *Right:* ONE vertically. *Overprint:* Red ONE. *Engraver:* Bald, Cousland & Co. *Comments:* H-RI-425-A5, Durand-3. Altered from $1 Southern Bank of Georgia, Bainbridge, Georgia. 18__. 1850s.

Rarity: *None known*

$1 • W-RI-010-001-A020

Center: Cows drinking in stream. *Comments:* H-RI-425-A10, Durand-6. 1850s.

Rarity: *None known*

$1 • W-RI-010-001-A030

Left: 1 / Two allegorical women flanking shield / ONE. *Center:* Ship, Three allegorical women reclining around shield surmounted by eagle. *Right:* 1 / Two farmers and dog. *Engraver:* Danforth, Wright & Co. *Comments:* H-RI-425-A15, Durand-4. Altered from $1 Bank of Washtenaw, Washtenaw, Michigan. 1850s.

Rarity: *None known*

$1 • W-RI-010-001-A040

Left: ONE / Reaper under tree. *Center:* Sheep, Horses drinking from well. *Right:* 1 / Sailor with spyglass. *Engraver:* Danforth, Wright & Co. *Comments:* H-Unlisted, Durand-5. Altered from $1 Commercial Bank of New Jersey, Perth Amboy, New Jersey series. July 10, 1856. 1850s.

Rarity: URS-3

$2 • W-RI-010-002-N010

Center: Woman leaning on shield. *Comments:* H-RI-425-N5, Durand-12. Altered or spurious. 1850s.

Rarity: *None known*

$2 • W-RI-010-002-A050

Left: 2 / Farmer plowing. *Center:* Men loading wagon with sheaves, Men cradling and binding. *Right:* 2 / Two floating cherubs with caduceus and sheaf. *Tint:* Red-brown 2s / TWO DOLLARS. *Engraver:* Danforth, Wright & Co. *Comments:* H-RI-425-A25, Durand-9. Altered from $2 Southern Bank of Georgia, Bainbridge, Georgia. March 1, 1858. 1850s.

Rarity: *None known*

$2 • W-RI-010-002-A060

Left: TWO / Woman feeding fowl. *Center:* Sailing ship, Steamship. *Right:* 2 / Indian woman with spear. *Engraver:* Danforth, Wright & Co. *Comments:* H-RI-425-A30, Durand-11. Altered from $2 Commercial Bank of New Jersey, Perth Amboy, New Jersey series. July 10, 1856. 1850s.

Rarity: *None known*

$2 • W-RI-010-002-A070

Left: 2 / Blacksmith by forge. *Center:* Farmer feeding swine, Two horses. *Bottom center:* 2 on die. *Right:* 2 / Farmer carrying corn stalks. *Overprint:* Red. *Engraver:* Toppan, Carpenter & Co. *Comments:* H-RI-425-A35, Durand-10. Altered from W-RI-1630-002-G020. Aug. 6, 1855. 1850s.

Rarity: *None known*

$3 • W-RI-010-003-A080

Left: 3 / Steamship. *Center:* Justice / Shield surmounted by eagle / Liberty. *Right:* 3 / Train of cars. *Overprint:* Red THREE. *Engraver:* Baldwin, Bald & Cousland / Bald, Cousland & Co. *Comments:* H-RI-425-A40, Durand-14. Altered from W-RI-1500-003-G030. 18__. 1850s.

Rarity: *None known*

$5 • W-RI-010-005-A090

Left: 5 / FIVE / FIVE. *Center:* Indian woman, Five gold dollars, Three cherubs, Frontiersman. *Right:* 5 / Female portrait / FIVE. *Overprint:* FIVE. *Engraver:* Rawdon, Wright, Hatch & Edson. *Comments:* H-RI-425-A45, Durand-17. Altered from $5 Farmers and Merchants Bank of Memphis, Memphis, Tennessee. 1850s.

Rarity: *None known*

ANTHONY VILLAGE, RHODE ISLAND

Located in the eastern part of Coventry, Anthony Village was named after the Anthony family who built the first mill in the area. The state's textile industry had its inception here during the 19th century. The mill villages that were created as a result were populated mostly by French-Canadian and Irish immigrants who worked in the factories, while others became farmers.

See also Coventry, Rhode Island.

Coventry Bank
1850–1865
W-RI-020

History: The Coventry Bank was incorporated in May 1850. It was formed as both a convenience and a business venture, catering to the mill workers who lived in the area. Its capital was $75,000 in 1853 but had decreased to $68,050 by 1855. By 1860 it had increased again to $100,000. Circulation was reported to be $26,530 in 1851 and $32,946 in 1863. Specie in 1857 was $2,134.87.

In 1865 the interests of the Coventry Bank were succeeded by the Coventry National Bank.

See also listing under Coventry, W-RI-230.

Numismatic Commentary: Genuine, circulated issues from this bank are very hard to locate. Seemingly, this bank did not issue $3 notes, as none are known, although this was a standard denomination for banks of the era.

VALID ISSUES

$1 • W-RI-020-001-G010
Left: 1 / Woman seated with spool, Factories. *Center:* Three women reclining in clouds. *Bottom center:* Anchor on shield. *Right:* 1 / George Washington on horseback. *Engraver:* Toppan, Carpenter, Casilear & Co. *Comments:* H-RI-10-G2, Durand-18. 18__. 1850s.
Rarity: *None known*

$1 • W-RI-020-001-G010a
Overprint: Red panel outlining white ONE. *Engraver:* Toppan, Carpenter, Casilear & Co. / ABNCo. monogram. *Comments:* H-RI-10-G2b, Durand-19. Similar to W-RI-020-001-G010 but with additional engraver imprint. 18__. 1850s–1860s.
Rarity: *None known*

$2 • W-RI-020-002-G020
Left: Three women with anchor looking upward / TWO. *Center:* Woman leaning on shield bearing anchor, Ships. *Bottom center:* Gears. *Right:* 2 / Portrait of Benjamin Franklin. *Engraver:* Toppan, Carpenter, Casilear & Co. *Comments:* H-RI-10-G4, Durand-20. 18__. 1850s.
Rarity: *None known*

$2 • W-RI-020-002-G020a   CJF

Overprint: Red panel outlining white TWO. *Engraver:* Toppan, Carpenter, Casilear & Co. / ABNCo. monogram. *Comments:* H-RI-10-G4b, Durand-21. Similar to W-RI-020-002-G020 but with additional engraver imprint. 18__. 1850s–1860s.
Rarity: URS-3
VF $1,200

$5 • W-RI-020-005-G030
Left: 5 / Woman standing. *Center:* Eagle with shield / FIVE. *Right:* 5 / Helmeted man with pole and cap. *Engraver:* Toppan, Carpenter, Casilear & Co. *Comments:* H-RI-10-G6, Durand-26. 18__. 1850s.
Rarity: *None known*

$5 • W-RI-020-005-G040
Left: 5 / Woman seated. *Center:* Woman on strongbox, Child and dog. *Bottom center:* Sheaf and plow. *Right:* Indian woman seated as Liberty. *Engraver:* Toppan, Carpenter, Casilear & Co. *Comments:* H-RI-10-G8, Durand-24. 18__. 1850s.
Rarity: *None known*

$5 • W-RI-020-005-G040a
Overprint: Red panel outlining white FIVE. *Engraver:* Toppan, Carpenter, Casilear & Co. / ABNCo. monogram. *Comments:* H-RI-10-G8a, Durand-25. Similar to W-RI-020-005-G030 but with additional engraver imprint. 18__. 1850s–1860s.
Rarity: *None known*

$10 • W-RI-020-010-G050
Left: 10 / Man seated with tablet. *Center:* Commerce seated / Female portrait. *Bottom center:* Dog and strongbox. *Right:* Three women standing with arms clasped. *Engraver:* Toppan, Carpenter, Casilear & Co. *Comments:* H-RI-10-G10, Durand-30. 18__. 1850s–1860s.
Rarity: *None known*

$20 • W-RI-020-020-G060
Left: 20 / Train. *Center:* Cherubs flanking seated Justice. *Bottom center:* Steamship. *Right:* 20 / Ceres. *Engraver:* Toppan, Carpenter, Casilear & Co. *Comments:* H-RI-10-G12, Durand-33. 18__. 1850s–1860s.
Rarity: *None known*

$50 • W-RI-020-050-G070
Left: 50 / Ceres / 50. *Center:* Commerce and Industry. *Bottom center:* Train. *Right:* 50 / Boy gathering corn. *Engraver:* Toppan, Carpenter, Casilear & Co. *Comments:* H-RI-10-G14, Durand-34. 18__. 1850s–1860s.
Rarity: *None known*

$100 • W-RI-020-100-G080
Left: Sailor seated / 100. *Center:* Woman and cherub in clouds. *Bottom center:* Gears. *Right:* 100 / Ship / 100. *Engraver:* Toppan, Carpenter, Casilear & Co. *Comments:* H-RI-10-G16, Durand-35. 18__. 1850s–1860s.
Rarity: *None known*

NON-VALID ISSUES

$3 • W-RI-020-003-R010
Engraver: Toppan, Carpenter, Casilear & Co. *Comments:* H-RI-10-R3, Durand-22. Raised from W-RI-020-001-G010. 1850s.
Rarity: *None known*

$3 • W-RI-020-003-R020
Engraver: Toppan, Carpenter, Casilear & Co. *Comments:* H-Unlisted, Durand-23. Raised from W-RI-020-002-G020. 1850s.
Rarity: URS-3

$5 • W-RI-020-005-C030
Engraver: Toppan, Carpenter, Casilear & Co. *Comments:* H-RI-10-C6, Durand-27. Counterfeit of W-RI-020-005-G030. 18__. 1850s.
Rarity: URS-2
VF $250

$5 • W-RI-020-005-R030
Engraver: Toppan, Carpenter, Casilear & Co. *Comments:* H-Unlisted, Durand-28. Raised from W-RI-020-001-G010. 1850s.
Rarity: URS-3

$5 • W-RI-020-005-R040
Engraver: Toppan, Carpenter, Casilear & Co. *Comments:* H-RI-10-R6, Durand-29. Raised from W-RI-020-002-G020. 1850s.
Rarity: *None known*

$10 • W-RI-020-010-R050
Engraver: Toppan, Carpenter, Casilear & Co. *Comments:* H-RI-10-R10, Durand-31. Raised from W-RI-020-001-G010. 18__. 1850s–1860s.
Rarity: *None known*

$10 • W-RI-020-010-R060

Engraver: Toppan, Carpenter, Casilear & Co. *Comments:* H-RI-10-R11, Durand-32. Raised from W-RI-020-002-G020. 1850s.

Rarity: *None known*

ASHAWAY, RHODE ISLAND

Ashaway is a village in the town of Hopkinton, which separated from Westerly in 1757.

See also Hopkinton and Westerly, Rhode Island.

Ashaway Bank
1855–1865
W-RI-030

History: The Ashaway Bank was chartered in 1855 in Hopkinton. Authorized capital was $75,000, where it remained throughout the bank's existence. Specie was listed at $1,442.80 in 1857 and circulation was valued at $14,839, where it remained until 1863. In 1864 it doubled to $35,325. In May 1865, the bank's address changed to Ashaway, a district of Hopkinton. Its business was succeeded by the Ashaway National Bank.

See also listing under Hopkinton, W-RI-440.

VALID ISSUES

$2 • W-RI-030-002-G010

CJF

Overprint: Red TWO. *Comments:* H-Unlisted, Durand-37. July 9th, 1855. 1850s–1860s.

Rarity: URS-3
F $1,000; **VF** $2,500

BRISTOL, RHODE ISLAND

Named after Bristol, England, this seaport town was one of Rhode Island's five state capitals until 1854. Boat-building and other sea-related industries made up the commerce for the town, as did manufacturing.

The first battle in King Philip's War took place in the area later called Bristol. After the conflict, the town was officially settled in 1680. It was originally a part of Massachusetts until it was transferred to Rhode Island in 1747. During the Revolutionary War, Bristol was attacked twice. On October 7, 1775, British troops sailed into Bristol and demanded supplies. The town was bombarded when the residents refused to cooperate, and a second attack occurred there three years later.

Bank of Bristol
1800–1865
W-RI-045

History: The Bank of Bristol was chartered in June 1800 as a holding company for the Bristol Insurance Company. It also stored government deposits for the area. The bank opened on December 25 of that year. William Bradford was the bank's founding president, and its first cashier was Joseph Rawson. The bank's capital was divided into 800 shares of $100 each, amounting to $80,000. The same was raised to $120,000 by December 1813, and by 1847 it was $150,000. This value remained constant through 1864. Circulation was listed at almost $19,000 between 1849 and 1860, decreasing to $12,955 in 1862. Specie amounted to $3,148.03 in 1857.

The Bank of Bristol went into voluntary liquidation in 1865.[7]

Numismatic Commentary: The earliest of this bank's issues were printed from a copper plate engraved by William Hamlin. These are extremely hard to locate. Many other issues show an Indian (Philip of Mount Hope) with a bow in hand. Reprints of the original notes have the words "Rhode Island" to the left and right of the vignette.

VALID ISSUES

$1 • W-RI-045-001-G010

CC

Engraver: William Hamlin. *Comments:* H-RI-20-G4, Durand-43. 18__. 1800s–1810s.

Rarity: URS-3
VF $750; **EF** $1,000

$1 • W-RI-045-001-G020

Left: ONE / 1. *Center:* 1 / Philip of Mount Hope / Indian man standing, Mountain / 1. *Right:* RHODE ISLAND vertically. *Engraver:* Murray, Draper & Fairman. *Comments:* H-RI-20-G8, Durand-44. 18__. 1810s–1860s.

Rarity: URS-1
Proof $2,000

$1 • W-RI-045-001-G020a

Center: 1 / RHODE ISLAND / Philip of Mount Hope / Indian man standing, Mountain / 1. *Engraver:* Murray, Draper & Fairman. *Comments:* H-RI-20-G8a. Similar to W-RI-045-001-G020. 18__. 1810s–1860s.

Rarity: URS-3
VF $450; **Proof** $1,200

$2 • W-RI-045-002-G030   CC

Engraver: William Hamlin. *Comments:* H-RI-20-G12, Durand-45. 18__. 1800s–1810s.
Rarity: URS-3
VF $450

$2 • W-RI-045-002-G040

Left: II / 2. *Center:* 2 / Philip of Mount Hope / 2. *Engraver:* Murray, Draper, Fairman & Co. *Comments:* H-RI-20-G16, Durand-46. 18__. 1810s–1860s.
Rarity: *None known*

$2 • W-RI-045-002-G040a   CC

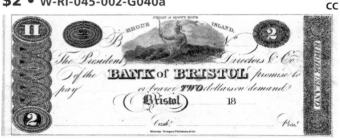

Engraver: Murray, Draper, Fairman & Co. *Comments:* H-RI-20-G16a. Similar to W-RI-045-002-G040. 18__. 1810s–1860s.
Rarity: URS-1
Proof $2,000

$3 • W-RI-045-003-G050   CC

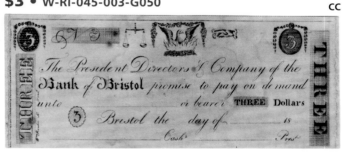

Engraver: William Hamlin. *Comments:* H-RI-20-G20, Durand-47. 18__. 1800s–1810s.
Rarity: URS-2
VF $1,050; Proof $1,500

$3 • W-RI-045-003-G060

Left: III / 3. *Center:* 3 / Philip of Mount Hope / 3. *Engraver:* Murray, Draper, Fairman & Co. *Comments:* H-RI-20-G24, Durand-48. 18__. 1810s–1860s.
Rarity: URS-3
Proof $1,200

$3 • W-RI-045-003-G060a   SBG

Engraver: Murray, Draper, Fairman & Co. *Comments:* H-RI-20-G24a. Similar to W-RI-045-003-G060. 18__. 1810s–1860s.
Rarity: URS-1
VF $450; Proof $1,500

$5 • W-RI-045-005-G070

Left: V FIVE V vertically. *Center:* Woman seated with 5 / 5 / Ship under sail. *Bottom center:* FIVE. *Right:* FIVE vertically. *Comments:* H-RI-20-G28, Durand-50. 1800s–1810s.
Rarity: URS-3
VF $550

$5 • W-RI-045-005-G080

Left: V / 5. *Center:* 5 / Philip of Mount Hope / 5. *Right:* RHODE ISLAND vertically. *Engraver:* Murray, Draper, Fairman & Co. *Comments:* H-RI-20-G32, Durand-51. 18__. 1810s–1860s.
Rarity: URS-3
VF $550

$5 • W-RI-045-005-G080a   CC

Engraver: Murray, Draper, Fairman & Co. *Comments:* H-RI-20-G32a. Similar to W-RI-045-005-G080. 18__. 1810s–1860s.
Rarity: URS-1
Proof $1,500

$10 • W-RI-045-010-G090

Left: TEN / 10. *Center:* 10 / Philip of Mount Hope / Indian man standing, Mountain / 10. *Right:* RHODE ISLAND vertically. *Engraver:* Murray, Draper, Fairman & Co. *Comments:* H-RI-20-G36, Durand-54. 18__. 1810s–1860s.
Rarity: *None known*

$20 • W-RI-045-020-G100

Left: TWENTY / 20. *Center:* 20 / Philip of Mount Hope / Indian man standing, Mountain / 20. *Right:* RHODE ISLAND vertically. *Engraver:* Murray, Draper, Fairman & Co. *Comments:* H-RI-20-G40, Durand-57. 18__. 1810s–1860s.
Rarity: *None known*

$30 • W-RI-045-030-G110

CC

Engraver: Murray, Draper, Fairman & Co. *Comments:* H-RI-20-G44, Durand-59. 18__. 1810s–1860s.

Rarity: URS-1
Proof $4,000

$50 • W-RI-045-050-G120

Left: FIFTY / 50. *Center:* 50 / Philip of Mount Hope / Indian man standing, Mountain / 50. *Right:* RHODE ISLAND vertically. *Engraver:* Murray, Draper, Fairman & Co. *Comments:* H-RI-20-G48, Durand-60. 18__. 1810s–1860s.

Rarity: *None known*

Uncut Sheets

$1-$2-$3-$5 • W-RI-045-001.002.003.005-US010

Vignette(s): ($1) Plow, Beehive, Phoenix. *($2)* Philip of Mount Hope. *($3)* Philip of Mount Hope. *($5)* Philip of Mount Hope. *Comments:* H-RI-20-G4, G16, G24, G32. 18__. 1810s–1860s.

Rarity: —
Selected auction price: Heritage,
January 2010, Lot 12903, Unc $2,070

Non-Valid Issues

$3 • W-RI-045-003-C060a

Comments: H-RI-20-C24a, Durand-49. Counterfeit of W-RI-045-003-G060a. 18__. 1841.

Rarity: *None known*

$5 • W-RI-045-005-C070

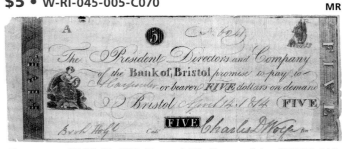

MR

Comments: H-RI-20-C28, Durand-52. Counterfeit of W-RI-045-005-G070. 1800s–1810s.

Rarity: URS-5
F $250; **VF** $1,500

$5 • W-RI-045-005-R010

Engraver: Murray, Draper, Fairman & Co. *Comments:* H-RI-20-R2, Durand-53. Raised from W-RI-045-001-G020. 18__. 1810s–1860s.

Rarity: *None known*

$10 • W-RI-045-010-R020

Engraver: Murray, Draper, Fairman & Co. *Comments:* H-RI-20-R4, Durand-55. Raised from W-RI-045-001-G020. 18__. 1810s–1860s.

Rarity: *None known*

$10 • W-RI-045-010-N010

Center: Spread eagle. *Comments:* H-RI-20-N5, Durand-56. 1810s–1860s.

Rarity: *None known*

$20 • W-RI-045-020-R030

Engraver: Murray, Draper, Fairman & Co. *Comments:* H-RI-20-R6, Durand-58. Raised from W-RI-045-001-G020. 18__. 1810s–1860s.

Rarity: *None known*

$50 • W-RI-045-050-R040

Engraver: Murray, Draper, Fairman & Co. *Comments:* H-RI-20-R8, Durand-61. Raised from W-RI-045-001-G020. 18__. 1810s–1860s.

Rarity: *None known*

Bristol Union Bank
1823–1831
W-RI-060

History: The Bristol Union Bank was chartered on October 28, 1823, with $50,000 in authorized capital. The rate of discount on its notes in the marketplace was five to eight percent at one point.

In 1830 this bank moved to Tiverton, and in 1831 its name was changed to the Fall River Union Bank, W-RI-1480.

Numismatic Commentary: All of this bank's notes were engraved and printed by Reed, Stiles, & Co. Genuine notes are hard to find. The $5 note shows an early scene of downtown Bristol.

Valid Issues

$1 • W-RI-060-001-G010

Left: ONE on dies vertically. *Center:* ONE / View of Bristol from the forest / 1. *Right:* RHODE ISLAND on dies vertically. *Comments:* H-RI-25-G4, Durand-2207. Jan. 1, 1824.

Rarity: URS-3
Proof $1,500

$2 • W-RI-060-002-G020

Left: 2 on dies vertically. *Center:* TWO / Harbor view / 2 / TWO. *Right:* RHODE ISLAND on dies vertically. *Comments:* H-RI-25-G8, Durand-2208. Jan. 1, 1824.

Rarity: URS-3
Proof $1,500

Collectors and Researchers:

If you have new information about any banks or notes listed in this volume, contact Whitman Publishing, Attn: Obsolete Paper Money, 3101 Clairmont Road, Suite G, Atlanta, GA 30329.

$3 • **W-RI-060-003-G030**

SBG

Comments: H-RI-25-G12, Durand-2209. Jan.y 1st, 1824.
Rarity: URS-3
Proof $1,700

$5 • **W-RI-060-005-G040**

Left: 5 on V on dies vertically. **Center:** FIVE / View of Bristol / 5. **Right:** RHODE ISLAND on dies vertically. **Comments:** H-RI-25-G16, Durand-2210. Jan. 1, 1824.
Rarity: URS-3
Proof $1,500

Non-Valid Issues

$10 • **W-RI-060-010-R010**

Comments: H-RI-25-R5, Durand-2211. Raised from W-RI-060-001-G010. Jan. 1, 1824.
Rarity: *None known*

Commercial Bank
1809–1869
W-RI-070

History: The Commercial Bank was incorporated in February 1809. One of the unusual clauses of its charter dictated that the bank directors were to serve on no other bank board. William D'Wolf was the bank's first president, and John Wardwell was its first cashier.

The capital was stated as $50,000 in 1813 and was raised to $75,000 by 1847. The same was reduced to $52,500 in May 1849. Circulation that year was $17,461. It increased to $22,628 between 1857 and 1863. Specie was reported to be $2,185.09 in 1857.

The bank failed by 1869, after the note-issuing era for state-chartered banks had ended.

Numismatic Commentary: This bank served the community for 60 years. Examples of its notes from many decades can still be found today. An interesting classical vignette, "Phoebus in the Chariot of the Sun," appears on a $100 issue. Non-valid issues are also plentiful.

Remaining in the American Bank Note Co. archives as of 2003 was a $1-$2-$5-$10 face plate and a $1-$2-$5-$10 tint plate.

Valid Issues

$1 • **W-RI-070-001-G010**

Left: ONE vertically / Eagle with shield on chest bearing 1. **Center:** ONE / Allegorical figure, barrels, bales. **Bottom center:** 1 in wreath. **Right:** State motto. **Comments:** H-RI-30-G2, Durand-62. 18__. 1809–1810s.
Rarity: URS-3
Proof $750

$1 • **W-RI-070-001-G010a**

Right: 1 / RHODE ISLAND / State motto. **Comments:** H-RI-30-G2a. Similar to W-RI-070-001-G010. 18__. 1820s.
Rarity: URS-3
VF $450

$1 • **W-RI-070-001-G020**

Left: ONE / Bust of George Washington / ONE. **Center:** 1 / Two blacksmiths at anvil in front of forge / 1 / Panel outlining white ONE. **Right:** ONE / Woman / ONE. **Engraver:** New England Bank Note Co. **Comments:** H-RI-30-G6. 18__. 1840s.
Rarity: *None known*

$1 • **W-RI-070-001-G030**

QDB

Engraver: New England Bank Note Co. **Comments:** H-RI-30-G7, Durand-63. 18__. 1840s–1860s.
Rarity: URS-1
VF $1,500

$1 • **W-RI-070-001-G040**

Left: ONE on 1 / Sailor. **Center:** Wharf. **Right:** 1 / Portrait of girl. **Tint:** Green panel and 1 / 1. **Engraver:** American Bank Note Co. **Comments:** H-RI-30-G9a, Durand-64. Proprietary Proofs exist. 18__. 1860s.
Rarity: URS-3
VF $1,500

$1.25 • **W-RI-070-001.25-G050**

Left: 1 25/100 / Train / 1 25/100. **Center:** Ship and sailing vessels on sea. **Right:** 1 25/100 / Eagle. **Engraver:** New England Bank Note Co. **Comments:** H-RI-30-G13, Durand-67. 18__. 1830s–1840s.
Rarity: URS-3
VF $750

$1.50 • **W-RI-070-001.50-G060**

Left: 1 Doll. 50 Cts. vertically. **Center:** Eagle on rock / $1 50/100. **Right:** 1 50/100 / Justice. **Engraver:** New England Bank Note Co. **Comments:** H-RI-30-G14, Durand-68. 18__. 1830s–1840s.
Rarity: *None known*

$1.75 • **W-RI-070-001.75-G070**

Left: $1.75 Cts / Hebe watering eagle / 1 75/100. **Center:** Three sloops at sea. **Right:** Agriculture, 1 75/100. **Engraver:** New England Bank Note Co. **Comments:** H-RI-30-G15, Durand-69. 18__. 1830s–1840s.
Rarity: *None known*

$2 • **W-RI-070-002-G080**

Left: TWO vertically. **Center:** TWO / Allegorical figure, Barrels, bales, and buildings. **Right:** State motto / 2. **Comments:** H-RI-30-G18, Durand-70. 18__. 1809–1810s.
Rarity: URS-3
VF $450

$2 • W-RI-070-002-G080a

Right: 2 / State motto / 2. *Comments:* H-RI-30-G18a. Similar to W-RI-070-002-G080. 18__. 1820s.

Rarity: URS-3
VF $450

$2 • W-RI-070-002-G090

Left: TWO / Woman with hand on cheek / 2. *Center:* 2 / Woman giving drink to one of two seated men / 2 / Panel outlining white TWO. *Right:* TWO / Female portrait. *Engraver:* New England Bank Note Co. *Comments:* H-RI-30-G21. 18__. 1840s.

Rarity: *None known*

$2 • W-RI-070-002-G100

Left: TWO / Farmer in field / TWO. *Center:* 2 / Naval engagement, ships of war, men in boats / 2. *Bottom center:* Anchor and HOPE on shield *Right:* 2 / Male portrait. *Engraver:* New England Bank Note Co. *Comments:* H-RI-30-G22, Durand-72. 18__. 1840s–1850s.

Rarity: *None known*

$2 • W-RI-070-002-G110   CJF

Engraver: New England Bank Note Co. *Comments:* H-RI-30-G26, Durand-71. 18__. 1860s.

Rarity: URS-3
VF $1,000

$2 • W-RI-070-002-G120   SBG

Tint: Green panel of 2s. *Back:* Green. *Engraver:* American Bank Note Co. *Comments:* H-RI-30-G28a, Durand-73. Proof. Proprietary Proofs exist. May 1st, 1866. 1860s.

Rarity: URS-3
VF $1,700; **Proof** $1,500

$2 • W-RI-070-002-G130

Center: 2 / Allegorical woman holding urn / 2. *Right:* TWO / Sailor / TWO. *Overprint:* Red TWO. *Comments:* H-Unlisted, Durand-78. 1850s–1860s.

Rarity: URS-3

$3 • W-RI-070-003-G140

Left: THREE vertically. *Center:* THREE DOL.S / Justice seated by bales, Barrels and Ships. *Bottom center:* 3. *Right:* Eagle with shield. *Comments:* H-RI-30-G32, Durand-79. 18__. 1809–1810s.

Rarity: URS-3
VF $450

$3 • W-RI-070-003-G140a

Right: 3 / Eagle with shield. *Comments:* H-RI-30-G32a. Similar to W-RI-070-003-G140. 18__. 1820s.

Rarity: URS-3
VF $450

$3 • W-RI-070-003-G150

Left: THREE vertically / 3. *Center:* Wharf scene. *Right:* 3 / THREE / Train / 3. *Engraver:* New England Bank Note Co. *Comments:* H-RI-30-G34, Durand-80. 18__. 1840s–1860s.

Rarity: URS-3
VF $550

$3 • W-RI-070-003-G160

Left: THREE / Man standing with sickle / 3 on THREE. *Center:* 3 / Woman with eagle / 3. *Right:* THREE / Sailor standing with pail / 3 on THREE. *Comments:* H-Unlisted. 1840s–1860s.

Rarity: —

$5 • W-RI-070-005-G170

Left: FIVE vertically / Shield with anchor. *Center:* Liberty seated / 5. *Bottom center:* 5. *Right:* Eagle with shield bearing 5. *Comments:* H-RI-30-G38, Durand-86. 18__. 1809–1810s.

Rarity: URS-3
VF $450

$5 • W-RI-070-005-G170a

Right: 5 / Eagle with shield bearing 5. *Comments:* H-RI-30-G38a. Similar to W-RI-070-005-G170. 18__. 1820s.

Rarity: *None known*

$5 • W-RI-070-005-G180

Left: 5 / FIVE / 5. *Center:* V / Eagle / V. *Right:* 5 / FIVE / 5. *Engraver:* New England Bank Note Co. *Comments:* H-RI-30-G42, Durand-65. 18__. 1840s.

Rarity: URS-3
VF $550

$5 • W-RI-070-005-G190

Left: Eagle on shield and anchor, Factories and ships / FIVE. *Center:* V / Woman and cherub. *Right:* 5 / Girl with basket of flowers. *Engraver:* New England Bank Note Co. *Comments:* H-RI-30-G44, Durand-88. 18__. 1850s–1860s.

Rarity: *None known*

$5 • W-RI-070-005-G190a

Overprint: Red FIVE. *Engraver:* New England Bank Note Co. *Comments:* H-Unlisted, Durand-90. Similar to W-RI-070-005-G190. 18__. 1850s–1860s.

Rarity: URS-3

$5 • W-RI-070-005-G200

Left: 5 / Liberty with child at her feet. *Center:* 5 / Portrait of General Ambrose Burnside / 5. *Right:* 5 / Woman seated with spyglass. *Tint:* Green panel and 5, 5. *Back:* Green. *Engraver:* American Bank Note Co. *Comments:* H-RI-30-G46a, Durand-87. 18__. 1860s.

Rarity: —

Selected auction price: Heritage, September 2011, Lot 15801, Choice Unc $575

$10 • W-RI-070-010-G210

SBG

Comments: H-RI-30-G50, Durand-96. 18__. 1809–1810s.

Rarity: URS-3
Proof $900

$10 • W-RI-070-010-G210a

Left: 10 / TEN vertically / State arms. *Center:* TEN / Allegorical woman reclining with cornucopia. *Bottom center:* 10. *Right:* Eagle with shield bearing 10. *Comments:* H-RI-30-G51, Durand-97. Similar to W-RI-070-010-G210. 18__. 1820s.

Rarity: URS-3
Proof $750

$10 • W-RI-070-010-G220

Left: Mechanic seated with tools, train and building / TEN. *Center:* X. *Right:* 10 / Reaper standing with sheaf on knee. *Engraver:* New England Bank Note Co. *Comments:* H-RI-30-G54, Durand-98. 18__. 1840s–1850s.

Rarity: URS-3
VF $750

$10 • W-RI-070-010-G220a

Tint: Red panel and TEN. *Engraver:* New England Bank Note Co. *Comments:* H-RI-30-G54a. Similar to W-RI-070-010-G220. 18__. 1850s.

Rarity: URS-3
VF $750

$10 • W-RI-070-010-G220b

Tint: Red panel and TEN. *Engraver:* New England Bank Note Co. / ABNCo. monogram. *Comments:* H-RI-30-G54b. Similar to W-RI-070-010-G220 but with additional engraver imprint. 18__. 1850s–1860s.

Rarity: *None known*

$10 • W-RI-070-010-G230

CJF

Back: Green. *Engraver:* American Bank Note Co. *Comments:* H-RI-30-G56a, Durand-99. 18__. 1860s.

Rarity: URS-3
VF $1,500

$20 • W-RI-070-020-G240

CJF

Engraver: New England Bank Note Co. *Comments:* H-RI-30-G60, Durand-105. 18__. 1840s–1860s.

Rarity: URS-1
VF $1,500

$50 • W-RI-070-050-G250

Left: FIFTY / Eagle with shield / DOLLARS vertically. *Center:* 50 / Sailing ship. *Engraver:* P. Maverick. *Comments:* H-RI-30-G61, Durand-107. 18__. 1809–1810s.

Rarity: URS-3
VF $450

$50 • W-RI-070-050-G260

Left: FIFTY / Allegorical figure / FIFTY. *Center:* 50 / Man restraining prancing horse / 50. *Right:* FIFTY / Allegorical figure / FIFTY. *Engraver:* New England Bank Note Co. *Comments:* H-RI-30-G63, Durand-108. 18__. 1840s–1860s.

Rarity: URS-3
VF $450

$100 • W-RI-070-100-G270

Left: 100 / Eagle / 100. *Center:* "Phoebus in Chariot of the Sun". *Right:* C / Portrait of George Washington / C. *Engraver:* New England Bank Note Co. *Comments:* H-RI-30-G66, Durand-109. 18__. 1850s–1860s.

Rarity: *None known*

NON-VALID ISSUES

$1 • W-RI-070-001-C010

Comments: H-RI-30-C2. Counterfeit of W-RI-070-001-G010. 18__. 1820s.

Rarity: *None known*

$1 • W-RI-070-001-A010
Left: ONE / Reaper standing under tree. *Center:* Three horses drinking at well. *Right:* 1 / Sailor with spyglass. *Engraver:* Danforth, Wright & Co. *Comments:* H-RI-30-A5, Durand-65. Altered from $1 Commercial Bank of New Jersey, Perth Amboy, New Jersey series. July 10, 1856.
Rarity: URS-3
VF $250

$1 • W-RI-070-001-A020
Comments: H-Unlisted, Durand-66. Altered from a higher-denomination Commercial Bank of Millington, Millington, Maryland. 18__. 1840s.
Rarity: URS-3
VF $100

$1.25 • W-RI-070-001.25-A030
Left: 1 25/100 / Train / 1 25/100. *Center:* Ships and sailing ships on ocean / $1.25 Cts. *Right:* 1 25/100 / Eagle. *Engraver:* New England Bank Note Co. *Comments:* H-RI-30-A10. Altered from $1.25 Roxbury Bank, Roxbury, Massachusetts, or from notes of other failed banks using the same plate. 18__. 1850s.
Rarity: URS-3
VF $375

$1.50 • W-RI-070-001.50-A040
Left: 1 Doll 50 Cts. vertically. *Center:* Eagle on rock in ocean / $1 50/100. *Right:* 1 50/100 / Justice. *Engraver:* New England Bank Note Co. *Comments:* H-RI-30-A11. Altered from $1.50 Roxbury Bank, Roxbury, Massachusetts, or from notes of other failed banks using the same plate. 18__. 1850s.
Rarity: *None known*

$1.75 • W-RI-070-001.75-A050
Left: $1.75 Cts. / Hebe watering eagle / 1 75/100. *Center:* Three sloops at sea. *Right:* $1.75 Cts. / Woman seated with grain, Dog / 1 75/100. *Engraver:* New England Bank Note Co. *Comments:* H-RI-30-A12. Altered from $1.75 Roxbury Bank, Roxbury, Massachusetts, or from notes of other failed banks using the same plate. 18__. 1850s.
Rarity: *None known*

$2 • W-RI-070-002-C080
Comments: H-RI-30-C18, Durand-74. Counterfeit of W-RI-070-002-G080. 18__. 1820s.
Rarity: URS-3
VF $250

$2 • W-RI-070-002-A060
Left: 2 / Farm scene, Man on horse / TWO. *Center:* Train passing cliffs, Men working. *Right:* 2 / Vessels near shore. *Engraver:* New England Bank Note Co. *Comments:* H-RI-30-A25, Durand-75. Altered from $2 Commercial Bank, Gratiot, Michigan. 18__. 1840s.
Rarity: URS-3
VF $250

$2 • W-RI-070-002-A070
Left: TWO / Woman feeding chickens. *Center:* Steamship and sailing ship. *Right:* 2 / Indian woman by a stream. *Engraver:* Danforth, Wright & Co. *Comments:* H-RI-30-A30, Durand-76. Altered from $2 Commercial Bank of New Jersey, Perth Amboy, New Jersey series. 18__. 1850s.
Rarity: *None known*

$2 • W-RI-070-002-A080
Comments: H-Unlisted, Durand-77. Altered from a higher-denomination Commercial Bank of Millington, Millington, Maryland. 18__. 1840s.
Rarity: URS-3
VF $100

$3 • W-RI-070-003-C140

CJF

Comments: H-RI-30-C32, Durand-81. Counterfeit of W-RI-070-003-G140. 18__. 1820s.
Rarity: URS-3
VF $250

$3 • W-RI-070-003-A090
Left: 3 / Portrait of George Washington / THREE. *Center:* Steamship and other vessels. *Right:* 3 / Hebe watering eagle. *Engraver:* New England Bank Note Co. *Comments:* H-RI-30-A40, Durand-82. Altered from $3 Commercial Bank, Gratiot, Michigan. 18__. 1840s.
Rarity: *None known*

$3 • W-RI-070-003-A100
Left: Two men and woman / THREE. *Center:* Woman holding key with arm around eagle / State arms of New Jersey. *Right:* 3 / Woman standing beside bale, barrel, and anchor. *Comments:* H-Unlisted, Durand-83. Altered from $3 Commercial Bank of Perth Amboy, Perth Amboy, New Jersey. 18__. 1850s.
Rarity: URS-3
F $75

$3 • W-RI-070-003-A110
Left: 3 / Train / 3. *Center:* THREE / Sailing ship / THREE. *Right:* 3 / "George Washington at Dorchester Heights". *Comments:* H-Unlisted, Durand-84. Altered from $5 Commercial Bank of Gratiot, Gratiot, Michigan. 18__. 1840s.
Rarity: URS-3
F $75

$3 • W-RI-070-003-A120
Comments: H-Unlisted, Durand-85. Altered from higher-denomination Commercial Bank of Millington, Millington, Maryland. 18__. 1840s.
Rarity: URS-3

$3 • W-RI-070-003-N010
Left: 3 / Train / 3. *Center:* THREE / Sailing ship / THREE. *Right:* 3 / "George Washington at Dorchester Heights". *Comments:* H-RI-30-N5, Durand-84. Altered from $5 Commercial Bank of Gratiot, Gratiot, Michigan. 18__. 1840s.
Rarity: *None known*

$5 • W-RI-070-005-C170a
Comments: H-RI-30-C38a. Counterfeit of W-RI-070-005-G170a. 18__. 1810.
Rarity: URS-3
VF $250

$5 • W-RI-070-005-C190
Engraver: New England Bank Note Co. *Comments:* H-RI-30-C44. Counterfeit of W-RI-070-005-G190. 18__. 1850s.
Rarity: URS-3
VF $250

$5 • W-RI-070-005-A130
Left: FIVE / Cornucopia / Woman standing. *Center:* 5 / Reaping scene, Farm and mill / V. *Right:* FIVE / Cornucopia / Woman standing. *Engraver:* Draper, Underwood, Bald & Spencer. *Comments:* H-RI-30-A45. Altered from $5 Commercial Bank of Millington, Millington, Maryland. 18__. 1840s.
Rarity: *None known*

$5 • W-RI-070-005-A140
Left: FIVE vertically. *Center:* 5 / Amphitrite and Neptune in shell drawn by sea horses / 5. *Right:* V / Canal scene / V. *Engraver:* Rawdon, Wright, Hatch & Co. *Comments:* H-RI-30-A50, Durand-92. Altered from $5 Commercial Bank of Millington, Millington, Maryland. 18__. 1852.
Rarity: URS-3
VF $250

$5 • W-RI-070-005-A140a
Center: 5 / Spread eagle on rock in ocean / 5. *Comments:* H-Unlisted, Durand-93. Similar to W-RI-070-005-A140. 18__. 1852.
Rarity: URS-3

$5 • W-RI-070-005-A150
Left: 5 / Train / 5. *Center:* FIVE / Sailing ship / FIVE. *Right:* 5 / "George Washington at Dorchester Heights". *Comments:* H-RI-30-A55, Durand-89. Altered from $5 Commercial Bank, Gratiot, Michigan. 18__. 1840s.
Rarity: URS-3
VF $250

$5 • W-RI-070-005-A150a
Overprint: Red FIVE. *Comments:* H-RI-30-A55a. Similar to W-RI-070-005-A150. 18__. 1850s.
Rarity: URS-3
VF $250

$5 • W-RI-070-005-A160
Left: 5 / Ship under sail. *Center:* Whaling scene, men in boat. *Right:* 5 / Portrait of sailor. *Engraver:* Danforth, Wright & Co. *Comments:* H-RI-30-A60, Durand-91. Altered from $5 Commercial Bank of New Jersey, Perth Amboy, New Jersey. 18__. 1850s.
Rarity: *None known*

$5 • W-RI-070-005-A170
Left: Men driving cattle across river / 5. *Center:* 5 / Men haying, Wagon and oxen. *Right:* 5. *Tint:* Brown-orange lathework outlining white 5. *Engraver:* Bald, Cousland & Co. *Comments:* H-RI-30-A65, Durand-94. Altered from $5 Pioneer Association, La Fayette, Indiana. 18__. 1850s.
Rarity: *None known*

$10 • W-RI-070-010-C220a
Engraver: New England Bank Note Co. *Comments:* H-RI-30-C54a, Durand-100. Counterfeit of W-RI-070-010-G220a. 18__. 1850s.
Rarity: *None known*

$10 • W-RI-070-010-C220b   CC

Tint: Red panel and TEN. *Engraver:* New England Bank Note Co. / ABNCo. monogram. *Comments:* H-RI-30-C54b. Counterfeit of W-RI-070-010-G220b. 186_. 1860s.
Rarity: URS-1
F $900

$10 • W-RI-070-010-AR010
Left: TEN / Reaper standing under tree. *Center:* Three horses drinking at well. *Right:* 10 / Sailor with spyglass. *Engraver:* Danforth, Wright & Co. *Comments:* H-RI-30-AR80, Durand-104. Altered and raised from $1 Commercial Bank of New Jersey, Perth Amboy, New Jersey series. 18__. 1850s.
Rarity: *None known*

$10 • W-RI-070-010-A180
Left: TEN / Fortuna standing. *Center:* Gears / Sailing ship / Produce. *Right:* 10 / Wharf scene. *Comments:* H-Unlisted, Durand-101. Altered from $10 Commercial Bank, Gratiot, Michigan. 18__. 1840s.
Rarity: URS-3
F $90

$10 • W-RI-070-010-A190
Left: X / Bacchus medallion head / 10. *Center:* 10 on die / Woman seated by sea with pen and scroll / Mercury offering money bag / Neptune in sea chariot / 10 on die. *Right:* 10 / Bacchus medallion head / X. *Engraver:* Rawdon, Wright, Hatch & Co. *Comments:* H-RI-30-A70, Durand-102. Altered from $10 Commercial Bank of Millington, Millington, Maryland. 18__. 1840s.
Rarity: URS-3
VF $250

$10 • W-RI-070-010-A200
Left: TEN / Helmeted woman standing with lyre. *Center:* Gears / Sailing ship / Produce. *Right:* 10 / Wharf scene. *Engraver:* New England Bank Note Co. *Comments:* H-RI-30-A75. Altered from $10 Commercial Bank, Gratiot, Michigan. 18__. 1840s.
Rarity: *None known*

$10 • W-RI-070-010-A210

Left: TEN vertically. *Center:* 10 on die / Liberty, Spinning wheel and shield / 10 on die. *Right:* Diagonal X on panel. *Comments:* H-Unlisted, Durand-103. Altered from $1 Commercial Bank of New Jersey, Perth Amboy, New Jersey. 18__. 1850s.

Rarity: URS-3

F $90

$20 • W-RI-070-020-A220

Left: 20 / Female medallion head / 20. *Center:* Eagle / Justice and Liberty flanking shield surmounted by eagle / Ships. *Right:* 20 / Female medallion head / 20. *Engraver:* Draper, Underwood, Bald & Spencer. *Comments:* H-RI-30-A85, Durand-106. Altered from $20 Commercial Bank of Millington, Millington, Maryland. 18__. 1840s.

Rarity: URS-1

Commercial Bank of Bristol
1840s
W-RI-080

History: A non-existent bank represented only by notes altered from those of other banks. The notes were intended to pass for those of the Commercial Bank, W-RI-070.

ISSUES

$10 • W-RI-080-010-A010

Left: TEN vertically. *Center:* 10 / Woman seated / 10. *Bottom center:* Female portrait. *Right:* Die / X on die / Die. *Engraver:* Rawdon, Wright, Hatch & Co. *Comments:* H-RI-31-A10. Altered from $10 Commercial Bank of Millington, Millington, Maryland. 18__. 1840s.

Rarity: URS-3

VF $200

Eagle Bank
1818–1865
W-RI-090

History: The Eagle Bank was chartered in February 1818. By 1848 its capital was $50,000, and by 1850 it had increased to $75,000. It was reduced to $50,000 by 1860. Circulation in 1848 was $36,207, and specie was $2,986.03 in 1857. In 1850 rumors circulated to the effect that the public might be defrauded by the action of the bank's management, and the General Assembly appointed a committee to investigate. In 1851 the Suffolk Bank clearing house refused to handle the bank's notes.[8] All eventually turned out well, however, and the bank continued in business.

The interests of the Eagle Bank were succeeded by the Eagle National Bank in 1865.

Numismatic Commentary: The title on some of the PSSP / New England Bank Note Co. issues reads: "The Eagle Bank of Bristol, RI." All notes from this bank are extremely rare. Uncut sheets are reported to exist.

VALID ISSUES

$1 • W-RI-090-001-G010   SBG

Engraver: Reed. *Comments:* H-RI-35-G4, Durand-110. First issue. Proof. 18__. 1818–1820s.

Rarity: URS-3

VF $250; **Proof** $1,600

$1 • W-RI-090-001-G020

Left: 1 / Minerva standing with 1 / 1. *Center:* ONE / Commerce seated with caduceus and cornucopia, Plow and ships / ONE. *Bottom center:* Ruling machine. *Right:* 1 / Eagle / 1. *Engraver:* PSSP. *Comments:* H-RI-35-G6. 18__. 1830s.

Rarity: —

Selected auction price: Stack's Bowers Galleries, January 2012, Lot 5173, Unc $2,587

$1 • W-RI-090-001-G030

Left: 1 / Woman wearing bonnet, standing by pail / ONE. *Center:* Machinery and merchandise flanking Ceres holding sickle and rake, Factories and harbor / ONE / Panel outlining white ONE. *Bottom center:* Ruling machine. *Right:* 1 / Ship / ONE. *Engraver:* PSSP / New England Bank Note Co. *Comments:* H-RI-35-G8. 18__. 1830s–1840s.

Rarity: *None known*

$1 • W-RI-090-001-G040   SBG

Engraver: Danforth & Hufty. *Comments:* H-RI-35-G10, Durand-111. Proof. January 1st, 1848. 1840s.

Rarity: URS-3

Proof $1,200

$2 • W-RI-090-002-G050

BH

Engraver: Reed. *Comments:* H-RI-35-G13. 18__. 1818–1820s.

Rarity: URS-3

Proof $750

$2 • W-RI-090-002-G060

Left: 2 / Hebe watering eagle / 2. *Center:* 2 / Plow, Commerce seated on shore, Cornucopia / 2. *Bottom center:* Woman swimming. *Right:* 2 / Justice standing / 2. *Engraver:* PSSP. *Comments:* H-RI-35-G14. 18__. 1830s.

Rarity: *None known*

$2 • W-RI-090-002-G070

Left: 2 / Woman standing with staff, Cornucopia / TWO. *Center:* TWO / Machinery and merchandise flanking Ceres holding sickle and rake, Factories and harbor / Panel outlining white TWO. *Right:* 2 / Woman wearing hat, Trees / TWO. *Engraver:* PSSP / New England Bank Note Co. *Comments:* H-RI-35-G15. 18__. 1830s–1840s.

Rarity: *None known*

$2 • W-RI-090-002-G080

SBG

Engraver: Danforth & Hufty. *Comments:* H-RI-35-G16, Durand-112. January 1st, 1848. 1840s.

Rarity: URS-3

Proof $1,200

$2 • W-RI-090-002-G080a

CC

Overprint: Red TWO. *Engraver:* Danforth & Hufty. *Comments:* H-Unlisted, Durand-Unlisted. Similar to W-RI-090-002-G080. January 1st, 18__. 1850s.

Rarity: URS-3

F $350; **VF** $1,200

$3 • W-RI-090-003-G090

SBG

Engraver: Reed. *Comments:* H-RI-35-G18, Durand-113. First issue. 18__. 1818–1820s.

Rarity: URS-3

Proof $750

$3 • W-RI-090-003-G100

Left: 3 / Eagle on rock / 3. *Center:* 3 / Commerce with caduceus and cornucopia, Plow, Ships / 3. *Right:* 3 / Woman standing with cornucopia / 3. *Engraver:* PSSP. *Comments:* H-RI-35-G20. 18__. 1830s.

Rarity: *None known*

$3 • W-RI-090-003-G110

Left: 3 / Beehive and foliage / THREE. *Center:* Machinery and merchandise flanking Ceres holding sickle and rake, Factories and harbor / THREE / Panel outlining white THREE. *Right:* 3 on THREE / Two reapers / 3 on THREE. *Engraver:* PSSP / New England Bank Note Co. *Comments:* H-RI-35-G22. 18__. 1830s–1840s.

Rarity: *None known*

$5 • W-RI-090-005-G120

Left: FIVE FIVE FIVE vertically. *Center:* 5 / Eagle with shield bearing 5 / 5. *Bottom center:* FIVE. *Right:* 5 FIVE DOLLARS 5 vertically. *Engraver:* Reed. *Comments:* H-RI-35-G24, Durand-115. First issue. 18__. 1818–1820s.

Rarity: URS-3

Proof $500

$5 • W-RI-090-005-G130

Left: Panel bearing FIVE / Plenty and Minerva seated / V. *Center:* FIVE / Allegorical woman / FIVE / Panel of microletters. *Right:* 5 / Eagle / 5. *Engraver:* PSSP. *Comments:* H-RI-35-G26. 18__. 1830s.

Rarity: *None known*

$5 • W-RI-090-005-G140

Left: 5 / Blacksmith at anvil / FIVE. *Center:* Mercury standing with 5, Cornucopia and merchandise, Factories and ship / V / Panel outlining white FIVE. *Right:* 5 / Ceres kneeling / FIVE. *Engraver:* Danforth & Hufty. *Comments:* H-RI-35-G28. Jan. 1, 1848. 1840s.

Rarity: *None known*

$5 • W-RI-090-005-G150

CC

Engraver: Danforth & Hufty. *Comments:* H-RI-35-G30, Durand-116. January 1st, 18__. 1840s–1850s.
Rarity: URS-3
Proof $1,200

$5 • W-RI-090-005-G150a

CC

Overprint: Red FIVE. *Engraver:* Danforth & Hufty. *Comments:* H-Unlisted, Durand-Unlisted. Similar to W-RI-090-005-G150. January 1st, 18__. 1850s.
Rarity: URS-3
VF $400

$10 • W-RI-090-010-G160
Left: Panel with TEN / Manhattan spilling water jug / TEN. *Center:* TEN / Ceres seated / TEN / Panel of microletters. *Right:* 10 / Portrait of Indian / 10. *Engraver:* PSSP. *Comments:* H-RI-35-G32. 18__. 1830s.
Rarity: *None known*

$10 • W-RI-090-010-G170
Left: 10 / Farmer sowing / TEN. *Center:* Helmeted man holding anchor and shield bearing 10, Merchandise, factories, and ship / Canal scene / Panel outlining white TEN. *Right:* 10 / Ship / TEN. *Back:* Black lathework and bank name. *Engraver:* PSSP / New England Bank Note Co. *Comments:* H-RI-35-G34a, Durand-118. 18__. 1830s–1840s.
Rarity: URS-3
VF $350

$20 • W-RI-090-020-G180
Left: 20 XX 20 vertically. *Center:* 20 / Liberty sitting on bales / 20. *Right:* TWENTY on lathework dies. *Back:* Brown-orange. *Engraver:* PSSP / New England Bank Note Co. *Comments:* H-RI-35-G36a, Durand-121. 18__. 1830s–1840s.
Rarity: *None known*

$50 • W-RI-090-050-G190
Left: 50 / Goddess of Plenty, Ship / 50. *Center:* FIFTY DOLLARS / 50. *Right:* FIFTY vertically. *Back:* Brown-orange. *Engraver:* PSSP / New England Bank Note Co. *Comments:* H-RI-35-G38a, Durand-124. 18__. 1830s–1850s.
Rarity: URS-3
VF $500

$100 • W-RI-090-100-G200
Left: C / Portrait of George Washington / C. *Center:* 100 / Manhattan pouring water from jug, Ship / 100. *Right:* ONE HUNDRED vertically. *Back:* Brown-orange. *Engraver:* PSSP / New England Bank Note Co. *Comments:* H-RI-35-G40a, Durand-125. 18__. 1830s–1850s.
Rarity: URS-3
VF $500

Uncut Sheets
$1-$1-$2-$5 • W-RI-090-001.001.002.005-US010
Vignette(s): (*$1*) Indian family overlooking cliff, Ships and city / Spread eagle / Ruling machine / Liberty, eagle, and shield. (*$1*) Indian family overlooking cliff, Ships and city / Spread eagle / Ruling machine / Liberty, eagle, and shield. (*$2*) Liberty standing / Eagle in clouds / Woman swimming / Two allegorical figures with shield bearing 2. (*$5*) Blacksmith at anvil / Mercury standing with 5, Cornucopia and merchandise, Factories and ship / Ceres kneeling. *Engraver:* Danforth & Hufty. *Comments:* H-RI-35-G10, G10, G16, G30. Variously dated January 1st, 1848, January 1st, 1848, January 1st, 1848, January 1st, 18__. 1840s.
Rarity: URS-3
Proof $2,500

$1-$2-$3-$5 • W-RI-090-001.002.003.005-US020
Vignette(s): (*$1*) Eagle with shield bearing 1. (*$2*) Eagle bearing 2 / Woman swimming. (*$3*) Eagle with shield bearing 3. (*$5*) Eagle with shield bearing 5. *Engraver:* Reed. *Comments:* H-RI-35-G4, G13, G18, G24. 18__. 1818–1820s.
Rarity: URS-3
Proof $2,500

NON-VALID ISSUES
$3 • W-RI-090-003-A010
Left: 3 / Steamship. *Center:* Justice, Shield surmounted by eagle, Liberty. *Right:* 3 / Train. *Overprint:* Red THREE. *Engraver:* Baldwin, Bald & Cousland / Bald, Cousland & Co. *Comments:* H-RI-35-A5, Durand-114. Altered from W-RI-1500-003-G030a. 18__. 1850s.
Rarity: *None known*

$5 • W-RI-090-005-R010
Engraver: Danforth & Hufty. *Comments:* H-RI-35-R5, Durand-117. Raised from W-RI-090-001-G040. Jan. 1, 1848. 1840s.
Rarity: *None known*

$10 • W-RI-090-010-R020
Engraver: Danforth & Hufty. *Comments:* H-RI-35-R6, Durand-119. Raised from W-RI-090-001-G040. Jan. 1, 1848. 1840s.
Rarity: URS-3
VF $200

$10 • W-RI-090-010-A020
Left: 10 / Portrait of George Washington held by cherub / 10. *Center:* X / Spread eagle and American shield / X. *Right:* 10 / Indian and woman / 10. *Engraver:* Terry, Pelton & Co. *Comments:* H-RI-35-A10, Durand-120. Altered from $10 Citizens Bank, Augusta, Maine, or from notes of other failed banks using the same plate. 18__. 1850s.
Rarity: URS-3
VF $200

$10 • W-RI-090-010-N010

Center: Indian with tomahawk. *Engraver:* Murray, Draper, Fairman & Co. *Comments:* H-RI-35-N5. 18___. 1810s–1860s.

Rarity: *None known*

$20 • W-RI-090-020-A030

Left: 20 / 20. *Center:* 20 / Philip of Mount Hope / 20. *Right:* RHODE ISLAND vertically. *Comments:* H-RI-35-A15, Durand-122. Altered from W-RI-045-002-G040a. 1810s–1860s.

Rarity: *None known*

$20 • W-RI-090-020-N020

Center: Woman, tools. *Right:* Steamboat. *Comments:* H-RI-35-N10, Durand-123. 1810s–1860s.

Rarity: *None known*

Freemans Bank
1850s
W-RI-100

History: A non-existent bank represented only by notes altered from those of other banks. The notes were intended to pass for those of the Freemens Bank, W-RI-110.

ISSUES

$1 • W-RI-100-001-A010

Left: ONE / 1. *Center:* 1 / Two women seated with shield, 1. *Bottom center:* Cattle. *Right:* 1 / Portrait of George Washington / ONE. *Engraver:* Terry, Pelton & Co. *Comments:* H-RI-39-A5. Altered from $1 Citizens Bank, Augusta, Maine, or from notes of other failed banks using the same plate. 18___. 1840s–1860s.

Rarity: URS-3
VF $200

$10 • W-RI-100-010-A020   SI

Engraver: Terry, Pelton & Co. *Comments:* H-RI-39-A10. 18___. 1840s.

Rarity: URS-3
VF $200

Freemens Bank
1817–1865
W-RI-110

History: The Freemens Bank was incorporated in 1817. Its office was located on lower State Street. Charles Collins served as its first president, and John West served as its first cashier. Circulation in 1818 was listed at $3,142, increasing to $36,939 in 1849 and to $25,453 in 1857. The capital in 1831 was valued at $67,000. On Saturday, November 22, 1862, the bank was entered by burglars using false keys, and more than $20,000 worth of bills, bonds, and securities was stolen. Notice was given to holders of bonds and securities, and the certificates were invalidated. Paper money imprinted with the bank name amounted to about $14,000, including $3,200 in uncut sheets signed by the president but not the cashier. A printing plate made by Abner Reed decades earlier was used to create a new issue of notes, now with a green overprint. Issues of the designs had been stolen but were no longer paid out. A "German" attempted to exchange $1,000 in bills in New York City, but he ran away and left the bills behind when a teller, who had heard of the robbery, questioned him.

The business of the bank was succeeded by the First National Bank of Bristol, chartered on June 16, 1865.

Numismatic Commentary: In February 1863, the Freemens Bank started issuing notes with a green pattern printed on the back to take the place of the older designs that had been stolen, as noted above. These notes were very distinct from the previous issue of notes that were stolen in the robbery. As such, they are particularly interesting to collect.

VALID ISSUES

$1 • W-RI-110-001-G010   CC

Engraver: Reed. *Comments:* H-RI-40-G2, Durand-126. 18___. 1817–1820s.

Rarity: URS-3
Proof $600

$1 • W-RI-110-001-G010a

Left: 1 RHODE ISLAND 1 vertically. *Center:* 1 / Spread eagle on rock / 1. *Bottom center:* ONE. *Right:* 1 ONE 1 vertically. *Overprint:* Red ONE. *Engraver:* Reed. *Comments:* H-RI-40-G2a, Durand-127. Similar to W-RI-110-001-G010. 18___. 1850s.

Rarity: URS-6
VF $300

$1 • W-RI-110-001-G010b   CC

Overprint: Ornate red ONE. *Engraver:* Reed / ABNCo. monogram. *Comments:* H-Unlisted, Durand-Unlisted. Similar to W-RI-110-001-G010 but with additional engraver imprint. 18__. 1860s.
Rarity: URS-6
VF $300

$1 • W-RI-110-001-G010c   CC, CC

Overprint: Green 1, ONE, 1. *Back:* Green lathework. *Engraver:* Reed / ABNCo. monogram. *Comments:* H-RI-40-G2c, Durand-128. Similar to W-RI-110-001-G010 but with additional engraver imprint. 18__. 1860s.
Rarity: URS-3
F $400; **VF** $450

$1 • W-RI-110-001-G020
Left: 1 / Two Indians / ONE. *Center:* 1 / Knowledge, Justice, and Liberty / 1. *Bottom center:* Cattle. *Right:* 1 / Portrait of George Washington / ONE. *Engraver:* Terry, Pelton & Co. *Comments:* H-RI-40-G6, Durand-129. Beware of altered notes of the same design. 18__. 1840s.
Rarity: *None known*

$2 • W-RI-110-002-G030
Left: 2 RHODE ISLAND 2 vertically. *Center:* 2 / Spread eagle on rock / 2. *Right:* 2 TWO 2 vertically. *Engraver:* Reed. *Comments:* H-RI-40-G10, Durand-131. 18__. 1817–1820s.
Rarity: URS-3
Proof $500

$2 • W-RI-110-002-G030a
Overprint: Red TWO. *Engraver:* Reed. *Comments:* H-RI-40-G10a, Durand-132. Similar to W-RI-110-002-G030. 18__. 1850s.
Rarity: URS-6
VF $250

$2 • W-RI-110-002-G030b   CC

Overprint: Ornate red TWO. *Engraver:* Reed / ABNCo. monogram. *Comments:* H-RI-40-G10b. Similar to W-RI-110-002-G030 but with additional engraver imprint. 18__. 1850s–1860s.
Rarity: URS-3
VF $350

$2 • W-RI-110-002-G030c   QDB, QDB

Overprint: Green 2, TWO, 2. *Back:* Green lathework. *Engraver:* Reed / ABNCo. monogram. *Comments:* H-RI-40-G10c, Durand-133. Similar to W-RI-110-002-G030 but with additional engraver imprint. 18__. 1860s.
Rarity: URS-5
VF $250

$2 • W-RI-110-002-G040
Left: TWO / Portrait of cherub / 2. *Center:* 2 / Ceres giving grain to seated Liberty, Ships / 2. *Bottom center:* Anchor and implements. *Right:* 2 / Female portrait / TWO. *Engraver:* Terry, Pelton & Co. *Comments:* H-RI-40-G14, Durand-134. Beware of altered notes of the same design. 18__. 1840s.
Rarity: *None known*

$3 • W-RI-110-003-G050   CC

Engraver: Reed. *Comments:* H-RI-40-G18, Durand-139. 18__.
1817–1820s.

Rarity: URS-2

Proof $1,700

$3 • W-RI-110-003-G050a

Left: 3 RHODE ISLAND 3 vertically. *Center:* 3 / Eagle / 3. *Bottom center:* THREE. *Right:* 3 THREE 3 vertically. *Overprint:*
Red THREE. *Engraver:* Reed. *Comments:* H-RI-40-G18a,
Durand-138. Similar to W-RI-110-003-G050. 18__. 1850s.

Rarity: URS-6

VF $250

$3 • W-RI-110-003-G050b

Overprint: Red THREE. *Engraver:* Reed / ABNCo. monogram.
Comments: H-RI-40-G18b. Similar to W-RI-110-003-G050 but
with additional engraver imprint. 18__. 1850s–1860s.

Rarity: URS-3

VF $250

$3 • W-RI-110-003-G050c   CC, CC

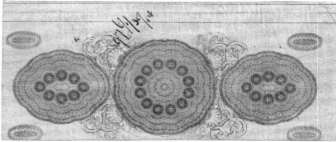

Overprint: Green 3, THREE, 3. *Back:* Green lathework.
Engraver: Reed / ABNCo. monogram. *Comments:* H-RI-40-
G18c, Durand-137. Similar to W-RI-110-003-G050 but with
additional engraver imprint. 18__. 1860s.

Rarity: URS-5

VF $450

$3 • W-RI-110-003-G060

Left: 3 / Allegorical woman with trident and shield bearing
THREE / THREE. *Center:* Female portrait / Ceres and Justice
flanking shield bearing anchor surmounted by eagle / Portrait of
cherub. *Bottom center:* Anchor and implements. *Right:* 3 /
Ceres seated in grain field / THREE. *Engraver:* Terry, Pelton &
Co. *Comments:* H-RI-40-G22, Durand-140. Beware of altered
notes of the same design. 18__. 1840s.

Rarity: *None known*

$5 • W-RI-110-005-G070   BH

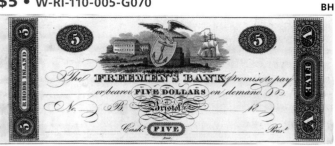

Engraver: Reed. *Comments:* H-RI-40-G26, Durand-142. Proof.
18__. 1817–1820s.

Rarity: URS-3

Proof $650

$5 • W-RI-110-005-G070a

Left: 5 RHODE ISLAND 5 vertically. *Center:* 5 / Spread eagle
on shield bearing anchor, Ship and buildings / 5. *Right:* V FIVE
V vertically. *Overprint:* Red FIVE. *Engraver:* Reed. *Comments:*
H-RI-40-G26a, Durand-143. Similar to W-RI-110-005-G070.
18__. 1850s.

Rarity: *None known*

$5 • W-RI-110-005-G070b

Overprint: Red FIVE. *Engraver:* Reed / ABNCo. monogram.
Comments: H-RI-40-G26b. Similar to W-RI-110-005-G070 but
with additional engraver imprint. 18__. 1850s–1860s.

Rarity: *None known*

How to Read the Whitman Numbering System

$1 • W-RI-010-001-G010a

Denomination: Value of the note shown.

W: Whitman number. This number is a sortable code unique
to each bank and note.

RI: Abbreviation for the state under study.

010: Numerical designation specific to each bank.

001: The denomination in dollars.

G010a: G indicates a good or valid note. Other categories are
indicated thus: C (counterfeit); R (raised); S (spurious); N
(not-attributed); A (altered). Numbers are assigned starting
with 010, 020, et seq. Terminal letters following the number
indicate variations of a note: a series of different colored overprints, tints, payees, etc., all on the same design of note. For
more information, see the "How to Use This Book" section at
the front of the volume, page xiv.

$5 • W-RI-110-005-G070c   QDB, QDB

Overprint: Green 5, FIVE, 5. *Back:* Green lathework. *Engraver:* Reed / ABNCo. monogram. *Comments:* H-RI-40-G26c, Durand-144. Similar to W-RI-110-005-G070 but with additional engraver imprint. 18__. 1860s.

Rarity: URS-3
VF $500

$5 • W-RI-110-005-G080

Left: FIVE / Portrait of Benjamin Franklin / V. *Center:* 5 / Three allegorical women / 5. *Right:* V / Portrait of Marquis de Lafayette / FIVE. *Engraver:* Terry, Pelton & Co. *Comments:* H-RI-40-G30, Durand-145. 18__. 1840s.

Rarity: *None known*

$5 • W-RI-110-005-G090   TD

Overprint: Red FIVE. *Engraver:* New England Bank Note Co. *Comments:* H-RI-40-G32, Durand-146. 18__. 1860s.

Rarity: URS-6
VF $300

$10 • W-RI-110-010-G100

Left: X RHODE ISLAND X vertically. *Center:* 10 / Justice, Sailboat and factories / 10. *Right:* TEN 10 TEN vertically. *Engraver:* Reed. *Comments:* H-RI-40-G34. 18__. 1817–1820s.

Rarity: URS-3
Proof $500

$10 • W-RI-110-010-G100a

Overprint: Red X, TEN, X. *Engraver:* Reed. *Comments:* H-RI-40-G34a, Durand-150. Similar to W-RI-110-010-G100. 18__. 1850s.

Rarity: *None known*

$10 • W-RI-110-010-G100b

Overprint: Green X, TEN, X. *Back:* Green lathework. *Engraver:* Reed / ABNCo. monogram. *Comments:* H-RI-40-G34c, Durand-151. Similar to W-RI-110-010-G100 but with additional engraver imprint. 18__. 1860s.

Rarity: URS-5
VF $250

$10 • W-RI-110-010-G110

Left: 10 / Portrait of George Washington held by cherub / 10. *Center:* X / Spread eagle and American shield / X. *Bottom center:* Ship. *Right:* 10 / Indian and woman / 10. *Engraver:* Terry, Pelton & Co. *Comments:* H-RI-40-G40, Durand-152. Beware of altered notes of the same design. 18__. 1840s.

Rarity: *None known*

$10 • W-RI-110-010-G120   CJF

Overprint: Red TEN. *Engraver:* New England Bank Note Co. *Comments:* H-RI-40-G42, Durand-153. 18__. 1860s.

Rarity: URS-3
VF $300

$20 • W-RI-110-020-G130

Left: 20 RHODE ISLAND 20 vertically. *Center:* 20 / Liberty / 20. *Right:* 20 TWENTY 20 vertically. *Engraver:* Reed. *Comments:* H-RI-40-G46, Durand-155. 18__. 1817–1820s.

Rarity: URS-3
Proof $500

$20 • W-RI-110-020-G130a

Overprint: Red TWENTY. *Engraver:* Reed. *Comments:* H-RI-40-G46a, Durand-156. Similar to W-RI-110-020-G130. 18__. 1850s.

Rarity: *None known*

$20 • W-RI-110-020-G130b

Overprint: Red TWENTY. *Engraver:* Reed / ABNCo. monogram. *Comments:* H-RI-40-G46b. Similar to W-RI-110-020-G130 but with additional engraver imprint. 18__. 1850s–1860s.

Rarity: *None known*

$20 • W-RI-110-020-G130c

Overprint: Green 20 / 20. *Back:* Green lathework. *Engraver:* Reed / ABNCo. monogram. *Comments:* H-RI-40-G46c, Durand-157. Similar to W-RI-110-020-G130 but with additional engraver imprint. 18__. 1860s.

Rarity: URS-3
VF $350

$20 • **W-RI-110-020-G140**

Left: XX / Three sailors, one getting out of boat, Ship / XX. *Center:* Scene with horses / Indian man and woman / Beehive. *Bottom center:* Anchor. *Right:* 20 / Man standing, Man picking up sheaf / 20. *Engraver:* Terry, Pelton & Co. *Comments:* H-RI-40-G50, Durand-158. Beware of altered notes of the same design. 18__. 1840s.

Rarity: *None known*

$50 • **W-RI-110-050-G150**

Left: 50 / Liberty by shield / 50. *Center:* Hebe watering eagle. *Bottom center:* Anchor and implements. *Right:* 50 / Farmer holding grain / 50. *Engraver:* Terry, Pelton & Co. *Comments:* H-RI-40-G54, Durand-160. Beware of altered notes of the same design. 18__. 1840s.

Rarity: *None known*

$50 • **W-RI-110-050-G160**

Left: FIFTY / Allegorical figure / FIFTY. *Center:* 50 / Man restraining prancing horse / 50. *Right:* FIFTY / Allegorical figure / FIFTY. *Engraver:* New England Bank Note Co. *Comments:* H-RI-40-G56, Durand-161. 18__. 1850s–1860s.

Rarity: *None known*

$100 • **W-RI-110-100-G170**

Left: ONE HUNDRED on 100 / Portrait of William Henry Harrison. *Center:* Wharf scene, Men loading wagon with barrels. *Right:* ONE HUNDRED on 100 / Portrait of Christopher Columbus. *Engraver:* New England Bank Note Co. *Comments:* H-RI-40-G60, Durand-163. 18__. 1850s–1860s.

Rarity: *None known*

Non-Valid Issues

$1 • **W-RI-110-001-A010**

Comments: H-Unlisted, Durand-130. Altered from $1 Citizens Bank, Augusta, Maine. This note was printed from a general plate used by several banks. 18__. 1840s.

Rarity: URS-3
F $90

$2 • **W-RI-110-002-A020**

Left: Female reclining on column and tables. *Center:* Spread eagle standing on shield. *Bottom center:* Horse. *Right:* Man picking corn. *Engraver:* Toppan, Carpenter, Casilear & Co. *Comments:* H-RI-40-A5, Durand-136. Altered from $2 Freemen's Bank, Washington, D.C. 18__. 1850s.

Rarity: *None known*

$2 • **W-RI-110-002-A030**

Left: TWO / Portrait of cherub / 2. *Center:* 2 / Ceres giving grain to seated Liberty / 2. *Bottom center:* Anchor and implements. *Right:* 2 / Female portrait / TWO. *Engraver:* Terry, Pelton & Co. *Comments:* H-RI-40-A10. Altered from $2 Citizens Bank, Augusta, Maine, or from notes of other failed banks using the same plate. This bank also issued legitimate notes from this plate, W-RI-110-002-G040. 18__. 1840s.

Rarity: *None known*

$2 • **W-RI-110-002-A040**

Comments: H-Unlisted, Durand-135. Altered from $2 Citizens Bank, Augusta, Maine. This note was printed from a general plate used by several banks. 18__. 1840s.

Rarity: URS-3
F $90

$3 • **W-RI-110-003-A050**

Engraver: Terry, Pelton & Co. *Comments:* H-RI-40-A15, Durand-141. Altered from $3 Citizens Bank, Augusta, Maine, or from notes of other failed banks using the same plate. This note was printed from a general plate used by several banks. This bank also issued legitimate notes from this plate, W-RI-110-003-G060. 18__. 1840s.

Rarity: *None known*

$5 • **W-RI-110-005-A060**

Left: Soldier with flag standing in front of cannon / FIVE. *Center:* 5 / Industry. *Right:* 5 / Milkmaid and cows. *Engraver:* Toppan, Carpenter, Casilear & Co. *Comments:* H-RI-40-A18, Durand-149. Altered from $5 Freeman's Bank, Augusta, Maine. 18__. 1850s.

Rarity: URS-3
VF $300

$5 • **W-RI-110-005-A070**

Engraver: Terry, Pelton & Co. *Comments:* H-RI-40-A20, Durand-147. Altered from $5 Citizens Bank, Augusta, Maine, or from notes of other failed banks using the same plate. This note was printed from a general plate used by several banks. This bank also issued legitimate notes from this plate, W-RI-110-005-G080. 18__. 1840s.

Rarity: URS-3
VF $150

$5 • **W-RI-110-005-A080**

Left: 5 / Farmer and family resting under tree. *Center:* Portrait of Benjamin Franklin. *Right:* 5 / Woodsman felling tree, Children and oxen. *Overprint:* Red V / V. *Comments:* H-RI-40-A25, Durand-148. Altered from W-RI-1630-005-G040. Aug. 6, 1855. 1850s.

Rarity: *None known*

$10 • **W-RI-110-010-A090**

Comments: H-Unlisted, Durand-154. Altered from $10 Citizens Bank, Augusta, Maine. This note was printed from a general plate used by several banks. 18__. 1840s.

Rarity: URS-3
VF $150

$20 • **W-RI-110-020-A100**

Engraver: Terry, Pelton & Co. *Comments:* H-RI-40-A35, Durand-159. Altered from $20 Citizens Bank, Augusta, Maine, or from notes of other failed banks using the same plate. This note was printed from a general plate used by several banks. This bank also issued legitimate notes from this plate, W-RI-110-020-G140. 18__. 1840s.

Rarity: URS-3
VF $250

$50 • **W-RI-110-050-A110**

Engraver: Terry, Pelton & Co. *Comments:* H-RI-40-A40, Durand-162. Altered from $50 Citizens Bank, Augusta, Maine, or from notes of other failed banks using the same plate. This note was printed from a general plate used by several banks. This bank also issued legitimate notes from this plate, W-RI-110-050-G150. 18__. 1840s.

Rarity: *None known*

Mount Hope Bank
1818–1832
W-RI-120

History: The Mount Hope Bank was chartered in October 1818. In 1832 the *American Annual Register* reported that the bank "has made no discounts [loans to customers], and is winding up its concerns." In 1833 its bills traded at a discount of five to eight percent, after which they became worthless.

Numismatic Commentary: It is fitting that some of this bank's notes show a vignette of a Native American in a canoe. Mount Hope, an area of Bristol, was the seat of influence for the Native American chief King Philip. Another note shows the Arkwright Mill, an early textile manufacturer in Coventry. Remainder notes are fairly easy to come by, and four-note sheets are also available.

VALID ISSUES

$1 • W-RI-120-001-G010
Left: Lathework panel bearing 1 RHODE ISLAND 1 vertically. **Center:** ONE / Indian paddling canoe / 1. **Right:** Lathework panel bearing 1 / 1 vertically. **Engraver:** Graphic Co. **Comments:** H-RI-45-G2, Durand-165. 18__. 1818–1820s.
Rarity: URS-8
VF $175

$1 • W-RI-120-001-G020

Engraver: Reed & Pelton. **Comments:** H-RI-45-G4, Durand-164. Remainder. 18__. 1820s–1830s.
Rarity: URS-8
VF $200; **Unc-Rem** $700

$1 • W-RI-120-001-G030
Engraver: Reed & Stiles. **Comments:** H-Unlisted, Durand-Unlisted. 1820s–1830s.
Rarity: *None known*

$1 • W-RI-120-001-G040
Engraver: Reed & Pelton. **Comments:** H-Unlisted, Durand-Unlisted. 1820s–1830s.
Rarity: *None known*

$2 • W-RI-120-002-G050
Left: Lathework panel bearing 2 RHODE ISLAND 2 vertically. **Center:** 2. **Right:** Lathework panel bearing 2 / 2 vertically. **Engraver:** Graphic Co. **Comments:** H-RI-45-G6, Durand-166. 18__. 1818–1820s.
Rarity: URS-8
VF $175

$2 • W-RI-120-002-G060

Engraver: Reed & Pelton. **Comments:** H-RI-45-G8, Durand-166. 18__. 1820s–1830s.
Rarity: URS-8
VF $175; **Unc-Rem** $125

$2 • W-RI-120-002-G070
Engraver: Reed & Stiles. **Comments:** H-Unlisted, Durand-Unlisted. 1820s–1830s.
Rarity: *None known*

$2 • W-RI-120-002-G080
Engraver: Reed & Pelton. **Comments:** H-Unlisted, Durand-Unlisted. 1820s–1830s.
Rarity: *None known*

$3 • W-RI-120-003-G090

Engraver: Graphic Co. **Comments:** H-RI-45-G10, Durand-167. 18__. 1818–1820s.
Rarity: URS-7
VF $200; **Proof** $1,200

$5 • W-RI-120-005-G100

Engraver: Graphic Co. **Comments:** H-RI-45-G12, Durand-168. 18__. 1818–1820s.
Rarity: URS-7
VF $200

$10 • W-RI-120-010-G110

QDB

Engraver: Graphic Co. *Comments:* H-RI-45-G14, Durand-169. 18___. 1818–1820s.

Rarity: URS-6
VF $200

$20 • W-RI-120-020-G120

Left: Lathework panel bearing 20 TWENTY DOLLARS 20 vertically. *Center:* 20 / Commerce and Ceres with shield of Hope / 20. *Bottom center:* XX on TWENTY. *Right:* Lathework panel bearing XX RHODE ISLAND XX vertically. *Engraver:* Reed & Pelton. *Comments:* H-RI-45-G16, Durand-170. 18___. 1820s.

Rarity: URS-5
VF $250

$50 • W-RI-120-050-G130

CC

Engraver: Reed & Stiles. *Comments:* H-RI-45-G18. 182_. 1820s.

Rarity: URS-1
VF $2,000; **CU** $1,200

$100 • W-RI-120-100-G140

Left: 100 / ONE HUNDRED vertically / 100. *Center:* Ship, Anchor on shield, Ship. *Bottom center:* 100. *Right:* 100 / RHODE ISLAND vertically / 100. *Engraver:* Reed & Stiles. *Comments:* H-RI-45-G20, Durand-171. 182_. 1820s.

Rarity: URS-3
Proof $500

$500 • W-RI-120-500-G150

Left: 500 FIVE HUNDRED 500 vertically. *Center:* 500 / Woman reclining, pointing, Two women in water / 500. *Right:* D RHODE ISLAND D vertically. *Comments:* H-RI-45-G24, Durand-172. 1820s.

Rarity: URS-3
Proof $800

$500 • W-RI-120-500-G160

Left: 500 FIVE HUNDRED 500 vertically. *Center:* 500 / Woman reclining, pointing, Two women in water / 500. *Right:* D RHODE ISLAND D vertically. *Comments:* H-RI-45-G28. 1820s–1830s.

Rarity: URS-3
Proof $800

Uncut Sheets

$1-$1-$2-$2 • W-RI-120-001.001.002.002-US010

Engraver: Reed & Stiles. *Comments:* All unlisted in Haxby. No description available. 1820s–1830s.

Rarity: *None known*

$1-$1-$2-$2 • W-RI-120-001.001.002.002-US020

Engraver: Reed & Pelton. *Comments:* All unlisted in Haxby. No description available. 1820s–1830s.

Rarity: *None known*

Pokanoket Bank
1855
W-RI-130

History: The Pokanoket Bank was chartered in May 1855 but was never organized and did not open for business. Its charter was later forfeited.

BURRILLVILLE, RHODE ISLAND

Burrillville was originally a part of Gloucester until it separated in 1806. It was named after the Honorable James Burrill, the attorney general of the state at the time. The town lies on the northwestern corner of Rhode Island and is bounded by the states of Massachusetts and Connecticut and the towns of Gloucester and Smithfield. The villages within Burrillville include Oakland, Mapleville, Bridgeton, Pascoag, Wallum Lake, Nasonville, Glendale, and Harrisville.

The town thrived by means of agriculture and products such as apples, corn, rye, oats, potatoes, butter, cheese, beef, and pork. Lumbering also brought employment for those who cut hoop-poles, shaved shingles, and hewed ship timber. Quarries existed nearby and brought an additional form of commerce to the area.

The town was officially incorporated on November 17, 1806. In 1844 disputes over boundaries between Massachusetts and Gloucester reduced the land of the town when a large tract was given to Massachusetts.

See also Gloucester and Pascoag, Rhode Island.

Burrillville Bank
1820–1832
W-RI-140

History: The Burrillville Bank was incorporated in 1818 but didn't open for business until about 1820. Abraham Baker was its first president and C. Lawson its first cashier. In 1830 John L. Clark, who made a fortune in the lottery business in Providence, gained control of the bank and became president. He hand-picked the directors and operated in a questionable manner. In 1832 it was charged that he had absconded with funds, but he was never convicted on this count. He did, however, over-issue currency. The bank failed soon afterward. It was widely stated that the bank was a fraud but, for some reason, the blame was centered on others than Clark. He committed suicide in July 1836.

An investigation into the Burrillville Bank led to the discovery that only $6,000 of capital had ever been paid in, and these had been in stock notes.[9] It was found that the institution had been fraudulent from the beginning. The bank was a complete loss for its stockholders. Newspapers of the era stated that the currency became worthless. However, a later account, probably incorrect, stated that the notes were redeemed at face-value for a total of $49,000.[10] As is often the case for early banks, facts are scarce.

Numismatic Commentary: The notes with the PSSP design are more plentiful in the marketplace than the notes engraved by A. B. & C. Durand, Wright & Co. Finding a nice, mid- to high-grade note should not be a problem.

Remaining in the American Bank Note Co. archives as of 2003 was a $1-$1-$2-$3 tint plate, probably mislabeled, as in the early 1830s such color protectors would not have been used.

VALID ISSUES

$1 • W-RI-140-001-G010

Engraver: A. B. & C. Durand, Wright & Co. **Comments:** H-RI-50-G2, Durand-173. 18__. 1820s–1830s.
Rarity: URS-3
Proof $500

$1 • W-RI-140-001-G020
Center: Alternating flower garlands and gridwork segments. **Engraver:** PSSP. **Comments:** H-RI-50-G4, Durand-174. 18__. 1830s.
Rarity: URS-7
VG $80

$1 • W-RI-140-001-G020a

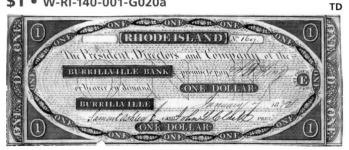

Engraver: PSSP. **Comments:** H-RI-50-G6. Similar to W-RI-140-001-G020. 18__. 1830s.
Rarity: URS-7
F $100

$2 • W-RI-140-002-G030

Engraver: A. B. & C. Durand, Wright & Co. **Comments:** H-RI-50-G8, Durand-175. 18__. 1820s–1830s.
Rarity: URS-3
Proof $1,000

$2 • W-RI-140-002-G040
Center: Alternating flower garlands and gridwork segments. **Engraver:** PSSP. **Comments:** H-RI-50-G10, Durand-176. 18__. 1830s.
Rarity: URS-6
VF $100

$2 • W-RI-140-002-G040a

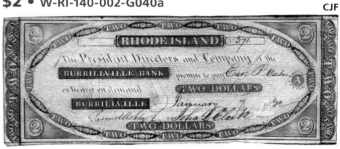

Engraver: PSSP. **Comments:** H-RI-50-G12. Similar to W-RI-140-002-G040. 18__. 1830s.
Rarity: URS-6
VF $100

$3 • W-RI-140-003-G050

Engraver: A. B. & C. Durand, Wright & Co. **Comments:** H-RI-50-G14, Durand-177. 18__. 1820s–1830s.
Rarity: URS-3
Proof $900

$3 • W-RI-140-003-G060
Center: Alternating flower garlands and gridwork segments. **Engraver:** PSSP. **Comments:** H-RI-50-G16, Durand-178. 18__. 1830s.
Rarity: URS-3
VF $150

$3 • **W-RI-140-003-G060a**　　　　TD

Engraver: PSSP. *Comments:* H-RI-50-G18. Similar to W-RI-140-003-G060. 18__. 1830s.
Rarity: URS-3
VG $115

$5 • **W-RI-140-005-G070**

Left: 5 / Eagle and serpent / 5. *Right:* Woman being drawn by horse in chariot / 5. *Engraver:* A. B. & C. Durand, Wright & Co. *Comments:* H-Unlisted, Durand-180. 18__. 1820s–1830s.
Rarity: URS-3

$5 • **W-RI-140-005-G080**　　　　CJF

Engraver: PPSP. *Comments:* H-RI-50-G20. 18__. 1820s.
Rarity: URS-3
VF $150

$5 • **W-RI-140-005-G090**　　　　QDB

Engraver: PSSP. *Comments:* H-RI-50-G22, Durand-181. 18__. 1830s.
Rarity: URS-7
VG $90; **VF** $125; **AU** $150

$10 • **W-RI-140-010-G100**

Left: Conjoined lathework circles bearing TEN vertically. *Center:* 10 / Four allegorical women under tree, Village, Farm and harbor / 10. *Right:* Conjoined lathework circles bearing TEN vertically. *Engraver:* PSSP. *Comments:* H-RI-50-G24. 18__. 1820s.
Rarity: URS-6
VF $150

$10 • **W-RI-140-010-G110**　　　　CJF

Engraver: PSSP. *Comments:* H-RI-50-G26, Durand-182. 18__. 1830s.
Rarity: URS-6
EF $135

$20 • **W-RI-140-020-G120**　　　　CC

Engraver: PSSP. *Comments:* H-RI-50-G30, Durand-183. 18__. 1830s.
Rarity: URS-5
Unc-Rem $500

$50 • **W-RI-140-050-G130**　　　　CC

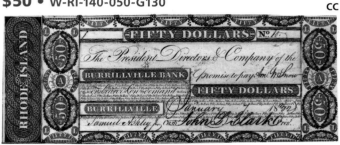

Engraver: PSSP. *Comments:* H-RI-50-G34, Durand-184. 18__. 1830s.
Rarity: URS-3
VF $400; **AU** $1,100

$100 • **W-RI-140-100-G140**

Left: Lathework flower garlands and gridwork segments. *Center:* Alternating flower garlands and gridwork segments. *Right:* 100 / 100 vertically. *Engraver:* PSSP. *Comments:* H-RI-50-G38. 18__. 1820s–1830s.
Rarity: *None known*

NON-VALID ISSUES

$1 • W-RI-140-001-S010

CJF

Comments: H-Unlisted, Durand-Unlisted. 18__. 1820s.
Rarity: URS-3

$3 • W-RI-140-003-S020

Left: Lathework panel bearing THREE vertically. *Right:* Lathework panel bearing THREE vertically. *Comments:* H-RI-50-S2, Durand-179. Similar to W-RI-140-003-G060. Pink paper. 18__. 1820s.

Rarity: URS-3
VF $150

Burrillville Agricultural Bank
1815–1818
W-RI-150

History: Chartered in 1815 in the village of Slatersville, the Burrillville Agricultural Bank did not open until February 1818. On June 18 of the same year, the charter was amended to change the title to the Burrillville Agricultural and Manufacturers Bank, W-RI-160.

See also listing under Slatersville, W-RI-1320.

Numismatic Commentary: The denominations and designs of this bank's issues are unknown, but if made, were probably of the Perkins type.

Burrillville Agricultural and Manufacturers Bank
1818–1822
W-RI-160

History: The Burrillville Agricultural and Manufacturers Bank was originally titled the Burrillville Agricultural Bank, W-RI-150. On June 18, 1818, the charter was amended to change the name. In October 1822, the bank was again modified to become the Village Bank, W-RI-1410.

See also listing under Slatersville, W-RI-1330, and Smithfield, W-RI-1333.

Numismatic Commentary: The few notes recorded for this bank are of a Perkins variant design. The imprint reads: Perkins Patent Steel Plate (PPSP). This variation occurred at about the same time Jacob Perkins left his company to move to England (see volume 1 of this series for his biography).

VALID ISSUES

$2 • W-RI-160-002-G010

Left: Panel with TWO / TWO vertically. *Center:* 11 / 11. *Bottom center:* TWO / 2. *Right:* Panel with TWO / TWO vertically. *Engraver:* PPSP. *Comments:* H-RI-52-G12. 18__. 1820s.
Rarity: *None known*

$3 • W-RI-160-003-G020

Left: Panel with THREE / THREE vertically. *Center:* 111 / 111. *Bottom center:* THREE / 3. *Right:* Panel with THREE / THREE vertically. *Engraver:* PPSP. *Comments:* H-RI-52-G14. 18__. 1820s.
Rarity: *None known*

Granite Bank
1851–1865
W-RI-170

History: The Granite Bank was incorporated in June 1833 as the Pascoag Bank, W-RI-180, in the village of Pascoag. The authorized starting capital was $50,000. Its title was changed to the Granite Bank in June 1851. In 1857 its capital was $60,000, bills in circulation amounted to $23,136, and specie totaled $4,063.57. In 1862 its capital was the same, but circulation was $36,267.[11]

After July 5, 1865, the interests of the bank were succeeded by the Pascoag National Bank.

See also listing under Pascoag, W-RI-690.

Pascoag Bank
1833–1851
W-RI-180

History: The Pascoag Bank was incorporated in Pascoag Village in June 1833. Its charter was amended to change the name to the Granite Bank, W-RI-170, in June 1851.[12]

See also listing under Pascoag, W-RI-700.

CAROLINA MILLS, RHODE ISLAND

A village near Charlestown and Richmond, Carolina Mills lies close on the Pawcatuck River in Washington County. A wooden dam and a grist mill were built in 1802 on the river that passed through the village, and later a cotton mill was erected. At this early time, housing for employees was in nearby Charlestown, and most buildings for the mill were located in Richmond.

During the early 19th century, the settlement included a school, a church, a bank, stores, a smithy, a meeting hall, and a post office. In 1843 the local mill was purchased by Rowland G. Hazard, who renamed it in honor of his wife. The village adopted the same name and officially became Carolina Mills. In 1862 the Carolina Mills Company transferred from making cotton textiles to woolen materials.

Washington County Bank
1856–1865
W-RI-190

History: This bank was incorporated in Richmond in 1856 and went into operation on August 12 that same year. R.G. Hazard was its president and J.H. Babcock its cashier. Authorized capital was set at $50,000. Bills in circulation were listed at $16,122, and specie totaled $1,458.41. The name of the location was changed to Carolina Mills in 1863, after which the bank moved to Charlestown. It closed in 1865.

See also listing under Richmond, W-RI-1280.

Numismatic Commentary: Collectors can find examples of attractive 1850s and early 1860s notes with variants of both red and green overprints available. High-grade notes should not be too hard to locate.

Remaining in the American Bank Note Co. archives as of 2003 was a $1-$2-$1-$5 tint plate.

VALID ISSUES

$1 • W-RI-190-001-G010
Left: 1 / Man feeding horse. *Center:* Portrait of George Washington. *Right:* 1 / Girl feeding chickens. *Engraver:* Toppan, Carpenter & Co. *Comments:* H-RI-430-G2a, Durand-185. 18__. 1850s.
Rarity: *None known*

$1 • W-RI-190-001-G010a   TD

Overprint: Red 1, 1. *Engraver:* Toppan, Carpenter & Co. *Comments:* H-Unlisted, Durand-Unlisted. Similar to W-RI-190-001-G010. 18__. 1850s–1860s.
Rarity: URS-7
F $125; **VF** $200

$1 • W-RI-190-001-G010b
Overprint: Red 1, 1. *Engraver:* American Bank Note Co. *Comments:* H-RI-430-G2b, Durand-186. Similar to W-RI-190-001-G010 but with different date and engraver imprint. Jan.y 1, 186_. 1860s.
Rarity: URS-7
VF $150

$1 • W-RI-190-001-G010c
Overprint: Green 1, 1. *Engraver:* American Bank Note Co. *Comments:* H-RI-430-G2c, Durand-187. Similar to W-RI-190-001-G010 but with different date and engraver imprint. Jan.y 1, 186_. 1860s.
Rarity: URS-8
F $110; **VF** $150

$1 • W-RI-190-001-G010d   CC

Overprint: Green 1, 1. *Engraver:* American Bank Note Co. *Comments:* H-RI-430-G2d, Durand-188. Similar to W-RI-190-001-G010 but with different date and engraver imprint. Jan.y 2nd, 186_. 1860s.
Rarity: URS-8
VF $250; **EF** $400

$2 • W-RI-190-002-G020
Left: 2 / Two men building. *Center:* Male portrait / Man seated with horses / Male portrait. *Right:* 2 / Portrait of George Washington. *Engraver:* Toppan, Carpenter & Co. *Comments:* H-Unlisted, Durand-189. 18__. 1850s.
Rarity: URS-3

$2 • W-RI-190-002-G020a
Overprint: Red TWO. *Engraver:* Toppan, Carpenter & Co. *Comments:* H-RI-430-G4a, Durand-190. Similar to W-RI-190-002-G020. 18__. 1850s.
Rarity: *None known*

$2 • W-RI-190-002-G020b   CC

Overprint: Red TWO. *Engraver:* American Bank Note Co. *Comments:* H-RI-430-G4b. Similar to W-RI-190-002-G020 but with different date and engraver imprint. Jan.y 2nd, 186_. 1860s.
Rarity: URS-7
VF $150

$2 • W-RI-190-002-G020c   CJF

Overprint: Green TWO. *Engraver:* American Bank Note Co. *Comments:* H-RI-430-G4c, Durand-191. Similar to W-RI-190-002-G020 but with different date and engraver imprint. Jan.y 2nd, 186_. 1860s.

Rarity: URS-8
VG $95; **VF** $150

$2 • W-RI-190-002-G020d   ANS

Overprint: Green 2, 2. *Engraver:* American Bank Note Co. *Comments:* H-RI-430-G4d, Durand-192. Similar to W-RI-190-002-G020 but with different date and engraver imprint. Jan.y 2nd, 186_. 1860s.

Rarity: URS-6
VF $150

$3 • W-RI-190-003-G030

Left: Two farmers, Woman holding child, 3. *Center:* Female portrait. *Right:* Scene in blacksmith shop, 3. *Overprint:* Likely red 3, 3. *Engraver:* Unverified, but likely Toppan, Carpenter & Co. *Comments:* H-RI-430-G6a, Durand-193. 18__. 1850s.

Rarity: *None known*

$3 • W-RI-190-003-G030a

Overprint: Likely red 3, 3. *Engraver:* Unverified, but likely American Bank Note Co. *Comments:* H-RI-430-G6b. Similar to W-RI-190-003-G030 but with different date and engraver imprint. Jan. 1, 186_. 1860s.

Rarity: *None known*

$5 • W-RI-190-005-G040

Left: 5 / Militia men throwing up breastwork. *Center:* Revolutionary War soldier, Shield bearing bust of George Washington, Liberty, Two Indians. *Right:* 5 / Girl with cow and calf. *Engraver:* Toppan, Carpenter & Co. *Comments:* H-RI-430-G8a, Durand-194. 18__. 1850s.

Rarity: *None known*

$5 • W-RI-190-005-G040a

Overprint: Red 5 / 5. *Engraver:* American Bank Note Co. *Comments:* H-RI-430-G8b, Durand-195. Similar to W-RI-190-005-G040 but with different date and engraver imprint. Jan.y 2, 186_. 1860s.

Rarity: URS-7
VF $150

$5 • W-RI-190-005-G040b   CJF

Overprint: Green 5, 5. *Engraver:* American Bank Note Co. *Comments:* H-RI-430-G8c, Durand-196. Similar to W-RI-190-005-G040 but with different date and engraver imprint. Jan.y 2nd, 186_. 1860s.

Rarity: URS-8
F $150; **VF** $300

$5 • W-RI-190-005-G040c

Overprint: Green V / V. *Engraver:* American Bank Note Co. *Comments:* H-RI-430-G8d, Durand-197. Similar to W-RI-190-005-G040 but with different date and engraver imprint. Jan. 1, 186_. 1860s.

Rarity: URS-6
F $170

$10 • W-RI-190-010-G050

Left: 10 / Liberty and shield / U.S. Capitol. *Center:* Two men, Indian and family. *Right:* 10. *Engraver:* Unverified, but likely Toppan, Carpenter & Co. *Comments:* H-RI-430-G10a, Durand-198. 18__. 1850s.

Rarity: URS-3
VF $300

$10 • W-RI-190-010-G050a

Overprint: Red TEN. *Engraver:* Unverified, but likely American Bank Note Co. *Comments:* H-RI-430-G10b, Durand-199. Similar to W-RI-190-010-G050 but with different date and engraver imprint. Jan. 2, 186_. 1860s.

Rarity: *None known*

$50 • W-RI-190-050-G060

Left: 50 / Blacksmith. *Center:* Cattle. *Right:* 50 / Train. *Engraver:* Unverified, but likely Toppan, Carpenter & Co. *Comments:* H-RI-430-G12, Durand-203. 18__. 1850s.

Rarity: *None known*

$50 • W-RI-190-050-G060a

Engraver: Unverified, but likely American Bank Note Co. *Comments:* H-RI-430-G12b. Similar to W-RI-190-050-G060 but with different date and engraver imprint. Jan. 1, 186_. 1860s.

Rarity: *None known*

NON-VALID ISSUES

$10 • **W-RI-190-010-A010**
Center: Corn gathering scene. *Comments:* H-RI-430-N5, Durand-200. 1850s–1860s.

Rarity: *None known*

$10 • **W-RI-190-010-A020**
Center: Eagle / Men harvesting grain. *Comments:* H-RI-430-N10, Durand-201. 1850s–1860s.

Rarity: *None known*

$20 • **W-RI-190-020-A030**
Center: Eagle. *Comments:* H-RI-430-N15, Durand-202. 1850s–1860s.

Rarity: *None known*

CENTREVILLE, RHODE ISLAND

Centreville is one of the villages of West Warwick, which was known as Warwick during the 19th century. The first textile mill in the area was founded in 1809 by Christopher Lippitt, and subsequent mills were erected. Other villages in the town included Arctic, Crompton, Riverpoint, Natick, and Phenix.

See also Warwick, Rhode Island.

Centreville Bank
1828–1865
W-RI-200

History: The Centreville Bank was incorporated in June 1828. The capital was $25,000 in 1831 and $100,000 in 1855. Circulation was $28,026.25 in 1849; specie was at $4,603.95. The capital was $100,000 in 1856. The bank saw a circulation of $25,247 in 1857, which increased to $53,657 in 1862. Specie amounted to $2,824.79 in 1857.

The business of the Centreville Bank was succeeded by the Centreville National Bank in June 1865.

See also listing under Warwick, W-RI-1570.

CHEPACHET, RHODE ISLAND

Chepachet is one of the villages of Gloucester and was originally settled by the Pequot and Nipmuc Indians. The name means "where rivers meet" in the native language. The American Revolution saw Newport Loyalists exiled here, and in 1842 the Dorr Rebellion saw its conclusion in Chepachet, when non-landowners won voting rights in the state Constitution.

See also Gloucester, Rhode Island.

Franklin Bank
1818–1868
W-RI-210

History: The Franklin Bank was chartered in February 1818 by a group from the Gloucester village of Chepachet. Jesse Tourtellot served as its first president, and Cyril Cook was its first cashier. Its authorized capital was $50,000, which was reduced to $38,000 by 1849 and increased again to $50,000 by 1855. Circulation was $24,689 in 1849, $28,131.50 in 1857, and $32,085 by 1863. Specie amounted to $2,176.09 in 1857.

This bank was successful and continued to do business until the national banking system arose, in which it did not participate. It was closed down in 1868, and its capital and surplus were distributed to the stockholders.[13]

See also listing under Gloucester, W-RI-420.

Numismatic Commentary: Genuine notes are hard to find, but many non-valid issues are available. Some non-valid notes with a Reed imprint are printed on colored paper from green to blue.

VALID ISSUES

$1 • **W-RI-210-001-G010**
Left: 1 / ONE ONE ONE / 1. *Center:* 1 / Allegorical woman leaning on shield bearing ONE, pointing to coach and horses / 1. *Right:* 1 RHODE ISLAND 1 vertically. *Engraver:* Reed. *Comments:* H-RI-55-G2, Durand-204. 18__. 1818–1820s

Rarity: *None known*

$1 • **W-RI-210-001-G020**
Left: Narrow panel of lathework circle segments. *Center:* 1 / 1 / Flower garlands and gridwork segments / 1 / 1. *Right:* Narrow panel of lathework circle segments. *Engraver:* PSSP. *Comments:* H-RI-55-G6, Durand-205. 18__. 1820s–1830s.

Rarity: *None known*

$1 • **W-RI-210-001-G030**
Left: 1 / Minerva with 1 / 1. *Center:* ONE / Commerce, Ship and plow / ONE. *Right:* 1 / Eagle / 1. *Engraver:* PSSP. *Comments:* H-RI-55-G8, Durand-206. 18__. 1830s.

Rarity: *None known*

$1 • **W-RI-210-001-G040**
Left: ONE vertically. *Center:* Steamboat and other vessels / 1. *Right:* ONE / Indian woman seated / ONE. *Engraver:* New England Bank Note Co. *Comments:* H-RI-55-G10, Durand-207. 18__. 1840s.

Rarity: *None known*

$1 • **W-RI-210-001-G050**
Left: Commerce seated, Train, vessels, and canal lock. *Center:* 1 bearing "Signing of the Declaration of Independence" / 1. *Right:* 1 / Woman with apron of grain. *Engraver:* New England Bank Note Co. *Comments:* H-RI-55-G12, Durand-208. 18__. 1850s.

Rarity: *None known*

$2 • **W-RI-210-002-G060**
Left: 2 / TWO TWO TWO / 2. *Center:* 2 / Justice, River, bridge, and factories / 2. *Bottom center:* 2. *Right:* 2 RHODE ISLAND 2 vertically. *Engraver:* Reed. *Comments:* H-RI-55-G16, Durand-210. 18__. 1818–1820s.

Rarity: *None known*

$2 • **W-RI-210-002-G070**
Left: Narrow panel of lathework circle segments. *Center:* 2 / 2 / Alternating flower garlands and gridwork segments / 2 / 2. *Right:* Narrow panel of lathework circle segments. *Engraver:* PSSP. *Comments:* H-RI-55-G20, Durand-211. 18__. 1820s–1830s.

Rarity: *None known*

$2 • **W-RI-210-002-G080**
Left: 2 / Hebe watering eagle / 2. *Center:* 2 / Commerce, Cornucopia and plow / 2. *Right:* 2 / Justice / 2. *Engraver:* PSSP. *Comments:* H-RI-55-G22, Durand-212. 18__. 1830s.

Rarity: *None known*

$2 • W-RI-210-002-G090

Left: 2 / TWO / 2. *Center:* Ship and other vessels / 2. *Right:* TWO / Woman drawing water from well / TWO. *Engraver:* New England Bank Note Co. *Comments:* H-RI-55-G24, Durand-213. 18__. 1840s.

Rarity: *None known*

$2 • W-RI-210-002-G100

Left: Men driving sheep into stream. *Center:* 2 bearing "Signing of the Declaration of Independence" / 2. *Right:* TWO / Woman with flowers / TWO. *Engraver:* New England Bank Note Co. *Comments:* H-RI-55-G26, Durand-214. 18__. 1850s.

Rarity: *None known*

$3 • W-RI-210-003-G110

Engraver: Reed. *Comments:* H-RI-55-G30, Durand-216. 18__. 1818–1820s.

Rarity: URS-1
VF $4,000

$3 • W-RI-210-003-G120

Engraver: PSSP. *Comments:* H-RI-55-G34, Durand-217. 18__. 1820s–1830s.

Rarity: URS-3
VF $125

$3 • W-RI-210-003-G130

Engraver: PSSP. *Comments:* H-RI-55-G36, Durand-218. 18__. 1830s.

Rarity: URS-1
VF $950

$3 • W-RI-210-003-G140

Left: THREE vertically. *Center:* Reaping scene / 3. *Right:* THREE / Steamboat / 3 on THREE. *Engraver:* New England Bank Note Co. *Comments:* H-RI-55-G38, Durand-219. 18__. 1840s.

Rarity: *None known*

$3 • W-RI-210-003-G150

Left: Man on horseback, Boy, dog, and cattle / 3. *Center:* 3. *Right:* 3 on THREE / Woman with flowers / THREE. *Engraver:* New England Bank Note Co. *Comments:* H-RI-55-G40, Durand-220. 18__. 1850s.

Rarity: *None known*

$5 • W-RI-210-005-G160

Left: Lathework chain bearing RHODE ISLAND vertically / 5 / 5. *Center:* 5 / 5 / Alternating flower garlands and gridwork segments / 5 / 5. *Right:* 5 / 5. *Engraver:* PSSP. *Comments:* H-RI-55-G44. 18__. 1820s.

Rarity: *None known*

$5 • W-RI-210-005-G160a

Engraver: PSSP. *Comments:* H-RI-55-G46. Similar to W-RI-210-005-G160. 18__. 1820s–1830s.

Rarity: *None known*

$5 • W-RI-210-005-G170

Left: RHODE ISLAND vertically. *Center:* 5 / Blacksmith / V. *Right:* 5 / Allegorical figure / 5. *Engraver:* PSSP. *Comments:* H-RI-55-G48, Durand-221. 18__. 1830s.

Rarity: *None known*

$5 • W-RI-210-005-G180

Left: Panel with FIVE / Plenty and Minerva seated / V. *Center:* FIVE / Allegorical woman seated / FIVE / Panel of microletters. *Right:* 5 / Eagle / 5. *Engraver:* PSSP. *Comments:* H-RI-55-G50. 18__. 1830s.

Rarity: *None known*

$5 • W-RI-210-005-G190

Left: FIVE vertically. *Center:* Woman unveiling shield bearing 5 / V. *Right:* 5 / Sailing ship. *Engraver:* New England Bank Note Co. *Comments:* H-RI-55-G52, Durand-222. 18__. 1840s.

Rarity: *None known*

$5 • W-RI-210-005-G200

Left: Eagle and shield / FIVE. *Center:* V containing woman with cornucopia and cherub. *Right:* 5 / Girl with basket. *Engraver:* New England Bank Note Co. *Comments:* H-RI-55-G54, Durand-223. 18__. 1850s.

Rarity: *None known*

$10 • W-RI-210-010-G210

Left: Lathework chain bearing RHODE ISLAND / 10 / 10 vertically. *Center:* Alternating flower garlands and gridwork segments. *Right:* 10 / 10 vertically. *Engraver:* PSSP. *Comments:* H-RI-55-G58. 18__. 1820s.

Rarity: *None known*

$10 • W-RI-210-010-G210a

Engraver: PSSP. *Comments:* H-RI-55-G60. Similar to W-RI-210-010-G210. 18__. 1820s–1830s.

Rarity: *None known*

$10 • W-RI-210-010-G220

Left: Panel with TEN / Manhattan spilling water jug / TEN. *Center:* TEN / Ceres seated / TEN / Panel of microletters. *Right:* Panel with 10 / Portrait of Indian / 10. *Engraver:* PSSP. *Comments:* H-RI-55-G64. 18__. 1830s.
Rarity: *None known*

$10 • W-RI-210-010-G230

Left: 10 / X / 10. *Center:* Farmer with plow and oxen / 10. *Right:* TEN / Allegorical woman with lyre and cornucopia. *Engraver:* New England Bank Note Co. *Comments:* H-RI-55-G66, Durand-225. 18__. 1840s.
Rarity: *None known*

$10 • W-RI-210-010-G240

Left: Train, Vulcan seated with tools, Building / TEN. *Center:* X. *Right:* 10 / Farmer with sickle and sheaf. *Engraver:* New England Bank Note Co. *Comments:* H-RI-55-G68, Durand-226. 18__. 1850s.
Rarity: *None known*

$10 • W-RI-210-010-G250

Left: X / Indian with bow. *Center:* Steamer and other vessels / X. *Right:* 10 / Woman with sheaf. *Engraver:* PSSP / New England Bank Note Co. *Comments:* H-RI-55-G70, Durand-227. Beware of altered notes similar to the genuine. 18__. 1850s.
Rarity: *None known*

$10 • W-RI-210-010-G250a

Overprint: Red TEN. *Engraver:* PSSP / New England Bank Note Co. *Comments:* H-RI-55-G70a, Durand-228. Similar to W-RI-210-010-G250. 18__. 1850s.
Rarity: *None known*

$20 • W-RI-210-020-G260

Left: Lathework chain bearing RHODE ISLAND / 20 / 20 vertically. *Center:* Alternating flower garlands and gridwork segments. *Right:* 20 / 20 vertically. *Engraver:* PSSP. *Comments:* H-RI-55-G74. 18__. 1820s–1830s.
Rarity: *None known*

$20 • W-RI-210-020-G270

Left: 20 / XX vertically / 20. *Center:* 20 / Woman seated with scales, Sheaf and bales, Men plowing, Ship. *Right:* TWENTY vertically. *Engraver:* PSSP / New England Bank Note Co. *Comments:* H-RI-55-G76. 18__. 1830s.
Rarity: *None known*

$20 • W-RI-210-020-G280

Left: Steamboat / XX / Train. *Center:* Liberty, Justice, and Knowledge with eagle / 20. *Right:* XX / Milkmaid. *Engraver:* PSSP / New England Bank Note Co. *Comments:* H-RI-55-G78, Durand-230. Beware of altered notes of the same design. 18__. 1840s.
Rarity: *None known*

$20 • W-RI-210-020-G290

Left: 20 / Woman seated with book on lap. *Center:* XX / Eagle / XX. *Right:* 20 / Ship. *Engraver:* New England Bank Note Co. *Comments:* H-RI-55-G80, Durand-231. 18__. 1850s.
Rarity: *None known*

$50 • W-RI-210-050-G300

Left: Lathework chain bearing RHODE ISLAND / 50 / 50 vertically. *Center:* Alternating flower garlands and gridwork segments. *Right:* 50 / 50 vertically. *Engraver:* PSSP. *Comments:* H-RI-55-G84. 18__. 1820s–1830s.
Rarity: *None known*

$50 • W-RI-210-050-G310

Left: 50 / Woman standing with ankles crossed, staff, Cornucopia and anchor / 50. *Center:* FIFTY DOLLARS / 50. *Right:* FIFTY vertically. *Engraver:* PSSP / New England Bank Note Co. *Comments:* H-RI-55-G86. 18__. 1830s.
Rarity: *None known*

$50 • W-RI-210-050-G320

Left: 50 / Steamboat and schooner. *Center:* Harvesting scene, Farmers, hay / 50. *Right:* L / Justice. *Engraver:* New England Bank Note Co. *Comments:* H-RI-55-G88, Durand-233. 18__. 1840s.
Rarity: *None known*

$50 • W-RI-210-050-G330

Left: FIFTY / Woman with wreath and flowers / FIFTY. *Center:* 50 / Man restraining prancing horse / 50. *Right:* FIFTY / Woman with cornucopia / FIFTY. *Engraver:* New England Bank Note Co. *Comments:* H-RI-55-G90, Durand-234. 18__. 1850s.
Rarity: *None known*

$100 • W-RI-210-100-G340

Left: Lathework chain bearing RHODE ISLAND / 100 / 100 vertically. *Center:* Alternating flower garlands and gridwork segments. *Right:* 100 / 100 vertically. *Engraver:* PSSP. *Comments:* H-RI-55-G94. 18__. 1820s–1830s.
Rarity: *None known*

$100 • W-RI-210-100-G350

Left: Lathework panel with C / Portrait of George Washington / C. *Center:* 100 / Manhattan reclining pouring water, Ship / 100. *Right:* Lathework panel bearing ONE HUNDRED vertically. *Engraver:* PSSP / New England Bank Note Co. *Comments:* H-RI-55-G96. 18__. 1830s.
Rarity: *None known*

$100 • W-RI-210-100-G360

Left: ONE HUNDRED across 100 / Portrait of William Henry Harrison. *Center:* Wharf scene. *Right:* ONE HUNDRED across 100 / Portrait of Christopher Columbus. *Engraver:* New England Bank Note Co. *Comments:* H-RI-55-G98, Durand-235. 18__. 1840s.
Rarity: *None known*

$100 • W-RI-210-100-G370

Left: 100 / Eagle / 100. *Center:* C / "Phoebus in Chariot of the Sun" / 100. *Right:* C / Portrait of George Washington / C. *Engraver:* New England Bank Note Co. *Comments:* H-RI-55-G100, Durand-236. 18__. 1850s.
Rarity: *None known*

NON-VALID ISSUES

$1 • W-RI-210-001-C010

CJF

Engraver: Reed. *Comments:* H-RI-55-C2, Durand-209. Counterfeit of W-RI-210-001-G010. 18___. 1820s.
Rarity: URS-3
VF $100

$2 • W-RI-210-002-C060

CJF

Engraver: Reed. *Comments:* H-RI-55-C16, Durand-215. Counterfeit of W-RI-210-002-G060. 18___. 1819–1821.
Rarity: URS-5
VF $200

$2 • W-RI-210-002-C060a

CJF

Engraver: Reed. *Comments:* H-Unlisted, Durand-Unlisted. Similar to W-RI-210-002-C060. Printed on blue paper. 18___. 1819–1820s.
Rarity: URS-4
F $250

$2 • W-RI-210-002-C060b

SI

Engraver: Reed. *Comments:* H-Unlisted, Durand-Unlisted. Similar to W-RI-210-002-C060. Printed on green paper. 18___. 1819–1820s.
Rarity: URS-4
F $250

$5 • W-RI-210-005-S010

Left: Liberty. *Center:* 5 / Reclining allegorical figure. *Right:* FIVE / Portrait of Benjamin Franklin. *Engraver:* Spencer, Hufty & Danforth. *Comments:* H-RI-55-S5, Durand-224. July 15, 18___. 1850s.
Rarity: URS-3
VF $100

$10 • W-RI-210-010-A010

CC

Overprint: Red TEN. *Engraver:* PSSP / New England Bank Note Co. *Comments:* H-RI-55-A5, Durand-229. Altered from W-RI-1300-010-G080, or from notes of other failed banks using the same plate. Genuine notes of this design were issued, W-RI-210-010-G250. 18___. 1830s–1850s.
Rarity: URS-5
VF $350

$20 • W-RI-210-020-A020

Engraver: New England Bank Note Co. *Comments:* H-RI-55-A10, Durand-232. Altered from W-RI-1300-020-G090, or from notes of other failed banks using the same plate. Genuine notes of this design were issued, W-RI-210-020-G280. 18___. 1840s–1850s.
Rarity: *None known*

COVENTRY, RHODE ISLAND

Coventry was originally a part of Warwick when it was first settled in the early 18th century. Farmers populated the area by 1741, and they petitioned the General Assembly to incorporate the district as a town. It was named after the English city of Coventry.

During the 18th century, Coventry was an agricultural community. The first mill built in the nearby village of Anthony—the mill operated from 1872 to 1874—brought the Industrial Revolution to the area, causing the eastern portion of Coventry to become heavily industrialized. The western part of town remained rural. French-Canadian and Irish immigrants took up residence in the mill villages.

See also Anthony Village, Rhode Island.

Bank of Kent
1818–1867
W-RI-220

History: The Bank of Kent was chartered in June 1818 with $50,000 authorized capital. This was during a time of great expansion in the Rhode Island manufacturing industry, and there was a greater need for financial resources. The bank's founding president and cashier were Caleb Fiske and Silvanus Hopkins, respectively. Capital was $30,000 in 1848 and was raised to $50,000 by 1855, where it remained through 1864. Circulation in 1863 amounted to $10,266. The same was listed at $14,695 from 1857 through 1860, decreasing to $10,266 by 1862. Specie totaled $1,836.34 in 1857. The directors and stockholders did not apply for a national bank charter, and the institution closed in 1867.[14]

Numismatic Commentary: Genuine notes from this bank are available in the marketplace. At least one uncut sheet from the engraving firm of Terry, Pelton & Co. is known. Some of the vignettes include women working at looms, a textile machine, a view of a local factory, and a young Oliver Hazard Perry.

VALID ISSUES

$1 • W-RI-220-001-G010   CJF

Engraver: Reed. **Comments:** H-RI-60-G2, Durand-237. 18__. 1818–1820s.
> **Rarity:** URS-1
> **VF** $600; **EF** $1,200

$1 • W-RI-220-001-G020
Left: ONE vertically. **Center:** 1 / Two women working in factory / 1. **Bottom center:** Shield with anchor / ONE. **Right:** ONE / Portrait of Commodore Oliver Hazard Perry / ONE. **Engraver:** Terry, Pelton & Co. **Comments:** H-RI-60-G6, Durand-238. 18__. 1830s–1840s.
> **Rarity:** *None known*

$1 • W-RI-220-001-G020a
Overprint: Red ONE. **Engraver:** Terry, Pelton & Co. **Comments:** H-RI-60-G6a, Durand-239. Similar to W-RI-220-001-G020. 18__. 1850s.
> **Rarity:** URS-6
> **VF** $300

$1 • W-RI-220-001-G030
Left: 1 / Justice. **Center:** 1 / Industry / 1. **Right:** 1 / State arms. **Comments:** H-RI-60-G8, Durand-240. 18__. 1860s.
> **Rarity:** *None known*

$1.50 • W-RI-220-001.50-G040
Center: Textile machinery. **Engraver:** Reed. **Comments:** H-RI-60-G11, Durand-242. 18__. 1810s–1820s.
> **Rarity:** URS-3
> **VF** $300

$2 • W-RI-220-002-G050
Left: TWO 2 TWO vertically. **Center:** 2 / Ceres, City / 2. **Bottom center:** TWO. **Right:** 2 RHODE ISLAND 2 vertically. **Engraver:** Reed. **Comments:** H-RI-60-G14, Durand-243. 18__. 1818–1820s.
> **Rarity:** URS-3
> **VF** $300

$2 • W-RI-220-002-G060
Left: TWO vertically. **Center:** 2 / Village and buildings / 2 / TWO. **Bottom center:** Shield with anchor. **Right:** TWO / Portrait of Benjamin Franklin / TWO. **Engraver:** Terry, Pelton & Co. **Comments:** H-RI-60-G18, Durand-244. 18__. 1830s–1840s.
> **Rarity:** *None known*

$2 • W-RI-220-002-G060a
Overprint: Red TWO. **Engraver:** Terry, Pelton & Co. **Comments:** H-RI-60-G18a, Durand-245. Similar to W-RI-220-002-G060. 18__. 1850s.
> **Rarity:** URS-3
> **VF** $300

$2 • W-RI-220-002-G070
Left: 2 / Girl with dove. **Center:** Two allegorical women seated on bales, Factories. **Right:** 2 / Mechanic, anvil, and hammer. **Comments:** H-RI-60-G20, Durand-246. 18__. 1860s.
> **Rarity:** *None known*

$3 • W-RI-220-003-G080   SBG

Engraver: Reed. **Comments:** H-RI-60-G22, Durand-248. Proof. 18__. 1818–1820s.
> **Rarity:** URS-3
> **VF** $300; **Proof** $2,000

$5 • W-RI-220-005-G090
Left: FIVE vertically. **Center:** 5 on die / Building with water and boat, People / 5 on die / FIVE over FIVE. **Bottom center:** Shield with anchor. **Right:** FIVE / Portrait of George Washington / FIVE. **Engraver:** Terry, Pelton & Co. **Comments:** H-RI-60-G28, Durand-250. 18__. 1830s–1840s.
> **Rarity:** *None known*

$5 • **W-RI-220-005-G090a**

Overprint: Red FIVE. *Engraver:* Terry, Pelton & Co. *Comments:* H-RI-60-G28a, Durand-251. Similar to W-RI-220-005-G090. 18__. 1850s.

Rarity: URS-3
VF $300

$5 • **W-RI-220-005-G100**

Left: Two frightened horses, Cattle in stream / 5. *Center:* 5. *Right:* 5 / Woman, Spinning wheel, Factory. *Comments:* H-RI-60-G30, Durand-252. 18__. 1860s.

Rarity: *None known*

$5 • **W-RI-220-005-G100a**

Overprint: Red FIVE. *Comments:* H-Unlisted, Durand-254. Similar to W-RI-220-005-G100. 18__. 1860s.

Rarity: URS-3
F $90

$5 • **W-RI-220-005-G110**

Left: Factories and village / 5. *Center:* 5. *Right:* FIVE / Portrait of George Washington / FIVE. *Comments:* H-Unlisted, Durand-255. 18__. 1830s–1840s.

Rarity: URS-6

$5 • **W-RI-220-005-G110a**

Overprint: Red FIVE. *Comments:* H-Unlisted, Durand-256. Similar to W-RI-220-005-G110. 18__. 1850s.

Rarity: URS-5

$5 • **W-RI-220-005-G110b**

Tint: Red. *Comments:* H-Unlisted, Durand-257. Similar to W-RI-220-005-G110. 18__. 1850s.

Rarity: URS-6

$10 • **W-RI-220-010-G120**

Left: Panel with TEN / Manhattan spilling water jug / TEN. *Center:* TEN / Ceres seated / TEN / Panel of microletters. *Right:* Panel with 10 / Portrait of Indian / 10. *Engraver:* PSSP. *Comments:* H-RI-60-G32. 18__. 1830s.

Rarity: *None known*

$10 • **W-RI-220-010-G130**

Left: 10, X, 10. *Center:* Man with oxen, 10. *Right:* TEN / Woman standing with cornucopia. *Engraver:* New England Bank Note Co. *Comments:* H-RI-60-G34, Durand-259. 18__. 1840s–1850s.

Rarity: *None known*

$10 • **W-RI-220-010-G130a**

Overprint: Red TEN. *Engraver:* New England Bank Note Co. *Comments:* H-RI-60-G34a, Durand-258. Similar to W-RI-220-010-G130. 18__. 1850s.

Rarity: URS-3
VF $400

$10 • **W-RI-220-010-G130b**   CC

Overprint: Red TEN. *Engraver:* New England Bank Note Co. / ABNCo. monogram. *Comments:* H-RI-60-G34b. Similar to W-RI-220-010-G130 but with additional engraver imprint. 18__. 1850s–1860s.

Rarity: URS-5
VF $300; **AU** $600

$20 • **W-RI-220-020-G140**

Left: 20 / XX vertically / 20. *Center:* 20 / Woman seated with scales, Sheaf and bales, Men plowing, Ship / 20. *Right:* TWENTY vertically. *Engraver:* PSSP / New England Bank Note Co. *Comments:* H-RI-60-G36. 18__. 1830s.

Rarity: *None known*

$20 • **W-RI-220-020-G150**

Left: 20 / Woman seated. *Center:* XX / Eagle / XX. *Right:* 20 / Sailing vessel. *Engraver:* New England Bank Note Co. *Comments:* H-RI-60-G38, Durand-261. 18__. 1840s–1850s.

Rarity: *None known*

$20 • **W-RI-220-020-G150a**

Overprint: Red TWENTY. *Engraver:* New England Bank Note Co. *Comments:* H-RI-60-G38a, Durand-260. Similar to W-RI-220-020-G150. 18__. 1850s.

Rarity: URS-3
VF $400

$20 • **W-RI-220-020-G150b**   CC

Overprint: Red TWENTY. *Engraver:* New England Bank Note Co. / ABNCo. monogram. *Comments:* H-RI-60-G38b, Durand-260. Similar to W-RI-220-020-G150 but with additional engraver imprint. Remainder. 18__. 1850s–1860s.

Rarity: URS-4
AU $400

$50 • **W-RI-220-050-G160**

Left: 50 / Woman standing with ankles crossed, staff, Cornucopia and anchor / 50. *Center:* FIFTY DOLLARS / 50. *Right:* FIFTY vertically. *Engraver:* PSSP / New England Bank Note Co. *Comments:* H-RI-60-G40. 18__. 1830s.

Rarity: *None known*

$50 • W-RI-220-050-G170
Left: FIFTY / Woman holding flowers and wreath / FIFTY. *Center:* 50 / Man restraining horse / 50. *Right:* FIFTY / Woman standing / FIFTY. *Engraver:* New England Bank Note Co. *Comments:* H-RI-60-G42, Durand-263. 18__. 1840s–1850s.
Rarity: *None known*

$50 • W-RI-220-050-G170a CC

Overprint: Red FIFTY. *Engraver:* New England Bank Note Co. *Comments:* H-RI-60-G42a, Durand-262. Similar to W-RI-220-050-G170. 18__. 1850s.
Rarity: URS-3
VF $400

$100 • W-RI-220-100-G180
Left: Lathework panel with C / Portrait of George Washington / C. *Center:* 100 / Manhattan reclining pouring water, Ship / 100. *Right:* Lathework panel with ONE HUNDRED vertically. *Engraver:* PSSP / New England Bank Note Co. *Comments:* H-RI-60-G44. 18__. 1830s–1840s.
Rarity: *None known*

$100 • W-RI-220-100-G190
Left: 100 / Eagle / 100. *Center:* C / "Phoebus in Chariot of the Sun" / 100. *Right:* C / Portrait of George Washington / C. *Engraver:* New England Bank Note Co. *Comments:* H-RI-60-G46, Durand-264. 18__. 1840s–1850s.
Rarity: *None known*

$100 • W-RI-220-100-G190a CC

Overprint: Red HUNDRED. *Comments:* H-Unlisted, Durand-265. Similar to W-RI-220-100-G190. 18__. 1840s–1850s.
Rarity: URS-3
VF $450; **AU** $500

Uncut Sheets
$1-$1-$2-$5 • W-RI-220-001.001.002.005-US010
Vignette(s): *($1)* Two women working in factory / Shield with anchor / Portrait of Commodore Oliver Hazard Perry. *($1)* Two women working in factory / Shield with anchor / Portrait of Commodore Oliver Hazard Perry. *($2)* Village and buildings / Shield with anchor / Portrait of Benjamin Franklin. *($5)* Building with water and boat, People / Shield with anchor / Portrait of George Washington. *Overprint(s):* Red. *Engraver:* Terry, Pelton & Co. *Comments:* H-RI-60-G6a, G6a, G18a, G28a. 18__. 1850s.
Rarity: URS-3
VF $2,000

NON-VALID ISSUES
$1 • W-RI-220-001-C010
Engraver: Reed. *Comments:* H-RI-60-C2, Durand-241. Counterfeit of W-RI-220-001-G010. 18__. 1820s.
Rarity: URS-3
VF $250

$2 • W-RI-220-002-C050 CJF

Engraver: Reed. *Comments:* H-RI-60-C14, Durand-247. Counterfeit of W-RI-220-002-G050. 18__. 1820s.
Rarity: URS-3
VF $250

$3 • W-RI-220-003-C080
Engraver: Reed. *Comments:* H-RI-60-C22, Durand-249. Counterfeit of W-RI-220-003-G080. 18__. 1810s.
Rarity: URS-3
VF $300

$5 • W-RI-220-005-S010 SI

Engraver: Toppan, Carpenter, Casilear & Co. *Comments:* H-RI-60-S5. Spurious design imitating a rough verbal description of W-RI-220-005-G090. May 1st, 185_. 1850s.
Rarity: URS-6
VF $125

$5 • W-RI-220-005-S010a

Left: 5 on die. *Center:* Building / 5 bearing FIVE DOLLARS. *Bottom center:* Shield bearing state arms. *Right:* FIVE / Portrait of George Washington / FIVE. *Overprint:* Red FIVE. *Engraver:* Toppan, Carpenter, Casilear & Co. *Comments:* H-RI-60-S5a. Similar to W-RI-220-005-S010. May 1, 1856.

Rarity: URS-6
VF $250

$5 • W-RI-220-005-A010

Left: FIVE / State arms of Michigan. *Center:* Farmer, sailor, and mechanic. *Right:* 5 / Portrait of Franklin Pierce. *Engraver:* Danforth, Wright & Co. *Comments:* H-RI-60-A5, Durand-253. Altered from $5 Bank of Washtenaw, Washtenaw, Michigan series. 1850s.

Rarity: *None known*

Coventry Bank
1850–1865
W-RI-230

History: The Coventry Bank was incorporated in May 1850, formed as a convenience and a business venture to serve mill workers who lived in the area. Its capital was $75,000 in 1853, decreased to $68,050 by 1855, and increased to $100,000 by 1860. Circulation was $26,530 in 1851 and $32,946 in 1863. Specie in 1857 was $2,134.87.

In 1865 the business of the Coventry Bank was succeeded by the Coventry National Bank.

See also listing under Anthony Village, W-RI-020.

CRANSTON, RHODE ISLAND

Men from Warwick purchased land in 1662 that included what would later become Cranston. In 1714, after years of controversy and border disputes, the southern and western lines of Cranston were firmly established. It was incorporated as a town in 1754 and separated from Providence. Throughout the 19th century, however, much of Cranston was redistributed back to Providence.

Immigrants from Ireland, Canada, Italy, Germany, Sweden, Greece, and Armenia arrived during the Industrial Revolution to work in the textile mills. An ideal harbor and falls from the Pawtuxet River provided water power in Cranston's village of Pawtuxet.

See also Pawtuxet and Providence, Rhode Island.

Cranston Bank
1818–1865
W-RI-240

History: The Cranston Bank was incorporated in February 1818. Sylvester Wicks was the bank's first president, and Jeremiah Knight was its first cashier. Similar to the activity of many other banks, the Cranston Bank profited by issuing large quantities of notes and shipping them at a discount to distant locations with the expectation that many would never be redeemed.

Capital was listed at $25,000 between 1849 and 1855. By 1857 it had increased to $37,500. Circulation was $10,367 in 1857 but had decreased to $9,807 by 1862. Specie was $1,017.59 in 1857.

The bank was moved to Providence in 1850 and to Olneyville in 1865. It was closed that year.

Also see listings under Olneyville, W-RI-685, and Providence, W-RI-885.

Numismatic Commentary: Genuine, signed notes are hard to find. Some reprint Proofs may be found in the marketplace as well as altered notes. Sheets of the reprints may become available from time to time.

VALID ISSUES

$1 • W-RI-240-001-G010

SBG

Engraver: Reed. *Comments:* H-RI-65-G3, Durand-266. 18__. 1818–1820s.

Rarity: URS-3
Proof $500

$1 • W-RI-240-001-G010a

CJF

Engraver: Reed. *Comments:* H-RI-65-G3a. Similar to W-RI-240-001-G010. Reprint. 18__. 1820s–1830s.

Rarity: URS-3
Proof $500

$1 • W-RI-240-001-G020

Left: 1 / Portrait of George Washington. *Center:* Female portrait / 1 / Female portrait. *Right:* 1 / Portrait of Benjamin Franklin. *Engraver:* New England Bank Note Co. *Comments:* H-RI-65-G7, Durand-267. 18__. 1840s–1850s.

Rarity: *None known*

$2 • W-RI-240-002-G030

Left: TWO / Two seated Indians, Falls / TWO. *Center:* 2 / Three allegorical figures / 2. *Bottom center:* Cattle. *Right:* TWO / Portrait of George Washington / TWO. *Engraver:* Terry, Pelton & Co. *Comments:* H-RI-65-G12, Durand-268. 18__. 1840s–1850s.

Rarity: *None known*

$3 • W-RI-240-003-G040

CC

Engraver: Reed. *Comments:* H-RI-65-G16, Durand-269. 18__. 1810s–1820s.

Rarity: URS-3
Proof $500

$3 • W-RI-240-003-G040a

Left: 3 THREE 3 vertically. *Bottom center:* 3. *Right:* 3 RHODE ISLAND 3 vertically. *Engraver:* Reed. *Comments:* H-RI-65-G16a. Similar to W-RI-240-003-G040. Reprint. 18__. 1820s.

Rarity: URS-3
Proof $75

$3 • W-RI-240-003-G050

Left: THREE vertically. *Center:* Farmer in field, Spread eagle, Shield and 3. *Bottom center:* Train. *Right:* THREE / Portrait of girl / 3. *Engraver:* Terry, Pelton & Co. *Comments:* H-RI-65-G20, Durand-270. 18__. 1840s–1850s.

Rarity: *None known*

$5 • W-RI-240-005-G060

QDB

Engraver: Reed. *Comments:* H-RI-65-G24, Durand-273. 18__. 1818–1820s.

Rarity: URS-3
Proof $600

$5 • W-RI-240-005-G060a

QDB

Engraver: Reed. *Comments:* H-RI-65-G24a. Similar to W-RI-240-005-G060. Reprint. 18__. 1820s–1830s.

Rarity: URS-3
Proof $75

$5 • W-RI-240-005-G070

Left: 5 / Portrait of Benjamin Franklin. *Center:* Female portrait / Eagle / Liberty, Justice, and Knowledge / Ship / Cupid. *Right:* 5 / "George Washington at Dorchester Heights". *Engraver:* Terry, Pelton & Co. *Comments:* H-RI-65-G28, Durand-274. 18__. 1830s–1850s.

Rarity: URS-3
Proof $500

$10 • W-RI-240-010-G080

Left: X / Indian with bow. *Center:* Steamboat, schooner, boats, distant city / X. *Right:* 10 / Girl holding sheaf. *Engraver:* New England Bank Note Co. *Comments:* H-RI-65-G32, Durand-277. 18__. 1840s–1850s.

Rarity: *None known*

$20 • W-RI-240-020-G090

Left: 20 / Woman with book on lap, opening chest. *Center:* XX / Eagle / XX. *Right:* 20 / Ship. *Engraver:* New England Bank Note Co. *Comments:* H-RI-65-G34, Durand-281. 18__. 1840s–1860s.

Rarity: *None known*

$50 • W-RI-240-050-G100

Left: FIFTY / Woman holding wreath and flowers / FIFTY. *Center:* 50 / Man restraining prancing horse / 50. *Right:* FIFTY / Woman with cornucopia / FIFTY. *Engraver:* New England Bank Note Co. *Comments:* H-RI-65-G36, Durand-283. 18__. 1840s–1850s.

Rarity: *None known*

$100 • W-RI-240-100-G110

CJF

Engraver: New England Bank Note Co. *Comments:* H-RI-65-G38, Durand-285. 18__. 1840s–1860s.

Rarity: URS-1
VF $1,000

Uncut Sheets

$1-$1-$3-$5 • W-RI-240-001.001.003.005-US010

Vignette(s): ($1) Woman seated, Building. ($1) Woman seated, Building. ($3) Woman seated with 3. ($5) Allegorical figure seated, Mill. *Engraver:* Reed. *Comments:* H-RI-65-G3, G3, G16, G24. 18__. 1818–1820s.

Rarity: URS-3
Proof $2,500

$1-$1-$3-$5 • W-RI-240-001.001.003.005-US010a

Overprint(s): Red. *Engraver:* Reed. *Comments:* H-RI-65-G3a, G3a, G16a, G24a. Similar to W-RI-240-001.001.003.005-US010. Reprint. 18__. 1820s–1830s.

Rarity: URS-3
Proof $250

NON-VALID ISSUES

$3 • W-RI-240-003-C040a

TD

Engraver: Reed. *Comments:* H-RI-65-C16a, Durand-271. Counterfeit of W-RI-240-003-G040a. 18__. 1820s–1830s.
Rarity: URS-3
VF $125

$3 • W-RI-240-003-C050

Engraver: Terry, Pelton & Co. *Comments:* H-RI-65-C20, Durand-272. Counterfeit of W-RI-240-003-G050. 18__. 1840s–1850s.
Rarity: *None known*

$5 • W-RI-240-005-C070

Engraver: Terry, Pelton & Co. *Comments:* H-RI-65-C28. Counterfeit of W-RI-240-005-G070. 18__. 1840s–1850s.
Rarity: *None known*

$5 • W-RI-240-005-A010

Left: 5 / Two Indians / 5. *Center:* 5 / Literature, Justice, and Liberty / 5. *Right:* 5 / Portrait of George Washington / 5. *Engraver:* Terry, Pelton & Co. *Comments:* H-RI-65-A5, Durand-275. Altered from $1 Citizens Bank of Augusta, Augusta, Maine, or from notes of other failed banks using the same plate. 18__. 1840s.
Rarity: *None known*

$5 • W-RI-240-005-A020

Left: FIVE / Portrait of Benjamin Franklin / V. *Center:* 5 / Three allegorical women / 5. *Right:* V / Portrait of Marquis de Lafayette / FIVE. *Engraver:* Terry, Pelton & Co. *Comments:* H-RI-65-A10, Durand-276. Altered from $5 Citizens Bank of Augusta, Augusta, Maine, or from notes of other failed banks using the same plate. 18__. 1844.
Rarity: *None known*

$10 • W-RI-240-010-S010

Left: 10 / Indian with raised tomahawk. *Center:* Man on horse / Three allegorical women. *Bottom center:* Train. *Right:* 10 / Female portrait / 10. *Engraver:* Terry, Pelton & Co. *Comments:* H-RI-65-S5. 18__. 1841.
Rarity: URS-3
VF $125

$10 • W-RI-240-010-A030

Left: 10 / Portrait of George Washington held by cherub / 10. *Center:* X / E PLURIBUS UNUM / Spread eagle with shield and arrows / X. *Right:* 10 / Indian / 10. *Engraver:* Terry, Pelton & Co. *Comments:* H-RI-65-A15, Durand-279. Altered from $10 Citizens Bank of Augusta, Augusta, Maine, or from notes of other failed banks using the same plate. 18__. 1840s.
Rarity: *None known*

$10 • W-RI-240-010-A040

Left: X / Man in canal boat, Shrubbery and houses / Beehive / X. *Center:* Indian with raised tomahawk, Dog and deer. *Right:* Farmer, grain, and tree / Farmer harrowing with two horses, House. *Engraver:* Terry, Pelton & Co. *Comments:* H-RI-65-A20, Durand-280. Altered from $20 East Bridgewater Bank, East Bridgewater, Massachusetts. 1840s.
Rarity: *None known*

$10 • W-RI-240-010-N010

Left: 10 / RHODE ISLAND / Man with gun. *Center:* Men with animals / Two women and man with plow / Ships. *Right:* 10 / Female portrait / 10. *Comments:* H-Unlisted, Durand-278. 1840s.
Rarity: *None known*

$20 • W-RI-240-020-A050

CJF

Engraver: Terry, Pelton & Co. *Comments:* H-RI-65-A25, Durand-282. Altered from $20 East Bridgewater Bank, East Bridgewater, Massachusetts. 18__. 1840s.
Rarity: URS-1
VF $125

$50 • W-RI-240-050-A060

Left: 50 / Man in canal boat, Shrubbery and houses / Beehive / 50. *Center:* Indian with raised tomahawk, Dog and deer. *Right:* Farmer, grain, and tree / Farmer harrowing with two horses, House. *Comments:* H-Unlisted, Durand-284. Altered from $20 East Bridgewater Bank, East Bridgewater, Massachusetts. 1840s.
Rarity: URS-3

Elmwood Bank
1854–1867
W-RI-250

History: The Elmwood Bank was incorporated in May 1854. Its authorized capital was $55,350, which was reduced to $40,000 by June 1855. It was increased to $82,650 by 1857 and remained at that amount through 1864. The founding president was William V. Daboll. He was accompanied by cashier Daniel L. Rawson, who was replaced in 1857 by C.H. Bassett. Circulation was reported to be $10,600 from 1857 to 1860. Specie in 1857 totaled $1,478.08. In 1858 real estate security was $1,000. Circulation in 1862 was $19,500.

The bank closed in 1867.

See also listing under Elmwood, W-RI-350.

Numismatic Commentary: All genuine notes show an engraving of a village scene with the home of the bank president, William V. Daboll, on Elmwood Avenue in Cranston. An unusual aspect of this bank's currency is that none of its notes have been found to be altered or raised.[15]

VALID ISSUES

$1 • W-RI-250-001-G010

CC

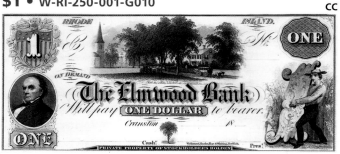

Engraver: Wellstood, Hanks, Hay & Whiting. **Comments:** H-RI-70-G2, Durand-286. 18__. 1850s.
Rarity: URS-3
Proof $2,500

$1 • W-RI-250-001-G010a

CJF

Overprint: Red ONE. **Engraver:** Wellstood, Hanks, Hay & Whiting. **Comments:** H-RI-70-G2a, Durand-287. Similar to W-RI-250-001-G010. 18__. 1850s.
Rarity: URS-2
VF $1,500

$1 • W-RI-250-001-G010b

Overprint: Red ONE. **Engraver:** Wellstood, Hanks, Hay & Whiting / ABNCo. monogram. **Comments:** H-RI-70-G2b. Similar to W-RI-250-001-G010 but with additional engraver imprint. 18__. 1850s–1860s.
Rarity: *None known*

$2 • W-RI-250-002-G020

Left: Home of William Daboll / 2 on shield. **Center:** Portrait of Franklin Pierce. **Right:** II / Woman holding 2. **Engraver:** Wellstood, Hanks, Hay & Whiting. **Comments:** H-RI-70-G4, Durand-288. 18__. 1850s.
Rarity: URS-2
Proof $2,500

$2 • W-RI-250-002-G020a

Overprint: Red TWO. **Engraver:** Wellstood, Hanks, Hay & Whiting. **Comments:** H-RI-70-G4a, Durand-289. Similar to W-RI-250-002-G020. 18__. 1850s.
Rarity: URS-3
VF $750

$2 • W-RI-250-002-G020b

CC

Overprint: Red TWO. **Engraver:** Wellstood, Hanks, Hay & Whiting / ABNCo. monogram. **Comments:** H-RI-70-G4b. Similar to W-RI-250-002-G020 but with additional engraver imprint. 18__. 1850s–1860s.
Rarity: URS-2
VF $1,300

$3 • W-RI-250-003-G030

Left: Home of William Daboll / 3 on shield. **Center:** Male portrait. **Right:** 3 on die / Woman seated holding 3. **Comments:** H-Unlisted, Durand-290. Model Proof for an unissued $3 bill. 1850s–1860s.
Rarity: URS-3

$5 • W-RI-250-005-G040

Left: FIVE / Woman standing, Man seated beneath tree. **Center:** 5 on die / Home of William Daboll. **Right:** 5 / Woman standing. **Engraver:** Wellstood, Hanks, Hay & Whiting. **Comments:** H-RI-70-G6, Durand-291. 18__. 1850s.
Rarity: URS-1
Proof $2,500

$5 • W-RI-250-005-G040a

Overprint: Red FIVE. **Engraver:** Wellstood, Hanks, Hay & Whiting. **Comments:** H-RI-70-G6a, Durand-292. Similar to W-RI-250-005-G040. 18__. 1850s–1860s.
Rarity: URS-3
VF $750

$5 • W-RI-250-005-G040b

Overprint: Red FIVE. **Engraver:** Wellstood, Hanks, Hay & Whiting / ABNCo. monogram. **Comments:** H-RI-70-G6b. Similar to W-RI-250-005-G040 but with additional engraver imprint. 18__. 1860s.
Rarity: *None known*

$10 • W-RI-250-010-G050

SBG

Engraver: Wellstood, Hanks, Hay & Whiting. **Comments:** H-RI-70-G8, Durand-293. 18__. 1850s.
Rarity: URS-2
Proof $3,900

$10 • W-RI-250-010-G050a

Left: TEN / Liberty with pole, cap, and X / TEN on 10. *Center:* Home of William Daboll. *Bottom center:* Tree. *Right:* 10 / X bearing TEN, Milkmaid and cow. *Overprint:* Red TEN. *Engraver:* Wellstood, Hanks, Hay & Whiting. *Comments:* H-RI-70-G8a, Durand-294. Similar to W-RI-250-010-G050. 18__. 1850s.

Rarity: *None known*

$10 • W-RI-250-010-G050b

Overprint: Red TEN. *Engraver:* Wellstood, Hanks, Hay & Whiting / ABNCo. monogram. *Comments:* H-RI-70-G8b. Similar to W-RI-250-010-G050 but with additional engraver imprint. 18__. 1860s.

Rarity: *None known*

$50 • W-RI-250-050-G060

Left: 50 / Female portrait. *Center:* Home of William Daboll. *Bottom center:* 50. *Right:* Three men holding 50. *Engraver:* Wellstood, Hanks, Hay & Whiting. *Comments:* H-RI-70-G10, Durand-295. 18__. 1850s–1860s.

Rarity: URS-1
Proof $2,500

$100 • W-RI-250-100-G070

Left: 100 / Female portrait and sheaves in C. *Center:* Sickle and shield / Two women. *Bottom center:* Tree. *Right:* 100 / Home of William Daboll / 100. *Engraver:* Wellstood, Hanks, Hay & Whiting. *Comments:* H-RI-70-G12, Durand-296. 18__. 1850s–1860s.

Rarity: URS-1
Proof $2,500

Uncut Sheets

$5-$5-$10-$10 • W-RI-250-005.005.010.010-US010

Vignette(s): *($5)* Woman standing, Man seated beneath tree / Home of William Daboll / Woman standing. *($5)* Woman standing, Man seated beneath tree / Home of William Daboll / Woman standing. *($10)* Liberty / Home of William Daboll / Tree / Milkmaid and cow. *($10)* Liberty / Home of William Daboll / Tree / Milkmaid and cow. *Engraver:* Wellstood, Hanks, Hay & Whiting. *Comments:* H-RI-70-G6, G6, G8, G8. 1850s.

Rarity: URS-1
Proof $7,500

CUMBERLAND, RHODE ISLAND

Cumberland was the site of the first settlement in Rhode Island. It was founded by William Blackstone from Shawmut, Massachusetts. The land was originally a part of Rehoboth, which was called Wannamoisett by the natives. In 1746 it was divided from Attleborough and renamed Cumberland.

In the early years, tar was manufactured from pine-tree pitch, and by 1797 a mill for sawing marble was established, a precursor to later mineral industries. Textile mills became important, the first being established in 1810 in the Cumberland village of Woonsocket. Other industries included metal manufacturing, lumber, and shipbuilding.

See also Woonsocket, Rhode Island.

Citizens Bank
1851–1865
W-RI-260

History: The Citizens Bank was incorporated in May 1851. Notes with the Cumberland imprint were issued in 1851 and 1852. The bank's location was changed in 1853 to Woonsocket, a small village in the Cumberland area. This village was incorporated as the town of Woonsocket in 1867.

The bank's capital in 1857 was $56,950. Circulation was $24,003, which increased to $27,797 by 1862. Specie amounted to $2,031.14 in 1857.

The business of the Citizens Bank was succeeded by the Citizens National Bank, chartered on April 1, 1865.

See also listing under Woonsocket, W-RI-1670.

Numismatic Commentary: This bank had the unfortunate distinction of having its circulation seemingly increased by the appearance of notes which were readily altered from the Citizens Bank of Washington, D.C. Apparently, much of the issue of notes from this bankrupt D.C. bank was altered to represent the Citizens Bank, Cumberland.[16]

VALID ISSUES

$1 • W-RI-260-001-G010

Left: 1 / Portrait of George Washington. *Center:* Allegorical figure / 1 / Allegorical figure. *Right:* 1 / Portrait of Benjamin Franklin. *Engraver:* New England Bank Note Co. *Comments:* H-RI-75-G2, Durand-2583. 18__. 1850s.

Rarity: *None known*

How to Read the Whitman Numbering System
$1 • W-RI-010-001-G010a

Denomination: Value of the note shown.

W: Whitman number. This number is a sortable code unique to each bank and note.

RI: Abbreviation for the state under study.

010: Numerical designation specific to each bank.

001: The denomination in dollars.

G010a: G indicates a good or valid note. Other categories are indicated thus: C (counterfeit); R (raised); S (spurious); N (not-attributed); A (altered). Numbers are assigned starting with 010, 020, et seq. Terminal letters following the number indicate variations of a note: a series of different colored overprints, tints, payees, etc., all on the same design of note. For more information, see the "How to Use This Book" section at the front of the volume, page xiv.

$2 • W-RI-260-002-G020

Left: 2 / Portrait of Christopher Columbus. *Center:* Allegorical figure / 2 / Allegorical figure. *Right:* 2 / Male portrait. *Engraver:* New England Bank Note Co. *Comments:* H-RI-75-G4, Durand-2585. 18__. 1850s.

Rarity: *None known*

$3 • W-RI-260-003-G030

Left: 3 / George Washington with his horse. *Center:* Allegorical figure / 3 / Allegorical figure. *Right:* 3 / Vulcan with hammer. *Engraver:* New England Bank Note Co. *Comments:* H-RI-75-G6, Durand-2587. 18__. 1850s.

Rarity: *None known*

$5 • W-RI-260-005-G040

Left: Eagle on shield / FIVE. *Center:* V / Woman and cherub. *Right:* 5 / Girl with basket of flowers. *Engraver:* New England Bank Note Co. *Comments:* H-RI-75-G8, Durand-2589. 18__. 1850s.

Rarity: *None known*

Non-Valid Issues

$1 • W-RI-260-001-A010

Left: ONE vertically. *Center:* 1 / Woman standing by anvil / 1. *Right:* Indian and sailor holding flag / ONE. *Engraver:* Wellstood, Hanks, Hay & Whiting. *Comments:* H-RI-75-A5, Durand-2584. Altered from $1 Citizens Bank, Washington, D.C. 18__. 1850s.

Rarity: *None known*

$2 • W-RI-260-002-A020

CJF

Engraver: Wellstood, Hanks, Hay & Whiting. *Comments:* H-RI-75-A10, Durand-2586. Altered from $2 Citizens Bank of Washington, D.C. Nov.r 3d, 1852.

Rarity: URS-5
VF $200

$3 • W-RI-260-003-A030

Left: THREE vertically. *Center:* 3 / Mechanic standing, Train / 3. *Right:* Farmer carrying basket of corn / 3. *Engraver:* Wellstood, Hanks, Hay & Whiting. *Comments:* H-RI-75-A15, Durand-2588. Altered from $3 Citizens Bank, Washington, D.C. 18__. 1850s.

Rarity: URS-3
VF $350

$5 • W-RI-260-005-A040

CJF

Engraver: Wellstood, Hanks, Hay & Whiting. *Comments:* H-RI-75-A20, Durand-2590. Altered from $5 Citizens Bank of Washington, D.C. Nov.r 3d, 1852.

Rarity: URS-3
VF $200

$10 • W-RI-260-010-A050

Left: TEN vertically. *Center:* 10 / Liberty with arm on X / 10. *Bottom center:* Steamboat. *Right:* TEN / Indian kneeling on rocks / TEN. *Engraver:* Wellstood, Hanks, Hay & Whiting. *Comments:* H-RI-75-A25, Durand-2591. Altered from $10 Citizens Bank, Washington, D.C. 18__. 1850s.

Rarity: *None known*

$20 • W-RI-260-020-A060

Left: TWENTY vertically. *Center:* 20 / Man reading in front of building / 20 / TWENTY. *Right:* TWENTY / Woman standing with shield, Woman reclining with globe. *Comments:* H-Unlisted, Durand-2592. Altered from $2 Citizens Bank, Washington, D.C. 18__. 1850s.

Rarity: URS-3

$50 • W-RI-260-050-A070

Comments: H-Unlisted, Durand-2593. Altered from an unknown denomination of the Citizens Bank, Washington, D.C. 18__. 1850s.

Rarity: URS-3
F $125

Cumberland Bank
1823–1865
W-RI-270

History: This institution was chartered in 1822 and incorporated in January 1823. Its authorized capital was $75,000. The Amos Cook House, a large, two-story structure in the center of the village, was the office for this bank in the early days.[17]

The stock was increased several times, and in 1850 it was $75,000, with 1,500 shares valued at $50 each.[18] Circulation in 1849 was $49,911, but it decreased to $31,952 by 1857. It rose again to $53,572 by December 1863. In 1855 capital was $125,000. Specie amounted to $2,225 in 1857.

After September 30, 1865, the Cumberland Bank closed its affairs and its business was succeeded by the Cumberland National Bank.

Numismatic Commentary: Genuine notes are hard to find, but counterfeits are readily available in the marketplace. Colored paper was used for at least some of its notes. Counterfeiters noticed this and followed suit.

VALID ISSUES

$1 • **W-RI-270-001-G010**

Left: 1 on ONE / RHODE ISLAND / 1 on ONE vertically. *Center:* 1 on ONE / Woman standing under tree with 1 / 1 on ONE. *Right:* Inverted 1 / Scene / Inverted 1. *Engraver:* Horton, Providence. *Comments:* H-RI-80-G3, Durand-297. 18__. 1820s.

Rarity: *None known*

$1 • **W-RI-270-001-G010a**

Engraver: Horton, Providence. *Comments:* H-RI-80-G3a, Durand-300. Similar to W-RI-270-001-G010 but printed on blue paper. 18__. 1820s.

Rarity: *None known*

$1 • **W-RI-270-001-G010b**

Engraver: Horton, Providence. *Comments:* H-RI-80-G3b, Durand-301. Similar to W-RI-270-001-G010 but printed on pink paper. 18__. 1820s.

Rarity: *None known*

$1 • **W-RI-270-001-G020**   CJF

Overprint: Red ONE. *Engraver:* New England Bank Note Co. *Comments:* H-RI-80-G6, Durand-298. 18__. 1830s–1860s.

Rarity: URS-1
VF $1,000

$2 • **W-RI-270-002-G030**

Left: 2 / RHODE ISLAND, TWO / 2 vertically. *Center:* TWO on die bearing anchor / Industry / TWO on die bearing anchor. *Bottom center:* Ship's hull. *Right:* TWO 2 TWO vertically. *Engraver:* Horton, Providence. *Comments:* H-RI-80-G10, Durand-302. 18__. 1820s.

Rarity: URS-3
VF $275

$2 • **W-RI-270-002-G030a**

Engraver: Horton, Providence. *Comments:* H-RI-80-G10a, Durand-305. Similar to W-RI-270-002-G030 but printed on blue paper. 18__. 1820s.

Rarity: *None known*

$2 • **W-RI-270-002-G040**

Left: 2 / TWO / 2. *Center:* Ship and other vessels / 2. *Right:* TWO / Woman at well / TWO. *Engraver:* New England Bank Note Co. *Comments:* H-RI-80-G13, Durand-303. 18__. 1840s–1860s.

Rarity: *None known*

$3 • **W-RI-270-003-G050**

Left: 3 RHODE ISLAND 3 vertically. *Center:* 3 on THREE on die / Allegorical figure with shield of Hope and 3 / 3 on THREE on die. *Bottom center:* Boat. *Right:* 3 / Female portrait / 3. *Engraver:* Horton, Providence. *Comments:* H-RI-80-G17, Durand-306. 18__. 1820s.

Rarity: *None known*

$3 • **W-RI-270-003-G050a**

Engraver: Horton, Providence. *Comments:* H-RI-80-G17a, Durand-309. Similar to W-RI-270-003-G050 but printed on blue paper. 18__. 1820s.

Rarity: *None known*

$3 • **W-RI-270-003-G060**

Left: THREE vertically. *Center:* Reaping scene / 3. *Right:* THREE / Steamboat / 3 on THREE. *Engraver:* New England Bank Note Co. *Comments:* H-RI-80-G20, Durand-307. 18__. 1840s–1860s.

Rarity: *None known*

$5 • **W-RI-270-005-G070**

Left: 5 / Blacksmith at anvil / FIVE. *Center:* Mercury standing with 5, Cornucopia and merchandise, Factories and ship / V / Panel outlining white FIVE. *Right:* 5 / Ceres kneeling / FIVE. *Engraver:* PSSP / New England Bank Note Co. *Comments:* H-RI-80-G24, Durand-311. 18__. 1830s.

Rarity: *None known*

$5 • **W-RI-270-005-G080**

Left: FIVE vertically. *Center:* Woman raising curtain from shield bearing 5 / V. *Right:* 5 / Ship. *Engraver:* New England Bank Note Co. *Comments:* H-RI-80-G26, Durand-311. 18__. 1840s–1860s.

Rarity: *None known*

$10 • **W-RI-270-010-G090**

Left: 10 / Farmer sowing / TEN. *Center:* Mercury standing with 10 / Merchandise, factories, and ship / Canal scene / Panel outlining white TEN. *Right:* 10 / Ship / TEN. *Engraver:* PSSP / New England Bank Note Co. *Comments:* H-RI-80-G32. 18__. 1830s.

Rarity: *None known*

$10 • **W-RI-270-010-G100**

Left: 10 / X / 10. *Center:* Farmer with plow and oxen / 10. *Right:* TEN / Woman standing with lyre and cornucopia. *Engraver:* New England Bank Note Co. *Comments:* H-RI-80-G34, Durand-313. 18__. 1840s–1860s.

Rarity: *None known*

$20 • **W-RI-270-020-G110**

Left: 20 / Woman with book on lap, opening chest. *Center:* XX / Eagle / XX. *Right:* 20 / Ship. *Engraver:* New England Bank Note Co. *Comments:* H-RI-80-G38, Durand-316. 18__. 1840s–1860s.

Rarity: *None known*

$50 • **W-RI-270-050-G120**

Left: FIFTY / Woman standing with wreath and flowers / FIFTY. *Center:* 50 / Man restraining prancing horse / 50. *Right:* FIFTY / Woman standing with cornucopia / FIFTY. *Engraver:* New England Bank Note Co. *Comments:* H-RI-80-G42, Durand-317. 18__. 1840s–1860s.

Rarity: *None known*

NON-VALID ISSUES

$1 • **W-RI-270-001-C010**

SI

Engraver: Horton, Providence. *Comments:* H-RI-80-C3, Durand-299. Counterfeit of W-RI-270-001-G010. 18__. 1820s.
Rarity: URS-5
VF $350

$1 • **W-RI-270-001-C010a**

CJF

Engraver: Horton, Providence. *Comments:* H-RI-80-C3a, Durand-300. Counterfeit of W-RI-270-001-G010a. 18__. 1820s.
Rarity: URS-5
VF $350

$1 • **W-RI-270-001-C010b**
Engraver: Horton, Providence. *Comments:* H-RI-80-C3b, Durand-301. Counterfeit of W-RI-270-001-G010b. 18__. 1820s.
Rarity: URS-5
VF $350

$2 • **W-RI-270-002-C030**

CJF

Engraver: Horton, Providence. *Comments:* H-RI-80-C10, Durand-304. Counterfeit of W-RI-270-002-G030. 18__. 1820s.
Rarity: URS-5
VF $350

$2 • **W-RI-270-002-C030a**
Engraver: Horton, Providence. *Comments:* H-RI-80-C10a, Durand-305. Counterfeit of W-RI-270-002-G030a. 18__. 1820s.
Rarity: URS-5
VF $350

$3 • **W-RI-270-003-C050**
Engraver: Horton, Providence. *Comments:* H-RI-80-C17, Durand-308. Counterfeit of W-RI-270-003-G050. 18__. 1820s.
Rarity: *None known*

$3 • **W-RI-270-003-C050a**
Engraver: Horton, Providence. *Comments:* H-RI-80-C17a, Durand-309. Counterfeit of W-RI-270-003-G050a. 18__. 1820s.
Rarity: URS-5
VF $350

$3 • **W-RI-270-003-A010**
Left: 3 / Steamboat. *Center:* Justice, Shield surmounted by eagle, Liberty. *Right:* 3 / Train. *Overprint:* Red THREE. *Engraver:* Baldwin, Bald & Cousland / Bald, Cousland & Co. *Comments:* H-RI-80-A5, Durand-310. Altered from W-RI-1500-003-G030a. 18__. 1850s.
Rarity: *None known*

$5 • **W-RI-270-005-S010**
Center: Woman with sheaf of wheat, Train. *Comments:* H-Unlisted, Durand-312. 1850s.
Rarity: *None known*

$5 • **W-RI-270-005-N010**
Center: Ceres seated, Train. *Comments:* H-RI-80-N5. 18__. 1840s.
Rarity: *None known*

$10 • **W-RI-270-010-S020**
Left: Man seated with hammer, anvil, wheel. *Comments:* H-Unlisted, Durand-315. 1850s.
Rarity: URS-3

$10 • **W-RI-270-010-A020**
Left: Train and men working / Portrait of Benjamin Franklin. *Center:* Four allegorical figures. *Right:* 10 on die / 10 on die. *Engraver:* New England Bank Note Co. *Comments:* H-RI-80-A10, Durand-314. Altered from $10 Globe Bank, Bangor, Maine. 18__. 1830s.
Rarity: URS-3
VF $350

$10 • **W-RI-270-010-N020**
Left: Medallion head. *Center:* Eagle and ship. *Right:* TEN. *Comments:* H-RI-80-N10. 18__. 1850s.
Rarity: *None known*

$10 • **W-RI-270-010-N030**
Center: Mechanic seated. *Comments:* H-RI-80-N15. 18__. 1850s.
Rarity: *None known*

Railroad Bank
1851–1865
W-RI-280

History: The Railroad Bank was incorporated in Cumberland in May 1851. Shortly thereafter, the bank was moved to Woonsocket, and a Woonsocket imprint was used on the bank's notes. The likely source of the bank's name came from the opening of the Providence and Worcester Railroad in 1847, supplanting the obsolete Blackstone Canal. Edward Harris, the bank's president, was the founder and owner of the Harris Woolen Company. He was also the founder of the public library in Woonsocket.[19] William Metcalf served as the bank's first cashier and was succeeded by Reuben G. Randall.

The bank's capital was $100,000 in 1855. By 1857 it was $105,600. Bills in circulation were at $25,432, and specie totaled $1,584.73. From 1857 to 1860 capital was $103,850, and in 1862 it was reported to be $106,700. Circulation reached $54,382 by 1862.

The business of the Railroad Bank was succeeded by the First National Bank of Woonsocket, chartered on July 7, 1865.

See also listing under Woonsocket, W-RI-1700.

Numismatic Commentary: Genuine notes with the Cumberland imprint are extremely hard to locate. Genuine notes with the Woonsocket imprint are only a little less difficult. There is a much better chance of locating a non-genuine example from the Woonsocket location.

All notes of this bank were engraved by the New England Bank Note Co.

VALID ISSUES

$1 • W-RI-280-001-G010
Left: ONE vertically / 1. *Center:* Agricultural scene / 1. *Right:* 1 / Ship / ONE. *Comments:* H-RI-85-G2, Durand-2649. 18__. 1850s.
Rarity: *None known*

$2 • W-RI-280-002-G020
Left: TWO vertically / 2. *Center:* Spread eagle on bale / 2. *Right:* 2 / TWO / Schooner. *Comments:* H-RI-85-G4, Durand-2650. 18__. 1850s.
Rarity: *None known*

$3 • W-RI-280-003-G030
Left: THREE vertically / 3. *Center:* Wharf scene / 3. *Right:* 3 / THREE / Train. *Comments:* H-RI-85-G6, Durand-2651. 18__. 1850s.
Rarity: *None known*

$10 • W-RI-280-010-G040
Left: 10 / X / 10. *Center:* Farmer with plow and oxen / 10. *Right:* TEN / Woman standing with lyre and cornucopia. *Comments:* H-RI-85-G10, Durand-2652. 18__. 1850s.
Rarity: *None known*

$20 • W-RI-280-020-G050
Left: 20 / Knowledge. *Center:* XX / Eagle / XX. *Right:* 20 / Sailing ship. *Comments:* H-RI-85-G12, Durand-2653. 18__. 1850s.
Rarity: *None known*

$50 • W-RI-280-050-G060
Left: FIFTY / Woman standing with wreath and flowers / FIFTY. *Center:* 50 / Man restraining prancing horse / 50. *Right:* FIFTY / Woman standing with cornucopia / FIFTY. *Comments:* H-RI-85-G14, Durand-2654. 18__. 1850s.
Rarity: *None known*

$100 • W-RI-280-100-G070
Left: ONE HUNDRED on 100 / Portrait of William Henry Harrison. *Center:* Wharf scene, Men loading wagon with barrels. *Right:* ONE HUNDRED on 100 / Portrait of Christopher Columbus. *Comments:* H-RI-85-G16, Durand-2655. 18__. 1850s.
Rarity: *None known*

Woonsocket Falls Bank
1828–1865
W-RI-290

History: Incorporated in June 1828 at Woonsocket, the Woonsocket Falls Bank was known as the Woonsocket Bank to local residents. At that time, Woonsocket was a small settlement along the eastern shore of the Blackstone River in the town of Cumberland.[20]

In 1831 capital was $51,269, circulation totaled $8,649, and specie was $2,541.11. Capital was $100,000 in 1848, $122,950.60 in 1849, and $100,000 in 1850. There were 2,000 shares valued at $50 each. Circulation grew from $31,332 in 1857 to $95,740 in 1863. Specie totaled $3,988.33 in 1857.

The interests of the Woonsocket Falls Bank were succeeded by the Woonsocket National Bank, chartered on July 1, 1865.

See also listing under Woonsocket, W-RI-1720.

Numismatic Commentary: This bank issued notes from two different addresses. The earlier series, from Cumberland, are the harder to locate. The later series have many denominations showing foot traffic traversing the bridge over the "falls." A few examples of high-denomination notes have appeared in the marketplace over the past decade or so.

VALID ISSUES

$1 • W-RI-290-001-G010
Left: 1 / Woman wearing bonnet, standing by pail / ONE. *Center:* Machinery and merchandise flanking Ceres holding sickle and rake, Factories and harbor / ONE / Panel outlining white ONE. *Right:* 1 / Ship / ONE. *Engraver:* PSSP / New England Bank Note Co. *Comments:* H-RI-90-G2. 18__. 1830s–1840s.
Rarity: *None known*

$1 • W-RI-290-001-G020
Left: ONE / 1. *Center:* Agricultural scene / 1. *Right:* 1 / Ship / ONE. *Engraver:* New England Bank Note Co. *Comments:* H-RI-90-G4, Durand-2707. 18__. 1840s–1850s.
Rarity: *None known*

$1.25 • W-RI-290-001.25-G030
Left: 1 25/100 / Train / 1 25/100. *Center:* Sloop and other vessels at sea / $1.25 Cts. *Right:* 1 25/100 / Eagle. *Engraver:* New England Bank Note Co. *Comments:* H-RI-90-G6. 18__. 1830s.
Rarity: *None known*

$1.50 • W-RI-290-001.50-G040
Left: 1 Doll. 50 Cts. vertically. *Center:* Eagle on rock in ocean / $1 50/100. *Right:* 1 50/100 / Justice. *Engraver:* New England Bank Note Co. *Comments:* H-RI-90-G7. 18__. 1830s.
Rarity: *None known*

$1.75 • W-RI-290-001.75-G050
Left: $1.75 Cts / Hebe watering eagle / 1 75/100. *Center:* Three sloops at sea. *Right:* $1.75 Cts / Woman seated with grain, Dog / 1 75/100. *Engraver:* New England Bank Note Co. *Comments:* H-RI-90-G8. 18__. 1830s.
Rarity: *None known*

$2 • W-RI-290-002-G060

Left: 2 / Woman standing with staff, Cornucopia / TWO. *Center:* TWO / Machinery and merchandise flanking Ceres holding sickle and rake, Factories and harbor / Panel outlining white TWO. *Right:* 2 / Woman wearing hat, Trees / TWO. *Engraver:* PSSP / New England Bank Note Co. *Comments:* H-RI-90-G10. 18__. 1830s–1840s.

Rarity: *None known*

$2 • W-RI-290-002-G070

Left: TWO / 2. *Center:* Spread eagle, Iron castings, cannon balls, machinery, 2. *Right:* 2 / TWO / Schooner. *Engraver:* PSSP / New England Bank Note Co. *Comments:* H-RI-90-G12, Durand-2708. 18__. 1840s–1850s.

Rarity: *None known*

$3 • W-RI-290-003-G080

Left: THREE / Beehive and foliage / THREE. *Center:* Machinery and merchandise flanking Ceres holding sickle and rake, Factories and harbor / THREE / Panel outlining white THREE. *Right:* 3 / THREE / Train. *Engraver:* PSSP / New England Bank Note Co. *Comments:* H-RI-90-G16. 18__. 1840s–1850s.

Rarity: *None known*

$3 • W-RI-290-003-G090

Left: THREE / 3. *Center:* Sailor and bales, Wharf scene / 3. *Right:* 3 / THREE / Train. *Engraver:* New England Bank Note Co. *Comments:* H-RI-90-G18, Durand-2709. 18__. 1840s–1850s.

Rarity: *None known*

$5 • W-RI-290-005-G100

Left: Eagle on shield and anchor / FIVE. *Center:* V containing woman with cornucopia and cherub. *Right:* 5 / Girl with basket. *Engraver:* New England Bank Note Co. *Comments:* H-RI-90-G24, Durand-2710. 18__. 1850s.

Rarity: *None known*

$10 • W-RI-290-010-G110

Left: Mechanic with tools, Train and building / TEN. *Center:* X. *Right:* 10 / Farmer with sheaf. *Engraver:* New England Bank Note Co. *Comments:* H-RI-90-G30, Durand-2711. 18__. 1850s.

Rarity: *None known*

$20 • W-RI-290-020-G120

Left: 20 / Woman. *Center:* XX / Eagle / XX. *Right:* 20 / Ship. *Engraver:* New England Bank Note Co. *Comments:* H-RI-90-G36, Durand-2712. 18__. 1840s–1850s.

Rarity: *None known*

$50 • W-RI-290-050-G130

Left: FIFTY / Woman standing with wreath and flowers / FIFTY. *Center:* 50 / Man restraining prancing horse / 50. *Right:* FIFTY / Woman standing with cornucopia / FIFTY. *Engraver:* New England Bank Note Co. *Comments:* H-RI-90-G42. 18__. 1840s–1850s.

Rarity: *None known*

$50 • W-RI-290-050-G130a

Engraver: New England Bank Note Co. / ABNCo. monogram. *Comments:* H-RI-90-G42a, Durand-2713. Similar to W-RI-290-050-G130 but with additional engraver imprint. 18__. 1850s–1860s.

Rarity: URS-3
Proof $800

$100 • W-RI-290-100-G140

Left: ONE HUNDRED across 100 / Portrait of William Henry Harrison. *Center:* Wharf scene. *Right:* ONE HUNDRED across 100 / Portrait of Christopher Columbus. *Engraver:* New England Bank Note Co. *Comments:* H-RI-90-G46, Durand-2714. 18__. 1840s–1850s.

Rarity: *None known*

$100 • W-RI-290-100-G140a

Engraver: PSSP / New England Bank Note Co. *Comments:* H-RI-90-G46a. Similar to W-RI-290-100-G140 but with additional engraver imprint. 18__. 1850s–1860s.

Rarity: *None known*

NON-VALID ISSUES

$2 • W-RI-290-002-A010

Left: 2 / Laureate woman with grain and sheaves. *Center:* Train, hill, and steamship. *Right:* TWO / Woman with harp / TWO. *Back:* Orange dies bearing 2s. *Engraver:* W.L. Ormsby / Baker & Duyckink. *Comments:* H-RI-90-A10, Durand-2721. Altered from $2 Crawfordsville, Logansport and Northern Indiana Railroad Company, Logansport, Indiana. 185_. 1859.

Rarity: *None known*

$2 • W-RI-290-002-A020

Left: TWO and 2 / State arms of Michigan. *Center:* Woodsmen felling and cutting trees. *Right:* 2 / Ceres. *Engraver:* Danforth, Wright & Co. *Comments:* H-RI-90-A15, Durand-2722. Altered from $2 Bank of Washtenaw, Washtenaw, Michigan series. 1850s.

Rarity: *None known*

$2 • W-RI-290-002-A030

Left: 2 / Farmer plowing. *Center:* Men cradling, binding, and loading wagon with sheaves. *Right:* 2 / Two floating cherubs with caduceus and sheaf. *Comments:* H-Unlisted, Durand-2723. Altered from $2 Southern Bank of Georgia, Bainbridge, Georgia. 1850s.

Rarity: URS-3
F $90

$5 • W-RI-290-005-N010

Left: 5 / Steamboat / Woman. *Center:* 5 / Three women / 5. *Right:* FIVE vertically. *Comments:* H-RI-90-N5, Durand-2730. 1850s.

Rarity: *None known*

$5 • W-RI-290-005-AR010

Overprint: Red panel outlining white FIVE. *Engraver:* Toppan, Carpenter & Co. *Comments:* H-RI-90-AR5, Durand-2727. Altered and raised from W-RI-1720-001-G010. Jan. 1, 18__. 1860s.

Rarity: *None known*

$5 • W-RI-290-005-AR020

Left: 5 / Train / 5. *Center:* Train / Ceres by sheaf / Canal. *Right:* FIVE / Ceres holding grain overhead. *Back:* Circles made up of 5s bearing five portraits of George Washington. *Engraver:* W.L. Ormsby / Baker & Duyckink. *Comments:* H-RI-90-AR20, Durand-2728. Altered and raised from $5 Crawfordsville, Logansport and Northern Indiana Railroad Company, Logansport, Indiana. 185_. 1859.

Rarity: *None known*

$5 • W-RI-290-005-AR030

Left: Portrait of Henry Clay / V. *Center:* Farmer feeding hogs. *Right:* 5 / Farmer carrying basket of corn. *Overprint:* Red FIVE. *Engraver:* Wellstood, Hay & Whiting. *Comments:* H-RI-90-AR25, Durand-2729. Altered and raised from $5 Thames bank, Laurel, Indiana. Aug. 12, 1856.

Rarity: *None known*

$10 • W-RI-290-010-AR040

Left: 10 / Two women flanking shield bearing tree / 10. *Center:* Woman, Eagle, Shield, Two women. *Right:* 10 / Two men walking. *Overprint:* Red ONE. *Engraver:* Danforth, Wright & Co. *Comments:* H-RI-90-A30, Durand-2734. Altered and raised from $1 Bank of Washtenaw, Washtenaw, Michigan. 185_. 1859.

Rarity: *None known*

$10 • W-RI-290-010-A040

Left: 10 / Hebe seated with Liberty pole and watering eagle. *Center:* Steamboat loaded with cotton. *Bottom center:* Shield. *Right:* 10 / Female portrait / TEN. *Engraver:* Rawdon, Wright, Hatch & Edson. *Comments:* H-RI-90-A35, Durand-2735. Altered from $10 Farmers & Merchants Bank of Memphis, Tennessee series. 1850s.

Rarity: *None known*

East Greenwich, Rhode Island

East Greenwich in Kent County was originally part of the larger town of Greenwich, which was formed in 1677 and named after Greenwich, England. It was initially inhabited by the Pequot Indians. The town was renamed Yornana in 1686. In 1700 the Greenwich name was resumed.

The rural portion of the town was separated in 1741 to become West Greenwich. The rest of the town became East Greenwich and was bordered by Exeter, West Greenwich, North Kingstown, Potowomut, and Warwick. Naval facilities were established there.

The cove of East Greenwich provided a haven for fishermen, and the production of textiles, brushes, and machinery also contributed to the economy. Shipbuilding had its part in the industry of the town as well.

Bank of New England
1853 AND 1854
W-RI-300

History: The Bank of New England was incorporated in 1853. However, the General Assembly of Rhode Island passed an act voiding its charter, and it expired in January 1854.[21]

Numismatic Commentary: No notes are known from this bank, but there is the possibility that Proofs were made in anticipation of the institution going into business.

Greenwich Bank
1856–1865
W-RI-315

History: The Greenwich Bank was incorporated in May 1856 with an authorized capital of $50,000. The bank had $32,090 of paid-in capital by the time it started business. From 1860 to 1864 the same was $62,500. Circulation from 1857 to 1860 was $23,701. In 1862 it was $39,005. Specie in 1857 was $1,981.23.

The interests of the Greenwich Bank were succeeded by the Greenwich National Bank, chartered on July 8, 1865.

Numismatic Commentary: Notes from this bank are very rare. Almost all issues are unknown today, with the $1 being the only denomination that seems to show up, and only at widely spaced intervals.

Valid Issues

$1 • W-RI-315-001-G010   SBG

Engraver: Danforth, Wright & Co. *Comments:* H-Unlisted, Durand-Unlisted. Proof. 18__. 1850s.

Rarity: URS-3
VF $2,000

$1 • W-RI-315-001-G010a

Left: 1 on die / ONE on 1 on die. *Center:* 1 / Sailor seated with anchor and scales leaning against capstan, Boats / 1. *Right:* 1 on die / Train. *Overprint:* Red 1, 1. *Engraver:* Danforth, Wright & Co. *Comments:* H-RI-95-G2a, Durand-318. Similar to W-RI-315-001-G010. 18__. 1850s.

Rarity: URS-3
VF $1,500
Selected auction price: Heritage, June 2010, Lot 12564, VG $575

$1 • W-RI-315-001-G010b   SBG

Overprint: Red panel outlining white ONE. *Engraver:* American Bank Note Co. *Comments:* H-RI-95-G2c, Durand-319. Similar to W-RI-315-001-G010 but with different engraver imprint. 18__. 1860s.

Rarity: URS-3
VF $1,500; **Proof** $4,200

$2 • W-RI-315-002-G020

Left: 2 / Man holding child on knee. *Center:* Family and Indian family flanking shield bearing 2. *Right:* Two allegorical figures. *Overprint:* Red 2, 2. *Engraver:* Danforth, Wright & Co. *Comments:* H-RI-95-G4a, Durand-320. 18__. 1850s.

Rarity: *None known*

$2 • W-RI-315-002-G020a

Overprint: Red panel outlining white TWO. *Engraver:* American Bank Note Co. *Comments:* H-RI-95-G4c, Durand-321. Similar to W-RI-315-002-G020 but with different engraver imprint. 18__. 1860s.

Rarity: *None known*

$5 • W-RI-315-005-G030

Left: FIVE / State arms / 5. *Center:* "Signing of the Declaration of Independence" / Portrait of George Washington. *Right:* 5 on medallion head / Portrait of Christopher Columbus. *Overprint:* Red 5, 5. *Engraver:* Danforth, Wright & Co. *Comments:* H-RI-95-G6a, Durand-324. 18__. 1850s.

Rarity: *None known*

$5 • W-RI-315-005-G030a

Overprint: Red panel outlining white FIVE. *Engraver:* American Bank Note Co. *Comments:* H-RI-95-G6c, Durand-325. Similar to W-RI-315-005-G030 but with different engraver imprint. 18__. 1860s.

Rarity: *None known*

$10 • W-RI-315-010-G040

Left: X / Liberty, Eagle. *Center:* View of town, public square, houses, and churches. *Right:* 10 / Portrait of girl. *Engraver:* Danforth, Wright & Co. *Comments:* H-RI-95-G8, Durand-328. 18__. 1850s.

Rarity: *None known*

$20 • W-RI-315-020-G050

Left: XX / Milkmaid. *Center:* Train under bridge. *Right:* 20 / Farmer plowing. *Engraver:* Danforth, Wright & Co. *Comments:* H-RI-95-G10, Durand-331. 18__. 1850s.

Rarity: *None known*

$50 • W-RI-315-050-G060

Left: Two women, Sailor, mechanic, harbor, and city. *Center:* 50 / 50 / Anchor on shield. *Right:* FIFTY / Two women, farmer, oxen. *Engraver:* Danforth, Wright & Co. *Comments:* H-RI-95-G12, Durand-334. 18__. 1850s.

Rarity: *None known*

Uncut Sheets

$1-$1-$2-$5 • W-RI-315-001.001.002.005-US010

Vignette(s): (*$1*) Sailor seated with anchor and scales leaning against capstan, Boats / Train. (*$1*) Sailor seated with anchor and scales leaning against capstan, Boats / Train. (*$2*) Man holding child on knee / Family and Indian family flanking shield bearing 2 / Two allegorical figures. (*$5*) State arms / "Signing of the Declaration of Independence" / Portrait of George Washington / 5 on medallion head / Portrait of Christopher Columbus. *Engraver:* Danforth, Wright & Co. *Comments:* All unlisted in Haxby. 18__. 1850s.

Rarity: URS-3
VF $3,000

$10-$10-$20-$50 • W-RI-315-010.010.020.050-US020

Vignette(s): (*$10*) Liberty, Eagle / View of town, public square, houses, and churches / Portrait of girl. (*$10*) Liberty, Eagle / View of town, public square, houses, and churches / Portrait of girl. (*$20*) Milkmaid / Train under bridge / Farmer plowing. (*$50*) Two women, Sailor, mechanic, harbor, and city / Anchor on shield / Two women, farmer, oxen. *Engraver:* Danforth, Wright & Co. *Comments:* H-RI-95-G8, G8, G10, G12. 18__. 1850s.

Rarity: URS-3
VF $3,000

Non-Valid Issues

$3 • W-RI-315-003-R010

Engraver: Danforth, Wright & Co. *Comments:* H-RI-95-R2, Durand-322. Raised from W-RI-315-001-G010. 18__. 1850s.

Rarity: *None known*

$3 • W-RI-315-003-A010

Left: 3 / Wheelwrights at work. *Center:* Man watering horse at trough, Two farmers, Flock of sheep. *Right:* 3 / Girl feeding chickens. *Overprint:* Red 3, 3. *Engraver:* Toppan, Carpenter & Co. *Comments:* H-RI-95-A5, Durand-323. Altered from W-RI-1630-003-G030. Aug. 6, 1855.

Rarity: *None known*

$5 • W-RI-315-005-R020

Engraver: Danforth, Wright & Co. *Comments:* H-RI-95-R4, Durand-326. Raised from W-RI-315-001-G010 series. 18__. 1850s.

Rarity: *None known*

$5 • W-RI-315-005-R030

Engraver: Danforth, Wright & Co. *Comments:* H-RI-95-R6, Durand-327. Raised from W-RI-315-002-G020 series. 18__. 1850s.

Rarity: *None known*

$10 • W-RI-315-010-R040

Engraver: Danforth, Wright & Co. *Comments:* H-RI-95-R10, Durand-329. Raised from W-RI-315-001-G010 series. 18__. 1850s.

Rarity: *None known*

$10 • W-RI-315-010-R050

Engraver: Danforth, Wright & Co. *Comments:* H-RI-95-R12, Durand-330. Raised from W-RI-315-002-G020 series. 18__. 1850s.

Rarity: *None known*

$20 • W-RI-315-020-R060

Engraver: Danforth, Wright & Co. *Comments:* H-RI-95-R16, Durand-332. Raised from W-RI-315-001-G010 series. 18__. 1850s.

Rarity: *None known*

$20 • W-RI-315-020-R070

Engraver: Danforth, Wright & Co. *Comments:* H-RI-95-R18, Durand-333. Raised from W-RI-315-002-G020 series. 18__. 1850s.

Rarity: *None known*

Rhode Island Central Bank
1805–1857
W-RI-330

History: Chartered in October 1805, the Rhode Island Central Bank served the town of East Greenwich for 53 years before it fell into the hands of criminals.

In 1805 the bank had $60,000 in authorized capital which was raised to $81,960 by 1848 and again to $117,138.72 by 1856. A circulation of $28,257 was listed in the *Annual Report* of 1849. By 1855 the bank had placed a large quantity of notes in commerce, a fraudulent over-issue. In early 1856 the bank stopped redeeming its notes, which soon became nearly worthless. Trading in them was continued by exchange brokers later, who sold them at pennies on the dollar to fraudsters who altered them with imprints of other banks.

Numismatic Commentary: There seems to be an ample supply of notes from this bank. Obtaining two to three different issues should not be hard.

Remaining in the American Bank Note Co. archives as of 2003 was a $1-$1-$2-$3 face plate and a $5-$5-$5-$10 face plate.

VALID ISSUES

$1 • W-RI-330-001-G010
Left: ONE vertically. *Center:* 1 / 1 / Alternating flower garlands and gridwork segments / Anchor on shield / 1 / 1. *Comments:* H-RI-100-G2, Durand-347. 18__. 1805–1810s.
Rarity: *None known*

$1 • W-RI-330-001-G020   SBG

Engraver: Horton, Providence. **Comments:** H-RI-100-G4, Durand-348. 18__. 1820s.
Rarity: URS-3
Proof $1,800

$1 • W-RI-330-001-G030   SBG

Engraver: Fairman, Draper, Underwood & Co. **Comments:** H-RI-100-G6, Durand-349. Proof. 18__. 1820s–1830s.
Rarity: URS-3
VF $800; **Proof** $1,300

$1 • W-RI-330-001-G040
Left: ONE / Sailor standing. *Center:* Ceres seated by plow / 1. *Bottom center:* State arms. *Right:* Sailing ship / ONE. *Engraver:* Rawdon, Wright, Hatch & Edson. *Comments:* H-RI-100-G10, Durand-350. 18__. 1850s.
Rarity: URS-3
Proof $500

$1 • W-RI-330-001-G040a
Overprint: Red ONE. *Engraver:* Rawdon, Wright, Hatch & Edson. *Comments:* H-RI-100-G10a, Durand-351. Similar to W-RI-330-001-G040. 18__. 1850s.
Rarity: *None known*

$1 • W-RI-330-001-G040b   CC

Overprint: Red ONE. *Engraver:* Rawdon, Wright, Hatch & Edson. *Comments:* H-RI-100-G10b. Similar to W-RI-330-001-G040 but with different date. July 4th, 1855. 1850s.
Rarity: URS-6
VF $150

$1 • W-RI-330-001-G040c   CJF

Overprint: Blue ONE. *Engraver:* Rawdon, Wright, Hatch & Edson. *Comments:* H-RI-100-G10c, Durand-352. Similar to W-RI-330-001-G040 but with different date. July 4th, 1855. 1850s.
Rarity: URS-6
VF $200

$2 • W-RI-330-002-G050
Left: TWO vertically. *Center:* 2 / 2 / Alternating flower garlands and gridwork segments / Anchor on shield / 2 / 2. *Comments:* H-RI-100-G14, Durand-354. 18__. 1805–1810s.
Rarity: *None known*

$2 • W-RI-330-002-G060

SI

Engraver: Horton, Providence. **Comments:** H-RI-100-G16, Durand-355. 18__. 1820s.

Rarity: URS-3
Proof $1,000

$2 • W-RI-330-002-G070

SBG

Engraver: Fairman, Draper, Underwood & Co. **Comments:** H-RI-100-G18, Durand-356. Third issue. Proof. 18__. 1820s–1830s.

Rarity: URS-1
VF $1,500; **Proof** $2,200

$2 • W-RI-330-002-G080

Left: TWO / Two girls. **Center:** Farmer, Shield bearing agricultural scene, Milkmaid. **Right:** 2 / Hope with anchor. **Engraver:** Rawdon, Wright, Hatch & Edson. **Comments:** H-RI-100-G22, Durand-357. 18__. 1850s.

Rarity: URS-6
VF $200

$2 • W-RI-330-002-G080a

Overprint: Red TWO. **Engraver:** Rawdon, Wright, Hatch & Edson. **Comments:** H-RI-100-G22a, Durand-358. Similar to W-RI-330-002-G080. 18__. 1850s.

Rarity: *None known*

$2 • W-RI-330-002-G080b

CJF

Overprint: Red TWO. **Engraver:** Rawdon, Wright, Hatch & Edson. **Comments:** H-RI-100-G22b. Similar to W-RI-330-002-G080 but with different date. July 4th, 1855. 1850s.

Rarity: URS-6
VF $200

$2 • W-RI-330-002-G080c

Overprint: Blue TWO. **Engraver:** Rawdon, Wright, Hatch & Edson. **Comments:** H-RI-100-G22c, Durand-359. Similar to W-RI-330-002-G080 but with different date. July 4, 1855.

Rarity: *None known*

$3 • W-RI-330-003-G090

Left: THREE vertically. **Center:** 3 / 3 / Alternating flower garlands and gridwork segments / Anchor on shield / 3 / 3. **Comments:** H-Unlisted, Durand-361. 18__. 1805–1810s.

Rarity: *None known*

$3 • W-RI-330-003-G100

Comments: H-RI-100-G26, Durand-363. No description available. Third issue. 18__. 1805–1810s.

Rarity: *None known*

$3 • W-RI-330-003-G110

Left: THREE / Female portrait / THREE vertically. **Center:** 3 / Woman reclining with sickle, 3, Sheaf / 3. **Bottom center:** Shield and 3. **Right:** 3 / RHODE ISLAND / 3 vertically. **Engraver:** Horton, Providence. **Comments:** H-RI-100-G28, Durand-362. 18__. 1820s.

Rarity: URS-3
Proof $1,000

$3 • W-RI-330-003-G120

SBG

Engraver: Fairman, Draper, Underwood & Co. **Comments:** H-RI-100-G30. Third issue. Proof. 18__. 1820s–1830s.

Rarity: URS-1
Proof $1,400

$3 • W-RI-330-003-G130

Left: THREE / Woman with flowers. **Center:** Indian, Shield bearing river scene, Woodsman / 3. **Right:** Justice / THREE. **Engraver:** Rawdon, Wright, Hatch & Edson. **Comments:** H-RI-100-G34, Durand-364. 18__. 1850s.

Rarity: URS-3
Proof $750

$3 • W-RI-330-003-G130a

Overprint: Red THREE. **Engraver:** Rawdon, Wright, Hatch & Edson. **Comments:** H-RI-100-G34a, Durand-365. Similar to W-RI-330-003-G130. 18__. 1850s.

Rarity: URS-6
VF $200

$3 • W-RI-330-003-G130b · CC

Overprint: Red THREE. *Engraver:* Rawdon, Wright, Hatch & Edson. *Comments:* H-RI-100-G34b. Similar to W-RI-330-003-G130 but with different date. July 4th, 1855. 1850s.

Rarity: URS-6
F $105; **VF** $200

$3 • W-RI-330-003-G130c

Overprint: Blue THREE. *Engraver:* Rawdon, Wright, Hatch & Edson. *Comments:* H-RI-100-G34c, Durand-366. Similar to W-RI-330-003-G130 but with different date. July 4, 1855.

Rarity: *None known*

$5 • W-RI-330-005-G140

Left: FIVE vertically. *Center:* 5 / 5 / Alternating flower garlands and gridwork segments / Anchor on shield / 5 / 5. *Comments:* H-RI-100-G38, Durand-367. 18__. 1805–1810s.

Rarity: *None known*

$5 • W-RI-330-005-G150

Left: FIVE / Portrait of George Washington / FIVE vertically. *Center:* FIVE on 5 / Liberty with shield of Hope / FIVE on 5. *Bottom center:* 5. *Right:* 5 / RHODE ISLAND / 5 vertically. *Engraver:* Horton. Prov. *Comments:* H-RI-100-G40, Durand-368. 18__. 1820s.

Rarity: URS-3
Proof $1,000

$5 • W-RI-330-005-G160

Left: Panel with FIVE / Plenty and Minerva seated / V. *Center:* FIVE / Allegorical woman seated / FIVE / Panel of microletters. *Right:* 5 / Eagle / 5. *Engraver:* PSSP. *Comments:* H-RI-100-G42. 18__. 1830s.

Rarity: *None known*

$5 • W-RI-330-005-G170 · CC

Engraver: Toppan, Carpenter, Casilear & Co. *Comments:* H-RI-100-G46, Durand-369. 18__. 1850s.

Rarity: URS-3
Proof $1,400

$5 • W-RI-330-005-G170a · SI

Overprint: Red large 5, 5. *Engraver:* Toppan, Carpenter, Casilear & Co. *Comments:* H-RI-100-G46a, Durand-370. Similar to W-RI-330-005-G170. 18__. 1850s.

Rarity: URS-6
VF $200

$5 • W-RI-330-005-G170b · CC

Overprint: Red small 5, 5. *Engraver:* Toppan, Carpenter, Casilear & Co. *Comments:* H-RI-100-G46b. Similar to W-RI-330-005-G170 but with different date. October 1, 1855. 1850s.

Rarity: URS-6
VG $95; **F** $125; **VF** $200

$5 • W-RI-330-005-G170c

Left: 5 / Female portrait. *Center:* Man, woman, and child. *Right:* 5 / Portrait of George Washington. *Overprint:* Red smaller 5, 5. *Engraver:* Toppan, Carpenter, Casilear & Co. *Comments:* H-RI-100-G46c. Similar to W-RI-330-005-G170 but with different date. Oct. 1, 1855.

Rarity: URS-6
VF $200

$10 • W-RI-330-010-G180

Left: 10 / Female portrait. *Center:* Sailing vessels / TEN / Eagle. *Right:* 10 / Portrait of William Penn. *Engraver:* Toppan, Carpenter, Casilear & Co. *Comments:* H-RI-100-G52, Durand-374. 18__. 1850s.

Rarity: URS-3
Proof $750

Collectors and Researchers:

If you have new information about any banks or notes listed in this volume, contact Whitman Publishing, Attn: Obsolete Paper Money, 3101 Clairmont Road, Suite G, Atlanta, GA 30329.

$10 • W-RI-330-010-G180a

CC

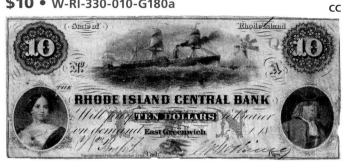

Overprint: Red TEN. *Engraver:* Toppan, Carpenter, Casilear & Co. *Comments:* H-RI-100-G52a, Durand-375. Similar to W-RI-330-010-G180. 18__. 1850s.
Rarity: URS-1
VF $500

$10 • W-RI-330-010-G180b

NJW

Overprint: Red TEN. *Engraver:* Toppan, Carpenter, Casilear & Co. *Comments:* H-RI-100-G52b. Similar to W-RI-330-010-G180 but with engraved date. October 1, 1855. 1850s.
Rarity: URS-5
F $175; **VF** $200

$20 • W-RI-330-020-G190

Left: 20 / XX vertically / 20. *Center:* 20 / Woman seated with scales, Sheaf and bales, Men plowing, Ship / 20. *Right:* TWENTY vertically. *Engraver:* PSSP / New England Bank Note Co. *Comments:* H-RI-100-G54. 18__. 1830s.
Rarity: *None known*

$20 • W-RI-330-020-G200

Left: 20 / Woman seated with book on lap, opening chest. *Center:* XX / Eagle on rock / XX. *Right:* 20 / Ship in harbor. *Engraver:* New England Bank Note Co. *Comments:* H-RI-100-G56, Durand-378. 18__. 1840s–1850s.
Rarity: *None known*

$50 • W-RI-330-050-G210

Left: 50 / Cornucopia, Woman standing with ankles crossed, Staff, Anchor. *Center:* FIFTY DOLLARS / 50. *Right:* FIFTY vertically. *Engraver:* PSSP / New England Bank Note Co. *Comments:* H-RI-100-G58. 18__. 1830s.
Rarity: *None known*

$50 • W-RI-330-050-G220

Left: FIFTY / Woman standing with wreath and flowers / FIFTY. *Center:* 50 / Man restraining prancing horse / 50. *Right:* FIFTY / Woman standing with cornucopia / FIFTY. *Engraver:* New England Bank Note Co. *Comments:* H-RI-100-G60, Durand-380. 18__. 1840s–1850s.
Rarity: *None known*

$100 • W-RI-330-100-G230

Left: Lathework panel with C / Portrait of George Washington / C. *Center:* 100 / Manhattan reclining pouring water, Ship / 100. *Right:* Lathework panel with ONE HUNDRED vertically. *Engraver:* PSSP / New England Bank Note Co. *Comments:* H-RI-100-G62. 18__. 1830s.
Rarity: *None known*

$100 • W-RI-330-100-G240

Left: RHODE ISLAND vertically. *Center:* 100 / Mercury with bag of coins / 100. *Right:* 100 / Spread eagle on rock in sea / 100. *Comments:* H-RI-100-G64, Durand-381. 18__. 1840s–1850s.
Rarity: *None known*

NON-VALID ISSUES

$1 • W-RI-330-001-C010

Comments: H-RI-100-C2, Durand-353. Counterfeit of W-RI-330-001-G010. 18__. 1810s.
Rarity: URS-3
VF $150

$2 • W-RI-330-002-C050

CJF

Comments: H-RI-100-C14, Durand-360. Counterfeit of W-RI-330-002-G050. 18__. 1810s.
Rarity: URS-3
VF $150

$5 • W-RI-330-005-C140

CJF

Comments: H-RI-100-C38, Durand-371. Counterfeit of W-RI-330-005-G140. 18__. 1800s.
Rarity: URS-3
VF $150

$5 • W-RI-330-005-R010

Overprint: Red FIVE. *Engraver:* Rawdon, Wright, Hatch & Edson. *Comments:* H-RI-100-R5, Durand-372. Raised from W-RI-330-001-G040b. July 4, 1855.
Rarity: URS-3
VF $150

$5 • W-RI-330-005-S010

cc

Engraver: Rawdon, Wright, Hatch & Edson. **Comments:** H-RI-100-S5, Durand-373. 18__. 1850s.
Rarity: URS-6
VF $150

$10 • W-RI-330-010-R020

Comments: H-Unlisted, Durand-376. Raised from W-RI-330-001-G040. 1850s.
Rarity: *None known*

$10 • W-RI-330-010-S020

Left: 10 / Canal scene / X. **Center:** Liberty with shield bearing 10. **Right:** 10 / Lovers kissing / X. **Engraver:** Danforth, Bald & Co. **Comments:** H-RI-100-S10, Durand-377. 18__. 1856.
Rarity: *None known*

$20 • W-RI-330-020-R030

Comments: H-Unlisted, Durand-379. Raised from W-RI-330-002-G080. 1850s.
Rarity: URS-3

Rhode Island Exchange Bank
1852–1860
W-RI-340

History: The Rhode Island Exchange Bank was incorporated in May 1852. The books for subscriptions were opened on November 24 at the Rhode Island Central Bank. Capital in 1855 was $46,100, but it was raised to $60,000 by 1856. Circulation was $29,464 in 1857, and specie was $1,387.13 the same year. In February 1860, it was learned that cashier Daniel C. Kenyon had defaulted to the extent of $72,000. On February 10, the bank failed. Kenyon was arrested and sentenced to eight years in prison, a rare instance of prosecution of a bank official (in this era most got off scot-free). The public was allowed to present currency for redemption until August 1, 1860, and receive partial face-value. After that, the notes were worthless.[22]

Numismatic Commentary: There are many handsomely engraved notes from this bank in the marketplace. Some picture factory looms tended by women. Others show a scene of East Greenwich from the waters of Narragansett Bay.

VALID ISSUES

$1 • W-RI-340-001-G010

Left: Woman holding 1 / 1. **Center:** Women working at textile machines / ONE. **Bottom center:** Eagle. **Right:** Woman holding 1 / 1. **Engraver:** Toppan, Carpenter, Casilear & Co. **Comments:** H-RI-105-G2, Durand-382. 18__. 1850s.
Rarity: *None known*

$1 • W-RI-340-001-G010a

Overprint: Red ONE. **Engraver:** Toppan, Carpenter, Casilear & Co. **Comments:** H-RI-105-G2a, Durand-383. Similar to W-RI-340-001-G010. 18__. 1850s.
Rarity: *None known*

$1 • W-RI-340-001-G010b

cc

Overprint: Red script ONE. **Engraver:** Toppan, Carpenter, Casilear & Co. **Comments:** H-RI-105-G2b, Durand-384. Similar to W-RI-340-001-G010. 18__. 1850s.
Rarity: URS-6
VF $200

$1 • W-RI-340-001-G010c

Overprint: Red script ONE. **Engraver:** Toppan, Carpenter, Casilear & Co. / ABNCo. monogram. **Comments:** H-RI-105-G2c. Similar to W-RI-340-001-G010 but with additional engraver imprint. 18__. 1850s.
Rarity: URS-6
VG $110; **VF** $200

$1 • W-RI-340-001-G020

cc

Tint: Red micro ONEs and dies bearing ONEs. **Engraver:** Wellstood, Hay & Whiting. **Comments:** H-RI-105-G4a, Durand-385. Remainder. Jany 1st, 18__. 1859.
Rarity: URS-6
VF $500; **Proof** $2,700

$1 • W-RI-340-001-G020a
CC

Tint: Red micro ONEs and dies bearing ONEs / Red-brown outlining white ONE. *Engraver:* Wellstood, Hay & Whiting. *Comments:* H-RI-105-G4b. Similar to W-RI-340-001-G020. Jany 1st, 18__. 1859.

Rarity: URS-6
VF $300

$2 • W-RI-340-002-G030
Left: 2 / Woman tending machine. *Center:* Ceres, Shield bearing state arms, Liberty. *Right:* 2 / Train. *Engraver:* Toppan, Carpenter, Casilear & Co. *Comments:* H-RI-105-G6, Durand-386. 18__. 1850s.

Rarity: *None known*

$2 • W-RI-340-002-G030a
Overprint: Red TWO. *Engraver:* Toppan, Carpenter, Casilear & Co. *Comments:* H-RI-105-G6a, Durand-387. Similar to W-RI-340-002-G030. 18__. 1850s.

Rarity: URS-5
VF $300

$2 • W-RI-340-002-G030b
QDB

Overprint: Red script TWO. *Engraver:* Toppan, Carpenter, Casilear & Co. *Comments:* H-RI-105-G6b, Durand-388. Similar to W-RI-340-002-G030. 18__. 1850s.

Rarity: URS-5
VF $450

$2 • W-RI-340-002-G030c
Overprint: Red script TWO. *Engraver:* Toppan, Carpenter, Casilear & Co. / ABNCo. monogram. *Comments:* H-RI-105-G6c. Similar to W-RI-340-002-G030 but with additional engraver imprint. 18__. 1850s.

Rarity: *None known*

$2 • W-RI-340-002-G040
CC

Tint: Red micro TWOs and dies bearing 2 / TWO. *Engraver:* Wellstood, Hay & Whiting. *Comments:* H-RI-105-G8a, Durand-389. Remainder. Jany 1st, 18__. 1859.

Rarity: URS-6
VF $300; **Unc-Rem** $500; **Proof** $2,700

$2 • W-RI-340-002-G040a
Left: Two women holding shield bearing 2 / 2. *Center:* Sailboats in harbor / TWO. *Bottom center:* Anchor on shield. *Right:* TWO / Woman holding 2. *Tint:* Brown-orange micro TWOs outlining white TWO and die bearing 2. *Engraver:* Wellstood, Hay & Whiting. *Comments:* H-RI-105-G8b, Durand-389. Similar to W-RI-340-002-G040. Jan. 1, 18__. 1859.

Rarity: URS-6
VF $300

$3 • W-RI-340-003-G050
Left: 3 / Allegorical woman and sailor with flag. *Center:* Train on bridge, Town. *Right:* 3 / Ceres. *Engraver:* Toppan, Carpenter, Casilear & Co. *Comments:* H-RI-105-G10, Durand-390. 18__. 1850s.

Rarity: *None known*

$3 • W-RI-340-003-G050a
Overprint: Red THREE. *Engraver:* Toppan, Carpenter, Casilear & Co. *Comments:* H-RI-105-G10a, Durand-391. Similar to W-RI-340-003-G050. 18__. 1850s.

Rarity: *None known*

$3 • W-RI-340-003-G050b
Overprint: Red script THREE. *Engraver:* Toppan, Carpenter, Casilear & Co. *Comments:* H-RI-105-G10b, Durand-392. Similar to W-RI-340-003-G050. 18__. 1850s.

Rarity: *None known*

$3 • W-RI-340-003-G050c
Overprint: Red script THREE. *Engraver:* Toppan, Carpenter, Casilear & Co. / ABNCo. monogram. *Comments:* H-RI-105-G10c. Similar to W-RI-340-003-G050 but with additional engraver imprint. 18__. 1850s.

Rarity: *None known*

$5 • W-RI-340-005-G060
Left: Indian / 5. *Center:* Woman seated with basket, Sailboats / FIVE. *Bottom center:* Plow. *Right:* 5 / Female portrait. *Engraver:* Toppan, Carpenter, Casilear & Co. *Comments:* H-RI-105-G12, Durand-393. 18__. 1850s.

Rarity: *None known*

$5 • W-RI-340-005-G060a

Overprint: Red FIVE. *Engraver:* Toppan, Carpenter, Casilear & Co. *Comments:* H-RI-105-G12a, Durand-394. Similar to W-RI-340-005-G060. 18__. 1850s.

Rarity: *None known*

$5 • W-RI-340-005-G060b

Overprint: Red script FIVE. *Engraver:* Toppan, Carpenter, Casilear & Co. *Comments:* H-RI-105-G12b, Durand-395. Similar to W-RI-340-005-G060. 18__. 1850s.

Rarity: URS-6
VF $495

$10 • W-RI-340-010-G070

Left: 10 / Mason holding level against wall. *Center:* Spread eagle on tree limb, Train, Bridge and canal. *Right:* 10 / George Washington on horseback. *Engraver:* Toppan, Carpenter, Casilear & Co. *Comments:* H-RI-105-G14, Durand-396. 18__. 1850s.

Rarity: *None known*

$10 • W-RI-340-010-G070a

Overprint: Red TEN. *Engraver:* Toppan, Carpenter, Casilear & Co. *Comments:* H-RI-105-G14a, Durand-397. Similar to W-RI-340-010-G070. 18__. 1850s.

Rarity: URS-3
VF $350

$10 • W-RI-340-010-G070b

Overprint: Red script TEN. *Engraver:* Toppan, Carpenter, Casilear & Co. *Comments:* H-RI-105-G14b, Durand-398. Similar to W-RI-340-010-G070. 18__. 1850s.

Rarity: *None known*

$20 • W-RI-340-020-G080

SBG

Engraver: Wellstood, Hanks, Hay & Whiting. *Comments:* H-RI-105-G16, Durand-402. Proof. January 1st, 18__. 1850s.

Rarity: URS-2
Proof $4,800

$50 • W-RI-340-050-G090

Left: Three men holding die bearing 50. *Center:* Cherub / Portrait of girl / Cherub. *Bottom center:* Anchor on shield. *Right:* 50 / Portrait of Benjamin Franklin. *Engraver:* Wellstood, Hanks, Hay & Whiting. *Comments:* H-RI-105-G18, Durand-403. Jan. 1, 18__. 1850s.

Rarity: URS-1
Proof $3,000

Uncut Sheets

$1-$2 • W-RI-340-001.002-US010

CC

Engraver: Wellstood, Hanks, Hay & Whiting. *Comments:* H-RI-105-G4a, G8a. Remainder. Jany 1st, 18__. 1850s.

Rarity: URS-1
Unc-Rem $1,000; **Proof** $5,400

Non-Valid Issues

$10 • W-RI-340-010-R010

Engraver: Toppan, Carpenter, Casilear & Co. *Comments:* H-RI-105-R5, Durand-399. Raised from W-RI-340-001-G010 series. 18__. 1850s.

Rarity: *None known*

$10 • W-RI-340-010-R020

Engraver: Toppan, Carpenter, Casilear & Co. *Comments:* H-RI-105-R10, Durand-400. Raised from W-RI-340-002-G030 series. 18__. 1850s.

Rarity: *None known*

$10 • W-RI-340-010-S010

TD

Tint: Red TEN. *Engraver:* Danforth, Bald & Co. *Comments:* H-RI-105-S5a, Durand-401. 18__. 1856.

Rarity: URS-5
VF $250

ELMWOOD, RHODE ISLAND

Elmwood is a southern neighborhood of Providence. It was named by Joseph J. Cooke, who purchased the land in 1843. He and other developers planted elm trees framing the suburban community's wide streets.

The area was comprised mostly of farmland until the mid-19th century brought about industrial development. Manufacturing and shipping took root, and the remaining farms were eventually divided.

See also Providence, Rhode Island.

Elmwood Bank
1854–1867
W-RI-350

History: The Elmwood Bank was incorporated in May 1854. Its authorized capital was $55,350, which was reduced to $40,000 by June 1855. It was increased to $82,650 by 1857 and remained at that amount through 1864. The founding president was William V. Daboll. He was accompanied by cashier Daniel L. Rawson, who was replaced in 1857 by C.H. Bassett. Circulation was reported to be $10,600 from 1857 to 1860. Specie in 1857 totaled $1,478.08. In 1858 real estate security was $1,000. Circulation in 1862 was $19,500.

The bank closed in 1867.

See also listing under Cranston, W-RI-250.

EXETER, RHODE ISLAND

Named after a city in England, the town of Exeter was formed in 1742. It was part of land that initially made up North Kingstown. Villages within Exeter include Exeter, Liberty, Fisherville, Tripps Corner, Pine Hill, Black Plain, and Millville. West and East Greenwich lie to the north, and the state of Connecticut borders the town on the west. The earliest industries of Exeter depended on the woodlands, which yielded large quantities of timber.

Exeter Bank
1833–1865
W-RI-360

History: The Exeter Bank was chartered in June 1833 with an authorized capital of $50,000. Capital ranged from $21,330 in 1848 to $35,844 in 1857. Circulation amounted to $12,054 in 1857 and $15,884 in 1863. Specie was valued at $1,340.45 in 1857.

The bank closed in 1865, after which its notes were redeemed at face value for a time.

Numismatic Commentary: The Rawdon, Wright & Hatch engraving company was the sole supplier of paper money for this bank. One might encounter some notes with the words "Counterfeit" or "Worthless" dubbed in on the signature lines. These descriptors were evidently placed to deter use of the notes in commerce after either the bank or the courts sequestered them. At least one uncut sheet remains with these interesting notations.

VALID ISSUES

$1 • W-RI-360-001-G010
Left: ONE on three dies / Ships / 1. *Center:* 1 / Indian / 1 / Man with eagle / 1. *Bottom center:* Ceres. *Right:* ONE / Woman seated with shield bearing anchor / 1. *Engraver:* Rawdon, Wright, Hatch & Co. *Comments:* H-RI-110-G4, Durand-404. 18__. 1830s–1850s.
Rarity: URS-6
VF $400

$1 • W-RI-360-001-G010a
Overprint: Red ONE. *Engraver:* Rawdon, Wright, Hatch & Co. *Comments:* H-RI-110-G4a, Durand-410. Similar to W-RI-360-001-G010. 18__. 1850s–1860s.
Rarity: *None known*

$2 • W-RI-360-002-G020
Left: TWO / Ceres seated by shield bearing 2 / 2. *Center:* 2 / Cherub kneeling and cutting 2 on stone / 2. *Bottom center:* Eagle and cup. *Right:* Woman standing with column / TWO. *Engraver:* Rawdon, Wright, Hatch & Co. *Comments:* H-RI-110-G8, Durand-410. 18__. 1830s–1850s.
Rarity: URS-3
VF $400

$2 • W-RI-360-002-G020a
Overprint: Red TWO. *Engraver:* Rawdon, Wright, Hatch & Co. *Comments:* H-RI-110-G8a. Similar to W-RI-360-002-G020. 18__. 1830s–1850s.
Rarity: *None known*

$3 • W-RI-360-003-G030   TD

Engraver: Rawdon, Wright, Hatch & Co. *Comments:* H-RI-110-G12, Durand-412. 18__. 1830s–1850s.
Rarity: URS-3
VF $750

$3 • W-RI-360-003-G030a
Left: 3 / Portrait of George Washington / 3. *Center:* 3 / Hebe watering eagle / 3 / THREE DOLLARS on three dies. *Bottom center:* 3. *Right:* 3 / Portrait of DeWitt Clinton / 3. *Overprint:* Red THREE. *Engraver:* Rawdon, Wright, Hatch & Co. *Comments:* H-RI-110-G12a. Similar to W-RI-360-003-G030. 18__. 1850s–1860s.
Rarity: *None known*

$5 • W-RI-360-005-G040
Left: FIVE / Woman and eagle / V. *Center:* 5 / Ceres / 5. *Right:* FIVE vertically. *Engraver:* Rawdon, Wright, Hatch & Co. *Comments:* H-RI-110-G16, Durand-415. 18__. 1830s–1850s.
Rarity: URS-3
VF $500

$5 • W-RI-360-005-G040a

Overprint: Red FIVE. *Engraver:* Rawdon, Wright, Hatch & Co. *Comments:* H-RI-110-G16a, Durand-416. Similar to W-RI-360-005-G040. 18__. 1850s–1860s.

Rarity: *None known*

$10 • W-RI-360-010-G050

Left: 10 / Liberty with shield of Hope / 10. *Center:* TEN / Agricultural implements, beehive, cornucopia / TEN. *Bottom center:* Cherub riding stag. *Right:* 10. *Engraver:* Rawdon, Wright, Hatch & Co. *Comments:* H-RI-110-G20, Durand-419. 18__. 1830s–1850s.

Rarity: *None known*

$10 • W-RI-360-010-G050a

QDB

Overprint: Red TEN. *Engraver:* Rawdon, Wright, Hatch & Co. *Comments:* H-RI-110-G20a, Durand-420. Similar to W-RI-360-010-G050. 18__. 1850s–1860s.

Rarity: URS-3
VF $950

$10 • W-RI-360-010-G060

Center: Woman and vessel. *Bottom center:* Indian and canoe. *Comments:* H-Unlisted, Durand-422. 1850s–1860s.

Rarity: URS-3

Uncut Sheets

$1-$1-$2-$3 • W-RI-360-001.001.002.003-US010

Vignette(s): *($1)* Ships / Indian / Man with eagle / Ceres / Woman seated with shield bearing anchor. *($1)* Ships / Indian / Man with eagle / Ceres / Woman seated with shield bearing anchor. *($2)* Ceres seated by shield / Cherub kneeling and cutting 2 on stone / Eagle and cup / Woman standing with column. *($3)* Portrait of George Washington / Hebe watering eagle / Portrait of DeWitt Clinton. *Engraver:* Rawdon, Wright, Hatch & Co. *Comments:* H-RI-110-G4, G4, G8, G12. 18__. 1850s–1860s.

Rarity: URS-3
VF $3,000

Non-Valid Issues

$1 • W-RI-360-001-A010

Left: ONE vertically. *Center:* Reaper seated under tree / Portrait of Daniel Webster / ONE / ONE across 1. *Right:* ONE vertically. *Engraver:* Danforth, Wright & Co. *Comments:* H-RI-110-A5, Durand-406. Altered from $1 Exeter Bank, 2nd, Exeter, New Hampshire. Dec. 3, 1855.

Rarity: *None known*

$1 • W-RI-360-001-A020

Left: 1 / Woman wearing bonnet / ONE. *Center:* Machinery and merchandise flanking Ceres holding rake and sickle, Factories and harbor / ONE. *Right:* 1 / Ship / ONE. *Engraver:* New England Bank Note Co. *Comments:* H-RI-110-A10, Durand-405. Altered from $1 Washington County Bank, Calais, Maine, or from notes of other failed banks using the same plate. 18__. 1850s.

Rarity: *None known*

$1.25 • W-RI-360-001.25-A030

Left: 1 25/100 / Train / 1 25/100. *Center:* Sailing ships in the bay / $1.25 Cts. *Right:* 1 25/100 / Spread eagle. *Engraver:* New England Bank Note Co. *Comments:* H-RI-110-A15, Durand-407. Altered from $1.25 Roxbury Bank, Roxbury, Massachusetts, or from notes of other failed banks using the same plate. 18__. 1850s.

Rarity: *None known*

$1.50 • W-RI-360-001.50-A040

Left: 1 DOLL. 50 Cts vertically. *Center:* Spread eagle / $1 50/100. *Right:* 1 50/100 / Justice. *Engraver:* New England Bank Note Co. *Comments:* H-RI-110-A20, Durand-408. Altered from $1.50 Roxbury Bank, Roxbury, Massachusetts, or from notes of other failed banks using the same plate. 18__. 1850s.

Rarity: *None known*

$1.75 • W-RI-360-001.75-A050

Left: $1.75 Cts / Liberty and eagle / 1 75/100. *Center:* Three sloops at sea. *Right:* $1.75 Cts / Agriculture / 1 75/100. *Engraver:* New England Bank Note Co. *Comments:* H-RI-110-A25, Durand-409. Altered from $1.75 Roxbury Bank, Roxbury, Massachusetts, or from notes of other failed banks using the same plate. 18__. 1850s.

Rarity: *None known*

$2 • W-RI-360-002-A060

Left: 2 / Woman standing with staff / TWO. *Center:* Machinery and merchandise flanking Ceres holding rake and sickle, Factories and harbor / TWO. *Right:* 2 / Female portrait / TWO. *Engraver:* New England Bank Note Co. *Comments:* H-RI-110-A30, Durand-411. Altered from $2 Washington County Bank, Calais, Maine, or from notes of other failed banks using the same plate. 18__. 1850s.

Rarity: *None known*

$3 • W-RI-360-003-A070

Left: THREE / Beehive and foliage / THREE. *Center:* Machinery and merchandise flanking Ceres holding rake and sickle, Factories and harbor / THREE. *Right:* 3 on THREE / Two reapers / 3 on THREE. *Engraver:* New England Bank Note Co. *Comments:* H-RI-110-A40, Durand-413. Altered from $3 Washington County Bank, Calais, Maine, or from notes of other failed banks using the same plate. 18__. 1850s.

Rarity: *None known*

$3 • W-RI-360-003-A080

Left: 3 / Two children with toy boats / THREE. *Center:* River scene with raft, Buildings and falls. *Right:* 3 / Three allegorical figures with shield and scales / THREE. *Engraver:* New England Bank Note Co. *Comments:* H-RI-110-A35, Durand-414. Altered from $3 Stillwater Canal Bank, Orono, Maine. 18__. 1850s.

Rarity: *None known*

$5 • W-RI-360-005-A090

Left: Indian standing with rifle / 5. *Center:* V / Train backed up to wharf, People, dock, water, and boat. *Bottom center:* Indian in canoe. *Right:* Minerva standing with spear and shield. *Comments:* H-RI-110-A50, Durand-418. Altered from $5 Bank of Lower Canada, Quebec, Canada. 18__. 1830s.

Rarity: *None known*

$5 • W-RI-360-005-A100

Left: 5 / Cattle / FIVE. *Center:* River scene with raft, Buildings and falls. *Right:* FIVE / Milkmaid. *Engraver:* New England Bank Note Co. *Comments:* H-RI-110-A45, Durand-417. Altered from $5 Stillwater Canal Bank, Orono, Maine. 18__. 1850s.

Rarity: *None known*

$10 • W-RI-360-010-A110

Left: TEN / Justice standing with balance. *Center:* River scene, Log raft and docks, Warehouses / Panel outlining white TEN. *Right:* 10 / Woman / TEN. *Engraver:* New England Bank Note Co. *Comments:* H-RI-110-A55. Altered from $10 Stillwater Canal Bank, Orono, Maine. 18__. 1850s.

Rarity: *None known*

$10 • W-RI-360-010-A120

Left: Lathework panel with TEN vertically. *Center:* 10 / Mercury seated on shore with caduceus, Ship / 10. *Bottom center:* British arms. *Right:* Minerva standing with spear and shield / TEN. *Comments:* H-RI-110-A60, Durand-421. Altered from $10 Bank of Lower Canada, Quebec, Canada. 18__. 1850s.

Rarity: *None known*

FALL RIVER, RHODE ISLAND

Named after the cascades in the Quequechan River, which has eight waterfalls, the area that is known as Fall River was once inhabited by the Pokanoket Wampanoag tribe. Quequechan is believed to mean "falling river." It was originally located entirely in Rhode Island.

In early times Fall River was made up of Freetown to the north, and Tiverton, Rhode Island, to the south, until February 26, 1803, when it was incorporated as a town on its own. A year later it changed its name to Troy, which continued for 30 years until it changed back to Fall River on February 12, 1834. In 1856 the town of Tiverton decided to split from Fall River, and in 1861 the U.S. Supreme Court moved the boundary of the state line, placing Fall River entirely within Massachusetts.

Saw mills, grist mills, and fulling mills were the early forms of industry in Fall River. On July 2, 1843, a massive fire destroyed 291 buildings across the center of town, leaving 200 families homeless and destroying shops, the custom house, post office, hotels, churches, and banks. A fund of $50,000 for the aid of the struggling victims was donated by people in towns including Boston, Cambridge, Providence, and New Bedford. Textiles were a major industry under the influence of nearby Rhode Island developments. The Fall River Iron Works, as well as spinning mills, cotton manufactories, woolen manufactories, thread mills, a twine mill, a loom-making firm, and a linen manufactory were also located here. Coal and iron from Europe were also imported in Fall River.

See also Tiverton, Rhode Island, and Fall River, Massachusetts.

Fall River Union Bank
1823–1860 • 1860–1864
W-RI-370 • W-MA-1560

History: The Fall River Union Bank was incorporated as the Bristol Union Bank, W-RI-060, in 1823 with an authorized capital of $200,000. The location was changed to Tiverton, Rhode Island, in 1830, and the title was changed to the Fall River Union Bank in 1831.

The bank's capital was $199,512 in 1848, divided into 2,000 shares valued at $100 each. Bills in circulation totaled $68,128 in 1849. By 1857 capital had been decreased to $99,500. The bank was located in a building on the corner of South Main and Rodman streets.

The Fall River Union Bank became a Massachusetts bank in 1860 as a result of the boundary change which took place at the January session of the legislatures of the two states involved. A portion of Tiverton, Rhode Island, became part of Fall River, and all of Fall River, Rhode Island, became part of Massachusetts. Notes were imprinted at Fall River, Massachusetts, beginning in 1860.

In January 1863, the bank's circulation was $42,666. The business of the Fall River Union Bank was succeeded by the First National Bank of Fall River, chartered in February 1864.

See also listings under Tiverton, W-RI-1480, and Massachusetts.

Numismatic Commentary: All issues bearing the imprint of Fall River in Massachusetts are relatively unknown. Any example is a rare prize.

VALID ISSUES
Notes With Rhode Island Address

$2 • W-RI-370-002-G005   CJF

Overprint: Red TWO. *Engraver:* New England Bank Note Co. *Comments:* H-Unlisted, Durand-Unlisted. 18__. 1858–1860s.

Rarity: —

$50 • W-RI-370-050-G010

Left: FIFTY / Grain, fruit, and flowers / 50. *Center:* 50 / Three allegorical women, Eagle and ship. *Right:* FIFTY on 50 / Blacksmith. *Engraver:* New England Bank Note Co. / ABNCo. monogram. *Comments:* H-RI-495-G70, Durand-2229. 18__. 1858–1860s.

Rarity: —

$100 • W-RI-370-100-G020

Left: C / Men and fishing boats / 100. *Center:* Eagle on bale, Cornucopia, Flowers, Fruit / 100. *Right:* 100 / Ceres / 100. *Engraver:* New England Bank Note Co. / ABNCo. monogram. *Comments:* H-RI-495-G72, Durand-2231. 18__. 1858–1860s.

Rarity: —

$500 • W-RI-370-500-G030

Left: Indian in canoe / 500. *Center:* 500. *Right:* 500 / Justice. *Engraver:* New England Bank Note Co. / ABNCo. monogram. *Comments:* H-RI-495-G74, Durand-2233. 18__. 1858–1860s.

Rarity: —

Notes With Massachusetts Address

$1 • W-MA-1560-001-G010

Left: Man on horse, Boy with hand on one of four cows, Houses / 1. *Center:* 1 / Dolphin. *Right:* ONE / Indian man with bow and arrow / 1. *Engraver:* American Bank Note Co. *Comments:* H-MA-570-G2. Similar to $1 Fall River Union Bank, Rhode Island, but with different state. 1862–1864.

Rarity: —

$2 • W-MA-1560-002-G020

Left: Train, dock, and ships, Depot and men / 2 bearing female portrait / 2. *Center:* 2 bearing female portrait. *Right:* 2 / Portrait of George Washington and horse / TWO. *Engraver:* American Bank Note Co. *Comments:* H-MA-570-G4. Similar to $2 Fall River Union Bank, Rhode Island, but with different state. 1862–1864.

Rarity: —

$5 • W-MA-1560-005-G030

Left: Indian man paddling canoe on river / V in FIVE. *Center:* V. *Right:* 5 / Spread eagle perched on shield bearing 5. *Engraver:* American Bank Note Co. *Comments:* H-MA-570-G6. 1862–1864.

Rarity: URS-5

F $300

$10 • W-MA-1560-010-G040

Left: Mechanic seated on boiler working bellows / X. *Center:* X. *Right:* TEN / Portrait of George Washington / TEN. *Engraver:* American Bank Note Co. *Comments:* H-MA-570-G8. Similar to $10 Fall River Union Bank, Rhode Island, but with different state. 1862–1864.

Rarity: —

$20 • W-MA-1560-020-G050

Left: Woman reclining on rock with eagle and sheaf / 20. *Center:* TWENTY and 20 / Female portrait. *Right:* 20 / Portrait of Benjamin Franklin. *Engraver:* American Bank Note Co. *Comments:* H-MA-570-G10. 1862–1864.

Rarity: —

$50 • W-MA-1560-050-G060

Left: FIFTY / Sheaves and fruit / 50. *Center:* 50 / Three women seated with eagle, pole and cap, shield, scales, and book. *Right:* FIFTY across 50 / Train, Vulcan seated with tools. *Engraver:* New England Bank Note Co. / American Bank Note Co. *Comments:* H-MA-570-G12. Similar to $50 Fall River Union Bank, Rhode Island, but with different state. 1862–1864.

Rarity: —

$100 • W-MA-1560-100-G070

Left: C / Men with fishing boat at shore / 100. *Center:* Cornucopia, Eagle perched on bale, Sheaf / 100. *Right:* 100 / Ceres / 100. *Engraver:* New England Bank Note Co. / American Bank Note Co. *Comments:* H-MA-570-G14. Similar to $100 Fall River Union Bank, Rhode Island, but with different state. 1862–1864.

Rarity: —

$500 • W-MA-1560-500-G080

Left: Indian paddling canoe, Forest and mountains / 500 / D D. *Bottom center:* 500. *Right:* 500 / Justice. *Engraver:* New England Bank Note Co. / American Bank Note Co. *Comments:* H-MA-570-G16. Similar to $500 Fall River Union Bank, Rhode Island, but with different state. 1862–1864.

Rarity: —

Pocasset Bank
1854–1860 • 1860–1865
W-RI-380 • W-MA-1590

History: The Pocasset Bank was incorporated in May 1854 with an authorized capital of $200,000. The official address was Tiverton, Rhode Island, but "Main Street, Fall River" was given on some reports, that section being in Rhode Island at the time. After a boundary change between Tiverton and Fall River was put into effect in the 1860 January session of the two state legislatures involved, the institution became a Massachusetts bank when Fall River became a part of Massachusetts.

The bank's circulation was $67,033 in 1860 and $82,007 in 1863. Real estate was valued at $100, and specie was listed at $4,830.48.

The business of the bank was succeeded by the Pocasset National Bank, chartered on December 31, 1864. The state bank began winding up its affairs in early 1865.

See also listings under Tiverton, W-RI-1490, and Massachusetts.

Numismatic Commentary: Genuine notes from this bi-state bank are hard to locate. Notes from the Rhode Island address are more plentiful. Some of the vignettes show Weetamoe, an Indian queen, escaping on a raft of logs from English pursuers. She perished in the waters of the Narragansett Bay when the raft overturned.

As of 2003 there was a $1-$1-$2-$5 tint plate remaining at the American Bank Note Co. archives.

VALID ISSUES
Notes with Rhode Island Address

$1 • W-RI-380-001-G010

CC

Overprint: Red 1. *Engraver:* Wellstood, Hanks, Hay & Whiting / ABNCo. monogram. *Comments:* H-RI-500-G20a, Durand-433. 18__. 1850s.

Rarity: URS-7
F $150

$1 • W-RI-380-001-G010a

Overprint: Blue 1. *Engraver:* Wellstood, Hanks, Hay & Whiting / ABNCo. monogram. *Comments:* H-RI-500-G20b, Durand-434. Similar to W-RI-380-001-G010. 18__. 1850s.

Rarity: —

$2 • W-RI-380-002-G020

RD

Engraver: Wellstood, Hanks, Hay & Whiting / ABNCo. monogram. *Comments:* H-Unlisted. 18__. 1850s.

Rarity: URS-7
F $150

$2 • W-RI-380-002-G020a

CC

Overprint: Red 2. *Engraver:* Wellstood, Hanks, Hay & Whiting / ABNCo. monogram. *Comments:* H-RI-500-G22a, Durand-435. Similar to W-RI-380-002-G020. 18__. 1850s.

Rarity: URS-7
F $150

$2 • W-RI-380-002-G020b

MK

Overprint: Blue 2. *Engraver:* Wellstood, Hanks, Hay & Whiting / ABNCo. monogram. *Comments:* H-RI-500-G22b, Durand-436. Similar to W-RI-380-002-G020. 18__. 1850s.

Rarity: URS-4
G $300; F $500

$2 • W-RI-380-002-G030

Left: TWO on 2 / Indian woman. *Center:* Cow and calf in stream, Sheep and house. *Right:* 2 / Portrait of two girls. *Comments:* H-RI-500-G24, Durand-437. 18__. 1860s.

Rarity: —

$5 • W-RI-380-005-G040

Left: FIVE / Reverses of three U.S. and two Spanish-U.S. silver dollars. *Center:* 5 / Indian woman poling raft. *Bottom center:* Men loading wagon with hay. *Right:* FIVE across 5 / FIVE. *Overprint:* Red 5. *Engraver:* Wellstood, Hanks, Hay & Whiting / ABNCo. monogram. *Comments:* H-RI-500-G26a, Durand-440. 18__. 1850s.

Rarity: —

$5 • W-RI-380-005-G040a

Overprint: Blue 5. *Engraver:* Wellstood, Hanks, Hay & Whiting / ABNCo. monogram. *Comments:* H-RI-500-G26b, Durand-441. Similar to W-RI-380-005-G040. 18__. 1850s.

Rarity: —

$10 • W-RI-380-010-G050

Left: 10 / Stonecutter at work, Marble quarry. *Right:* 10 / Indian woman poling raft. *Engraver:* Wellstood, Hanks, Hay & Whiting. *Comments:* H-Unlisted, Durand-442. 1850s.

Rarity: —

$20 • W-RI-380-020-G060

Left: 20 / Indian woman poling raft. *Bottom center:* Anchor on shield. *Right:* Justice in clouds / 20. *Engraver:* Wellstood, Hanks, Hay & Whiting. *Comments:* H-Unlisted, Durand-443. 1850s.

Rarity: —

$50 • W-RI-380-050-G070

Left: 50 / Farm scene, Woman standing, Man seated at lunch. *Bottom center:* 50. *Right:* Indian woman poling raft / 50. *Engraver:* Wellstood, Hanks, Hay & Whiting. *Comments:* H-Unlisted, Durand-444. 1850s.

Rarity: —

$100 • W-RI-380-100-G080

Left: 100 / Sailing ship. *Center:* C / Indian woman poling raft. *Right:* 100 / Farmer sharpening scythe. *Engraver:* Wellstood, Hanks, Hay & Whiting. *Comments:* H-Unlisted, Durand-445. 1850s.

Rarity: —

$500 • W-RI-380-500-G090

Left: 500 / Warship under sail, Ship. *Center:* D. *Right:* 500 / Indian woman poling raft. *Engraver:* Wellstood, Hanks, Hay & Whiting. *Comments:* H-Unlisted, Durand-446. 1850s.

Rarity: —

$1,000 • W-RI-380-1000-G100

Left: Indian woman poling raft / 1000. *Center:* M. *Right:* 1000 / Indian seated smoking pipe, Indian woman, Canoe and wigwam. *Engraver:* Wellstood, Hanks, Hay & Whiting. *Comments:* H-Unlisted, Durand-447. 1850s.

Rarity: —

Notes with Massachusetts Address

$1 • W-MA-1590-001-G010

Engraver: American Bank Note Co. *Comments:* H-MA-585-G2a. Similar to W-RI-380-001-G010 but with different state and imprint. 18__. 1860s.

Rarity: —

$2 • W-MA-1590-002-G020

Engraver: American Bank Note Co. *Comments:* H-MA-585-G4a. Similar to W-RI-380-002-G020 but with different state and imprint. 18__. 1860s.

Rarity: —

$2 • W-MA-1590-002-G030   CJF

Tint: Green. *Engraver:* American Bank Note Co. *Comments:* H-MA-585-G6a. Similar to W-RI-380-002-G030 but with different state and imprint. March 4, 1862.

Rarity: URS-2
VF $1,500

$5 • W-MA-1590-005-G040   CJF

Overprint: Green 5 / FIVE / 5. *Engraver:* Wellstood, Hanks, Hay & Whiting / ABNCo. monogram. *Comments:* H-MA-585-G8a. Similar to W-RI-380-005-G040 but with different state and imprint. March 4, 1862. 1860s.

Rarity: URS-2
VF $1,500

$10 • W-MA-1590-010-G050

Engraver: American Bank Note Co. *Comments:* H-MA-585-G10. Similar to W-RI-380-010-G050 but with different state and imprint. 18__. 1860s.

Rarity: —

$20 • W-MA-1590-020-G060

Engraver: American Bank Note Co. *Comments:* H-MA-585-G12a. Similar to W-RI-380-020-G060 but with different state and imprint. 18__. 1860s.

Rarity: —

$50 • W-MA-1590-050-G070

Engraver: American Bank Note Co. *Comments:* H-MA-585-G14a. Similar to W-RI-380-050-G070 but with different state and imprint. 18__. 1860s.

Rarity: —

$100 • W-MA-1590-100-G080

Engraver: American Bank Note Co. *Comments:* H-MA-585-G16a. Similar to W-RI-380-100-G080 but with different state and imprint. 18__. 1860s.

Rarity: —

$500 • W-MA-1590-500-G090

Engraver: American Bank Note Co. *Comments:* H-MA-585-G18a. Similar to W-RI-380-500-G090 but with different state and imprint. 18__. 1860s.

Rarity: —

$1,000 • W-MA-1590-1000-G100

Engraver: American Bank Note Co. *Comments:* H-MA-585-G20. Similar to W-RI-380-1000-G100 but with different state and imprint. 18__. 1860s.

Rarity: —

Non-Valid Issues
Notes with Rhode Island Address

$2 • W-RI-380-002-C020a   CC

Overprint: Red 2. *Engraver:* Wellstood, Hanks, Hay & Whiting / ABNCo. monogram. *Comments:* H-RI-500-C22a, Durand-438. Counterfeit of W-RI-380-002-G020a. 18__. 1850s.

Rarity: URS-8
VF $150

$2 • W-RI-380-002-C020b

Engraver: Wellstood, Hanks, Hay & Whiting / ABNCo. monogram. *Comments:* H-RI-500-C22b, Durand-439. Counterfeit of W-RI-380-002-G020b. 18__. 1850s.

Rarity: URS-7
VF $150

Notes with Massachusetts Address

$2 • W-MA-1590-002-C020
Engraver: American Bank Note Co. *Comments:* H-MA-585-C4a. Counterfeit of W-MA-1590-002-G020. 18__. 1860s.
Rarity: —

$5 • W-MA-1590-005-C040
Engraver: American Bank Note Co. *Comments:* H-MA-585-C8. Counterfeit of W-MA-1590-005-G040. 18__. 1860s.
Rarity: URS-7
VG $100; **VF** $175

$5 • W-MA-1590-005-A010   CJF

Overprint: Red FIVE. *Engraver:* Bald, Cousland & Co. / Baldwin, Bald & Cousland. *Comments:* H-MA-585-A5. 18__. 1860s.
Rarity: URS-7
VG $100; **VF** $225

Tiverton Bank
1855–1857
W-RI-390

History: The Tiverton Bank was incorporated in May 1855 and commenced business in December 1856. Its authorized capital was $50,000.

The bank had a very brief existence, as it was forced to close at the end of 1857 due to the financial panic that year. The bank was managed by out-of-state owners with capital made up of

---

How to Read the Whitman Numbering System
$1 • W-RI-010-001-G010a

Denomination: Value of the note shown.

W: Whitman number. This number is a sortable code unique to each bank and note.

RI: Abbreviation for the state under study.

010: Numerical designation specific to each bank.

001: The denomination in dollars.

G010a: G indicates a good or valid note. Other categories are indicated thus: C (counterfeit); R (raised); S (spurious); N (not-attributed); A (altered). Numbers are assigned starting with 010, 020, et seq. Terminal letters following the number indicate variations of a note: a series of different colored overprints, tints, payees, etc., all on the same design of note. For more information, see the "How to Use This Book" section at the front of the volume, page xiv.

---

bogus bank notes. At one point the cashier took bank funds to New York City. The entire operation was fraudulent.

See also listing under Tiverton, W-RI-1500.

Numismatic Commentary: Genuine notes are fairly plentiful in today's marketplace.

Remaining in the American Bank Note Co. archives as of 2003 was a $1-$1-$2-$3 tint plate and a $5-$5-$10-$20 tint plate.

VALID ISSUES

$5 • W-RI-390-005-G010   CC

Tint: Red-brown outlining white 5, V, 5. *Engraver:* Bald, Cousland & Co. *Comments:* H-RI-505-G18a, Durand-2247. Remainder. Aug.t 1st, 1857. 1850s.
Rarity: URS-6
VF $300; **Proof** $750

$10 • W-RI-390-010-G020   SBG

Tint: Orange outlining white 10, TEN. *Engraver:* Bald, Cousland & Co. *Comments:* H-RI-505-G20b, Durand-2248. Proof. 18__. 1850s.
Rarity: URS-4
Proof $900

$20 • W-RI-390-020-G030   TD

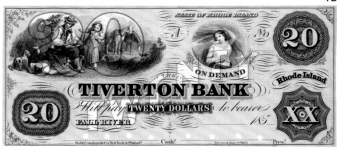

Tint: Orange outlining white 20, TWENTY. *Engraver:* Bald, Cousland & Co. *Comments:* H-RI-505-G22b, Durand-2249. Proof. 185_. 1850s.
Rarity: URS-4
Proof $1,000

Uncut Sheets
$5-$5-$10-$20 •
W-RI-390-005.005.010.020-US010

SBG

Engraver: Bald, Cousland & Co. *Comments:* H-RI-505-G18a, G18a, G20b, G22b. Variously dated Aug.t 1st, 1857, Aug.t 1st, 1857, 18__, 185_. 1850s.

Rarity: URS-3
Proof $3,000

FOSTER, RHODE ISLAND

In 1662 British colonists purchased the land that would become Foster from the natives who lived there. At the time it was called West Quanaug. In 1730 the area was incorporated with Scituate, Rhode Island. In 1781 the town was renamed after Theodore Foster, a U.S. senator. The town is bordered by the towns of Coventry, Killingly, Sterling, Gloucester, and Scituate, and the state of Connecticut.

Commerce was conducted in products such as corn, rye, oats, potatoes, butter, cheese, and hay. The villages within Foster were Hopkins Mills, Foster Center, Clayville, Moosup Valley, North Foster, and Mount Vernon. In 1782 the population

consisted of 1,763 residents. In 1820 it was at its largest with a population of 2,900.

Mount Vernon Bank
1823–1859
W-RI-400

History: The Mount Vernon Bank was incorporated in 1823 in the town of Foster. Almost half of the directors did not actually reside in Foster but lived in Providence.[23] Circulation in 1849 was listed at $36,160.

Banker's Magazine reported a robbery that occurred at this bank in 1852:

> The Mount Vernon Bank, at Foster, Rhode Island, was entered between Saturday, the 4th of September, and the following Monday morning, and robbed of $10,300 in bills of the bank. About $7,000 were of the denomination of $50, and numbered mostly from No. 400 to 500, $2,000 of which had never been put in circulation. The remainder were in bills of $10, $20, and $100. The bank has issued the following advertisement: "Caution. —The Mount Vernon Bank, of Foster, hereby cautions the public against receiving bills of the bank of the denomination of $20, $50, and $100, issued prior to this date. All parties holding bills of those denominations, which have been put in circulation by the bank, are informed that said bills will be redeemed on presentation at their counter. By order of the Directors, R.G. Place, *Cashier. Mount Vernon Bank, Foster,* September 6, 1852."[24]

In 1854 the bank moved to Providence, where it remained for the duration of its existence. Notes with both the Foster and Providence imprints were circulated. In Providence the bank was located at 87 Westminster Street. Capital was set at $60,000 and raised to $92,778 by 1856.

This bank failed in 1859.

See also listing under Providence, W-RI-1100.

Numismatic Commentary: Except for the highest denominations, notes printed with the Providence address are readily available, while their earlier counterparts dated at Foster are very hard to locate. Most of the issues are handsomely engraved and pleasant to view.

VALID ISSUES
$1 • W-RI-400-001-G010
Left: 1. *Center:* ONE DOLLAR in lathework panel vertically / ONE. *Right:* 1. *Engraver:* Rawdon, Wright, Hatch & Co. *Comments:* H-RI-115-G2. 18__. 1823.

Rarity: URS-3
Proof $2,000

$1 • W-RI-400-001-G020
Left: 1. *Center:* 1 / ONE. *Right:* 1. *Engraver:* Rawdon, Wright, Hatch & Co. *Comments:* H-RI-115-G4, Durand-1679. 18__. 1830s–1840s.

Rarity: URS-3
Proof $2,000

$2 • W-RI-400-002-G030

Left: 2. *Center:* 2 / TWO. *Right:* 2. *Engraver:* Rawdon, Wright, Hatch & Co. *Comments:* H-RI-115-G12, Durand-1680. 18__. 1823.

Rarity: URS-3
Proof $2,000

$2 • W-RI-400-002-G040

Left: 2. *Center:* TWO DOLLARS in lathework panel vertically / TWO. *Right:* 2. *Engraver:* Rawdon, Wright, Hatch & Co. *Comments:* H-RI-115-G14. 18__. 1830s.

Rarity: URS-3
Proof $2,000

$5 • W-RI-400-005-G050

Left: 5. *Center:* 5 / FIVE. *Right:* 5. *Engraver:* Rawdon, Wright, Hatch & Co. *Comments:* H-RI-115-G26, Durand-1681. 18__. 1830s–1840s.

Rarity: URS-3
Proof $2,000

$5 • W-RI-400-005-G060

Engraver: Rawdon, Wright, Hatch & Co. *Comments:* H-Unlisted, Durand-Unlisted. Proof. 18__. 1850s.

Rarity: URS-1
Proof $2,000

$10 • W-RI-400-010-G070

Left: 10. *Center:* 10 / TEN. *Right:* 10. *Engraver:* Rawdon, Wright, Hatch & Co. *Comments:* H-RI-115-G32, Durand-1682. 18__. 1830s–1840s.

Rarity: URS-3
Proof $2,000

$10 • W-RI-400-010-G080

Engraver: Rawdon, Wright, Hatch & Co. *Comments:* H-Unlisted, Durand-Unlisted. 18__. 1850s.

Rarity: URS-1
VF $1,600; Proof $2,000

$20 • W-RI-400-020-G090

Left: 20. *Center:* 20 / TWENTY. *Right:* 20. *Engraver:* Rawdon, Wright, Hatch & Co. *Comments:* H-RI-115-G38, Durand-1683. 18__. 1830s.

Rarity: URS-3
Proof $2,000

$20 • W-RI-400-020-G100

Left: XX / Portrait of Benjamin Franklin / 20. *Center:* Marquis de Lafayette standing with hat and cane. *Right:* 20. *Engraver:* Rawdon, Wright, Hatch & Co. *Comments:* H-RI-115-G40. 18__. 1830s–1840s.

Rarity: URS-3
Proof $2,000

$20 • W-RI-400-020-G110

SBG

Engraver: Rawdon, Wright, Hatch & Co. *Comments:* H-Unlisted, Durand-Unlisted. Proof. 18__. 1850s.

Rarity: URS-3
Proof $2,000

$50 • W-RI-400-050-G120

Left: 50 / Sailing ship / 50. *Center:* 50 / Statue of George Washington / 50. *Right:* Portrait of cherub / 50 / Portrait of cherub. *Overprint:* Red FIFTY. *Engraver:* Rawdon, Wright, Hatch & Co. *Comments:* H-RI-115-G44. 18__. 1830s–1840s.

Rarity: URS-3
Proof $2,000

$100 • W-RI-400-100-G130

Left: Cherub flying with basket of flowers. *Center:* Goddess of Plenty seated, Mercury and griffin on strongbox. *Bottom center:* Eagle. *Right:* C / 100. *Engraver:* Rawdon, Wright, Hatch & Co. *Comments:* H-RI-115-G48. 18__. 1830s–1840s.

Rarity: URS-3
Proof $2,000

GLOUCESTER, RHODE ISLAND

Gloucester, also spelled Glocester, was settled in 1706 as a part of Providence but separated in 1731. It was named after the Duke of Gloucester, Henry Stuart. In 1806 the northern section of town separated to become Burrillville, and during the American Revolution, Newport Loyalists were exiled to Gloucester.

In 1841 the Dorr Rebellion against the state originated in Gloucester. Agriculture made up the primary industry for the town, including hay, corn, potatoes, beef, fruit, pork, oats, and rye. In the early 19th century, a brickyard existed here, as well as an oil works, a hat factory, a potash factory, a distillery, a tannery, a nail and tool factory, and various mills for woolen and cotton cloth. In 1838 gold was discovered on the Page farm, and some mining took place.

See also Burrillville and Chepachet, Rhode Island.

Farmers Exchange Bank
1804–1809
W-RI-410

History: This bank was the most publicized fraud of its era. Conceived by Andrew Dexter, an exchange broker in Boston, it was criminally operated from the beginning. The Farmers Exchange Bank was chartered in February 1804 with an authorized capital of $100,000. The capital was divided into 2,000 shares of $50 each, payable in seven installments of specie. Only a fraction of that amount was ever actually paid in. The rest of the payments were simply loans to the directors, and the final two installments were not paid at all. The actual amount of capital was only $3,081.11.

The bank issued at least $760,265 in bills, some of which were redeemed in exchange for others. Dexter desired to keep the flood of bills secret, and the cashier of the bank was directed to sign them privately and mostly at night. Many of these bills were distributed with the offer that if they were held, six percent interest would be paid, but specie would be paid if they were redeemed.

By 1809 the fraud was exposed. The bank collapsed, and its bills became worthless.

See state introduction for more information.

Numismatic Commentary: Bills dated in 1806 were printed by William Hamlin of Providence. Soon afterward, a flood of paper money was printed for this bank by the Jacob Perkins company in Newburyport, Massachusetts, allowing today's collector the opportunity to easily obtain multiple denominations. While not especially pretty to look at, these bills are historic in that the process with which they were engraved and printed, Perkins' Patent Stereotype Steel Plate (PSSP), revolutionized his bank-note plant by speeding up the engraving process in order to service a greater number of banks more quickly and at a lower cost than his competition (see volume 1 of this series for detailed information about Perkins).

VALID ISSUES
$1 • W-RI-410-001-G010

MR

Engraver: Hamlin. **Comments:** H-RI-120-G2, Durand-448. 18__. 1804–1808.
Rarity: URS-8
VF $100

$1 • W-RI-410-001-G020

CJF

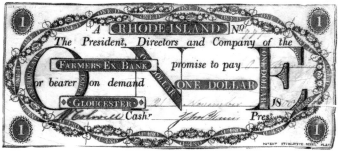

Engraver: PSSP. **Comments:** H-RI-120-G4, Durand-449. 18__. 1807–1809.
Rarity: URS-10
F $100

$2 • W-RI-410-002-G030

Left: TWO vertically. **Center:** Oxen / 2 / TWO / 2 / Farmer hoeing. **Engraver:** Hamlin. **Comments:** H-RI-120-G6, Durand-450. 18__. 1804–1808.
Rarity: URS-8
VF $100

$2 • W-RI-410-002-G040

TD

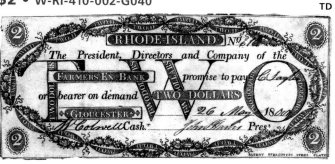

Engraver: PSSP. **Comments:** H-RI-120-G8, Durand-451. 18__. 1807–1809.
Rarity: URS-10
VG $50; **VF** $100

$3 • W-RI-410-003-G050

CC

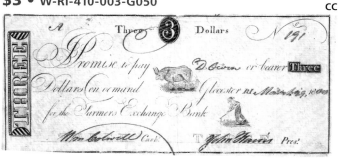

Engraver: Hamlin. **Comments:** H-RI-120-G10, Durand-452. 18__. 1806–1808.
Rarity: URS-7
VF $350

$3 • W-RI-410-003-G060   CJF

Engraver: PSSP. *Comments:* H-RI-120-G12, Durand-453. 18__.
1807–1809.

Rarity: URS-10
VF $100

$5 • W-RI-410-005-G070   MR

Engraver: Hamlin. *Comments:* H-RI-120-G14, Durand-454.
18__. 1804–1808.

Rarity: URS-5
VF $200

$5 • W-RI-410-005-G080   BM

Engraver: Perkins. *Comments:* H-RI-120-G16, Durand-455.
18__. 1806–1808.

Rarity: URS-10
F $50; VF $100

$5 • W-RI-410-005-G080a   ANS

Engraver: Perkins. *Comments:* H-RI-120-G18. Similar to
W-RI-410-005-G080. 18__. Circa 1806 and 1807.

Rarity: —
VG $34; F $42; VF $45; EF $50

$10 • W-RI-410-010-G090   CC

Engraver: Perkins. *Comments:* H-RI-120-G20, Durand-456.
18__. 1806–1808.

Rarity: URS-10
VF $75

$10 • W-RI-410-010-G090a   CJF

Engraver: Perkins. *Comments:* H-RI-120-G22. Similar to
W-RI-410-010-G090. 18__. 1808.

Rarity: URS-10
VF $75

Franklin Bank
1818–1868
W-RI-420

History: The Franklin Bank was chartered in February 1818 by
a group from the Gloucester village of Chepachet. Jesse Tourtellot served as its first president, and Cyril Cook was its first
cashier. Its authorized capital was $50,000, which was reduced
to $38,000 by 1849 and increased again to $50,000 by 1855.
Circulation was $24,689 in 1849, $28,131.50 in 1857, and
$32,085 by 1863. Specie amounted to $2,176.09 in 1857.

This bank was successful and continued to do business until
the national banking system arose, in which it did not participate. It was closed down in 1868, and its capital and surplus
were distributed to the stockholders.[25]

See also listing under Chepachet, W-RI-210.

GREENVILLE, RHODE ISLAND
Greenville is a small village in the town of Smithfield. Named
after Revolutionary War general Nathanael Greene, the town
was settled in the 17th century. It became known for its extensive apple orchards.

Exchange Bank
1863–1865
W-RI-425

History: Around 1863 the Smithfield Exchange Bank, W-RI-430, became known as the Exchange Bank. In 1865 its interests were succeeded by the National Exchange Bank of Greenville. See also listing under Smithfield, W-RI-1335.

NON-VALID ISSUES
$2 • W-RI-425-002-A010

CC

Tint: Red panel of microletters, 2 on die, and outlined red 2. **Engraver:** Wellstood, Hay & Whiting. **Comments:** H-Unlisted. Sept. 10th, 1857. 1850s.

Rarity: URS-8
VF $200

Smithfield Exchange Bank
1822–1863
W-RI-430

History: The Smithfield Exchange Bank was organized in June 1822 in a room of the Greenville Tavern. The authorized capital was $40,000, which was reduced to $30,000 in 1845, raised to $60,000 in 1856, and raised again to $100,000 by December 1862. The first president was Daniel Winsor, and the first cashier was Nicholas Winsor. By 1856 Owen Battey had succeeded Daniel Winsor as president, and William Winsor had succeeded Nicholas Winsor as cashier.

The location of the bank was moved to another place in the village around 1856. Bills in circulation amounted to $56,662 in 1857, with specie at $3,247.23. In 1863 circulation was $60,298. It became known as the Exchange Bank, W-RI-425, the same year.

See also listing under Smithfield, W-RI-1380.

Numismatic Commentary: Genuine notes issued from either of the two addresses are hard to locate. Most of the known examples are Proofs.

VALID ISSUES
$1 • W-RI-430-001-G010

SBG

Engraver: Danforth & Hufty. **Comments:** H-RI-465-G50, Durand-467. July 4th, 1848.
Rarity: URS-3
Proof $2,000

$1 • W-RI-430-001-G010a
Left: ONE / Portrait of George Washington / 1. **Center:** Milkmaid seated, Cows / 1 bearing ONE ONE. **Right:** 1 / Portrait of Martha Washington / ONE. **Engraver:** Danforth & Hufty. **Comments:** H-RI-465-G50a. Similar to W-RI-430-001-G010 but with different date. July 4, 18__. 1850s.
Rarity: URS-3
Proof $2,000

$2 • W-RI-430-002-G020
Left: 2 / State arms / TWO. **Center:** Man hammering, Cooper working on barrel, 2. **Right:** TWO / Portrait of Benjamin Franklin / TWO on medallion head. **Engraver:** Danforth & Hufty. **Comments:** H-RI-465-G52, Durand-473. July 4th, 1848.
Rarity: *None known*

$2 • W-RI-430-002-G020a

CJF

Engraver: Danforth & Hufty. **Comments:** H-RI-465-G52a. Similar to W-RI-430-002-G020 but with different date. July 4th, 18__. 1850s.
Rarity: URS-2
Proof $2,000

$5 • W-RI-430-005-G030
Left: 5 / Shield bearing anchor / FIVE. **Center:** Portrait of Zachary Taylor / 5 / Female portrait. **Right:** 5 / Portrait of Kate Sevier / 5. **Engraver:** Danforth & Hufty. **Comments:** H-RI-465-G54, Durand-479. July 4th, 1848.
Rarity: *None known*

$5 • W-RI-430-005-G030a
Engraver: Danforth & Hufty. **Comments:** H-RI-465-G54a. Similar to W-RI-430-005-G030 but with different date. July 4, 18__. 1850s.
Rarity: URS-3
Proof $2,000

$10 • W-RI-430-010-G040

Left: "Signing of the Declaration of Independence" / X. *Center:* X. *Right:* 10 / Train, Man with wheelbarrow. *Engraver:* New England Bank Note Co. *Comments:* H-RI-465-G58, Durand-482. 18__. 1850s.

Rarity: *None known*

$10 • W-RI-430-010-G050   CC

Engraver: Danforth & Hufty / ABNCo. monogram. *Comments:* H-Unlisted. July __, 18__. 1850s.

Rarity: URS-8
VF $200

$20 • W-RI-430-020-G060

Left: 20 / Woman seated with book on lap, opening chest. *Center:* XX / Eagle on rock / XX. *Right:* 20 / Ship in harbor. *Engraver:* New England Bank Note Co. *Comments:* H-RI-465-G60, Durand-484. Similar to W-RI-1380-020-G190 but with different city. 18__. 1850s.

Rarity: *None known*

$50 • W-RI-430-050-G070

Left: FIFTY / Woman standing with wreath and flowers / FIFTY. *Center:* 50 / Man restraining prancing horse / 50. *Right:* FIFTY / Woman standing with cornucopia / FIFTY. *Engraver:* New England Bank Note Co. *Comments:* H-RI-465-G62, Durand-485. Similar to W-RI-1380-050-G210 but with different city. 18__. 1850s.

Rarity: *None known*

$100 • W-RI-430-100-G080

Left: ONE HUNDRED across 100 / Portrait of William Henry Harrison. *Center:* Wharf scene. *Right:* ONE HUNDRED across 100 / Portrait of Christopher Columbus. *Engraver:* New England Bank Note Co. *Comments:* H-RI-465-G64, Durand-486. Similar to W-RI-1380-100-G230 but with different city. 18__. 1850s.

Rarity: *None known*

Uncut Sheets

$1-$1-$2-$5 • W-RI-430-001.001.002.005-US010

Vignette(s): *($1)* Portrait of George Washington / Milkmaid seated, Cows / Portrait of Martha Washington. *($1)* Portrait of George Washington / Milkmaid seated, Cows / Portrait of Martha Washington. *($2)* Tree / Man hammering, Cooper working on barrel / Portrait of Benjamin Franklin / TWO on medallion head. *($5)* Shield bearing anchor / Portrait of Zachary Taylor / Female portrait / Portrait of Kate Sevier. *Engraver:* Danforth & Hufty. *Comments:* H-RI-465-G50, G50, G52, G54. July 4th, 1848.

Rarity: URS-3
Proof $8,000

Non-Valid Issues

$1.25 • W-RI-430-001.25-A010   CJF

Engraver: New England Bank Note Co. *Comments:* H-RI-465-A5, Durand-470. Altered from $1.25 Roxbury Bank, Roxbury, Massachusetts, or from notes of other failed banks using the same plate. Proof. 18__. 1853.

Rarity: URS-3
F $150; **VF** $250

$1.50 • W-RI-430-001.50-A020   CC

Engraver: New England Bank Note Co. *Comments:* H-RI-465-A10, Durand-471. Altered from $1.50 Roxbury Bank, Roxbury, Massachusetts, or from notes of other failed banks using the same plate. 18__. 1853.

Rarity: URS-3
VF $250

HOPKINTON, RHODE ISLAND

Originally a part of Westerly in the early days, Hopkinton separated as a town on March 14, 1757. It was named after Stephen Hopkins, who signed the Declaration of Independence and also became governor of Rhode Island. Several industrial villages were encompassed in the borders of Hopkinton, including Ashaway. Each village was named after a mill.

See also Ashaway and Westerly, Rhode Island.

Ashaway Bank
1855–1865
W-RI-440

History: The Ashaway Bank was chartered in 1855 in Hopkinton. Its authorized capital was $75,000, where it remained throughout the bank's existence. Specie was listed at $1,442.80 in 1857 and circulation was valued at $14,839, where it remained until 1863. In 1864 it doubled to $35,325. In May 1865, the bank's address changed to Ashaway, a district of Hopkinton. Its business was succeeded by the Ashaway National Bank.

See also listing under Ashaway, W-RI-030.

Numismatic Commentary: Genuine notes from this small village bank are very hard to locate.

VALID ISSUES

$1 • W-RI-440-001-G010

Left: ONE / Farmer seated under tree. *Center:* Indian seated, Plow, grain, cabin. *Right:* 1 / Female portrait. *Engraver:* Danforth, Wright & Co. *Comments:* H-RI-15-G2, Durand-36. July 9, 1855. 1850s–1860s.

        Rarity: *None known*

$2 • W-RI-440-002-G020

Left: Two horses, Train / 2. *Right:* 2 / Woman seated, Two men standing. *Engraver:* Danforth, Wright & Co. *Comments:* H-RI-15-G4, Durand-37. July 9, 1855. 1850s–1860s.

        Rarity: *None known*

$3 • W-RI-440-003-G030

Left: Ceres kneeling, Minerva standing. *Center:* 3 on DOLLARS, Two seated women, one pointing at ship. *Right:* 3 / Two men, Dog. *Engraver:* Danforth, Wright & Co. *Comments:* H-RI-15-G6, Durand-38. 18__. 1850s–1860s.

        Rarity: *None known*

$5 • W-RI-440-005-G040

Left: Portrait of Daniel Webster / 5. *Center:* Man on horseback, Two boys driving cattle. *Right:* 5 / Indian woman and papoose. *Engraver:* Danforth, Wright & Co. *Comments:* H-RI-15-G8, Durand-39. July 9, 1855. 1850s–1860s.

        Rarity: *None known*

$10 • W-RI-440-010-G050

Left: Portrait of Indian chief / X. *Center:* Ceres reclining on chest and gazing at city. *Right:* 10 / Woman at well. *Engraver:* Danforth, Wright & Co. *Comments:* H-RI-15-G10, Durand-41. 18__. 1850s–1860s.

        Rarity: *None known*

$50 • W-RI-440-050-G060

Left: FIFTY / Portrait of Liberty surrounded by 14 stars / 50. *Center:* 50. *Right:* 50 / 50. *Engraver:* Danforth, Wright & Co. *Comments:* H-RI-15-G12, Durand-42. 18__. 1850s–1860s.

        Rarity: *None known*

Uncut Sheets

$1-$1-$2-$5 • W-RI-440-001.001.002.005-US010

Vignette(s): ($1) Farmer seated under tree / Indian seated, Plow, grain, cabin / Female portrait. *($1)* Farmer seated under tree / Indian seated, Plow, grain, cabin / Female portrait. *($2)* Two horses / Train / Woman seated, Two men standing. *($5)* Portrait of Daniel Webster / Man on horseback, Two boys driving cattle / Indian woman and papoose. *Engraver:* Danforth, Wright & Co. *Comments:* H-RI-15-G2, G2, G4, G8. July 9, 1855.

        Rarity: *None known*

$3-$10 • W-RI-440-003.010-US020

Vignette(s): ($3) Ceres kneeling, Minerva standing / Two seated women, one pointing at ship / Two men, Dog. *($10)* Portrait of Indian chief / Ceres reclining on chest and gazing at city / Woman at well. *Engraver:* Danforth, Wright & Co. *Comments:* H-RI-15-G6, G10. Partial sheet. 18__. 1850s–1860s.

        Rarity: *None known*

NON-VALID ISSUES

$5 • W-RI-440-005-N010

Center: Cattle drinking, Man on horseback. *Comments:* H-Unlisted, Durand-40. 18__. 1850s–1860s.

        Rarity: URS-3

Hopkinton Bank
1851–1859
W-RI-450

History: The Hopkinton Bank was organized on August 5, 1851. In an endeavor to make large dividends, this bank speculated heavily in Western land securities. The failure of these profits to materialize led to the downfall of the bank.[26]

The capital was $100,000 in 1855 and $109,600 in 1857, but the bank was unable to redeem its largely inflated circulation. The condition, however, was not entirely due to speculation, as the widespread suspension of specie payments by most of the banks of Rhode Island on September 28, 1857, was also an influence. The Hopkinton Bank went into receivership in 1857 and closed in 1859.

See also listing under Westerly, W-RI-1590.

Richmond Bank
1856–1866
W-RI-460

History: The Richmond Bank was chartered in May 1856 with an authorized capital of $50,000. By 1857 the figure had doubled. Later, the bank had an address in Alton, a village within Richmond. In 1860 the capital amount was back at the original $50,000. Circulation averaged at $31,000, and specie totaled $1,293.17 in 1857.[27]

In 1865 the bank was located in Hopkinton, and by 1866 the bank had closed its affairs. Its business was succeeded by the First National Bank of Hopkinton, chartered in 1865.

See also listings under Alton, W-RI-010, and Richmond, W-RI-1270.

JOHNSTON, RHODE ISLAND

Johnston was originally a part of Providence but was incorporated into a separate township on March 6, 1759. It was named after August Johnston, who was the attorney general of the colony. The town is bounded on the north by Smithfield and on the east by the Woonasquatucket River. Cranston and Scituate make up its other borders to the south and west.

Agriculture provided the principal income for the area, with corn, hay, oats, potatoes, and barley for malting being the most prominent. Orchards were also spread throughout the town. There were also cotton factories, woolen businesses, and a chemical works.

Rhode Island Agricultural Bank
1823–1844
W-RI-470

History: The Rhode Island Agricultural Bank was chartered in 1823. In 1843 the bank was placed under an injunction. It stopped redeeming bills on March 1, 1844, and later failed.

Numismatic Commentary: Genuine issues available today are mostly the products of the Rawdon & Wright engraving firm. An interesting and historical vignette appears on one of the issues: the $3 note shows a ship being set on fire while stranded on a sand bar. The perpetrators can be seen rowing away in smaller boats. This action, "The Burning of the *Gaspee*," a British revenue ship, was the first overt challenge to British authority prior to the Revolutionary War.

VALID ISSUES

$1 • W-RI-470-001-G010

CJF

Engraver: Horton. **Comments:** H-RI-135-G2, Durand-487. Printed on blue paper. 18__. 1820s.
Rarity: URS-3
VF $400

$1 • W-RI-470-001-G020

CJF

Engraver: Rawdon, Wright & Co. **Comments:** H-RI-135-G4, Durand-488. Remainder. 18__. 1830s–1840s.
Rarity: URS-7
AU $54; **CU** $70

$2 • W-RI-470-002-G030

Comments: H-RI-135-G10, Durand-489. No description available. 18__. 1820s.
Rarity: *None known*

$2 • W-RI-470-002-G040

CJF

Engraver: Rawdon, Wright & Co. **Comments:** H-RI-135-G12, Durand-489. Remainder. 18__. 1830s–1840s.
Rarity: URS-7
F $150; **AU** $75; **CU** $80

$3 • W-RI-470-003-G050

Comments: H-RI-135-G16, Durand-489. No description available. 18__. 1820s.
Rarity: *None known*

$3 • W-RI-470-003-G060

CJF

Engraver: Rawdon, Wright & Co. **Comments:** H-RI-135-G18, Durand-500. 18__. 1830s–1840s.
Rarity: URS-8
EF $100; **Unc-Rem** $150; **CU** $200

$5 • W-RI-470-005-G070

Comments: H-RI-135-G22. No description available. 18__. 1820s.
Rarity: *None known*

$5 • W-RI-470-005-G080

CJF

Engraver: Rawdon, Wright & Co. **Comments:** H-RI-135-G24, Durand-501. 18__. 1830s–1840s.
Rarity: URS-8
VF $150; **CU** $75

$10 • W-RI-470-010-G090

Comments: H-RI-135-G28. No description available. 18__. 1820s.
Rarity: *None known*

$10 • W-RI-470-010-G100

CJF

Engraver: Rawdon, Wright & Co. **Comments:** H-RI-135-G30, Durand-502. Remainder. 18__. 1830s–1840s.
Rarity: URS-6
AU $115; **CU** $150

$20 • W-RI-470-020-G110

Comments: H-RI-135-G34. No description available. 18__. 1820s.
Rarity: *None known*

$20 • W-RI-470-020-G120

CJF

Engraver: Rawdon, Wright & Co. **Comments:** H-RI-135-G36, Durand-503. 18__. 1830s–1840s.
Rarity: URS-6
VF $150; **CU** $95

KINGSTON, RHODE ISLAND

Originally known as Little Rest, the town was named Kingston in 1826. From 1752 until 1894, Kingston was the county seat for Washington County until a new courthouse was constructed in West Kingston.

See also North Kingstown, South Kingston, and South Kingstown, Rhode Island.

Note that these towns have slightly different spellings.

Landholders Bank
1818–1866
W-RI-480

History: The Landholders Bank was incorporated in February 1818 in the Kingston village of South Kingston (later South Kingstown), one of the largest towns in the state. John B. Dockray was the bank's founding president, and Thomas R. Wells was the first cashier.

In 1850 the capital was $100,000, divided into 2,000 shares worth $50 each.[28] By 1856 the same had risen to $150,000, where it remained until 1862. It was then decreased to $105,000. In 1857 circulation totaled $40,785, and specie amounted to $2,273.86.

The interests of the Landholders Bank were succeeded by the National Landholders Bank, chartered on May 17, 1865.

See also listings under South Kingston, W-RI-1420, and South Kingstown, W-RI-1440.

Numismatic Commentary: Bank notes signed at two locations can be found. The earlier issues by Reed, Stiles & Co. show the South Kingston location, while the ornate notes of Rawdon, Wright & Hatch and the New England Bank Note Co. are found dated at Kingston. One issue shows a vignette titled "The Landing of Roger Williams," memorializing a historic event and the founding of the State of Rhode Island.

VALID ISSUES

$1 • W-RI-480-001-G010

Left: 1 / Woman and Indian flanking shield bearing anchor / 1. **Center:** 1 / "The Landing of Roger Williams" / 1. **Bottom center:** Shield bearing anchor. **Right:** Woman in 1. **Engraver:** Rawdon, Wright & Hatch. **Comments:** H-RI-485-G20a, Durand-2174. 18__. 1830s–1850s.
Rarity: URS-3
VF $800

$1 • W-RI-480-001-G010a

CJF

Overprint: Red ONE. **Back:** Red CHECK. **Engraver:** Rawdon, Wright & Hatch. **Comments:** H-RI-485-G20b, Durand-2175. Similar to W-RI-480-001-G010. 18__. 1830s–1850s.
Rarity: URS-3
VF $1,500

$1.25 • W-RI-480-001.25-G020

Comments: H-RI-485-G22. No description available. 18__. 1830s.
Rarity: *None known*

$1.50 • W-RI-480-001.50-G030

Comments: H-RI-485-G24. No description available. 18__. 1830s.
Rarity: *None known*

$1.75 • W-RI-480-001.75-G040

Comments: H-RI-485-G26. No description available. 18__. 1830s.
Rarity: *None known*

$2 • W-RI-480-002-G050

CC

Back: Red CHECK. **Engraver:** Rawdon, Wright & Hatch. **Comments:** H-RI-485-G28a, Durand-2177. 18__. 1850s.
Rarity: URS-2
F $850; **VF** $1,000

$2 • W-RI-480-002-G050a

Left: TWO / Portrait of George Washington / TWO. **Center:** 2 / Minerva and Justice flanking 2 / 2. **Bottom center:** Shield bearing anchor. **Right:** 2 / Ceres seated / 2. **Overprint:** Red TWO. **Back:** Red CHECK. **Engraver:** Rawdon, Wright & Hatch. **Comments:** H-RI-485-G28b, Durand-2178. Similar to W-RI-480-002-G050. 18__. 1850s.
Rarity: *None known*

$3 • W-RI-480-003-G060

Left: 3 / Female portrait / 3. **Center:** 3 / Train and landscape / 3. **Right:** THREE / Portrait / 3. **Back:** Red CHECK. **Engraver:** Rawdon, Wright & Hatch. **Comments:** H-RI-485-G30a, Durand-2180. 18__. 1840s–1850s.
Rarity: *None known*

$3 • W-RI-480-003-G060a

Overprint: Red THREE. **Back:** Red CHECK. **Engraver:** Rawdon, Wright & Hatch. **Comments:** H-RI-485-G30b, Durand-2181. Similar to W-RI-480-003-G060. 18__. 1850s.
Rarity: *None known*

$5 • W-RI-480-005-G070

Left: FIVE vertically. **Center:** Woman raising curtain from shield bearing 5 / V. **Right:** 5 / Sailing ship. **Back:** Red CHECK. **Engraver:** New England Bank Note Co. **Comments:** H-RI-485-G32, Durand-2185. 18__. 1840s–1850s.
Rarity: *None known*

$5 • W-RI-480-005-G080

Left: Ceres seated with rake, sickle, and implements on dock / V on FIVE. **Center:** Indian woman seated in V. **Right:** 5 / Portrait of George Washington. **Engraver:** New England Bank Note Co. **Comments:** H-Unlisted, Durand-2186. 18__. 1850s–1860s.
Rarity: URS-3
F $350

$5 • W-RI-480-005-G080a

CJF

Overprint: Red FIVE. **Back:** Red CHECK. **Engraver:** New England Bank Note Co. **Comments:** H-RI-485-G34, Durand-2187. Similar to W-RI-480-005-G080. 18__. 1850s–1860s.
Rarity: URS-3
VF $750

$10 • W-RI-480-010-G090

Left: 10 / X / 10. **Center:** Farmer and oxen / 10. **Right:** TEN / Goddess of Plenty. **Back:** Red CHECK. **Engraver:** New England Bank Note Co. **Comments:** H-RI-485-G36, Durand-2193. 18__. 1840s–1850s.
Rarity: *None known*

$10 • W-RI-480-010-G090a

Overprint: Red TEN. **Back:** Red CHECK. **Engraver:** New England Bank Note Co. / ABNCo. monogram. **Comments:** H-RI-485-G36a, Durand-2194. Similar to W-RI-480-010-G090 but with additional engraver imprint. 18__. 1850s–1860s.
Rarity: *None known*

$20 • W-RI-480-020-G100

Left: 20 / XX vertically / 20. **Center:** 20 / Woman seated with scales, Sheaf and bales, Men plowing, Ship / 20. **Right:** TWENTY vertically. **Back:** Congreve. **Engraver:** PSSP / New England Bank Note Co. **Comments:** H-RI-485-G38. 18__. 1830s.
Rarity: *None known*

$20 • W-RI-480-020-G110

Left: 20 / Woman seated with book on lap, opening chest. **Center:** XX / Eagle / XX. **Right:** 20 / Ship. **Engraver:** New England Bank Note Co. **Comments:** H-RI-485-G40, Durand-2197. 18__. 1840s–1850s.
Rarity: *None known*

$20 • W-RI-480-020-G110a

Overprint: Red TWENTY. **Back:** Red CHECK. **Comments:** H-Unlisted, Durand-2198. Similar to W-RI-480-020-G110. 18__. 1840s–1850s.
Rarity: URS-3
VF $750

$20 • W-RI-480-020-G120

Left: Woman standing with eagle / 20. **Center:** TWENTY across 20 / Female portrait. **Right:** 20 / Portrait of Benjamin Franklin. **Overprint:** Red TWENTY. **Back:** Red CHECK. **Engraver:** New England Bank Note Co. / ABNCo. monogram. **Comments:** H-RI-485-G42. 18__. 1850s–1860s.
Rarity: *None known*

$50 • W-RI-480-050-G130

Left: 50 / Woman standing with ankles crossed, Staff, Cornucopia and anchor / 50. *Center:* FIFTY DOLLARS / 50. *Right:* FIFTY vertically. *Back:* Congreve. *Engraver:* PSSP / New England Bank Note Co. *Comments:* H-RI-485-G44. 18___. 1830s.

Rarity: *None known*

$50 • W-RI-480-050-G140

Left: FIFTY / Woman standing with wreath and flowers / FIFTY. *Center:* 50 / Man restraining prancing horse / 50. *Right:* FIFTY / Woman standing with cornucopia / FIFTY. *Engraver:* New England Bank Note Co. *Comments:* H-RI-485-G46, Durand-2201. 18___. 1840s–1850s.

Rarity: *None known*

$50 • W-RI-480-050-G150

Left: FIFTY / Grain, fruit, and flowers / 50. *Center:* 50 / Justice, Liberty, and Commerce. *Right:* FIFTY on 50 / Blacksmith / FIFTY on 50. *Comments:* H-Unlisted, Durand-2202. 18___. 1850s–1860s.

Rarity: URS-3

$50 • W-RI-480-050-G150a

Overprint: Red FIFTY. *Back:* Red CHECK. *Engraver:* New England Bank Note Co. / ABNCo. monogram. *Comments:* H-RI-485-G48a, Durand-2203. Similar to W-RI-480-050-G150 but with additional engraver imprint. 18___. 1850s–1860s.

Rarity: *None known*

$100 • W-RI-480-100-G160

Left: C / Men and boats / 100. *Center:* Eagle on bale / 100. *Right:* 100 / Ceres / 100. *Comments:* H-Unlisted, Durand-2205. 18___. 1850s–1860s.

Rarity: URS-3
VF $750

$100 • W-RI-480-100-G160a

Overprint: Red HUNDRED. *Back:* Red CHECK. *Engraver:* New England Bank Note Co. / ABNCo. monogram. *Comments:* H-RI-485-G50a, Durand-2206. Similar to W-RI-480-100-G160 but with additional engraver imprint. 18___. 1850s–1860s.

Rarity: *None known*

$100 • W-RI-480-100-G170

Left: ONE HUNDRED on 100 / Portrait of William Henry Harrison. *Center:* Wharf scene, men loading wagon with barrels. *Right:* ONE HUNDRED on 100 / Portrait of Christopher Columbus. *Engraver:* New England Bank Note Co. *Comments:* H-RI-485-G52, Durand-2204. 18___. 1840s–1850s.

Rarity: *None known*

Non-Valid Issues

$3 • W-RI-480-003-R010

Engraver: Rawdon, Wright & Hatch. *Comments:* H-RI-485-R5, Durand-2182. Raised from W-RI-480-001-G010 series. 18___. 1850s.

Rarity: *None known*

$3 • W-RI-480-003-R020

Comments: H-Unlisted, Durand-2183. Raised from W-RI-480-002-G050. 18___. 1850s.

Rarity: URS-3

$5 • W-RI-480-005-R030

Engraver: Rawdon, Wright & Hatch. *Comments:* H-RI-485-R10, Durand-2189. Raised from W-RI-480-001-G010 series. 18___. 1850s.

Rarity: *None known*

$5 • W-RI-480-005-R040

Engraver: Rawdon, Wright & Hatch. *Comments:* H-RI-485-R12, Durand-2190. Raised from W-RI-480-002-G050 series. 18___. 1850s.

Rarity: *None known*

$5 • W-RI-480-005-A010

Left: V. *Center:* Horses running / Liberty and Ceres flanking shield surmounted by horse's head. *Bottom center:* Sleeping dog. *Right:* 5 / Portrait of girl. *Overprint:* Red FIVE. *Engraver:* Bald, Cousland & Co. / Baldwin, Bald & Cousland. *Comments:* H-RI-485-A15, Durand-2191. Altered from $5 Bank of Morgan, Morgan, Georgia. 18___. 1850s.

Rarity: *None known*

$10 • W-RI-480-010-R050

Engraver: Rawdon, Wright & Hatch. *Comments:* H-RI-485-R15, Durand-2195. Raised from W-RI-480-001-G010 series. 18___. 1850s.

Rarity: *None known*

$10 • W-RI-480-010-R060

Engraver: Rawdon, Wright & Hatch. *Comments:* H-RI-485-R17, Durand-2196. Raised from W-RI-480-002-G050 series. 18___. 1850s.

Rarity: *None known*

$20 • W-RI-480-020-R070

Engraver: Rawdon, Wright & Hatch. *Comments:* H-RI-485-R20, Durand-2199. Raised from W-RI-480-001-G010 series. 18___. 1850s.

Rarity: *None known*

$20 • W-RI-480-020-R080

Engraver: Rawdon, Wright & Hatch. *Comments:* H-RI-485-R22, Durand-2200. Raised from W-RI-480-002-G050 series. 18___. 1850s.

Rarity: *None known*

Newport, Rhode Island

Newport is located on Aquidneck Island and was founded in 1639 by settlers seeking religious freedom. Quakers and Jews came here to escape persecution. In the mid-19th century, Newport became a resort getaway for the wealthy. The area received its initial riches from whaling, and 17 oil and candle manufactories were opened. The famed Goddard and Townsend furniture was constructed here. Ships, barrels, rum, chocolate, textiles, clothes, bottles, hats, and shoes were also produced. During the 17th and 18th centuries, piracy found an active port in the town. Those who were apprehended were hanged in Newport and buried on nearby Goat Island.

Aquidneck Bank
1854–1865
W-RI-490

History: The Aquidneck Bank was incorporated in May 1854, but it had released its bills in anticipation, and they were already in circulation by that time. The Aquidneck Bank became the eighth bank in the town, making a combined capital of about $800,000.[29] William Bradford was the bank's first president, and Joseph Rawson was its first cashier.

The bank had $68,377 in circulation and $4,316.73 in specie in 1856. Capital rose slightly to $123,750, as did the bank's specie to total $6,228.67. In 1858 circulation had decreased to $56,421. By 1862 capital had increased to $183,600, and circulation was $77,783.

On November 25, 1865, the business of this bank was succeeded by the Aquidneck National Bank.

Numismatic Commentary: Interesting and historic vignettes are found on issues from this bank. Some of the issues show both Spanish and American dollar-size coins amounting to the exact value of the note. Spanish coins were legal-tender until September 1859. Also, "The Death of King Philip" is shown on the $2 note.

VALID ISSUES

$1 • W-RI-490-001-G010   SBG

Overprint: Red ONE. **Engraver:** Wellstood, Hanks, Hay & Whiting. **Comments:** H-RI-140-G2, Durand-Unlisted. 18__. 1850s.

Rarity: URS-3
VF $400; **EF** $900

$1 • W-RI-490-001-G010a   QDB, QDB

Overprint: Red panel outlining ONE. **Engraver:** Wellstood, Hanks, Hay & Whiting / ABNCo. monogram. **Comments:** H-RI-140-G2b, Durand-504. Similar to W-RI-490-001-G010 but with additional engraver imprint. 18__. 1860s.

Rarity: URS-3
VF $400; **EF** $900
Selected auction price: Stack's Bowers Galleries, September 2009, EF $829

$2 • W-RI-490-002-G020

Left: 2 / Horse-drawn cart / 2. **Center:** "The Death of King Philip" / TWO. **Bottom center:** Tower. **Right:** 2 / Two reverses of U.S. silver dollars. **Engraver:** Wellstood, Hanks, Hay & Whiting. **Comments:** H-RI-140-G4. 18__. 1850s.

Rarity: URS-3
Proof $5,000

$2 • W-RI-490-002-G020a

Overprint: Red panel outlining white TWO. **Engraver:** Wellstood, Hanks, Hay & Whiting / ABNCo. monogram. **Comments:** H-RI-140-G4b, Durand-505. Similar to W-RI-490-002-G020 but with additional engraver imprint. July 1, 18__. 1860s.

Rarity: URS-3
VF $3,500

$5 • W-RI-490-005-G030

Left: FIVE / Five U.S. silver dollars. **Center:** View of Newport, Steamboat. **Bottom center:** Old mill. **Right:** 5 / 5, Indians, Waterfalls, Bridge and train. **Engraver:** Wellstood, Hanks, Hay & Whiting. **Comments:** H-RI-140-G6, Durand-Unlisted. 18__. 1850s.

Rarity: URS-3
Proof $2,500

$5 • W-RI-490-005-G030a   CJF

Overprint: Red panel outlining FIVE. **Engraver:** Wellstood, Hanks, Hay & Whiting / ABNCo. monogram. **Comments:** H-RI-140-G6b, Durand-508. Similar to W-RI-490-005-G030 but with additional engraver imprint. July 1st, 18__. 1860s.

Rarity: URS-3
VF $500

$10 • W-RI-490-010-G040   CC

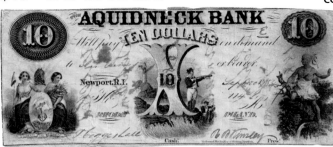

Engraver: Wellstood, Hanks, Hay & Whiting. **Comments:** H-RI-140-G8, Durand-510. 18__. 1850s.

Rarity: URS-3
VF $700

$20 • W-RI-490-020-G050

QDB

Overprint: Red TWENTY. *Engraver:* Wellstood, Hanks, Hay & Whiting. *Comments:* H-RI-140-G10, Durand-512. 18__. 1850s.

Rarity: URS-3

Unc-Rem $1,000

$50 • W-RI-490-050-G060

Left: Steamship / 50. *Center:* Portrait of Daniel Webster. *Bottom center:* Anchor on shield. *Right:* 50 / Ship. *Engraver:* Wellstood, Hanks, Hay & Whiting. *Comments:* H-RI-140-G12, Durand-513. 18__. 1850s.

Rarity: URS-1

Proof $4,000

$100 • W-RI-490-100-G070

Left: C / Two allegorical figures. *Center:* 100 / Portrait of Christopher Columbus / 100. *Right:* C. *Engraver:* Wellstood, Hanks, Hay & Whiting. *Comments:* H-RI-140-G14, Durand-514. 18__. 1850s.

Rarity: *None known*

Non-Valid Issues

$2 • W-RI-490-002-S010

Center: Indians. *Comments:* H-Unlisted, Durand-506. Photograph passed as a note. 1850s.

Rarity: URS-3

F $75

$2 • W-RI-490-002-N010

Center: Indians. *Comments:* H-RI-140-N5, Durand-507. 1850s.

Rarity: *None known*

$5 • W-RI-490-005-N020

Center: Indians. *Comments:* H-RI-140-N10, Durand-509. 1850s.

Rarity: *None known*

$10 • W-RI-490-010-N030

Center: Indians. *Comments:* H-RI-140-N15, Durand-511. 1850s.

Rarity: *None known*

Bank of Rhode Island
1795–1865
W-RI-505

History: The Bank of Rhode Island, the second oldest bank in the state, was chartered and incorporated in October 1795. The bank opened for business at the residence of Moses Seixas, who was the first cashier. The bank's founding president was Christopher Champlin. The starting authorized capital was $100,000, which was reduced to $80,000 in October 1833.

The business of the Bank of Rhode Island was succeeded by the National Bank of Rhode Island, chartered on August 21, 1865.

Numismatic Commentary: Genuine notes are hard but not impossible to locate. Collectors may find a whaling vignette along with Commodore Perry on one note, while another shows General Washington reading a dispatch in wartime. It has not been ascertained for certain, but clues in the vignette point to this being a scene at Dorchester Heights. Another vignette shows action during the Battle of Lexington.

Valid Issues

$1 • W-RI-505-001-G010

Left: UNIT 1 DOLLAR vertically. *Center:* Hand pointing / ONE / Anchor / ONE. *Right:* 1 / 1 on diamond vertically. *Comments:* H-RI-170-G4, Durand-516. 18__. 1810s–1820s.

Rarity: *None known*

$1 • W-RI-505-001-G010a

SBG

Comments: H-RI-170-G5. Similar to W-RI-505-001-G010. 1830s.

Rarity: URS-3

VF $550

$1 • W-RI-505-001-G020

CJF

Engraver: Rawdon, Wright, Hatch & Edson. *Comments:* H-RI-170-G8, Durand-517. 18__. 1840s.

Rarity: URS-3

F $250

$1 • W-RI-505-001-G020a

Left: ONE on three dies / Shield bearing anchor surmounted by eagle / ONE. *Center:* 1 / Whaling scene / 1. *Bottom center:* Woman with wreath of flowers. *Right:* ONE / Portrait of Commodore Oliver Hazard Perry / 1. *Engraver:* Rawdon, Wright, Hatch & Edson. *Comments:* H-RI-170-G8a. Similar to W-RI-505-001-G020 but with different engraver imprint. 18__. 1840s–1860s.

Rarity: *None known*

$1 • W-RI-505-001-G030
Comments: H-Unlisted, Durand-515. No description available. First issue. 1810s–1820s.
Rarity: *None known*

$2 • W-RI-505-002-G040
Left: Panel with TWO D vertically. *Center:* TWO / Anchor / TWO. *Right:* 2 / 2 vertically. *Comments:* H-RI-170-G12. 18__. 1810s–1820s.
Rarity: *None known*

$2 • W-RI-505-002-G050
Comments: H-Unlisted, Durand-519. No description available. First issue. 1810s–1820s.
Rarity: *None known*

$2 • W-RI-505-002-G060
Left: UNIT 2 DOLLARS vertically. *Center:* Hand pointing / TWO / Anchor / TWO. *Right:* 2 / 2 on diamond vertically. *Comments:* H-Unlisted, Durand-520. 18__. 1810s–1820s.
Rarity: URS-3

$2 • W-RI-505-002-G070
Left: 2 / Man seated with scroll and pen / TWO. *Center:* 2 / Woman with crown and shield / 2. *Bottom center:* Ship. *Right:* 2 / Woman with eagle and bust of George Washington / TWO. *Engraver:* Rawdon, Wright, Hatch & Co. *Comments:* H-RI-170-G16, Durand-521. Occasionally bank engravers signed their work. The vignette on the left was signed by A.B. Durand, and the vignette on the right was signed by E. Fertwelon. 18__. 1830s–1840s.
Rarity: *None known*

$2 • W-RI-505-002-G070a
Engraver: Rawdon, Wright, Hatch & Edson. *Comments:* H-RI-170-G16a, Durand-521. Similar to W-RI-505-002-G070 but with different engraver imprint. 18__. 1840s–1860s.
Rarity: URS-3
VF $350

$3 • W-RI-505-003-G080
Comments: H-Unlisted, Durand-523. No description available. First issue. 18__. 1810s–1820s.
Rarity: *None known*

$3 • W-RI-505-003-G090
Left: UNIT 3 DOLLARS vertically. *Center:* Hand pointing / THREE / Anchor / THREE. *Right:* 3 / 3 on diamond vertically. *Comments:* H-RI-170-G20, Durand-524. 18__. 1810s–1820s.
Rarity: URS-3

$3 • W-RI-505-003-G100
Left: IN GOD WE TRUST, Woman standing, 3. *Center:* 3 / Woman lassoing steer / 3. *Bottom center:* Mercury. *Right:* 3 / Ship and passengers / 3. *Engraver:* Rawdon, Wright, Hatch & Co. *Comments:* H-RI-170-G24, Durand-525. 18__. 1830s–1840s.
Rarity: *None known*

$3 • W-RI-505-003-G100a

CC

Engraver: Rawdon, Wright, Hatch & Edson. *Comments:* H-RI-170-G24a. Similar to W-RI-505-003-G100 but with different engraver imprint. 18__. 1840s–1860s.
Rarity: URS-3
VF $750

$5 • W-RI-505-005-G110
Left: FIVE DOL vertically. *Center:* Hand pointing / FIVE / Anchor, Ribbon and branches / FIVE. *Right:* 5 / V vertically. *Comments:* H-RI-170-G28. 18__. 1810s–1820s.
Rarity: *None known*

$5 • W-RI-505-005-G120
Comments: H-Unlisted, Durand-527. No description available. First issue. 1810s–1820s.
Rarity: *None known*

$5 • W-RI-505-005-G130
Left: UNIT 5 DOLLARS vertically. *Center:* Hand pointing / FIVE / Anchor / FIVE. *Right:* 5 / 5 on diamond vertically. *Comments:* H-Unlisted, Durand-528. 18__. 1810s–1820s.
Rarity: URS-3

$5 • W-RI-505-005-G140
Left: FIVE / Allegorical woman and eagle / 5. *Center:* 5 / Vulcan seated / 5. *Bottom center:* Lion's head. *Right:* FIVE / Archimedes raising the world with lever / 5. *Engraver:* Rawdon, Wright, Hatch & Co. *Comments:* H-RI-170-G32, Durand-529. 18__. 1830s–1840s.
Rarity: *None known*

$5 • W-RI-505-005-G140a
Engraver: Rawdon, Wright, Hatch & Edson. *Comments:* H-RI-170-G32a. Similar to W-RI-505-005-G140 but with different engraver imprint. 18__. 1840s–1860s.
Rarity: *None known*

$10 • W-RI-505-010-G150
Left: TEN DOL vertically. *Center:* Hand pointing / TEN / Anchor, Branches / TEN. *Right:* 10 / X vertically. *Comments:* H-RI-170-G36, Durand-536. 18__. 1810s–1820s.
Rarity: *None known*

$10 • W-RI-505-010-G160
Comments: H-Unlisted, Durand-534. No description available. First issue. 1810s–1820s.
Rarity: *None known*

$10 • W-RI-505-010-G170
Left: UNIT 10 DOLLARS vertically. *Center:* Hand pointing / TEN / Anchor / TEN. *Right:* 10 / 10 on diamond vertically. *Comments:* H-Unlisted, Durand-535. 18__. 1810s–1820s.
Rarity: URS-3

$10 • W-RI-505-010-G180

Left: TEN / Allegorical woman seated and Mercury flying in clouds / 10. *Center:* 10 / Ship under sail / 10. *Bottom center:* Anchor on shield. *Right:* TEN / View of stone mill / X. *Engraver:* Rawdon, Wright, Hatch & Co. *Comments:* H-RI-170-G40, Durand-536. 18__. 1830s–1840s.

Rarity: *None known*

$10 • W-RI-505-010-G190

Center: Ship, Mercury, British arms. *Comments:* H-Unlisted, Durand-540. 1830s–1840s.

Rarity: URS-3

$20 • W-RI-505-020-G200

Left: XX / Portrait of George Washington. *Center:* George Washington on horse reading message, soldiers, cannon. *Right:* 20 / Portrait of Henry Clay. *Tint:* Red lathework. *Engraver:* American Bank Note Co. *Comments:* H-RI-170-G46a, Durand-541. 18__. 1860s.

Rarity: URS-2
Proof $4,000

$20 • W-RI-505-020-G210

Center: Ship, Mercury, British arms. *Comments:* H-Unlisted, Durand-545. 1830s–1840s.

Rarity: URS-3

$30 • W-RI-505-030-G220

Left: Justice seated on box. *Center:* "The Landing of Roger Williams". *Right:* White die with scalloped edges / Portrait of Daniel Webster. *Tint:* Red lathework. *Engraver:* American Bank Note Co. *Comments:* H-RI-170-G50a, Durand-546. 18__. 1860s.

Rarity: URS-2
Proof $8,000

$50 • W-RI-505-050-G230

Left: FIFTY vertically. *Center:* State arms on shield / 50. *Right:* 50 / L. *Engraver:* Rawdon, Wright, Hatch & Co. *Comments:* H-RI-170-G54, Durand-547. 18__. 1830s–1850s.

Rarity: *None known*

$50 • W-RI-505-050-G240   CC

Tint: Green lathework. *Engraver:* American Bank Note Co. *Comments:* H-RI-170-G56a, Durand-548. 18__. 1860s.

Rarity: URS-2
Proof $8,000
Selected auction price: Stack's Bowers Galleries, March 2013, Proof $8,400

$100 • W-RI-505-100-G250

Left: 100 DOLLARS vertically. *Center:* State arms on shield / 100. *Right:* 100 / C. *Engraver:* Rawdon, Wright, Hatch & Co. *Comments:* H-RI-170-G60, Durand-551. 18__. 1830s–1850s.

Rarity: *None known*

$100 • W-RI-505-100-G260   SBG

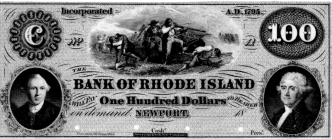

Tint: Green lathework. *Engraver:* American Bank Note Co. *Comments:* H-RI-170-G62a, Durand-552. 18__. 1860s.

Rarity: URS-2
Proof $8,000

Uncut Sheets

$20-$30 • W-RI-505-020.030-US010

Vignette(s): *($20)* Portrait of George Washington / George Washington on horse reading message, soldiers, cannon / Portrait of Henry Clay. *($30)* Justice seated on box / "The Landing of Roger Williams" / Portrait of Daniel Webster. *Engraver:* American Bank Note Co. *Comments:* H-RI-170-G46a, G50a. 18__. 1860s.

Rarity: URS-1
Proof $10,000

NON-VALID ISSUES

$1 • W-RI-505-001-C010

Comments: H-RI-170-C4. Counterfeit of W-RI-505-001-G010. 18__. 1831.

Rarity: URS-3
VF $200

$1 • W-RI-505-001-C010a

Comments: H-Unlisted, Durand-518. Counterfeit of W-RI-505-001-G010a. 1830s.

Rarity: URS-3

$2 • W-RI-505-002-C040

Comments: H-RI-170-C12. Counterfeit of W-RI-505-002-G040. 18__. 1831.

Rarity: URS-3
VF $200

$2 • W-RI-505-002-C060

Comments: H-Unlisted, Durand-522. Counterfeit of W-RI-505-002-G060. 1810s–1820s.

Rarity: URS-3

$3 • W-RI-505-003-A010

Left: 3 / Portrait of George Washington / THREE. *Center:* Woman seated on wharf with caduceus, Ship. *Bottom center:* Strongbox and cornucopia with coins. *Right:* 3 / Mechanic, sailor, and farmer standing with 3. *Overprint:* THREE. *Engraver:* Rawdon, Wright, Hatch & Edson. *Comments:* H-RI-170-A5. Altered from $3 Farmers and Merchants Bank, Memphis, Tennessee series. 1850s.

Rarity: *None known*

$3 • W-RI-505-003-A020
Left: 3 / Portrait of George Washington / THREE. *Center:* Allegorical woman pointing to ship. *Right:* 3 / Mechanic, sailor, and farmer with 3. *Overprint:* Red or blue THREE. *Comments:* H-Unlisted, Durand-526. Altered from $3 Farmers & Merchants Bank of Memphis, Memphis, Tennessee. 1850s.
Rarity: URS-3

$5 • W-RI-505-005-C110
Comments: H-RI-170-C28. Counterfeit of W-RI-505-005-G110. 18__. 1811.
Rarity: URS-3
VF $200

$5 • W-RI-505-005-C130
Comments: H-Unlisted, Durand-530. Counterfeit of W-RI-505-005-G130. 1810s–1820s.
Rarity: URS-3

$5 • W-RI-505-005-R010
Engraver: Rawdon, Wright, Hatch & Edson. *Comments:* H-RI-170-R5, Durand-531. Raised from W-RI-505-001-G020a. 18__. 1850s.
Rarity: *None known*

$5 • W-RI-505-005-R020
Engraver: Rawdon, Wright, Hatch & Edson. *Comments:* H-RI-170-R10, Durand-532. Raised from W-RI-505-002-G070a. 18__. 1850s.
Rarity: *None known*

$5 • W-RI-505-005-N010
Left: Indian. *Center:* Railroad and train. *Right:* Indian. *Comments:* H-Unlisted, Durand-533. Altered or spurious. 18__. 1850s.
Rarity: URS-3
F $75

$5 • W-RI-505-005-A030
Left: Indian standing with rifle / 3. *Center:* V / Train backed up to wharf, People, Train. *Bottom center:* Indian in canoe. *Right:* Minerva standing with spear and shield. *Comments:* H-RI-170-A10. Altered from $5 Bank of Lower Canada, Quebec, Canada. 18__. 1830s.
Rarity: *None known*

$10 • W-RI-505-010-C150
Comments: H-RI-170-C36. Counterfeit of W-RI-505-010-G150. 18__. 1811.
Rarity: URS-3
VF $200

$10 • W-RI-505-010-R030
Engraver: Rawdon, Wright, Hatch & Edson. *Comments:* H-RI-170-R15, Durand-537. Raised from W-RI-505-001-G020a. 18__. 1850s.
Rarity: *None known*

$10 • W-RI-505-010-R040
Engraver: Rawdon, Wright, Hatch & Edson. *Comments:* H-RI-170-R20, Durand-538. Raised from W-RI-505-002-G070a. 18__. 1850s.
Rarity: *None known*

$10 • W-RI-505-010-N020
Center: Girl and boy. *Comments:* H-RI-170-N5. 18__. 1850s.
Rarity: *None known*

$10 • W-RI-505-010-A040
Left: 10 / Justice. *Center:* Indian family looking at plow. *Right:* 10 / Woman reclining with cornucopia. *Back:* Ten orange dies bearing Xs. *Engraver:* W.L. Ormsby. *Comments:* H-RI-170-A15, Durand-539. Altered from $10 Farmers and Drovers Bank, Petersburg, Indiana. Oct. 1, 1858.
Rarity: *None known*

$10 • W-RI-505-010-A050
Left: Lathework panel with TEN vertically. *Center:* 10 / Mercury seated on shore with caduceus, Ship / 10. *Bottom center:* British arms. *Right:* Minerva standing with spear and shield / TEN. *Comments:* H-RI-170-A20. Altered from $10 Bank of Lower Canada, Quebec, Canada. 18__. 1850s.
Rarity: *None known*

$20 • W-RI-505-020-R050
Engraver: Rawdon, Wright, Hatch & Edson. *Comments:* H-RI-170-R25, Durand-542. Raised from W-RI-505-001-G020a. 18__. 1850s.
Rarity: *None known*

$20 • W-RI-505-020-R060
Engraver: Rawdon, Wright, Hatch & Edson. *Comments:* H-RI-170-R30, Durand-543. Raised from W-RI-505-002-G070a. 18__. 1850s.
Rarity: *None known*

$20 • W-RI-505-050-A060
Left: 20 / Sailor on wharf. *Center:* Portrait of George Washington. *Right:* 20 / Ceres. *Overprint:* Red 20. *Comments:* H-RI-170-A25, Durand-544. Altered from W-RI-1630-020-G060. 18__. 1855.
Rarity: *None known*

$50 • W-RI-505-050-R070
Engraver: Rawdon, Wright, Hatch & Edson. *Comments:* H-RI-170-R35, Durand-549. Raised from W-RI-505-001-G020a. 18__. 1850s.
Rarity: *None known*

$50 • W-RI-505-050-R080
Engraver: Rawdon, Wright, Hatch & Edson. *Comments:* H-RI-170-R40, Durand-550. Raised from W-RI-505-002-G070a. 18__. 1850s.
Rarity: *None known*

Eagle Bank
1820s
W-RI-520

History: The Eagle Bank in Newport was a spurious bank. The Eagle banks located in Providence and in Bristol provided a good opportunity for racketeers to pass fraudulent bank notes. Both of these banks were chartered in 1818, about the time these spurious notes appeared.

Issues
$5 • W-RI-520-005-G010
Center: 5 on die / Spread eagle on globe / Portrait of George Washington / 5 on die. *Right:* Lathework bearing V vertically. *Comments:* H-RI-145-G6, Durand-559. 18__. 1824.
Rarity: URS-3
VF $350

Merchants Bank
1817–1902
W-RI-530

History: The Merchants Bank was incorporated in February 1817 and was the fourth bank established in what was at that time one of two capital cities of Rhode Island, the other being Providence. Samuel Whitehorne was president until 1844, when N.S. Ruggles took his place. Thomas H. Mumford was the bank's first cashier.

The capital was $100,000 for the duration of the bank's existence. Circulation ranged from $33,013 in 1849 to $42,801 in 1863. Specie was reported to be $7,023.24 in 1838 and $3,123.66 in 1857. The bank continued under a state charter until after the note-issuing era ended in July 1866. It closed in 1902.

Numismatic Commentary: Examples of genuine notes are readily available in the marketplace. The bank used various engravers during its lifetime. One historic note shows the mysterious stone tower near the center of the town. A little research brings out many theories of its origin.

VALID ISSUES

$1 • W-RI-530-001-G010
Engraver: P. Maverick. *Comments:* H-RI-150-G2. No description available. 18__. 1817–1820s.
Rarity: *None known*

$1 • W-RI-530-001-G020
Left: 1 / RHODE ISLAND / 1. *Center:* 1 / ONE DOLLAR / 1. *Bottom center:* 1. *Right:* 1 / ONE / 1. *Engraver:* Leney & Rollinson. *Comments:* H-RI-150-G4, Durand-561. 18__. 1820s–1830s.
Rarity: *None known*

$1 • W-RI-530-001-G030
Center: View of paper mill, Eagle. *Right:* Cherub supporting 1. *Comments:* H-RI-150-G6, Durand-562. 18__. 1830s–1840s.
Rarity: *None known*

$1 • W-RI-530-001-G040

BM

Engraver: New England Bank Note Co. / Rawdon, Wright, Hatch & Edson. *Comments:* H-RI-150-G8, Durand-563. 18__. 1850s.
Rarity: URS-6
VF $250

$1 • W-RI-530-001-G040a
Left: 1 / Sailor standing. *Center:* Steamboat, Ceres holding 1, Train. *Right:* 1 / Liberty holding 1 atop cornucopia of coins. *Tint:* Red-orange lathework. *Engraver:* New England Bank Note Co. / Rawdon, Wright, Hatch & Edson. *Comments:* H-RI-150-G8a. Similar to W-RI-530-001-G040. Remainder. 18__. 1850s–1860s.
Rarity: URS-7
AU $195

$1 • W-RI-530-001-G040b
CC

Overprint: Red 1, 1, and ONE. *Engraver:* New England Bank Note Co. / Rawdon, Wright, Hatch & Edson. *Comments:* H-RI-150-G8b, Durand-564. Similar to W-RI-530-001-G040. 18__. 1860s.
Rarity: URS-7
VF $250

$1.50 • W-RI-530-001.50-G050
Left: 1.50 / RHODE ISLAND vertically / 1.50. *Center:* 1 1/2 / 1.50 / 1.50. *Bottom center:* 1.50. *Right:* 1.50. *Engraver:* Leney & Rollinson. *Comments:* H-RI-150-G10, Durand-567. 18__. 1820s.
Rarity: URS-3
VF $400

$2 • W-RI-530-002-G060
Left: TWO vertically. *Center:* 2 / Sailing vessels / 2. *Right:* 2 vertically. *Engraver:* P. Maverick. *Comments:* H-RI-150-G14, Durand-574. 18__. 1817–1820s.
Rarity: URS-3
VF $250

$2 • W-RI-530-002-G070
Left: 2 / RHODE ISLAND / 2. *Center:* TWO DOLLARS / 2. *Bottom center:* 2. *Right:* TWO vertically. *Engraver:* Leney & Rollinson. *Comments:* H-RI-150-G16, Durand-568. 18__. 1820s–1830s.
Rarity: *None known*

$2 • W-RI-530-002-G080
SBG

Engraver: P. Maverick. *Comments:* H-RI-150-G18, Durand-569. 18__. 1830s–1840s.
Rarity: URS-1
VF $2,500

$2 • W-RI-530-002-G090
Left: TWO / Indian. *Center:* Farmers driving sheep across river / TWO TWO. *Right:* 2 / Two girls. *Engraver:* New England Bank Note Co. / Rawdon, Wright, Hatch & Edson. *Comments:* H-RI-150-G20, Durand-570. 18__. 1850s.
Rarity: URS-5
VF $250

$2 • W-RI-530-002-G090a   CC

Tint: Red-orange lathework. *Engraver:* New England Bank Note Co. / Rawdon, Wright, Hatch & Edson. *Comments:* H-RI-150-G20a. Similar to W-RI-530-002-G090. Remainder. 18__. 1850s–1860s.

Rarity: URS-5

EF $325; **AU** $500

$2 • W-RI-530-002-G090b   CC

Overprint: Red TWO. *Engraver:* New England Bank Note Co. / Rawdon, Wright, Hatch & Edson. *Comments:* H-RI-150-G20b, Durand-571. Similar to W-RI-530-002-G090. 18__. 1860s.

Rarity: URS-6

VF $250

$2 • W-RI-530-002-G100

Center: Woman, Agricultural implements. *Right:* Indian. *Comments:* H-Unlisted, Durand-573. 1820s–1830s.

Rarity: URS-3

$3 • W-RI-530-003-G110

Left: 3 / RHODE ISLAND / 3. *Center:* 3 / THREE DOLLARS / 3. *Bottom center:* 3. *Right:* THREE vertically. *Engraver:* Leney & Rollinson. *Comments:* H-RI-150-G22, Durand-576. 18__. 1820s–1830s.

Rarity: *None known*

$3 • W-RI-530-003-G120   TD

Engraver: New England Bank Note Co. / Rawdon, Wright, Hatch & Edson. *Comments:* H-RI-150-G26, Durand-577. 18__. 1850s.

Rarity: URS-1

VF $450

$3 • W-RI-530-003-G120a

Left: 3 / Minerva with anchor. *Center:* Three men seated with coins, scythe, and rake / THREE THREE. *Right:* 3 / Liberty standing with pole and cap watering eagle. *Tint:* Red-orange lathework. *Engraver:* New England Bank Note Co. / Rawdon, Wright, Hatch & Edson. *Comments:* H-RI-150-G26a. Similar to W-RI-530-003-G120. Remainder. 18__. 1850s–1860s.

Rarity: URS-3

AU $240

$3 • W-RI-530-003-G120b   ANS

Overprint: Red THREE. *Engraver:* New England Bank Note Co. / Rawdon, Wright, Hatch & Edson. *Comments:* H-RI-150-G26b, Durand-578. Similar to W-RI-530-003-G120. 18__. 1860s.

Rarity: URS-5

VF $250

$5 • W-RI-530-005-G130

Engraver: P. Maverick. *Comments:* H-RI-150-G28. No description available. 18__. 1817–1820s.

Rarity: *None known*

$5 • W-RI-530-005-G140

Left: V / RHODE ISLAND / V. *Center:* 5 / FIVE DOLLARS / V. *Bottom center:* V. *Right:* FIVE vertically. *Engraver:* Leney & Rollinson. *Comments:* H-RI-150-G30, Durand-584. 18__. 1820s–1830s.

Rarity: *None known*

$5 • W-RI-530-005-G150

Left: RHODE ISLAND vertically. *Center:* 5 / View of the State House / 5. *Right:* FIVE vertically. *Comments:* H-RI-150-G34, Durand-585. 18__. 1830s–1840s.

Rarity: *None known*

$5 • W-RI-530-005-G160

Left: 5 / Female portrait / FIVE. *Center:* Train, Allegorical figure, Steamboat. *Right:* 5 / Five allegorical figures supporting 5. *Engraver:* Rawdon, Wright, Hatch & Edson / New England Bank Note Co. *Comments:* H-RI-150-G36, Durand-586. 18__. 1850s.

Rarity: *None known*

$5 • W-RI-530-005-G160a

Overprint: Red FIVE. *Comments:* H-Unlisted, Durand-587. Similar to W-RI-530-005-G160. 18__. 1850s.

Rarity: URS-3

$5 • W-RI-530-005-G170

Left: Woman. *Center:* Indian, Train. *Right:* Woman. *Comments:* H-Unlisted, Durand-591. 1820s–1830s.

Rarity: URS-3

$10 • W-RI-530-010-G180

Engraver: P. Maverick. *Comments:* H-RI-150-G40. No description available. 18__. 1817–1820s.

Rarity: *None known*

$10 • W-RI-530-010-G190

Left: X / RHODE ISLAND / X. *Center:* 10 / TEN DOLLARS / X. *Right:* TEN vertically. *Engraver:* Leney & Rollinson. *Comments:* H-RI-150-G42, Durand-594. 18__. 1820s–1830s.

Rarity: *None known*

$10 • W-RI-530-010-G200

Left: 10 / Triton supporting cornucopia / Steamship. *Center:* Steamboat / Minerva reclining / State arms / Sheaf, plow / Train. *Right:* 10 / Eagle / TEN. *Engraver:* Rawdon, Wright, Hatch & Edson / New England Bank Note Co. *Comments:* H-RI-150-G46, Durand-595. 18__. 1850s.

Rarity: *None known*

$10 • W-RI-530-010-G210

Center: Two allegorical figures and griffin on chest. *Comments:* H-Unlisted, Durand-598. 1820s–1830s.

Rarity: URS-3

$20 • W-RI-530-020-G220

Left: TWENTY / Two Indians. *Center:* TWENTY on lathework panel. *Right:* Indian woman and Ceres / 20. *Engraver:* Rawdon, Wright, Hatch & Edson / New England Bank Note Co. *Comments:* H-RI-150-G50, Durand-599. 18__. 1850s.

Rarity: *None known*

$20 • W-RI-530-020-G220a

Engraver: Danforth, Wright & Co. *Comments:* H-Unlisted, Durand-Unlisted. Similar to W-RI-530-020-G220 but with different engraver imprint. 18__. 1850s.

Rarity: *None known*

$50 • W-RI-530-050-G230

Engraver: P. Maverick. *Comments:* H-RI-150-G54. No description available. 18__. 1817–1830s.

Rarity: *None known*

$50 • W-RI-530-050-G240

Left: RHODE ISLAND vertically. *Center:* 50 / Medallion head of Commodore Oliver Hazard Perry / 50. *Right:* FIFTY vertically. *Comments:* H-RI-150-G58, Durand-603. 18__. 1830s–1840s.

Rarity: *None known*

$50 • W-RI-530-050-G250

Left: 50 / Woman and three children, Globe. *Center:* Steamship under sail, Ship anchored. *Right:* 50 / Train / 50. *Engraver:* Rawdon, Wright, Hatch & Edson / New England Bank Note Co. *Comments:* H-RI-150-G60, Durand-602. 18__. 1850s.

Rarity: *None known*

$50 • W-RI-530-050-G250a

Engraver: Danforth, Wright & Co. *Comments:* H-Unlisted, Durand-Unlisted. Similar to W-RI-530-050-G250 but with different engraver imprint. 18__. 1850s.

Rarity: *None known*

$100 • W-RI-530-100-G260

SBG

Engraver: Danforth, Wright & Co. *Comments:* H-RI-150-G64, Durand-606. 18__. 1850s.

Rarity: URS-1
VF $5,000; **Proof** $7,500
Selected auction price: Stack's Bowers Galleries, March 2013, Proof $7,261

Uncut Sheets
$20-$50-$100 • W-RI-530-020.050.100-US010

Vignette(s): *($20)* Two Indians / Indian woman and Ceres. *($50)* Woman and three children, Globe / Steamship under sail, Ship anchored / Train. *($100)* Train / Ship / Woman. *Engraver:* Danforth, Wright & Co. *Comments:* H-Unlisted, H-Unlisted, H-RI-150-G64. 18__. 1850s.

Rarity: *None known*

Non-Valid Issues
$1 • W-RI-530-001-A010

Left: 1 / Portrait of William Henry Harrison. *Center:* Men catching cattle. *Bottom center:* Indian in canoe. *Right:* Indian with bow. *Comments:* H-RI-150-A5, Durand-565. Altered from $1 Merchants Bank, Mankato City, Minnesota. Sept. 1, 185_. 1850s.

Rarity: *None known*

$1 • W-RI-530-001-A020

ANS

Overprint: Red ONE. *Comments:* H-RI-150-A10, Durand-566. Altered from $1 Merchants Bank, Stillwater, Minnesota. October 20th, 1854. 1850s.

Rarity: URS-5
F $125

$1.50 • W-RI-530-001.50-C050

Engraver: Leney & Rollinson. *Comments:* H-RI-150-C10. Counterfeit of W-RI-530-001.50-G050. 18__. 1820s.

Rarity: URS-3

$2 • W-RI-530-002-C060   TD

Engraver: P. Maverick. *Comments:* H-RI-150-C14. Counterfeit of W-RI-530-002-G060. 18__. 1820s.

Rarity: URS-3
VF $200

$2 • W-RI-530-002-S010

Left: 2. *Center:* Man seated, Temple. *Bottom center:* Steamboat. *Comments:* H-Unlisted, Durand-575. 1820s.

Rarity: URS-3

$2 • W-RI-530-002-A030

Left: 2 / Agriculture and Commerce, Ship and shield. *Right:* Portrait of Zachary Taylor. *Engraver:* W.L. Ormsby. *Comments:* H-RI-150-A15, Durand-572. Altered from $2 Merchants Bank, Fort Leavenworth, Kansas. 185_. 1850s.

Rarity: URS-3
VF $250

$2 • W-RI-530-002-A040

Left: 2 / TWO / 2. *Center:* 2 / Ceres seated, Train on bridge, Sheaf and canal lock. *Bottom center:* Road, trees, sign post. *Right:* Indian man / 2. *Comments:* H-RI-150-A20. Altered from $2 Merchants Bank, Stillwater, Minnesota. Oct. 20, 1854. 1850s.

Rarity: *None known*

$3 • W-RI-530-003-N010

Center: Ceres, sheaf, cows. *Comments:* H-RI-150-N15, Durand-581. 1820s.

Rarity: *None known*

$3 • W-RI-530-003-N020

Left: 3. *Center:* Man seated, Temple. *Bottom center:* Steamboat. *Comments:* H-RI-150-N20, Durand-582. 1820s.

Rarity: *None known*

$3 • W-RI-530-003-N030

Center: Two women seated. *Comments:* H-RI-150-N25. 1820s.

Rarity: *None known*

$3 • W-RI-530-003-N040

Left: 3. *Center:* THREE DOLLARS / THREE on die / THREE DOLLARS. *Right:* 3 on die. *Tint:* Orange and THREE. *Engraver:* New England Bank Note Co. *Comments:* H-RI-150-S5, Durand-583. Altered or spurious. Jan. 1, 1859. 1850s.

Rarity: URS-3
VF $350

$3 • W-RI-530-003-A050

Left: 3 / Medallion head. *Center:* Vulcan at forge. *Right:* 3 / Portrait of William Henry Harrison. *Engraver:* W.L. Ormsby. *Comments:* H-RI-150-A25, Durand-579. Altered from $3 Merchants Bank, Fort Leavenworth, Kansas. 185_. 1850s.

Rarity: *None known*

$3 • W-RI-530-003-A060

Left: 3 / Agriculture and Commerce, Ship and shield. *Right:* 3 / Portrait of Zachary Taylor. *Comments:* H-Unlisted, Durand-580. Altered from $2 Merchants Bank, Fort Leavenworth, Kansas. 1850s.

Rarity: URS-3

$5 • W-RI-530-005-R010

Comments: H-RI-150-R5. Raised from W-RI-530-001-G030. 18__. 1830s.

Rarity: *None known*

$5 • W-RI-530-005-S020   BM

Engraver: Toppan, Carpenter & Co. *Comments:* H-RI-150-S10, Durand-593. Spurious plate used for banks in several states. 18__. 1850s.

Rarity: URS-5
VF $200

$5 • W-RI-530-005-N050

Center: Two allegorical figures and griffin on chest. *Comments:* H-RI-150-S15, Durand-589. Altered or spurious. 1820s.

Rarity: *None known*

$5 • W-RI-530-005-N060

Left: 5. *Center:* Man seated, Temple. *Bottom center:* Steamboat. *Comments:* H-RI-150-N30, Durand-592. 1820s.

Rarity: *None known*

$5 • W-RI-530-005-N070

Center: Neptune in chariot drawn by sea horses. *Comments:* H-Unlisted, Durand-590. Altered or spurious. 1820s.

Rarity: URS-3

$5 • W-RI-530-005-A070

Left: 5 / Allegorical woman leaning on shield. *Center:* Ceres and Liberty. *Right:* 5 / Portrait of Zachary Taylor. *Engraver:* W.L. Ormsby. *Comments:* H-RI-150-A30, Durand-588. Altered from $5 Merchants Bank, Fort Leavenworth, Kansas. 185_. 1857.

Rarity: URS-5
VF $250

$10 • W-RI-530-010-R020

Comments: H-RI-150-R10, Durand-596. Raised from W-RI-530-001-G030. 18__. 1830s.

Rarity: *None known*

$10 • W-RI-530-010-A080

Left: X / Arm and hammer, Spread eagle. *Center:* Allegorical woman with spinning wheel / 10. *Right:* Medallion head of George Washington flanked by fruit and flowers. *Engraver:* W.L. Ormsby. *Comments:* H-RI-150-A35, Durand-597. Altered from $10 Merchants Bank, Fort Leavenworth, Kansas. 185_. 1850s.

Rarity: *None known*

$20 • W-RI-530-020-R030

Comments: H-Unlisted, Durand-600. Raised from W-RI-530-001-G030. 1830s–1840s.

Rarity: URS-3

$20 • W-RI-530-020-N080

Center: Two allegorical figures and griffin on chest. *Comments:* H-RI-150-S20, Durand-601. Altered or spurious. 1820s–1830s.

Rarity: *None known*

$50 • W-RI-530-050-R040

Comments: H-RI-150-R15, Durand-604. Raised from W-RI-530-001-G030. 18__. 1830s.

Rarity: *None known*

$50 • W-RI-530-050-N090

Center: Two allegorical figures and griffin on chest. *Comments:* H-RI-150-S40, Durand-605. Altered or spurious. 1820s–1830s.

Rarity: *None known*

New England Commercial Bank
1818–1860
W-RI-540

History: The New England Commercial Bank was incorporated in February 1818 and in due course opened its office at 193 Thames Street. William Ennis was the founding president, and W.T. Dellingham was the first cashier. Authorized capital was set at $75,000, where it remained for the duration of the bank's existence. In 1850 there were 1,500 shares worth $50 each. Circulation was $19,885 in 1857. Specie amounted to $3,370.70 in 1838 and $3,007.72 in 1857. Real estate was valued at $5,500.

The New England Commercial Bank went into voluntary liquidation in 1914, although it issued no new notes after 1860.[30]

Numismatic Commentary: This bank's notes are probably the most available of any Rhode Island bank. Many sheets and remainders of various issues still exist. However, any signed and dated genuine note is truly a rare find.

VALID ISSUES

$1 • W-RI-540-001-G010

Engraver: N. & S.S. Jocelyn. *Comments:* H-RI-155-G2, Durand-607. Proof. 1818–1820s.

Rarity: URS-2
VG $100; **Proof** $2,900
Selected auction price: Stack's Bowers Galleries, November 2008, Proof $2,845

$1 • W-RI-540-001-G020

Engraver: PSSP. *Comments:* H-RI-155-G6, Durand-608. Remainder. 18__. 1820s–1830s.

Rarity: URS-10
CU $50

$1 • W-RI-540-001-G030

Left: 1 / Woman wearing bonnet, standing by pail / ONE. *Center:* Machinery and merchandise flanking Ceres holding sickle and rake, Factories and harbor / ONE. *Right:* 1 / Ship / ONE. *Engraver:* PSSP / New England Bank Note Co. *Comments:* H-RI-155-G10. 18__. 1830s–1840s.

Rarity: *None known*

$1 • W-RI-540-001-G040

Left: ONE vertically. *Center:* Ships in bay / 1. *Right:* ONE / Indian woman / ONE. *Engraver:* New England Bank Note Co. *Comments:* H-RI-155-G12, Durand-609. 18__. 1840s–1850s.

Rarity: URS-3
VF $400

$1 • W-RI-540-001-G050

Engraver: New England Bank Note Co. *Comments:* H-RI-155-G14, Durand-610. 18__. 1850s.

Rarity: URS-3
VF $600

$1 • W-RI-540-001-G060

Overprint: Green ONE. *Engraver:* New England Bank Note Co. / ABNCo. monogram. *Comments:* H-RI-155-G16a, Durand-611. Remainder. 18__. 1860s.

Rarity: URS-10
CU $45

$1.25 • W-RI-540-001.25-G070

Left: 1 25/100 / Train / 1 25/100. *Center:* Sailing ships in bay / $1.25 Cts. *Right:* 1 25/100 / Spread eagle. *Engraver:* New England Bank Note Co. *Comments:* H-RI-155-G18, Durand-613. 18__. 1830s.

Rarity: *None known*

$1.50 • W-RI-540-001.50-G080

Left: 1 Doll. 50 Cts. vertically. *Center:* Eagle / $1 50/100. *Right:* 1 50/100 with coins / Woman standing. *Engraver:* New England Bank Note Co. *Comments:* H-RI-155-G20, Durand-614. 18__. 1830s.

Rarity: URS-3
VF $400

$1.75 • W-RI-540-001.75-G090

Left: $1.75 Cts / Liberty and eagle / 1 75/100. *Center:* Three sloops at sea. *Right:* $1.75 Cts. / Woman seated with grain, Dog / 1 75/100. *Engraver:* New England Bank Note Co. *Comments:* H-RI-155-G22, Durand-615. 18__. 1830s.

Rarity: *None known*

$2 • W-RI-540-002-G100

Engraver: N. & S.S. Jocelyn. *Comments:* H-RI-155-G26, Durand-616. First issue. 18__. 1818–1820s.

Rarity: URS-3
Proof $500

$2 • W-RI-540-002-G110

CC

Engraver: PSSP. *Comments:* H-RI-155-G32, Durand-617. Remainder. 18__. 1820s–1830s.

Rarity: URS-10
VF $1,000; **Unc-Rem** $60

$2 • W-RI-540-002-G120

TD

Engraver: PSSP / New England Bank Note Co. *Comments:* H-RI-155-G36, Durand-618. Remainder. 18__. 1830s–1840s.

Rarity: URS-10
VF $1,000; **Unc-Rem** $45

$2 • W-RI-540-002-G130

Left: 2 / TWO / 2. *Center:* Sailing vessels / 2. *Right:* TWO / Milkmaid standing / TWO. *Engraver:* New England Bank Note Co. *Comments:* H-RI-155-G38, Durand-619. 18__. 1840s–1850s.

Rarity: URS-3
VF $400

$2 • W-RI-540-002-G140

Left: 2 / Portrait of Christopher Columbus. *Center:* Goddess of Plenty / 2 / Portrait of Justice. *Right:* 2 / Male portrait. *Engraver:* New England Bank Note Co. *Comments:* H-RI-155-G40, Durand-620. 18__. 1850s.

Rarity: URS-3
VF $400

$2 • W-RI-540-002-G150

CC

Overprint: Green TWO. *Engraver:* New England Bank Note Co. / ABNCo. monogram. *Comments:* H-RI-155-G44a, Durand-621. Remainder. 18__. 1860s.

Rarity: URS-10
VF $1,000; **Unc-Rem** $50

$3 • W-RI-540-003-G160

Left: 3. *Right:* 3. *Engraver:* PSSP. *Comments:* H-RI-155-G50, Durand-622. There are no known intact specimens of this note, although there are numerous sheets containing the fractional part. For some reason all the sheets were cut, destroying the top and bottom of the sheet. Similar in appearance to early Perkins issues with "watermelon" motif. 18__. 1820s–1830s.

Rarity: *None known*

$3 • W-RI-540-003-G170

Left: THREE vertically. *Center:* Man reaping and woman with sheaf / 3. *Right:* THREE and steamship / 3 on THREE. *Engraver:* New England Bank Note Co. *Comments:* H-RI-155-G56, Durand-623. 18__. 1840s–1850s.

Rarity: *None known*

$3 • W-RI-540-003-G180

Left: 3 / George Washington with horse. *Center:* Female portrait / 3 / Portrait of girl. *Right:* 3 / Vulcan. *Engraver:* New England Bank Note Co. *Comments:* H-RI-155-G58, Durand-624. 18__. 1850s.

Rarity: *None known*

$3 • W-RI-540-003-G190

RMS

Overprint: Green THREE. *Engraver:* New England Bank Note Co. / ABNCo. monogram. *Comments:* H-RI-155-G60a, Durand-625. 18__. 1860s.

Rarity: URS-10
VF $1,000; **Unc-Rem** $50

$5 • W-RI-540-005-G200

Left: Commerce with shield bearing 5, Cherub, Ships. *Center:* 5 on die. *Bottom center:* Anchor on shield. *Right:* V / RHODE ISLAND / V vertically. *Engraver:* N. & S.S. Jocelyn. *Comments:* H-RI-155-G64, Durand-626. 18__. 1818–1820s.

Rarity: URS-3
Proof $500

$5 • W-RI-540-005-G210

Left: 5 / Portrait of George Washington / 5. *Center:* Panel of microletters. *Right:* V / Portrait of Marquis de Lafayette / 5. *Engraver:* PSSP. *Comments:* H-RI-155-G66. 18__. 1820s–1830s.

Rarity: *None known*

$5 • W-RI-540-005-G220

TD

Engraver: New England Bank Note Co. / PSSP. *Comments:* H-RI-155-G70, Durand-627. 18__. 1830s–1840s.

Rarity: URS-10
VF $1,000; **Unc-Rem** $50

$5 • W-RI-540-005-G230

Left: Spread eagle on American shield and anchor, Factories and ships / FIVE. *Center:* V bearing allegorical woman and cherub. *Right:* 5 / Young girl with basket of flowers. *Engraver:* New England Bank Note Co. *Comments:* H-RI-155-G76, Durand-628. 18__. 1850s.

Rarity: URS-3
VF $250

$5 • W-RI-540-005-G230a

CC

Overprint: Green FIVE. *Engraver:* New England Bank Note Co. / ABNCo. monogram. *Comments:* H-RI-155-G76b, Durand-629. Similar to W-RI-540-005-G230 but with additional engraver imprint. Remainder. 18__. 1860s.

Rarity: URS-10
VF $1,000; **Unc-Rem** $65

$10 • W-RI-540-010-G240

Left: 10 / Portrait of George Washington / 10. *Center:* Panel of microletters. *Right:* 10 / Portrait of Marquis de Lafayette / 10. *Engraver:* PSSP. *Comments:* H-RI-155-G80. 18__. 1820s–1830s.

Rarity: *None known*

$10 • W-RI-540-010-G250

CC

Engraver: PSSP / New England Bank Note Co. *Comments:* H-RI-155-G82, Durand-630. Remainder. 18__. 1830s–1840s.

Rarity: URS-10
VF $1,000; **Unc-Rem** $65

How to Read the Whitman Numbering System

$1 • W-RI-010-001-G010a

Denomination: Value of the note shown.

W: Whitman number. This number is a sortable code unique to each bank and note.

RI: Abbreviation for the state under study.

010: Numerical designation specific to each bank.

001: The denomination in dollars.

G010a: G indicates a good or valid note. Other categories are indicated thus: C (counterfeit); R (raised); S (spurious); N (not-attributed); A (altered). Numbers are assigned starting with 010, 020, et seq. Terminal letters following the number indicate variations of a note: a series of different colored overprints, tints, payees, etc., all on the same design of note. For more information, see the "How to Use This Book" section at the front of the volume, page xiv.

$10 • W-RI-540-010-G260

CC

Engraver: New England Bank Note Co. *Comments:* H-RI-155-G86, Durand-631. 18__. 1850s.

Rarity: URS-3

VF $1,000

$10 • W-RI-540-010-G260a

CC

Overprint: Green TEN. *Engraver:* New England Bank Note Co. / ABNCo. monogram. *Comments:* H-RI-155-G86b, Durand-632. Similar to W-RI-540-010-G260 but with additional engraver imprint. Remainder. 18__. 1860s.

Rarity: URS-10

VF $1,000; **Unc-Rem** $65

$50 • W-RI-540-050-G270

CC

Engraver: Perkins. *Comments:* H-RI-155-G92, Durand-633. Remainder. 18__. 1820s–1830s.

Rarity: URS-10

VF $1,500; **Unc-Rem** $80

$50 • W-RI-540-050-G280

CC

Engraver: PSSP / New England Bank Note Co. *Comments:* H-RI-155-G94, Durand-634. 18__. 1830s–1840s.

Rarity: URS-10

Unc-Rem $90

$50 • W-RI-540-050-G290

Left: FIFTY / Woman standing with wreath and flowers / FIFTY. *Center:* 50 / Man holding horse / 50. *Right:* FIFTY / Woman standing with cornucopia / FIFTY. *Engraver:* New England Bank Note Co. *Comments:* H-RI-155-G96, Durand-635. 18__. 1850s.

Rarity: *None known*

$50 • W-RI-540-050-G300

CC

Overprint: Green FIFTY. *Engraver:* New England Bank Note Co. / ABNCo. monogram. *Comments:* H-RI-155-G98a, Durand-636. Remainder. 18__. 1860s.

Rarity: URS-10

CU $200

$100 • W-RI-540-100-G310

CC

Engraver: Perkins. *Comments:* H-RI-155-G104, Durand-637. 18__. 1820s–1830s.

Rarity: URS-10

VF $1,500; **Unc-Rem** $70

$100 • W-RI-540-100-G320

SBG

Engraver: PSSP / New England Bank Note Co. *Comments:* H-RI-155-G106, Durand-638. Remainder. 18___. 1830s–1840s.

Rarity: URS-10

Unc-Rem $125

$100 • W-RI-540-100-G330

Left: ONE HUNDRED on 100 / Portrait of William Henry Harrison. *Center:* Wharf scene. *Right:* ONE HUNDRED on 100 / Portrait of Christopher Columbus. *Engraver:* New England Bank Note Co. *Comments:* H-RI-155-G108, Durand-639. 18___. 1850s.

Rarity: *None known*

$100 • W-RI-540-100-G340

QDB

Overprint: Green HUNDRED. *Engraver:* New England Bank Note Co. / ABNCo. monogram. *Comments:* H-RI-155-G110a, Durand-640. 18___. 1860s.

Rarity: URS-10

Unc-Rem $200

Uncut Sheets

$1-$1-$2-$3 • W-RI-540-001.001.002.003-US005

Vignette(s): *($1)* Dock and implements / Woman reclining against bale / Farming implements. *($1)* Dock and implements / Woman reclining against bale / Farming implements. *($2)* George Washington on horseback / Woman with cornucopia / George Washington on horseback. *($3)* Portrait of cherub / Woman with shield bearing 3 / Portrait of cherub. *Engraver:* New England Bank Note Co. / ABNCo. monogram. *Comments:* All unlisted in Haxby. 18___. 1860s.

Rarity: URS-10

$3-$2-$1-$1 • W-RI-540-003.002.001.001-US010

Vignette(s): *($3)* 3 / 3. *($2)* 2 / 2. *($1)* Portrait of George Washington / Two children with bales and barrels / Male portrait. *($1)* Portrait of George Washington / Two children with bales and barrels / Male portrait. *Engraver:* PSSP. *Comments:* H-RI-155-G50, G32, G6, G6. Found with the top of the $3 and the bottom of the $1 cut off. 18___. 1820s–1830s.

Rarity: URS-10

$5-$10 • W-RI-540-005.010-US020

Vignette(s): *($5)* Blacksmith / Man with shield bearing 5, Fruit and anchor, Sailing ship / Girl seated. *($10)* Farmer sowing / Mercury with shield bearing 10 / Merchandise, factories, and ships / Canal scene / Ships under sail. *Engraver:* PSSP / New England Bank Note Co. *Comments:* H-RI-155-G70, G82. 18___. 1830s–1840s.

Rarity: URS-10

$10-$5-$5-$5 • W-RI-540-010.005.005.005-US030

Vignette(s): *($10)* Man with cog wheel / Man standing with cane. *($5)* Spread eagle on American shield and anchor, Factories and ships / V containing allegorical woman and cherub / Young girl with basket of flowers. *($5)* Spread eagle on American shield and anchor, Factories and ships / V containing allegorical woman and cherub / Young girl with basket of flowers. *($5)* Spread eagle on American shield and anchor, Factories and ships / V containing allegorical woman and cherub / Young girl with basket of flowers. *Engraver:* New England Bank Note Co. / ABNCo. monogram. *Comments:* H-RI-155-G86b, G76b, G76b, G76b. 18___. 1860s.

Rarity: URS-10

$50-$100 • W-RI-540-050.100-US040

Vignette(s): *($50)* RHODE ISLAND vertically / 50, 50 on two ovals. *($100)* RHODE ISLAND vertically. *Engraver:* PSSP. *Comments:* H-RI-155-G92, G104. 18___. 1820s–1830s.

Rarity: URS-10

$50-$100 • W-RI-540-050.100-US050

Vignette(s): *($50)* Sheaves and fruit / Liberty, Justice, and Knowledge / Vulcan. *($100)* Men in boat / Eagle atop package / Woman with veil of flowers. *Engraver:* New England Bank Note Co. / ABNCo. monogram. *Comments:* H-RI-155-G98a, G110a. 18___. 1820s–1830s.

Rarity: URS-10

$100-$50 • W-RI-540-100.050-US060

QDB

Engraver: PSSP / New England Bank Note Co. *Comments:* H-RI-155-G106, G94. 18___. 1830s–1840s.

Rarity: URS-8

VF $200

Non-Valid Issues
$1 • W-RI-540-001-C010

CC

Engraver: N. & S.S. Jocelyn. *Comments:* H-RI-155-C2, Durand-612. Counterfeit of W-RI-540-001-G010. 1820s.
Rarity: URS-3
VF $100

Newport Bank
1803–1865
W-RI-550

History: The Newport Bank was incorporated in 1803 with $120,000 in authorized capital, which remained constant throughout the bank's existence. Constant Taber and John R. Shearman served as founding president and cashier, respectively. In the 1830s it was a "pet bank," or depository of federal funds. Circulation in 1849 was listed at $32,439. There were 2,000 shares valued at $60 each. In 1856 the bank was located at Washington Square. Circulation was reported to be $55,056 in 1857 and $61,038 in 1862. Specie was $4,121.79 in 1857.

In 1865 the business of the Newport Bank was succeeded by the Newport National Bank.

Numismatic Commentary: On several occasions this bank featured Christopher Columbus and the discovery of America on its notes. Another note carries the vignette of the "Ocean House," a resort home on famous Bellevue Avenue.

Valid Issues
$1 • W-RI-550-001-G010

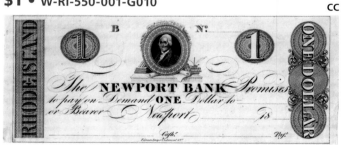

CC

Engraver: Fairman, Draper, Underwood & Co. *Comments:* H-RI-160-G10, Durand-641. First issue. Proof. 18__. 1820s–1830s.
Rarity: URS-1
Proof $1,900
Selected auction price: Stack's Bowers Galleries, November 2008, Proof $1,890

$1 • W-RI-550-001-G020
Comments: H-Unlisted, Durand-642. No description available. Second issue. 18__. 1820s–1830s.
Rarity: *None known*

$1 • W-RI-550-001-G030

CC

Engraver: Rawdon, Wright, & Hatch. *Comments:* H-RI-160-G14, Durand-643. 18__. 1840s–1850s.
Rarity: URS-3
VF $300

$1 • W-RI-550-001-G030a
Engraver: Rawdon, Wright, Hatch & Edson. *Comments:* H-RI-160-G14a. Similar to W-RI-550-001-G030 but with different engraver imprint. 18__. 1850s–1860s.
Rarity: URS-3
VF $300

$2 • W-RI-550-002-G040
Comments: H-Unlisted, Durand-646. No description available. First issue. 1820s–1830s.
Rarity: *None known*

$2 • W-RI-550-002-G050

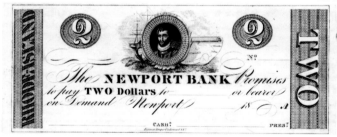

SBG

Engraver: Fairman, Draper, Underwood & Co. *Comments:* H-RI-160-G20, Durand-647. Proof. 18__. 1820s–1830s.
Rarity: URS-1
Proof $2,000

$2 • W-RI-550-002-G060

CC

Engraver: Rawdon, Wright, & Hatch. *Comments:* H-RI-160-G24, Durand-648. 18__. 1840s–1850s.
Rarity: URS-3
VF $1,000
Selected auction price: Stack's Bowers Galleries, January 2011, VF $1,000

$2 • W-RI-550-002-G060a

Left: TWO / Medallion head / TWO. *Center:* 2 / Women standing beside 2 / 2 / TWO. *Bottom center:* Shield bearing anchor. *Right:* Cherub on 2 / Cherub on 2. *Engraver:* Rawdon, Wright, Hatch & Edson. *Comments:* H-RI-160-G24a. Similar to W-RI-550-002-G060 but with different engraver imprint. 18__. 1850s–1860s.
Rarity: *None known*

$5 • W-RI-550-005-G070

CC

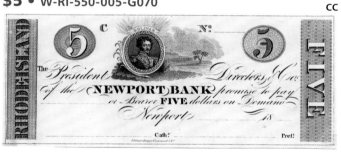

Comments: H-Unlisted, Durand-651. First issue. Proof. 18__. 1820s–1830s.
Rarity: URS-3
Proof $1,000

$5 • W-RI-550-005-G080

Comments: H-Unlisted, Durand-652. No description available. Second issue. 1820s–1830s.
Rarity: *None known*

$5 • W-RI-550-005-G090

CJF

Engraver: Rawdon, Wright, Hatch & Edson. *Comments:* H-RI-160-G30, Durand-653. 18__. 1840s–1850s.
Rarity: URS-3
VF $1,100

$5 • W-RI-550-005-G090a

Left: 5 / FIVE on medallion head / V. *Center:* Sailing vessels. *Bottom center:* Shield bearing anchor. *Right:* FIVE / "Ocean House" / FIVE. *Engraver:* Rawdon, Wright, Hatch & Edson. *Comments:* H-RI-160-G30a. Similar to W-RI-550-005-G090 but with different engraver imprint. 18__. 1850s–1860s.
Rarity: URS-3
VF $300

$10 • W-RI-550-010-G100

Comments: H-Unlisted, Durand-656. No description available. First issue. 1820s–1830s.
Rarity: *None known*

$10 • W-RI-550-010-G110

Comments: H-Unlisted, Durand-657. No description available. Second issue. 1820s–1830s.
Rarity: *None known*

$10 • W-RI-550-010-G120

Left: Panel with 10 / Medallion head / TEN. *Center:* Eagle on shield, Steamship, U.S. Capitol. *Bottom center:* Anchor on shield. *Right:* Deer / 10 / Buffalo. *Engraver:* Rawdon, Wright, Hatch & Co. *Comments:* H-RI-160-G36. 18__. 1840s–1850s.
Rarity: *None known*

$10 • W-RI-550-010-G120a

Engraver: Rawdon, Wright, Hatch & Edson. *Comments:* H-RI-160-G36a. Similar to W-RI-550-010-G120 but with different engraver imprint. 18__. 1850s–1860s.
Rarity: *None known*

$20 • W-RI-550-020-G130

Left: Sailing ship / Scales on shield / Plow. *Center:* 20 on die between TWENTY and DOLLARS / Sheep. *Right:* 20 / XX. *Engraver:* Hamlin. *Comments:* H-RI-160-G40, Durand-661. First issue. 18__. 1800s.
Rarity: URS-3
VF $250

$30 • W-RI-550-030-G140

Left: THIRTY, 30, DOLLARS vertically / Pitcher / Scale / Anchor. *Center:* THIRTY DOLLARS / Sheep. *Right:* 30 / Spread eagle. *Engraver:* Hamlin. *Comments:* H-RI-160-G44, Durand-662. 18__. 1800s.
Rarity: URS-3
VF $750

$50 • W-RI-550-050-G150

Comments: H-Unlisted, Durand-663. No description available. First issue. 1820s–1830s.
Rarity: *None known*

$50 • W-RI-550-050-G160

Left: 50 / Medallion head / 50. *Center:* Justice / Rising sun on shield / Cherub. *Right:* FIFTY / Minerva / 50. *Engraver:* Rawdon, Wright, Hatch & Co. *Comments:* H-RI-160-G50, Durand-664. 18__. 1840s–1850s.
Rarity: *None known*

$50 • W-RI-550-050-G160a

Engraver: Rawdon, Wright, Hatch & Edson. *Comments:* H-RI-160-G50a. Similar to W-RI-550-050-G160 but with different engraver imprint. 18__. 1850s–1860s.

Rarity: *None known*

$100 • W-RI-550-100-G170

Comments: H-Unlisted, Durand-665. No description available. First issue. 1820s–1830s.

Rarity: *None known*

$100 • W-RI-550-100-G180

Left: 100 / Medallion head / 100. *Center:* Shipping scene, City. *Right:* 100 / Eagle / 100. *Engraver:* Rawdon, Wright, Hatch & Co. *Comments:* H-RI-160-G56, Durand-666. 18__. 1840s–1850s.

Rarity: *None known*

$100 • W-RI-550-100-G180a

Engraver: Rawdon, Wright, Hatch & Edson. *Comments:* H-RI-160-G56a. Similar to W-RI-550-100-G180 but with different engraver imprint. 18__. 1850s–1860s.

Rarity: URS-3
VF $300

Uncut Sheets

$1-$1-$2-$10 • W-RI-550-001.001.002.010-US010

Vignette(s): *($1)* Male portrait. *($1)* Male portrait. *($2)* Portrait of Christopher Columbus. *($10)* No description available. *Engraver:* Fairman, Draper, Underwood & Co. *Comments:* H-RI-160-G10, G10, G20, H-Unlisted. 18__. 1820s–1830s.

Rarity: *None known*

$50-$5-$5-$5 • W-RI-550-050.005.005.005-US020

Engraver: Fairman, Draper, Underwood & Co. *Comments:* All unlisted in Haxby. No description available. 18__. 1820s–1830s.

Rarity: *None known*

NON-VALID ISSUES

$1 • W-RI-550-001-C010

Engraver: Fairman, Draper, Underwood & Co. *Comments:* H-RI-160-C10, Durand-644. Counterfeit of W-RI-550-001-G010. 18__. 1830s.

Rarity: *None known*

$1 • W-RI-550-001-S010

Left: 1 RHODE ISLAND 1 vertically. *Center:* 1 on ONE / Ceres / 1 on ONE. *Right:* 1 / 1. *Comments:* H-RI-160-S5, Durand-645. 18__. 1820s.

Rarity: URS-3
VF $150

$2 • W-RI-550-002-S020

BM

Engraver: Terry, Pelton & Co. *Comments:* H-RI-160-S10, Durand-649. Similar to W-RI-550-002-G050. 18__. 1830s.

Rarity: URS-3
VF $200

$2 • W-RI-550-002-S020a

Engraver: Terry, Pelton & Co. *Comments:* H-RI-160-S10a, Durand-650. Similar to W-RI-550-002-S020. 18__. 1830s.

Rarity: URS-3
VF $300

$5 • W-RI-550-005-R010

Comments: H-RI-160-R5, Durand-654. Raised from W-RI-550-001-G030 series. 18__. 1850s.

Rarity: *None known*

$5 • W-RI-550-005-A010

Left: 5 / Cattle / FIVE. *Center:* River scene, Log raft, docks. *Right:* FIVE / Milkmaid with pail and stool. *Engraver:* New England Bank Note Co. *Comments:* H-RI-160-A5, Durand-655. Altered from $5 Stillwater Canal Bank, Orono, Maine. 18__. 1840s.

Rarity: *None known*

$10 • W-RI-550-010-R020

Comments: H-RI-160-R10, Durand-659. Raised from W-RI-550-001-G030 series. 18__. 1850s.

Rarity: *None known*

$10 • W-RI-550-010-S030

Left: Portrait of William Henry Harrison. *Center:* Blacksmith resting hands on hammer, Train. *Tint:* Green outlining TEN. *Engraver:* Rawdon, Wright, Hatch & Edson / ABNCo. monogram. *Comments:* H-RI-160-S15, Durand-658. May 1, 1862. 1860s.

Rarity: URS-3
VF $300

$10 • W-RI-550-010-S030a

Tint: Orange outlining X, X / TEN. *Engraver:* Rawdon, Wright, Hatch & Edson / ABNCo. monogram. *Comments:* H-RI-160-S15a. Similar to W-RI-550-010-S030. May 1, 1862. 1860s.

Rarity: URS-3
VF $300

$10 • W-RI-550-010-A020

Left: TEN / Justice. *Center:* River scene, Log raft, docks. *Right:* 10 / Woman / TEN. *Engraver:* New England Bank Note Co. *Comments:* H-RI-160-A10, Durand-660. Altered from $10 Stillwater Canal Bank, Orono, Maine $. 18__. 1840s.

Rarity: *None known*

Newport Exchange Bank
1834–1865
W-RI-560

History: The Newport Exchange Bank was incorporated in January 1834. In 1836 the bank commissioners made note that "the directors of the Newport Exchange Bank had made large purchases of paper in New York, as well as in Providence, and recommended that the practice of discounting abroad should be corrected by the legislature."[31] Capital was $60,000 in February 1848, with 1,200 shares worth $50 each. Circulation ranged from $18,583 in 1857 to $26,922 in 1863. Specie was $7,822.33 in 1838 and $2,199.97 in 1857. The bank's office was located at 158 Thames Street in 1856.

The business of the Newport Exchange Bank was succeeded by the National Exchange Bank of Newport in 1865.

Numismatic Commentary: Genuine notes are very hard to locate. Only the $50 denomination is usually found in the marketplace. For some collectors, doubts persist as to the authenticity of these notes. Some view these as Proof issues, while others claim them to be only remainders. The paper composition lies somewhere between the soft paper used for Proofs and the stronger paper used for circulation issues.

VALID ISSUES

$1 • **W-RI-560-001-G010**
Left: ONE / Justice, Shield surmounted by an eagle, Commerce / 1. *Center:* Shield, Woman seated and Neptune in chariot drawn by seahorses. *Right:* 1 / Two cherubs and two dolphins / 1. *Engraver:* Rawdon, Wright, Hatch & Edson. *Comments:* H-RI-165-G3, Durand-667. 18__. 1830s–1850s.

Rarity: URS-3
Proof $500

$2 • **W-RI-560-002-G020**
Left: TWO / Liberty / TWO. *Center:* 2 / Ship / Mercury seated / 2. *Right:* Indian / TWO. *Engraver:* Rawdon, Wright, Hatch & Edson. *Comments:* H-RI-165-G8, Durand-668. 18__. 1830s–1850s.

Rarity: URS-3
Proof $500

$3 • **W-RI-560-003-G030**
Left: Woman seated with eagle / 3. *Center:* 3 / Steamboat / 3. *Right:* THREE / Justice / 3. *Engraver:* Rawdon, Wright, Hatch & Edson. *Comments:* H-RI-165-G12, Durand-670. 18__. 1830s–1850s.

Rarity: URS-3
Proof $500

$5 • **W-RI-560-005-G040**
Left: FIVE / Ceres / 5. *Center:* 5 / Allegorical figure in clouds / 5. *Right:* FIVE / Mercury flying in clouds / 5. *Engraver:* Rawdon, Wright, Hatch & Edson. *Comments:* H-RI-165-G14, Durand-671. 18__. 1830s–1860s.

Rarity: URS-3
Proof $500

$10 • **W-RI-560-010-G050**
Left: 10 on stone / Cherub engraving 10 on stone / 10. *Center:* Woman and vessels / Shield / Portrait of Commodore Oliver Hazard Perry. *Right:* X / Justice. *Engraver:* Rawdon, Wright, Hatch & Edson. *Comments:* H-RI-165-G16, Durand-674. 18__. 1830s–1860s.

Rarity: URS-3
Proof $600

$20 • **W-RI-560-020-G060**
Left: TWENTY vertically. *Center:* XX / Neptune and Venus in shell drawn by sea horses / XX. *Right:* 20 / Cherub and basket of flowers / 20. *Engraver:* Rawdon, Wright, Hatch & Edson. *Comments:* H-RI-165-G18, Durand-677. 18__. 1830s–1860s.

Rarity: *None known*

$50 • **W-RI-560-050-G070**   CC

Engraver: Rawdon, Wright, Hatch & Co. *Comments:* H-RI-165-G20, Durand-678. 18__. 1830s–1860s.

Rarity: URS-5
VF $375; **Unc-Rem** $500; **Proof** $800
Selected auction price: Stack's Bowers Galleries,
March 2009, Proof $770

Uncut Sheets

$1-$1-$2-$3 • **W-RI-560-001.001.002.003-US010**
Vignette(s): (*$1*) Justice / Shield surmounted by eagle / Commerce / Shield, Woman seated and Neptune in chariot drawn by seahorses / Two cherubs and two dolphins. (*$1*) Justice / Shield surmounted by eagle / Commerce / Shield, Woman seated and Neptune in chariot drawn by seahorses / Two cherubs and two dolphins. (*$2*) Liberty / Ship / Mercury seated / Indian. (*$3*) Woman seated with eagle / Steamboat / Justice. *Engraver:* Rawdon, Wright, Hatch & Edson. *Comments:* H-RI-165-G3, G3, G8, G12. 18__. 1830s–1850s.

Rarity: URS-3
Proof $1,200

$5-$5-$10-$10 • **W-RI-560-005.005.010.010-US020**
Vignette(s): (*$5*) Ceres / Allegorical figure in clouds / Mercury flying in clouds. (*$5*) Ceres / Allegorical figure in clouds / Mercury flying in clouds. (*$10*) Cherub engraving 10 on stone / Woman and vessels / Shield / Portrait of Commodore Oliver Hazard Perry / Justice. (*$10*) Cherub engraving 10 on stone / Woman and vessels / Shield / Portrait of Commodore Oliver Hazard Perry / Justice. *Engraver:* Rawdon, Wright, Hatch & Edson. *Comments:* H-RI-165-G14, G14, G16, G16. 18__. 1830s–1860s.

Rarity: URS-3
Proof $1,500

NON-VALID ISSUES

$2 • W-RI-560-002-N010

Left: Woman. *Center:* Shield / Woman reclining. *Right:* Woman. *Comments:* H-RI-165-S5, Durand-669. Altered or spurious. 1830s–1850s.

Rarity: *None known*

$5 • W-RI-560-005-S010

Left: Portrait of William Henry Harrison / Woman. *Center:* Vulcan resting on hammer and anvil, Train. *Comments:* H-RI-165-S10, Durand-673. 1830s–1850s.

Rarity: *None known*

$5 • W-RI-560-005-A010

Left: 5 / Cattle / FIVE. *Center:* River scene, Log raft, docks, and warehouses. *Right:* FIVE / Milkmaid standing with pail and stool. *Engraver:* New England Bank Note Co. *Comments:* H-RI-165-A5, Durand-672. Altered from $5 Stillwater Canal Bank, Orono, Maine. 18__. 1830s–1850s.

Rarity: *None known*

$10 • W-RI-560-010-S020

Left: Portrait of William Henry Harrison / Woman. *Center:* Vulcan resting on hammer and anvil, Train. *Comments:* H-RI-165-S15, Durand-676. 1830s–1850s.

Rarity: *None known*

$10 • W-RI-560-010-A020

Left: TEN / Justice. *Center:* River scene, Log raft, Docks and warehouses. *Right:* 10 / Bust of woman / TEN. *Engraver:* New England Bank Note Co. *Comments:* H-RI-165-A10, Durand-675. Altered from $10 Stillwater Canal Bank, Orono, Maine. 18__. 1830s–1850s.

Rarity: *None known*

Rhode Island Union Bank
1804–1881
W-RI-570

History: The Rhode Island Union Bank was incorporated in 1804. Samuel Elam and John L. Boss served as the founding president and cashier, respectively. In 1826 its capital was $200,000, which was reduced to $150,000 in 1847 and increased again to $165,000 in 1849. The bank was located at 178 Thames Street in 1856.

Circulation was $22,325 in 1826. This value increased dramatically to $128,706 in 1857 and then fell to $39,339 in 1862. Specie in 1857 amounted to $3,780.47.

No new currency was issued after 1866. By 1872 only $2,140 face value remained unredeemed. The business of the Rhode Island Union Bank was succeeded by the Union National Bank in 1881.

Numismatic Commentary: Various denominations of genuine notes are available in the marketplace. On one issue, the coastal paddle-wheeler *Newport* is portrayed, while on another the child portrait of Dr. Alfred L. Elwyn as painted by Thomas Sully is shown. This engraving of Elwyn also appears on at least one issue of Confederate currency, which is unusual in that he was an abolitionist.

VALID ISSUES

$1 • W-RI-570-001-G010

Engraver: P. Maverick. *Comments:* H-RI-175-G2, Durand-687. No description available. 18__. 1800s–1810s.

Rarity: *None known*

$1 • W-RI-570-001-G020

Center: Woman, Scenery, Clasped hands. *Engraver:* P. Maverick. *Comments:* H-RI-175-G4, Durand-688. 18__. 1810s–1820s.

Rarity: *None known*

$1 • W-RI-570-001-G030

CC

Engraver: Durand & Co. *Comments:* H-RI-175-G8, Durand-689. 18__. 1840s–1850s.

Rarity: URS-8
VG $50; **EF** $70

$1 • W-RI-570-001-G030a

TD

Overprint: Red ONE. *Engraver:* Durand & Co. *Comments:* H-RI-175-G8a, Durand-690. Similar to W-RI-570-001-G030. 18__. 1850s.

Rarity: URS-8
VF $150

$1 • W-RI-570-001-G030b

CC

Overprint: Green ONE. *Engraver:* Durand & Co. / ABNCo. monogram. *Comments:* H-RI-175-G8b, Durand-691. Similar to W-RI-570-001-G030 but with additional engraver imprint. 18__. 1850s–1860s.

Rarity: URS-8
VF $150

$1 • W-RI-570-001-G040

CC, CC

Back: Green. **Engraver:** American Bank Note Co. **Comments:** H-RI-175-G10a, Durand-692. Jan.y 10th, 18__. 1865 and 1866.
Rarity: URS-7
VF $200

$2 • W-RI-570-002-G050

Left: 2 TWO 2 vertically. **Center:** Die with clasped hands / TWO DOLLARS / Plow. **Right:** 2 TWO 2 vertically. **Engraver:** P. Maverick. **Comments:** H-RI-175-G14, Durand-694. 18__. 1800s–1810s.
Rarity: *None known*

$2 • W-RI-570-002-G060

Center: View of the Redwood Library in Newport / Die with clasped hands. **Engraver:** P. Maverick. **Comments:** H-RI-175-G16, Durand-695. 1810s–1820s.
Rarity: *None known*

$2 • W-RI-570-002-G070

SBG

Engraver: Durand & Co. **Comments:** H-RI-175-G20, Durand-696. Remainder. 18__. 1840s–1850s.
Rarity: URS-6
VF $150; **Proof** $1,250
Selected auction price: Stack's Bowers Galleries, March 2013, Proof $1,200

$2 • W-RI-570-002-G070a

SI

Overprint: Red TWO. **Engraver:** Durand & Co. **Comments:** H-RI-175-G20a, Durand-697. Similar to W-RI-570-002-G070. 18__. 1850s.
Rarity: URS-6
VF $150

$2 • W-RI-570-002-G070b

BM

Overprint: Green TWO. **Engraver:** Durand & Co. / ABNCo. monogram. **Comments:** H-RI-175-G20b, Durand-698. Similar to W-RI-570-002-G070 but with additional engraver imprint. 18__. 1850s–1860s.
Rarity: URS-6
VF $150

$2 • W-RI-570-002-G080

CC, CC

Engraver: American Bank Note Co. **Comments:** H-RI-175-G22a, Durand-699. Jan.y 10th, 18__. 1865 and 1866.
Rarity: URS-5
VF $300

$3 • W-RI-570-003-G090

Left: THREE DOLL'S vertically. *Center:* Clasped hands / Windmill. *Bottom center:* 3. *Right:* THREE DOLL'S vertically. *Engraver:* P. Maverick. *Comments:* H-RI-175-G26. 18__. 1800s–1810s.

Rarity: *None known*

$3 • W-RI-570-003-G100

Engraver: P. Maverick. *Comments:* H-RI-175-G28, Durand-703. No description available. First issue. 18__. 1810s–1820s.

Rarity: *None known*

$5 • W-RI-570-005-G110

Center: Figure of Solon / Die with clasped hands. *Engraver:* P. Maverick. *Comments:* H-RI-175-G32, Durand-705. 18__. 1810s–1820s.

Rarity: *None known*

$5 • W-RI-570-005-G120

Engraver: Durand & Co. *Comments:* H-RI-175-G36, Durand-706. Remainder. 18__. 1840s–1850s.

Rarity: URS-7
VF $150; CU $735; **Proof** $950
Selected auction price: Stack's Bowers Galleries, March 2013, Proof $900

$5 • W-RI-570-005-G120a

Overprint: Red FIVE. *Engraver:* Durand & Co. *Comments:* H-RI-175-G36a, Durand-707. Similar to W-RI-570-005-G120. 18__. 1850s.

Rarity: URS-7
VF $200

$5 • W-RI-570-005-G120b

Overprint: Green FIVE. *Engraver:* Durand & Co. / ABNCo. monogram. *Comments:* H-RI-175-G36b, Durand-708. Similar to W-RI-570-005-G120 but with additional engraver imprint. 18__. 1850s–1860s.

Rarity: URS-7
VF $200

$5 • W-RI-570-005-G130

Back: Green. *Engraver:* American Bank Note Co. *Comments:* H-RI-175-G38a, Durand-709. Jan.y 10th, 18__. 1865.

Rarity: URS-5
VF $400
Selected auction price: Stack's Bowers Galleries, March 2013, VF $266

$10 • W-RI-570-010-G145

Center: View of bank / Die with clasped hands. *Engraver:* P. Maverick. *Comments:* H-RI-175-G42, Durand-715. 18__. 1810s–1820s.

Rarity: *None known*

$10 • W-RI-570-010-G160

Comments: H-RI-175-G44. No description available. 18__. 1830s–1840s.

Rarity: *None known*

$10 • **W-RI-570-010-G170**
Left: 10 / X / 10. *Center:* Farmer with plow and oxen / 10. *Right:* TEN / Goddess of Plenty with lyre, Cornucopia. *Engraver:* New England Bank Note Co. *Comments:* H-RI-175-G46, Durand-716. 18__. 1840s–1850s. **Rarity:** *None known*

$10 • **W-RI-570-010-G180**   CC

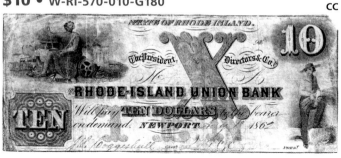

Overprint: Red TEN. *Engraver:* New England Bank Note Co. *Comments:* H-RI-175-G48a, Durand-717. 186_. 1860s.
Rarity: URS-3
VF $300

$10 • **W-RI-570-010-G180a**
Overprint: Red ornate TEN. *Engraver:* New England Bank Note Co. / ABNCo. monogram. *Comments:* H-RI-175-G48b. Similar to W-RI-570-010-G180 but with additional engraver imprint. 18__. 1860s.
Rarity: *None known*

$10 • **W-RI-570-010-G190**
Left: X. *Center:* "Signing of the Declaration of Independence" / Portrait of George Washington. *Bottom center:* 10. *Right:* TEN over X / Man leaning on capstan. *Engraver:* American Bank Note Co. *Comments:* H-RI-175-G50a, Durand-718. Jan. 10, 18__. 1865 and 1866.
Rarity: URS-3
VF $400

$20 • **W-RI-570-020-G200**
Left: 20 / Woman. *Center:* XX / Eagle / XX. *Right:* 20 / Ship. *Engraver:* New England Bank Note Co. *Comments:* H-RI-175-G56, Durand-725. 18__. 1840s–1850s.
Rarity: *None known*

$20 • **W-RI-570-020-G200a**
Overprint: Red XX / XX. *Engraver:* New England Bank Note Co. *Comments:* H-RI-175-G56a, Durand-726. Similar to W-RI-570-020-G200. 18__. 1850s.
Rarity: *None known*

$20 • **W-RI-570-020-G200b**
Overprint: Red XX / XX. *Engraver:* New England Bank Note Co. / ABNCo. monogram. *Comments:* H-RI-175-G56b. Similar to W-RI-570-020-G200 but with additional engraver imprint. 18__. 1860s.
Rarity: *None known*

$20 • **W-RI-570-020-G210**   CC

Engraver: American Bank Note Co. *Comments:* H-RI-175-G58a, Durand-727. Jan. 10th, 18__. 1865.
Rarity: URS-3
VF $2,500
Selected auction price: Stack's Bowers Galleries, January 2011, $1,896

$50 • **W-RI-570-050-G220**
Left: FIFTY / Woman standing with wreath and flowers / FIFTY. *Center:* 50 / Man holding horse / 50. *Right:* FIFTY / Woman standing with cornucopia / FIFTY. *Engraver:* New England Bank Note Co. *Comments:* H-RI-175-G62, Durand-729. 18__. 1840s–1860s.
Rarity: *None known*

$100 • **W-RI-570-100-G230**
Left: ONE HUNDRED across 100 / Portrait of William Henry Harrison. *Center:* Wharf scene, men loading wagon with barrels. *Right:* ONE HUNDRED across 100 / Portrait of Christopher Columbus. *Engraver:* New England Bank Note Co. *Comments:* H-RI-175-G66, Durand-730. 18__. 1840s–1860s.
Rarity: *None known*

Uncut Sheets

$1-$1-$2-$5 • **W-RI-570-001.001.002.005-US010**
Vignette(s): *($1)* Portrait of boy / Ship in stormy sea / Clasped hands. *($1)* Portrait of boy / Ship in stormy sea / Clasped hands. *($2)* Tall ships / Portrait of General Nathanael Greene / Clasped hands. *($5)* Indian seated with bow, Dog and horse / Hope and cherub raising drapery and revealing anchor / Bust. *Engraver:* Durand & Co. *Comments:* H-RI-175-G8, G8, G20, G36. 18__. 1850s.
Rarity: URS-3
VF $1,000

Non-Valid Issues

$1 • **W-RI-570-001-C010**
Engraver: P. Maverick. *Comments:* H-RI-175-C2, Durand-693. Counterfeit W-RI-570-001-G010. 18__. 1810s.
Rarity: *None known*

$2 • **W-RI-570-002-C050**
Engraver: P. Maverick. *Comments:* H-RI-175-C14, Durand-700. Counterfeit of W-RI-570-002-G050. 18__. 1815.
Rarity: URS-3
VF $200

$2 • W-RI-570-002-C060

Engraver: P. Maverick. *Comments:* H-RI-175-C16, Durand-701. Counterfeit of W-RI-570-002-G060. 18__. 1831.

Rarity: *None known*

$2 • W-RI-570-002-N010

Center: Two women and state arms / Village. *Comments:* H-Unlisted, Durand-702. Altered or spurious. 1840s–1850s.

Rarity: URS-3

$3 • W-RI-570-003-C090

SBG

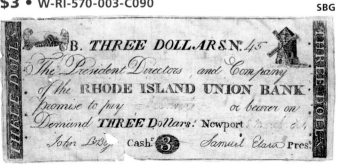

Comments: H-RI-175-C26. Counterfeit of W-RI-570-003-G090. 18__. 1800s.

Rarity: URS-3
VF $500

$3 • W-RI-570-003-A010

Left: 3 / Train / 3. *Center:* FIVE / Ship under sail / FIVE. *Right:* 3 / George Washington and his horse. *Engraver:* New England Bank Note Co. *Comments:* H-RI-175-A5, Durand-704. Altered from $5 Commercial Bank, Gratiot, Michigan. 18__. 1840s.

Rarity: URS-3
VF $200

$5 • W-RI-570-005-C120

Engraver: Durand & Co. *Comments:* H-RI-175-C36, Durand-710. Counterfeit of W-RI-570-005-G120. 18__. 1850s.

Rarity: *None known*

$5 • W-RI-570-005-S010

Left: FIVE vertically. *Center:* 5 / Animals / 5 / FIVE. *Bottom center:* Ship. *Right:* FIVE vertically. *Overprint:* Red FIVE. *Engraver:* Draper, Underwood, Bald & Spencer. *Comments:* H-RI-175-S5. From a modified plate originally for a fraudulent $5 of the non-existent Farmers Bank, Mount Holly, New Jersey. 18__. 1830s.

Rarity: URS-3
VF $200

$5 • W-RI-570-005-N020

Center: Ceres, Sheaf. *Comments:* H-RI-175-N5, Durand-714. 1830s–1850s.

Rarity: URS-3
F $250

$5 • W-RI-570-005-N030

Center: Ceres. *Comments:* H-RI-175-N10. 1840s–1850s.

Rarity: *None known*

$5 • W-RI-570-005-N040

Center: Drover on horseback with cattle. *Bottom center:* Steamboat. *Comments:* H-Unlisted, Durand-713. Altered or spurious. 1840s–1850s.

Rarity: URS-3

$5 • W-RI-570-005-A020

Left: 5 / Train / 5. *Center:* FIVE / Ship under sail / FIVE. *Right:* 5 / George Washington and his horse. *Engraver:* New England Bank Note Co. *Comments:* H-RI-175-A10, Durand-711. Altered from $5 Commercial Bank, Gratiot, Michigan. 18__. 1840s.

Rarity: *None known*

$5 • W-RI-570-005-A030

Left: Indian. *Center:* Railroad, Train. *Bottom center:* Indian in canoe. *Right:* Minerva standing with spear and shield. *Comments:* H-RI-175-A15, Durand-712. Altered from $5 Bank of Lower Canada, Quebec, Canada. 18__. 1830s.

Rarity: *None known*

$10 • W-RI-570-010-C160

Comments: H-RI-175-C44. No description available. Counterfeit of W-RI-570-010-G160. 18__. 1844.

Rarity: *None known*

$10 • W-RI-570-010-C180a

Engraver: New England Bank Note Co. / ABNCo. monogram. *Comments:* H-RI-175-C48b, Durand-719. Counterfeit of W-RI-570-010-G180a. 18__. 1860s.

Rarity: *None known*

$10 • W-RI-570-010-R010

Engraver: American Bank Note Co. *Comments:* H-RI-175-R10, Durand-720. Raised from W-RI-570-001-G040. Jan. 10, 18__. 1865.

Rarity: URS-3
VF $200

$10 • W-RI-570-010-R020

Engraver: American Bank Note Co. *Comments:* H-RI-175-R15, Durand-721. Raised from W-RI-570-005-G130. Jan. 10, 18__. 1860s.

Rarity: *None known*

$10 • W-RI-570-010-R030

Comments: H-Unlisted, Durand-722. Raised from W-RI-570-005-G130. Jan.y 10th, 18__. 1865.

Rarity: URS-3

$10 • W-RI-570-010-R040

ANS

Engraver: P. Maverick. *Comments:* H-Unlisted, Durand-Unlisted. Raised from $1. 180_. 1800s.

Rarity: URS-3
VF $200

$10 • W-RI-570-010-A040

SI

Overprint: Red TEN. **Comments:** H-Unlisted, Durand-724. 186_. 1860s.

Rarity: URS-3
VF $100

$10 • W-RI-570-010-A050

CC

Engraver: New England Bank Note Co. **Comments:** H-RI-175-A20, Durand-723. Altered from $10 Commercial Bank, Gratiot, Michigan. 18__. 1842.

Rarity: URS-3
VF $150

$20 • W-RI-570-020-R050

Engraver: Durand & Co. **Comments:** H-RI-175-R5, Durand-728. Raised from W-RI-570-001-G030. 18__. 1850s.

Rarity: *None known*

Traders Bank
1836–1865
W-RI-580

History: The Traders Bank was incorporated in 1836. Borden Wood served as its first president, and R.B. Cranston was the founding cashier. The capital was $60,000 in 1848. This value was increased to $110,000 in 1857 and to $116,960 in 1860. Circulation ranged from $38,017.50 in 1849 to $53,173 in 1863.

    The interests of the Traders Bank were succeeded by the First National Bank of Newport on May 1, 1865.

Numismatic Commentary: Genuine notes from this bank are very hard to locate. Few have surfaced, to date. Many non-valid issues are still available in the marketplace.

VALID ISSUES

$1 • W-RI-580-001-G010

Left: 1 / Woman wearing bonnet, standing by pail. **Center:** Machinery and merchandise flanking Ceres holding sickle and rake, Factories and harbor / ONE / Panel outlining white ONE. **Right:** 1 / Ship / ONE. **Engraver:** PSSP / New England Bank Note Co. **Comments:** H-RI-180-G2. 18__. 1830s–1840s.

Rarity: *None known*

$1 • W-RI-580-001-G020

Left: 1 / Cherub and flowers / 1. **Center:** Train / Agricultural implements / City. **Right:** ONE / Farmer with axe and sickle / ONE. **Comments:** H-RI-180-G4, Durand-731. 18__. 1840s.

Rarity: *None known*

$1 • W-RI-580-001-G030

Left: Commerce seated with lyre, leaning on barrel / 1. **Center:** 1 bearing "Signing of the Declaration of Independence". **Right:** 1 / Ceres with elbow on fence, apron full of grain / 1. **Overprint:** Red ONE. **Engraver:** New England Bank Note Co. **Comments:** H-RI-180-G8a, Durand-732. 18__. 1850s–1860s.

Rarity: *None known*

$1.25 • W-RI-580-001.25-G040

Left: 1 25/100 / Train / 1 25/100. **Center:** Sloop and other vessels at sea / $1.25 Cts. **Right:** 1 25/100 / Eagle. **Engraver:** New England Bank Note Co. **Comments:** H-RI-180-G10. 18__. 1830s.

Rarity: *None known*

$1.50 • W-RI-580-001.50-G050

Left: 1 Doll. 50 Cts. vertically. **Center:** Eagle on rock in ocean / $1 50/100. **Right:** 1 50/100 / Justice. **Engraver:** New England Bank Note Co. **Comments:** H-RI-180-G11. 18__. 1830s.

Rarity: *None known*

$1.75 • W-RI-580-001.75-G060

Left: $1.75 Cts / Hebe watering eagle / 1 75/100. **Center:** Three sloops at sea **Right:** $1.75 Cts / Woman seated with grain, Dog / 1 75/100. **Engraver:** New England Bank Note Co. **Comments:** H-RI-180-G12. 18__. 1830s.

Rarity: *None known*

$2 • W-RI-580-002-G070

Left: 2 / Woman standing with staff, Cornucopia / TWO. **Center:** TWO / Machinery and merchandise flanking Ceres holding sickle and rake, Factories and harbor / Panel outlining white TWO. **Right:** 2 / Woman wearing hat, Trees / TWO. **Engraver:** PSSP / New England Bank Note Co. **Comments:** H-RI-180-G14, Durand-734. 18__. 1830s–1840s.

Rarity: *None known*

$2 • W-RI-580-002-G080

Left: 2 / TWO / 2. **Center:** Ships at sea / 2. **Right:** TWO / Woman at well / TWO. **Comments:** H-RI-180-G16, Durand-734. 18__. 1840s.

Rarity: *None known*

$2 • W-RI-580-002-G090

Left: Horse running / 2. **Center:** 1 bearing "Signing of the Declaration of Independence". **Right:** TWO / Woman / TWO. **Overprint:** Red TWO. **Engraver:** New England Bank Note Co. **Comments:** H-RI-180-G20a, Durand-735. 18__. 1850s–1860s.

Rarity: URS-3
VF $300

$3 • **W-RI-580-003-G100**

Left: THREE / Beehive / THREE. *Center:* Machinery and merchandise flanking Ceres holding sickle and rake, Factories and harbor / Panel outlining white THREE. *Right:* THREE on 3 / Two reapers / THREE on 3. *Engraver:* PSSP / New England Bank Note Co. *Comments:* H-RI-180-G22, Durand-738. 18__. 1830s–1840s. **Rarity:** *None known*

$3 • **W-RI-580-003-G110**

Left: 3 / Medallion head / 3. *Center:* Ceres seated, Farmer plowing. *Right:* 3 / Venus bathing. *Comments:* H-RI-180-G24, Durand-739. 18__. 1840s. **Rarity:** *None known*

$5 • **W-RI-580-005-G120**

Left: 5 / Blacksmith at anvil / FIVE. *Center:* Mercury standing with 5, Cornucopia and merchandise, Factories and ship / V / Panel outlining white FIVE. *Right:* 5 / Ceres kneeling / FIVE. *Engraver:* PSSP / New England Bank Note Co. *Comments:* H-RI-180-G28. 18__. 1830s. **Rarity:** *None known*

$5 • **W-RI-580-005-G130**

Left: FIVE vertically. *Center:* Woman unveiling shield bearing 5 / V. *Right:* 5 / Sailing ship. *Engraver:* New England Bank Note Co. *Comments:* H-RI-180-G32, Durand-740. 18__. 1840s. **Rarity:** *None known*

$5 • **W-RI-580-005-G140**

Left: FIVE across V. *Center:* Ceres seated, Town and harbor / Indian woman seated in V. *Right:* 5 / Portrait of George Washington. *Overprint:* Red FIVE. *Engraver:* New England Bank Note Co. *Comments:* H-RI-180-G36, Durand-741. 18__. 1850s. **Rarity:** *None known*

$10 • **W-RI-580-010-G150**

Left: X / Indian with bow. *Center:* Steamboat, schooner, boats, and city / X. *Right:* 10 / Woman with sheaf. *Engraver:* New England Bank Note Co. *Comments:* H-RI-180-G40, Durand-749. Beware of altered notes of same design. 18__. 1830s–1850s. **Rarity:** *None known*

$10 • **W-RI-580-010-G160**

Left: 10 / X / 10. *Center:* Farmer with plow and oxen / 10. *Right:* 10 / Ceres. *Engraver:* New England Bank Note Co. *Comments:* H-RI-180-G44, Durand-748. 18__. 1850s. **Rarity:** *None known*

$10 • **W-RI-580-010-G170**

Left: 10 / Female portrait / TEN. *Center:* Allegorical woman between 1 and 0. *Right:* 10 / Female portrait / TEN. *Engraver:* Rawdon, Wright, Hatch & Edson. *Comments:* H-RI-180-G48, Durand-750. 18__. 1860s. **Rarity:** *None known*

$20 • **W-RI-580-020-G180**

Left: 20 / XX vertically / 20. *Center:* 20 / Woman seated with scales, Sheaf and bales, Men plowing and ship / 20. *Right:* TWENTY vertically. *Engraver:* PSSP / New England Bank Note Co. *Comments:* H-RI-180-G52, Durand-754. 18__. 1830s. **Rarity:** *None known*

$20 • **W-RI-580-020-G190**

Left: 20 / Woman. *Center:* XX / Eagle / XX. *Right:* 20 / Ship. *Engraver:* New England Bank Note Co. *Comments:* H-RI-180-G56, Durand-753. 18__. 1840s–1850s. **Rarity:** *None known*

$50 • **W-RI-580-050-G200**

Left: 50 / Woman standing with ankles crossed, Staff, Cornucopia and anchor. *Center:* FIFTY DOLLARS / 50. *Right:* FIFTY vertically. *Engraver:* PSSP / New England Bank Note Co. *Comments:* H-RI-180-G60, Durand-756. 18__. 1830s. **Rarity:** *None known*

$50 • **W-RI-580-050-G210**

Left: FIFTY / Woman standing with wreath and flowers / FIFTY. *Center:* 50 / Man holding horse / 50. *Right:* FIFTY / Woman standing with cornucopia / FIFTY. *Engraver:* New England Bank Note Co. *Comments:* H-RI-180-G64, Durand-755. 18__. 1840s–1850s. **Rarity:** *None known*

$100 • **W-RI-580-100-G220**

Left: Lathework panel with C / Portrait of George Washington / C. *Center:* 100 / Manhattan reclining pouring water, Ship / 100. *Right:* Lathework panel with ONE HUNDRED vertically. *Engraver:* PSSP / New England Bank Note Co. *Comments:* H-RI-180-G68, Durand-757. 18__. 1830s **Rarity:** *None known*

$100 • **W-RI-580-100-G230**

Left: ONE HUNDRED across 100 / Portrait of William Henry Harrison. *Center:* Wharf scene. *Right:* ONE HUNDRED across 100 / Portrait of Christopher Columbus. *Engraver:* New England Bank Note Co. *Comments:* H-RI-180-G72, Durand-757. 18__. 1840s–1850s. **Rarity:** *None known*

NON-VALID ISSUES

$1 • **W-RI-580-001-A010**

Left: Woman with flowers / ONE across 1. *Center:* Reaper seated beside grain cradle, Harvesting scene. *Right:* ONE / Indian overlooking city / ONE. *Overprint:* Red ONE. *Engraver:* New England Bank Note Co. / Rawdon, Wright, Hatch & Edson. *Comments:* H-RI-180-A5, Durand-733. Altered from $1 Waubeek Bank, DeSoto, Nebraska. 1857. **Rarity:** URS-3 **VF** $200

$2 • **W-RI-580-002-A020**

Left: 2 / Reverses of U.S. silver dollar and Spanish silver dollar. *Center:* Farmer and woman by well. *Right:* 2 / Allegorical woman with hand on 2. *Overprint:* Red TWO. *Engraver:* Wellstood, Hay & Whiting. *Comments:* H-RI-180-A10, Durand-736. Altered from $2 Thames Bank, Laurel, Indiana. 1850s. **Rarity:** *None known*

$2 • **W-RI-580-002-A030**

Left: Two girls carrying sheaves / 2. *Center:* Sailor, Shield surmounted by badger, Mechanic. *Right:* 2 / Allegorical woman and Indian. *Overprint:* Red TWO. *Engraver:* New England Bank Note Co. / Rawdon, Wright, Hatch & Edson. *Comments:* H-RI-180-A15, Durand-737. Altered from $2 Waubeek Bank, Desoto, Nebraska. 1857. **Rarity:** *None known*

$5 • **W-RI-580-005-N010**

Center: Country scene, Man, mill. *Comments:* H-RI-180-N8, Durand-747. 1830s–1840s.

Rarity: *None known*

$5 • **W-RI-580-005-N020**

Center: Portrait of Benjamin Franklin / Canal lock, two horses, man sitting with girl standing. *Comments:* H-Unlisted, Durand-746. Altered or spurious. 1830s–1840s.

Rarity: URS-3

$5 • **W-RI-580-005-A040**

Center: Eagle, ship, and city. *Engraver:* New England Bank Note Co. *Comments:* H-RI-180-N5. Likely altered from W-RI-1300-005-G070, or from notes of other failed banks using the same plate. 1830s–1840s.

Rarity: *None known*

$5 • **W-RI-580-005-A050**

Left: Male portrait / V. *Center:* Man feeding pigs, Dog. *Right:* 5 / Man carrying basket of corn. *Overprint:* Red FIVE. *Engraver:* Wellstood, Hay & Whiting. *Comments:* H-RI-180-A20, Durand-744. Altered from $5 Thames Bank, Laurel, Indian. Jan. 12, 185_. 1853.

Rarity: URS-3
VF $200

$5 • **W-RI-580-005-A060**

SI

Engraver: Terry, Pelton & Co. *Comments:* H-RI-180-A25, Durand-745. Altered from $5 Citizens Bank, Augusta, Maine, or from notes of other failed banks using the same plate. 18__. 1840s.

Rarity: URS-3
VF $250

$5 • **W-RI-580-005-A070**

Left: 5 / Portrait of Henry Clay. *Center:* Steamboat. *Right:* 5 / Portrait of George Washington. *Overprint:* Red FIVE. *Engraver:* New England Bank Note Co. / Rawdon, Wright, Hatch & Edson. *Comments:* H-RI-180-A30, Durand-742. Altered from $5 Waubeek Bank, De Soto, Nebraska. 1857.

Rarity: URS-3
VF $250

$5 • **W-RI-580-005-A080**

Left: 5 / FIVE / 5. *Center:* V / Spread eagle, Ships and city / V. *Right:* 5 / FIVE / 5. *Comments:* H-Unlisted, Durand-743. Altered from W-RI-1300-005-G070. 1830s–1840s.

Rarity: URS-3

$10 • **W-RI-580-010-C170**

Engraver: Rawdon, Wright, Hatch & Edson. *Comments:* H-RI-180-C48, Durand-751. Counterfeit of W-RI-580-010-G170. 18__. 1860s.

Rarity: *None known*

$10 • **W-RI-580-010-A090**

Left: 10 / Liberty with shield and eagle. *Center:* Industry. *Right:* X on shield / Portrait of George Washington. *Comments:* H-Unlisted, Durand-752. Altered from W-RI-1300-010-G080. 1830s–1840s.

Rarity: URS-3

$10 • **W-RI-580-010-A100**

Engraver: New England Bank Note Co. *Comments:* H-RI-180-A35, Durand-749. Altered from W-RI-1300-010-G080, or from notes of other failed banks using the same plate. 18__. 1856.

Rarity: URS-3
VF $200

$20 • **W-RI-580-020-A110**

Left: Steamship / XX / Coaches. *Center:* Eagle / Three allegorical figures / 20. *Right:* XX / Woman standing. *Comments:* H-Unlisted, Durand-754. Altered from W-RI-1300-020-G090. 1830s–1840s.

Rarity: URS-3

$20 • **W-RI-580-020-A120**

Left: 20 / XX vertically / 20. *Center:* 20 / Woman seated with scales, Sheaf and bales, Men plowing, Ship / 20. *Right:* TWENTY vertically. *Engraver:* New England Bank Note Co. *Comments:* H-RI-180-A38. Altered from W-RI-1300-020-G090, or from notes of other failed banks using the same plate. 18__. 1830s–1840s.

Rarity: *None known*

$50 • **W-RI-580-050-A130**

Left: 50 / Liberty standing by shield bearing anchor, Fruit / 50. *Center:* L / Hebe watering eagle / L. *Bottom center:* Anchor and implements. *Right:* 50 / Farmer with sheaf / 50. *Engraver:* Terry, Pelton & Co. *Comments:* H-RI-180-A40, Durand-756. Altered from $50 Citizens Bank, Augusta, Maine, or from notes of other failed banks using the same plate. 18__. 1840s.

Rarity: *None known*

How to Read the Whitman Numbering System

$1 • **W-RI-010-001-G010a**

Denomination: Value of the note shown.

W: Whitman number. This number is a sortable code unique to each bank and note.

RI: Abbreviation for the state under study.

010: Numerical designation specific to each bank.

001: The denomination in dollars.

G010a: G indicates a good or valid note. Other categories are indicated thus: C (counterfeit); R (raised); S (spurious); N (not-attributed); A (altered). Numbers are assigned starting with 010, 020, et seq. Terminal letters following the number indicate variations of a note: a series of different colored overprints, tints, payees, etc., all on the same design of note. For more information, see the "How to Use This Book" section at the front of the volume, page xiv.

NORTH KINGSTOWN, RHODE ISLAND

Kings Towne was founded in 1674 on land that included what would later become North Kingstown (also spelled Kingston), South Kingstown, Exeter, and Narragansett. In 1722 it split into the North and South regions, and in 1742 the town of Exeter separated from North Kingstown.

During the 18th century, North Kingstown was primarily agricultural in nature, although shipbuilding and fishing also took place to a significant extent. In the early 19th century, during the Industrial Revolution, several mills and mill villages were established. Villages in North Kingstown included Wickford, Wickford Landing, Wickford Junction, West Wickford, South Wickford, Lafayette, East Lafayette, Davisville, Bellville, Slocumville, Annaquatucket, Oak Hill, Sandy Hill Mills, Peirce's Mills, Narragansett, Shady Lea, Silver Spring, Allenton, Hamilton, Scrabbletown, Saundrestown, Shermantown, and Swamptown—a lengthy roster.

See also Kingston, South Kingston, South Kingstown, and Wickford, Rhode Island.

Note that these towns have slightly different spellings.

Narragansett Bank
1805–1865
W-RI-590

History: The Narragansett Bank was chartered and incorporated in 1805 with $60,000 in authorized capital. The same had dropped to $50,000 by 1850. The bank had a circulation of $27,647 in 1849, which was reduced to $17,704 by 1857 and increased to $32,354 in 1863. Specie amounted to $2,076.75 in 1857.

In 1865 the bank's charter was surrendered, and its capital was combined with that of the North Kingston Bank, W-RI-600. The combination was succeeded by the Wickford National Bank, chartered October 17, 1865.[32]

See also listing under Wickford, W-RI-1640.

North Kingston Bank
1819–1865
W-RI-600

History: The North Kingston Bank was chartered in 1818 as the South Kingston Bank, W-RI-1430, at a location called Little Rest, the present location of the South Kingstown village of Kingston. After holding a few meetings and being unable to induce investors to purchase its stock for the raising of capital, the location was abandoned. The charter was amended in 1819, the name was changed to the North Kingston Bank, and the location was moved to the North Kingstown village of Wickford. The North Kingston Bank had $75,000 in capital in 1849 along with $42,605 of bills in circulation. Specie totaled $2,043.22 in 1857.

The founding president was Daniel Champlin, with Pardon T. Hammond as cashier. Later, Lieutenant Governor John J.

Reynolds, born in North Kingstown on December 7, 1812, became a director at the age of 24. He then became president in 1851 upon the death of his father. He remained president until the bank became a National bank in 1865.[33]

The assets of the North Kingston Bank were combined with the Narragansett Bank, W-RI-590, to form the Wickford National Bank, chartered on October 17, 1865.

See also listing under Wickford, W-RI-1650.

Numismatic Commentary: Genuine notes are very hard to locate, but non-valid issues present themselves in the marketplace fairly frequently.

The Farmers Bank of Wickford failed in 1857, and its entire issue of notes was altered to fraudulently represent this bank.

North Kingstown Exchange Bank
1847 AND 1848
W-RI-610

History: The North Kingstown Exchange Bank was incorporated in 1847; its charter was repealed before the bank opened for business. Apparently, the organizers were well-prepared for its eventual opening, as plates had been ordered for bank notes in anticipation, and a full complement of denominations had been planned. At least one set of Proof notes was printed for inspection by the bank's officers.[34]

Numismatic Commentary: Remaining in the American Bank Note Co. archives as of 2003 was a $10-$20-$50-$100 face plate and a $1-$2-$3-$5 face plate. All notes of this bank were engraved by Rawdon, Wright, Hatch & Edson.

VALID ISSUES

$1 • W-RI-610-001-G010
Left: ONE / Woman holding flowers being carried on the shoulders of two men / ONE. *Center:* Cherub on 1 / Ceres holding 1 / Cherub on 1. *Bottom center:* Anchor on shield. *Right:* ONE / Justice holding scales overhead / ONE. *Comments:* H-RI-185-G2, Durand-758. 18__. 1840s.
> **Rarity:** URS-3
> **Proof** $500

$2 • W-RI-610-002-G020
Left: 2 / Female portrait. *Center:* Cherub on 2 / Ceres holding grain, Plow and sheaf, Train crossing bridge / Cherub on 2. *Bottom center:* Man seated on plow. *Right:* TWO. *Comments:* H-RI-185-G4, Durand-759. 18__. 1840s.
> **Rarity:** URS-3
> **Proof** $500

$3 • W-RI-610-003-G030
Left: THREE / Female portrait / THREE. *Center:* Allegorical woman holding pen with scroll and globe. *Bottom center:* Cornucopia. *Right:* 3 / Sailor standing. *Comments:* H-RI-185-G6, Durand-760. 18__. 1840s.
> **Rarity:** URS-3
> **Proof** $500

$5 • W-RI-610-005-G040

Left: 5 / Female portrait / FIVE. *Center:* Liberty standing next to shield bearing 5 / Eagle. *Bottom center:* V bearing cherub. *Right:* 5 / Justice and Minerva with 5 and cornucopia of coins. *Comments:* H-RI-185-G8, Durand-761. 18__. 1840s.

Rarity: URS-3
Proof $500

$10 • W-RI-610-010-G050

Left: Deer / 10 / Bison. *Center:* 1, Allegorical woman with cornucopia and key, 0. *Bottom center:* Sheaf and plow. *Right:* 10 / Milkmaid churning. *Comments:* H-RI-185-G10, Durand-762. 18__. 1840s.

Rarity: URS-3
Proof $500

$20 • W-RI-610-020-G060

Left: TWENTY / Minerva with spear. *Center:* 20 / 2, Allegorical woman holding rake, 0. *Bottom center:* Sheaf and plow. *Right:* 20. *Comments:* H-RI-185-G12, Durand-763. 18__. 1840s.

Rarity: URS-3
Proof $500

$50 • W-RI-610-050-G070

Left: 50 / Vulcan seated with scroll and sledge. *Center:* Liberty with eagle and shield, City. *Bottom center:* Strongbox and dog with key. *Right:* 50 / Allegorical woman with rake and produce. *Comments:* H-RI-185-G14, Durand-764. 18__. 1840s.

Rarity: URS-3
Proof $500

$100 • W-RI-610-100-G080

Left: 100 / Allegorical woman with produce and flowers. *Center:* Portrait of George Washington flanked by coats of arms, flags, drums. *Bottom center:* Ceres seated. *Right:* 100 / Spread eagle on American shield. *Comments:* H-RI-185-G16, Durand-765. 18__. 1840s.

Rarity: URS-3
Proof $600

Uncut Sheets

$1-$2-$3-$5 • W-RI-610-001.002.003.005-US010

Vignette(s): *($1)* Woman holding flowers being carried on the shoulders of two men / Cherub on 1 / Ceres holding 1 / Cherub on 1 / Anchor on shield / Justice holding scales overhead. *($2)* Female portrait / Cherub on 2 / Ceres holding grain, Plow and sheaf, Train crossing bridge / Cherub on 2 / Man seated on plow. *($3)* Female portrait / Allegorical woman holding pen with scroll and globe / Cornucopia / Sailor standing. *($5)* Female portrait / Liberty standing next to shield bearing 5 / Eagle / V bearing cherub / Justice and Minerva with 5 and cornucopia of coins. *Engraver:* Rawdon, Wright, Hatch & Edson. *Comments:* H-RI-185-G2, G4, G6, G8. 18__. 1840s.

Rarity: URS-3
Proof $2,500

$10-$20-$50-$100 •

W-RI-610-010.020.050.100-US020

Vignette(s): *($10)* Deer / Bison / Allegorical woman with cornucopia and key / Sheaf and plow / Milkmaid churning. *($20)* Minerva with spear / Allegorical woman holding rake / Sheaf and plow. *($50)* Vulcan seated with scroll and sledge / Liberty with eagle and shield, City / Strongbox and dog with key / Allegorical woman with rake and produce. *($100)* Allegorical woman with produce and flowers / Portrait of George Washington flanked by coats of arms, flags, drums / Ceres seated / Spread eagle on American shield. *Engraver:* Rawdon, Wright, Hatch & Edson. *Comments:* H-RI-185-G10, G12, G14, G16. 18__. 1840s.

Rarity: URS-3
Proof $2,500

NORTH PROVIDENCE, RHODE ISLAND

Providence was established as a territory in 1636 under the name Providence Plantation. By 1730 the town had divided and Smithfield, Scituate, and Gloucester were incorporated as their own towns. Cranston was annexed in 1754, followed by Johnston in 1759. In 1765 North Providence split and was incorporated as its own town. Throughout the next century, parts of the area were parceled back to Providence, and in 1874 the eastern section of North Providence was combined with its village of Pawtucket.

See also Pawtucket and Providence, Rhode Island.

Manufacturers Bank
1813–1865
W-RI-620

History: The Manufacturers Bank was incorporated in the village of Pawtucket in the town of North Providence in October 1813. It was chartered in 1814. Samuel Slater, a manufacturing pioneer and credited as being the father of the American Industrial Revolution for establishing British textile technology in the United States, was one of the 13 members of the board of directors. He served as president from 1819 until 1831, when he retired due to ill health.[35]

A slowdown of business in Pawtucket in 1829 caused significant losses to the bank. This convinced the management to remove the bank to Providence in June 1831. In 1850 capital was $453,100, and by 1851 it had risen to $500,000. Circulation that year was $67,273.

The interests of the bank were succeeded by the Manufacturers National Bank, chartered on June 16, 1865.

See also listings under Pawtucket, W-RI-720, and Providence, W-RI-1030.

Numismatic Commentary: Genuine notes are hard to locate. Some examples seen show various textile machinery. Occasionally a counterfeit $3 note showing a primitive loom becomes available, a nice reminder of the early textile industry in New England.

VALID ISSUES

$1 • W-RI-620-001-G010
Engraver: Unverified, but likely Murray, Draper, Fairman &
Co. *Comments:* H-RI-190-G2, Durand-1503. No description
available. 18__. 1810s–1820s.

Rarity: *None known*

$2 • W-RI-620-002-G020
Engraver: Unverified, but likely Murray, Draper, Fairman &
Co. *Comments:* H-RI-190-G8, Durand-1504. No description
available. 18__. 1810s–1820s.

Rarity: *None known*

$3 • W-RI-620-003-G030
Left: THREE vertically. *Center:* 3 / Man working loom / 3.
Right: RHODE ISLAND vertically. *Engraver:* Murray, Draper,
Fairman & Co. *Comments:* H-RI-190-G10, Durand-1505. 181_.
1810s–1820s.

Rarity: *None known*

$5 • W-RI-620-005-G040   SBG

Engraver: Murray, Draper, Fairman & Co. *Comments:* H-RI-
190-G12, Durand-1507. Proof. 181_. 1810s–1820s.

Rarity: URS-3
Proof $3,000
Selected auction price: Stack's Bowers Galleries,
March 2013, Proof $2,900

NON-VALID ISSUES

$3 • W-RI-620-003-C030   CJF

Engraver: Murray, Draper, Fairman & Co. *Comments:* H-RI-
190-C10, Durand-1506. Counterfeit of W-RI-620-003-G030.
18__. 1824–1829.

Rarity: URS-6
VF $350

New England Pacific Bank
1818–1865
W-RI-630

History: The New England Pacific Bank was incorporated in
October 1818. Capital was authorized at $50,000. The same
rose to $107,200 by 1850. In 1854 the bank applied for a further
increase in capital, and by 1862 it was $185,150. Circulation
was $74,669 in 1862.

The New England Pacific Bank was not legally organized,
and in 1820 it was sold to parties outside the state. The legislature passed amendments to its charter in 1826, and the bank had
a subsequent honorable career.[36]

Due to heavy losses, the bank was suffering in Smithfield,
and it opened an office of discount and deposit in Pawtucket.
After the move to Pawtucket, the notes were imprinted North
Providence as the village of Pawtucket was in the northern corner of North Providence.

The capital ranged from $105,550 in 1848 to $185,150 in
1862. Its circulation at its lowest was $33,178.75 and at its
highest $74,669. Specie was reported to be $2,457.31 in 1857.

The Pacific National Bank assumed the business of the New
England Pacific Bank after it was chartered on June 27, 1865.

See also listing under Smithfield, W-RI-1350.

Numismatic Commentary: Collectors should be able to locate
a genuine example or two in a reasonable amount of time. Some
of the non-valid issues are easier to find.

VALID ISSUES

$1 • W-RI-630-001-G010
Left: ONE vertically. *Center:* 1 bearing ONE / Farm scene / 1
bearing ONE. *Right:* 1 / Justice. *Engraver:* Rawdon, Wright,
Hatch & Edson. *Comments:* H-RI-455-G22, Durand-770. 18__.
1840s–1850s.

Rarity: *None known*

$1 • W-RI-630-001-G010a   CC

Overprint: Red ONE. *Engraver:* Rawdon, Wright, Hatch &
Edson. *Comments:* H-RI-455-G22a, Durand-771. Similar to
W-RI-630-001-G010. 18__. 1850s.

Rarity: URS-3
VF $900
Selected auction price: Heritage,
April–May 2011, Lot 15309, VF $805

$1 • W-RI-630-001-G020

Left: Commerce leaning on barrel, Train and boat. *Center:* 1 / "Signing of the Declaration of Independence". *Right:* 1 / Girl with sheaf. *Overprint:* Red ONE. *Engraver:* New England Bank Note Co. / ABNCo. monogram. *Comments:* H-RI-455-G24, Durand-772. 18__. 1860s.

Rarity: URS-3
VF $300

$1.25 • W-RI-630-001.25-G030

Left: 1 25/100 / Train / 1 25/100. *Center:* Sloop and other vessels at sea / $1.25 Cts. *Right:* 1 25/100 / Eagle. *Engraver:* New England Bank Note Co. *Comments:* H-RI-455-G26. 18__. 1830s.

Rarity: *None known*

$1.50 • W-RI-630-001.50-G040

Left: 1 Doll. 50 Cts. vertically. *Center:* Eagle on rock in ocean / $1 50/100. *Right:* 1 50/100 / Justice. *Engraver:* New England Bank Note Co. *Comments:* H-RI-455-G27. 18__. 1830s.

Rarity: *None known*

$1.75 • W-RI-630-001.75-G050

Left: $1.75 Cts. / Hebe watering eagle / 1 75/100. *Center:* Three sloops at sea. *Right:* $1.75 Cts / Dog, Woman seated with grain / 1 75/100. *Engraver:* New England Bank Note Co. *Comments:* H-RI-455-G28. 18__. 1830s.

Rarity: *None known*

$2 • W-RI-630-002-G060

Left: TWO vertically. *Center:* Steamboat, Agriculture and Manufacturing, Train. *Bottom center:* Anchor on shield. *Right:* 2 / Indian woman / 2. *Engraver:* Rawdon, Wright, Hatch & Edson. *Comments:* H-RI-455-G30, Durand-773. 18__. 1840s–1850s.

Rarity: *None known*

$2 • W-RI-630-002-G060a

Overprint: Red TWO. *Engraver:* Rawdon, Wright, Hatch & Edson. *Comments:* H-RI-455-G30a, Durand-774. Similar to W-RI-630-002-G060. 18__. 1850s.

Rarity: *None known*

$2 • W-RI-630-002-G070

Left: Men driving sheep into stream / 2. *Center:* 2 / "Signing of the Declaration of Independence". *Right:* TWO / Woman with wreath / TWO. *Overprint:* Red TWO. *Engraver:* New England Bank Note Co. / ABNCo. monogram. *Comments:* H-RI-455-G32, Durand-775. 18__. 1860s.

Rarity: *None known*

$3 • W-RI-630-003-G080

Left: THREE vertically. *Center:* THREE DOLLARS on 3 / Farmers and milkmaids / THREE DOLLARS on 3. *Bottom center:* Shield bearing anchor. *Right:* 3 / Portrait of girl / 3. *Engraver:* Rawdon, Wright, Hatch & Edson. *Comments:* H-RI-455-G38, Durand-777. 18__. 1840s–1850s.

Rarity: *None known*

$3 • W-RI-630-003-G080a

CC

Overprint: Red THREE. *Engraver:* Rawdon, Wright, Hatch & Edson. *Comments:* H-RI-455-G38a, Durand-778. Similar to W-RI-630-003-G080. 18__. 1850s.

Rarity: URS-3
VF $900

$3 • W-RI-630-003-G090

Left: Farmer and cattle, Load of hay / 3. *Center:* 3. *Right:* THREE and 3 / Woman with flowers / THREE. *Overprint:* Red THREE. *Engraver:* New England Bank Note Co. / ABNCo. monogram. *Comments:* H-RI-455-G40, Durand-779. 18__. 1860s.

Rarity: *None known*

$5 • W-RI-630-005-G100

Left: Spread eagle on shield / FIVE. *Center:* V / Allegorical figure and cherub. *Right:* 5 / Girl with basket of flowers. *Engraver:* New England Bank Note Co. *Comments:* H-RI-455-G44, Durand-781. Beware of altered notes of the same design as the genuine. 18__. 1850s.

Rarity: *None known*

$5 • W-RI-630-005-G110

Left: Woman seated with rake and shield, Ship / V on FIVE. *Center:* Woman seated in V / FIVE. *Right:* 5 / Portrait of George Washington. *Overprint:* Red FIVE. *Engraver:* New England Bank Note Co. / ABNCo. monogram. *Comments:* H-RI-455-G46, Durand-782. 18__. 1860s.

Rarity: URS-3
VF $350

$10 • W-RI-630-010-G120

Left: Vulcan seated / TEN. *Center:* X. *Right:* 10 / Reaper with sickle and sheaf. *Engraver:* New England Bank Note Co. *Comments:* H-RI-455-G50, Durand-785. 18__. 1850s.

Rarity: *None known*

$10 • W-RI-630-010-G130

Left: "Signing of the Declaration of Independence" / X. *Center:* X. *Right:* 10 / Train at station. *Overprint:* Red TEN. *Engraver:* New England Bank Note Co. / ABNCo. monogram. *Comments:* H-RI-455-G54, Durand-786. 18__. 1860s.

Rarity: URS-3
VF $500

$20 • W-RI-630-020-G140

Left: 20 / Minerva. *Center:* Agriculture standing between 2 and 0. *Right:* 20 / Ceres / 20. *Engraver:* Rawdon, Wright, Hatch & Edson. *Comments:* H-RI-455-G56, Durand-791. 18__. 1850s.

Rarity: *None known*

$20 • W-RI-630-020-G150

Left: Liberty and eagle / 20. *Center:* TWENTY across 20 / Female portrait. *Right:* 20 / Portrait of Benjamin Franklin. *Overprint:* Red TWENTY. *Engraver:* New England Bank Note Co. / ABNCo. monogram. *Comments:* H-RI-455-G58, Durand-792. 18__. 1860s.

Rarity: *None known*

$50 • W-RI-630-050-G160

Left: 50 / Minerva. *Center:* Ceres and Vulcan seated. *Right:* 50 / Cherub steering sailboat / 50. *Engraver:* Rawdon, Wright, Hatch & Edson. *Comments:* H-RI-455-G62, Durand-793. 18__. 1850s.

Rarity: *None known*

$50 • W-RI-630-050-G170

Left: FIFTY / Sheaves and fruit / 50. *Center:* 50 / Three allegorical women with eagle. *Right:* FIFTY across 50 / Vulcan. *Overprint:* Red FIFTY. *Engraver:* New England Bank Note Co. / ABNCo. monogram. *Comments:* H-RI-455-G64, Durand-794. 18__. 1860s.

Rarity: *None known*

$100 • W-RI-630-100-G180

Left: 100 / Vulcan seated. *Center:* Spread eagle on tree limb, Canal scene and train. *Right:* 100 / Ceres. *Overprint:* Red HUNDRED. *Comments:* H-Unlisted, Durand-795. 18__. 1860s.

Rarity: URS-3
VF $450

$100 • W-RI-630-100-G190

Left: C / Men and boats / 100. *Center:* Eagle on bale / 100. *Bottom center:* 100. *Right:* 100 / Ceres / 100. *Overprint:* Red HUNDRED. *Engraver:* Rawdon, Wright, Hatch & Edson. *Comments:* H-RI-455-G68, Durand-796. 18__. 1850s.

Rarity: *None known*

$500 • W-RI-630-500-G200

Left: Farm scene / 500. *Center:* 500 / D. *Right:* 500 vertically. *Engraver:* Rawdon, Wright, Hatch & Edson. *Comments:* H-RI-455-G74, Durand-797. 18__. 1850s.

Rarity: *None known*

Non-Valid Issues

$2 • W-RI-630-002-A010

Left: Ceres standing / 2. *Center:* 2 / Moneta seated, open book on lap, opening chest / 2. *Bottom center:* State arms. *Right:* Fortuna standing / 2. *Engraver:* Draper, Toppan, Longacre & Co. *Comments:* H-RI-455-A2, Durand-776. Altered from $2 Calhoun County Bank, Marshall, Michigan. 18__. 1850s.

Rarity: *None known*

$3 • W-RI-630-003-A020

Left: 3 / Steamboat. *Center:* Justice / Shield surmounted by eagle / Liberty. *Right:* 3 / Train of cars. *Overprint:* Red THREE. *Engraver:* Baldwin, Bald & Cousland / Bald, Cousland & Co. *Comments:* H-RI-455-A5, Durand-780. Altered from W-RI-1500-003-G030a. 18__. 1850s.

Rarity: *None known*

$5 • W-RI-630-005-R010

Engraver: Rawdon, Wright, Hatch & Edson. *Comments:* H-RI-455-R10, Durand-783. Raised from W-RI-630-001-G010. 18__. 1850s.

Rarity: *None known*

$5 • W-RI-630-005-A030   CC

Engraver: New England Bank Note Co. *Comments:* H-RI-455-A10, Durand-784. Genuine notes of this design were issued. 18__. 1850s.

Rarity: URS-3
VF $300

$10 • W-RI-630-010-S010

Left: Farmer with sheaf of grain / TEN. *Center:* Vulcan seated at forge. *Right:* X / 10. *Engraver:* Rawdon, Wright, Hatch & Edson. *Comments:* H-RI-455-S5, Durand-788. May 1st, 1862.

Rarity: URS-3
VF $200

$10 • W-RI-630-010-S010a   CC

Tint: Green outlining TEN. *Engraver:* Rawdon, Wright, Hatch & Edson. *Comments:* H-RI-455-S5a, Durand-789. Similar to W-RI-630-010-S010. May 1st, 1862.

Rarity: URS-3
VF $350

$10 • W-RI-630-010-S010b

Tint: Orange outlining TEN and X X. *Engraver:* Rawdon, Wright, Hatch & Edson. *Comments:* H-RI-455-S5b, Durand-790. Similar to W-RI-630-010-S010. May 1st, 1862.

Rarity: URS-3
VF $250

$10 • W-RI-630-010-A040   CC

Overprint: Red X, X. *Comments:* H-RI-455-A15, Durand-787. Altered from W-RI-1630-010-G050. 18__. 1850s.

Rarity: URS-3
VF $300

North Providence Bank
1834–1867
W-RI-640

History: The North Providence Bank was incorporated at the North Providence village of Pawtucket on October 31, 1834. However, the notes from this bank have the North Providence address, despite the fact that the *Rhode Island Register* reported the bank's location as being in Pawtucket.

The bank's first president and cashier were Urian Benedict and D. Wilkinson, respectively. The bank suspended specie payment in 1840. Capital was $81,250 in 1848 and $135,000 in 1856. Circulation amounted to $25,327 in 1849, rising up to $32,928 in 1862. Specie was reported to be $4,193.20 in 1857.

The bank failed in 1867.

Numismatic Commentary: The standout note from this bank is the $5 issue bearing a vignette showing the "Battle of Lake Erie." Notes with historical vignettes are always popular, and with this bank both the genuine and counterfeit are available to the collector.

VALID ISSUES

$1 • W-RI-640-001-G010
Left: ONE / Woman standing next to fountain / ONE. *Center:* Indian man raising tomahawk, Dog and slain deer / Portrait of girl. *Right:* ONE / Woman holding eagle / ONE. *Engraver:* Terry, Pelton & Co. *Comments:* H-RI-195-G2, Durand-798. First issue. 18__. 1830s–1840s.
Rarity: URS-3
Proof $500

$1 • W-RI-640-001-G010a

Engraver: Terry, Pelton & Co. *Comments:* H-RI-195-G4, Durand-799. Similar to W-RI-640-001-G010 but with different date. Second issue. 18__. 1840s–1850s.
Rarity: URS-3
VF $800; **Proof** $1,000

$1 • W-RI-640-001-G010b
Overprint: Red ONE. *Engraver:* Terry, Pelton & Co. / ABNCo. monogram. *Comments:* H-RI-195-G4a, Durand-800. Similar to W-RI-640-001-G010 but with additional engraver imprint. 18__. 1850s–1860s.
Rarity: URS-3
VF $400

$2 • W-RI-640-002-G020
Left: Men. *Center:* Eagle. *Right:* Ceres. *Comments:* H-Unlisted, Durand-802. 1830s–1840s.
Rarity: URS-3

$2 • W-RI-640-002-G030

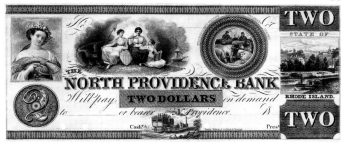

Engraver: Terry, Pelton & Co. *Comments:* H-RI-195-G6, Durand-803. 18__. 1830s–1840s.
Rarity: URS-3
Proof $1,200
Selected auction price: Stack's Bowers Galleries, November 2008, Proof $1,126

$2 • W-RI-640-002-G030a

Overprint: Red TWO. *Engraver:* Terry, Pelton & Co. *Comments:* H-Unlisted, Durand-Unlisted. Similar to W-RI-640-002-G030. 18__. 1860s.
Rarity: URS-3
F $600; **VF** $750

$2 • W-RI-640-002-G040
Center: 2 / Liberty, Justice, and Knowledge / Two men buying cattle. *Engraver:* Terry, Pelton & Co. *Comments:* H-RI-195-G8. 18__. 1840s–1850s.
Rarity: URS-3
Proof $750

$2 • W-RI-640-002-G040a
Overprint: Red TWO. *Engraver:* Terry, Pelton & Co. / ABNCo. monogram. *Comments:* H-RI-195-G8a, Durand-804. Similar to W-RI-640-002-G040 but with additional engraver imprint. 18__. 1850s–1860s.
Rarity: *None known*

$5 • W-RI-640-005-G050
Left: 5 / Blacksmith at anvil / FIVE. *Center:* Mercury standing with 5, Cornucopia and merchandise, Factories and ship / V / Panel outlining white FIVE. *Right:* 5 / Ceres kneeling / FIVE. *Engraver:* PSSP / New England Bank Note Co. *Comments:* H-RI-195-G10. 18__. 1830s.
Rarity: *None known*

$5 • W-RI-640-005-G060
Left: FIVE vertically. *Center:* 5 / "Battle of Lake Erie" / Portrait of girl. *Bottom center:* Beaver. *Right:* 5 / Waterfall next to building / 5. *Engraver:* Terry, Pelton & Co. *Comments:* H-RI-195-G12, Durand-807. This note illustrates Thomas Birch's famous painting of Perry's victory on Lake Erie, when he is being transferred to the *Niagara*. 18__. 1830s.
Rarity: URS-3
Proof $500

$5 • W-RI-640-005-G070

Left: FIVE vertically. *Center:* 5 / "Battle of Lake Erie" / 5. *Right:* 5 / Waterfall and building / 5. *Engraver:* Terry, Pelton & Co. *Comments:* H-RI-195-G14, Durand-808. 18__. 1830s–1850s.

Rarity: URS-3

Proof $500

$5 • W-RI-640-005-G070a

Overprint: Red FIVE. *Engraver:* Terry, Pelton & Co. / ABNCo. monogram. *Comments:* H-RI-195-G14a, Durand-809. Similar to W-RI-640-005-G070 but with additional engraver imprint. 18__. 1850s–1860s.

Rarity: URS-3

$10 • W-RI-640-010-G080

Engraver: PSSP / New England Bank Note Co. *Comments:* H-RI-195-G16. No description available. 18__. 1830s–1860s.

Rarity: *None known*

$10 • W-RI-640-010-G090

Left: 10 on X / Commerce seated with shield bearing TEN. *Center:* Steamboat and schooners in harbor. *Right:* 10 on X / Ceres. *Engraver:* Terry, Pelton & Co. *Comments:* H-RI-195-G18, Durand-811. 18__. 1830s–1840s.

Rarity: URS-3

Proof $600

$10 • W-RI-640-010-G090a   QDB

Engraver: Terry, Pelton & Co. *Comments:* H-RI-195-G20, Durand-812. Similar to W-RI-640-010-G090 but with different date. 18__. 1840s–1850s.

Rarity: URS-3

Proof $750

$20 • W-RI-640-020-G100

Left: 20 / XX / 20. *Center:* Farmers plowing, Justice seated, Ship. *Right:* TWENTY vertically. *Engraver:* PSSP / New England Bank Note Co. *Comments:* H-RI-195-G24, Durand-814. 18__. 1830s–1860s.

Rarity: *None known*

$50 • W-RI-640-050-G110

Left: 50 / Commerce, Staff, Cornucopia and anchor / 50. *Center:* FIFTY DOLLARS / 50. *Right:* FIFTY vertically. *Engraver:* PSSP / New England Bank Note Co. *Comments:* H-RI-195-G28, Durand-815. 18__. 1830s–1860s.

Rarity: *None known*

$100 • W-RI-640-100-G120

Left: ONE HUNDRED on 100 / Portrait of William Henry Harrison. *Center:* Wharf scene. *Right:* ONE HUNDRED on 100 / Portrait of Christopher Columbus. *Engraver:* New England Bank Note Co. *Comments:* H-RI-195-G32, Durand-816. 18__. 1840s–1860s.

Rarity: *None known*

$500 • W-RI-640-500-G130

Left: 500. *Center:* Indian paddling canoe / 500. *Right:* 500 / Justice. *Engraver:* New England Bank Note Co. *Comments:* H-RI-195-G36, Durand-817. 18__. 1840s–1860s.

Rarity: *None known*

$1,000 • W-RI-640-1000-G140

Left: 1000. *Center:* Eagle on cliff / 1000. *Right:* 1000 / Indian woman with bow and arrows. *Engraver:* New England Bank Note Co. *Comments:* H-RI-195-G40, Durand-818. 18__. 1840s–1860s.

Rarity: *None known*

NON-VALID ISSUES

$1 • W-RI-640-001-N010

Left: ONE / Female portrait / ONE. *Center:* Woman and eagle, Ship. *Right:* ONE / Female portrait / ONE. *Comments:* H-RI-195-N5, Durand-801. 1830s–1840s.

Rarity: *None known*

$2 • W-RI-640-002-A010

Left: Sailor standing by bale / 2. *Center:* Two women seated with bolts of fabric. *Right:* TWO / Mercury / 2. *Engraver:* Wellstood, Hanks, Hay & Whiting. *Comments:* H-RI-195-A5, Durand-805. Altered from $2 Merchants Exchange Bank, Anacostia, D.C. Jan. 2, 1854. 1850s.

Rarity: URS-3

VF $200

$3 • W-RI-640-003-A020

Left: THREE / Mercury in clouds holding caduceus and cornucopia of coins. *Center:* Globe, Allegorical woman with shield bearing pine tree and bull, Sheaves. *Right:* 3. *Overprint:* Red THREE. *Engraver:* Wellstood, Hanks, Hay & Whiting. *Comments:* H-RI-195-A10, Durand-806. Altered from $3 Merchants Exchange Bank, Anacostia, D.C. series. Jan. 2, 1854. 1850s.

Rarity: URS-3

VF $200

$5 • W-RI-640-005-R010

Engraver: Terry, Pelton & Co. *Comments:* H-RI-195-R2, Durand-810. Raised from W-RI-640-001-G010. 18__. 1840s.

Rarity: *None known*

$10 • W-RI-640-010-AR010

Left: 10 / Farmer and family resting. *Center:* Portrait of Benjamin Franklin. *Right:* 10 / Woodsman felling tree, Oxen, children. *Overprint:* Red V, V. *Comments:* H-RI-195-A15, Durand-813. Altered and raised from W-RI-1630-005-G040. Aug. 6, 1855. 1850s.

Rarity: URS-3

Peoples Bank
1846–1865
W-RI-650

History: The Peoples Bank was incorporated in 1846 in the North Providence village of Pawtucket. C.F. Manchester was its founding president, and J.S. Tourtellot was its first cashier. Capital was $50,000 in February 1848 until it rose to $150,000

in 1855 and again to $175,000 in 1857. In 1849 circulation was $40,583. Specie was $2,593.36 in 1857.

The business of the bank was succeeded by the First National Bank of Pawtucket, chartered on February 27, 1865.

Numismatic Commentary: With a little patience, genuine notes from this bank should become available in the market-place. The notes with a red tint are especially handsome.

Remaining in the American Bank Note Co. archives as of 2003 was a $1-$1-$1-$2 tint plate.

VALID ISSUES

$1 • W-RI-650-001-G010   CC

Engraver: Danforth, Bald & Co. **Comments:** H-RI-200-G4, Durand-819. January 1st, 18__. 1850s.
Rarity: URS-3
Proof $500

$1 • W-RI-650-001-G010a
Overprint: Red 1, ONE, 1. **Engraver:** Danforth, Bald & Co. **Comments:** H-RI-200-G4b, Durand-820. Similar to W-RI-650-001-G010. Jan. 1, 18__. 1850s–1860s.
Rarity: URS-6
VF $300

$1 • W-RI-650-001-G010b   CC

Tint: Red-brown outlining 1, 1, white ONE on die, Serial number. **Engraver:** Danforth, Bald & Co. / ABNCo. monogram. **Comments:** H-RI-200-G4c, Durand-821. Similar to W-RI-650-001-G010 but with additional engraver imprint. January 1st, 18__. 1860s.
Rarity: URS-5
VF $700
Selected auction price: Stack's Bowers Galleries, May 2008, VF $664

$2 • W-RI-650-002-G020   CC

Engraver: Danforth, Bald & Co. **Comments:** H-RI-200-G8, Durand-824. January 1st, 18__. 1850s.
Rarity: URS-3
Proof $800
Selected auction price: Stack's Bowers Galleries, July 2008, Proof $741

$2 • W-RI-650-002-G020a
Left: Medallion head of William Shakespeare / TWO over 2 on die. **Center:** Ceres and Commerce. **Right:** 2 / Liberty, eagle, and shield. **Overprint:** Red 2, TWO, 2. **Engraver:** Danforth, Bald & Co. / American Bank Note Co. **Comments:** H-RI-200-G8b, Durand-825. Similar to W-RI-650-002-G020 but with additional engraver imprint. Jan. 1, 18__. 1860s.
Rarity: *None known*

$2 • W-RI-650-002-G020b
Tint: Red-brown. **Engraver:** Danforth, Bald & Co. / ABNCo. monogram. **Comments:** H-RI-200-G8c, Durand-826. Similar to W-RI-650-002-G020 but with additional engraver imprint. Jan. 1, 18__. 1860s.
Rarity: *None known*

$3 • W-RI-650-003-G030
Left: 3 / Mechanic. **Center:** Ceres, plow, and train. **Right:** 3 / Sailor. **Comments:** H-Unlisted, Durand-830. 1850s–1860s.
Rarity: URS-3

$5 • W-RI-650-005-G040
Left: 5 / Woman seated looking at eagle. **Center:** Three women. **Right:** 5 / Train. **Engraver:** Danforth, Wright & Co. **Comments:** H-RI-200-G12, Durand-833. Jan. 1, 18__. 1850s.
Rarity: URS-3
Proof $500

$5 • W-RI-650-005-G040a
Overprint: Red 5, FIVE. **Engraver:** Danforth, Wright & Co. **Comments:** H-RI-200-G12a, Durand-832. Similar to W-RI-650-005-G040. Jan. 1, 18__. 1850s.
Rarity: *None known*

$5 • W-RI-650-005-G040b
Overprint: Red 5, FIVE. **Engraver:** Danforth, Bald & Co. / ABNCo. monogram. **Comments:** H-RI-200-G12b. Similar to W-RI-650-005-G040 but with different engraver imprint. Jan. 1, 18__. 1860s.
Rarity: URS-3
VF $300

$5 • W-RI-650-005-G040c

QDB

Overprint: Red 5, FIVE, Serial number. *Engraver:* American Bank Note Co. *Comments:* H-RI-200-G12c. Similar to W-RI-650-005-G040 but with different engraver imprint. January 1st, 18__. 1860s.

Rarity: URS-3
VF $450
Selected auction price: Heritage,
June 2010, Lot 12565, Choice Fine $920

$5 • W-RI-650-005-G040d

Tint: Red-brown. *Engraver:* Danforth, Wright & Co. *Comments:* H-Unlisted, Durand-834. Similar to W-RI-650-005-G040. 18__. 1860s.
Rarity: URS-3

$5 • W-RI-650-005-G050

Left: 5 / Mechanic. *Center:* Ceres, plow, and train. *Right:* 5 / Sailor. *Comments:* H-Unlisted, Durand-837. 1850s–1860s.
Rarity: URS-3

$10 • W-RI-650-010-G060

Left: X / Portrait of Franklin Pierce / 10. *Center:* State arms on shield. *Right:* 10 / Cattle, train, bridge. *Engraver:* Danforth, Bald & Co. *Comments:* H-RI-200-G16, Durand-839. Jan. 1, 18__. 1850s.
Rarity: URS-3
Proof $500

$10 • W-RI-650-010-G060a

Overprint: Red X, TEN, X. *Engraver:* Danforth, Wright & Co. *Comments:* H-RI-200-G16a, Durand-840. Similar to W-RI-650-010-G060 but with different engraver imprint. Jan. 1, 18__. 1850s.
Rarity: *None known*

$10 • W-RI-650-010-G060b

CC

Overprint: Red X, TEN, X. *Engraver:* Danforth, Wright & Co. / ABNCo. monogram. *Comments:* H-RI-200-G16b. Similar to W-RI-650-010-G060 but with different engraver imprint. January 1st, 18__. 1850s–1860s.
Rarity: URS-3
VF $600

$10 • W-RI-650-010-G060c

Overprint: Red X, TEN, X. *Engraver:* American Bank Note Co. *Comments:* H-RI-200-G16c. Similar to W-RI-650-010-G060 but with different engraver imprint. Jan. 1, 18__. 1860s.
Rarity: *None known*

$10 • W-RI-650-010-G060d

Tint: Red-brown. *Engraver:* Danforth, Wright & Co. *Comments:* H-Unlisted, Durand-841. Similar to W-RI-650-010-G060 but with different engraver imprint. Jan. 1, 18__. 1860s.
Rarity: URS-3

$20 • W-RI-650-020-G070

Left: 20 / Minerva standing. *Center:* 2, Allegorical woman, 0. *Right:* 20 / Ceres / 20. *Engraver:* Rawdon, Wright, Hatch & Edson. *Comments:* H-RI-200-G18, Durand-844. 18__. 1850s–1860s.
Rarity: *None known*

$20 • W-RI-650-020-G080

Left: 20 / Mechanic. *Center:* Ceres, plow, and train. *Right:* 20 / Sailor. *Comments:* H-Unlisted, Durand-846. 1850s–1860s.
Rarity: URS-3

$50 • W-RI-650-050-G090

Left: 50 / Minerva. *Center:* Agriculture and Industry. *Right:* 50 / Cherub steering sailboat / 50. *Engraver:* Rawdon, Wright, Hatch & Edson. *Comments:* H-RI-200-G20, Durand-847. 18__. 1850s–1860s.
Rarity: *None known*

$100 • W-RI-650-100-G100

Left: 100 / Vulcan. *Center:* Spread eagle on tree limb. *Bottom center:* 100. *Right:* 100 / Ceres. *Overprint:* Red HUNDRED. *Engraver:* Rawdon, Wright, Hatch & Edson. *Comments:* H-RI-200-G22, Durand-848. 18__. 1850s–1860s.
Rarity: *None known*

$500 • W-RI-650-500-G110

Left: 500. *Center:* Indian paddling canoe / 500. *Right:* 500 / Justice. *Engraver:* New England Bank Note Co. *Comments:* H-RI-200-G24, Durand-849. 18__. 1850s–1860s.
Rarity: *None known*

$1,000 • W-RI-650-1000-G120

Left: 1000. *Center:* Eagle on cliff / 1000. *Right:* 1000 / Indian woman with bow and arrows. *Engraver:* New England Bank Note Co. *Comments:* H-RI-200-G26, Durand-50. 18__. 1850s–1860s.
Rarity: *None known*

Uncut Sheets

$1-$1-$1-$2 • W-RI-650-001.001.001.002-US010

Vignette(s): ($1) Portrait of George Washington / Three women around shield bearing anchor / Female portrait with sheaf. *($1)* Portrait of George Washington / Three women around shield bearing anchor / Female portrait with sheaf. *($1)* Portrait of George Washington / Three women around shield bearing anchor / Female portrait with sheaf. *($2)* Medallion head of William Shakespeare / Ceres and Commerce / Liberty, eagle, and shield. *Engraver:* Danforth, Bald & Co. *Comments:* H-RI-200-G4, G4, G4, G8. January 1st, 18__. 1850s.

Rarity: URS-3
Proof $2,500
Selected auction price: Lyn Knight,
June 2008, Lot 3160, CU $2,800

Non-Valid Issues

$1 • W-RI-650-001-A010

Left: 1 / Sailing ship. *Center:* Three men forging iron / 1. *Right:* 1 / Ceres and Indian woman. *Engraver:* Danforth, Bald & Co. *Comments:* H-RI-200-A5, Durand-822. Altered from $1 Peoples Bank, Washington, D.C. Dec. 1, 1852.

Rarity: URS-3
VF $250

$1 • W-RI-650-001-A020

Left: ONE / Woman holding cornucopia of flowers standing by 1. *Center:* Capitol / Eagle on U.S. shield / Steamship. *Right:* 1 on medallion U.S. shield / Portrait of George Washington. *Engraver:* Wellstood, Hanks, Hay & Whiting. *Comments:* H-RI-200-A10, Durand-823. Altered from $1 Peoples Bank of North America, Georgetown, D.C. 18__. 1850s.

Rarity: *None known*

$2 • W-RI-650-002-N010

Center: Two women, one pointing to ship. *Right:* Woman, eagle, and shield. *Comments:* H-RI-200-N10, Durand-828. 1850s.

Rarity: *None known*

$2 • W-RI-650-002-A030

Left: TWO / 2 / Mechanic. *Center:* 2 on shield / Ceres. *Bottom center:* Strongbox. *Right:* 2 / Sailor. *Engraver:* Danforth, Bald & Co. *Comments:* H-RI-200-A12, Durand-827. Altered from $2 Peoples Bank, Washington, D.C. Dec. 1, 1852.

Rarity: *None known*

$3 • W-RI-650-003-N020

Center: Two women, one pointing to ship. *Right:* Woman, eagle, and shield. *Comments:* H-RI-200-N15, Durand-831. 1850s.

Rarity: *None known*

$3 • W-RI-650-003-A040

Left: 3 / Portrait of Daniel Webster. *Center:* Ceres and Liberty flanking shield surmounted by eagle. *Right:* THREE on 3 / Female portrait. *Engraver:* New England Bank Note Co. *Comments:* H-RI-200-A15, Durand-829. Altered from $3 Waubeek Bank, DeSoto, Nebraska. 1857.

Rarity: URS-3
VF $300

$5 • W-RI-650-005-A050

Left: 5 / Woman with shield bearing scene, Tools. *Center:* Ceres and Liberty. *Right:* 5 / Portrait of Zachary Taylor. *Engraver:* W.L. Ormsby. *Comments:* H-RI-200-A20, Durand-836. Altered from $5 Merchants Bank, Fort Leavenworth, Kansas. 185_. 1850s.

Rarity: *None known*

$5 • W-RI-650-005-A060

Left: 5 / Sailing ship. *Center:* Three men forging iron / 5. *Bottom center:* Woman swimming. *Right:* 5 / Ceres and Indian woman. *Engraver:* Danforth, Bald & Co. *Comments:* H-RI-200-A25, Durand-835. Altered from $1 Peoples Bank, Washington, D.C. 1850s.

Rarity: *None known*

$5 • W-RI-650-005-A070

Left: 5 / Cherub holding portrait of George Washington / 5. *Center:* 5 / Spread eagle and shield / 5. *Right:* 5 / Indian and woman / 5. *Comments:* H-Unlisted, Durand-838. Altered from $10 Citizens Bank, Augusta, Maine. 1850s–1860s.

Rarity: URS-3

$10 • W-RI-650-010-AR010

Left: 10 / Sailing ship. *Center:* Three men forging iron /10. *Bottom center:* Woman swimming. *Right:* 10 / Ceres and Indian woman. *Engraver:* Danforth, Bald & Co. *Comments:* H-RI-200-AR5, Durand-842. Altered and raised from $1 Peoples Bank, Washington, D.C. Dec. 1, 1852.

Rarity: URS-3
VF $250

$10 • W-RI-650-010-A080

Left: 10 / Cherub holding portrait of George Washington / 10. *Center:* X / Spread eagle and shield / X. *Right:* 10 / Indian and woman / 10. *Engraver:* Terry, Pelton & Co. *Comments:* H-RI-200-A30, Durand-843. Altered from $10 Citizens Bank, Augusta, Maine, or from notes of other failed banks using the same plate. 18__. 1848.

Rarity: URS-3
VF $200

$20 • W-RI-650-020-AR020

Left: 20 / Sailing ship. *Center:* Three men forging iron / 20. *Right:* 20 / Ceres and Indian woman. *Engraver:* Danforth, Bald & Co. *Comments:* H-RI-200-AR10, Durand-845. Altered from $1 Peoples Bank, Washington, D.C. Dec. 1, 185_. 1856.

Rarity: URS-3
VF $250

Slater Bank
1855–1865
W-RI-660

History: The Slater Bank was incorporated at the village of Pawtucket in North Providence in 1855 with $100,000 in authorized capital. The bank was named after Samuel Slater, the aforementioned pioneer in cotton-manufacturing, using techniques developed in England. The capital was increased to $150,000 by 1857. The bank's circulation was around $35,000 at that time, and specie amounted to $3,514.07.

The business of the Slater Bank was succeeded by the Slater National Bank, chartered on March 3, 1865.

See also listing under Pawtucket, W-RI-730.

VALID ISSUES

$1 • W-RI-660-001-G010

Left: 1 / Woman seated with 1. *Center:* View of the Pawtucket Falls and mills. *Bottom center:* Anchor on shield. *Right:* 1 / Portrait of Samuel Slater. *Engraver:* Wellstood, Hanks, Hay & Whiting. *Comments:* H-Unlisted, Durand-851. 18__. 1850s.

Rarity: URS-3

$1 • W-RI-660-001-G010a

Overprint: Red ONE. *Engraver:* Wellstood, Hanks, Hay & Whiting. *Comments:* H-RI-205-G2a, Durand-852. Similar to W-RI-660-001-G010. 18__. 1850s.

Rarity: URS-3

VF $750

$1 • W-RI-660-001-G010b

QDB

Overprint: Red panel outlining white ONE. *Engraver:* Wellstood, Hanks, Hay & Whiting / ABNCo. monogram. *Comments:* H-Unlisted, Durand-Unlisted. Similar to W-RI-660-001-G010 but with additional engraver imprint. January 5th, 186_. 1860s.

Rarity: URS-2

VF $850; **EF** $1,000

$1 • W-RI-660-001-G010c

Overprint: Green ONE. *Engraver:* Wellstood, Hanks, Hay & Whiting / ABNCo. monogram. *Comments:* H-RI-205-G2b, Durand-853. Similar to W-RI-660-001-G010 but with additional engraver imprint. 18__. 1860s.

Rarity: URS-3

VF $750

$1 • W-RI-660-001-G010d

Tint: Blue panel vertically. *Engraver:* Wellstood, Hanks, Hay & Whiting / ABNCo. monogram. *Comments:* H-RI-205-G2c, Durand-854. Similar to W-RI-660-001-G010 but with additional engraver imprint. 186_. 1860s.

Rarity: URS-3

VF $750

$2 • W-RI-660-002-G020

SBG

Engraver: Wellstood, Hanks, Hay & Whiting. *Comments:* H-Unlisted, Durand-855. Proof. 18__. 1850s.

Rarity: URS-2

VF $750; **Proof** $5,200

Selected auction price: Stack's Bowers Galleries, March 2013, Proof $5,140

$2 • W-RI-660-002-G020a

Left: TWO / 2 with allegorical figure. *Center:* View of the Pawtucket Falls and mills. *Right:* 2 / Portrait of Samuel Slater. *Overprint:* Red TWO. *Engraver:* Wellstood, Hanks, Hay & Whiting. *Comments:* H-RI-205-G4a, Durand-856. Similar to W-RI-660-002-G020. 18__. 1850s.

Rarity: URS-3

VF $750

$2 • W-RI-660-002-G020b

Overprint: Green TWO. *Engraver:* Wellstood, Hanks, Hay & Whiting / ABNCo. monogram. *Comments:* H-RI-205-G4b, Durand-857. Similar to W-RI-660-002-G020 but with additional engraver imprint. 18__. 1850s–1860s.

Rarity: *None known*

$2 • W-RI-660-002-G020c

Tint: Blue panel vertically. *Engraver:* Wellstood, Hanks, Hay & Whiting / ABNCo. monogram. *Comments:* H-RI-205-G4c, Durand-858. Similar to W-RI-660-002-G020 but with additional engraver imprint. 186_. 1860s.

Rarity: *None known*

$5 • W-RI-660-005-G030

SBG

Engraver: Wellstood, Hanks, Hay & Whiting. *Comments:* H-Unlisted, Durand-859. Proof. 18__. 1850s.

Rarity: URS-2

VF $750; **Proof** $6,700

Selected auction price: Stack's Bowers Galleries, March 2013, Proof $6,650

$5 • W-RI-660-005-G030a

Left: View of the Pawtucket Falls and mills / V surrounded by women. *Center:* Portrait of Samuel Slater. *Right:* 5 / Industry. *Overprint:* Red FIVE. *Engraver:* Wellstood, Hanks, Hay & Whiting. *Comments:* H-RI-205-G6a, Durand-860. Similar to W-RI-660-005-G030. 18__. 1850s.

Rarity: URS-3
VF $750

$5 • W-RI-660-005-G030b

Overprint: Green FIVE. *Engraver:* Wellstood, Hanks, Hay & Whiting / ABNCo. monogram. *Comments:* H-RI-205-G6b, Durand-861. Similar to W-RI-660-005-G030 but with additional engraver imprint. 18__. 1850s–1860s.

Rarity: URS-3
VF $750

$5 • W-RI-660-005-G030c

Tint: Blue panel vertically. *Engraver:* Wellstood, Hanks, Hay & Whiting / ABNCo. monogram. *Comments:* H-Unlisted, Durand-862. Similar to W-RI-660-005-G030 but with additional engraver imprint. 186_. 1860s.

Rarity: URS-3

$10 • W-RI-660-010-G040   CC

Engraver: Wellstood, Hanks, Hay & Whiting. *Comments:* H-Unlisted, Durand-864. Proof. 18__. 1850s.

Rarity: URS-1
Proof $2,900
Selected auction price: Stack's Bowers Galleries, January 2011, Proof $2,844

$10 • W-RI-660-010-G040a

Left: 10 / Portrait of Samuel Slater. *Center:* View of the Pawtucket Falls and mills. *Right:* 10 / TEN on X, Woman and cow. *Overprint:* Red X / X. *Engraver:* Wellstood, Hanks, Hay & Whiting. *Comments:* H-RI-205-G8a, Durand-865. Similar to W-RI-660-010-G040. 18__. 1850s.

Rarity: *None known*

$10 • W-RI-660-010-G040b

Overprint: Green X / X. *Engraver:* Wellstood, Hanks, Hay & Whiting / ABNCo. monogram. *Comments:* H-RI-205-G8b, Durand-866. Similar to W-RI-660-010-G040 but with additional engraver imprint. 18__. 1850s–1860s.

Rarity: *None known*

$10 • W-RI-660-010-G040c

Tint: Blue panel vertically. *Engraver:* Wellstood, Hanks, Hay & Whiting / ABNCo. monogram. *Comments:* H-Unlisted, Durand-867. Similar to W-RI-660-010-G040 but with additional engraver imprint. 186_. 1860s.

Rarity: URS-3
VF $800

$50 • W-RI-660-050-G050

Left: 50 / Cherub / Mechanic. *Center:* Farmer and woman at well. *Bottom center:* Anchor on shield. *Right:* 50 / Cherub / Portrait of Samuel Slater. *Engraver:* Wellstood, Hanks, Hay & Whiting. *Comments:* H-RI-205-G10, Durand-869. 18__. 1850s.

Rarity: *None known*

$50 • W-RI-660-050-G050a   SBG

Overprint: Red L / L. *Engraver:* Wellstood, Hanks, Hay & Whiting. *Comments:* H-Unlisted. Similar to W-RI-660-050-G050. Proof. 18__. 1850s.

Rarity: URS-1
VF $900; **Proof** $9,200
Selected auction price: Stack's Bowers Galleries, March 2013, Proof $9,076

$100 • W-RI-660-100-G060

Left: C / Portrait of Samuel Slater. *Center:* Liberty and eagle. *Bottom center:* Anchor on shield. *Right:* 100 / Woman with liberty cap, Factories. *Engraver:* Wellstood, Hanks, Hay & Whiting. *Comments:* H-RI-205-G12, Durand-870. 18__. 1850s.

Rarity: *None known*

$100 • W-RI-660-100-G060a   QDB

Overprint: Red 100. *Engraver:* Wellstood, Hanks, Hay & Whiting. *Comments:* H-Unlisted. Similar to W-RI-660-100-G060. Proof. 18__. 1850s.

Rarity: URS-1
VF $900; **Proof** $9,500

$500 • W-RI-660-500-G070

Left: 500 / Male portrait. *Center:* Fame blowing trumpet. *Bottom center:* Anchor on shield. *Right:* 500 / Blacksmith. *Engraver:* Wellstood, Hanks, Hay & Whiting. *Comments:* H-RI-205-G14, Durand-871. 18__. 1850s.

Rarity: *None known*

Non-Valid Issues

$5 • W-RI-660-005-A010

Left: 5 / FIVE / FIVE. *Center:* Indian woman and frontiersman reclining with three cherubs playing over five gold dollars. *Bottom center:* Steamboat. *Right:* 5 / Female portrait / FIVE. *Overprint:* FIVE. *Engraver:* Rawdon, Wright, Hatch & Edson. *Comments:* H-RI-205-A5, Durand-863. Altered from $5 Farmers & Merchants Bank of Memphis, Memphis, Tennessee series. 1850s.

Rarity: *None known*

$10 • W-RI-660-010-R010

Comments: H-Unlisted, Durand-868. Raised from W-RI-660-001-G010. 1850s.

Rarity: URS-3

North Scituate, Rhode Island

North Scituate is a village within Scituate, Rhode Island.
See also Scituate, Rhode Island.

Citizens Union Bank
1833–1865
W-RI-670

History: The Citizens Union Bank was chartered in January 1833 in Scituate with $50,000 in authorized capital. Josiah Westcott served as its founding president, and David H. Braman was the first cashier. In 1835 the plates of this bank fell into the hands of racketeers. Counterfeits of all the notes of this bank were common.[37] As a result, the bank failed in 1836, but it redeemed its bills in full and later gained an infusion of funds which allowed it to reopen for business.[38] The bank's capital had increased to $55,675 by 1857. It had bills in circulation amounting to $19,638, which rose to $28,972 by 1862. Specie totaled $2,186.53 in 1857.

The interests of the Citizens Union Bank were succeeded by the Scituate National Bank, chartered on September 7, 1865.

See also listing under Scituate, W-RI-1290.

Hamilton Bank
1841–1851
W-RI-680

History: The Hamilton Bank was incorporated as the Scituate Bank, W-RI-1310, in 1818, but it was forced to liquidate due to out-of-state fraud. The bank reopened in January 1841, and the title was changed to the Hamilton Bank under president Luther C. Harris. That year the bank was robbed of a large number of

its unsigned notes. These notes were later put into circulation with forged signatures, and the bank refused to redeem them. The bank maintained a precarious existence until June 1849, when it was forced into receivership yet again. All claims against the bank were required to be presented before June 1852.[39]

See also listing under Scituate, W-RI-1300.

Numismatic Commentary: Few genuine notes are available in today's marketplace, but non-valid issues are plentiful.

Valid Issues

$1 • W-RI-680-001-G010

CC

Engraver: Danforth & Hufty. *Comments:* H-RI-440-G20, Durand-2128. 18__. 1840s.

Rarity: URS-5
VG $75; **VF** $150

$2 • W-RI-680-002-G020

CC

Engraver: Danforth & Hufty. *Comments:* H-RI-440-G22, Durand-2129. 18__. 1840s.

Rarity: URS-5
VF $200

$3 • W-RI-680-003-G030

Left: THREE / Farmer / THREE. *Center:* 3 / Ceres seated, Eagle, beehive, flowers / 3. *Right:* Sailor standing. *Comments:* H-Unlisted, Durand-2130. 1840s.

Rarity: URS-3

$5 • W-RI-680-005-G040

Left: 5 / FIVE / 5. *Center:* V / Spread eagle, Anchor, boxes, bales, plow, Vessels / V. *Right:* 5 / FIVE / 5. *Comments:* H-Unlisted, Durand-2131. 1840s.

Rarity: URS-3

$5 • W-RI-680-005-G050

QDB

Engraver: Danforth & Hufty. **Comments:** H-RI-440-G24, Durand-2132. 18___. 1840s.

Rarity: URS-5
VG $200; **VF** $350

$5 • W-RI-680-005-G050a

Left: 5 / Portrait of Daniel Webster. **Center:** FIVE on medallion head / "Signing of the Declaration of Independence". **Bottom center:** V / Arm and hammer / V. **Right:** 5 / Medallion head / 5. **Comments:** H-Unlisted, Durand-2133. Similar to W-RI-680-005-G050. 1840s.

Rarity: URS-3

$10 • W-RI-680-010-G060

CC

Engraver: Danforth & Hufty. **Comments:** H-RI-440-G26, Durand-2134. 18___. 1840s.

Rarity: URS-3
Proof $950

$10 • W-RI-680-010-G070

Left: X / Indian with bow. **Center:** Harbor scene, steamship, sloop / X. **Right:** 10 / Girl with flowers. **Comments:** H-Unlisted, Durand-2135. 1840s.

Rarity: URS-3

Uncut Sheets
$1-$1-$1-$2 • W-RI-680-001.001.001.002-US010

Vignette(s): ($1) 1 on medallion head of Daniel Webster / Male portrait / Two horses / Medallion head of William Shakespeare / Eagle / Woman standing. **($1)** 1 on medallion head of Daniel Webster / Male portrait / Two horses / Medallion head of William Shakespeare / Eagle / Woman standing. **($1)** 1 on medallion head of Daniel Webster / Male portrait / Two horses / Medallion head of William Shakespeare / Eagle / Woman standing. **($2)** Portrait of John Adams / Woman with headdress leaning on shield holding staff / Train / Portrait of Zachary Taylor. **Engraver:** Danforth & Hufty. **Comments:** H-RI-440-G20, G20, G20, G22. 18___. 1840s.

Rarity: URS-3
Proof $2,500

$10-$5 • W-RI-680-010.005-US020

Vignette(s): ($10) Woman with pole and cap holding shield, Eagle / Industry seated next to anvil / Arm and hammer / Portrait of George Washington. **($5)** Portrait of General Ambrose Burnside / FIVE on medallion head / "Signing of the Declaration of Independence" / Arm and hammer / Medallion head. **Engraver:** Danforth & Hufty. **Comments:** H-RI-440-G26, G24. 18___. 1840s.

Rarity: URS-3
Proof $1,200

NORTH SHOREHAM, RHODE ISLAND

North Shoreham encompasses the entirety of Block Island, which lies in the Atlantic Ocean 13 miles south of the Rhode Island coast. The Niantic Indians used to inhabit the land and called it "Manisses." English settlers first arrived in 1661 when the island was still a part of Massachusetts. Later it was ceded to Rhode Island in 1672. The island was snared by the British during the War of 1812, but they were thwarted when they found that all of the livestock and food had been moved to Stonington, Connecticut.

By the middle of the 19th century, steam technology brought newfound opulence to Block Island. Before it had been a place for fishermen to cast their nets, but it was soon remade into a summer getaway for factory workers and residents of the cities. A handful of devastating shipwrecks occurred off of Block Island throughout the years, including the *Palantine,* which caught fire and sank in 1738, and the *Warrior,* which wrecked in the same place in 1831. A fortuitous shipwreck brought coal to the island, inspiring the islanders to replace peat and make coal the major fuel source after 1846.

Island Bank
1854
W-RI-683

History: The Island Bank was incorporated on Block Island in January 1854. The bank was never organized and its charter was forfeited. As such, it is unlikely that notes were printed. However Proofs could exist if they were printed in anticipation.

OLNEYVILLE, RHODE ISLAND

Olneyville is a neighborhood in Providence.

Settlement began in the early 18th century, when the area had its inception as a center of trade with a Narragansett village nearby. Christopher Olney established a grist mill and a paper mill on the Woonasquatucket River, and the area was named after him. He was a captain during the Revolutionary War as well as a farmer. A forge, a foundry, and other small industries arose in Olneyvill in the time following the war. The arrival of the railroad in the 19th century helped to develop Olneyville into a mill district, attracting immigrant workers.

See also Providence, Rhode Island.

Cranston Bank
1818–1865
W-RI-685

History: The Cranston Bank was incorporated in February 1818. Sylvester Wicks was the bank's first president, and Jeremiah Knight was its first cashier. Similar to the activity of many other banks, the Cranston Bank profited by issuing large quantities of notes and shipping them at a discount to distant locations with the expectation that many would never be redeemed.

Capital was listed at $25,000 between 1849 and 1855. By 1857 it had increased to $37,500. Circulation was $10,367 in 1857 but had decreased to $9,807 by 1862. Specie was $1,017.59 in 1857.

The bank moved to Providence in 1850 and to Olneyville in 1865. It was closed that year.

Also see listings under Cranston, W-RI-240, and Providence, W-RI-885.

PASCOAG, RHODE ISLAND

Pascoag is a village within Burrillville, one of eight. It began industry with a saw mill and various other businesses, and later it became a textile manufacturing town.

See also Burrillville, Rhode Island.

Granite Bank
1851–1865
W-RI-690

History: The Granite Bank was incorporated in June 1833 as the Pascoag Bank, W-RI-180, in the village of Pascoag. The authorized starting capital was $50,000. Its title was changed to the Granite Bank in June 1851. In 1857 its capital was $60,000, bills in circulation amounted to $23,136, and specie totaled $4,063.57. In 1862 its capital was the same, but circulation was $36,267.[40]

After July 5, 1865, the interests of the bank were succeeded by the Pascoag National Bank.

See also listing under Burrillville, W-RI-170.

Numismatic Commentary: Named after the bedrock beneath much of Rhode Island's farms, the Granite Bank is similar to many other Rhode Island banks in that genuine notes are very hard to locate. Various issues of non-valid notes are available to at least partially fill that void.

VALID ISSUES

5¢ • W-RI-690-00.05-G010
Center: 5. *Comments:* H-Unlisted, Durand-876. Square note. 1850s–1860s.
Rarity: URS-3
VF $500

10¢ • W-RI-690-00.10-G020
Center: 10. *Comments:* H-Unlisted, Durand-877. Square note. 1850s–1860s.
Rarity: URS-3
VF $500

25¢ • W-RI-690-00.25-G030
Center: 25. *Comments:* H-Unlisted, Durand-878. Square note. 1850s–1860s.
Rarity: URS-3
VF $500

50¢ • W-RI-690-00.50-G040
Center: 50. *Comments:* H-Unlisted, Durand-879. Square note. 1850s–1860s.
Rarity: URS-3
VF $500

$1 • W-RI-690-001-G050
Left: 1 / Portrait of George Washington. *Center:* Female portrait / 1 / Portrait of girl. *Right:* 1 / Portrait of Benjamin Franklin. *Engraver:* New England Bank Note Co. *Comments:* H-RI-210-G2, Durand-880. 18__. 1850s.
Rarity: *None known*

$1 • W-RI-690-001-G060
Left: 1 / Bales, barrels, cornucopia / 1. *Center:* 1 / Commerce / 1. *Right:* 1 / Agricultural implements. *Engraver:* New England Bank Note Co. / ABNCo. monogram. *Comments:* H-RI-210-G4a, Durand-881. 18__. 1850s.
Rarity: *None known*

$2 • W-RI-690-002-G070
Left: 2 / Portrait of Christopher Columbus. *Center:* Ceres / 2 / Justice. *Right:* 2 / Male portrait. *Engraver:* New England Bank Note Co. *Comments:* H-RI-210-G6, Durand-883. 18__. 1850s–1860s.
Rarity: *None known*

$2 • W-RI-690-002-G080
Left: 2 / Wheelwright at work. *Center:* Flock of sheep, Man watering horse at trough, Two farmers. *Right:* 2 / Girl feeding chickens. *Comments:* H-Unlisted, Durand-884. 1850s–1860s.
Rarity: URS-3
VF $300

$3 • W-RI-690-003-G090
Left: 3 / George Washington on horseback. *Center:* Female portrait / 3 / Female portrait. *Right:* 3 / Vulcan standing with sledge. *Engraver:* New England Bank Note Co. *Comments:* H-RI-210-G8, Durand-885. 18__. 1850s–1860s.
Rarity: *None known*

$5 • W-RI-690-005-G100
Left: FIVE / Eagle and shield. *Center:* V / Woman and cherub. *Right:* 5 / Girl with basket of flowers. *Engraver:* New England Bank Note Co. *Comments:* H-RI-210-G10, Durand-888. 18__. 1850s.
Rarity: *None known*

$5 • W-RI-690-005-G100a
Engraver: New England Bank Note Co. / ABNCo. monogram. *Comments:* H-RI-210-G10b. Similar to W-RI-690-005-G100 but with additional engraver imprint. 18__. 1850s–1860s.
Rarity: *None known*

$10 • W-RI-690-010-G110
Left: Vulcan seated / TEN. *Center:* X. *Right:* 10 / Farmer. *Engraver:* New England Bank Note Co. *Comments:* H-RI-210-G12, Durand-892. 18__. 1850s.
Rarity: *None known*

$10 • W-RI-690-010-G110a

Engraver: New England Bank Note Co. / ABNCo. monogram. *Comments:* H-RI-210-G12b. Similar to W-RI-690-010-G110 but with additional engraver imprint. 18__. 1850s–1860s.

Rarity: *None known*

$20 • W-RI-690-020-G120

Left: 20 / Minerva. *Center:* 2, Woman seated, 0. *Right:* 20 / Ceres / 20. *Engraver:* Rawdon, Wright, Hatch & Edson. *Comments:* H-RI-210-G14, Durand-893. 18__. 1850s–1860s.

Rarity: *None known*

$50 • W-RI-690-050-G130

Left: 50 / Minerva. *Center:* Ceres and Vulcan. *Right:* 50 / Cherub steering sailboat / 50. *Engraver:* Rawdon, Wright, Hatch & Edson. *Comments:* H-RI-210-G16, Durand-894. 18__. 1850s–1860s

Rarity: *None known*

$100 • W-RI-690-100-G140

Left: 100 / Vulcan seated. *Center:* Spread eagle on tree limb. *Bottom center:* 100. *Right:* 100 / Woman seated with rake. *Engraver:* Rawdon, Wright, Hatch & Edson. *Comments:* H-RI-210-G18, Durand-895. 18__. 1850s–1860s.

Rarity: *None known*

NON-VALID ISSUES

$1 • W-RI-690-001-N010

Center: 1 / Woman seated / 1. *Comments:* H-RI-210-N5, Durand-882. 1850s.

Rarity: *None known*

$3 • W-RI-690-003-S010

Center: Female portrait / 3 / Female portrait / Portrait of George Washington. *Comments:* H-RI-210-S5, Durand-887. Similar to W-RI-690-003-G090. 1850s.

Rarity: *None known*

$3 • W-RI-690-003-A010

Left: 3 / Wheelwrights at work. *Center:* Flock of sheep, Man watering horse at trough, Two farmers. *Right:* 3 / Girl feeding chickens. *Overprint:* Red 3, 3. *Engraver:* Toppan, Carpenter, Casilear & Co. *Comments:* H-RI-210-A5, Durand-886. Altered from W-RI-1630-003-G030. Aug. 6, 1855.

Rarity: *None known*

$5 • W-RI-690-005-A020

Left: Drove of horses. *Center:* Two allegorical figures. *Right:* 5 / Portrait of girl. *Overprint:* Red FIVE. *Engraver:* Bald, Cousland & Co. / Baldwin, Bald & Cousland. *Comments:* H-RI-210-A10, Durand-890. Altered from $5 Bank of Morgan, Morgan, Georgia. 18__. 1850s.

Rarity: URS-3

VF $300

$5 • W-RI-690-005-A030

Left: V / Male portrait. *Center:* Side-wheel steamer. *Right:* 5 / Portrait of George Washington. *Overprint:* Red FIVE. *Engraver:* New England Bank Note Co. / Rawdon, Wright, Hatch & Edson. *Comments:* H-RI-210-A15, Durand-889. Altered from $5 Waubeek Bank, DeSoto, Nebraska. 1857.

Rarity: URS-3

VF $300

$5 • W-RI-690-005-A040

Left: 5 / Two children with grapes. *Center:* Two allegorical women flanking anvil. *Right:* 5 / Men driving sheep into river. *Overprint:* Red FIVE. *Engraver:* Rawdon, Wright, Hatch & Edson / New England Bank Note Co. *Comments:* H-RI-210-A20, Durand-891. Altered from W-RI-1630-005-G040. 18__. 1850s.

Rarity: *None known*

Pascoag Bank
1833–1851
W-RI-700

History: The Pascoag Bank was incorporated in Pascoag Village in June 1833. Its charter was amended to change the name of the bank to the Granite Bank, W-RI-690, in June 1851.[41]

See also listing under Burrillville, W-RI-180.

Numismatic Commentary: This bank was predecessor to the Granite Bank, and genuine notes from it are also very hard to locate. The $3 issue of the PSSP design is the note that most often becomes available.

VALID ISSUES

$1 • W-RI-700-001-G010

Left: 1 / Eagle / 1. *Center:* 1 / Woman seated with plow, Sailboats / 1. *Right:* 1 / Woman standing / 1. *Engraver:* PSSP. *Comments:* H-RI-215-G2, Durand-872. 18__. 1834–1840s.

Rarity: *None known*

$1.25 • W-RI-700-001.25-G020

Left: 1 25/100 / Train / 1 25/100. *Center:* Sloop and other vessels at sea / $1.25 Cts. *Right:* 1 25/100 / Eagle. *Engraver:* New England Bank Note Co. *Comments:* H-RI-215-G4, Durand-880. 18__. 1830s.

Rarity: *None known*

$1.50 • W-RI-700-001.50-G030

Left: 1 Doll. 50 Cts. vertically. *Center:* Eagle on rock in ocean / $1 50/100. *Right:* 1 50/100 / Justice. *Engraver:* New England Bank Note Co. *Comments:* H-RI-215-G5. 18__. 1830s.

Rarity: *None known*

$1.75 • W-RI-700-001.75-G040

Left: $1.75 Cts / Hebe watering eagle / 1 75/100. *Center:* Three sloops at sea. *Right:* $1.75 Cts / Woman seated with grain, Dog / 1 75/100. *Engraver:* New England Bank Note Co. *Comments:* H-RI-215-G6. 18__. 1830s.

Rarity: *None known*

$2 • W-RI-700-002-G050

Left: 2 / Eagle / 2. *Center:* 2 / Woman seated with plow, Sailboats / 2. *Right:* 2 / Woman standing / 2. *Engraver:* PSSP. *Comments:* H-RI-215-G8, Durand-873. 18__. 1834–1840s.

Rarity: *None known*

$3 • W-RI-700-003-G060

Left: 3 / Eagle / 3. *Center:* 3 / Woman seated with plow, Sailboats / 3. *Right:* 3 / Woman standing / 3. *Engraver:* PSSP. *Comments:* H-RI-215-G14, Durand-874. 18__. 1834–1840s.

Rarity: URS-3

VF $500

$5 • W-RI-700-005-G070

Left: Panel with FIVE / Plenty and Minerva seated / V. *Center:* FIVE / Allegorical woman seated / FIVE. *Right:* Panel with 10 / Portrait of Indian / 10. *Engraver:* PSSP. *Comments:* H-RI-215-G20, Durand-875. 18__. 1834–1840s.

Rarity: *None known*

$10 • W-RI-700-010-G080

Left: Panel with TEN / Manhattan and spilling water jug / TEN. *Center:* TEN / Ceres seated / TEN / Panel of microletters. *Right:* Panel with 10 / Portrait of Indian / 10. *Engraver:* PSSP / New England Bank Note Co. *Comments:* H-RI-215-G26. 18__. 1830s–1840s.

Rarity: *None known*

$20 • W-RI-700-020-G090

Left: 20 / XX vertically / 20. *Center:* 20 / Woman seated with scales, Sheaf and bales, Men plowing, Ship. *Right:* TWENTY vertically. *Engraver:* PSSP / New England Bank Note Co. *Comments:* H-RI-215-G30. 18__. 1830s–1840s.

Rarity: *None known*

PAWTUCKET, RHODE ISLAND

Pawtucket, a village within North Providence, means "little falls" in the native tongue, referring to the 50-foot falls of the local river. It was originally known as Rehoboth in 1651 and was comprised of 600 acres, a part of Massachusetts. In 1671 Joseph Jenks settled across the river and erected a forge and shop. In the same place, Samuel Slater opened the country's first cotton mill in 1793. Iron workers produced farm tools, anchors, cannons, and muskets. A dozen cotton mills, a print works, and manufacturers of cotton machinery, bobbins, spools, shoes, boots, ships, carriages, chairs, and cabinets were also located here. In 1862 the entire area was ceded to Rhode Island.

See also Pawtucket, Massachusetts, Providence, and North Providence, Rhode Island.

Farmers and Mechanics Bank
1822–1829
W-RI-710

History: The Farmers and Mechanics Bank was incorporated in 1822 with an authorized capital of $200,000 to serve the large textile industry in the Pawtucket area. This bank was heavily dependent upon the Wilkinson family, one of the most important factory owners in the city. The bank failed in 1829 due to excessive loans made to the failed Wilkinson business. The bank managed to pay all of its creditors, but the stockholders lost all of their investment. No loss was sustained by the holders of its bills.[42]

Under the old charter, the new Phenix Bank, W-RI-1160, was formed with an address in Providence.[43]

Numismatic Commentary: Genuine notes with the Pawtucket address are extremely hard to locate. Only a few specimens are known today.

VALID ISSUES

$1 • W-RI-710-001-G010

Left: RHODE ISLAND on curved banner vertically. *Center:* 1 / Blacksmith and man at anvil / 1. *Bottom center:* ONE. *Right:* Scene / 1 vertically. *Engraver:* Graphic Co. *Comments:* H-RI-220-G4a, Durand-896. May 1st, 1823.

Rarity: URS-3

VF $500

$2 • W-RI-710-002-G020

Left: RHODE ISLAND on curved banner vertically. *Center:* 2 / Blacksmith and man at anvil / 2. *Bottom center:* TWO. *Right:* Scene / 2 vertically. *Engraver:* Graphic Co. *Comments:* H-RI-220-G8a, Durand-897. May 1st, 1823.

Rarity: *None known*

$3 • W-RI-710-003-G030

Left: RHODE ISLAND on curved banner vertically. *Center:* 3 / Blacksmith and man at anvil / 3. *Bottom center:* THREE. *Right:* Scene / 3 vertically. *Engraver:* Graphic Co. *Comments:* H-RI-220-G12a, Durand-898. May 1st, 1823.

Rarity: *None known*

$5 • W-RI-710-005-G040 TD

Engraver: Graphic Co. *Comments:* H-Unlisted, Durand-Unlisted. Repaired note. May 1st, 1823.

Rarity: URS-1

VF $750

Manufacturers Bank
1813–1865
W-RI-720

History: The Manufacturers Bank was incorporated in the village of Pawtucket in the town of North Providence in October 1813. It was chartered in 1814. Samuel Slater was one of the 13 members of the board of directors. He served as president from 1819 until 1831, when he retired due to ill health.[44]

A slowdown of business in Pawtucket in 1829 caused significant losses to the bank. This convinced the management to remove the bank to Providence in June 1831. In 1850 capital was $453,100, and by 1851 it had risen to $500,000. Circulation that year was $67,273.

The interests of the bank were succeeded by the Manufacturers National Bank, chartered on June 16, 1865.

See also listings under North Providence, W-RI-620, and Providence, W-RI-1030.

Slater Bank
1855–1865
W-RI-730

History: The Slater Bank was incorporated at the village of Pawtucket in North Providence in 1855 with $100,000 in authorized capital. The bank was named after Samuel Slater, whose name is associated with several banks. The capital was increased to $150,000 by 1857. The bank's circulation was around $35,000 at that time, and specie amounted to $3,514.07.

The business of the Slater Bank was succeeded by the Slater National Bank, chartered on March 3, 1865.

See also listing under North Providence, W-RI-660.

Numismatic Commentary: Most of this bank's issues show a vignette of textile mills surrounding the falls of a river. The male portrait is that of Samuel Slater, the man Andrew Jackson named "The Father of the American Industrial Revolution." Genuine notes appear at auction only on occasion.

Pawtuxet, Rhode Island

The Sononoce Pawtuxet tribe, a part of the Narragansett Indian nation, called this place "Little Falls" in their native tongue. In 1662 men from Warwick purchased the land west of the Providence Purchase, including what would later become Cranston.

Pawtuxet Village spans land that is in both Cranston and Warwick. In the 18th century, water power from the Pawtuxet River gave rise to mills, and soon the town had become a prime shipping port for trade with the West Indies. The town was destroyed by fire in King Philip's War, but it was rebuilt and was a busy seaport by the time of the American Revolution. In the 19th century, the shipping industry gave way to the textile industry, and mill villages were erected on either end of the Pawtuxet Falls. The Rhodes-on-the-Pawtuxet casino, dance hall, and canoe center was opened.

See also Cranston, Rhode Island.

Pawtuxet Bank
1814–1882
W-RI-740

History: The Pawtuxet Bank was incorporated at Pawtuxet in October 1814. The founding president was James Rhodes, and Samuel E. Gardiner was the first cashier. Its location was changed to Providence in June 1845. In 1856 it was located at 41 Westminster Street.

The capital of the bank was $118,387 in 1848, $129,850 in 1849, and $150,000 by 1855. Circulation was $51,278 in 1849, but it was reduced to $14,445 by 1857. Specie totaled $2,413.55 the same year.

The Pawtuxet Bank continued as a state bank until it was liquidated in 1882. The original bank building is still standing today.

See also listing under Providence, W-RI-1140.

Numismatic Commentary: Genuine notes dated at Pawtuxet are scarce. The earlier issues by Reed surface more often than the later issues by Terry Pelton & Co. Issues dated in Providence are also scarce.

Valid Issues

$1 • W-RI-740-001-G010
Left: ONE vertically. *Center:* 1 / Woman seated next to beehive / 1. *Bottom center:* ONE. *Right:* RHODE ISLAND vertically. *Engraver:* Reed. *Comments:* H-RI-225-G2, Durand-1774. 181_. 1810s.
Rarity: —
VF $200

$1 • W-RI-740-001-G010a
Center: ONE. *Engraver:* Reed. *Comments:* H-RI-225-G2a, Durand-1775. Similar to W-RI-740-001-G010. 182_. 1820s.
Rarity: *None known*

$1 • W-RI-740-001-G020 SBG

Engraver: Reed. *Comments:* H-RI-225-G4. Similar to W-RI-740-001-G010 but with varying end panels. Proof. 181_. 1810s.
Rarity: URS-3
Proof $350
Selected auction price: Stack's Bowers Galleries, November 2013, AU $940

$1 • W-RI-740-001-G020a
Center: ONE. *Engraver:* Reed. *Comments:* H-RI-225-G4a. Similar to W-RI-740-001-G020. 182_. 1820s.
Rarity: *None known*

$1 • W-RI-740-001-G030 CC

Engraver: Reed. *Comments:* H-RI-225-G6. Similar to W-RI-740-001-G010 but with varying end panels. 181_. 1810s.
Rarity: URS-3
Proof $350

$1 • W-RI-740-001-G030a

CC

Engraver: Reed. *Comments:* H-RI-225-G6a. Similar to W-RI-740-001-G030 but with engraved ONE. 182_. 1820s.
Rarity: URS-2
VF $350

$1 • W-RI-740-001-G040
Engraver: Unverified, but likely Terry, Pelton & Co. *Comments:* H-RI-225-G12. No description available. 18__. 1830s–1845.
Rarity: *None known*

$2 • W-RI-740-002-G050
Left: TWO vertically. *Center:* 2 / Justice seated / 2. *Bottom center:* TWO across 2. *Right:* RHODE ISLAND vertically. *Engraver:* Reed. *Comments:* H-RI-225-G14, Durand-1778. 181_. 1810s.
Rarity: URS-3
Proof $350

$2 • W-RI-740-002-G060
Engraver: Unverified, but likely Terry, Pelton & Co. *Comments:* H-RI-225-G18. No description available. 18__. 1830s–1845.
Rarity: *None known*

$3 • W-RI-740-003-G070
Left: THREE vertically. *Center:* 3 / Hope with shield bearing anchor / 3. *Bottom center:* Building. *Right:* RHODE ISLAND vertically. *Comments:* H-RI-225-G22, Durand-1780. 181_. 1810s.
Rarity: URS-3
Proof $350

$3 • W-RI-740-003-G080
Engraver: Unverified, but likely Terry, Pelton & Co. *Comments:* H-RI-225-G26. No description available. 18__. 1830s–1845.
Rarity: *None known*

$4 • W-RI-740-004-G090
Left: FOUR vertically. *Center:* 4 / IV, Commerce and Industry, IV. *Bottom center:* IV. *Right:* RHODE ISLAND vertically. *Engraver:* Reed. *Comments:* H-RI-225-G30, Durand-1781. 18__. 1810s.
Rarity: *None known*

$5 • W-RI-740-005-G100
Left: FIVE vertically. *Center:* 5 / Hope, Commerce. *Bottom center:* V. *Right:* RHODE ISLAND vertically. *Engraver:* Reed. *Comments:* H-RI-225-G34, Durand-1782. 181_. 1810s.
Rarity: URS-3
Proof $350

$5 • W-RI-740-005-G100a
Center: 5 / Hope / 5 / Commerce. *Comments:* H-Unlisted, Durand-1783. Similar to W-RI-740-005-G100. 181_. 1810s.
Rarity: URS-3

$5 • W-RI-740-005-G110
Engraver: Unverified, but likely Terry, Pelton & Co. *Comments:* H-RI-225-G36. No description available. 18__. 1830s–1845.
Rarity: *None known*

$10 • W-RI-740-010-G120
Left: TEN vertically. *Center:* 10 with Industry / 10 with Hope. *Bottom center:* X. *Right:* RHODE ISLAND vertically. *Engraver:* Reed. *Comments:* H-RI-225-G40, Durand-1784. 181_. 1810s.
Rarity: URS-3
Proof $350

$10 • W-RI-740-010-G130
Left: Panel with TEN. *Center:* X / Ceres and Justice flanking shield bearing anchor and surmounted by eagle / Cattle, sheep, and two men. *Bottom center:* Cattle. *Right:* 10 / Sailing ship and steamboat / 10. *Engraver:* Terry, Pelton & Co. *Comments:* H-RI-225-G44, Durand-1784. 18__. 1830s–1845.
Rarity: URS-1
Proof $900

$20 • W-RI-740-020-G140
Left: Panel with TWENTY vertically. *Center:* Cow and calf lying down / Two men shearing sheep, Man standing, Trees, Building. *Bottom center:* State arms. *Right:* XX / Sailing ship and steamboat / XX. *Engraver:* Terry, Pelton & Co. *Comments:* H-RI-225-G50. 18__. 1830s–1845.
Rarity: *None known*

NON-VALID ISSUES

$1 • W-RI-740-001-C010
Engraver: Reed. *Comments:* H-RI-225-C2, Durand-1776. Counterfeit of W-RI-740-001-G010. 18__. 1810s.
Rarity: URS-3
VF $175

$1 • W-RI-740-001-C010a
Engraver: Reed. *Comments:* H-Unlisted, Durand-1777. Counterfeit of W-RI-740-001-G010a. 182_. 1820s.
Rarity: URS-3

$1 • W-RI-740-001-C030a
Engraver: Reed. *Comments:* H-RI-225-C6a, Durand-1777. Counterfeit of W-RI-740-001-G030a. 18__. 1820s.
Rarity: URS-3
VF $175

$2 • W-RI-740-002-C050
Engraver: Reed. *Comments:* H-RI-225-C14, Durand-1779. Counterfeit of W-RI-740-002-G050. 18__. 1810s.
Rarity: URS-3
VF $175

$10 • W-RI-740-010-A010
Left: 10 / Portrait of George Washington held by cherub / 10. *Center:* X / Spread eagle with shield and arrows, E PLURIBUS UNUM / X. *Right:* 10 / Indian and woman / 10. *Engraver:* Terry, Pelton & Co. *Comments:* H-RI-225-A5, Durand-1793. Altered from $10 Citizens Bank, Augusta, Maine, or from notes of other failed banks using the same plate. 18__. 1840s.
Rarity: URS-3
VF $175

PEACEDALE, RHODE ISLAND

Peacedale, also spelled Peace Dale, is a village of South Kingstown. It is sometimes grouped with the village of Wakefield as a census-designated place and identified as Wakefield-Peacedale. It was founded in 1800 by Rowland Hazard, who was the pioneer of textile-carding machines in Rhode Island. By 1814 Hazard was one of the first manufacturers to use narrow-width power looms. He was also the first woolen manufacturer to house all manufacturing processes in one building.

In 1845 one of the mill buildings was destroyed by fire, but it was quickly replaced by new mills that had state-of-the-art features, including hydropower systems. Woolen shawls and other high-quality woolen materials were manufactured here. There was a stone waving mill, a store, a post office, and a public hall.

Peacedale Bank
1853
W-RI-750

History: The Peacedale Bank was incorporated in May 1853 with an authorized capital of $50,000. This bank did not open for business. It is not known if Proof notes were made.

PHENIX, RHODE ISLAND

The Warwick village of Phenix (today West Warwick) was originally called Roger Williams Village, named after the Roger Williams mill (whose namesake was the founder of the Providence Plantation) that was destroyed by fire in 1821. It was rebuilt and renamed the Phenix Manufacturing Company. The village was also renamed since the mill was the main industry for the area. As it was reborn from the ashes of the old, the village was also given new life and named Phenix Village.

Phenix Bank
1835–1865
W-RI-760

History: The Phenix Bank was incorporated in 1835. It had $200,000 capital in 1848, which was increased to $306,900 in 1857 and again to $417,250 in 1860. It finally reached a high of $437,400 in 1863. Samuel B. Wheaton was president in 1848, followed by Edward Pearce from 1857 to 1864. Benjamin White, a numismatist, was cashier from 1848 to 1864.

The Phenix Bank was succeeded by the Phenix National Bank, chartered on July 17, 1865.

Phenix Village Bank
1856–1865
W-RI-770

History: The Phenix Village Bank was incorporated in May 1856. The bank was formed to meet the needs of the local textile industry and its employees. William B. Spencer served as the bank's founding president, and Henry D. Brown was its first cashier.

Capital was $63,250 in 1857 and varied little throughout the bank's existence. Bills in circulation amounted to $20,712, which rose slightly to $24,735 by 1862. Specie totaled $2,471.36 in 1857. In 1875 the bank's capital was only $50,000.

The business of this bank was succeeded by the Phenix National Bank of Providence, chartered on July 17, 1865—the same day the Phenix National Bank was chartered.

Numismatic Commentary: A trove of cancelled and cut-out notes appeared on the market during the early 1980s. These evidently were bank-cancelled notes stored away for some unknown reason and finally released into the marketplace, giving the collector the chance to put together a set of some six to eight notes, many with the scene of Phenix Village.

VALID ISSUES
$1 • W-RI-770-001-G010   CC

Tint: Red-brown panels and dies outlining ONEs. **Engraver:** Danforth, Wright & Co. **Comments:** H-RI-230-G2a, Durand-899. 18__. 1856–1860s.

Rarity: URS-5
F $250; **Proof** $2,000

How to Read the Whitman Numbering System
$1 • W-RI-010-001-G010a

Denomination: Value of the note shown.

W: Whitman number. This number is a sortable code unique to each bank and note.

RI: Abbreviation for the state under study.

010: Numerical designation specific to each bank.

001: The denomination in dollars.

G010a: G indicates a good or valid note. Other categories are indicated thus: C (counterfeit); R (raised); S (spurious); N (not-attributed); A (altered). Numbers are assigned starting with 010, 020, et seq. Terminal letters following the number indicate variations of a note: a series of different colored overprints, tints, payees, etc., all on the same design of note. For more information, see the "How to Use This Book" section at the front of the volume, page xiv.

$2 • W-RI-770-002-G020

CC

Tint: Red-brown panels and dies outlining TWOs. *Engraver:* Danforth, Wright & Co. *Comments:* H-RI-230-G4a, Durand-901. 18__. 1856–1860s.

Rarity: URS-5
F $250; **VF** $400; **Proof** $2,000

$3 • W-RI-770-003-G030

CC

Tint: Red-brown panels outlining white THREEs. *Engraver:* Danforth, Wright & Co. *Comments:* H-RI-230-G6a, Durand-902. 18__. 1856–1860s.

Rarity: URS-3
F $600

$5 • W-RI-770-005-G040

SBG

Tint: Red-brown outlining white 5. *Engraver:* Danforth, Wright & Co. *Comments:* H-RI-230-G8a, Durand-903. 18__. 1856–1860s.

Rarity: URS-3
VF $250; **Proof** $3,500
Selected auction price: Heritage, April 2008, Lot 12511, Gem New $2,300

$10 • W-RI-770-010-G050

SBG

Tint: Red-brown panels outlining white TEN and Xs. *Engraver:* Danforth, Wright & Co. *Comments:* H-RI-230-G10a, Durand-904. 18__. 1856–1860s.

Rarity: URS-2
Proof $5,500
Selected auction price: Stack's Bowers Galleries, March 2013, Proof $5,446

$50 • W-RI-770-050-G060

QDB

Tint: Red-brown dies and panel outlining white FIFTY DOLLARS. *Engraver:* Danforth, Wright & Co. *Comments:* H-RI-230-G12a, Durand-905. 18__. 1856–1860s.

Rarity: URS-1
VF $500; **Proof** $5,200
Selected auction price: Stack's Bowers Galleries, September 2009, Proof $5,034

$100 • W-RI-770-100-G070

SBG

Tint: Red-brown dies and panel bearing ONE HUNDRED. *Engraver:* Danforth, Wright & Co. *Comments:* H-RI-230-G14a, Durand-906. 18__. 1856–1860s.

Rarity: URS-1
VF $1,200; **Proof** $5,500

Uncut Sheets

$1-$1-$2-$3 • W-RI-770-001.001.002.003-US010
Vignette(s): *($1)* Male portrait / View of Phenix Village and falls. *($1)* Male portrait / View of Phenix Village and falls. *($2)* Male portrait / View of Phenix Village and falls. *($3)* View of Phenix Village and falls. *Engraver:* Danforth, Wright & Co. *Comments:* H-RI-230-G2a, G2a, G4a, G6a. 18__. 1856–1860s.

Rarity: URS-3
Proof $4,000

$5-$5-$5-$10 • W-RI-770-005.005.005.010-US020
Vignette(s): *($5)* Man tending machinery / Male portrait. *($5)* Man tending machinery / Male portrait. *($5)* Man tending machinery / Male portrait. *($10)* Men at work in foundry / Male portrait. *Engraver:* Danforth, Wright & Co. *Comments:* H-RI-230-G8a, G8a, G8a, G10a. 18__. 1856–1860s.

Rarity: URS-3
Proof $4,000

$50-$100 • W-RI-770-050.100-US030
Vignette(s): *($50)* View of Phenix Manufacturing Company. *($100)* Male portrait. *Engraver:* Danforth, Wright & Co. *Comments:* H-RI-230-G12a, G14a. 18__. 1856–1860s.

Rarity: URS-1
Proof $10,000

Non-Valid Issues

$1 • W-RI-770-001-A010
Left: 1 / Milkmaid standing. *Center:* Two cows, Horse and cows. *Bottom center:* Obverse of U.S. gold dollar. *Right:* ONE / Girl / 1. *Overprint:* Red ONE. *Engraver:* Wellstood, Hay & Whiting. *Comments:* H-RI-230-A5, Durand-900. Altered from $1 Thames Bank, Laurel, Indiana. 1850s.

Rarity: *None known*

Providence, Rhode Island

The modern-day capital of Rhode Island (Newport was also a capital city until 1900), Providence is located at the mouth of the Providence River and the head of the Narragansett Bay. In 1636 it was founded by Roger Williams, who secured the title from the Narragansett tribe. The area was known as the Providence Plantation at that time.

The local economy was primarily agricultural in nature, but distilleries in Providence transformed West Indian sugar and molasses, which were also important in commerce, into rum. Providence was one of the first cities in the country to industrialize, producing silverware and jewelry that became famous nationally. In 1835 the railroad came to Providence, trade increased, and in this era, many European immigrants arrived to work.

See also North Providence, Rhode Island.

American Bank
1833–1865
W-RI-780

History: The American Bank was incorporated in October 1833. Henry P. Franklin was the first president, and Daniel C. Cushing was the first cashier. The capital was $55,600 in 1849, increasing dramatically to $530,000 by 1850. It was listed as $1,000,000 in June 1855 and $2,000,000 in 1856. Circulation was $59,394 in 1849. This increased to $135,866 by 1857 and again to $487,768 by 1862. In 1852 the amount of loans given was $871,886. Specie was valued at $10,006 that year, and bank notes totaled $15,046.[45] The bank's specie had increased to $20,288.05 by 1857.

The business of the American Bank was succeeded by the American National Bank, chartered on July 20, 1865.

Numismatic Commentary: The marketplace offers a plentiful supply of notes from this bank. Both genuine and non-valid issues are relative easy to locate. Some of the issues have interesting scenes, such as a $1 note with Niagara Falls in the background of the central vignette, a $5 note with silver dollars equal to the worth of the note shown in the central vignette, and an eagle with wingtips that reach almost to the edges of the note.

Valid Issues

$1 • W-RI-780-001-G010

SBG

Engraver: Chas. Toppan & Co. *Comments:* H-RI-240-G4, Durand-907. 18__. 1830s–1840s.

Rarity: URS-3
Proof $400

$1 • W-RI-780-001-G020
Left: 1 / Woman painting on pedestal, Cog wheel. *Center:* Woman seated with shield and fasces. *Right:* 1 / Male portrait. *Engraver:* Toppan, Carpenter, Casilear & Co. *Comments:* H-RI-240-G6, Durand-908. 18__. 1850s.

Rarity: *None known*

$1 • W-RI-780-001-G020a

TD

Overprint: Ornate red ONE. *Engraver:* Toppan, Carpenter, Casilear & Co. *Comments:* H-RI-240-G6a, Durand-909. Similar to W-RI-780-001-G020. 18__. 1850s.

Rarity: URS-2
VF $800

$1 • W-RI-780-001-G020b

Overprint: Red ONE. *Engraver:* Toppan, Carpenter, Casilear & Co. / ABNCo. monogram. *Comments:* H-RI-240-G6b. Similar to W-RI-780-001-G020 but with different date and additional engraver imprint. May 1, 1858.

Rarity: URS-3

VF $300

$1 • W-RI-780-001-G020c   CC

Overprint: Red ONE. *Engraver:* American Bank Note Co. *Comments:* H-RI-240-G6c. Similar to W-RI-780-001-G020 but with different date and engraver imprint. Sept. 1st, 1862.

Rarity: URS-3

VF $1,200

Selected auction price: Stack's Bowers Galleries, January 2010, VF $1,126

$1 • W-RI-780-001-G030

Left: ONE / Woman standing by column / ONE. *Center:* 1 / Woman with vase of flowers. *Right:* ONE / Steamboats / ONE *Comments:* H-Unlisted, Durand-912. 18__. 1830s–1840s.

Rarity: URS-3

$2 • W-RI-780-002-G040   CC

Engraver: Chas. Toppan & Co. *Comments:* H-RI-240-G10, Durand-913. 18__. 1830s–1840s.

Rarity: URS-3

Proof $1,200

Selected auction price: Stack's Bowers Galleries, March 2013, Proof $1,334

$2 • W-RI-780-002-G050

Left: Portrait of Henry P. Franklin / 2. *Center:* Steamboat and other ships in bay. *Right:* 2 / Allegorical figure with shield. *Engraver:* Toppan, Carpenter, Casilear & Co. *Comments:* H-RI-240-G12, Durand-914. 18__. 1850s.

Rarity: *None known*

$2 • W-RI-780-002-G050a

Overprint: Red TWO. *Engraver:* Toppan, Carpenter, Casilear & Co. *Comments:* H-RI-240-G12a, Durand-915. Similar to W-RI-780-002-G050. 18__. 1850s.

Rarity: *None known*

$2 • W-RI-780-002-G050b

Overprint: Red TWO. *Engraver:* Toppan, Carpenter, Casilear & Co. / ABNCo. monogram. *Comments:* H-RI-240-G12b. Similar to W-RI-780-002-G050 but with different date and additional engraver imprint. May 1, 1858.

Rarity: *None known*

$2 • W-RI-780-002-G050c

Overprint: Red TWO. *Engraver:* American Bank Note Co. *Comments:* H-RI-240-G12c. Similar to W-RI-780-002-G050 but with different date and engraver imprint. Sept. 1, 1862.

Rarity: URS-3

VF $300

$3 • W-RI-780-003-G060   SBG

Engraver: Chas. Toppan & Co. *Comments:* H-RI-240-G16, Durand-918. 18__. 1830s–1840s.

Rarity: URS-2

Proof $1,900

Selected auction price: Stack's Bowers Galleries, March 2013, Proof $1,815

$3 • W-RI-780-003-G070

Left: 3 / 3. *Center:* Two women working at looms / 3. *Right:* Portrait of Henry P. Franklin. *Engraver:* Unverified, but likely Toppan, Carpenter, Casilear & Co. *Comments:* H-RI-240-G18, Durand-919. 18__. Circa 1850s.

Rarity: *None known*

$3 • W-RI-780-003-G070a

Overprint: Red THREE. *Engraver:* Unverified, but likely Toppan, Carpenter, Casilear & Co. *Comments:* H-RI-240-G18a, Durand-920. Similar to W-RI-780-003-G070. 18__. 1850s.

Rarity: *None known*

$3 • W-RI-780-003-G080

Center: Two allegorical women / Sailing vessels / 3. *Engraver:* Durand and Co. *Comments:* H-Unlisted, Durand-921. 1830s–1840s.

Rarity: URS-3

$5 • W-RI-780-005-G090
SBG

Engraver: Chas. Toppan & Co. *Comments:* H-RI-240-G22, Durand-922. 18__. 1830s–1840s.

Rarity: URS-3
Proof $500

$5 • W-RI-780-005-G100
CC

Overprint: Red V, V. *Engraver:* American Bank Note Co. *Comments:* H-RI-240-G24, Durand-923. Sept. 10th, 1860. 1860s.

Rarity: URS-2
VF $1,500

$5 • W-RI-780-005-G110

Left: 5 / Portrait of Henry P. Franklin. *Center:* Steamship, Vessels. *Bottom center:* Eagle on branch. *Right:* 5 / Woman seated in 5. *Engraver:* Unverified, but likely Toppan, Carpenter, Casilear & Co. *Comments:* H-RI-240-G26, Durand-924. 18__. 1850s.

Rarity: *None known*

$5 • W-RI-780-005-G110a

Overprint: Red FIVE. *Engraver:* Toppan, Carpenter, Casilear & Co. *Comments:* H-RI-240-G26a, Durand-925. Similar to W-RI-780-005-G110. 18__. 1850s.

Rarity: *None known*

$5 • W-RI-780-005-G110b

Overprint: Red FIVE. *Engraver:* Toppan, Carpenter, Casilear & Co. / ABNCo. monogram. *Comments:* H-RI-240-G26b. Similar to W-RI-780-005-G110 but with different date and additional engraver imprint. May 1, 1858.

Rarity: URS-3
VF $500

$5 • W-RI-780-005-G120
CC

Overprint: Red FIVE. *Engraver:* Rawdon, Wright, Hatch & Edson. *Comments:* H-RI-240-G28a, Durand-926. June 1st, 185_. 1858.

Rarity: URS-3
VF $1,100

$5 • W-RI-780-005-G130
SBG

Overprint: Red FIVE. *Engraver:* Rawdon, Wright, Hatch & Edson. *Comments:* H-RI-240-G30a, Durand-927. June 1st, 185_. 1850s.

Rarity: URS-2
VF $5,800
Selected auction price: Stack's Bowers Galleries, March 2013, Proof $5,748

$10 • W-RI-780-010-G140
SBG

Engraver: Chas. Toppan & Co. *Comments:* H-RI-240-G32, Durand-933. 18__. 1830s–1840s.

Rarity: URS-3
Proof $1,200

$10 • W-RI-780-010-G150

Left: Portrait of Benjamin Franklin / 10. *Center:* X. *Right:* X / 10 / Commerce and Liberty flanking shield bearing anchor. *Engraver:* Toppan, Carpenter, Casilear & Co. *Comments:* H-RI-240-G34, Durand-934. 18__. 1850s.

Rarity: *None known*

$10 • **W-RI-780-010-G150a**

Overprint: Red TEN. *Engraver:* Unverified, but likely Toppan, Carpenter, Casilear & Co. *Comments:* H-RI-240-G34a, Durand-935. Similar to W-RI-780-010-G150. 18__. 1850s.

Rarity: *None known*

$20 • **W-RI-780-020-G160**   SBG

Engraver: Chas. Toppan & Co. *Comments:* H-RI-240-G35, Durand-942. 18__. 1830s–1840s.

Rarity: URS-2
Proof $2,000
Selected auction price: Stack's Bowers Galleries, March 2013, Proof $1,936

$20 • **W-RI-780-020-G170**

Left: 20 / Indian man seated. *Center:* Columbia draped in American flag / 20. *Right:* 20 / Indian woman seated. *Engraver:* Unverified, but likely Rawdon, Wright, Hatch & Edson. *Comments:* H-RI-240-G36, Durand-940. 18__. 1850s.

Rarity: *None known*

$20 • **W-RI-780-020-G170a**

Overprint: Red 20. *Engraver:* Unverified, but likely Rawdon, Wright, Hatch & Edson. *Comments:* H-RI-240-G36a, Durand-941. Similar to W-RI-780-020-G170. 18__. 1850s.

Rarity: *None known*

$20 • **W-RI-780-020-G170b**

Overprint: Red 20. *Engraver:* American Bank Note Co. *Comments:* H-RI-240-G36c. Similar to W-RI-780-020-G170 but with different date and engraver imprint. Sept. 1, 1862.

Rarity: URS-3
VF $500

$50 • **W-RI-780-050-G180**   SBG

Engraver: Chas. Toppan & Co. *Comments:* H-RI-240-G38, Durand-943. 18__. 1830s–1840s.

Rarity: URS-1
Proof $2,200
Selected auction price: Stack's Bowers Galleries, March 2013, Proof $2,057

$50 • **W-RI-780-050-G180a**

Left: 50 / Industry / 50. *Center:* Steamer ship / Allegorical figure, George Washington on shield surmounted by eagle on globe, Allegorical figure / Steamer ship. *Bottom center:* Anchor on shield. *Right:* 50 / Industry / 50. *Overprint:* Red 50. *Engraver:* Unverified, but likely Toppan, Carpenter, Casilear & Co. *Comments:* H-RI-240-G38a, Durand-943. Similar to W-RI-780-050-G180 but with different engraver imprint. 18__. 1850s.

Rarity: *None known*

$100 • **W-RI-780-100-G190**   CJF

Engraver: Chas. Toppan & Co. *Comments:* H-RI-240-G40, Durand-944. 18__. 1830s–1840s.

Rarity: URS-1
Proof $2,300

$100 • **W-RI-780-100-G190a**

Left: 100 / Justice / 100. *Center:* 100 / Justice, Angel / 100. *Bottom center:* Anchor on shield. *Right:* 100 / Justice / 100. *Overprint:* Red 100. *Engraver:* Chas. Toppan & Co. *Comments:* H-RI-240-G40a. Similar to W-RI-780-100-G190. 18__. 1850s.

Rarity: *None known*

$500 • **W-RI-780-500-G200**

Left: 500 / Portrait of Benjamin Franklin. *Center:* Liberty, shield, eagle. *Bottom center:* Anchor on shield. *Right:* 500 / D. *Engraver:* Unverified, but likely Toppan, Carpenter, Casilear & Co. *Comments:* H-RI-240-G42, Durand-946. 18__. 1850s.

Rarity: *None known*

$1,000 • **W-RI-780-1000-G210**

Left: Eagle with shield. *Center:* Portrait of Henry P. Franklin. *Right:* 1000 / M. *Engraver:* Toppan, Carpenter, Casilear & Co. *Comments:* H-RI-240-G44, Durand-947. 18__. 1850s.

Rarity: URS-3
Proof $5,000

Post Note

$1 • **W-RI-780-001-G220**

Left: POST NOTE vertically. *Center:* 1 on medallion head / Woman seated with sheaf / 1 on medallion head. *Right:* 1 / Figure standing / ONE. *Engraver:* Chas. Toppan & Co. *Comments:* H-RI-240-G60. 18__. 1830s.

Rarity: URS-3
Proof $300

Uncut Sheets

$1-$1-$2-$3 • W-RI-780-001.001.002.003-US010

Vignette(s): ($1) Men in boat / Allegorical woman seated, Factory with water wheel / Anchor on shield / Steamboats. *($1)* Men in boat / Allegorical woman seated, Factory with water wheel / Anchor on shield / Steamboats. *($2)* Eagle and shield / Agriculture, Commerce, and Manufacturing / Eagle and shield. *($3)* Portrait of George Washington / Female portrait / Indian in canoe, Scenery / Female portrait / Anchor on shield / Portrait of Marquis de Lafayette. *Engraver:* Chas. Toppan & Co. *Comments:* H-RI-240-G4, G4, G10, G16. 18__. 1830s–1840s.

Rarity: URS-3
Proof $1,700

$5-$5-$10-$50 • W-RI-780-005.005.010.050-US020

Vignette(s): ($5) Portrait of George Washington / "Washington Crossing the Delaware" / Portrait of Benjamin Franklin. *($5)* Portrait of George Washington / "Washington Crossing the Delaware" / Portrait of Benjamin Franklin. *($10)* Medallion head / Trains / Anchor on shield / Medallion head. *($50)* Industry / Allegorical figure / George Washington on shield surmounted by eagle on globe / Allegorical figure / Anchor on shield / Industry. *Engraver:* Chas. Toppan & Co. *Comments:* H-RI-240-G22, G22, G32, G38. 18__. 1830s–1840s.

Rarity: URS-3
Proof $1,700

$20-$20-$100-$1 • W-RI-780-020.020.100.001-US030

Vignette(s): ($20) Portrait of girl / Commerce / Hebe and eagle / Commerce / Anchor on shield / Portrait of boy. *($20)* Portrait of girl / Commerce / Hebe and eagle / Commerce / Anchor on shield / Portrait of boy. *($100)* Justice / Justice, Angel / Anchor on shield / Justice. *($1)* Woman seated with sheaf / Figure standing. *Engraver:* Chas. Toppan & Co. *Comments:* H-RI-240-G35, G35, G40, G60. Last note is a post note. 18__. 1830s–1840s.

Rarity: URS-3
Proof $1,700

Non-Valid Issues

$1 • W-RI-780-001-S010

Left: ONE / Woman standing, Urn of flowers / 1. *Center:* 1 / Woman seated, Urn of flowers / 1. *Right:* ONE / Steamboats / ONE. *Comments:* H-RI-240-S5. 1850s.

Rarity: *None known*

$1 • W-RI-780-001-A010

Left: 1 / Justice standing / ONE. *Center:* 1 on medallion head / Ceres standing with sheaf and sickle / 1 on medallion head. *Right:* 1 / Woman standing with staff / ONE. *Engraver:* Underwood, Bald, Spencer & Hufty. *Comments:* H-RI-240-A5, Durand-910. Altered from $1 Bank of Superior, Superior, Michigan. 18__. 1830s–1840s.

Rarity: URS-3
VF $250

$1 • W-RI-780-001-A020

Left: 1 / Portrait of George Washington / 1. *Center:* Medallion head bearing 1 / Sleeping child and dog, Man / Medallion head bearing 1. *Right:* 1 / Woman and child / 1. *Engraver:* Draper, Toppan, Underwood & Co. / Underwood, Bald, Spencer & Hufty. *Comments:* H-RI-240-A10, Durand-911. Altered from $1 Tenth Ward Bank, New York City, New York. 18__. 1840s.

Rarity: *None known*

$2 • W-RI-780-002-N010

Left: Woman with shield bearing 2. *Right:* Real Estate Pledged / Woman with shield bearing 2. *Comments:* H-RI-240-N5. 1830s–1840s.

Rarity: *None known*

$2 • W-RI-780-002-N020

Center: Commerce / Liberty. *Comments:* H-Unlisted, Durand-917. Altered or spurious. 1830s–1840s.

Rarity: URS-3

$2 • W-RI-780-002-A030

Left: 2 / Liberty standing. *Center:* 2 on medallion head / Ceres, Indian woman and sailor / 2 on medallion head. *Right:* 2 / Minerva standing. *Comments:* H-Unlisted, Durand-916. Altered from $2 Bank of Superior, Superior, Michigan. 1830s–1840s.

Rarity: URS-3

$3 • W-RI-780-003-N030

Left: Two women. *Center:* Sailing ships. *Right:* 3. *Comments:* H-RI-240-N15. 1830s–1840s.

Rarity: *None known*

$5 • W-RI-780-005-R010

Engraver: American Bank Note Co. *Comments:* H-RI-240-R6c, Durand-928. Raised from W-RI-780-001-G020c. Sept. 1, 1862.

Rarity: URS-3
VF $250

$5 • W-RI-780-005-N040

Center: Two women / Sailing vessels. *Comments:* H-RI-240-N20, Durand-931. 1830s–1840s.

Rarity: *None known*

$5 • W-RI-780-005-N050

Left: Medallion head. *Center:* Two women seated flanking shield. *Right:* Medallion head. *Comments:* H-RI-240-N25, Durand-932. 1830s–1840s.

Rarity: *None known*

$5 • W-RI-780-005-A040

Left: 5 / V / 5. *Center:* V on star / Steamship and sailing ships. *Right:* 5 on V / FIVE / Train. *Engraver:* Boston Bank Note Co. *Comments:* H-RI-240-A15, Durand-930. Altered from $5 Bank of Owasso, Owasso, Michigan. 18__. 1840s.

Rarity: URS-3
VF $250

$5 • W-RI-780-005-A050

Left: FIVE / Roman senator with scroll / 5. *Center:* FIVE on helmeted medal / Sheaf / Woman with infant / FIVE on helmeted medal. *Bottom center:* Train. *Right:* FIVE / Woman with book / 5. *Engraver:* Draper, Underwood & Co. / Underwood, Bald, Spencer & Hufty. *Comments:* H-RI-240-A20, Durand-929. Altered from $5 Tenth Ward Bank, New York City, New York. 18__. 1840s.

Rarity: *None known*

$10 • W-RI-780-010-N060

Left: Woman with agricultural implements. *Center:* Woman seated. *Right:* Male portrait. *Comments:* H-RI-240-N30, Durand-939. 1830s–1840s.

Rarity: *None known*

$10 • W-RI-780-010-A060

Left: 10 / Portrait of George Washington held by cherub / 10. *Center:* X / Spread eagle with shield / X. *Bottom center:* Ship. *Right:* 10 / Indian / 10. *Engraver:* Terry, Pelton & Co. *Comments:* H-RI-240-A25, Durand-936. Altered from $10 Citizens Bank, Augusta, Maine, or from notes of other failed banks using the same plate. 18__. 1840s.

Rarity: *None known*

$10 • W-RI-780-010-A070

Left: 10 / Sailor with U.S. flag / X. *Center:* Diagonal 10 on medal / "Signing of the Declaration of Independence" / Diagonal 10 on medal. *Bottom center:* Eagle. *Right:* X / "Pat Lyon at the Forge" / 10. *Engraver:* Draper, Underwood & Co. / Underwood, Bald, Spencer & Hufty. *Comments:* H-RI-240-A30, Durand-938. Altered from $10 Tenth Ward Bank, New York City, New York. 18__. 1840s.

Rarity: *None known*

$10 • W-RI-780-010-A080

Left: 10 / Agriculture and Justice flanking shield bearing anchor. *Center:* Man standing over boy gathering corn, Horse-drawn wagon. *Right:* 10 / Portrait of girl with ringlets. *Overprint:* Red X, X. *Comments:* H-RI-240-A35, Durand-937. Altered from W-RI-1630-010-G050. 18__. 1855.

Rarity: *None known*

$100 • W-RI-780-100-A090

Left: HUNDRED / Justice holding sword and balance / 100. *Center:* 100 / Allegorical woman and Justice flanking shield bearing rising sun, Train on bridge, Ships / 100. *Right:* Panel bearing ONE HUNDRED vertically. *Engraver:* Unverified, but likely Draper, Toppan & Co. *Comments:* H-RI-240-A50, Durand-945. Altered from $100 Tenth Ward Bank, New York City, New York. 18__. 1840s.

Rarity: *None known*

Arcade Bank
1831–1865
W-RI-790

History: The Arcade Bank was incorporated in June 1831 and a few years later became one of the "pet banks" of the Jackson administration. Charles Dyer and Thomas J. Stead served as the first president and cashier, respectively. The institution was located in the Arcade, a complex of stores and offices. In 1833 the bank speculated heavily by sending vast amounts of notes out of state, where it was hard for them to be redeemed. In the same year, the directors who had encouraged this caper forfeited their shares and were liable for prosecution.[46] The capital between 1833 and 1837 was $200,000, rising to $500,000 by 1849. This amount was raised still further to $1,000,000 by 1856. Bills in circulation were $31,744 in 1835, $70,000 in 1836, and $58,662 in 1857. Specie that same year totaled $6,500.

In 1865 the business of the Arcade Bank was succeeded by the Rhode Island National Bank, chartered on April 6, 1865.

Numismatic Commentary: Genuine notes are very scarce. Many of these issues show a vignette of the Arcade Building, the first shopping mall in the United States. The north and south entrances are distinctly different in appearance.

VALID ISSUES

$1 • W-RI-790-001-G010   CJF

Engraver: Rawdon, Wright & Co. *Comments:* H-RI-245-G4, Durand-948. 18__. 1830s–1840s.

Rarity: URS-3
Proof $1,000

$1 • W-RI-790-001-G020

Left: ONE vertically. *Center:* 1 / View of the northern entrance to the Arcade / 1. *Right:* Beehive / Female portrait / Shield. *Engraver:* Toppan, Carpenter & Co. *Comments:* H-RI-245-G6, Durand-949. 18__. 1840s–1850s.

Rarity: URS-3
Proof $1,000

$1 • W-RI-790-001-G020a

Overprint: Red ONE. *Engraver:* Toppan, Carpenter & Co. *Comments:* H-RI-245-G6c, Durand-950. Similar to W-RI-790-001-G020 but with additional text "Incorporated 1831" and "CAPITAL $1,000,000". 18__. 1850s–1860s.

Rarity: *None known*

$2 • W-RI-790-002-G030

Left: 2 / TWO / 2. *Center:* 2 / View of the southern entrance to the Arcade / 2. *Right:* 2 / TWO / 2. *Engraver:* Rawdon, Wright & Co. *Comments:* H-RI-245-G10, Durand-952. 18__. 1830s–1840s.

Rarity: *None known*

$2 • W-RI-790-002-G040

Left: TWO vertically. *Center:* 2 / View of the northern entrance to the Arcade / 2. *Bottom center:* Anchor on shield. *Right:* Beehive / Indian maid / Shield. *Engraver:* Toppan, Carpenter & Co. *Comments:* H-RI-245-G12, Durand-953. 18__. 1840s–1850s.

Rarity: URS-3
Proof $1,000

$2 • **W-RI-790-002-G040a**

CC

Overprint: Red TWO. **Engraver:** Toppan, Carpenter & Co. **Comments:** H-RI-245-G12c, Durand-954. Similar to W-RI-790-002-G040 but with additional text "Incorporated 1831" and "CAPITAL $1,000,000". 18__. 1850s–1860s.
Rarity: URS-3
VF $500

$2 • **W-RI-790-002-G050**

Center: Seated giant. **Comments:** H-Unlisted, Durand-955. 1840s–1850s.
Rarity: *None known*

$3 • **W-RI-790-003-G060**

Left: 3 / Portrait of George Washington / 3. **Center:** 3 on die / View of the southern entrance to the Arcade. **Bottom center:** Shield bearing anchor. **Right:** 3 / Portrait of Commodore Oliver Hazard Perry / 3. **Engraver:** Rawdon, Wright & Co. **Comments:** H-RI-245-G16, Durand-956. 18__. 1830s–1840s.
Rarity: URS-3
Proof $1,000

$3 • **W-RI-790-003-G070**

CJF

Engraver: Toppan, Carpenter & Co. **Comments:** H-RI-245-G18, Durand-957. 18__. 1840s–1850s.
Rarity: URS-3
Proof $1,000

$3 • **W-RI-790-003-G070a**

Left: THREE vertically. **Center:** 3 / View of the northern entrance to the Arcade / 3. **Right:** Ceres / THREE. **Overprint:** Red THREE. **Engraver:** Toppan, Carpenter & Co. **Comments:** H-RI-245-G18b, Durand-958. Similar to W-RI-790-003-G070 but with additional text "Incorporated 1831" and "CAPITAL $1,000,000". 18__. 1850s–1860s.
Rarity: URS-3
VF $500

$5 • **W-RI-790-005-G080**

Left: 5 / Woman with shield bearing 5 / 5. **Center:** 5 / View of the southern entrance to the Arcade / 5. **Right:** FIVE vertically. **Engraver:** Rawdon, Wright & Co. **Comments:** H-RI-245-G22, Durand-960. 18__. 1830s–1840s.
Rarity: URS-3
Proof $1,000

$5 • **W-RI-790-005-G090**

Left: Female portrait. **Center:** 5 / View of the northern entrance to the Arcade / 5. **Bottom center:** Anchor on shield. **Right:** Spread eagle. **Engraver:** Toppan, Carpenter & Co. **Comments:** H-RI-245-G24, Durand-961. 18__. 1840s–1850s.
Rarity: *None known*

$5 • **W-RI-790-005-G090a**

Overprint: Red FIVE. **Engraver:** Toppan, Carpenter & Co. **Comments:** H-Unlisted, Durand-962. Similar to W-RI-790-005-G090. 1840s–1850s.
Rarity: URS-3

$5 • **W-RI-790-005-G090b**

Overprint: Red FIVE. **Engraver:** Toppan, Carpenter & Co. **Comments:** H-RI-245-G24c, Durand-963. Similar to W-RI-790-005-G090 but with additional text "Incorporated 1831" and "CAPITAL $1,000,000". 18__. 1850s–1860s.
Rarity: URS-3
VF $500

$10 • **W-RI-790-010-G100**

Left: Portrait of Marquis de Lafayette / 10 / Portrait of Robert Fulton. **Center:** 10 / View of the northern entrance to the Arcade / 10. **Right:** Portrait of Chief Justice John Marshall / TEN / Portrait of Benjamin Franklin. **Engraver:** Draper, Toppan, Longacre & Co. **Comments:** H-RI-245-G28, Durand-966. 18__. 1840s.
Rarity: URS-3
Proof $750

$20 • **W-RI-790-020-G110**

Left: XX / Woman / XX. **Center:** Sheaf / Three allegorical figures / Beehive / 20. **Bottom center:** Star. **Right:** 20 / Drover and cattle / 20. **Engraver:** Draper, Toppan, Longacre & Co. **Comments:** H-RI-245-G32, Durand-969. 18__. 1840s.
Rarity: *None known*

$50 • **W-RI-790-050-G120**

Left: Man. **Center:** 50 / Globe, ship. **Bottom center:** Anchor on shield. **Right:** 50 / Male portrait / 50. **Engraver:** Unverified, but likely Draper, Toppan, Longacre & Co. **Comments:** H-RI-245-G34, Durand-971. 18__. 1840s–1850s.
Rarity: *None known*

$100 • **W-RI-790-100-G130**

Left: 100 / Portrait / 100. **Center:** 100 / Man on horseback / 100. **Bottom center:** Anchor on shield. **Right:** 100 / Portrait / 100. **Engraver:** Unverified, but likely Draper, Toppan, Longacre & Co. **Comments:** H-RI-245-G36, Durand-972. 18__. 1840s–1850s.
Rarity: *None known*

$500 • W-RI-790-500-G140

Left: Indian paddling canoe, Trees and mountains / 500. *Center:* 500 / Justice. *Engraver:* New England Bank Note Co. *Comments:* H-RI-245-G38, Durand-973. 18__. 1850s.

Rarity: *None known*

$1,000 • W-RI-790-1000-G150

Left: Eagle on cliff overlooking sea. *Center:* 1000. *Right:* 1000 / Indian maid. *Engraver:* New England Bank Note Co. *Comments:* H-RI-245-G40, Durand-974. 18__. 1850s.

Rarity: *None known*

Uncut Sheets

$1-$1-$2-$3 • W-RI-790-001.001.002.003-US010

Vignette(s): ($1) View of the northern entrance to the Arcade / Beehive / Female portrait / Shield. *($1)* View of the northern entrance to the Arcade / Beehive / Female portrait / Shield. *($2)* View of the northern entrance to the Arcade / Anchor on shield / Beehive / Indian maid / Shield. *($3)* View of the northern entrance to the Arcade / Ceres. *Engraver:* Toppan, Carpenter & Co. *Comments:* H-RI-245-G6, G6, G12, G18. 18__. 1840s–1850s.

Rarity: URS-3
Proof $3,500

Non-Valid Issues

$1 • W-RI-790-001-A010

Left: 1 / Woman holding infant / 1. *Center:* Medallion head bearing 1 / Sleeping child and dog, Man reaping / Medallion head bearing 1. *Bottom center:* Eagle. *Right:* 1 / Portrait of George Washington. *Engraver:* Draper, Underwood & Co. / Underwood, Bald, Spencer & Hufty. *Comments:* H-RI-245-A5, Durand-951. Altered from $1 Tenth Ward Bank, New York City, New York. Similar to genuine but with left and right vignettes switched. 18__. 1840s.

Rarity: *None known*

$2 • W-RI-790-002-A020

Left: 2 on die. *Center:* Manhattan reclining with urn and staff / 2. *Right:* Woman, Panel of wheat and corn ears. *Engraver:* Durand & Co. *Comments:* H-RI-245-A10. Altered from $2 Globe Bank, New York City, New York. 18__. 1840.

Rarity: *None known*

$3 • W-RI-790-003-C070a

Engraver: Toppan, Carpenter & Co. *Comments:* H-RI-245-C18b, Durand-959. Counterfeit of W-RI-790-003-G070a. 18__. 1855.

Rarity: URS-3
VF $350

$5 • W-RI-790-005-A030

Left: 5 / Cattle / FIVE. *Center:* River scene, Raft and docks, Warehouses. *Right:* FIVE / Milkmaid. *Engraver:* PSSP / New England Bank Note Co. *Comments:* H-RI-245-A15, Durand-965. Altered from $5 Stillwater Canal Bank, Orono, Maine. 18__. 1840s.

Rarity: *None known*

$5 • W-RI-790-005-A040

CC

Engraver: Danforth, Underwood & Co. / Underwood, Bald, Spencer & Hufty. *Comments:* H-RI-245-A20, Durand-964. Altered from $5 Tenth Ward Bank, New York City, New York. 18__. 1840s.

Rarity: URS-3
VF $150

$10 • W-RI-790-010-A050

Left: 10 / Sailor with U.S. flag / X. *Center:* Diagonal 10 on medallion head / "Signing of the Declaration of Independence" / Diagonal 10 on medallion head. *Bottom center:* Eagle. *Right:* X / "Pat Lyon at the Forge" / 10. *Engraver:* Draper, Underwood & Co. / Underwood, Bald, Spencer & Hufty. *Comments:* H-RI-245-A25, Durand-967. Altered from $10 Tenth Ward Bank, New York City, New York. 18__. 1840s.

Rarity: *None known*

$10 • W-RI-790-010-A060

Left: TEN / Justice. *Center:* River scene, Raft and docks, Warehouses. *Right:* 10 / Woman / TEN. *Engraver:* PSSP / New England Bank Note Co. *Comments:* H-RI-245-A30, Durand-968. Altered from $10 Stillwater Canal Bank of Orono, Maine. 18__. 1840s.

Rarity: *None known*

$20 • W-RI-790-020-A070

Left: 20 / Train / XX. *Center:* Diagonal 20 on medallion head / "Pat Lyon at the Forge" / Diagonal 20 on medallion head. *Right:* 20 / Cattle / XX. *Engraver:* Draper, Underwood & Co. / Underwood, Bald, Spencer & Hufty. *Comments:* H-RI-245-A35, Durand-970. Altered from $20 Tenth Ward Bank, New York City, New York. 18__. 1840s.

Rarity: *None known*

$20 • W-RI-790-020-A080

Left: Anchor, Hope seated on shore. *Center:* 20 / Warehouse, Ships in harbor. *Right:* 20. *Engraver:* Durand & Co. *Comments:* H-RI-245-A40. Altered from $20 Globe Bank, New York City, New York. 18__. 1840.

Rarity: *None known*

Atlantic Bank
1853–1882
W-RI-800

History: The Atlantic Bank was organized on June 6, 1853, and incorporated the same year. In 1853 Caleb Gerald Burrows was president, accompanied by C.M. Stone as cashier. Hiram Hill took over the presidency from 1853 to 1874.[47] The bank was located at 48 Broad Street in 1856.

The capital ranged from a low of $101,300 in June 1855 to a high of $144,800 in 1856. Circulation ranged from $27,209 in 1857 to $66,889 in 1862 to an extreme low of $1,074 in 1874. The bank's specie was $2,780.15 in 1857.

The Atlantic Bank remained a state bank until it obtained a charter as the Atlantic National Bank in 1882. No notes were issued after 1866.

Numismatic Commentary: Genuine notes are very hard to locate. Any surviving examples of such are Proof notes. No signed and dated examples have been encountered. Non-valid examples are available.

VALID ISSUES

$1 • W-RI-800-001-G010
Left: ONE / Two women / ONE. *Center:* Ships. *Bottom center:* Portrait of boy. *Right:* 1 / Eagle on water / ONE. *Engraver:* Wellstood, Hanks, Hay & Whiting. *Comments:* H-RI-250-G2, Durand-975. 18__. 1850s.

Rarity: *None known*

$1 • W-RI-800-001-G010a

Overprint: Green panel outlining white ONE. *Engraver:* Wellstood, Hanks, Hay & Whiting / ABNCo. monogram. *Comments:* H-RI-250-G2a, Durand-976. Similar to W-RI-800-001-G010 but with additional engraver imprint and text "Patented 30 June 1857". 18__. 1850s–1860s.

Rarity: URS-3
Proof $1,000

$1 • W-RI-800-001-G020
Center: Woman, Eagle on shield, Train, Woman. *Comments:* H-Unlisted, Durand-977. 1850s–1860s.

Rarity: URS-3

$2 • W-RI-800-002-G030
Left: 2 / Cherub with cornucopia / TWO. *Center:* Woman seated with shield bearing anchor, Ship. *Bottom center:* Portrait of boy. *Right:* 2 / TWO / Cherub. *Engraver:* Wellstood, Hanks, Hay & Whiting. *Comments:* H-RI-250-G4, Durand-978. 18__. 1850s.

Rarity: *None known*

$2 • W-RI-800-002-G030a

Overprint: Green panel outlining white TWO. *Engraver:* Wellstood, Hanks, Hay & Whiting / ABNCo. monogram. *Comments:* H-RI-250-G4a, Durand-979. Similar to W-RI-800-002-G030 but with additional engraver imprint and text "Patented 30 June 1857". 18__. 1850s–1860s.

Rarity: URS-3
Proof $6,200
Selected auction price: Stack's Bowers Galleries, March 2013, Proof $6,051

$5 • W-RI-800-005-G040
Left: FIVE on V / Two allegorical figures / 5. *Center:* Clipper ship, steamboat, vessels. *Bottom center:* Portrait of girl. *Right:* FIVE / Ship under sail, Sailor seated by bales / 5. *Engraver:* Wellstood, Hanks, Hay & Whiting. *Comments:* H-RI-250-G6, Durand-982. 18__. 1850s.

Rarity: *None known*

$10 • W-RI-800-010-G050
Left: 10 / 10 on X, Two sailors, boat, rocks, and lighthouse. *Center:* Industry, Agriculture, and Commerce. *Bottom center:* Portrait of boy. *Right:* 10 / Girl standing on rocky shore. *Engraver:* Wellstood, Hanks, Hay & Whiting. *Comments:* H-RI-250-G8, Durand-985. 18__. 1850s.

Rarity: *None known*

$10 • W-RI-800-010-G050a

Engraver: Wellstood, Hanks, Hay & Whiting. *Comments:* H-Unlisted, Durand-Unlisted. Similar to W-RI-800-010-G050 but with different central vignette. 18__. 1850s.

Rarity: URS-1
Unc-Rem $450; **Proof** $6,000
Selected auction price: Stack's Bowers Galleries, March 2013, Proof $5,446

$50 • W-RI-800-050-G060

Left: 50 vertically / Justice / FIFTY. *Center:* Industry, Agriculture, and Commerce. *Right:* 50 / Sailor. *Comments:* H-Unlisted, Durand-986. 1850s–1860s.

Rarity: URS-3

$50 • W-RI-800-050-G060a

Overprint: Red FIFTY. *Engraver:* Wellstood, Hanks, Hay & Whiting. *Comments:* H-RI-250-G10a, Durand-987. Similar to W-RI-800-050-G060. 18__. 1850s.

Rarity: URS-1
Proof $3,000

$100 • W-RI-800-100-G070

SBG

Comments: H-Unlisted, Durand-988. 18__. 1850s.

Rarity: URS-1
Proof $8,000
Selected auction price: Stack's Bowers Galleries,
March 2013, Proof $7,866

$100 • W-RI-800-100-G070a

Left: Allegorical figure holding shield bearing arm and hammer / 100 / Sailor. *Center:* Cherub / Sailor / Cherub. *Bottom center:* Portrait of boy. *Right:* 100 / Ceres. *Overprint:* Red 100. *Engraver:* Wellstood, Hanks, Hay & Whiting. *Comments:* H-RI-250-G12a, Durand-989. Similar to W-RI-800-100-G070. 18__. 1850s.

Rarity: URS-1
Proof $6,000

Uncut Sheets

$1-$1-$1-$2 • W-RI-800-001.001.001.002-US010

Vignette(s): *($1)* Two women / Ships / Portrait of girl / Eagle on water. *($1)* Two women / Ships / Portrait of girl / Eagle on water. *($1)* Two women / Ships / Portrait of girl / Eagle on water. *($2)* Cherub with cornucopia / Woman seated with shield bearing anchor, Ship / Portrait of girl / Cherub. *Engraver:* Wellstood, Hanks, Hay & Whiting / ABNCo. monogram. *Comments:* H-RI-250-G2a, G2a, G2a, G4a. 18__. 1850s–1860s.

Rarity: URS-3
Proof $3,500

$50-$100 • W-RI-800-050.100-US020

Vignette(s): *($50)* Justice / Industry, Agriculture, and Commerce / Sailor. *($100)* Allegorical figure and sailor / Cherub / Sailor / Cherub / Portrait of girl / Ceres. *Engraver:* Wellstood, Hanks, Hay & Whiting. *Comments:* H-RI-250-G10a, G12a. 18__. 1850s.

Rarity: URS-3
Proof $2,500

Non-Valid Issues

$1 • W-RI-800-001-S010

Left: 1 / Woman seated on anchor. *Center:* Eagle on U.S. shield, Train. *Bottom center:* Sheaf and plow. *Right:* ONE / Indian woman pulling arrow from quiver. *Comments:* H-RI-250-S5, Durand-981. 185_. 1850s.

Rarity: *None known*

$2 • W-RI-800-002-N010

Center: Steamship and sailing vessels. *Comments:* H-RI-250-N5, Durand-980. 1850s.

Rarity: *None known*

$3 • W-RI-800-003-A010

Left: 3 / Steamship. *Center:* Justice, Shield surmounted by eagle, Liberty. *Right:* 3 / Train. *Overprint:* Red THREE. *Engraver:* Baldwin, Bald & Cousland / Bald, Cousland & Co. *Comments:* H-RI-250-A5, Durand-981. Altered from W-RI-1500-003-G030a. 18__. 1850s.

Rarity: *None known*

$5 • W-RI-800-005-S020

Center: Portraits of five presidents on V surmounted by eagle and two flags / 5. *Comments:* H-RI-250-S10, Durand-984. 1850s.

Rarity: *None known*

$5 • W-RI-800-005-N020

Left: Woman. *Center:* Spread eagle, Ships. *Right:* Ship under sail. *Comments:* H-RI-250-N10, Durand-983. 1850s.

Rarity: *None known*

Atlas Bank
1854–1867
W-RI-810

History: The Atlas Bank was chartered in May 1854. Henry J. Angell served as its first president, and Harvey F. Payton was its first cashier. It commenced business in August. Authorized capital was set at $100,000. The bank was located at North Main Street on the corner of Smith Avenue.

Bills in circulation totaled $25,603 in 1854, which decreased to $16,782 by 1862. Specie was listed at $3,872 in 1857.

The bank closed in 1867.

Numismatic Commentary: Genuine notes are hard to locate. A popular note in this series is the $1 note showing a cherub rolling a silver dollar to the left and a very popular image of Santa Claus about to go up the chimney.

Valid Issues

$1 • W-RI-810-001-G010

Left: 1 / Cherub as fountain. *Center:* Cherub rolling silver dollar. *Bottom center:* Woman seated. *Right:* 1 / Santa Claus. *Overprint:* Red ONE. *Engraver:* New England Bank Note Co. / Rawdon, Wright, Hatch & Edson. *Comments:* H-RI-255-G2a, Durand-990. A coveted Santa Claus note. 18__. 1850s.

Rarity: URS-5
Proof $5,000

$1 • **W-RI-810-001-G010a**

CC

Overprint: Red ONE. *Engraver:* New England Bank Note Co. / Rawdon, Wright, Hatch & Edson / ABNCo. monogram. *Comments:* H-RI-255-G2b, Durand-991. Similar to W-RI-810-001-G010 but with additional engraver imprint. 18__. 1850s–1860s.

Rarity: URS-5

Proof $5,700

Selected auction price: Heritage, January 2012, Proof $5,634

$1 • **W-RI-810-001-G010b**

SBG

Overprint: Green ONE. *Engraver:* New England Bank Note Co. / Rawdon, Wright, Hatch & Edson / ABNCo. monogram. *Comments:* H-Unlisted, Durand-Unlisted. Similar to W-RI-810-001-G010 but with additional engraver imprint. 18__. 1850s–1860s.

Rarity: URS-3

F $9,000

Selected auction price: Heritage, January 2012, F $9,000

$2 • **W-RI-810-002-G020**

Left: Hunter / 2. *Center:* Milkmaid seated, Cows. *Right:* 2 / Female portrait. *Overprint:* Red TWO. *Engraver:* New England Bank Note Co. / Rawdon, Wright, Hatch & Edson. *Comments:* H-RI-255-G4a, Durand-992. 18__. 1850s.

Rarity: *None known*

$2 • **W-RI-810-002-G020a**

CC

Overprint: Red TWO. *Engraver:* New England Bank Note Co. / Rawdon, Wright, Hatch & Edson / ABNCo. monogram. *Comments:* H-RI-255-G4b, Durand-993. Similar to W-RI-810-002-G020 but with additional engraver imprint. 18__. 1850s–1860s.

Rarity: URS-2

F $750; **VF** $1,500

$2 • **W-RI-810-002-G020b**

Overprint: Green TWO. *Engraver:* New England Bank Note Co. / Rawdon, Wright, Hatch & Edson / ABNCo. monogram. *Comments:* H-Unlisted. Similar to W-RI-810-002-G020 but with additional engraver imprint. 18__. 1850s–1860s.

Rarity: *None known*

$3 • **W-RI-810-003-G030**

Left: 3 / Indian girl. *Center:* Cherubs sporting with dolphin in water, Allegorical woman seated on rock. *Right:* 3 / Cherub on the back of dolphin. *Overprint:* Red THREE. *Engraver:* New England Bank Note Co. / Rawdon, Wright, Hatch & Edson. *Comments:* H-RI-255-G6a, Durand-994. 18__. 1850s.

Rarity: *None known*

$3 • **W-RI-810-003-G030a**

Overprint: Red THREE. *Engraver:* New England Bank Note Co. / Rawdon, Wright, Hatch & Edson / ABNCo. monogram. *Comments:* H-RI-255-G6b, Durand-995. Similar to W-RI-810-003-G030 but with additional engraver imprint. 18__. 1850s–1860s.

Rarity: *None known*

$5 • **W-RI-810-005-G040**

Left: FIVE / Minerva. *Center:* Train. *Right:* 5 / Female portrait / 5. *Overprint:* Red FIVE. *Engraver:* New England Bank Note Co. / Rawdon, Wright, Hatch & Edson. *Comments:* H-RI-255-G8a, Durand-996. 18__. 1850s.

Rarity: *None known*

$5 • **W-RI-810-005-G040a**

Engraver: New England Bank Note Co. / Rawdon, Wright, Hatch & Edson / ABNCo. monogram. *Comments:* H-RI-255-G8b, Durand-997. Similar to W-RI-810-005-G040 but with additional engraver imprint. 18__. 1850s–1860s.

Rarity: *None known*

$10 • **W-RI-810-010-G050**

Left: Sailor / 10. *Center:* Industry. *Bottom center:* Farmers loading hay. *Right:* 10 / Hope seated. *Engraver:* New England Bank Note Co. / Rawdon, Wright, Hatch & Edson. *Comments:* H-RI-255-G10, Durand-999. 18__. 1850s.

Rarity: *None known*

$10 • **W-RI-810-010-G050a**

Engraver: New England Bank Note Co. / Rawdon, Wright, Hatch & Edson / ABNCo. monogram. *Comments:* H-RI-255-G10b. Similar to W-RI-810-010-G050 but with additional engraver imprint. 18__. 1850s–1860s.

Rarity: *None known*

$20 • **W-RI-810-020-G060**

Left: Sailor / 20. *Center:* Justice and Prosperity flanking shield surmounted by eagle. *Right:* 20 / Liberty. *Engraver:* New England Bank Note Co. / Rawdon, Wright, Hatch & Edson. *Comments:* H-RI-255-G12, Durand-1000. 18__. 1850s.

Rarity: *None known*

$50 • W-RI-810-050-G070

CJF

Engraver: New England Bank Note Co. / Rawdon, Wright, Hatch & Edson. *Comments:* H-RI-255-G14, Durand-1001. 18__. 1850s.
Rarity: URS-1
VF $2,500

$100 • W-RI-810-100-G080

Left: Female portrait / 100. *Center:* Agriculture and Commerce, Strongbox, sheaf, and steamship. *Right:* 100 / Archimedes raising world with lever. *Engraver:* New England Bank Note Co. / Rawdon, Wright, Hatch & Edson. *Comments:* H-RI-255-G16, Durand-1002. 18__. 1850s.
Rarity: *None known*

NON-VALID ISSUES

$5 • W-RI-810-005-A010

Left: 5 / FIVE / FIVE. *Center:* Indian woman and frontiersman flanking five gold dollars, Three cherubs. *Bottom center:* Steamboat. *Right:* 5 / Female portrait / FIVE. *Overprint:* FIVE. *Engraver:* Rawdon, Wright, Hatch & Edson. *Comments:* H-RI-255-A5, Durand-998. Altered from $5 Farmers and Mechanics Bank of Memphis, Memphis, Tennessee series. 1850s.
Rarity: *None known*

Bank of America
1851–1890
W-RI-820

History: The Bank of America was incorporated in May 1851 and began business in July. Adnah Sackett and L.B. Frieze were its first president and cashier, respectively. It commenced business in July with $50,000 in authorized capital. The bank was located on Weybosset Street.

The capital was $195,600 by 1857. Bills in circulation totaled $33,217 at the same date, with specie at $4,199.34. By 1862 circulation was $122,352. No notes were issued after 1866.

The business of the Bank of America was taken over by the Mutual Trust and Deposit Co. of Providence in 1890 to become the Bank of America Loan and Trust Co.

Numismatic Commentary: Genuine notes are easily attainable thanks to a hoard of uncut sheets that was dispersed in the late 20th century. Such sheets are still available in the marketplace. Genuine signed and dated notes from a different series are available as well.

Remaining in the American Bank Note Co. archives as of 2003 was a $10-$20-$50-$100 face plate.

VALID ISSUES

$1 • W-RI-820-001-G010

Left: 1 / Portrait of Christopher Columbus. *Center:* Seaport, Liberty seated, Eagle and shield, Train. *Right:* 1 / Girl carrying grain. *Engraver:* Toppan, Carpenter, Casilear & Co. *Comments:* H-RI-235-G2, Durand-1003. 18__. 1850s–1860s.
Rarity: URS-3
Proof $500

$1 • W-RI-820-001-G010a

QDB

Overprint: Red ONE. *Comments:* H-Unlisted, Durand-1004. Similar to W-RI-820-001-G010. 18__. 1850s–1860s.
Rarity: URS-3
F $250

$1 • W-RI-820-001-G010b

CC

Tint: Green panel. *Engraver:* National Bank Note Co. *Comments:* H-RI-235-G4a. Similar to W-RI-820-001-G010. 18__. 1860s.
Rarity: URS-10
VF $150; **CU** $75

$2 • W-RI-820-002-G020

Left: 2 on die / History writing on tablet leaning on pedestal. *Center:* Woman reclining on packages, Sailing ship. *Right:* 2 on die / Portrait of Thomas Jefferson. *Engraver:* Toppan, Carpenter, Casilear & Co. *Comments:* H-RI-235-G6. 18__. 1850s–1860s.
Rarity: URS-3
Proof $500

$2 • W-RI-820-002-G020a

CJF

Overprint: Red TWO. *Engraver:* Toppan, Carpenter, Casilear & Co. *Comments:* H-Unlisted, Durand-1007. Similar to W-RI-820-002-G020. 18__. 1850s–1860s.

Rarity: URS-5
VF $400

$2 • W-RI-820-002-G020b

CC

Tint: Green panel. *Engraver:* National Bank Note Co. *Comments:* H-RI-235-G8a, Durand-1006. Similar to W-RI-820-002-G020. 18__. 1860s.

Rarity: URS-10
VF $200; **Unc-Rem** $90

$2 • W-RI-820-002-G030

Left: TWO / Liberty. *Center:* Portrait of Thomas Jefferson / Liberty with shield. *Right:* 2 / Eagle on shield / 2. *Comments:* H-Unlisted, Durand-1008. 1850s–1860s.

Rarity: URS-3

$3 • W-RI-820-003-G040

Left: 3 / Justice. *Center:* Portrait of Indian woman. *Bottom center:* Eagle. *Right:* 3 / Ship under sail. *Engraver:* Toppan, Carpenter, Casilear & Co. *Comments:* H-RI-235-G10, Durand-1010. 18__. 1850s–1860s.

Rarity: URS-3
Proof $500

$5 • W-RI-820-005-G050

Left: Eagle on shield / 5. *Center:* Portrait of George Washington. *Bottom center:* Steamship. *Right:* 5 / State arms. *Engraver:* Toppan, Carpenter, Casilear & Co. *Comments:* H-Unlisted, Durand-1014. 18__. 1850s.

Rarity: URS-3

$5 • W-RI-820-005-G050a

Overprint: Red FIVE. *Engraver:* Toppan, Carpenter, Casilear & Co. *Comments:* H-RI-235-G12a, Durand-1013. Similar to W-RI-820-005-G050. 18__. 1850s.

Rarity: *None known*

$5 • W-RI-820-005-G050b

Overprint: Red FIVE. *Engraver:* Toppan, Carpenter, Casilear & Co. / ABNCo. monogram. *Comments:* H-RI-235-G12b. Similar to W-RI-820-005-G050 but with additional engraver imprint. 18__. 1850s–1860s.

Rarity: *None known*

$5 • W-RI-820-005-G060

TD

Tint: Green panel. *Engraver:* National Bank Note Co. *Comments:* H-RI-235-G14a, Durand-1012. 18__. 1860s.

Rarity: URS-10
VF $200; **Unc-Rem** $100

$10 • W-RI-820-010-G070

Left: 10 / TEN. *Center:* Woman seated with cap, pole, and shield. *Right:* 10 on die / Dollars. *Engraver:* Unverified, but likely Toppan, Carpenter, Casilear & Co. *Comments:* H-RI-235-G16, Durand-1019. 18__. 1850s.

Rarity: *None known*

$10 • W-RI-820-010-G080

QDB

Tint: Green panels. *Engraver:* National Bank Note Co. *Comments:* H-RI-235-G18a, Durand-1018. 18__. 1860s.

Rarity: URS-8
VF $350; **Unc-Rem** $150

$20 • W-RI-820-020-G090

Left: 20 / Train. *Center:* Cherub, Justice, Cherub. *Right:* 20 / Ceres. *Engraver:* Toppan, Carpenter, Casilear & Co. *Comments:* H-RI-235-G20, Durand-1021. 18__. 1850s.

Rarity: *None known*

$20 • W-RI-820-020-G090a

CC

Overprint: Red TWENTY. **Engraver:** Toppan, Carpenter, Casilear & Co. **Comments:** H-Unlisted, Durand-Unlisted. Similar to W-RI-820-020-G090. 18__. 1860s.

Rarity: URS-1

F $600; **VF** $1,500

$50 • W-RI-820-050-G100

Left: 50 / Female portrait / 50. **Center:** Industry and Commerce. **Right:** 50 / Boy gathering corn. **Engraver:** Unverified, but likely Toppan, Carpenter, Casilear & Co. **Comments:** H-RI-235-G22, Durand-1022. 18__. 1850s.

Rarity: *None known*

$100 • W-RI-820-100-G110

Left: 100 / Sailor. **Center:** Woman and cherubs soaring above city. **Right:** 100 / Ship / 100. **Engraver:** Unverified, but likely Toppan, Carpenter, Casilear & Co. **Comments:** H-RI-235-G24, Durand-1024. 18__. 1850s.

Rarity: *None known*

Uncut Sheets

$1-$1-$1-$2 • W-RI-820-001.001.001.002-US010

Vignette(s): **($1)** Male portrait / Seaport / Liberty seated, Eagle and shield / Train / Girl carrying grain. **($1)** Male portrait / Seaport / Liberty seated, Eagle and shield / Train / Girl carrying grain. **($1)** Male portrait / Seaport / Liberty seated, Eagle and shield / Train / Girl carrying grain. **($2)** History writing on tablet leaning on pedestal / Woman reclining on packages, Sailing ship / Male portrait. **Tint(s):** Green. **Engraver:** National Bank Note Co. **Comments:** H-RI-235-G4a, G4a, G4a, G8a. 18__. 1860s.

Rarity: URS-10

VF $250

$5-$5-$5-$10 • W-RI-820-005.005.005.010-US020

Vignette(s): **($5)** Woman standing with wreath / Male portrait / Anchor. **($5)** Woman standing with wreath / Male portrait / Anchor. **($5)** Woman standing with wreath / Male portrait / Anchor. **($10)** Male portrait / Woman seated with cap, pole, and shield. **Tint(s):** Green. **Engraver:** National Bank Note Co. **Comments:** H-RI-235-G14a, G14a, G14a, G18a. 18__. 1860s.

Rarity: URS-10

VF $250

Non-Valid Issues

$1 • W-RI-820-001-A010

CJF

Engraver: Toppan & Co. **Comments:** H-RI-235-A5, Durand-1005. Altered from $1 Pennsylvania Savings Bank, Philadelphia, Pennsylvania. 185_. 1852.

Rarity: URS-5

VF $150

$2 • W-RI-820-002-A020

CC

Engraver: Rawdon, Wright, Hatch & Edson. **Comments:** H-RI-235-A10. Handwritten 94 over 51 in date. Oct. 19th, 1851. 1850s.

Rarity: URS-3

F $200

$2 • W-RI-820-002-N010

Center: Liberty / Neptune / Eagle. **Comments:** H-RI-235-N5, Durand-1009. 1850s.

Rarity: *None known*

$3 • W-RI-820-003-A030

Left: 3 / Portrait of George Washington / THREE. **Center:** Liberty standing next to portrait of George Washington / Eagle and shield. **Bottom center:** Anchor on shield. **Right:** 3 / Liberty standing. **Engraver:** Rawdon, Wright, Hatch & Edson. **Comments:** H-RI-235-A15, Durand-1011. Altered from $3 Bank of America, Georgetown, D.C. Oct. 19, 185_. 1850s.

Rarity: *None known*

$5 • W-RI-820-005-C050b

Overprint: Red FIVE. *Engraver:* Toppan, Carpenter, Casilear & Co. / ABNCo. monogram. *Comments:* H-RI-235-C12b, Durand-1015. Counterfeit of W-RI-820-005-G050b. 18__. 1861.

Rarity: URS-3
VF $200

$5 • W-RI-820-005-R010

Engraver: National Bank Note Co. *Comments:* H-RI-235-R4, Durand-1016. Raised from W-RI-820-001-G010b. 18__. 1860s.
Rarity: *None known*

$5 • W-RI-820-005-A040

Left: Men driving cattle into stream / 5. *Center:* Five men haying, Wagon and oxen. *Right:* 5. *Engraver:* Bald, Cousland & Co. *Comments:* H-RI-235-A20, Durand-1017. Altered from $5 Pioneer Association, La Fayette, Indiana. 18__. 1850s.
Rarity: *None known*

$10 • W-RI-820-010-R020

Engraver: National Bank Note Co. *Comments:* H-RI-235-R5, Durand-1020. Raised from W-RI-820-001-G010b. 18__. 1860s.
Rarity: *None known*

$50 • W-RI-820-050-N020

Center: Train. *Comments:* H-RI-235-N10, Durand-1023. 1850s.
Rarity: *None known*

Bank of Commerce
1851–1865
W-RI-830

History: The Bank of Commerce was incorporated in May 1851 and commenced business on July 8, when the first installment of 20 percent of its capital had been paid. It was located at Market Square in 1863. Amos D. Smith and Joseph H. Bourne were the first president and cashier, respectively. The bank had a close association with the Merchants Insurance Company, which needed a ready source of capital in the event of an unexpected large claim.[48] In 1855 the bank's capital was $1,000,000, which increased over the years to $1,708,900.

Figures given in 1857 were reported as $101,859 worth of bills in circulation and specie valued at $50,398.47. Circulation was up to $173,074 by 1862.

The interests of the Bank of Commerce were succeeded by the National Bank of Commerce, chartered on August 1, 1865.

Numismatic Commentary: Genuine notes are hard to locate. Non-valid examples are in the marketplace in abundance.

VALID ISSUES

$1 • W-RI-830-001-G010

Left: 1 / Sailor with spyglass. *Center:* Commerce seated. *Right:* 1 / History writing on tablet. *Engraver:* Toppan, Carpenter, Casilear & Co. *Comments:* H-RI-275-G2, Durand-1025. 18__. 1850s.
Rarity: *None known*

$1 • W-RI-830-001-G010a

Overprint: Red panel outlining white ONE. *Engraver:* Toppan, Carpenter, Casilear & Co. *Comments:* H-RI-275-G2a, Durand-1026. Similar to W-RI-830-001-G010. 18__. 1850s.
Rarity: *None known*

$1 • W-RI-830-001-G010b

Overprint: Red panel outlining white ONE. *Engraver:* Toppan, Carpenter, Casilear & Co. / ABNCo. monogram. *Comments:* H-RI-275-G2b, Durand-1026. Similar to W-RI-830-001-G010 but with additional engraver imprint. 18__. 1860s.
Rarity: URS-6
VF $300

$2 • W-RI-830-002-G020

Left: Indian on rock / 2. *Center:* Two ships, Schooner under sail. *Right:* 2 / Ceres. *Engraver:* Toppan, Carpenter, Casilear & Co. *Comments:* H-RI-275-G4, Durand-1028. 18__. 1850s.
Rarity: URS-3
Proof $500

$2 • W-RI-830-002-G020a

Overprint: Red panel outlining white TWO. *Engraver:* Toppan, Carpenter, Casilear & Co. *Comments:* H-RI-275-G4a, Durand-1029. Similar to W-RI-830-002-G020. 18__. 1850s.
Rarity: *None known*

$2 • W-RI-830-002-G020b

Overprint: Red panel outlining white TWO. *Engraver:* Toppan, Carpenter, Casilear & Co. / ABNCo. monogram. *Comments:* H-RI-275-G4b, Durand-1029. Similar to W-RI-830-002-G020 but with additional engraver imprint. 18__. 1860s.
Rarity: *None known*

$3 • W-RI-830-003-G030

Engraver: Toppan, Carpenter, Casilear & Co. *Comments:* H-RI-275-G6, Durand-1032. 18__. 1850s.
Rarity: URS-1
Proof $2,500

$3 • W-RI-830-003-G030a
Overprint: Red panel outlining white THREE. *Engraver:* Toppan, Carpenter, Casilear & Co. *Comments:* H-RI-275-G6a, Durand-1033. Similar to W-RI-830-003-G030. 18__. 1850s.
Rarity: *None known*

$3 • W-RI-830-003-G030b
Overprint: Red panel outlining white THREE. *Engraver:* Toppan, Carpenter, Casilear & Co. / ABNCo. monogram. *Comments:* H-RI-275-G6b. Similar to W-RI-830-003-G030 but with additional engraver imprint. 18__. 1860s.
Rarity: URS-3
VF $400

$5 • W-RI-830-005-G040
Left: FIVE / Steamship, Ships. *Center:* Portrait of Henry Clay. *Right:* 5 / Goddess of Plenty. *Engraver:* Toppan, Carpenter, Casilear & Co. *Comments:* H-RI-275-G8, Durand-1036. 18__. 1850s.
Rarity: URS-3
Proof $500

$5 • W-RI-830-005-G040a
Overprint: Red panel outlining white FIVE. *Engraver:* Toppan, Carpenter, Casilear & Co. *Comments:* H-RI-275-G8a, Durand-1037. Similar to W-RI-830-005-G040. 18__. 1850s.
Rarity: *None known*

$5 • W-RI-830-005-G040b   CJF

Overprint: Red panel outlining white FIVE. *Engraver:* Toppan, Carpenter, Casilear & Co. / ABNCo. monogram. *Comments:* H-RI-275-G8b. Similar to W-RI-830-005-G040 but with additional engraver imprint. 18__. 1860s.
Rarity: URS-3
VF $400

$10 • W-RI-830-010-G050
Left: Harbor view / 10. *Center:* 10. *Right:* TEN / Justice seated. *Engraver:* Toppan, Carpenter, Casilear & Co. *Comments:* H-RI-275-G10, Durand-1040. 18__. 1850s.
Rarity: *None known*

$10 • W-RI-830-010-G050a
Overprint: Red panel outlining white TEN. *Engraver:* Toppan, Carpenter, Casilear & Co. *Comments:* H-RI-275-G10a. Similar to W-RI-830-010-G050. 18__. 1850s.
Rarity: *None known*

$10 • W-RI-830-010-G050b
Overprint: Red panel outlining white TEN. *Engraver:* Toppan, Carpenter, Casilear & Co. / ABNCo. monogram. *Comments:* H-RI-275-G10b. Similar to W-RI-830-010-G050 but with additional engraver imprint. 18__. 1860s.
Rarity: *None known*

$50 • W-RI-830-050-G060
Left: 50 / Cherub seated. *Center:* Commerce seated. *Bottom center:* Anchor on shield. *Right:* 50 / Cherub seated. *Engraver:* Toppan, Carpenter, Casilear & Co. *Comments:* H-RI-275-G12, Durand-1042. 18__. 1850s.
Rarity: *None known*

$100 • W-RI-830-100-G070   CC

Engraver: Toppan, Carpenter, Casilear & Co. *Comments:* H-RI-275-G14, Durand-1043. 18__. 1850s.
Rarity: URS-3
Proof $2,000

$500 • W-RI-830-500-G080
Left: Liberty on throne, Village / D. *Center:* Portrait of George Washington. *Right:* 500. *Engraver:* Toppan, Carpenter, Casilear & Co. *Comments:* H-RI-275-G16, Durand-1044. 18__. 1850s.
Rarity: URS-3
Proof $1,000

$1,000 • W-RI-830-1000-G090   SBG

Engraver: Toppan, Carpenter, Casilear & Co. *Comments:* H-RI-275-G18, Durand-1045. 18__. 1850s.
Rarity: URS-1
Proof $10,000

NON-VALID ISSUES

$1 • W-RI-830-001-S010
Left: ONE / Portrait of William Henry Harrison. *Center:* Mercury seated with sailor pointing out to sea / 1. *Bottom center:* Steamboat. *Right:* George Washington standing / ONE. *Engraver:* Toppan, Carpenter & Co. *Comments:* H-RI-275-S5, Durand-1038. May 1, 1856.
Rarity: *None known*

$1 • W-RI-830-001-N010
Center: Man pointing to sea. *Comments:* H-Unlisted, Durand-1027. 18__. 1850s.
Rarity: URS-3

$2 • W-RI-830-002-N020

Center: Woman / Train / Bust of George Washington. *Comments:* H-RI-275-N5, Durand-1030. 18__. 1850s.

Rarity: *None known*

$2 • W-RI-830-002-N030

Center:: Two women seated with sheaf and sickle, Train. *Comments:* H-Unlisted, Durand-1031. 18__. 1850s.

Rarity: URS-3

$3 • W-RI-830-003-S020

CJF

Engraver: Toppan, Carpenter, Casilear & Co. *Comments:* H-RI-275-S10, Durand-1034. Spurious design imitating a rough verbal description of W-RI-830-003-G030. July 1, 18__. 1856.

Rarity: URS-5
VF $115

$3 • W-RI-830-003-N040

Center: Woman, boxes, ship. *Comments:* H-RI-275-N10, Durand-1035. Altered or spurious. 18__. 1850s.

Rarity: *None known*

$5 • W-RI-830-005-N050

CC

Comments: H-RI-275-N15, Durand-1039. 18__. 1850s.

Rarity: URS-3
F $300

$5 • W-RI-830-005-A010

Left: V / Portrait of Henry Clay. *Center:* Steamboat. *Right:* 5 / Portrait of George Washington. *Overprint:* Red FIVE. *Engraver:* New England Bank Note Co. / Rawdon, Wright, Hatch & Edson. *Comments:* H-RI-275-A5, Durand-1038. Altered from $5 Waubeek Bank, De Soto, Nebraska. 1857.

Rarity: *None known*

$10 • W-RI-830-010-N060

Left: Woman. *Center:* Eagle / Ship. *Right:* 10 / Ship. *Comments:* H-RI-275-N20, Durand-1041. Altered or spurious. 18__. 1850s.

Rarity: *None known*

Bank of North America
1823–1865
W-RI-840

History: The Bank of North America was incorporated in 1823. Cyrus Butler was the bank's founding president, and John Taylor was its first cashier. The bank had $448,100 in capital by 1848. From 1857 to 1863 its capital was $860,000. The bank's circulation was at $56,800 in 1852, increasing to $95,800 by 1857 and to $140,600 by 1863. Deposits in 1852 amounted to $60,048. Specie totaled $22,000 in 1857. The bank was located in the N.A. Building on Weybosset Street.

The business of the Bank of North America was succeeded by the National Bank of North America, chartered on April 17, 1865. Two of the bank's presidents, Elisha Harris and Seth Padelford, were governors of Rhode Island.

Numismatic Commentary: Genuine issues are scarce and take time to locate. A rare marriage of engravers is presented with a series of notes from this bank: the engraving firm of Reed & Pelton makes an appearance on some issues. Reed & Pelton worked together for just a short time in the late 1830s and produced very few issues for various banks.

VALID ISSUES

$1 • W-RI-840-001-G010

Left: Die / 1 on die vertically / Die. *Center:* ONE / Two women seated with sheaf, Spinning wheel, Sickle, Ship, Building / ONE. *Bottom center:* Die. *Right:* Die / RHODE ISLAND on die vertically / Die. *Payee:* Seth Wheaton. *Engraver:* PSSP / Reed & Pelton. *Comments:* H-RI-365-G2, Durand-1046. First issue. 182_. 1820s–1840s.

Rarity: URS-3
Proof $350

$1 • W-RI-840-001-G010a

Center: ONE / Three women seated with sheaf, Spinning wheel, Sickle, Ship, Building / ONE. *Payee:* Nicholas Brown. *Engraver:* Reed & Pelton. *Comments:* H-RI-365-G2a. Similar to W-RI-840-001-G010 but with different engraved payee. 182_. 1820s.

Rarity: URS-3
Proof $350

$1 • W-RI-840-001-G020

Left: Indian standing / ONE. *Center:* 1 / Railway station, Wharf, Steamboat. *Right:* 1 / ONE on medallion head. *Engraver:* Rawdon, Wright & Hatch. *Comments:* H-RI-365-G6, Durand-1047. 18__. 1840s–1850s.

Rarity: *None known*

$1 • W-RI-840-001-G020a

Overprint: Red ONE. *Engraver:* Rawdon, Wright & Hatch. *Comments:* H-RI-365-G6a, Durand-1048. Similar to W-RI-840-001-G020. 18__. 1850s–1860s.

Rarity: URS-3
VF $400

$1 • W-RI-840-001-G030

SI

Engraver: Wellstood, Hanks, Hay & Whiting. *Comments:* H-Unlisted, Durand-Unlisted. 18__. 1850s.
Rarity: URS-1
VF $800

$1 • W-RI-840-001-G040

Left: 1 / Fame blowing trumpet. *Center:* Liberty seated on globe, Eagle and cherub. *Right:* 1 / Male portrait. *Back:* Bank of North America across ONE / 1 on die containing two allegorical figures. *Engraver:* Wellstood, Hanks, Hay & Whiting. *Comments:* H-RI-365-G8, Durand-1049. 18__. 1850s.
Rarity: URS-1
Proof $3,000

$1 • W-RI-840-001-G040a

Engraver: Wellstood, Hanks, Hay & Whiting / ABNCo. monogram. *Comments:* H-RI-365-G8a, Durand-1049. Similar to W-RI-840-001-G040 but with additional engraver imprint. 18__. 1850s–1860s.
Rarity: URS-3
VF $350

$2 • W-RI-840-002-G050

CC

Engraver: Reed & Pelton. *Comments:* H-RI-365-G10, Durand-1051. 182_. 1820s–1840s.
Rarity: URS-3
Proof $500

$2 • W-RI-840-002-G060

Left: TWO vertically. *Center:* 2 / Liberty beside shield / TWO. *Bottom center:* Dog's head. *Right:* 2 / TWO on medallion head. *Engraver:* Rawdon, Wright & Hatch. *Comments:* H-RI-365-G12, Durand-1052. 18__. 1840s–1850s.
Rarity: *None known*

$2 • W-RI-840-002-G060a

Overprint: Red TWO. *Engraver:* Rawdon, Wright & Hatch. *Comments:* H-RI-365-G12a, Durand-1053. Similar to W-RI-840-002-G060. 18__. 1850s–1860s.
Rarity: *None known*

$2 • W-RI-840-002-G070

Left: 2 / Woman seated with child, pole and cap. *Center:* Male portrait. *Right:* 2. *Back:* Bank of North America across TWO / 2 on die containing two allegorical figures. *Engraver:* Wellstood, Hanks, Hay & Whiting. *Comments:* H-RI-365-G14, Durand-1054. 18__. 1850s.
Rarity: *None known*

$2 • W-RI-840-002-G070a

Engraver: Wellstood, Hanks, Hay & Whiting / ABNCo. monogram. *Comments:* H-RI-365-G14a. Similar to W-RI-840-002-G070 but with additional engraver imprint. 18__. 1850s–1860s.
Rarity: URS-3

$2 • W-RI-840-002-G070b

QDB, QDB

Back: Bank of North America across TWO / 2s on dies containing allegorical figures. *Engraver:* American Bank Note Co. *Comments:* H-Unlisted. Similar to W-RI-840-002-G070 but with different engraver imprint. January 1st, 1863.
Rarity: URS-2
VF $2,000

$3 • W-RI-840-003-G080

Left: 3. *Center:* 3 / Indian princess surrounded by flags, Drum. *Right:* THREE / Farmer / THREE. *Comments:* H-RI-365-G18, Durand-1056. This was the only $3 issued. 18__. 1860s.
Rarity: *None known*

$5 • W-RI-840-005-G090

SBG

Engraver: Reed & Pelton. *Comments:* H-RI-365-G20, Durand-1058. First issue. 182_. 1820s–1840s.
Rarity: URS-3
Proof $1,700

$5 • **W-RI-840-005-G100**

Left: FIVE / Liberty seated. *Center:* FIVE on 5 / Sailor in boat. *Bottom center:* Steamship. *Right:* 5 on shield / Portrait of Benjamin Franklin. *Engraver:* Wellstood, Hanks, Hay & Whiting. *Comments:* H-RI-365-G24, Durand-1059. 18__. 1850s.

Rarity: URS-3
Proof $1,500

$5 • **W-RI-840-005-G110**

Left: Three dies vertically. *Center:* Woman seated with 5. *Bottom center:* Die. *Right:* Three dies vertically. *Comments:* H-Unlisted, Durand-1061. 18__. 1850s.

Rarity: URS-3

$10 • **W-RI-840-010-G120**

Engraver: Reed & Pelton. *Comments:* H-RI-365-G26. No description available. 182_. 1820s.

Rarity: *None known*

$10 • **W-RI-840-010-G130**

Left: Three dies / X over 10 on die. *Center:* 10 / Two women seated / X over 10. *Bottom center:* Die. *Right:* Three dies / RHODE ISLAND across die. *Comments:* H-Unlisted, Durand-1063. 18__. 1850s.

Rarity: URS-3

$10 • **W-RI-840-010-G140**   SBG

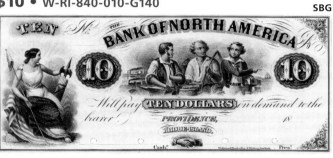

Engraver: Wellstood, Hanks, Hay & Whiting. *Comments:* H-RI-365-G30, Durand-1064. Proof. 18__. 1850s.

Rarity: URS-1
Proof $5,000
Selected auction price: Stack's Bowers Galleries, March 2013, Proof $4,841

$50 • **W-RI-840-050-G150**

Left: 50 / Indian princess. *Center:* Eagle and shield on rock in sea. *Right:* 50 / Knowledge seated on scroll holding pen and book. *Comments:* H-RI-365-G36, Durand-1073. 18__. 1850s.

Rarity: *None known*

$100 • **W-RI-840-100-G160**

Left: 100 / Cherub with cornucopia / 100. *Center:* Ships, Spread eagle on shield, Ships. *Right:* 100 / Cherub with cornucopia / 100. *Comments:* H-RI-365-G39, Durand-1077. 18__. 1850s.

Rarity: *None known*

$500 • **W-RI-840-500-G170**

Left: 500 / Spread eagle on shield / 500. *Center:* Seated Liberty and shield / D. *Right:* 500 / Two allegorical figures. *Comments:* H-RI-365-G42, Durand-1079. 18__. 1850s.

Rarity: URS-1

$1,000 • **W-RI-840-1000-G180**

Left: Woman holding olive branch and sword / 1000. *Center:* Globe showing map of North America. *Right:* Woman with flowers and cornucopia / 1000. *Comments:* H-RI-365-G44, Durand-1080. 18__. 1850s.

Rarity: URS-1

Uncut Sheets

$1-$1 • **W-RI-840-001.001-US010**

Vignette(s): *($1)* Three women seated with sheaf, Spinning wheel, Sickle, Ship, Building. *($1)* Three women seated with sheaf, Spinning wheel, Sickle, Ship, Building. *Engraver:* Reed & Pelton. *Comments:* H-RI-365-G2a, G2a. 182_. 1820s.

Rarity: URS-3
Proof $800

$2-$5 • **W-RI-840-002.005-US020**

Vignette(s): *($2)* Hope and Knowledge. *($5)* Woman standing with staff / Woman seated with shield bearing FIVE. *Engraver:* Reed & Pelton. *Comments:* H-RI-365-G10, G20. 182_. 1820s–1840s.

Rarity: URS-3
Proof $800

Non-Valid Issues

$1 • **W-RI-840-001-C010**

Engraver: Reed & Pelton. *Comments:* H-RI-365-C2, Durand-1050. Counterfeit of W-RI-840-001-G010. 182_. 1820s.

Rarity: URS-3
VF $250

$1 • **W-RI-840-001-A010**

Left: ONE on die supported by cherub riding on dolphin / ONE. *Center:* 1 / Sailor with quadrant, Ceres with sickle and sheaf seated on sacks. *Right:* ONE / Portrait of George Washington / ONE. *Overprint:* Red ONE. *Engraver:* Wellstood, Hanks, Hay & Whiting. *Comments:* H-RI-365-A5. Altered from $1 Mechanics Bank, Georgetown, D.C. 18__. 1850s.

Rarity: *None known*

$2 • **W-RI-840-002-A020**

Left: TWO / Justice / 2. *Center:* Eagle on shield. *Right:* 2 / TWO / Male portrait. *Comments:* H-Unlisted, Durand-1055. Altered from $2 Peoples Bank of North America, Georgetown, D.C. 18__. 1850s.

Rarity: URS-3

$3 • **W-RI-840-003-S010**   CC

Comments: H-RI-365-S5, Durand-1057. 182_. 1820s.

Rarity: URS-3
VF $375

$5 • W-RI-840-005-C090

Engraver: Reed & Pelton. *Comments:* H-RI-365-C20. Counterfeit of W-RI-840-005-G090. 182_. 1820s.

Rarity: *None known*

$5 • W-RI-840-005-S020   CC

Engraver: Rawdon, Wright & Hatch. *Comments:* H-RI-365-S10, Durand-1062. 18__. 1830s.

Rarity: URS-3
VF $200

$5 • W-RI-840-005-N010

Left: Indian. *Center:* Train. *Right:* Indian. *Comments:* H-RI-365-N5. 18__. 1850s.

Rarity: *None known*

$5 • W-RI-840-005-A030

Left: FIVE / Minerva standing with spear, helmet, and shield / FIVE. *Center:* Three allegorical women reclining with sheaf, pole and cap, globe, and quadrant / FIVE. *Right:* 5 / Portrait of George Washington. *Engraver:* Danforth, Bald & Co. *Comments:* H-RI-365-A10, Durand-1059. Altered from $5 Columbia Bank, Washington, D.C. 18__. 1850s.

Rarity: *None known*

$5 • W-RI-840-005-A040

Left: 10 / Woman with scroll. *Center:* X / Three allegorical women. *Right:* 10 / Cattle, Telegraph pole. *Comments:* H-Unlisted, Durand-1060. Altered from $10 Columbia Bank, Washington, D.C. 18__. 1850s.

Rarity: URS-3

$10 • W-RI-840-010-R010

Engraver: Reed & Pelton. *Comments:* H-RI-365-R4, Durand-1065. Raised from W-RI-840-001-G010. 182_. 1820s.

Rarity: URS-3
VF $200

$10 • W-RI-840-010-R020

Engraver: Reed & Pelton. *Comments:* H-RI-365-R5, Durand-1066. Raised from W-RI-840-002-G050. 182_. 1820s.

Rarity: *None known*

$10 • W-RI-840-010-R030

Engraver: Wellstood, Hanks, Hay & Whiting. *Comments:* H-RI-365-R10, Durand-1067. Raised from W-RI-840-001-G040. 18__. 1850s.

Rarity: *None known*

$10 • W-RI-840-010-N020

Left: Woman, flag. *Center:* Farmer, sailor, and mechanic. *Comments:* H-RI-365-N10, Durand-1069. 18__. 1850s.

Rarity: *None known*

$10 • W-RI-840-010-A050   CC

Engraver: Underwood, Bald, Spencer & Hufty. *Comments:* H-RI-365-A15, Durand-1070. Altered from $10 Bank of Vicksburg, Vicksburg, Mississippi. 18__. 1850s.

Rarity: URS-3
VF $200

$10 • W-RI-840-010-A060

Left: 10 / Justice. *Center:* Indian family, Woman pointing at plow. *Right:* 10 / Woman reclining on cornucopia. *Back:* Ten orange dies with Xs. *Engraver:* Unverified, but likely W.L. Ormsby. *Comments:* H-RI-365-A20, Durand-1068. Altered from $10 Farmers and Drovers Bank, Petersburg, Indiana. 1850s.

Rarity: *None known*

$20 • W-RI-840-020-N030

Center: Woman, Bale of goods, Shield. *Comments:* H-RI-365-N20, Durand-1071. Altered or spurious. 18__. 1850s.

Rarity: *None known*

$20 • W-RI-840-020-A070

Left: 20 / Sailor standing on wharf, leaning on capstan. *Center:* Medallion portrait of George Washington. *Right:* 20 / Ceres seated with sheaf and sickle. *Overprint:* Red 20. *Comments:* H-RI-365-A25, Durand-1072. Altered from W-RI-1630-020-G060. 18__. 1855.

Rarity: *None known*

$50 • W-RI-840-050-R040

Engraver: Reed & Pelton. *Comments:* H-RI-365-R15, Durand-1074. Raised from W-RI-840-005-G090. 18__. 1820s.

Rarity: *None known*

$50 • W-RI-840-050-R050

Engraver: Wellstood, Hanks, Hay & Whiting. *Comments:* H-RI-365-R20, Durand-1075. Raised from W-RI-840-005-G100. 18__. 1850s.

Rarity: *None known*

$50 • W-RI-840-050-N040

Center: Hope sitting on anchor with fluke raised. *Comments:* H-RI-365-N25, Durand-1076. 18__. 1850s.

Rarity: *None known*

$100 • W-RI-840-100-R060

Engraver: Reed & Pelton. *Comments:* H-RI-365-R25, Durand-1078. Raised from W-RI-840-005-G090. 18__. 1820s.

Rarity: *None known*

Bank of the Republic
1854–1856
W-RI-850

History: The Bank of the Republic was incorporated in May 1854 with an authorized capital of $100,000. Nathaniel A. Eddy was the bank's first president, and Charles M. Howlet was its first cashier. The officers speculated heavily by sending vast amounts of notes out of state, which made it difficult for the notes to ever be redeemed, thereby leaving the bank with immediate profit. Capital was mainly in the form of promissory notes. The bank had little in the way of real assets and failed in 1856.

Numismatic Commentary: This bank failed and left plenty of its notes behind, thus giving collectors a good chance at acquiring a selection. $5 notes have been observed at least twice, possibly three times, with a #1 serial number—indicating multiple starts of the serial sequence within a short period of time.

The imprint of the American Bank Note Co. was used from 1854 to 1858 in conjunction with a separate entity—Jocelyn, Draper, Welsh & Co.

VALID ISSUES

$1 • W-RI-850-001-G010 SBG

Engraver: Jocelyn, Draper, Welsh & Co. / American Bank Note Co. **Comments:** H-RI-385-G2, Durand-1081. The portrait of Washington is as painted by Gilbert Stuart. 18__. 1850s.
Rarity: URS-3
Proof $500

$1 • W-RI-850-001-G010a CC

Overprint: Red 1, 1. **Engraver:** Jocelyn, Draper, Welsh & Co. / American Bank Note Co. **Comments:** H-RI-385-G2a, Durand-1082. Similar to W-RI-850-001-G010. 18__. 1855.
Rarity: URS-12
VF $75

$2 • W-RI-850-002-G020

Left: TWO / Commerce with American shield. *Center:* 2 / Liberty and Agriculture holding shield of Hope. *Right:* 2 / TWO. *Engraver:* Jocelyn, Draper, Welsh & Co. / American Bank Note Co. *Comments:* H-RI-385-G4, Durand-1083. 18__. 1854–1856.
Rarity: URS-3
Proof $400

$2 • W-RI-850-002-G020a CJF

Overprint: Red TWO. **Engraver:** Jocelyn, Draper, Welsh & Co. / American Bank Note Co. **Comments:** H-RI-385-G4a, Durand-1084. Similar to W-RI-850-002-G020. 18__. 1855 and 1856.
Rarity: URS-12
VF $52

$3 • W-RI-850-003-G030 SBG

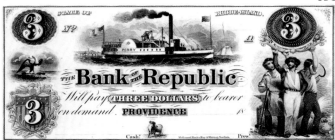

Engraver: Wellstood, Hanks, Hay & Whiting. **Comments:** H-Unlisted, Durand-1085. Proof. 18__. 1854–1856.
Rarity: URS-1
Proof $2,700
Selected auction price: Stack's Bowers Galleries, March 2013, Proof $2,662

$3 • W-RI-850-003-G030a CJF

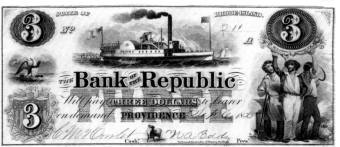

Overprint: Red THREE. **Engraver:** Wellstood, Hanks, Hay & Whiting. **Comments:** H-RI-385-G6a, Durand-1086. Similar to W-RI-850-003-G030. 18__. 1854–1856.
Rarity: URS-10
VF $150

$5 • W-RI-850-005-G040

Left: FIVE / Woman standing with cornucopia. *Center:* U.S. Capitol / Die. *Right:* 5 / Female portrait / 5. *Engraver:* Jocelyn, Draper, Welsh & Co. / American Bank Note Co. *Comments:* H-RI-385-G8, Durand-1087. U.S. Capitol as depicted in a drawing by Thomas U. Girard. 18__. 1854–1856.

Rarity: URS-3
Proof $400

$5 • W-RI-850-005-G040a   CJF

Overprint: Red FIVE. *Engraver:* Jocelyn, Draper, Welsh & Co. / American Bank Note Co. *Comments:* H-RI-385-G8a, Durand-1088. Similar to W-RI-850-005-G040. 18__. 1854–1856.

Rarity: URS-12
VG $40; VF $70

$10 • W-RI-850-010-G050

Left: 10 / Portrait of Benjamin Franklin / TEN through DOLLARS. *Center:* Farmer and woman at well. *Right:* 10 / Spread eagle on shield. *Engraver:* Wellstood, Hanks, Hay & Whiting. *Comments:* H-RI-385-G10a, Durand-1089. 18__. 1854–1856.

Rarity: URS-10
VG $55; VF $85

$10 • W-RI-850-010-G050a   CJF

Overprint: Red TEN. *Engraver:* Wellstood, Hanks, Hay & Whiting. *Comments:* H-Unlisted, Durand-1090. Similar to W-RI-850-010-G050. 18__. 1854–1856.

Rarity: URS-10
VF $100

$50 • W-RI-850-050-G060   SBG

Engraver: Wellstood, Hanks, Hay & Whiting. *Comments:* H-RI-385-G14, Durand-1091. Proof. 18__. 1854–1856.

Rarity: URS-1
Proof $4,500
Selected auction price: Stack's Bowers Galleries, March 2013, Proof $4,538

$100 • W-RI-850-100-G070

Left: 100 / Woman and shield. *Center:* Liberty and eagle. *Bottom center:* Female portrait. *Right:* 100 / C. *Engraver:* Wellstood, Hanks, Hay & Whiting. *Comments:* H-RI-385-G16, Durand-1092. 18__. 1854–1856.

Rarity: *None known*

Uncut Sheets
$1-$1-$2-$5 • W-RI-850-001.001.002.005-US010

Vignette(s): ($1) Eagle / Portrait of George Washington. *($1)* Eagle / Portrait of George Washington. *($2)* Commerce with American shield / Liberty and Agriculture holding shield of Hope. *($5)* Woman standing with cornucopia / U.S. Capitol / Female portrait. *Engraver:* Jocelyn, Draper, Welsh & Co. / American Bank Note Co. *Comments:* H-RI-385-G2, G2, G4, G8. 18__. 1854–1856.

Rarity: URS-10
VF $200

Bank of the United States {2nd} (branch)
1817–1836
W-RI-860

History: The second Bank of the United States was chartered in 1816 for a duration of 20 years. Its capital was $35,000,000, of which the United States owned $7,000,000. Branch banks in several large cities were opened during 1816 and 1817 in direct competition with state banks.

How to Read the Whitman Numbering System
$1 • W-RI-010-001-G010a

Denomination: Value of the note shown.

W: Whitman number. This number is a sortable code unique to each bank and note.

RI: Abbreviation for the state under study.

010: Numerical designation specific to each bank.

001: The denomination in dollars.

G010a: G indicates a good or valid note. Other categories are indicated thus: C (counterfeit); R (raised); S (spurious); N (not-attributed); A (altered). Numbers are assigned starting with 010, 020, et seq. Terminal letters following the number indicate variations of a note: a series of different colored overprints, tints, payees, etc., all on the same design of note. For more information, see the "How to Use This Book" section at the front of the volume, page xiv.

The Providence branch was established in 1817. The directors appointed by the president and the Senate were Saul Alley, Peter Wagner, John T. Sullivan, Hugh M. Eldry, and Henry G. Gilpin.[49] Although some branches in other states overburdened themselves with speculation, the branch in Providence was an exception. In 1827 the Providence branch had an increase of $100,000 in capital.[50]

In 1834 the Providence branch president was Philip Allen, accompanied by N. Weituman Jr. as cashier.[51] The bank's charter expired in 1836.

Numismatic Commentary: In addition to notes, "drafts" resembling bank notes were issued. Some financial capers may have been practiced with these drafts.

VALID ISSUES

$5 • **W-RI-860-005-G010**

CJF

Engraver: Murray, Draper, Fairman & Co. *Comments:* H-US2-G828, Durand-1093. 18__. 1830s.

Rarity: URS-3
VF $400

$5 • **W-RI-860-005-G020**
Left: FIVE vertically. *Center:* 5 / Eagle perched on shield, Ships / V. *Right:* FIVE vertically. *Engraver:* Fairman, Draper, Underwood & Co. *Comments:* H-US2-G830. 1810s–1830s.

Rarity: URS-3
VF $400

$10 • **W-RI-860-010-G030**
Left: Portraits. *Center:* 10 / Eagle perched on shield, Ship / 10. *Right:* Portraits. *Engraver:* Murray, Draper, Fairman & Co. *Comments:* H-US2-G834. 1810s–1830s.

Rarity: *None known*

$10 • **W-RI-860-010-G040**
Left: TEN vertically. *Center:* 10 / Eagle perched on shield, Ships / X. *Right:* TEN vertically. *Engraver:* Fairman, Draper, Underwood & Co. *Comments:* H-US2-G836. 1810s–1830s.

Rarity: *None known*

$20 • **W-RI-860-020-G050**
Left: Portraits. *Center:* 20 / Eagle perched on shield, Ship / 20. *Right:* Portraits. *Engraver:* Murray, Draper, Fairman & Co. *Comments:* H-US2-G840. 1810s–1830s.

Rarity: *None known*

$20 • **W-RI-860-020-G060**
Left: Portraits. *Center:* 20 / Eagle perched on shield, Ship / 20. *Right:* Portraits. *Engraver:* Fairman, Draper, Underwood & Co. *Comments:* H-US2-G842. 1810s–1830s.

Rarity: *None known*

$20 • **W-RI-860-020-G070**
Left: 20 vertically. *Center:* 20 / Eagle perched on shield, Ship / 20. *Right:* XX vertically. *Engraver:* Draper, Underwood, Bald & Spencer. *Comments:* H-US2-G844. 1810s–1830s.

Rarity: *None known*

$50 • **W-RI-860-050-G080**
Left: Portraits. *Center:* 50 / Eagle perched on shield, Ship / 50. *Right:* Portraits. *Engraver:* Murray, Draper, Fairman & Co. *Comments:* H-US2-G848. 1810s–1830s.

Rarity: *None known*

$50 • **W-RI-860-050-G090**
Left: Eagle / Portrait of Martha Washington / Minerva. *Center:* 50 / Eagle perched on shield, Ship / 50. *Right:* Eagle / Portrait of Benjamin Franklin / Female portrait. *Engraver:* Fairman, Draper, Underwood & Co. *Comments:* H-US2-G850. 1810s–1830s.

Rarity: *None known*

$50 • **W-RI-860-050-G100**
Left: L / Male portrait / 50. *Center:* 50 / Eagle perched on shield / L. *Right:* 50 / Male portrait / L. *Engraver:* Draper, Underwood, Bald & Spencer. *Comments:* H-US2-G852. 1810s–1830s.

Rarity: *None known*

$100 • **W-RI-860-100-G110**
Left: Portraits. *Center:* 100 / Eagle perched on shield, Ship / 100. *Right:* Portraits. *Engraver:* Murray, Draper, Fairman & Co. *Comments:* H-US2-G856. 1810s–1830s.

Rarity: *None known*

$100 • **W-RI-860-100-G120**
Left: Eagle / Portrait of George Washington / Minerva. *Center:* 100 / Eagle perched on shield, Ship / 100. *Right:* Eagle / Portrait of Benjamin Franklin / Female portrait. *Engraver:* Fairman, Draper, Underwood & Co. *Comments:* H-US2-G858. 1810s–1830s.

Rarity: *None known*

$100 • **W-RI-860-100-G130**
Left: 100 / Male portrait / C. *Center:* 100 / Eagle perched on shield / 100. *Right:* C / Male portrait / 100. *Engraver:* Draper, Underwood, Bald & Spencer. *Comments:* H-US2-G860. 1810s–1830s.

Rarity: *None known*

NON-VALID ISSUES

$5 • **W-RI-860-005-C010**
Left: Portraits. *Center:* Eagle perched on shield, Ship, Nymphs holding frame bearing 5. *Bottom center:* 5. *Right:* Portraits. *Engraver:* Murray, Draper, Fairman & Co. *Comments:* H-US2-C828, Durand-1094. Counterfeit of W-RI-860-005-G010. 1810s–1830s.

Rarity: URS-5

$10 • **W-RI-860-010-C030**
Left: Portraits. *Center:* 10 / Eagle perched on shield, Ship / 10. *Right:* Portraits. *Engraver:* Murray, Draper, Fairman & Co. *Comments:* H-US2-C834. Counterfeit of W-RI-860-010-G030. 1810s–1830s.

Rarity: *None known*

$20 • W-RI-860-020-C050
Left: Portraits. *Center:* 20 / Eagle perched on shield, Ship / 20. *Right:* Portraits. *Engraver:* Murray, Draper, Fairman & Co. *Comments:* H-US2-C840. Counterfeit of W-RI-860-020-G050. 1810s–1830s.
　　　　　　Rarity: *None known*

$50 • W-RI-860-050-C090
Left: Eagle / Portrait of Martha Washington / Minerva. *Center:* 50 / Eagle perched on shield, Ship / 50. *Right:* Eagle / Portrait of Benjamin Franklin / Female portrait. *Engraver:* Fairman, Draper, Underwood & Co. *Comments:* H-US2-C850. Counterfeit of W-RI-860-050-G090. 1810s–1830s.
　　　　　　Rarity: *None known*

$100 • W-RI-860-100-C110
Left: Portraits. *Center:* 100 / Eagle perched on shield, Ship / 100. *Right:* Portraits. *Engraver:* Murray, Draper, Fairman & Co. *Comments:* H-US2-C856. Counterfeit of W-RI-860-100-G110. 1810s–1830s.
　　　　　　Rarity: *None known*

$100 • W-RI-860-100-C120
Left: Eagle / Portrait of George Washington / Minerva. *Center:* 100 / Eagle perched on shield, Ship / 100. *Right:* Eagle / Portrait of Benjamin Franklin / Female portrait. *Engraver:* Fairman, Draper, Underwood & Co. *Comments:* H-US2-C858. Counterfeit of W-RI-860-100-G120. 1810s–1830s.
　　　　　　Rarity: *None known*

Blackstone Canal Bank
1831–1865
W-RI-870

History: The Blackstone Canal Bank was incorporated as a fiscal agent for the Blackstone Canal Company in 1831. Nicholas Brown was the bank's founding president, and T.B. Fenner was its first cashier. The canal and the bank were named after the Reverend William Blackstone, who arrived in the Narragansett Bay region nearly two years earlier than Providence founder Roger Williams.[52] The bank was located at 6 What Cheer Building from 1856 to 1863.

In 1834 the bank was separated from the Canal Company in order to survive, and its charter was amended.[53] The capital in 1848 was $437,425, which increased to $500,000 by 1852. Circulation was $93,985 in 1849 and more than doubled to $254,800 by 1852. Selected figures for 1852 included: deposits $124,853; money due banks $15,834; profits $38,440.[54] Specie was $10,100 in 1857.

The business of the Blackstone Canal Bank was succeeded by the Blackstone Canal National Bank in 1865.

Numismatic Commentary: A few uncut sheets from this bank have been cut up to supply collectors with individual notes. Obtaining a genuine signed and dated note remains a challenge. One colorful note shows a portrait of General Burnside, the man whose facial hair gave us the descriptive word "sideburns."

VALID ISSUES

$1 • W-RI-870-001-G010　　　　SBG

Engraver: Draper, Underwood, Bald & Spencer. *Comments:* H-RI-260-G4. 18__. 1830s.
　　　　Rarity: URS-1
　　　　Proof $1,000

$1 • W-RI-870-001-G020　　　　QDB

Engraver: New England Bank Note Co. *Comments:* H-RI-260-G8, Durand-1095. Remainder. 18__. 1830s–1840s.
　　　　Rarity: URS-3
　　　　VF $400; **Proof** $1,200

$1 • W-RI-870-001-G030
Left: 1 / Portrait of George Washington / 1. *Center:* 1 / Angel blowing trumpet / 1. *Bottom center:* Shield bearing anchor. *Right:* 1 / Bust of Alexander Hamilton / 1. *Engraver:* Toppan, Carpenter & Co. *Comments:* H-RI-260-G10, Durand-1096. 18__. 1840s–1850s.
　　　　Rarity: URS-6
　　　　VF $400

$1 • W-RI-870-001-G030a　　　　CJF

Engraver: Toppan, Carpenter & Co. *Comments:* H-RI-260-G10a, Durand-1097. Similar to W-RI-870-001-G030. 18__. 1850s.
　　　　Rarity: URS-6
　　　　VG $400; **Proof** $750
Selected auction price: Stack's Bowers Galleries, January 2010, Proof $563

$1 • W-RI-870-001-G030b

CJF

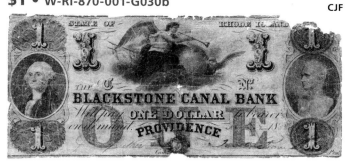

Overprint: Red ONE. *Engraver:* Toppan, Carpenter & Co. *Comments:* H-RI-260-G10b, Durand-1098. Similar to W-RI-870-001-G030. 18___. 1850s.

Rarity: URS-6
VF $400

$1 • W-RI-870-001-G040

CJF

Tint: Green panel. *Engraver:* National Bank Note Co. *Comments:* H-RI-260-G12a, Durand-1099. Jan. 1st, 186_. 1860s.

Rarity: URS-3
VF $2,000

$1.25 • W-RI-870-001.25-G050

Left: 1 25/100 / 100 / Train / 1 25/100. *Center:* Sloop and other vessels at sea / $1.25 Cts. *Right:* 1 25/100 / Eagle. *Engraver:* New England Bank Note Co. *Comments:* H-RI-260-G14. 18___. 1830s.

Rarity: *None known*

$1.50 • W-RI-870-001.50-G060

Left: 1 Doll. 50 Cts. vertically. *Center:* Eagle on rock in ocean / $1 50/100. *Right:* 1 50/100 / Justice. *Engraver:* New England Bank Note Co. *Comments:* H-RI-260-G15. 18___. 1830s.

Rarity: *None known*

$1.75 • W-RI-870-001.75-G070

Left: $1.75 Cts / Hebe watering eagle / 1 75/100. *Center:* Three sloops at sea. *Right:* $1.75 Cts / Woman seated with grain, Dog / 1 75/100. *Engraver:* New England Bank Note Co. *Comments:* H-RI-260-G16. 18___. 1830s.

Rarity: *None known*

$2 • W-RI-870-002-G080

SBG

Engraver: Draper, Underwood, Bald & Spencer. *Comments:* H-RI-260-G20, Durand-1101. 18___. 1830s.

Rarity: URS-3
VF $175; **Proof** $3,000
Selected auction price: Stack's Bowers Galleries, March 2013, Proof $2,904

$2 • W-RI-870-002-G090

QDB

Engraver: New England Bank Note Co. *Comments:* H-RI-260-G22. Proof. 18___. 1830s–1840s.

Rarity: URS-1
Proof $1,500

$2 • W-RI-870-002-G100

Left: 2 / Portrait of Chief Justice John Marshall. *Center:* Two women seated with packages, Ships. *Bottom center:* Shield bearing anchor. *Right:* 2 / Woman seated with headdress and shield, Cap and pole. *Engraver:* Toppan, Carpenter & Co. *Comments:* H-RI-260-G24, Durand-1102. 18___. 1840s–1850s.

Rarity: URS-6
VF $250

$2 • W-RI-870-002-G100a

CJF

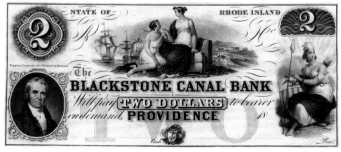

Engraver: Toppan, Carpenter & Co. *Comments:* H-RI-260-G24a, Durand-1103. Similar to W-RI-870-002-G100. 18___. 1850s.

Rarity: URS-6
VF $300; **Proof** $1,000

$2 • W-RI-870-002-G100b

Bottom center: Shield bearing anchor / TWO. *Overprint:* Red TWO. *Engraver:* Toppan, Carpenter & Co. *Comments:* H-RI-260-G24b, Durand-1104. Similar to W-RI-870-002-G100. 18__. 1850s.

Rarity: *None known*

$2 • W-RI-870-002-G110

Left: 2 / Blacksmith holding hammer. *Center:* Steamship, City. *Right:* 2 / Woman standing with arm on bale. *Tint:* Green panel vertically. *Engraver:* National Bank Note Co. *Comments:* H-RI-260-G26a, Durand-1105. Jan. 1, 186_. 1860s.

Rarity: *None known*

$2 • W-RI-870-002-G120

Left: 2 / Male portrait. *Center:* Sailing ships, Two allegorical figures. *Bottom center:* Shield bearing anchor / TWO. *Right:* 2 / Liberty. *Comments:* H-Unlisted, Durand-1107. 18__. 1850s.

Rarity: URS-3

$3 • W-RI-870-003-G130

Left: 3 / Minerva seated. *Center:* Agriculture and Commerce. *Right:* 3 / Industry. *Comments:* H-Unlisted, Durand-1110. 18__. 1850s.

Rarity: URS-3

$3 • W-RI-870-003-G140　　　　SBG

Engraver: Draper, Underwood, Bald & Spencer. *Comments:* H-Unlisted, Durand-Unlisted. 18__. 1830s.

Rarity: URS-1

Proof $3,400

Selected auction price: Stack's Bowers Galleries, March 2013, Proof $3,388

$5 • W-RI-870-005-G150

Left: 5 / Minerva resting on shield. *Center:* Shield bearing anchor flanked by seated Agriculture and Commerce. *Bottom center:* Bale and cogwheel. *Right:* 5 / Industry seated. *Engraver:* Unverified, but likely Toppan, Carpenter & Co. *Comments:* H-RI-260-G30, Durand-1114. 18__. 1840s–1850s.

Rarity: *None known*

$5 • W-RI-870-005-G160　　　　SBG

Engraver: Draper, Underwood, Bald & Spencer. *Comments:* H-Unlisted, Durand-Unlisted. 18__. 1830s.

Rarity: URS-3

Proof $750

$10 • W-RI-870-010-G170

Left: 10 / Female portrait. *Center:* Blacksmith seated / 10. *Bottom center:* Anchor on shield. *Right:* TEN / Indian girl standing. *Engraver:* Unverified, but likely Toppan, Carpenter & Co. *Comments:* H-RI-260-G36, Durand-1115. 18__. 1840s–1850s.

Rarity: *None known*

$10 • W-RI-870-010-G180　　　　SBG

Engraver: Draper, Underwood, Bald & Spencer. *Comments:* H-Unlisted, Durand-Unlisted. 18__. 1830s.

Rarity: URS-1

Proof $3,000

Selected auction price: Stack's Bowers Galleries, March 2013, Proof $2,904

$50 • W-RI-870-050-G190

Left: 50 FIFTY 50 vertically. *Center:* 50 / Commerce seated / 50. *Bottom center:* Anchor on shield. *Right:* 50. *Engraver:* Unverified, but likely Toppan, Carpenter & Co. *Comments:* H-RI-260-G40, Durand-1121. 18__. 1840s–1850s.

Rarity: *None known*

$50 • W-RI-870-050-G200

SBG

Engraver: Draper, Underwood, Bald & Spencer. *Comments:* H-Unlisted. 18__. 1830s.

Rarity: URS-1
Proof $3,700

$100 • W-RI-870-100-G210

Left: Lathework panel with C / Portrait of George Washington / C. *Center:* 100 / Manhattan reclining pouring water, Ship / 100. *Right:* Lathework panel with ONE HUNDRED vertically. *Engraver:* PSSP / New England Bank Note Co. *Comments:* H-RI-260-G42. 18__. 1830s–1840s.

Rarity: *None known*

$100 • W-RI-870-100-G220

Left: 100 HUNDRED 100 vertically. *Center:* 100 / Hope seated / 100. *Bottom center:* Steamship. *Right:* ONE HUNDRED vertically. *Engraver:* Unverified, but likely Toppan, Carpenter & Co. *Comments:* H-RI-260-G44, Durand-1125. 18__. 1840s–1850s.

Rarity: *None known*

$500 • W-RI-870-500-G230

Left: 500 / 500 vertically / 500. *Center:* 500 / Woman seated with shield bearing D, Fasces, cornucopia, lyre, and sheaf / 500. *Right:* 500 / D / 500. *Engraver:* PSSP / New England Bank Note Co. *Comments:* H-RI-260-G46. 18__. 1830s.

Rarity: *None known*

$500 • W-RI-870-500-G240

Left: D / Mason. *Center:* View of U.S. Capitol. *Right:* 500 / Train. *Engraver:* Unverified, but likely Toppan, Carpenter & Co. *Comments:* H-RI-260-G48, Durand-1126. 18__. 1840s–1850s.

Rarity: *None known*

$1,000 • W-RI-870-1000-G250

Left: THOUSAND vertically. *Center:* 1000 / Woman standing with lyre, Cornucopia / 1000. *Right:* 1000 / Anchor, bales. *Engraver:* PSSP / New England Bank Note Co. *Comments:* H-RI-260-G50. 18__. 1830s.

Rarity: *None known*

$1,000 • W-RI-870-1000-G260

Left: M / Two ships under sail. *Center:* Ship, Steamship under sail, Ship. *Right:* 1000 / Anchor, bales. *Engraver:* Unverified, but likely Toppan, Carpenter & Co. *Comments:* H-RI-260-G52, Durand-1127. 18__. 1840s–1850s.

Rarity: *None known*

Uncut Sheets

$1-$1-$1-$2 • W-RI-870-001.001.001.002-US010

Vignette(s): *($1)* Portrait of George Washington / Angel blowing trumpet / Shield bearing anchor / Bust of Alexander Hamilton. *($1)* Portrait of George Washington / Angel blowing trumpet / Shield bearing anchor / Bust of Alexander Hamilton. *($1)* Portrait of George Washington / Angel blowing trumpet / Shield bearing anchor / Bust of Alexander Hamilton. *($2)* Portrait of Chief Justice John Marshall / Two women seated with packages, Ships / Shield bearing anchor / Woman seated with headdress and shield, Cap and pole. *Engraver:* Toppan, Carpenter & Co. *Comments:* H-RI-260-G10, G10, G10, G24. 18__. 1840s–1850s.

Rarity: URS-3
Proof $2,500

$1-$1-$1-$2 • W-RI-870-001.001.001.002-US010a

Engraver: Toppan, Carpenter & Co. *Comments:* H-RI-260-G10a, G10a, G10a, G24a. Similar to W-RI-870-001.001.001.002-US010. 18__. 1840s–1850s.

Rarity: URS-3
Proof $2,500

$1-$1-$2-$3 • W-RI-870-001.001.002.003-US020

Vignette(s): *($1)* Three women seated with statues. *($1)* Three women seated with statues. *($2)* Man and woman seated with grain. *($3)* Minerva seated / Agriculture and Commerce / Industry. *Engraver:* Draper, Underwood, Bald & Spencer. *Comments:* H-RI-260-G4, G4, G20, Unlisted. 18__. 1830s.

Rarity: *None known*

$5-$5-$10-$50 • W-RI-870-005.005.010.050-US030

Vignette(s): *($5)* People seated under tree / Woman seated on anchor / Woman seated with cornucopia. *($5)* People seated under tree / Woman seated on anchor / Woman seated with cornucopia. *($10)* Ship passing through canal lock / Ceres and sailor flanking lathework panel with TEN / Warehouse. *($50)* Three women seated by ocean. *Engraver:* Draper, Underwood, Bald & Spencer. *Comments:* All unlisted in Haxby. 18__. 1830s.

Rarity: *None known*

NON-VALID ISSUES

$1 • W-RI-870-001-A010

Left: 1 / Woman standing with basket / ONE. *Center:* Woman seated holding rake and sickle, Train, Ships, Factories / ONE. *Right:* 1 / Ships / 1. *Engraver:* New England Bank Note Co. *Comments:* H-RI-260-A5, Durand-1100. Altered from $1 Stillwater Canal Bank, Orono, Maine, or from notes of other failed banks using the same plate. 18__. 1830s.

Rarity: *None known*

$2 • W-RI-870-002-C100a

Engraver: Toppan, Carpenter & Co. *Comments:* H-RI-260-C24a, Durand-1106. Counterfeit of W-RI-870-002-G100a. 18__. 1850s.

Rarity: URS-3
VF $300

$3 • W-RI-870-003-C130

Comments: H-Unlisted, Durand-1111. Counterfeit of W-RI-870-003-G130. Done poorly by lithography. 1830s.

Rarity: URS-3

$3 • W-RI-870-003-R010

Engraver: National Bank Note Co. *Comments:* H-RI-260-R12, Durand-1108. Raised from W-RI-870-001-G040. Jan. 1, 186_. 1860s.

Rarity: *None known*

$3 • W-RI-870-003-N010

Left: 3 THREE 3 vertically. *Center:* 3 / Two women and man / 3 *Right:* 3 THREE 3 vertically. *Comments:* H-Unlisted. 1830s.

Rarity: —

$3 • W-RI-870-003-A020

Left: 3 / Two boys playing by tub / THREE. *Center:* River scene, Log raft, and docks, Warehouses / THREE. *Right:* 3 / Three women seated with shield, balance, and book / THREE. *Engraver:* PSSP / New England Bank Note Co. *Comments:* H-RI-260-A10, Durand-1100. Altered from $3 Stillwater Canal Bank, Orono, Maine. 18__. 1830s.

Rarity: *None known*

$5 • W-RI-870-005-R020

Engraver: National Bank Note Co. *Comments:* H-RI-260-R13, Durand-1112. Raised from W-RI-870-001-G040. Jan. 1, 186_. 1860s.

Rarity: *None known*

$5 • W-RI-870-005-N020

Left: Woman. *Center:* Two women. *Right:* Woman. *Comments:* H-RI-260-N5. 1830s.

Rarity: *None known*

$5 • W-RI-870-005-A030

Left: 5 / Two cows / FIVE. *Center:* Boats, Houses along shore with long wharves. *Right:* FIVE / Woman standing. *Engraver:* PSSP / New England Bank Note Co. *Comments:* H-RI-260-A15, Durand-1113. Altered from $5 Stillwater Canal Bank, Orono, Maine. Bank title misspelled "Providence." 18__. 1830s.

Rarity: URS-3
VF $250

$10 • W-RI-870-010-C170

Comments: H-RI-260-C36, Durand-1116. Counterfeit of W-RI-870-010-G170. 18__. 1850s.

Rarity: *None known*

$10 • W-RI-870-010-R030

Engraver: National Bank Note Co. *Comments:* H-RI-260-R14, Durand-1117. Raised from W-RI-870-001-G040. Jan. 1, 186_. 1860s.

Rarity: URS-3
VF $350

$10 • W-RI-870-010-AR010

Comments: H-Unlisted, Durand-1118. The word German word *zehn* (ten) in the center of the bill may be detected by holding the bill to a light. 1830s.

Rarity: URS-3

$10 • W-RI-870-010-A040

Left: TEN / Justice standing. *Center:* River scene with raft, buildings, and falls. *Right:* 10 / Female bust / TEN. *Engraver:* PSSP / New England Bank Note Co. *Comments:* H-RI-260-A20, Durand-1119. Altered from $10 Stillwater Canal Bank, Orono, Maine. 18__. 1830s.

Rarity: *None known*

$20 • W-RI-870-020-A050

Left: 20 / Woman resting scroll and arm on chest. *Center:* Indian woman reclining on cliff, Canal locks and city. *Right:* 20 / Train. *Overprint:* Red TWENTY. *Engraver:* Danforth, Bald & Co. *Comments:* H-RI-260-A25, Durand-1120. Altered from $20 Columbia Bank, Washington, D.C. 18__. 1850s.

Rarity: *None known*

$50 • W-RI-870-050-R040

Engraver: National Bank Note Co. *Comments:* H-RI-260-R16, Durand-1122. Raised from W-RI-870-001-G040. Jan. 1, 186_. 1860s.

Rarity: *None known*

$50 • W-RI-870-050-R050

Center: Woman sitting. *Comments:* H-Unlisted, Durand-1124. Raised from $5. Red ink used to disguise the alterations. 1830s.

Rarity: URS-3

$50 • W-RI-870-050-A060

Comments: H-Unlisted, Durand-1123. Raised from unknown denomination of the Stillwater Canal Bank, Orono, Maine. 1830s.

Rarity: URS-3

Butchers and Drovers Bank
1853–1890
W-RI-880

History: The Butchers and Drovers Bank was chartered in May 1853. Benjamin B. Knight and J.S. Tourtellot served as the first president and cashier, respectively. It was located at 25 Broad Street in 1855 and Weybosset Street in 1863.

The capital ranged from $242,300 in 1855 to $246,450 in 1862. Bills in circulation ranged from $433,343 in 1855 to $156,097 in 1862 and 1863. Specie was $3,120.62 in 1857. In 1874 fractional currency totaled $892.33.

This bank continued to operate as a state bank until it was liquidated in 1890. No notes were issued after 1866.

Numismatic Commentary: Notes from this bank are very hard to locate. Assembling a set is a daunting experience.

VALID ISSUES

$1 • W-RI-880-001-G010

SBG

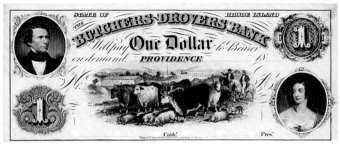

Engraver: Toppan, Carpenter, Casilear & Co. *Comments:* H-RI-265-G2a, Durand-1146. 18__. 1850s.

Rarity: URS-1
Proof $1,400
Selected auction price: Stack's Bowers Galleries, March 2013, Proof $1,331

$1 • W-RI-880-001-G010a

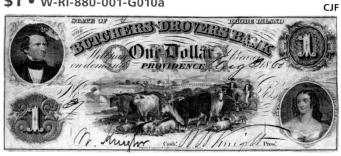

CJF

Overprint: Red ONE. **Engraver:** Toppan, Carpenter, Casilear & Co. **Comments:** H-Unlisted, Durand-1147. Similar to W-RI-880-001-G010. 18__. 1860s.

Rarity: URS-3
VF $1,000

$2 • W-RI-880-002-G020

Left: 2 / Portrait of Stephen A. Douglas / TWO. **Center:** Drove of cattle and sheep. **Right:** 2 / Female portrait / TWO. **Engraver:** Toppan, Carpenter, Casilear & Co. **Comments:** H-RI-265-G4a, Durand-1148. 18__. 1850s.

Rarity: *None known*

$2 • W-RI-880-002-G020a

Overprint: Red TWO. **Engraver:** Toppan, Carpenter, Casilear & Co. **Comments:** H-Unlisted, Durand-1149. Similar to W-RI-880-002-G020. 18__. 1850s.

Rarity: URS-3

$5 • W-RI-880-005-G030

QDB

Engraver: Toppan, Carpenter, Casilear & Co. **Comments:** H-RI-265-G6a, Durand-1151. 18__. 1850s.

Rarity: URS-1
Proof $2,000

$5 • W-RI-880-005-G030a

Left: Three sea nymphs floating on water and holding cherub / 5 on shield. **Right:** 5 / Portrait of Lewis Cass. **Overprint:** Red FIVE. **Engraver:** Toppan, Carpenter, Casilear & Co. **Comments:** H-Unlisted, Durand-1152. Similar to W-RI-880-005-G030. 18__. 1850s.

Rarity: URS-3

$10 • W-RI-880-010-G040

Left: 10 / Men driving cattle. **Center:** Women flanking shield bearing anchor surmounted by horse's head. **Bottom center:** Beehive. **Right:** 10 / Portrait of Andrew Jackson. **Overprint:** Red TEN. **Engraver:** Toppan, Carpenter, Casilear & Co. **Comments:** H-RI-265-G8a, Durand-1156. 18__. 1850s.

Rarity: URS-3
VF $400

$10 • W-RI-880-010-G050

CC

Engraver: Toppan, Carpenter, Casilear & Co. **Comments:** H-RI-265-G10, Durand-1154. Possibly never issued. 18__. 1850s.

Rarity: URS-3
Proof $1,300

$10 • W-RI-880-010-G050a

Left: 10 / Men driving cattle. **Center:** Women flanking shield bearing anchor surmounted by horse's head. **Bottom center:** Beehive. **Right:** 10 / Portrait of Benjamin Franklin. **Overprint:** Red TEN. **Engraver:** Toppan, Carpenter, Casilear & Co. **Comments:** H-Unlisted, Durand-1155. Similar to W-RI-880-010-G050. 18__. 1850s.

Rarity: URS-3

$50 • W-RI-880-050-G060

Left: Commerce / 50. **Center:** Portrait of Henry Clay. **Right:** 50 / Anchor, bale, box, and barrel. **Overprint:** Red FIFTY. **Engraver:** Toppan, Carpenter, Casilear & Co. **Comments:** H-RI-265-G12a, Durand-1161. 18__. 1850s.

Rarity: *None known*

$100 • W-RI-880-100-G070

Left: Indian / 100. **Center:** Marine view. **Right:** 100 / Portrait of Daniel Webster. **Overprint:** Red HUNDRED. **Engraver:** Toppan, Carpenter, Casilear & Co. **Comments:** H-RI-265-G14a, Durand-1162. 18__. 1850s.

Rarity: *None known*

NON-VALID ISSUES

$3 • W-RI-880-003-R010

Engraver: Toppan, Carpenter, Casilear & Co. **Comments:** H-RI-265-R5, Durand-1150. Raised from W-RI-880-002-G020. 18__. 1850s.

Rarity: *None known*

$5 • W-RI-880-005-A010

Left: Men driving cattle across river / 5. **Center:** 5 / Five men gathering hay, Oxen, wagon. **Right:** 5. **Tint:** Brown-orange lathework. **Engraver:** Bald, Cousland & Co. **Comments:** H-RI-265-A5. Altered from $5 Pioneer Association, La Fayette, Indiana. 18__. 1850s.

Rarity: *None known*

$10 • W-RI-880-010-R020

Engraver: Toppan, Carpenter, Casilear & Co. **Comments:** H-RI-265-R10, Durand-1157. Raised from W-RI-880-001-G010. 18__. 1850s.

Rarity: *None known*

$10 • W-RI-880-010-R030

Engraver: Toppan, Carpenter, Casilear & Co. *Comments:* H-RI-265-R12, Durand-1158. Raised from W-RI-880-002-G020. 18__. 1850s.

Rarity: *None known*

$10 • W-RI-880-010-N010

Center: Man and dog / Man and woman, Wagon of hay / Man and dog. *Comments:* H-RI-26-N5, Durand-1159. 18__. 1850s.

Rarity: *None known*

$10 • W-RI-880-010-N020

Center: Woman with staff, Man. *Comments:* H-RI-265-N10, Durand-1160. 18__. 1850s.

Rarity: *None known*

Cranston Bank
1818–1865
W-RI-885

History: The Cranston Bank was incorporated in February 1818. Sylvester Wicks was the bank's first president, and Jeremiah Knight was its first cashier. Similar to the activity of many other banks, the Cranston Bank profited by issuing large quantities of notes and shipping them at a discount to distant locations with the expectation that many would never be redeemed.

Capital was listed at $25,000 between 1849 and 1855. By 1857 it had increased to $37,500. Circulation was $10,367 in 1857 but had decreased to $9,807 by 1862. Specie was $1,017.59 in 1857.

The bank was moved to Providence in 1850 and to Olneyville in 1865. It was closed that year.

Also see listings under Cranston, W-RI-240, and Olneyville, W-RI-685.

City Bank
1833–1865
W-RI-890

History: The City Bank was incorporated in June 1833 during an era of great expansion in the Providence area. Anthony B. Arnold served as its first president, and William R. Watson was its first cashier. It was located at 41 Westminster Street in 1864. The same year, *Banker's Magazine* reported this: "This bank has withdrawn from the Suffolk bank arrangement, and now redeems its notes at its own counter."

The capital was given as $200,000 in 1848 and raised to $300,000 by 1855. The circulation was $44,450.25. In September 1853, the amount of fractional bills issued by the bank was $33,460.50. Circulation in 1857 reached $61,135, rising to $84,653 in 1862. Specie was at $5,095.61 the same year.

The City Bank wound down its affairs after its interests were succeeded by the City National Bank, chartered on July 12, 1865.

Numismatic Commentary: The most frequently encountered notes from this bank are the Proof issues and the $1 American Bank Note Co. issue. Other genuine notes are very hard to locate. A view of the actual bank building is shown on the $2 issue engraved by the American Bank Note Co.

VALID ISSUES

$1 • W-RI-890-001-G010

Left: ONE / Female portrait / ONE. *Center:* 1 / Eagle on tree limb / 1. *Bottom center:* Steamship. *Right:* ONE / Man shearing sheep, Woman standing nearby / ONE. *Engraver:* Unverified, but likely Rawdon, Wright & Hatch. *Comments:* H-RI-270-G4, Durand-1163. 18__. 1840s–1850s.

Rarity: *None known*

$1 • W-RI-890-001-G020

CJF

Tint: Green panel. *Engraver:* American Bank Note Co. *Comments:* H-RI-270-G8a, Durand-1164. Jan. 1st, 1861.

Rarity: URS-3

VF $750

$1 • W-RI-890-001-G030

Left: Portrait of Benjamin Franklin. *Center:* Portrait of girl. *Right:* Portrait of George Washington. *Comments:* H-Unlisted, Durand-1167. 1840s–1850s.

Rarity: URS-3

VF $400

$2 • W-RI-890-002-G040

CC

Engraver: Rawdon, Wright & Hatch. *Comments:* H-RI-270-G12, Durand-1171. 18__. 1840s–1850s.

Rarity: URS-3

VF $1,000

$2 • W-RI-890-002-G050

Left: Ceres / 2. *Center:* Children, Cattle. *Right:* 2 / Building. *Tint:* Green panel. *Engraver:* American Bank Note Co. *Comments:* H-RI-270-G16a, Durand-1172. Jan. 1, 1861.

Rarity: URS-3

VF $400

$3 • W-RI-890-003-G060   SBG

Tint: Green panel and 3 / 3. *Engraver:* American Bank Note Co. *Comments:* H-RI-270-G20, Durand-1175. Proof. Jan. 1st, 1861.

Rarity: URS-1

VF $400; **Proof** $9,000

Selected auction price: Stack's Bowers Galleries, March 2013, Proof $9,076

$5 • W-RI-890-005-G070

Left: 5 / Female portrait / 5. *Center:* 5 / Liberty and eagle in V / 5. *Right:* FIVE / Industry / 5. *Engraver:* Unverified, but likely Rawdon, Wright & Hatch. *Comments:* H-RI-270-G24, Durand-1177. 18__. 1840s–1850s.

Rarity: *None known*

$5 • W-RI-890-005-G080

Left: Pilot boat / 5. *Center:* Sailor with trumpet on vessel. *Right:* 5 / Allegorical figure with V on shield. *Tint:* Green panel. *Engraver:* American Bank Note Co. *Comments:* H-RI-270-G28a, Durand-1178. Jan. 1, 1861.

Rarity: *None known*

$10 • W-RI-890-010-G090

Left: 10 / Ceres seated / X. *Center:* Ships and other vessels / Cherub on X. *Bottom center:* Sailing vessel. *Right:* 10 / Justice / X. *Engraver:* Rawdon, Wright & Hatch. *Comments:* H-RI-270-G32, Durand-1181. 18__. 1840s–1850s.

Rarity: URS-3

Proof $500

$10 • W-RI-890-010-G100   CC

Tint: Green panel. *Engraver:* American Bank Note Co. *Comments:* H-RI-270-G36a, Durand-1182. Jan. 1st, 1861.

Rarity: URS-2

Proof $4,000

$50 • W-RI-890-050-G110   SBG

Engraver: Rawdon, Wright & Hatch. *Comments:* H-RI-270-G42, Durand-1187. 18__. 1830s–1850s.

Rarity: URS-2

Proof $5,200

Selected auction price: Stack's Bowers Galleries, March 2013, Proof $5,143

$50 • W-RI-890-050-G120   CC

Tint: Green panel of Ls and dies bearing white L / L. *Engraver:* American Bank Note Co. *Comments:* H-RI-270-G44a, Durand-1188. Jan. 1st, 1861.

Rarity: URS-2

Proof $4,000

$100 • W-RI-890-100-G130

Left: 100 / Portrait of Commodore Oliver Hazard Perry / 100. *Center:* Ship under construction. *Right:* 100 / Portrait of girl / 100. *Engraver:* Rawdon, Wright & Hatch. *Comments:* H-RI-270-G48, Durand-1192. 18__. 1830s–1850s.

Rarity: URS-3

Proof $600

$100 • W-RI-890-100-G140

Left: C / 100. *Center:* C / Ceres, Vessels / C. *Right:* 100 / Eagle. *Tint:* Green panel. *Engraver:* American Bank Note Co. *Comments:* H-RI-270-G52a, Durand-1193. Jan. 1, 1861.

Rarity: URS-3

VF $350

$500 • W-RI-890-500-G150

Left: Indian paddling canoe, Trees and mountains / 500. *Center:* 500. *Right:* 500 / Justice. *Engraver:* New England Bank Note Co. *Comments:* H-RI-270-G56, Durand-1194. 18__. 1840s–1850s.

Rarity: *None known*

$500 • W-RI-890-500-G160

Left: Portrait of Benjamin Franklin / 500. *Center:* "The Landing of Roger Williams". *Right:* 500 / D. *Tint:* Green panel. *Engraver:* American Bank Note Co. *Comments:* H-RI-270-G60a, Durand-1195. Jan. 1, 1861.

Rarity: URS-3

Proof $1,500

$1,000 • W-RI-890-1000-G170

Left: Eagle on cliff / 1000. *Center:* 1000. *Right:* 1000 / Indian girl. *Engraver:* New England Bank Note Co. *Comments:* H-RI-270-G64, Durand-1196. 18__. 1840s–1850s.

Rarity: *None known*

$1,000 • W-RI-890-1000-G180

Left: Portrait of George Washington / 1000. *Center:* Goddess of Plenty, Vessels. *Right:* 1000 / M. *Engraver:* American Bank Note Co. *Comments:* H-RI-270-G68a, Durand-1197. Jan. 1, 1861.

Rarity: URS-3

Proof $3,500

NON-VALID ISSUES

$1 • W-RI-890-001-C010

Engraver: Unverified, but likely Rawdon, Wright & Hatch. *Comments:* H-RI-270-C4, Durand-1165. Counterfeit of W-RI-890-001-G010. 18__. 1850s.

Rarity: *None known*

$1 • W-RI-890-001-S010

Left: 1 / Portrait of George Washington. *Center:* 1 / Female portrait / 1 / ONE. *Right:* 1 / Portrait of Benjamin Franklin. *Comments:* H-RI-270-S5, Durand-1190. The plate was probably first used for spurious notes of the Lynn Mechanics Bank, Lynn, Massachusetts. 1850s.

Rarity: *None known*

$1 • W-RI-890-001-A010

Left: ONE / Knowledge. *Center:* 1 / Train, hill, and steamship with ONEs. *Right:* ONE / Liberty. *Engraver:* W.L. Ormsby. *Comments:* H-RI-270-A5, Durand-1166. Altered from $1 Potomac River Bank, Georgetown, D.C. 185_. 1850s.

Rarity: *None known*

$1.25 • W-RI-890-001.25-A020

Left: 1 25/100 / Train / 1 25/100. *Center:* Sailing ships in bay / $1.25 Cts. *Right:* 1 25/100 / Spread eagle. *Engraver:* New England Bank Note Co. *Comments:* H-RI-270-G9, Durand-1168. Altered from $1.25 Roxbury Bank, Roxbury, Massachusetts. 18__. 1850s.

Rarity: URS-3

VF $350

$1.50 • W-RI-890-001.50-A030

CJF

Engraver: New England Bank Note Co. *Comments:* H-RI-270-G10, Durand-1169. Altered from $1.50 Roxbury Bank, Roxbury, Massachusetts. 18__. 1850s.

Rarity: URS-3

VF $400

$1.75 • W-RI-890-001.75-A040

CJF

Engraver: New England Bank Note Co. *Comments:* H-RI-270-G11, Durand-1170. Altered from $1.75 Roxbury Bank, Roxbury, Massachusetts 18__. 1850s.

Rarity: URS-3

VF $350

$2 • W-RI-890-002-S020

CC

Engraver: Rawdon, Wright & Hatch. *Comments:* H-RI-270-S10, Durand-1174. 18__. 1837.

Rarity: URS-6

VG $95

$2 • W-RI-890-002-A050

Left: TWO / Justice / TWO. *Center:* 2 / TWO on medallion head / Train, hill, and steamship, TWOs. *Right:* TWO / Liberty. *Engraver:* W.L. Ormsby. *Comments:* H-RI-270-A25. Altered from $2 Potomac River Bank, Georgetown, D.C. 185_. 1850s.

Rarity: *None known*

$3 • W-RI-890-003-S030

CC

Engraver: Rawdon, Wright & Hatch. *Comments:* H-RI-270-S15, Durand-1176. May 1st, 1847.

Rarity: URS-5

VG $140

$5 • W-RI-890-005-R010

Engraver: American Bank Note Co. *Comments:* H-RI-270-R6, Durand-1180. Raised from W-RI-890-001-G020. Jan. 1, 1861.

Rarity: *None known*

$5 • W-RI-890-005-S040

CJF

Engraver: Rawdon, Wright & Hatch. *Comments:* H-RI-270-S20, Durand-1179. Spurious in rough imitation of W-RI-890-005-G070. May 1st, 1849.

Rarity: URS-6
VG $80

$10 • W-RI-890-010-R020

Engraver: American Bank Note Co. *Comments:* H-RI-270-R10, Durand-1183. Raised from W-RI-890-001-G020. Jan. 1, 1861.

Rarity: *None known*

$10 • W-RI-890-010-R030

Engraver: American Bank Note Co. *Comments:* H-RI-270-R16, Durand-1184. Raised from W-RI-890-002-G050. Jan. 1, 1861.

Rarity: *None known*

$10 • W-RI-890-010-S050

Center: Portrait of George Washington / Portrait of girl / Portrait of Benjamin Franklin. *Comments:* H-RI-270-S25, Durand-1185. Altered or spurious. 1850s.

Rarity: *None known*

$20 • W-RI-890-020-N010

Center: Woman / Eagle. *Comments:* H-RI-270-N5, Durand-1186. Altered or spurious. 1850s.

Rarity: *None known*

$50 • W-RI-890-050-R040

Comments: H-Unlisted, Durand-1189. Raised from W-RI-890-001-G020. Jan. 1st, 1861.

Rarity: URS-3

$50 • W-RI-890-050-N020

Center: Woman, eagle, table, and eagle grasping arrows. *Comments:* H-RI-270-N10, Durand-1191. 1850s.

Rarity: *None known*

$50 • W-RI-890-050-A060

Comments: H-RI-270-A30, Durand-1190. Altered and raised from $1. 1850s.

Rarity: *None known*

Commercial Bank
1833–1865
W-RI-900

History: The Commercial Bank was incorporated in 1833. Its founding president and cashier were Richmond Bullock and David Andrews, respectively. In 1864 the bank was located at 11 Market Square. The capital was $326,950 in 1848, $639,000 in 1855, $736,900 in 1857, and $950,000 in 1863. Circulation

was at $39,139 in 1849 and reached $1,000,000 by 1864. Specie was listed at $6,251.60 in 1857.

The business of the Commercial Bank was succeeded by the Commercial National Bank, chartered on June 21, 1865.

Numismatic Commentary: Notes from this bank are elusive. Fortunately, some beautiful issues engraved by the National Bank Note Co. appear from time to time. Some of the red-tinted $1 notes have been raised to a higher denomination and appear in the marketplace on occasion.

VALID ISSUES

$1 • W-RI-900-001-G010

Comments: H-RI-276-G4, Durand-1198. No description available. 18__. 1830s.

Rarity: *None known*

$1 • W-RI-900-001-G020

Left: ONE / Farmer gathering corn / ONE. *Center:* 1 / Sailor steering ship / 1. *Right:* ONE / Indian woman / ONE. *Engraver:* Draper, Toppan & Co. *Comments:* H-RI-276-G6, Durand-1198. 18__. 1830s–1850s.

Rarity: URS-3
Proof $400

$1 • W-RI-900-001-G030

PEM

Tint: Red-orange panel and border. *Engraver:* National Bank Note Co. *Comments:* H-RI-276-G8a, Durand-1199. 186_. 1860s.

Rarity: URS-4
VF $350; **Proof** $4,000

$2 • W-RI-900-002-G040

Comments: H-RI-276-G12, Durand-1201. No description available. 18__. 1830s.

Rarity: *None known*

$2 • W-RI-900-002-G050

SBG

Engraver: Toppan, Carpenter & Co. *Comments:* H-RI-276-G14, Durand-1201. Proof. January 1st, 18__. 1830s–1850s.

Rarity: URS-1
Proof $1,400
Selected auction price: Stack's Bowers Galleries, August 2011, Proof $1,304

$2 • W-RI-900-002-G060   CC

Tint: Red-orange panels and TWO. *Engraver:* National Bank Note Co. *Comments:* H-RI-276-G16a, Durand-1202. 186_. 1860s.
Rarity: URS-4
VF $350; **Proof** $2,000

$3 • W-RI-900-003-G070
Comments: H-RI-276-G22, Durand-1206. No description available. 18__. 1830s. **Rarity:** *None known*

$3 • W-RI-900-003-G080   CC

Engraver: Draper, Toppan & Co. *Comments:* H-RI-276-G24, Durand-1206. Proof. 18__. 1830s–1850s.
Rarity: URS-3
Proof $1,000

$5 • W-RI-900-005-G090
Left: 5 / Allegorical woman holding bolt of fabric / 5. *Center:* Steamboat, City. *Right:* FIVE vertically. *Engraver:* Rawdon, Wright & Hatch. *Comments:* H-RI-276-G34, Durand-1209. 18__. 1830s–1850s.
Rarity: URS-3
VF $400

$5 • W-RI-900-005-G100
Left: 5 / Male portrait. *Center:* Three sailors on wharf. *Right:* 5 / Portrait of girl. *Comments:* H-RI-276-G36, Durand-1210. 18__. 1850s–1860s.
Rarity: *None known*

$10 • W-RI-900-010-G110
Left: 10 / Ship under sail / 10. *Center:* Spread eagle, Liberty seated. *Bottom center:* Anchor and barrels. *Right:* 10 / Indian and Liberty flanking shield bearing view of mill / X. *Engraver:* Unverified, but likely Rawdon, Wright & Hatch. *Comments:* H-RI-276-G42, Durand-1218. 18__. 1830s–1850s.
Rarity: *None known*

$10 • W-RI-900-010-G120   CC

Comments: H-RI-276-G44, Durand-1219. Proof. January 1st, 18__. 1850s–1860s.
Rarity: URS-2
Proof $1,000

$20 • W-RI-900-020-G130   CC

Engraver: Rawdon, Wright, Hatch & Co. *Comments:* H-RI-276-G50, Durand-1226. 18__. 1830s–1850s.
Rarity: URS-2
Proof $1,800

$20 • W-RI-900-020-G140
Left: XX / Farmer. *Center:* Horses, goat, and sheep at well. *Right:* 20 / Sailor. *Comments:* H-Unlisted, Durand-1228. 1830s–1850s.
Rarity: URS-3

$50 • W-RI-900-050-G150
Left: 50 / Ceres / 50. *Center:* Minerva, Shield surmounted by eagle, Justice / 50. *Right:* FIFTY vertically. *Engraver:* Unverified, but likely Rawdon, Wright & Hatch. *Comments:* H-RI-276-G54, Durand-1230. 18__. 1830s–1850s.
Rarity: *None known*

$100 • W-RI-900-100-G160
Left: Hope supporting anchor / 100. *Center:* Minerva, Shield surmounted by eagle, Justice / 50. *Bottom center:* Woman reclining. *Right:* Hope standing / 100. *Engraver:* Rawdon, Wright & Hatch. *Comments:* H-RI-276-G58, Durand-1231. 18__. 1830s–1860s.
Rarity: *None known*

$500 • W-RI-900-500-G170
Left: Statue of George Washington / 500. *Center:* Woman with shield and eagle. *Bottom center:* Eagle with chicks in nest. *Right:* Woman leaning on pillar / 500. *Engraver:* Rawdon, Wright & Hatch. *Comments:* H-RI-276-G62, Durand-1232. 18__. 1830s–1860s.
Rarity: URS-3
Proof $800

Non-Valid Issues

$1 • W-RI-900-001-A010

Left: ONE / Farmer. *Center:* Horses, goats, and sheep at well. *Right:* 1 / Sailor. *Overprint:* Red ONE. *Engraver:* Danforth, Wright & Co. *Comments:* H-RI-276-A5, Durand-1200. Altered from $1 Commercial Bank, Perth Amboy, New Jersey series. July 10, 1856.

Rarity: URS-3
VF $250

$2 • W-RI-900-002-A020

Left: 2 / Man on horse, Boy, dog, and cow / TWO. *Center:* Train passing cliffs, Men. *Right:* 2 / Vessels near shore. *Engraver:* New England Bank Note Co. *Comments:* H-RI-276-A10, Durand-1203. Altered from $2 Commercial Bank, Gratiot, Michigan. 18__. 1840s.

Rarity: *None known*

$2 • W-RI-900-002-A030

CJF

Overprint: Red TWO. *Engraver:* Danforth, Wright & Co. *Comments:* H-RI-276-A15, Durand-1204. Altered from $2 Commercial Bank, Perth Amboy, New Jersey series. July 10th, 1856.

Rarity: URS-6
VF $150

$2 • W-RI-900-002-A040

Left: TWO / Woman / TWO. *Center:* 2 / Indian with slain deer / 2. *Right:* TWO / Sailor with anchor / TWO. *Engraver:* Terry, Pelton & Co. *Comments:* H-RI-276-A20, Durand-1205. Altered from $2 Pennsylvania Savings Bank, Philadelphia. 18__. 1851.

Rarity: *None known*

$3 • W-RI-900-003-C080

Engraver: Draper, Toppan & Co. *Comments:* H-RI-276-C24, Durand-1207. Counterfeit of W-RI-900-003-G080. This note is a lithograph facsimile with the word "Providence" badly executed. 18__. 1840s.

Rarity: *None known*

$3 • W-RI-900-003-A050

CJF

Engraver: New England Bank Note Co. *Comments:* H-RI-276-A25, Durand-1208. Altered from $3 Commercial Bank, Gratiot, Michigan. 18__. 1840s.

Rarity: URS-3
VF $150

$5 • W-RI-900-005-R010

Engraver: National Bank Note Co. *Comments:* H-RI-276-R10, Durand-1211. Raised from W-RI-900-001-G030. 186_. 1860s.

Rarity: URS-3
VF $200

$5 • W-RI-900-005-N010

Center: Three women, Strongbox, Ship. *Bottom center:* Arm and hammer. *Right:* Milkmaids. *Comments:* H-RI-276-N5, Durand-1216. 1840s.

Rarity: *None known*

$5 • W-RI-900-005-N020

Center: Woman, Spinning wheel. *Comments:* H-RI-276-N10, Durand-1217. 1840s.

Rarity: *None known*

$5 • W-RI-900-005-A060

Left: Men driving cattle across river / 5. *Center:* 5 / Five men gathering hay, Oxen, wagon. *Right:* 5. *Tint:* Brown-orange lathework outlining white 5. *Engraver:* Bald, Cousland & Co. *Comments:* H-RI-276-A30, Durand-1215. Altered from $5 Pioneer Association, La Fayette, Indiana. 18__. 1850s.

Rarity: *None known*

$5 • W-RI-900-005-A070

Left: FIVE vertically. *Center:* 5 / Amphitrite and Neptune in shell drawn by sea horses / 5. *Bottom center:* Steamboat. *Right:* V / Canal / V. *Engraver:* Rawdon, Wright & Hatch. *Comments:* H-RI-276-A35, Durand-1214. Altered from $5 Commercial Bank of Millington, Millington, Maryland. 18__. 1840s.

Rarity: *None known*

$5 • W-RI-900-005-A080

Left: 5 / Train / 5. *Center:* FIVE / Ship / FIVE. *Right:* 5 / "George Washington at Dorchester Heights". *Engraver:* New England Bank Note Co. *Comments:* H-RI-276-A40, Durand-1213. Altered from $5 Commercial bank, Gratiot, Michigan. 18__. 1840s.

Rarity: *None known*

$5 • W-RI-900-005-A090
Left: 5 / Ship under sail. *Center:* Whaling scene, Men in boat, Ship. *Right:* 5 / Sailor. *Engraver:* Danforth, Wright & Co. *Comments:* H-RI-276-A45, Durand-1212. Altered from $5 Commercial Bank of New Jersey, Perth Amboy, New Jersey series. July 10, 1856.
Rarity: *None known*

$10 • W-RI-900-010-R020
Engraver: Draper, Toppan & Co. *Comments:* H-RI-276-R6, Durand-1220. Raised from W-RI-900-001-G020. 18__. 1850s.
Rarity: *None known*

$10 • W-RI-900-010-R030
Engraver: National Bank Note Co. *Comments:* H-RI-276-R12, Durand-1221. Raised from W-RI-900-001-G030. 186_. 1860s.
Rarity: URS-3
VF $200

$10 • W-RI-900-010-R040
Engraver: National Bank Note Co. *Comments:* H-RI-276-R20, Durand-1222. Raised from W-RI-900-002-G060. 186_. 1860s.
Rarity: *None known*

$10 • W-RI-900-010-N030
Center: Woman, Spinning wheel. *Comments:* H-RI-276-N15, Durand-1225. 1840s.
Rarity: *None known*

$10 • W-RI-900-010-A100
Center: 10 / Woman seated, Shield, house / 10. *Bottom center:* Portrait. *Comments:* H-Unlisted, Durand-1224. Altered from $10 Commercial Bank, Millington, Maryland. 1840s.
Rarity: URS-3

$10 • W-RI-900-010-A110
Left: X / Medallion head of Bacchus / 10. *Center:* 10 / Mercury flying / Woman seated on wharf / Neptune and sea horses / 10. *Right:* 10 / Medallion head of Bacchus / X. *Engraver:* Rawdon, Wright & Hatch. *Comments:* H-RI-276-A50. Altered from $10 Commercial Bank of Millington, Millington, Maryland. 18__. 1840s.
Rarity: *None known*

$10 • W-RI-900-010-A120
Left: TEN / Fortuna standing. *Center:* Gears / Sailing ship / Produce. *Right:* 10 / Wharf scene. *Engraver:* New England Bank Note Co. *Comments:* H-RI-276-A55. Altered from $10 Commercial Bank, Gratiot, Michigan. 18__. 1840s.
Rarity: *None known*

$20 • W-RI-900-020-R050
Engraver: National Bank Note Co. *Comments:* H-RI-276-R22, Durand-1227. Raised from W-RI-900-002-G060. 186_. 1860s.
Rarity: *None known*

$20 • W-RI-900-020-S010
Left: 20 / Spread eagle. *Center:* Liberty and merchandise, Ship / 20. *Right:* Spread eagle / 20. *Engraver:* Danforth & Hufty. *Comments:* H-RI-276-S5, Durand-1229. 18__. 1850s.
Rarity: URS-3
VF $200

Commercial Bank of Rhode Island
1850s
W-RI-910

History: A non-existent bank represented only by notes altered from those of other banks.

ISSUES
$20 • W-RI-910-020-AR010
Left: XX / Man seated. *Center:* Horses, Bales. *Right:* 20 / Man seated. *Engraver:* Danforth, Wright & Co. *Comments:* H-RI-278-AR5. July 10, 1856.
Rarity: URS-3
VF $200

Continental Bank
1853–1865
W-RI-920

History: The Continental Bank was chartered in May 1853. Benjamin R. Almy was the first president, and Albert G. Durfee was the first cashier. It was located at 8 What Cheer Street. The capital was $222,950 throughout its existence. Its circulation was $43,678 in 1857, increasing to $133,114 by 1862. Specie was listed at $2,424.71 in 1857.

The business of the Continental Bank was succeeded by the Fourth National Bank of Providence, chartered on January 31, 1865.

Numismatic Commentary: Certain issues from this bank have a vignette of a train just having crossed the Rockville Bridge on the Susquehanna River, above Harrisburg in distant Pennsylvania. The bridge had the reputation of being the longest stone arch bridge in the United States. It was replaced in 1877.

VALID ISSUES
$1 • W-RI-920-001-G010
Left: 1 / Anchor, box, bale, and barrel. *Center:* Train, Train crossing bridge spanning river. *Right:* 1 / Female portrait. *Overprint:* Red ONE. *Engraver:* Toppan, Carpenter, Casilear & Co. *Comments:* H-RI-280-G2a. 18__. 1850s–1860s.
Rarity: *None known*

$1 • W-RI-920-001-G010a
Overprint: Red panel outlining white ONE. *Engraver:* Toppan, Carpenter, Casilear & Co. / ABNCo. monogram. *Comments:* H-RI-280-G2b, Durand-1233. Similar to W-RI-920-001-G010 but with additional engraver imprint. 18__. 1860s.
Rarity: URS-6
VF $400

$1 • W-RI-920-001-G010b   QDB

Overprint: Red panel outlining white ONE. *Engraver:* American Bank Note Co. *Comments:* H-Unlisted, Durand-Unlisted. Similar to W-RI-920-001-G010 but with different engraver imprint. 18__. 1860s.

Rarity: URS-4
F $400; **VF** $750; **Unc-Rem** $2,000

$2 • W-RI-920-002-G020

Left: Train, Train crossing bridge spanning river / 2. *Center:* Portrait of Daniel Webster. *Right:* 2 / Eagle and shield. *Overprint:* Red TWO. *Engraver:* Toppan, Carpenter, Casilear & Co. *Comments:* H-RI-280-G4a. 18__. 1850s–1860s.

Rarity: URS-6
VF $400

$2 • W-RI-920-002-G020a   CJF

Overprint: Red panel outlining white TWO. *Engraver:* Toppan, Carpenter, Casilear & Co. / ABNCo. monogram. *Comments:* H-RI-280-G4b, Durand-1234. Similar to W-RI-920-002-G020 but with additional engraver imprint. 18__. 1860s.

Rarity: URS-6
VF $400

$3 • W-RI-920-003-G030

Left: Three allegorical women with anchor on cliff / THREE. *Center:* Man, woman, and baby. *Right:* 3 / Commerce seated. *Overprint:* Red 3, 3. *Engraver:* Toppan, Carpenter, Casilear & Co. *Comments:* H-RI-280-G6a. 18__. 1850s.

Rarity: *None known*

$3 • W-RI-920-003-G030a   CC

Overprint: Red 3, 3. *Engraver:* Toppan, Carpenter, Casilear & Co. / ABNCo. monogram. *Comments:* H-RI-280-G6b, Durand-1235. Similar to W-RI-920-003-G030 but with additional engraver imprint. 18__. 1860s.

Rarity: URS-5
VF $1,000

$5 • W-RI-920-005-G040

Left: 5 / Indian. *Center:* "Surrender of Cornwallis at Yorktown". *Right:* 5 / Portrait of George Washington. *Overprint:* Red FIVE. *Engraver:* Toppan, Carpenter, Casilear & Co. *Comments:* H-RI-280-G8a, Durand-1236. 18__. 1850s.

Rarity: *None known*

$5 • W-RI-920-005-G040a

Overprint: Red panel outlining white FIVE. *Engraver:* Toppan, Carpenter, Casilear & Co. / ABNCo. monogram. *Comments:* H-RI-280-G8b, Durand-1236. Similar to W-RI-920-005-G040 but with additional engraver imprint. 18__. 1860s.

Rarity: URS-3
VF $400

$10 • W-RI-920-010-G050

Left: Portrait of John Jay / Medallion bust of George Washington. *Center:* 10 / Woman seated with eagle atop globe. *Right:* 10 / Portrait of John Hancock. *Overprint:* Red X, TEN. *Engraver:* Toppan, Carpenter, Casilear & Co. *Comments:* H-RI-280-G10a. 18__. 1850s.

Rarity: *None known*

$10 • W-RI-920-010-G050a   CJF

Overprint: Red X, TEN. *Engraver:* American Bank Note Co. *Comments:* H-RI-280-G10b, Durand-1239. Similar to W-RI-920-010-G050 but with different engraver imprint. 18__. 1860s.

Rarity: URS-3
VF $750

$20 • W-RI-920-020-G060

SBG

Engraver: Toppan, Carpenter, Casilear & Co. *Comments:* H-RI-280-G12, Durand-1243. 18___. 1850s–1860s.
Rarity: URS-3
VF $900

$50 • W-RI-920-050-G070

Left: 50 / Ship. *Center:* Commerce seated. *Right:* 50 / Portrait of Millard Fillmore. *Engraver:* Toppan, Carpenter, Casilear & Co. *Comments:* H-RI-280-G14, Durand-1244. 18___. 1850s–1860s.
Rarity: *None known*

$100 • W-RI-920-100-G080

Left: 100 / Female portrait. *Center:* Brig, Spread eagle on rock in sea, Warship. *Right:* 100 / History. *Engraver:* Toppan, Carpenter, Casilear & Co. *Comments:* H-RI-280-G16, Durand-1245. 18___. 1850s–1860s.
Rarity: *None known*

$500 • W-RI-920-500-G090

Left: 500 / Portrait of Henry Clay. *Center:* Steamship, Vessels. *Right:* 500 / Sailor. *Engraver:* Toppan, Carpenter, Casilear & Co. *Comments:* H-RI-280-G18, Durand-1246. 18___. 1850s–1860s.
Rarity: *None known*

NON-VALID ISSUES

$5 • W-RI-920-005-R010

CC

Overprint: Red panel outlining white FIVE. *Engraver:* Toppan, Carpenter, Casilear & Co. / ABNCo. monogram. *Comments:* H-RI-280-R3, Durand-1237. Raised from W-RI-920-001-G010 series. 18___. 1860s.
Rarity: URS-3
VF $300

$5 • W-RI-920-005-A010

Left: Running horses / V. *Center:* Liberty and Ceres flanking shield surmounted by horse's head. *Right:* 5 / Portrait of girl shading her eyes. *Overprint:* Red FIVE. *Engraver:* Bald, Cousland & Co. / Baldwin, Bald & Cousland. *Comments:* H-RI-280-A10, Durand-1238. Altered from $5 Bank of Morgan, Morgan, Georgia. 18___. 1850s.
Rarity: *None known*

$10 • W-RI-920-010-R020

Overprint: Red TEN. *Engraver:* Toppan, Carpenter, Casilear & Co. *Comments:* H-RI-280-R4, Durand-1240. Raised from W-RI-920-001-G010 series. March 1, 18___. 1850s.
Rarity: URS-3
VF $200

$10 • W-RI-920-010-R030

Engraver: Toppan, Carpenter, Casilear & Co. / ABNCo. monogram. *Comments:* H-RI-280-R8, Durand-1241. Raised from W-RI-920-002-G020 series. 18___. 1860s.
Rarity: *None known*

$10 • W-RI-920-010-AR010

Center: Ship at sea. *Comments:* H-RI-280-A5, Durand-1242. Altered and raised from $1 bill. 1850s.
Rarity: *None known*

Eagle Bank
1818–1865
W-RI-930

History: The Eagle Bank was chartered in February 1818. Wheeler Martin served as the bank's founding president, and John Lippitt was its first cashier. The office was located at 23 Market Square in 1863.

The capital of the Eagle Bank was $400,000 in 1848. The same was raised to $500,000 in 1855. Circulation was at $38,827.50 in 1849, $32,992 in 1857, and $56,497 in 1862. Specie was valued at $2,691.67 in 1857.

The business of the Eagle Bank was succeeded by the National Eagle Bank, chartered on April 17, 1865.

Numismatic Commentary: The opportunity to secure a genuine note from this bank does not present itself very often. The bank used multiple engravers to design its notes, from Peter Maverick to the American Bank Note Co., but few bills remain today. Collectors of historical portraits should be pleased to find that one

How to Read the Whitman Numbering System
$1 • W-RI-010-001-G010a

Denomination: Value of the note shown.

W: Whitman number. This number is a sortable code unique to each bank and note.

RI: Abbreviation for the state under study.

010: Numerical designation specific to each bank.

001: The denomination in dollars.

G010a: G indicates a good or valid note. Other categories are indicated thus: C (counterfeit); R (raised); S (spurious); N (not-attributed); A (altered). Numbers are assigned starting with 010, 020, et seq. Terminal letters following the number indicate variations of a note: a series of different colored overprints, tints, payees, etc., all on the same design of note. For more information, see the "How to Use This Book" section at the front of the volume, page xiv.

issue bears an image of Abraham Lincoln, whose image appears on only a few notes issued by state-chartered banks in America.

Remaining in the American Bank Note Co. archives as of 2003 was a $1-$1-$2-$5 tint plate.

VALID ISSUES

$1 • W-RI-930-001-G010

Left: ONE vertically. *Right:* RHODE ISLAND vertically. *Engraver:* P. Maverick. *Comments:* H-RI-285-G2, Durand-1250. 18___. 1818–1820s.
Rarity: *None known*

$1 • W-RI-930-001-G020

SBG

Engraver: Draper, Toppan & Longacre. *Comments:* H-RI-285-G6, Durand-1251. Proof. 18___. 1840s–1850s.
Rarity: URS-3
VF $350; **Proof** $2,200
Selected auction price: Stack's Bowers Galleries, March 2013, Proof $2,057

$1 • W-RI-930-001-G030

Left: ONE on 1 / Stonecutters, Bust of Thomas H. Watts. *Center:* Spread eagle on rock. *Right:* ONE / Two children. *Tint:* Red-orange 1 / 1 and panel of 1s. *Engraver:* American Bank Note Co. *Comments:* H-RI-285-G8a. Mar. 4, 186_. 1860s.
Rarity: URS-3
VF $500

$1 • W-RI-930-001-G030a

CJF

Tint: Green dies outlining white 1 / 1 and panel of dies bearing 1s. *Engraver:* American Bank Note Co. *Comments:* H-RI-285-G8b, Durand-1252. Similar to W-RI-930-001-G030. March 4th, 186_. 1860s.
Rarity: URS-3
Proof $1,500

$1.50 • W-RI-930-001.50-G040

CJF

Engraver: P. Maverick / Durand & Co. *Comments:* H-RI-285-G12, Durand-1253. July 1st, 1837.
Rarity: URS-3
VF $500

$2 • W-RI-930-002-G055

Left: TWO vertically. *Right:* RHODE ISLAND vertically. *Engraver:* P. Maverick. *Comments:* H-RI-285-G16, Durand-1254. 18___. 1818–1820s.
Rarity: *None known*

$2 • W-RI-930-002-G070

Left: TWO / Train / TWO. *Center:* 2 / Female portrait / 2. *Bottom center:* Anchor on shield. *Right:* TWO / Steamboat / TWO. *Engraver:* Unverified, but likely Draper, Toppan, Longacre & Co. *Comments:* H-RI-285-G20, Durand-1255. 18___. 1840s–1850s.
Rarity: *None known*

$2 • W-RI-930-002-G080

Left: America. *Center:* 2 / Spread eagle on rock / 2. *Right:* 2 / 2. *Tint:* Red-orange 2 / 2 and panel. *Engraver:* American Bank Note Co. *Comments:* H-RI-285-G22a, Durand-1256. Mar. 4, 186_. 1860s.
Rarity: URS-3
VF $500

$2 • W-RI-930-002-G080a

Tint: Green 2 / 2 and panel. *Engraver:* American Bank Note Co. *Comments:* H-Unlisted. Similar to W-RI-930-002-G080. Mar. 4, 186_. 1860s.
Rarity: —

$3 • W-RI-930-003-G090

Left: THREE vertically. *Center:* 3 / Hope standing / III. *Bottom center:* Anchor. *Right:* RHODE ISLAND vertically. *Engraver:* P. Maverick. *Comments:* H-RI-285-G24, Durand-1257. First issue. 18___. 1818–1820s.
Rarity: *None known*

$3 • W-RI-930-003-G100

Left: Spread eagle on limb. *Center:* 3 / Two allegorical figures / 3. *Bottom center:* Anchor on shield. *Right:* Female portrait. *Engraver:* Unverified, but likely Draper, Toppan, Longacre & Co. *Comments:* H-RI-285-G28, Durand-1258. 18___. 1840s–1850s.
Rarity: *None known*

$5 • W-RI-930-005-G110   CC

Engraver: P. Maverick. *Comments:* H-RI-285-G34, Durand-1261. 18__. 1818–1830s.

Rarity: URS-2

F $250

$5 • W-RI-930-005-G120

Left: 5 / Man holding dividers on scroll, Two stonecutters / 5. *Center:* V. *Bottom center:* Woman seated. *Right:* 5 / Commerce seated, Vessels / 5. *Engraver:* Unverified, but likely Draper, Toppan, Longacre & Co. *Comments:* H-RI-285-G36, Durand-1262. 18__. 1840s–1850s.

Rarity: *None known*

$5 • W-RI-930-005-G130

Left: FIVE / Woman seated. *Center:* 5 / Portrait of Abraham Lincoln / FIVE. *Right:* 5 / Eagle. *Tint:* Orange panel and 5 / 5. *Engraver:* American Bank Note Co. *Comments:* H-RI-285-G38a, Durand-1263. Mar. 4, 186_. 1860s.

Rarity: URS-3

Proof $3,500

$10 • W-RI-930-010-G140

Left: TEN vertically. *Center:* Neptune in chariot drawn by two sea horses / X. *Right:* RHODE ISLAND vertically. *Engraver:* P. Maverick / Durand & Co. *Comments:* H-RI-285-G44, Durand-1268. 18__. 1818–1830s.

Rarity: *None known*

$10 • W-RI-930-010-G150

Left: X / X. *Center:* Eagle, globe / X / Liberty. *Bottom center:* Dog. *Right:* X / X. *Engraver:* Unverified, but likely Draper, Toppan, Longacre & Co. *Comments:* H-RI-285-G46, Durand-1269. 18__. 1840s–1850s.

Rarity: *None known*

$20 • W-RI-930-020-G160

Left: RHODE ISLAND vertically. *Center:* 20 / Anchor and scroll bearing In God We Hope / 20. *Bottom center:* Anchor. *Right:* TWENTY vertically. *Engraver:* P. Maverick / Durand & Co. *Comments:* H-RI-285-G50, Durand-1272. 18__. 1818–1850s.

Rarity: *None known*

$50 • W-RI-930-050-G170

Left: RHODE ISLAND vertically. *Center:* 50 / Ship and sloop at sea, Lighthouse / 50. *Bottom center:* Anchor on shield. *Right:* FIFTY vertically. *Engraver:* P. Maverick / Durand & Co. *Comments:* H-RI-285-G54, Durand-1276. 18__. 1818–1850s.

Rarity: *None known*

$100 • W-RI-930-100-G180

Left: RHODE ISLAND vertically. *Center:* 100 / Spread eagle on anchor leaning against rock bearing In God We Hope / 100. *Bottom center:* Anchor on shield. *Right:* ONE HUNDRED vertically. *Engraver:* P. Maverick / Durand & Co. *Comments:* H-RI-285-G58, Durand-1278. 18__. 1818–1850s.

Rarity: *None known*

NON-VALID ISSUES

$1.50 • W-RI-930-001.50-A010   CC

Engraver: Terry, Pelton & Co. *Comments:* H-Unlisted, Durand-Unlisted. 18__. 1820s.

Rarity: URS-2

VG $350

$3 • W-RI-930-003-C090   CC

Engraver: P. Maverick. *Comments:* H-RI-285-C24, Durand-1259. Counterfeit of W-RI-930-003-G090. 18__. 1810s–1820s.

Rarity: URS-3

VF $350

$3 • W-RI-930-003-R010

Engraver: Draper, Toppan, Longacre & Co. *Comments:* H-RI-285-R5, Durand-1260. Raised from W-RI-930-001-G020. 18__. 1850s.

Rarity: *None known*

$5 • W-RI-930-005-R020

Engraver: American Bank Note Co. *Comments:* H-Unlisted, Durand-1264. Raised from W-RI-930-001-G030a. 186_. 1860s.

Rarity: URS-3

$5 • W-RI-930-005-R030

Left: Woman. *Center:* Train. *Right:* Medallion head. *Comments:* H-RI-285-N5. Raised from $1. 1850s.

Rarity: *None known*

$5 • W-RI-930-005-S010   cc

Engraver: Rawdon, Wright & Hatch. *Comments:* H-RI-285-S5, Durand-1267. 18__. 1852.

Rarity: URS-3
VF $200

$5 • W-RI-930-005-AR010
Left: FIVE / Indian family overlooking cliff / Ships. *Center:* Spread eagle. *Right:* 5 / Liberty, eagle, and shield. *Engraver:* Danforth & Hufty. *Comments:* H-RI-285-AR5, Durand-1265. Altered from W-RI-090-001-G040. Jan. 1, 1848.

Rarity: *None known*

$5 • W-RI-930-005-AR020
Engraver: Danforth & Hufty. *Comments:* H-RI-285-AR6, Durand-1266. Altered and raised from W-RI-090-003-G100. Jan. 1, 1848.

Rarity: *None known*

$10 • W-RI-930-010-R040
Engraver: American Bank Note Co. *Comments:* H-Unlisted, Durand-1270. Raised from W-RI-930-001-G030a. 186_. 1860s.

Rarity: URS-3

$10 • W-RI-930-010-A020
Left: TEN / Indian family overlooking cliff / Ships. *Center:* Spread eagle. *Right:* 10 / Liberty, eagle, and shield. *Comments:* H-Unlisted, Durand-1271. Altered from W-RI-090-001-G040. 1850s.

Rarity: URS-3

$20 • W-RI-930-020-R050
Engraver: Unverified, but likely Draper, Toppan, Longacre & Co. *Comments:* H-Unlisted, Durand-1273. Raised from W-RI-930-002-G070. 1840s–1850s.

Rarity: URS-3
VF $125

$20 • W-RI-930-020-R060
Engraver: Unverified, but likely Draper, Toppan, Longacre & Co. *Comments:* H-RI-285-R10, Durand-1274. Raised from W-RI-930-003-G100. 18__. 1850s.

Rarity: *None known*

$20 • W-RI-930-020-AR030
Left: Die / Male portrait. *Center:* 20 / Spread eagle and shield / 20. *Bottom center:* Portrait of girl. *Right:* Die / Plow vertically / Die. *Engraver:* Terry, Pelton & Co. *Comments:* H-RI-285-AR8, Durand-1275. This note was raised from a $1 and the appearance changed by pasting the described vignettes on both sides. 18__. 1830s.

Rarity: URS-3
VF $150

$50 • W-RI-930-050-AR040
Left: ONE / Indian family overlooking cliff / Ships. *Center:* Spread eagle. *Bottom center:* Loom. *Right:* 50 / Liberty, eagle, and shield. *Engraver:* Danforth & Hufty. *Comments:* H-RI-285-AR10, Durand-1277. Altered and raised from W-RI-090-001-G040. Jan. 1, 1848.

Rarity: *None known*

Exchange Bank
1801–1865
W-RI-940

History: Chartered and incorporated in 1801, the Exchange Bank had a close association with the Washington Insurance Company, which needed a ready source of capital in the event of an unexpected large claim.[55] The bank had an authorized capital of $400,000, which increased to $500,000 in 1848. The circulation of the bank was $66,300 in 1849, $44,700 in 1857, and $72,300 in 1862. Specie was reported at $4,788.06 in 1857. It was located at 55 Westminster Street in 1863.

In 1865 the business of the Exchange Bank was succeeded by the National Exchange Bank.

Numismatic Commentary: This bank was one of Rhode Island's oldest banking institutions. Their notes were obtained through various engraving firms, and many are available in the marketplace. One amusing $5 issue shows the engraving of half an eagle on a shield as the center vignette. This was meant to correlate to the value of a $5 gold piece that is still referred to as a "half eagle."

VALID ISSUES

$1 • W-RI-940-001-G010
Left: ONE vertically. *Center:* Plow, ONE / 1 / D / 1. *Right:* Woman standing with anchor / ONE. *Comments:* H-RI-290-G2, Durand-1279. First issue. 18__. 1800s.

Rarity: *None known*

$1 • W-RI-940-001-G010a
Center: 1 / 1 / Script ONE. *Comments:* H-Unlisted, Durand-1280. Similar to W-RI-940-001-G010. 18__. 1800s.

Rarity: URS-3
VF $200

$1 • W-RI-940-001-G020   cc

Comments: H-RI-290-G4, Durand-1281. 18__. 1800s–1810s.

Rarity: URS-1
F $450

$1 • W-RI-940-001-G020a
Center: 1 / 1 / Script ONE. *Comments:* H-RI-290-G4a. Similar to W-RI-940-001-G020. 18__. 1800s.
Rarity: *None known*

$1 • W-RI-940-001-G030
Left: 1 ONE 1 vertically. *Center:* 1 / Hope seated on rocks with anchor / 1. *Right:* ONE vertically. *Engraver:* Leney & Rollinson. *Comments:* H-RI-290-G6, Durand-1282. 18__. 1810s–1820s.
Rarity: *None known*

$1 • W-RI-940-001-G040   CC

Engraver: Reed, Stiles & Co. *Comments:* H-RI-290-G7a. 18__. 1820s.
Rarity: URS-3
Proof $600

$1 • W-RI-940-001-G050   CJF

Engraver: Rawdon, Wright & Hatch. *Comments:* H-RI-290-G9, Durand-1283. 18__. 1830s–1840s.
Rarity: URS-3
VG $250

$1 • W-RI-940-001-G060
Center: Indian. *Comments:* H-RI-290-G10. 18__. 1840s.
Rarity: *None known*

$1 • W-RI-940-001-G070
Left: 1 / Train / ONE. *Center:* Group of milkmaids. *Right:* 1 / Venus bathing / ONE. *Comments:* H-Unlisted, Durand-1284. 1800s.
Rarity: URS-3

$1 • W-RI-940-001-G080
Left: ONE / Allegorical woman holding 1 / ONE. *Center:* Cherub, Male portrait, Cherub. *Bottom center:* Anchor on shield. *Right:* ONE / Farmer reclining with basket, Flock of sheep / 1. *Engraver:* Wellstood, Hanks, Hay & Whiting. *Comments:* H-RI-290-G12, Durand-1285. 18__. 1850s.
Rarity: URS-3
Proof $300

$1 • W-RI-940-001-G080a
Overprint: Red 1. *Engraver:* Wellstood, Hanks, Hay & Whiting. *Comments:* H-RI-290-G12a, Durand-1286. Similar to W-RI-940-001-G080. 18__. 1850s.
Rarity: URS-3
VF $250; **Proof** $3,200
Selected auction price: Stack's Bowers Galleries, March 2013, Proof $3,146

$1 • W-RI-940-001-G080b
Overprint: Red 1. *Engraver:* Wellstood, Hanks, Hay & Whiting / ABNCo. monogram. *Comments:* H-RI-290-G12b. Similar to W-RI-940-001-G080 but with additional engraver imprint. 18__. 1850s–1860s.
Rarity: *None known*

$1 • W-RI-940-001-G080c   CJF

Overprint: Red ONE. *Engraver:* Wellstood, Hanks, Hay & Whiting / ABNCo. monogram. *Comments:* H-Unlisted, Durand-Unlisted. Similar to W-RI-940-001-G080 but with additional engraver imprint. 18__. 1850s–1860s.
Rarity: URS-3
VF $600

$2 • W-RI-940-002-G090
Left: TWO vertically. *Center:* 2 / Farmer plowing with oxen, Houses. *Right:* 2. *Comments:* H-RI-290-G16. 18__. 1800s.
Rarity: *None known*

$2 • W-RI-940-002-G100
Left: TWO vertically. *Center:* 2 / 2. *Comments:* H-RI-290-G18, Durand-1292. 18__. 1800s.
Rarity: *None known*

$2 • W-RI-940-002-G110   CC

Comments: H-RI-290-G20, Durand-1293. 18__. 1810s–1820s.
Rarity: URS-3
Proof $1,200
Selected auction price: Stack's Bowers Galleries, March 2013, Proof $1,149

$2 • **W-RI-940-002-G120**

SBG

Engraver: Reed & Stiles. *Comments:* H-RI-290-G22, Durand-1294. 18__. 1820s.

Rarity: URS-3
Proof $1,500
Selected auction price: Stack's Bowers Galleries, March 2013, Proof $1,452

$2 • **W-RI-940-002-G130**

Left: 2 / Ship and steamboats, City / 2. *Center:* Griffin on strongbox, Woman holding key and receiving horn of plenty from Mercury / TWO. *Bottom center:* Anchor on shield. *Right:* 2 / Justice with state arms / TWO. *Engraver:* Unverified, but likely Rawdon, Wright & Hatch. *Comments:* H-RI-290-G24, Durand-1295. 18__. 1830s–1840s.

Rarity: *None known*

$2 • **W-RI-940-002-G140**

Left: 2 / Portrait of Daniel Webster. *Center:* Portrait between two cherubs / Industry. *Right:* 2 / TWO. *Engraver:* Wellstood, Hanks, Hay & Whiting. *Comments:* H-RI-290-G26, Durand-1296. 18__. 1850s.

Rarity: URS-3
Proof $1,100

$2 • **W-RI-940-002-G140a**

Overprint: Red 2. *Engraver:* Wellstood, Hanks, Hay & Whiting. *Comments:* H-RI-290-G26a, Durand-1297. Similar to W-RI-940-002-G140. 18__. 1850s.

Rarity: *None known*

$2 • **W-RI-940-002-G140b**

Overprint: Red 2. *Engraver:* Wellstood, Hanks, Hay & Whiting / ABNCo. monogram. *Comments:* H-RI-290-G26b. Similar to W-RI-940-002-G140 but with additional engraver imprint. 18__. 1850s–1860s.

Rarity: URS-3
VF $250

$2 • **W-RI-940-002-G150**

Left: TWO vertically. *Center:* 2. *Right:* 2. *Comments:* H-Unlisted, Durand-1291. First issue. 1800s.

Rarity: URS-3

$3 • **W-RI-940-003-G160**

Left: THREE vertically. *Comments:* H-RI-290-G30, Durand-1301. First issue. 18__. 1800s.

Rarity: *None known*

$3 • **W-RI-940-003-G170**

Left: THREE vertically. *Center:* Die bearing horse / 3 / THREE / 3. *Right:* THREE / Hope standing with anchor. *Comments:* H-RI-290-G32, Durand-1302. 18__. 1800s.

Rarity: *None known*

$3 • **W-RI-940-003-G180**

CJF

Engraver: Leney & Rollinson. *Comments:* H-RI-290-G34, Durand-1303. Type of third issue. 18__. 1810s.

Rarity: URS-1
Proof $500

$3 • **W-RI-940-003-G190**

CC

Engraver: Reed, Stiles & Co. *Comments:* H-RI-290-G35. 18__. 1820s.

Rarity: URS-3
Proof $500
Selected auction price: Spink-Smythe, July 2008, Proof $340

$3 • **W-RI-940-003-G200**

Center: Eagle holding banner bearing E PLURIBUS UNUM. *Comments:* H-RI-290-G37, Durand-1309. 18__. 1830s.

Rarity: *None known*

$5 • **W-RI-940-005-G210**

Left: FIVE vertically. *Center:* FIVE / 5 / Half Eagle coin / FIVE / 5. *Right:* Die bearing standing man / FIVE. *Comments:* H-RI-290-G40, Durand-1311. 18__. 1800s–1820s.

Rarity: *None known*

$5 • **W-RI-940-005-G220**

Left: FIVE vertically. *Center:* 5 / Hope seated, Ship / V. *Right:* FIVE vertically. *Comments:* H-RI-290-G41, Durand-1310. 18__. 1810s–1820s.

Rarity: URS-3
Proof $300

$5 • **W-RI-940-005-G230**

Comments: H-RI-290-G43, Durand-1312. No description available. 18__. 1830s–1840s.

Rarity: *None known*

$5 • W-RI-940-005-G240

CJF

Engraver: Rawdon, Wright & Hatch. *Comments:* H-RI-290-G44, Durand-1312. 18__. 1850s.

Rarity: URS-1
VF $800

$5 • W-RI-940-005-G250

CJF

Engraver: Terry, Pelton & Co. *Comments:* H-Unlisted, Durand-Unlisted. Proof. 18__. 1830s–1850s.

Rarity: URS-2
Proof $1,200

$10 • W-RI-940-010-G260

Left: 10. *Center:* Reaper with sickle, plough, rake, and sheaf of grain / 10. *Right:* 10 / Two men carrying woman on their shoulders. *Engraver:* Wellstood, Hanks, Hay & Whiting. *Comments:* H-RI-290-G48, Durand-1323. 18__. 1850s.

Rarity: *None known*

$50 • W-RI-940-050-G270

Left: 50 / Woman standing with ankles crossed, Staff, Cornucopia and anchor / 50. *Center:* FIFTY DOLLARS / 50. *Right:* FIFTY vertically. *Engraver:* PSSP / New England Bank Note Co. *Comments:* H-RI-290-G50. 18__. 1830s.

Rarity: *None known*

$50 • W-RI-940-050-G280

Left: Woman floating in air holding distaff / FIFTY. *Center:* 50 / Male portrait / 50. *Bottom center:* Anchor on shield. *Right:* Ceres soaring in air / FIFTY. *Engraver:* Wellstood, Hanks, Hay & Whiting. *Comments:* H-RI-290-G52, Durand-1327. 18__. 1850s.

Rarity: *None known*

$100 • W-RI-940-100-G290

Left: Lathework panel bearing C / Portrait of George Washington / C. *Center:* 100 / Manhattan reclining pouring water, Ship / 100. *Right:* Lathework panel bearing ONE HUNDRED vertically. *Engraver:* PSSP / New England Bank Note Co. *Comments:* H-RI-290-G54. 18__. 1830s.

Rarity: *None known*

$100 • W-RI-940-100-G300

Left: 100 / Cherub / C. *Center:* New York's Crystal Palace. *Bottom center:* Anchor on shield. *Right:* 100 / Cherub / Male portrait. *Engraver:* Wellstood, Hanks, Hay & Whiting. *Comments:* H-RI-290-G56, Durand-1329. 18__. 1850s.

Rarity: *None known*

$500 • W-RI-940-500-G310

Left: 500 / 500 vertically / 500. *Center:* 500 / Woman seated with shield bearing D, Fasces, cornucopia, lyre, and sheaf / 500. *Right:* 500 / D / 500. *Engraver:* PSSP / New England Bank Note Co. *Comments:* H-RI-290-G58. 18__. 1830s.

Rarity: *None known*

$500 • W-RI-940-500-G320

Left: Sailor / 500. *Center:* Cherub, Male portrait, Cherub. *Bottom center:* Anchor on shield. *Right:* 500 / Justice. *Engraver:* Wellstood, Hanks, Hay & Whiting. *Comments:* H-RI-290-G60, Durand-1330. 18__. 1850s.

Rarity: *None known*

$1,000 • W-RI-940-1000-G330

Left: THOUSAND vertically. *Center:* 1000 / Woman standing with legs crossed, Lyre, Cornucopia / 1000. *Right:* 1000 / M / 1000. *Engraver:* PSSP / New England Bank Note Co. *Comments:* H-RI-290-G62. 18__. 1830s.

Rarity: *None known*

$1,000 • W-RI-940-1000-G340

SBG

Engraver: Wellstood, Hanks, Hay & Whiting. *Comments:* H-RI-290-G64, Durand-1331. 18__. 1850s.

Rarity: URS-1
Proof $2,000

Non-Valid Issues

$1 • W-RI-940-001-C010

Comments: H-Unlisted, Durand-1287. Counterfeit of W-RI-940-001-G010. 1800s.

Rarity: URS-3

$1 • W-RI-940-001-C010a

Comments: H-Unlisted, Durand-1288. Counterfeit of W-RI-940-001-G010a. 1800s.

Rarity: URS-3

$1 • **W-RI-940-001-C020**   CJF

Comments: H-RI-290-C4, Durand-1289. Counterfeit of W-RI-940-001-G020. 18__. 1800s.
Rarity: URS-3
VF $150

$1 • **W-RI-940-001-C020a**
Comments: H-RI-290-C4a. Counterfeit of W-RI-940-001-G020a. 18__. 1800s.
Rarity: URS-3
VF $250

$1 • **W-RI-940-001-S010**
Left: 1 on panel vertically. *Center:* 1 / Woman with scroll / 1. *Right:* 1 on panel vertically. *Engraver:* Rawdon, Wright & Hatch. *Comments:* H-RI-290-S5, Durand-1290. 18__. 1840s.
Rarity: URS-3
VF $250

$2 • **W-RI-940-002-C090**
Comments: H-RI-290-C16. Counterfeit of W-RI-940-002-G090. 18__. 1800s.
Rarity: URS-3
VF $150

$2 • **W-RI-940-002-C100**
Comments: H-RI-290-C18, Durand-1299. Counterfeit of W-RI-940-002-G100. 18__. 1800s.
Rarity: URS-3
VF $150

$2 • **W-RI-940-002-C150**
Comments: H-Unlisted, Durand-1298. Counterfeit of W-RI-940-002-G150. 1800s.
Rarity: URS-3

$2 • **W-RI-940-002-S020**   CC

Engraver: American Bank Note Co. *Comments:* H-RI-290-S10, Durand-1300. Jany 2nd, 185_. 1854.
Rarity: URS-5
VF $150

$3 • **W-RI-940-003-C160**
Comments: H-Unlisted, Durand-1304. Counterfeit of W-RI-940-003-G160. 1800s.
Rarity: URS-3

$3 • **W-RI-940-003-C170**   NJW

Comments: H-RI-290-C32, Durand-1305. Counterfeit of W-RI-940-003-G170. 18__. 1800s.
Rarity: URS-3
VF $150

$3 • **W-RI-940-003-C180**
Engraver: Leney & Rollinson. *Comments:* H-RI-290-C34, Durand-1306. Counterfeit of W-RI-940-003-G180. 18__. 1810s.
Rarity: URS-3
VF $200

$3 • **W-RI-940-003-S030**
Center: Eagle holding banner bearing E PLURIBUS UNUM. *Comments:* H-RI-290-S15. 1830s.
Rarity: *None known*

$3 • **W-RI-940-003-A010**
Left: 3 / Steamship. *Center:* Justice, Shield surmounted by eagle, Liberty. *Right:* 3 / Train. *Overprint:* Red THREE. *Engraver:* Baldwin, Bald & Cousland / Bald, Cousland & Co. *Comments:* H-RI-290-A5, Durand-1307. Altered from W-RI-1500-003-G030a. 18__. 1850s.
Rarity: *None known*

$3 • **W-RI-940-003-A020**
Left: 3. *Center:* Farming scene with overseer on horse. *Right:* 3 / Female portrait. *Engraver:* Toppan, Carpenter, Casilear & Co. *Comments:* H-RI-290-A10, Durand-1308. Altered from $3 Exchange Bank, Bangor, Maine. 18__. 1850s.
Rarity: *None known*

$5 • **W-RI-940-005-C210**
Comments: H-RI-290-C40, Durand-1315. Counterfeit of W-RI-940-005-G210. 18__. 1820s.
Rarity: URS-3
VF $150

$5 • **W-RI-940-005-C220**
Comments: H-Unlisted, Durand-1314. Counterfeit of W-RI-940-005-G220. 1800s.
Rarity: URS-3

$5 • **W-RI-940-005-R010**
Comments: H-RI-290-R6, Durand-1313. Raised from W-RI-940-001-G060. 18__. 1840s–1850s.
Rarity: *None known*

$5 • W-RI-940-005-S040

Left: Bank front / 5. *Center:* 5 / Woman, globe, harp / 5. *Bottom center:* Arm and hammer. *Right:* "George Washington at Dorchester Heights" / 5. *Engraver:* Toppan, Carpenter & Co. *Comments:* H-RI-290-S20, Durand-1318. From a modified, fraudulent plate originally for a $5 of the Mechanics Bank, Philadelphia, Pennsylvania. 18__. 1850s.

Rarity: *None known*

$5 • W-RI-940-005-N010

Center: Liberty and steamboat. *Comments:* H-RI-290-N5, Durand-1320. Altered or spurious. 1840s–1850s.

Rarity: *None known*

$5 • W-RI-940-005-N020

Center: 5 / Three women / 5. *Comments:* H-RI-290-N10, Durand-1321. Altered or spurious. 1800s.

Rarity: *None known*

$5 • W-RI-940-005-N030

Engraver: Rawdon, Wright & Hatch. *Comments:* H-RI-290-N15. No description available. 1800s.

Rarity: *None known*

$5 • W-RI-940-005-A030

Left: 5 on die / 5 on die. *Center:* Two women floating in clouds with eagle and shield. *Right:* 5 on die / 5 on die. *Engraver:* W.L. Ormsby. *Comments:* H-RI-290-A15, Durand-1317. Altered from a spurious $5 of the Exchange Bank, Hartford, Connecticut. Dec. 1, 1856.

Rarity: *None known*

$5 • W-RI-940-005-A040

Left: Dog's head and key. *Center:* Men cutting grain in wheat field. *Right:* 5 / Female portrait. *Engraver:* W.L. Ormsby. *Comments:* H-RI-290-A20, Durand-1319. Altered from $5 Farmers and Drovers Bank, Petersburg, Indiana. Oct. 1, 1858.

Rarity: *None known*

$5 • W-RI-940-005-A050

Left: Three women supporting 5. *Center:* Eagle and shield / Reclining Indian woman with flags / 5. *Bottom center:* Steamboat. *Right:* 5 / Indian with gun. *Engraver:* Toppan, Carpenter, Casilear & Co. *Comments:* H-RI-290-A25, Durand-1316. Altered from $5 Exchange Bank, Bangor, Maine. 18__. 1850s.

Rarity: *None known*

$10 • W-RI-940-010-R020

Comments: H-RI-290-R8, Durand-1324. Raised from W-RI-940-001-G060. 18__. 1840s–1850s.

Rarity: *None known*

$10 • W-RI-940-010-N040

Left: Sailor. *Center:* Three women reclining in clouds. *Right:* Woman with grain on her back. *Comments:* H-RI-290-N20, Durand-1326. 1840s–1850s.

Rarity: *None known*

$10 • W-RI-940-010-A060

Center: 10 / 10 / Indian hunting buffalo / 10 / 10. *Engraver:* Danforth, Wright & Co. *Comments:* H-RI-290-A30, Durand-1325. Altered from $10 Exchange Bank, Hartford, Connecticut. Dec. 1, 1856.

Rarity: URS-3
VF $250

$50 • W-RI-940-050-R030

Center: Liberty and steamboat. *Comments:* H-Unlisted, Durand-1328. Raised from $5. 1840s–1850s.

Rarity: URS-3

Fox River Bank
1850s
W-RI-950

History: The Fox River Bank was located in Dundee, Illinois. The J.A. Carpenter Company made this note payable in Providence, Rhode Island, in order to spread the issue out of state. It would have taken weeks, maybe even months for the note to travel the distance between Providence and Dundee. The firm had free use of its funds during the time lag. This was a common practice during the era.[56]

ISSUES

$2 • W-RI-950-002-N010   cc

Engraver: Toppan, Carpenter, Casilear & Co. *Comments:* H-Unlisted, Durand-1332. 18__. 1850s.

Rarity: URS-3
G $300; **VF** $400

Franklin Bank
1820s
W-RI-960

History: A non-existent bank represented only by spurious notes.

Numismatic Commentary: Spurious $5 notes with the likeness of Benjamin Franklin were circulated, supposedly from this bank, but probably not in Rhode Island. This fraud was detected, and some bills were collected, after which they were likely bundled together and stored away. They evidently got wet and were stained. Almost all issues that are available to the collector exhibit this stain mark diagonally on the right side on the note.

ISSUES

$5 • W-RI-960-005-S010

CJF

Engraver: Murray, Draper, Fairman & Co. *Comments:* H-RI-300-G5, Durand-1333. 18__. 1824.

Rarity: URS-6

VF $200

Globe Bank
1831–1865
W-RI-970

History: The Globe Bank was incorporated in 1831 and served as a fiscal agent for the New York and Stonington Railroad Company. The bank handled the company's payroll. It was located at 56 Westminster Street. The capital for the bank was $409,200 in 1848, increasing to $600,000 by 1855. Figures for 1852 included: loans $647,307; specie $1,764; bank notes $4,081.[57] Circulation was $69,150 in 1857, with specie at $2,939.74. By 1862 circulation had risen to $257,839.

The business of the Globe Bank was succeeded by the National Globe Bank in 1865. There was an unrelated Globe Bank, W-RI-1340, located in Smithfield.

Numismatic Commentary: All genuine notes from this bank are hard to locate. Some notes show Archimedes lifting the world with the aid of a fulcrum and lever. Others show Atlas supporting the world on his shoulders, and another shows the globe in the heavens surrounded by allegorical figures. These are some of the more interesting vignettes to be found among Rhode Island banks.

VALID ISSUES

$1 • W-RI-970-001-G010

Left: Lathework panel bearing ONE / D / ONE vertically. *Center:* 1 / 1 / Alternating flower garlands and gridwork segments / 1 / 1. *Right:* Lathework panel bearing ONE / D / ONE vertically. *Engraver:* PSSP. *Comments:* H-RI-305-G2, Durand-1335. 18__. 1830s.

Rarity: *None known*

$1 • W-RI-970-001-G020

BH

Engraver: Rawdon, Wright, Hatch & Co. *Comments:* H-RI-305-G4, Durand-1336. 18__. 1830s.

Rarity: URS-1

Proof $5,000

$1 • W-RI-970-001-G030

CC

Engraver: Rawdon, Wright & Hatch. *Comments:* H-RI-305-G6, Durand-1337. 18__. Circa 1839.

Rarity: URS-3

VF $350; **Proof** $1,600

Selected auction price: Stack's Bowers Galleries, June 2010, Proof $1,540

$1 • W-RI-970-001-G030a

Engraver: Rawdon, Wright & Hatch. *Comments:* H-RI-305-G6a, Durand-1338. Similar to W-RI-970-001-G030 but with additional ONEs. 18__. 1840s.

Rarity: URS-5

VF $350

$1 • W-RI-970-001-G040

Left: 1 on medallion shield / Cherub with cornucopia. *Center:* Four allegorical figures on globe bearing ONE and supported on the shoulders of Atlas, Father Time, and Knowledge reclining. *Right:* 1 on medallion shield / Cherub with cornucopia. *Engraver:* Wellstood, Hanks, Hay & Whiting. *Comments:* H-RI-305-G8, Durand-1339. 18__. 1850s.

Rarity: URS-1

Proof $7,000

$1 • W-RI-970-001-G040a

Overprint: Green 1 / 1. *Engraver:* Wellstood, Hanks, Hay & Whiting. *Comments:* H-RI-305-G8a. Similar to W-RI-970-001-G040. 18__. 1850s.

Rarity: URS-3

VF $350

$1 • W-RI-970-001-G040b

Overprint: Green ONE / ONE. *Engraver:* Wellstood, Hanks, Hay & Whiting. *Comments:* H-RI-305-G8b, Durand-1340. Similar to W-RI-970-001-G040. 18__. 1860s.

Rarity: *None known*

$1 • W-RI-970-001-G040c

CC

Overprint: Green ONE / ONE. *Engraver:* Wellstood, Hanks, Hay & Whiting / ABNCo. monogram. *Comments:* H-RI-305-G8c. Similar to W-RI-970-001-G040 but with additional engraver imprint. 18__. 1860s.

Rarity: URS-3
VF $750; **Proof** $3,100
Selected auction price: Stack's Bowers Galleries, June 2010, Proof $3,081

$2 • W-RI-970-002-G050

CC

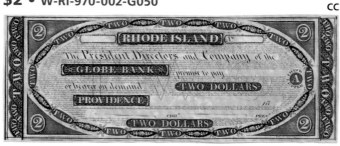

Engraver: PSSP. *Comments:* H-RI-305-G12, Durand-1341. 18__. 1830s.

Rarity: URS-2
Proof $700
Selected auction price: Stack's Bowers Galleries, January 2010, Proof $652

$2 • W-RI-970-002-G060

Left: 2 / TWO vertically / 2. *Center:* 2 / Archimedes lifting world with lever / 2. *Bottom center:* Eagle. *Right:* TWO. *Engraver:* Rawdon, Wright, Hatch & Co. *Comments:* H-RI-305-G14, Durand-1342. 18__. 1830s.

Rarity: *None known*

$2 • W-RI-970-002-G070

Center: TWO on 2 / Archimedes lifting world with lever / TWO on 2. *Bottom center:* Dog and strongbox. *Right:* 2 on lathework vertically. *Engraver:* Rawdon, Wright & Hatch. *Comments:* H-RI-305-G16, Durand-1343. 18__. Circa 1839.

Rarity: *None known*

$2 • W-RI-970-002-G070a

Engraver: Rawdon, Wright & Hatch. *Comments:* H-RI-305-G16a, Durand-1344. Similar to W-RI-970-002-G070 but with additional TWOs. 18__. 1840s.

Rarity: *None known*

$2 • W-RI-970-002-G080

Left: Shield bearing 2 / Cherub. *Center:* Woman and man reclining / Atlas supporting globe bearing THREE with four allegorical women on top / Woman and man reclining. *Right:* Shield bearing 2 / Cherub. *Engraver:* Wellstood, Hanks, Hay & Whiting. *Comments:* H-RI-305-G18, Durand-1345. 18__. 1850s.

Rarity: URS-2
VF $350; **Proof** $2,000

$2 • W-RI-970-002-G080a

Overprint: Green 2 / 2. *Engraver:* Wellstood, Hanks, Hay & Whiting. *Comments:* H-RI-305-G18a. Similar to W-RI-970-002-G080. 18__. 1850s.

Rarity: URS-5
VG $1,450
Selected auction price: Stack's Bowers Galleries, January 2010, VG $1,422

$2 • W-RI-970-002-G080b

CC

Overprint: Green TWO / TWO. *Engraver:* Wellstood, Hanks, Hay & Whiting. *Comments:* H-RI-305-G18b, Durand-1346. Similar to W-RI-970-002-G080. 18__. 1860s.

Rarity: URS-5
VF $350

$2 • W-RI-970-002-G080c

Overprint: Green TWO / TWO. *Engraver:* Wellstood, Hanks, Hay & Whiting / ABNCo. monogram. *Comments:* H-RI-305-G18c. Similar to W-RI-970-002-G080 but with additional engraver imprint. 18__. 1860s.

Rarity: URS-5
VF $350

$3 • W-RI-970-003-G090

Left: Lathework panel bearing THREE vertically. *Center:* 3 / 3 / Alternating flower garlands and gridwork segments / 3 / 3. *Right:* Lathework panel bearing THREE vertically. *Comments:* H-RI-305-G22, Durand-1349. 1830s.

Rarity: URS-3
Proof $300

$3 • W-RI-970-003-G100

Left: 3 / THREE vertically / 3. *Center:* 3 / Archimedes lifting globe with lever / 3. *Bottom center:* Eagle. *Right:* THREE. *Comments:* H-RI-305-G24, Durand-1350. 1850s.

Rarity: *None known*

$3 • W-RI-970-003-G110

Center: 3 / Archimedes lifting globe with lever / 3. *Bottom center:* Dog and strongbox. *Right:* 3 on lathework vertically. *Comments:* H-RI-305-G26, Durand-1351. 1850s.

Rarity: *None known*

$3 • **W-RI-970-003-G110a**

Comments: H-RI-305-G26a, Durand-1352. Similar to W-RI-970-003-G110 but with additional THREEs. 1850s–1860s.

Rarity: *None known*

$3 • **W-RI-970-003-G120**

Left: Shield bearing 3 / Cherub. *Center:* Woman and man reclining / Atlas supporting globe bearing THREE with four allegorical women on top / Woman and man reclining. *Right:* Shield bearing 3 / Cherub. *Engraver:* Wellstood, Hanks, Hay & Whiting. *Comments:* H-RI-305-G28, Durand-1354. 18__. 1850s.

Rarity: URS-2

VF $350; **Proof** $3,000

$3 • **W-RI-970-003-G120a**

Overprint: Green 3 / 3. *Engraver:* Wellstood, Hanks, Hay & Whiting. *Comments:* H-RI-305-G28a, Durand-1353. Similar to W-RI-970-003-G120. 18__. 1850s.

Rarity: URS-3

VF $350

$3 • **W-RI-970-003-G120b**   CC

Overprint: Green ornate 3 / 3. *Engraver:* Wellstood, Hanks, Hay & Whiting / ABNCo. monogram. *Comments:* H-RI-305-G28b. Similar to W-RI-970-003-G120 but with additional engraver imprint. 18__. 1860s.

Rarity: URS-3

F $1,250

$5 • **W-RI-970-005-G130**

Left: Lathework chain bearing RHODE ISLAND vertically / 5 / 5. *Center:* Alternating flower garlands and grid segments, Spiral lathework lines. *Right:* 5 / 5. *Engraver:* PSSP. *Comments:* H-RI-305-G30, Durand-1357. 18__. 1830s.

Rarity: *None known*

$5 • **W-RI-970-005-G140**   CC

Comments: H-RI-305-G34, Durand-1358. Proof. 18__. 1830s–1840s.

Rarity: URS-2

Proof $3,400

$5 • **W-RI-970-005-G150**   CJF

Overprint: Red FIVE. *Comments:* H-RI-305-G36, Durand-1359. 18__. 1840s–1850s.

Rarity: URS-1

VF $800; **Proof** $2,000

$5 • **W-RI-970-005-G160**

Left: FIVE vertically. *Center:* Atlas supporting globe with allegorical women on top. *Bottom center:* Shield bearing anchor. *Right:* FIVE over 5 / FIVE over 5. *Comments:* H-RI-305-G38, Durand-1360. 18__. 1840s–1850s.

Rarity: *None known*

$5 • **W-RI-970-005-G160a**

Tint: Red-brown and 5. *Engraver:* Wellstood, Hanks, Hay & Whiting. *Comments:* H-RI-305-G40a, Durand-1361. Similar to W-RI-970-005-G160. 18__. 1850s.

Rarity: URS-3

VF $350

$5 • **W-RI-970-005-G160b**   CJF

Tint: Red-brown panel, microlettering, and die bearing white 5. *Engraver:* Wellstood, Hanks, Hay & Whiting / ABNCo. monogram. *Comments:* H-RI-305-G40b. Similar to W-RI-970-005-G160 but with additional engraver imprint. 18__. 1850s–1860s.

Rarity: URS-3

VF $3,000

$5 • **W-RI-970-005-G170**   CC

Engraver: Rawdon, Wright, Hatch & Co. *Comments:* H-Unlisted, Durand-Unlisted. Note the title is engraved "The Globe Bank In The City Of Providence". 18__. 1840s–1850s.

Rarity: URS-1

Proof $2,500

$10 • **W-RI-970-010-G180**

Left: Lathework chain bearing RHODE ISLAND / 10 / 10 vertically. *Center:* Alternating flower garlands and gridwork segments, TEN DOLLARS with spiral lathework lines. *Right:* 10 / 10 vertically. *Engraver:* PSSP. *Comments:* H-RI-305-G42. 18__. 1830s.

Rarity: *None known*

$10 • **W-RI-970-010-G190**   CC

Engraver: New England Bank Note Co. *Comments:* H-RI-305-G46, Durand-1365. 18__. 1830s.

Rarity: URS-2
Proof $6,600
Selected auction price: Stack's Bowers Galleries,
January 2011, Proof $6,500

$10 • **W-RI-970-010-G200**

Left: Sailor with hand on capstan / 10. *Center:* Train, Canal / Commerce reclining on bale, City and ships. *Right:* 10. *Comments:* H-RI-305-G48, Durand-1366. 18__. 1840s.

Rarity: *None known*

$10 • **W-RI-970-010-G210**

Left: X / 10 / X. *Center:* Atlas supporting globe with allegorical women on top. *Bottom center:* Anchor on shield. *Right:* TEN vertically. *Comments:* H-RI-305-G50, Durand-1367. 18__. 1850s.

Rarity: *None known*

$10 • **W-RI-970-010-G220**

Left: TEN vertically. *Center:* Atlas supporting globe with allegorical women on top. *Bottom center:* Anchor on shield. *Right:* X / X. *Tint:* Red-brown and 10. *Engraver:* Wellstood, Hay & Whiting. *Comments:* H-RI-305-G52a, Durand-1368. 18__. 1850s.

Rarity: *None known*

$10 • **W-RI-970-010-G220a**   CC

Tint: Red-brown panel, microlettering, and die bearing white 10. *Engraver:* Wellstood, Hay & Whiting / ABNCo. monogram. *Comments:* H-RI-305-G52b. Similar to W-RI-970-010-G220 but with additional engraver imprint. 18__. 1850s–1860s.

Rarity: URS-3
VF $4,000; Proof $7,900
Selected auction price: Stack's Bowers Galleries,
May 2008, Proof $7,800

$20 • **W-RI-970-020-G230**

Left: Lathework chain bearing RHODE ISLAND / 20 / 20 vertically. *Center:* Alternating flower garlands and gridwork segments. *Right:* 20 / 20 vertically. *Engraver:* PSSP. *Comments:* H-RI-305-G54. 18__. 1820s–1830s.

Rarity: *None known*

$50 • **W-RI-970-050-G240**

Left: Lathework chain bearing RHODE ISLAND / 50 / 50 vertically. *Center:* Alternating flower garlands and gridwork segments. *Right:* 50 / 50 vertically. *Engraver:* PSSP. *Comments:* H-RI-305-G58. 18__. 1820s–1830s.

Rarity: *None known*

$50 • **W-RI-970-050-G250**

Left: 50 / Minerva. *Center:* Agriculture and Industry. *Right:* 50 / Cherub steering sailboat / 50. *Engraver:* New England Bank Note Co. *Comments:* H-RI-305-G60, Durand-1378. 18__. 1850s.

Rarity: *None known*

$50 • **W-RI-970-050-G260**   CC

Tint: Green dies bearing white 50s. *Engraver:* American Bank Note Co. *Comments:* H-RI-305-G62a, Durand-1379. November 1st, 18__. 1860s.

Rarity: URS-1
VF $500; Proof $11,600
Selected auction price: Stack's Bowers Galleries,
January 2011, Proof $11,500

$100 • **W-RI-970-100-G270**

Left: Lathework chain bearing RHODE ISLAND / 100 / 100 vertically. *Center:* Alternating flower garlands and gridwork segments. *Right:* 100 / 100 vertically. *Engraver:* PSSP. *Comments:* H-RI-305-G64. 18__. 1820s–1830s.

Rarity: *None known*

$100 • **W-RI-970-100-G280**

Left: ONE HUNDRED across 100 / Portrait of William Henry Harrison. *Center:* Wharf scene, Men loading wagon with barrels. *Right:* ONE HUNDRED across 100 / Portrait of Christopher Columbus. *Engraver:* New England Bank Note Co. *Comments:* H-RI-305-G68, Durand-1380. 18__. 1840s.

Rarity: *None known*

$100 • **W-RI-970-100-G290**

Left: 100 / Vulcan seated with sledge and anchor. *Center:* Eagle on limb, Train on bridge, Canal locks / C. *Bottom center:* 100 *Right:* 100 / Ceres seated, Cornucopia. *Engraver:* Rawdon, Wright, Hatch & Edson. *Comments:* H-RI-305-G70, Durand-1381. 18__. 1850s.

Rarity: *None known*

$100 • **W-RI-970-100-G290a**

Overprint: Red HUNDRED. *Engraver:* Rawdon, Wright, Hatch & Edson. *Comments:* H-RI-305-G70a. Similar to W-RI-970-100-G290. 18__. 1860s.

Rarity: *None known*

$100 • **W-RI-970-100-G300**

Left: 100 / Anchor, bales. *Center:* Two women flanking shield bearing state arms. *Right:* 100 / Woman with hand on globe. *Tint:* Green and 100s. *Engraver:* American Bank Note Co. *Comments:* H-RI-305-G72a, Durand-1382. 18__. 1860s.

Rarity: *None known*

$500 • **W-RI-970-500-G310**

Left: 500 / Portrait of George Washington. *Center:* Agriculture and Manufacturing. *Right:* 500 / Industry. *Engraver:* Unverified, but likely New England Bank Note Co. *Comments:* H-RI-305-G76a, Durand-1384. 18__. 1850s.

Rarity: *None known*

$1,000 • **W-RI-970-1000-G320**

Left: Justice. *Center:* 1000 / 1000 / 1000. *Tint:* Green. *Engraver:* Unverified, but likely New England Bank Note Co. *Comments:* H-RI-305-G78a, Durand-1385. 18__. 1850s.

Rarity: *None known*

Non-Valid Issues

$2 • **W-RI-970-002-A010**

Left: 2 on die. *Center:* Manhattan reclining with water urn / 2. *Right:* Woman with wheat and ears of corn. *Engraver:* Durand & Co. *Comments:* H-RI-305-A5, Durand-1347. Altered from $2 Globe Bank, New York City, New York. 1840.

Rarity: *None known*

$2 • **W-RI-970-002-A020**

Left: 2 / Portrait of William Penn. *Center:* Train at station. *Right:* 2 / Mechanic. *Overprint:* Red TWO. *Engraver:* New England Bank Note Co. *Comments:* H-RI-305-A6, Durand-1348. Altered from W-RI-1580-002-G120a. 18__. 1850s.

Rarity: *None known*

$3 • **W-RI-970-003-A030**

Left: 3 on die. *Center:* Manhattan reclining with water urn / 3. *Right:* 3 on die on panel of wheat and ears of corn. *Engraver:* Durand & Co. *Comments:* H-RI-305-A10, Durand-1355. Altered from $3 Globe Bank, New York City, New York. 1840.

Rarity: *None known*

$3 • **W-RI-970-003-A040**

Left: Panel bearing lathework circles / Two cherubs with scroll / Panel bearing lathework circles. *Center:* 3 / Indian seated with box, Dog / 3. *Right:* Lathework panel bearing THREE vertically. *Engraver:* Durand & Co. *Comments:* H-RI-305-A15, Durand-1356. Altered from $3 Globe Bank, New York, New York. 18__. 1840s.

Rarity: *None known*

$5 • **W-RI-970-005-R010**

Engraver: Wellstood, Hanks, Hay & Whiting. *Comments:* H-RI-305-R5, Durand-1362. Raised from W-RI-970-001-G040. 18__. 1850s.

Rarity: *None known*

$5 • **W-RI-970-005-A050**

Left: Fleet of sailing ships at sea / 5. *Center:* Four allegorical figures seated on globe. *Right:* 5 / Allegorical figure with shield bearing 5. *Engraver:* New England Bank Note Co. *Comments:* H-RI-305-A20, Durand-1364. Altered from $5 Globe Bank, Bangor, Maine. 18__. 1840s.

Rarity: *None known*

$5 • **W-RI-970-005-A060**

Left: Indian man seated on stump with dog. *Center:* Sailing vessel in harbor next to building / 5 on die. *Right:* FIVE / Corn and wheat. *Engraver:* Durand & Co. *Comments:* H-RI-305-A25, Durand-1363. Altered from $5 Globe Bank, New York City, New York. 1840.

Rarity: URS-3

VF $250

$10 • **W-RI-970-010-R020**

Engraver: Rawdon, Wright & Hatch. *Comments:* H-RI-305-R10, Durand-1369. Raised from W-RI-970-001-G030. 18__. 1830s.

Rarity: *None known*

$10 • **W-RI-970-010-R030**

Engraver: Wellstood, Hanks, Hay & Whiting. *Comments:* H-RI-305-R15, Durand-1370. Raised from W-RI-970-001-G040. 18__. 1850s.

Rarity: *None known*

$10 • **W-RI-970-010-R040**

Engraver: Wellstood, Hanks, Hay & Whiting. *Comments:* H-RI-305-R20, Durand-1371. Raised from W-RI-970-002-G080. 18__. 1850s.

Rarity: *None known*

$10 • **W-RI-970-010-R050**

Engraver: Wellstood, Hanks, Hay & Whiting. *Comments:* H-RI-305-R25, Durand-1372. Raised from W-RI-970-003-G120. 18__. 1850s.

Rarity: *None known*

$10 • **W-RI-970-010-R060**

Engraver: Wellstood, Hanks, Hay & Whiting. *Comments:* H-RI-305-R30, Durand-1373. Raised from W-RI-970-005-G160a. 18__. 1850s.

Rarity: *None known*

$10 • **W-RI-970-010-AR010**

Left: Fleet of sailing ships at sea / 10. *Center:* Four allegorical figures seated on globe. *Right:* 10. *Comments:* H-Unlisted, Durand-1374. Altered and raised from $5 Globe Bank, Bangor, Maine. 1850s.

Rarity: URS-3

VF $125

$10 • **W-RI-970-010-A070**

Left: Train / Portrait of Benjamin Franklin. *Center:* Four allegorical figures seated on globe. *Right:* 10. *Engraver:* New England Bank Note Co. *Comments:* H-RI-305-A30, Durand-1375. Altered from $10 Globe Bank, Bangor, Maine. 18__. 1840s.

Rarity: *None known*

$10 • **W-RI-970-010-A080**

Left: Artist resting on easel. *Center:* X / Harbor scene, Sailing ships, building. *Right:* 10 / Medallion head / 10. *Engraver:* Durand & Co. *Comments:* H-RI-305-A35, Durand-1376. Altered from $10 Globe Bank, New York City, New York. 1840.

Rarity: *None known*

$20 • W-RI-970-020-AR020

Left: Fleet of sailing ships at sea / 20. **Center:** Four allegorical figures seated on globe. **Right:** 20 / Allegorical figure with shield bearing 20. **Comments:** H-Unlisted, Durand-1377. Altered and raised from $5 Globe Bank, Bangor, Maine. 1850s.

Rarity: URS-3

$100 • W-RI-970-100-C290a

Engraver: Rawdon, Wright, Hatch & Edson. **Comments:** H-RI-305-C70a, Durand-1383. Counterfeit of W-RI-970-100-G290a. 18__. 1860s.

Rarity: *None known*

Grocers and Producers Bank
1853–1879
W-RI-980

History: The Grocers and Producers Bank was incorporated in May 1853. It was located at 32 Westminster Street. Figures for 1857 included: capital $153,800; bills in circulation $67,350; specie $3,371.78.[58] Circulation had increased to $89,462 by 1862, but only $1,848 was unredeemed by 1872. The Grocers and Producers Bank remained a state bank throughout the note-issuing period, continuing until it went into receivership in 1879 and closed for fraud.[59]

Numismatic Commentary: Lower-denomination notes are available signed and dated, while the higher denominations are most likely remainders without signatures.

Remaining in the American Bank Note Co. archives as of 2003 was a $1-$1-$1-$2 face plate and a $5-$5-$5-$10 face plate.

VALID ISSUES

$1 • W-RI-980-001-G010   CC

Overprint: Red ONE. **Engraver:** Wellstood, Hanks, Hay & Whiting. **Comments:** H-RI-310-G2a. 18__. 1850s.

Rarity: URS-2
VG $300

$1 • W-RI-980-001-G010a   SBG

Overprint: Green 1, 1. **Engraver:** American Bank Note Co. **Comments:** H-RI-310-G2c, Durand-1386. Similar to W-RI-980-001-G010. 18__. 1860s.

Rarity: URS-5
EF $595

$2 • W-RI-980-002-G020

Left: 2 / Blacksmith leaning over anvil / TWO. **Center:** 2. **Right:** 2 / Girl / TWO. **Overprint:** Likely 2 / 2. **Engraver:** Wellstood, Hanks, Hay & Whiting. **Comments:** H-RI-310-G4a, Durand-1388. 18__. 1850s.

Rarity: *None known*

$2 • W-RI-980-002-G030

Left: 2 / Boy sifting coal / TWO. **Center:** 2. **Right:** 2 / Girl / TWO. **Overprint:** Likely 2 / 2. **Engraver:** Wellstood, Hanks, Hay & Whiting. **Comments:** H-RI-310-G6a, Durand-1387. 18__. 1850s.

Rarity: *None known*

$2 • W-RI-980-002-G030a

Overprint: Green 2 / 2. **Engraver:** American Bank Note Co. **Comments:** H-RI-310-G6c, Durand-1387. Similar to W-RI-980-002-G030 but with different engraver imprint. 18__. 1860s.

Rarity: URS-3
VF $350

$2 • W-RI-980-002-G040

Center: Woman, Agricultural implements. **Comments:** H-Unlisted, Durand-1389. 1850s.

Rarity: URS-3

$5 • W-RI-980-005-G050   SBG

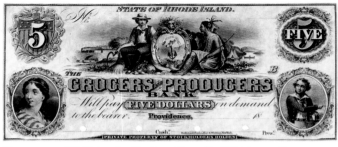

Engraver: Wellstood, Hanks, Hay & Whiting. **Comments:** H-Unlisted, Durand-Unlisted. Proof. 18__. 1850s.

Rarity: URS-2
Proof $3,400
Selected auction price: Stack's Bowers Galleries, March 2013, Proof $3,350

$5 • W-RI-980-005-G050a

Left: 5 / Man with scythe. *Center:* Farmer, State arms, Indian. *Right:* FIVE on 5 / Sailor. *Overprint:* Likely 5 / 5. *Engraver:* Wellstood, Hanks, Hay & Whiting. *Comments:* H-RI-310-G8a, Durand-1391. Similar to W-RI-980-005-G050. 18__. 1850s.

Rarity: URS-1

$5 • W-RI-980-005-G050b

CC

Overprint: Green FIVE. *Engraver:* American Bank Note Co. *Comments:* H-Unlisted, Durand-Unlisted. Similar to W-RI-980-005-G050 but with different engraver imprint. 18__. 1860s.

Rarity: URS-3
VF $750

$5 • W-RI-980-005-G060

Left: 5 / Female portrait. *Center:* Farmer, State arms, Indian. *Right:* FIVE on 5 / Sailor. *Comments:* H-Unlisted. 1850s.

Rarity: —

$5 • W-RI-980-005-G060a

Overprint: Likely 5 / 5. *Engraver:* Wellstood, Hanks, Hay & Whiting. *Comments:* H-RI-310-G10a, Durand-1390. Similar to W-RI-980-005-G060. 18__. 1850s.

Rarity: *None known*

$5 • W-RI-980-005-G070

Center: Three women, Goods, factories, and steamer. *Comments:* H-Unlisted, Durand-1393. 1850s.

Rarity: URS-3

$10 • W-RI-980-010-G080

SBG

Engraver: Wellstood, Hanks, Hay & Whiting. *Comments:* H-Unlisted. Proof. 18__. 1850s.

Rarity: URS-1
Proof $4,250
Selected auction price: Stack's Bowers Galleries, March 2013, Proof $4,234

$10 • W-RI-980-010-G080a

QDB

Overprint: Red TEN. *Engraver:* Wellstood, Hanks, Hay & Whiting. *Comments:* H-RI-310-G12a, Durand-1394. Similar to W-RI-980-010-G080. 18__. 1850s–1860s.

Rarity: URS-1
VF $350; **Proof** $2,500

$10 • W-RI-980-010-G090

Center: Three women, Goods, factories, and steamer. *Comments:* H-Unlisted, Durand-1396. 1850s.

Rarity: URS-3

$50 • W-RI-980-050-G100

SBG

Engraver: Wellstood, Hanks, Hay & Whiting. *Comments:* H-Unlisted, Durand-Unlisted. Proof. 18__. 1850s–1860s.

Rarity: URS-2
Proof $6,100
Selected auction price: Stack's Bowers Galleries, March 2013, Proof $6,051

$50 • W-RI-980-050-G100a

CC

Overprint: Red FIFTY. *Engraver:* Wellstood, Hanks, Hay & Whiting. *Comments:* H-RI-310-G14a, Durand-1399. Similar to W-RI-980-050-G100. 18__. 1850s–1860s.

Rarity: URS-3
VF $650

$100 • W-RI-980-100-G110

SBG

Engraver: Wellstood, Hanks, Hay & Whiting. *Comments:* H-Unlisted. Proof. 18__. 1850s.

Rarity: URS-1
Proof $6,700
Selected auction price: Stack's Bowers Galleries, March 2013, Proof $6,650

$100 • W-RI-980-100-G110a

QDB

Overprint: Red HUNDRED. *Engraver:* Wellstood, Hanks, Hay & Whiting. *Comments:* H-RI-310-G16a, Durand-1400. Similar to W-RI-980-100-G110. 18__. 1850s–1860s.

Rarity: URS-1
VF $5,000

$500 • W-RI-980-500-G120

QDB

Overprint: Red 500. *Engraver:* Wellstood, Hanks, Hay & Whiting. *Comments:* H-RI-310-G18a, Durand-1401. 18__. 1850s–1860s.

Rarity: URS-1
VF $1,200; **Proof** $8,000

Non-Valid Issues

$5 • W-RI-980-005-R010

Engraver: Wellstood, Hanks, Hay & Whiting. *Comments:* H-RI-310-R5, Durand-1392. Raised from W-RI-980-001-G010 series. 18__. 1850s.

Rarity: *None known*

$10 • W-RI-980-010-R020

Engraver: Wellstood, Hanks, Hay & Whiting. *Comments:* H-RI-310-R10, Durand-1395. Raised from W-RI-980-001-G010 series. 18__. 1850s.

Rarity: *None known*

$20 • W-RI-980-020-R030

Engraver: Wellstood, Hanks, Hay & Whiting. *Comments:* H-RI-310-R15, Durand-1397. Raised from W-RI-980-001-G010 series. 18__. 1850s.

Rarity: *None known*

$20 • W-RI-980-020-N010

Center: Three women, Goods, factories, and steamer. *Comments:* H-Unlisted, Durand-1398. 1850s.

Rarity: URS-3

High Street Bank
1828–1930
W-RI-990

History: Incorporated in 1828, the High Street Bank has the distinction of being a state bank that continued in operation during the entire state bank and National bank periods without changing its charter or conforming to the general practices of the time.[60] It was located at 154 High Street in 1863 and 846 Westminster Street in 1904.

Capital was $120,000 in 1848 and increased to $150,000 by 1850. Circulation amounted to $26,179 in 1857. Specie totaled $3,128,96 the same year. The bank's real estate was valued at $30,000 at this time plus $15,000 for the banking house. Cash on hand totaled $28,487.95. No currency was issued after 1865.

This bank remained in business until 1930, when it then became the High Street Bank and Trust Company. Today it is known as the Citizens Bank.

Numismatic Commentary: There in no shortage of spurious notes from this bank in the marketplace, but genuine notes, signed and dated, are hard to find.

Valid Issues

$1 • W-RI-990-001-G010

Center: Alternating flower garlands and gridwork segments. *Engraver:* PSSP. *Comments:* H-RI-315-G2, Durand-1402. 18__. 1820s–1830s.

Rarity: *None known*

$1 • W-RI-990-001-G020

Left: ONE, 1. *Center:* Farm scene / 1. *Right:* Ship, 1 / ONE. *Engraver:* New England Bank Note Co. *Comments:* H-RI-315-G6, Durand-1402. 18__. 1840s.

Rarity: *None known*

$1 • W-RI-990-001-G030

Left: 1 / Portrait of George Washington. *Center:* Woman seated with lyre / 1 / Woman seated with lyre. *Right:* 1 / Portrait of Benjamin Franklin. *Engraver:* New England Bank Note Co. *Comments:* H-RI-315-G8, Durand-1403. 18__. 1850s.

Rarity: *None known*

$1 • W-RI-990-001-G040
Left: 1 / Portrait of Henry Clay. *Center:* George Washington reading dispatches, Officers, soldiers. *Right:* 1 / Eagle on shield. *Engraver:* American Bank Note Co. *Comments:* H-RI-315-G10, Durand-1404. 18__. 1860s.
Rarity: *None known*

$2 • W-RI-990-002-G050
Center: Alternating flower garlands and gridwork segments. *Engraver:* PSSP. *Comments:* H-RI-315-G12. 18__. 1820s–1830s.
Rarity: *None known*

$2 • W-RI-990-002-G060
Left: TWO / 2. *Center:* Spread eagle on bale, Cannon balls and machinery / 2. *Right:* 2 / TWO / Schooner. *Engraver:* New England Bank Note Co. *Comments:* H-RI-315-G16, Durand-1405. 18__. 1840s.
Rarity: *None known*

$2 • W-RI-990-002-G070
Left: 2 / Portrait of Christopher Columbus. *Center:* Woman seated with cornucopia / 2 / Justice seated / TWO, TWO. *Right:* 2 / Portrait. *Engraver:* New England Bank Note Co. *Comments:* H-RI-315-G18, Durand-1408. 18__. 1850s.
Rarity: *None known*

$2 • W-RI-990-002-G080
Left: 2 / Ceres. *Center:* Cows in stream, Children on bank. *Right:* 2 / Portrait of Benjamin Franklin. *Engraver:* American Bank Note Co. *Comments:* H-RI-315-G20, Durand-1407. 18__. 1860s.
Rarity: *None known*

$3 • W-RI-990-003-G090
Center: Alternating flower garlands and gridwork segments. *Engraver:* PSSP. *Comments:* H-RI-315-G22. 18__. 1820s–1830s.
Rarity: *None known*

$3 • W-RI-990-003-G100
Left: THREE / Wharf scene / 3. *Center:* Bales, Sailor standing with hat in hand, Harbor / 3. *Right:* 3 / THREE / Train. *Engraver:* New England Bank Note Co. *Comments:* H-RI-315-G26, Durand-1409. 18__. 1840s.
Rarity: *None known*

$3 • W-RI-990-003-G110
Left: 3 / George Washington standing by horse. *Center:* Female portrait / Female portrait. *Right:* 3 / Blacksmith. *Engraver:* New England Bank Note Co. *Comments:* H-RI-315-G28, Durand-1410. 18__. 1850s.
Rarity: *None known*

$3 • W-RI-990-003-G120
Left: 3 / Two blacksmiths at work. *Center:* Portrait of George Washington. *Right:* 3 / Man dressing leather. *Engraver:* American Bank Note Co. *Comments:* H-RI-315-G30, Durand-1411. 18__. 1860s.
Rarity: *None known*

$5 • W-RI-990-005-G130
Center: Alternating flower garlands and gridwork segments. *Engraver:* PSSP. *Comments:* H-RI-315-G32. 18__. 1820s–1830s.
Rarity: *None known*

$5 • W-RI-990-005-G140
Left: FIVE vertically. *Center:* Allegorical woman raising curtain from shield bearing 5. *Right:* 5 / Ship. *Engraver:* New England Bank Note Co. *Comments:* H-RI-315-G36, Durand-1414. 18__. 1840s.
Rarity: *None known*

$5 • W-RI-990-005-G150
Left: FIVE. *Center:* Spread eagle on shield / Liberty and cherub with V. *Right:* 5 / Girl with basket of flowers. *Engraver:* New England Bank Note Co. *Comments:* H-RI-315-G38, Durand-1413. 18__. 1850s.
Rarity: *None known*

$5 • W-RI-990-005-G150a
Overprint: Red FIVE. *Engraver:* New England Bank Note Co. / ABNCo. monogram. *Comments:* H-RI-315-G38a, Durand-1413. Similar to W-RI-990-005-G150 but with additional engraver imprint. 18__. 1850s–1860s.
Rarity: *None known*

$10 • W-RI-990-010-G160
Center: Alternating flower garlands and gridwork segments. *Engraver:* PSSP. *Comments:* H-RI-315-G40. 18__. 1820s–1830s.
Rarity: *None known*

$10 • W-RI-990-010-G170
Left: 10 / X / 10. *Center:* Farmer with plow and oxen. *Right:* TEN / Goddess of Plenty. *Engraver:* New England Bank Note Co. *Comments:* H-RI-315-G44, Durand-1415. 18__. 1840s.
Rarity: *None known*

$10 • W-RI-990-010-G180
Left: Train, Mechanic seated with tools, Building / TEN. *Center:* X / TEN. *Right:* 10 / Reaper standing with sheaf. *Engraver:* New England Bank Note Co. *Comments:* H-RI-315-G46, Durand-1416. 18__. 1850s.
Rarity: *None known*

$10 • W-RI-990-010-G180a
Overprint: Red TEN. *Engraver:* New England Bank Note Co. / ABNCo. monogram. *Comments:* H-RI-315-G46a, Durand-1416. Similar to W-RI-990-010-G180 but with additional engraver imprint. 18__. 1850s–1860s.
Rarity: URS-3
VF $400

$20 • W-RI-990-020-G190
Center: Alternating flower garlands and gridwork segments. *Engraver:* PSSP. *Comments:* H-RI-315-G47, Durand-1418. 18__. 1820s–1830s.
Rarity: *None known*

$20 • W-RI-990-020-G200
Left: 20 / Woman. *Center:* XX / Eagle / XX. *Right:* 20 / Ship. *Engraver:* New England Bank Note Co. *Comments:* H-RI-315-G50, Durand-1418. 18__. 1840s–1850s.
Rarity: *None known*

$20 • W-RI-990-020-G210
Left: Liberty and eagle / 20. *Center:* 20 / Female portrait. *Right:* 20 / Portrait of Benjamin Franklin. *Engraver:* New England Bank Note Co. / ABNCo. monogram. *Comments:* H-RI-315-G52a, Durand-1419. 18__. 1850s–1860s.
Rarity: URS-3
Proof $1,500

$50 • W-RI-990-050-G220

Center: Alternating flower garlands and gridwork segments. *Engraver:* PSSP. *Comments:* H-RI-315-G53, Durand-1420. 18__. 1820s–1830s.

Rarity: *None known*

$50 • W-RI-990-050-G230

Left: FIFTY / Woman standing with cornucopia / FIFTY. *Center:* 50 / Man holding horse / 50. *Right:* FIFTY / Allegorical figure / FIFTY. *Engraver:* New England Bank Note Co. *Comments:* H-RI-315-G56, Durand-1420. 18__. 1840s–1850s.

Rarity: *None known*

$50 • W-RI-990-050-G240

CJF

Overprint: Red FIFTY. *Engraver:* New England Bank Note Co. *Comments:* H-RI-315-G58a, Durand-1421. 18__. 1850s–1860s.

Rarity: URS-1
VF $2,000

$100 • W-RI-990-100-G250

Center: Alternating flower garlands and gridwork segments. *Engraver:* PSSP. *Comments:* H-RI-315-G59, Durand-1422. 18__. 1820s–1830s.

Rarity: *None known*

$100 • W-RI-990-100-G260

Left: ONE HUNDRED across 100 / Portrait of William Henry Harrison. *Center:* Wharf scene. *Right:* ONE HUNDRED across 100 / Portrait of Christopher Columbus. *Engraver:* New England Bank Note Co. *Comments:* H-RI-315-G62, Durand-1422. 18__. 1840s–1850s.

Rarity: *None known*

$100 • W-RI-990-100-G270

CC

Engraver: New England Bank Note Co. / ABNCo. monogram. *Comments:* H-RI-315-G64a, Durand-1423. 18__. 1850s–1860s.

Rarity: URS-1
Proof $3,500

$100 • W-RI-990-100-G280

Left: 100 / Portrait of George Washington held by cherub / 100. *Center:* C / Spread eagle with shield and arrows, E PLURIBUS UNUM / C. *Right:* 100 / Indian / 100. *Comments:* H-Unlisted, Durand-1424. 1850s–1860s.

Rarity: URS-3

$500 • W-RI-990-500-G290

Left: 500. *Center:* Indian paddling canoe / 500. *Right:* 500 / Justice. *Engraver:* New England Bank Note Co. / ABNCo. monogram. *Comments:* H-RI-315-G68a, Durand-1425. 18__. 1860s.

Rarity: *None known*

Non-Valid Issues

$2 • W-RI-990-002-S010

CC

Engraver: Rawdon, Wright, Hatch & Edson. *Comments:* H-RI-315-S5. Spurious design imitating rough verbal description of W-RI-990-002-G070. March 10th, 18__. 1861.

Rarity: URS-6
VF $90

$3 • W-RI-990-003-S020

CC

Overprint: Red THREE. *Engraver:* Rawdon, Wright, Hatch & Edson. *Comments:* H-RI-315-S10, Durand-1412. This note is a close similarity to W-RI-990-003-G110. However, the vignettes of George Washington and the blacksmith are slightly different. Jan. 1st, 1859.

Rarity: URS-5
VF $100

$3 • W-RI-990-003-S020a

CC

Overprint: Red THREE, 3, THREE. *Engraver:* Rawdon, Wright, Hatch & Edson. *Comments:* H-Unlisted, Durand-Unlisted. Similar to W-RI-990-003-S020. Jan. 1st, 1859. 1850s.

Rarity: URS-3
VF $350

$10 • W-RI-990-010-A010

Left: 10 / Portrait of George Washington held by cherub / 10. **Center:** X / Spread eagle with shield and arrows, E PLURIBUS UNUM / X. **Bottom center:** Ship. **Right:** 10 / Indian / 10. **Engraver:** Terry, Pelton & Co. **Comments:** H-RI-315-A5, Durand-1417. Altered from $10 Citizens Bank, Augusta, Maine, or from notes of other failed banks using the same plate. 18__. 1840s.

Rarity: *None known*

$100 • W-RI-990-100-AR010

Center: C / Two blacksmiths at work / C. **Comments:** H-RI-315-A10. Altered and raised. 1840s.

Rarity: *None known*

Jackson Bank
1854–1895
W-RI-1000

History: The Jackson Bank was organized in June 1854. All the notes of this bank have a portrait of Andrew Jackson on their face.

The authorized capital was $170,000 in 1855, $220,100 in 1857, and $233,400 in 1860. Circulation was $39,606 in 1857, rising up to $86,397 in 1862. Specie amounted to just $3,923.52 in 1857. The bank was located at 25 Weybosset Street in 1862.

The Jackson Bank remained a state bank until it was liquidated in 1895.

Numismatic Commentary: Genuine notes are hard to find. Beware of $1 notes that have been raised to a higher denomination.

VALID ISSUES

$1 • W-RI-1000-001-G010

QDB

Engraver: Toppan, Carpenter, Casilear & Co. **Comments:** H-RI-320-G2, Durand-1427. 18__. 1850s.

Rarity: URS-3
Proof $1,000

$1 • W-RI-1000-001-G010a

Left: 1 / Militia men and drummer boy. **Center:** Portrait of Andrew Jackson. **Right:** 1 / Blacksmith holding sledge. **Overprint:** Red 1 / 1. **Engraver:** Toppan, Carpenter, Casilear & Co. / ABNCo. monogram. **Comments:** H-RI-320-G2a, Durand-1428. Similar to W-RI-1000-001-G010 but with additional engraver imprint. 18__. 1850s–1860s.

Rarity: URS-3
VG $950

$2 • W-RI-1000-002-G020

Left: 2 / Militia men throwing up breastwork. **Center:** Portrait of Andrew Jackson. **Right:** 2 / Solider standing by cannon holding flag. **Engraver:** Toppan, Carpenter, Casilear & Co. **Comments:** H-RI-320-G4, Durand-1429. 18__. 1850s.

Rarity: URS-2
Proof $1,500

$2 • W-RI-1000-002-G020a

Overprint: Red 2 / 2. **Engraver:** Toppan, Carpenter, Casilear & Co. / ABNCo. monogram. **Comments:** H-RI-320-G4a, Durand-1430. Similar to W-RI-1000-002-G020 but with additional engraver imprint. 18__. 1850s–1860s.

Rarity: *None known*

$5 • W-RI-1000-005-G030

Left: 5 / Two Indians on horseback hunting buffaloes. **Center:** Portrait of Andrew Jackson. **Right:** 5 / Yoke of oxen, Two children, Man felling tree. **Engraver:** Toppan, Carpenter, Casilear & Co. **Comments:** H-RI-320-G6, Durand-1431. 18__. 1850s.

Rarity: *None known*

$5 • W-RI-1000-005-G030a

Overprint: Red 5 / 5. **Engraver:** Toppan, Carpenter, Casilear & Co. / ABNCo. monogram. **Comments:** H-RI-320-G6a, Durand-1432. Similar to W-RI-1000-005-G030 but with additional engraver imprint. 18__. 1850s–1860s.

Rarity: *None known*

$10 • W-RI-1000-010-G040

Left: X / Battle of New Orleans / Portrait of Zachary Taylor. **Right:** 10 / Portrait of General Winfield Scott. **Engraver:** Toppan, Carpenter, Casilear & Co. **Comments:** H-RI-320-G8, Durand-1434. 18__. 1850s.

Rarity: *None known*

How to Read the Whitman Numbering System
$1 • W-RI-010-001-G010a

Denomination: Value of the note shown.

W: Whitman number. This number is a sortable code unique to each bank and note.

RI: Abbreviation for the state under study.

010: Numerical designation specific to each bank.

001: The denomination in dollars.

G010a: G indicates a good or valid note. Other categories are indicated thus: C (counterfeit); R (raised); S (spurious); N (not-attributed); A (altered). Numbers are assigned starting with 010, 020, et seq. Terminal letters following the number indicate variations of a note: a series of different colored overprints, tints, payees, etc., all on the same design of note. For more information, see the "How to Use This Book" section at the front of the volume, page xiv.

$10 • W-RI-1000-010-G040a

Overprint: Red. *Engraver:* Toppan, Carpenter, Casilear & Co. /ABNCo. monogram. *Comments:* H-RI-320-G8a, Durand-1435. Similar to W-RI-1000-010-G040 but with additional engraver imprint. 18__. 1850s–1860s.

Rarity: *None known*

$100 • W-RI-1000-100-G050

Left: C / C. *Center:* View of New York harbor, Ships and steamships, City. *Bottom center:* Anchor on shield. *Right:* 100 / Portrait of Andrew Jackson. *Engraver:* Unverified, but likely Toppan, Carpenter, Casilear & Co. *Comments:* H-RI-320-G10, Durand-1438. 18__. 1850s–1860s.

Rarity: *None known*

NON-VALID ISSUES

$5 • W-RI-1000-005-R010

Overprint: Red 5 / 5. *Engraver:* Toppan, Carpenter, & Co. / ABNCo. monogram. *Comments:* H-RI-320-R5, Durand-1433. Raised from W-RI-1000-001-G010a. 18__. 1860s.

Rarity: URS-3
VF $250

$10 • W-RI-1000-010-R020

Engraver: Toppan, Carpenter, Casilear & Co. / ABNCo. monogram. *Comments:* H-RI-320-R10, Durand-1436. Raised from W-RI-1000-001-G010a. 18__. 1860s.

Rarity: *None known*

$20 • W-RI-1000-020-R030

Engraver: Toppan, Carpenter, Casilear & Co. / ABNCo. monogram. *Comments:* H-RI-320-R15, Durand-1437. Raised from W-RI-1000-001-G010a. The bank issued no $20 bills. 18__. 1860s.

Rarity: *None known*

Liberty Bank
1854–1883
W-RI-1010

History: The Liberty Bank was incorporated in 1854. The starting capital was authorized at $100,000. Its office was at 3 Canal Street. Figures for 1857 were: capital $121,150; bills in circulation $23,983; specie $3,527.91. Circulation was up to $41,970 by 1862, but it fell to only $1,007 in 1876.

The Liberty Bank remained in operation as a state bank until it was liquidated in 1883.

Numismatic Commentary: Genuine notes of the lower denominations appear occasionally in the marketplace. The $5

denomination shows "The Landing of Roger Williams," and the $100 denomination shows "The Surrender of Cornwallis at Yorktown."

Remaining in the American Bank Note Co. archives as of 2003 was a $100 face plate, a $100-$100 face plate, a broken $1-$1-$1-$2 face plate, and a $5-$5-$5-$10 face plate.

VALID ISSUES

$1 • W-RI-1010-001-G010

Left: 1 / Man with gun and dog. *Center:* 1 / Men trying to calm horse, Man lying on ground / 1. *Right:* 1 / Girl. *Engraver:* Toppan, Carpenter, Casilear & Co. *Comments:* H-RI-325-G2, Durand-1439. 18__. 1850s.

Rarity: URS-3

$1 • W-RI-1010-001-G010a

Overprint: Red 1, 1. *Engraver:* Toppan, Carpenter, Casilear & Co. *Comments:* H-RI-325-G2a, Durand-1440. Similar to W-RI-1010-001-G010. 18__. 1850s.

Rarity: URS-3
VF $350

$1 • W-RI-1010-001-G010b

Overprint: Red 1, 1. *Engraver:* Toppan, Carpenter, Casilear & Co. / ABNCo. monogram. *Comments:* H-RI-325-G2b. Similar to W-RI-1010-001-G010 but with additional engraver imprint. 18__. 1850s–1860s.

Rarity: URS-3
VF $350

$1 • W-RI-1010-001-G010c

Engraver: American Bank Note Co. *Comments:* H-Unlisted, Durand-Unlisted. Similar to W-RI-1010-001-G010 but with different engraver imprint. 18__. 1860s.

Rarity: URS-3
VF $1,200; **Proof** $1,000

$2 • W-RI-1010-002-G020

Engraver: Toppan, Carpenter, Casilear & Co. *Comments:* H-RI-325-G4, Durand-1442. 18__. 1850s.

Rarity: URS-3
VF $400; **Proof** $1,400

$2 • W-RI-1010-002-G020a

Left: 2 / Portrait of girl. *Right:* 2 / Drover bargaining for cow, Cows and sheep. *Overprint:* Red TWO. *Engraver:* Toppan, Carpenter, Casilear & Co. *Comments:* H-RI-325-G4a, Durand-1443. Similar to W-RI-1010-002-G020. 18__. 1850s.

Rarity: *None known*

$2 • W-RI-1010-002-G020b

Engraver: American Bank Note Co. *Comments:* H-RI-325-G4b, Durand-1441. Similar to W-RI-1010-002-G020 but with different engraver imprint. 18__. 1860s.

Rarity: URS-3

$2 • W-RI-1010-002-G030   CC

Engraver: American Bank Note Co. *Comments:* H-RI-325-G6, Durand-1444. 18__. 1850s.

Rarity: URS-3
VF $1,500; **Proof** $2,100
Selected auction price: Stack's Bowers Galleries, March 2013, Proof $2,050

$5 • W-RI-1010-005-G040

Left: 5 / Sailor by capstan. *Center:* 5 / "The Landing of Roger Williams" / 5. *Right:* 5 / Female portrait. *Engraver:* Toppan, Carpenter, Casilear & Co. *Comments:* H-RI-325-G8, Durand-1447. 18__. 1850s.

Rarity: *None known*

$5 • W-RI-1010-005-G040a

Overprint: Red. *Engraver:* Toppan, Carpenter, Casilear & Co. *Comments:* H-RI-325-G8a, Durand-1447. Similar to W-RI-1010-005-G040. 18__. 1850s.

Rarity: *None known*

$10 • W-RI-1010-010-G050

Left: 10 / Anchor, box. *Center:* Liberty seated in clouds / Eagle and Indian woman. *Bottom center:* Eagle. *Right:* 10 / Portrait of George Washington / TEN. *Engraver:* Toppan, Carpenter, Casilear & Co. *Comments:* H-RI-325-G10, Durand-1450. 18__. 1850s–1860s.

Rarity: *None known*

$50 • W-RI-1010-050-G060

Left: 50 / Male portrait. *Center:* Spread eagle on shield. *Bottom center:* Eagle. *Right:* 50 / Indian woman as Liberty. *Engraver:* Toppan, Carpenter, Casilear & Co. *Comments:* H-RI-325-G12, Durand-1458. 18__. 1850s–1860s.

Rarity: *None known*

$50 • W-RI-1010-050-G060a   CC

Engraver: American Bank Note Co. *Comments:* H-Unlisted, Durand-Unlisted. Similar to W-RI-1010-050-G060 but with different engraver imprint. 18__. 1850s–1860s.

Rarity: URS-1
EF $1,000; **Proof** $2,000

$100 • W-RI-1010-100-G070

Left: 100. *Center:* "Surrender of Cornwallis at Yorktown". *Right:* 100 / Spread eagle. *Engraver:* Toppan, Carpenter, Casilear & Co. *Comments:* H-RI-32-G14, Durand-1461. 18__. 1850s–1860s.

Rarity: *None known*

Uncut Sheets

$1-$1-$1-$2 • W-RI-1010-001.001.001.002-US010

Vignette(s): (*$1*) Man with gun and dog / Men trying to calm horse, Figure lying on ground / Girl. (*$1*) Man with gun and dog / Men trying to calm horse, Figure lying on ground / Girl. (*$1*) Man with gun and dog / Men trying to calm horse, Figure lying on ground / Girl. (*$2*) Portrait of girl / Drover bargaining for cow, Cows and sheep. *Overprint(s):* Red. *Engraver:* Toppan, Carpenter, Casilear & Co. *Comments:* H-RI-325-G2a, G2a, G2a, G4a. 18__. 1850s.

Rarity: URS-3
VF $2,000

Non-Valid Issues

$2 • W-RI-1010-002-C020   SI

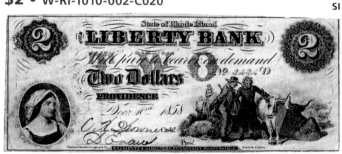

Overprint: Red TWO. *Engraver:* Toppan, Carpenter, Casilear & Co. *Comments:* H-RI-325-C4, Durand-1445. Approximate counterfeit of W-RI-1010-002-G020. Dec. 10th, 1858.

Rarity: URS-7
VG $35; **VF** $150

$2 • W-RI-1010-002-C020b

CC

Overprint: Blue TWO. *Engraver:* Toppan, Carpenter, Casilear & Co. *Comments:* H-RI-325-C4b, Durand-1446. Approximate counterfeit of W-RI-1010-002-G020b. Dec. 10th, 1858.

Rarity: URS-7
VF $150

$5 • W-RI-1010-005-R010

Engraver: Toppan, Carpenter, Casilear & Co. *Comments:* H-Unlisted, Durand-1448. Raised from W-RI-1010-001-G010. 1850s.

Rarity: URS-3

$5 • W-RI-1010-005-R020

Engraver: Toppan, Carpenter, Casilear & Co. *Comments:* H-Unlisted, Durand-1449. Raised from W-RI-1010-002-G020. 1850s.

Rarity: URS-3

$10 • W-RI-1010-010-R030

Engraver: Toppan, Carpenter, Casilear & Co. *Comments:* H-RI-325-R5, Durand-1451. Raised from W-RI-1010-001-G010 series. 18__. 1850s.

Rarity: *None known*

$10 • W-RI-1010-010-R040

Engraver: Toppan, Carpenter, Casilear & Co. *Comments:* H-RI-325-R10, Durand-1452. Raised from W-RI-1010-002-G020. Dec. 10th, 1858.

Rarity: URS-3
VF $150

$10 • W-RI-1010-010-R050

Engraver: Toppan, Carpenter, Casilear & Co. *Comments:* H-Unlisted, Durand-1453. Raised from W-RI-1010-002-G020. 1850s.

Rarity: URS-3

$10 • W-RI-1010-010-N010

Center: Two children on bank, Cows in stream. *Comments:* H-Unlisted, Durand-1454. Altered or spurious. 1850s.

Rarity: URS-3

$10 • W-RI-1010-010-N020

Center: Child with bird's nest. *Comments:* H-Unlisted, Durand-1455. Altered or spurious. 1850s.

Rarity: URS-3

$20 • W-RI-1010-020-R060

Engraver: Toppan, Carpenter, Casilear & Co. *Comments:* H-Unlisted, Durand-1456. Raised from W-RI-1010-001-G010. 1850s.

Rarity: URS-3

$20 • W-RI-1010-020-R070

Engraver: Toppan, Carpenter, Casilear & Co. *Comments:* H-Unlisted, Durand-1457. Raised from W-RI-1010-002-G020. 1850s.

Rarity: URS-3

$50 • W-RI-1010-050-R080

Engraver: Toppan, Carpenter, Casilear & Co. *Comments:* H-Unlisted, Durand-1459. Raised from W-RI-1010-001-G010. 1850s.

Rarity: URS-3

$50 • W-RI-1010-050-R090

Engraver: Toppan, Carpenter, Casilear & Co. *Comments:* H-Unlisted, Durand-1460. Raised from W-RI-1010-002-G020. 1850s.

Rarity: URS-3

Lime Rock Bank
1859–1865
W-RI-1020

History: The Lime Rock Bank was incorporated as the Smithfield Lime Rock Bank, W-RI-1390, on January 29, 1823. The bank moved to Providence in May 1847. In January 1859, the title of the bank was changed to the Lime Rock Bank. Figures for 1852 were given as: capital $151,850; circulation $61,622; deposits $40,350; money due banks $65; profits $3,716.[61] By 1862 the capital had been increased to $228,900, and circulation was at $82,106.

The business of the Lime Rock Bank was succeeded by the Lime Rock National Bank, chartered on June 7, 1865.

Numismatic Commentary: While notes from this bank during its early years as the Smithfield Lime Rock Bank appear in the market place from time to time, notes from the re-invented bank at Providence are extremely scarce.

VALID ISSUES

$1 • W-RI-1020-001-G010

CJF

Overprint: Red panel outlining white ONE. *Comments:* H-RI-330-G2, Durand-1490. 1860s.

Rarity: URS-1
VF $700; **Proof** $2,000

$2 • W-RI-1020-002-G020

Left: 2 / Man and woman with guns. *Center:* Portrait of girl. *Right:* 2 / Man and boy plowing. *Comments:* H-RI-330-G4, Durand-1491. 1860s.

Rarity: *None known*

$3 • W-RI-1020-003-G030

Left: Three allegorical figures supporting 3. *Center:* Ship, Sailor by bales with spyglass. *Right:* 3 / Horses frightened by train. *Comments:* H-RI-330-G6, Durand-1492. 1860s.

Rarity: *None known*

$5 • W-RI-1020-005-G040

Left: 5 / 5. *Center:* Mechanic, wheels, tools. *Right:* FIVE / Liberty / FIVE. *Comments:* H-RI-330-G8, Durand-1494. 1860s.

Rarity: *None known*

$10 • W-RI-1020-010-G050

Left: X / 10. *Center:* Agriculture and Commerce. *Right:* 10 / Mason holding level. *Comments:* H-RI-330-G10, Durand-1496. 1860s.

Rarity: *None known*

$20 • W-RI-1020-020-G060

Left: 20 / Minerva. *Center:* 2, Woman seated, 0. *Right:* 20 / Woman reclining on cornucopia / 20. *Comments:* H-RI-330-G12, Durand-1499. 1860s.

Rarity: *None known*

$50 • W-RI-1020-050-G070

Left: 50. *Center:* Steamship and other vessels. *Right:* 50 / Female portrait. *Engraver:* Unverified, but likely American Bank Note Co. *Comments:* H-RI-330-G14, Durand-1500. 1860s.

Rarity: *None known*

$100 • W-RI-1020-100-G080

Left: Female portrait. *Center:* Marine view, Sailing ships. *Right:* 100. *Engraver:* Unverified, but likely American Bank Note Co. *Comments:* H-RI-330-G16, Durand-1502. 1860s.

Rarity: *None known*

NON-VALID ISSUES

$3 • W-RI-1020-003-R010

Comments: H-Unlisted, Durand-1493. Raised from W-RI-1020-001-G010. 1860s.

Rarity: URS-3
VF $150

$5 • W-RI-1020-005-C040

Comments: H-RI-330-C8, Durand-1495. Counterfeit of W-RI-1020-005-G040. 1860s.

Rarity: URS-3
VF $125

$10 • W-RI-1020-010-N010

Center: Woman in loose robe. *Right:* Ceres. *Comments:* H-Unlisted, Durand-1498. Altered or spurious. 1860s.

Rarity: URS-3
VF $125

$10 • W-RI-1020-010-A010

Left: 10 / Hunter and dog. *Center:* Boys catching horse. *Right:* 10 / Portrait of girl. *Comments:* H-Unlisted, Durand-1497. Altered from W-RI-1010-001-G010. 1860s.

Rarity: URS-3
VF $150

$50 • W-RI-1020-050-A020

Left: 50 / Woman and horse. *Center:* Milkmaid and cows. *Right:* 50 / Blacksmith by forge. *Overprint:* Red FIFTY. *Comments:* H-Unlisted, Durand-1501. Altered from W-RI-1580-050-G310a. 1860s.

Rarity: URS-3
VF $150

Manufacturers Bank
1813–1865
W-RI-1030

History: The Manufacturers Bank was incorporated in the village of Pawtucket in the town of North Providence in October 1813. Samuel Slater was one of the 13 members of the board of directors. He served as president from 1819 until 1831, when he retired due to ill health.[62] A slowdown of business in Pawtucket in 1829 caused significant losses to the bank. This convinced the management to remove the bank to Providence in June 1831.

Capital was $453,100 in 1848 and increased to $500,000 in 1855. Loans amounted to $659,306 in 1852, bank notes were worth $2,015, and specie totaled $13,745. Circulation was at a low of $35,592 in 1857 and had risen to $56,945 by 1862. Specie was $5,876.55 in 1857.

The interests of the bank were succeeded by the Manufacturers National Bank, chartered on June 16, 1865.

See also listings under North Providence, W-RI-620, and Pawtucket, W-RI-720.

Numismatic Commentary: There are many non-valid notes in the marketplace but few genuine from this bank.

VALID ISSUES

$1 • W-RI-1030-001-G010

Engraver: Rawdon, Wright, Hatch & Edson. *Comments:* H-RI-190-G20, Durand-1508. No description available. 18__. 1840s.

Rarity: *None known*

$1 • W-RI-1030-001-G020

Left: 1. *Center:* Industry / 1. *Right:* ONE / Portrait of girl. *Overprint:* Red ONE. *Engraver:* Rawdon, Wright, Hatch & Edson. *Comments:* H-RI-190-G22a, Durand-1509. 18__. 1850s–1860s.

Rarity: URS-3
VF $300

$1.25 • W-RI-1030-001.25-G030

Engraver: New England Bank Note Co. *Comments:* H-RI-190-G23. No description available. 18__. 1830s.

Rarity: *None known*

$1.75 • W-RI-1030-001.75-G040

Engraver: New England Bank Note Co. *Comments:* H-RI-190-G25. No description available. 18__. 1830s.

Rarity: *None known*

$2 • W-RI-1030-002-G050

Left: 2 / Female portrait. *Center:* Liberty, Shield bearing 2, Spread eagle / TWO. *Right:* 2 / Female portrait. *Engraver:* Rawdon, Wright, Hatch & Edson. *Comments:* H-RI-190-G26, Durand-1513. 18__. 1840s.

Rarity: URS-3
Proof $500

$2 • W-RI-1030-002-G050a

Engraver: Rawdon, Wright, Hatch & Edson / ABNCo. monogram. *Comments:* H-RI-190-G26a. Similar to W-RI-1030-002-G050 but with additional engraver imprint. 18__. 1840s–1850s.

Rarity: *None known*

$2 • W-RI-1030-002-G060

Left: 2. *Center:* Industry. *Right:* TWO / Female portrait. *Engraver:* Rawdon, Wright, Hatch & Edson. *Comments:* H-RI-190-G28a, Durand-1514. 18__. 1850s–1860s.

Rarity: *None known*

$3 • W-RI-1030-003-G070

Left: 3 / Allegorical woman. *Center:* THREE / Liberty seated with cornucopia and U.S. shield. *Right:* 3 / Justice holding balance overhead. *Engraver:* Rawdon, Wright, Hatch & Co. *Comments:* H-RI-190-G34, Durand-1517. 18__. 1840s.

Rarity: URS-3

Proof $500

$3 • W-RI-1030-003-G070a

Engraver: Rawdon, Wright, Hatch & Edson / ABNCo. monogram. *Comments:* H-RI-190-G34a. Similar to W-RI-1030-003-G070 but with additional engraver imprint. 18__. 1840s–1850s.

Rarity: *None known*

$5 • W-RI-1030-005-G080

Left: 5 / Man seated by table / FIVE. *Center:* FIVE / Commerce seated holding pen, Globe, ship, train. *Right:* 5 / Minerva standing, globe and owl. *Engraver:* Rawdon, Wright, Hatch & Co. *Comments:* H-RI-190-G38, Durand-1518. 18__. 1840s.

Rarity: URS-3

Proof $500

$5 • W-RI-1030-005-G080a

Engraver: Rawdon, Wright, Hatch & Edson / ABNCo. monogram. *Comments:* H-RI-190-G38a. Similar to W-RI-1030-005-G080 but with additional engraver imprint. 18__. 1840s–1850s.

Rarity: *None known*

$10 • W-RI-1030-010-G090

Left: 10 on lathework strip vertically. *Center:* Horse towing canal boat, Bridge, building / X. *Right:* TEN / Industry seated by cogwheel and column. *Engraver:* Rawdon, Wright, Hatch & Co. *Comments:* H-RI-190-G42, Durand-1523. 18__. 1840s.

Rarity: *None known*

$10 • W-RI-1030-010-G100

Left: TEN / Farmer plowing / TEN. *Center:* 10 / Industry seated, Shield and cornucopia / 10. *Right:* TEN / Farmer sowing. *Comments:* H-Unlisted, Durand-1526. 1840s.

Rarity: URS-3

$20 • W-RI-1030-020-G110

CJF

Engraver: Rawdon, Wright, & Hatch. *Comments:* H-RI-190-G46, Durand-1527. Proof. 18__. 1840s.

Rarity: URS-1

Proof $2,000

$50 • W-RI-1030-050-G120

Engraver: New England Bank Note Co. *Comments:* H-RI-190-G48. No description available. 18__. 1830s.

Rarity: *None known*

$50 • W-RI-1030-050-G130

Left: 50. *Center:* Canal boat with cotton bales, Factory and other buildings / FIFTY. *Right:* 50 / Man with tablet. *Engraver:* Rawdon, Wright, Hatch & Co. *Comments:* H-RI-190-G50, Durand-1528. 18__. 1840s.

Rarity: *None known*

$100 • W-RI-1030-100-G140

Engraver: New England Bank Note Co. *Comments:* H-RI-190-G52. No description available. 18__. 1830s.

Rarity: *None known*

$100 • W-RI-1030-100-G150

Left: 100 / Woman / 100. *Center:* Canal boat with cotton bales, Factory and other buildings. *Right:* 100 / Vulcan. *Engraver:* Rawdon, Wright, Hatch & Co. *Comments:* H-RI-190-G54, Durand-1529. 18__. 1840s.

Rarity: *None known*

$500 • W-RI-1030-500-G160

Left: 500. *Center:* Allegorical woman seated on sheaves pointing to farm scene / 500 / D. *Right:* 500 vertically. *Engraver:* Rawdon, Wright, Hatch & Edson. *Comments:* H-RI-190-G56, Durand-1530. 18__. 1860s.

Rarity: *None known*

$1,000 • W-RI-1030-1000-G170

Left: Laocoon and sons strangled by serpents / 1000. *Center:* THOUSAND / Train. *Right:* 1000 / Vessels / 1000. *Engraver:* Rawdon, Wright, Hatch & Edson. *Comments:* H-RI-190-G58, Durand-1531. 18__. 1860s.

Rarity: *None known*

Non-Valid Issues

$1 • W-RI-1030-001-S010

CC

Comments: H-RI-190-S5, Durand-1512. 18__. 1860s.

Rarity: URS-5

F $280

$1 • W-RI-1030-001-A010

Left: Justice and Liberty with eagle and shield / 1. *Center:* Cherub / 1 on medallion shield / Cherub. *Right:* Mercury in clouds, ONE. *Overprint:* Red ONE. *Engraver:* Wellstood, Hanks, Hay & Whiting. *Comments:* H-RI-190-A5, Durand-1510. Altered from $1 Manufacturers Bank, Georgetown, D.C. 18__. 1850s.

Rarity: *None known*

$1 • W-RI-1030-001-A020   CC

Engraver: Rawdon, Wright & Hatch. ***Comments:*** H-RI-190-A10, Durand-1511. Dec.r 1st, 18__. 1853.

Rarity: URS-5

VF $275

$2 • W-RI-1030-002-A030   CC

Engraver: Rawdon, Wright & Hatch. ***Comments:*** H-RI-190-A12, Durand-1515. Dec.r 1st, 1840.

Rarity: URS-3

VF $275

$2 • W-RI-1030-002-A040   CC

Overprint: Red TWO. ***Engraver:*** Wellstood, Hanks, Hay & Whiting. ***Comments:*** H-RI-190-A15, Durand-1516. Altered from $2 Manufacturers Bank, Georgetown, D.C. 18__. 1850s.

Rarity: URS-5

VF $275

$5 • W-RI-1030-005-R010

Comments: H-Unlisted, Durand-1519. Raised from W-RI-1030-001-G020. 1850s–1860s.

Rarity: URS-3

$5 • W-RI-1030-005-N010

Left: FIVE / Farmer plowing / FIVE. ***Center:*** 5 / Allegorical woman seated with shield and cornucopia / 5. ***Right:*** FIVE / Farmer sowing / FIVE. ***Engraver:*** Unverified, but likely Rawdon, Wright & Hatch. ***Comments:*** H-RI-190-N12. Possibly altered and raised. 1850s.

Rarity: *None known*

$5 • W-RI-1030-005-N020   CC

Engraver: Durand, Perkins & Co. ***Comments:*** H-RI-190-N15, Durand-1522. Spurious note supposedly signed by Samuel Slater in 1842. Slater died in 1835. 18__. 1840s.

Rarity: URS-5

VF $300

$5 • W-RI-1030-005-A050   CC

Engraver: Draper, Toppan, Longacre & Co. ***Comments:*** H-RI-190-A20, Durand-1521. Altered from $5 Calhoun County Bank, Marshall, Michigan. 18__. 1857.

Rarity: URS-3

VF $200

$5 • W-RI-1030-005-A060   CC

Engraver: Rawdon, Wright & Hatch. ***Comments:*** H-RI-190-A25, Durand-1520. Altered from $5 Bank of Gallipolis, Gallipolis, Ohio. 18__. 1840s–1850s.

Rarity: URS-3

VF $300

$10 • W-RI-1030-010-A070

Left: 10 / TEN on X. ***Center:*** Boy and horses, Sheep. ***Right:*** 10 / Stonecutter. ***Tint:*** Red. ***Engraver:*** J. Sage & Sons. ***Comments:*** H-RI-190-A28, Durand-1525. Altered from $10 Manufacturers Bank, Hartford, Indiana. 1858.

Rarity: *None known*

$10 • W-RI-1030-010-A080

Left: TEN vertically. *Center:* Liberty on wharf, Shield. *Right:* 10 / Steamboat / X. *Engraver:* Rawdon, Wright & Hatch. *Comments:* H-RI-190-A30, Durand-1524. Altered from $10 Bank of Gallipolis, Gallipolis, Ohio. 18__. 1840s–1850s.

Rarity: *None known*

Marine Bank
1856–1864
W-RI-1040

History: The Marine Bank was incorporated in 1856 and commenced operations on September 7 of that year. The bank was located at 13 Market Street in 1864.

Figures for 1857 included: bills in circulation $17,646; specie $2,041.32; capital $250,000. Circulation was up to $31,178 by 1862.

The business of the bank was succeeded by the Third National Bank of Providence, chartered on December 20, 1864.

Numismatic Commentary: Some of the beautiful notes of this bank include vignettes of whaling and "The Launching of the *Adriatic*," a ship that was a popular side-wheeler on the East Coast. The opportunity to secure a genuine note does not present itself as often as the spurious and raised issues.

VALID ISSUES

$1 • W-RI-1040-001-G010

Left: ONE / Sailor holding flag. *Center:* Sailing ships in harbor. *Right:* 1 / Anchor, box, barrel, and bale. *Overprint:* Red ONE. *Engraver:* Toppan, Carpenter & Co. *Comments:* H-RI-335-G2a, Durand-1532. 18__. 1850s.

Rarity: URS-3
Proof $500

$1 • W-RI-1040-001-G010a

Overprint: Red ONE. *Engraver:* American Bank Note Co. *Comments:* H-Unlisted, Durand-Unlisted. Similar to W-RI-1040-001-G010 but with different engraver imprint. 18__. 1860s.

Rarity: URS-2
F $1,000

$2 • W-RI-1040-002-G020

Left: Sailor and Agriculture. *Center:* 2 / Death struggles of whale, Two boats. *Right:* 2 / Commerce seated. *Overprint:* Red TWO. *Engraver:* Toppan, Carpenter & Co. *Comments:* H-RI-335-G4a, Durand-1533. 18__. 1850s.

Rarity: URS-3
Proof $900

$3 • W-RI-1040-003-G030

Left: Three girls with anchor. *Center:* Steamship and boats in harbor. *Right:* 3 / Commerce seated. *Overprint:* Red THREE. *Engraver:* Toppan, Carpenter & Co. *Comments:* H-RI-335-G6a, Durand-1535. 18__. 1856–1860s.

Rarity: URS-3
Proof $900

$5 • W-RI-1040-005-G040

Engraver: Toppan, Carpenter & Co. *Comments:* H-RI-335-G8, Durand-1538. 18__. 1850s.

Rarity: URS-3
Proof $5,500
Selected auction price: Stack's Bowers Galleries, March 2013, Proof $5,400

$5 • W-RI-1040-005-G050

Left: 5 / Portrait of George Washington / 5. *Center:* 5 / St. George slaying dragon / 5. *Right:* 5 / FIVE. *Comments:* H-Unlisted, Durand-1540. 1850s.

Rarity: URS-3

$5 • W-RI-1040-005-G060

Center: Woman holding sheaf and trident. *Comments:* H-Unlisted, Durand-1541. 1850s.

Rarity: URS-3

$10 • W-RI-1040-010-G070

Engraver: Toppan, Carpenter & Co. *Comments:* H-RI-335-G10, Durand-1542. 18__. 1850s.

Rarity: URS-2
Proof $4,300
Selected auction price: Stack's Bowers Galleries, March 2013, Proof $4,200

$10 • W-RI-1040-010-G080

Left: Portrait of George Washington. *Center:* St. George slaying dragon. *Comments:* H-Unlisted, Durand-1543. 1850s.

Rarity: URS-3

$20 • W-RI-1040-020-G090

Left: Portrait of George Washington. *Center:* St. George slaying dragon. *Comments:* H-Unlisted, Durand-1545. 1850s.

Rarity: URS-3

$50 • W-RI-1040-050-G100

Left: 50 / Female portrait. *Center:* Village, Boats in harbor. *Right:* 50 / Eagle. *Engraver:* Toppan, Carpenter & Co. *Comments:* H-RI-335-G12, Durand-1547. 18__. 1856–1860s.

Rarity: URS-3
Proof $900

$100 • W-RI-1040-100-G110

Left: 100 / Man leaning on capstan. *Center:* Angel blowing trumpet. *Right:* 100 / Portrait of George Washington. *Engraver:* Toppan, Carpenter & Co. *Comments:* H-RI-335-G14, Durand-1548. 18__. 1856–1860s.

Rarity: URS-3
Proof $500

$500 • W-RI-1040-500-G120

Left: 500 / Woman reclining with eagle, shield, and pole and cap. *Center:* D / Portrait of boy. *Right:* 500 / Woman reclining with cherub. *Comments:* H-Unlisted, Durand-1549. Model Proof of an unissued note. 1850s.

Rarity: URS-1
Proof $800

$1,000 • W-RI-1040-1000-G130

Left: 1000. *Center:* 1000 / Man with sickle, Man with compass. *Bottom center:* Shield on anchor. *Right:* 1000. *Comments:* H-Unlisted, Durand-1550. Model Proof of an unissued note. 1850s.

Rarity: URS-1
Proof $800

Uncut Sheets

$50-$100 • W-RI-1040-050.100-US010

Vignette(s): ($50) Female portrait / Village, Boats in harbor / Eagle. *($100)* Man leaning on capstan / Angel blowing trumpet / Portrait of George Washington. *Engraver:* Toppan, Carpenter & Co. *Comments:* H-RI-335-G12, G14. 18__. 1856–1860s.

Rarity: URS-3
Proof $1,500

Non-Valid Issues

$2 • W-RI-1040-002-S010

Center: Three women, Ship. *Comments:* H-RI-335-S5, Durand-1534. 1850s.

Rarity: None known

$3 • W-RI-1040-003-S020

Center: Three women, Ship. *Comments:* H-RI-335-S10, Durand-1536. 1850s.

Rarity: None known

$3 • W-RI-1040-003-S030

Left: Portrait of George Washington. *Center:* St. George slaying dragon. *Back:* Orange. *Engraver:* Bald, Adams & Co. *Comments:* H-RI-335-S15a, Durand-1537. May 1, 185_. 1857.

Rarity: URS-3
VF $250

$5 • W-RI-1040-005-A010

Left: 5 / Portrait of George Washington. *Center:* Steamboat. *Right:* V / Portrait of Henry Clay. *Overprint:* Red FIVE. *Engraver:* New England Bank Note Co. / Rawdon, Wright, Hatch & Edson. *Comments:* H-RI-335-A5, Durand-1539. Altered from $5 Waubeek Bank, De Soto, Nebraska. 1857.

Rarity: None known

$10 • W-RI-1040-010-N010

Center: Woman holding sheaf and trident. *Comments:* H-RI-335-N5, Durand-1544. 1850s.

Rarity: None known

$20 • W-RI-1040-020-N020

Center: Woman holding sheaf and trident. *Comments:* H-RI-335-N10, Durand-1546. 1850s.

Rarity: None known

Mechanics Bank
1823–1865
W-RI-1050

History: The Mechanics Bank was incorporated on June 30, 1823, with an authorized capital of $100,000. By 1825 capital had increased to $250,000, and by July 1827 it was $500,000, where it remained constant through 1864. Circulation of the bank was $47,318 in 1849, $59,123 in 1852, and $102,658 in 1862. Deposits in 1852 amounted to $27,488, money due banks $14,495, and profits $14,670. Specie totaled $5,122.91 in 1857. Its address was 27 South Main Street in 1863.

The business of the Mechanics Bank was succeeded by the Mechanics National Bank, chartered on April 14, 1865.

Numismatic Commentary: Signed and dated genuine notes are very hard to locate. Proofs and remainder single notes seem to be the only issues available in today's marketplace.

Valid Issues

$1 • W-RI-1050-001-G010   SBG

Engraver: A. B. & C. Durand & Wright. *Comments:* H-RI-340-G4, Durand-1551. 18__. 1820s.

Rarity: URS-3
Proof $1,000
Selected auction price: Spink, April 2009, Proof $975

$1 • W-RI-1050-001-G020

Left: Vulcan with hammer, anvil, and wheel / ONE. *Center:* Eagle and shield. *Bottom center:* Anchor and shield. *Right:* 1 / Male portrait. *Comments:* H-RI-340-G8, Durand-1552. 18__. 1840s.

Rarity: None known

$1 • W-RI-1050-001-G030

Left: ONE vertically. *Center:* Eagle, State arms, Eagle. *Bottom center:* Anchor and shield. *Right:* ONE vertically. *Engraver:* Unverified, but likely Toppan, Carpenter & Co. *Comments:* H-RI-340-G10, Durand-1553. 18__. 1850s.

Rarity: *None known*

$1.25 • W-RI-1050-001.25-G040

Left: 1 25/100 / Train / 1 25/100. *Center:* Sloop and other vessels at sea / $1.25 Cts. *Right:* 1 25/100 / Eagle. *Engraver:* New England Bank Note Co. *Comments:* H-RI-340-G11. 18__. 1830s.

Rarity: *None known*

$1.50 • W-RI-1050-001.50-G050

Left: 1 Doll. 50 Cts. vertically. *Center:* Eagle on rock in ocean / $1 50/100. *Right:* 1 50/100 / Justice. *Engraver:* New England Bank Note Co. *Comments:* H-RI-340-G12. 18__. 1830s.

Rarity: *None known*

$1.75 • W-RI-1050-001.75-G060

Left: $1.75 Cts. / Hebe watering eagle / 1 75/100. *Center:* Three sloops at sea. *Right:* $1.75 Cts. / Dog / Woman seated with grain / 1 75/100. *Engraver:* New England Bank Note Co. *Comments:* H-RI-340-G13. 18__. 1830s.

Rarity: *None known*

$2 • W-RI-1050-002-G070   SBG

Engraver: A. B. & C. Durand & Wright. *Comments:* H-RI-340-G14, Durand-1556. 18__. 1820s.

Rarity: URS-3
Proof $1,000

$2 • W-RI-1050-002-G080

Left: 2 / Male portrait. *Center:* Allegorical woman leaning on shield bearing state arms. *Bottom center:* Anchor on shield. *Right:* 2 / Male portrait. *Comments:* H-RI-340-G18, Durand-1557. 18__. 1840s.

Rarity: URS-3
VF $200

$2 • W-RI-1050-002-G090

Left: TWO vertically. *Center:* Eagle, State arms, Eagle. *Right:* TWO vertically. *Engraver:* Unverified, but likely Toppan, Carpenter & Co. *Comments:* H-RI-340-G20, Durand-1558. 18__. 1850s.

Rarity: *None known*

$5 • W-RI-1050-005-G100

Left: FIVE on lathework vertically. *Center:* 5 / Liberty seated, Eagle on globe / 5. *Bottom center:* Cog wheel. *Right:* FIVE on lathework vertically. *Overprint:* FIVE. *Engraver:* Toppan, Carpenter & Co. *Comments:* H-RI-340-G26, Durand-1567. 18__. 1840s.

Rarity: URS-3
Proof $1,000

$5 • W-RI-1050-005-G110

Left: FIVE vertically. *Center:* Eagle, State arms, Eagle. *Right:* FIVE vertically. *Engraver:* Unverified, but likely Toppan, Carpenter & Co. *Comments:* H-RI-340-G28, Durand-1568. 18__. 1850s.

Rarity: *None known*

$10 • W-RI-1050-010-G120   SBG

Engraver: Toppan, Carpenter & Co. *Comments:* H-RI-340-G32, Durand-1578. 18__. 1850s.

Rarity: URS-3
Proof $1,600
Selected auction price: Stack's Bowers Galleries, March 2013, Proof $1,573

$10 • W-RI-1050-010-G130

Left: 10 / Portrait of George Washington / TEN. *Center:* 10 / Liberty and eagle / 10. *Right:* TEN / Allegorical woman. *Comments:* H-Unlisted, Durand-1581. 1850s.

Rarity: URS-3

$20 • W-RI-1050-020-G140   SBG

Engraver: Toppan, Carpenter & Co. *Comments:* H-RI-340-G36, Durand-1582. 18__. 1850s.

Rarity: URS-3
Proof $1,800

$50 • W-RI-1050-050-G150

Left: 50 / Woman standing with ankles crossed, Staff, Cornucopia and anchor / 50. *Center:* FIFTY DOLLARS / 50. *Right:* FIFTY vertically. *Engraver:* PSSP / New England Bank Note Co. *Comments:* H-RI-340-G38. 18__. 1830s.

Rarity: *None known*

$50 • W-RI-1050-050-G160

Left: FIFTY / Allegorical figure / FIFTY. *Center:* 50 / Man holding horse / 50. *Right:* FIFTY / Allegorical figure / FIFTY. *Engraver:* New England Bank Note Co. *Comments:* H-RI-340-G40, Durand-1583. 18__. 1840s–1850s.

Rarity: *None known*

$100 • **W-RI-1050-100-G170**

Left: Lathework panel bearing C / Portrait of George Washington / C. *Center:* 100 / Manhattan reclining pouring water, Ship / 100. *Right:* Lathework panel bearing ONE HUNDRED vertically. *Engraver:* PSSP / New England Bank Note Co. *Comments:* H-RI-340-G42. 18__. 1830s.

Rarity: *None known*

$100 • **W-RI-1050-100-G180**

Engraver: PSSP / New England Bank Note Co. *Comments:* H-RI-340-G44. 18__. 1830s.

Rarity: *None known*

$500 • **W-RI-1050-100-G190**

Left: 500 / 500 vertically / 500. *Center:* 500 / Woman seated with shield bearing D, Fasces, cornucopia, lyre, and sheaf / 500. *Right:* 500 / D / 500. *Engraver:* PSSP / New England Bank Note Co. *Comments:* H-RI-340-G46, Durand-1584. 18__. 1830s.

Rarity: *None known*

$500 • **W-RI-1050-500-G200**

Left: Woman on sheaves pointing to farming scene / 500. *Center:* 500 / D. *Right:* 500 vertically. *Engraver:* Rawdon, Wright, Hatch & Edson. *Comments:* H-RI-340-G48, Durand-1585. 18__. 1840s–1850s.

Rarity: *None known*

$1,000 • **W-RI-1050-1000-G210**

Left: THOUSAND vertically. *Center:* 1000 / Woman standing with legs crossed, Lyre, Cornucopia / 1000. *Right:* 1000 / M / 1000. *Engraver:* PSSP / New England Bank Note Co. *Comments:* H-RI-340-G50. 18__. 1830s.

Rarity: *None known*

$1,000 • **W-RI-1050-1000-G220**

Left: Laocoon and sons strangled by serpents / 1000. *Center:* THOUSAND / Train. *Right:* 1000 / Vessels / 1000. *Engraver:* Rawdon, Wright, Hatch & Edson. *Comments:* H-RI-340-G52, Durand-1586. 18__. 1840s–1850s.

Rarity: *None known*

Uncut Sheets

$10-$20 • **W-RI-1050-010.020-US010**

Vignette(s): *($10)* Arm and hammer / Allegorical figure / State arms surmounted by eagle / Allegorical figure / Portrait of George Washington. *($20)* Portrait of Christopher Columbus / Mechanic seated on cornice / Anchor on shield / Portrait of Benjamin Franklin. *Engraver:* Toppan, Carpenter & Co. *Comments:* H-RI-340-G32, G36. 18__. 1850s.

Rarity: URS-3
Proof $1,000

Non-Valid Issues

$1 • **W-RI-1050-001-N010**

Left: Indian. *Center:* Blacksmith. *Right:* Indian. *Comments:* H-RI-340-N5, Durand-1555. 1850s.

Rarity: *None known*

$1 • **W-RI-1050-001-A010**   CC

Engraver: Durand & Co. *Comments:* H-RI-340-A5, Durand-1554. 185_. 1851.

Rarity: URS-5
VF $150

$2 • **W-RI-1050-002-C080**

Comments: H-Unlisted, Durand-1559. Counterfeit of W-RI-1050-002-G080. 18__. 1840s.

Rarity: URS-3

$2 • **W-RI-1050-002-N020**

Left: Sailor holding flag. *Center:* Ships. *Right:* Woman with wreath. *Comments:* H-RI-340-N10, Durand-1562. 1850s.

Rarity: *None known*

$2 • **W-RI-1050-002-A020**

Left: TWO and 2 / State arms. *Center:* Men felling and cutting trees. *Right:* 2 / Ceres. *Engraver:* Danforth, Wright & Co. *Comments:* H-RI-340-A10, Durand-1560. Altered from $2 Bank of Washtenaw, Ann Arbor, Michigan series. 1850s.

Rarity: *None known*

$2 • **W-RI-1050-002-A030**

Left: 2 / Portrait of George Washington / TWO. *Center:* Allegorical woman, U.S. shield, Sheaf. *Right:* TWO above TWO / Mercury in clouds. *Engraver:* Wellstood, Hanks, Hay & Whiting. *Comments:* H-RI-340-A15, Durand-1561. Altered from $2 Mechanics Bank, Georgetown, D.C. 18__. 1852.

Rarity: URS-3
VF $200

$2 • **W-RI-1050-002-A040**

Left: 2 / Portrait of Benjamin Franklin. *Center:* Train. *Bottom center:* U.S. shield. *Right:* Minerva seated / 2. *Overprint:* TWO. *Engraver:* Rawdon, Wright, Hatch & Edson. *Comments:* H-RI-340-A20, Durand-1562. Altered from $2 Farmers & Merchants Bank of Memphis, Memphis, Tennessee series. 1850s.

Rarity: *None known*

$3 • **W-RI-1050-003-S010**

Left: Portrait of George Washington. *Center:* Liberty standing and woman seated flanking shield surmounted by horse's head. *Right:* Portrait of Thomas Jefferson. *Engraver:* Draper, Toppan & Co. *Comments:* H-RI-340-S5, Durand-1565. June 17, 18__. 1840s.

Rarity: *None known*

$3 • W-RI-1050-003-N030

Center: Two women, horse's head. *Comments:* H-RI-340-N15, Durand-1564. 1850s.

Rarity: *None known*

$3 • W-RI-1050-003-A050   CC

Overprint: Red THREE. *Engraver:* Wellstood, Hanks, Hay & Whiting. *Comments:* H-RI-340-A25, Durand-1563. Altered from $3 Mechanics Bank, Georgetown, D.C. 18__. 1850s.

Rarity: URS-3
F $200

$3 • W-RI-1050-003-A060

Left: Two cherubs playing in clouds. *Center:* 3 / Indian seated with bow, Dog / 3. *Right:* Panel bearing THREE vertically. *Engraver:* Durand & Co. *Comments:* H-RI-340-A30, Durand-1566. Altered from $3 Globe Bank, New York, New York. 18__. 1840.

Rarity: *None known*

$5 • W-RI-1050-005-R010

Engraver: A. B. & C. Durand & Wright. *Comments:* H-RI-340-R5, Durand-1571. Raised from W-RI-1050-001-G010. 18__. 1820s–1830s.

Rarity: *None known*

$5 • W-RI-1050-005-S020   SI

Engraver: Toppan, Carpenter & Co. *Comments:* H-Unlisted, Durand-Unlisted. From a modified, fraudulent plate originally for a counterfeit $5 of the Mechanics Bank, Philadelphia, Pennsylvania. 18__. 1856.

Rarity: URS-4

$5 • W-RI-1050-005-S020a   CC

Overprint: Red FIVE. *Engraver:* Toppan, Carpenter & Co. *Comments:* H-RI-340-S10a, Durand-1576. From a modified, fraudulent plate originally for a counterfeit $5 of the Mechanics Bank, Philadelphia, Pennsylvania. Similar to W-RI-1050-005-S020. 18__. 1855.

Rarity: URS-4
VF $150

$5 • W-RI-1050-005-S030   CC

Engraver: New England Bank Note Co. *Comments:* H-RI-340-S15, Durand-1575. July 15th, 1853.

Rarity: URS-4
VF $200

$5 • W-RI-1050-005-S040

Left: 5. *Center:* Portraits of five presidents in V, Eagle and flags. *Right:* 5 / Ship under sail. *Comments:* H-RI-340-S20, Durand-1577. 1850s.

Rarity: *None known*

$5 • W-RI-1050-005-N040

Left: FIVE DOLLARS vertically. *Center:* Goddess of Plenty, Money chest. *Right:* FIVE vertically. *Comments:* H-RI-340-N20, Durand-1569. 1850s.

Rarity: *None known*

$5 • W-RI-1050-005-A070

Left: Woman standing. *Center:* Cherub / 5 / Cherub. *Bottom center:* Steamship. *Right:* Portrait. *Comments:* H-RI-340-N25, Durand-1574. Altered from $5 Mechanics Bank, Washington, D.C. 1850s.

Rarity: *None known*

$5 • W-RI-1050-005-A080

Left: FIVE / Man with spear / V. *Center:* 5 / Woman with cog wheel / 5. *Bottom center:* Arm and hammer. *Right:* V / Blacksmith with anvil / V. *Engraver:* Rawdon, Wright & Hatch. *Comments:* H-RI-340-A35, Durand-1572. Altered from $5 Mechanics Bank, Montreal, Canada. 18__. 1837.

Rarity: URS-3
VF $150

$5 • W-RI-1050-005-A090

Left: FIVE / Portrait of Benjamin Franklin / FIVE. *Center:* Three allegorical women, Portrait of George Washington, Two allegorical women. *Right:* 5 / Portrait of Andrew Jackson / 5. *Engraver:* Danforth, Wright & Co. *Comments:* H-RI-340-A40, Durand-1573. Altered from $5 Mechanics Bank of Memphis, Memphis, Tennessee series. 1850s.

Rarity: *None known*

$10 • W-RI-1050-010-N050

Center: X / Vulcan at forge / X. *Comments:* H-RI-340-N30. 1850s.

Rarity: *None known*

$10 • W-RI-1050-010-A100

Left: 10 across TEN across X / Man tending machine. *Center:* X. *Right:* 10 across TEN across X / Men at work in foundry. *Engraver:* Danforth, Wright & Co. *Comments:* H-RI-340-A45, Durand-1579. Altered from $10 Mechanics Bank of Memphis, Memphis, Tennessee series. 1850s.

Rarity: *None known*

$10 • W-RI-1050-010-A110

Left: 10 / Allegorical woman with shield / 10. *Center:* X / Vulcan and two women / X. *Right:* TEN / Cherub writing on tablet / TEN. *Engraver:* Rawdon, Wright & Hatch. *Comments:* H-RI-340-A50, Durand-1580. Altered from $10 Mechanics Bank, Montreal, Canada. 18__. 1830s.

Rarity: *None known*

Mechanics and Manufacturers Bank
1827–1865
W-RI-1060

History: The Mechanics and Manufacturers Bank was incorporated in 1827. The bank was located at 24 Westminster Street in 1856 and 207 N. Main Street in 1863.

The following was printed in 1851:

> Rhode Island. —The Mechanics and Manufacturers' Bank of Providence has had an injunction laid upon it, and a receiver appointed, in consequence of an examination made by commissioners appointed by the Governor of Rhode Island.
>
> The examination showed that the Cashier, A.W. Snow, was a defaulter to the amount of upwards of $70,000,— and criminal proceedings were forthwith instituted against him.
>
> The public, however, need have no apprehension as to the safety of the bill-holders unless the condition of the bank has greatly changed for the worse since the last return, which was made in October, 1847 . . . the capital is $186,150. So that if half the capital stock should have been lost, still the public is secure, and not only the bills, but the deposits, will be paid in full. It would appear, therefore, that there need be no alarm among the bill-holders.[63]

The officers of the bank salvaged the institution. Capital was $255,700 in 1855. Circulation was $27,569.50.[64] Figures for 1857 included: capital $288,900; bills in circulation $38,957; specie $4,500. Circulation was $136,700 in 1862.

The business of the bank was succeeded by the Fifth National Bank of Providence, chartered on April 12, 1865.

Numismatic Commentary: Some banks would redeem and then punch-cancel their notes before disposing of them. Some of these cancelled issues, however, were saved and survived. Many issues of this bank show cancellation holes or cut-outs. Genuine signed and dated notes are worth more, but without a choice, collectors may have to settle for a cancelled note. This bank's issues include a popular Santa Claus vignette on a $1 issue.

VALID ISSUES

$1 • W-RI-1060-001-G010   CC

Engraver: N. & S.S. Jocelyn / Fairman, Draper, Underwood & Co. *Comments:* H-RI-345-G2, Durand-1587. 18__. 1827–1830s.

Rarity: URS-3
Proof $400

$1 • W-RI-1060-001-G020   CC

Engraver: Draper, Toppan & Co. *Comments:* H-RI-345-G4, Durand-1588. 18__. 1830s–1850s.

Rarity: URS-2
VF $750

$1 • W-RI-1060-001-G030

Left: 1 / Woman seated. *Center:* Santa Claus in sleigh being driven by reindeer. *Right:* 1 / Woman leaning on 1. *Overprint:* Red ONE. *Engraver:* Rawdon, Wright, Hatch & Edson / New England Bank Note Co. *Comments:* H-RI-345-G6a, Durand-1589. A coveted Santa Claus note. 18__. 1850s–1860s.

Rarity: URS-5
VF $4,000

$1 • W-RI-1060-001-G030a

Overprint: Red ONE. *Engraver:* Rawdon, Wright, Hatch & Edson / New England Bank Note Co. / ABNCo. monogram. *Comments:* H-RI-345-G6b. Similar to W-RI-1060-001-G030 but with additional engraver imprint. A coveted Santa Claus note. 18__. 1860s.

Rarity: URS-5
VF $4,000

$1.25 • W-RI-1060-001.25-G040

Left: 1 25/100 / Train / 1 25/100. *Center:* Sailing ships in bay / $1.25 Cts. *Right:* 1 25/100 / Spread eagle. *Engraver:* New England Bank Note Co. *Comments:* H-RI-345-G8. 18__. 1830s.

Rarity: None known

$1.50 • W-RI-1060-001.50-G050

Left: 1 DOLL. 50 Cts. vertically. *Center:* Eagle on rock in ocean / $1 50/100. *Right:* Justice / 1 / 50/100. *Engraver:* New England Bank Note Co. *Comments:* H-RI-345-G9. 18__. 1830s.

Rarity: None known

$1.75 • W-RI-1060-001.75-G060

Left: $1.75 Cts. / Liberty and eagle / 1 75/100. *Center:* Three sloops at sea. *Right:* $1.75 Cts. / Agriculture and dog / 1 75/100. *Engraver:* New England Bank Note Co. *Comments:* H-RI-345-G10. 18__. 1830s.

Rarity: None known

$2 • W-RI-1060-002-G070   SBG

Engraver: Draper, Toppan & Co. *Comments:* H-RI-345-G12, Durand-1593. 18__. 1830s–1850s.

Rarity: URS-1
Proof $2,100
Selected auction price: Stack's Bowers Galleries, March 2013, Proof $2,050

$2 • W-RI-1060-002-G080

Left: Liberty, 2, Justice / 2. *Right:* 2 / Ceres seated. *Overprint:* Red TWO. *Engraver:* Rawdon, Wright, Hatch & Edson / New England Bank Note Co. *Comments:* H-RI-345-G14a, Durand-1594. 18__. 1850s–1860s.

Rarity: URS-5
VF $150

$2 • W-RI-1060-002-G080a   TD

Overprint: Red TWO. *Engraver:* Rawdon, Wright, Hatch & Edson / New England Bank Note Co. / ABNCo. monogram. *Comments:* H-RI-345-G14b. Similar to W-RI-1060-002-G080 but with additional engraver imprint. 18__. 1860s.

Rarity: URS-3
VF $250

$2 • W-RI-1060-002-G090

Left: II / Portrait / II. *Center:* 2 / Horse and rider / 2 / Woman holding TWO. *Right:* TWO DOLLARS vertically. *Comments:* H-Unlisted. 1830s–1850s.

Rarity: —

$3 • W-RI-1060-003-G100

Engraver: New England Bank Note Co. *Comments:* H-RI-345-G18. No description available. 18__. 1830s–1840s.

Rarity: None known

$3 • W-RI-1060-003-G110

Left: Portrait of Daniel Webster / 3. *Center:* THREE / THREE. *Right:* 3 / 3 with three allegorical women / 3. *Overprint:* Red 3. *Engraver:* Rawdon, Wright, Hatch & Edson / New England Bank Note Co. *Comments:* H-RI-345-G20a, Durand-1595. 18__. 1850s.

Rarity: None known

$3 • W-RI-1060-003-G110a   CC

Overprint: Red 3. *Engraver:* Rawdon, Wright, Hatch & Edson / New England Bank Note Co. / ABNCo. monogram. *Comments:* H-RI-345-G20b. Similar to W-RI-1060-003-G110 but with additional engraver imprint. 18__. 1850s–1860s.

Rarity: URS-3
VF $600

$5 • W-RI-1060-005-G120   SBG

Engraver: N. & S.S. Jocelyn / Fairman, Draper, Underwood & Co. *Comments:* H-RI-345-G22, Durand-1597. 18__. 1827–1830s.

Rarity: URS-3
Proof $1,300
Selected auction price: Stack's Bowers Galleries, November 2008, Proof $1,300

$5 • W-RI-1060-005-G130

Left: 5 / Woman seated in V / FIVE. *Center:* 5 / Five figures grouped around 5 / 5. *Right:* 5 / Ceres seated in 5 / FIVE. *Engraver:* New England Bank Note Co. *Comments:* H-RI-345-G26, Durand-1598. 18__. 1830s–1850s.

Rarity: None known

$5 • W-RI-1060-005-G140

Left: Five allegorical figures with 5 / 5. *Center:* 5. *Right:* 5 / Portrait of boy. *Overprint:* Red FIVE and 5. *Engraver:* Rawdon, Wright, Hatch & Edson / New England Bank Note Co. *Comments:* H-RI-345-G28a, Durand-1599. 18__. 1850s–1860s.
Rarity: *None known*

$5 • W-RI-1060-005-G140a

Overprint: Red FIVE and 5. *Engraver:* Rawdon, Wright, Hatch & Edson / New England Bank Note Co. / ABNCo. monogram. *Comments:* H-RI-345-G28b. Similar to W-RI-1060-005-G140 but with additional engraver imprint. 18__. 1860s.
Rarity: URS-3
VF $350

$10 • W-RI-1060-010-G150

Left: Panel bearing TEN / Manhattan spilling water jug / TEN. *Center:* TEN / Ceres seated / TEN / Panel of microletters. *Right:* Panel bearing 10 / Portrait of Indian / 10. *Engraver:* PSSP. *Comments:* H-RI-345-G31. 18__. 1830s.
Rarity: *None known*

$10 • W-RI-1060-010-G160

Left: 10 / Farmer sowing / 10. *Center:* Mercury standing, Ships, Canal scene. *Right:* 10 / Ship and other vessels, Lighthouse / TEN. *Engraver:* New England Bank Note Co. *Comments:* H-RI-345-G32, Durand-1600. 18__. 1830s–1850s.
Rarity: *None known*

$10 • W-RI-1060-010-G170

Left: X / Bale, Cogwheel / X. *Center:* Man reclining with shield bearing plow, Sheaf and train, Two deer / TEN. *Right:* 10 / Female portrait. *Overprint:* Red TEN. *Engraver:* Rawdon, Wright, Hatch & Edson / New England Bank Note Co. *Comments:* H-RI-345-G34a, Durand-1601. 18__. 1850s–1860s.
Rarity: URS-3
VF $600

$20 • W-RI-1060-020-G180

Left: 20 / XX vertically / 20. *Center:* 20 / Men plowing / Woman seated with scales, Sheaf and bales / Ship. *Right:* TWENTY vertically. *Engraver:* PSSP / New England Bank Note Co. *Comments:* H-RI-345-G36. 18__. 1830s.
Rarity: *None known*

$20 • W-RI-1060-020-G190

Left: Steamer / XX / Train. *Center:* Eagle / Liberty, Justice, and Science / Ship. *Right:* XX / Milkmaid. *Engraver:* New England Bank Note Co. *Comments:* H-RI-345-G38, Durand-1602. Beware of altered notes of the same design as the genuine. 18__. 1830s–1850s.
Rarity: *None known*

$20 • W-RI-1060-020-G200

Left: XX / Portrait of girl. *Center:* Commerce seated with globe, Sailing vessel. *Right:* 20 / Bale, barrel, and anchor. *Overprint:* TWENTY. *Engraver:* Rawdon, Wright, Hatch & Edson / New England Bank Note Co. *Comments:* H-RI-345-G40, Durand-1603. 18__. 1850s–1860s.
Rarity: URS-3
VF $600

$50 • W-RI-1060-050-G210

Left: 50 / Woman standing with ankles crossed, Staff, Cornucopia and anchor / 50. *Center:* FIFTY DOLLARS / 50. *Right:* FIFTY vertically. *Engraver:* PSSP / New England Bank Note Co. *Comments:* H-RI-345-G42. 18__. 1830s.
Rarity: *None known*

$50 • W-RI-1060-050-G220

Left: 50 / Steamer and schooner. *Center:* Harvesting scene. *Right:* 1 / Justice. *Engraver:* New England Bank Note Co. *Comments:* H-RI-345-G44, Durand-1605. 18__. 1830s–1850s.
Rarity: *None known*

$50 • W-RI-1060-050-G230

Left: 50 / 50. *Center:* Scene in boiler yard, Men working on boilers. *Right:* 50 / Female portrait. *Engraver:* Unverified, but likely Rawdon, Wright, Hatch & Edson / New England Bank Note Co. *Comments:* H-RI-345-G46, Durand-1606. 18__. 1850s–1860s.
Rarity: *None known*

$100 • W-RI-1060-100-G240

Left: Lathework panel bearing C / Portrait of George Washington / C. *Center:* 100 / Manhattan reclining pouring water, Ship / 100. *Right:* Lathework panel bearing ONE HUNDRED vertically. *Engraver:* PSSP / New England Bank Note Co. *Comments:* H-RI-345-G48. 18__. 1830s.
Rarity: *None known*

$100 • W-RI-1060-100-G250

Left: 100 / Eagle / 100. *Center:* C / "Phoebus in Chariot of the Sun" / 100. *Right:* C / Portrait of George Washington / C. *Engraver:* New England Bank Note Co. *Comments:* H-RI-345-G50, Durand-1607. 18__. 1830s–1850s.
Rarity: *None known*

$100 • W-RI-1060-100-G260

Left: 100 / Fountain. *Center:* Globe and ships, Liberty seated, Eagle. *Right:* 100 / 100. *Engraver:* New England Bank Note Co. *Comments:* H-RI-345-G52, Durand-1608. 18__. 1850s–1860s.
Rarity: *None known*

$500 • W-RI-1060-500-G270

Left: 500. *Center:* Indian paddling canoe / 500. *Right:* 500 / Justice. *Engraver:* New England Bank Note Co. *Comments:* H-RI-345-G54, Durand-1609. 18__. 1850s–1860s.
Rarity: *None known*

$1,000 • W-RI-1060-1000-G280

Left: 1000. *Center:* Eagle on cliff / 1000. *Right:* 1000 / Indian woman. *Engraver:* New England Bank Note Co. *Comments:* H-RI-345-G56, Durand-1610. 18__. 1850s–1860s.
Rarity: *None known*

NON-VALID ISSUES

$1.25 • W-RI-1060-001.25-A010   CC

Engraver: New England Bank Note Co. **Comments:** H-RI-345-A5, Durand-1590. Altered from $1.25 Roxbury Bank, Roxbury, Massachusetts, or from notes of other failed banks using the same plate. 18__. 1830s.

Rarity: URS-3

G $170; **VF** $250

$1.50 • W-RI-1060-001.50-A020

Left: 1 DOLL. 50 Cts. vertically. **Center:** Spread eagle / $1 50/100. **Right:** 1 50/100 / Justice. **Engraver:** New England Bank Note Co. **Comments:** H-RI-345-A10, Durand-1591. Altered from $1.50 Roxbury Bank, Roxbury, Massachusetts, or from notes of other failed banks using the same plate. 18__. 1850s.

Rarity: URS-3

VF $250

$1.75 • W-RI-1060-001.75-A030   SI

Engraver: New England Bank Note Co. **Comments:** H-RI-345-A15, Durand-1592. Altered from $1.75 Roxbury Bank, Roxbury, Massachusetts, or from notes of other failed banks using the same plate. 18__. 1850s.

Rarity: URS-3

VF $250

$3 • W-RI-1060-003-N010

Center: Woman seated on shield. **Comments:** H-RI-345-N5, Durand-1596. 1850s.

Rarity: *None known*

$20 • W-RI-1060-020-A040

Left: Steamer / XX / Train. **Center:** Eagle / Liberty, Justice, and Science / Ship. **Right:** XX / Milkmaid. **Engraver:** New England Bank Note Co. **Comments:** H-RI-345-A20, Durand-1604. Altered from W-RI-1300-020-G090, or from notes of other failed banks using the same plate. Genuine notes of this design were issued, W-RI-1060-020-G190. 18__. 1850s.

Rarity: URS-3

VF $200

Mercantile Bank
1854–1865
W-RI-1070

History: The Mercantile Bank was incorporated in 1854 and commenced business early in July of that year. Authorized capital was set at $100,000. Circulation was $38,561 in 1857 but was only $1,894 in 1862. Specie amounted to $2,095.87 in 1857. It was located on Westminster Street.

In 1865 the business of the Mercantile Bank was succeeded by the First National Bank.

Numismatic Commentary: Genuine notes are hard to locate. The $1 and $2 notes are the most likely to become available.

VALID ISSUES

$1 • W-RI-1070-001-G010   CC

Overprint: Red 1 / 1. **Engraver:** Toppan, Carpenter & Co. **Comments:** H-RI-350-G2a, Durand-1611. 18__. 1850s.

Rarity: URS-2

VF $850

$1 • W-RI-1070-001-G010a

Left: 1 / Female portrait. **Center:** Sailor standing by ship's gunwale. **Right:** 1 / Venus seated in shell. **Overprint:** Likely red ONE. **Engraver:** Toppan, Carpenter & Co. / ABNCo. monogram. **Comments:** H-RI-350-G2b. Similar to W-RI-1070-001-G010 but with additional engraver imprint. 185_. 1850s.

Rarity: *None known*

$2 • W-RI-1070-002-G020

Left: 2 / Mechanic with anvil. **Right:** 2 / Men, women, and children waving at passing train. **Overprint:** Red 2. **Engraver:** Toppan, Carpenter & Co. **Comments:** H-RI-350-G4a. 185_. 1850s.

Rarity: *None known*

$2 • W-RI-1070-002-G020a   CJF

Overprint: Red 2. **Engraver:** Toppan, Carpenter & Co. / ABNCo. monogram. **Comments:** H-RI-350-G4b, Durand-1612. Similar to W-RI-1070-002-G020 but with additional engraver imprint. 185_. 1850s.

Rarity: URS-2

VF $1,000

$3 • W-RI-1070-003-G030

Left: 3 / Mercury. *Center:* Scene in blacksmith shop. *Right:* 3 / Blacksmith standing. *Overprint:* Red THREE. *Engraver:* Toppan, Carpenter & Co. *Comments:* H-RI-350-G6a, Durand-1613. 185_. 1850s.

Rarity: URS-2
VF $1,000

$3 • W-RI-1070-003-G030a

Overprint: Red THREE. *Engraver:* Toppan, Carpenter & Co. / ABNCo. monogram. *Comments:* H-RI-350-G6b. Similar to W-RI-1070-003-G030 but with additional engraver imprint. 185_. 1850s.

Rarity: *None known*

$5 • W-RI-1070-005-G040

Left: 5 / Sailor leaning on capstan. *Center:* Sailing ships / FIVE. *Right:* 5 / Woman holding sheaf. *Overprint:* Red FIVE. *Engraver:* Toppan, Carpenter & Co. *Comments:* H-RI-350-G8a, Durand-1615. 18__. 1850s.

Rarity: URS-3
VF $250

$5 • W-RI-1070-005-G040a

Overprint: Red FIVE. *Engraver:* Toppan, Carpenter & Co. / ABNCo. monogram. *Comments:* H-RI-350-G8b. Similar to W-RI-1070-005-G040 but with additional engraver imprint. 18__. 1850s–1860s.

Rarity: *None known*

$10 • W-RI-1070-010-G050

Left: Cattle by stream / 10. *Right:* 10 / Female portrait. *Overprint:* Likely red TEN. *Engraver:* Toppan, Carpenter & Co. *Comments:* H-RI-350-G10a, Durand-1617. 18__. 1850s.

Rarity: *None known*

$20 • W-RI-1070-020-G060

Left: 20 / Anchor and merchandise. *Center:* Warship and merchant ship under sail. *Right:* 20 / Train. *Overprint:* Likely red 20 or TWENTY. *Engraver:* Toppan, Carpenter & Co. *Comments:* H-RI-350-G12a, Durand-1620. 18__. 1850s.

Rarity: *None known*

$50 • W-RI-1070-050-G070

Left: 50 / Jupiter. *Right:* 50 / Man carrying corn stalks. *Overprint:* Likely red 50 or FIFTY. *Engraver:* Toppan, Carpenter & Co. *Comments:* H-RI-350-G14a, Durand-1623. 18__. 1850s.

Rarity: *None known*

$100 • W-RI-1070-100-G080

Left: Portrait of Benjamin Franklin / Portrait of Christopher Columbus / Portrait of Benjamin Franklin. *Bottom center:* 100. *Right:* 100 / Cherub, Portrait of George Washington, Cherub. *Overprint:* Likely red 100 or HUNDRED. *Engraver:* Toppan, Carpenter & Co. *Comments:* H-RI-350-G16a, Durand-1624. 18__. 1850s.

Rarity: *None known*

$500 • W-RI-1070-500-G090

Left: 500 / Portrait of Daniel Webster. *Center:* Mechanic and sailor, Bale. *Right:* 500 / Portrait of George Washington. *Engraver:* Toppan, Carpenter & Co. *Comments:* H-RI-350-G18a, Durand-1625. 18__. 1850s.

Rarity: *None known*

Non-Valid Issues

$3 • W-RI-1070-003-S010

Left: Panel bearing 3 vertically. *Center:* Medallion head / Reaper lying by stalks of wheat / Medallion head. *Right:* THREE / Sailor on mast / THREE. *Engraver:* Danforth, Spencer & Hufty. *Comments:* H-RI-350-S5, Durand-1614. May 1, 18__. 1854.

Rarity: URS-3
VF $200

$5 • W-RI-1070-005-A010

Left: FIVE / Minerva standing / FIVE. *Center:* Three allegorical women reclining with sheaf, pole and cap, globe and quadrant. *Right:* 5 / Portrait of George Washington. *Engraver:* Danforth, Bald & Co. *Comments:* H-RI-350-A5, Durand-1616. Altered from $5 Columbia Bank, Washington, D.C. 185_. 1850s.

Rarity: URS-3
VF $250

$10 • W-RI-1070-010-AR010

Left: TEN / Minerva standing / TEN. *Center:* Three allegorical women reclining with sheaf, pole and cap, globe and quadrant. *Right:* 10 / Portrait of George Washington. *Comments:* H-Unlisted, Durand-1618. Altered and raised from $5 Columbia Bank, Washington, D.C. 1850s.

Rarity: URS-3
VF $150

$10 • W-RI-1070-010-A020

Left: Woman resting on scroll and chest. *Center:* X on U.S. shield / Three allegorical women on shore, one pointing to ship. *Right:* 10 / Cattle, poles, train, and bridge. *Overprint:* Red TEN. *Comments:* H-Unlisted, Durand-1619. Altered from $10 Columbia Bank, Washington, D.C. 1850s.

Rarity: URS-3
VF $150

$10 • W-RI-1070-010-A030

Left: 10 / Woman seated. *Center:* X / Three women standing / *Right:* 10 / Scene with trees. *Overprint:* Red TEN. *Engraver:* Danforth, Bald & Co. *Comments:* H-RI-350-A10. Altered from $10 Columbia Bank, Washington, D.C. 185_. 1856.

Rarity: URS-3
VF $250

$20 • W-RI-1070-020-R010

Comments: H-RI-350-R5, Durand-1621. Raised from W-RI-1070-002-G020 series. 185_. 1850s.

Rarity: *None known*

$20 • W-RI-1070-020-AR020

Left: TWENTY / Minerva standing / TWENTY. *Center:* Three allegorical women reclining with sheaf, pole and cap, globe and quadrant. *Right:* 20 / Portrait of George Washington. *Comments:* H-Unlisted, Durand-1622. Altered and raised from $5 Columbia Bank, Washington, D.C. 1850s.

Rarity: URS-3
VF $150

Merchants Bank
1818–1865
W-RI-1080

History: The Merchants Bank, incorporated in 1818, became one of the strongest banks in the country. It was the sole depository for the city of Providence for a long time. This bank also was connected with the Suffolk Bank of Boston, the central clearing house for most of the New England banks. Because of its reputation for stability, the bank's notes were frequently counterfeited.[65]

The capital of the Merchants Bank was $500,000 in 1849 and $815,200 in 1860. Circulation was listed at $28,765 in 1849. 1857 included these figures: capital $770,850; bills in circulation $16,534; specie $27,500. Circulation increased dramatically to $125,991 by 1862.

The business of the bank was succeeded by the Merchants National Bank of Providence, chartered on April 24, 1865.

Numismatic Commentary: This bank made good use of color on many of its notes. Quite a few different issues may be found in today's marketplace. Many altered and spurious notes may also be found.

VALID ISSUES
$1 • W-RI-1080-001-G010

SBG

Engraver: Leney & Rollinson. **Comments:** H-RI-355-G2, Durand-1626. Note the title is printed "The Merchants' Bank In Providence". 18__. 1818–1830s.
Rarity: URS-3
Proof $1,150
Selected auction price: Stack's Bowers Galleries, March 2013, Proof $1,149

$1 • W-RI-1080-001-G020

Left: 1 / Portrait of Benjamin Franklin / ONE. **Center:** Sailing ship. **Bottom center:** Anchor on shield. **Right:** 1 / Sailor standing. **Engraver:** Rawdon, Wright & Hatch. **Comments:** H-RI-355-G6, Durand-1627. 18__. 1840s–1860.
Rarity: URS-3
VF $350

$1 • W-RI-1080-001-G030

SBG

Tint: Green panel and border of 1s. **Engraver:** National Bank Note Co. **Comments:** H-RI-355-G8a, Durand-1628. Note the title is printed "The Merchants' Bank In Providence". Jan.y 1st, 186_. 1860s.
Rarity: URS-3
VF $1,250; **Proof** $5,200

$2 • W-RI-1080-002-G040

SBG

Engraver: Leney & Rollinson. **Comments:** H-RI-355-G10, Durand-1638. Note the title is printed "The Merchants' Bank In Providence". 18__. 1818–1830s.
Rarity: URS-3
Proof $1,600
Selected auction price: Stack's Bowers Galleries, November 2008, Proof $1,541

$2 • W-RI-1080-002-G050

Left: 2 / Portrait of George Washington / TWO. **Center:** Spread eagle on tree limb. **Bottom center:** Anchor on shield. **Right:** 2 / Justice. **Engraver:** Rawdon, Wright & Hatch. **Comments:** H-RI-355-G14, Durand-1639. 18__. 1840s–1860.
Rarity: *None known*

$2 • W-RI-1080-002-G060

QDB

Tint: Green panel and frames of 2s. **Engraver:** National Bank Note Co. **Comments:** H-RI-355-G16a, Durand-1640. Note the title is printed "The Merchants' Bank In Providence". Proof. Jan.y 1st, 186_. 1860s.
Rarity: URS-3
VF $750; **Proof** $2,500

$3 • W-RI-1080-003-G070   SBG

Engraver: Leney & Rollinson. *Comments:* H-RI-355-G18, Durand-1646. Note the title is printed "The Merchants' Bank In Providence". 18__. 1818–1830s.
Rarity: URS-3
Proof $1,600
Selected auction price: Stack's Bowers Galleries, March 2013, Proof $1,573

$3 • W-RI-1080-003-G080

Left: Vulcan, Sledge, wheel, and anvil / 3. *Center:* Indian / Spread eagle on globe over city / Ceres. *Right:* 3 / Portrait of Indian princess. *Comments:* H-RI-355-G22, Durand-1647. 1830s.
Rarity: *None known*

$3 • W-RI-1080-003-G090

Left: Vulcan, Sledge, wheel, and anvil / THREE. *Center:* Indian / Spread eagle on globe over city / Ceres. *Right:* 3 / 3. *Tint:* Orange THREE and die with 3. *Engraver:* National Bank Note Co. *Comments:* H-RI-355-G24a, Durand-1648. 18__. 1860s.
Rarity: URS-3
VF $500

$3 • W-RI-1080-003-G100

Left: 3 / THREE / 3. *Center:* 3 / Ceres. *Right:* Portrait of Indian / 3. *Comments:* H-Unlisted, Durand-1654. 1830s.
Rarity: URS-3

$5 • W-RI-1080-005-G110   SBG

Engraver: Leney & Rollinson. *Comments:* H-RI-355-G26, Durand-1655. Note the title is printed "The Merchants' Bank In Providence". 18__. 1818–1830s.
Rarity: URS-3
Proof $1,200
Selected auction price: Spink-Smythe, July 2008, Proof $1,100

$5 • W-RI-1080-005-G120   CC

Engraver: Rawdon, Wright, Hatch & Co. *Comments:* H-RI-355-G28, Durand-1656. 18__. 1830s–1840s.
Rarity: URS-1
Proof $1,200

$5 • W-RI-1080-005-G130

Left: Three women on cliff / FIVE. *Center:* Harbor view, vessels, city. *Right:* 5 on shield / Female portrait. *Engraver:* Toppan, Carpenter & Co. *Comments:* H-RI-355-G30, Durand-1657. 18__. 1850s.
Rarity: *None known*

$5 • W-RI-1080-005-G140

Left: Three women on cliff / FIVE. *Center:* Harbor view, vessels, city. *Right:* 5 / V. *Tint:* Orange FIVE and die. *Engraver:* Toppan, Carpenter & Co. / National Bank Note Co. *Comments:* H-RI-355-G32a, Durand-1658. 18__. 1860s.
Rarity: URS-3
VF $500

$5 • W-RI-1080-005-G150

Left: FIVE vertically. *Center:* 5 / Spread eagle on shield. *Right:* Indian woman standing / FIVE. *Overprint:* Red FIVE. *Comments:* H-Unlisted, Durand-1665. 1830s.
Rarity: URS-3

$10 • W-RI-1080-010-G160   SBG

Engraver: Leney & Rollinson. *Comments:* H-RI-355-G34, Durand-1666. Note the title is printed "The Merchants' Bank In Providence". 18__. 1818–1830s.
Rarity: URS-3
Proof $1,350
Selected auction price: Stack's Bowers Galleries, March 2013, Proof $1,331

$10 • W-RI-1080-010-G170

Left: TEN / Woman seated / 10. *Center:* X / 10. *Bottom center:* Cherub on deer. *Right:* TEN / Manhattan pouring water out of urn / X. *Engraver:* Rawdon, Wright, Hatch & Co. *Comments:* H-RI-355-G36, Durand-1667. 18__. 1830s–1840s.
Rarity: URS-3
Proof $750

$10 • W-RI-1080-010-G180

Left: Agriculture and sailor holding flag. *Center:* Commerce seated, Anchor and shield, Vessels. *Right:* 10 / Liberty. *Engraver:* Unverified, but likely Toppan, Carpenter, Casilear & Co. *Comments:* H-RI-355-G38, Durand-1668. 18__. 1850s–1860s.

Rarity: *None known*

$50 • W-RI-1080-050-G190

Left: Allegorical figure holding shield bearing 50. *Center:* 50 / Portrait of Henry Clay. *Bottom center:* Anchor on shield. *Right:* Allegorical figure holding shield bearing 50 / 50. *Engraver:* Unverified, but likely Toppan, Carpenter, Casilear & Co. *Comments:* H-RI-355-G42, Durand-1674. 18__. 1850s–1860s.

Rarity: *None known*

$100 • W-RI-1080-100-G200

Left: ONE HUNDRED vertically. *Center:* 100 / Commerce, Vessels / 100. *Right:* ONE HUNDRED vertically. *Engraver:* Unverified, but likely Toppan, Carpenter, Casilear & Co. *Comments:* H-RI-355-G46, Durand-1675. 18__. 1850s–1860s.

Rarity: *None known*

$500 • W-RI-1080-500-G210

Left: Ship under sail, Steamer / 500. *Center:* Portrait of Benjamin Franklin. *Right:* 500 on scrollwork. *Engraver:* Unverified, but likely Toppan, Carpenter, Casilear & Co. *Comments:* H-RI-355-G48, Durand-1676. 18__. 1850s–1860s.

Rarity: *None known*

$1,000 • W-RI-1080-1000-G220

Left: 1000. *Center:* Allegorical woman, Cog wheel, steamer, train, depot / 1000. *Right:* ONE THOUSAND vertically. *Engraver:* Unverified, but likely Toppan, Carpenter, Casilear & Co. *Comments:* H-RI-355-G50, Durand-1677. 18__. 1850s–1860s.

Rarity: *None known*

Post Notes

$___ • W-RI-1080-___-G230

Engraver: Leney & Rollinson. *Comments:* H-RI-355-G60. Denomination filled in by hand. 18__. 1810s–1820s.

Rarity: URS-3
Proof $350

Non-Valid Issues

$1 • W-RI-1080-001-C010

Engraver: Leney & Rollinson. *Comments:* H-RI-355-C2, Durand-1629. Counterfeit of W-RI-1080-001-G010. 18__. 1820s.

Rarity: *None known*

$1 • W-RI-1080-001-N010

Left: Portrait of cherub / 1 / Portrait of cherub. *Center:* 1 / Liberty resting on shield bearing eagle / 1. *Right:* ONE / Angel writing on stone tablet / ONE. *Comments:* H-RI-355-N5, Durand-1634. 1830s.

Rarity: URS-3
VF $150

$1 • W-RI-1080-001-A010

Left: ONE on 1 / Spread eagle and shield / ONE. *Center:* Basket of produce / Reaper with cradle. *Right:* 1 / Indian woman with 1. *Overprint:* Red or blue ONE. *Comments:* H-Unlisted, Durand-1632. Altered from $1 Merchants Bank, Mankato City, Minnesota. 1830s.

Rarity: URS-3

$1 • W-RI-1080-001-A020   CC

Engraver: Rawdon, Wright, Hatch & Edson. *Comments:* H-RI-355-A5, Durand-1630. Altered from $1 Merchants Bank, Washington, D.C. Jan. 1st, 1859.

Rarity: URS-6
F $110

$1 • W-RI-1080-001-A030

Left: ONE / People and horse cart. *Center:* Train at station, People and buildings. *Right:* 1 / Girl shading eyes with hand. *Comments:* H-RI-355-A10, Durand-1633. Altered from $1 Bank of Greensborough, Greensborough, Georgia series. 1850s.

Rarity: *None known*

$1 • W-RI-1080-001-A040

Left: 1 / Portrait of William Henry Harrison. *Center:* Bust of Mercury / Man on horse lassoing steer. *Right:* 1 / Indian with bow. *Comments:* H-RI-355-A15, Durand-1631. Altered from $1 Merchants Bank, Mankato City, Minnesota. Sept. 1, 185_. 1850s.

Rarity: *None known*

$1 • W-RI-1080-001-A050   PEM

Comments: H-RI-355-A20. Altered from $1 Merchants Bank, Stillwater, Minnesota. October 20th, 1854.

Rarity: URS-6
VF $200

$1 • W-RI-1080-001-A060

Left: 1 / Spread eagle / ONE. *Center:* Man / ONE. *Bottom center:* Dog. *Right:* 1 / Woman with 1. *Engraver:* Rawdon, Wright, Hatch & Edson. *Comments:* H-RI-355-A25. Altered from $1 Farmers & Merchants Bank of Memphis, Memphis, Tennessee. Aug. 1, 1854.

Rarity: URS-5
VF $200

$1.25 • W-RI-1080-001.25-A070

BM

Engraver: New England Bank Note Co. **Comments:** H-RI-355-A30, Durand-1635. Altered from $1.25 Roxbury Bank, Roxbury, Massachusetts, or from notes of other failed banks using the same plate. 18__. 1853.

Rarity: URS-5

VF $250

$1.50 • W-RI-1080-001.50-A080

Left: 1 DOLL. 50 Cts. vertically. **Center:** Spread eagle on rock in ocean / $1 50/100. **Right:** 1 50/100 / Justice. **Engraver:** New England Bank Note Co. **Comments:** H-RI-355-A31, Durand-1636. Altered from $1.50 Roxbury Bank, Roxbury, Massachusetts, or from notes of other failed banks using the same plate. 18__. 1850s.

Rarity: *None known*

$1.75 • W-RI-1080-001.75-A090

Left: $1.75 Cts. / Hebe watering eagle / 1 75/100. **Center:** Three sloops at sea. **Right:** $1.75 Cts. / Agriculture / 1 75/100. **Engraver:** New England Bank Note Co. **Comments:** H-RI-355-A32, Durand-1637. Altered from $1.75 Roxbury Bank, Roxbury, Massachusetts, or from notes of other failed banks using the same plate. 18__. 1850s.

Rarity: *None known*

$2 • W-RI-1080-002-C040

Engraver: Leney & Rollinson. **Comments:** H-RI-355-C10, Durand-1641. Counterfeit of W-RI-1080-002-G040. 18__. 1820s.

Rarity: *None known*

$2 • W-RI-1080-002-N020

Center: Sailing ship. **Comments:** H-RI-355-N10. 1850s.

Rarity: *None known*

$2 • W-RI-1080-002-A100

Left: 2 / Shield, Commerce and Ceres, Ship. **Right:** 2 / Portrait of Zachary Taylor. **Engraver:** W.L. Ormsby. **Comments:** H-RI-355-A35, Durand-1642. Altered from $2 Merchants Bank, Ft. Leavenworth, Kansas. 18__. 1850s.

Rarity: *None known*

$2 • W-RI-1080-002-A110

Left: Indian brave on horse. **Center:** Spread eagle / Ceres. **Right:** 2 / Deer on hill. **Comments:** H-RI-355-A40, Durand-1643. Altered from $2 Merchants Bank, Mankato City, Minnesota. Sept. 1, 185_. 1850s.

Rarity: *None known*

$2 • W-RI-1080-002-A120

Left: 2 / TWO / 2. **Center:** 2 / Ceres. **Right:** Indian / 2. **Comments:** H-RI-355-A45, Durand-1645. Altered from $2 Merchants Bank, Stillwater, Minnesota. Oct. 20, 185_. 1850s.

Rarity: URS-5

VF $200

$2 • W-RI-1080-002-A130

Left: 2 / Portrait of Benjamin Franklin / TWO. **Center:** Station, Train. **Right:** 2 / Minerva with 2 / TWO. **Overprint:** TWO. **Engraver:** Rawdon, Wright, Hatch & Edson. **Comments:** H-RI-355-A50, Durand-1644. Altered from $2 Farmers & Merchants Bank of Memphis, Memphis, Tennessee series. 1850s.

Rarity: *None known*

$3 • W-RI-1080-003-N030

Left: 3 / Female. **Center:** Ceres. **Right:** 3 / Ships. **Comments:** H-RI-355-N15, Durand-1653. 1850s.

Rarity: *None known*

$3 • W-RI-1080-003-A140

Left: 3 / Portrait of Andrew Jackson. **Center:** 3 / Coats of arms surrounding Indian woman with bow / 3. **Right:** THREE / Ceres / 3. **Overprint:** Red THREE. **Engraver:** Rawdon, Wright, Hatch & Edson. **Comments:** H-RI-355-A55, Durand-1649. Altered from $3 Merchants Bank, Washington, D.C. Jan. 1, 1859.

Rarity: URS-3

VF $200

$3 • W-RI-1080-003-A150

Left: 3 / Helmeted medallion head. **Center:** Mechanic by forge, Anvil and wheelwright. **Right:** 3 / Portrait of William Henry Harrison. **Engraver:** W.L. Ormsby. **Comments:** H-RI-355-A60, Durand-1650. Altered from $3 Merchants Bank, Ft. Leavenworth, Kansas. 185_. 1850s.

Rarity: *None known*

$3 • W-RI-1080-003-A160

Left: 3 on die. **Center:** Manhattan reclining with urn. **Right:** 3 on die on panel of wheat and ears of corn. **Engraver:** Durand & Co. **Comments:** H-RI-355-A65, Durand-1651. Altered from $3 Globe Bank, New York City, New York. 1840.

Rarity: *None known*

$3 • W-RI-1080-003-A170

Left: 3 / Portrait of George Washington / THREE. **Center:** Allegorical woman on wharf. **Bottom center:** Strongbox and cornucopia with coins. **Right:** 3 / Mechanic, sailor, and farmer with 3. **Overprint:** THREE. **Engraver:** Rawdon, Wright, Hatch & Edson. **Comments:** H-RI-355-A70, Durand-1652. Altered from $3 Farmers & Merchants Bank of Memphis, Memphis, Tennessee series. 1850s.

Rarity: *None known*

$5 • W-RI-1080-005-C110   CC

Engraver: Leney & Rollinson. *Comments:* H-RI-355-C26, Durand-1659. Counterfeit of W-RI-1080-005-G110. Note the title is printed "The Merchants' Bank In Providence". 18__. 1820s–1830s.

Rarity: URS-5
VF $150

$5 • W-RI-1080-005-S010

Left: 5 / Allegorical man. *Center:* Steamship. *Right:* 5 / Ceres. *Engraver:* Bald, Adams & Co. *Comments:* H-RI-355-S5, Durand-1664. Altered from $5 Merchants Bank, Stillwater, Minnesota. 18__. 1850s.

Rarity: URS-3
VF $200

$5 • W-RI-1080-005-N040

Center: Woman. *Comments:* H-Unlisted, Durand-1663. Altered or spurious. 1850s.
Rarity: *None known*

$5 • W-RI-1080-005-A180

Center: Wild horses. *Comments:* H-Unlisted, Durand-1662. 1850s.
Rarity: *None known*

$5 • W-RI-1080-005-A190

Left: 5 / Allegorical woman seated on rocks, Tools, shield, and river scene. *Center:* Ceres and Liberty. *Right:* 5 / Portrait of Zachary Taylor. *Engraver:* W.L. Ormsby. *Comments:* H-RI-355-A75, Durand-1660. Altered from $5 Merchants Bank, Mankato City, Fort Leavenworth, Kansas. 185_. 1850s.
Rarity: *None known*

$5 • W-RI-1080-005-A200

Left: Indian woman holding bow / FIVE. *Center:* Eagle / Indian watching train. *Bottom center:* Indian in canoe. *Right:* 5 / Allegorical woman seated on hay. *Comments:* H-RI-355-A80, Durand-1661. Altered from $5 Merchants Bank, Mankato City, Minnesota. Sept. 1, 185_. 1850s.
Rarity: *None known*

$10 • W-RI-1080-010-C160

Engraver: Leney & Rollinson. *Comments:* H-RI-355-C34, Durand-1669. Counterfeit of W-RI-1080-010-G160. 18__. 1818 and 1819.

Rarity: URS-3
VF $150

$10 • W-RI-1080-010-A210

Left: Indian woman holding bow / TEN. *Center:* Eagle / Indian watching train. *Right:* 10 / Allegorical woman seated on hay. *Comments:* H-Unlisted, Durand-1672. Altered from $5 Merchants Bank, Mankato, Minnesota. 1850s.

Rarity: URS-3

$10 • W-RI-1080-010-A220

Left: X / Spread eagle on shield bearing arm and hammer. *Center:* Allegorical woman beside spinning wheel / 10. *Right:* Panel of fruit and flowers bearing medallion head of George Washington. *Engraver:* W.L. Ormsby. *Comments:* H-RI-355-A90, Durand-1670. Altered from $10 Merchants Bank, Ft. Leavenworth, Kansas. 185_. 1850s.
Rarity: *None known*

$10 • W-RI-1080-010-A230

Left: X / Portrait of William Henry Harrison. *Center:* Farmer plowing with oxen / Bust of Mercury. *Bottom center:* Indian in canoe. *Right:* X / Indian with bow. *Comments:* H-RI-355-A95, Durand-1671. Altered from $10 Merchants Bank, Mankato, Minnesota. Sept. 1, 185_. 1850s.
Rarity: *None known*

$10 • W-RI-1080-010-A240

Center: Woman, Shield. *Bottom center:* Woman seated. *Right:* Steamboat. *Engraver:* Rawdon, Wright & Hatch. *Comments:* H-RI-355-A100, Durand-1673. Altered from $10 Bank of Gallipolis, Gallipolis, Ohio. 18__. 1840s.
Rarity: *None known*

Moshassuck Bank
1856
W-RI-1090

History: The Moshassuck Bank was incorporated in 1856, but it was never organized and did not open for business.

> The Legislature of Rhode Island, at its late session, chartered the following new banks: Marine Bank, Providence; Northern Bank, Providence; Moshassuck Bank [an existing ABNCo. plate reads Moshausic Bank], Providence; Pokanoket Bank, Bristol; Richmond Bank, Richmond;

How to Read the Whitman Numbering System
$1 • W-RI-010-001-G010a

Denomination: Value of the note shown.

W: Whitman number. This number is a sortable code unique to each bank and note.

RI: Abbreviation for the state under study.

010: Numerical designation specific to each bank.

001: The denomination in dollars.

G010a: G indicates a good or valid note. Other categories are indicated thus: C (counterfeit); R (raised); S (spurious); N (not-attributed); A (altered). Numbers are assigned starting with 010, 020, et seq. Terminal letters following the number indicate variations of a note: a series of different colored overprints, tints, payees, etc., all on the same design of note. For more information, see the "How to Use This Book" section at the front of the volume, page xiv.

Washington County Bank, Richmond; and the Greenwich Bank, Greenwich.[66]

The bank's charter was forfeited in 1919.

Numismatic Commentary: Remaining in the American Bank Note Co. archives as of 2003 was a $1-$1-$2-$3 face plate imprinted "Moshausic Bank," which may have been the original spelling. It is likely that Proofs were at one time printed for this location, but none are known to exist.

Mount Vernon Bank
1823–1859
W-RI-1100

History: The Mount Vernon Bank was incorporated in 1823 in the town of Foster. Almost half of the directors did not actually reside in Foster but lived in Providence.[67] Circulation in 1849 was listed at $36,160.

In 1854 the bank moved to Providence, where it remained for the duration of its existence. Notes with both the Foster and Providence imprints were circulated. In Providence the bank was located at 87 Westminster Street. Capital was set at $60,000 and raised to $92,778 by 1856.

This bank failed in 1859.

See also listing under Foster, W-RI-400.

VALID ISSUES

$1 • W-RI-1100-001-G010   SI

Engraver: Rawdon, Wright, Hatch & Edson. **Comments:** H-RI-115-G50. 18__. 1840s–1850s.
Rarity: URS-3
VF $125; **Proof** $500

$1 • W-RI-1100-001-G010a   ANS

Overprint: Red ONE. **Engraver:** Rawdon, Wright, Hatch & Edson. **Comments:** H-RI-115-G50a, Durand-1684. Similar to W-RI-1100-001-G010. 18__. 1850s.
Rarity: URS-8
F $70; **VF** $125; **CU** $200

$1 • W-RI-1100-001-G020   QDB

Overprint: Red ONE. **Engraver:** New England Bank Note Co. / Rawdon, Wright, Hatch & Edson. **Comments:** H-RI-115-G52a, Durand-1685. 18__. 1850s.
Rarity: URS-4
VF $300; **EF** $500

$2 • W-RI-1100-002-G030
Left: 2 / Portrait of Liberty / 2. **Center:** 2 / Farmer, Bull on shield surmounted by beehive, Hunter. **Right:** Two cherubs on 2 / Medallion head. **Engraver:** Rawdon, Wright, Hatch & Edson. **Comments:** H-RI-115-G54, Durand-1686. Remainder. 18__. 1840s–1850s.
Rarity: URS-8
CU $850

$2 • W-RI-1100-002-G030a   NJW

Overprint: Red TWO. **Engraver:** Rawdon, Wright, Hatch & Edson. **Comments:** H-RI-115-G54a. Similar to W-RI-1100-002-G030. 18__. 1850s.
Rarity: URS-4
F $105; **Unc-Rem** $250

$3 • W-RI-1100-003-G040   NJW

Overprint: Red 3. **Engraver:** New England Bank Note Co. / Rawdon, Wright, Hatch & Edson. **Comments:** H-RI-115-G56, Durand-1687. Center vignette from a painting by Landseer. 18__. 1850s.
Rarity: URS-8
EF $300; **Unc-Rem** $350

$5 • W-RI-1100-005-G050

Left: 5 / V / 5. *Center:* Liberty standing / FIVE / FIVE. *Right:* 5 / Drover and cattle / 5. *Engraver:* Rawdon, Wright, Hatch & Co. *Comments:* H-RI-115-G58, Durand-1689. 18__. 1850s.

Rarity: *None known*

$5 • W-RI-1100-005-G060   CJF

Overprint: Red 5. *Engraver:* New England Bank Note Co. / Rawdon, Wright, Hatch & Edson. *Comments:* H-RI-115-G60, Durand-1688. 18__. 1850s.

Rarity: URS-7

F $95; **VF** $175; **Unc-Rem** $425

$10 • W-RI-1100-010-G070

Left: TEN / Portrait of George Washington / TEN. *Center:* Hope standing with anchor / 10. *Right:* 10. *Engraver:* Rawdon, Wright, Hatch & Co. *Comments:* H-RI-115-G62, Durand-1692. 18__. 1850s.

Rarity: *None known*

$10 • W-RI-1100-010-G080   CJF

Overprint: Red TEN. *Engraver:* New England Bank Note Co. / Rawdon, Wright, Hatch & Edson. *Comments:* H-RI-115-G64, Durand-1691. 18__. 1850s.

Rarity: URS-7

VF $200; **Unc-Rem** $450

$20 • W-RI-1100-020-G090   CC

Engraver: Rawdon, Wright, Hatch & Co. *Comments:* H-RI-115-G66, Durand-1694. 18__. 1850s.

Rarity: URS-4

VF $450; **EF** $700

$20 • W-RI-1100-020-G090a

Overprint: Red TWENTY. *Engraver:* Rawdon, Wright, Hatch & Co. *Comments:* H-RI-115-G66a. Similar to W-RI-1100-020-G090. 18__. 1850s.

Rarity: *None known*

$50 • W-RI-1100-050-G100

Left: 50 / Sailing ship / 50. *Center:* 50 / Statue of George Washington / 50. *Right:* Portrait of cherub / 50 / Portrait of cherub. *Engraver:* Rawdon, Wright, Hatch & Co. *Comments:* H-RI-115-G68. 18__. 1850s.

Rarity: *None known*

$50 • W-RI-1100-050-G100a

Overprint: Red FIFTY. *Engraver:* Rawdon, Wright, Hatch & Co. *Comments:* H-RI-115-G68a, Durand-1695. Similar to W-RI-1100-050-G100. 18__. 1850s.

Rarity: URS-5

VF $350

$100 • W-RI-1100-100-G110   CC

Engraver: New England Bank Note Co. *Comments:* H-RI-115-G70, Durand-1696. 18__. 1850s.

Rarity: URS-3

VF $750; **AU** $900

$100 • W-RI-1100-100-G110a   CC

Overprint: Red HUNDRED. *Engraver:* New England Bank Note Co. *Comments:* H-RI-115-G70a. Similar to W-RI-1100-100-G110. 18__. 1850s.

Rarity: URS-3

VF $1,000; **AU** $1,800

Non-Valid Issues

$5 • W-RI-1100-005-R010

Engraver: New England Bank Note Co. / Rawdon, Wright, Hatch & Edson. *Comments:* H-RI-115-R15, Durand-1690. Raised from W-RI-1100-001-G020. 18__. 1850s.

Rarity: *None known*

$10 • W-RI-1100-010-R020

Engraver: New England Bank Note Co. / Rawdon, Wright, Hatch & Edson. *Comments:* H-RI-115-R20, Durand-1693. Raised from W-RI-1100-001-G020. 18__. 1850s.

Rarity: *None known*

National Bank
1833–1865
W-RI-1110

History: The National Bank was incorporated in 1833 at a time when the industrialization of Providence was accelerating. The bank had its offices at 11 Market Square. During the Panic of 1837 the bank was forced to suspend specie payments, but the bank recovered and payment resumed. In 1850 the capital was $120,000, and in 1857 it was $320,500. In 1854 the president was George W. Hallet, and the cashier was E. Bourne. In 1857 circulation was $83,496.75, and specie amounted to $9,164.71.[68]

The business of the National Bank was succeeded by the Old National Bank, chartered on May 15, 1865.

Numismatic Commentary: During the bank's 32-year life as a state-chartered corporation, it used at least eight different engravers to print its notes. Collectors can find quite a bit of diversity with the vignettes. Nautical to heraldic to patriotic scenes may be found.

The imprint of the American Bank Note Co. was used from 1854 to 1858 in conjunction with a separate entity—Jocelyn, Draper, Welsh & Co.

VALID ISSUES

$1 • W-RI-1110-001-G010

Left: 1 / Minerva standing with 1 / 1. *Center:* ONE / Plow, Commerce seated with caduceus and cornucopia, Ships / ONE. *Right:* 1 / Eagle / 1. *Engraver:* PSSP. *Comments:* H-RI-360-G2. 18__. 1830s.

Rarity: *None known*

$1 • W-RI-1110-001-G020

Left: ONE / Portrait of George Washington. *Center:* Liberty, eagle, and shield. *Right:* ONE / Portrait of Benjamin Franklin. *Engraver:* Rawdon, Wright, Hatch & Co. *Comments:* H-RI-360-G4, Durand-1697. 18__. 1830s.

Rarity: *None known*

$1 • W-RI-1110-001-G030

Left: ONE / Spread eagle and shield / 1. *Center:* Naval engagement. *Bottom center:* Anchor on shield. *Right:* 1 / Spread eagle and shield / ONE. *Engraver:* Rawdon, Wright, Hatch & Co. *Comments:* H-RI-360-G6, Durand-1698. 18__. 1830s.

Rarity: *None known*

$1 • W-RI-1110-001-G040

SBG

Engraver: Draper, Toppan & Co. *Comments:* H-RI-360-G8, Durand-1699. 184_. 1840s.

Rarity: URS-3
Proof $3,200
Selected auction price: Stack's Bowers Galleries, March 2013, Proof $3,146

$1 • W-RI-1110-001-G040a

Left: 1 bearing ONE DOLLAR / Woman gathering grapes. *Center:* Spread eagle, Ships / ONE. *Bottom center:* Shield bearing anchor. *Right:* 1 bearing ONE DOLLAR / Sailor standing. *Engraver:* Draper, Toppan & Co. *Comments:* H-RI-360-G8a, Durand-1700. Similar to W-RI-1110-001-G040. 184_. 1840s.

Rarity: URS-3
VF $400

$1 • W-RI-1110-001-G040b

Center: Spread eagle, Ships / ONE. *Engraver:* Toppan, Carpenter & Co. *Comments:* H-RI-360-G8b. Similar to W-RI-1110-001-G040 but with different engraver imprint. 184_. 1840s.

Rarity: URS-3
VF $400

$1 • W-RI-1110-001-G050

SBG

Engraver: Toppan, Carpenter & Co. *Comments:* H-RI-360-G10, Durand-1701. 18__. 1850s.

Rarity: URS-3
VF $400; **Proof** $2,500

$1 • W-RI-1110-001-G050a

Overprint: Red ONE. *Engraver:* Toppan, Carpenter & Co. *Comments:* H-RI-360-G10a, Durand-1702. Similar to W-RI-1110-001-G050. 18__. 1850s.

Rarity: *None known*

$1 • W-RI-1110-001-G060   SBG

Tint: Red-orange lathework, microlettering, ONE, and outlining white 1 / 1. *Engraver:* Jocelyn, Draper, Welsh & Co. / American Bank Note Co. *Comments:* H-RI-360-G12a, Durand-1703. 18__. 1850s–1860s.

Rarity: URS-2
EF $600; **Proof** $4,500

$1 • W-RI-1110-001-G060a

Tint: Green outlining white ONE and 1 / 1. *Engraver:* American Bank Note Co. *Comments:* H-RI-360-G12b, Durand-1704. Similar to W-RI-1110-001-G060 but with different date and engraver imprint. Sept. 1, 186_. 1860s.

Rarity: URS-3
VG $650; **VF** $700

$1 • W-RI-1110-001-G070

Left: ONE on 1 / Portrait of Henry Clay. *Center:* 1 on ONE DOLLAR / America crushing Secession. *Right:* ONE on 1 / Eagle on rock. *Engraver:* Unverified, but likely American Bank Note Co. *Comments:* H-RI-360-G14, Durand-1705. 1860s.

Rarity: *None known*

$1.25 • W-RI-1110-001.25-G080

Left: 1 25/100 / Train / 1 25/100. *Center:* Sloop and other vessels at sea / $1.25 Cts. *Right:* 1 25/100 / Eagle. *Engraver:* New England Bank Note Co. *Comments:* H-RI-360-G16. 18__. 1830s.

Rarity: *None known*

$1.50 • W-RI-1110-001.50-G090

Left: 1 Doll 50 Cts. vertically. *Center:* Eagle on rock in ocean / $1 50/100. *Right:* 1 50/100 / Justice. *Engraver:* New England Bank Note Co. *Comments:* H-RI-360-G17. 18__. 1830s.

Rarity: *None known*

$1.75 • W-RI-1110-001.75-G100

Left: $1.75 Cts. / Hebe watering eagle / 1 75/100. *Center:* Three sloops at sea. *Right:* $1.75 Cts. / Dog / Woman seated with grain / 1 75/100. *Engraver:* New England Bank Note Co. *Comments:* H-RI-360-G18. 18__. 1830s.

Rarity: *None known*

$2 • W-RI-1110-002-G110

Left: 2 / Hebe watering eagle / 2. *Center:* 2 / Commerce seated on shore, Plow and cornucopia / 2. *Right:* 2 / Justice standing / 2. *Engraver:* PSSP. *Comments:* H-RI-360-G20. 18__. 1830s.

Rarity: *None known*

$2 • W-RI-1110-002-G120

Left: Male portrait. *Center:* 2 / Goddess of Plenty, Train / 2. *Bottom center:* Dog, strongbox, and key. *Right:* Portrait of Benjamin Franklin. *Engraver:* Rawdon, Wright, Hatch & Co. *Comments:* H-RI-360-G22, Durand-1708. 18__. 1830s.

Rarity: *None known*

$2 • W-RI-1110-002-G130   CC

Engraver: Draper, Toppan & Co. *Comments:* H-RI-360-G24, Durand-1709. 184_. 1840s.

Rarity: URS-2
Proof $2,500

$2 • W-RI-1110-002-G130a

Left: 2 / Spread eagle on shield. *Center:* Temple, Architecture and Agriculture, Ships / TWO. *Right:* 2 / Spread eagle on shield. *Engraver:* Draper, Toppan & Co. *Comments:* H-RI-360-G24a, Durand-1710. Similar to W-RI-1110-002-G130. 184_. 1840s.

Rarity: *None known*

$2 • W-RI-1110-002-G130b

Center: Temple, Architecture and Agriculture, Ships / TWO. *Engraver:* Toppan, Carpenter & Co. *Comments:* H-RI-360-G24b. Similar to W-RI-1110-002-G130 but with different engraver imprint. 184_. 1840s.

Rarity: *None known*

$2 • W-RI-1110-002-G140

Left: TWO on 2 / Eagle perched on shield. *Center:* Sailing ship / TWO. *Bottom center:* Shield bearing anchor. *Right:* TWO on 2 / Eagle perched on shield. *Engraver:* Toppan, Carpenter & Co. *Comments:* H-RI-360-G26, Durand-1711. 18__. 1850s.

Rarity: URS-3
Proof $600

$2 • W-RI-1110-002-G140a   CJF

Overprint: Red TWO. *Engraver:* Toppan, Carpenter & Co. *Comments:* H-RI-360-G26a, Durand-1712. Similar to W-RI-1110-002-G140. 18__. 1850s.

Rarity: URS-3
VF $500

$2 • W-RI-1110-002-G150

CJF

Tint: Red-orange lathework, microlettering, and outlining white 2 / 2. *Engraver:* Jocelyn, Draper, Welsh & Co. / American Bank Note Co. *Comments:* H-RI-360-G28a, Durand-1713. 18__. 1850s–1860s.

Rarity: URS-2
Proof $3,000

$2 • W-RI-1110-002-G150a

Tint: Green outlining white 2 / 2. *Engraver:* American Bank Note Co. *Comments:* H-RI-360-G28b, Durand-1714. Similar to W-RI-1110-002-G150 but with different date and engraver imprint. Sept. 1, 186_. 1860s.

Rarity: URS-3
VF $500

$3 • W-RI-1110-003-G160

Left: 3 / Eagle on rock / 3. *Center:* 3 / Plow, Commerce seated with caduceus and cornucopia, Ships / 3 / Panel bearing THREE. *Right:* 3 / Woman standing with cornucopia / 3. *Engraver:* PSSP. *Comments:* H-RI-360-G30. 18__. 1830s.

Rarity: *None known*

$3 • W-RI-1110-003-G170

SBG

Engraver: Toppan, Carpenter & Co. *Comments:* H-RI-360-G36, Durand-1717. 18__. 1850s.

Rarity: URS-2
Proof $3,200
Selected auction price: Stack's Bowers Galleries, March 2013, Proof $3,146

$3 • W-RI-1110-003-G180

Left: THREE / Sailor / DOLLARS. *Center:* 3 / Man and boy viewing bust of George Washington / 3. *Right:* 3 / Camp scene. *Engraver:* Unverified, but likely American Bank Note Co. *Comments:* H-RI-360-G38, Durand-1718. 18__. 1860s.

Rarity: *None known*

$5 • W-RI-1110-005-G190

SBG

Engraver: Toppan, Carpenter & Co. *Comments:* H-RI-360-G44, Durand-1722. 18__. 1840s.

Rarity: URS-2
Proof $2,700
Selected auction price: Stack's Bowers Galleries, October 2010, Proof $2,608

$5 • W-RI-1110-005-G200

CC

Engraver: Toppan, Carpenter & Co. *Comments:* H-RI-360-G45, Durand-1734. Jan.y 1st, 18__. 1850s.

Rarity: URS-3
F $250; **Proof** $2,000

$5 • W-RI-1110-005-G210

Left: 5 / Indian on rock. *Center:* Steamboat and other ships. *Right:* Indian overlooking precipice / 5. *Comments:* H-RI-360-G46, Durand-1723. 18__. 1850s.

Rarity: *None known*

$5 • W-RI-1110-005-G220

Left: 5 / Charging soldier. *Center:* Spread eagle on shield, Mortar, balls. *Right:* 5 / Allegorical woman with spyglass. *Tint:* Green panel vertically. *Engraver:* American Bank Note Co. *Comments:* H-RI-360-G48a, Durand-1724. July 1, 186_. 1860s.

Rarity: URS-3
VF $750

$10 • W-RI-1110-010-G230

Left: Panel bearing TEN / Manhattan spilling water jug / TEN. *Center:* TEN / Ceres seated / TEN / Panel of microletters. *Right:* Panel bearing 10 / Portrait of Indian / 10. *Engraver:* Toppan, Carpenter & Co. *Comments:* H-RI-360-G52. 18__. 1840s.

Rarity: *None known*

$10 • W-RI-1110-010-G240

Left: TENs on 10 / Portrait of Christopher Columbus. *Center:* Spread eagle, Anchor, cogwheel, and ships. *Right:* TENs on 10 / Portrait of George Washington. *Engraver:* Toppan, Carpenter & Co. *Comments:* H-RI-360-G58, Durand-1736. Jan.y 1st, 18__. 1840s–1850s.

Rarity: URS-3
Proof $500

$10 • W-RI-1110-010-G240a

CJF

Overprint: Red TEN. *Engraver:* Toppan, Carpenter & Co. / ABNCo. monogram. *Comments:* H-RI-360-G58a. Similar to W-RI-1110-010-G240 but with additional engraver imprint. Jan.y 1st, 18__. 1840s–1850s.

Rarity: URS-3
VG $75; **VF** $275

$10 • W-RI-1110-010-G240b

Overprint: Red TEN. *Engraver:* Toppan, Carpenter & Co. / ABNCo. monogram. *Comments:* H-RI-360-G58b. Similar to W-RI-1110-010-G240 but with additional engraver imprint. Jan. 1, 18__. 1860s.

Rarity: *None known*

$10 • W-RI-1110-010-G250

Left: Spread eagle on rock / X. *Center:* TEN DOLLARS. *Right:* 10 / Female portrait. *Tint:* 10 on green die. *Engraver:* Unverified, but likely American Bank Note Co. *Comments:* H-RI-360-G60a, Durand-1737. Jan. 1, 186_. 1860s.

Rarity: *None known*

$20 • W-RI-1110-020-G260

CC

Engraver: Rawdon, Wright & Hatch. *Comments:* H-RI-360-G66, Durand-1742. 18__. 1840s.

Rarity: URS-2
Proof $2,200
Selected auction price: Spink-Smythe, April 2009, Proof $2,099

$50 • W-RI-1110-050-G270

Left: 50 / Woman standing with ankles crossed, Staff, Cornucopia and anchor / 50. *Center:* FIFTY DOLLARS / 50. *Right:* FIFTY vertically. *Engraver:* PSSP / New England Bank Note Co. *Comments:* H-RI-360-G70. 18__. 1830s.

Rarity: *None known*

$50 • W-RI-1110-050-G280

Left: Soldier with flag standing by cannon / FIFTY. *Center:* Portrait of John Quincy Adams. *Right:* 50. *Engraver:* Toppan, Carpenter & Co. *Comments:* H-RI-360-G74, Durand-1745. 18__. 1850s.

Rarity: URS-3
Proof $1,000

$50 • W-RI-1110-050-G280a

Tint: Green L / L. *Comments:* H-RI-360-G74a, Durand-1746. Similar to W-RI-1110-050-G280. 18__. 1860s.

Rarity: *None known*

$100 • W-RI-1110-100-G290

Left: Lathework panel bearing C / Portrait of George Washington / C. *Center:* 100 / Manhattan reclining pouring water, Ship / 100. *Right:* Lathework panel bearing ONE HUNDRED vertically. *Engraver:* PSSP / New England Bank Note Co. *Comments:* H-RI-360-G78. 18__. 1830s.

Rarity: *None known*

$100 • W-RI-1110-100-G300

Left: Woman seated with pole and cap holding shield, Capitol building / 100. *Center:* Portrait of George Washington. *Right:* 100. *Engraver:* Toppan, Carpenter & Co. *Comments:* H-RI-360-G82, Durand-1747. 18__. 1850s.

Rarity: URS-3
Proof $1,500

$100 • W-RI-1110-100-G300a

Tint: Green C / C. *Comments:* H-RI-360-G82a, Durand-1748. Similar to W-RI-1110-100-G300. 18__. 1860s.

Rarity: *None known*

$500 • W-RI-1110-500-G310

Left: 500 / 500 vertically / 500. *Center:* 500 / Woman seated with shield bearing D, Fasces, cornucopia, lyre, and sheaf / 500. *Right:* 500 / D / 500. *Engraver:* PSSP / New England Bank Note Co. *Comments:* H-RI-360-G86. 18__. 1850s.

Rarity: *None known*

$500 • W-RI-1110-500-G320

Left: 500 / Justice. *Center:* Spread eagle on shield. *Right:* 500 / Liberty. *Engraver:* Toppan, Carpenter & Co. *Comments:* H-RI-360-G88, Durand-1749. 18__. 1850s.

Rarity: *None known*

$500 • W-RI-1110-500-G320a

SBG

Overprint: Red D / D. *Engraver:* Jocelyn, Draper, Welsh & Co. / American Bank Note Co. *Comments:* H-Unlisted, Durand-Unlisted. Similar to W-RI-1110-500-G320 but with different engraver imprint. 18__. 1860s.

Rarity: URS-1
Proof $17,000
Selected auction price: Stack's Bowers Galleries, March 2013, Proof $16,943

$1,000 • W-RI-1110-1000-G330

Left: THOUSAND vertically. *Center:* 1000 / Woman standing with legs crossed, Lyre, cornucopia / 1000. *Right:* 1000 / M / 1000. *Engraver:* PSSP / New England Bank Note Co. *Comments:* H-RI-360-G92. 18___. 1850s.

Rarity: *None known*

$1,000 • W-RI-1110-1000-G340

Left: Liberty, U.S. Capitol / 1000. *Center:* Portrait of George Washington. *Right:* 1000. *Engraver:* Toppan, Carpenter & Co. *Comments:* H-RI-360-G94, Durand-1750. 18___. 1850s.

Rarity: *None known*

Uncut Sheets

$1-$1-$1-$2 • W-RI-1110-001.001.001.002-US010

Vignette(s): ($1) Woman seated / Spread eagle, Ships / Shield bearing anchor / Woman with pole and cap, Shield. *($1)* Woman seated / Spread eagle, Ships / Shield bearing anchor / Woman with pole and cap, Shield. *($1)* Woman seated / Spread eagle, Ships / Shield bearing anchor / Woman with pole and cap, Shield. *($2)* Eagle perched on shield / Sailing ship / Shield bearing anchor / Eagle perched on shield. *Engraver:* Toppan, Carpenter & Co. *Comments:* H-RI-360-G10, G10, G10, G26. 18___. 1850s.

Rarity: URS-3
Proof $2,500

$1-$1-$1-$2 • W-RI-1110-001.001.001.002-US020

Vignette(s): ($1) Portrait of Henry Clay / Factories / Spread eagle on shield / Farming / Portrait of George Washington. *($1)* Portrait of Henry Clay / Factories / Spread eagle on shield / Farming / Portrait of George Washington. *($1)* Portrait of Henry Clay / Factories / Spread eagle on shield / Farming / Portrait of George Washington. *($2)* Justice / George Washington on horseback, Two officers, Tent with American flag / Spread eagle on shield. *Tint(s):* Red-orange. *Engraver:* Jocelyn, Draper, Welsh & Co. / American Bank Note Co. *Comments:* H-RI-360-G12a, G12a, G12a, G28a. 18___. 1850s–1860s.

Rarity: URS-3
Proof $3,500

Non-Valid Issues

$1 • W-RI-1110-001-C040

Engraver: Draper, Toppan & Co. *Comments:* H-RI-360-C8, Durand-1706. Counterfeit of W-RI-1110-001-G040. 184_. 1840s.

Rarity: *None known*

$1 • W-RI-1110-001-C050

Engraver: Toppan, Carpenter & Co. *Comments:* H-RI-360-C10, Durand-1707. Counterfeit of W-RI-1110-001-G050. 18___. 1850s.

Rarity: *None known*

$2 • W-RI-1110-002-C130

CC

Engraver: Draper, Toppan & Co. *Comments:* H-RI-360-C24, Durand-1715. Counterfeit of W-RI-1110-002-G130. 184_. 1840s.

Rarity: URS-5
VF $150

$2 • W-RI-1110-002-N010

Center: Spread eagle on shield. *Comments:* H-RI-360-N5, Durand-1716. Altered or spurious. 1840s–1850s.

Rarity: *None known*

$3 • W-RI-1110-003-S010

CJF

Engraver: Toppan, Carpenter & Co. *Comments:* H-RI-360-S5, Durand-1721. Spurious design imitating a rough verbal description of W-RI-1110-003-G170. 18___. 1857.

Rarity: URS-6
VF $150

$3 • W-RI-1110-003-A010

Left: Eagle on U.S. shield / 3. *Center:* 3 / Portrait of George Washington. *Right:* 3 / Mercury with cornucopia and caduceus. *Overprint:* THREE. *Engraver:* Wellstood, Hanks, Hay & Whiting. *Comments:* H-RI-360-A5, Durand-1719. Altered from $3 Mechanics Bank, Georgetown, D.C. 18___. 1850s.

Rarity: *None known*

$3 • W-RI-1110-003-A020

Left: 3 / Portrait of George Washington / THREE. *Center:* Commerce beckoning to ship. *Right:* 3 / Mechanic, sailor, and farmer with 3. *Overprint:* THREE. *Engraver:* Rawdon, Wright, Hatch & Edson. *Comments:* H-RI-360-A10, Durand-1720. Altered from $3 Farmers & Merchants Bank, Memphis, Tennessee. 1850s.

Rarity: URS-3
VF $250

$5 • W-RI-1110-005-C200

CJF

Engraver: Toppan, Carpenter & Co. *Comments:* H-RI-360-C45. Counterfeit of W-RI-1110-005-G200. Jan.y 1st, 18__. 1850s.

Rarity: URS-5
VF $150

$5 • W-RI-1110-005-S020

Left: 5. *Center:* Factories / FIVE DOLLARS on 5. *Right:* FIVE / Portrait of George Washington / FIVE. *Engraver:* Toppan, Carpenter & Co. *Comments:* H-RI-360-S10, Durand-1732. May 1st, 185_. 1858.

Rarity: URS-5
VF $150

$5 • W-RI-1110-005-S020a

Overprint: Red FIVE. *Engraver:* Toppan, Carpenter & Co. *Comments:* H-RI-360-S10a, Durand-1733. Similar to W-RI-1110-005-S020. May 1st, 185_. 1858.

Rarity: URS-5
VF $150

$5 • W-RI-1110-005-S020b

CJF

Tint: Red outlining white FIVE. *Engraver:* Toppan, Carpenter & Co. *Comments:* H-RI-360-S10b, Durand-1731. Similar to W-RI-1110-005-S020. May 1st, 185_. 1858.

Rarity: URS-5
VG $85; **VF** $150

$5 • W-RI-1110-005-N020

Center: Train and cars, Houses and bridge. *Right:* Indian and child. *Comments:* H-RI-360-N15, Durand-1730. 1840s–1850s.

Rarity: *None known*

$5 • W-RI-1110-005-N030

Center: Indian hunting, Flying figures, Gold dollar. *Right:* Woman. *Comments:* H-RI-360-N20. 1840s–1850s.

Rarity: *None known*

$5 • W-RI-1110-005-A030

Left: 5 / Female portrait / 5. *Center:* Man reclining with sickle, sheaf, and cornucopia in V. *Right:* 5 / Female portrait / FIVE. *Overprint:* Red 5 / 5 or FIVE. *Engraver:* Danforth, Bald & Co. *Comments:* H-RI-360-A12, Durand-1729. Altered from $5 Eastern Bank, West Killingly, Connecticut series. 18__. 1850s.

Rarity: URS-3
VF $150

$5 • W-RI-1110-005-A040

Left: FIVE / Minerva standing / FIVE. *Center:* Liberty and two allegorical women. *Right:* 5 / Portrait of George Washington. *Engraver:* Danforth, Bald & Co. *Comments:* H-RI-360-A15, Durand-1725. Altered from $5 Columbia Bank, Washington, D.C. 18__. 1850s.

Rarity: *None known*

$5 • W-RI-1110-005-A050

Left: FIVE / Laureate woman with arm on shield bearing 5. *Center:* Train / Allegorical woman in clouds with eagle and shield / 5. *Right:* FIVE / Liberty. *Engraver:* W.L. Ormsby. *Comments:* H-RI-360-A20, Durand-1728. Altered from $5 Potomac River Bank, Georgetown, D.C. 18__. 1850s.

Rarity: *None known*

$5 • W-RI-1110-005-A060

Left: 5 / Farm family. *Center:* Portrait of Benjamin Franklin. *Right:* 5 / Woodsman and cattle. *Overprint:* Red V / V. *Comments:* H-RI-360-A25, Durand-1726. Altered from W-RI-1630-005-G040. Aug. 6, 1855.

Rarity: *None known*

$5 • W-RI-1110-005-A070

Left: 5 / FIVE / FIVE. *Center:* Indian woman, Man and three cherubs with five silver dollars / FIVE. *Bottom center:* Steamboat. *Right:* 5 / Female portrait / FIVE. *Overprint:* Red FIVE. *Engraver:* Rawdon, Wright, Hatch & Edson. *Comments:* H-RI-360-A30, Durand-1727. Altered from $5 Farmers & Merchants Bank, Memphis, Tennessee. 1850s.

Rarity: URS-5
VF $150

$5 • W-RI-1110-005-A070a

Overprint: Blue. *Engraver:* Rawdon, Wright, Hatch & Edson. *Comments:* H-Unlisted, Durand-Unlisted. Similar to W-RI-1110-005-A070. Altered from $5 Farmers & Merchants Bank, Memphis, Tennessee. 1850s.

Rarity: —

$10 • W-RI-1110-010-C240a

Engraver: Toppan, Carpenter & Co. *Comments:* H-RI-360-C58a, Durand-1738. Counterfeit of W-RI-1110-010-G240a. Jan. 1, 18__. 1860s.

Rarity: URS-5
VF $150

$10 • W-RI-1110-010-C240b

Engraver: Toppan, Carpenter & Co. / ABNCo. monogram. *Comments:* H-RI-360-C58b. Counterfeit of W-RI-1110-010-G240b. Jan. 1, 18__. 1860s.

Rarity: *None known*

$10 • **W-RI-1110-010-A080**

Left: 10 / Woman with scroll. *Center:* X on shield / Three allegorical women viewing ship. *Right:* 10 / Train on bridge, Cattle. *Overprint:* Red TEN. *Engraver:* Danforth, Bald & Co. *Comments:* H-RI-360-A35, Durand-1739. Altered from $10 Columbia Bank, Washington, D.C. 18__. 1850s.

Rarity: URS-3

$10 • **W-RI-1110-010-A090**   CJF

Overprint: Red X / X. *Comments:* H-RI-360-A40, Durand-1740. Altered from W-RI-1630-010-G050. Right edge of note torn. 18__. 1850s.

Rarity: URS-3
Proof $75

$10 • **W-RI-1110-010-A100**   ANS

Engraver: Rawdon, Wright & Hatch. *Comments:* H-RI-360-A42, Durand-1741. 18__. 1840s.

Rarity: URS-3
VG $90; **VF** $250

$20 • **W-RI-1110-020-N040**

Left: XX. *Center:* Men shooting buffalo. *Right:* 20 / Portrait. *Comments:* H-RI-360-N30, Durand-1744. 1840s–1850s.

Rarity: *None known*

$20 • **W-RI-1110-020-A110**

Left: Men driving cattle into stream / XX. *Center:* Reaper, Shield bearing pine tree and deer, Sailor. *Right:* 20 / Male portrait. *Overprint:* Red TWENTY. *Engraver:* Bald, Cousland & Co. / Baldwin, Bald & Cousland. *Comments:* H-RI-360-A45, Durand-1743. Altered from $20 Bank of Morgan, Morgan, Georgia. 18__. 1850s.

Rarity: *None known*

Northern Bank
1850s
W-RI-1120

History: A non-existent bank represented only by notes altered from those of other banks. They were intended to pass for the Northern Bank in Providence, W-RI-1130.

ISSUES

$1 • **W-RI-1120-001-A010**

Left: 1 / Cattle, Train. *Center:* Woman with cows. *Right:* 1 / Female portrait. *Tint:* Red-brown 1s and panel outlining white ONE DOLLAR. *Engraver:* Danforth, Wright & Co. *Comments:* H-RI-369-A5, Durand-1754. Altered from $1 Southern Bank of Georgia, Georgia. March 1, 1858.

Rarity: URS-5
VF $150

Northern Bank in Providence
1856–1882
W-RI-1130

History: The Northern Bank in Providence was incorporated in 1856. It was located on Weybosset Street. In 1857 the capital was $228,200, bills in circulation totaled $49,206, and specie amounted to $2,374.85. Circulation had increased to $144,217 by 1862. The bank continued under its state charter until it closed in 1882. By 1874 only $1,479 in currency was outstanding.

Numismatic Commentary: One $5 issue shows a vignette of "Dr. Kane's Arctic Expedition," while a $10 denomination shows "Major Waldron's Terrible Fight." Issues from this bank are not plentiful but do turn up in the marketplace from time to time.

VALID ISSUES

$1 • **W-RI-1130-001-G010**

Left: ONE / Mercury in clouds. *Center:* Hope leaning on shield, Ships. *Right:* 1 / Ceres. *Engraver:* Toppan, Carpenter & Co. *Comments:* H-RI-369-G2, Durand-1751. 18__. 1850s.

Rarity: *None known*

$1 • **W-RI-1130-001-G010a**

Overprint: Red ONE. *Engraver:* Toppan, Carpenter & Co. / ABNCo. monogram. *Comments:* H-RI-370-G2b, Durand-1752. Similar to W-RI-1130-001-G010 but with additional engraver imprint. 18__. 1850s–1860s.

Rarity: URS-3
VF $400

$1 • **W-RI-1130-001-G010b**   TD

Overprint: Red ONE. *Engraver:* American Bank Note Co. *Comments:* H-Unlisted, Durand-Unlisted. Similar to W-RI-1130-001-G010 but with different engraver imprint. 18__. 1860s.

Rarity: URS-3
VF $600

$1 • W-RI-1130-001-G010c

Overprint: Green panel outlining white ONE. *Engraver:* American Bank Note Co. *Comments:* H-RI-370-G2c, Durand-1753. Similar to W-RI-1130-001-G010 but with different date and engraver imprint. July 1, 1862.

Rarity: URS-3
VF $400

$2 • W-RI-1130-002-G020

Left: TWO / Allegorical woman. *Center:* Spread eagle on U.S. shield. *Right:* 2 / Farmer with corn. *Engraver:* Toppan, Carpenter & Co. *Comments:* H-RI-370-G4, Durand-1756. 18__. 1850s.

Rarity: *None known*

$2 • W-RI-1130-002-G020a

Overprint: Red TWO. *Engraver:* Toppan, Carpenter & Co. / ABNCo. monogram. *Comments:* H-RI-370-G4b, Durand-1757. Similar to W-RI-1130-002-G020 but with additional engraver imprint. 18__. 1850s–1860s.

Rarity: URS-3
VF $400

$2 • W-RI-1130-002-G020b CJF

Overprint: Green panel outlining TWO. *Engraver:* American Bank Note Co. *Comments:* H-RI-370-G4c, Durand-1758. Similar to W-RI-1130-002-G020 but with different date and engraver imprint. July 1st, 1862.

Rarity: URS-3
VF $750

$3 • W-RI-1130-003-G030

Left: THREE / Justice. *Center:* Steamship and other vessels. *Right:* 3 / Girl feeding chickens. *Engraver:* Toppan, Carpenter & Co. *Comments:* H-RI-370-G6, Durand-1759. 18__. 1850s.

Rarity: *None known*

$3 • W-RI-1130-003-G030a

Overprint: Red THREE. *Engraver:* Toppan, Carpenter & Co. /ABNCo. monogram. *Comments:* H-RI-370-G6b, Durand-1760. Similar to W-RI-1130-003-G030 but with additional engraver imprint. 18__. 1850s–1860s.

Rarity: *None known*

$3 • W-RI-1130-003-G030b

Overprint: Green panel outlining THREE. *Engraver:* American Bank Note Co. *Comments:* H-RI-370-G6c, Durand-1761. Similar to W-RI-1130-003-G030 but with different date and engraver imprint. July 1, 1862.

Rarity: *None known*

$5 • W-RI-1130-005-G040

Center: "Dr. Kane's Arctic Expedition". *Right:* 5 / Woman feeding cows. *Engraver:* Toppan, Carpenter & Co. *Comments:* H-RI-370-G8, Durand-1764. 18__. 1850s.

Rarity: URS-3
Proof $3,000

$5 • W-RI-1130-005-G040a

Overprint: Red FIVE. *Engraver:* Toppan, Carpenter & Co. / ABNCo. monogram. *Comments:* H-RI-370-G8b, Durand-1763. Similar to W-RI-1130-005-G040 but with additional engraver imprint. 18__. 1850s–1860s.

Rarity: *None known*

$5 • W-RI-1130-005-G040b CC

Tint: Green counters. *Engraver:* American Bank Note Co. *Comments:* H-RI-370-G8c, Durand-1762. Similar to W-RI-1130-005-G040 but with different date and engraver imprint. July 1st, 1862.

Rarity: URS-3
F $1,900
Selected auction price: Stack's Bowers Galleries, January 2011, F $1,896

$10 • W-RI-1130-010-G050 CJF

Engraver: Toppan, Carpenter & Co. *Comments:* H-RI-370-G10, Durand-1767. 18__. 1850s.

Rarity: URS-3
Proof $3,000

$50 • W-RI-1130-050-G060

Left: 50 / Beaver. *Center:* Farmers at lunch. *Right:* 50 / Dogs hunting. *Engraver:* Toppan, Carpenter & Co. *Comments:* H-RI-370-G12, Durand-1770. 18__. 1850s.

Rarity: *None known*

$100 • W-RI-1130-100-G070

Left: 100 / Deer. *Center:* Surveyors. *Right:* Men building railroad. *Engraver:* Toppan, Carpenter & Co. *Comments:* H-RI-370-G14, Durand-1771. 18__. 1850s.

Rarity: *None known*

$500 • W-RI-1130-500-G080

Left: 500 / Bull. *Center:* Horses at trough. *Right:* 500 / Indian. *Engraver:* Toppan, Carpenter & Co. *Comments:* H-RI-370-G16, Durand-1772. 18__. 1850s.

Rarity: *None known*

$1,000 • W-RI-1130-1000-G090

Left: 1000 / Indian on horseback. *Center:* "Signing of the First Constitution" on the Mayflower. *Right:* 1000 / Dog and strongbox. *Engraver:* Toppan, Carpenter & Co. *Comments:* H-RI-370-G18, Durand-1773. 18__. 1850s.

Rarity: *None known*

NON-VALID ISSUES

$1 • W-RI-1130-001-N010

Center: Indian woman seated with shield and bow and arrows, Cotton bales. *Comments:* H-RI-370-N5, Durand-1755. Altered or spurious. 1850s.

Rarity: *None known*

$5 • W-RI-1130-005-R010

Comments: H-Unlisted, Durand-1765. Raised from W-RI-1130-001-G010. 1850s.

Rarity: URS-3

$5 • W-RI-1130-005-N020

Center: Indian woman seated with shield and bow and arrows, Cotton bales. *Comments:* H-RI-370-N10, Durand-1766. Altered or spurious. 1850s.

Rarity: *None known*

$10 • W-RI-1130-010-R020

Engraver: Toppan, Carpenter & Co. *Comments:* H-RI-370-R5. Raised from W-RI-1130-001-G010 series. 18__. 1850s.

Rarity: *None known*

$10 • W-RI-1130-010-R030

Center: Indian woman seated with shield and bow and arrows, Cotton bales. *Comments:* H-RI-370-N20, Durand-1769. Raised from W-RI-1130-001-N010. 1850s.

Rarity: *None known*

$10 • W-RI-1130-010-N030

Center: Indian woman seated with shield and bow and arrows, Cotton bales. *Comments:* H-RI-370-N15, Durand-1768. Altered or spurious. 1850s.

Rarity: *None known*

Pawtuxet Bank
1814–1882
W-RI-1140

History: The Pawtuxet Bank was incorporated at Pawtuxet in October 1814. The founding president was James Rhodes, and Samuel E. Gardiner was the first cashier. Its location was changed to Providence in June 1845. In 1856 it was located at 41 Westminster Street.

The capital of the bank was $118,387 in 1848, $129,850 in 1849, and $150,000 by 1855. Circulation was $51,278 in 1849, but it was reduced to $14,445 by 1857. Specie totaled $2,413.55 the same year.

The Pawtuxet Bank continued as a state bank until it was liquidated in 1882. The original bank building is still standing today.

See also listing under Pawtuxet, W-RI-740.

VALID ISSUES

$1 • W-RI-1140-001-G010

Left: Indian, State arms, Woodcutter / 1. *Center:* 1. *Bottom center:* Plow and sheaf. *Right:* 1 / Bull's head. *Engraver:* Rawdon, Wright, Hatch & Edson. *Comments:* H-RI-225-G56, Durand-1785. 18__. 1840s–1850s.

Rarity: *None known*

$1 • W-RI-1140-001-G010a

Overprint: Red ONE. *Engraver:* Rawdon, Wright, Hatch & Edson. *Comments:* H-RI-225-G56a. Similar to W-RI-1140-001-G010. 18__. 1850s.

Rarity: URS-3

VF $400

$1 • W-RI-1140-001-G010b   SI

Overprint: Red ONE. *Engraver:* American Bank Note Co. *Comments:* H-RI-225-G56c. Similar to W-RI-1140-001-G010 but with different engraver imprint. 18__. 1860s.

Rarity: URS-1

VF $1,000

$1 • W-RI-1140-001-G020   CJF

Engraver: New England Bank Note Co. *Comments:* H-Unlisted. 18__. 1840s.

Rarity: URS-1

VG $300; **VF** $500

$2 • W-RI-1140-002-G030

Left: Woman with eagle and shield / 2. *Center:* 2. *Bottom center:* Shield bearing anchor. *Right:* TWO / Sailing vessel. *Engraver:* Rawdon, Wright, Hatch & Edson. *Comments:* H-RI-225-G60. 18__. 1840–1850s.

Rarity: *None known*

$2 • W-RI-1140-002-G030a

Overprint: Red TWO. *Engraver:* Rawdon, Wright, Hatch & Edson. *Comments:* H-RI-225-G60a, Durand-1786. Similar to W-RI-1140-002-G030. 18__. 1850s.

Rarity: *None known*

$2 • W-RI-1140-002-G030b

CJF

Overprint: Red TWO. *Engraver:* American Bank Note Co. *Comments:* H-RI-225-G60c. Similar to W-RI-1140-002-G030 but with different engraver imprint. 18__. 1860s.

Rarity: URS-1
VF $1,250

$3 • W-RI-1140-003-G040

Left: THREE / Farmer and milkmaid / 3. *Center:* Medallion head / 3 / Medallion head. *Right:* 3 / Female portrait. *Engraver:* Rawdon, Wright, Hatch & Edson. *Comments:* H-RI-225-G64, Durand-1787. 18__. 1840s–1850s.

Rarity: *None known*

$3 • W-RI-1140-003-G040a

Overprint: Red THREE. *Engraver:* Rawdon, Wright, Hatch & Edson. *Comments:* H-RI-225-G64a. Similar to W-RI-1140-003-G040. 18__. 1850s.

Rarity: *None known*

$3 • W-RI-1140-003-G040b

Overprint: Red THREE. *Engraver:* American Bank Note Co. *Comments:* H-RI-225-G64c. Similar to W-RI-1140-003-G040 but with different engraver imprint. 18__. 1860s.

Rarity: *None known*

$5 • W-RI-1140-005-G050

Left: Steamboat and other vessels / FIVE. *Center:* Ceres seated in V. *Right:* 5 / Sailor. *Engraver:* Rawdon, Wright, Hatch & Edson. *Comments:* H-RI-225-G68. 18__. 1840s–1850s.

Rarity: *None known*

$5 • W-RI-1140-005-G050a

Overprint: Red FIVE. *Engraver:* Rawdon, Wright, Hatch & Edson. *Comments:* H-RI-225-G68a, Durand-1788. Similar to W-RI-1140-005-G050. 18__. 1850s.

Rarity: *None known*

$5 • W-RI-1140-005-G050b

TD

Overprint: Red FIVE. *Engraver:* Rawdon, Wright, Hatch & Edson / New England Bank Note Co. *Comments:* H-Unlisted, Durand-Unlisted. Similar to W-RI-1140-005-G050 but with additional engraver imprint and different date. Jan.y __, 18__. 1860s.

Rarity: URS-1
VF $1,250

$5 • W-RI-1140-005-G050c

Overprint: Red FIVE. *Engraver:* American Bank Note Co. *Comments:* H-RI-225-G68c. Similar to W-RI-1140-005-G050 but with different engraver imprint. 18__. 1860s.

Rarity: *None known*

$10 • W-RI-1140-010-G060

Left: 10 / X / 10. *Center:* 10 / Yoke of oxen, Farmer. *Right:* TEN / Goddess of Plenty. *Engraver:* New England Bank Note Co. *Comments:* H-RI-225-G72, Durand-1789. 18__. 1840s–1850s.

Rarity: *None known*

$10 • W-RI-1140-010-G070

Left: 10 / Female portrait / TEN. *Center:* Allegorical figure between 1 and 0. *Right:* 10 / Female portrait / TEN. *Engraver:* Rawdon, Wright, Hatch & Edson. *Comments:* H-RI-225-G74, Durand-1790. 18__. 1850s–1860s.

Rarity: *None known*

$10 • W-RI-1140-010-G080

Left: TEN vertically. *Center:* Die with X / Shield of Hope surmounted by eagle flanked by Justice and Agriculture, Farmers, sheep, and cattle. *Right:* 10 / Sailing ship and steamship / 10. *Comments:* H-Unlisted, Durand-1791. 1850s.

Rarity: URS-3

$20 • W-RI-1140-020-G090

Left: TWENTY vertically. *Center:* Cows lying down, Sheep and shepherd. *Right:* XX / Sailing ship and steamboat / XX. *Engraver:* Terry, Pelton & Co. *Comments:* H-RI-225-G78, Durand-1795. 18__. 1840s.

Rarity: *None known*

$20 • W-RI-1140-020-G100

SI

Engraver: New England Bank Note Co. **Comments:** H-RI-225-G80, Durand-1794. A note of this design exists from the Pawtuxet Bank, Providence, Massachusetts, apparently an error. 18__. 1840s–1860s.

Rarity: URS-1
Proof $1,500

$50 • W-RI-1140-050-G110

Left: Minerva / 50. **Center:** Ceres and Vulcan seated. **Right:** 50 / Cherub steering sailboat / 50. **Engraver:** Rawdon, Wright, Hatch & Edson. **Comments:** H-RI-225-G84, Durand-1796. 18__. 1850s–1860s.

Rarity: *None known*

$100 • W-RI-1140-100-G120

Left: 100 / Vulcan seated. **Center:** Spread eagle on tree limb, Canal scene and train. **Right:** 100 / Ceres. **Overprint:** Red HUNDRED. **Engraver:** Rawdon, Wright, Hatch & Edson. **Comments:** H-RI-225-G88a, Durand-1797. 18__. 1850s–1860s.

Rarity: *None known*

NON-VALID ISSUES

$10 • W-RI-1140-010-R010

Engraver: Rawdon, Wright, Hatch & Edson. **Comments:** H-RI-225-R5, Durand-1792. Raised from W-RI-1140-001-G010. 18__. 1850s.

Rarity: *None known*

$100 • W-RI-1140-100-C120

CJF

Overprint: Red HUNDRED. **Engraver:** Rawdon, Wright, Hatch & Edson. **Comments:** H-RI-225-C88a, Durand-1798. Counterfeit of W-RI-1140-100-G120. 18__. 1860s.

Rarity: URS-5
VF $250

Phenix Bank
1840s–1850s
W-RI-1150

History: A non-existent bank represented only by notes altered from those of other banks. The notes were intended to pass for those of Phenix Bank of Providence, W-RI-1160.

ISSUES

$1 • W-RI-1150-001-A010

QDB

Overprint: Red ONE. **Engraver:** Wellstood, Hay & Whiting. **Comments:** H-RI-374-A5, Durand-1801. Altered from $1 Thames Bank, Laurel, Indiana. August12th, 185_. 1859.

Rarity: URS-6
VF $500

$1 • W-RI-1150-001-A020

Left: ONE / Two Indians / 1. **Center:** 1 / Liberty, Justice, and Knowledge / 1. **Right:** 1 / Portrait of George Washington / ONE. **Engraver:** Terry, Pelton & Co. **Comments:** H-RI-374-A10, Durand-1802. 18__. 1830s–1840s.

Rarity: *None known*

$2 • W-RI-1150-002-AR010

Left: 2 / Milkmaid with bucket. **Center:** Cows and horse, Train. **Bottom center:** Obverse of U.S. gold dollar. **Right:** TWO / Girl / 2. **Overprint:** Red TWO. **Engraver:** Wellstood, Hay & Whiting. **Comments:** H-RI-374-AR15, Durand-1806. Altered and raised from $1 Thames Bank, Laurel, Indiana. 1850s.

Rarity: *None known*

$2 • W-RI-1150-002-A030

Left: Justice, Ceres, and Commerce / 2. **Center:** 2. **Right:** 2 / Vulcan by cogwheel. **Overprint:** Red TWO. **Comments:** H-Unlisted, Durand-1805. 1850s.

Rarity: URS-5

$2 • W-RI-1150-002-A040

Left: TWO / Portrait of cherub / 2. **Center:** 2 / Ceres and Liberty, Ships / 2. **Right:** 2 / Portrait of cherub / TWO. **Engraver:** Terry, Pelton & Co. **Comments:** H-RI-374-A20, Durand-1807. Altered from $2 Citizens Bank, Augusta, Maine, or from notes of other failed banks using the same plate. 18__. 1830s–1840s.

Rarity: *None known*

$5 • **W-RI-1150-005-A050**

Left: Portrait of Henry Clay / V. *Center:* Farmer feeding hogs. *Bottom center:* Dog. *Right:* 5 / Farmer carrying basket of corn. *Overprint:* Red FIVE. *Engraver:* Wellstood, Hay & Whiting. *Comments:* H-RI-374-A30, Durand-1815. Altered from $5 Thames Bank, Laurel, Indiana. Aug. 12, 185_. 1859.

Rarity: URS-5
VF $150

$5 • **W-RI-1150-005-A060**

Left: FIVE / Portrait of Benjamin Franklin / V. *Center:* 5 / Two allegorical women, Agricultural items, Ship. *Bottom center:* Anchor and implements. *Right:* V / Portrait of Marquis de Lafayette / FIVE. *Engraver:* Terry, Pelton & Co. *Comments:* H-RI-374-A35, Durand-1816. Altered from $5 Citizens Bank, Augusta, Maine, or from notes of other failed banks using the same plate. 18__. 1830s–1840s.

Rarity: *None known*

$5 • **W-RI-1150-005-A070**

Left: 5 / Portrait of George Washington held by cherub / 5. *Center:* Spread eagle and shield. *Right:* 5 / Indian and settler woman. *Comments:* H-Unlisted, Durand-1817. Altered from $10 Citizens Bank, Augusta, Maine. 1850s.

Rarity: URS-3

$10 • **W-RI-1150-010-A080**

Left: 10 / Portrait of George Washington held by cherub / 10. *Center:* X / Spread eagle and shield / X. *Right:* 10 / Indian and settler woman / 10. *Engraver:* Terry, Pelton & Co. *Comments:* H-RI-374-A40, Durand-1822. Altered from $10 Citizens Bank, Augusta, Maine. 18__. 1830s–1840s.

Rarity: *None known*

$20 • **W-RI-1150-020-A090**

Left: XX / Rowboat / XX. *Center:* Plowing scene, Woman and Indian, Beehive. *Right:* XX / Harvest scene / XX. *Engraver:* Terry, Pelton & Co. *Comments:* H-RI-374-A45, Durand-1825. Altered from $20 Citizens Bank, Augusta, Maine, or from notes of other failed banks using the same plate. 18__. 1830s–1840s.

Rarity: *None known*

Phenix Bank of Providence
1833–1865
W-RI-1160

History: The Farmers and Mechanics Bank, W-RI-710, which failed in 1829, was reorganized as the Phenix Bank of Providence and moved to Providence. There, a new institution was formed under the forfeited charter and commenced business.[69] The capital of the bank was $300,000 in 1855 and $380,000 by 1857. Circulation was $70,389 in 1857. Specie amounted to $6,690.82.

The business of the Phenix Bank of Providence was succeeded by the National Phenix Bank, chartered on May 18, 1865.

Numismatic Commentary: Genuine signed and dated notes are available in the marketplace, and some Proof notes have also come available.

VALID ISSUES

$1 • **W-RI-1160-001-G010**

Engraver: Terry, Pelton & Co. *Comments:* H-RI-375-G4, Durand-1799. No description available. First issue. 18__. 1830s–1840s.

Rarity: *None known*

$1 • **W-RI-1160-001-G020**

SBG

Engraver: Toppan, Carpenter, Casilear & Co. *Comments:* H-RI-375-G6. 18__. 1850s.

Rarity: URS-2
Proof $2,000
Selected auction price: Stack's Bowers Galleries, March 2013, Proof $1,900

$1 • **W-RI-1160-001-G020a**

Overprint: Red ONE. *Engraver:* Toppan, Carpenter, Casilear & Co. *Comments:* H-RI-375-G6a, Durand-1800. Similar to W-RI-1160-001-G020. 18__. 1850s.

Rarity: *None known*

$1 • **W-RI-1160-001-G020b**

Overprint: Red ONE. *Engraver:* Toppan, Carpenter, Casilear & Co. / ABNCo. monogram. *Comments:* H-RI-375-G6b. Similar to W-RI-1160-001-G020 but with additional engraver imprint. 18__. 1850s–1860s.

Rarity: *None known*

$1 • **W-RI-1160-001-G020c**

CC

Overprint: Red ONE. *Engraver:* American Bank Note Co. *Comments:* H-RI-375-G6c. Similar to W-RI-1160-001-G020 but with different engraver imprint. 18__. 1860s.

Rarity: URS-3
VF $1,350
Selected auction price: Stack's Bowers Galleries, January 2011, VF $1,300

$2 • W-RI-1160-002-G030　　　CJF

Engraver: Terry, Pelton & Co. **Comments:** H-RI-375-G10, Durand-1804. 18__. 1830s–1840s.
Rarity: URS-3
VF $900

$2 • W-RI-1160-002-G040

Left: Justice, Ceres, and Commerce / 2. **Center:** 2. **Right:** 2 / Vulcan by cogwheel. **Engraver:** Toppan, Carpenter, Casilear & Co. **Comments:** H-RI-375-G12. 18__. 1850s.
Rarity: *None known*

$2 • W-RI-1160-002-G040a

Overprint: Red TWO. **Engraver:** Toppan, Carpenter, Casilear & Co. **Comments:** H-RI-375-G12a. Similar to W-RI-1160-002-G040. 18__. 1850s.
Rarity: *None known*

$2 • W-RI-1160-002-G040b

Engraver: Toppan, Carpenter, Casilear & Co. / ABNCo. monogram. **Comments:** H-RI-375-G12b. Similar to W-RI-1160-002-G040 but with additional engraver imprint. 18__. 1850s–1860s.
Rarity: *None known*

$2 • W-RI-1160-002-G040c　　　CJF

Overprint: Red TWO. **Engraver:** American Bank Note Co. **Comments:** H-RI-375-G12c, Durand-1805. Similar to W-RI-1160-002-G040 but with different engraver imprint. 18__. 1860s.
Rarity: URS-3
VF $400

$3 • W-RI-1160-003-G050

Engraver: Terry, Pelton & Co. **Comments:** H-RI-375-G16. No description available. 18__. 1830s–1840s.
Rarity: *None known*

$3 • W-RI-1160-003-G060　　　SBG

Engraver: Toppan, Carpenter, Casilear & Co. **Comments:** H-RI-375-G18. 18__. 1850s.
Rarity: URS-2
Proof $1,950
Selected auction price: Stack's Bowers Galleries, March 2013, Proof $1,936

$3 • W-RI-1160-003-G060a

Overprint: Red THREE. **Engraver:** Toppan, Carpenter, Casilear & Co. **Comments:** H-RI-375-G18a, Durand-1809. Similar to W-RI-1160-003-G060. 18__. 1850s.
Rarity: URS-3
VF $400

$3 • W-RI-1160-003-G060b

Overprint: Red THREE. **Engraver:** Toppan, Carpenter, Casilear & Co. / ABNCo. monogram. **Comments:** H-RI-375-G18b. Similar to W-RI-1160-003-G060 but with additional engraver imprint. 18__. 1850s–1860s.
Rarity: *None known*

$3 • W-RI-1160-003-G060c

Overprint: Red THREE. **Engraver:** American Bank Note Co. **Comments:** H-RI-375-G18c. Similar to W-RI-1160-003-G060 but with different engraver imprint. 18__. 1860s.
Rarity: *None known*

$5 • W-RI-1160-005-G070　　　CC

Engraver: Terry, Pelton & Co. **Comments:** H-RI-375-G22, Durand-1813. 18__. 1830s–1840s.
Rarity: URS-3
Proof $750

$5 • W-RI-1160-005-G080

Left: V / Three sailors on shore, Boat / V. **Center:** FIVE on die / Train. **Bottom center:** Phoenix. **Right:** V / "Battle of Lake Erie" / V. **Engraver:** Terry, Pelton & Co. **Comments:** H-RI-375-G24, Durand-1812. 18__. 1830s–1840s.
Rarity: URS-3
VF $400

$5 • **W-RI-1160-005-G090**

Left: FIVE / Ceres / FIVE. *Center:* Spread eagle on shield / 5. *Right:* 5 / Liberty. *Engraver:* Toppan, Carpenter, Casilear & Co. *Comments:* H-RI-375-G28. 18__. 1850s.

Rarity: *None known*

$5 • **W-RI-1160-005-G090a**

Overprint: Red FIVE. *Engraver:* Toppan, Carpenter, Casilear & Co. *Comments:* H-RI-375-G28a, Durand-1814. Similar to W-RI-1160-005-G090. 18__. 1850s.

Rarity: *None known*

$5 • **W-RI-1160-005-G090b**

Overprint: Red FIVE. *Engraver:* Toppan, Carpenter, Casilear & Co. / ABNCo. monogram. *Comments:* H-RI-375-G28b. Similar to W-RI-1160-005-G090 but with additional engraver imprint. 18__. 1860s.

Rarity: URS-3
VF $400

$10 • **W-RI-1160-010-G100**   SBG

Engraver: Terry, Pelton & Co. *Comments:* H-RI-375-G32, Durand-1819. 18__. 1830s–1840s.

Rarity: URS-3
Proof $750

$10 • **W-RI-1160-010-G110**   CJF

Engraver: Toppan, Carpenter, Casilear & Co. *Comments:* H-RI-375-G36, Durand-1820. 18__. 1850s.

Rarity: URS-3
Proof $750

$10 • **W-RI-1160-010-G110a**

Left: X / Portrait of George Washington / 10. *Center:* 10 / Liberty, eagle, and shield. *Bottom center:* Phoenix. *Right:* 10 / Commerce. *Overprint:* Red TEN. *Engraver:* Toppan, Carpenter, Casilear & Co. *Comments:* H-RI-375-G36a, Durand-1821. Similar to W-RI-1160-010-G110. 18__. 1850s.

Rarity: *None known*

$10 • **W-RI-1160-010-G110b**   CC

Overprint: Red TEN. *Engraver:* Toppan, Carpenter, Casilear & Co. / ABNCo. monogram. *Comments:* H-RI-375-G36b. Similar to W-RI-1160-010-G110 but with additional engraver imprint. 18__. 1860s.

Rarity: URS-3
VF $900
Selected auction price: Stack's Bowers Galleries, January 2010, VF $889

$20 • **W-RI-1160-020-G120**

Engraver: Terry, Pelton & Co. *Comments:* H-RI-375-G38. No description available. 18__. 1830s–1840s.

Rarity: *None known*

$20 • **W-RI-1160-020-G130**   CJF

Engraver: Toppan, Carpenter, Casilear & Co. *Comments:* H-RI-375-G40, Durand-1824. 18__. 1850s–1860s.

Rarity: URS-3
VF $400; **Proof** $1,900
Selected auction price: Spink-Smythe, April 2009, Proof $1,852

$50 • **W-RI-1160-050-G140**   CC

Engraver: Terry, Pelton & Co. *Comments:* H-RI-375-G44, Durand-1826. 18__. 1830s–1840s.

Rarity: URS-3
Proof $1,200
Selected auction price: Spink-Smythe, April 2009, Proof $1,173

$50 • W-RI-1160-050-G150

SBG

Engraver: Toppan, Carpenter, Casilear & Co. *Comments:* H-RI-375-G46, Durand-1827. 18__. 1850s–1860s.
Rarity: URS-3
Proof $2,200
Selected auction price: Stack's Bowers Galleries, October 2011, Proof $2,132

$100 • W-RI-1160-100-G160

SBG

Engraver: Terry, Pelton & Co. *Comments:* H-RI-375-G50, Durand-1829. 18__. 1830s–1840s.
Rarity: URS-3
Proof $500

$100 • W-RI-1160-100-G170

SBG

Engraver: Toppan, Carpenter, Casilear & Co. *Comments:* H-RI-375-G52, Durand-1830. 18__. 1850s–1860s.
Rarity: URS-2
Proof $4,300
Selected auction price: Stack's Bowers Galleries, March 2013, Proof $4,235

$500 • W-RI-1160-500-G180

Left: Sailing ship / D. *Center:* 500 on die / 500. *Bottom center:* Female portrait. *Right:* Sailor seated on bale, Spyglass. *Engraver:* Toppan, Carpenter, Casilear & Co. *Comments:* H-RI-375-G54, Durand-1831. 18__. 1850s–1860s.
Rarity: *None known*

Uncut Sheets

$5-$10 • W-RI-1160-005.010-US010

CC

Engraver: Terry, Pelton & Co. *Comments:* H-RI-375-G22, G32. 18__. 1830s–1840s.
Rarity: URS-1
Proof $3,500

Non-Valid Issues

$1 • W-RI-1160-001-N010

Center: Sailing ship. *Comments:* H-RI-375-N5, Durand-1803. Altered or spurious. 1850s.
Rarity: *None known*

$2 • W-RI-1160-002-N020

Center: Man and ship. *Comments:* H-RI-375-N10, Durand-1808. Altered or spurious. 1850s.
Rarity: *None known*

$3 • W-RI-1160-003-N030

Center: Man and ship. *Comments:* H-RI-375-N15, Durand-1811. Altered or spurious. 1850s.
Rarity: *None known*

$5 • W-RI-1160-005-N040

Center: Man and ship. *Comments:* H-RI-375-N18, Durand-1818. Altered or spurious. 1850s.
Rarity: *None known*

$10 • W-RI-1160-010-N050

Center: Man and ship. *Comments:* H-RI-375-N20, Durand-1823. Altered or spurious. 1850s.
Rarity: *None known*

$50 • W-RI-1160-050-N060

Center: Man and ship. *Comments:* H-RI-375-N25, Durand-1828. Altered or spurious. 1850s.
Rarity: *None known*

Phoenix Bank
1840s
W-RI-1165

History: A non-existent bank represented only by fraudulent notes or notes altered from those of other banks.

Issues

$3 • W-RI-1165-003-A010

CJF

Engraver: Terry, Pelton & Co. *Comments:* H-RI-374-A25, Durand-1810. Altered from $3 Citizens Bank, Augusta, Maine. 18__. 1841.

Rarity: URS-3
VF $250

Providence Bank
1791–1865
W-RI-1170

History: The Providence Bank, the oldest bank in Rhode Island and the fifth oldest bank in the country, was incorporated in October 1791. It had a close association with the Providence Insurance Company, and the bank was relied on to supply capital for unexpected large claims, usually from the shipping industry.

The birth of the Providence Bank had its inception when Jabez Bowen, John Brown, and John Jenks, as well as other merchants, endeavored to found a bank in Providence in 1784. Plans were made and subscriptions were solicited through advertisements and other means. The necessary capital was not raised, and the plans were abandoned for a time. Seven years later, the ever-active John Brown was still pursuing the idea of a bank for the city of Providence.

In 1791 the plans for the bank were presented to the city and adopted. The directors chose a location on Hopkins Street.[70] The bank remained at this location until 1801, when it moved to South Main Street, where it remained for the next 125 years.

Authorized capital was $400,000 in 1791, increased to $450,000 in 1813, and was up to $500,000 by 1848. Circulation was reported at $128,300 in 1849, $112,253 in 1857, and $170,673 in 1862. Specie was reported to be $41,050.37 in 1857.

The business of the long-lived Providence Bank was succeeded by the Providence National Bank in 1865.

Numismatic Commentary: 56 genuine issues have been recorded for this issuer. There is plenty of opportunity to locate some of these issues in the marketplace.

Remaining in the American Bank Note Co. archives as of 2003 was a $1-$1-$2-$3 tint plate and a $10-$10-$10-$20 tint plate.

Valid Issues

$1 • W-RI-1170-001-G010

Center: 1 / 1 / ONE, Eagle on anchor / 1 / 1. *Comments:* H-RI-380-G10, Durand-1833. 18__. 1800s–1810s.
Rarity: *None known*

$1 • W-RI-1170-001-G020

QDB

Engraver: Leney & Rollinson. *Comments:* H-RI-380-G14, Durand-1834. 18__. 1810s–1820s.
Rarity: URS-3
Proof $1,400
Selected auction price: Spink-Smythe, April 2009, Proof $1,358

$1 • W-RI-1170-001-G030

SBG

Engraver: Durand, Perkins & Co. *Comments:* H-RI-380-G16, Durand-1835. 18__. 1820s–1830s.
Rarity: URS-3
VF $500; **Proof** $1,400

$1 • W-RI-1170-001-G030a

Engraver: Durand, Perkins & Co. *Comments:* H-RI-380-G16a, Durand-1836. Similar to W-RI-1170-001-G030 but with "Incorporated in 1791". 18__. 1830s.
Rarity: URS-3
VF $1,000

$1 • W-RI-1170-001-G040

Left: ONE / 1 / ONE. *Center:* Man seated on rock, Ship under sail. *Bottom center:* Anchor on shield. *Right:* 1 / Indian, State arms, Woman / 1. *Engraver:* Rawdon, Wright, Hatch & Co. *Comments:* H-RI-380-G20, Durand-1837. 18__. 1840s.
Rarity: *None known*

$1 • W-RI-1170-001-G050

Left: 1 / Woman seated. *Center:* Woman reclining with shield bearing anchor, Houses. *Right:* ONE / Woman seated with bolt of cloth. *Engraver:* Wellstood, Hanks, Hay & Whiting. *Comments:* H-RI-380-G22, Durand-1838. 185_. 1850s.
Rarity: URS-3
Proof $600

$1 • W-RI-1170-001-G050a

Overprint: Red ONE. *Engraver:* Wellstood, Hanks, Hay & Whiting. *Comments:* H-RI-380-G22a, Durand-1839. Similar to W-RI-1170-001-G050. 185_. 1850s.
Rarity: URS-3
VF $350

$1 • W-RI-1170-001-G050b

CJF

Tint: Green ONE. *Engraver:* American Bank Note Co. *Comments:* H-RI-380-G22c, Durand-1840. Similar to W-RI-1170-001-G050 but with different date and engraver imprint. August 1st, 1863.

Rarity: URS-3
VF $500

$2 • W-RI-1170-002-G060

Comments: H-Unlisted, Durand-1842. No description available. 1850s.

Rarity: *None known*

$2 • W-RI-1170-002-G070

Engraver: Wellstood, Hanks, Hay & Whiting. *Comments:* H-RI-380-G24, Durand-1843. No description available. 18__. 1800s–1810s.

Rarity: *None known*

$2 • W-RI-1170-002-G080

Comments: H-Unlisted, Durand-1844. No description available. 1810s–1820s.

Rarity: *None known*

$2 • W-RI-1170-002-G090

Left: 2 TWO 2 vertically. *Center:* 2 / Printing press / 2. *Bottom center:* 2. *Right:* TWO vertically. *Engraver:* Leney & Rollinson. *Comments:* H-RI-380-G26. 18__. 1810s–1820s.

Rarity: URS-3
Proof $1,200

$2 • W-RI-1170-002-G100

Left: 2 / Scene vertically / 2. *Right:* 2 / Woman seated with shield bearing anchor / 2. *Engraver:* Durand, Perkins & Co. *Comments:* H-RI-380-G28. 18__. 1820s–1830s.

Rarity: URS-3
Proof $1,200

$2 • W-RI-1170-002-G110

Left: Figure in 2. *Center:* Liberty, State arms. *Bottom center:* Anchor on shield. *Right:* TWO / 2 / TWO. *Engraver:* Rawdon, Wright & Hatch. *Comments:* H-RI-380-G30, Durand-1845. 18__. 1840s–1850s.

Rarity: *None known*

$2 • W-RI-1170-002-G120

CC

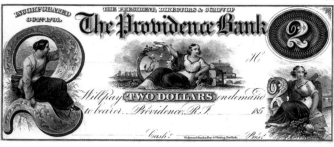

Engraver: Wellstood, Hanks, Hay & Whiting. *Comments:* H-RI-380-G32, Durand-1846. 185_. 1850s.

Rarity: URS-1
Proof $2,200

$2 • W-RI-1170-002-G120a

CC

Overprint: Red TWO. *Engraver:* Wellstood, Hanks, Hay & Whiting. *Comments:* H-RI-380-G32a, Durand-1847. Similar to W-RI-1170-002-G120. 185_. 1850s.

Rarity: URS-3
Proof $1,700
Selected auction price: Stack's Bowers Galleries, January 2011, Proof $1,658

$2 • W-RI-1170-002-G120b

Tint: Green TWO. *Engraver:* American Bank Note Co. *Comments:* H-RI-380-G32c, Durand-1848. Similar to W-RI-1170-002-G120 but with different date and engraver imprint. Aug. 1, 1863.

Rarity: *None known*

$3 • W-RI-1170-003-G130

Comments: H-Unlisted, Durand-1850. No description available. 1810s–1820s.

Rarity: *None known*

$3 • W-RI-1170-003-G140

Comments: H-Unlisted, Durand-1851. No description available. 1810s–1820s.

Rarity: *None known*

$3 • W-RI-1170-003-G150

Comments: H-Unlisted, Durand-1852. No description available. 1810s–1820s.

Rarity: *None known*

$3 • W-RI-1170-003-G160

Left: III THREE III vertically. *Center:* 3 / Loom / 3. *Bottom center:* 3. *Right:* THREE vertically. *Engraver:* Leney & Rollinson. *Comments:* H-RI-380-G36. 18__. 1810s–1820s.

Rarity: URS-3
Proof $1,200

$3 • W-RI-1170-003-G170

Left: III / 3 / III. *Center:* Allegorical woman, State arms. *Bottom center:* 3. *Right:* Allegorical figure in 3. *Engraver:* Rawdon, Wright & Hatch. *Comments:* H-RI-380-G40, Durand-1853. 18__. 1840s–1850s.

Rarity: *None known*

$3 • W-RI-1170-003-G180

SI

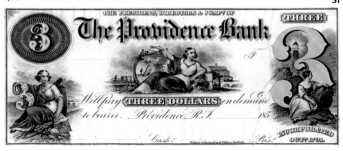

Engraver: Wellstood, Hanks, Hay & Whiting. *Comments:* H-RI-380-G42, Durand-1854. 185_. 1850s.

Rarity: URS-1
Proof $1,200

$3 • W-RI-1170-003-G180a

SBG

Overprint: Red THREE. *Engraver:* Wellstood, Hanks, Hay & Whiting. *Comments:* H-RI-380-G42a, Durand-1855. Similar to W-RI-1170-003-G180. 185_. 1850s.

Rarity: URS-3
Proof $800

$3 • W-RI-1170-003-G180b

Tint: Green THREE. *Engraver:* American Bank Note Co. *Comments:* H-RI-380-G42c, Durand-1856. Similar to W-RI-1170-003-G180 but with different date and engraver imprint. Aug. 1, 1863.

Rarity: *None known*

$5 • W-RI-1170-005-G190

Left: FIVE D vertically. *Center:* 5 / Sailing ship / FIVE D / Plow. *Right:* 5 vertically. *Comments:* H-RI-380-G48, Durand-1858. 18__. 1800s.

Rarity: *None known*

$5 • W-RI-1170-005-G200

Left: 5 FIVE 5 vertically. *Center:* Woman seated / FIVE / D / 5. *Right:* 5 / Anchor / FIVE. *Comments:* H-RI-380-G52. 18__. 1810s.

Rarity: *None known*

$5 • W-RI-1170-005-G210

Left: FIVE vertically. *Center:* FIVE / 5 / Anchor, Woman seated by barrel. *Right:* FIVE / 5 / FIVE. *Comments:* H-RI-380-G54. 1810s.

Rarity: *None known*

$5 • W-RI-1170-005-G220

Left: FIVE vertically. *Center:* 5 / Woman seated on bale. *Right:* 5 / Anchor / FIVE. *Comments:* H-Unlisted, Durand-1859. 1810s.

Rarity: URS-3

$5 • W-RI-1170-005-G230

Left: FIVE vertically. *Center:* Anchor / FIVE / 5 on die. *Right:* FIVE over 5 / FIVE. *Comments:* H-Unlisted, Durand-1860. 1810s.

Rarity: URS-3

$5 • W-RI-1170-005-G240

Left: V FIVE V vertically. *Center:* 5 / Farming implements / V. *Bottom center:* 5 on die. *Right:* FIVE vertically. *Engraver:* Leney & Rollinson. *Comments:* H-RI-380-G58, Durand-1861. 18__. 1830s.

Rarity: *None known*

$5 • W-RI-1170-005-G250

Left: 5 / Man with helmet and cornucopia / FIVE. *Center:* Woman and cherub flanking 5 / FIVE / 5 on die. *Bottom center:* Shield with anchor. *Right:* FIVE / Woman standing with pole / FIVE. *Comments:* H-Unlisted, Durand-1862. 1830s.

Rarity: URS-3

$5 • W-RI-1170-005-G250a

Engraver: Rawdon, Wright & Hatch. *Comments:* H-RI-380-G62, Durand-1863. Similar to W-RI-1170-005-G250. 18__. 1840s–1850s.

Rarity: *None known*

$5 • W-RI-1170-005-G250b

Overprint: Red FIVE. *Engraver:* Rawdon, Wright & Hatch. *Comments:* H-RI-380-G62a, Durand-1865. Similar to W-RI-1170-005-G250. 18__. 1850s.

Rarity: URS-3
VF $400

$5 • W-RI-1170-005-G260

Left: FIVE / V and three allegorical women / 5. *Center:* Commerce, State arms. *Right:* FIVE / 5 and V on shield surmounted by two cherubs. *Engraver:* Wellstood, Hanks, Hay & Whiting. *Comments:* H-RI-380-G64, Durand-1864. 18__. 1850s.

Rarity: URS-3
Proof $400

$5 • W-RI-1170-005-G260a

Tint: Green FIVE. *Engraver:* Wellstood, Hanks, Hay & Whiting. *Comments:* H-Unlisted, Durand-1866. Similar to W-RI-1170-005-G260. 1850s.

Rarity: URS-3

$5 • W-RI-1170-005-G270

Left: 5. *Center:* Two sailboats. *Right:* 5. *Tint:* Green. *Engraver:* National Bank Note Co. *Comments:* H-RI-380-G66a, Durand-1867. Possibly never issued. 186_. 1860s.

Rarity: URS-3
Proof $4,000

$5 • W-RI-1170-005-G270a

Tint: Micro 5s and FIVEs. *Comments:* H-Unlisted, Durand-1868. Similar to W-RI-1170-005-G270. 1860s.

Rarity: URS-3

$5 • W-RI-1170-005-G280　　　　　　CC

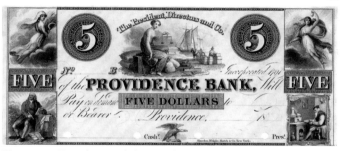

Engraver: Rawdon, Wright, Hatch & Co. *Comments:* H-Unlisted. 18__. 1860s.

Rarity: URS-2
Proof $1,500

$10 • W-RI-1170-010-G290

Left: TEN vertically. *Center:* 10 / Barrel, plow, and ship, Shield bearing anchor. *Right:* 10. *Comments:* H-RI-380-G68, Durand-1875. 18__. 1800s.

Rarity: URS-3

$10 • W-RI-1170-010-G300

Left: TEN vertically. *Center:* Dragon / TEN on die. *Right:* TEN on die / 10 / Anchor. *Comments:* H-RI-380-G70, Durand-1876. 18__. 1800s.

Rarity: *None known*

$10 • W-RI-1170-010-G310

Left: 10 on die. *Center:* Commerce, State arms. *Right:* 10 on die. *Comments:* H-Unlisted, Durand-1877. 1800s.

Rarity: URS-3

$10 • W-RI-1170-010-G320

Left: 10 / Indian woman with bow and quiver. *Center:* Cherub holding gold coin, Money, chest, cornucopia. *Right:* TEN / Minerva standing with left arm on shield / TEN. *Comments:* H-Unlisted, Durand-1878. Coin shown is a $10 gold piece representative of the denomination. 1800s.

Rarity: URS-3

$10 • W-RI-1170-010-G330

Left: 10 / Indian woman with bow and quiver / TEN. *Center:* TEN DOLLARS / Cherub holding gold coin, Money, chest, cornucopia / TEN DOLLARS. *Bottom center:* Anchor on shield. *Right:* 10 / Minerva standing with left arm on shield / TEN. *Engraver:* Unverified, but likely Rawdon, Wright & Hatch. *Comments:* H-RI-380-G76, Durand-1879. Coin shown is a $10 gold piece representative of the denomination. 18__. 1840s–1850s.

Rarity: *None known*

$10 • W-RI-1170-010-G340

Left: X / Woman holding scroll bearing Incorporated Oct. 1791 / X. *Center:* TEN DOLLARS across 10 on TEN. *Right:* 10 / Anchor of Hope. *Tint:* Panel and frame. *Engraver:* Wellstood, Hanks, Hay & Whiting. *Comments:* H-RI-380-G78, Durand-1880. 185_. 1850s.

Rarity: URS-3
Proof $350

$10 • W-RI-1170-010-G350

Left: X / Woman holding scroll / X. *Center:* TEN DOLLARS over 10. *Right:* 10. *Engraver:* American Bank Note Co. *Comments:* H-RI-380-G80a. March 4, 1861. 1860s.

Rarity: URS-3
Proof $2,000

$20 • W-RI-1170-020-G360

Left: Goddess of Plenty, Spread eagle. *Center:* XX / Ceres beside column / XX. *Bottom center:* Eagle. *Right:* Liberty / 20 / Spread eagle. *Comments:* H-RI-380-G90, Durand-1884. 18__. 1850s.

Rarity: *None known*

$20 • W-RI-1170-020-G370　　　　　　JF

Tint: Red 20 on green die outlining white TWENTY on red panel of microlettering. *Engraver:* American Bank Note Co. *Comments:* H-RI-380-G92, Durand-1885. March 4th, 1861.

Rarity: URS-3
Proof $4,000

$50 • W-RI-1170-050-G380

Left: FIFTY vertically. *Center:* State arms surmounted by wreath. *Right:* 50 / State arms / 50. *Comments:* H-RI-380-G98, Durand-1887. 18__. 1850s.

Rarity: *None known*

$50 • W-RI-1170-050-G390　　　　　　SBG

Comments: H-RI-380-G98, Durand-1887. 18__. 1850s.

Rarity: URS-1
Proof $3,700
Selected auction price: Stack's Bowers Galleries, March 2013, Proof $3,630

$100 • W-RI-1170-100-G400

Left: ONE HUNDRED vertically. *Center:* Liberty, State arms surmounted by wreath, Minerva. *Right:* 100 / State arms / 100. *Comments:* H-RI-380-G104, Durand-1889. 18__. 1850s.

Rarity: *None known*

$100 • W-RI-1170-100-G405

CC

Engraver: Fairman, Draper, Underwood & Co. *Comments:* H-Unlisted. 18__. 1800s.

Rarity: URS-1
Proof $2,500
Selected auction price: Stack's Bowers Galleries, October 2008, Proof $2,137

$500 • W-RI-1170-500-G410

Left: D / 500 on medallion head. *Center:* Allegorical figure and cherubs in clouds over city. *Bottom center:* 500. *Right:* 500 / 500 on medallion head / 500. *Comments:* H-RI-380-G108, Durand-1891. 18__. 1850s–1860s.

Rarity: URS-1
Proof $4,000

$1,000 • W-RI-1170-1000-G420

Left: 1000 vertically. *Center:* Liberty, State arms surmounted by wreath, Minerva. *Right:* 1000 across M / 1000 on medallion head. *Comments:* H-RI-380-G112, Durand-1893. 18__. 1850s–1860s.

Rarity: *None known*

Post Notes

$50 • W-RI-1170-050-G430

Comments: H-Unlisted. No description available. 18__. 1820s.

Rarity: *None known*

$100 • W-RI-1170-100-G440

Comments: H-Unlisted. No description available. 18__. 1820s.

Rarity: *None known*

$500 • W-RI-1170-500-G450

Comments: H-Unlisted. No description available. 18__. 1820s.

Rarity: *None known*

Uncut Sheets

$2-$2-$2-$3 • W-RI-1170-002.002.002.003-US010

Vignette(s): ($2) Milkmaid seated in 2 / State arms / Commerce seated / Industry holding 2. ($2) Milkmaid seated in 2 / State arms / Commerce seated / Industry holding 2. ($2) Milkmaid seated in 2 / State arms / Commerce seated / Industry holding 2. ($3) Agriculture / State arms / Commerce seated / THREE / Lighthouse and rocks seen through 3, Woman seated. *Comments:* H-RI-380-G32a, G32a, G32a, G42a. 185_. 1850s.

Rarity: URS-3
Proof $4,000

Post Note Sheets

$100-$50-$500 • W-RI-1170-100.050.500-US020

Vignette(s): No description available. *Engraver:* Fairman, Draper, Underwood & Co. *Comments:* All unlisted in Haxby. 18__. 1820s.

Rarity: *None known*

$500-$100-$50 • W-RI-1170-500.100.050-US030

Vignette(s): No description available. *Engraver:* Fairman, Draper, Underwood & Co. *Comments:* All unlisted in Haxby. 18__. 1820s.

Rarity: *None known*

Non-Valid Issues

$1 • W-RI-1170-001-C010

Comments: H-RI-380-C10. Counterfeit of W-RI-1170-001-G010. 18__. 1811.

Rarity: URS-3
VF $150

$1 • W-RI-1170-001-S010

CC

Comments: H-RI-380-S5, Durand-1841. 18__. 1830s.

Rarity: URS-5
VF $150

How to Read the Whitman Numbering System

$1 • W-RI-010-001-G010a

Denomination: Value of the note shown.

W: Whitman number. This number is a sortable code unique to each bank and note.

RI: Abbreviation for the state under study.

010: Numerical designation specific to each bank.

001: The denomination in dollars.

G010a: G indicates a good or valid note. Other categories are indicated thus: C (counterfeit); R (raised); S (spurious); N (not-attributed); A (altered). Numbers are assigned starting with 010, 020, et seq. Terminal letters following the number indicate variations of a note: a series of different colored overprints, tints, payees, etc., all on the same design of note. For more information, see the "How to Use This Book" section at the front of the volume, page xiv.

$1 • W-RI-1170-001-A010

Left: 1 / Woman wearing bonnet, standing by pail / ONE. *Center:* Machinery and merchandise flanking Ceres holding sickle and rake, Factories and harbor / ONE. *Right:* 1 / Ship / ONE. *Engraver:* New England Bank Note Co. *Comments:* H-RI-380-A5. Altered from $1 Washington County Bank, Calais, Maine, or from notes of other failed banks using the same notes. 18__. 1830s.

Rarity: *None known*

$2 • W-RI-1170-002-N010

Left: 2. *Center:* Woman, eagle, ship. *Right:* Ship. *Comments:* H-RI-380-N5, Durand-1849. Altered or spurious. 1830s.

Rarity: URS-3

$3 • W-RI-1170-003-N020

Left: 2. *Center:* Woman, eagle, ship. *Right:* Ship. *Comments:* H-RI-380-N10, Durand-1857. 1830s.

Rarity: *None known*

$5 • W-RI-1170-005-C190

SBG

Comments: H-RI-380-C48, Durand-1870. Counterfeit of W-RI-1170-005-G190. 18__. 1800s.

Rarity: URS-3
VF $150

$5 • W-RI-1170-005-C200

CJF

Comments: H-RI-380-C52. Counterfeit of W-RI-1170-005-G200. 18__. 1812.

Rarity: URS-3
VF $150

$5 • W-RI-1170-005-C210

Comments: H-RI-380-C54. Counterfeit of W-RI-1170-005-G210. 1813.

Rarity: *None known*

$5 • W-RI-1170-005-C230

Comments: H-Unlisted, Durand-1871. Counterfeit of W-RI-1170-005-G230. 1830s.

Rarity: URS-3

$5 • W-RI-1170-005-C240

TD

Engraver: Leney & Rollinson. *Comments:* H-RI-380-C58. Counterfeit of W-RI-1170-005-G240. 18__. 1820s–1830s.

Rarity: URS-3
VF $150

$5 • W-RI-1170-005-R010

Engraver: Durand, Perkins & Co. *Comments:* H-RI-380-R5, Durand-1872. Raised from W-RI-1170-001-G030 series. 18__. 1830s.

Rarity: *None known*

$5 • W-RI-1170-005-N030

Left: 5. *Center:* Woman, eagle, ship. *Right:* Ship. *Comments:* H-RI-380-N15, Durand-1874. Altered or spurious. 1830s.

Rarity: URS-3

$5 • W-RI-1170-005-N040

Center: 5 / Male portrait / 5. *Comments:* H-RI-380-N20. 1830s.

Rarity: *None known*

$5 • W-RI-1170-005-N050

Center: Train. *Comments:* H-RI-380-N25. 1830s.

Rarity: *None known*

$5 • W-RI-1170-005-A020

Left: V on FIVE / Farm family. *Center:* Men on log raft, Man in skiff. *Right:* 5 / Two women. *Tint:* Green-yellow. *Engraver:* Danforth, Wright & Co. *Comments:* H-RI-380-A10, Durand-1873. Altered from $5 Brownville Bank and Land Company, Omaha, Nebraska series. Sept. 1, 1857.

Rarity: *None known*

$10 • W-RI-1170-010-C290

Comments: H-RI-380-C68, Durand-1881. Counterfeit of W-RI-1170-010-G290. 18__. 1801.

Rarity: URS-3
VF $150

$10 • W-RI-1170-010-C300

NJW

Comments: H-RI-380-C70, Durand-1882. Counterfeit of W-RI-1170-010-G300. 18__. 1806.

Rarity: URS-5
VF $150

$10 • W-RI-1170-010-R020

Engraver: Durand, Perkins & Co. *Comments:* H-RI-380-R10, Durand-1883. Raised from W-RI-1170-001-G030 series. 18__. 1840s.

Rarity: *None known*

$20 • W-RI-1170-020-R030

Comments: H-Unlisted, Durand-1886. Raised from W-RI-1170-002-G120. 185_. 1850s.

Rarity: URS-3

$50 • W-RI-1170-050-R040

Engraver: Durand, Perkins & Co. *Comments:* H-RI-380-R15, Durand-1888. Raised from W-RI-1170-001-G030 series. 18__. 1850s.

Rarity: *None known*

$100 • W-RI-1170-100-R050

Engraver: Durand, Perkins & Co. *Comments:* H-RI-380-R20, Durand-1890. Raised from W-RI-1170-001-G030 series. 18__. 1850s.

Rarity: *None known*

$500 • W-RI-1170-500-S020

Left: 500 / Artists at work. *Center:* Portrait of George Washington / Allegorical woman, Beehive, Allegorical woman. *Bottom center:* 500. *Right:* 500 / Portrait of Martha Washington. *Comments:* H-RI-380-S10, Durand-1892. 1830s.

Rarity: *None known*

Roger Williams Bank
1803–1865
W-RI-1180

History: The Roger Williams Bank was incorporated in 1803. It was chartered as a direct result of political influence. President Thomas Jefferson assisted the bank due to the affiliations of its directors with his party. The members were all in good political standing with the Jefferson administration, and thus all the government deposits held by the Providence Bank were transferred to this bank and held there until 1817.[71]

The capital of the bank was $150,000 in 1803. By 1849 it was $499,950, rising again to $500,000 in 1857. In 1850 there were 6,666 shares of $75 each.[72] Circulation was at $65,352 in 1849 and $87,554 in 1862. Deposits amounted to $109,067, and money due banks was $19,646 in 1852. The bank was located at 23 Market Square in 1863.

The business of the Roger Williams Bank was succeeded by the Roger Williams National Bank, chartered on August 7, 1865.

Numismatic Commentary: Notes from this bank are elusive. The issues with large red overprints are the hardest to locate.

Remaining in the American Bank Note Co. archives as of 2003 was a $1-$1-$1-$2 face plate and a $3-$3-$5-$10 face plate.

VALID ISSUES

$1 • W-RI-1180-001-G010

Comments: H-RI-420-G2, Durand-1899. No description available. 18__. 1800s–1810s.

Rarity: *None known*

$1 • W-RI-1180-001-G020

Comments: H-Unlisted. No description available. 18__. 1800s–1810s.

Rarity: *None known*

$1 • W-RI-1180-001-G030   SBG

Engraver: Draper, Toppan, Longacre & Co. *Comments:* H-RI-420-G6, Durand-1900. Proprietary Proofs exist. 18__. 1830s–1850s.

Rarity: URS-3
Proof $1,700
Selected auction price: Spink-Smythe, April 2009, Proof $1,600

$1 • W-RI-1180-001-G030a   CJF

Engraver: Draper, Toppan, Longacre & Co. *Comments:* H-Unlisted, Durand-Unlisted. Similar to W-RI-1180-001-G030. Proof. 18__. 1830s–1850s.

Rarity: URS-3
F $1,000

$1 • W-RI-1180-001-G040   CJF

Tint: Red ONE and die outlining white 1. *Engraver:* National Bank Note Co. *Comments:* H-RI-420-G8a, Durand-1901. 186_. 1860s.

Rarity: URS-3
VF $1,500; **Proof** $3,000

$1 • **W-RI-1180-001-G050**

NJW

Engraver: Draper, Toppan, Longacre & Co. **Comments:** H-Unlisted, Durand-Unlisted. 18__. 1830s–1850s.

Rarity: URS-2
VF $1,250; **Proof** $1,500

$2 • **W-RI-1180-002-G060**

Left: TWO vertically. **Center:** Justice holding scales seated under tree / 2. **Right:** 2 vertically. **Comments:** H-RI-420-G12, Durand-1903. 18__. 1800s–1810s.

Rarity: *None known*

$2 • **W-RI-1180-002-G070**

CJF

Engraver: Draper, Toppan, Longacre & Co. **Comments:** H-RI-420-G16, Durand-1904. Proprietary Proofs exist. 18__. 1830s–1850s.

Rarity: URS-3
Proof $1,000

$2 • **W-RI-1180-002-G070a**

CJF

Overprint: Red TWO, TWO. **Engraver:** Toppan, Longacre & Co. / ABNCo. monogram. **Comments:** H-Unlisted, Durand-Unlisted. Similar to W-RI-1180-002-G070 but with different engraver imprint. 18__. 1860s.

Rarity: URS-3
VF $900

$2 • **W-RI-1180-1280-002-G080**

Left: 2 / TWO DOLLARS. **Center:** Two seated women, Woman placing wreath on bust of George Washington. **Right:** 2 / TWO DOLLARS. **Tint:** Red 2s. **Engraver:** National Bank Note Co. **Comments:** H-RI-420-G18a, Durand-1905. 186_. 1860s.

Rarity: URS-3
Proof $1,500

$2 • **W-RI-1180-1280-002-G080a**

CC

Tint: Red dies. **Engraver:** National Bank Note Co. **Comments:** H-Unlisted, Durand-Unlisted. Similar to W-RI-1180-1280-002-G080. 186_. 1860s.

Rarity: URS-3
Proof $4,700

$3 • **W-RI-1180-003-G090**

Comments: H-RI-420-G22, Durand-1907. No description available. 18__. 1800s–1810s.

Rarity: *None known*

$3 • **W-RI-1180-003-G100**

Comments: H-Unlisted. No description available. 18__. 1800s–1810s.

Rarity: *None known*

$3 • **W-RI-1180-003-G110**

Left: Male portrait. **Center:** 3 / Hope reclining, Anchor, ship / 3. **Right:** Anchor. **Engraver:** Draper, Toppan, Longacre & Co. **Comments:** H-RI-420-G26, Durand-1908. 18__. 1830s–1850s.

Rarity: *None known*

$3 • **W-RI-1180-003-G120**

NJW

Engraver: Draper, Toppan, Longacre & Co. **Comments:** H-Unlisted, Durand-Unlisted. 18__. 1830s–1850s.

Rarity: URS-3
Proof $1,100

$5 • **W-RI-1180-005-G130**

Left: FIVE vertically. **Center:** Olive tree. **Right:** 5 on die. **Comments:** H-RI-420-G30, Durand-1910. 18__. 1800s–1810s.

Rarity: *None known*

$5 • **W-RI-1180-005-G140**
Left: Male portrait. *Center:* 5 / Hope reclining with anchor / 5.
Right: Eagle. *Engraver:* Draper, Toppan, Longacre & Co.
Comments: H-RI-420-G34, Durand-1911. 18__. 1830s–1850s.
Rarity: URS-3
Proof $1,000

$5 • **W-RI-1180-005-G150**
Left: Male portrait. *Center:* 5 / Hope reclining with anchor / 5.
Right: State arms. *Comments:* H-Unlisted, Durand-1912. 1830s–
1850s.
Rarity: URS-3

$5 • **W-RI-1180-005-G160**   CC

Engraver: Toppan, Carpenter, Casilear & Co. *Comments:*
H-RI-420-G36, Durand-1913. 18__. 1850s–1860s.
Rarity: URS-3
Proof $2,900
Selected auction price: Stack's Bowers Galleries,
March 2013, Proof $2,904

$5 • **W-RI-1180-005-G160a**   CJF

Overprint: Red FIVE. *Engraver:* Toppan, Carpenter, Casilear &
Co. *Comments:* H-Unlisted, Durand-Unlisted. Similar to W-RI-
1180-005-G160. 18__. 1850s–1860s.
Rarity: URS-3
VF $900

$5 • **W-RI-1180-005-G160b**
Overprint: Red FIVE. *Engraver:* Toppan, Carpenter, Casilear
& Co. / ABNCo. monogram. *Comments:* H-RI-420-G36a,
Durand-1914. Similar to W-RI-1180-005-G160 but with addi-
tional engraver imprint. 18__. 1860s.
Rarity: *None known*

$10 • **W-RI-1180-010-G170**
Comments: H-RI-420-G40, Durand-1917. No description avail-
able. 18__. 1800s–1810s.
Rarity: *None known*

$10 • **W-RI-1180-010-G180**
Left: Male portrait. *Center:* 10 / Neptune seated / 10. *Right:*
Eagle on tree limb. *Engraver:* Draper, Toppan, Longacre & Co.
Comments: H-RI-420-G44, Durand-1918. 18__. 1830s–1850s.
Rarity: *None known*

$10 • **W-RI-1180-010-G180a**
Overprint: Red X / X. *Comments:* H-Unlisted, Durand-1919.
Similar to W-RI-1180-010-G180. 1830s–1850s.
Rarity: URS-3

$10 • **W-RI-1180-010-G190**   CC

Engraver: Toppan, Carpenter, Casilear & Co. *Comments:* H-RI-
420-G46, Durand-1920. 18__. 1850s.
Rarity: URS-2
Proof $2,600

$10 • **W-RI-1180-010-G190a**
Overprint: Red X / X. *Engraver:* Toppan, Carpenter, Casilear &
Co. *Comments:* H-RI-420-G46a, Durand-1921. Similar to W-RI-
1180-010-G190. 18__. 1850s.
Rarity: URS-3
Proof $1,000

$20 • **W-RI-1180-020-G200**
Comments: H-RI-420-G50, Durand-1923. No description avail-
able. 18__. 1800s–1830s.
Rarity: *None known*

$20 • **W-RI-1180-020-G210**
Left: 20. *Center:* Commerce, Steamer, State arms, Farmer. *Bot-
tom center:* Woman seated. *Right:* 20 / Female portrait. *Engraver:*
Unverified, but likely Draper, Toppan, Longacre & Co. *Com-
ments:* H-RI-420-G54, Durand-1924. 18__. 1830s–1850s.
Rarity: *None known*

$50 • **W-RI-1180-050-G220**
Comments: H-RI-420-G57, Durand-1926. No description avail-
able. 18__. 1800s.
Rarity: *None known*

$50 • **W-RI-1180-050-G230**
Left: 50 / Neptune in shell. *Bottom center:* Indian. *Right:* 50 /
Sailor standing. *Engraver:* Draper, Toppan, Longacre & Co.
Comments: H-RI-420-G60, Durand-1927. 18__. 1830s–1850s.
Rarity: *None known*

$100 • **W-RI-1180-100-G240**
Comments: H-RI-420-G62, Durand-1928. No description avail-
able. 18__. 1800s.
Rarity: *None known*

$100 • **W-RI-1180-100-G250**
Left: 100 / Marine view. *Center:* Female portrait. *Right:* 100 /
Indian on rock. *Engraver:* Draper, Toppan, Longacre & Co.
Comments: H-RI-420-G64, Durand-1929. 18__. 1830s–1850s.
Rarity: *None known*

$500 • **W-RI-1180-500-G260**

Left: D / Medallion head. *Center:* Commerce and Manufacturing. *Right:* 500 / Medallion head of George Washington. *Engraver:* Unverified, but likely Draper, Toppan, Longacre & Co. *Comments:* H-RI-420-G68, Durand-1930. 1830s–1850s.

Rarity: *None known*

$1,000 • **W-RI-1180-1000-G270**

Left: Ceres / 1000. *Center:* Marine view. *Right:* Justice / 1000. *Engraver:* Unverified, but likely Draper, Toppan, Longacre & Co. *Comments:* H-RI-420-G72, Durand-1931. 18__. 1830s–1850s.

Rarity: *None known*

Uncut Sheets

$1-$3 • **W-RI-1180-001.003-US010**

Vignette(s): No description available. *Engraver:* Unverified, but likely Draper, Toppan, Longacre & Co. *Comments:* All unlisted in Haxby. 18__. 1830s–1850s.

Rarity: *None known*

NON-VALID ISSUES

$1 • **W-RI-1180-001-C010**

Comments: H-RI-420-C2, Durand-1902. Counterfeit of W-RI-1180-001-G010. 18__. 1824.

Rarity: *None known*

$2 • **W-RI-1180-002-C060**

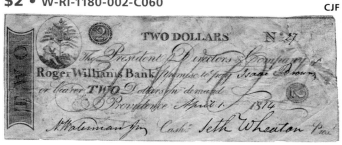

CJF

Comments: H-RI-420-C12, Durand-1906. Counterfeit of W-RI-1180-002-G060. 18__. 1814.

Rarity: URS-3
VF $200

$3 • **W-RI-1180-003-C090**

Comments: H-RI-420-C22, Durand-1909. Counterfeit of W-RI-1180-003-G090. 18__. 1837.

Rarity: *None known*

$5 • **W-RI-1180-005-C130**

Comments: H-RI-420-C30, Durand-1915. Counterfeit of W-RI-1180-005-G130. 18__. 1814.

Rarity: URS-3
VF $150

$5 • **W-RI-1180-005-R010**

Engraver: Draper, Toppan, Longacre & Co. *Comments:* H-RI-420-R5, Durand-1916. Raised from W-RI-1180-001-G030. 18__. 1840s.

Rarity: *None known*

$10 • **W-RI-1180-010-R020**

Engraver: Draper, Toppan, Longacre & Co. *Comments:* H-RI-420-R10, Durand-1922. Raised from W-RI-1180-001-G030. 18__. 1840s.

Rarity: *None known*

$20 • **W-RI-1180-020-R030**

Engraver: Draper, Toppan, Longacre & Co. *Comments:* H-RI-420-R15, Durand-1925. Raised from W-RI-1180-001-G030. 18__. 1840s.

Rarity: *None known*

Smithfield Lime Rock Bank
1823–1859
W-RI-1190

History: The Smithfield Lime Rock Bank was incorporated on January 29, 1823, in Smithfield. The bank's address was 8 What Cheer Building. Its location changed to Providence in May 1847. Capital of the bank was $100,100 in 1848 and $228,700 in 1856. Bills in circulation were $50,797, and specie amounted to $2,983.95 in 1857.

In January 1859, the title of the bank was changed to the Lime Rock Bank, W-RI-1020.

See also listing under Smithfield, W-RI-1390.

VALID ISSUES

$1 • **W-RI-1190-001-G010**

Left: ONE / Woman holding 1 / ONE. *Center:* 1 / Woman seated with scales and anvil / 1. *Bottom center:* Shield with anchor. *Right:* ONE / Portrait of George Washington / ONE. *Comments:* H-RI-470-G40, Durand-1478. 1820s–1850s.

Rarity: URS-3
F $450

$1 • **W-RI-1190-001-G010a**

Overprint: Red ONE. *Comments:* H-RI-470-G40a, Durand-1479. Similar to W-RI-1190-001-G010. 1820s–1850s.

Rarity: URS-3
F $450

$2 • **W-RI-1190-002-G020**

Left: TWO / Ceres and cherub / TWO. *Center:* Spread eagle on rock in sea. *Right:* 2 / Boy with sheaf. *Comments:* H-RI-470-G42, Durand-1480. 1820s–1850s.

Rarity: URS-3
F $450

$2 • **W-RI-1190-002-G020a**

Overprint: Red TWO. *Comments:* H-RI-470-G42a, Durand-1481. Similar to W-RI-1190-002-G020. 1820s–1850s.

Rarity: URS-3
F $450

$3 • **W-RI-1190-003-G030**

Left: Three allegorical figures supporting 3. *Center:* Ship, Sailor by bales with spyglass. *Right:* 3 / Horses frightened by train / THREE vertically. *Comments:* H-RI-470-G44, Durand-1482. 1820s–1850s.

Rarity: URS-3
F $450

$3 • W-RI-1190-003-G030a

Overprint: Red THREE. *Comments:* H-RI-470-G44a, Durand-1483. Similar to W-RI-1190-003-G030. 1820s–1850s.

Rarity: *None known*

$5 • W-RI-1190-005-G040

Left: FIVE / Woman with compass / 5. *Center:* 5 / Five cherubs with 5 / 5. *Right:* FIVE vertically. *Comments:* H-RI-470-G46, Durand-1484. 1820s–1850s.

Rarity: URS-3
F $500

$5 • W-RI-1190-005-G050

Left: 5 / 5. *Center:* Mechanic, wheels, tools. *Right:* FIVE / Liberty / FIVE. *Comments:* H-RI-470-G48, Durand-1485. 1820s–1850s.

Rarity: *None known*

$10 • W-RI-1190-010-G060

Left: X / X. *Center:* Agriculture and Commerce. *Right:* 10 / Mason holding level. *Comments:* H-RI-470-G50, Durand-1486. 1820s–1850s.

Rarity: *None known*

$20 • W-RI-1190-020-G070

Left: 20 / Minerva. *Center:* Woman seated between 2 and 0. *Bottom center:* XX. *Right:* 20 / Woman reclining on cornucopia / 20. *Engraver:* New England Bank Note Co. *Comments:* H-RI-470-G52, Durand-1487. 18__. 1860s.

Rarity: *None known*

$50 • W-RI-1190-050-G080

Left: 50 / Minerva. *Center:* Ceres, Cornucopia, Vulcan. *Right:* 50 / Cherub in sailboat / 50. *Comments:* H-RI-470-G54, Durand-1488. 1820s–1850s.

Rarity: *None known*

$100 • W-RI-1190-100-G090

Left: 100 / Vulcan. *Center:* Train, Spread eagle on tree limb, Canal locks. *Right:* 100 / Ceres. *Comments:* H-RI-470-G56, Durand-1489. 1820s–1850s.

Rarity: *None known*

State Bank
1850–1893
W-RI-1200

History: The State Bank was incorporated in May 1850 with an authorized capital of $100,000. In 1854 the president was J.P. Merriam, and the cashier was T.H. Rhodes. Capital was $150,000 in 1855. Circulation was at a low of $33,526 in 1862 and a high of $45,226 in 1857. Specie was $2,191.75 in 1857. No new notes were issued after the mid-1860s.

The State Bank was liquidated in 1893.

Numismatic Commentary: Many of this bank's issues have a vignette of the Old State House in Providence. All genuine notes are very scarce.

VALID ISSUES

$1 • W-RI-1200-001-G010

CJF

Engraver: Toppan, Carpenter, Casilear & Co. *Comments:* H-RI-390-G2, Durand-1932. 18__. 1850s.

Rarity: URS-3
Proof $1,500

$2 • W-RI-1200-002-G020

CJF

Engraver: Toppan, Carpenter, Casilear & Co. *Comments:* H-RI-390-G4, Durand-1935. 18__. 1850s.

Rarity: URS-3
Proof $1,500

$3 • W-RI-1200-003-G030

CC

Engraver: Toppan, Carpenter, Casilear & Co. *Comments:* H-RI-390-G6, Durand-1937. 18__. 1850s.

Rarity: URS-3
Proof $1,500

$5 • W-RI-1200-005-G040

CC

Engraver: Toppan, Carpenter, Casilear & Co. **Comments:** H-RI-390-G8, Durand-1939. 18__. 1850s.

Rarity: URS-3
Proof $1,500

$10 • W-RI-1200-010-G050

Left: 10 / Three women on rock, one standing with hand on anchor / TEN. **Center:** Hope seated with shield bearing state arms. **Right:** 10 / Old State House. **Engraver:** Toppan, Carpenter, Casilear & Co. **Comments:** H-RI-390-G10, Durand-1943. 18__. 1850s.

Rarity: *None known*

$20 • W-RI-1200-020-G060

Left: Agriculture and sailor. **Center:** Agriculture, Commerce. **Right:** 20 / Old State House. **Engraver:** Toppan, Carpenter, Casilear & Co. **Comments:** H-RI-390-G12, Durand-1946. 18__. 1850s.

Rarity: URS-3
Proof $1,500

$50 • W-RI-1200-050-G070

Left: 50 / Female portrait. **Center:** Hope reclining on shield bearing anchor, Ships. **Right:** 50 / Female portrait. **Engraver:** Toppan, Carpenter, Casilear & Co. **Comments:** H-RI-390-G14, Durand-1948. 18__. 1850s.

Rarity: *None known*

$100 • W-RI-1200-100-G080

Left: Old State House. **Center:** Eagle and shield. **Right:** 100 / Female portrait. **Engraver:** Toppan, Carpenter, Casilear & Co. **Comments:** H-RI-390-G16, Durand-1950. 18__. 1850s.

Rarity: *None known*

$500 • W-RI-1200-500-G090

Left: Indian woman / 500. **Center:** Three allegorical figures, Train and ships. **Bottom center:** Eagle. **Right:** 500 / 500. **Engraver:** Toppan, Carpenter, Casilear & Co. **Comments:** H-RI-390-G18, Durand-1951. 18__. 1850s.

Rarity: *None known*

$1,000 • W-RI-1200-1000-G100

Left: M / 1000. **Center:** Commerce and Agriculture, Canal scene. **Right:** 1000 / 1000. **Engraver:** Toppan, Carpenter, Casilear & Co. **Comments:** H-RI-390-G20, Durand-1952. 18__. 1850s.

Rarity: *None known*

Uncut Sheets

$3-$20 • W-RI-1200-003.020-US010

Vignette(s): ($3) State House / Woman seated with shield bearing anchor / Eagle / Female portrait. **($20)** Agriculture and sailor / Agriculture, Commerce / Old State House. **Engraver:** Toppan, Carpenter, Casilear & Co. **Comments:** H-RI-390-G6, G12. 18__. 1850s.

Rarity: URS-3
Proof $3,500

Non-Valid Issues

$1 • W-RI-1200-001-S010

CJF

Engraver: Draper, Toppan & Co. **Comments:** H-RI-390-S5. From a modified, fraudulent plate originally for a counterfeit $1 of the State Bank of Indiana. July 1st, 1850.

Rarity: URS-7
VF $150

$1 • W-RI-1200-001-A010

SBG

Engraver: New England Bank Note Co. **Comments:** H-RI-390-N5, Durand-1933. Altered from W-RI-220-001-G010. July 2, 18__. 1850s.

Rarity: URS-3
VG $200; **VF** $400

$1 • W-RI-1200-001-S020

Left: ONE / Allegorical figure / ONE. **Center:** Blacksmith shop. **Right:** ONE / Portrait of Christopher Columbus / ONE. **Comments:** H-RI-390-N10, Durand-1934. 18__. 1850s.

Rarity: *None known*

$2 • W-RI-1200-002-A020

Left: Two girls carrying sheaves / 2. **Center:** Sailor and mechanic flanking shield surmounted by badger. **Right:** 2 / Liberty standing and Indian woman kneeling. **Overprint:** Red TWO. **Engraver:** Rawdon, Wright, Hatch & Edson / New England Bank Note Co. **Comments:** H-RI-390-A5, Durand-1936. Altered from $2 Waubeek Bank, DeSoto, Nebraska. 1857.

Rarity: URS-6
VF $150

$3 • W-RI-1200-003-S030
Center: Blacksmith seated. *Comments:* H-Unlisted, Durand-1938. 18__. 1850s.
Rarity: URS-3
F $175

$5 • W-RI-1200-005-R010
Engraver: Toppan, Carpenter, Casilear & Co. *Comments:* H-RI-390-R5, Durand-1940. Raised from W-RI-1200-001-G010. 18__. 1850s.
Rarity: *None known*

$5 • W-RI-1200-005-R020
Engraver: Toppan, Carpenter, Casilear & Co. *Comments:* H-RI-390-R10, Durand-1941. Raised from W-RI-1200-002-G020. 18__. 1850s.
Rarity: *None known*

$5 • W-RI-1200-005-S040
Left: 5 / Sailor seated with sextant / FIVE. *Center:* Steamboat, Woman seated by shield, Factories. *Right:* 5 / Woman seated / FIVE. *Engraver:* Wellstood, Hanks & Co. *Comments:* H-RI-390-S10. 18__. 1850s.
Rarity: *None known*

$5 • W-RI-1200-005-S050
Left: Sailor. *Center:* Woman, Shield and military objects. *Right:* Woman with hammer and dividers. *Comments:* H-Unlisted, Durand-1942. 18__. 1850s.
Rarity: *None known*

$10 • W-RI-1200-010-R030
Engraver: Toppan, Carpenter, Casilear & Co. *Comments:* H-RI-390-R15, Durand-1944. Raised from W-RI-1200-001-G010. 18__. 1850s.
Rarity: *None known*

$10 • W-RI-1200-010-A030
Left: 10 / Agriculture and Commerce with shield of Hope. *Center:* Farmers gathering corn, Wagon and horses. *Right:* 10 / Portrait of girl. *Overprint:* Red X / X. *Engraver:* Unverified, but likely Toppan, Carpenter & Co. *Comments:* H-RI-390-A10, Durand-1945. Altered from W-RI-1630-010-G050. 18__. 1850s.
Rarity: URS-6
VF $150

$20 • W-RI-1200-020-R040
Engraver: Toppan, Carpenter, Casilear & Co. *Comments:* H-RI-390-R20, Durand-1947. Raised from W-RI-1200-001-G010. 18__. 1850s.
Rarity: URS-5
VF $150

$50 • W-RI-1200-050-R050
Engraver: Toppan, Carpenter, Casilear & Co. *Comments:* H-RI-390-R25, Durand-1949. Raised from W-RI-1200-001-G010. 18__. 1850s.
Rarity: URS-3
VF $200

Collectors and Researchers:

If you have new information about any banks or notes listed in this volume, contact Whitman Publishing, Attn: Obsolete Paper Money, 3101 Clairmont Road, Suite G, Atlanta, GA 30329.

Traders Bank
1836–1865
W-RI-1210

History: The Traders Bank of Providence was incorporated in June 1836. A bank opened in Newport with the same name and in the same year. This coincidence afforded counterfeiters a golden opportunity due to the natural confusion regarding the source of the Traders Bank notes.[73] In 1848 the capital of the Providence-based bank was $200,000. Its circulation at that time was $57,100; the same was at a low of $36,996 in 1857. Figures for 1852 included these: deposits $39,953; money due banks $7,848; profits $11,470. The bank applied for an increase in capital in 1854. However, records show that the request was not approved. Specie was $3,127.69 in 1857.

The business of the Traders Bank was succeeded by the Traders National Bank, chartered on June 7, 1865.

Numismatic Commentary: Quite a few issues from this bank appear in the marketplace, but few are genuine. However, a certain series of bills offers collectors a chance to obtain some unusual denominations, such as the $1.25, $1.50 and $1.75 notes engraved by the firm of Terry, Pelton and Co.

VALID ISSUES

$1 • W-RI-1210-001-G010
Left: ONE / Wharf scene / ONE. *Center:* Griffin on strongbox, Ceres seated, Mercury. *Bottom center:* Clasped hands. *Right:* ONE / Liberty seated / ONE. *Engraver:* Unverified, but likely Rawdon, Wright & Hatch. *Comments:* H-RI-395-G2, Durand-1953. 18__. 1830s–1840s.
Rarity: *None known*

$1 • W-RI-1210-001-G020
Left: 1 / Female portrait. *Center:* Allegorical figure supporting 1 / 1. *Right:* ONE / Agriculture and sailor. *Engraver:* Rawdon, Wright, Hatch & Edson. *Comments:* H-RI-395-G4, Durand-1954. 18__. 1840s–1850s.
Rarity: *None known*

$1 • W-RI-1210-001-G020a
CJF

Engraver: Rawdon, Wright, Hatch & Edson / ABNCo. monogram. *Comments:* H-RI-395-G4a. Similar to W-RI-1210-001-G020 but with additional engraver imprint. 18__. 1850s–1860s.
Rarity: URS-3
VF $1,000

$1 • W-RI-1210-001-G020b

CC

Overprint: Red ONE. **Engraver:** Rawdon, Wright, Hatch & Edson / ABNCo. monogram. **Comments:** H-Unlisted. Similar to W-RI-1210-001-G020 but with additional engraver imprint. 18__. 1850s–1860s.
Rarity: URS-3
VF $1,250

$1.25 • W-RI-1210-001.25-G030

Left: $1 25/100 / Samson and the lion. **Center:** Indians / $1 25/100. **Right:** 1 DOLL. 25 Cts. vertically. **Engraver:** Terry, Pelton & Co. **Comments:** H-RI-395-G6, Durand-1956. 18__. Circa 1837.
Rarity: URS-3
VF $1,100
Selected auction price: Stack's Bowers Galleries, January 2010, VF $1,067

$1.50 • W-RI-1210-001.50-G040

Engraver: Terry, Pelton & Co. **Comments:** H-RI-395-G7. No description available. 18__. Circa 1837.
Rarity: *None known*

$1.75 • W-RI-1210-001.75-G050

Engraver: Terry, Pelton & Co. **Comments:** H-RI-395-G8. 18__. Circa 1837.
Rarity: URS-3
VF $500; **Proof** $2,500

$2 • W-RI-1210-002-G060

Left: St. George slaying dragon / 2. **Center:** Winged allegorical figure, Neptune in cart drawn by sea horses. **Bottom center:** Cherub on deer. **Right:** 2 / Hercules battling with Hydra. **Engraver:** Unverified, but likely Rawdon, Wright & Hatch. **Comments:** H-RI-395-G10, Durand-1957. 18__. 1830s–1840s.
Rarity: *None known*

$2 • W-RI-1210-002-G070

Left: Milkmaid and farmer / 2. **Center:** Liberty, Shield bearing state arms, Spread eagle. **Bottom center:** Ox. **Right:** 2 / Sailor. **Engraver:** Rawdon, Wright, Hatch & Edson. **Comments:** H-RI-395-G12, Durand-1958. 18__. 1840s–1850s.
Rarity: *None known*

$2 • W-RI-1210-002-G070a

Engraver: Rawdon, Wright, Hatch & Edson / ABNCo. monogram. **Comments:** H-RI-395-G12a. Similar to W-RI-1210-002-G070 but with additional engraver imprint. 18__. 1850s–1860s.
Rarity: *None known*

$3 • W-RI-1210-003-G080

Left: 3 / Drovers and cattle / 3. **Center:** Three Indians, Dog and slain deer. **Bottom center:** Urn. **Right:** 3 / George Washington and horse. **Engraver:** Terry, Pelton & Co. **Comments:** H-RI-395-G14, Durand-1962. 18__. 1836–1840s.
Rarity: URS-3
VF $300

$3 • W-RI-1210-003-G090

Left: THREE / Hope by lighthouse, Ship. **Center:** 3 / Ship under sail. **Right:** 3 / Two children. **Tint:** Green 3 on die and panel outlining white THREE. **Engraver:** American Bank Note Co. **Comments:** H-RI-395-G18a, Durand-1963. 18__. 1860s.
Rarity: URS-3
Proof $2,500

$5 • W-RI-1210-005-G100

Left: V / Launching of ship / V. **Center:** Agricultural implements and products. **Bottom center:** Steamboat. **Right:** V / Liberty and eagle / V. **Engraver:** Unverified, but likely Rawdon, Wright & Hatch. **Comments:** H-RI-395-G22, Durand-1965. 18__. 1830s–1850s.
Rarity: *None known*

$5 • W-RI-1210-005-G110

Left: V / Female portrait. **Center:** Sailor seated by anchor and boat, Ship. **Right:** 5 / Eagle on shield. **Tint:** Green. **Engraver:** American Bank Note Co. **Comments:** H-RI-395-G26a, Durand-1966. 18__. 1860s.
Rarity: *None known*

$10 • W-RI-1210-010-G120

Left: TEN DOLLARS / Vulcan, Ceres and Mercury, Anvil / 10. **Center:** X / Ox / X. **Bottom center:** Eagle. **Right:** TEN / Drover and cattle / 10. **Engraver:** Unverified, but likely Rawdon, Wright & Hatch. **Comments:** H-RI-395-G30, Durand-1976. 18__. 1830s–1850s.
Rarity: *None known*

$20 • W-RI-1210-020-G130

Left: XX / Ship on stocks / XX. **Center:** Wharf scene. **Bottom center:** Train. **Right:** 20 / Indian and Commerce / XX. **Engraver:** Terry, Pelton & Co. **Comments:** H-RI-395-G34, Durand-1982. 18__. 1840s–1850s.
Rarity: *None known*

$50 • W-RI-1210-050-G140

Left: FIFTY vertically. **Center:** Wharf scene. **Right:** 50 / Two cobblers at work / 50. **Engraver:** Terry, Pelton & Co. **Comments:** H-RI-395-G38, Durand-1985. 18__. 1830s–1850s.
Rarity: URS-3
Proof $2,500

$100 • W-RI-1210-100-G150

Left: ONE HUNDRED vertically. **Center:** C on die / Woman standing with globe / C on die. **Right:** 100 / Figure / 100. **Engraver:** Terry, Pelton & Co. **Comments:** H-RI-395-G40, Durand-1988. 18__. 1830s–1850s.
Rarity: URS-3
Proof $2,500

NON-VALID ISSUES

$1 • W-RI-1210-001-C020
Comments: H-Unlisted, Durand-1955. Counterfeit of W-RI-1210-001-G020. Photographic. 1830s–1850s.
Rarity: URS-3
F $100

$2 • W-RI-1210-002-N010
Center: Sailor seated on barrel. *Comments:* H-RI-395-N5, Durand-1961. Altered or spurious. 1830s–1850s.
Rarity: *None known*

$2 • W-RI-1210-002-A010
Left: 2 / Reverses of silver dollar and Spanish Pillar dollar. *Center:* Man and woman by well. *Bottom center:* Bull. *Right:* 2 / Allegorical woman with 2. *Overprint:* Red TWO. *Engraver:* Wellstood, Hay & Whiting. *Comments:* H-RI-395-A5, Durand-1960. Altered from $2 Thames Bank, Laurel, Indiana. 1850s.
Rarity: *None known*

$2 • W-RI-1210-002-A020
Left: Woman / 2 on seal. *Center:* Man and woman seated / TWO. *Right:* 2 / Woman standing with flag and shield, Woman kneeling. *Overprint:* Red TWO. *Engraver:* New England Bank Note Co. / Rawdon, Wright, Hatch & Edson. *Comments:* H-RI-395-A10, Durand-1959. Altered from $2 Waubeek Bank, De Soto, Nebraska. 1857.
Rarity: URS-7
VF $100

$3 • W-RI-1210-003-A030
Left: 3 / Female portrait. *Center:* Three cherubs and three silver dollars. *Right:* 3 / Wagon of hay. *Overprint:* Red THREE. *Engraver:* Rawdon, Wright, Hatch & Edson / New England Bank Note Co. *Comments:* H-RI-395-A15, Durand-1964. Altered from W-RI-1580-003-G190a. 18__. 1850s.
Rarity: *None known*

$5 • W-RI-1210-005-R010
Engraver: Rawdon, Wright, Hatch & Edson. *Comments:* H-RI-395-R5, Durand-1967. Raised from W-RI-1210-001-G020 series. 18__. 1850s.
Rarity: *None known*

$5 • W-RI-1210-005-N020
Left: Portrait of Benjamin Franklin. *Center:* Canal lock, Two horses, Man and woman. *Comments:* H-RI-395-N10, Durand-1972. Altered or spurious. 1830s–1850s.
Rarity: *None known*

$5 • W-RI-1210-005-N030
Center: Country scene, Man, mill. *Comments:* H-RI-395-N15, Durand-1973. Altered or spurious. 1830s–1850s.
Rarity: *None known*

$5 • W-RI-1210-005-N040
Center: Woman holding 5, Sheaf, Train. *Comments:* H-RI-395-N20, Durand-1974. Altered or spurious. 1830s–1850s.
Rarity: *None known*

$5 • W-RI-1210-005-N050
Center: Shield between two men. *Comments:* H-Unlisted, Durand-1975. Altered or spurious. 1830s–1850s.
Rarity: URS-3
F $75

$5 • W-RI-1210-005-A040
Left: Portrait of Henry Clay / V. *Center:* Farmer feeding hogs. *Bottom center:* Dog lying down. *Right:* 5 / Farmer carrying basket of corn. *Overprint:* Red FIVE. *Engraver:* Wellstood, Hay & Whiting. *Comments:* H-RI-395-A20, Durand-1968. Altered from $5 Thames Bank, Laurel, Indiana. 1850s.
Rarity: *None known*

$5 • W-RI-1210-005-A050
SI

Engraver: Terry, Pelton & Co. *Comments:* H-RI-395-A25, Durand-1970. Altered from $5 Citizens Bank, Augusta, Maine, or from notes of other failed banks using the same plate. 18__. 1840s.
Rarity: URS-3
VF $150

$5 • W-RI-1210-005-AR010
Left: FIVE / Portrait of cherub / 5. *Center:* 5 / Ceres and Liberty / 5. *Bottom center:* Anchor and implements. *Right:* 5 / Female portrait / FIVE. *Engraver:* Terry, Pelton & Co. *Comments:* H-RI-395-AR30, Durand-1969. Altered and raised from $2 Citizens Bank, Augusta, Maine, or from notes of other failed banks using the same plate. 18__. 1830s–1850s.
Rarity: *None known*

$5 • W-RI-1210-005-A060
Left: V / Portrait of Henry Clay. *Center:* Steamboat. *Right:* 5 / Portrait of George Washington. *Overprint:* Red FIVE. *Engraver:* New England Bank Note Co. / Rawdon, Wright, Hatch & Edson. *Comments:* H-RI-395-A35, Durand-1971. Altered from $5 Waubeek Bank, De Soto, Nebraska. 1857.
Rarity: *None known*

$10 • W-RI-1210-010-R020
Engraver: Rawdon, Wright, Hatch & Edson. *Comments:* H-RI-395-R6, Durand-1977. Raised from W-RI-1210-001-G020 series. 18__. 1850s.
Rarity: *None known*

$10 • W-RI-1210-010-N060
Left: Steamboat, ships. *Center:* Two allegorical women. *Right:* Allegorical woman. *Comments:* H-RI-395-N25, Durand-1980. Altered or spurious. 1830s–1850s.
Rarity: *None known*

$10 • W-RI-1210-010-N070
Center: Men lassoing wild horse. *Comments:* H-RI-395-N30, Durand-1978. Altered or spurious. 1830s–1850s.
Rarity: *None known*

$10 • W-RI-1210-010-N080
Center: Woman with key seated between 1 and 0. *Comments:* H-RI-395-N35, Durand-1979. Altered or spurious. 1830s–1850s.
Rarity: *None known*

$10 • W-RI-1210-010-N090
Left: Indian. *Center:* Steamboat, ships. *Right:* Woman. *Comments:* H-Unlisted, Durand-1981. Altered or spurious. 1830s–1850s.
Rarity: URS-3
F $75

$20 • W-RI-1210-020-N100
Center: Woman, Shield, Military objects. *Comments:* H-RI-395-N45, Durand-1984. Altered or spurious. 1830s–1850s.
Rarity: *None known*

$20 • W-RI-1210-020-A070

Comments: H-RI-395-N40, Durand-1983. 18__. 1850s.
Rarity: URS-1
F $75

$50 • W-RI-1210-050-N110
Center: Woman, Shield, Military objects. *Comments:* H-RI-395-N50, Durand-1987. Altered or spurious. 1830s–1850s.
Rarity: *None known*

$50 • W-RI-1210-050-A080
Left: 50 / Allegorical woman, Shield bearing anchor surmounted by bowl of fruit / 50. *Center:* L / Hebe pouring drink for eagle / L. *Bottom center:* Anchor and implements. *Right:* 50 / Farmer holding grain / 50. *Engraver:* Terry, Pelton & Co. *Comments:* H-RI-395-A40, Durand-1986. Altered from $50 Citizens Bank, Augusta, Maine, or from notes of other failed banks using the same plate. 18__. 1830s–1850s.
Rarity: *None known*

Union Bank
1814–1890
W-RI-1220

History: The Union Bank was chartered in 1814 with an authorized capital of $500,000. Circulation was at a high of $94,240 in 1862 and a low of $39,714 in 1857. Specie was $7,500 that same year. The bank continued under its state charter until it closed in 1890. No notes were issued after the mid-1860s.

Numismatic Commentary: Genuine notes from this bank are not abundant but appear on occasion. One has a popular vignette, "The Landing of Roger Williams."

VALID ISSUES

$1 • W-RI-1220-001-G010

Engraver: Leney & Rollinson. *Comments:* H-RI-400-G2, Durand-1989. 18__. 1810s–1830s.
Rarity: URS-3
VF $250

$1 • W-RI-1220-001-G020
Comments: H-Unlisted, Durand-1990. No description available. 1810s–1830s.
Rarity: *None known*

$1 • W-RI-1220-001-G030
Left: 1 / Medallion head / 1. *Center:* 1 / Woman seated / 1 / ONE. *Right:* Woman in 1. *Engraver:* Rawdon, Wright & Hatch. *Comments:* H-RI-400-G5. 18__. 1840s.
Rarity: URS-3
Proof $1,000

$1 • W-RI-1220-001-G040
Left: Justice / 1. *Center:* Commerce, Ships. *Right:* 1 / Woman with spyglass. *Engraver:* Toppan, Carpenter, Casilear & Co. *Comments:* H-RI-400-G6, Durand-1991. 18__. 1850s.
Rarity: URS-3
VF $400

$1 • W-RI-1220-001-G040a

Overprint: Red ONE. *Engraver:* Toppan, Carpenter, Casilear & Co. / ABNCo. monogram. *Comments:* H-RI-400-G6b, Durand-1992. Similar to W-RI-1220-001-G040 but with additional engraver imprint. 18__. 1850s–1860s.
Rarity: URS-3
VG $750

$1 • W-RI-1220-001-G040b
Overprint: Red ONE. *Engraver:* American Bank Note Co. *Comments:* H-RI-400-G6c. Similar to W-RI-1220-001-G040 but with different engraver imprint. 18__. 1860s.
Rarity: *None known*

$2 • W-RI-1220-002-G050

Left: TWO vertically. *Center:* 2 / Hope with anchor / 2. *Right:* 2 TWO 2 vertically. *Engraver:* Leney & Rollinson. *Comments:* H-RI-400-G10, Durand-1994. 18__. 1814–1820s.

Rarity: URS-3
Proof $350

$2 • W-RI-1220-002-G060

CJF

Engraver: Rawdon, Wright & Hatch. *Comments:* H-RI-400-G13, Durand-1995. 18__. 1840s.

Rarity: URS-3
F $1,200; **VF** $2,500

$2 • W-RI-1220-002-G070

Left: TWO / Milkmaid seated / TWO. *Center:* Justice, Agriculture, and Commerce. *Bottom center:* Anchor on shield. *Right:* 2 / Ship / TWO. *Engraver:* Toppan, Carpenter, Casilear & Co. *Comments:* H-RI-400-G14, Durand-1996. 18__. 1850s.

Rarity: *None known*

$2 • W-RI-1220-002-G070a

SI

Overprint: Red TWO. *Engraver:* Toppan, Carpenter, Casilear & Co. / ABNCo. monogram. *Comments:* H-RI-400-G14b, Durand-1997. Similar to W-RI-1220-002-G070 but with additional engraver imprint. 18__. 1860s.

Rarity: URS-2
VF $750

$2 • W-RI-1220-002-G070b

Overprint: Red TWO. *Engraver:* American Bank Note Co. *Comments:* H-RI-400-G14c. Similar to W-RI-1220-002-G070 but with different engraver imprint. 18__. 1860s.

Rarity: *None known*

$3 • W-RI-1220-003-G080

CJF

Engraver: Leney & Rollinson. *Comments:* H-RI-400-G18, Durand-2001. 18__. 1810s–1830s.

Rarity: URS-3
VF $350; **Proof** $1,900

$3 • W-RI-1220-003-G090

Comments: H-Unlisted, Durand-2002. No description available. 1810s–1830s.

Rarity: *None known*

$3 • W-RI-1220-003-G100

Left: State arms / Indian man, Woman standing / State arms. *Center:* 3 / Woman reclining / 3 / THREE. *Bottom center:* Clasped hands. *Right:* Woman in 3. *Engraver:* Rawdon, Wright & Hatch. *Comments:* H-RI-400-G21. 18__. 1840s.

Rarity: URS-3
Proof $500

$3 • W-RI-1220-003-G110

Left: Three allegorical figures, Anchor. *Center:* Sailing ship, lighthouse. *Bottom center:* Anchor on shield. *Right:* 3 / Portrait of George Washington. *Engraver:* Toppan, Carpenter, Casilear & Co. *Comments:* H-RI-400-G22, Durand-2003. 18__. 1850s.

Rarity: *None known*

$3 • W-RI-1220-003-G110a

Overprint: Red THREE. *Engraver:* Toppan, Carpenter, Casilear & Co. / ABNCo. monogram. *Comments:* H-RI-400-G22b, Durand-2004. Similar to W-RI-1220-003-G110 but with additional engraver imprint. 18__. 1860s.

Rarity: *None known*

$3 • W-RI-1220-003-G110b

Overprint: Red THREE. *Engraver:* American Bank Note Co. *Comments:* H-RI-400-G22c. Similar to W-RI-1220-003-G110 but with different engraver imprint. 18__. 1860s.

Rarity: *None known*

$5 • W-RI-1220-005-G120

Left: V FIVE V vertically. *Center:* 5 on die / Woman seated pointing at ship / V on die. *Bottom center:* Box. *Right:* FIVE vertically. *Engraver:* Leney & Rollinson. *Comments:* H-RI-400-G26, Durand-2008. First issue. 18__. 1814.

Rarity: URS-3
Proof $350

$5 • W-RI-1220-005-G130

Comments: H-Unlisted, Durand-2009. No description available. 1810s–1830s.

Rarity: *None known*

$5 • W-RI-1220-005-G140

Left: Ceres / 5. *Center:* Ceres seated on plow. ***Bottom center:*** Anchor on shield. *Right:* 5 / Steamboat. *Engraver:* Unverified, but likely Toppan, Carpenter, Casilear & Co. *Comments:* H-RI-400-G30, Durand-2010. 18__. 1850s.

Rarity: *None known*

$5 • W-RI-1220-005-G140a

Overprint: Red FIVE. *Engraver:* Toppan, Carpenter, Casilear & Co. / ABNCo. monogram. *Comments:* H-RI-400-G30b, Durand-2011. Similar to W-RI-1220-005-G140 but with additional engraver imprint. 18__. 1860s.

Rarity: URS-3
VF $950

$5 • W-RI-1220-005-G140b

Overprint: Red FIVE. *Engraver:* American Bank Note Co. *Comments:* H-RI-400-G30c. Similar to W-RI-1220-005-G140 but with different engraver imprint. 18__. 1860s.

Rarity: *None known*

$10 • W-RI-1220-010-G150

Left: TEN vertically. *Center:* 10 / Allegorical figure / 10. *Right:* TEN vertically. *Engraver:* Leney & Rollinson. *Comments:* H-RI-400-G34, Durand-2020. 18__. 1814.

Rarity: *None known*

$10 • W-RI-1220-010-G160

Left: X / Portrait of Benjamin Franklin / 10. *Center:* Steamship and other vessels. *Right:* 10 / Fine Arts. *Engraver:* Toppan, Carpenter, Casilear & Co. *Comments:* H-RI-400-G38, Durand-2021. 18__. 1850s.

Rarity: *None known*

$10 • W-RI-1220-010-G160a

Overprint: Red TEN. *Engraver:* Toppan, Carpenter, Casilear & Co. / ABNCo. monogram. *Comments:* H-RI-400-G38b, Durand-2022. Similar to W-RI-1220-010-G160 but with additional engraver imprint. 18__. 1860s.

Rarity: *None known*

$10 • W-RI-1220-010-G160b   CJF

Overprint: Red TEN. *Engraver:* American Bank Note Co. *Comments:* H-RI-400-G38c. Similar to W-RI-1220-010-G160 but with different engraver imprint. 18__. 1860s.

Rarity: URS-2
VF $750

$50 • W-RI-1220-050-G170

Left: 50 L 50 vertically. *Center:* 50 / Ship on stocks / Allegorical figure on tablet bearing 50 / 50. *Right:* L RHODE ISLAND L vertically. *Engraver:* Unverified, but likely Toppan, Carpenter, Casilear & Co. *Comments:* H-RI-400-G42, Durand-2029. 18__. 1850s.

Rarity: *None known*

$100 • W-RI-1220-100-G180

Left: 100 C 100 vertically. *Center:* 100 / Shield bearing state arms / 100. ***Bottom center:*** 100. *Right:* C RHODE ISLAND C vertically. *Engraver:* Unverified, but likely Toppan, Carpenter, Casilear & Co. *Comments:* H-RI-400-G46, Durand-2030. 18__. 1850s.

Rarity: *None known*

$500 • W-RI-1220-500-G190   SBG

Engraver: Reed. *Comments:* H-RI-400-G50, Durand-2031. Proof. 18__. 1850s.

Rarity: URS-1
Proof $6,700
Selected auction price: Stack's Bowers Galleries, March 2013, Proof $6,656

Uncut Sheets

$1-$1-$2-$3 • W-RI-1220-001.001.002.003-US010

Vignette(s): (*$1*) Medallion head / Woman seated / Woman in 1. (*$1*) Medallion head / Woman seated / Woman in 1. (*$2*) Woman / "The Landing of Roger Williams" / Clasped hands inside wreath / Woman standing in 2. (*$3*) State arms / Indian man, Woman standing / State arms / Woman reclining / Clasped hands / Woman in 3. *Engraver:* Rawdon, Wright & Hatch. *Comments:* H-RI-400-G5, G5, G13, G21. 18__. 1840s.

Rarity: URS-3
Proof $2,000

NON-VALID ISSUES

$1 • W-RI-1220-001-C010

Engraver: Leney & Rollinson. *Comments:* H-RI-400-C2. Counterfeit of W-RI-1220-001-G010. 18__. 1842.

Rarity: URS-3
VF $150

$2 • W-RI-1220-002-N010

Left: 2 / TWO. *Center:* Eagle on shield. *Right:* Portrait of George Washington. *Comments:* H-RI-400-N5, Durand-1999. Altered or spurious. 1840s.

Rarity: *None known*

$2 • W-RI-1220-002-N020

Center: Vulcan with sledge, Train. *Comments:* H-RI-400-N10, Durand-2000. Altered or spurious. 1840s.

Rarity: *None known*

$2 • W-RI-1220-002-A010

Left: 2 on die. *Center:* Manhattan with water urn / 2. *Right:* Panel of wheat and corn bearing female portrait. *Engraver:* Durand & Co. *Comments:* H-RI-400-A5, Durand-1998. Altered from $2 Globe Bank, New York City, New York. 1840.

Rarity: *None known*

$3 • **W-RI-1220-003-S010**

Left: 3 on die. *Center:* 3 on die / Woman standing with scales next to shield bearing eagle, Ship / 3 on die. *Bottom center:* Plow and beehive. *Right:* THREE / Sailing vessel / THREE. *Comments:* H-Unlisted, Durand-2006. 1840s.

Rarity: URS-3

F $100

$3 • **W-RI-1220-003-N030**

Center: Vulcan with sledge, Train. *Comments:* H-RI-400-N15, Durand-2007. Altered or spurious. 1840s.

Rarity: *None known*

$3 • **W-RI-1220-003-A020**

Left: 3 on die. *Center:* Manhattan with water urn / 3. *Right:* Panel of wheat and corn bearing die with 3. *Engraver:* Durand & Co. *Comments:* H-RI-400-A10, Durand-2005. Altered from $3 Globe Bank, New York City, New York. 1840.

Rarity: *None known*

$5 • **W-RI-1220-005-C120**

Engraver: Leney & Rollinson. *Comments:* H-RI-400-C26, Durand-2012. Counterfeit of W-RI-1220-005-G120. 18__. 1842.

Rarity: URS-3

F $100

$5 • **W-RI-1220-005-R010**

Engraver: Toppan, Carpenter, Casilear & Co. *Comments:* H-RI-400-R5, Durand-2013. Raised from W-RI-1220-001-G040 series. 18__. 1850s.

Rarity: *None known*

$5 • **W-RI-1220-005-S020**   SI, SI

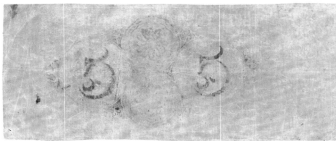

Back: Brown-orange 5, 5 on dies. *Engraver:* Toppan, Carpenter & Co. *Comments:* H-RI-400-S5, Durand-2019. From a modified, fraudulent plate originally for W-RI-1110-005-C200. 185_. 1856.

Rarity: URS-6

VF $150

$5 • **W-RI-1220-005-S030**

Left: Lathework panel bearing FIVE vertically. *Center:* Drover, cattle. *Right:* Lathework panel bearing FIVE vertically. *Engraver:* Draper, Underwood, Bald & Spencer. *Comments:* H-RI-400-S10, Durand-2017. Altered or spurious. The non-existent Farmers Bank, Mount Holly, New Jersey, initially used this design. 18__. 1850s.

Rarity: *None known*

$5 • **W-RI-1220-005-N040**

Center: Vulcan with sledge, Train. *Comments:* H-RI-400-N20, Durand-2018. Altered or spurious. 1840s.

Rarity: *None known*

$5 • **W-RI-1220-005-A030**

Left: V / Portrait of Henry Clay. *Center:* Steamboat. *Right:* 5 / Portrait of George Washington. *Overprint:* Red FIVE. *Engraver:* New England Bank Note Co. / Rawdon, Wright, Hatch & Edson. *Comments:* H-RI-400-A15, Durand-2014. Altered from $5 Waubeek Bank, De Soto, Nebraska. 1857.

Rarity: *None known*

$5 • **W-RI-1220-005-A040**   CJF

Engraver: Durand & Co. *Comments:* H-RI-400-A20, Durand-2015. Altered from $5 Globe Bank, New York City, New York series. April __, 1840.

Rarity: URS-3

F $300

$5 • **W-RI-1220-005-A050**

Left: FIVE / Laureate woman with shield bearing 5. *Center:* Train / Allegorical woman in clouds with eagle and shield / 5. *Right:* FIVE / Liberty. *Engraver:* W.L. Ormsby. *Comments:* H-RI-400-A22, Durand-2016. Altered from $5 Potomac River Bank, Georgetown, D.C. 18__. 1850s.

Rarity: *None known*

$10 • **W-RI-1220-010-C150**

Engraver: Leney & Rollinson. *Comments:* H-RI-400-C34, Durand-2023. Counterfeit of W-RI-1220-010-G150. 18__. 1840s.

Rarity: *None known*

$10 • **W-RI-1220-010-R020**

Comments: H-RI-400-R6, Durand-2024. Raised from W-RI-1220-001-G040 series. 18__. 1850s.

Rarity: *None known*

$10 • **W-RI-1220-010-N050**

Center: Vulcan with sledge, Train. *Comments:* H-RI-400-N25, Durand-2027. Altered or spurious. 1840s.

Rarity: *None known*

$10 • W-RI-1220-010-AR010

Center: Blacksmith and two women. *Comments:* H-RI-400-A25, Durand-2026. Altered and raised from $2. 1840s.

Rarity: *None known*

$10 • W-RI-1220-010-A060   CC

Overprint: Red X / X. *Comments:* H-RI-400-A30, Durand-2025. Altered from W-RI-1630-010-G050. 18__. 1855.

Rarity: URS-4
F $200

$20 • W-RI-1220-020-R030

Engraver: Toppan, Carpenter, Casilear & Co. *Comments:* H-RI-400-R7, Durand-2028. Raised from W-RI-1220-001-G040 series. No genuine $20 notes have been reported from this bank. 18__. 1850s.

Rarity: *None known*

Union Bank of Providence
1850s
W-RI-1230

History: A non-existent bank represented only by notes altered from those of other banks. The notes were intended to pass for those of the Union Bank, W-RI-1220.

ISSUES

$3 • W-RI-1230-003-A010   CJF

Engraver: Rawdon, Wright & Hatch. *Comments:* H-RI-401-G4. May 1st, 1847.

Rarity: URS-3
F $300

Westminster Bank
1854–1923
W-RI-1240

History: The Westminster Bank was incorporated in 1854. It was located at 42 Weybosset Street in 1864, 56 Weybosset in 1886, and 73 Westminster Street in 1916.

Capital was $101,300 in 1855. Selected figures for 1857 included: bills in circulation $41,937; specie $3,675.48. Circulation reached $70,028 by 1862 but was only $1,070 in 1874. Specie was a mere $122.74 at that time but had risen to $127,104.77 by 1914.

The bank remained open as a state bank until 1923, but it did not issue any notes after the mid-1860s.

Numismatic Commentary: Collectors should be able to acquire a few issues from this bank without too much difficulty. One $5 note shows a panoramic vignette of the railroad station in the heart of the city.

VALID ISSUES

$1 • W-RI-1240-001-G010

Left: 1 / Male portrait. *Center:* Rural scene, Farmers at lunch. *Right:* 1 / Beehive. *Overprint:* Likely red ONE. *Engraver:* Toppan, Carpenter, Casilear & Co. *Comments:* H-RI-405-G2a, Durand-2032. 18__. 1850s.

Rarity: *None known*

$1 • W-RI-1240-001-G010a   CJF

Overprint: Red panel outlining white ONE. *Engraver:* American Bank Note Co. *Comments:* H-RI-405-G2c, Durand-2033. Similar to W-RI-1240-001-G010 but with different engraver imprint. 18__. 1860s.

Rarity: URS-3
VF $750

$2 • W-RI-1240-002-G020

Left: 2 / Male portrait. *Center:* Two allegorical figures. *Right:* 2 / Female portrait. *Overprint:* Likely red TWO. *Engraver:* Toppan, Carpenter, Casilear & Co. *Comments:* H-RI-405-G4a, Durand-2035. 18__. 1850s.

Rarity: *None known*

$2 • W-RI-1240-002-G020a

Overprint: Red panel outlining white TWO. *Engraver:* American Bank Note Co. *Comments:* H-RI-405-G4c, Durand-2036. Similar to W-RI-1240-002-G020 but with different engraver imprint. 18__. 1860s.

Rarity: *None known*

$5 • W-RI-1240-005-G030

Left: 5 / Male portrait. *Center:* View of Providence Railroad Station. *Right:* 5 / Male portrait. *Overprint:* Likely red FIVE. *Engraver:* Toppan, Carpenter, Casilear & Co. *Comments:* H-RI-405-G6a, Durand-2037. 18__. 1850s.

Rarity: *None known*

$5 • W-RI-1240-005-G030a

CJF

Overprint: Red panel outlining white FIVE. *Engraver:* American Bank Note Co. *Comments:* H-RI-405-G6c, Durand-2038. Similar to W-RI-1240-005-G030 but with different engraver imprint. 18__. 1860s.

Rarity: URS-7
EF $200; **CU** $300

$10 • W-RI-1240-010-G045

CC

Engraver: Toppan, Carpenter, Casilear & Co. *Comments:* H-Unlisted, Durand-Unlisted. Proof. 18__. 1850s.

Rarity: URS-1
Proof $2,100
Selected auction price: Stack's Bowers Galleries, March 2013, Proof $2,013

$10 • W-RI-1240-010-G045a

Overprint: Likely red TEN. *Engraver:* Toppan, Carpenter, Casilear & Co. *Comments:* H-RI-405-G8a, Durand-2041. Similar to W-RI-1240-010-G045. 18__. 1850s.

Rarity: *None known*

$10 • W-RI-1240-010-G045b

CJF

Overprint: Red panel outlining white TEN. *Engraver:* American Bank Note Co. *Comments:* H-RI-405-G8c, Durand-2042. Similar to W-RI-1240-010-G045 but with different engraver imprint. 18__. 1860s.

Rarity: URS-6
VF $300; **Unc-Rem** $400

$20 • W-RI-1240-020-G060

CC

Engraver: Toppan, Carpenter, Casilear & Co. *Comments:* H-Unlisted. 18__. 1850s.

Rarity: URS-6
VF $300

$20 • W-RI-1240-020-G060a

Left: Man on horse, Goats, Two men / 20. *Center:* Female portrait. *Right:* 20 on die / Male portrait. *Overprint:* Red TWENTY. *Engraver:* Toppan, Carpenter, Casilear & Co. *Comments:* H-RI-405-G10a, Durand-2044. Similar to W-RI-1240-020-G060. 18__. 1850s–1860s.

Rarity: URS-2
Proof $2,500

$20 • W-RI-1240-020-G060b

CJF

Overprint: Red panel outlining white TWENTY. *Engraver:* American Bank Note Co. *Comments:* H-RI-405-G10c, Durand-2045. Similar to W-RI-1240-020-G060 but with different engraver imprint. 18__. 1860s.

Rarity: URS-6
VF $325; **Unc-Rem** $400

$50 • W-RI-1240-050-G070

Left: 50 / Male portrait. *Center:* Portrait of John Quincy Adams / Commerce seated / Portrait of John Adams. *Right:* 50 / Female portrait. *Overprint:* Likely red FIFTY. *Engraver:* Toppan, Carpenter, Casilear & Co. *Comments:* H-RI-405-G12a, Durand-2046. 18__. 1850s.

Rarity: *None known*

$50 • W-RI-1240-050-G070a

CJF

Overprint: Red panel outlining white FIFTY. *Engraver:* American Bank Note Co. *Comments:* H-RI-405-G12c, Durand-2047. Similar to W-RI-1240-050-G070 but with different engraver imprint. 18__. 1860s.

Rarity: URS-1
VG $1,500

$100 • W-RI-1240-100-G080

Left: 100 / Herd of horses. *Right:* 100 / Male portrait. *Overprint:* Likely red. *Engraver:* Toppan, Carpenter, Casilear & Co. *Comments:* H-RI-405-G14a, Durand-2048. 18__. 1850s.

Rarity: *None known*

$100 • W-RI-1240-100-G080a

CJF

Overprint: Red panel outlining white C, 100, C. *Engraver:* American Bank Note Co. *Comments:* H-RI-405-G14c, Durand-2049. Similar to W-RI-1240-100-G080 but with different engraver imprint. 18__. 1860s.

Rarity: URS-3
VF $750

$500 • W-RI-1240-500-G090

Left: FIVE HUNDRED vertically. *Center:* Woman and Indian man flanking eagle / Male portrait. *Right:* 500 in wreath / Woman and three men seated. *Engraver:* Toppan, Carpenter, Casilear & Co. *Comments:* H-RI-405-G16, Durand-2050. 18__. 1850s.

Rarity: *None known*

$500 • W-RI-1240-500-G090a

CJF

Engraver: American Bank Note Co. *Comments:* H-RI-405-G16b. Similar to W-RI-1240-500-G090 but with different engraver imprint. 18__. 1860s.

Rarity: URS-1
Unc-Rem $900; **Proof** $2,500

Uncut Sheets

$5-$5-$10-$20 • W-RI-1240-005.005.010.020-US010

Vignette(s): *($5)* Male portrait / View of Providence / Male portrait. *($5)* Male portrait / View of Providence / Male portrait. *($10)* Ship / Two male portraits / Sailing ship. *($20)* Man on horse and animals / Female portrait / Male portrait. *Engraver:* American Bank Note Co. *Comments:* H-RI-405-G6c, G6c, G8c, G10c. 18__. 1860s.

Rarity: URS-8
Proof $800

Non-Valid Issues

$1 • W-RI-1240-001-A010

CJF

Engraver: Draper, Toppan, Longacre & Co. *Comments:* H-RI-405-A5, Durand-2034. Altered from $1 Calhoun County Bank, Marshall, Michigan. 18__. 1830s–1850s.

Rarity: URS-7
VF $250

$5 • W-RI-1240-005-R010

Comments: H-RI-405-R4, Durand-2039. Raised from W-RI-1240-001-G010 series. 18__. 1850s–1860s.

Rarity: *None known*

$5 • W-RI-1240-005-R020

CJF

Comments: H-Unlisted, Durand-Unlisted. Raised from W-RI-1240-002-G020 series. 18__. 1850s–1860s.
Rarity: URS-1
F $250

$5 • W-RI-1240-005-S010

CJF

Engraver: Danforth, Wright & Co. *Comments:* H-RI-405-S5, Durand-2040. 18__. 1830s–1850s.
Rarity: URS-6
VF $135

$10 • W-RI-1240-010-R030
Comments: H-RI-405-R6, Durand-2043. Raised from W-RI-1240-001-G010 series. 18__. 1850s–1860s.
Rarity: *None known*

Weybosset Bank
1831–1865
W-RI-1250

History: The Weybosset Bank was chartered and incorporated in 1831 as a direct result of the expansion of industry in the area. Several new companies and manufactories needed accommodation, and several banks were formed to answer the call.[74]

The capital of the Weybosset Bank was $325,000 in 1848 and increased to $400,000 by 1856. Bills in circulation amounted to $41,094.25 in 1849, $59,524 in 1857, and $268,631 in 1862. Specie totaled $5,577.71 in 1857.

The amount of fractional bills issued by the bank in September 1853 was $119,000. In February 1854, the same was $68,347. The bank was located at 55 Westminster Street in 1856.

The business of the Weybosset Bank was succeeded by the Weybosset National Bank, chartered on May 20, 1865.

Numismatic Commentary: Some issues from this bank are exceptionally interesting, such as the note with the vignette of an Indian spearing a bison and three different unusual denominations. Most genuine issues are hard to locate.

VALID ISSUES
$1 • W-RI-1250-001-G010

CC

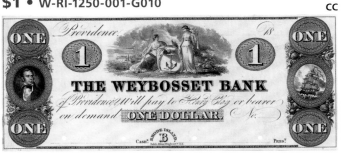

Engraver: Balch, Stiles, Wright & Co. *Comments:* H-RI-410-G2, Durand-2051. 18__. 1830s.
Rarity: URS-3
Proof $1,200
Selected auction price: Spink-Smythe, April 2009, Proof $1,111

$1 • W-RI-1250-001-G020

CJF

Engraver: Boston Bank Note Co. *Comments:* H-RI-410-G4, Durand-2052. 18__. 1840s–1850s.
Rarity: URS-3
VF $400

$1 • W-RI-1250-001-G030
Left: 1 on die / Woman with veil. *Center:* Men and Indians / Male portrait. *Right:* 1 on die / Portrait of William Rhodes. *Engraver:* Toppan, Carpenter, Casilear & Co. *Comments:* H-RI-410-G6, Durand-2053. 18__. 1850s.
Rarity: *None known*

$1 • W-RI-1250-001-G030a
Overprint: Red ONE. *Engraver:* Toppan, Carpenter, Casilear & Co. / ABNCo. monogram. *Comments:* H-RI-410-G6b, Durand-2055. Similar to W-RI-1250-001-G030 but with additional engraver imprint. 18__. 1850s.
Rarity: URS-3
VF $400

$1 • W-RI-1250-001-G030b   CJF

Overprint: Red 1 / 1. *Engraver:* Toppan, Carpenter, Casilear & Co. / ABNCo. monogram. *Comments:* H-RI-410-G6c, Durand-2054. Similar to W-RI-1250-001-G030 but with additional engraver imprint. 18__. 1860s.
Rarity: URS-3
VF $750

$1.25 • W-RI-1250-001.25-G040   CJF

Engraver: New England Bank Note Co. *Comments:* H-RI-410-G7. 18__. 1850s.
Rarity: URS-2
VF $1,000

$1.50 • W-RI-1250-001.50-G050
Left: 1 Doll 50 Cts. vertically. *Center:* Eagle on rock in ocean / $1 50/100. *Right:* 1 50/100 / Justice. *Engraver:* New England Bank Note Co. *Comments:* H-RI-410-G8. 18__. 1850s.
Rarity: *None known*

$1.75 • W-RI-1250-001.75-G060
Left: $1.75 Cts. / Hebe watering eagle / 1 75/100. *Center:* Three sloops at sea. *Right:* $1.75 Cts. / Woman seated with grain, Dog / 1 75/100. *Engraver:* New England Bank Note Co. *Comments:* H-RI-410-G9. 18__. 1850s.
Rarity: *None known*

$2 • W-RI-1250-002-G070
Left: 2 / TWO. *Center:* Ships, Sailor seated on bale, Ships. *Bottom center:* Eagle. *Right:* TWO / State arms. *Engraver:* Balch, Stiles, Wright & Co. *Comments:* H-RI-410-G10, Durand-2059. 18__. 1830s.
Rarity: *None known*

$2 • W-RI-1250-002-G080
Left: RHODE ISLAND vertically. *Center:* Goddess of Plenty opening money chest. *Bottom center:* Eagle. *Right:* Stars bearing 2. *Engraver:* Boston Bank Note Co. *Comments:* H-RI-410-G12, Durand-2060. 18__. 1840s–1850s.
Rarity: *None known*

$2 • W-RI-1250-002-G090
Left: 2 / Female portrait. *Center:* "John Eliot preaching to the Indians". *Right:* 2 / Portrait of William Rhodes. *Engraver:* Toppan, Carpenter, Casilear & Co. *Comments:* H-RI-410-G14, Durand-2061. 18__. 1850s.
Rarity: URS-3
VF $900

$2 • W-RI-1250-002-G090a
Overprint: Red TWO. *Engraver:* Toppan, Carpenter, Casilear & Co. / ABNCo. monogram. *Comments:* H-RI-410-G14b, Durand-2063. Similar to W-RI-1250-002-G090 but with additional engraver imprint. 18__. 1850s–1860s.
Rarity: *None known*

$2 • W-RI-1250-002-G090b
Overprint: Red 2 / 2. *Engraver:* Toppan, Carpenter, Casilear & Co. / ABNCo. monogram. *Comments:* H-RI-410-G14c, Durand-2062. Similar to W-RI-1250-002-G090 but with additional engraver imprint. 18__. 1860s.
Rarity: *None known*

$5 • W-RI-1250-005-G100   CC

Engraver: Balch, Stiles, Wright & Co. *Comments:* H-RI-410-G16, Durand-2068. 18__. 1830s.
Rarity: URS-2
Proof $1,100

$5 • W-RI-1250-005-G110
Left: 5 / Woman with pole and cap and headdress. *Center:* Portrait of George Washington / Sailing vessel / Portrait of John Quincy Adams. *Right:* 5 / Woman. *Engraver:* Toppan, Carpenter & Co. *Comments:* H-RI-410-G20, Durand-2070. 18__. 1840s–1850s.
Rarity: URS-3
Proof $1,200

$5 • **W-RI-1250-005-G110a**
Engraver: Toppan, Carpenter & Co. *Comments:* H-RI-410-G20a, Durand-2069. Similar to W-RI-1250-005-G110 but with different date. April 1st, 18___. 1850s.
Rarity: URS-3

$5 • **W-RI-1250-005-G125**
CJF

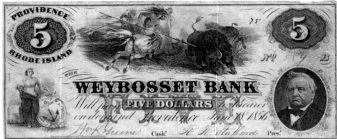

Overprint: Red FIVE. *Engraver:* Toppan, Carpenter & Co. *Comments:* H-RI-410-G22a, Durand-2070. June 18, 1856.
Rarity: URS-3
VF $750

$10 • **W-RI-1250-010-G140**
Left: Spread eagle on rock in sea / TEN. *Center:* 10 / Cornucopia, wand, barrels, Ship / 10. *Right:* George Washington standing. *Comments:* H-RI-410-G26, Durand-2078. 1850s.
Rarity: *None known*

$10 • **W-RI-1250-010-G150**
Left: Female portrait. *Center:* Commerce. *Right:* Male portrait. *Comments:* H-RI-410-G28, Durand-2079. 1850s.
Rarity: *None known*

$10 • **W-RI-1250-010-G160**
SBG

Engraver: Toppan, Carpenter & Co. *Comments:* H-RI-410-G30, Durand-2080. 18___. 1840s–1850s.
Rarity: URS-3
Proof $750

$20 • **W-RI-1250-020-G170**
Engraver: Balch, Stiles, Wright & Co. *Comments:* H-RI-410-G32, Durand-2084. No description available. 18___. 1830s.
Rarity: *None known*

$50 • **W-RI-1250-050-G180**
Left: FIFTY vertically. *Center:* 50 / Ship, Commerce. *Bottom center:* L. *Right:* 50 / Shield of Hope / 50. *Engraver:* Balch, Stiles, Wright & Co. *Comments:* H-RI-410-G34, Durand-2087. 18___. 1830s–1860s.
Rarity: URS-3
Proof $350

$100 • **W-RI-1250-100-G190**
Left: Eagle on rock / 100. *Center:* 100 / Allegorical woman reclining on shield bearing anchor. *Right:* 100 / Male portrait / 100. *Engraver:* Toppan, Carpenter, Casilear & Co. *Comments:* H-RI-410-G38, Durand-2088. 18___. 1850s.
Rarity: *None known*

$500 • **W-RI-1250-500-G200**
Left: 500. *Center:* Commerce, Portrait of Millard Fillmore. *Bottom center:* Female portrait. *Right:* 500. *Engraver:* Toppan, Carpenter, Casilear & Co. *Comments:* H-RI-410-G42, Durand-2089. 18___. 1850s.
Rarity: URS-3
Proof $2,500

Uncut Sheets
$5-$5-$10-$10 • **W-RI-1250-005.005.010.010-US010**
Vignette(s): *($5)* Woman with pole and cap and headdress / Portrait of George Washington / Sailing vessel / Portrait of John Quincy Adams / Woman. *($5)* Woman with pole and cap and headdress / Portrait of George Washington / Sailing vessel / Portrait of John Quincy Adams / Woman. *($10)* Portrait of William Henry Harrison / Female portrait / Dog with strongbox / Female portrait / Eagle / Portrait of Henry Clay. *($10)* Portrait of William Henry Harrison / Female portrait / Dog with strongbox / Female portrait / Eagle / Portrait of Henry Clay. *Engraver:* Toppan, Carpenter & Co. *Comments:* H-RI-410-G20, G20, G30, G30. 18___. 1840s–1850s.
Rarity: URS-3
Proof $2,000

NON-VALID ISSUES
$1.25 • **W-RI-1250-001.25-A010**
Left: 1 25/100 / Train / 1 25/100. *Center:* Sailing ships in bay / $1.25 Cts. *Right:* 1 25/100 / Spread eagle. *Engraver:* New England Bank Note Co. *Comments:* H-RI-410-A5, Durand-2056. Altered from $1.25 Roxbury Bank, Roxbury, Massachusetts, or from notes of other failed banks using the same plate. 18___. 1850s.
Rarity: *None known*

$1.50 • **W-RI-1250-001.50-A020**
Left: 1 Doll. 50 Cts. vertically. *Center:* Eagle on rock / $1 50/100. *Right:* 1 50/100 / Woman standing. *Engraver:* New England Bank Note Co. *Comments:* H-RI-410-A10, Durand-2057. Altered from $1.50 Roxbury Bank, Roxbury, Massachusetts, or from notes of other failed banks using the same plate. 18___. 1850s.
Rarity: URS-5
VF $300

$1.75 • **W-RI-1250-001.75-A030**
Left: $1.75 Cts. / Liberty and eagle / 1 75/100. *Center:* Three sloops at sea. *Right:* $1.75 Cts. / Agriculture / 1 75/100. *Engraver:* New England Bank Note Co. *Comments:* H-RI-410-A15, Durand-2058. Altered from $1.75 Roxbury Bank, Roxbury, Massachusetts, or from notes of other failed banks using the same plate. 18___. 1850s.
Rarity: *None known*

$2 • W-RI-1250-002-C090

Comments: H-Unlisted, Durand-2064. Counterfeit of W-RI-1250-002-G090. Early photograph reproduction. 1850s.

Rarity: URS-3

F $200

$3 • W-RI-1250-003-R010

Engraver: Boston Bank Note Co. *Comments:* H-RI-410-R5, Durand-2065. Raised from W-RI-1250-001-G020. No genuine $3 bills have been reported from this bank. 18__. 1840s.

Rarity: *None known*

$3 • W-RI-1250-003-S010

Left: Woman / 3. *Center:* 3 on die / Train / 3 on die. *Right:* Indian with gun and raised tomahawk / 3. *Engraver:* New England Bank Note Co. *Comments:* H-RI-410-S5, Durand-2067. 18__. 1837.

Rarity: URS-3

VF $150

$3 • W-RI-1250-003-A040

Left: THREE / Beehive and foliage / THREE. *Center:* Ceres with machinery and merchandise, Factories and harbor / THREE. *Right:* 3 on THREE / Two reapers / 3 on THREE. *Engraver:* PSSP / New England Bank Note Co. *Comments:* H-RI-410-A20, Durand-2066. Altered from $3 Washington County Bank, Calais, Maine, or from notes of other failed banks using the same plate. 18__. 1850s.

Rarity: URS-3

VF $150

$5 • W-RI-1250-005-C110a

CJF

Engraver: Toppan, Carpenter & Co. *Comments:* H-RI-410-C20a. Counterfeit of W-RI-1250-005-G110a. April 1st, 18__. 1860 and 1861.

Rarity: URS-8

VG $65; VF $150

$5 • W-RI-1250-005-C120

Comments: H-Unlisted, Durand-2071. Counterfeit of W-RI-1250-005-G120. 1850s.

Rarity: URS-6

$5 • W-RI-1250-005-R020

Engraver: Boston Bank Note Co. *Comments:* H-RI-410-R10, Durand-2072. Raised from W-RI-1250-001-G020. 18__. 1840s.

Rarity: *None known*

$5 • W-RI-1250-005-R030

Engraver: Toppan, Carpenter, Casilear & Co. *Comments:* H-RI-410-R15, Durand-2073. Raised from W-RI-1250-001-G030 series. 18__. 1850s.

Rarity: *None known*

$5 • W-RI-1250-005-N010

Left: Blacksmith. *Center:* Woman beside 5. *Right:* Woman and flowers. *Comments:* H-RI-410-N5, Durand-2076. Altered or spurious. 1850s.

Rarity: *None known*

$5 • W-RI-1250-005-N020

Left: Blacksmith. *Center:* Ship, anchor. *Right:* Woman. *Comments:* H-RI-410-N10, Durand-2077. Altered or spurious. 1850s.

Rarity: *None known*

$5 • W-RI-1250-005-N030

Center: Three mechanics. *Comments:* H-Unlisted, Durand-2075. Altered or spurious. 1850s.

Rarity: URS-3

F $100

$5 • W-RI-1250-005-A050

Left: FIVE / State arms vertically. *Center:* Three men. *Right:* 5 / Portrait of Franklin Pierce. *Engraver:* Danforth, Wright & Co. *Comments:* H-RI-410-A25. Altered from $5 Bank of Washtenaw, Ann Arbor, Michigan series. 1850s.

Rarity: *None known*

$5 • W-RI-1250-005-A060

Left: 5 / Blacksmith at anvil / FIVE. *Center:* Mercury holding shield bearing 5 / Sailing vessel / V on die / FIVE. *Right:* 5 / Ceres seated / FIVE. *Engraver:* PSSP / New England Bank Note Co. *Comments:* H-RI-410-A30, Durand-2074. Altered from $5 Washington County Bank, Calais, Maine. 18__. 1850s.

Rarity: *None known*

$10 • W-RI-1250-010-R030

Engraver: Toppan, Carpenter, Casilear & Co. *Comments:* H-RI-410-R20, Durand-2081. Raised from W-RI-1250-001-G030 series. 18__. 1850s.

Rarity: *None known*

$10 • W-RI-1250-010-N040

Left: Indian. *Center:* Steamboat. *Right:* Woman. *Comments:* H-Unlisted, Durand-2083. Altered or spurious. 1850s.

Rarity: URS-3

F $90

$10 • W-RI-1250-010-A070

Left: 10 / Man standing / TEN. *Center:* Man holding shield bearing 10 / Ship / X on die / TEN. *Right:* 10 / Sailing vessel / TEN. *Engraver:* PSSP / New England Bank Note Co. *Comments:* H-RI-410-A35, Durand-2082. Altered from $10 Oxford Bank, Fryeburg, Maine, or from notes of other failed banks using the same plate. 18__. 1850s.

Rarity: URS-3

VF $150

$10 • W-RI-1250-010-A080

Left: 10 / Hebe seated with Liberty pole and watering eagle. *Center:* Steamboat loaded with cotton. *Bottom center:* Shield. *Right:* 10 / Female portrait / TEN. *Engraver:* Rawdon, Wright, Hatch & Edson. *Comments:* H-RI-410-A40. Altered from $10 Farmers & Merchants Bank of Memphis, Memphis, Tennessee series. 1850s.

Rarity: *None known*

$20 • **W-RI-1250-020-R040**

Comments: H-Unlisted, Durand-2084. Raised from W-RI-1250-001-G030. 1850s.

Rarity: URS-3

$20 • **W-RI-1250-020-R050**

Left: XX / Female portrait. *Center:* "John Eliot preaching to the Indians". *Right:* 20 / Male portrait. *Engraver:* Toppan, Carpenter, Casilear & Co. *Comments:* H-RI-410-R25, Durand-2085. Raised from W-RI-1250-002-G090. 18__. 1850s.

Rarity: URS-3

VF $200

$20 • **W-RI-1250-020-A090**

Left: 20 / XX / 20. *Center:* 20 / Justice on wharf with bales and merchandise, Ship / 20. *Right:* Oval. *Comments:* H-Unlisted, Durand-2086. Altered from $20 Washington County Bank, Calais, Maine. 1850s.

Rarity: URS-3

F $75

What Cheer Bank
1853–1866
W-RI-1260

History: The What Cheer Bank was incorporated in May 1853. Its unusual name is derived from an Indian phrase. In 1636, in an attempt to escape religious persecution in the Massachusetts Bay Colony, Roger Williams and others crossed the Seekonk River. When he arrived, the Narragansett Indians greeted him with "What Cheer, Netop!" This term became famous and in later years was used to name many businesses, including one in Gold Rush California.

The bank's capital was $159,150 in 1857. By 1863 it was $160,400. Circulation was at $29,304 in 1857 and had increased to $66,775 in 1862. Specie amounted to $2,489.12 in 1857. The bank was located at 4 Union Building in 1860.

The bank ceased business in 1866.

Numismatic Commentary: The note most likely to be found is the $2 spurious issue with the portraits of John Marshall and Elias Boudinot.

Valid Issues

$1 • **W-RI-1260-001-G010**

Left: 1 / Industry. *Center:* Indian seated on cliff, River and city. *Right:* 1 / Female portrait. *Overprint:* Red ONE. *Engraver:* Toppan, Carpenter, Casilear & Co. *Comments:* H-RI-415-G2a, Durand-2091. 18__. 1850s.

Rarity: URS-3

VF $500

$1 • **W-RI-1260-001-G010a**

CC

Engraver: Toppan, Carpenter, Casilear & Co. / ABNCo. monogram. *Comments:* H-Unlisted. Similar to W-RI-1260-001-G010 but with additional engraver imprint. 18__. 1850s–1860s.

Rarity: URS-2

F $1,700

Selected auction price: Lynn Knight, July 2008, F $1,657

$1 • **W-RI-1260-001-G010b**

Overprint: Red ONE. *Engraver:* Toppan, Carpenter, Casilear & Co. / ABNCo. monogram. *Comments:* H-RI-415-G2b. Similar to W-RI-1260-001-G010 but with additional engraver imprint. 18__. 1850s–1860s.

Rarity: URS-1

$2 • **W-RI-1260-002-G020**

Left: 2 / Fine Arts. *Center:* Two horses and colt running in field. *Right:* 2 / Female portrait. *Overprint:* Red TWO. *Engraver:* Toppan, Carpenter, Casilear & Co. *Comments:* H-RI-415-G4a, Durand-2092. 18__. 1850s.

Rarity: *None known*

$2 • **W-RI-1260-002-G020a**

Overprint: Red TWO. *Engraver:* Toppan, Carpenter, Casilear & Co. / ABNCo. monogram. *Comments:* H-RI-415-G4b, Durand-2092. Similar to W-RI-1260-002-G020 but with additional engraver imprint. 18__. 1850s–1860s.

Rarity: URS-3

VF $750

$2 • **W-RI-1260-002-G020b**

SBG

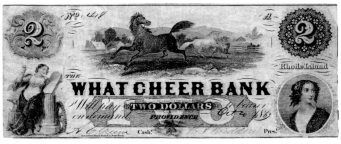

Overprint: Green panel outlining white TWO. *Engraver:* American Bank Note Co. *Comments:* H-Unlisted, Durand-Unlisted. Similar to W-RI-1260-002-G020 but with different engraver imprint. 18__. 1860s.

Rarity: URS-2

VF $1,900

Selected auction price: Stack's Bowers Galleries, August 2012, VF $1,895

$5 • W-RI-1260-005-G030

Left: Female portrait / 5. *Center:* Liberty, State arms surmounted by eagle, Justice. *Bottom center:* Steamboat. *Right:* 5 / Indian seated. *Overprint:* Red FIVE. *Engraver:* Toppan, Carpenter, Casilear & Co. *Comments:* H-RI-415-G6a, Durand-2095. 18__. 1850s.

Rarity: *None known*

$5 • W-RI-1260-005-G030a

Overprint: Red FIVE. *Engraver:* Toppan, Carpenter, Casilear & Co. / ABNCo. monogram. *Comments:* H-RI-415-G6b, Durand-2096. Similar to W-RI-1260-005-G030 but with additional engraver imprint. 18__. 1850s–1860s.

Rarity: *None known*

$10 • W-RI-1260-010-G040

Left: 10 / Portrait of Daniel Webster. *Center:* Cattle. *Bottom center:* Portrait of Indian. *Right:* 10 / Anchor and bales. *Engraver:* Toppan, Carpenter, Casilear & Co. *Comments:* H-RI-415-G8, Durand-2097. 18__. 1850s.

Rarity: *None known*

$50 • W-RI-1260-050-G050

Left: FIFTY / Goddess of Plenty. *Center:* Three sea nymphs floating in water supporting cherub. *Right:* 50 / Portrait of Henry Clay. *Engraver:* Toppan, Carpenter, Casilear & Co. *Comments:* H-RI-415-G12, Durand-2100. 18__. 1850s.

Rarity: *None known*

$100 • W-RI-1260-100-G060

Left: 100 / Henry Clay seated with dog. *Center:* Liberty seated between two columns, Eagle and shield, Train and town. *Right:* 100 / Ship, Commerce seated with spyglass. *Engraver:* Toppan, Carpenter, Casilear & Co. *Comments:* H-RI-415-G14, Durand-2101. 18__. 1850s.

Rarity: *None known*

NON-VALID ISSUES

$2 • W-RI-1260-002-S010

CJF

Engraver: Danforth, Wright & Co. *Comments:* H-RI-415-S5, Durand-2093. 18__. 1861.

Rarity: URS-7
F $110; **VF** $150

$3 • W-RI-1260-003-R010

ANS

Engraver: Toppan, Carpenter, Casilear & Co. / ABNCo. monogram. *Comments:* H-RI-415-R5, Durand-2094. Raised from W-RI-1260-001-G010b. The bank issued no $3 bills. 18__. 1860s.

Rarity: URS-3
VF $350

$5 • W-RI-1260-005-R020

Engraver: Toppan, Carpenter, Casilear & Co. / ABNCo. monogram. *Comments:* H-RI-415-R10. Raised from W-RI-1260-001-G010b. 18__. 1860s.

Rarity: *None known*

$10 • W-RI-1260-010-R030

Engraver: Toppan, Carpenter, Casilear & Co. / ABNCo. monogram. *Comments:* H-RI-415-R15, Durand-2098. Raised from W-RI-1260-001-G010b. 18__. 1860s.

Rarity: *None known*

$10 • W-RI-1260-010-R040

Engraver: Toppan, Carpenter, Casilear & Co. / ABNCo. monogram. *Comments:* H-RI-415-R20, Durand-2099. Raised from W-RI-1260-002-G020a. 18__. 1860s.

Rarity: *None known*

RICHMOND, RHODE ISLAND

The land that was integrated as Richmond by the General Assembly was originally inhabited by the Narragansett tribe. In May 1669, the area was organized under the name of Westerly. It was made up of land that later separated into four towns: Westerly, Charlestown, Richmond, and Hopkinton. Charlestown separated from Westerly in 1738, and Richmond followed suit, separating from Charlestown on August 18, 1747. It is thought to have been named after Edward Richmond, the attorney general for the colony in the late 1670s.

Farming and agriculture made up the primary commercial activity for the town, including dairy, wool, poultry, and cranberries. Industry followed after, powered by water from the local streams. Sawmills and textile mills flourished as a result.

Richmond had a population of 508 in 1748. This figure reached as high as 1,830 by 1865.

See also Alton, Rhode Island.

Richmond Bank
1856–1866
W-RI-1270

History: The Richmond Bank was chartered in May 1856 with an authorized capital of $50,000. By 1857 the figure had doubled. Later, the bank had an address in Alton, another village within Richmond. In 1860 the capital amount was back at the original $50,000. Circulation averaged at $31,000, and specie totaled $1,293.17 in 1857.[75]

In 1865 the bank was located in Hopkinton. Its business was succeeded by the First National Bank of Hopkinton, chartered in 1865.

See also listings under Alton, W-RI-010, and Hopkinton, W-RI-460.

Washington County Bank
1856–1865
W-RI-1280

History: This bank was incorporated in Richmond in 1856 and went into operation on August 12 the same year. R.G. Hazard was its first president and J.H. Babcock its first cashier. Capital was set at $50,000. In an early account, bills in circulation were listed at $16,122, and specie totaled $1,458.41. The name of the location was changed to Carolina Mills in 1863, after which the bank moved to Charlestown. It closed in 1865.

See also listing under Carolina Mills, W-RI-190.

Numismatic Commentary: Collectors can find examples of attractive 1850s–1860s notes with variants of both red and green overprints available. High-grade notes should not be too hard to locate.

Remaining in the American Bank Note Co. archives as of 2003 was a $1-$2-$1-$5 tint plate.

SCITUATE, RHODE ISLAND

Settled in 1710 by immigrants from a town of the same name in Massachusetts, the area of Scituate was first known as "Satuit," which means "cold brook" in the native tongue of the Indians who resided there. The town separated from Providence in 1731. The first moderator of Scituate was Stephen Hopkins, who became governor of Rhode Island and also signed the Declaration of Independence.

Villages that made up Scituate included North Scituate, Hope, Ashland, Clayville, Elmdale, Fiskeville, Glenn Rock, Harrisdale, Jackson, Kent, Ponaganset, Potterville, Richmond, Rockland, Saundersville, and South Scituate. Foster separated in 1781.

See also North Scituate, Rhode Island.

Citizens Union Bank
1833–1865
W-RI-1290

History: The Citizens Union Bank was chartered in January 1833 in Scituate with $50,000 in authorized capital. Josiah Westcott served as its founding president, and David H. Braman was the first cashier. In 1835 the plates of this bank fell into the hands of racketeers. As a result, the bank failed in 1836, but it redeemed its bills in full. Later it was reorganized, given an infusion of capital, and reopened for business.[76] The bank's capital had increased to $55,675 by 1857. It had bills in circulation amounting to $19,638, which rose to $28,972 by 1862. Specie totaled $2,186.53 in 1857.

The interests of the Citizens Union Bank were succeeded by the Scituate National Bank, chartered on September 7, 1865.

See also listing under North Scituate, W-RI-670.

Numismatic Commentary: Genuine notes are hard to find. One historical issue bears an interesting vignette of William Tell with a crossbow, shooting an apple off of the head of his son. Another shows "The Signing of the First Constitution" (Mayflower Compact) while on board the Mayflower. Another unusual vignette used by this bank could be considered a "borrowed" vignette that was exclusively engraved for the Bank of North America in Philadelphia (incorporated in 1781). On a $20 issue, an allegorical female appears at the front of the bank building offering General George Washington a sack of coins to support the Continental Army. This vignette appeared on a $50 issue of the Bank of North America in Philadelphia.

Remaining in the American Bank Note Co. archives as of 2003 was a $1-$1-$3-$5 face plate.

VALID ISSUES
$1 • W-RI-1290-001-G010

CC

Comments: H-RI-435-G2, Durand-2102. Proof. 18__. 1830s.
Rarity: URS-3
Proof $1,200
Selected auction price: Spink-Smythe,
April 2009, Proof $1,173

$1 • W-RI-1290-001-G020
Left: ONE vertically. **Center:** Train / ONE / 1. **Right:** ONE / Ships / ONE. **Engraver:** Terry, Pelton & Co. **Comments:** H-RI-435-G4, Durand-2103. Contemporary, unauthorized printings from the genuine plate have been reported. 18__. 1830s.
Rarity: URS-3
Proof $400

$1 • W-RI-1290-001-G030

Left: 1 / Commerce / 1. *Center:* Liberty, Shield, Eagle. *Bottom center:* Female portrait. *Right:* 1 / Ceres / ONE. *Engraver:* Draper, Toppan & Co. *Comments:* H-RI-435-G6, Durand-2104. 18__. 1840s–1850s.

Rarity: URS-3
Proof $400

$2 • W-RI-1290-002-G040

Left: TWO / Farmer / TWO. *Center:* 2 / Battle at sea / 2. *Bottom center:* Anchor on shield. *Right:* 2 / Portrait of officer. *Comments:* H-RI-435-G10, Durand-2107. 18__. 1840s–1850s.

Rarity: *None known*

$2 • W-RI-1290-002-G050

CJF

Engraver: Toppan, Carpenter & Co. *Comments:* H-RI-435-G12, Durand-2108. 18__. 1860s.

Rarity: URS-1
VF $7,500

$2 • W-RI-1290-002-G060

Left: TWO vertically / 2. *Center:* Spread eagle, iron castings, cannon balls. *Right:* 2 / TWO / Schooner and another boat. *Engraver:* New England Bank Note Co. *Comments:* H-RI-435-G14, Durand-2109. 18__. 1860s.

Rarity: *None known*

$3 • W-RI-1290-003-G070

Left: THREE vertically. *Center:* Men and animals / Two women seated with shield bearing anchor / THREE. *Bottom center:* Train. *Right:* 3 / Female portrait. *Engraver:* Terry, Pelton & Co. *Comments:* H-RI-435-G18, Durand-2112. Contemporary, unauthorized printings from the genuine plate have been reported. 18__. 1830s.

Rarity: URS-3
VF $200

$3 • W-RI-1290-003-G070a

Comments: H-Unlisted, Durand-2110. Similar to W-RI-1290-003-G070. 1830s.

Rarity: URS-3

$3 • W-RI-1290-003-G080

Left: 3 / Commerce seated. *Center:* Fame in clouds blowing trumpet, Eagle and globe. *Right:* 3 / Three cherubs. *Engraver:* Draper, Toppan & Co. *Comments:* H-RI-435-G22, Durand-2111. 18__. 1840s–1850s.

Rarity: URS-3
Proof $400

$5 • W-RI-1290-005-G090

Left: FIVE vertically. *Center:* Men and animals / Two women seated with shield bearing anchor. *Right:* Female portrait. *Engraver:* Terry, Pelton & Co. *Comments:* H-RI-435-G26, Durand-2113. 18__. 1830s.

Rarity: *None known*

$5 • W-RI-1290-005-G100

Left: 5 / Ceres seated. *Center:* Five allegorical figures grouped around 5. *Right:* 5 / Portrait of Indian woman. *Engraver:* Draper, Toppan & Co. *Comments:* H-RI-435-G30, Durand-2114. 18__. 1830s–1850s.

Rarity: URS-3
Proof $400

$5 • W-RI-1290-005-G110

SBG

Comments: H-Unlisted, Durand-Unlisted. 18__. 1830s–1850s.

Rarity: URS-3
EF $500
Selected auction price: Stack's Bowers Galleries, March 2013, EF $484

$10 • W-RI-1290-010-G120

CC

Engraver: Chas. Toppan & Co. *Comments:* H-RI-435-G34, Durand-2117. 18__. 1830s–1850s.

Rarity: URS-3
Proof $1,200

$10 • W-RI-1290-010-G120a

Comments: H-Unlisted, Durand-Unlisted. Similar to W-RI-1290-010-G120 but with "stockholders private property holden" statement. 18__. 1830s–1850s.

Rarity: —

$20 • W-RI-1290-020-G130   CC

Engraver: Chas. Toppan & Co. *Comments:* H-RI-435-G38, Durand-2119. 18__. 1830s–1850s.

Rarity: URS-2
Proof $1,900

$20 • W-RI-1290-020-G130a

Comments: H-Unlisted, Durand-Unlisted. Similar to W-RI-1290-020-G130 but with "stockholders private property holden" statement. 18__. 1830s–1850s.

Rarity: —

$50 • W-RI-1290-050-G140

Left: FIFTY vertically. *Center:* L / Rural scene, Load of hay, men with rakes and forks / L. *Right:* 50 / Man and cattle / 50. *Comments:* H-RI-435-G40, Durand-2121. 18__. 1830s–1850s.

Rarity: *None known*

$100 • W-RI-1290-100-G150

Left: 100 / Woman, Man and horse / 100. *Center:* Steamboat, Ship and sloop. *Right:* 100 / Three allegorical figures / 100. *Comments:* H-RI-435-G42, Durand-2122. 18__. 1830s–1850s.

Rarity: *None known*

Uncut Sheets

$10-$20 • W-RI-1290-010.020-US010

Vignette(s): ($10) Portrait of George Washington / William Tell shooting apple off son's head / Shield bearing anchor / "Washington Crossing the Delaware". *($20)* Eagle on shield / George Washington on horseback receiving scroll from Liberty / Portrait of Marquis de Lafayette. *Engraver:* Chas. Toppan & Co. *Comments:* H-RI-435-G34, G38. 18__. 1830s–1850s.

Rarity: URS-3
Proof $3,500

$10-$20 • W-RI-1290-010.020-US010a

Comments: All unlisted in Haxby. Similar to W-RI-1290-010.020-US010 but with "stockholders private property holden" statement. 1830s–1850s.

Rarity: URS-3

Non-Valid Issues

$1 • W-RI-1290-001-C010

Comments: H-RI-435-C2, Durand-2105. Counterfeit of W-RI-1290-001-G010. 18__. 1830s.

Rarity: URS-3
F $100

$1 • W-RI-1290-001-C020

Comments: H-Unlisted, Durand-2106. Counterfeit of W-RI-1290-001-G020. Unauthorized printing from a genuine plate. 1830s.

Rarity: URS-3
F $125

$5 • W-RI-1290-005-C090

Comments: H-Unlisted, Durand-2115. Counterfeit of W-RI-1290-005-G090. Unauthorized printed from a genuine plate. 1830s.

Rarity: URS-3
F $125

$5 • W-RI-1290-005-A010

Left: 5 / Indian with bow. *Center:* Harbor scene, steamship, sloop / 5. *Right:* 5 / Girl with flowers. *Comments:* H-Unlisted, Durand-2116. Altered from W-RI-1300-005-G070, or from notes of other failed banks using the same plate. 1830s.

Rarity: URS-3
F $150

$10 • W-RI-1290-010-A020

Left: X / Indian with bow. *Center:* Harbor scene, steamship, sloop / X. *Right:* 10 / Girl with flowers. *Engraver:* New England Bank Note Co. *Comments:* H-RI-435-A5, Durand-2118. Altered from W-RI-1300-010-G080, or from notes of other failed banks using the same plate. 18__. 1840s–1850s.

Rarity: *None known*

$20 • W-RI-1290-020-A030

Left: Steamboat / XX / Train. *Center:* Liberty, Justice, and Knowledge with eagle / 20. *Right:* XX / Milkmaid. *Engraver:* New England Bank Note Co. *Comments:* H-RI-435-A10, Durand-2120. Altered from W-RI-1300-020-G090, or from notes of other failed banks using the same plate. 18__. 1840s–1850s.

Rarity: *None known*

Hamilton Bank
1841–1851
W-RI-1300

History: The Hamilton Bank was incorporated as the Scituate Bank, W-RI-1310, in 1818, but it was forced to liquidate due to fraud committed by out-of-state stockholders. The bank was reorganized and reopened in January 1841. At that time the title was changed to the Hamilton Bank under president Luther C. Harris. In that year the bank was robbed of a large number of its unsigned notes. These bills were later put into circulation with forged signatures, and the bank refused to redeem them. The bank maintained a precarious existence until June 1849, when it was forced into receivership yet again. All claims against the bank were required to be presented before June 1852.[77]

See also listing under North Scituate, W-RI-680.

Numismatic Commentary: Genuine notes from this bank are not easy to locate. All the genuine issues dated at Scituate were engraved by the New England Bank Note Co.

VALID ISSUES

$1 • W-RI-1300-001-G010

TD

Comments: H-RI-440-G2, Durand-2136. 18__. 1840s.
Rarity: URS-3
VF $300

$1 • W-RI-1300-001-G020
Comments: H-Unlisted, Durand-2123. No description available. 18__. 1840s.
Rarity: *None known*

$2 • W-RI-1300-002-G030
Left: TWO / Portrait of girl / 2. *Center:* 2 / Woman giving drink to resting workers / 2. *Right:* TWO / Portrait of girl / 2. *Comments:* H-RI-440-G4, Durand-2138. 18__. 1840s.
Rarity: URS-3
VF $300

$2 • W-RI-1300-002-G040
Comments: H-Unlisted, Durand-2124. No description available. 1840s.
Rarity: *None known*

$3 • W-RI-1300-003-G050
Left: Farmer with scythe. *Center:* 3 / Woman placing garland on eagle / 3. *Right:* THREE / Sailor on wharf / 3 across THREE. *Comments:* H-RI-440-G6, Durand-2140. 18__. 1840s.
Rarity: URS-3
VF $300

$3 • W-RI-1300-003-G060
Comments: H-Unlisted, Durand-2126. Similar to Durand-2127. 1840s.
Rarity: URS-3
VF $300

$5 • W-RI-1300-005-G070

QDB

Comments: H-RI-440-G8, Durand-2141. 18__. 1840s–1850s.
Rarity: URS-3
VF $300

$10 • W-RI-1300-010-G080
Left: X / Indian with bow. *Center:* Steamboat and other vessels, City / X. *Right:* 10 / Woman with bonnet. *Comments:* H-RI-440-G10, Durand-2142. 18__. 1840s.
Rarity: *None known*

$20 • W-RI-1300-020-G090
Left: Steamboat / XX / Train. *Center:* Liberty, Justice, and Knowledge / 20. *Right:* XX / Milkmaid. *Comments:* H-RI-440-G12, Durand-2143. 18__. 1840s.
Rarity: *None known*

$50 • W-RI-1300-050-G100
Left: 50 / Steamboat and schooner. *Center:* Men, hay, rake. *Right:* L / Justice. *Comments:* H-Unlisted, Durand-2144. 1840s.
Rarity: URS-3
VF $300

NON-VALID ISSUES

$1 • W-RI-1300-001-S010

QDB

Comments: H-RI-440-S5, Durand-2137. July 1st, 1850.
Rarity: URS-5
VF $125

$2 • W-RI-1300-002-C040
Comments: H-Unlisted, Durand-2125. Counterfeit of W-RI-1300-002-G040. March 1821.
Rarity: URS-3

$2 • W-RI-1300-002-S020
Left: 2 / Woman with sickle. *Center:* Man in field with horse and plow, Trees / 2 on die. *Bottom center:* Eagle. *Right:* TWO / Truth. *Comments:* H-RI-440-S10, Durand-2139. July 1, 1850.
Rarity: URS-5
VF $300

$3 • W-RI-1300-003-C060
Left: 3 / Medallion head / 3 vertically. *Center:* 3 over THREE / Three women with sheep / 3. *Bottom center:* Shield bearing medallion head. *Right:* 3 RHODE ISLAND 3 vertically. *Comments:* H-Unlisted, Durand-2127. Early counterfeit. Counterfeit of W-RI-1300-003-G060. 1840s.
Rarity: URS-3
VF $90

Scituate Bank
1818–1841
W-RI-1310

History: The Scituate Bank was incorporated in 1818. The commissioners discovered in 1836 that controlling interest had been sold to out-of-state parties, who had given promissory notes to the bank for $49,361 while it held promissory notes of residents for only $2,047. Its specie had been secretly removed. New plates had been prepared and $43,000 of bills had been printed, of which $36,328 were found in the bank. After liquidation in 1841, followed by a reorganization and infusion of capital, the name of the institution was changed to the Hamilton Bank, W-RI-1300.[78]

Numismatic Commentary: Genuine notes may be hard to find, although some Proof issues do appear in the marketplace from time to time.

VALID ISSUES

$1 • W-RI-1310-001-G010
Left: Female portrait. *Center:* Three women seated with sheep. *Bottom center:* Female portrait. *Right:* RHODE ISLAND. *Engraver:* Horton, Providence. *Comments:* H-RI-445-G2. 18__. 1818–1820s.
Rarity: *None known*

$1 • W-RI-1310-001-G020
Engraver: New England Bank Note Co. *Comments:* H-RI-445-G5. No description available. 18__. 1830s.
Rarity: *None known*

$2 • W-RI-1310-002-G030
Left: Female portrait. *Center:* Three women seated with sheep. *Bottom center:* Female portrait. *Right:* RHODE ISLAND. *Engraver:* Horton, Providence. *Comments:* H-RI-445-G6. 18__. 1818–1820s.
Rarity: *None known*

$2 • W-RI-1310-002-G040
Left: TWO / Milkmaid standing with stool. *Center:* 2 / Spread eagle standing on rock / TWO / Panel of microlettering outlining white TWO. *Right:* 2 / Woman seated with book / TWO. *Engraver:* New England Bank Note Co. *Comments:* H-RI-445-G9. 18__. 1830s.
Rarity: URS-3
VF $200

$3 • W-RI-1310-003-G050
Left: 3 / Female portrait / 3 vertically. *Center:* 3 on THREE on die / Three women seated with sheep and 3 / 3 on die. *Bottom center:* Female portrait. *Right:* 3 RHODE ISLAND 3 vertically. *Engraver:* Horton, Providence. *Comments:* H-RI-445-G10. 18__. 1818–1820s.
Rarity: URS-3
F $270

$3 • W-RI-1310-003-G060
Left: Portrait of Thomas Jefferson. *Center:* 3 / Man standing next to shield bearing anchor / THREE / THREE. *Right:* 3 / Portrait of George Washington / THREE. *Engraver:* New England Bank Note Co. *Comments:* H-RI-445-G14. 18__. 1830s.
Rarity: URS-3
VF $300

$5 • W-RI-1310-005-G070
Left: 5 / Male portrait / FIVE. *Center:* 5 / Eagle, Women flanking shield bearing anchor, Cornucopia, anchor, Ships / 5. *Right:* 5 / Portrait of Andrew Jackson / FIVE. *Engraver:* New England Bank Note Co. *Comments:* H-RI-445-G18. 18__. 1830s.
Rarity: *None known*

$10 • W-RI-1310-010-G080
Left: 10 / Female portrait / 10. *Center:* Scene / Woman standing. *Bottom center:* Female portrait. *Right:* X / Indian with tomahawk. *Engraver:* Terry, Pelton & Co. *Comments:* H-RI-445-G24. 18__. 1830s.
Rarity: URS-3
Proof $500

$50 • W-RI-1310-050-G090
Left: FIFTY vertically. *Center:* L on die / Three women / L on die. *Bottom center:* Steamboat. *Right:* 50 / Portrait of Commodore Oliver Hazard Perry / 50. *Engraver:* Terry, Pelton & Co. *Comments:* H-RI-445-G32. 18__. 1830s.
Rarity: URS-3
Proof $500

NON-VALID ISSUES

$2 • W-RI-1310-002-C030
Engraver: Horton, Providence. *Comments:* H-RI-445-C6. Counterfeit of W-RI-1310-002-G030. 18__. 1821.
Rarity: *None known*

$3 • W-RI-1310-003-C050

CC

Engraver: Horton, Providence. *Comments:* H-RI-445-C10. Counterfeit of W-RI-1310-003-G050. 18__. 1827–1837.
Rarity: URS-3
VF $200

$3 • W-RI-1310-003-A010

TD

Engraver: PPSP. *Comments:* H-Unlisted. 18__. 1810s.
Rarity: URS-1

$5 • W-RI-1310-005-C070

SI

Engraver: New England Bank Note Co. **Comments:** H-Unlisted. Counterfeit of W-RI-1310-005-G070. 18__. 1830s.
Rarity: URS-1
VF $750

SLATERSVILLE, RHODE ISLAND

America's first planned industrial village, Slatersville is a village of Smithfield. It was established in Providence in 1636. Years later in 1790, Samuel Slater made a replica of an English cotton-spinning machine in the town that bears his name, leading to the first successful cotton mill in the United States. The machinery was built in Pawtucket, Rhode Island, in 1793.

By 1803 the Slater brothers had bought the land and water rights to Slatersville. A stone mill was opened in 1807. This was quickly followed by a cotton mill and housing for workers, creating a "Mill Village." The first mill was destroyed in 1826 by a fire, but it was replaced by another mill that still stands today. The mills were powered by the Slatersville reservoir, which spans 170 acres.

A small town rose up around the mills, and soon industrial villages were springing up all around Rhode Island. It became known as the Rhode Island System. Throughout the 19th century such activity was duplicated up and down the Blackstone River.

Burrillville Agricultural Bank
1815–1818
W-RI-1320

History: Originally chartered in 1815 in the village of Slatersville, the Burrillville Agricultural Bank did not open until February 1818. On June 18 of the same year, the charter was amended to change the title of the bank to the Burrillville Agricultural and Manufacturers Bank, W-RI-1330.

See also listing under Burrillville, W-RI-150.

Numismatic Commentary: The denominations and designs of bank issues under this title are unknown, but if they were made, they were probably of the Perkins type.

Burrillville Agricultural and Manufacturers Bank
1818–1822
W-RI-1330

History: The Burrillville Agricultural and Manufacturers Bank was originally the Burrillville Agricultural Bank, W-RI-1320. On June 18, 1818, the charter was amended to change the name as noted above. In October 1822, the bank was again modified to become the Village Bank, W-RI-1410.

See also listing under Burrillville, W-RI-160, and Smithfield, W-RI-1333.

SMITHFIELD, RHODE ISLAND

The land that was granted by Roger Williams and dedicated as Smithfield was originally a hunting and fishing ground for the Wampanoag tribe. It was called Wionkhiege at the time.

In 1730 Smithfield, Gloucester, and Scituate separated from Providence. Smithfield was made up of fewer than 500 residents and was 73 square miles in area. It later divided into the two separate towns of North Smithfield and Lincoln.

Manufacturing was the main industry for Smithfield during the early 19th century, including textiles and foundries as well as cotton manufacturing. The first textile mill was built in 1810 on the Mill River in the nearby village of Woonsocket. Limestone was discovered and yielded large quarries for stone that was processed into lime. The lime was shipped to distant places, including throughout the South, along with whetstones and white-stones for the making of furnaces and hearths. The settlement was sometimes referred to as Smithfield Bank, perhaps in relation to a bank of that name located there.

See also Woonsocket, Rhode Island.

Burrillville Agricultural and Manufacturers Bank
1818–1822
W-RI-1333

History: The Burrillville Agricultural and Manufacturers Bank was originally the Burrillville Agricultural Bank, W-RI-1320. On June 18, 1818, the charter was amended to change the name. In October 1822, the bank was again modified to become the Village Bank, W-RI-1410.

See also listing under Burrillville, W-RI-160, and Slatersville, W-RI-1330.

Numismatic Commentary: The few notes recorded for this address imprint are of a Perkins variant design. The imprint reads: Perkins Patent Steel Plate (PPSP). This variation occurred at about the same time Jacob Perkins moved to England.

VALID ISSUES

$1 • W-RI-1333-001-G010

CJF

Engraver: PPSP. *Comments:* H-RI-52-G10. 18__. 1819–1821.
Rarity: URS-3
VF $250

Exchange Bank
1863–1865
W-RI-1335

History: Around 1863 the Smithfield Exchange Bank, W-RI-1380, became known as the Exchange Bank. In 1865 its interests were succeeded by the National Exchange Bank of Greenville.
See also listing under Smithfield, W-RI-425.

Globe Bank
1844–1865
W-RI-1340

History: On March 12, 1844, the name of the Providence County Bank, W-RI-1360, was changed to the Globe Bank, and the location was moved to Globe Village, a part Smithfield. The location was again changed to Woonsocket opposite the Harrison Mill in 1855. The bank had an authorized capital of $50,000 in 1848. This was raised to $75,000 by 1849 and to $100,000 by 1855. Bills in circulation totaled $40,585 in 1849, decreased to $27,192 by 1860, and increased again to $63,208 by 1862. The president was Spencer Mowry, accompanied by cashier S. Newton.

The business of the Globe Bank was succeeded by the National Globe Bank, chartered on June 23, 1865. There was an unrelated Globe Bank, W-RI-970, located in Providence.
See also listing under Woonsocket, W-RI-1680.

Numismatic Commentary: Genuine notes from the Globe Bank with the Smithfield address are a welcome find for the Rhode Island collector.

Remaining in the American Bank Note Co. archives as of 2003 was a $10 face plate. It was the same plate used for the Globe Bank of Smithfield and a bank in Keene, New Hampshire. During a robbery $10,000 in unsigned $10, $20, $50, and $100 bills were stolen from the bank. These denominations may therefore appear with forged signatures.

VALID ISSUES

$1 • W-RI-1340-001-G010
Left: ONE / Girl / ONE. *Center:* 1 / Woman seated / 1. *Bottom center:* Shield. *Right:* Woman standing in 1. *Comments:* H-Unlisted. 1840s–1860s.
Rarity: —

$1 • W-RI-1340-001-G020
Left: Justice / 1. *Center:* View of public building. *Right:* 1 / Portrait of Henry Clay. *Comments:* H-RI-450-G2, Durand-2610. 18__. 1840s–1860s.
Rarity: *None known*

$2 • W-RI-1340-002-G030
Left: TWO. *Center:* Steamship at sea, Sailing vessel. *Right:* 2 / Girl holding grain. *Comments:* H-RI-450-G4, Durand-2611. 18__. 1840s–1860s.
Rarity: *None known*

$3 • W-RI-1340-003-G040
Left: Liberty / 3. *Center:* Farm view, Group of men haying. *Right:* 3 / 3. *Comments:* H-RI-450-G6, Durand-2615. 18__. 1840s–1860s.
Rarity: *None known*

$5 • W-RI-1340-005-G050
Left: Water spouting from fountain / 5. *Center:* Ocean view, Two steamships, Sailing vessel. *Right:* 5 / Female portrait. *Comments:* H-RI-450-G8, Durand-2617. 18__. 1840s–1860s.
Rarity: *None known*

$10 • W-RI-1340-010-G060
Left: Two girls / 10. *Center:* Oxen drawing load of wheat, Man on horse, House. *Right:* 10 / Indian girl. *Comments:* H-RI-450-G10, Durand-2621. 18__. 1840s–1860s.
Rarity: *None known*

$10 • W-RI-1340-010-G070
Center: Globe on man's shoulders, Woman, Train. *Comments:* H-Unlisted, Durand-2625. 1840s–1860s.
Rarity: *None known*

$20 • W-RI-1340-020-G080
Left: 20 / Globe, Neptune seated in shell, Vessels. *Right:* XX / Squaw. *Comments:* H-RI-450-G12, Durand-2626. 18__. 1840s–1860s.
Rarity: *None known*

$50 • W-RI-1340-050-G090
Left: 50 / Globe, Man and two cherubs astride eagle. *Right:* 50 / Portrait of Daniel Webster. *Comments:* H-RI-450-G14, Durand-2629. 18__. 1840s–1860s.
Rarity: *None known*

$100 • W-RI-1340-100-G100
Left: C. *Center:* Harbor and shipping / C. *Right:* 100 / Girl with wheat. *Comments:* H-RI-450-G16, Durand-2630. 18__. 1840s–1860s.
Rarity: *None known*

$500 • W-RI-1340-500-G110
Left: Forest scene, Indian in canoe / 500. *Center:* 500. *Right:* 500 / Justice. *Engraver:* New England Bank Note Co. *Comments:* H-RI-450-G18, Durand-2632. 18__. 1840s–1860s.
Rarity: *None known*

$1,000 • W-RI-1340-1000-G120

Left: Spread eagle on cliff overlooking ocean / 1000. *Center:* 1000. *Right:* 1000 / Indian girl. *Engraver:* New England Bank Note Co. *Comments:* H-Unlisted, Durand-2633. 18__. 1840s–1860s.

Rarity: URS-3
F $1,600

NON-VALID ISSUES

$2 • W-RI-1340-002-S010

Center: Neptune. *Comments:* H-RI-450-N5, Durand-2614. 1840s–1860s.

Rarity: *None known*

$2 • W-RI-1340-002-N010

Left: TWO / Girl / TWO. *Center:* Justice / 2 / Liberty. *Right:* Ceres standing in 2. *Engraver:* New England Bank Note Co. *Comments:* H-RI-450-N8, Durand-2613. Altered or spurious. 18__. 1846.

Rarity: URS-3
VF $250

$2 • W-RI-1340-002-A010

Left: 2 on die. *Center:* Manhattan reclining with water urn / 2. *Right:* Woman on panel of wheat and corn. *Engraver:* Durand & Co. *Comments:* H-RI-450-A5, Durand-2612. Altered from $2 Globe Bank, New York City, New York. 1840.

Rarity: *None known*

$3 • W-RI-1340-003-A020

Left: 3 on die. *Center:* Manhattan reclining with water urn / 3. *Right:* 3 on die on panel of wheat and corn. *Engraver:* Durand & Co. *Comments:* H-RI-450-A10, Durand-2616. Altered from $3 Globe Bank, New York City, New York. 1840.

Rarity: URS-3
VF $200

$5 • W-RI-1340-005-R010

Comments: H-RI-450-R4, Durand-2618. Raised from W-RI-1340-001-G020. 18__. 1840s–1860s.

Rarity: *None known*

$5 • W-RI-1340-005-A030

Left: Dog, Indian on rock. *Center:* Warehouse, Ships in harbor / 5. *Right:* FIVE on die on panel of wheat and fruit. *Engraver:* Durand & Co. *Comments:* H-RI-450-A15, Durand-2619. Altered from $5 Globe Bank, New York City, New York series. 1840.

Rarity: *None known*

$5 • W-RI-1340-005-A040

Left: Sailing ships at sea / 5. *Center:* Four women seated on globe. *Right:* 5 / Woman standing with shield bearing 5. *Engraver:* New England Bank Note Co. *Comments:* H-RI-450-A20, Durand-2620. Altered from $5 Globe Bank, Bangor, Maine. 18__. 1840s.

Rarity: *None known*

$10 • W-RI-1340-010-R020

Comments: H-RI-450-R6, Durand-2622. Raised from W-RI-1340-001-G020. 18__. 1840s–1860s.

Rarity: *None known*

$10 • W-RI-1340-010-A050

Left: Train / Portrait of Benjamin Franklin. *Center:* Four women seated on globe. *Right:* 10 / 10. *Engraver:* New England Bank Note Co. *Comments:* H-RI-450-A25, Durand-2623. Altered from $10 Globe Bank, Bangor, Maine. 18__. 1840s.

Rarity: *None known*

$10 • W-RI-1340-010-A060

Left: Artist. *Center:* X / Warehouse, Ships in harbor. *Right:* 10 / Medallion head / 10. *Engraver:* New England Bank Note Co. *Comments:* H-RI-450-A30, Durand-2624. Altered from $10 Globe Bank, New York City, New York. 18__. 1840s.

Rarity: *None known*

$20 • W-RI-1340-020-R030

Comments: H-Unlisted, Durand-2627. Raised from W-RI-1340-001-G020. 1840s–1860s.

Rarity: URS-3
VF $200

$20 • W-RI-1340-020-N020

Center: Steamship in storm. *Comments:* H-RI-450-N10, Durand-2627. 1840s–1860s.

Rarity: *None known*

$20 • W-RI-1340-020-N030

Center: Steamship in storm. *Comments:* H-Unlisted, Durand-2628. Altered or spurious. 1840s–1860s.

Rarity: URS-3
VF $100

$100 • W-RI-1340-100-S020

Left: 100 on shield / Allegorical man. *Center:* Spread eagle on tree limb. *Right:* Allegorical woman / 100 on shield. *Overprint:* Red HUNDRED. *Comments:* H-RI-450-S5, Durand-2631. 1840s–1860s.

Rarity: *None known*

New England Pacific Bank
1818–1865
W-RI-1350

History: The New England Pacific Bank was incorporated in October 1818. Capital was authorized at $50,000. The same rose to $107,200 by 1850. In 1854 the bank applied for a further increase in capital, and by 1862 it was $185,150. Circulation was $74,669 in 1862.

Due to heavy losses, the bank was suffering in Smithfield, and it opened an office of discount and deposit in Pawtucket, seeking a more favorable business climate. After the move to Pawtucket, its notes were imprinted North Providence as the village of Pawtucket was in the northern corner of North Providence.

The Pacific National Bank assumed the business of the New England Pacific Bank after it was chartered on June 27, 1865.

See also listing under North Providence, W-RI-630.

VALID ISSUES
Payable at Office of Discount and Deposit, Pawtucket

$1 • W-RI-1350-001-G010
Left: Portrait of George Washington / Die / Portrait of George Washington. *Center:* ONE / Man seated at table / 1. *Bottom center:* Plow and implements. *Right:* 1 / Portrait of William Penn / Die. *Engraver:* A. B. & C. Durand & Wright. *Comments:* H-RI-455-G3, Durand-766. 18__. 1820s.
Rarity: URS-3
Proof $300

$2 • W-RI-1350-002-G020   SBG

Comments: H-RI-455-G6, Durand-767. Proof. 18__. 1810s–1820s.
Rarity: URS-2
Proof $2,200
Selected auction price: Stack's Bowers Galleries, March 2013, Proof $2,178

$3 • W-RI-1350-003-G030
Engraver: A. B. & C. Durand & Wright. *Comments:* H-RI-455-G9, Durand-768. No description available. 1810s–1820s.
Rarity: *None known*

$5 • W-RI-1350-005-G040
Left: Portrait of William Penn / 5 / Portrait of William Penn. *Center:* FIVE / Manhattan reclining and pouring water from jug / 5. *Bottom center:* Shield bearing anchor. *Right:* 5 / Portrait of Benjamin Franklin. *Engraver:* A. B. & C. Durand & Wright. *Comments:* H-RI-455-G12, Durand-769. 18__. 1820s.
Rarity: URS-3
Proof $300

Providence County Bank
1834–1844
W-RI-1360

History: The Providence County Bank was incorporated in January 1834. During an 1844 robbery, criminals escaped with a large quantity of unsigned notes. This prompted the bank directors to change the location of the bank to Globe Village, a part of the village of Woonsocket in Smithfield. On March 12, 1844, the name of the Providence County Bank was changed to the Globe Bank, W-RI-1680.

Numismatic Commentary: This remains a very hard bank to collect. Notes engraved by Rawdon, Wright & Hatch are the issues collectors will encounter.

VALID ISSUES

$1 • W-RI-1360-001-G010
Left: ONE / Female portrait / ONE. *Center:* 1 / Woman seated, Cog wheel / 1. *Bottom center:* Shield bearing anchor. *Right:* Woman in 1. *Engraver:* Rawdon, Wright & Hatch. *Comments:* H-RI-460-G4. 18__. 1840s.
Rarity: URS-3
Proof $2,000

$2 • W-RI-1360-002-G020
Left: TWO / Female portrait / TWO. *Center:* 2 / Woman standing beside 2 / 2. *Bottom center:* Shield bearing anchor. *Right:* Woman in 2. *Engraver:* Rawdon, Wright & Hatch. *Comments:* H-RI-460-G8. 18__. 1840s.
Rarity: URS-3
Proof $2,000

$3 • W-RI-1360-003-G030
Left: 3 / Female portrait / 3. *Center:* 3 / Women flanking shield surmounted by eagle / 3. *Bottom center:* Shield bearing anchor. *Right:* Woman standing in 3. *Engraver:* Rawdon, Wright & Hatch. *Comments:* H-RI-460-G12. 18__. 1840s.
Rarity: URS-3
Proof $2,000

$5 • W-RI-1360-005-G040
Left: 5 / Female portrait / 5. *Center:* 5 with cherubs / Woman next to shield holding pole and cap / 5 with cherubs. *Bottom center:* Shield bearing anchor. *Right:* George Washington in 5. *Comments:* H-RI-460-G16, Durand-2605. 1840s.
Rarity: URS-3
Proof $2,000

$10 • W-RI-1360-010-G050
Comments: H-Unlisted, Durand-2606. No description available. 1840s.
Rarity: *None known*

$10 • W-RI-1360-010-G060
Left: 10 / Farmer sowing / TEN. *Center:* Mercury standing with 10, Merchandise, factories, and ship / Canal scene / Panel outlining white TEN. *Right:* 10 / Ship / TEN. *Engraver:* New England Bank Note Co. *Comments:* H-RI-460-G18. 18__. 1830s–1840s.
Rarity: *None known*

$20 • W-RI-1360-020-G070
Comments: H-Unlisted, Durand-2607. No description available. 1840s.
Rarity: *None known*

$20 • W-RI-1360-020-G080
Left: 20 / XX vertically / 20. *Center:* 20 / Woman seated with scales, Sheaf and bales, Men plowing, Ship / 20. *Right:* TWENTY vertically. *Engraver:* PSSP / New England Bank Note Co. *Comments:* H-RI-460-G20. 18__. 1830s–1840s.
Rarity: *None known*

$50 • W-RI-1360-050-G090
Comments: H-Unlisted, Durand-2608. No description available. 1840s.
Rarity: *None known*

$50 • W-RI-1360-050-G100

Left: 50 / Woman standing with ankles crossed, Staff, Cornucopia and anchor / 50. *Center:* FIFTY DOLLARS / 50. *Right:* FIFTY vertically. *Engraver:* PSSP / New England Bank Note Co. *Comments:* H-RI-460-G22. 18__. 1830s–1840s.

Rarity: *None known*

$100 • W-RI-1360-100-G110

Comments: H-Unlisted, Durand-2609. No description available. 1840s.

Rarity: *None known*

$100 • W-RI-1360-100-G120

Left: Lathework panel bearing C / Portrait of George Washington / C. *Center:* 100 / Manhattan reclining pouring water, Ship / 100. *Right:* Lathework panel bearing ONE HUNDRED vertically. *Engraver:* PSSP / New England Bank Note Co. *Comments:* H-RI-460-G24. 18__. 1830s–1840s.

Rarity: *None known*

Uncut Sheets

$1-$2-$3-$5 • W-RI-1360-001.002.003.005-US010

Vignette(s): *($1)* Female portrait / Woman seated, Cog wheel Shield bearing anchor / Woman in 1. *($2)* Female portrait / Woman standing beside 2 / Shield bearing anchor / Woman in 2. *($3)* Female portrait / Women flanking shield surmounted by eagle / Shield bearing anchor / Woman standing in 3. *($5)* Female portrait / 5 with cherubs / Woman next to shield holding pole and cap / 5 with cherubs / Shield bearing anchor / George Washington in 5. *Comments:* H-RI-460-G4, G8, G12, G16. 18__. 1840s.

Rarity: URS-3

Proof $8,000

Smithfield Bank
1800s–1820s
W-RI-1370

History: Little appears in print regarding the Smithfield Bank. In 1806 several notices were published of dangerous counterfeits of the bank. The Smithfield Bank had an authorized capital of $60,000 in 1813. Its president was Owen Battey, and its cashier was William Winsor. In 1829 Smithfield Bank bills were listed as a currency preferred for investment by other Rhode Island banks.

Smithfield Exchange Bank
1822–1863
W-RI-1380

History: The Smithfield Exchange Bank was incorporated in June 1822 in a room of the Greenville Tavern. The authorized capital was $40,000, which was reduced to $30,000 in 1845, raised to $60,000 in 1856, and raised again to $100,000 by December 1862. The first president was Daniel Winsor, and the first cashier was Nicholas Winsor. By 1856 Owen Battey had succeeded Daniel Winsor as president, and William Winsor had succeeded Nicholas Winsor as cashier.

The location of the bank was moved to another place in the village around 1856. Bills in circulation amounted to $56,662 in 1857, with specie at $3,247.23. In 1863 circulation was $60,298. It became known as the Exchange Bank, W-RI-1335, the same year.

See also listing under Greenville, W-RI-430.

VALID ISSUES

$1 • W-RI-1380-001-G010

Left: 1 on ONE / RHODE ISLAND / 1 on ONE vertically. *Center:* 1 on die / Liberty, Shield bearing state arms, Ceres / 1 on die. *Right:* Helmeted head / 1 / Two mermaids / 1 / Bearded head vertically. *Engraver:* Horton, Providence. *Comments:* H-RI-465-G2, Durand-457. 18__. 1820s.

Rarity: *None known*

$1 • W-RI-1380-001-G020

Engraver: A. B. & C. Durand & Wright. *Comments:* H-RI-465-G4, Durand-458. January 1st, 1826.

Rarity: URS-1

Proof $2,000

How to Read the Whitman Numbering System
$1 • W-RI-010-001-G010a

Denomination: Value of the note shown.

W: Whitman number. This number is a sortable code unique to each bank and note.

RI: Abbreviation for the state under study.

010: Numerical designation specific to each bank.

001: The denomination in dollars.

G010a: G indicates a good or valid note. Other categories are indicated thus: C (counterfeit); R (raised); S (spurious); N (not-attributed); A (altered). Numbers are assigned starting with 010, 020, et seq. Terminal letters following the number indicate variations of a note: a series of different colored overprints, tints, payees, etc., all on the same design of note. For more information, see the "How to Use This Book" section at the front of the volume, page xiv.

$1 • **W-RI-1380-001-G020a**
Engraver: A. B. & C. Durand & Wright. *Comments:* H-RI-465-G4a. Similar to W-RI-1380-001-G020 but with different date and possible addition of "RHODE ISLAND". Jan. 1, 18__. 1830s–1840s.
Rarity: *None known*

$1 • **W-RI-1380-001-G030**
Left: 1 / Woman wearing bonnet, standing by pail / ONE. *Center:* Machinery and merchandise flanking Ceres holding sickle and rake, Factories and harbor / ONE / Panel outlining white ONE. *Right:* 1 / Ship / ONE. *Engraver:* PSSP / New England Bank Note Co. *Comments:* H-RI-465-G6. 18__. 1830s.
Rarity: *None known*

$1.25 • **W-RI-1380-001.25-G040**
Left: 1 25/100 / Train / 1 25/100. *Center:* Sloop and other vessels at sea / $1.25 Cts. *Right:* 1 25/100 / Eagle. *Engraver:* New England Bank Note Co. *Comments:* H-RI-465-G9. 18__. 1830s.
Rarity: *None known*

$1.50 • **W-RI-1380-001.50-G050**
Left: 1 Doll. 50 Cts. vertically. *Center:* Eagle on rock in ocean / $1 50/100. *Right:* 1 50/100 / Justice. *Engraver:* New England Bank Note Co. *Comments:* H-RI-465-G10. 18__. 1830s.
Rarity: *None known*

$1.75 • **W-RI-1380-001.75-G060**
Left: $1.75 Cts. / Hebe watering eagle / 1 75/100. *Center:* Three sloops at sea. *Right:* $1.75 Cts. / Woman seated with grain, Dog / 1 75/100. *Engraver:* New England Bank Note Co. *Comments:* H-RI-465-G11. 18__. 1830s.
Rarity: *None known*

$2 • **W-RI-1380-002-G070**
Engraver: Horton, Providence. *Comments:* H-RI-465-G12, Durand-460. No description available. First issue. 18__. 1820s.
Rarity: *None known*

$2 • **W-RI-1380-002-G080**
Left: Die / Portrait of George Washington / Die. *Center:* 2 / Sea serpents / Woman waving drapery. *Bottom center:* Shield bearing anchor. *Right:* Die / Portrait of Benjamin Franklin / Die. *Engraver:* A. B. & C. Durand & Wright. *Comments:* H-RI-465-G14, Durand-461. Jan. 1, 1826.
Rarity: URS-3
Proof $500

$2 • **W-RI-1380-002-G080a**
Engraver: A. B. & C. Durand & Wright. *Comments:* H-RI-465-G14a. Similar to W-RI-1380-002-G080 but with different date and possible addition of "RHODE ISLAND". Jan. 1, 18__. 1830s–1840s.
Rarity: *None known*

$2 • **W-RI-1380-002-G090**
Left: 2 / Woman standing with staff, Cornucopia / TWO. *Center:* TWO / Machinery and merchandise flanking Ceres holding sickle and rake, Factories and harbor / Panel outlining white TWO. *Right:* 2 / Woman wearing hat, Trees / TWO. *Engraver:* PSSP / New England Bank Note Co. *Comments:* H-RI-465-G16. 18__. 1830s.
Rarity: *None known*

$3 • **W-RI-1380-003-G100**
Engraver: Horton, Providence. *Comments:* H-RI-465-G18, Durand-462. No description available. First issue. 18__. 1820s.
Rarity: *None known*

$3 • **W-RI-1380-003-G110**

SBG

Payee: DeWitt Clinton. *Engraver:* A. B. & C. Durand & Wright. *Comments:* H-RI-465-G20, Durand-463. January 1st, 1826.
Rarity: URS-2
Proof $2,100
Selected auction price: Stack's Bowers Galleries, March 2013, Proof $2,057

$3 • **W-RI-1380-003-G110a**
Engraver: A. B. & C. Durand & Wright. *Comments:* H-RI-465-G21, Durand-464. Similar to W-RI-1380-003-G110 but with different date and additional 3s. Jan. 1, 18__. 1830s–1840s.
Rarity: URS-3
VF $700

$3 • **W-RI-1380-003-G120**
Left: THREE / Beehive and foliage / THREE. *Center:* Machinery and merchandise flanking Ceres holding sickle and rake, Factories and harbor / THREE / Panel outlining white THREE. *Right:* 3 on THREE / Two reapers / 3 on THREE. *Engraver:* PSSP / New England Bank Note Co. *Comments:* H-RI-465-G22. 18__. 1830s.
Rarity: *None known*

$5 • **W-RI-1380-005-G130**
Engraver: Horton, Providence. *Comments:* H-RI-465-G24. No description available. 18__. 1820s.
Rarity: *None known*

$5 • **W-RI-1380-005-G140**

CJF

Engraver: A. B. & C. Durand & Wright. *Comments:* H-RI-465-G26, Durand-465. Jan.y 1st, 1826.
Rarity: URS-3
Proof $1,200

$5 • W-RI-1380-005-G140a

Engraver: A. B. & C. Durand & Wright. *Comments:* H-RI-465-G26a. Similar to W-RI-1380-005-G140 but with different date. Jan. 1, 18__. 1830s. **Rarity:** *None known*

$5 • W-RI-1380-005-G150

Left: 5 / Blacksmith at anvil / FIVE. *Center:* Mercury standing with 5, Cornucopia and merchandise, Factories and ship / V / Panel outlining white FIVE. *Right:* 5 / Ceres kneeling / FIVE. *Engraver:* PSSP / New England Bank Note Co. *Comments:* H-RI-465-G28. 18__. 1830s.
Rarity: *None known*

$10 • W-RI-1380-010-G160

Left: 10 / Farmer sowing / TEN. *Center:* Mercury standing with 10, Merchandise, Factories and ship / Canal scene / Panel outlining white TEN. *Right:* 10 / Ship / TEN. *Engraver:* PSSP / New England Bank Note Co. *Comments:* H-RI-465-G32. 18__. 1830s.
Rarity: *None known*

$10 • W-RI-1380-010-G170

Left: Panel bearing 10 / X / 10. *Center:* Allegorical male standing by oxen and plow / 10. *Right:* TEN / Woman standing with lyre, Cornucopia. *Engraver:* New England Bank Note Co. *Comments:* H-RI-465-G34. 18__. 1840s.
Rarity: *None known*

$20 • W-RI-1380-020-G180

Left: 20 / XX vertically / 20. *Center:* 20 / Woman seated with scales, Sheaf and bales, Men plowing, Ship. *Right:* TWENTY vertically. *Engraver:* PSSP / New England Bank Note Co. *Comments:* H-RI-465-G38. 18__. 1830s.
Rarity: *None known*

$20 • W-RI-1380-020-G190

Left: 20 / Woman seated with book on lap, opening chest. *Center:* XX / Eagle on rock / XX. *Right:* 20 / Ship in harbor. *Engraver:* New England Bank Note Co. *Comments:* H-RI-465-G40. 18__. 1840s.
Rarity: *None known*

$50 • W-RI-1380-050-G200

Left: 50 / Woman standing with ankles crossed, Staff, Cornucopia and anchor / 50. *Center:* FIFTY DOLLARS / 50. *Right:* FIFTY vertically. *Engraver:* PSSP / New England Bank Note Co. *Comments:* H-RI-465-G42. 18__. 1830s.
Rarity: *None known*

$50 • W-RI-1380-050-G210

Left: FIFTY / Woman standing with wreath and flowers / FIFTY. *Center:* 50 / Man restraining prancing horse / 50. *Right:* FIFTY / Woman standing with cornucopia / FIFTY. *Engraver:* New England Bank Note Co. *Comments:* H-RI-465-G44. 18__. 1840s.
Rarity: *None known*

$100 • W-RI-1380-100-G220

Left: Lathework panel bearing C / Portrait of George Washington / C. *Center:* 100 / Manhattan reclining pouring water, Ship / 100. *Right:* Lathework panel bearing ONE HUNDRED vertically. *Engraver:* PSSP / New England Bank Note Co. *Comments:* H-RI-465-G46. 18__. 1830s–1840s.
Rarity: *None known*

$100 • W-RI-1380-100-G230

Left: ONE HUNDRED across 100 / Portrait of William Henry Harrison. *Center:* Wharf scene. *Right:* ONE HUNDRED across 100 / Portrait of Christopher Columbus. *Engraver:* New England Bank Note Co. *Comments:* H-RI-465-G48. 18__. 1840s.
Rarity: *None known*

Non-Valid Issues

$1 • W-RI-1380-001-C010

Engraver: Horton, Providence. *Comments:* H-RI-465-C2, Durand-459. Counterfeit of W-RI-1380-001-G010. 18__. 1825.
Rarity: URS-3
VF $150

$1 • W-RI-1380-001-N010

Center: Ships at sea. *Comments:* H-RI-465-N5, Durand-469. Altered or spurious. 1840s.
Rarity: *None known*

$1 • W-RI-1380-001-A010

Left: 1 on medallion head / Portrait of Daniel Webster. *Center:* Horses frightened by train / Medallion head of William Shakespeare. *Right:* ONE / Allegorical woman / ONE. *Engraver:* Danforth & Hufty. *Comments:* H-RI-465-A3, Durand-468. Altered from W-RI-680-001-G010. 18__. Circa 1850.
Rarity: *None known*

$1.75 • W-RI-1380-001.75-A020

Left: $1.75 Cts. / Hebe watering eagle / 1 75/100. *Center:* Three sloops at sea. *Right:* Agriculture / 1 75/100. *Engraver:* New England Bank Note Co. *Comments:* H-RI-465-A15, Durand-472. Altered from $1.75 Roxbury Bank, Roxbury, Massachusetts, or from notes of other failed banks using the same plate. 18__. 1850s.
Rarity: *None known*

$2 • W-RI-1380-002-S010

Left: TWO / Ship / 2. *Center:* Train on bridge / Two women seated / Strongbox. *Right:* 2 / Laureate woman leaning on shield bearing 2. *Comments:* H-RI-465-S5, Durand-474. 18__. 1860s.
Rarity: *None known*

$2 • W-RI-1380-002-N020

Center: Woman and strongbox. *Right:* Woman. *Comments:* H-Unlisted, Durand-475. 1840s.
Rarity: *None known*

$2 • W-RI-1380-002-N030

Center: Ships at sea. *Comments:* H-RI-465-N10, Durand-477. 1840s.
Rarity: *None known*

$2 • W-RI-1380-002-N040

Left: Woman. *Center:* Train. *Bottom center:* Male portrait. *Right:* Woman. *Comments:* H-RI-465-N15, Durand-474. 1840s.
Rarity: *None known*

$2 • W-RI-1380-002-N050

Left: Two girls. *Center:* Indian man and woman in canoe. *Right:* Mercury with 2. *Comments:* H-RI-465-N20, Durand-476. 18__. 1856.
Rarity: *None known*

$3 • W-RI-1380-003-A030

Left: 3 / Steamship. *Center:* Justice, Shield surmounted by eagle, Liberty. *Right:* 3 / Train. *Overprint:* Red THREE. *Engraver:* Baldwin, Bald & Cousland / Bald, Cousland & Co. *Comments:* H-RI-465-A20, Durand-478. Altered from W-RI-1500-003-G030a. 18__. 1850s.

Rarity: *None known*

$5 • W-RI-1380-005-N060

Center: Ships at sea. *Comments:* H-RI-465-N25, Durand-481. Altered or spurious. 1840s.

Rarity: *None known*

$5 • W-RI-1380-005-A040

Left: 5 / Portrait of Andrew Jackson / FIVE. *Center:* Liberty, Eagle on shield of Hope, Justice. *Right:* 5 / Female portrait / FIVE. *Engraver:* Baldwin, Bald & Cousland / Bald, Cousland & Co. *Comments:* H-RI-465-A25, Durand-480. Altered from W-RI-1500-005-G040a. 18__. 1850s.

Rarity: URS-3
VG $70; **VF** $150

$10 • W-RI-1380-010-N070

Center: Train. *Comments:* H-Unlisted, Durand-483. Altered or spurious. 1840s.

Rarity: *None known*

$10 • W-RI-1380-010-A050

Left: Train / X / Steamboat. *Center:* 10 / Ceres / 10. *Right:* 10 on orate die. *Engraver:* Rawdon, Wright & Hatch. *Comments:* H-RI-465-A30, Durand-466. Altered from $10 Farmers and Mechanics Bank, Pontiac, Michigan. 18__. 1840s.

Rarity: *None known*

Smithfield Lime Rock Bank
1823–1859
W-RI-1390

History: The Smithfield Lime Rock Bank was incorporated on January 29, 1823, at Smithfield. Its location changed to Providence in May 1847. Capital of the bank was $100,100 in 1848 and $228,700 in 1856. Bills in circulation were $50,797, and specie amounted to $2,983.95 in 1857.

In January 1859, the title of the bank was changed to the Lime Rock Bank, W-RI-1020.

See also listing under Providence, W-RI-1190.

VALID ISSUES

$1 • W-RI-1390-001-G010

Left: 1 RHODE ISLAND 1 vertically. *Center:* 1 / Bull / ONE on 1 / 1. *Right:* 1 / Lathework panel vertically / 1. *Engraver:* Graphic Co. *Comments:* H-RI-470-G2. 1820s–1830s.

Rarity: *None known*

$1 • W-RI-1390-001-G010a

Engraver: Graphic Co. *Comments:* H-RI-470-G2a. Similar to W-RI-1390-001-G010 but with different date. April 1, 1839.

Rarity: URS-3
VF $350

$1 • W-RI-1390-001-G020

Left: ONE / Industry / 1. *Center:* 1 / Spread eagle on shield / 1. *Right:* Minerva standing / 1. *Comments:* H-RI-470-G4, Durand-1463. 1830s.

Rarity: URS-3

$1 • W-RI-1390-001-G030

CC

Engraver: Draper, Toppan & Co. *Comments:* H-RI-470-G6, Durand-1464. 18__. 1840s.

Rarity: URS-4
Proof $1,300
Selected auction price: Spink-Smythe, April 2009, Proof $1,296

$2 • W-RI-1390-002-G040

Left: 2 RHODE ISLAND 2 vertically. *Center:* 2 / Milkmaid milking cow / 2. *Right:* 2 / Lathework panel vertically / 2. *Engraver:* Graphic Co. *Comments:* H-RI-470-G8. 1820s–1830s.

Rarity: *None known*

$2 • W-RI-1390-002-G040a

Engraver: Graphic Co. *Comments:* H-RI-470-G8a. Similar to W-RI-1390-002-G040 but with different date. April 1, 1839.

Rarity: URS-3
VF $350

$2 • W-RI-1390-002-G050

Left: 2 / Steamship and rowboat / 2. *Center:* Portrait of Marquis de Lafayette / Building, Commerce and Ceres, Wagon and horses / Portrait of George Washington. *Right:* 2 / Train / 2. *Comments:* H-RI-470-G10, Durand-1467. 1830s.

Rarity: URS-3
VF $400

$2 • W-RI-1390-002-G060

SBG

Engraver: Draper, Toppan & Co. *Comments:* H-RI-470-G12, Durand-1468. 18__. 1840s.

Rarity: URS-3
VF $400; **Proof** $1,200
Selected auction price: Stack's Bowers Galleries, March 2013, Proof $1,028

$3 • W-RI-1390-003-G070

Comments: H-RI-470-G14, Durand-1469. No description available. 1820s–1830s.

Rarity: *None known*

$3 • W-RI-1390-003-G080

Left: Indian / THREE. *Center:* Livestock, Man on horseback, Man. *Right:* THREE / Woman seated / 3. *Comments:* H-RI-470-G16, Durand-1470. Second issue. 1830s.

Rarity: URS-3

VF $500

$3 • W-RI-1390-003-G090

Left: Three allegorical figures supporting 3. *Center:* Ship, Sailor by bales with spyglass. *Right:* 3 / Horses frightened by train, 3. *Engraver:* Unverified, but likely American Bank Note Co. *Comments:* H-RI-470-G18, Durand-1471. 1840s.

Rarity: *None known*

$5 • W-RI-1390-005-G100

Left: V / RHODE ISLAND vertically / V. *Center:* 5 / Train / 5 / 5. *Right:* 5. *Engraver:* Graphic Co. *Comments:* H-RI-470-G20. 1820s–1830s.

Rarity: *None known*

$5 • W-RI-1390-005-G100a

Engraver: Graphic Co. *Comments:* H-RI-470-G20a. Similar to W-RI-1390-005-G100 but with different date. April 1, 1839.

Rarity: URS-3

VF $350

$5 • W-RI-1390-005-G110

Left: 5 / Spread eagle on shield / 5. *Center:* 5 / Commerce seated with dog, Bank building and wagon / 5. *Right:* FIVE vertically. *Comments:* H-RI-470-G22, Durand-1474. 1830s.

Rarity: URS-3

VF $500

$5 • W-RI-1390-005-G120

Left: FIVE / Woman with compass / 5. *Center:* 5 / Five cherubs grouped around 5 / 5. *Right:* FIVE vertically. *Comments:* H-RI-470-G24, Durand-1475. 1840s.

Rarity: URS-3

VF $450; **Proof** $700

$10 • W-RI-1390-010-G130

Left: 10 / Farmer sowing. *Center:* Mercury with oval bearing 10, Merchandise, factories, cornucopia, anchor. *Right:* FIFTY vertically. *Engraver:* New England Bank Note Co. *Comments:* H-RI-470-G30, Durand-1477. 1830s–1840s.

Rarity: *None known*

$50 • W-RI-1390-050-G140

Left: 50 / Woman standing, cornucopia, anchor / 50. *Center:* FIFTY DOLLARS, 50. *Right:* FIFTY vertically. *Engraver:* New England Bank Note Co. / PSSP. *Comments:* H-RI-470-G34. 1830s–1840s.

Rarity: *None known*

$100 • W-RI-1390-100-G150

Left: C / Portrait of George Washington / C. *Center:* 100 / Manhattan pouring water, Ship / 100. *Right:* ONE HUNDRED vertically. *Engraver:* New England Bank Note Co. / PSSP. *Comments:* H-RI-470-G36. 1830s–1840s.

Rarity: *None known*

$500 • W-RI-1390-500-G160

Left: 500 / 500 vertically. *Center:* 500 / Woman standing with shield bearing D, cornucopia, lyre, and sheaf. *Right:* 500 / D / 500 vertically. *Engraver:* New England Bank Note Co. / PSSP. *Comments:* H-RI-470-G38. 1830s–1840s.

Rarity: *None known*

Non-Valid Issues

$1 • W-RI-1390-001-C020

Comments: H-RI-470-C4, Durand-1465. Counterfeit of W-RI-1390-001-G020. 1840s.

Rarity: *None known*

$3 • W-RI-1390-003-C070

Comments: H-Unlisted, Durand-1472. Counterfeit of W-RI-1390-003-G070. 1830s–1850s.

Rarity: *None known*

$5 • W-RI-1390-005-A010

Left: FIVE vertically. *Center:* 5 / Farmer plowing and farmer sowing. *Right:* V / 5 / V. *Comments:* H-Unlisted, Durand-1476. Altered from $5 Farmers and Mechanics Bank, Pontiac, Michigan. 1830s–1850s.

Rarity: URS-3

F $100

$5 • W-RI-1390-005-A020

Left: FIVE vertically. *Center:* Farmer plowing with two horses / 5 on die / Farmer sowing, Team pulling harrow. *Bottom center:* Pledge. *Right:* V / 5 / V. *Engraver:* Rawdon, Wright & Hatch. *Comments:* H-RI-470-A5. Altered from $5 Farmers & Mechanics Bank at Pontiac, Pontiac, Michigan. 18__. 1840s.

Rarity: *None known*

$10 • W-RI-1390-010-N010

Center: Boys catching horse. *Comments:* H-RI-470-N5. 1830s–1850s.

Rarity: *None known*

$10 • W-RI-1390-010-A030

Left: Diagonal X / TEN. *Center:* Woman leaning on rock, Train / Ceres with sheaf on back. *Right:* 10 / Portrait of George Washington. *Overprint:* Red TEN. *Engraver:* Bald, Cousland & Co. / Baldwin, Bald & Cousland. *Comments:* H-RI-470-A10. Altered from $10 Southern Bank of Georgia, Bainbridge, Georgia. 18__. 1860s.

Rarity: *None known*

$50 • W-RI-1390-050-A040

Left: 50 / Woman feeding white horse. *Center:* Cattle, Milkmaid seated, Cattle. *Right:* 50 / Blacksmith standing by anvil. *Overprint:* Red FIFTY. *Engraver:* Rawdon, Wright, Hatch & Edson / New England Bank Note Co. *Comments:* H-RI-470-A15. Altered from W-RI-1580-050-G310a. 18__. 1850s.

Rarity: *None known*

Smithfield Union Bank
1805–1865
W-RI-1400

History: The Smithfield Union Bank was incorporated in 1805 in Smithfield with an authorized capital of $50,000. In 1852 the bank moved to the city of Woonsocket to take advantage of the profits from the burgeoning textile industry in that city.

The business of the Smithfield Union Bank was succeeded by the National Union Bank of Woonsocket in 1865.

See also listing under Woonsocket, W-RI-1710.

Numismatic Commentary: Genuine notes from this bank are hard to find. One issue, an early half-dollar note shown below, is a denomination rarity for Rhode Island banks.

VALID ISSUES

50¢ • W-RI-1400-00.50-G010

CJF

Comments: H-RI-475-G4, Durand-2673. Very rare denomination for a Rhode Island bank note. 18__. 1800s.

Rarity: URS-3
VF $350

$1 • W-RI-1400-001-G020

Engraver: Hamlin. **Comments:** H-RI-475-G8, Durand-2674. No description available. 18__. 1800s.

Rarity: *None known*

$1 • W-RI-1400-001-G030

CC

Engraver: PSSP. **Comments:** H-RI-475-G10, Durand-2676. 18__. 1807–1809.

Rarity: URS-3
VF $200

$1 • W-RI-1400-001-G040

Left: Panel bearing ONE / ONE vertically. **Center:** 1 on die / RHODE ISLAND / 1 on die. **Bottom center:** 1 on die. **Right:** Panel bearing ONE / ONE vertically. **Engraver:** PSSP. **Comments:** H-RI-475-G12, Durand-2675. 18__. 1810s–1820s.

Rarity: *None known*

$1 • W-RI-1400-001-G050

Left: 1 / Woman wearing bonnet, standing by pail / ONE. **Center:** Machinery and merchandise flanking Ceres holding sickle and rake, Factories and harbor / ONE / Panel outlining white ONE. **Right:** 1 / Ship / ONE. **Engraver:** PSSP / New England Bank Note Co. **Comments:** H-RI-475-G16. 18__. 1830s.

Rarity: *None known*

$1 • W-RI-1400-001-G060

Left: ONE vertically. **Center:** Sloop and other vessels. **Right:** ONE / Indian woman seated with bow and arrow / ONE. **Engraver:** New England Bank Note Co. **Comments:** H-RI-475-G20. 18__. 1840s–1850s.

Rarity: *None known*

$2 • W-RI-1400-002-G070

Engraver: Hamlin. **Comments:** H-RI-475-G28, Durand-2680. No description available. 18__. 1800s.

Rarity: *None known*

$2 • W-RI-1400-002-G080

Center: 2 / 2 / Alternating flower garlands and gridwork segments bearing TWO / 2 / 2. **Engraver:** PSSP. **Comments:** H-RI-475-G30, Durand-2681. 18__. 1807–1809.

Rarity: *None known*

$2 • W-RI-1400-002-G090

Left: Panel bearing TWO / TWO vertically. **Center:** Alternating flower garlands and gridwork segments. **Bottom center:** 2 on oval. **Right:** Panel bearing TWO / TWO vertically. **Engraver:** PSSP. **Comments:** H-RI-475-G34, Durand-2682. 18__. 1810s–1820s.

Rarity: *None known*

$2 • **W-RI-1400-002-G100**
Left: 2 / Woman standing with staff, Cornucopia / TWO. *Center:* TWO / Ceres seated holding sickle and rake, Machinery and merchandise, Factories and harbor / Panel outlining white TWO. *Bottom center:* 2 on die. *Right:* 2 / Woman wearing hat, Trees / TWO. *Engraver:* PSSP / New England Bank Note Co. *Comments:* H-RI-475-G38. 18__. 1830s.
Rarity: *None known*

$2 • **W-RI-1400-002-G110**
Engraver: PSSP / New England Bank Note Co. *Comments:* H-RI-475-G42. No description available. 18__. 1830s.
Rarity: *None known*

$3 • **W-RI-1400-003-G120**
Left: THREE vertically. *Center:* 3 on die / Liberty with pole and cap. *Right:* 3 on die. *Engraver:* Hamlin. *Comments:* H-RI-475-G46, Durand-2684. 18__. 1800s.
Rarity: *None known*

$3 • **W-RI-1400-003-G130**
Center: 3 / 3 / Alternating flower garlands and gridwork segments bearing THREE / 3 / 3. *Engraver:* PSSP. *Comments:* H-RI-475-G50, Durand-2685. 18__. 1807–1809.
Rarity: *None known*

$3 • **W-RI-1400-003-G140**
Left: Panel bearing THREE / THREE vertically. *Center:* Alternating flower garlands and gridwork segments bearing THREE. *Bottom center:* 3 on die. *Right:* Panel bearing THREE / THREE vertically. *Engraver:* PSSP. *Comments:* H-RI-475-G52, Durand-2686. 18__. 1810s–1820s.
Rarity: *None known*

$3 • **W-RI-1400-003-G150**
Left: THREE / Beehive and foliage / THREE. *Center:* Machinery and merchandise flanking Ceres holding sickle and rake, Factories and harbor / THREE / Panel outlining white THREE. *Right:* 3 on THREE / Two reapers / 3 on THREE. *Engraver:* PSSP / New England Bank Note Co. *Comments:* H-RI-475-G56. 18__. 1830s.
Rarity: *None known*

$3 • **W-RI-1400-003-G160**
Left: THREE vertically. *Center:* Man reaping with sickle, Woman standing with hat and sheaf / 3. *Right:* THREE / Steamship / 3 on THREE. *Engraver:* New England Bank Note Co. *Comments:* H-RI-475-G60. 18__. 1840s–1850s.
Rarity: *None known*

$5 • **W-RI-1400-005-G170**
Left: 5 / FIVE / 5 vertically. *Center:* 5 on die / Ceres. *Right:* 5 on die. *Engraver:* Hamlin. *Comments:* H-RI-475-G64, Durand-2687. 18__. 1800s.
Rarity: *None known*

$5 • **W-RI-1400-005-G180**
Comments: H-Unlisted, Durand-2688. No description available. 1800s.
Rarity: *None known*

$5 • **W-RI-1400-005-G190**
Left: Gridwork panel bearing RHODE ISLAND / 5 / 5 vertically. *Center:* Alternating flower garlands and gridwork segments. *Right:* 5 / 5 vertically. *Comments:* H-RI-475-G66, Durand-2689. 18__. 1806 and 1807.
Rarity: *None known*

$5 • **W-RI-1400-005-G190a**
Center: Alternating flower garlands and gridwork segments bearing rose-covered FIVE. *Comments:* H-RI-475-G68. Similar to W-RI-1400-005-G190. 18__. 1808 and 1809.
Rarity: *None known*

$5 • **W-RI-1400-005-G190b**
Center: Alternating flower garlands and gridwork segments bearing rose-covered FIVE. *Engraver:* PSSP. *Comments:* H-RI-475-G70. Similar to W-RI-1400-005-G190. 18__. 1809–1820s.
Rarity: *None known*

$5 • **W-RI-1400-005-G190c**
Center: Alternating flower garlands and gridwork segments bearing rose-covered FIVE. *Engraver:* PSSP. *Comments:* H-RI-475-G72. Similar to W-RI-1400-005-G190. 18__. 1820s.
Rarity: *None known*

$5 • **W-RI-1400-005-G200**
Left: 5 / Blacksmith at anvil / FIVE. *Center:* Mercury standing with 5, Cornucopia and merchandise, Factories and ship / V / Panel outlining white FIVE. *Right:* 5 / Ceres kneeling / FIVE. *Engraver:* PSSP / New England Bank Note Co. *Comments:* H-RI-475-G76. 18__. 1830s.
Rarity: *None known*

$5 • **W-RI-1400-005-G210**
Left: FIVE vertically. *Center:* Woman unveiling shield bearing 5 / V. *Right:* 5 / Sailing ship. *Engraver:* New England Bank Note Co. *Comments:* H-RI-475-G80. 18__. 1840s–1850s.
Rarity: *None known*

$7 • **W-RI-1400-007-G220**
Left: Panel bearing 7 / SEVEN / 7 vertically. *Center:* 7 / Hope resting on anchor. *Right:* 7. *Engraver:* Hamlin. *Comments:* H-RI-475-G84, Durand-2691. 18__. 1800s.
Rarity: *None known*

$10 • **W-RI-1400-010-G230**
Left: Gridwork panel bearing RHODE ISLAND / 10 / 10 vertically. *Center:* Alternating flower garlands and gridwork segments. *Right:* 10 / 10 vertically. *Comments:* H-RI-475-G88, Durand-2623. 18__. 1806 and 1807.
Rarity: *None known*

$10 • **W-RI-1400-010-G230a**
Center: Alternating flower garlands and gridwork segments bearing rose-covered TEN. *Comments:* H-RI-475-G90. Similar to W-RI-1400-010-G230. 18__. 1808 and 1809.
Rarity: *None known*

$10 • **W-RI-1400-010-G230b**
Center: Alternating flower garlands and gridwork segments bearing rose-covered TEN. *Engraver:* PSSP. *Comments:* H-RI-475-G92. Similar to W-RI-1400-010-G230. 18__. 1809–1820s.
Rarity: *None known*

$10 • **W-RI-1400-010-G230c**

Center: Alternating flower garlands and gridwork segments bearing rose-covered TEN. *Engraver:* PSSP. *Comments:* H-RI-475-G94. Similar to W-RI-1400-010-G230. 18__. 1820s.

Rarity: *None known*

$10 • **W-RI-1400-010-G240**

Left: 10 / Farmer sowing / TEN. *Center:* Mercury standing with 10, Merchandise, Factories and ship / Canal scene / Panel outlining white TEN. *Right:* 10 / Ship / 10. *Engraver:* PSSP / New England Bank Note Co. *Comments:* H-RI-475-G98. 18__. 1830s.

Rarity: *None known*

$10 • **W-RI-1400-010-G250**

Left: Panel bearing 10 / X / 10. *Center:* Allegorical male standing by oxen and plow / 10. *Right:* TEN / Woman standing with lyre, Cornucopia. *Engraver:* New England Bank Note Co. *Comments:* H-RI-475-G102. 18__. 1840s–1850s.

Rarity: *None known*

$20 • **W-RI-1400-020-G260**

Left: Panel bearing TWENTY vertically. *Center:* 20 / Woman standing with upraised distaff and bouquet. *Right:* 20. *Engraver:* Hamlin. *Comments:* H-RI-475-G106. 18__. 1800s.

Rarity: *None known*

$20 • **W-RI-1400-020-G270**

Left: Gridwork panel bearing RHODE ISLAND / 20 / 20 vertically. *Center:* Alternating flower garlands and gridwork segments. *Right:* 20 / 20 vertically. *Comments:* H-RI-475-G110. 18__. 1806–1809.

Rarity: *None known*

$20 • **W-RI-1400-020-G270a**

Engraver: PSSP. *Comments:* H-RI-475-G112. Similar to W-RI-1400-020-G270. 18__. 1809–1820s.

Rarity: *None known*

$20 • **W-RI-1400-020-G270b**

Engraver: PSSP. *Comments:* H-RI-475-G114. Similar to W-RI-1400-020-G270. 18__. 1820s–1830s.

Rarity: *None known*

$20 • **W-RI-1400-020-G280**

Left: 20 / Woman seated with book on lap, opening chest. *Center:* XX / Eagle on rock / XX. *Right:* 20 / Ship in harbor. *Engraver:* New England Bank Note Co. *Comments:* H-RI-475-G116. 18__. 1840s–1850s.

Rarity: *None known*

$50 • **W-RI-1400-050-G290**

Left: Lathework chain bearing RHODE ISLAND / 50 / 50 vertically. *Center:* Alternating flower garlands and gridwork segments. *Right:* 50 / 50 vertically. *Engraver:* PSSP. *Comments:* H-RI-475-G120. 18__. 1820s–1830s.

Rarity: *None known*

$50 • **W-RI-1400-050-G300**

Left: FIFTY / Woman standing with wreath and flowers / FIFTY. *Center:* 50 / Man restraining prancing horse / 50. *Right:* FIFTY / Woman standing with cornucopia / FIFTY. *Engraver:* New England Bank Note Co. *Comments:* H-RI-475-G126. 18__. 1840s–1850s.

Rarity: *None known*

$100 • **W-RI-1400-100-G310**

Left: Lathework chain bearing RHODE ISLAND / 100 / 100 vertically. *Center:* Alternating flower garlands and gridwork segments. *Right:* 100 / 100 vertically. *Engraver:* PSSP. *Comments:* H-RI-475-G130. 18__. 1820s–1830s.

Rarity: *None known*

$100 • **W-RI-1400-100-G320**

Left: ONE HUNDRED on 100 / Portrait of William Henry Harrison. *Center:* Wharf scene, Men loading wagon with barrels. *Right:* ONE HUNDRED on 100 / Portrait of Christopher Columbus. *Engraver:* New England Bank Note Co. *Comments:* H-RI-475-G132. 18__. 1840s–1850s.

Rarity: *None known*

Uncut Sheets

$3-$1-$5-$7 • **W-RI-1400-003.001.005.007-US010**

Vignette(s): *($3)* Liberty with pole and cap. *($1)* No description available. *($5)* Ceres. *($7)* Hope resting on anchor. *Comments:* H-RI-475-G46, G8, G64, G84. 18__. 1800s.

Rarity: *None known*

Non-Valid Issues

$1.25 • **W-RI-1400-001.25-A010**

CJF

Engraver: New England Bank Note Co. *Comments:* H-RI-475-A5, Durand-2677. Altered from $1.25 Roxbury Bank, Roxbury, Massachusetts, or from notes of other failed banks using the same plate. 18__. 1800s.

Rarity: URS-3

VF $500

$1.50 • **W-RI-1400-001.50-A020**

Left: 1 DOLL. 50 Cts. vertically. *Center:* Spread eagle / $1 50/100. *Right:* 1 50/100 / Justice. *Engraver:* New England Bank Note Co. *Comments:* H-RI-475-A10, Durand-2678. Altered from $1.50 Roxbury Bank, Roxbury, Massachusetts, or from notes of other failed banks using the same plate. 18__. 1800s.

Rarity: *None known*

$1.75 • **W-RI-1400-001.75-A030**

Left: $1.75 Cts. / Liberty and eagle / 1 75/100. *Center:* Three sloops at sea. *Right:* $1.75 Cts. / Agriculture / 1 75/100. *Engraver:* New England Bank Note Co. *Comments:* H-RI-475-A15, Durand-2679. Altered from $1.75 Roxbury Bank, Roxbury, Massachusetts, or from notes of other failed banks using the same plate. 18__. 1800s.

Rarity: *None known*

$2 • W-RI-1400-002-A040

CJF

Engraver: Draper, Toppan, Longacre & Co. *Comments:* H-RI-475-A20, Durand-2683. Altered from $2 Calhoun County Bank, Marshall, Michigan. 18___. 1850s.
Rarity: URS-4
VF $200

$3 • W-RI-1400-003-C120
Engraver: Hamlin. *Comments:* H-RI-475-C46. Counterfeit of W-RI-1400-003-G120. 18___. 1800s.
Rarity: URS-3
VF $250

$5 • W-RI-1400-005-C170
Engraver: Hamlin. *Comments:* H-RI-475-C64. Counterfeit of W-RI-1400-005-G170. 18___. 1800s.
Rarity: URS-3
VF $250

$5 • W-RI-1400-005-A050
Left: FIVE vertically. *Center:* Farmer plowing with two horses / 5 on die / Farmer sowing, team pulling harrow. *Right:* V / 5 / V. *Engraver:* Rawdon, Wright & Hatch. *Comments:* H-RI-475-A25, Durand-2690. Altered from $5 Farmers & Mechanics Bank at Pontiac, Pontiac, Michigan. 18___. 1850s.
Rarity: *None known*

$7 • W-RI-1400-007-C220

MR

Engraver: Hamlin. *Comments:* H-RI-475-C84, Durand-2692. Counterfeit of W-RI-1400-007-G220 with an early vignette of Hope. 18___. 1800s.
Rarity: URS-3
VF $250

$10 • W-RI-1400-010-A060
Left: TEN / Portrait of Chief Justice John Marshall / 10. *Center:* 10 / Train / 10. *Right:* TEN / Portrait of George Washington / 10. *Engraver:* Draper, Toppan, Longacre & Co. *Comments:* H-RI-475-A30, Durand-2693. Altered from $10 Calhoun County Bank, Marshall, Michigan. 18___. 1850s.
Rarity: *None known*

$20 • W-RI-1400-020-C260
Engraver: Hamlin. *Comments:* H-RI-475-C106. Counterfeit of W-RI-1400-020-G260. 18___. 1800s.
Rarity: URS-3
VF $250

Village Bank
1822–1865
W-RI-1410

History: The Village Bank was formerly the Burrillville Agricultural and Manufacturing Bank, W-RI-160. Its location was sometimes cited under Slatersville, W-RI-1330. It became the Village Bank in October 1822.

The Suffolk Bank, Boston, reported on January 30, 1838, that bills of this bank would not be received.[79] The authorized capital of the bank was $50,000, rising to $60,000 by 1849 with 1,200 shares valued at $50 each. By 1855 the capital was $100,000. Bills in circulation totaled $23,841 in 1857, with specie at $1,462.48.

The business of the Village Bank was succeeded by the First National Bank of Smithfield in 1865.

Numismatic Commentary: Genuine notes from the Village Bank appear in the marketplace and with patience are collectible. The two issues of PSSP design are very hard to locate.

VALID ISSUES
$1 • W-RI-1410-001-G010
Left: 1 on eagle / Portrait of George Washington / 1. *Center:* Two cherubs with goods, Cornucopia and beehive. *Right:* 1 on eagle / Portrait of Marquis de Lafayette / 1. *Engraver:* PSSP / New England Bank Note Co. *Comments:* H-RI-480-G4, Durand-2148. 18___. 1820s–1830s.
Rarity: *None known*

$1 • W-RI-1410-001-G020
Left: 1 / Woman wearing bonnet, standing by pail / ONE. *Center:* Ceres seated holding sickle and rake, Machinery and merchandise, Factories and harbor. *Right:* 1 / Ship / ONE. *Engraver:* PSSP / New England Bank Note Co. *Comments:* H-RI-480-G6. 18___. 1830s–1840s.
Rarity: *None known*

$1 • W-RI-1410-001-G030
Left: 1 / Portrait of George Washington. *Center:* Woman / 1 / Woman. *Right:* 1 / Portrait of Benjamin Franklin. *Engraver:* New England Bank Note Co. *Comments:* H-RI-480-G8, Durand-2149. 18___. 1850s.
Rarity: *None known*

$1 • W-RI-1410-001-G040
Left: 1 / Liberty. *Center:* Cherub rolling silver dollar, Train. *Right:* 1 / Commerce and Manufacturing. *Engraver:* Unverified, but likely Rawdon, Wright, Hatch & Edson / New England Bank Note Co. *Comments:* H-RI-480-G10, Durand-2150. 18___. 1850s.
Rarity: *None known*

$2 • W-RI-1410-002-G050

Left: 2 on eagle / Portrait of George Washington / 2. *Center:* Two cherubs with goods, Cornucopia and beehive. *Right:* 2 on eagle / Portrait of Marquis de Lafayette / 2. *Engraver:* PSSP. *Comments:* H-RI-480-G12, Durand-2151. 18__. 1820s–1830s.

Rarity: *None known*

$2 • W-RI-1410-002-G060

Left: 2 / Woman standing with staff, Cornucopia / TWO. *Center:* TWO / Machinery and merchandise flanking Ceres holding sickle and rake, Factories and harbor / Panel outlining white TWO. *Right:* 2 / Woman wearing hat, Trees / TWO. *Engraver:* PSSP / New England Bank Note Co. *Comments:* H-RI-480-G16. 18__. 1830s–1840s.

Rarity: *None known*

$2 • W-RI-1410-002-G070

Left: 2 / Portrait of Christopher Columbus. *Center:* Goddess of Plenty / 2 / Justice. *Right:* 2 / Male portrait. *Engraver:* New England Bank Note Co. *Comments:* H-RI-480-G18, Durand-2152. 18__. 1850s.

Rarity: *None known*

$2 • W-RI-1410-002-G080

Left: 2 / Farmer with cradle and grain. *Center:* Two cherubs with two silver dollars. *Right:* 2 / Portrait of girl reading. *Engraver:* Unverified, but likely Rawdon, Wright, Hatch & Edson / New England Bank Note Co. *Comments:* H-RI-480-G20, Durand-2153. 18__. 1850s.

Rarity: *None known*

$3 • W-RI-1410-003-G090

Left: 3 on eagle / Portrait of George Washington / 3. *Center:* Two cherubs with goods, Cornucopia and beehive. *Right:* 3 on eagle / Portrait of Marquis de Lafayette / 3. *Engraver:* PSSP. *Comments:* H-RI-480-G22, Durand-2156. 18__. 1820s–1830s.

Rarity: *None known*

$3 • W-RI-1410-003-G100

Left: THREE / Beehive and foliage / THREE. *Center:* Machinery and merchandise flanking Ceres holding sickle and rake, Factories and harbor / THREE / Panel outlining white THREE. *Right:* 3 on THREE / Two reapers / 3 on THREE. *Engraver:* PSSP / New England Bank Note Co. *Comments:* H-RI-480-G26. 18__. 1830s–1840s.

Rarity: *None known*

$3 • W-RI-1410-003-G110

Left: 3 / George Washington with horse. *Center:* Female portrait / 3 / Portrait of girl. *Right:* 3 / Vulcan. *Engraver:* New England Bank Note Co. *Comments:* H-RI-480-G28, Durand-2157. 18__. 1850s.

Rarity: *None known*

$3 • W-RI-1410-003-G120

Left: THREE / Minerva. *Center:* Three cherubs and three silver dollars. *Right:* 3 / Sailor holding oar. *Engraver:* Rawdon, Wright, Hatch & Edson / New England Bank Note Co. *Comments:* H-RI-480-G30, Durand-2158. 18__. 1850s.

Rarity: *None known*

$3 • W-RI-1410-003-G120a   CC

Overprint: Red THREE. *Engraver:* Rawdon, Wright, Hatch & Edson / New England Bank Note Co. / ABNCo. monogram. *Comments:* H-Unlisted, Durand-Unlisted. Similar to W-RI-1410-003-G120 but with additional engraver imprint. 18__. 1850s.

Rarity: URS-2
VF $1,400

Selected auction price: Stack's Bowers Galleries, May 2008, VF $1,329

$3 • W-RI-1410-003-G125   CJF

Engraver: New England Bank Note Co. *Comments:* H-Unlisted, Durand-Unlisted. 18__. 1850s.

Rarity: URS-2
VF $1,200

$5 • W-RI-1410-005-G130

Left: 5 / Portrait of George Washington / 5. *Center:* RHODE ISLAND. *Right:* 5 / Portrait of Marquis de Lafayette / 5. *Engraver:* PSSP. *Comments:* H-RI-480-G34, Durand-2162. 18__. 1828–1830s.

Rarity: URS-3
VF $400

$5 • W-RI-1410-005-G140

Left: 5 / Five figures grouped around V. *Center:* Five cherubs and five silver dollars. *Right:* 5 / Woman feeding horse. *Engraver:* Unverified, but likely Rawdon, Wright, Hatch & Edson / New England Bank Note Co. *Comments:* H-RI-480-G40, Durand-2163. 18__. 1850s.

Rarity: *None known*

Collectors and Researchers:

If you have new information about any banks or notes listed in this volume, contact Whitman Publishing, Attn: Obsolete Paper Money, 3101 Clairmont Road, Suite G, Atlanta, GA 30329.

$10 • W-RI-1410-010-G150

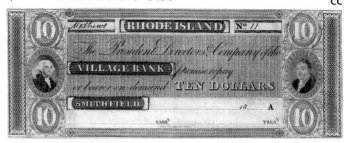

cc

Engraver: PSSP. *Comments:* H-RI-480-G44, Durand-2166. 18__. 1828–1830s.

Rarity: URS-3
VF $750; **Proof** $1,000

$10 • W-RI-1410-010-G160

Left: Woman with flowers / TEN. *Center:* Train, depot, Harbor and shipping. *Right:* X / Indian woman. *Engraver:* Unverified, but likely Rawdon, Wright, Hatch & Edson / New England Bank Note Co. *Comments:* H-RI-480-G50, Durand-2167. 18__. 1850s.

Rarity: *None known*

$20 • W-RI-1410-020-G170

Left: Lathework chain bearing RHODE ISLAND / 20 / 20 vertically. *Center:* Alternating flower garlands and gridwork segments. *Right:* 20 / 20 vertically. *Engraver:* PSSP. *Comments:* H-RI-480-G54. 18__. 1820s–1830s.

Rarity: *None known*

$20 • W-RI-1410-020-G180

Left: 20 / Woman seated with book on lap, opening chest. *Center:* XX / Eagle / XX. *Right:* 20 / Ship. *Engraver:* New England Bank Note Co. *Comments:* H-RI-480-G58, Durand-2170. 18__. 1840s–1850s.

Rarity: *None known*

$50 • W-RI-1410-050-G190

Left: Lathework chain bearing RHODE ISLAND / 50 / 50 vertically. *Center:* Alternating flower garlands and gridwork segments. *Right:* 50 / 50 vertically. *Engraver:* PSSP. *Comments:* H-RI-480-G62. 18__. 1820s–1830s.

Rarity: *None known*

$50 • W-RI-1410-050-G200

Left: FIFTY / Allegorical figure / FIFTY. *Center:* 50 / Man holding horse / 50. *Right:* FIFTY / Woman standing with cornucopia / FIFTY. *Engraver:* New England Bank Note Co. *Comments:* H-RI-480-G66, Durand-2171. 18__. 1840s–1850s.

Rarity: *None known*

$100 • W-RI-1410-100-G210

Left: Lathework chain bearing RHODE ISLAND / 100 / 100 vertically. *Center:* Alternating flower garlands and gridwork segments. *Right:* 100 / 100 vertically. *Engraver:* PSSP. *Comments:* H-RI-480-G70. 18__. 1820s–1830s.

Rarity: *None known*

$100 • W-RI-1410-100-G220

Left: ONE HUNDRED across 100 / Portrait of William Henry Harrison. *Center:* Wharf scene. *Right:* ONE HUNDRED across 100 / Portrait of Christopher Columbus. *Engraver:* New England Bank Note Co. *Comments:* H-RI-480-G74, Durand-2172. 18__. 1840s–1850s.

Rarity: *None known*

Non-Valid Issues

$2 • W-RI-1410-002-A010

Left: 2 / Farmer plowing. *Center:* Men loading wagon with sheaves, Men cradling and binding. *Right:* 2 / Two cherubs with sheaf and caduceus. *Tint:* Red-brown 2s and TWO DOLLARS. *Engraver:* Danforth, Wright & Co. *Comments:* H-RI-480-A5, Durand-2154. Altered from $2 Southern Bank of Georgia, Bainbridge, Georgia. March 1, 1858.

Rarity: URS-3
VF $150

$2 • W-RI-1410-002-A020

Left: Die containing state arms of Michigan / TWO and 2. *Center:* Men cutting trees. *Right:* Ceres, 2. *Engraver:* Danforth, Wright & Co. *Comments:* H-RI-480-A10, Durand-2155. Altered from $2 Bank of Washtenaw, Washtenaw, Michigan series. 1850s.

Rarity: URS-3
VF $150

$3 • W-RI-1410-003-S010

Center: Train. *Right:* Woman standing with shield bearing 3. *Engraver:* Danforth, Underwood & Co. *Comments:* H-RI-480-S5, Durand-2161. 18__. 1850s.

Rarity: *None known*

$3 • W-RI-1410-003-AR010

Left: 3 / Farmer plowing. *Center:* Men loading wagon with sheaves, Men cradling and binding. *Right:* 3 / Two cherubs with sheaf and caduceus. *Tint:* Red-brown 3s and THREE DOLLARS. *Engraver:* Danforth, Wright & Co. *Comments:* H-RI-480-A15, Durand-2159. Altered and raised from $2 Southern Bank of Georgia, Bainbridge, Georgia. March 1, 1858.

Rarity: *None known*

$3 • W-RI-1410-003-A030

Left: 3 / Woman with harp. *Center:* Sailor and bales, Wharf, ship, warehouse, merchandise, Eagle and shield. *Right:* 3 / Portrait of Marquis de Lafayette / THREE. *Engraver:* New England Bank Note Co. *Comments:* H-RI-480-A18, Durand-2160. Altered from $3 Lafayette Bank, Boston, Massachusetts. 18__. 1850s.

Rarity: *None known*

$5 • W-RI-1410-005-S020

Left: V / Picture of ox / V. *Center:* 5 / Ceres / 5. *Right:* FIVE vertically. *Comments:* H-RI-480-S10, Durand-2165. 18__. 1845.

Rarity: URS-3
VF $150

$5 • W-RI-1410-005-A040

Left: 5 / FIVE / FIVE. *Center:* Three cherubs on five gold dollars, Frontiersman and Indian woman. *Right:* 5 / Female portrait / FIVE. *Overprint:* FIVE. *Engraver:* Rawdon, Wright, Hatch & Edson. *Comments:* H-RI-480-A20, Durand-2164. Altered from $5 Farmers & Merchants Bank of Memphis, Memphis, Tennessee. 1850s.

Rarity: URS-3
VF $150

$10 • W-RI-1410-010-S030

CC

Engraver: Underwood, Bald, Spencer & Hufty. **Comments:** H-RI-480-S15, Durand-2169. 18__. 1846.

Rarity: URS-4

VF $300

$10 • W-RI-1410-010-A050

Left: 10 / Portrait of George Washington held by cherub / 10. **Center:** 10 / Spread eagle and shield, E PLURIBUS UNUM / 10. **Right:** 10 / Indian / 10. **Engraver:** Terry, Pelton & Co. **Comments:** H-RI-480-A25, Durand-2168. Altered from $10 Citizens Bank, Augusta, Maine, or from notes of other failed banks using the same plate. 18__. 1850s.

Rarity: *None known*

SOUTH KINGSTON, RHODE ISLAND

The village of South Kingston, adjacent to the town of Wakefield, was distinct from the village of North Kingston (also spelled North Kingstown) for many years. In the late 19th century, both were incorporated into the larger area of South Kingstown.

In 1675 South Kingston was a base for the most famous Wampanoag chief, Metacomet, who was also known as King Philip and fought what became known as King Philip's War against the early colonists. Metacomet bivouacked his tribe for the winter on an island in the middle of the swamp of South Kingston. His fortifications would have been impenetrable had he not been betrayed by his tribesman, Peter, who led the English through his defenses. The English massacred a great number of Wampanoag before being driven back, and Metacomet led his tribe away. This battle was the turning point of his losing King Philip's War.

The General Assembly of Rhode Island held its October sessions in South Kingston beginning in the 1750s and continuing through part of the 19th century. Later South Kingston was incorporated into the larger area of South *Kingstown.*

See also Kingston, North Kingstown, and South Kingstown, Rhode Island.

Note that these towns have slightly different spellings.

Landholders Bank
1818–1866
W-RI-1420

History: The Landholders Bank was incorporated in February 1818 in the Kingston village of South Kingston (later South Kingstown), one of the largest towns in the state. John B. Dockray was the bank's founding president, and Thomas R. Wells was the first cashier.

In 1850 the capital was $100,000. By 1856 the same had risen to $150,000, where it remained until 1862. It was then decreased to $105,000. In 1857 circulation totaled $40,785, and specie amounted to $2,273.86.

The interests of the Landholders Bank were succeeded by the National Landholders Bank, chartered on May 17, 1865.

See also listing under Kingston, W-RI-480, and South Kingstown, W-RI-1440.

South Kingston Bank
1818 AND 1819
W-RI-1430

History: The South Kingston Bank was chartered in October 1818 in the village of Little Rest, which later became part of South Kingston. However, the area was unable to provide ready capital, and in 1819 the charter was amended to change the name to the North Kingston Bank, W-RI-600, located in North Kingstown.

Numismatic Commentary: The denominations and designs of this bank's note issues are unknown but were probably of the Perkins type.[80]

SOUTH KINGSTOWN, RHODE ISLAND

South Kingstown encompasses the villages of Kingston, West Kingston, Peace Dale, and Wakefield. South *Kingston* was an earlier village that was incorporated into this larger region later on. The area was incorporated as Kings Town in 1674 on land that was once occupied by the Narragansett Indians, who used the land to hunt, fish, and grow corn. The town was officially formed in 1722 and split into two parts—Kings Towne and North Kingstown.

Livestock, flax, vegetables, and dairy provided much of the income for South Kingstown. The products were traded to the West Indies and other areas. By 1800 the Wakefield Manufacturing Company was in operation in town. The Narragansett Pacer was bred here as a swift saddle horse, first drawing carriages of export items and later competing in horse races. Pacers were ridden by George Washington and Paul Revere, but the breed later became extinct. It is considered the ancestor of many gaited horses in the United States.

See also Kingston, North Kingstown, and South Kingston, Rhode Island.

Note that these towns have slightly different spellings.

Landholders Bank
1818–1866
W-RI-1440

History: The Landholders Bank was incorporated in February 1818 in the Kingston village of South Kingston (later South Kingstown), one of the largest towns in the state.[81] John B. Dockray was the bank's founding president, and Thomas R. Wells was the first cashier. Capital was $100,000 in 1848. By 1855 the same had been increased to $150,000, and in 1863 it was $105,000.

The interests of the Landholders Bank were succeeded by the National Landholders Bank, chartered on May 17, 1865.

See also listing under Kingston, W-RI-480, and South Kingston, W-RI-1420.

VALID ISSUES

$1 • W-RI-1440-001-G010

SBG

Engraver: Reed. *Comments:* H-RI-485-G2, Durand-2173. 18__. 1818–1830s.

Rarity: URS-3
Proof $750

$2 • W-RI-1440-002-G020

QDB

Engraver: Reed. *Comments:* H-RI-485-G10, Durand-2174. Proof. 18__. 1818–1830s.

Rarity: URS-3
Proof $1,000

$3 • W-RI-1440-003-G030

Left: 3 3 3 vertically. *Center:* 3 / Woman seated / 3. *Bottom center:* THREE. *Right:* 3 RHODE ISLAND 3 vertically. *Engraver:* Reed. *Comments:* H-RI-485-G12. 18__. 1818–1830s.

Rarity: *None known*

$5 • W-RI-1440-005-G040

Left: V 5 V vertically. *Center:* 5 / Woman pointing to village holding shield bearing 5 / 5. *Right:* 5 RHODE ISLAND 5 vertically. *Engraver:* Reed. *Comments:* H-RI-485-G14, Durand-2184. First issue. 18__. 1818–1830s.

Rarity: *None known*

$10 • W-RI-1440-010-G050

Left: 10 TEN 10 vertically. *Center:* 10 / Shepherdess and sheep, House / 10. *Right:* 10 RHODE ISLAND 10 vertically. *Engraver:* Reed, Stiles & Co. *Comments:* H-RI-485-G16, Durand-2192. 18__. 1820s–1840s.

Rarity: URS-3
Proof $300

Uncut Sheets

$1-$1-$1-$2 • W-RI-1440-001.001.001.002-US010

Vignette(s): *($1)* Woman with staff and plow. *($1)* Woman with staff and plow. *($1)* Woman with staff and plow. *($2)* Milkmaid and cow, House. *Engraver:* Reed. *Comments:* H-RI-485-G2, G2, G2, G10. 18__. 1818–1830s.

Rarity: URS-3
Proof $1,500

NON-VALID ISSUES

$2 • W-RI-1440-002-C020

Engraver: Reed. *Comments:* H-RI-485-C10, Durand-2179. Counterfeit of W-RI-1440-002-G020. 18__. 1818–1830s.

Rarity: URS-3
VF $150

$3 • W-RI-1440-003-C030

Engraver: Reed. *Comments:* H-RI-485-C12, Durand-2176. Counterfeit of W-RI-1440-003-G030. 18__. 1820s.

Rarity: URS-3
VF $150

$5 • W-RI-1440-005-C040

SI

Comments: H-RI-485-C14, Durand-2188. Counterfeit of W-RI-1440-005-G040. 18__. 1810s–1820s.

Rarity: URS-4
VF $200

$5 • W-RI-1440-005-R010

Comments: H-Unlisted, Durand-2189. Raised from W-RI-1440-002-G020. 18__. 1818–1830s.

Rarity: URS-3

$5 • W-RI-1440-005-R020

Comments: H-Unlisted, Durand-2190. Raised from W-RI-1440-002-G020. 18__. 1818–1830s.

Rarity: URS-3
VF $100

$5 • W-RI-1440-005-A010

Left: V. *Center:* Liberty and Ceres flanking shield surmounted by horse's head / Running horses. *Right:* 5 / Portrait of girl. *Comments:* H-Unlisted, Durand-2191. Altered from $5 Bank of Morgan, Morgan, Georgia. 1810s–1820s.

Rarity: URS-3
VF $90

Wakefield Bank
1834–1865
W-RI-1450

History: The Wakefield Bank was incorporated in October 1834. The authorized capital of the bank was $50,000. The capital was increased to $99,500 by 1855 and again in 1857 to $100,000, where it remained through 1862. Circulation was $19,109 in 1849, $14,745 in 1860, and $29,318 in 1863. Specie was $2,520.90 in 1857.

The interests of the Wakefield Bank were succeeded by the Wakefield National Bank on April 27, 1865.

See also listing under Wakefield, W-RI-1530.

SOWAMSET, RHODE ISLAND

The first record of the name Sowamset is found in the patent granted to Plymouth settlers in 1629, regarding it "as the utmost limits of the said place commonly called Pokenocutt *alias* Sowamsett."[82] The name could possibly derive from the native word for "southwest," although there was also a pond not far away that was known as Assowamset, which could also be attributed as the source.

Sowamset was bought from the Massasoit tribe in 1653.[83] It was incorporated as the town of Warren in 1747. By 1770 Barrington had separated from the town, and from 1764 to 1770 the College of Rhode Island had its seat in Sowamset. Cotton, braid, and twine were manufactured here, and the industries were continued long after the bank-note–issuing era ended.

See also Warren, Rhode Island.

Sowamset Bank
1854–1865
W-RI-1465

History: The Sowamset Bank was incorporated in June 1854 and commenced operations on August 6, 1855. The authorized capital was $50,000 until 1857, when it increased to $200,000. Only $67,500 was actually paid in. Later that year it was reported to be $66,950, and in 1860 it was $71,300. Bills in circulation at that time totaled $23,154. In 1862 capital was slightly higher at $71,500, and circulation had nearly doubled to $43,836.

The business of the Sowamset Bank was succeeded by the First National Bank of Warren, chartered on December 30, 1864.

See also listing under Warren, W-RI-1550.

TIVERTON, RHODE ISLAND

Incorporated by English colonists in 1694, Tiverton was initially a part of Massachusetts. In 1746 it was annexed to Rhode Island during a boundary dispute, and it was incorporated as a town the next year. During the Revolutionary War, Tiverton was a haven for colonists fleeing British occupation and also a location for the mustering of Colonial forces.

Farming, fishing, and boat construction occurred in Tiverton, along with the manufacture of menhaden oil, which derives from fish. Cotton and woolen mills were built in 1811. In 1856 the northern section of the town separated from Tiverton and was called Fall River. On March 1, 1862, a case between Rhode Island and Massachusetts led to Fall River becoming a part of Massachusetts.

See also Fall River, Rhode Island, and Fall River, Massachusetts.

Fall River Union Bank
1831–1860
W-RI-1480

History: The Fall River Union Bank was incorporated as the Bristol Union Bank, W-RI-060, in 1823 with an authorized capital of $200,000. The location of the bank was changed to Tiverton, Rhode Island, in 1830, and the title was changed to the Fall River Union Bank in 1831.

The bank's capital was $199,512 in 1848, divided into 2,000 shares valued at $100 each. Bills in circulation totaled $68,128 in 1849. By 1857 capital had decreased to $99,500. The bank was located in a building on the corner of South Main and Rodman streets.

The Fall River Union Bank became a Massachusetts bank in 1860 as a result of the boundary change which took place at the January session of the Houses of the two states involved. A portion of Tiverton, Rhode Island, became part of Fall River, and all of Fall River, Rhode Island, became part of Massachusetts. Notes are dated at Fall River, Massachusetts, beginning in 1860.

See also listing under Fall River, W-RI-370.

Numismatic Commentary: Genuine notes with the Tiverton address are hard to locate. Altered notes with this address also exist.

VALID ISSUES

$1 • **W-RI-1480-001-G010**
Comments: H-RI-495-G4. No description available. 18__. 1830s.
Rarity: *None known*

$1 • **W-RI-1480-001-G020**
Engraver: New England Bank Note Co. *Comments:* H-RI-495-G6. No description available. 18__. 1830s.
Rarity: *None known*

$1 • **W-RI-1480-001-G030**
Left: 1. *Center:* Man on horseback, Boy, Cows, House / 1 / Dolphin. *Right:* ONE / Indian / 1. *Comments:* H-RI-495-G10, Durand-2212. 18__. 1840s–1850s.
Rarity: *None known*

$1.25 • **W-RI-1480-001.25-G040**   CJF

Engraver: New England Bank Note Co. *Comments:* H-RI-495-G11. 18__. 1850s.
Rarity: URS-6
VF $250

$1.50 • W-RI-1480-001.50-G050

Left: 1 Doll. 50 Cts. vertically. *Center:* Perched eagle / $1 50/100. *Right:* 1 50/100 / Man standing. *Engraver:* New England Bank Note Co. *Comments:* H-RI-495-G12. 18__. 1850s.

Rarity: URS-5

VF $250

$1.75 • W-RI-1480-001.75-G060

Left: $1.75 Cts. / Man and eagle / 1 75/100. *Center:* Sailing vessels. *Right:* $1.75 Cts. / Woman leaning on boxes / 1 75/100. *Engraver:* New England Bank Note Co. *Comments:* H-RI-495-G13. 18__. 1850s.

Rarity: URS-5

VF $250

$2 • W-RI-1480-002-G070

Comments: H-RI-495-G14. No description available. 18__. 1830s.

Rarity: *None known*

$2 • W-RI-1480-002-G080

Engraver: Unverified, but likely New England Bank Note Co. *Comments:* H-RI-495-G16. No description available. 18__. 1830s.

Rarity: *None known*

$2 • W-RI-1480-002-G090

Left: 2. *Center:* Train depot and men, Pier, steamship, vessels / 2 / Female portrait. *Right:* 2 / George Washington beside his horse / TWO. *Comments:* H-RI-495-G20, Durand-2217. 18__. 1840s–1850s.

Rarity: *None known*

$5 • W-RI-1480-005-G100

Comments: H-RI-495-G24. No description available. 18__. 1830s.

Rarity: *None known*

$5 • W-RI-1480-005-G110

Engraver: Unverified, but likely New England Bank Note Co. *Comments:* H-RI-495-G26. No description available. 18__. 1830s.

Rarity: *None known*

$5 • W-RI-1480-005-G120

Left: V on FIVE. *Center:* Indian paddling canoe / V. *Bottom center:* Dog and strongbox. *Right:* 5 / Spread eagle on shield. *Comments:* H-RI-495-G30, Durand-2220. 18__. 1840s–1850s.

Rarity: *None known*

$10 • W-RI-1480-010-G130

Comments: H-RI-495-G34. No description available. 18__. 1830s.

Rarity: *None known*

$10 • W-RI-1480-010-G140

Engraver: Unverified, but likely New England Bank Note Co. *Comments:* H-RI-495-G36. No description available. 18__. 1830s.

Rarity: *None known*

$10 • W-RI-1480-010-G150

Left: X. *Center:* Blacksmith shop / X. *Right:* TEN / Portrait of George Washington / TEN. *Comments:* H-RI-495-G40, Durand-2224. 18__. 1840s–1850s.

Rarity: *None known*

$20 • W-RI-1480-020-G160

Comments: H-RI-495-G44. No description available. 18__. 1840s–1850s.

Rarity: *None known*

$20 • W-RI-1480-020-G170

Left: 20 / Woman. *Center:* XX / Eagle / XX. *Right:* 20 / Ship. *Engraver:* New England Bank Note Co. *Comments:* H-RI-495-G48, Durand-2226. 18__. 1840s–1850s.

Rarity: *None known*

$50 • W-RI-1480-050-G180

Left: FIFTY / Allegorical figure / FIFTY. *Center:* 50 / Man restraining prancing horse / 50. *Right:* FIFTY / Allegorical figure / FIFTY. *Engraver:* New England Bank Note Co. *Comments:* H-RI-495-G54, Durand-2228. 18__. 1840s–1850s.

Rarity: *None known*

$100 • W-RI-1480-100-G190

Left: ONE HUNDRED across 100 / Portrait of William Henry Harrison. *Center:* Wharf scene. *Right:* ONE HUNDRED across 100 / Portrait of Christopher Columbus. *Engraver:* New England Bank Note Co. *Comments:* H-RI-495-G58, Durand-2230. 18__. 1840s–1850s.

Rarity: *None known*

$500 • W-RI-1480-500-G200

Left: 500. *Center:* Harvest scene. *Right:* 500. *Engraver:* New England Bank Note Co. *Comments:* H-RI-495-G62, Durand-2232. 18__. 1840s–1850s.

Rarity: *None known*

NON-VALID ISSUES

$1 • W-RI-1480-001-A010   CC

Engraver: New England Bank Note Co. / PSSP. *Comments:* H-RI-495-A5, Durand-2213. Altered from $1 Washington County Bank, Calais, Maine, or from notes of other failed banks using the same plate. 18__. 1840s–1850s.

Rarity: URS-3

VF $150

$1.25 • W-RI-1480-001.25-A020   CC

Comments: H-Unlisted, Durand-2214. Altered from $1.25 Roxbury Bank, Roxbury, Massachusetts. 18__. 1800s.

Rarity: URS-5

VF $100

$1.50 • **W-RI-1480-001.50-A030**

CC

Comments: H-Unlisted, Durand-2215. Altered from $1.50 Roxbury Bank, Roxbury, Massachusetts. 18__. 1830s.
Rarity: URS-5
VF $100

$1.75 • **W-RI-1480-001.75-A040**

CC

Comments: H-Unlisted, Durand-2216. Altered from $1.75 Roxbury Bank, Roxbury, Massachusetts. 18__. 1830s.
Rarity: URS-5
VF $150

$2 • **W-RI-1480-002-A050**

Left: 2 / Woman with horn of plenty, Anchor / TWO. **Center:** Ceres, Machinery and merchandise, Factories and harbor. **Right:** 2 / Female portrait / TWO. **Engraver:** New England Bank Note Co. **Comments:** H-RI-495-A10, Durand-2218. Altered from $2 Washington County Bank, Calais, Maine, or from notes of other failed banks using the same plate. 18__. 1840s–1850s.
Rarity: *None known*

$3 • **W-RI-1480-003-A060**

CC

Engraver: New England Bank Note Co. / PSSP. **Comments:** H-RI-495-A15, Durand-2219. Altered from $3 Washington County Bank, Calais, Maine, or from notes of other failed banks using the same plate. No genuine $3 bills have been reported from this bank. 18__. 1840s–1850s.
Rarity: URS-3
VF $150

$5 • **W-RI-1480-005-A070**

Engraver: New England Bank Note Co. **Comments:** H-RI-495-A20. Altered from $5 Washington County Bank, Calais, Maine. 18__. 1840s–1850s.
Rarity: *None known*

$5 • **W-RI-1480-005-A080**

Left: V on FIVE / Man holding child while woman and child look on. **Center:** Men, raft, and boat. **Right:** 5 / Two women with wheat. **Engraver:** Danforth, Wright & Co. **Comments:** H-RI-495-A25, Durand-2223. Altered from $5 Brownville Bank, Omaha City, Nebraska series. Sept. 1, 1857.
Rarity: *None known*

$5 • **W-RI-1480-005-A090**

CC

Engraver: PSSP / New England Bank Note Co. **Comments:** H-RI-495-A30, Durand-2221. Altered from $5 Stillwater Canal Bank, Orono, Maine. 18__. 1840s.
Rarity: URS-4
VF $200

$10 • **W-RI-1480-010-A100**

CC

Engraver: PSSP / New England Bank Note Co. **Comments:** H-RI-495-A35, Durand-2225. Altered from $10 Stillwater Canal Bank, Orono, Maine. 18__. 1830s.
Rarity: URS-3
VF $200

Pocasset Bank
1854–1860
W-RI-1490

History: The Pocasset Bank was incorporated in May 1854 with an authorized capital of $200,000. The official address was Tiverton, Rhode Island, but "Main Street, Fall River" was given on some reports, that section being in Rhode Island at the time. After a boundary change between Tiverton and Fall River was put into effect in the January 1860 session of the two state legislatures involved, the institution became a Massachusetts bank when Fall River became a part of Massachusetts that year.

See also listing under Fall River, W-RI-380.

Numismatic Commentary: The Indian maiden poling a raft is thought to represent "Weetamoe," the Indian sachem who drowned while trying to evade capture by the English. Most of the notes dated at Fall River with the Indian sachem are well-done counterfeits. Genuine notes are hard to find, but counterfeits are available.

Remaining in the American Bank Note Co. archives as of 2003 was a $1-$1-$2-$5 tint plate.

VALID ISSUES

$1 • W-RI-1490-001-G010

Engraver: Wellstood, Hanks, Hay & Whiting. **Comments:** H-RI-500-G2. 18__. 1850s.
Rarity: URS-1
Proof $1,200

$1 • W-RI-1490-001-G010a

Overprint: Red 1. **Engraver:** Wellstood, Hanks, Hay & Whiting. **Comments:** H-RI-500-G2a, Durand-423. Similar to W-RI-1490-001-G010. 18__. 1850s.
Rarity: *None known*

$2 • W-RI-1490-002-G020

Left: TWO on 2 / Indian queen of Pocasset crossing river on raft. **Bottom center:** Clasped hands. **Right:** 2 / Reverse of silver dollar and Spanish American dollar. **Engraver:** Wellstood, Hanks, Hay & Whiting. **Comments:** H-RI-500-G4. 18__. 1850s.
Rarity: URS-3
Proof $1,250

$2 • W-RI-1490-002-G020a

Overprint: Red 2. **Engraver:** Wellstood, Hanks, Hay & Whiting. **Comments:** H-RI-500-G4a, Durand-424. Similar to W-RI-1490-002-G020. 18__. 1850s.
Rarity: *None known*

$5 • W-RI-1490-005-G030

Engraver: Wellstood, Hanks, Hay & Whiting. **Comments:** H-RI-500-G6. 18__. 1850s.
Rarity: URS-3
Proof $2,400
Selected auction price: Stack's Bowers Galleries, January 2008, Proof $2,356

$5 • W-RI-1490-005-G030a

Overprint: Red 5. **Engraver:** Wellstood, Hanks, Hay & Whiting. **Comments:** H-RI-500-G6a, Durand-425. Similar to W-RI-1490-005-G030. 18__. 1850s.
Rarity: *None known*

$10 • W-RI-1490-010-G040

Left: 10 / Stonecutter at work in quarry. **Right:** 10 / Indian queen of Pocasset crossing river on raft. **Engraver:** Wellstood, Hanks, Hay & Whiting. **Comments:** H-RI-500-G8, Durand-427. 18__. 1850s.
Rarity: URS-3
Proof $2,500

$20 • W-RI-1490-020-G050

Left: 20 / Indian queen of Pocasset crossing river on raft. **Center:** TWENTY DOLLARS / 20 / Justice soaring in clouds. **Bottom center:** Anchor on shield. **Engraver:** Wellstood, Hanks, Hay & Whiting. **Comments:** H-RI-500-G10, Durand-428. 18__. 1850s.
Rarity: URS-3
Proof $2,500

$50 • W-RI-1490-050-G060

Engraver: Wellstood, Hanks, Hay & Whiting. **Comments:** H-RI-500-G12, Durand-429. 18__. 1850s.
Rarity: URS-1
Proof $4,000
Selected auction price: Stack's Bowers Galleries, June 2010, Proof $3,851

$100 • W-RI-1490-100-G070

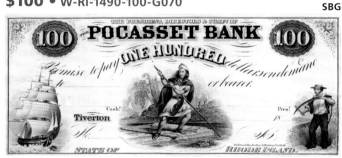

Engraver: Wellstood, Hanks, Hay & Whiting. **Comments:** H-RI-500-G14, Durand-430. 18__. 1850s.
Rarity: URS-1
Proof $5,800
Selected auction price: Stack's Bowers Galleries, March 2013, Proof $5,748

$500 • W-RI-1490-500-G080

Left: 500 / Ship under sail, Ship. *Center:* D / Indian queen of Pocasset crossing river on raft. *Right:* 500. *Engraver:* Wellstood, Hanks, Hay & Whiting. *Comments:* H-RI-500-G16, Durand-431. 18__. 1850s.

Rarity: URS-1

$1,000 • W-RI-1490-1000-G090

Left: Indian queen of Pocasset crossing river on raft / 1000. *Center:* M. *Right:* 1000 / Indian smoking pipe, Indian woman, Wigwam. *Engraver:* Wellstood, Hanks, Hay & Whiting. *Comments:* H-RI-500-G18, Durand-432. 18__. 1850s.

Rarity: URS-1

NON-VALID ISSUES

$1 • W-RI-1490-001-N010

Center: Cattle in stream, Horses. *Comments:* H-RI-500-N5. 1850s.

Rarity: *None known*

$5 • W-RI-1490-005-A010

Left: 5 / V / 5. *Center:* Man with child, Horses and dog. *Right:* 5 / V / 5. *Engraver:* Bald, Cousland & Co. / Baldwin, Bald & Cousland. *Comments:* H-RI-500-A5. Altered from $5 Southern Bank of Georgia, Bainbridge, Georgia. 18__. 1850s.

Rarity: URS-3
VF $600

$5 • W-RI-1490-005-A020

Left: 5 / Portrait of Andrew Jackson. *Center:* 5 / Liberty, Anchor on shield surmounted by eagle, Justice / 5. *Right:* 5 / Female portrait. *Overprint:* Red FIVE. *Engraver:* Baldwin, Bald & Cousland / Bald, Cousland & Co. *Comments:* H-RI-500-A10, Durand-426. Altered from $5 Tiverton Bank, Tiverton, Rhode Island. 18__. 1850s.

Rarity: URS-3
VF $600

Tiverton Bank
1855–1857
W-RI-1500

History: The Tiverton Bank was incorporated in May 1855 and commenced business in December 1856. Its authorized capital was $50,000.

The bank had a very brief existence, as it was forced to close at the end of 1857 due to the financial panic that year. The bank was managed by out-of-state owners with capital made up of bogus bank notes. At one point the cashier took bank funds to New York City. The entire operation was fraudulent.

See also listing under Fall River, W-RI-390.

VALID ISSUES

$1 • W-RI-1500-001-G010

Engraver: Baldwin, Bald & Cousland / Bald, Cousland & Co. **Comments:** H-RI-505-G2, Durand-2234. 18__. 1850s.

Rarity: URS-2
Proof $1,500

$1 • W-RI-1500-001-G010a

Overprint: Red ONE. **Engraver:** Baldwin, Bald & Cousland / Bald, Cousland & Co. **Comments:** H-RI-505-G2a, Durand-2235. Similar to W-RI-1500-001-G010. 18__. 1850s.

Rarity: URS-9
VF $150

$2 • W-RI-1500-002-G020

Engraver: Baldwin, Bald & Cousland / Bald, Cousland & Co. **Comments:** H-RI-505-G4, Durand-2236. 18__. 1850s.

Rarity: URS-2
Proof $1,000

$2 • W-RI-1500-002-G020a

Overprint: Red TWO. **Engraver:** Baldwin, Bald & Cousland / Bald, Cousland & Co. **Comments:** H-RI-505-G4a, Durand-2237. Similar to W-RI-1500-002-G020. 18__. 1850s.
Rarity: URS-9
VF $100

$3 • W-RI-1500-003-G030

Engraver: Baldwin, Bald & Cousland / Bald, Cousland & Co. **Comments:** H-RI-505-G6, Durand-2238. 18__. 1850s.
Rarity: URS-2
Proof $1,200

$3 • W-RI-1500-003-G030a

Overprint: Red THREE. **Engraver:** Baldwin, Bald & Cousland / Bald, Cousland & Co. **Comments:** H-RI-505-G6a, Durand-2239. Similar to W-RI-1500-003-G030. 18__. 1850s.
Rarity: URS-9
VF $150

$5 • W-RI-1500-005-G040

Engraver: Baldwin, Bald & Cousland / Bald, Cousland & Co. **Comments:** H-RI-505-G8, Durand-2240. 18__. 1850s.
Rarity: URS-3
Proof $1,000

$5 • W-RI-1500-005-G040a

Overprint: Red FIVE. **Engraver:** Baldwin, Bald & Cousland / Bald, Cousland & Co. **Comments:** H-RI-505-G8a, Durand-2241. Similar to W-RI-1500-005-G040. 18__. 1850s.
Rarity: URS-9
VF $150; **AU** $300

$10 • W-RI-1500-010-G050

Engraver: Baldwin, Bald & Cousland / Bald, Cousland & Co. **Comments:** H-RI-505-G10, Durand-2243. 18__. 1850s.
Rarity: URS-3
Proof $1,200

$10 • W-RI-1500-010-G050a
SI

Overprint: Red TEN. **Engraver:** Baldwin, Bald & Cousland / Bald, Cousland & Co. **Comments:** H-RI-505-G10a, Durand-2244. Similar to W-RI-1500-010-G050. 18__. 1850s.

Rarity: URS-8

VF $200

$20 • W-RI-1500-020-G060

Left: Man with horses, Children and bear cub / 20. **Center:** Ceres. **Right:** 20 / RHODE ISLAND / XX. **Engraver:** Baldwin, Bald & Cousland / Bald, Cousland & Co. **Comments:** H-RI-505-G12, Durand-2245. 185_. 1850s.

Rarity: *None known*

$20 • W-RI-1500-020-G060a
MK

Overprint: Red XX. **Engraver:** Baldwin, Bald & Cousland / Bald, Cousland & Co. **Comments:** H-RI-505-G12a, Durand-2246. Similar to W-RI-1500-020-G060. 185_. 1850s.

Rarity: URS-6

VF $250; **EF** $450

How to Read the Whitman Numbering System

$1 • W-RI-010-001-G010a

Denomination: Value of the note shown.

W: Whitman number. This number is a sortable code unique to each bank and note.

RI: Abbreviation for the state under study.

010: Numerical designation specific to each bank.

001: The denomination in dollars.

G010a: G indicates a good or valid note. Other categories are indicated thus: C (counterfeit); R (raised); S (spurious); N (not-attributed); A (altered). Numbers are assigned starting with 010, 020, et seq. Terminal letters following the number indicate variations of a note: a series of different colored over-prints, tints, payees, etc., all on the same design of note. For more information, see the "How to Use This Book" section at the front of the volume, page xiv.

Uncut Sheets

$1-$1-$2-$3 • W-RI-1500-001.001.002.003-US010
SBG

Engraver: Bald, Cousland & Co. / Baldwin, Bald & Cousland. **Comments:** H-RI-505-G2, G2, G4, G6. 18__. 1850s.

Rarity: URS-2

Proof $1,500

Selected auction price: Lyn Knight, June 2012, Lot 712, AU $1,000

$5-$5-$10-$10 • W-RI-1500-005.005.010.020-US020

Vignette(s): **($5)** Male portrait / Two women seated with anchor, Pole and cap / Female portrait. **($5)** Male portrait / Two women seated with anchor, Pole and cap / Female portrait. **($10)** Ceres, Farm and harvest / Portrait of Daniel Webster. **($10)** Ceres, Farm and harvest / Portrait of Daniel Webster. **Engraver:** Bald, Cousland & Co. / Baldwin, Bald & Cousland. **Comments:** H-RI-505-G8, G8, G10, G10. 1850s.

Rarity: URS-3

Proof $1,500

NON-VALID ISSUES

$5 • W-RI-1500-005-R010

Engraver: Baldwin, Bald & Cousland / Bald, Cousland & Co. *Comments:* H-RI-505-R4, Durand-2242. Raised from W-RI-1500-001-G010a. 18__. 1850s.

Rarity: *None known*

WAKEFIELD, RHODE ISLAND

Settled in the 18th century, Wakefield has a prime location on the Saugatucket River and the Post Road. It grew to be an important part of the textile industry after 1807 with the establishment of a carding mill. The population in 1822 was merely 60. When Peace Dale nearby became a manufacturing town, with factories located there and near other water-power sites, Wakefield became the center of commerce.

Bank of the South County
1851–1860
W-RI-1510

History: Incorporated in 1851, the Bank of the South County suspended payment in 1857 but later resumed, albeit in an impaired position. It continued to operate until September 1860.[84] Its failure was caused by heavy speculation in weak Western land securities and an inflated circulation of currency.

Numismatic Commentary: All notes are found imprinted with the Wakefield address. The issues of this bank which are available in the marketplace offer an array of beautifully engraved vignettes, including some unusual denominations of $4, $15, and $25.

Remaining in the American Bank Note Co. archives as of 2003 was a $10-$25 face plate and a $1-$1 face plate.

VALID ISSUES

$1 • W-RI-1510-001-G010

SBG

Engraver: Toppan, Carpenter, Casilear & Co. *Comments:* H-RI-515-G2, Durand-2250. 18__. 1850s.

Rarity: URS-3
VF $150; **Proof** $800
Selected auction price: Stack's Bowers Galleries, March 2013, Proof $726

$1 • W-RI-1510-001-G010a

Left: Female portrait / 1. *Center:* Farmer, house, and trees. *Right:* ONE on 1 / Portrait of Andrew Jackson. *Overprint:* Red ONE. *Engraver:* Toppan, Carpenter, Casilear & Co. *Comments:* H-RI-515-G2a, Durand-2251. Similar to W-RI-1510-001-G010. 18__. 1850s.

Rarity: URS-6
VF $150

$1 • W-RI-1510-001-G010b

CC

Overprint: Red ornate ONE and plate letters. *Engraver:* Toppan, Carpenter, Casilear & Co. *Comments:* H-RI-515-G2b, Durand-2253. Similar to W-RI-1510-001-G010. 18__. 1850s.

Rarity: URS-6
VF $200

$1 • W-RI-1510-001-G010c

Overprint: Red block ONE. *Engraver:* Toppan, Carpenter, Casilear & Co. *Comments:* H-RI-515-G2c, Durand-2252. Similar to W-RI-1510-001-G010. 18__. 1850s.

Rarity: URS-6
VF $150

$2 • W-RI-1510-002-G020

Left: TWO / Industry. *Center:* Train, Blacksmith and ship's carpenter, Sailing ship. *Right:* 2 / Female portrait / TWO. *Engraver:* Toppan, Carpenter, Casilear & Co. *Comments:* H-RI-515-G4, Durand-2254. 18__. 1850s.

Rarity: URS-5
VF $200

$2 • W-RI-1510-002-G020a

Overprint: Red TWO. *Engraver:* Toppan, Carpenter, Casilear & Co. *Comments:* H-RI-515-G4a, Durand-2257. Similar to W-RI-1510-002-G020. 18__. 1850s.

Rarity: *None known*

$2 • W-RI-1510-002-G020b

QDB

Overprint: Red ornate TWO. *Engraver:* Toppan, Carpenter, Casilear & Co. *Comments:* H-RI-515-G4b, Durand-2255. Similar to W-RI-1510-002-G020. 18__. 1850s.

Rarity: URS-5
VF $200

$2 • **W-RI-1510-002-G020c**

Overprint: Red block TWO. *Engraver:* Toppan, Carpenter, Casilear & Co. *Comments:* H-RI-515-G4c, Durand-2256. Similar to W-RI-1510-002-G020. 18__. 1850s.

Rarity: URS-5
VF $200

$4 • **W-RI-1510-004-G030**

CJF

Engraver: Toppan, Carpenter, Casilear & Co. *Comments:* H-RI-515-G6, Durand-2258. 18__. 1850s.

Rarity: URS-3
Proof $3,500

$5 • **W-RI-1510-005-G040**

SBG

Engraver: Toppan, Carpenter, Casilear & Co. *Comments:* H-RI-515-G8, Durand-2259. 18__. 1851–1856.

Rarity: URS-3
VF $250; Proof $1,500
Selected auction price: Stack's Bowers Galleries, March 2013, Proof $1,452

$5 • **W-RI-1510-005-G040a**

CC

Overprint: Red V / V. *Engraver:* Toppan, Carpenter, Casilear & Co. *Comments:* H-RI-515-G8a, Durand-2260. Similar to W-RI-1510-005-G040. 18__. 1850s.

Rarity: URS-4
VF $600

$5 • **W-RI-1510-005-G040b**

Left: 5 / Female portrait / 5. *Center:* Industry standing in V. *Right:* Portrait of Rachel Jackson. *Overprint:* Red FIVEs. *Engraver:* Toppan, Carpenter, Casilear & Co. *Comments:* H-RI-515-G8b, Durand-2261. Similar to W-RI-1510-005-G040. 18__. 1856.

Rarity: URS-3
VF $500

$5 • **W-RI-1510-005-G040c**

Overprint: Red 5 / 5. *Engraver:* Toppan, Carpenter, Casilear & Co. *Comments:* H-RI-515-G8c, Durand-2262. Similar to W-RI-1510-005-G040. 18__. 1850s.

Rarity: URS-3
VF $500

$10 • **W-RI-1510-010-G050**

Left: 10 / Man seated reading tablet. *Center:* Agriculture / Female portrait. *Bottom center:* Dog and strongbox. *Right:* 10 / Three women standing. *Engraver:* Toppan, Carpenter, Casilear & Co. *Comments:* H-RI-515-G10, Durand-2264. 18__. 1850s.

Rarity: URS-3
VF $250

$15 • **W-RI-1510-015-G060**

CC

Engraver: Toppan, Carpenter, Casilear & Co. *Comments:* H-RI-515-G12, Durand-2267. 18__. 1850s.

Rarity: URS-2
Proof $5,000

$20 • **W-RI-1510-020-G070**

Left: 20 / Train. *Center:* Eagle, Liberty seated, Cherub holding melon, Child seated. *Bottom center:* Steamship. *Right:* 20 / Ceres. *Engraver:* Unverified, but likely Toppan, Carpenter, Casilear & Co. *Comments:* H-RI-515-G14, Durand-2268. 18__. 1850s.

Rarity: *None known*

$25 • **W-RI-1510-025-G080**

Left: 25 / Liberty with U.S. shield. *Center:* View of blacksmith shop. *Right:* 25 / Commerce with spyglass. *Engraver:* Toppan, Carpenter, Casilear & Co. *Comments:* H-RI-515-G16, Durand-2269. 18__. 1850s.

Rarity: URS-2
Proof $5,000

$50 • **W-RI-1510-050-G090**

Left: 50 / Female portrait / 50. *Center:* Ship, Two women seated with wheel and anvil, Buildings. *Bottom center:* Train. *Right:* 50 / Boy standing with pole and fish. *Engraver:* Unverified, but likely Toppan, Carpenter, Casilear & Co. *Comments:* H-RI-515-G18, Durand-2270. 18__. 1850s.

Rarity: *None known*

$100 • W-RI-1510-100-G100

Left: 100 / Sailor. *Center:* Angel carrying figure in clouds over city. *Bottom center:* Three spools of cotton and wheels. *Right:* 100 / Ship / 100. *Engraver:* Unverified, but likely Toppan, Carpenter, Casilear & Co. *Comments:* H-RI-515-G20, Durand-2271. 18__. 1850s.

Rarity: *None known*

NON-VALID ISSUES

$5 • W-RI-1510-005-C040

Engraver: Unverified, but likely Toppan, Carpenter, Casilear & Co. *Comments:* H-RI-515-C8. Counterfeit of W-RI-1510-005-G040 series. 18__. 1850s.

Rarity: *None known*

$5 • W-RI-1510-005-R010

Engraver: Toppan, Carpenter, Casilear & Co. *Comments:* H-RI-515-R4, Durand-2263. Raised from W-RI-1510-001-G010 series. 18__. 1850s.

Rarity: *None known*

$10 • W-RI-1510-010-R020

Engraver: Toppan, Carpenter, Casilear & Co. *Comments:* H-RI-515-R5, Durand-2265. Raised from W-RI-1510-001-G010 series. 18__. 1850s.

Rarity: *None known*

$10 • W-RI-1510-010-R030

Engraver: Toppan, Carpenter, Casilear & Co. *Comments:* H-RI-515-R12, Durand-2266. Raised from W-RI-1510-002-G020 series. 18__. 1850s.

Rarity: *None known*

$20 • W-RI-1510-020-R040

Engraver: Toppan, Carpenter, Casilear & Co. *Comments:* H-RI-515-R13, Durand-2268. Raised from W-RI-1510-002-G020 series. 18__. 1850s.

Rarity: *None known*

Peoples Exchange Bank
1853–1865
W-RI-1520

History: The Peoples Exchange Bank was incorporated in 1853 in Wakefield. Capital was $41,670 in 1855, increasing to $70,000 by 1857. The circulation of the bank was $24,388 in 1857, with $13,782.22 worth of specie.

The business of the Peoples Exchange Bank was succeeded by the National Exchange Bank, chartered in 1865.

Numismatic Commentary: Genuine notes from this bank are very hard to locate.

VALID ISSUES

$1 • W-RI-1520-001-G010

CJF

Engraver: New England Bank Note Co. / Rawdon, Wright, Hatch & Edson. *Comments:* H-RI-510-G2, Durand-2272. 18__. 1850s.

Rarity: URS-3
VF $1,250

$1 • W-RI-1520-001-G010a

CC

Overprint: Red ONE. *Engraver:* New England Bank Note Co. / Rawdon, Wright, Hatch & Edson. *Comments:* H-Unlisted, Durand-Unlisted. Similar to W-RI-1520-001-G010. 18__. 1850s.

Rarity: URS-3
G $250; **VG** $350

$2 • W-RI-1520-002-G020

Left: Man lying down, Men / 2 on die. *Center:* 2. *Right:* 2 / Three women. *Engraver:* New England Bank Note Co. / Rawdon, Wright, Hatch & Edson. *Comments:* H-RI-510-G4, Durand-2273. 18__. 1850s.

Rarity: URS-3
VF $500

$3 • W-RI-1520-003-G030

Left: 3. *Center:* 3. *Right:* 3 / Three men / 3. *Engraver:* New England Bank Note Co. / Rawdon, Wright, Hatch & Edson. *Comments:* H-RI-510-G6, Durand-2274. 18__. 1850s.

Rarity: *None known*

$5 • W-RI-1520-005-G040

Left: 5. *Center:* Commerce seated, Train and bridge. *Right:* 5 / Five figures with 5. *Engraver:* New England Bank Note Co. / Rawdon, Wright, Hatch & Edson. *Comments:* H-RI-510-G8, Durand-2275. 18__. 1850s.

Rarity: *None known*

$10 • W-RI-1520-010-G050

Left: 10. *Center:* Four cows, Milkmaid. *Right:* 10 / Eagle / TEN. *Engraver:* New England Bank Note Co. / Rawdon, Wright, Hatch & Edson. *Comments:* H-RI-510-G10, Durand-2276. 18__. 1850s.

Rarity: *None known*

$20 • W-RI-1520-020-G060

Left: 20. *Center:* Woman, Man seated, Two farmers, load of hay drawn by oxen. *Right:* 20 / Ceres. *Engraver:* New England Bank Note Co. / Rawdon, Wright, Hatch & Edson. *Comments:* H-RI-510-G12, Durand-2277. 18__. 1850s–1860s.

Rarity: *None known*

$50 • W-RI-1520-050-G070

Left: 50. *Center:* Man plowing, cart, horse, and trees / Agriculture, Cattle. *Right:* 50 / Ship on stocks. *Engraver:* New England Bank Note Co. / Rawdon, Wright, Hatch & Edson. *Comments:* H-RI-510-G14, Durand-2278. 18__. 1850s–1860s.

Rarity: *None known*

$100 • W-RI-1520-100-G080

Left: 100 / Goddess of Plenty, Bags of coins. *Center:* Men driving sheep into stream, Factories. *Right:* 100 / Woman with rake. *Engraver:* New England Bank Note Co. / Rawdon, Wright, Hatch & Edson. *Comments:* H-RI-510-G16, Durand-2279. 18__. 1850s–1860s.

Rarity: *None known*

Wakefield Bank
1834–1865
W-RI-1530

History: The Wakefield Bank was incorporated in October 1834. The authorized capital of the bank was $50,000. The capital was increased to $99,500 by 1855 and again in 1857 to $100,000, where it remained through 1862. Circulation was $19,109 in 1849, $14,745 in 1860, and $29,318 in 1863. Specie was $2,520.90 in 1857.

The interests of the Wakefield Bank were succeeded by the Wakefield National Bank on April 27, 1865.

See also listing under South Kingstown, W-RI-1450.

VALID ISSUES

$1 • W-RI-1530-001-G010

Left: ONE / Cattle / 1. *Center:* 1 / Indian in canoe / 1. *Right:* 1 / Four ONEs / 1. *Engraver:* Rawdon, Wright & Hatch. *Comments:* H-RI-520-G2, Durand-2280. 18__. 1834–1840s.

Rarity: *None known*

$1 • W-RI-1530-001-G020

TD

Engraver: New England Bank Note Co. *Comments:* H-RI-520-G4, Durand-2281. 18__. 1840s–1850s.

Rarity: URS-3
F $400; **VF** $1,500

$1 • W-RI-1530-001-G030

Left: ONE over 1 / ONE vertically / ONE over 1. *Center:* Two women seated with anvil / ONE. *Right:* 1 / Female portrait. *Overprint:* Red ONE. *Engraver:* Rawdon, Wright, Hatch & Edson / New England Bank Note Co. *Comments:* H-RI-520-G6a, Durand-2282. Jan. 1, 18__. 1850s–1860s.

Rarity: URS-3
VF $500

$2 • W-RI-1530-002-G040

Left: Reapers, Factory and canal view. *Center:* Portrait of George Washington / 2. *Right:* TWO / Ship at sea / 2. *Engraver:* Rawdon, Wright & Hatch. *Comments:* H-RI-520-G8, Durand-2283. 18__. 1834–1840s.

Rarity: *None known*

$2 • W-RI-1530-002-G050

Left: 2 / TWO / 2. *Center:* Schooner and other ships. *Right:* TWO / Woman drawing water from well / TWO. *Engraver:* New England Bank Note Co. *Comments:* H-RI-520-G10, Durand-2284. 18__. 1840s–1850s.

Rarity: URS-2
VF $1,500

$2 • W-RI-1530-002-G060

Left: 2 / Men shearing sheep. *Center:* 2 / Commerce and Industry, Anvil, anchor / 2. *Right:* 2 / Men washing sheep. *Engraver:* Rawdon, Wright, Hatch & Edson / New England Bank Note Co. *Comments:* H-RI-520-G12, Durand-2285. Jan. 1, 18__. 1850s–1860s.

Rarity: *None known*

$3 • W-RI-1530-003-G070

Left: Train / 3 / Schooner and ship. *Center:* 3 / Milkmaid churning / 3. *Right:* THREE / Cattle / 3. *Engraver:* Rawdon, Wright & Hatch. *Comments:* H-RI-520-G14, Durand-2287. 18__. 1834–1840s.

Rarity: *None known*

$3 • W-RI-1530-003-G080

Left: THREE vertically. *Center:* Reaping scene / 3. *Right:* THREE / Steamboat / 3 on THREE. *Engraver:* New England Bank Note Co. *Comments:* H-RI-520-G16, Durand-2288. 18__. 1840s–1850s.

Rarity: URS-3
VF $500

$5 • W-RI-1530-005-G090

Left: 5 / Vulcan and Commerce / V. *Center:* Archimedes raising world with lever. *Right:* 5 / Ceres with sheaf and cattle / FIVE. *Engraver:* Rawdon, Wright & Hatch. *Comments:* H-RI-520-G18, Durand-2290. 18__. 1834–1840s.

Rarity: *None known*

$5 • W-RI-1530-005-G100

Left: FIVE across 5. *Center:* Indian woman seated in V / Ceres on wharf with implements of manufacturing and commerce. *Right:* 5 / Portrait of George Washington. *Engraver:* New England Bank Note Co. *Comments:* H-RI-520-G20, Durand-2291. 18__. 1850s.

Rarity: *None known*

$10 • W-RI-1530-010-G110

Left: Indian with bow / 10. *Center:* X / Jupiter in chariot drawn by horses / X. *Bottom center:* Ceres. *Right:* 10 / Farmer / TEN. *Engraver:* Rawdon, Wright & Hatch. *Comments:* H-RI-520-G22, Durand-2294. 18__. 1834–1840s.

Rarity: *None known*

$10 • W-RI-1530-010-G120

Left: X. *Center:* "Signing of the Declaration of Independence" / X. *Right:* 10 / Train passing building. Man with wheelbarrow. *Engraver:* New England Bank Note Co. *Comments:* H-RI-520-G24, Durand-2295. 18__. 1850s.

Rarity: *None known*

$20 • W-RI-1530-020-G130

Left: 20 / Farmer plowing with two horses / 20. *Center:* 20 / Group of milkmaids and farmers. *Right:* 20 / Ship / XX. *Engraver:* Rawdon, Wright & Hatch. *Comments:* H-RI-520-G26, Durand-2298. 18__. 1834–1850s.

Rarity: URS-3
VF $500

$50 • W-RI-1530-050-G140

Left: 50 / Female portrait / 50. *Center:* Woodsman, Bull's head, Hunter / 50. *Engraver:* Rawdon, Wright & Hatch. *Comments:* H-RI-520-G28, Durand-2299. 18__. 1834–1850s.

Rarity: *None known*

$100 • W-RI-1530-100-G150

Left: 100 / Liberty / 100. *Center:* C / Ships / C. *Right:* 100 / Justice / 100. *Engraver:* Rawdon, Wright & Hatch. *Comments:* H-RI-520-G30, Durand-2300. 18__. 1834–1850s.

Rarity: *None known*

$100 • W-RI-1530-100-G160

Left: 100 / Vulcan. *Center:* Spread eagle on tree limb / Canal scene. *Bottom center:* 100. *Right:* 100 / Ceres. *Engraver:* Rawdon, Wright, Hatch & Edson. *Comments:* H-RI-520-G32, Durand-2301. 18__. 1850s.

Rarity: *None known*

Non-Valid Issues

$2 • W-RI-1530-002-A010

Left: Two men with basket of cotton. *Center:* Dog's head / Allegorical woman floating over ocean with grain and cornucopia. *Right:* 2 / Indian with tomahawk. *Engraver:* Baldwin, Bald & Cousland / Bald, Cousland & Co. *Comments:* H-RI-520-A5, Durand-2286. Altered from $2 Bank of Morgan, Morgan, Georgia. 18__. 1857.

Rarity: URS-3
VF $250

$3 • W-RI-1530-003-N010

Center: One man reaping, Girl with sheaf. *Comments:* H-RI-520-N5, Durand-2289. Altered or spurious. 1850s.

Rarity: *None known*

$5 • W-RI-1530-005-S010

Center: Ceres seated, Sickle, rake / Indian woman on V. *Engraver:* New England Bank Note Co. *Comments:* H-RI-520-S5, Durand-2293. May 1, 18__. 1860s.

Rarity: *None known*

$5 • W-RI-1530-005-A020

Left: FIVE / Minerva standing / FIVE. *Center:* Ceres, Liberty, and allegorical woman. *Right:* 5 / Portrait of George Washington. *Engraver:* Danforth, Bald & Co. *Comments:* H-RI-520-A10, Durand-2292. Altered from $5 Columbia Bank, Washington, D.C. 18__. 1850s.

Rarity: *None known*

$10 • W-RI-1530-010-N020

Center: Liberty. *Right:* Indian. *Comments:* H-RI-520-N15, Durand-2297. Altered or spurious. 18__. 1844.

Rarity: *None known*

$10 • W-RI-1530-010-A030

Left: 10 / Portrait of George Washington held by cherub / 10. *Center:* X / Spread eagle and shield / X. *Bottom center:* Ship. *Right:* 10 / Indian / 10. *Engraver:* Terry, Pelton & Co. *Comments:* H-RI-520-A15, Durand-2296. Altered from $10 Citizens Bank, Augusta, Maine, or from notes of other failed banks using the same plate. 18__. 1850s.

Rarity: *None known*

Warren, Rhode Island

Warren was first explored in 1621. It was originally known as Sowams, or Sowamset, by the natives. A trading post from Plymouth Colony was established there in 1622. Roger Williams, after his banishment from Salem in 1636, fled to Sowams and was given protection by the Massasoit Indians before he settled in Providence.

In 1668 Sowams was incorporated as a township on land that became a part of Massachusetts. Later its name was changed to Warren. The land was ceded to Rhode Island in 1747. It was named after the British naval hero Admiral Sir Peter Warren.

Warren became an important whaling port with shipbuilding not far behind in terms of industry. Its vessels were well-known throughout the whaling and merchant industries as well as the West India trade. When the whaling industry declined in the middle of the 19th century, textiles became important in the commerce of the town. The first cotton mill was erected in 1847.

See also Sowamset, Rhode Island.

Hope Bank
1822–1865
W-RI-1540

History: The Hope Bank was incorporated in 1822. Capital was $125,000 in 1848. This was increased slightly to $130,000 by 1857. Circulation was $18,011 in 1848, but it rose to $20,579 by 1860.

The business was succeeded by the National Hope Bank, chartered on April 14, 1865.

Numismatic Commentary: Genuine notes from this bank are hard to locate. Recorded non-valid notes are similarly scarce.

Valid Issues

$1 • W-RI-1540-001-G010

Engraver: Horton, Providence. *Comments:* H-RI-525-G2, Durand-2302. No description available. 18__. 1820s.

Rarity: *None known*

$1 • W-RI-1540-001-G020

Left: 1 / Woman wearing bonnet, standing by pail / ONE. *Center:* Machinery and merchandise flanking Ceres holding sickle and rake, Factories and harbor / ONE / Panel outlining white ONE. *Right:* 1 / Ship / ONE. *Engraver:* PSSP / New England Bank Note Co. *Comments:* H-RI-525-G4. 18__. 1830s–1840s.

Rarity: *None known*

$1 • W-RI-1540-001-G030

CJF

Engraver: New England Bank Note Co. *Comments:* H-RI-525-G6, Durand-2303. 18__. 1840s–1850s.

Rarity: URS-2
VF $1,500

$1 • W-RI-1540-001-G030a

Overprint: Red ONE. *Engraver:* New England Bank Note Co. *Comments:* H-RI-525-G6a. Similar to W-RI-1540-001-G030. 18__. 1850s.

Rarity: *None known*

$1 • W-RI-1540-001-G040

Left: Male portrait / 1. *Center:* Two trains, Train crossing bridge. *Right:* 1 / Female portrait. *Comments:* H-RI-525-G8, Durand-2304. 18__. 1850s–1860s.

Rarity: *None known*

$2 • W-RI-1540-002-G050

Left: TWO / RHODE ISLAND / TWO vertically. *Center:* TWOs and 2s / Woman seated near bay / TWOs and 2s with cherub. *Bottom center:* Two men in boat. *Right:* 2 / Woman standing / 2. *Engraver:* Horton, Providence. *Comments:* H-RI-525-G12, Durand-2306. 18__. 1820s. 1850s–1860s.

Rarity: *None known*

$2 • W-RI-1540-002-G060

Left: 2 / Woman standing with staff, Cornucopia / TWO. *Center:* TWO / Machinery and merchandise flanking Ceres holding sickle and rake, Factories and harbor / Panel outlining white TWO. *Right:* 2 / Woman wearing hat, Trees / TWO. *Engraver:* PSSP / New England Bank Note Co. *Comments:* H-RI-525-G14. 18__. 1830s–1840s.

Rarity: *None known*

$2 • W-RI-1540-002-G070

Left: 2 / TWO / 2. *Center:* Ships and other vessels. *Right:* TWO / Woman drawing water from well / TWO. *Engraver:* New England Bank Note Co. *Comments:* H-RI-525-G16, Durand-2307. 18__. 1840s–1850s.

Rarity: *None known*

$2 • W-RI-1540-002-G070a

Overprint: Red TWO. *Engraver:* New England Bank Note Co. *Comments:* H-RI-525-G16a. Similar to W-RI-1540-002-G070. 18__. 1850s.

Rarity: *None known*

$2 • W-RI-1540-002-G080

Left: Male portrait / 2. *Center:* Two cherubs with swords and two silver dollars. *Right:* 2 / Female portrait. *Comments:* H-RI-525-G18, Durand-2308. 18__. 1850s–1860s.

Rarity: *None known*

$3 • W-RI-1540-003-G090

Engraver: Horton, Providence. *Comments:* H-RI-525-G22, Durand-2312. No description available. 18__. 1820s.

Rarity: *None known*

$3 • W-RI-1540-003-G100

Left: THREE / Beehive and foliage / THREE. *Center:* Ceres seated holding sickle and rake, Machinery and merchandise, Factories and harbor / Panel outlining white THREE. *Right:* 3 on THREE / Two reapers / 3 on THREE. *Engraver:* New England Bank Note Co. / PSSP. *Comments:* H-RI-525-G24. 18__. 1830s–1840s.

Rarity: *None known*

$3 • W-RI-1540-003-G110

Left: THREE vertically. *Center:* Man reaping with sickle, woman standing with hat and sheaf / 3. *Right:* THREE / Steamboat / 3 on THREE. *Engraver:* New England Bank Note Co. *Comments:* H-RI-525-G26, Durand-2313. 18__. 1840s–1850s.

Rarity: *None known*

$3 • W-RI-1540-003-G110a

Overprint: Red THREE. *Engraver:* New England Bank Note Co. *Comments:* H-RI-525-G26a. Similar to W-RI-1540-003-G110. 18__. 1850s.

Rarity: *None known*

$3 • W-RI-1540-003-G120

Left: 3 / Male portrait / THREE. *Center:* Milkmaid milking cow, Cow lying down. *Right:* 3 / Female portrait. *Comments:* H-RI-525-G28, Durand-2314. 18__. 1850s–1860s.

Rarity: *None known*

$5 • W-RI-1540-005-G130

Engraver: Horton, Providence. *Comments:* H-RI-525-G32, Durand-2316. No description available. 18__. 1820s.

Rarity: *None known*

$5 • W-RI-1540-005-G140

Left: 5 / Blacksmith at anvil / FIVE. *Center:* Mercury standing with 5, Cornucopia and merchandise, Factories and ship / V / Panel outlining white FIVE. *Right:* 5 / Ceres kneeling / FIVE. *Engraver:* PSSP / New England Bank Note Co. *Comments:* H-RI-525-G34. 18__. 1830s–1840s.

Rarity: *None known*

$5 • W-RI-1540-005-G150

Left: FIVE vertically. *Center:* Woman raising drapery from shield bearing 5 / V. *Right:* 5 / Sailing ship. *Engraver:* New England Bank Note Co. *Comments:* H-RI-525-G36, Durand-2317. 18__. 1840s–1850s.

Rarity: *None known*

$5 • W-RI-1540-005-G160

Left: V on FIVE. *Center:* Indian girl seated in V / Manufacturing, Commerce, and Agriculture. *Right:* 5 / Portrait of George Washington. *Overprint:* Red FIVE. *Engraver:* New England Bank Note Co. *Comments:* H-RI-525-G38, Durand-2318. 18__. 1850s.

Rarity: *None known*

$5 • W-RI-1540-005-G170

Left: Soldier with sword / FIVE. *Center:* Man and woman / 5. *Right:* Justice standing / FIVE. *Comments:* H-RI-525-G40, Durand-2319. 18__. 1850s–1860s.

Rarity: *None known*

$10 • W-RI-1540-010-G180

Left: 10 / X / 10. *Center:* Farmer with primitive plow and oxen / 10. *Right:* TEN / Woman standing with lyre, Cornucopia. *Engraver:* New England Bank Note Co. *Comments:* H-RI-525-G46, Durand-2320. 18__. 1840s–1850s.

Rarity: *None known*

$10 • W-RI-1540-010-G190

Left: Portrait / X. *Center:* Commerce seated, Bales and barrels. *Right:* 10 / Indian woman. *Comments:* H-RI-525-G48, Durand-2321. 18__. 1850s–1860s.

Rarity: *None known*

$50 • W-RI-1540-050-G200

Left: 50 / Woman standing with ankles crossed, Staff, Cornucopia and anchor / 50. *Center:* FIFTY DOLLARS / 50. *Right:* FIFTY vertically. *Engraver:* New England Bank Note Co. / PSSP. *Comments:* H-RI-525-G52. 18__. 1830s.

Rarity: *None known*

$50 • W-RI-1540-050-G210

Left: 50 / Steamboat and other vessels. *Center:* Farm scene / 50. *Right:* L / Justice. *Engraver:* New England Bank Note Co. *Comments:* H-RI-525-G54, Durand-2322. 18__. 1840s.

Rarity: *None known*

$50 • W-RI-1540-050-G220

Left: 50 / Minerva. *Center:* Vulcan and Ceres seated. *Right:* 50 / Cherub steering sailboat / 50. *Engraver:* Rawdon, Wright, Hatch & Edson. *Comments:* H-RI-525-G56, Durand-2323. 18__. 1850s.

Rarity: *None known*

$100 • W-RI-1540-100-G230

Left: Lathework panel bearing C / Portrait of George Washington / C. *Center:* 100 / Manhattan reclining pouring water, Ship / 100. *Right:* Lathework panel bearing ONE HUNDRED vertically. *Engraver:* New England Bank Note Co. / PSSP. *Comments:* H-RI-525-G60. 18__. 1830s.

Rarity: *None known*

$100 • W-RI-1540-100-G240

Left: 100 / Spread eagle / 100. *Center:* C / "Phoebus in Chariot of the Sun" / 100. *Right:* C / Portrait of George Washington / C. *Engraver:* New England Bank Note Co. *Comments:* H-RI-525-G62, Durand-2324. 18__. 1840s.

Rarity: *None known*

$100 • W-RI-1540-100-G250

Left: 100 / Vulcan seated. *Center:* Spread eagle on tree branch / Canal scene. *Right:* 100 / Ceres seated. *Engraver:* Rawdon, Wright, Hatch & Edson. *Comments:* H-RI-525-G64, Durand-2325. 18__. 1850s.

Rarity: *None known*

$100 • W-RI-1540-100-G260

Left: 100 / Male portrait. *Center:* Three sailing vessels at sea. *Right:* 100 / Two children. *Comments:* H-RI-525-G66, Durand-2326. 18__. 1860s.

Rarity: *None known*

NON-VALID ISSUES

$1 • W-RI-1540-001-C030

Comments: H-Unlisted, Durand-2305. Counterfeit of W-RI-1540-001-G030. 18__. 1840s–1850s.

Rarity: URS-3

F $100

$2 • W-RI-1540-002-C050

Engraver: Horton, Providence. *Comments:* H-RI-525-C12, Durand-2309. Counterfeit of W-RI-1540-002-G050. 18__. 1820s.

Rarity: URS-3

VF $300

$2 • W-RI-1540-002-S010

Left: Portrait. *Center:* Train, canal, bridge, and city. *Right:* Male portrait. *Comments:* H-Unlisted, Durand-2311. 1820s.

Rarity: URS-3

F $100

$2 • W-RI-1540-002-A010

Left: 2 / Female portrait / 2. *Center:* Rowboat and steamboat / Portrait of Marquis de Lafayette. *Bottom center:* Harbor scene, Three men in boat. *Right:* 2 / Cow and calf lying down / 2. *Engraver:* Boston Bank Note Co. *Comments:* H-RI-525-A5, Durand-2310. Altered from $2 Bank of Owasso, Owasso, Michigan. 18__. 1840s. **Rarity:** *None known*

$3 • W-RI-1540-003-A020

Left: THREE vertically. *Center:* Rowboat, sailing ship, steamboat, and sloop in harbor, Hills / Boy and cow. *Bottom center:* Train. *Right:* 3 / Portrait of Commodore Oliver Hazard Perry. *Engraver:* Boston Bank Note Co. *Comments:* H-RI-525-A10, Durand-2315. Altered from $3 Bank of Owasso, Owasso, Michigan. 18__. 1840s. **Rarity:** *None known*

Sowamset Bank
1854–1865
W-RI-1550

History: The Sowamset Bank was incorporated in June 1854 and commenced operations on August 6, 1855. The authorized capital was $50,000 until 1857, when it increased to $200,000. Only $67,500 was actually paid in. Later that year it was reported to be $66,950, and in 1860 it was $71,300. Bills in circulation at that time totaled $23,154. In 1862 capital was slightly higher at $71,500, and circulation had nearly doubled to $43,836.

The business of the Sowamset Bank was succeeded by the First National Bank of Warren, chartered on December 30, 1864.

See also listing under Sowamset, W-RI-1465.

VALID ISSUES

$1 • W-RI-1550-001-G010

Left: 1 / Sailing vessel / 1. *Center:* Woman seated, pointing / ONE. *Bottom center:* Sailing vessel. *Right:* 1 on die / Indian man holding 1. *Comments:* H-Unlisted, Durand-2327. 1854–1860s.

Rarity: URS-3

VF $800

$1 • W-RI-1550-001-G010a
Overprint: Red ONE. *Engraver:* New England Bank Note Co. / Rawdon, Wright, Hatch & Edson. *Comments:* H-RI-530-G2a, Durand-2328. Similar to W-RI-1550-001-G010. 18__. 1854–1860s.
Rarity: URS-3
VF $800

$2 • W-RI-1550-002-G020
Left: TWO / Train, Steamship / TWO. *Center:* Drove of wild horses. *Right:* 2 / Indian girl holding corn and 2. *Comments:* H-Unlisted, Durand-2329. 1854–1860s.
Rarity: URS-3
VF $150

$2 • W-RI-1550-002-G020a   cc

Overprint: Red TWO. *Engraver:* New England Bank Note Co. / Rawdon, Wright, Hatch & Edson. *Comments:* H-RI-530-G4a, Durand-2330. Similar to W-RI-1550-002-G020. 18__. 1850s–1860s.
Rarity: URS-3
F $600; VF $1,500

$3 • W-RI-1550-003-G030
Left: Ship / THREE. *Center:* Puritans trading with Indians. *Bottom center:* Men loading hay. *Right:* 3 / Portrait of Indian girl. *Comments:* H-Unlisted, Durand-2332. 1854–1860s.
Rarity: URS-3
VF $900

$3 • W-RI-1550-003-G030a
Overprint: Red THREE. *Engraver:* New England Bank Note Co. / Rawdon, Wright, Hatch & Edson. *Comments:* H-RI-530-G6a, Durand-2333. Similar to W-RI-1550-003-G030. 18__. 1850s–1860s.
Rarity: *None known*

$5 • W-RI-1550-005-G040
Left: Steamship and other vessels / V. *Right:* 5 on FIVE / Allegorical figure / FIVE. *Comments:* H-Unlisted, Durand-2335. 1854–1860s.
Rarity: URS-3
VF $800

$5 • W-RI-1550-005-G040a
Overprint: Red FIVE. *Engraver:* New England Bank Note Co. / Rawdon, Wright, Hatch & Edson. *Comments:* H-RI-530-G8a, Durand-2336. Similar to W-RI-1550-005-G040. 18__. 1850s–1860s.
Rarity: URS-3
VF $500

$10 • W-RI-1550-010-G050
Left: Sailor / 10. *Center:* Liberty and eagle soaring in clouds. *Right:* X / Female portrait. *Comments:* H-Unlisted, Durand-2339. 1854–1860s.
Rarity: URS-3
VF $800

$10 • W-RI-1550-010-G050a
Overprint: Red TEN. *Engraver:* New England Bank Note Co. / Rawdon, Wright, Hatch & Edson. *Comments:* H-RI-530-G10a, Durand-2340. Similar to W-RI-1550-010-G050. 18__. 1850s–1860s.
Rarity: *None known*

$50 • W-RI-1550-050-G060
Left: 50 / Man with rake and fork, Dog. *Center:* Train, Farm scene. *Right:* 50 / Two women, one with dinner horn. *Engraver:* Unverified, but likely New England Bank Note Co. / Rawdon, Wright, Hatch & Edson. *Comments:* H-RI-530-G12, Durand-2342. 18__. 1850s.
Rarity: *None known*

$100 • W-RI-1550-100-G070
Left: Liberty / 100. *Center:* Whaling in the Arctic regions. *Right:* 100 / Sailor with capstan. *Engraver:* Unverified, but likely New England Bank Note Co. / Rawdon, Wright, Hatch & Edson. *Comments:* H-RI-530-G14, Durand-2343. 18__. 1850s.
Rarity: *None known*

Non-Valid Issues

$2 • W-RI-1550-002-A010
Center: Spread eagle on shield. *Comments:* H-Unlisted, Durand-2331. 1854–1860s.
Rarity: *None known*

$3 • W-RI-1550-003-A020
Center: Spread eagle on shield. *Comments:* H-RI-530-A5, Durand-2334. 1854–1860s.
Rarity: *None known*

$5 • W-RI-1550-005-R010
Engraver: New England Bank Note Co. / Rawdon, Wright, Hatch & Edson. *Comments:* H-RI-530-R5, Durand-2337. Raised from W-RI-1550-001-G010 series. 18__. 1850s.
Rarity: *None known*

$5 • W-RI-1550-005-S010
Center: Eagle and shield, Portrait of George Washington. *Comments:* H-RI-530-N5, Durand-2338. 1854–1860s.
Rarity: *None known*

$10 • W-RI-1550-010-R020
Engraver: New England Bank Note Co. / Rawdon, Wright, Hatch & Edson. *Comments:* H-RI-530-R10, Durand-2341. Raised from W-RI-1550-010-G010 series. 18__. 1850s.
Rarity: *None known*

Warren Bank
1803–1865
W-RI-1560

History: The Warren Bank was incorporated as a holding company for the Warren Insurance Company in October 1803. Capital was $68,000 in that year, rising to $85,000 by 1813, $135,000 by 1848, and $200,000 by 1855. Circulation was at $48,042.25 in 1849, $28,981.75 in 1857, and $37,271 in 1862. Specie totaled $2,590.88 in 1857.

On August 1, 1865, the Warren Bank surrendered its charter and its business was succeeded by the National Warren Bank.[85]

Numismatic Commentary: Genuine notes are hard to locate. One interesting vignette can be observed on both a genuine and counterfeit $3 bill. W-RI-1560-003-C110 has a vignette of Capricorn in the style of a goat, the tenth sign of the Zodiac. It is unusual to find Zodiac symbols on bank notes. There may be only a few others on all the rest of the issues for banks in the United States.

VALID ISSUES

$1 • W-RI-1560-001-G010   CC

Comments: H-RI-535-G2, Durand-2344. ____. 1800s.
Rarity: URS-1
Proof $900

$1 • W-RI-1560-001-G020
Left: ONE vertically. *Center:* 1 on die / Woman leaning against parcels. *Bottom center:* ONE D. *Right:* 1 on die. *Comments:* H-RI-535-G4, Durand-2345. 18__. 1820s.
Rarity: *None known*

$1 • W-RI-1560-001-G030
Left: ONE vertically. *Center:* Sloop and other vessels / 1. *Right:* ONE / Indian woman with bow and arrows / ONE. *Engraver:* New England Bank Note Co. *Comments:* H-RI-535-G8, Durand-2346. 18__. 1840s.
Rarity: *None known*

$1 • W-RI-1560-001-G040
Left: ONE / Liberty by shield. *Center:* Indian reclining on shield, Eagle soaring, Deer. *Right:* 1 / Female portrait. *Comments:* H-RI-535-G10, Durand-2347. 18__. 1850s.
Rarity: *None known*

$1.25 • W-RI-1560-001.25-G050
Left: 1 25/100 / Train / 1 25/100. *Center:* Sloop and other vessels at sea / $1.25 Cts. *Right:* 1 25/100 / Eagle. *Engraver:* New England Bank Note Co. *Comments:* H-RI-535-G12. 18__. 1830s.
Rarity: *None known*

$1.50 • W-RI-1560-001.50-G060
Left: 1 Doll. 50 Cts. vertically. *Center:* Eagle on rock in ocean / $1 50/100. *Right:* 1 50/100 / Justice. *Engraver:* New England Bank Note Co. *Comments:* H-RI-535-G13. 18__. 1830s.
Rarity: *None known*

$1.75 • W-RI-1560-001.75-G070
Left: $1.75 Cts. / Hebe watering eagle / 1 75/100. *Center:* Three sloops at sea. *Right:* $1.75 Cts. / Yeoman standing with grain, Dog / 1 75/100. *Engraver:* New England Bank Note Co. *Comments:* H-RI-535-G14. 18__. 1830s.
Rarity: *None known*

$2 • W-RI-1560-002-G080
Comments: H-RI-535-G18, Durand-2350. No description available. 18__. 1800s.
Rarity: *None known*

$2 • W-RI-1560-002-G090
Left: 2 / TWO / 2. *Center:* Sailing ship, Vessels / Ornate 2. *Right:* TWO / Woman drawing water from well / TWO. *Engraver:* New England Bank Note Co. *Comments:* H-RI-535-G22, Durand-2351. 18__. 1840s.
Rarity: *None known*

$2 • W-RI-1560-002-G100
Left: 2. *Center:* Liberty seated holding portrait of George Washington and crowning eagle with wreath. *Right:* 2 / Fountain. *Comments:* H-RI-535-G24, Durand-2352. 18__. 1850s.
Rarity: *None known*

$3 • W-RI-1560-003-G110
Left: THREE vertically. *Center:* 3 on die / Capricorn / 3 on die. *Bottom center:* 3 on die. *Comments:* H-RI-535-G28, Durand-2355. 18__. 1800s.
Rarity: *None known*

$3 • W-RI-1560-003-G120
Left: THREE vertically. *Center:* Man reaping with sickle, Woman standing with hat and sheaf. *Right:* THREE / Steamship / 3 on THREE. *Engraver:* New England Bank Note Co. *Comments:* H-RI-535-G32, Durand-2356. 18__. 1840s.
Rarity: *None known*

$3 • W-RI-1560-003-G130
Left: 3 / Mercury soaring in clouds / THREE. *Center:* Justice with wreath, eagle, and shield. *Right:* 3 / Goddess of Plenty / THREE. *Comments:* H-RI-535-G34, Durand-2357. 18__. 1850s.
Rarity: *None known*

$5 • W-RI-1560-005-G140   CC

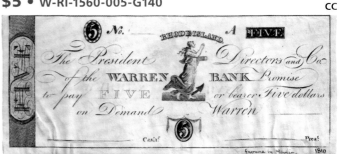

Engraver: Hamlin. *Comments:* H-RI-535-G38, Durand-2360. ____. 1800s–1810s.
Rarity: URS-1
Proof $1,200

$5 • W-RI-1560-005-G150
Left: FIVE vertically. *Center:* Woman unveiling shield bearing 5 / V. *Right:* 5 / Sailing ship. *Engraver:* New England Bank Note Co. *Comments:* H-RI-535-G42, Durand-2361. 18__. 1840s.
Rarity: *None known*

$5 • W-RI-1560-005-G160
Left: 5 / Train / 5. *Center:* Shipyard and wharf. *Right:* 5 / Cherub and dolphin. *Comments:* H-RI-535-G44, Durand-2362. 18__. 1850s.
Rarity: *None known*

$10 • W-RI-1560-010-G170
Comments: H-Unlisted, Durand-2364. No description available. 1850s.
Rarity: *None known*

$10 • W-RI-1560-010-G180
Left: TEN vertically. *Center:* 1 / 1. *Comments:* H-RI-535-G48. 18__. 1800s–1810s.
Rarity: *None known*

$10 • W-RI-1560-010-G190
Left: 10 / X / 10. *Center:* Man with plow and oxen / 10. *Right:* TEN / Goddess of Plenty. *Engraver:* New England Bank Note Co. *Comments:* H-RI-535-G54, Durand-2365. 18__. 1840s.
Rarity: *None known*

$10 • W-RI-1560-010-G200
Left: 10. *Center:* Harvest scene. *Right:* X / Sea horses / TEN. *Comments:* H-RI-535-G56, Durand-2366. 18__. 1850s.
Rarity: *None known*

$20 • W-RI-1560-020-G210
Left: 20 / Woman. *Center:* XX / Eagle. *Right:* 20 / Ship. *Engraver:* New England Bank Note Co. *Comments:* H-RI-535-G58, Durand-2368. 18__. 1840s–1850s.
Rarity: *None known*

$20 • W-RI-1560-020-G220
Left: XX / Justice and strongbox. *Center:* Male portrait. *Right:* 20 / Milkmaid churning. *Tint:* Red 20 and TWENTY on die and 20 DOLLARS. *Comments:* H-RI-535-G60a, Durand-2369. 1840s–1850s.
Rarity: *None known*

$50 • W-RI-1560-050-G230
Left: FIFTY / Woman standing with wreath and flowers / FIFTY. *Center:* 50 / Man holding horse / 50. *Right:* FIFTY / Woman standing with cornucopia / FIFTY. *Engraver:* New England Bank Note Co. *Comments:* H-RI-535-G64, Durand-2370. 18__. 1840s–1850s.
Rarity: *None known*

$50 • W-RI-1560-050-G240
Left: FIFTY / Girl with sheaf. *Center:* Male portrait. *Right:* FIFTY / Liberty. *Tint:* Red 50 and FIFTY on die and 50 DOLLARS. *Comments:* H-RI-535-G66a, Durand-2371. 1840s–1850s.
Rarity: *None known*

$50 • W-RI-1560-050-G250
Left: FIFTY / Woman writing on tablet with child. *Center:* Woman reclining with globe and books. *Right:* 50 / Female portrait. *Comments:* H-RI-535-G68, Durand-2372. 1840s–1850s.
Rarity: *None known*

$100 • W-RI-1560-100-G260
Left: ONE HUNDRED on 100 / Portrait of Christopher Columbus. *Center:* Wharf scene. *Right:* ONE HUNDRED on 100 / Portrait of William Henry Harrison. *Engraver:* New England Bank Note Co. *Comments:* H-RI-535-G72, Durand-2373. 18__. 1840s–1850s.
Rarity: *None known*

$100 • W-RI-1560-100-G270
Left: 100 / Farmer, dog. *Center:* Male portrait. *Right:* 100 / Female portrait. *Tint:* Red C and ONE HUNDRED on die and C DOLLARS. *Comments:* H-RI-535-G74a, Durand-2374. 1840s–1850s.
Rarity: *None known*

$100 • W-RI-1560-100-G280
Left: C / Woman and shield. *Center:* Ship under sail. *Right:* 100 / Anchor and rock. *Comments:* H-RI-535-G76, Durand-2375. 1840s–1850s.
Rarity: *None known*

NON-VALID ISSUES

$1 • W-RI-1560-001-C010

SI

Comments: H-RI-535-C2, Durand-2348. Counterfeit of W-RI-1560-001-G010. 18__. 1804.
Rarity: URS-5
VF $250

$1 • W-RI-1560-001-C020
Comments: H-RI-535-C4, Durand-2349. Counterfeit of W-RI-1560-001-G020. 18__. 1820s.
Rarity: URS-3
VF $300

$2 • W-RI-1560-002-C100
Comments: H-RI-535-C24. Counterfeit of W-RI-1560-002-G100. 18__. 1808–1811.
Rarity: URS-3
VF $250

$2 • W-RI-1560-002-S010

SI

Tint: Red-orange TWO. *Engraver:* American Bank Note Co. *Comments:* H-RI-535-S5a, Durand-2354. 185_. 1859.
Rarity: URS-6
VF $200

$2 • W-RI-1560-002-N010

Center: Sailor seated on barrel and man sitting on bars of lead. *Right:* Two women. *Comments:* H-RI-535-N5, Durand-2353. Altered or spurious. 1840s–1850s.

Rarity: *None known*

$3 • W-RI-1560-003-C110

CJF

Comments: H-RI-535-C28, Durand-2358. Counterfeit of W-RI-1560-003-G110. 18__. 1800s.

Rarity: URS-3
VF $350

$3 • W-RI-1560-003-S020

Left: THREE vertically. *Center:* 3 / Woman leaning on package, Ship / 3 / THREE. *Bottom center:* Printing press. *Right:* THREE / Scene with ships / THREE on 3. *Engraver:* New England Bank Note Co. *Comments:* H-RI-535-S10, Durand-2359. 186_. 1861.

Rarity: URS-3
VF $200

$5 • W-RI-1560-005-A010

Left: 5 / V / 5. *Center:* V on star / Sloop, steamboat. *Right:* 5 / FIVE / Train. *Engraver:* Boston Bank Note Co. *Comments:* H-RI-535-A5, Durand-2363. Altered from $5 Bank of Owasso, Owasso, Michigan. 18__. 1840s–1850s.

Rarity: URS-3
VF $200

$10 • W-RI-1560-010-C170

Comments: H-Unlisted, Durand-2367. Counterfeit of W-RI-1560-010-G170. 1840s–1850s.

Rarity: *None known*

$10 • W-RI-1560-010-C180

Comments: H-RI-535-C48. Counterfeit of W-RI-1560-010-G180. 18__. 1820s.

Rarity: *None known*

WARWICK, RHODE ISLAND

Founded by Samuel Gorton in 1642, Warwick included land that would later become Coventry and West Warwick. In 1648 the name was changed from Shawhomett to Warwick. The township was destroyed during King Philip's War but was soon rebuilt. Warwick was where the first shot was fired at the beginning of the Revolutionary War.

Merchants in Warwick imported molasses from the Caribbean which they brewed into rum. By the middle of the 19th century, commerce had changed, and locally manufactured textiles and regional crops were traded to Asia.

See also Centreville, Rhode Island.

Centreville Bank
1828–1865
W-RI-1570

History: The Centreville Bank was incorporated in June 1828. The capital was $25,000 in 1831 and $100,000 in 1855. Circulation was $28,026.25 in 1849; specie was at $4,603.95. The capital was $100,000 in 1856. The bank saw a circulation of $25,247 in 1857, which increased to $53,657 in 1862. Specie amounted to $2,824.79 in 1857.

The business of the Centreville Bank was succeeded by the Centreville National Bank in June 1865.

See also listing under Centreville, W-RI-200.

VALID ISSUES

$1 • W-RI-1570-001-G010

Left: Portrait of George Washington. *Center:* Cherubs, bales. *Right:* Portrait of Marquis de Lafayette. *Engraver:* PSSP. *Comments:* H-RI-540-G2, Durand-2376. 18__. 1820s–1830s.

Rarity: *None known*

$1 • W-RI-1570-001-G020

CC

Engraver: Rawdon, Wright, Hatch & Co. *Comments:* H-RI-540-G6, Durand-2377. 18__. 1830s–1850s.

Rarity: URS-3
F $800

Selected auction price: Stack's Bowers Galleries, January 2011, F $770

$1 • W-RI-1570-001-G030

Left: 1 / Indian on cliff. *Center:* Dog, key, strongbox, and money bags. *Right:* 1 / Farmer carrying hay. *Engraver:* Toppan, Carpenter, Casilear & Co. *Comments:* H-RI-540-G8, Durand-2378. 18__. 1850s.

Rarity: URS-3
VF $300

$1 • W-RI-1570-001-G030a

TD

Overprint: Red ONE. *Engraver:* Toppan, Carpenter, Casilear & Co. *Comments:* H-RI-540-G8a, Durand-2379. Similar to W-RI-1570-001-G030. 18__. 1850s–1860s.
Rarity: URS-3
VF $350

$2 • W-RI-1570-002-G040

Left: Portrait of George Washington. *Right:* Portrait of Marquis de Lafayette. *Engraver:* PSSP. *Comments:* H-RI-540-G12, Durand-2383. 18__. 1828–1830s.
Rarity: URS-3
VF $150

$2 • W-RI-1570-002-G050

Left: Pelican and chicks. *Center:* Portrait of George Washington / Agriculture and Justice flanking shield bearing 2 / Portrait of Marquis de Lafayette. *Bottom center:* Cherub riding deer. *Right:* 2 / Agriculture / TWO. *Engraver:* Rawdon, Wright & Hatch. *Comments:* H-RI-540-G16, Durand-2384. 18__. 1830s–1850s.
Rarity: URS-3
Proof $500

$2 • W-RI-1570-002-G060

SBG

Engraver: Toppan, Carpenter, Casilear & Co. *Comments:* H-RI-540-G18, Durand-2385. 18__. 1850s.
Rarity: URS-3
Proof $2,300
Selected auction price: Stack's Bowers Galleries, March 2013, Proof $2,299

$2 • W-RI-1570-002-G060a

Left: 2 / Justice. *Center:* Eagle and U.S. shield. *Bottom center:* Cogwheel. *Right:* 2 / Commerce. *Overprint:* Red TWO. *Engraver:* Toppan, Carpenter, Casilear & Co. *Comments:* H-RI-540-G18a, Durand-2386. Similar to W-RI-1570-002-G060. 18__. 1850s–1860s.
Rarity: *None known*

$3 • W-RI-1570-003-G070

Left: Portrait of George Washington. *Right:* Portrait of Marquis de Lafayette. *Engraver:* PSSP. *Comments:* H-RI-540-G22, Durand-2389. 18__. 1820s–1830s.
Rarity: *None known*

$3 • W-RI-1570-003-G080

Engraver: Rawdon, Wright, Hatch & Co. *Comments:* H-RI-540-G24, Durand-2390. No description available. 18__. 1830s–1850s.
Rarity: *None known*

$3 • W-RI-1570-003-G090

Left: 3 / Ceres reclining. *Center:* Ceres seated on shield bearing anchor, Train crossing bridge. *Right:* 3 / Indian reclining. *Engraver:* Toppan, Carpenter, Casilear & Co. *Comments:* H-RI-540-G26, Durand-2391. 18__. 1850s.
Rarity: URS-3
Proof $500

$3 • W-RI-1570-003-G090a

Overprint: Red THREE. *Engraver:* Toppan, Carpenter, Casilear & Co. *Comments:* H-RI-540-G26a, Durand-2392. Similar to W-RI-1570-003-G090. 18__. 1850s–1860s.
Rarity: *None known*

$5 • W-RI-1570-005-G100

Left: Portrait of George Washington. *Right:* Portrait of Marquis de Lafayette. *Engraver:* PSSP. *Comments:* H-RI-540-G30, Durand-2397. 18__. 1828–1830s.
Rarity: URS-3
VF $250

$5 • W-RI-1570-005-G110

Engraver: Rawdon, Wright, Hatch & Co. *Comments:* H-Unlisted, Durand-2398. No description available. 1820s–1830s.
Rarity: *None known*

$5 • W-RI-1570-005-G120

Left: 5 / Male portrait. *Center:* Boys trying to catch horse. *Right:* 5 / Male portrait. *Engraver:* Toppan, Carpenter, Casilear & Co. *Comments:* H-RI-540-G36, Durand-2399. 18__. 1850s.
Rarity: *None known*

$5 • W-RI-1570-005-G120a

CJF

Overprint: Red V / V. *Engraver:* Toppan, Carpenter, Casilear & Co. *Comments:* H-RI-540-G36a, Durand-2400. Similar to W-RI-1570-005-G120. 18__. 1850s–1860s.
Rarity: URS-1
VF $850

$10 • W-RI-1570-010-G130

Left: Portrait of George Washington. *Right:* Portrait of Marquis de Lafayette. *Engraver:* PSSP. *Comments:* H-RI-540-G40, Durand-2405. 18__. 1820s–1830s.

Rarity: *None known*

$10 • W-RI-1570-010-G140

Left: 10 / Male portrait. *Center:* Blacksmith shoeing horse, Two men. *Right:* 10 / Male portrait. *Engraver:* Toppan, Carpenter, Casilear & Co. *Comments:* H-RI-540-G46, Durand-2406. 18__. 1850s.

Rarity: *None known*

$10 • W-RI-1570-010-G140a

CJF

Overprint: Red X / X. *Engraver:* Toppan, Carpenter, Casilear & Co. *Comments:* H-RI-540-G46a, Durand-2407. Similar to W-RI-1570-010-G140. 18__. 1850s–1860s.

Rarity: URS-3
VF $500

$20 • W-RI-1570-020-G150

Left: Portrait of George Washington. *Right:* Portrait of Marquis de Lafayette. *Engraver:* PSSP. *Comments:* H-RI-540-G50, Durand-2410. 18__. 1820s–1830s.

Rarity: *None known*

$50 • W-RI-1570-050-G160

Left: Portrait of George Washington. *Right:* Portrait of Marquis de Lafayette. *Engraver:* PSSP. *Comments:* H-RI-540-G54, Durand-2411. 18__. 1820s–1830s.

Rarity: *None known*

$50 • W-RI-1570-050-G170

Left: 50 / Male portrait. *Center:* Three boys gathering corn and loading cart. *Right:* 50 / Male portrait. *Engraver:* Toppan, Carpenter, Casilear & Co. *Comments:* H-RI-540-G58, Durand-2412. 18__. 1850s.

Rarity: *None known*

$100 • W-RI-1570-100-G180

Left: Portrait of George Washington. *Right:* Portrait of Marquis de Lafayette. *Engraver:* PSSP. *Comments:* H-RI-540-G62, Durand-2414. 18__. 1820s–1830s.

Rarity: *None known*

$100 • W-RI-1570-100-G190

Left: 100 / Male portrait. *Center:* Drove of horses in field. *Right:* 100 / Male portrait. *Engraver:* Toppan, Carpenter, Casilear & Co. *Comments:* H-RI-540-G66, Durand-2415. 18__. 1850s.

Rarity: *None known*

NON-VALID ISSUES

$1 • W-RI-1570-001-N010

Center: Boatman floating down stream. *Comments:* H-RI-540-N5, Durand-2382. Altered or spurious. 1850s.

Rarity: *None known*

$1 • W-RI-1570-001-A010

Left: 1 / Cattle, telegraph poles, train. *Center:* Woman with two calves, Trees and river. *Right:* 1 / Female portrait. *Tint:* Red-brown 1s and panel outlining white ONE DOLLAR. *Engraver:* Danforth, Wright & Co. *Comments:* H-RI-540-A5, Durand-2381. Altered from $1 Southern Bank of Georgia, Bainbridge, Georgia. March 1, 1858.

Rarity: *None known*

$1 • W-RI-1570-001-A020

Left: ONE / Female portrait. *Center:* Portrait of girl / Oxen-drawn wagon of hay with two farmers. *Bottom center:* Ducks. *Right:* 1 / View of factories. *Overprint:* Red ONE. *Engraver:* Baldwin, Bald, Cousland & Co. / Bald, Cousland & Co. *Comments:* H-RI-540-A10, Durand-2380. Altered from W-RI-1500-001-G010a. 18__. 1850s.

Rarity: *None known*

$2 • W-RI-1570-002-A030

Left: 2 / Constitution, Monument. *Center:* Portrait of Andrew Jackson / Woman standing with shield bearing cotton plant. *Right:* 2 / Two Indians on cliff. *Overprint:* Red TWO. *Engraver:* Bald, Cousland & Co. *Comments:* H-RI-540-A15, Durand-2387. Altered from $2 Southern Bank of Georgia, Bainbridge, Georgia. 18__. 1850s.

Rarity: *None known*

$2 • W-RI-1570-002-A040

Left: 2 / Female portrait. *Center:* TWO over $ / Two women seated with shield bearing plow. *Bottom center:* Strongbox. *Right:* 2 / Train. *Engraver:* Danforth, Wright & Co. *Comments:* H-RI-540-A20, Durand-2388. Altered from $2 Bank of the Ohio Savings Institute, Tiffin, Ohio. 185_. 1850s.

Rarity: URS-3
VF $500

$2 • W-RI-1570-002-A050

SI

Engraver: Durand & Co. *Comments:* H-RI-540-A25. Altered from $2 Agricultural Bank, Montreal, Canada. 18__. 1840s.

Rarity: URS-3
VF $500

$3 • **W-RI-1570-003-N020**

Center: Sheaves and agricultural implements. *Right:* Woman, man, and dog. *Comments:* H-RI-540-N10, Durand-2396. 1850s.

Rarity: URS-3

VF $250

$3 • **W-RI-1570-003-N030**

Left: Male portrait / 3. *Center:* Women around shield surmounted by eagle. *Comments:* H-RI-540-N15, Durand-2395. 1850s.

Rarity: *None known*

$3 • **W-RI-1570-003-A060**

Left: 3 / Farmer standing. *Center:* 3 / Steamship / THREE. *Right:* 3 / Cherubs in 3. *Tint:* Green. *Engraver:* Danforth, Wright & Co. *Comments:* H-RI-540-A30, Durand-2393. Altered from $3 Brownville Bank & Land Co., Omaha City, Nebraska. Sept. 1, 1857.

Rarity: URS-3

VF $200

$3 • **W-RI-1570-003-A070**

Left: 3 / Female portrait. *Center:* Three cherubs and three silver dollars. *Right:* 3 / Wagon of hay. *Overprint:* Red THREE. *Engraver:* Rawdon, Wright, Hatch & Edson / New England Bank Note Co. *Comments:* H-RI-540-A35. Altered from W-RI-1580-003-G190a. 18__. 1858.

Rarity: URS-3

VF $200

$3 • **W-RI-1570-003-A080**

Left: 3 / Portrait of George Washington / THREE. *Center:* Commerce pointing to ship at sea. *Right:* 3 / Mechanic, sailor, and farmer standing with 3. *Overprint:* THREE. *Engraver:* Rawdon, Wright, Hatch & Edson. *Comments:* H-RI-540-A40, Durand-2394. Altered from $3 Farmers & Merchants Bank of Memphis, Tennessee. 1850s.

Rarity: URS-3

VF $500

$5 • **W-RI-1570-005-A090**

Center: Horses running / Liberty and Ceres flanking shield surmounted by horse's head. *Right:* 5 / Portrait of girl shading her eyes. *Overprint:* Red FIVE. *Engraver:* Baldwin, Bald, Cousland & Co. / Bald, Cousland & Co. *Comments:* H-RI-540-A45, Durand-2401. Altered from $5 Bank of Morgan, Morgan, Georgia. 18__. 1850s.

Rarity: *None known*

$5 • **W-RI-1570-005-A100**

Left: V on FIVE / Man, woman, children, and dog. *Center:* Men in rowboat, Campsite, Man working in field / FIVE. *Right:* 5 / Two women, one holding grain. *Tint:* Green lathework outlining white FIVE. *Engraver:* Danforth, Wright & Co. *Comments:* H-RI-540-A50, Durand-2403. Altered from $5 Brownville Bank and Land Company, Omaha City, Nebraska. Sept. 1, 1857.

Rarity: URS-3

VF $500

$5 • **W-RI-1570-005-A110**

Left: 5 / Two children. *Center:* Two allegorical women with anvil. *Right:* 5 / Men washing sheep in stream. *Overprint:* Red FIVE. *Engraver:* Rawdon, Wright, Hatch & Edson / New England Bank Note Co. *Comments:* H-RI-540-A55, Durand-2402. Altered from W-RI-1580-005-G240. 18__. 1850s.

Rarity: *None known*

$5 • **W-RI-1570-005-A120**

Left: 5 / Portrait of George Washington / FIVE. *Center:* Commerce pointing to ship at sea. *Right:* 5. *Overprint:* FIVE. *Comments:* H-Unlisted, Durand-2404. Altered from $3 Farmers & Merchants Bank of Memphis, Tennessee. 1850s.

Rarity: URS-3

VF $150

$10 • **W-RI-1570-010-R010**

Engraver: Rawdon, Wright & Hatch. *Comments:* H-RI-540-R6, Durand-2408. Raised from W-RI-1570-001-G020. 18__. 1850s.

Rarity: *None known*

$10 • **W-RI-1570-010-A130**

Left: 10 / Two women holding shield bearing anchor. *Center:* X / Two men and woman with horses / X. *Right:* 10 / Portrait of girl. *Engraver:* Unverified, but likely Toppan, Carpenter & Co. *Comments:* H-RI-540-A60, Durand-2409. Altered from W-RI-1630-010-G050. 18__. 1855.

Rarity: URS-3

VF $500

$50 • **W-RI-1570-050-A140**

Left: 50 / Girl and horse. *Center:* Milkmaid and cows. *Right:* 50 / Blacksmith standing. *Overprint:* Red FIFTY. *Engraver:* Rawdon, Wright, Hatch & Edson / New England Bank Note Co. *Comments:* H-RI-540-A65, Durand-2413. Altered from W-RI-1630-005-G040. 18__. 1850s.

Rarity: *None known*

Warwick Bank
1818–1859
W-RI-1580

History: The Warwick Bank was incorporated at Apponaug in 1818. Not long afterward, the location was changed to Warwick. Capital was $25,000 in 1848.[86] Circulation in 1849 was $5,547.

The operation of the bank became questionable, and after the books were audited, the Bank Commissioners suggested that the plates be stored in a city bank for safety.[87] When the plates could not be located, the bank was forced to close. The following report is quoted from *Clapp, Fuller and Browne's Bank Note Reporter and Counterfeit Detector* of March 1859:

> Warwick Bank, Rhode Island Perpetually Enjoined. In the Supreme Court of Providence, Rhode Island on Thursday, a decree was entered granting a perpetual injunction against the Warwick Bank, and appointing W. Hayes, Esquire receiver. The petition of the Bank Commissioners, on which this order is granted, states that the

plates of the bank, which, at the suggestion of the Commissioner, had been lodged in the American Bank, have been removed and are missing: that a large amount of bills have been put in circulation without a registry of the issue, and without security therefore; that the books of the bank do not show proper records of its proceedings; that its affairs are being so managed generally that the public, and those having funds in its custody, are in danger of being defrauded thereby.

Numismatic Commentary: Many examples across various denominations of this bank's later notes are still available. Some uncut sheets also remain. The early notes of the bank are very hard to find in the marketplace.

VALID ISSUES

$1 • W-RI-1580-001-G010

Left: 1 ONE 1 vertically. *Center:* 1 / Woman holding 1 bearing ONE / 1. *Bottom center:* ONE. *Right:* 1 RHODE ISLAND 1 vertically. *Engraver:* Reed. *Comments:* H-RI-545-G2, Durand-2416. 18__. 1818–1820s.

Rarity: URS-3
Proof $300

$1 • W-RI-1580-001-G020

Left: 1 / Woman wearing bonnet, standing by pail / ONE. *Center:* Machinery and merchandise flanking Ceres holding sickle and rake, Factories and harbor / ONE / Panel outlining white ONE. *Right:* 1 / Ship / ONE. *Engraver:* PSSP / New England Bank Note Co. *Comments:* H-RI-545-G8. 18__. 1830s–1840s.

Rarity: *None known*

$1 • W-RI-1580-001-G030

Left: ONE / Bust of George Washington / ONE. *Center:* 1 / Two blacksmiths at anvil in front of forge / 1 / Panel outlining white ONE. *Right:* ONE / Woman / ONE. *Engraver:* New England Bank Note Co. *Comments:* H-RI-545-G10, Durand-2417. 18__. 1840s–1850s.

Rarity: *None known*

$1 • W-RI-1580-001-G040

CC

Engraver: New England Bank Note Co. *Comments:* H-RI-545-G12, Durand-2418. 18__. 1850s.

Rarity: URS-4
F $170; **VF** $250

$1 • W-RI-1580-001-G050

QDB

Overprint: Red ONE. *Engraver:* New England Bank Note Co. *Comments:* H-RI-545-G14a, Durand-2419. 18__. 1850s.

Rarity: URS-8
VG $35; **VF** $125

$1 • W-RI-1580-001-G060

Left: ONE / Sailor. *Center:* Agricultural scene. *Right:* 1 / Train, bridge, and cattle. *Overprint:* Red ONE. *Engraver:* New England Bank Note Co. / Rawdon, Wright, Hatch & Edson. *Comments:* H-RI-545-G16a, Durand-2420. 18__. 1850s.

Rarity: *None known*

$1 • W-RI-1580-001-G060a

Overprint: Red ONE. *Engraver:* New England Bank Note Co. / Rawdon, Wright, Hatch & Edson / ABNCo. monogram. *Comments:* H-RI-545-G16b. Similar to W-RI-1580-001-G060 but with additional engraver imprint. 18__. 1858.

Rarity: URS-8
VF $125

$2 • W-RI-1580-002-G070

Left: 2 TWO 2 vertically. *Center:* 2 / Woman holding shield bearing 2 / Ship / 2. *Bottom center:* TWO. *Right:* 2 RHODE ISLAND 2 vertically. *Engraver:* Reed. *Comments:* H-RI-545-G20, Durand-2421. 18__. 1818–1820s.

Rarity: URS-3
Proof $300

$2 • W-RI-1580-002-G080

Left: 2 / Woman standing with staff, Cornucopia / TWO. *Center:* TWO / Machinery and merchandise flanking Ceres holding sickle and rake, Factories and harbor / Panel outlining white TWO. *Right:* 2 / Woman wearing hat, Trees / TWO. *Engraver:* PSSP / New England Bank Note Co. *Comments:* H-RI-545-G26. 18__. 1818–1820s.

Rarity: *None known*

$2 • W-RI-1580-002-G090

Left: TWO / Woman. *Center:* 2 / Woman giving drink to one of two men. *Right:* TWO / Ceres. *Engraver:* New England Bank Note Co. *Comments:* H-RI-545-G28, Durand-2422. 18__. 1840s–1850s.

Rarity: *None known*

$2 • **W-RI-1580-002-G100**

Engraver: New England Bank Note Co. **Comments:** H-RI-545-G30, Durand-2423. 18___. 1850s.

Rarity: URS-3
VF $900

$2 • **W-RI-1580-002-G110**

Overprint: Red TWO. **Engraver:** New England Bank Note Co. **Comments:** H-RI-545-G32a, Durand-2424. 18___. 1850s.

Rarity: URS-8
VG $60; **VF** $125

$2 • **W-RI-1580-002-G120**

Left: TWO on die / Male portrait. **Center:** Train / TWO. **Right:** 2 / Man seated. **Overprint:** Red TWO. **Engraver:** New England Bank Note Co. / Rawdon, Wright, Hatch & Co. **Comments:** H-RI-545-G34a. 18___. 1850s.

Rarity: *None known*

$2 • **W-RI-1580-002-G120a**

Overprint: Red TWO. **Engraver:** New England Bank Note Co. / Rawdon, Wright, Hatch & Edson / ABNCo. monogram. **Comments:** H-RI-545-G34b, Durand-2425. Similar to W-RI-1580-002-G120 but with additional engraver imprint. 18___. 1858.

Rarity: URS-8
VF $125

$3 • **W-RI-1580-003-G130**

Engraver: Reed. **Comments:** H-RI-545-G36, Durand-2426. No description available. 18___. 1818–1820s.

Rarity: *None known*

$3 • **W-RI-1580-003-G140**

Left: THREE / Beehive and foliage / THREE. **Center:** Machinery and merchandise flanking Ceres holding sickle and rake, Factories and harbor / THREE / Panel outlining white THREE. **Right:** 3 on THREE / Two reapers / 3 on THREE. **Engraver:** PSSP / New England Bank Note Co. **Comments:** H-RI-545-G42. 18___. 1818–1820s.

Rarity: *None known*

$3 • **W-RI-1580-003-G150**

Left: 3 THREE 3 vertically. **Center:** 3 / Allegorical woman / 3. **Right:** 3 RHODE ISLAND 3 vertically. **Comments:** H-Unlisted, Durand-2426. 1818–1820s.

Rarity: URS-3

$3 • **W-RI-1580-003-G160**

Left: THREE / Farmer with scythe / 3 on THREE. **Center:** 3 / Liberty and eagle / 3. **Right:** THREE / Sailor standing on wharf / 3 on THREE. **Engraver:** New England Bank Note Co. **Comments:** H-RI-545-G44, Durand-2427. 18___. 1840s–1850s.

Rarity: *None known*

$3 • **W-RI-1580-003-G170**

Left: 3 / "George Washington at Dorchester Heights". **Center:** Female portrait / 3 / Female portrait. **Right:** 3 / Vulcan with sledge. **Engraver:** New England Bank Note Co. **Comments:** H-RI-545-G46, Durand-2428. 18___. 1850s.

Rarity: *None known*

$3 • **W-RI-1580-003-G180**

Overprint: Red THREE. **Engraver:** New England Bank Note Co. **Comments:** H-RI-545-G48a, Durand-2429. 18___. 1850s.

Rarity: URS-7
VG $85; **VF** $150

$3 • **W-RI-1580-003-G190**

Left: 3 / Female portrait. **Center:** Three cherubs and three silver dollars. **Right:** 3 / Wagon of hay. **Overprint:** Red THREE. **Engraver:** New England Bank Note Co. / Rawdon, Wright, Hatch & Edson. **Comments:** H-RI-545-G50a, Durand-2430. 18___. 1850s.

Rarity: *None known*

$3 • **W-RI-1580-003-G190a**

Overprint: Red THREE. **Engraver:** New England Bank Note Co. / Rawdon, Wright, Hatch & Edson / ABNCo. monogram. **Comments:** H-RI-545-G50b. Similar to W-RI-1580-003-G190 but with additional engraver imprint. 18___. 1850s.

Rarity: URS-7
VF $125

$5 • **W-RI-1580-005-G200**

Left: 5 FIVE 5 vertically. **Center:** 5 / Allegorical woman / 5. **Right:** 5 RHODE ISLAND 5 vertically. **Engraver:** Reed. **Comments:** H-RI-545-G52, Durand-2431. 18___. 1818–1820s.

Rarity: URS-3
Proof $300

$5 • W-RI-1580-005-G210

Left: 5 / Blacksmith at anvil / FIVE. *Center:* Mercury standing with 5 / Cornucopia and merchandise, Factories and ship / V / Panel outlining white FIVE. *Right:* 5 / Ceres kneeling / FIVE. *Engraver:* PSSP / New England Bank Note Co. *Comments:* H-RI-545-G58. 18__. 1818–1820s.

Rarity: *None known*

$5 • W-RI-1580-005-G220

Left: FIVE 5 FIVE vertically. *Center:* 5 / Commerce holding 5 / 5. *Right:* V RHODE ISLAND V vertically. *Comments:* H-Unlisted, Durand-2432. 1818–1820s.

Rarity: URS-3

$5 • W-RI-1580-005-G230

Left: FIVE vertically. *Center:* Woman unveiling shield bearing 5 / V. *Right:* 5 / Sailing ship. *Engraver:* New England Bank Note Co. *Comments:* H-RI-545-G60, Durand-2433. 18__. 1840s–1850s.

Rarity: *None known*

$5 • W-RI-1580-005-G240

QDB

Overprint: Red FIVE. *Engraver:* New England Bank Note Co. / Rawdon, Wright, Hatch & Edson. *Comments:* H-RI-545-G62a, Durand-2434. 18__. 1858.

Rarity: URS-10
VF $100; **CU** $150

$10 • W-RI-1580-010-G250

Engraver: Reed. *Comments:* H-RI-545-G64. No description available. 1840s–1850s.

Rarity: *None known*

$10 • W-RI-1580-010-G260

Left: 10 / Farmer sowing / TEN. *Center:* Mercury standing with 10, Merchandise, Factories and ship / Canal scene / Panel outlining white TEN. *Right:* 10 / Ship / TEN. *Engraver:* PSSP / New England Bank Note Co. *Comments:* H-RI-545-G70. 18__. 1830s–1840s.

Rarity: *None known*

$10 • W-RI-1580-010-G270

Left: 10 X 10 vertically. *Center:* Allegorical man standing by oxen and plow / 10. *Right:* TEN / Woman standing with lyre, Cornucopia. *Engraver:* New England Bank Note Co. *Comments:* H-RI-545-G72, Durand-2436. 18__. 1840s–1850s.

Rarity: *None known*

$10 • W-RI-1580-010-G280

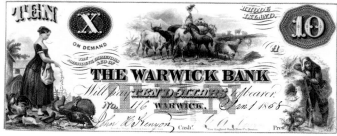

QDB

Overprint: Red TEN. *Engraver:* New England Bank Note Co. / Rawdon, Wright, Hatch & Edson. *Comments:* H-RI-545-G74a, Durand-2437. 18__. 1858.

Rarity: URS-9
VF $125; **CU** $195

$20 • W-RI-1580-020-G290

Left: 20 / Woman seated with book on lap, opening chest. *Center:* XX / Eagle / XX. *Right:* 20 / Ship. *Engraver:* New England Bank Note Co. *Comments:* H-RI-545-G82, Durand-2439. 18__. 1840s–1850s.

Rarity: *None known*

$20 • W-RI-1580-020-G300

QDB

Overprint: Red TWENTY. *Engraver:* New England Bank Note Co. / Rawdon, Wright, Hatch & Edson. *Comments:* H-RI-545-G84a, Durand-2440. 18__. 1858.

Rarity: URS-9
VF $200

$50 • W-RI-1580-050-G310

CC

Engraver: New England Bank Note Co. / Rawdon, Wright, Hatch & Edson. *Comments:* H-RI-545-G86. 18__. 1850s–1860s.

Rarity: URS-3
VG $250; **VF** $1,200

$50 • W-RI-1580-050-G310a

CC

Overprint: Red FIFTY. *Engraver:* New England Bank Note Co. / Rawdon, Wright, Hatch & Edson / ABNCo. monogram. *Comments:* H-RI-545-G86a. Similar to W-RI-1580-050-G310 but with additional engraver imprint. 18__. 1858.

Rarity: URS-8
VF $150; **AU** $195; **CU** $250

$50 • W-RI-1580-050-G310b

Left: 50 / Woman and horse. *Center:* Woman seated with basket, Cows. *Right:* 50 / Blacksmith standing with anvil. *Overprint:* Red FIFTY. *Engraver:* New England Bank Note Co. / Rawdon, Wright, Hatch & Edson / ABNCo. monogram. *Comments:* H-RI-545-G86b, Durand-2441. Similar to W-RI-1580-050-G310 but with additional engraver imprint and different date. 18__. 1859.

Rarity: URS-6
VF $150

Uncut Sheets

$5-$5-$10-$20 • W-RI-1580-005.005.010.020-US010

Vignette(s): *($5)* Two children / Two women seated with anvil / Men running sheep into river. *($5)* Two children / Two women seated with anvil / Men running sheep into river. *($10)* Woman feeding chickens / Horses / Man leaning on gun. *($20)* Woman seated on box / "Signing of the Declaration of Independence" / Portrait of Benjamin Franklin. *Engraver:* Rawdon, Wright, Hatch & Edson / New England Bank Note Co. *Comments:* H-RI-545-G62a, G62a, G74a, G84a. 18__. 1858.

Rarity: URS-10
Proof $350

$50 • W-RI-1580-050-US020

Vignette(s): *($50)* Woman and horse / Woman seated with basket, Cows / Blacksmith standing with anvil. *Overprint(s):* Red FIFTY. *Engraver:* New England Bank Note Co. / Rawdon, Wright, Hatch & Edson / ABNCo. monogram. *Comments:* H-RI-545-G86a. Sheet of one note. 18__. 1858.

Rarity: URS-3

Non-Valid Issues

$5 • W-RI-1580-005-A010

Left: FIVE / Portrait of Benjamin Franklin / V. *Center:* 5 / Three allegorical women. *Right:* V / Portrait of Marquis de Lafayette / FIVE. *Engraver:* Terry, Pelton & Co. *Comments:* H-RI-545-A5, Durand-2435. Altered from $5 Citizens Bank, Augusta, Maine, or from notes of other failed banks using the same plate. 18__. 1850s.

Rarity: None known

$10 • W-RI-1580-010-A020

Left: 10 / Portrait of George Washington held by cherub / 10. *Center:* X / E PLURIBUS UNUM / Spread eagle and shield / X. *Bottom center:* Ship. *Right:* 10 / Indian / 10. *Engraver:* Terry, Pelton & Co. *Comments:* H-RI-545-A10, Durand-2438. Altered from $10 Citizens Bank, Augusta, Maine, or from notes of other failed banks using the same plate. 18__. 1850s.

Rarity: None known

WESTERLY, RHODE ISLAND

Founded in 1669 by John Babcock, Westerly was first known as Misquamicut, which meant "a place for taking salmon." It was incorporated as the fifth town in the colony of Rhode Island. In 1686 the name was changed briefly to Haversham, a title which lasted only three years before it was changed back to Westerly. Later, Charlestown, Hopkinton—including the village of Ashaway—and Richmond were separated from Westerly.

Westerly was well-known for granite quarries that provided building materials for monuments and structures in neighboring towns and cities. The granite is blue with traces of red and pink and was sold as far south as Georgia. Many cemeteries used the granite from Westerly in their headstones.

See also Ashaway and Hopkinton, Rhode Island.

Hopkinton Bank
1851–1859
W-RI-1590

History: The Hopkinton Bank was organized on August 5, 1851. In an endeavor to make large dividends, this bank speculated heavily in Western land securities. The failure of these securities to materialize led to the downfall of the bank.[88]

The capital was $100,000 in 1855 and $109,600 in 1857, but the bank was unable to redeem its largely inflated circulation. The condition, however, was not entirely due to speculation, as the widespread suspension of specie payments by most of the banks of Rhode Island on September 28, 1857, also had a hand in matters. The Hopkinton Bank went into receivership in 1857 and closed in 1859.

See also listing under Hopkinton, W-RI-450.

Numismatic Commentary: It is a challenge to locate a genuine note from this bank. Bills were obtained from the New England Bank Note Co. and the firm of Danforth & Bald. The issues of this latter company are the ones most likely to appear in the marketplace.

Valid Issues

$1 • W-RI-1590-001-G010

Left: 1 / Portrait of George Washington. *Center:* Female portrait / 1 / Female portrait. *Right:* 1 / Portrait of Benjamin Franklin. *Engraver:* New England Bank Note Co. *Comments:* H-RI-130-G12, Durand-2442. 18__. 1850s.

Rarity: None known

$1 • **W-RI-1590-001-G020**   QDB

Back: Plain. *Engraver:* Danforth, Bald & Co. *Comments:* H-Unlisted, Durand-Unlisted. Proof. January 10th, 18__. 1850s.
Rarity: URS-4
EF $600; **Unc-Rem** $300; **Proof** $750

$1 • **W-RI-1590-001-G020a**   QDB, QDB

Back: Red 1 on panel outlining white ONE. *Engraver:* Danforth, Bald & Co. *Comments:* H-RI-130-G14a, Durand-2443. Similar to W-RI-1590-001-G020. January 10th, 18__. 1850s.
Rarity: URS-3
VF $400

$2 • **W-RI-1590-002-G030**

Left: 2 / Portrait of Christopher Columbus. *Center:* Agriculture / 2 / Justice. *Right:* 2 / Male portrait. *Engraver:* New England Bank Note Co. *Comments:* H-RI-130-G16, Durand-2444. 18__. 1850s.
Rarity: *None known*

$2 • **W-RI-1590-002-G040**   CC

Back: Red 2 on panel outlining white TWO. *Engraver:* Danforth, Bald & Co. *Comments:* H-RI-130-G18a, Durand-2445. January 10th, 18__. 1850s.
Rarity: URS-1
G $18; **Proof** $200

$3 • **W-RI-1590-003-G050**

Left: 3 / George Washington standing by horse. *Center:* Female portrait / 3 / Female portrait. *Right:* 3 / Vulcan. *Engraver:* New England Bank Note Co. *Comments:* H-RI-130-G20, Durand-2446. 18__. 1850s.
Rarity: *None known*

$3 • **W-RI-1590-003-G060**   SBG

Back: Plain. *Engraver:* Danforth, Bald & Co. *Comments:* H-Unlisted, Durand-Unlisted. Proof. 18__. 1850s.
Rarity: URS-3
VF $800; **Unc-Rem** $400; **Proof** $1,200

$3 • **W-RI-1590-003-G060a**

Left: 3. *Center:* Drover on horseback and boy driving swine / State arms. *Right:* 3 / Train. *Back:* Red 3 on panel outlining white THREE. *Engraver:* Danforth, Bald & Co. *Comments:* H-RI-130-G22a, Durand-2447. Similar to W-RI-1590-003-G060 but with different date. Jan. 10, 18__. 1850s.
Rarity: *None known*

$5 • **W-RI-1590-005-G070**   CJF

Engraver: New England Bank Note Co. *Comments:* H-RI-130-G24, Durand-2449. 18__. 1850s.
Rarity: URS-1

$5 • W-RI-1590-005-G080

SBG

Back: Plain. **Engraver:** Danforth, Bald & Co. **Comments:** H-Unlisted, Durand-Unlisted. Proof. January 10th, 18__. 1850s.
Rarity: URS-4
Proof $1,500

$5 • W-RI-1590-005-G080a

Left: Allegorical woman with U.S. shield on 5 / FIVE. **Center:** Three men. **Right:** 5 on FIVE on V / Portrait of George Washington. **Back:** Red 5 on panel outlining white FIVE. **Engraver:** Danforth, Bald & Co. **Comments:** H-RI-130-G26a, Durand-2450. Similar to W-RI-1590-005-G080. January 10th, 18__. 1850s.
Rarity: URS-3
VF $400

$10 • W-RI-1590-010-G090

Left: TEN. **Center:** Vulcan seated / X. **Right:** 10 / Reaper standing with sheaf. **Engraver:** New England Bank Note Co. **Comments:** H-RI-130-G28, Durand-2453. 18__. 1850s.
Rarity: *None known*

$10 • W-RI-1590-010-G100

SBG

Back: Plain. **Engraver:** Danforth, Bald & Co. **Comments:** H-Unlisted, Durand-Unlisted. Proof. 18__. 1850s.
Rarity: URS-5
Proof $1,500

$10 • W-RI-1590-010-G100a

Left: TEN. **Center:** Liberty and eagle, Mechanics / 10 on TEN on X. **Right:** 10 / Indian woman and Ceres. **Back:** Red 10 on panel outlining white TEN. **Engraver:** Danforth, Bald & Co. **Comments:** H-RI-130-G30a, Durand-2454. Similar to W-RI-1590-010-G100 but with different date. Jan. 10, 18__. 1850s.
Rarity: *None known*

$20 • W-RI-1590-020-G110

Left: 20 / Woman. **Center:** XX / Eagle / XX. **Right:** 20 / Ship. **Engraver:** New England Bank Note Co. **Comments:** H-RI-130-G32, Durand-2455. 18__. 1850s.
Rarity: *None known*

$50 • W-RI-1590-050-G120

Left: FIFTY / Woman standing with wreath and flowers / FIFTY. **Center:** 50 / Man holding horse / 50. **Right:** FIFTY / Woman standing with cornucopia / FIFTY. **Engraver:** New England Bank Note Co. **Comments:** H-RI-130-G34, Durand-2456. 18__. 1850s.
Rarity: *None known*

$100 • W-RI-1590-100-G130

Left: ONE HUNDRED across 100 / Portrait of William Henry Harrison. **Center:** Wharf scene, men loading wagon with barrels. **Right:** ONE HUNDRED across 100 / Portrait of Christopher Columbus. **Engraver:** New England Bank Note Co. **Comments:** H-RI-130-G36, Durand-2457. 18__. 1850s.
Rarity: *None known*

Uncut Sheets

$1-$1-$2-$5 • W-RI-1590-001.001.002.005-US010

Vignette(s): **($1)** Two Indian men / Three men and woman with farming implements / Three baskets on ground full of cotton next to tree. **($1)** Two Indian men / Three men and woman with farming implements / Three baskets on ground full of cotton next to tree. **($2)** Liberty standing / Train passing under bridge / State arms. **($5)** Allegorical woman with U.S. shield on 5 / Three men / Portrait of George Washington. **Engraver:** Danforth, Bald & Co. **Comments:** H-RI-130-G14a, G14a, G18a, G26a. January 10th, 18__. 1850s.
Rarity: URS-3
VF $2,000

$3-$10 • W-RI-1590-003.010-US020

Vignette(s): **($3)** Drover on horseback and boy driving swine / State arms / Train. **($10)** Liberty, Commerce, Agriculture, and Mechanics / Indian woman and Ceres. **Engraver:** Danforth, Bald & Co. **Comments:** All unlisted in Haxby. Jan. 10, 18__. 1850s.
Rarity: URS-3
VF $1,000

Non-Valid Issues

$3 • W-RI-1590-003-A010

Left: 3 / Portrait of Daniel Webster. **Center:** Ceres and Liberty flanking U.S. shield surmounted by eagle. **Right:** THREE on 3 / Female portrait. **Overprint:** Red THREE. **Engraver:** New England Bank Note Co. / Rawdon, Wright, Hatch & Edson. **Comments:** H-RI-130-A5, Durand-2448. Altered from $3 Waubeek Bank, DeSoto, Nebraska. 1857.
Rarity: *None known*

$5 • W-RI-1590-005-R010

Engraver: Danforth, Bald & Co. **Comments:** H-RI-130-R5, Durand-2451. Raised from W-RI-1590-001-G020 series. Jan. 10, 18__. 1850s.
Rarity: *None known*

$5 • W-RI-1590-005-R020

Engraver: Danforth, Bald & Co. **Comments:** H-RI-130-R10, Durand-2452. Raised from W-RI-1590-002-G040 series. Jan. 10, 18__. 1850s.
Rarity: *None known*

Niantic Bank
1854–1865
W-RI-1600

History: The Niantic Bank, named after an Indian tribe that occupied southwest Rhode Island, was incorporated in 1854. Capital was $200,000 in 1855 and $240,100 in 1857. Bills in circulation were $47,959 in 1857, and specie totaled $3,427.09 the same year. The Niantic Bank had $240,100 in capital as of December 1862 and a circulation of $106,099.

The business of the Niantic Bank was succeeded by the National Niantic Bank, chartered on February 18, 1865.

Numismatic Commentary: Collectors of bank notes who also like to see coins illustrated on their examples have a chance with the $1 issue from this bank. Other issues show an Indian family traveling in a canoe. In general, notes are hard to find, but not impossible.

Valid Issues

$1 • W-RI-1600-001-G010

Left: Two Indians on horses / 1 on die. **Center:** Reverse of silver dollar. **Bottom center:** 1. **Right:** 1 / Portrait of Daniel Webster / ONE. **Engraver:** Wellstood, Hanks, Hay & Whiting. **Comments:** H-RI-550-G2, Durand-2458. July 1st, 18__. 1850s.
Rarity: URS-3
Proof $700

$1 • W-RI-1600-001-G010a

Overprint: Red ONE. **Engraver:** Wellstood, Hanks, Hay & Whiting. **Comments:** H-RI-550-G2a, Durand-2459. Similar to W-RI-1600-001-G010. July 1st, 18__. 1850s.
Rarity: URS-3; URS-1
F $500; VF $1,000
Proof $2,500
Selected auction price: Stack's Bowers Galleries, January 2008, Proof $2,241

$1 • W-RI-1600-001-G010b

Overprint: Red panel outlining ONE. **Engraver:** Wellstood, Hanks, Hay & Whiting / ABNCo. monogram. **Comments:** H-RI-550-G2b, Durand-2460. Similar to W-RI-1600-001-G010 but with additional engraver imprint. July 1st, 18__. 1850s–1860s.
Rarity: URS-3
VF $500

$2 • W-RI-1600-002-G020

Left: TWO on 2 / ON DEMAND / Woman holding 2. **Center:** Man driving cattle and sheep / TWO. **Bottom center:** Clasped hands. **Right:** 2 / RHODE ISLAND / Man with sickle. **Engraver:** Wellstood, Hanks, Hay & Whiting. **Comments:** H-RI-550-G4, Durand-2461. July 1st, 18__. 1850s.
Rarity: URS-3
Proof $700

$2 • W-RI-1600-002-G020a

Overprint: Red TWO. **Engraver:** Wellstood, Hanks, Hay & Whiting. **Comments:** H-RI-550-G4a, Durand-2462. Similar to W-RI-1600-002-G020. July 1st, 18__. 1850s.
Rarity: URS-3
VF $500

$2 • W-RI-1600-002-G020b

Overprint: Red panel outlining white TWO. **Engraver:** Wellstood, Hanks, Hay & Whiting / ABNCo. monogram. **Comments:** H-RI-550-G4b, Durand-2463. Similar to W-RI-1600-002-G020 but with additional engraver imprint. July 1st, 18__. 1850s–1860s.
Rarity: URS-3
VF $500

$3 • W-RI-1600-003-G030

Engraver: Wellstood, Hanks, Hay & Whiting. **Comments:** H-RI-550-G6, Durand-2465. Proof. July 1st, 18__. 1850s.
Rarity: URS-2
Proof $1,000

$3 • W-RI-1600-003-G030a

Left: Sailing vessel / THREE on 3. **Center:** Two women with bolt of cloth. **Bottom center:** Shield bearing anchor. **Right:** III / Woman seated with 3 and lighthouse. **Overprint:** Red THREE. **Engraver:** Wellstood, Hanks, Hay & Whiting. **Comments:** H-RI-550-G6a, Durand-2466. Similar to W-RI-1600-003-G030. July 1st, 18__. 1850s.
Rarity: URS-3
VF $500

$3 • W-RI-1600-003-G030b

Overprint: Red panel outlining white THREE. **Engraver:** Wellstood, Hanks, Hay & Whiting / ABNCo. monogram. **Comments:** H-RI-550-G6b, Durand-2467. Similar to W-RI-1600-003-G030 but with additional engraver imprint. July 1st, 18__. 1850s–1860s.
Rarity: URS-3
VF $500

$5 • W-RI-1600-005-G040

Left: V / Indian woman seated. *Center:* Indian man and family in canoe / FIVE. *Right:* 5 / Man with basket of corn. *Engraver:* Wellstood, Hanks, Hay & Whiting. *Comments:* H-RI-550-G8, Durand-2468. July 1st, 18__. 1850s.

Rarity: URS-3

Proof $700

$5 • W-RI-1600-005-G040a

SBG

Overprint: Red FIVE. *Engraver:* Wellstood, Hanks, Hay & Whiting. *Comments:* H-RI-550-G8a, Durand-2469. Similar to W-RI-1600-005-G040. July 1st, 18__. 1850s.

Rarity: URS-3

Proof $3,400

Selected auction price: Stack's Bowers Galleries, March 2013, Proof $3,388

$5 • W-RI-1600-005-G040b

Overprint: Red panel outlining white FIVE. *Engraver:* Wellstood, Hanks, Hay & Whiting / ABNCo. monogram. *Comments:* H-RI-550-G8b, Durand-2470. Similar to W-RI-1600-005-G040 but with additional engraver imprint. July 1st, 18__. 1850s–1860s.

Rarity: *None known*

$10 • W-RI-1600-010-G050

Left: 10 on die / 10 on X. *Center:* Two women with shield / Mirror / TEN over TEN. *Bottom center:* Dog. *Right:* 10 on die / Woman with lighthouse. *Engraver:* Wellstood, Hanks, Hay & Whiting. *Comments:* H-RI-550-G10, Durand-2472. July 1st, 18__. 1850s.

Rarity: URS-3

Proof $1,500

$10 • W-RI-1600-010-G050a

CC

Overprint: Red TEN. *Engraver:* Wellstood, Hanks, Hay & Whiting. *Comments:* H-RI-550-G10a, Durand-2471. Similar to W-RI-1600-010-G050. July 1st, 18__. 1850s.

Rarity: URS-3

Proof $1,500

$10 • W-RI-1600-010-G050b

CJF

Overprint: Red panel outlining white TEN. *Engraver:* Wellstood, Hanks, Hay & Whiting / ABNCo. monogram. *Comments:* H-RI-550-G10b, Durand-2473. Similar to W-RI-1600-010-G050 but with additional engraver imprint. July 1st, 18__. 1850s–1860s.

Rarity: URS-2

$50 • W-RI-1600-050-G060

SBG

Engraver: Wellstood, Hanks, Hay & Whiting. *Comments:* H-RI-550-G12, Durand-2476. July 1st, 18__. 1850s.

Rarity: URS-1

Proof $4,900

Selected auction price: Stack's Bowers Galleries, March 2013, Proof $4,841

$50 • W-RI-1600-050-G060a

Left: Three men with farm implements holding up die bearing 50. *Center:* Portrait of Henry Clay / FIFTY. *Right:* 50 / Indian man. *Overprint:* Red L / L. *Engraver:* Wellstood, Hanks, Hay & Whiting. *Comments:* H-RI-550-G12a, Durand-2475. Similar to W-RI-1600-050-G060. July 1st, 18__. 1850s.

Rarity: URS-3

Proof $750

Uncut Sheets

$1-$1-$2-$5 • W-RI-1600-001.001.002.005-US010

Vignette(s): ($1) Two Indians on horses / Reverse of silver dollar / Portrait of Daniel Webster. *($1)* Two Indians on horses / Reverse of silver dollar / Portrait of Daniel Webster. *($2)* Woman holding 2 / Man driving cattle and sheep / Clasped hands / RHODE ISLAND / Man with sickle. *($5)* Indian woman seated / Indian woman and man in canoe / Man with basket of corn. *Engraver:* Wellstood, Hanks, Hay & Whiting. *Comments:* H-RI-550-G2, G2, G4, G8. July 1st, 18__. 1850s.

Rarity: URS-3

Proof $2,500

$10-$3-$5-$50 • W-RI-1600-010.003.005.050-US020
Vignette(s): *($10)* Two women with shield / Mirror / Dog / Woman with lighthouse. *($3)* Sailing vessel / Two women with bolt of cloth / Shield bearing anchor / Woman seated with 3 and lighthouse. *($5)* Indian woman seated / Indian woman and man in canoe / Man with basket of corn *($50)* Three men with farm implements holding up die bearing 50 / Portrait of Henry Clay / Indian man. *Engraver:* Wellstood, Hanks, Hay & Whiting. *Comments:* H-RI-550-G10, G6, G8, G12. July 1st, 18__. 1850s.
Rarity: URS-3
Proof $3,000

NON-VALID ISSUES

$2 • W-RI-1600-002-A010
Left: 2 / Reverse of silver dollar and pillar dollar. *Center:* Man and woman by well. *Bottom center:* Bull. *Right:* 2 / Allegorical woman with 2. *Overprint:* Red TWO. *Engraver:* Wellstood, Hanks, Hay & Whiting. *Comments:* H-RI-550-A5, Durand-2464. Altered from $2 Thames Bank, Laurel, Indiana. 1850s.
Rarity: *None known*

$10 • W-RI-1600-010-R010
Engraver: Wellstood, Hanks, Hay & Whiting. *Comments:* H-RI-550-R5, Durand-2474. Raised from W-RI-1600-001-G010 series. July 1, 18__. 1850s.
Rarity: *None known*

Phenix Bank
1818–1865
W-RI-1610

History: The Phenix Bank was incorporated in June 1818. In 1849 it had $100,000 in capital divided into 2,000 shares valued at $50 each.[89] By 1855 capital was $150,000.

In December 1850, the Phenix Bank was

> robbed of $16,000. Soon after, it suspended the issue of its bills and ordered new plates whose notes were dated January 1, 1851. The bank then refused to accept any of its old notes unless it could be proven that they were not stolen.[90]

A related account from *Banker's Magazine* reported:

> The Phenix Bank, Westerly, R.I., soon after it was robbed in December last, of sixteen thousand dollars, suspended the issue of its bills, and procured new plates, the emissions from which are dated January 1, 1850. The Bank having redeemed nearly all their old circulation, (with the exception of the *stolen money*), will hereafter redeem the *old bills*, at their counter, all of which are dated *previous* to January 1, 1850.

Bills in circulation were $17,425 from 1857 through 1860; the amount was $40,726 by 1862. Specie was $2,825.12 in 1857.

The business of the bank was succeeded by the Phenix National Bank, chartered on July 17, 1865.

Numismatic Commentary: In the early 21st century, a small hoard of notes from this bank became available to the marketplace. This included many higher denominations of $20 and $50 bills. At least two of this bank's notes show an engraving of the railroad bridge in Westerly, a local landmark.

VALID ISSUES

$1 • W-RI-1610-001-G010
Left: ONE, 1, ONE vertically. *Center:* 1 / Hope seated by anchor / 1. *Right:* 1 RHODE ISLAND 1 vertically. *Engraver:* Reed. *Comments:* H-RI-555-G2, Durand-2477. 18__. 1818–1820s.
Rarity: URS-3
Proof $300

$1 • W-RI-1610-001-G020
Engraver: Unverified, but likely Rawdon, Wright & Hatch. *Comments:* H-RI-555-G6, Durand-2478. No description available. 1818–1820s.
Rarity: *None known*

$1 • W-RI-1610-001-G025   CJF

Engraver: Terry, Pelton & Co. *Comments:* H-Unlisted, Durand-Unlisted. 18__. 1830s–1840s.
Rarity: URS-1
VF $500

$1 • W-RI-1610-001-G030   CC

Engraver: Toppan, Carpenter & Co. *Comments:* H-RI-555-G8, Durand-2479. January 1, 18__. 1840s.
Rarity: URS-3
VF $600

$1 • W-RI-1610-001-G040
Left: 1 / Portrait of George Washington / 1. *Center:* Ceres seated, Train and canal. *Right:* 1 / Portrait of Indian / 1. *Engraver:* Toppan, Carpenter, Casilear & Co. *Comments:* H-RI-555-G10, Durand-2480. January 1, 18__. 1850s.
Rarity: URS-3
VF $300

$1 • W-RI-1610-001-G040a

TD

Overprint: Green panel outlining white ONE. *Engraver:* Toppan, Carpenter, Casilear & Co. / ABNCo. monogram. *Comments:* H-Unlisted, Durand-Unlisted. Similar to W-RI-1610-001-G040 but with additional engraver imprint. January 1, 18__. 1860s.

Rarity: URS-3
VF $1,000

$2 • W-RI-1610-002-G050

SBG

Engraver: Reed. *Comments:* H-RI-555-G12, Durand-2484. 18__. 1818–1820s.

Rarity: URS-3
Proof $750

$2 • W-RI-1610-002-G060

Left: Lathework strip vertically. *Center:* 2 / Commerce resting on shield of Hope / 2. *Right:* TWO vertically. *Comments:* H-Unlisted, Durand-2485. 1818–1820s.

Rarity: URS-3

$2 • W-RI-1610-002-G070

Center: View of town hall, Railroad, canal, and country scene. *Right:* Portrait of Benjamin Franklin. *Engraver:* Unverified, but likely Rawdon, Wright & Hatch. *Comments:* H-RI-555-G16, Durand-2486. Remainder. 1818–1820s.

Rarity: URS-3
CU $195

$2 • W-RI-1610-002-G080

CC

Engraver: Toppan, Carpenter & Co. *Comments:* H-RI-555-G18, Durand-2487. Jan. 1, 18__. 1840s.

Rarity: URS-3
Proof $1,400

$2 • W-RI-1610-002-G090

Left: 2 / Portrait of John Quincy Adams / 2. *Center:* Steamship and distant ships. *Bottom center:* Phoenix. *Right:* 2 / Commerce with book and dividers / 2. *Engraver:* Toppan, Carpenter, Casilear & Co. *Comments:* H-RI-555-G20, Durand-2488. Jan. 1, 18__. 1850s.

Rarity: URS-3
VF $300

$3 • W-RI-1610-003-G100

Left: THREE 3 THREE vertically. *Center:* 3 / Hope resting against box containing 3 / 3. *Right:* 3 RHODE ISLAND 3 vertically. *Engraver:* Reed. *Comments:* H-RI-555-G22, Durand-2492. 18__. 1818–1820s.

Rarity: URS-3
Proof $300

$3 • W-RI-1610-003-G110

Left: 3 / Fine Arts. *Center:* Ceres and Indian reclining against globe surmounted by eagle. *Right:* 3 / Portrait of John Hancock. *Engraver:* Toppan, Carpenter, Casilear & Co. *Comments:* H-RI-555-G28, Durand-2493. Jan. 1, 18__. 1850s.

Rarity: URS-3
Proof $400

$5 • W-RI-1610-005-G120

Left: FIVE 5 FIVE vertically. *Center:* 5 / Woman holding 5 / 5. *Right:* V RHODE ISLAND V vertically. *Engraver:* Reed. *Comments:* H-RI-555-G32. 18__. 1818–1820s.

Rarity: URS-3
Proof $300

$5 • W-RI-1610-005-G130

SBG

Engraver: Toppan, Carpenter & Co. *Comments:* H-RI-555-G36, Durand-2495. January 1, 18__. 1840s.

Rarity: URS-3
VF $300; **Proof** $2,000

$5 • W-RI-1610-005-G140

Left: 5 / Portrait of Henry Clay / 5. *Center:* Train / Vulcan and Commerce / Ship. *Bottom center:* Phoenix. *Right:* 5 / Female portrait / V. *Engraver:* Unverified, but likely Toppan, Carpenter, Casilear & Co. *Comments:* H-RI-555-G38, Durand-2496. Jan. 1, 18__. 1850s.

Rarity: *None known*

$5 • W-RI-1610-005-G150

Left: 5 / Portrait of Henry Clay / 5. *Center:* Train / Vulcan and Commerce / Ship. *Bottom center:* Phoenix. *Right:* 5 / Female portrait / V. *Comments:* H-RI-555-G38a. 1850s.

Rarity: *None known*

$10 • **W-RI-1610-010-G160**

Left: 10 / Indian woman as Liberty. *Center:* Spread eagle with American flag. *Right:* 10 / Justice and eagle. *Engraver:* Toppan, Carpenter, Casilear & Co. *Comments:* H-RI-555-G46, Durand-2499. January 1, 18__. 1850s.

Rarity: URS-3

Proof $1,200

$10 • **W-RI-1610-010-G160a**

TD

Overprint: Red TEN. *Engraver:* Toppan, Carpenter, Casilear & Co. *Comments:* H-Unlisted, Durand-Unlisted. Similar to W-RI-1610-010-G160. January 1, 18__. 1850s.

Rarity: URS-3

VF $1,000

$20 • **W-RI-1610-020-G170**

Engraver: Unverified, but likely Rawdon, Wright & Hatch. *Comments:* H-RI-555-G54. No description available. 18__. 1830s–1840s.

Rarity: *None known*

$20 • **W-RI-1610-020-G175**

CJF

Engraver: Terry, Pelton & Co. *Comments:* H-Unlisted, Durand-Unlisted. 18__. 1840s.

Rarity: URS-2

VF $500

$20 • **W-RI-1610-020-G180**

CJF

Tint: Green panel outlining white TWENTY. *Engraver:* Toppan, Carpenter, Casilear & Co. / ABNCo. monogram. *Comments:* H-RI-555-G58, Durand-2501. January 1, 18__. 1860s.

Rarity: URS-2

$50 • **W-RI-1610-050-G190**

CJF

Tint: Green panel outlining white FIFTY. *Engraver:* Toppan, Carpenter, Casilear & Co. / ABNCo. monogram. *Comments:* H-RI-555-G64, Durand-2503. January 1, 18__. 1860s.

Rarity: URS-2

Uncut Sheets

$1-$1-$2-$5 • **W-RI-1610-001.001.002.005-US010**

Vignette(s): ($1) Woman holding up 1 bearing ONE / Portrait of George Washington / Eagle perched on cogwheels / Portrait of Thomas Jefferson, Ships / Eagle on crown / Portrait of William Henry Harrison. *($1)* Woman holding up 1 bearing ONE / Portrait of George Washington / Eagle perched on cogwheels / Portrait of Thomas Jefferson, Ships / Eagle on crown / Portrait of William Henry Harrison. *($2)* Woman with pen / Liberty / Shield / Spread eagle / Cornucopia of coins / Woman with pen. *($5)* Woman holding 5 bearing FIVE / Portrait of John Quincy Adams / Fame blowing trumpet with eagle / Portrait of James Monroe / Phoenix / Portrait of George Washington. *Engraver:* Toppan, Carpenter & Co. *Comments:* H-RI-555-G8, G8, G18, G36. January 1, 18__. 1840s.

Rarity: URS-3

Proof $1,600

Non-Valid Issues

$1 • **W-RI-1610-001-C010**

Engraver: Reed. *Comments:* H-RI-555-C2. Counterfeit of W-RI-1610-001-G010. 18__. 1818–1820s.

Rarity: URS-3

VF $125

$1 • **W-RI-1610-001-N010**

Center: Woman resting on barrel, Quadrant, sloop and brig. *Right:* Ceres. *Comments:* H-RI-555-N5, Durand-2483. Altered or spurious. 1820s.

Rarity: *None known*

$1 • **W-RI-1610-001-A010**

Left: ONE / Two Indians / 1. *Center:* 1 / Liberty, Justice, and Knowledge / 1. *Bottom center:* Cattle. *Right:* 1 / Portrait of George Washington / ONE. *Engraver:* Terry, Pelton & Co. *Comments:* H-RI-555-A5, Durand-2482. Altered from $2 Citizens Bank, Augusta, Maine, or from notes of other failed banks using the same plate. 18__. 1820s.

Rarity: *None known*

$2 • **W-RI-1610-002-C070**

Comments: H-Unlisted, Durand-210. Counterfeit of W-RI-1610-002-G070. 18__. 1818–1820s.

Rarity: URS-3

VF $110

$2 • W-RI-1610-002-S010   CC

Engraver: Rawdon, Wright & Hatch. *Comments:* H-RI-555-S5, Durand-2489. 18__. 1830s.

Rarity: URS-5

VF $100

$2 • W-RI-1610-002-N020

Left: Milkmaid. *Center:* Horse and cattle. *Right:* TWO / Portrait of child. *Comments:* H-RI-555-N10, Durand-2491. Altered or spurious. 1830s. Rarity: *None known*

$2 • W-RI-1610-002-A020

Left: TWO / Portrait of cherub / 2. *Center:* 2 / Ceres and Liberty / 2. *Right:* 2 / Female portrait / TWO. *Engraver:* Terry, Pelton & Co. *Comments:* H-RI-555-A10, Durand-2490. Altered from $2 Citizens Bank, Augusta, Maine, or from notes of other failed banks using the same plate. 18__. 1830s.

Rarity: *None known*

$3 • W-RI-1610-003-A030

Left: 3 / Allegorical woman with branch, Trident and THREE / THREE. *Center:* Portrait of cherub / Ceres and Justice flanking shield bearing anchor and surmounted by eagle / Portrait of cherub. *Right:* 3 / Ceres in field / 3. *Engraver:* Terry, Pelton & Co. *Comments:* H-RI-555-A15, Durand-2494. Altered from $3 Citizens Bank, Augusta, Maine, or from notes of other failed banks using the same plate. 18__. 1830s.

Rarity: *None known*

$5 • W-RI-1610-005-S020   CC

Overprint: Red FIVE. *Engraver:* Danforth, Bald & Co. *Comments:* H-RI-555-S10, Durand-2489. January 1, 18__. 1850s.

Rarity: URS-3

VF $150

$5 • W-RI-1610-005-N030

Left: 5 / Portrait of William Henry Harrison. *Center:* Ceres seated, Train and canal. *Right:* 5 / Allegorical figure. *Overprint:* Red FIVE. *Comments:* H-Unlisted, Durand-2498. Altered or spurious. 1850s.

Rarity: URS-3

F $90

$5 • W-RI-1610-005-AR010

Left: FIVE / Two Indians / 5. *Center:* 5 / Liberty, Justice, and Knowledge / 5. *Right:* 5 / Portrait of George Washington / FIVE. *Comments:* H-Unlisted, Durand-2497. Altered and raised from $1 Citizens Bank, Augusta, Maine. 1850s.

Rarity: URS-3

F $100

$5 • W-RI-1610-005-A040

Left: FIVE / Portrait of Benjamin Franklin / V. *Center:* 5 / Two allegorical women standing and one seated, Agricultural items and ship. *Bottom center:* Anchor and implements. *Right:* V / Portrait of Marquis de Lafayette / FIVE. *Engraver:* Terry, Pelton & Co. *Comments:* H-RI-555-A20. Altered from $5 Citizens Bank, Augusta, Maine, or from notes of other failed banks using the same plate. 18__. 1850s.

Rarity: *None known*

$10 • W-RI-1610-010-A050

Left: 10 / Portrait of George Washington held by cherub / 10. *Center:* X / Spread eagle and shield / X. *Bottom center:* Ship. *Right:* 10 / Indian and woman / 10. *Engraver:* Terry, Pelton & Co. *Comments:* H-RI-555-A25, Durand-2500. Altered from $10 Citizens Bank, Augusta, Maine, or from notes of other failed banks using the same plate. 18__. 1850s.

Rarity: *None known*

$20 • W-RI-1610-020-R010

Engraver: Unverified, but likely Rawdon, Wright & Hatch. *Comments:* H-RI-555-R5, Durand-2502. Raised from W-RI-1610-002-G070. 18__. 1830s–1840s.

Rarity: *None known*

Washington Bank
1800–1865
W-RI-1620

History: The Washington Bank was incorporated in June 1800 with $150,000 in authorized capital. It commenced business on August 22, located in one of the lower front rooms of the hotel owned by Paul Rhodes. A stone vault was built under the gravel hill on which the rear of the hotel stood.[91] This was the third bank established in Rhode Island.[92]

By 1862 circulation was at $63,292. During several of the early years of its existence, the business of the bank was very successful: the bills obtained a wide circulation, the loans of the bank were large for its capital and well-distributed, and the returns to the stockholders were ample. Some losses occurred when other banks were opened, increasing competition and lessening the profits.

The Washington Bank was succeeded by the Washington National Bank of Westerly, chartered on March 28, 1865.

Numismatic Commentary: This bank's first issues were engraved by Amos Doolittle, a copper-plate engraver best known for his four engravings of the Battle of Lexington. Doolittle's experiments with bank-note engraving were tepid at best. The bills he engraved for this bank were fairly crude, with each portrait of George Washington quite different in appearance. To be fair to Mr. Doolittle, all duplicated vignettes at that time had to be drawn by hand. The sideographic method of duplicating vignettes or portraits had not yet been invented. Consequently, each duplicate portrait on the sheet of bills he engraved appears a little different than the others.

The Washington Bank was another of the very few that issued fractional currency. The eight and sixteen cent notes were also denominated in shillings and pence. Reprints of genuine notes have been made.

VALID ISSUES

11¢/8d • **W-RI-1620-00.11/00.08-G010**
Center: 11 CENTS / EIGHT PENCE / Text. *Comments:* H-RI-560-G6, Durand-2504. Aug. 22, 1800.
Rarity: URS-1
VF $3,500

16¢/1s • **W-RI-1620-00.16/00.01-G020**
Comments: H-RI-560-G10, Durand-2505. No description available. Aug. 22, 1800.
Rarity: URS-1
VF $3,500

$1 • **W-RI-1620-001-G030**
Left: RHODE ISLAND vertically. *Center:* Portrait of George Washington. *Engraver:* Amos Doolittle. *Comments:* H-RI-560-G14, Durand-2506. 1800s.
Rarity: URS-6
VF $300

$1 • **W-RI-1620-001-G040**
Center: Portrait of George Washington, Guns and cannons. *Right:* RHODE ISLAND vertically. *Engraver:* P. Maverick. *Comments:* H-RI-560-G16, Durand-2507. 18__. 1820s.
Rarity: URS-3
Proof $1,000

$1 • **W-RI-1620-001-G050**
Left: 1 / ONE vertically / 1. *Center:* 1 / Sailboat / Portrait of George Washington / Train / 1. *Bottom center:* Steamboat. *Right:* ONE / Woman in niche. *Engraver:* Rawdon, Wright & Hatch. *Comments:* H-RI-560-G18, Durand-2508. 18__. 1830s.
Rarity: URS-3
VF $400

$1 • **W-RI-1620-001-G060**
Left: ONE vertically. *Center:* 1 / Farming scene / Portrait of George Washington / Industrial scene / 1. *Bottom center:* Arm and hammer. *Right:* Medallion head / ONE. *Engraver:* Unverified, but likely Rawdon, Wright & Hatch. *Comments:* H-RI-560-G20, Durand-2509. 18__. 1830s–1840s.
Rarity: *None known*

$1 • **W-RI-1620-001-G060a**
Engraver: Rawdon, Wright, Hatch & Edson. *Comments:* H-RI-560-G20a. Similar to W-RI-1620-001-G060 but with different engraver imprint. 18__. 1840s–1860s.
Rarity: URS-3
VF $750

$1 • **W-RI-1620-001-G060b**

CC

Engraver: Rawdon, Wright, Hatch & Edson. *Comments:* H-RI-560-G20b. Similar to W-RI-1620-001-G060 but with different date and engraver imprint. March 1st, 185_. 1850s.
Rarity: URS-3
VF $600

$2 • **W-RI-1620-002-G070**
Center: Portrait of George Washington, Guns and cannons. *Right:* RHODE ISLAND vertically. *Engraver:* P. Maverick. *Comments:* H-RI-560-G26, Durand-2510. 18__. 1820s.
Rarity: URS-3
Proof $1,000

$2 • **W-RI-1620-002-G080**
Left: TWO / Benjamin Franklin seated / TWO. *Center:* Sailboat / Portrait of George Washington / Train. *Bottom center:* Woman with flower garlands. *Right:* Statue of George Washington / TWO. *Engraver:* Rawdon, Wright & Hatch. *Comments:* H-RI-560-G28, Durand-2511. 18__. 1830s.
Rarity: URS-3
Proof $400

$2 • **W-RI-1620-002-G090**
Left: TWO vertically. *Center:* 2 / Dock scene, Portrait of George Washington, Train / 2. *Bottom center:* Arm and hammer. *Right:* Medallion head / TWO. *Engraver:* Rawdon, Wright, & Hatch. *Comments:* H-RI-560-G30, Durand-2512. 18__. 1830s–1840s.
Rarity: *None known*

$2 • **W-RI-1620-002-G090a**

CJF

Engraver: Rawdon, Wright, Hatch & Edson. *Comments:* H-RI-560-G30a. Similar to W-RI-1620-002-G090 but with different engraver imprint. 18__. 1840s–1860s.
Rarity: URS-1
VG $1,000

$2 • **W-RI-1620-002-G090b**
Engraver: Rawdon, Wright, Hatch & Edson. *Comments:* H-RI-560-G30b. Similar to W-RI-1620-002-G090 but with different date and engraver imprint. March 1, 185_. 1850s.
Rarity: *None known*

$3 • W-RI-1620-003-G100

Left: RHODE ISLAND vertically. *Center:* Portrait of George Washington. *Comments:* H-Unlisted, Durand-2514. 18__. 1800s.

Rarity: URS-6

$3 • W-RI-1620-003-G110

Left: Dies. *Center:* 3. *Right:* 3 / THREE DOLLARS / Portrait of George Washington. *Engraver:* Amos Doolittle. *Comments:* H-RI-560-G34, Durand-2514. 18__. 1800s.

Rarity: URS-6
VF $400

$3 • W-RI-1620-003-G120

Left: THREE vertically. *Center:* 3 on die / Portrait of George Washington, Guns and cannons / 3 on die. *Right:* RHODE ISLAND vertically. *Engraver:* P. Maverick. *Comments:* H-RI-560-G36, Durand-2515. 18__. 1820s.

Rarity: URS-3
Proof $300

$3 • W-RI-1620-003-G130

Left: THREE / Allegorical figure with eagle / 3. *Center:* Sailboat / Portrait of George Washington / Train. *Bottom center:* Eagle. *Right:* THREE / Ceres / THREE. *Engraver:* Rawdon, Wright & Hatch. *Comments:* H-RI-560-G38, Durand-2516. 18__. 1830s–1840s.

Rarity: URS-3
Proof $400

$3 • W-RI-1620-003-G130a

Engraver: Rawdon, Wright, Hatch & Edson. *Comments:* H-RI-560-G38a. Similar to W-RI-1620-003-G130 but with different engraver imprint. 18__. 1840s–1860s.

Rarity: *None known*

How to Read the Whitman Numbering System

$1 • W-RI-010-001-G010a

Denomination: Value of the note shown.

W: Whitman number. This number is a sortable code unique to each bank and note.

RI: Abbreviation for the state under study.

010: Numerical designation specific to each bank.

001: The denomination in dollars.

G010a: G indicates a good or valid note. Other categories are indicated thus: C (counterfeit); R (raised); S (spurious); N (not-attributed); A (altered). Numbers are assigned starting with 010, 020, et seq. Terminal letters following the number indicate variations of a note: a series of different colored overprints, tints, payees, etc., all on the same design of note. For more information, see the "How to Use This Book" section at the front of the volume, page xiv.

$5 • W-RI-1620-005-G140

QDB

Engraver: Amos Doolittle. *Comments:* H-RI-560-G42, Durand-2518. 18__. 1800s.

Rarity: URS-6
VF $300

$5 • W-RI-1620-005-G150

QDB

Engraver: PSSP. *Comments:* H-RI-560-G44, Durand-2519. 18__. 1808–1810s.

Rarity: URS-3
VF $200

$5 • W-RI-1620-005-G160

Left: Panel bearing FIVE vertically. *Center:* 5 / Portrait of George Washington, Military items / 5. *Right:* Panel bearing RHODE ISLAND vertically. *Engraver:* P. Maverick. *Comments:* H-RI-560-G46. 18__. 1820s.

Rarity: URS-3
Proof $300

$5 • W-RI-1620-005-G170

Left: FIVE vertically. *Center:* 5 / Sailboat / Portrait of George Washington / Train / 5. *Bottom center:* Eagle. *Right:* FIVE / Justice standing by eagle on shield / V. *Engraver:* Rawdon, Wright & Hatch. *Comments:* H-RI-560-G48. 18__. 1830s–1840s.

Rarity: URS-3
Proof $400

$5 • W-RI-1620-005-G170a

Engraver: Rawdon, Wright, Hatch & Edson. *Comments:* H-RI-560-G48a. Similar to W-RI-1620-005-G170 but with different engraver imprint. 18__. 1840s–1850s.

Rarity: *None known*

$5 • W-RI-1620-005-G170b

CJF

Engraver: American Bank Note Co. **Comments:** H-Unlisted. Similar to W-RI-1620-005-G170 but with different date and engraver imprint. May 1st, 1864. 1860s.
Rarity: URS-2

$5 • W-RI-1620-005-G180

Center: Portrait of George Washington, Guns and cannons. **Right:** RHODE ISLAND vertically. **Comments:** H-Unlisted, Durand-2520. 18__. 1820s.
Rarity: URS-5

$5 • W-RI-1620-005-G190

Left: FIVE vertically. **Center:** Sailboat / Portrait of George Washington / Train. **Right:** FIVE / Justice standing with eagle and shield / V. **Comments:** H-Unlisted, Durand-2521. 1820s.
Rarity: URS-3

$10 • W-RI-1620-010-G200

QDB

Engraver: Amos Doolittle. **Comments:** H-RI-560-G52, Durand-2525. 18__. 1800s.
Rarity: URS-5
VF $400

$10 • W-RI-1620-010-G210

Left: Anchor. **Center:** Text. **Engraver:** PSSP. **Comments:** H-RI-560-G54, Durand-2526. 18__. 1808–1810s.
Rarity: URS-3
VF $200

$10 • W-RI-1620-010-G220

Center: Portrait of George Washington, Guns and cannons. **Right:** RHODE ISLAND vertically. **Engraver:** P. Maverick. **Comments:** H-RI-560-G56, Durand-2527. 18__. 1820s.
Rarity: URS-3
Proof $300

$10 • W-RI-1620-010-G230

Left: X / Liberty with shield of Hope / 10. **Center:** 10 / Sailboat, Portrait of George Washington, Train / 10. **Bottom center:** Cherub riding on deer. **Right:** Allegorical figure leaning on pillar / X. **Engraver:** Rawdon, Wright & Hatch. **Comments:** H-RI-560-G58, Durand-2528. 18__. 1830s–1840s.
Rarity: URS-3
Proof $400

$10 • W-RI-1620-010-G230a

Engraver: Rawdon, Wright, Hatch & Edson. **Comments:** H-RI-560-G58a. Similar to W-RI-1620-010-G230 but with different engraver imprint. 18__. 1840s–1850s.
Rarity: *None known*

$10 • W-RI-1620-010-G230b

QDB

Engraver: American Bank Note Co. **Comments:** H-Unlisted. Similar to W-RI-1620-010-G230 but with different date and engraver imprint. May 1st, 1864. 1860s.
Rarity: URS-2
VF $1,250

$20 • W-RI-1620-020-G240

Left: TWENTY vertically. **Center:** Sailboat / Portrait of George Washington / Train. **Bottom center:** Eagle on rock. **Right:** 20 / Allegorical figure / 20. **Engraver:** Rawdon, Wright & Hatch. **Comments:** H-RI-560-G62, Durand-2531. 18__. 1830s–1860s.
Rarity: URS-3
Proof $300

$25 • W-RI-1620-025-G250

Left: RHODE ISLAND vertically. **Center:** 25 on die / Portrait of George Washington / 25. **Right:** 25 on die / Twenty-five Ds vertically. **Engraver:** Amos Doolittle. **Comments:** H-RI-560-G66, Durand-2532. 18__. 1800s.
Rarity: URS-3
VF $500

$50 • W-RI-1620-050-G260

Left: FIFTY vertically. **Center:** Sailboat / Portrait of George Washington / Train. **Bottom center:** Ceres seated. **Right:** 50 / Portrait of Benjamin Franklin / 50. **Engraver:** Rawdon, Wright & Hatch. **Comments:** H-RI-560-G70, Durand-2533. 18__. 1830s–1860s.
Rarity: URS-3
Proof $400

$100 • W-RI-1620-100-G270

Left: ONE HUNDRED vertically. **Center:** Sailboat / Portrait of George Washington / Train. **Bottom center:** Ship under full sail. **Right:** 100 / Justice / 100. **Engraver:** Rawdon, Wright & Hatch. **Comments:** H-RI-560-G74, Durand-2534. 18__. 1830s–1860s.
Rarity: URS-3
Proof $400

Uncut Sheets

$1-$1-$1-$1 • W-RI-1620-001.001.001.001-US010

Vignette(s): *($1)* Portrait of George Washington. *($1)* Portrait of George Washington. *($1)* Portrait of George Washington. *($1)* Portrait of George Washington. *Engraver:* Amos Doolittle. *Comments:* H-RI-560-G14, G14, G14, G14. Reprint. 1800s.
Rarity: URS-4
VF $500; **Unc-Rem** $1,000

$1-$1-$1-$2 • W-RI-1620-001.001.001.002-US020

Vignette(s): *($1)* Sailboat / Portrait of George Washington / Train / Steamboat / Woman in niche. *($1)* Sailboat / Portrait of George Washington / Train / Steamboat / Woman in niche. *($1)* Sailboat / Portrait of George Washington / Train / Steamboat / Woman in niche. *($2)* Benjamin Franklin seated / Sailboat / Portrait of George Washington / Train / Woman with flower garlands / Statue of George Washington. *Engraver:* Rawdon, Wright & Hatch. *Comments:* H-RI-560-G18, G18, G18, G28. 18__. 1830s.
Rarity: URS-3
Proof $2,000

$1-$1-$1-$5 • W-RI-1620-001.001.001.005-US030

Vignette(s): *($1)* Portrait of George Washington, Guns and cannons. *($1)* Portrait of George Washington, Guns and cannons. *($1)* Portrait of George Washington, Guns and cannons. *($5)* Portrait of George Washington, Guns and cannons. *Engraver:* P. Maverick. *Comments:* H-RI-560-G16, G16, G16, G46. 18__. 1820s.
Rarity: URS-3
Proof $2,000

$3-$3-$3-$25 • W-RI-1620-003.003.003.025-US040

Vignette(s): *($3)* Portrait of George Washington. *($3)* Portrait of George Washington. *($3)* Portrait of George Washington. *($25)* Portrait of George Washington. *Engraver:* Amos Doolittle. *Comments:* H-RI-560-G34, G34, G34, G66. Reprint. 18__. 1800s.
Rarity: URS-6
VF $500; **Unc-Rem** $1,000

$10-$3-$2-$1 • W-RI-1620-010.003.002.001-US050

Vignette(s): *($10)* Portrait of George Washington, Guns and cannons. *($3)* Portrait of George Washington, Guns and cannons. *($2)* Portrait of George Washington, Guns and cannons. *($1)* Portrait of George Washington, Guns and cannons. *Engraver:* P. Maverick. *Comments:* H-RI-560-G56, G36, G26, G16. 18__. 1820s.
Rarity: URS-3
Proof $2,000

$10-$5-$5-$5 • W-RI-1620-010.005.005.005-US060

Vignette(s): *($10)* Portrait of George Washington. *($5)* Portrait of George Washington. *($5)* Portrait of George Washington. *($5)* Portrait of George Washington. *Engraver:* Amos Doolittle. *Comments:* H-RI-560-G52, G42, G42, G42. Reprint. 18__. 1800s.
Rarity: URS-6
VF $500; **Unc-Rem** $1,000

$20-$20-$50-$100 •
W-RI-1620-020.020.050.100-US070

Vignette(s): *($20)* Sailboat / Portrait of George Washington / Train / Eagle on rock / Allegorical figure. *($20)* Sailboat / Portrait of George Washington / Train / Eagle on rock / Allegorical figure. *($50)* Sailboat / Portrait of George Washington / Train / Ceres seated / Portrait of Benjamin Franklin. *($100)* Sailboat / Portrait of George Washington / Train / Ship under full sail / Justice. *Engraver:* Rawdon, Wright & Hatch. *Comments:* H-RI-560-G62, G62, G70, G74. 18__. 1830s–1860s.
Rarity: URS-3
Proof $2,500

Non-Valid Issues

$2 • W-RI-1620-002-C070

Engraver: P. Maverick. *Comments:* H-RI-560-C26, Durand-2513. Counterfeit of W-RI-1620-002-G070. 18__. 1820s.
Rarity: URS-3
VF $200

$3 • W-RI-1620-003-C110   NJW

Engraver: Amos Doolittle. *Comments:* H-RI-560-C34. Counterfeit of W-RI-1620-003-G110. 18__. 1800s.
Rarity: URS-3
VF $250

$3 • W-RI-1620-003-C120   NJW

Engraver: P. Maverick. *Comments:* H-RI-560-C36, Durand-2517. Counterfeit of W-RI-1620-003-G120. 18__. 1820s–1830s.
Rarity: URS-5
VF $250

$5 • W-RI-1620-005-C170

Engraver: Rawdon, Wright & Hatch. *Comments:* H-RI-560-C48. Counterfeit of W-RI-1620-005-G170. 18__. 1840s
Rarity: *None known*

$5 • W-RI-1620-005-C180

Comments: H-Unlisted, Durand-2522. Counterfeit of W-RI-1620-005-G180. 18__. 1820s.
Rarity: URS-5
VF $100

$5 • W-RI-1620-005-N010

Center: Women flanking woman seated in 5. *Comments:* H-RI-560-N10, Durand-2524. Altered or spurious. 1820s.

Rarity: *None known*

$5 • W-RI-1620-005-A010

Left: FIVE / Ship. *Center:* 5 / Steamboat and other vessels / 5. *Right:* Diagonal FIVE / Portrait of George Washington. *Engraver:* Rawdon, Wright, Hatch & Edson. *Comments:* H-RI-560-A4, Durand-2523. Altered from $5 Washington Bank, Washington, D.C. 185_. 1850s. **Rarity:** *None known*

$10 • W-RI-1620-010-A020

Left: 10 / Portrait of George Washington held by cherub / 10. *Center:* X / Spread eagle and shield / X. *Bottom center:* Ship. *Right:* 10 / Indian and woman / 10. *Engraver:* Terry, Pelton & Co. *Comments:* H-RI-560-A5, Durand-2529. Altered from $10 Citizens Bank, Augusta, Maine, or from notes of other failed banks using the same plate. 18__. 1830s–1840s.

Rarity: *None known*

$10 • W-RI-1620-010-A030

Left: TEN / George Washington and horse / TEN. *Center:* 10 / Indian in canoe / 10. *Right:* TEN / Bust of George Washington / TEN. *Comments:* H-Unlisted, Durand-2530. Altered from $1 Washington Bank, Boston, Massachusetts. 1830s–1840s.

Rarity: URS-3

WICKFORD, RHODE ISLAND

Wickford, a village of North Kingstown, was named after Wickford in Essex, England. It was settled in 1637 when Roger Williams established a trading post on the land. The area was inhabited by the Narragansett tribe. Later, Richard Smith purchased the post in 1651. Wickford bloomed as a trading port and center for shipbuilding after King Philip's War. During the Revolutionary War, British troops attempted to raid Wickford, but they were rebuffed by the Wickford Gun, a cannon which had been commissioned by the General Assembly for self-defense.

The Washington Academy was founded in Wickford in 1800. By the late 1830s, the Providence and Stonington Railroad had bypassed the town, causing a decline in industry and commerce. Providence competed for shipping and trade, and the town's period of growth ended.

See also North Kingstown, Rhode Island.

Farmers Bank
1855–1858
W-RI-1630

History: The Farmers Bank was incorporated as the Wickford Bank, W-RI-1660, in 1854. The title was changed to the Farmers Bank in 1855. Capital was $30,000 in 1856.

This bank fell into the hands of out-of-state owners, and its capital was made up of mostly fraudulent notes. It also speculated heavily by sending vast amounts of notes out of state, which made them difficult to redeem and gave the bank extended use of the hard-currency funds.[93]

By 1857 the bank was in extreme difficulty. The *Banker's Magazine* reported this in 1858:

> The Farmers' Bank at Wickford suspended payment the last week in August. The 3d of September was assigned for the hearing of the application for an injunction against the bank, before Judge Shearman. In the morning a motion for a postponement was made in behalf of the bank. This the court denied, unless supported by evidence. In the afternoon the President and Cashier declined to be examined, and the injunction was made perpetual. Stephen T. Olney was appointed Receiver. The apprehension is, that the affairs of the bank will turn out badly. One of the reasons given by the commissioners in their petition was, that they had reason to believe that the circulation of the bank exceeded its capital. The president and cashier refused to be examined, and it was then believed that "the circulation of the bank exceeded its capital." One-third of the circulation was lost to the holders. In October, 1858, no payment of liabilities had been made.[94]

Numismatic Commentary: Today's collector can easily obtain an example of a note from the Farmers Bank. Some of the higher denominations lack an engraver's imprint.

Remaining in the American Bank Note Co. archives as of 2003 was a $1-$1-$2-$3 face plate.

VALID ISSUES

$1 • W-RI-1630-001-G010

TD

Overprint: Red ONE. *Engraver:* Toppan, Carpenter & Co. *Comments:* H-RI-565-G2a, Durand-2535. August 6th, 1855.

Rarity: URS-9
VG $45; **F** $100

$2 • W-RI-1630-002-G020

CC

Overprint: Red 2 / 2. *Engraver:* Toppan, Carpenter & Co. *Comments:* H-RI-565-G4a, Durand-2536. August 6th, 1855.

Rarity: URS-9
VG $65; **VF** $200

$3 • W-RI-1630-003-G030   TD

Overprint: Red 3 / 3. *Engraver:* Toppan, Carpenter & Co. *Comments:* H-RI-565-G6a, Durand-2537. August 6th, 1855.
Rarity: URS-8
VF $150

$5 • W-RI-1630-005-G040   CC

Overprint: Red V / V. *Engraver:* Toppan, Carpenter & Co. *Comments:* H-RI-565-G8a, Durand-2538. August 6th, 1855.
Rarity: URS-9
VF $150

$10 • W-RI-1630-010-G050   CC

Overprint: Red X / X. *Engraver:* Toppan, Carpenter & Co. *Comments:* H-RI-565-G10a, Durand-2539. 18__. 1855.
Rarity: URS-8
VF $150

$20 • W-RI-1630-020-G060   CC

Overprint: Red 2 / 0. *Comments:* H-RI-565-G12a, Durand-2540. 18__. 1855.
Rarity: URS-6
VF $300

Narragansett Bank
1805–1865
W-RI-1640

History: The Narragansett Bank was chartered and incorporated in 1805 with $60,000 in authorized capital. The same had dropped to $50,000 by 1850. The bank had a circulation of $27,647 in 1849, which was reduced to $17,704 by 1857 and increased to $32,354 in 1863. Specie amounted to $2,076.75 in 1857.

In 1865 the bank's charter was surrendered, and its capital was combined with that of the North Kingston Bank, W-RI-1650. The combination was succeeded by the Wickford National Bank, chartered October 17, 1865.[95]

See also listing under North Kingstown, W-RI-590.

Numismatic Commentary: Genuine notes are hard to locate, but non-valid issues are available in the marketplace. Some very early (1807 and 1808) counterfeit issues appear from time to time.

VALID ISSUES

$1 • W-RI-1640-001-G010
Left: ONE vertically. *Center:* Indian smoking pipe. *Bottom center:* Shield with anchor. *Comments:* H-RI-570-G2, Durand-2541. 18__. 1800s.
Rarity: *None known*

$1 • W-RI-1640-001-G020   SBG

Engraver: Rawdon, Wright & Hatch. *Comments:* H-RI-570-G6, Durand-2542. 18__. 1830s.
Rarity: URS-3
Proof $2,300
Selected auction price: Stack's Bowers Galleries, March 2013, Proof $2,299

$1 • W-RI-1640-001-G030
Left: ONE vertically / 1. *Center:* Farmer plowing / 1. *Right:* 1 / Indian standing. *Engraver:* Unverified, but likely Boston Bank Note Co. *Comments:* H-RI-570-G8, Durand-2543. 18__. 1830s–1860s.
Rarity: *None known*

$2 • W-RI-1640-002-G040
Comments: H-Unlisted, Durand-2547. First issue. 1800s.
Rarity: URS-3
VF $400

$2 • W-RI-1640-002-G050
Left: TWO vertically. *Center:* Reclining Indian. *Bottom center:* Colt. *Right:* 2 vertically. *Comments:* H-RI-570-G12. 18__. 1800s.
Rarity: *None known*

$2 • W-RI-1640-002-G060

Left: TWO / Indian man seated / TWO. *Center:* 2 / Woman seated with rake and grain, Tower / 2. *Bottom center:* Boat. *Right:* TWO / Woman standing with grain / TWO. *Engraver:* Rawdon, Wright & Hatch. *Comments:* H-RI-570-G16, Durand-2548. 18__. 1830s.

Rarity: URS-3

F $500

$2 • W-RI-1640-002-G070

Left: 2. *Center:* Cherub, Anchor on shield, Allegorical woman, Ships and train / 2. *Right:* 2 / Indian standing with bow and arrows. *Engraver:* Unverified, but likely Boston Bank Note Co. *Comments:* H-RI-570-G18, Durand-2549. 18__. 1830s–1860s.

Rarity: *None known*

$3 • W-RI-1640-003-G080

TD

Engraver: Rawdon, Wright & Hatch. *Comments:* H-RI-570-G24, Durand-2552. Proof specimen of a $3 bill as found on the stolen sheets. 18__. 1830s.

Rarity: URS-3

VF $600

$3 • W-RI-1640-003-G090

Left: Medallion head / 3. *Center:* Spread eagle on shield / 3. *Right:* THREE / Indian with bow. *Engraver:* Unverified, but likely Boston Bank Note Co. *Comments:* H-RI-570-G26, Durand-2553. 18__. 1830s–1860s.

Rarity: *None known*

$5 • W-RI-1640-005-G100

Left: FIVE vertically. *Center:* Minerva, V on shield, Indian. *Right:* FIVE vertically. *Engraver:* Unverified, but likely Rawdon, Wright & Hatch. *Comments:* H-RI-570-G30, Durand-2555. 18__. 1830s–1860s.

Rarity: *None known*

$10 • W-RI-1640-010-G110

Left: 10 on lathework strip. *Center:* 10 / Agriculture with eagle / X. *Bottom center:* Indian with headdress. *Right:* TEN / Woman standing. *Engraver:* Unverified, but likely Rawdon, Wright & Hatch. *Comments:* H-RI-570-G36, Durand-2560. 18__. 1830s–1860s.

Rarity: URS-3

Proof $500

$20 • W-RI-1640-020-G120

Left: TWENTY vertically. *Center:* 20 / Agriculture and Commerce / 20. *Right:* XX / Train / XX / 20. *Engraver:* Unverified, but likely Rawdon, Wright & Hatch. *Comments:* H-RI-570-G40, Durand-2562. 18__. 1830s–1860s.

Rarity: *None known*

$50 • W-RI-1640-050-G130

Left: FIFTY vertically. *Center:* Griffin and strongbox, Ceres receiving cornucopia from Mercury. *Right:* 50 / Steamboat / 50. *Engraver:* Unverified, but likely Rawdon, Wright & Hatch. *Comments:* H-RI-570-G44, Durand-2563. 18__. 1830s–1860s.

Rarity: *None known*

Non-Valid Issues

$1 • W-RI-1640-001-C010

Comments: H-RI-570-C2, Durand-2544. Counterfeit of W-RI-1640-001-G010. 18__. 1800s.

Rarity: URS-3

VF $400

$1 • W-RI-1640-001-N010

Center: Eagle and ship. *Comments:* H-RI-570-N5, Durand-2545. Altered or spurious. 1800s.

Rarity: *None known*

$1 • W-RI-1640-001-N020

Center: Three women, River and farm scene. *Comments:* H-RI-570-N10, Durand-2546. Altered or spurious. 1800s.

Rarity: *None known*

$2 • W-RI-1640-002-C040

Comments: H-Unlisted, Durand-2550. Counterfeit of W-RI-1640-002-G040. 1800s.

Rarity: *None known*

$2 • W-RI-1640-002-C050

MR

Comments: H-RI-570-C12. Counterfeit of W-RI-1640-002-G050. 18__. 1800s.

Rarity: URS-4

VF $600

$2 • W-RI-1640-002-A010

Left: 2 / Blacksmith by forge. *Center:* Farmer feeding swine, Two horses. *Right:* 2 / Farmer carrying corn stalks. *Overprint:* Red TWO. *Engraver:* Toppan, Carpenter & Co. *Comments:* H-RI-570-A3, Durand-2551. Altered from W-RI-1630-002-G020. Aug. 6, 1855.

Rarity: *None known*

$3 • W-RI-1640-003-A020

Left: 3 / Wheelwrights at work. *Center:* Flock of sheep, Rider watering horse at trough. *Right:* 3 / Girl feeding chickens. *Overprint:* Red 3 / 3. *Engraver:* Toppan, Carpenter & Co. *Comments:* H-RI-570-A5, Durand-2554. Altered from W-RI-1630-003-G030. Aug. 6, 1855.

Rarity: *None known*

$5 • W-RI-1640-005-A030

Left: 5 / V on FIVE / 5. *Center:* Three women floating in clouds. *Right:* FIVE / Portrait of Jenny Lind / FIVE. *Tint:* Orange dies outlining white 5s. *Engraver:* Danforth, Wright & Co. *Comments:* H-RI-570-A10, Durand-2559. Altered from $5 Arlington Bank, Washington, D.C. 18__. 1850s.

Rarity: *None known*

$5 • W-RI-1640-005-A040   SI

Tint: Orange dies outlining white 5s. *Engraver:* Danforth, Wright & Co. *Comments:* H-Unlisted, Durand-Unlisted. Altered from $5 Arlington Bank, Washington, D.C. 185_. 1850s.

Rarity: URS-3
F $150; **VF** $250

$5 • W-RI-1640-005-A050

Left: 5 / Reaper with dog / 5. *Center:* 5 / Cherub reclining with caduceus, Dog, strongbox / 5. *Bottom center:* State arms. *Right:* 5 / Milkmaid / 5. *Engraver:* Draper, Toppan, Longacre & Co. *Comments:* H-RI-570-A15, Durand-2557. Altered from $5 Calhoun County Bank, Marshall, Michigan. 18__. 1850s.

Rarity: *None known*

$5 • W-RI-1640-005-A060

Left: 5 / Farm family. *Center:* Portrait of Benjamin Franklin. *Right:* 5 / Woodsman and cattle. *Overprint:* Red V / V. *Engraver:* Toppan, Carpenter & Co. *Comments:* H-RI-570-A20, Durand-2556. Altered from W-RI-1630-005-G040. Aug. 6, 1855.

Rarity: *None known*

$5 • W-RI-1640-005-A070

Center: Woman standing with sheaf, Man kneeling binding sheaf. *Engraver:* W.L. Ormsby. *Comments:* H-RI-570-A25, Durand-2558. 1850s.

Rarity: *None known*

$10 • W-RI-1640-010-A080   ANS

Overprint: Red X / X. *Engraver:* Toppan, Carpenter & Co. *Comments:* H-RI-570-A30, Durand-2561. Altered from W-RI-1630-010-G050. 18__. 1850s.

Rarity: URS-5
VG $95; **VF** $150

North Kingston Bank
1819–1865
W-RI-1650

History: The North Kingston Bank was chartered in 1818 as the South Kingston Bank, W-RI-1430, at a location called Little Rest, the present location of the South Kingstown village of Kingston. After holding a few meetings and being unable to induce investors to purchase its stock for the raising of capital, planners abandoned the location. The charter was amended in 1819, the name was changed to the North Kingston Bank, and the location was moved to the North Kingstown village of Wickford. The North Kingston Bank had $75,000 in capital in 1849 along with $42,605 of bills in circulation. Specie totaled $2,043.22 in 1857.

The founding president was Daniel Champlin, with Pardon T. Hammond as cashier. Later, Lieutenant Governor John J. Reynolds, born in North Kingstown on December 7, 1812, became a director at the age of 24. He then became president in 1851 upon the death of his father. He remained in office until the bank merged its interests into a National bank in 1865.

The assets of the North Kingston Bank were combined with the Narragansett Bank, W-RI-1640, to form the Wickford National Bank, chartered on October 17, 1865.

See also listing under North Kingstown, W-RI-600.

VALID ISSUES

$1 • W-RI-1650-001-G010   BH

Engraver: Reed. *Comments:* H-RI-575-G2, Durand-2564. 18__. 1819–1820s.

Rarity: URS-3
Proof $700

$1 • W-RI-1650-001-G020   CJF

Engraver: Rawdon, Wright & Hatch. *Comments:* H-RI-575-G8, Durand-2564. 18__. 1850s.

Rarity: URS-1
VF $1,200

$1 • W-RI-1650-001-G030

QDB

Overprint: Red 1. *Engraver:* Toppan, Carpenter, Casilear & Co. *Comments:* H-RI-575-G10a, Durand-2565. 18__. 1850s.
Rarity: URS-3
Proof $1,000

$2 • W-RI-1650-002-G040

SBG

Engraver: Reed. *Comments:* H-RI-575-G14. 18__. 1819–1820s.
Rarity: URS-3
Proof $750

$2 • W-RI-1650-002-G050

Left: TWO / Sailing vessels / TWO. *Center:* Two allegorical figures, Wharf scene. *Bottom center:* Arm and hammer. *Right:* TWO / Hope seated / TWO. *Comments:* H-RI-575-G18, Durand-2566. 18__. 1850s.
Rarity: *None known*

$2 • W-RI-1650-002-G060

Left: 2 / Liberty and Ceres flanking shield of Hope / 2. *Right:* 2 / Portrait of George Washington / 2. *Overprint:* Red 2. *Engraver:* Toppan, Carpenter, Casilear & Co. *Comments:* H-RI-575-G20a, Durand-2567. 18__. 1850s.
Rarity: URS-3
Proof $1,000

$3 • W-RI-1650-003-G070

SBG

Engraver: Reed. *Comments:* H-RI-575-G24. 18__. 1819–1820s.
Rarity: URS-3
Proof $1,700
Selected auction price: Stack's Bowers Galleries, March 2013, Proof $1,694

$3 • W-RI-1650-003-G080

Left: THREE / Sailing vessels and men in rowboats / 3. *Center:* 3 / Venus and Neptune in shell drawn by sea horses / 3. *Bottom center:* Schooner. *Right:* THREE / Liberty and eagle / Portrait of George Washington / 3. *Comments:* H-RI-575-G28, Durand-2570. 18__. 1850s.
Rarity: *None known*

$3 • W-RI-1650-003-G090

Left: 3 / 3. *Center:* Gold coin / Liberty enthroned, Eagle, Sheaf and shield / Female portrait. *Right:* 3 / Portrait of Benjamin Franklin / 3. *Overprint:* Red 3. *Engraver:* Toppan, Carpenter, Casilear & Co. *Comments:* H-RI-575-G30a, Durand-2571. 18__. 1850s.
Rarity: *None known*

$5 • W-RI-1650-005-G100

Left: FIVE 5 FIVE vertically. *Center:* 5 / Allegorical woman seated on bale holding 5 / 5. *Bottom center:* Medallion head. *Right:* 5 RHODE ISLAND 5 vertically. *Engraver:* Reed. *Comments:* H-RI-575-G34, Durand-2574. 18__. 1819–1820s.
Rarity: URS-3
Proof $1,500

$5 • W-RI-1650-005-G110

Left: 5 / Train / 5. *Center:* Venus and Neptune in shell drawn by sea horses, Amphitrite and Neptune. *Right:* 5 / Cattle. *Engraver:* Rawdon, Wright, Hatch & Co. *Comments:* H-RI-575-G38, Durand-2575. 18__. 1830s–1850s.
Rarity: *None known*

$10 • W-RI-1650-010-G115

Engraver: Reed. *Comments:* H-RI-575-G40, Durand-2578. No description available. 18__. 1819–1820s.
Rarity: *None known*

$10 • W-RI-1650-010-G120

Left: 10 / Justice / 10. *Center:* X / Liberty seated by shield bearing eagle / 10. *Right:* TEN / Ten coins / TEN. *Engraver:* Rawdon, Wright, Hatch & Co. *Comments:* H-RI-575-G44, Durand-2578. 18__. 1830s–1850s.
Rarity: URS-3
Proof $1,500

$20 • W-RI-1650-020-G130

SBG

Engraver: Rawdon, Wright, Hatch & Co. *Comments:* H-Unlisted. 18__. 1830s–1850s.
Rarity: URS-1
Proof $4,500

$50 • W-RI-1650-050-G140

Left: 50 / Pelican and chicks / 50. *Center:* Allegorical woman, Indian and sailor flanking shield surmounted by eagle, Allegorical woman. *Right:* 50 / Pelican and chicks / 50. *Engraver:* Rawdon, Wright, Hatch & Co. *Comments:* H-RI-575-G50, Durand-2581. 18__. 1830s–1850s.
Rarity: *None known*

$100 • W-RI-1650-100-G150

Left: 100 / Liberty, eagle, and portrait of George Washington / 100. *Center:* 100 / Portrait of George Washington / 100. *Bottom center:* Eagle. *Right:* 100 / Sailing vessels / 100. *Engraver:* Rawdon, Wright, Hatch & Co. *Comments:* H-RI-575-G54, Durand-2582. 18__. 1830s–1850s.

Rarity: *None known*

NON-VALID ISSUES

$2 • W-RI-1650-002-A010

Left: 2 / Blacksmith standing by forge. *Center:* Farmer feeding swine, Two horses. *Right:* 2 / Farmer carrying corn stalks. *Overprint:* Red TWO. *Engraver:* Toppan, Carpenter & Co. *Comments:* H-RI-575-A5, Durand-2568. Altered from W-RI-1630-002-G020. Aug. 6, 1855.

Rarity: *None known*

$2 • W-RI-1650-002-A020

Left: 2 / Farmer and family resting. *Center:* Portrait of Benjamin Franklin. *Right:* 2 / Woodsman felling tree, Oxen, children. *Overprint:* Red 2 / 2. *Comments:* H-Unlisted, Durand-2569. Altered from W-RI-1630-005-G040. 1850s.

Rarity: URS-3

$3 • W-RI-1650-003-N010

Left: Sheep. *Center:* Man, horse, wagon. *Right:* Boy and man. *Comments:* H-RI-575-N5, Durand-2573. 1850s.

Rarity: *None known*

$3 • W-RI-1650-003-A030   ANS

Overprint: Red 3 / 3. *Engraver:* Toppan, Carpenter & Co. *Comments:* H-RI-575-A15, Durand-2572. Altered from W-RI-1630-003-G030. August 6th, 1855.

Rarity: URS-3
VF $500

$5 • W-RI-1650-005-N020

Center: Bridge / Indian. *Comments:* H-RI-575-N10, Durand-2577. 1850s.

Rarity: *None known*

$5 • W-RI-1650-005-A040

Left: 5 / Farmer and family resting. *Center:* Portrait of Benjamin Franklin. *Right:* 5 / Woodsman felling tree, Oxen, children. *Overprint:* Red V / V. *Comments:* H-RI-575-A20, Durand-2576. Altered from W-RI-1630-005-G040. Aug. 6, 1855.

Rarity: *None known*

$10 • W-RI-1650-010-A050   SI

Engraver: New England Bank Note Co. *Comments:* H-RI-575-A25, Durand-2580. Altered from $10 Commercial Bank, Gratiot Michigan. 18__. 1843.

Rarity: URS-4
VF $250

$10 • W-RI-1650-010-A060

Engraver: New England Bank Note Co. *Comments:* H-RI-575-A25a. Similar to W-RI-1650-010-A050 but with colored ink. 18__. 1843.

Rarity: *None known*

$10 • W-RI-1650-010-A070

Left: 10 / Justice / 10. *Center:* Farmers gathering corn, Wagon and horses. *Right:* 10 / Portrait of girl. *Overprint:* Red X / X. *Comments:* H-RI-575-A30, Durand-2579. Altered from W-RI-1630-010-G050. 18__. 1855.

Rarity: *None known*

Wickford Bank
1854 AND 1855
W-RI-1660

History: The Wickford Bank was incorporated in 1854. Although it is not certain, it can be inferred that if this bank issued notes, they were similar to those of its successor bank save for the title and a different date.

In 1855 the title of the bank was changed to the Farmers Bank, W-RI-1630.[96]

WOONSOCKET, RHODE ISLAND

A village of Cumberland, Woonsocket was made up of land on which three native tribes used to reside—the Nipmucs, the Wampanoags, and the Narragansetts. In 1661 Roger Williams purchased the area and referred to it as Niswosakit.

Woosocket Falls Village was founded in the 1820s. It was supplied with sufficient water power to become a primary location of textile mills, and the Industrial Revolution took root. The first textile mill was formed in 1810 on the Mill River in Woonsocket. By 1842 as many as 20 mills producing cotton fabric were located in Woonsocket. Six mill villages developed around the area.

The official town of Woonsocket was established in 1867, after the bank-note–issuing period ended, when the three villages of Cumberland—Woonsocket Falls, Social, and Jenckesville—joined together to become one entity. It was incorporated as a city in 1888.

See also Cumberland, Rhode Island.

Citizens Bank
1851–1865
W-RI-1670

History: The Citizens Bank was incorporated in May 1851. Notes with the Cumberland imprint were issued in 1851 and 1852. The bank's location was changed in 1853 to Woonsocket, a small village in the Cumberland area. This village was incorporated as the town of Woonsocket in 1867.

The bank's capital in 1857 was $56,950. Circulation was $24,003, which increased to $27,797 by 1862. Specie amounted to $2,031.14 in 1857.

The business of the Citizens Bank was succeeded by the Citizens National Bank, chartered on April 1, 1865.

See also listing under Cumberland, W-RI-260.

VALID ISSUES

$1 • W-RI-1670-001-G010   **SBG**

Engraver: Danforth, Bald & Co. **Comments:** H-RI-75-G20, Durand-2594. January 6th, 18__. 1850s–1860s.
Rarity: URS-2
Proof $2,000
Selected auction price: Stack's Bowers Galleries, June 2010, Proof $1,777

$2 • W-RI-1670-002-G020   **SBG**

Engraver: Danforth, Bald & Co. **Comments:** H-RI-75-G22, Durand-2595. January 6th, 18__. 1850s–1860s.
Rarity: URS-1
Proof $2,000

$3 • W-RI-1670-003-G030   **SBG**

Engraver: Danforth, Bald & Co. **Comments:** H-RI-75-G24, Durand-2596. January 6th, 18__. 1850s–1860s.
Rarity: URS-1
Proof $2,500
Selected auction price: Stack's Bowers Galleries, March 2013, Proof $2,420

$5 • W-RI-1670-005-G040   **SBG**

Engraver: Danforth, Bald & Co. **Comments:** H-RI-75-G26, Durand-2597. January 6th, 18__. 1850s–1860s.
Rarity: URS-3
Proof $2,000

$10 • W-RI-1670-010-G050
Left: 10 / Female portrait / TEN. **Center:** Ceres holding cornucopia and key seated between 1 and 0. **Right:** 10 / Female portrait / TEN. **Engraver:** Rawdon, Wright, Hatch & Edson. **Comments:** H-RI-75-G28, Durand-2598. 1850s–1860s.
Rarity: *None known*

$20 • W-RI-1670-020-G060
Left: 20 / Minerva. **Center:** Allegorical figure between 2 and 0. **Right:** 20 / Ceres / 20. **Engraver:** Rawdon, Wright, Hatch & Edson. **Comments:** H-RI-75-G30, Durand-2600. 1850s–1860s.
Rarity: *None known*

$50 • W-RI-1670-050-G070
Left: 50 / Minerva. **Center:** Vulcan and Ceres. **Bottom center:** 50. **Right:** 50 / Cherub steering sailboat / 50. **Engraver:** Rawdon, Wright, Hatch & Edson. **Comments:** H-RI-75-G32, Durand-2602. 1850s–1860s.
Rarity: *None known*

$100 • W-RI-1670-100-G080
Left: 100 / Vulcan. **Center:** Spread eagle on tree limb, Train and canal. **Right:** 100 / Agriculture. **Engraver:** Rawdon, Wright, Hatch & Edson. **Comments:** H-RI-75-G34, Durand-2604. 1850s–1860s.
Rarity: *None known*

Uncut Sheets

$5-$1-$2-$3 • W-RI-1670-005.001.002.003-US010

Vignette(s): ($5) Two women seated, Sailor and mechanic / Shield bearing anchor / Liberty and eagle. *($1)* Ceres seated, Town. *($2)* Eagle on shield / Two allegorical figures / Bull's head. *($3)* Train / Three allegorical figures in clouds / House and flag staff. *Engraver:* Danforth, Bald & Co. *Comments:* H-RI-75-G26, G20, G22, G24. January 6th, 18__. 1850s–1860s.

Rarity: *None known*

Non-Valid Issues

$10 • W-RI-1670-010-R010

Comments: H-RI-75-R3, Durand-2599. Raised from W-RI-1670-002-G020. 1850s–1860s.

Rarity: *None known*

$20 • W-RI-1670-020-R020

Comments: H-RI-75-R5, Durand-2601. Raised from W-RI-1670-002-G020. 1850s–1860s.

Rarity: *None known*

$50 • W-RI-1670-050-R030

Comments: H-RI-75-R7, Durand-2603. Raised from W-RI-1670-002-G020. 1850s–1860s.

Rarity: *None known*

Globe Bank
1844–1865
W-RI-1680

History: On March 12, 1844, the name of the Providence County Bank, W-RI-1360, was changed to the Globe Bank, and the location was moved to Globe Village, a part of Smithfield. The location was again changed to Woonsocket opposite the Harrison Mill in 1855. The bank had a capital of $50,000 in 1848. This was raised to $75,000 by 1849 and to $100,000 by 1855. Bills in circulation totaled $40,585 in 1849, decreased to $27,192 by 1860, and increased again to $63,208 by 1862. The first president was Spencer Mowry, and the first cashier was S. Newton.

The business of the Globe Bank was succeeded by the National Globe Bank on June 23, 1865. There was an unrelated Globe Bank, W-RI-970, located in Providence.

See also listing under Smithfield, W-RI-1340.

Producers Bank
1852–1865
W-RI-1690

History: The Producers Bank was incorporated in May 1852. Capital was $155,000 in 1855 and $200,000 in 1857. Circulation was $52,274 in 1857 and had increased to $63,098 by 1862. Specie was given at $5,503.78 in 1857.

The business of the Producers Bank was succeeded by the Producers National Bank in 1865.

Numismatic Commentary: Genuine notes from this bank are very hard to locate. Non-valid issues can occasionally be found in the marketplace.

Remaining in the American Bank Note Co. archives as of 2003 was a $100-$500 face plate, a $20-$50 face plate, and a single general back plate.

Valid Issues

$1 • W-RI-1690-001-G010

SBG

Engraver: Danforth, Bald & Co. *Comments:* H-RI-585-G3, Durand-2634. 18__. 1850s.

Rarity: URS-2
Proof $2,500

$2 • W-RI-1690-002-G020

SBG

Engraver: Danforth, Bald & Co. *Comments:* H-RI-585-G6, Durand-2636. 18__. 1850s.

Rarity: URS-2
Proof $2,100

$2 • W-RI-1690-002-G020a

Left: TWO / Portrait of Benjamin Franklin / TWO. *Center:* Liberty, Justice, and Truth, Shield surmounted by eagle. *Bottom center:* Dog, strongbox, and key. *Right:* TWO / Woman with rake and wheat / TWO. *Comments:* H-Unlisted, Durand-2638. Similar to W-RI-1690-002-G020 but without left portrait. 1850s.

Rarity: URS-3
F $125

$3 • W-RI-1690-003-G030

Left: 3 / Portrait of George Washington. *Center:* Two horses and train. *Bottom center:* Farm implements. *Right:* Female portrait. *Engraver:* Unverified, but likely Danforth, Bald & Co. *Comments:* H-RI-585-G9, Durand-2639. 18__. 1850s.

Rarity: *None known*

$5 • W-RI-1690-005-G040

Left: 5 / Train. *Center:* Horse, Anchor and shield surmounted by eagle, Horse. *Right:* Cattle. *Engraver:* Unverified, but likely Danforth, Bald & Co. *Comments:* H-RI-585-G12, Durand-2641. 18__. 1850s.

Rarity: *None known*

$10 • **W-RI-1690-010-G050**

Left: X / Female portrait / TEN. *Center:* Woman kneeling and supporting 1 and 0 / X on shield. *Right:* 10 / Two Indian women. *Engraver:* Unverified, but likely Danforth, Bald & Co. *Comments:* H-RI-585-G15, Durand-2643. 18__. 1850s.

Rarity: URS-3
Proof $1,200

$20 • **W-RI-1690-020-G060**

Left: Liberty / TWENTY. *Center:* 20 / Farmer plowing with oxen / Girl. *Right:* 20 / Ceres. *Engraver:* Unverified, but likely Danforth, Bald & Co. *Comments:* H-RI-585-G18, Durand-2644. 18__. 1850s.

Rarity: *None known*

$50 • **W-RI-1690-050-G070**

Left: Woman with medallion head resting on pillar. *Center:* 50 / Spread eagle on shield. *Right:* 50 / Portrait of George Washington. *Engraver:* Unverified, but likely Danforth, Bald & Co. *Comments:* H-RI-585-G21, Durand-2645. 18__. 1850s.

Rarity: *None known*

$100 • **W-RI-1690-100-G080**

Left: 100 / Man instructing child. *Center:* C. *Right:* 100 / Medallion head / 100. *Tint:* Brown lathework outlining white ONE HUNDRED. *Engraver:* Danforth, Bald & Co. *Comments:* H-RI-585-G24a, Durand-2646. 18__. 1850s–1860s.

Rarity: URS-3
VF $500

$500 • **W-RI-1690-500-G090**

Left: 500 / Artist. *Center:* Woman, Beehive, Woman. *Right:* 500 / Portrait of Martha Washington. *Engraver:* Danforth, Bald & Co. *Comments:* H-RI-585-G27, Durand-2647. 18__. 1850s.

Rarity: *None known*

Uncut Sheets

$1-$2-$3-$5 • **W-RI-1690-001.002.003.005-US010**

Vignette(s): *($1)* Liberty / Eagle / Indian viewing tools / Woman bathing / Mechanic's arm, hammer, and anvil. *($2)* Portrait of Benjamin Franklin / Liberty, Justice, and Truth, Shield surmounted by eagle / Dog, strongbox, and key / Agriculture. *($3)* Portrait of George Washington / Two horses and train / Farm implements / Female portrait. *($5)* Train / Horse, Anchor and shield surmounted by eagle, Horse / Cattle. *Engraver:* Danforth, Bald & Co. *Comments:* H-RI-585-G3, G6, G9, G12. 18__. 1850s.

Rarity: *None known*

$100-$500 • **W-RI-1690-100.500-US020**

Vignette(s): *($100)* Man instructing child / Medallion head. *($500)* Artist / Woman, Beehive, Woman / Portrait of Martha Washington. *Engraver:* Danforth, Bald & Co. *Comments:* H-RI-585-G24a, G27. 18__. 1850s.

Rarity: *None known*

NON-VALID ISSUES

$1 • **W-RI-1690-001-A010**

Left: 1 / Woman standing with basket / ONE. *Center:* Commerce / ONE. *Right:* 1 / Ships in bay / ONE. *Engraver:* New England Bank Note Co. *Comments:* H-RI-585-A5, Durand-2635. Altered from $1 Washington County Bank, Calais, Maine, or from notes of other failed banks using the same plate. 18__. 1850s.

Rarity: URS-3
VF $200

$2 • **W-RI-1690-002-A020**

Left: Woman with horn of plenty. *Center:* TWO / Commerce. *Right:* 2 / Portrait of girl / TWO. *Engraver:* New England Bank Note Co. *Comments:* H-RI-585-A10, Durand-2637. Altered from $2 Washington County Bank, Calais, Maine, or from notes of other failed banks using the same plate. 18__. 1850s.

Rarity: URS-3
VF $200

$3 • **W-RI-1690-003-A030**

Left: THREE / Beehive / THREE. *Center:* Woman with rake, shield, cog wheel / THREE. *Right:* 3 over THREE / Two men / 3 over THREE. *Engraver:* New England Bank Note Co. *Comments:* H-RI-585-A15, Durand-2640. Altered from $3 Washington County Bank, Calais, Maine, or from notes of other failed banks using the same plate. 18__. 1850s.

Rarity: URS-3
VF $200

$5 • **W-RI-1690-005-A040**

Comments: H-RI-585-A20, Durand-2642. No description available. Title and state very dark. 1850s.

Rarity: *None known*

$500 • **W-RI-1690-500-C090**

Engraver: Unverified, but likely Danforth, Bald & Co. *Comments:* H-RI-585-C27, Durand-2648. Counterfeit of W-RI-1690-500-G090. 18__. 1850s.

Rarity: *None known*

Railroad Bank
1851–1865
W-RI-1700

History: The Railroad Bank was incorporated in Cumberland in May 1851. Shortly thereafter, the bank was moved to Woonsocket, and a Woonsocket imprint was used on the bank's notes. The likely source of the bank's name came from the opening of the Providence and Worcester Railroad in 1847, taking business away from the Blackstone Canal. Edward Harris, the bank's president, was the founder and owner of the Harris Woolen Company. He was also the founder of the public library in Woonsocket.[97] William Metcalf served as the bank's first cashier and was succeeded by Reuben G. Randall.

The bank's capital was $100,000 in 1855. By 1857 it was $105,600. Bills in circulation were at $25,432, and specie totaled $1,584.73. From 1857 to 1860 capital was $103,850, and in 1862 it was reported to be $106,700. Circulation reached $54,382 by 1862.

The business of the Railroad Bank was succeeded by the First National Bank of Woonsocket, chartered on July 7, 1865.

See also listing under Cumberland, W-RI-280.

Numismatic Commentary: Genuine notes from the Woonsocket location are extremely hard to locate. There is a much better chance of locating a non-genuine example.

VALID ISSUES

$1 • W-RI-1700-001-G010
Left: 1 / Barrel, bales, ship / 1. *Center:* 1 / Commerce seated, Ship / 1. *Right:* 1 / Agricultural implements / 1. *Engraver:* New England Bank Note Co. / ABNCo. monogram. *Comments:* H-RI-85-G18a, Durand-2656. 18__. 1850s–1860s.
Rarity: *None known*

$2 • W-RI-1700-002-G020
Left: 2 / George Washington on horse / 2. *Center:* 2 / Allegorical woman standing by shield bearing 2, Cornucopia / 2. *Right:* 2 / George Washington on horse / 2. *Engraver:* New England Bank Note Co. / ABNCo. monogram. *Comments:* H-RI-85-G20a, Durand-2659. 18__. 1850s–1860s.
Rarity: *None known*

$2 • W-RI-1700-002-G030
Left: 2 / George Washington on horse / 2. *Center:* 2 / Woman standing with shield bearing 2 / 2. *Right:* 2 / George Washington on horse / 2. *Comments:* H-Unlisted, Durand-2660. 1850s–1860s.
Rarity: URS-3
VF $400

$3 • W-RI-1700-003-G040
Left: 3 / George Washington by horse. *Center:* Female portrait / 3 / Female portrait. *Right:* 3 / Vulcan standing with sledge. *Engraver:* New England Bank Note Co. *Comments:* H-RI-85-G24, Durand-2663. 18__. 1850s.
Rarity: *None known*

$3 • W-RI-1700-003-G050
Left: 3 / Portrait of cherub / 3. *Center:* 3 / Woman standing with lyre and shield bearing 3 / 3. *Right:* 3 / Portrait of cherub / 3. *Engraver:* New England Bank Note Co. / ABNCo. monogram. *Comments:* H-RI-85-G26a, Durand-2662. 18__. 1850s–1860s.
Rarity: URS-3
Proof $900

$5 • W-RI-1700-005-G060
Left: FIVE on 5. *Center:* Ceres seated with sickle / Factories and shipping / Agriculture and Commerce / Indian girl seated in V. *Right:* 5 / Portrait of George Washington. *Engraver:* New England Bank Note Co. *Comments:* H-RI-85-G28, Durand-2665. 18__. 1850s.
Rarity: *None known*

$5 • W-RI-1700-005-G060a
Overprint: Red V / V. *Comments:* H-Unlisted, Durand-2669. Similar to W-RI-1700-005-G060. 1850s.
Rarity: URS-3

$10 • W-RI-1700-010-G070
Left: X. *Center:* "Signing of the Declaration of Independence" / X. *Right:* 10 / Train passing building with steeple / Man with wheelbarrow. *Engraver:* New England Bank Note Co. *Comments:* H-RI-85-G30, Durand-2671. 18__. 1850s.
Rarity: *None known*

$500 • W-RI-1700-500-G080
Left: Indian in canoe, Forest. *Center:* 500. *Right:* 500 / Justice. *Engraver:* New England Bank Note Co. *Comments:* H-RI-85-G36, Durand-2672. 18__. 1850s.
Rarity: *None known*

NON-VALID ISSUES

$1 • W-RI-1700-001-N010
Left: Farmer. *Center:* Boating scene, Ox team on shore. *Right:* Male bust. *Comments:* H-RI-85-N5, Durand-2658. Altered or spurious. 1850s.
Rarity: *None known*

$1 • W-RI-1700-001-A010
Left: 1 / Anchor and bales. *Center:* Sailing ship, Steamboat, Dock. *Right:* 1 / Portrait of Zachary Taylor. *Overprint:* Red ONE. *Engraver:* Toppan, Carpenter, Casilear & Co. *Comments:* H-RI-85-A5, Durand-2657. Altered from $1 Erie and Kalamazoo Railroad Bank, Adrian, Michigan series. Aug. 1, 1853 or 1854.
Rarity: *None known*

$2 • W-RI-1700-002-N020
Left: Farmer. *Center:* Boating scene, ox team on shore. *Right:* Male bust. *Comments:* H-RI-85-N10, Durand-2661. Altered or spurious. 1850s.
Rarity: *None known*

$3 • W-RI-1700-003-A020
Left: 3 / Male portrait. *Center:* Women flanking shield / THREE. *Right:* THREE over 3 / Female portrait. *Overprint:* Red THREE. *Engraver:* New England Bank Note Co. / Rawdon, Wright, Hatch & Edson. *Comments:* H-RI-85-A15, Durand-2664. Altered from $3 Waubeek Bank, De Soto, Nebraska. 18__. 1857.
Rarity: URS-5
VF $350

$5 • W-RI-1700-005-S010

CJF

Engraver: New England Bank Note Co. *Comments:* H-RI-85-S5, Durand-2670. Roughly similar to W-RI-1700-005-G060. May 1, 18__. 1865.
Rarity: URS-3
VF $500

$5 • W-RI-1700-005-AR010

Left: 5 / Anchor and bales. *Center:* Sailing ship, steamboat, dock. *Right:* 5 / Portrait of Zachary Taylor. *Engraver:* Toppan, Carpenter, Casilear & Co. *Comments:* H-RI-85-AR20, Durand-2667. Altered from $1 Erie and Kalamazoo Railroad Bank, Adrian, Michigan series Aug. 1, 1853 or 1854.

Rarity: *None known*

$5 • W-RI-1700-005-AR020

Left: 5. *Center:* Train, Bridge. *Right:* 5 / Female portrait. *Engraver:* Toppan, Carpenter, Casilear & Co. *Comments:* H-RI-85-AR25, Durand-2666. Altered from $3 Erie and Kalamazoo Railroad Bank, Adrian, Michigan series. 185_ or Aug. 1, 1854.

Rarity: *None known*

$5 • W-RI-1700-005-AR030

Left: Ceres with shield bearing 5 / FIVE. *Center:* Portrait of Franklin Pierce. *Right:* Commerce with shield bearing 5 / FIVE. *Overprint:* Red 5 / 5. *Engraver:* Toppan, Carpenter, Casilear & Co. *Comments:* H-RI-85-AR30, Durand-2668. Altered from $5 Erie and Kalamazoo Railroad Bank, Adrian, Michigan. Aug. 1, 1853 or 1854.

Rarity: *None known*

Smithfield Union Bank
1805–1865
W-RI-1710

History: The Smithfield Union Bank was incorporated in 1805 in Smithfield with an authorized capital of $50,000. In 1852 the bank moved to the city of Woonsocket to take advantage of the profits from the burgeoning textile industry in that city.

The business of the Smithfield Union Bank was succeeded by the National Union Bank of Woonsocket in 1865.

See also listing under Smithfield, W-RI-1400.

VALID ISSUES

$1 • W-RI-1710-001-G010

Left: ONE vertically. *Center:* Steamboat and other vessels / 1. *Right:* ONE / Indian maiden with bow and arrows, ONE. *Engraver:* New England Bank Note Co. *Comments:* H-RI-475-G136, Durand-2694. 18__. 1850s.

Rarity: *None known*

$2 • W-RI-1710-002-G020

Left: 2 / TWO / 2. *Center:* Ship, vessels, and bay scene / 2. *Right:* TWO / Woman drawing water from well / TWO. *Engraver:* New England Bank Note Co. *Comments:* H-RI-475-G138, Durand-2695. 18__. 1850s.

Rarity: *None known*

$3 • W-RI-1710-003-G030

Left: THREE vertically. *Center:* Reaping scene. *Right:* THREE / Steamship / 3 on THREE. *Engraver:* New England Bank Note Co. *Comments:* H-RI-475-G140, Durand-2696. 18__. 1850s.

Rarity: *None known*

$5 • W-RI-1710-005-G040

Left: FIVE on lathework strip vertically. *Center:* Woman raising curtain from shield bearing 5. *Right:* 5 / Ship. *Comments:* H-Unlisted, Durand-2697. 1850s.

Rarity: URS-3

VF $500

$5 • W-RI-1710-005-G050

Left: V on FIVE. *Center:* Wharf scene / Agriculture, Farm implements and merchandise / Indian girl seated in V. *Right:* 5 / Portrait of George Washington. *Engraver:* New England Bank Note Co. *Comments:* H-RI-475-G142, Durand-2698. 18__. 1850s–1860s.

Rarity: *None known*

$10 • W-RI-1710-010-G060

Left: Vulcan seated with hammer, Anvil and wheel / TEN. *Center:* X. *Right:* 10 / Reaper standing with sheaf. *Engraver:* New England Bank Note Co. *Comments:* H-RI-475-G144, Durand-2699. 18__. 1850s–1860s.

Rarity: *None known*

$20 • W-RI-1710-020-G070

Left: 20 / Woman seated with book. *Center:* XX / Eagle / XX. *Right:* 20 / Ship. *Comments:* H-Unlisted, Durand-2700. 1850s.

Rarity: URS-3

VF $900

$50 • W-RI-1710-050-G080

Left: FIFTY / Allegorical figure / FIFTY. *Center:* 50 / Man holding restive horse / 50. *Right:* FIFTY / Allegorical figure / FIFTY. *Comments:* H-Unlisted, Durand-2701. 1850s.

Rarity: URS-3

$100 • W-RI-1710-100-G090

Left: ONE HUNDRED across 100 / Portrait of William Henry Harrison. *Center:* Wharf scene, Stores, Men loading covered wagon with barrels. *Right:* ONE HUNDRED across 100 / Portrait of Christopher Columbus. *Comments:* H-Unlisted, Durand-2702. 1850s.

Rarity: URS-3

VF $500

NON-VALID ISSUES

$2 • W-RI-1710-002-A010

Left: Ceres standing / 2. *Center:* 2 / Moneta seated / 2. *Bottom center:* State arms. *Right:* Fortuna standing / 2. *Engraver:* Draper, Toppan, Longacre & Co. *Comments:* H-RI-475-A50. Altered from $2 Calhoun County Bank, Marshall, Michigan. 18__. 1850s.

Rarity: URS-3

VF $200

Woonsocket Falls Bank
1828–1865
W-RI-1720

History: Incorporated in June 1828 at Woonsocket, the Woonsocket Falls Bank was known as the Woonsocket Bank to local residents. At that time, Woonsocket was a small settlement along the eastern shore of the Blackstone River in the town of Cumberland.[98]

In 1831 capital was $51,269, circulation totaled $8,649, and specie was $2,541.11. Capital was $100,000 in 1848, $122,950.60 in 1849, and $100,000 in 1850. There were 2,000 shares valued at $50 each. Circulation grew from $31,332 in 1857 to $95,740 in 1863. Specie totaled $3,988.33 in 1857.

The interests of the Woonsocket Falls Bank were succeeded by the Woonsocket National Bank, chartered on July 1, 1865.

See also listing under Cumberland, W-RI-290.

VALID ISSUES

$1 • W-RI-1720-001-G010
Left: 1 / Blacksmith by forge. *Center:* View of Woonsocket Falls. *Right:* 1 / Female portrait. *Engraver:* Toppan, Carpenter & Co. *Comments:* H-RI-90-G50, Durand-2715. Jan. 1, 18__. 1850s.
Rarity: *None known*

$1 • W-RI-1720-001-G010a
Tint: Yellow outlining white ONE. *Engraver:* Toppan, Carpenter & Co. *Comments:* H-RI-90-G50a, Durand-2716. Similar to W-RI-1720-001-G010. Jan. 1, 18__. 1850s–1860s.
Rarity: URS-3
VF $500

$1 • W-RI-1720-001-G010b
Tint: Red-brown outlining white ONE. *Engraver:* Toppan, Carpenter & Co. *Comments:* H-RI-90-G50b, Durand-2717. Similar to W-RI-1720-001-G010. Jan. 1, 18__. 1850s.
Rarity: *None known*

$2 • W-RI-1720-002-G020
Left: 2 / Portrait of Henry Clay. *Center:* View of Woonsocket Falls. *Right:* 2 / Female portrait. *Engraver:* Toppan, Carpenter & Co. *Comments:* H-RI-90-G52, Durand-2718. January 1st, 18__. 1850s.
Rarity: URS-3
Proof $3,000

$2 • W-RI-1720-002-G020a   QDB

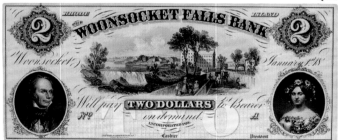

Tint: Yellow lathework and microlettering outlining white TWO. *Engraver:* Toppan, Carpenter & Co. *Comments:* H-RI-90-G52a, Durand-2719. Similar to W-RI-1720-002-G020. January 1st, 18__. 1850s.
Rarity: URS-3
Proof $3,000

$2 • W-RI-1720-002-G020b
Tint: Red-brown outlining white TWO. *Engraver:* Toppan, Carpenter & Co. *Comments:* H-RI-90-G52b, Durand-2720. Similar to W-RI-1720-002-G020. January 1st, 18__. 1850s.
Rarity: URS-3
Proof $3,000

$5 • W-RI-1720-005-G030
Left: 5 / Woman holding baby, Two farmers. *Right:* 5 / View of Woonsocket Falls. *Overprint:* Red 5. *Engraver:* Toppan, Carpenter & Co. *Comments:* H-RI-90-G54a, Durand-2724. January 1st, 18__. 1850s.
Rarity: URS-3
Proof $3,000

$5 • W-RI-1720-005-G030a
Tint: Yellow outlining white FIVE. *Engraver:* Toppan, Carpenter & Co. *Comments:* H-RI-90-G54b, Durand-2725. Similar to W-RI-1720-005-G030. January 1st, 18__. 1850s.
Rarity: URS-3
Proof $3,000

$5 • W-RI-1720-005-G030b   SBG

Tint: Red-brown lathework and microlettering outlining white FIVE. *Engraver:* Toppan, Carpenter & Co. *Comments:* H-RI-90-G54c, Durand-2726. Similar to W-RI-1720-005-G030. January 1st, 18__. 1850s.
Rarity: URS-3
Proof $6,100
Selected auction price: Stack's Bowers Galleries, March 2013, Proof $6,051

$10 • W-RI-1720-010-G040
Left: 10 / Portrait of girl. *Center:* View of Woonsocket Falls. *Right:* 10 / Woman feeding chickens. *Overprint:* Red TEN. *Engraver:* Toppan, Carpenter & Co. *Comments:* H-RI-90-G56a, Durand-2731. Jan. 1, 18__. 1850s.
Rarity: URS-3
Proof $3,000

$10 • W-RI-1720-010-G040a
Tint: Yellow outlining white TEN. *Engraver:* Toppan, Carpenter & Co. *Comments:* H-RI-90-G56b, Durand-2732. Similar to W-RI-1720-010-G040. Jan. 1, 18__. 1850s.
Rarity: URS-3
Proof $3,000

$10 • W-RI-1720-010-G040b
Tint: Red-brown outlining white TEN. *Engraver:* Toppan, Carpenter & Co. *Comments:* H-RI-90-G56c, Durand-2733. Similar to W-RI-1720-010-G040. Jan. 1, 18__. 1850s.
Rarity: URS-3
Proof $3,000

$20 • W-RI-1720-020-G050
Left: Female portrait / 20. *Center:* View of Woonsocket Falls. *Right:* 20 / Portrait of George Washington. *Engraver:* Toppan, Carpenter & Co. *Comments:* H-RI-90-G58, Durand-2736. Jan. 1, 18__. 1850s.
Rarity: URS-3
Proof $3,000

$20 • W-RI-1720-020-G050a

Overprint: Green TWENTY. *Engraver:* Toppan, Carpenter & Co. *Comments:* H-RI-90-G58a, Durand-2737. Similar to W-RI-1720-020-G050. Jan. 1, 18__. 1850s–1860s.

Rarity: *None known*

$50 • W-RI-1720-050-G060

CC

Engraver: Toppan, Carpenter & Co. *Comments:* H-RI-90-G60, Durand-2738. January 1st, 185_. 1850s.

Rarity: URS-1
Proof $3,500

$50 • W-RI-1720-050-G060a

Left: 50. *Center:* View of Woonsocket Falls / Female portrait. *Bottom center:* Sheep. *Right:* 50 / Portrait of boy. *Overprint:* Green FIFTY. *Engraver:* Toppan, Carpenter & Co. *Comments:* H-RI-90-G60a, Durand-2739. Similar to W-RI-1720-050-G060. January 1st, 185_. 1850s–1860s.

Rarity: *None known*

$100 • W-RI-1720-100-G070

SBG

Engraver: Toppan, Carpenter & Co. *Comments:* H-RI-90-G62, Durand-2740. January 1st, 18__. 1850s.

Rarity: URS-1
Proof $5,000

$100 • W-RI-1720-100-G070a

Left: 100 / View of Woonsocket Falls. *Right:* 100 / Ceres. *Overprint:* Green HUNDRED. *Engraver:* Toppan, Carpenter & Co. *Comments:* H-RI-90-G62a, Durand-2741. Similar to W-RI-1720-100-G070. January 1st, 18__. 1850s–1860s.

Rarity: URS-3
Proof $3,000

$500 • W-RI-1720-500-G080

CJF

Engraver: New England Bank Note Co. *Comments:* H-RI-90-G64, Durand-2742. 18__. 1850s.

Rarity: URS-3
Unc-Rem $2,500

$1,000 • W-RI-1720-1000-G090

CJF

Engraver: New England Bank Note Co. *Comments:* H-RI-90-G66, Durand-2743. 18__. 1850s.

Rarity: URS-3
Unc-Rem $2,500

NON-VALID ISSUES

$2 • W-RI-1720-002-A010

Left: 2 / Die with horse. *Center:* Farming scene, Hay wagon. *Right:* 2 on die / Cherub. *Tint:* Red-brown 2s and TWO DOLLARS. *Engraver:* Danforth, Wright & Co. *Comments:* H-Unlisted. Altered from $2 Southern Bank of Georgia, Bainbridge, Georgia. March 1, 1858.

Rarity: URS-6
VF $100

THE OBSOLETE BANK NOTES OF VERMONT

STATE BANKING IN VERMONT

Currency of Vermont: The Vermont State Bank

The Vermont State Bank was the first such institution in the state and also the first in the country to be organized and conducted by a state government. Incorporated in 1806 with Titus Hutchinson as the first president, it did business at Middlebury and Woodstock starting in 1807. In that year branches were opened at Burlington and Winchester. Before opening, each branch had to have $25,000 in coins in its vault. All assets and profits were the property of the state.

The Vermont State Bank experienced great difficulties, and in 1808 large quantities of counterfeit bills printed in Canada by Stephen Burroughs outnumbered legitimate notes in some areas. The State of Massachusetts, eager to protect its own interests, declared that Vermont notes were not valid there. Adding to the problem, rumors spread that notes of the Vermont State Bank were speculative and that the bank would fail. Following the federal Embargo Act of 1807 and the Non-Intercourse Act of 1808, which severely restricted maritime commerce, business in all of New England slowed greatly, and many businesses failed. To bolster confidence, the acts of 1809 and 1812 provided that the bank's currency could be used to pay real estate taxes. In 1812 the bank stopped issuing bills. The branches were closed that year and in 1813, and bills on hand were ordered to be burned. The redemption of notes continued for years afterward until the affairs of the bank were settled in 1845. By that time the state had incurred a loss of $200,000, but there was no loss to the holders of currency.[1]

State-Chartered Banks Formed

The first banks in Vermont to be formed by private stockholders were the Burlington and Windsor banks in 1818, followed by the Brattleboro Bank in 1821 and the Bank of Rutland in 1824. State regulations permitted banks to issue paper up to three times the amount of their capital, a generous figure, and required them to redeem the notes in specie (silver and gold coins) on demand.

During the next two decades, many other banks were chartered throughout the state. A legislative report giving the condition of banks as of April 1, 1828, showed 10 banks in operation with a combined paid-in capital of $321,216, specie and good bills (specie convertible) owned to the amount of $674,904, and currency in circulation at $949,844. Most banks had deposits for the redemption of their bills in Boston or in Troy, New York (close to Bennington, Vermont, across the state line). The Bank of Montpelier cleared its currency in New York City.

A few banks changed their names or evolved to become other banks. In Chelsea, the Bank of Orange County was established in 1827. Its charter expired in 1843, at which time its business was transferred to the newly chartered Orange County Bank, which operated until 1855. It was then succeeded by the second Orange County Bank. The Bank of Orange County at Irasburgh, titled so as not to be confused with the one in Chelsea, was formed in 1832. Its interests were succeeded by the Bank of Orleans, which variously spelled the town name on its currency as Irasburg and Irasburgh.

The location of a Vermont bank could not always be determined by its title. The Bank of Caledonia was in Danville, the Bank of Newbury was in Wells River, the Ascutney Bank did business in Windsor, and the Bank of Poultney was in West Poultney. The Bank of Bellows Falls was located in the village of that name in the town of Rockingham, and certain of its bills gave Rockingham as the address, not the village.

In 1831 a Safety Fund was set up by the state, and banks were required to contribute an amount equal to four and a half percent of their capital, payable in installments over a period of six years. Should the fund be depleted by paying the debts of failed banks, an additional tax would be levied, not to exceed three-quarters of one percent per year.

Without naming the bank, *Niles' Weekly Register*, November 14, 1835, carried this:

"A little monster." One of the state banks, in Vermont, having been suspected of a violation of its charter, a committee was appointed, by the legislature, to overhaul its affairs and report thereon to that body. In their report, the committee, among other developments of the mysteries of banking, state that "the banking room of this institution is in a wooden building occupied as a store—that the place of deposit for the notes, bills, papers and specie of the bank, is a wooden desk—and that the books of the bank consisted of one or two sheets of paper pinned or stitched together!"

The institution in question, the Essex Bank located in Guildhall, had a poor reputation but remained in operation. Two years later, in 1838 the Suffolk Bank in Boston stopped exchanging its bills. The situation became worse, and with $66,262 of bills in circulation, the bank closed in 1839 and officially failed in 1841, causing a loss to all involved. The assets of the Safety Fund were inadequate to cushion the fall. An investigation revealed that the officers had committed fraud. On these grounds, the state refused to redeem the bills, as the Safety Fund was intended to absorb normal business losses and failures due to unfortunate circumstances, not to compensate for criminal actions. Holders of Essex Bank bills were told to look to the bondsmen who had furnished security for the bank. This suggestion did not work.

The subsequent Banking Act of 1840 required that before a new bank could begin business, half of its capital had to be paid in specie. Modifications to the Safety Fund regulations were made in 1842. If a Vermont bank kept deposits in Boston for the prompt redemption of its bills at par, certain rules would be eased. This was a reference to the Suffolk Bank exchange system which had been in effect since 1824. By 1848 all but three Vermont banks had signed up for this clearing house service, and by 1850 membership was unanimous.

In 1841 there were 17 chartered banks operating in the state. New banks were authorized over the years. For example, in 1849 the Merchants Bank in Burlington, the Passumpsic Bank in St. Johnsbury, the Missisquoi Bank in Sheldon, and the Franklin County Bank at St. Albans Bay were all incorporated. Most banks were small and located in villages scattered throughout the state.

Bills bearing the imprint of the Commercial Bank, located in Poultney, circulated but were listed as fraudulent in *Thompson's Bank Note & Commercial Reporter* in 1850. There was no such bank. The same was true for the Green Mountain Bank of Rutland, also listed. The Jefferson Banking Company of Vermont was also fictitious. Its nicely engraved bills, designed by Edward Hulseman of New York City (perhaps best known as an engraver of dies for Hard Times tokens), bore no town name.

The Farmers Bank of Orwell, which operated legitimately in 1833 and continued until its business was succeeded by a national bank in 1864, was plagued by large quantities of counterfeits of its bills. The Farmers and Mechanics Bank of Burlington was another target for counterfeiters, who issued a wide range of denominations up to $100. All of the phony and spurious bills with Vermont imprints were made out-of-state

and mostly circulated in distant places. As such, these were not Vermont-based frauds.

This item is from the *Boston Atlas*, June 22, 1847:

> *Counterfeits.* A remittance was received yesterday at the Suffolk Bank, from the Bank of Burlington, Vt., of $900. There were four bills of $100 each, and two of $50 each, of the Shoe and Leather Dealers Bank, Boston, making $500. Then there were eight bills of $50 each, of the Massachusetts Bank, Boston.
>
> All of these bills had been altered from one dollar bills of the respective banks. The alterations are so well done that ninety-nine persons out of every hundred would not detect the cheat. The loss to the party who made the remittance is $886. We hope that the scoundrels who are flooding the country with their spurious notes may soon be detected.

Counterfeit and worthless bills had been a problem for a long time. Court dockets were filled with cases of people passing such currency. Many out-of-state bills of dubious worth circulated in Vermont, often received from distant buyers of cattle and agricultural products. Merchants typically received such bills at par and then passed them along to their customers, with the result that most became worn and ragged.

In 1852 the Free Banking Act provided that banks could be incorporated by 10 or more persons with a minimum of $50,000 in capital, which was not to exceed $200,000, and could issue bills against securities deposited with the state treasurer. Similar acts were passed by some other states and were intended to expand the banking system. After the Act passed, 13 banks were formed in Vermont, but all elected to comply with the stricter provisions of the Act of 1840, believing that it would be easier to attract capital if a bank appeared to have a stronger footing. By that time "free bank" was a term in American finance that often implied a weak or fraudulent structure.

There were many unsuccessful applications for bank charters in the early 1850s, a lengthy list including: the Waloomsic Bank (Bennington), the Peoples Bank (Brandon), the Bank of Cabot and the Eagle Bank (Castleton), the Western Vermont Bank (Fair Haven), the Fairfax Bank, the Hinesburg Bank, and the Bank of Lamoille (Johnson), the Bank at Newfane, the Bank of Richmond, and the Northern Bank of Vermont (St. Albans), and the Bank of South Hardwick, the Bank of Waterville, the West Randolph Bank, the Bank of Wilmington, and the Winooski Bank. Approval of charter petitions seems to have been reviewed with care, no doubt preventing the establishment of "paper mills" (as fraudulent issuers of large quantities of paper money were called).

The Panic of 1857 had very little effect on banks in the state, and, amazingly, only one suspended specie payments. After the National Banking Act of 1863, the directors of many banks elected to apply for charters to become national banks that assumed the businesses of the state banks. Old notes of the state banks continued to be redeemed for several years. By the mid-1860s, state authorities could look back on the note-issuing era and reflect that there had been very few problems.

Numismatic Comments

Notes of Vermont are especially appealing to collect, as the designs are quite varied. There are, to be sure, many of the Patent Stereotype Steel Plate (PSSP) issues in early years, but they quickly give way to a multiplicity of fascinating vignettes by Boston, Philadelphia, and New York engravers. Although several towns had multiple banks, most bills were issued by banks with small capital located in villages scattered throughout the state.

The earliest issues are those of the Vermont State Bank as described above. Large quantities of redeemed as well as undistributed notes remained in the hands of the state and later found their way into numismatic circles. Today, collecting a representative set of different denominations is easy enough to do, but the challenge can be heightened if early issues are wanted from the different branches.

For bank notes of the 1840s and 1850s, Proofs from the American Bank Note Co. archives, plus some modern proprietary Proofs, come on the market with some frequency, a remarkable contrast to before 1990, when such were great rarities. The Rawdon, Wright, Hatch & Edson $1, $2, $3, and $5 issues of the West River Bank of Jamaica, each with a vignette featuring Liberty Seated silver dollars, have been popular for a long time. As these existed in large quantities of remainder sheets, they are much less expensive than might be thought. Bills of St. Albans, usually seen in circulated grades, are varied. Some have an interesting link with the famous Confederate raid of 1864.

BELLOWS FALLS, VERMONT

The village of Bellows Falls, within the town of Rockingham, came into being when the first bridge across the Connecticut River—a waterwork extending 410 miles—was built in the area. The bridge was 360 feet long and was finished in 1785, opening a straight route from Boston to New Hampshire and from Vermont to Canada.

In 1791 a further canal and dam underwent construction, and the Bellows Falls Canal became the first of its kind in the United States. Completed in 1802, the waterway caused massive growth for the village, promoting development of water power and mills.

In 1802 the first paper mill was built, after which paper-making became one of the village's primary industries. Large quantities of logs from the upper reaches of Vermont and New Hampshire were floated down the Connecticut River to be processed in Bellows Falls and other locations. At the end of the century, Bellows Falls had become one of the largest paper manufacturing locations in the country. In 1833 the silk industry arrived as well, thriving for about a decade. This was anticipated to be a profit center for a number of Eastern towns. However, weather destroyed most of the mulberry trees which were the hosts for the worms, and the industry failed in the various locations in which it had been established.

In 1849 two railroads connected in Bellows Falls, resulting in even further growth to industry, including the manufacturing of dairy equipment. A textile mill was opened a decade later, as did factories that produced items from furniture to rifles.

See also Rockingham, Vermont.

Bank of Bellows Falls
1831–1866
W-VT-010

History: The Bank of Bellows Falls (sometimes also seen as the Bellows Falls Bank) was incorporated on November 9, 1831, with an authorized stock of $100,000, to begin operation when half of the capital was paid in. The first meeting of the incorporators took place on February 2, 1832, at the Mansion House on the Bellows Falls Square. Daniel Kellogg was elected president and William Henry was chosen as cashier. At the meeting the purchase of a lot on the west side of the Square was authorized, and within a few months a "small, one-story, brick building which served as the only banking house in Bellows Falls until 1875" was erected. Daniel Kellogg remained president until January 1837, when he was succeeded by Nathaniel Fullerton of Chester.

By 1837 the Bank of Bellows Falls was trading as the Bellows Falls Bank, although there was no corporate or legislative change, and there was no change in the officers. William Henry occupied the position of cashier until March 9, 1837, his resignation being occasioned by his election to Congress. He was succeeded by James H. Williams 1st.

Circulation for 1850 and 1851 was reported to be $120,256 and $134,262, respectively. By 1857 the capital was $100,000, circulation was $143,668, specie was $5,564, and real estate was valued at $6,200. In August 1859, circulation was $143,668. 1862 saw a circulation of $166,303.

On November 5, 1864, an attempt to rob the Bank of Bellows Falls was foiled. The robbers went through the window facing the town square and blew off part of the vault lock. They managed to pry open the outer door to the vault, but the inside door blocked them. They fled the scene, leaving behind some tools which had been stolen previously from the local blacksmith's shop. There were three further attempts to burglar the bank after the note-issuing period.

The business of the Bank of Bellows Falls was succeeded by the National Bank of Bellows Falls on June 12, 1866. On January 8, 1867, according to the law providing for the handling of retired bills, the directors of the national bank destroyed $144,000 worth of Bank of Bellows Falls notes in a bonfire.

See also listing under Rockingham, W-VT-600.

Numismatic Commentary: The Bank of Bellows Falls issued notes with this title in the 1850s and 1860s with the address of Bellows Falls. Earlier it also issued bills with the Bellows Falls Bank title and with the address of Rockingham, the town in which the Bank of Bellows Falls was located. Notes under both titles and addresses are very rare.

VALID ISSUES

$1 • W-VT-010-001-G010

CJF

Engraver: Rawdon, Wright, Hatch & Edson / New England Bank Note Co. **Comments:** H-VT-5-G2, Coulter-1. May 1st, 185_. 1850s.

Rarity: URS-2
F $1,000

$2 • W-VT-010-002-G020

Left: 2. **Center:** Train. **Bottom center:** Ox and tree. **Right:** TWO / Woman seated on bale, Cornucopia, Cherub and shield bearing 2. **Engraver:** Rawdon, Wright, Hatch & Edson / New England Bank Note Co. **Comments:** H-VT-5-G4, Coulter-2. May 1st, 185_. 1850s.

Rarity: URS-1
F $1,000

$5 • W-VT-010-005-G030

Left: Portrait of George Washington in 5 bearing FIVE. **Center:** Woman seated holding sickle, Farmers loading grain. **Bottom center:** Agricultural tools. **Right:** 5 / State arms. **Engraver:** Rawdon, Wright, Hatch & Edson / New England Bank Note Co. **Comments:** H-VT-5-G6, Coulter-4. May 1st, 185_. 1850s.

Rarity: URS-2
F $1,000

$5 • W-VT-010-005-G030a

CJF

Engraver: Rawdon, Wright, Hatch & Edson / New England Bank Note Co. / ABNCo. monogram. **Comments:** H-Unlisted, Coulter-Unlisted. Similar to W-VT-010-005-G030 but with different date and engraver imprint. May 1st, 186_. 1860s.

Rarity: URS-2
F $1,000

$10 • W-VT-010-010-G040

Left: Portrait of Benjamin Franklin in X, Female portrait. **Center:** Herd of cattle and sheep, Man on horse. **Right:** 10 / Justice. **Engraver:** Rawdon, Wright, Hatch & Edson / New England Bank Note Co. **Comments:** H-VT-5-G8, Coulter-7. May 1st, 185_. 1850s.

Rarity: None known

$20 • W-VT-010-020-G050

Left: Woman with cornucopia, Pole and cap / 20. **Center:** 20 / Ceres seated, Cows and house / 20. **Bottom center:** Cherub riding on deer. **Right:** 20 / Sheaf / 20. **Engraver:** Rawdon, Wright, Hatch & Edson / New England Bank Note Co. **Comments:** H-VT-5-G10, Coulter-10. May 1st, 185_. 1850s.

Rarity: None known

$50 • W-VT-010-050-G060

Left: 50 / State arms / 50. **Center:** Ship, Man seated with pole, Mechanical implements / 50. **Bottom center:** Eagle. **Right:** 50 / Two men and cattle / 50. **Engraver:** Rawdon, Wright, Hatch & Edson / New England Bank Note Co. **Comments:** H-VT-5-G12, Coulter-11. May 1st, 185_. 1850s.

Rarity: None known

$100 • W-VT-010-100-G070

Left: Portrait. **Center:** 100 / Wharf scene / 100. **Right:** Portrait. **Comments:** H-VT-5-G14, Coulter-12. 1850s–1860s.

Rarity: None known

NON-VALID ISSUES

$3 • W-VT-010-003-R010

Engraver: Rawdon, Wright, Hatch & Edson / New England Bank Note Co. **Comments:** H-VT-5-R5, Coulter-3. Raised from W-VT-010-002-G020. May 1st, 185_. 1850s.

Rarity: None known

$5 • W-VT-010-005-C030

Engraver: Rawdon, Wright, Hatch & Edson / New England Bank Note Co. **Comments:** H-Unlisted, Coulter-5. Counterfeit of W-VT-010-005-G030. 1850s.

Rarity: None known

$5 • W-VT-010-005-R020

Engraver: Rawdon, Wright, Hatch & Edson / New England Bank Note Co. **Comments:** H-VT-5-R10, Coulter-6. Raised from W-VT-010-002-G020. May 1st, 185_. 1850s.

Rarity: None known

$10 • W-VT-010-010-R030

Engraver: Rawdon, Wright, Hatch & Edson / New England Bank Note Co. **Comments:** H-VT-5-R15, Coulter-8. Raised from W-VT-010-002-G020. May 1st, 185_. 1850s.

Rarity: None known

$10 • W-VT-010-010-R040

Engraver: Rawdon, Wright, Hatch & Edson / New England Bank Note Co. **Comments:** H-VT-5-R20, Coulter-9. Raised from W-VT-010-002-G020. May 1st, 185_. 1850s.

Rarity: None known

BENNINGTON, VERMONT

Bennington is flanked by the Green Mountains and the Taconic Mountains. The abundant fishing and hunting were what originally drew the native tribes to this location, in addition to the numerous waterways that thread the land. In 1749 New Hampshire governor Benning Wentworth chartered the first town in the area, and he named it in honor of himself. The land was granted to William Williams and settlers mostly from Portsmouth, New Hampshire. They settled the land in 1761. This grant was contested by certain interests from the State of New York.

The Battle of Bennington was fought a few miles to the west over the border of New York during the Revolutionary War. General John Stark's men marched from New Hampshire through rugged woods to defeat 800 enemy troops. The battle was a direct prelude to the surrender at Saratoga, which contributed to the colonial success in the Revolution.

Bennington began to develop commercially in the early 19th century, and three distinct districts arose there: Old Bennington, Downtown Bennington, and North Bennington. Water power and natural resources were the primary means of industry for a long time, used to operate sawmills, gristmills, and paper mills. Pottery, iron, and textiles from Bennington became known across the country, and many of the mills of the era still stand today, employed currently in modern uses.

Bank of Bennington
1828–1841
W-VT-025

History: The Bank of Bennington was chartered in 1827 with $100,000 in authorized capital. By 1837 the amount of capital paid in was $94,970. Circulation at this time was $131,890. Specie was $9,711.40, and real estate was valued at $3,992.34.

In 1841 the bank's capital was $87,770, bills in circulation were $169,902, and real estate was valued at $3,992.34. The bank failed on August 25 the same year.

Numismatic Commentary: Notes of this bank are plentiful in the marketplace. Collectors can find odd denominations such as $4, $6, and $7 bills, as well as high-denomination $50 and $100 bills. Uncut sheets are available to a degree but are becoming increasingly scarce as collectors and dealers cut them apart for their single notes.

Remaining in the American Bank Note Co. archives as of 2003 was a $1-$1-$2-$5 face plate, a $50-$100 face plate, and a $5-$10-$10-$20 face plate.

VALID ISSUES
$1 • W-VT-025-001-G010

Left: ONE / Portrait of Marquis de Lafayette / ONE. *Center:* State arms / Liberty and Industry flanking shield. *Right:* Marquis de Lafayette standing with hat / ONE. *Engraver:* Rawdon, Clark & Co. *Comments:* H-VT-10-G2, Coulter-1. 18__. 1828–1840.
Rarity: URS-8
F $150

$2 • W-VT-025-002-G020
CJF

Engraver: Rawdon, Clark & Co. *Comments:* H-VT-10-G4, Coulter-2. 18__. 1828–1840.
Rarity: URS-8
F $150

$3 • W-VT-025-003-G030
CC

Engraver: Rawdon, Wright & Hatch. *Comments:* H-VT-10-G6, Coulter-3. 18__. 1830s.
Rarity: URS-7
VG $200; **Unc-Rem** $250

$4 • W-VT-025-004-G040
CJF

Engraver: Rawdon, Wright & Hatch. *Comments:* H-VT-10-G8, Coulter-4. 18__. 1830s.
Rarity: URS-6
VF $250; **Unc-Rem** $500; **CU** $595

$5 • W-VT-025-005-G050
CJF

Engraver: Rawdon, Clark & Co. *Comments:* H-VT-10-G10, Coulter-5. 18__. 1828–1840.
Rarity: URS-8
VF $75; **Unc-Rem** $100

$6 • W-VT-025-006-G060

TD

Engraver: Rawdon, Wright & Hatch. **Comments:** H-VT-10-G12, Coulter-6. 18___. 1830s.
Rarity: URS-5
CU $795

$7 • W-VT-025-007-G070

CJF

Engraver: Rawdon, Wright & Hatch. **Comments:** H-VT-10-G14, Coulter-7. Some notes are spuriously filled in. 18___. 1830s.
Rarity: URS-5
AU $400

$10 • W-VT-025-010-G080

CC

Engraver: Rawdon, Clark & Co. **Comments:** H-VT-10-G16, Coulter-8. 18___. 1828–1840.
Rarity: URS-8
Unc-Rem $75; **AU** $175

$20 • W-VT-025-020-G090

CC

Engraver: Rawdon, Clark & Co. **Comments:** H-VT-10-G18, Coulter-9. 18___. 1828–1840.
Rarity: URS-8
CU $110

$50 • W-VT-025-050-G100

CJF

Engraver: Rawdon, Wright & Hatch. **Comments:** H-VT-10-G20, Coulter-10. 18___. 1830s.
Rarity: URS-6
CU $250

$100 • W-VT-025-100-G110

CJF

Engraver: Rawdon, Wright & Hatch. **Comments:** H-VT-10-G22, Coulter-11. 18___. 1830s.
Rarity: URS-6
F $350; **Unc-Rem** $250; **CU** $400

How to Read the Whitman Numbering System

$1 • W-RI-010-001-G010a

Denomination: Value of the note shown.

W: Whitman number. This number is a sortable code unique to each bank and note.

RI: Abbreviation for the state under study.

010: Numerical designation specific to each bank.

001: The denomination in dollars.

G010a: G indicates a good or valid note. Other categories are indicated thus: C (counterfeit); R (raised); S (spurious); N (not-attributed); A (altered). Numbers are assigned starting with 010, 020, et seq. Terminal letters following the number indicate variations of a note: a series of different colored overprints, tints, payees, etc., all on the same design of note. For more information, see the "How to Use This Book" section at the front of the volume, page xiv.

Uncut Sheets

$1-$1-$2-$5 • W-VT-025-001.001.002.005-US010

Vignette(s): ($1) Portrait of Marquis de Lafayette / State arms / Liberty and Industry flanking shield / Marquis de Lafayette standing with hat. *($1)* Portrait of Marquis de Lafayette / State arms / Liberty and Industry flanking shield / Marquis de Lafayette standing with hat. *($2)* Male portrait / 2 with Justice and Industry / Portrait of Dewitt Clinton. *($5)* Portrait of Marquis de Lafayette / V surmounted by eagle, Justice and Liberty / Portrait of George Washington. *Engraver:* Rawdon, Clark & Co. *Comments:* H-VT-10-G2, G2, G4, G10. 18__. 1828–1840.

Rarity: URS-5

Unc-Rem $400; **AU** $700

$3-$4-$6-$7 • W-VT-025-003.004.006.007-US020

Vignette(s): ($3) Woman reclining in foliage / Woman standing. *($4)* Liberty and eagle / Woman seated receiving coins from Mercury in clouds, Griffin on strongbox. *($6)* Man shearing sheep, Woman / Cow / Benjamin Franklin seated. *($7)* Ceres and Vulcan, Mercury / Ceres standing beside pedestal / Farmer plowing. *Engraver:* Rawdon, Wright, Hatch & Co. *Comments:* H-VT-10-G6, G8, G12, G14. 18__. 1830s.

Rarity: URS-3

Unc-Rem $1,000; **AU** $1,500

$5-$10-$10-$20 • W-VT-025-005.010.010.020-US030

Vignette(s): ($5) Portrait of Marquis de Lafayette / V surmounted by eagle, Justice and Liberty / Portrait of George Washington. *($10)* Roman soldier on horse / Portrait of Benjamin Franklin / Portrait of George Washington. *($10)* Roman soldier on horse / Portrait of Benjamin Franklin / Portrait of George Washington. *($20)* Portrait of Benjamin Franklin / Justice standing, Shield and beehive / Portrait of DeWitt Clinton. *Engraver:* Rawdon, Clark & Co. *Comments:* H-VT-10-G10, G16, G16, G18. 18__. 1828–1840.

Rarity: URS-4

Unc-Rem $500; **AU** $450

$50-$100 • W-VT-025-050.100-US040

Vignette(s): ($50) Woman reclining in foliage / Woman with rake seated by shield. *($100)* Woman seated receiving coins from Mercury. *Engraver:* Rawdon, Wright, Hatch & Co. *Comments:* H-VT-10-G20, G22. 18__. 1830s.

Rarity: URS-4

Unc-Rem $450; **AU** $600

Non-Valid Issues

$10 • W-VT-025-010-R010

Engraver: Rawdon, Clark & Co. *Comments:* H-VT-10-R5. Raised from W-VT-025-001-G010. 18__. 1828–1840.

Rarity: *None known*

$20 • W-VT-025-020-R020

Engraver: Rawdon, Clark & Co. *Comments:* H-VT-10-R6. Raised from W-VT-025-001-G010. 18__. 1828–1830s.

Rarity: *None known*

Bank of Troy
1859
W-VT-040

History: Certain bills of the Bank of Troy, New York, were imprinted with the date October 15, 1859, and made payable in Bennington, Vermont. These were engraved by W.L. Ormsby, New York.[2] Vermont banks near the New York border often had large amounts of Bank of Troy notes on hand. Presumably, the bank had a redemption office in Bennington. This was probably due to the fact that the Manchester to Bennington-Pittsfield-Lenox-Stockbridge corridor was a summer retreat for Bostonians and the wealthy from Albany and Troy. The notes would have had a valid use in the Bennington area.

This is one of several instances in which a bank or entity in one state issued notes payable in another, although it was not chartered or officially authorized in the other state.

Valid Issues

$1 • W-VT-040-001-G010

TD

Comments: H-Unlisted, Coulter-Unlisted. Oct. 15th, 1859. 1859.

Rarity: URS-5

EF $200; **CU** $300

$5 • W-VT-040-005-G020

TD

Comments: H-Unlisted, Coulter-Unlisted. Oct. 15th, 1859. 1859.

Rarity: URS-5

EF $150; **Unc-Rem** $275

Uncut Sheets

$1-$5 • W-VT-040-001.005-US010

SBG

Comments: All unlisted in Haxby. Oct. 15th, 1859. 1859.

Rarity: URS-4

EF $450; **Unc-Rem** $550

Green Mountain Bank

1846 AND 1847

W-VT-050

History: The Green Mountain Bank was chartered on November 2, 1846. On October 25, 1847, its name was amended by an act of the Legislature to the Stark Bank, W-VT-060.

See also listing under Rutland, W-VT-625.

Stark Bank

1847–1868

W-VT-060

History: The Stark Bank was chartered on November 2, 1846, as the Green Mountain Bank, W-VT-050. On October 25, 1847, its name was amended by an act of the Legislature to the Stark Bank. The authorized starting capital was $50,000. In 1851 it had risen to $75,000.

In 1854 these figures were given: notes discounted $268,704; deposits in city banks $22,999; other resources $21,876; specie $6,849. In 1857 the capital was $47,400, bills in circulation totaled $26,445, specie was $2,279, and real estate was valued at $5,600.

The bank's charter expired on August 1, 1867. The outstanding circulation at this time was $4,696. The bank published a notice that it would not be liable to redeem its outstanding circulation after August 1, 1868.

Numismatic Commentary: Many of this bank's issues show a portrait of General John Stark, the hero of the Battle of Bennington. Genuine notes are hard to locate. Beware of raised notes.

Remaining in the American Bank Note Co. archives as of 2003 was a $5-$10 face plate, a $20-$50 face plate, and a $1-$1-$2-$5 face plate.

VALID ISSUES

$1 • W-VT-060-001-G010

CC

Engraver: Danforth & Hufty. *Comments:* H-VT-15-G2, Coulter-14. January __, 18__. 1847–1850s.

Rarity: URS-2

Proof $1,500

$1 • W-VT-060-001-G010a

Left: Liberty, shield, and eagle. *Center:* 1 on shield / Ceres seated. *Right:* 1 / Portrait of General John Stark. *Engraver:* American Bank Note Co. *Comments:* H-VT-15-G2b. Similar to W-VT-060-001-G010 but with different engraver imprint. January __, 18__. 1860s.

Rarity: URS-4

VF $500

$2 • W-VT-060-002-G020

Left: 2 / Portrait of Abby Hutchinson / 2. *Center:* Train passing around rocky point. *Right:* 2 / Portrait of General John Stark. *Engraver:* Danforth & Hufty. *Comments:* H-VT-15-G4, Coulter-16. January __, 18__. 1847–1850s.

Rarity: URS-4

VF $450; **Proof** $1,500

$2 • W-VT-060-002-G020a

CJF

Engraver: American Bank Note Co. *Comments:* H-VT-15-G4b. Similar to W-VT-060-002-G020 but with different engraver imprint. January __, 18__. 1860s.

Rarity: URS-2

F $1,000

$5 • W-VT-060-005-G030   TD

Engraver: Danforth & Hufty. **Comments:** H-VT-15-G6, Coulter-20. January __, 18__. 1847–1850s.
Rarity: URS-3
VF $400; **Proof** $1,500

$5 • W-VT-060-005-G030a

Left: FIVE / Portrait of General John Stark. **Center:** 5 / Man on horseback, dog, sheep, and mill. **Bottom center:** Wheelbarrow and sheaf. **Right:** 5 / Portrait of George Washington. **Engraver:** American Bank Note Co. **Comments:** H-VT-15-G6b. Similar to W-VT-060-005-G030 but with different engraver imprint. January __, 18__. 1860s.
Rarity: *None known*

$10 • W-VT-060-010-G040   CJF

Engraver: Danforth & Hufty. **Comments:** H-VT-15-G8, Coulter-25. January __, 18__. 1847–1850s.
Rarity: URS-3
Proof $1,250

$10 • W-VT-060-010-G040a

Left: X. **Center:** Portrait of General John Stark / Angel with cornucopia offering apple to woman. **Bottom center:** Two women flanking state arms. **Right:** 10. **Engraver:** American Bank Note Co. **Comments:** H-VT-15-G8b. Similar to W-VT-060-010-G040 but with different engraver imprint. January __, 18__. 1860s.
Rarity: URS-3
VF $800

$20 • W-VT-060-020-G050   CC

Engraver: Danforth & Hufty. **Comments:** H-VT-15-G10, Coulter-30. 18__. 1847–1850s.
Rarity: URS-2
Proof $2,000

$50 • W-VT-060-050-G060   CC

Engraver: Danforth & Hufty. **Comments:** H-VT-15-G12, Coulter-33. 18__. 1847–1850s.
Rarity: URS-1
Proof $2,500

$50 • W-VT-060-050-G060a

Left: Allegorical woman / 50. **Center:** "Presentation of the Declaration of Independence". **Right:** 50 / Portrait of General John Stark. **Engraver:** American Bank Note Co. **Comments:** H-VT-15-G12b. Similar to W-VT-060-050-G060 but with different engraver imprint. 18__. 1860s.
Rarity: *None known*

Uncut Sheets
$1-$1-$2-$5 • W-VT-060-001.001.002.005-US010

Vignette(s): **($1)** Liberty, shield, and eagle / Ceres seated / Portrait of General John Stark. **($1)** Liberty, shield, and eagle / Ceres seated / Portrait of General John Stark. **($2)** Portrait of Abby Hutchinson / Train passing around rocky point / Portrait of General John Stark. **($5)** Portrait of General John Stark / Man on horseback, Dog, sheep, and mill / Wheelbarrow and sheaf / Portrait of George Washington. **Engraver:** Danforth & Hufty. **Comments:** H-VT-15-G2, G2, G4, G6. January __, 18__. 1847–1850s.
Rarity: URS-3
Proof $3,000

$5-$10 • W-VT-060-005.010-US020
Vignette(s): ($5) Portrait of General John Stark / Man on horseback, Dog, sheep, and mill / Wheelbarrow and sheaf / Portrait of George Washington. *($10)* Portrait of General John Stark / Angel with cornucopia offering apple to woman / Two women flanking state arms. *Engraver:* Danforth & Hufty. *Comments:* H-VT-15-G6, G8. Partial sheet. January ___, 18___. 1847–1850s.
Rarity: URS-3
Proof $2,500

$20-$50 • W-VT-060-020.050-US030
Vignette(s): ($20) Ceres / Portrait of General John Stark / Three allegorical figures / Portrait of Daniel Webster. *($50)* Allegorical figure / "Presentation of the Declaration of Independence" / Portrait of General John Stark. *Engraver:* Danforth & Hufty. *Comments:* H-VT-15-G10, G12. Partial sheet. January ___, 18___. 1847–1850s.
Rarity: URS-2
Proof $3,000

Non-Valid Issues

$1 • W-VT-060-001-C010
Engraver: Danforth & Hufty. *Comments:* H-VT-15-C2, Coulter-15. Counterfeit of W-VT-060-001-G010. Photographic. January ___, 18___. 1847–1850s.
Rarity: *None known*

$2 • W-VT-060-002-S010

Engraver: Danforth & Hufty. *Comments:* H-VT-15-S5, Coulter-17. Spurious design imitating a rough verbal description of W-VT-060-002-G020. January ___, 18___. 1840s.
Rarity: URS-7
F $100

$3 • W-VT-060-003-R010
Comments: H-Unlisted, Coulter-18. Raised from W-VT-060-001-G010. January ___, 18___. 1847–1850s.
Rarity: *None known*

$3 • W-VT-060-003-N010
Center: Farmers gathering hay, Dog, children. *Comments:* H-Unlisted, Coulter-19. 1850s.
Rarity: *None known*

$5 • W-VT-060-005-R020
Engraver: Danforth & Hufty. *Comments:* H-VT-15-R3, Coulter-21. Raised from W-VT-060-001-G010. January ___, 18___. 1847–1850s.
Rarity: *None known*

$5 • W-VT-060-005-N020
Center: Three women, Strongbox, eagle. *Comments:* H-Unlisted, Coulter-22. 1850s.
Rarity: *None known*

$5 • W-VT-060-005-N030
Center: Woman with cornucopia. *Comments:* H-Unlisted, Coulter-23. 1850s.
Rarity: *None known*

$5 • W-VT-060-005-A010

Engraver: Rawdon, Wright & Hatch. *Comments:* H-VT-15-A5, Coulter-24. Altered from $5 Chippeway County Bank, Sault De St. Mary, Michigan. 18___. 1830s–1840s.
Rarity: URS-4
G $50

$10 • W-VT-060-010-R030
Engraver: Danforth & Hufty. *Comments:* H-VT-15-R4. Raised from W-VT-060-001-G010. January ___, 18___. 1847–1850s.
Rarity: *None known*

$10 • W-VT-060-010-S020

Engraver: Danforth & Hufty. *Comments:* H-VT-15-S10, Coulter-26. 18___. 1840s.
Rarity: URS-5
F $100

$10 • W-VT-060-010-N040
Center: Train, city, mountains. *Comments:* H-Unlisted, Coulter-29. 1850s.
Rarity: *None known*

$10 • W-VT-060-010-A020
Left: Train. *Center:* X in die / Neptune, Venus / X in die. *Bottom center:* Pledge. *Right:* Agricultural implements. *Engraver:* Rawdon, Wright & Hatch. *Comments:* H-VT-15-A10, Coulter-28. Altered from $10 Chippeway County Bank, Sault De St. Mary, Michigan. 18___. 1830s–1840s.
Rarity: URS-4
F $125

$20 • W-VT-060-020-R040

CC

Comments: H-VT-15-R5, Coulter-31. Raised from W-VT-060-001-G010. January __, 18__. 1830s.
Rarity: URS-4
F $125

$20 • W-VT-060-020-A030
Left: Eagle. *Center:* 20 / Agricultural implements, Train / 20. *Bottom center:* Pledge. *Right:* 20 on die / Eagle with shield / XX. *Engraver:* Rawdon, Wright & Hatch. *Comments:* H-VT-15-A15, Coulter-32. Altered from $20 Chippeway County Bank, Sault De St. Mary, Michigan. 18__. 1830s–1840s.
Rarity: *None known*

Walloomsac Bank
1854–1858
W-VT-070

History: The Walloomsac Bank was chartered on November 9, 1854, with an authorized starting capital of $100,000. $50,000 was required to be paid in before the bank could officially open. The bank failed to commence business by January 1, 1856, and its incorporation expired. However, on November 6, 1856, the Legislature revived the charter, extending the date of operation to January 1, 1858.

Numismatic Commentary: No notes of this bank are known to exist, but Proofs may have been made.

BETHEL, VERMONT
The first town to be chartered in the Republic of Vermont, Bethel was named after the biblical town of the same name, meaning "House of God." The first settler here was Benjamin Smith, who arrived in 1779 and was joined by more the following year. They built a fort as a defense against raids from Canadian Indian enemies during the Revolutionary War. Later the logs of the fort were used to build a dam and mills.

Bethel began quarrying while its population was still small, and soon Bethel white granite became widely renowned for its strength, color, and durability. Clear quartz, white feldspar, and black mica contributed to the stone's blue-white, spotted hue, and in the 19th century the stone was quarried by German and Irish immigrants who came to the town seeking work. The granite was used in such buildings as the Smithsonian Museum of Natural History and the American Bank Note Co. headquarters in New York.

In 1830 severe flooding washed away bridges, stores, mills, and factories. However, the locals rebuilt and were ready to welcome the Central Vermont Railroad by 1869, making the village a key location for trade and travel.

White River Bank
1851–1865
W-VT-080

History: The White River Bank was incorporated in 1850. By July 1851, 4,000 shares of stock had been subscribed for. The starting authorized capital was $75,000, $40,000 of which was required to be paid in before the bank could officially open. This figure remained the same through 1864. In August 1859, circulation was $74,487, specie was $3,209, and real estate was valued at $1,000. Circulation was at $85,343 in 1862.

The interests of the White River Bank were succeeded by the National White River Bank of Bethel, chartered March 31, 1865. The bank's liability to redeem its outstanding notes—a circulation of $1,820—expired on December 10, 1867.

Numismatic Commentary: All genuine notes were printed either by the New England Bank Note Co. or its successor, the American Bank Note Co. They are fairly hard to locate in the marketplace, but the New England Bank Note Co. issues turn up more often.

Remaining in the American Bank Note Co. archives as of 2003 was a $3-$5-$10-$20 face plate and a $3-$5-$10-$20 tint plate.

VALID ISSUES
$1 • W-VT-080-001-G010
Left: 1 / Portrait of George Washington. *Center:* Female portrait / 1 / Female portrait. *Right:* 1 / Portrait of Benjamin Franklin. *Engraver:* New England Bank Note Co. *Comments:* H-VT-20-G2, Coulter-1. 18__. 1850s.
Rarity: *None known*

$1 • W-VT-080-001-G020
Left: Woman seated resting on barrel / 1. *Center:* 1 bearing "Presentation of the Declaration of Independence". *Right:* 1 / Woman holding grain and leaning on fence. *Engraver:* New England Bank Note Co. *Comments:* H-VT-20-G4, Coulter-2. 18__. 1850s.
Rarity: *None known*

$1 • W-VT-080-001-G020a
Engraver: New England Bank Note Co. / ABNCo. monogram. *Comments:* H-VT-20-G4a. Similar to W-VT-080-001-G020 but with additional engraver imprint. 18__. 1850s.
Rarity: URS-4
VF $350

$1 • **W-VT-080-001-G020b**   TD

Overprint: Red ONE. *Engraver:* New England Bank Note Co. / ABNCo. monogram. *Comments:* H-Unlisted. Similar to W-VT-080-001-G020 but with additional engraver imprint. 18__. 1850s.
Rarity: URS-4
F $350; **VF** $450

$1 • **W-VT-080-001-G030**   TD

Tint: Green dies bearing white ONE and 1, ONE, 1. *Engraver:* American Bank Note Co. *Comments:* H-VT-20-G6, Coulter-3. July 1st, 1862.
Rarity: URS-3
F $750; **VF** $900

$2 • **W-VT-080-002-G040**   CC

Engraver: New England Bank Note Co. *Comments:* H-VT-20-G8, Coulter-4. 18__. 1850s.
Rarity: URS-3
F $500; **VF** $900

$2 • **W-VT-080-002-G050**

Left: Man, boy, and dog driving sheep across river / 2. *Center:* 2 bearing "Presentation of the Declaration of Independence". *Right:* TWO / Woman seated with garland of flowers / TWO. *Engraver:* New England Bank Note Co. *Comments:* H-VT-20-G10, Coulter-5. 18__. 1850s.
Rarity: *None known*

$2 • **W-VT-080-002-G050a**   CC

Overprint: Red TWO. *Engraver:* New England Bank Note Co. *Comments:* H-Unlisted. Similar to W-VT-080-002-G050. 18__. 1850s.
Rarity: URS-4
F $900

$2 • **W-VT-080-002-G050b**

Engraver: New England Bank Note Co. / ABNCo. monogram. *Comments:* H-VT-20-G10a. Similar to W-VT-080-002-G050 but with additional engraver imprint. 18__. 1850s–1860s.
Rarity: *None known*

$2 • **W-VT-080-002-G060**

Left: 2 / Two soldiers seated, Man beating drum. *Center:* 2 / TWO DOLLARS / 2. *Right:* 2 / Boy with bird's nest. *Tint:* Green die bearing white TWO. *Engraver:* American Bank Note Co. *Comments:* H-VT-20-G12, Coulter-6. 1862.
Rarity: *None known*

$3 • **W-VT-080-003-G070**

Left: 3 / George Washington on horseback. *Center:* Female portrait / 3 / Female portrait. *Right:* 3 / Blacksmith. *Engraver:* New England Bank Note Co. *Comments:* H-VT-20-G14, Coulter-8. 18__. 1850s.
Rarity: URS-3
F $750

$3 • **W-VT-080-003-G080**

Left: Farmer on horseback, Boy, cattle / 3. *Center:* 3. *Right:* 3 on THREE / Woman with basket of flowers / THREE. *Engraver:* New England Bank Note Co. *Comments:* H-VT-20-G16, Coulter-10. 18__. 1850s.
Rarity: *None known*

$3 • **W-VT-080-003-G080a**   CC

Overprint: Red THREE. *Engraver:* New England Bank Note Co. / ABNCo. monogram. *Comments:* H-VT-20-G16a. Similar to W-VT-080-003-G080 but with additional engraver imprint. 18__. 1850s–1860s.
Rarity: URS-3
F $750

$3 • W-VT-080-003-G090

Left: 3 / Female portrait. *Center:* Benjamin Franklin showing bust of George Washington to child. *Right:* 3 / Portrait of boy. *Tint:* Green dies bearing white THREEs. *Engraver:* American Bank Note Co. *Comments:* H-VT-20-G18, Coulter-11. 1862.
Rarity: *None known*

$5 • W-VT-080-005-G100   CC

Engraver: New England Bank Note Co. *Comments:* H-VT-20-G20, Coulter-13. 18__. 1850s.
Rarity: URS-5
F $350

$5 • W-VT-080-005-G100a

Left: Spread eagle on shield, Village and ship / FIVE. *Center:* Allegorical woman and cherub in V. *Right:* 5 / Girl with basket of flowers. *Engraver:* New England Bank Note Co. / ABNCo. monogram. *Comments:* H-VT-20-G20a. Similar to W-VT-080-005-G100 but with additional engraver imprint. 18__. 1850s–1860s.
Rarity: *None known*

$5 • W-VT-080-005-G110

Left: 5 / Soldier loading gun. *Center:* Liberty with eagle. *Right:* 5 / V on die. *Tint:* Green V / V. *Engraver:* American Bank Note Co. *Comments:* H-VT-20-G22, Coulter-14. 1862.
Rarity: *None known*

$10 • W-VT-080-010-G120

Left: Vulcan seated, Factory and building / TEN. *Center:* X. *Right:* 10 / Farmer holding sickle and sheaf. *Engraver:* New England Bank Note Co. *Comments:* H-VT-20-G24, Coulter-16. 18__. 1850s.
Rarity: *None known*

$10 • W-VT-080-010-G120a

Engraver: New England Bank Note Co. / ABNCo. monogram. *Comments:* H-VT-20-G24a. Similar to W-VT-080-010-G120 but with additional engraver imprint. 18__. 1850s–1860s.
Rarity: *None known*

$10 • W-VT-080-010-G130

Left: TEN on X / Niagara Falls / TEN on X. *Center:* George Washington reading dispatch, Officer writing on drum head. *Right:* 10 / Indian maid. *Tint:* Green X / X. *Engraver:* American Bank Note Co. *Comments:* H-VT-20-G26a, Coulter-17. 1862.
Rarity: *None known*

$20 • W-VT-080-020-G140

Left: 20 / Woman seated. *Center:* XX / Eagle / XX. *Right:* Brig / 20. *Engraver:* New England Bank Note Co. *Comments:* H-VT-20-G28, Coulter-18. 18__. 1850s.
Rarity: *None known*

$20 • W-VT-080-020-G150

Left: TWENTY / Allegorical figure / TWENTY. *Center:* Portrait of girl / XX / Portrait of girl. *Right:* 20 / Allegorical figure. *Tint:* Green XX. *Engraver:* American Bank Note Co. *Comments:* H-VT-20-G30a, Coulter-19. 1862.
Rarity: *None known*

$50 • W-VT-080-050-G160

Left: FIFTY / Woman standing / FIFTY. *Center:* Man holding restless horse by mane. *Right:* FIFTY / Woman standing with cornucopia / FIFTY. *Engraver:* New England Bank Note Co. *Comments:* H-VT-20-G32, Coulter-20. 18__. 1850s.
Rarity: *None known*

$100 • W-VT-080-100-G170

Left: ONE HUNDRED on 100 / Portrait of William Henry Harrison. *Center:* Wharf scene, Wagons, horses, men, vessels. *Right:* ONE HUNDRED on 100 / Portrait of Christopher Columbus. *Engraver:* New England Bank Note Co. *Comments:* H-VT-20-G34, Coulter-21. 18__. 1850s.
Rarity: *None known*

Non-Valid Issues

$3 • W-VT-080-003-S010   CJF

Overprint: Red 3 / 3. *Engraver:* New England Bank Note Co. *Comments:* H-VT-20-S5, Coulter-7. Jan. __, 185_. 1850s.
Rarity: URS-6
VG $75

$3 • W-VT-080-003-S010a   CC

Tint: Red outlining white THREE. *Comments:* H-VT-20-S5a, Coulter-9. Similar to W-VT-080-003-S010. Jan. __, 185_. 1850s.
Rarity: URS-5
F $125

$3 • W-VT-080-003-S020

ANS

Engraver: New England Bank Note Co. *Comments:* H-VT-20-S10, Coulter-Unlisted. 18__. 1850s.

Rarity: URS-8
F $60

$3 • W-VT-080-003-N010

Center: Woman resting on strongbox. *Comments:* H-Unlisted, Coulter-12. 1850s. **Rarity:** *None known*

$5 • W-VT-080-005-S030

Left: Eagle on shield and anchor, Factories and ships. *Center:* V bearing woman with cornucopia and cherub. *Right:* 5 / Girl with ringlets holding basket. *Engraver:* New England Bank Note Co. *Comments:* H-VT-20-S15, Coulter-Unlisted. 18__. 1850s.

Rarity: *None known*

$5 • W-VT-080-005-N020

Left: Portrait of Henry Clay. *Center:* Cattle, train, and tree. *Right:* Man with basket. *Comments:* H-Unlisted, Coulter-15. 1850s.

Rarity: *None known*

BRADFORD, VERMONT

Officially organized as a town on May 4, 1773, Bradford was settled by John Hosmer in 1765. The primary industries were agricultural in nature, but mills rose up around the falls of Waits River. By 1848 the Connecticut & Passumpsic Rivers Railroad had opened to Bradford.

In 1820 the Bradford Academy was chartered, and the Bradford Mills were built in 1847. The mills produced flour and feed and also performed other grinding jobs. At its highest production, the mill could grind 1,000 bushels a day. In 1859 the population of Bradford was 1,723, and industries included a foundry, a machine shop, two gristmills, three sawmills, a paper mill, a whetstone factory, and the manufacture of farm implements, wooden materials, and tinware. The sawmills mostly cut lumber from pine, spruce, ash, hemlock, and other hard woods, producing 500,000 board feet a year.

Bradford Bank
1853–1867
W-VT-090

History: The Bradford Bank was chartered in 1853 with $100,000 capital. By June 1855, capital was $50,000, rising to $100,000 as of May 1857. That same year circulation was $160,942, and specie was $4,491. In July 1859, circulation was $160,942.

On October 22, 1864, the majority of stockholders voted that it was "expedient to close up the affairs of said Bank, and to surrender the charter of the same at an early day." The charter had been authorized to endure for 23 years, but the bank had been doing business for a little more than ten years. The outstanding circulation as of July 1, 1867, was determined to be $3,206, the redemption of which was guaranteed by bonds which the Directors placed with the State Treasurer.

Numismatic Commentary: Genuine notes are available in the marketplace. Some of the denominations show coins in the vignettes.

VALID ISSUES

$1 • W-VT-090-001-G010

CJF

Overprint: Red ONE. *Engraver:* Rawdon, Wright, Hatch & Edson / New England Bank Note Co. *Comments:* H-VT-25-G2a, Coulter-1. April __, 18__. 1850s.

Rarity: URS-2
F $3,000

$1 • W-VT-090-001-G010a

Left: ONE / Justice and Minerva. *Center:* Lumberman, Gold dollar, Log cabin. *Right:* 1 bearing ONE / Indian woman. *Overprint:* Red ONE. *Engraver:* Rawdon, Wright, Hatch & Edson / New England Bank Note Co. / ABNCo. monogram. *Comments:* H-VT-25-G2b. Similar to W-VT-090-001-G010 but with additional engraver imprint. April __, 18__. 1850s–1860s.

Rarity: *None known*

$2 • W-VT-090-002-G020

Left: 2 / Liberty and eagle, Winged woman. *Center:* Milkmaid and boy, Cows, Two gold dollars. *Right:* 2 / Mermaid fountain. *Overprint:* Red TWO. *Engraver:* Rawdon, Wright, Hatch & Edson / New England Bank Note Co. *Comments:* H-VT-25-G4a, Coulter-3. April __, 18__. 1850s.

Rarity: *None known*

$2 • W-VT-090-002-G020a

Overprint: Red TWO. *Engraver:* Rawdon, Wright, Hatch & Edson / New England Bank Note Co. / ABNCo. monogram. *Comments:* H-VT-25-G4b. Similar to W-VT-090-002-G020 but with additional engraver imprint. April __, 18__. 1850s–1860s.

Rarity: *None known*

$3 • **W-VT-090-003-G030**   TD

Overprint: Red THREE. *Engraver:* Rawdon, Wright, Hatch & Edson / New England Bank Note Co. *Comments:* H-VT-25-G6a, Coulter-5. April __, 18__. 1850s.
Rarity: URS-2
F $1,250

$3 • **W-VT-090-003-G030a**

Left: Liberty seated in clouds watering eagle / 3. *Center:* Farmer, sailor, and mechanic, Three gold dollars. *Right:* 3 / Farmer seated with die bearing THREE. *Overprint:* Red THREE. *Engraver:* Rawdon, Wright, Hatch & Edson / New England Bank Note Co. / ABNCo. monogram. *Comments:* H-VT-25-G6b. Similar to W-VT-090-003-G030 but with additional engraver imprint. April __, 18__. 1850s.
Rarity: *None known*

$5 • **W-VT-090-005-G040**

Left: Farmer and milkmaid / 5. *Center:* Hunter, Indian woman, and three cherubs, Five gold dollars. *Right:* 5 / Male portrait. *Overprint:* Red FIVE. *Engraver:* Rawdon, Wright, Hatch & Edson / New England Bank Note Co. *Comments:* H-VT-25-G8a, Coulter-7. April __, 18__. 1850s.
Rarity: URS-4
VF $350

$5 • **W-VT-090-005-G040a**   CJF

Overprint: Red FIVE. *Engraver:* Rawdon, Wright, Hatch & Edson / New England Bank Note Co. / ABNCo. monogram. *Comments:* H-VT-25-G8b. Similar to W-VT-090-005-G040 but with additional engraver imprint. April __, 18__. 1850s–1860s.
Rarity: URS-2
F $1,250

$10 • **W-VT-090-010-G050**

Left: 10 / Two figures. *Center:* Allegorical figure, State arms, Allegorical figure. *Right:* X / Cherub riding dolphin. *Overprint:* Red TEN. *Engraver:* Rawdon, Wright, Hatch & Edson / New England Bank Note Co. *Comments:* H-VT-25-G10a, Coulter-10. April __, 18__. 1850s.
Rarity: *None known*

$10 • **W-VT-090-010-G050a**

Overprint: Red TEN. *Engraver:* Rawdon, Wright, Hatch & Edson / New England Bank Note Co. / ABNCo. monogram. *Comments:* H-VT-25-G10b. Similar to W-VT-090-010-G050 but with additional engraver imprint. April __, 18__. 1850s–1860s.
Rarity: *None known*

$20 • **W-VT-090-020-G060**

Left: Justice / XX. *Center:* Farmer and Indian, State arms, Farmer and Indian. *Right:* 20 / Plow and grain. *Overprint:* Red TWENTY. *Engraver:* Rawdon, Wright, Hatch & Edson / New England Bank Note Co. *Comments:* H-VT-25-G12a, Coulter-11. April __, 18__. 1850s.
Rarity: *None known*

$20 • **W-VT-090-020-G060a**

Overprint: Red TWENTY. *Engraver:* Rawdon, Wright, Hatch & Edson / New England Bank Note Co. / ABNCo. monogram. *Comments:* H-VT-25-G12b. Similar to W-VT-090-020-G060 but with additional engraver imprint. April __, 18__. 1850s–1860s.
Rarity: *None known*

$50 • **W-VT-090-050-G070**

Left: Plenty beside strongbox, Milkmaid, cows, Train, shipping, and factory / 50. *Right:* 50 / Portrait of Daniel Webster. *Overprint:* Red FIFTY. *Engraver:* Rawdon, Wright, Hatch & Edson / New England Bank Note Co. *Comments:* H-VT-25-G14a, Coulter-12. April __, 18__. 1850s.
Rarity: *None known*

$50 • **W-VT-090-050-G070a**   TD

Engraver: Rawdon, Wright, Hatch & Edson / New England Bank Note Co. / ABNCo. monogram. *Comments:* H-VT-25-G14b, Coulter-13. Similar to W-VT-090-050-G070 but with additional engraver imprint. April 1, 18__. 1850s–1860s.
Rarity: URS-2
VF $2,500

$100 • **W-VT-090-100-G080**

Left: 100 / Justice. *Center:* Woman, State arms surmounted by eagle, Woman. *Right:* 100 / Horses drawing load of hay. *Overprint:* Red HUNDRED. *Engraver:* Rawdon, Wright, Hatch & Edson / New England Bank Note Co. *Comments:* H-VT-25-G16a. April __, 18__. 1850s.
Rarity: *None known*

$100 • **W-VT-090-100-G080a**

Overprint: Red HUNDRED. *Engraver:* Rawdon, Wright, Hatch & Edson / New England Bank Note Co. / ABNCo. monogram. *Comments:* H-VT-25-G16b, Coulter-15. Similar to W-VT-090-100-G080 but with additional engraver imprint. April __, 18__. 1850s–1860s.
Rarity: *None known*

NON-VALID ISSUES

$1 • W-VT-090-001-A010
Left: 1 in die / Herd of cattle, bridge, train. *Center:* Girl, calves, canal boat, train. *Right:* Girl leaning on fence / 1 in die. *Engraver:* Danforth, Wright & Co. *Comments:* H-Unlisted, Coulter-2. Altered from Southern Bank of Bainbridge, Bainbridge, Georgia. 1850s.

Rarity: *None known*

$2 • W-VT-090-002-C020
Engraver: Rawdon, Wright, Hatch & Edson / New England Bank Note Co. *Comments:* H-VT-25-C4a. Counterfeit of W-VT-090-002-G020. April__, 18__. 1850s.

Rarity: *None known*

$2 • W-VT-090-002-N010
Left: 2 / Women. *Center:* Man, woman, cows, milk pails. *Comments:* H-Unlisted, Coulter-4. 1850s.

Rarity: *None known*

$3 • W-VT-090-003-S010
Left: George Washington on horse. *Center:* Woman / 3 / Woman. *Right:* Blacksmith. *Comments:* H-VT-25-S5, Coulter-6. 1850s.

Rarity: *None known*

$5 • W-VT-090-005-A020

Tint: Red-brown lathework outlining white 5. *Engraver:* Bald, Cousland & Co. *Comments:* H-VT-25-A10, Coulter-9. Altered from $5 Pioneer Association, Lafayette, Indiana. 18__. 1850s–1860s.

Rarity: URS-6
F $275

$50 • W-VT-090-050-C070a

Overprint: Red FIFTY. *Engraver:* Rawdon, Wright, Hatch & Edson / New England Bank Note Co. / ABNCo. monogram. *Comments:* H-VT-25-C14b. Counterfeit of W-VT-090-050-G070a. April __, 18__. 1850s–1860s.

Rarity: URS-5
F $350

$50 • W-VT-090-050-N020
Comments: H-Unlisted, Coulter-14. Imitation of W-VT-090-050-G070a. 1850s.

Rarity: *None known*

Bradford Bank of Bradford
1850s–1860s
W-VT-100

History: A non-existent bank represented only by notes altered from those of other banks. The notes were intended to pass for those of the Bradford Bank, W-VT-090.

ISSUES

$1 • W-VT-100-001-A010
Tint: Red-brown 1s and panel outlining white ONE DOLLAR. *Engraver:* Danforth, Wright & Co. *Comments:* H-VT-26-A5. Altered from $1 Southern Bank of Georgia, Bainbridge, Georgia. March 1, 18__. 1860s

Rarity: URS-5
F $125

$5 • W-VT-100-005-A020

Engraver: Rawdon, Wright, Hatch & Edson. *Comments:* H-VT-26-A10, Coulter-8. Altered from $5 Farmers and Merchants Bank, Memphis, Tennessee. May 10th, 1859.

Rarity: URS-6
F $100

BRANDON, VERMONT

Chartered in 1761, Brandon was settled on land that was full of natural resources, including productive farmland, rivers, timber, and minerals. Waterpower provided growth to many industries, including the production of iron ore and marble. In 1849 the railroad appeared in town, allowing the shipping of iron-made tools and products as well as paint, wooden goods, and marble.

The mid-19th century statesman Stephen A. Douglas was born in Brandon. Dairy, stockbreeding, and tourism slowly superseded the early industries of mining, and Brandon's village of Forest Dale housed an elementary school, a post office, and a pair of grocery stores.

Brandon Bank
1848–1864
W-VT-110

History: The Brandon Bank was chartered in 1848 with $50,000 in authorized capital. In 1852 its cashier was Lorenzo Bixby and the president was John A. Conant. In February 1854, the bank was rechartered and given an additional capital of $25,000. This value remained at $75,000 throughout the bank's existence.

Figures given in 1854 showed deposits in city banks at $27,055, specie at $8,357, and other resources at $1,521. Circulation was $55,687 in 1857, and specie totaled $2,754. In July 1862, circulation was $63,700.

The Brandon Bank was liquidated in 1864 and its business was succeeded by the Brandon National Bank, chartered March 26, 1864. Its charter expired on March 1, 1865, by proclamation of the Governor. The outstanding circulation as of July 1, 1867, was $2,167.

Numismatic Commentary: Genuine notes from this bank are very scarce. Collectors are most likely to come across a counterfeit issue more often than not. This bank is one of the very few in the New England states to have issued cashier notes that were probably given as change during times of hard money shortage. They are not merchant scrip.

VALID ISSUES

5¢ • W-VT-110-00.05-G010

CC

Overprint: Red 5. **Engraver:** American Bank Note Co. **Comments:** H-Unlisted, Coulter-1. January 1st, 1863.

Rarity: URS-7

VF $60

10¢ • W-VT-110-00.10-G020

CJF

Overprint: Red 10. **Engraver:** American Bank Note Co. **Comments:** H-Unlisted, Coulter-2. January 1st, 1863.

Rarity: URS-8

F $35

25¢ • W-VT-110-00.25-G030

CJF

Overprint: Red 25. **Engraver:** American Bank Note Co. **Comments:** H-Unlisted, Coulter-3. January 1st, 1863.

Rarity: URS-8

F $35

$1 • W-VT-110-001-G040

Left: Farm scene, Man, woman, three men, two oxen, men loading hay / 1. **Center:** 1. **Bottom center:** Machinery. **Right:** 1 / Portrait of Ceres / ONE. **Engraver:** New England Bank Note Co. **Comments:** H-VT-30-G2, Coulter-5. 18__. 1848–1850s.

Rarity: *None known*

$1 • W-VT-110-001-G040a

TD

Tint: Brown-orange lathework, panel of microlettering, and ONE. **Engraver:** Rawdon, Wright, Hatch & Edson / New England Bank Note Co. / ABNCo. monogram. **Comments:** H-VT-30-G2a. Similar to W-VT-110-001-G040 but with additional engraver imprint. 18__. 1850s–1860s.

Rarity: URS-2
VG $750

$2 • W-VT-110-002-G050

Left: Man, boy, and dog driving sheep across river / TWO. **Center:** 2. **Bottom center:** Sheaf and plow. **Right:** 2 / Blacksmith standing. **Engraver:** New England Bank Note Co. **Comments:** H-VT-30-G4, Coulter-6. 18__. 1848–1850s.

Rarity: *None known*

$2 • W-VT-110-002-G050a

TD

Tint: Brown-orange lathework, panel of microlettering, and TWO. **Engraver:** Rawdon, Wright, Hatch & Edson / New England Bank Note Co. / ABNCo. monogram. **Comments:** H-VT-30-G4a. Similar to W-VT-110-002-G050 but with additional engraver imprint. 18__. 1850s–1860s.

Rarity: URS-2
F $1,000

$3 • W-VT-110-003-G060

Left: Farmer plowing with two horses / 3. **Center:** 3. **Bottom center:** Train. **Right:** 3 / Stonecutter at work. **Engraver:** New England Bank Note Co. **Comments:** H-VT-30-G6, Coulter-8. 18__. 1848–1850s.

Rarity: *None known*

$3 • W-VT-110-003-G060a

Tint: Brown-orange. **Engraver:** New England Bank Note Co. / ABNCo. monogram. **Comments:** H-VT-30-G6a. Similar to W-VT-110-003-G060 but with additional engraver imprint. 18__. 1850s–1860s.

Rarity: *None known*

$5 • W-VT-110-005-G070

Left: Three cows, Farmer plowing with two oxen, Two men fishing / FIVE. **Center:** 5 / State arms. **Bottom center:** 5 on die. **Right:** 5 / Woman in clouds carrying flag, Three cherubs. **Engraver:** New England Bank Note Co. **Comments:** H-VT-30-G8, Coulter-9. 18__. 1848–1850s.

Rarity: *None known*

$5 • W-VT-110-005-G070a

Engraver: New England Bank Note Co. / ABNCo. monogram. **Comments:** H-VT-30-G8a. Similar to W-VT-110-005-G070 but with different date and additional engraver imprint. May 1st, 18__. 1850s–1860s.

Rarity: *None known*

$10 • W-VT-110-010-G080

CC

Engraver: Rawdon, Wright, Hatch & Edson / New England Bank Note Co. **Comments:** H-VT-30-G10, Coulter-15. 18__. 1848–1850s.

Rarity: URS-2
F $1,250

$10 • W-VT-110-010-G080a

Left: Two oxen drawing load of hay, Men on horseback / TEN. **Center:** X. **Right:** 10 / Two women. **Engraver:** New England Bank Note Co. / ABNCo. monogram. **Comments:** H-VT-30-G10a. Similar to W-VT-110-010-G080 but with additional engraver imprint. 18__. 1850s–1860s.

Rarity: *None known*

$20 • W-VT-110-020-G090

Left: 20 / Minerva standing. **Center:** Woman seated between 2 and 0 holding rake. **Right:** 20 / Woman reclining with cornucopia / 20. **Engraver:** Rawdon, Wright, Hatch & Edson. **Comments:** H-VT-30-G12, Coulter-16. 18__. 1848–1860s.

Rarity: *None known*

$50 • W-VT-110-050-G100

Left: 50 / Minerva. **Center:** Ceres and Vulcan seated with rake, hammer, and cornucopia. **Right:** 50 / Cherub steering sailboat / 50. **Engraver:** Rawdon, Wright, Hatch & Edson. **Comments:** H-VT-30-G14, Coulter-17. 18__. 1848–1860s.

Rarity: *None known*

$100 • W-VT-110-100-G110

Left: 100 / Vulcan seated. **Center:** Spread eagle on tree limb, Train on bridge, canal locks. **Bottom center:** 100. **Right:** 100 / Ceres seated with rake, Cornucopia. **Engraver:** Rawdon, Wright, Hatch & Edson. **Comments:** H-VT-30-G16, Coulter-18. 18__. 1848–1860s.

Rarity: *None known*

NON-VALID ISSUES

$1 • W-VT-110-001-N010
Center: Men, boys, sheep, and dog. *Comments:* H-Unlisted, Coulter-4. 1850s.
Rarity: *None known*

$2 • W-VT-110-002-C050

CJF

Engraver: New England Bank Note Co. *Comments:* H-VT-30-C4. Counterfeit of W-VT-110-002-G050. May 1st, 1858.
Rarity: URS-6
F $75

$2 • W-VT-110-002-N020
Engraver: New England Bank Note Co. *Comments:* H-Unlisted, Coulter-7. Imitation of W-VT-110-002-G050. Genuine note does not have "The President Directors & Co. of" over 2. May 1, 1858.
Rarity: *None known*

$5 • W-VT-110-005-C070a

CC

Engraver: New England Bank Note Co. / ABNCo. monogram. *Comments:* H-VT-30-C8a. Counterfeit of W-VT-110-005-G070a. May 1st, 18__. 1860s.
Rarity: URS-6
F $75

$5 • W-VT-110-005-R010
Engraver: New England Bank Note Co. *Comments:* H-VT-30-R5. Raised from W-VT-110-001-G040. 18__. 1848–1850s.
Rarity: *None known*

$5 • W-VT-110-005-R020
Engraver: New England Bank Note Co. *Comments:* H-VT-30-R10, Coulter-11. Raised from W-VT-110-002-G050. 18__. 1848–1850s.
Rarity: *None known*

$5 • W-VT-110-005-R030
Engraver: New England Bank Note Co. *Comments:* H-Unlisted, Coulter-12. Raised from W-VT-110-002-G050. May 1, 1858.
Rarity: *None known*

$5 • W-VT-110-005-N030
Engraver: New England Bank Note Co. / ABNCo. monogram. *Comments:* H-Unlisted, Coulter-10. Imitation of W-VT-110-005-G070. 1850s.
Rarity: *None known*

$5 • W-VT-110-005-N040
Left: Train. *Center:* Ship under sail. *Right:* Medallion head. *Comments:* H-VT-30-N5, Coulter-13. 1850s.
Rarity: *None known*

$5 • W-VT-110-005-N050
Center: Man and boys with dog running sheep across stream. *Comments:* H-Unlisted, Coulter-14. 1850s.
Rarity: *None known*

Peoples Bank
1821–1850s
W-VT-120

History: The Peoples Bank was incorporated on November 5, 1821, with an authorized capital of $100,000. In 1847 its capital was $75,000. By 1851 the same was valued at $150,000, and circulation was $156,193. In 1854 these figures were given: deposits in city banks $47,547; specie $4,227; other resources $7,785. Capital was $150,000 in 1855.

BRATTLEBORO, VERMONT

Originally a part of Fort Dummer, which was built to protect against raids by Indians, Brattleboro was chartered in 1753. It was named after William Brattle Jr., who was a colonel serving in the king's militia. He was a Harvard graduate, a lawyer, a preacher, a doctor, and a legislator. He never actually set foot in the town that was named after him.

Brattleboro's population grew throughout the 18th century. A gristmill and sawmill were erected there, and the stage coach route that passed through town stimulated the economy in the trade of grain, lumber, turpentine, tallow, and pork. Industry arrived in Brattleboro during the 19th century with the Vermont Valley railroad running straight through the town. Book publishing began here in 1805, and in the 1840s Brattleboro even took on a reputation as a resort town. Fresh springs with medicinal purposes were discovered and operated until 1871. The Estey Organ Company was also a prominent business during the time, manufacturing reed organs and distributing them as far as New Zealand.

Bank of Brattleboro
1821–1865
W-VT-130

History: The Bank of Brattleboro was chartered on November 5, 1821. Its capital was authorized at $100,000 with $75,000 paid in. Its charter expired on January 1, 1837, at which time it was renewed. In August 1845, circulation was $122,409. In October 1848, the capital was increased by $25,000, making the aggregate $100,000. In May 1857, capital was at $150,000, circulation was $174,882, specie was $11,376, and real estate was valued at $3,000.

The vote instructing the directors to take steps toward shutting down was passed on March 14, 1865, and the charter of the Vermont National Bank was granted on May 12, 1866. The outstanding circulation as of July 1, 1867, was $3,456, the redemption of which was guaranteed by the Vermont National Bank, which succeeded the business interests of the state bank.

Numismatic Commentary: Genuine notes are available in the marketplace. The New England Bank Note Co. engraved all of the later genuine notes, while the Graphic Co. produced the earlier notes.

VALID ISSUES

$1 • W-VT-130-001-G010   CC

Engraver: Graphic Co. *Comments:* H-VT-35-G2. Progressive Proof. 18__. 1820s–1830s.

Rarity: URS-3
Proof $750

$1 • W-VT-130-001-G020   CC

Comments: H-VT-35-G6, Coulter-1. 18__. 1830s.

Rarity: URS-3
VF $500

$1 • W-VT-130-001-G030

Left: Panel with ONE vertically. *Center:* Sloop and other vessels / 1. *Right:* ONE / Indian woman seated with bow and arrow / ONE. *Engraver:* New England Bank Note Co. *Comments:* H-VT-35-G10. 18__. 1840s–1850s.

Rarity: *None known*

$1 • W-VT-130-001-G040

Left: 1 / Portrait of George Washington. *Center:* Woman / 1. *Right:* 1 / Portrait of Benjamin Franklin. *Engraver:* New England Bank Note Co. *Comments:* H-VT-35-G12, Coulter-2. 18__. 1850s.

Rarity: *None known*

$1 • W-VT-130-001-G040a

Engraver: New England Bank Note Co. / ABNCo. monogram. *Comments:* H-Unlisted. Similar to W-VT-130-001-G040 but with additional engraver imprint. 18__. 1850s–1860s.

Rarity: *None known*

$1 • W-VT-130-001-G050   CC

Overprint: Red ONE. *Engraver:* New England Bank Note Co. / ABNCo. monogram. *Comments:* H-VT-35-G14a, Coulter-3. 18__. 1850s–1860s.

Rarity: URS-3
F $750

$2 • W-VT-130-002-G060

Left: 2 / TWO / 2. *Center:* Allegorical woman / 2 / Sailing ship and vessels / Allegorical woman. *Right:* TWO / Woman / TWO. *Engraver:* New England Bank Note Co. *Comments:* H-VT-35-G22, Coulter-4. 18__. 1840s–1850s.

Rarity: *None known*

$2 • W-VT-130-002-G070

Left: 2 / Portrait of Christopher Columbus. *Center:* Woman with cornucopia / 2 / Justice. *Right:* 2 / Portrait. *Engraver:* New England Bank Note Co. *Comments:* H-VT-35-G24, Coulter-5. 18__. 1850s.

Rarity: *None known*

$2 • W-VT-130-002-G080   CJF

Overprint: Red TWO. *Engraver:* New England Bank Note Co. *Comments:* H-VT-35-G26a, Coulter-6. 18__. 1850s–1860s.

Rarity: URS-3
F $750

$2 • W-VT-130-002-G080a

Left: 2 / George Washington with horse / 2. *Center:* 2 / Woman seated with 2 / 2. *Right:* 2 / George Washington with horse / 2. *Overprint:* Red TWO. *Engraver:* New England Bank Note Co. / ABNCo. monogram. *Comments:* H-Unlisted, Coulter-Unlisted. Similar to W-VT-130-002-G080 but with additional engraver imprint. 18__. 1850s–1860s.

Rarity: URS-3
VF $550

$3 • **W-VT-130-003-G090** CJF

Engraver: New England Bank Note Co. **Comments:** H-VT-35-G34. 18__. 1840s–1860s.

Rarity: URS-3
F $750

$3 • **W-VT-130-003-G100**

Left: 3 / George Washington with horse. **Center:** Female portrait / 3 / Female portrait. **Right:** 3 / Vulcan seated. **Engraver:** New England Bank Note Co. **Comments:** H-VT-35-G36, Coulter-12. 18__. 1850s. Rarity: *None known*

$3 • **W-VT-130-003-G110**

Left: 3 / Portrait of child / 3. **Center:** Woman seated beside 3. **Right:** 3 / Portrait of child / 3. **Overprint:** Red THREE. **Engraver:** New England Bank Note Co. **Comments:** H-VT-35-G38a, Coulter-11. 18__. 1850s–1860s.

Rarity: *None known*

$5 • **W-VT-130-005-G120**

Engraver: Graphic Co. **Comments:** H-VT-35-G40. No description available. 18__. 1820s.

Rarity: *None known*

$5 • **W-VT-130-005-G130**

Left: FIVE vertically. **Center:** Woman kneeling and unveiling shield bearing 5 / V. **Right:** 5 / Ship. **Engraver:** New England Bank Note Co. **Comments:** H-VT-35-G48, Coulter-17. 18__. 1840s–1850s. Rarity: *None known*

$5 • **W-VT-130-005-G140**

Left: Ceres seated with rake and shield, Buildings / V on FIVE. **Center:** Indian girl in V. **Right:** 5 / Portrait of George Washington. **Engraver:** New England Bank Note Co. **Comments:** H-VT-35-G50. 18__. 1840s–1850s.

Rarity: *None known*

$5 • **W-VT-130-005-G140a** CJF

Overprint: Red FIVE. **Engraver:** New England Bank Note Co. / ABNCo. monogram. **Comments:** H-Unlisted, Coulter-Unlisted. Similar to W-VT-130-005-G140 but with additional engraver imprint. 18__. 1850s–1860s.

Rarity: URS-3
F $750

$5 • **W-VT-130-005-G140b**

Overprint: Green FIVE. **Engraver:** New England Bank Note Co. / ABNCo. monogram. **Comments:** H-VT-35-G50b, Coulter-20. Similar to W-VT-130-005-G140 but with additional engraver imprint. 18__. 1850s–1860s.

Rarity: URS-2
VF $650

$5 • **W-VT-130-005-G150**

Left: FIVE. **Center:** Spread eagle on American shield / Vessels. **Right:** 5 / Girl with basket. **Overprint:** Red FIVE. **Engraver:** New England Bank Note Co. **Comments:** H-VT-35-G52a, Coulter-19. 18__. 1850s.

Rarity: *None known*

$10 • **W-VT-130-010-G160**

Engraver: Graphic Co. **Comments:** H-VT-35-G54. No description available. 18__. 1820s.

Rarity: *None known*

$10 • **W-VT-130-010-G170**

Left: X / 10 / X on lathework. **Center:** Farmer with plow and oxen / 10. **Right:** TEN / Woman holding rudder and cornucopia. **Engraver:** New England Bank Note Co. **Comments:** H-VT-35-G62, Coulter-23. 18__. 1840s–1850s.

Rarity: *None known*

$10 • **W-VT-130-010-G180**

Left: "Presentation of the Declaration of Independence" / X. **Center:** X. **Right:** 10 / Train and man with wheelbarrow. **Engraver:** New England Bank Note Co. **Comments:** H-VT-35-G64, Coulter-24. 18__. 1850s.

Rarity: *None known*

$10 • **W-VT-130-010-G180a** CC

Overprint: Red TEN. **Engraver:** New England Bank Note Co. **Comments:** H-Unlisted, Coulter-Unlisted. Similar to W-VT-130-010-G180. 18__. 1850s–1860s.

Rarity: URS-2
VF $2,500

$10 • **W-VT-130-010-G190**

Left: TEN. **Center:** Blacksmith seated / X. **Right:** 10 / Farmer with sheaf and sickle. **Overprint:** Red TEN. **Engraver:** New England Bank Note Co. **Comments:** H-VT-35-G66a, Coulter-22. 18__. 1850s. Rarity: *None known*

$20 • **W-VT-130-020-G200**

Left: 20 / Woman seated. **Center:** XX / Eagle / XX. **Right:** 20 / Ship. **Engraver:** New England Bank Note Co. **Comments:** H-VT-35-G72, Coulter-25. 18__. 1840s–1860s.

Rarity: *None known*

$50 • W-VT-130-050-G210

Left: FIFTY / Woman standing / FIFTY. *Center:* 50 / Man holding restless horse by mane / 50. *Right:* FIFTY / Woman standing / FIFTY. *Engraver:* New England Bank Note Co. *Comments:* H-VT-35-G78, Coulter-26. 18___. 1840s–1860s.

Rarity: *None known*

$100 • W-VT-130-100-G220

Left: ONE HUNDRED on 100 / Portrait of William Henry Harrison. *Center:* Wharf scene. *Right:* ONE HUNDRED on 100 / Portrait of Christopher Columbus. *Engraver:* New England Bank Note Co. *Comments:* H-VT-35-G84, Coulter-27. 18___. 1840s–1860s.

Rarity: *None known*

NON-VALID ISSUES

$2 • W-VT-130-002-N010

Center: Two women, Steamboat. *Comments:* H-Unlisted, Coulter-9. 1840s–1860s.

Rarity: *None known*

$2 • W-VT-130-002-A010

Left: Sailor standing by bale holding hat and quadrant. *Center:* Two women. *Bottom center:* Cornucopia. *Right:* TWO / Mercury with cornucopia and caduceus / 2. *Overprint:* Red TWO. *Engraver:* Wellstood, Hanks, Hay & Whiting. *Comments:* H-VT-35-A5, Coulter-10. Altered from $2 Merchants Exchange Bank, Anacostia, D.C. series. Jan. 2, 185_. 1850s.

Rarity: *None known*

$3 • W-VT-130-003-N020

Left: Man holding axe. *Center:* 3 / Steamboats, City. *Right:* Two cupids in 3. *Comments:* H-Unlisted, Coulter-13. 1840s–1860s.

Rarity: *None known*

$3 • W-VT-130-003-S010

Left: George Washington on horseback. *Center:* Female portrait / Three dies / 3 / Female portrait. *Right:* Blacksmith resting on anvil. *Comments:* H-VT-35-S10, Coulter-14. Jan. ___, 185_. 1850s.

Rarity: URS-6
F $150

$3 • W-VT-130-003-N030

Left: Figure with cornucopia. *Center:* Woman, Globe. *Comments:* H-Unlisted, Coulter-16. 1840s–1860s.

Rarity: *None known*

$3 • W-VT-130-003-A020

Left: Mercury. *Center:* Woman, Shield. *Bottom center:* Eagle *Right:* 3. *Overprint:* Red THREE. *Engraver:* Wellstood, Hanks, Hay & Whiting. *Comments:* H-VT-35-A10, Coulter-15. Altered from $3 Merchants Exchange Bank, Anacostia, D.C. series. Jan. 2, 185_. 1850s.

Rarity: URS-5
F $125

$5 • W-VT-130-005-N040

Comments: H-Unlisted, Coulter-18. Imitation of W-VT-130-003-A020. Jan. 2, 185_. 1850s.

Rarity: *None known*

$5 • W-VT-130-005-A030

Left: 5 / Ship. *Center:* Whaling scene. *Right:* 5 / Sailor at ship's wheel. *Engraver:* Danforth, Wright & Co. *Comments:* H-VT-35-A15, Coulter-21. Altered from $5 Commercial Bank of New Jersey, Perth Amboy, New Jersey series. July 10, 1856.

Rarity: *None known*

$10 • W-VT-130-010-R010

Engraver: Graphic Co. *Comments:* H-VT-35-R5. Raised from W-VT-130-001-G010. 18___. 1820s.

Rarity: URS-4
F $175

Brattleborough Bank
LATE 1830s
W-VT-140

History: A non-existent bank represented only by fraudulent notes intended to pass for the Bank of Brattleboro, W-VT-130.

ISSUES

$2 • W-VT-140-002-N010

Left: Justice / 2. *Center:* 2 / Two allegorical figures with griffin / 2. *Right:* Lathework. *Comments:* H-Unlisted, Coulter-7. 1840s–1860s.

Rarity: URS-3
F $300

$2 • W-VT-140-002-N010a

Comments: H-Unlisted, Coulter-8. Similar to W-VT-130-002-N010 but with "Brattleboro" instead of "Brattleborough." 1840s–1860s.

Rarity: *None known*

$2 • W-VT-140-002-A010

Comments: H-VT-36-G4. 18___. 1838.

Rarity: URS-4
F $150

Windham County Bank
1857–1864
W-VT-150

History: The Windham County Bank was chartered in 1856 with an authorized capital of $150,000. In 1857 its circulation was $97,237, and specie was $11,612. In January 1858, capital was $100,000. Circulation was $97,237 in August 1859, but by July 1862, it was $129,983. By 1861 the bank's capital was $150,000 again.

In March 1864, the stockholders agreed to convert their stock into capital stock in a national banking association. This was called the First National Bank of Brattleboro, which opened for business on June 30, 1864. The outstanding circulation of the Windham County Bank as of July 1, 1867, was reported to be $720, the redemption of which was guaranteed by the First National Bank of Brattleboro, which succeeded the business interests of the state bank.

Numismatic Commentary: If the $720 figure reported above is to be believed, there should not be many signed and dated genuine notes currently in the marketplace or in collections. However, these notes seem to be quite plentiful. Augmenting this fact are the issues of remainder notes in all their colors and beautiful graphics. Uncut sheets still appear from time to time.

Remaining in the American Bank Note Co. archives as of 2003 was a $3 tint plate, a $20-$50 tint plate, and a $100 tint plate.

VALID ISSUES

$1 • W-VT-150-001-G010   CC

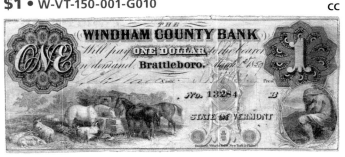

Tint: Red-brown overall lathework with 1. **Engraver:** Danforth, Wright & Co. **Comments:** H-VT-40-G2a, Coulter-39. March __, 18__. 1850s.

> **Rarity:** URS-8
> **Unc-Rem** $200

$1 • W-VT-150-001-G010a   TD

Tint: Green lathework with 1. **Engraver:** Danforth, Wright & Co. / ABNCo. monogram. **Comments:** H-VT-40-G2b, Coulter-40. Similar to W-VT-150-001-G010 but with additional engraver imprint. March __, 18__. 1860s.

> **Rarity:** URS-9
> **Unc-Rem** $200

$1 • W-VT-150-001-G020

Left: 1 / Male portrait. **Center:** Train. **Right:** 1 / Male portrait. **Comments:** H-Unlisted, Coulter-41. 1860s.

> **Rarity:** *None known*

$1 • W-VT-150-001-G030

Left: ONE / Indian on shield. **Center:** Die / ONEs. **Right:** Portrait of Judge Story. **Comments:** H-Unlisted, Coulter-42. 1860s.

> **Rarity:** *None known*

$2 • W-VT-150-002-G040   CJF

Tint: Red-brown lathework and microletters outlining white TWO. **Engraver:** Danforth, Wright & Co. **Comments:** H-VT-40-G4a, Coulter-43. March __, 18__. 1850s.

> **Rarity:** URS-8
> **Unc-Rem** $475

$2 • W-VT-150-002-G040a   CC

Tint: Green lathework and microletters outlining white TWO. **Engraver:** Danforth, Wright & Co. / ABNCo. monogram. **Comments:** H-VT-40-G4b, Coulter-44. Similar to W-VT-150-002-G040 but with additional engraver imprint. March __, 18__. 1860s.

> **Rarity:** URS-8
> **CU** $475

$2 • W-VT-150-002-G050

Left: 2 / Male portrait. **Center:** Spread eagle on limb, Shipping. **Right:** 2 / Female portrait. **Comments:** H-Unlisted, Coulter-45. 1860s.

> **Rarity:** *None known*

$2 • W-VT-150-002-G060

Left: Ship under sail. **Center:** Die / TWOs. **Right:** Portrait of Judge Story. **Comments:** H-Unlisted, Coulter-46. 1860s.

> **Rarity:** *None known*

$3 • W-VT-150-003-G070   CJF

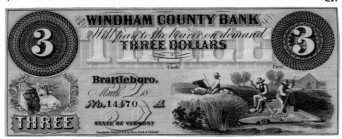

Tint: Red-brown overall lathework and microletters outlining white THREE, 3. **Engraver:** Danforth, Wright & Co. **Comments:** H-VT-40-G6a, Coulter-47. March __, 18__. 1850s.

> **Rarity:** URS-6
> **Unc-Rem** $400

$3 • W-VT-150-003-G080

Left: Male portrait. *Center:* Spread eagle on shield, Buildings. *Right:* Mercury soaring in clouds. *Comments:* H-Unlisted, Coulter-48. 1860s.

Rarity: *None known*

$5 • W-VT-150-005-G090

CJF

Tint: Red-brown overall lathework and microletters outlining white FIVE. *Engraver:* Danforth, Wright & Co. *Comments:* H-VT-40-G8a, Coulter-51. March __, 18__. 1857–1860s.

Rarity: URS-9
F $145; **Unc-Rem** $150

$5 • W-VT-150-005-G090a

CC

Tint: Green lathework and microletters outlining white FIVE. *Engraver:* Danforth, Wright & Co. / ABNCo. monogram. *Comments:* H-VT-40-G8b, Coulter-52. Similar to W-VT-150-005-G090 but with additional engraver imprint. March __, 18__. 1860s.

Rarity: URS-8
VF $150; **Unc-Rem** $300

$10 • W-VT-150-010-G100

CJF

Tint: Red-brown overall lathework and microletters outlining white TEN DOLLARS, White 10 and X on red dies. *Engraver:* Danforth, Wright & Co. *Comments:* H-VT-40-G10a, Coulter-54. March __, 18__. 1860s.

Rarity: URS-8
VF $250; **Unc-Rem** $400

$20 • W-VT-150-020-G110

CJF

Tint: Red-brown overall lathework. *Engraver:* Danforth, Wright & Co. *Comments:* H-VT-40-G12a. March __, 18__. 1850s.

Rarity: URS-5
VF $400; **Proof** $2,700

$20 • W-VT-150-020-G110a

CC

Tint: Green lathework. *Engraver:* Danforth, Wright & Co. / ABNCo. monogram. *Comments:* H-VT-40-G12b, Coulter-55. Similar to W-VT-150-020-G110 but with additional engraver imprint. March __, 18__. 1860s.

Rarity: URS-4
VF $1,100

$50 • W-VT-150-050-G120

CC

Tint: Red-brown lathework outlining FIFTY. *Engraver:* Danforth, Wright & Co. *Comments:* H-VT-40-G14a. March __, 18__. 1850s.

Rarity: URS-3
Proof $2,800

$50 • W-VT-150-050-G120a

CC

Tint: Green lathework outlining FIFTY. *Engraver:* Danforth, Wright & Co. / ABNCo. monogram. *Comments:* H-VT-40-G14b, Coulter-56. Similar to W-VT-150-050-G120 but with additional engraver imprint. March __, 18__. 1860s.

Rarity: URS-3
VF $650; **Proof** $1,900

$100 • W-VT-150-100-G130

Left: 100 / Portrait of George Washington. *Center:* Beehive flanked by allegorical women / ONE HUNDRED. *Right:* 100 / Portrait of Martha Washington. *Tint:* Red-brown lathework outlining white 100. *Engraver:* Danforth, Wright & Co. *Comments:* H-VT-40-G16a, Coulter-57. March __, 18__. 1850s.

Rarity: *None known*

$100 • W-VT-150-100-G130a

Tint: Green lathework outlining white 100. *Engraver:* Danforth, Wright & Co. / ABNCo. monogram. *Comments:* H-VT-40-G16b. Similar to W-VT-150-100-G130 but with additional engraver imprint. March __, 18__. 1860s.

Rarity: *None known*

Uncut Sheets

$1-$1-$2-$5 • W-VT-150-001.001.002.005-US010

Vignette(s): ($1) Three horses drinking from trough / Goats, sheep, and farmhouse / Man seated. *($1)* Three horses drinking from trough / Goats, sheep, and farmhouse / Man seated. *($2)* Farmer plowing with two horses / Cattle / Farming scene / Portrait of Christopher Columbus. *($5)* Portrait of Indian chief / Horses flanking shield bearing state arms surmounted by eagle / 5 on FIVE on shield. *Tint(s):* Red-brown. *Engraver:* Danforth, Wright & Co. *Comments:* H-VT-40-G2a, G2a, G4a, G8a. March __, 18__. 1850s.

Rarity: URS-5
Unc-Rem $800

$1-$1-$2-$5 • W-VT-150-001.001.002.005-US010a

Tint(s): Green. *Engraver:* Danforth, Wright & Co. / ABNCo. monogram. *Comments:* H-VT-40-G2b, G2b, G4b, G8b. Similar to W-VT-150-001.001.002.005-US010. March __, 18__. 1860s.

Rarity: URS-5
Unc-Rem $450

$1-$3-$5-$10 • W-VT-150-001.003.005.010-US020

Vignette(s): ($1) Three horses drinking from trough / Goats, sheep, and farmhouse / Man seated. *($3)* Bull's head / Three men and horses working reaping machine. *($5)* Portrait of Indian chief / Horses flanking shield bearing state arms surmounted by eagle / 5 on FIVE on shield. *($10)* Arts and Sciences. *Tint(s):* Red. *Engraver:* Danforth, Wright & Co. *Comments:* H-VT-40-G2a, G6a, G8a, G10a. March __, 18__. 1850s.

Rarity: URS-5
Unc-Rem $800

$20-$50 • W-VT-150-020.050-US030

Vignette(s): ($20) Milkmaid and cows / Two women seated near shield bearing agricultural implements. *($50)* Milkmaid / Blacksmith with hammer and anvil / Liberty seated. *Tint(s):* Red. *Engraver:* Danforth, Wright & Co. *Comments:* H-VT-40-G12a, G14a. March __, 18__. 1850s.

Rarity: URS-4
Unc-Rem $800

Non-Valid Issues

$3 • W-VT-150-003-S010

CJF

Tint: Red lathework outlining white 3. *Engraver:* Toppan, Carpenter & Co. *Comments:* H-VT-40-S5a, Coulter-50. June 16th, 18__. 1860s.

Rarity: URS-8
VF $75; **EF** $200

How to Read the Whitman Numbering System

$1 • W-RI-010-001-G010a

Denomination: Value of the note shown.

W: Whitman number. This number is a sortable code unique to each bank and note.

RI: Abbreviation for the state under study.

010: Numerical designation specific to each bank.

001: The denomination in dollars.

G010a: G indicates a good or valid note. Other categories are indicated thus: C (counterfeit); R (raised); S (spurious); N (not-attributed); A (altered). Numbers are assigned starting with 010, 020, et seq. Terminal letters following the number indicate variations of a note: a series of different colored overprints, tints, payees, etc., all on the same design of note. For more information, see the "How to Use This Book" section at the front of the volume, page xiv.

$3 • W-VT-150-003-N010

Center: Woman, Eagle on shield, Woman. *Comments:* H-Unlisted, Coulter-49. 1860s.

Rarity: *None known*

$5 • W-VT-150-005-A010

Left: 5 / State arms of Michigan / FIVE. *Center:* U.S. Capitol / General Zachary Taylor. *Right:* 5 / Liberty. *Engraver:* Danforth, Bald & Co. *Comments:* H-VT-40-A5, Coulter-53. Altered from $5 Government Stock Bank, Ann Arbor, Michigan. June 1, 185_. 1850s.

Rarity: URS-5
F $125

BURLINGTON, VERMONT

The largest city in the state of Vermont, Burlington is believed to have been named after Richard Boyle, the 3rd Earl of Burlington. Other possibilities include the Burling family of New York, who owned land in nearby towns. The land was awarded in 1763 to Samuel Willis and other settlers, but a permanent settlement was delayed by the Revolutionary War. In 1783 Stephen Lawrence arrived, and the town was organized in 1785.

Burlington was attacked in 1813 by the British, with no major effect on the outcome of the war. The town was ideally positioned on Lake Champlain to make it a port of entry and a center of trade during the 19th century. It competed particularly with the Champlain Canal, the Erie Canal, and the Chambly Canal. Steamboats brought freight and passengers, as did the Rutland & Burlington Railroad and the Vermont Central Railroad. Lumbering and manufacturing became important in Burlington, and the town was incorporated as a city in 1865.

Bank of Burlington
CIRCA 1819–1865
W-VT-160

History: The Bank of Burlington was incorporated on November 1, 1818, with $150,000 in authorized capital. The charter of the bank was extended three different times: first on November 5, 1830, then on November 8, 1847, and finally on November 20, 1861.

In September 1835, the Bank of Burlington redeemed all of its notes in denominations of $5 and upwards. It had a capital of $102,000 and a circulation of $98,687.

In June 1836, the bank was on the list of deposit banks discontinued under the Deposite Act of June 1836. In November 1836, circulation was at $184,233, and capital was $150,000. In February 1837, capital was $126,352. In September 1841, these figures were given: capital stock $150,000; bills in circulation $110,877; real estate $10,558.42.

In 1847 the *Boston Atlas* reported that $900 in counterfeits had been received by the Suffolk Bank as a remittance from the Bank of Burlington, all of which had been altered from $1 bills of various banks:

The alterations are so well done, that ninety-nine persons out of every hundred would not detect the cheat. The loss to the party who made the remittance, is $886. We hope that the scoundrels who are flooding the country with their spurious notes, may soon be detected.

By 1857 these figures were reported: bills in circulation $79,650; specie $10,245; real estate $9,000. Circulation was $103,912 in 1862.

In 1865 the business of the Bank of Burlington was succeeded by the First National Bank. The bank published notice that it would not be liable to redeem its outstanding bills after December 4, 1867.

Numismatic Commentary: This is a bank where expectations to obtain genuine issues are reasonable.

Remaining in the American Bank Note Co. archives as of 2003 was a $1-$1-$2-$3 face plate and a $5-$5-$10-$10 face plate.

VALID ISSUES

$1 • W-VT-160-001-G010

Engraver: Graphic Co. *Comments:* H-VT-45-G2. No description available. 18__. Circa 1819–1820s.

Rarity: *None known*

$1 • W-VT-160-001-G020   CC

Engraver: Durand & Wright. *Comments:* H-VT-45-G4. 18__. 1820s–1840s.

Rarity: URS-3
Proof $700

$1 • W-VT-160-001-G030   CC

Engraver: Danforth & Hufty. *Comments:* H-VT-45-G8. 18__. 1840s–1850s.

Rarity: URS-3
Proof $900

$1 • W-VT-160-001-G030a   CC

Overprint: Red ONE. **Engraver:** Danforth & Hufty. **Comments:** H-Unlisted. Similar to W-VT-160-001-G030. 18__. 1850s–1860s.
Rarity: URS-3
VF $700; **Proof** $1,000

$1 • W-VT-160-001-G030b   CJF, CJF

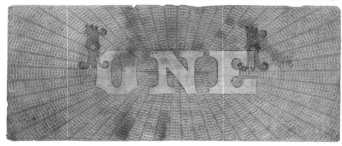

Overprint: Green 1, 1. **Back:** Red outlining white ONE. **Engraver:** American Bank Note Co. **Comments:** H-VT-45-G8c, Coulter-2. Similar to W-VT-160-001-G030 but with different date and engraver imprint. Feb. 1st, 1864.
Rarity: URS-3
VG $750

$2 • W-VT-160-002-G040
Engraver: Graphic Co. **Comments:** H-VT-45-G10. No description available. 18__. Circa 1819–1820s.
Rarity: None known

$2 • W-VT-160-002-G050   CC

Engraver: Durand & Wright. **Comments:** H-VT-45-G12, Coulter-5. 18__. 1820s–1840s.
Rarity: URS-4
F $250

$2 • W-VT-160-002-G060
Left: Die / Portrait of Benjamin Franklin / 2. **Center:** 2 / Roman, Building / 2. **Bottom center:** Steamboat. **Right:** TWO / Beehive / 2. **Engraver:** Durand & Wright. **Comments:** H-VT-45-G14, Coulter-1. 18__. 1820s–1840s.
Rarity: None known

$2 • W-VT-160-002-G070   CC

Engraver: Danforth & Hufty. **Comments:** H-VT-45-G18, Coulter-3. 18__. 1840s–1850s.
Rarity: URS-3
Proof $1,000

$2 • W-VT-160-002-G070a   CJF, CJF

Overprint: Green 2, 2. **Back:** Red outlining white TWO. **Engraver:** American Bank Note Co. **Comments:** H-Unlisted, Coulter-Unlisted. Similar to W-VT-160-002-G070 but with different date and engraver imprint. Feb. 1st, 1864.
Rarity: URS-3
VG $500

$3 • W-VT-160-003-G080
Comments: H-VT-45-G20. No description available. 1840s–1850s.
Rarity: None known

$3 • W-VT-160-003-G090

CC

Engraver: Durand & Wright. *Comments:* H-VT-45-G22. 18__. 1820s–1840s.

Rarity: URS-3
Proof $1,600

$3 • W-VT-160-003-G100

CJF

Engraver: Danforth & Hufty. *Comments:* H-VT-45-G26, Coulter-6. 18__. 1840s–1850s.

Rarity: URS-4
VG $200; **Proof** $1,000

$3 • W-VT-160-003-G100a

Left: THREE / Liberty, Shield and eagle / THREE. *Center:* Drover on horseback, Cattle and sheep. *Bottom center:* Dog with key and strongbox. *Right:* 3 / Woman with wheat and sickle / THREE. *Overprint:* Green. *Back:* Red. *Engraver:* American Bank Note Co. *Comments:* H-VT-45-G26c. Similar to W-VT-160-003-G100 but with different date and engraver imprint. Feb. 1, 1864.

Rarity: *None known*

$5 • W-VT-160-005-G110

CJF

Engraver: Graphic Co. *Comments:* H-VT-45-G28. 18__. Circa 1819–1820s.

Rarity: URS-3
F $750

$5 • W-VT-160-005-G120

Left: VERMONT vertically. *Center:* V / Building, Woman holding 5 strung as harp / 5. *Right:* 5 on die / 5 on die vertically. *Engraver:* Graphic Co. *Comments:* H-VT-45-G30. 18__. 1820s–1830s.

Rarity: *None known*

$5 • W-VT-160-005-G130

Left: 5 / Female portrait / FIVE. *Center:* Eagle on tree limb. *Bottom center:* Carding machine. *Right:* FIVE / Liberty / FIVE. *Engraver:* Danforth & Hufty. *Comments:* H-VT-45-G34, Coulter-8. 18__. 1840s–1850s.

Rarity: *None known*

$5 • W-VT-160-005-G130a

CJF

Overprint: Red FIVE. *Engraver:* Danforth & Hufty. *Comments:* H-Unlisted, Coulter-Unlisted. Similar to W-VT-160-005-G130. 18__. 1850s–1860s.

Rarity: URS-3
VF $750

$5 • W-VT-160-005-G130b

Engraver: American Bank Note Co. *Comments:* H-VT-45-G34b. Similar to W-VT-160-005-G130 but with different date and engraver imprint. Feb. 1, 1864.

Rarity: *None known*

$10 • W-VT-160-010-G140

Engraver: Graphic Co. *Comments:* H-VT-45-G36. No description available. 18__. 1820s–1830s.

Rarity: *None known*

$10 • W-VT-160-010-G150

Left: TEN / Train / TEN. *Center:* Woman sitting between 1 and 0 / Lake and steamer. *Bottom center:* Dog, key, and strongbox. *Right:* TEN / Cherub, hammer, and anvil / X. *Engraver:* Danforth & Hufty. *Comments:* H-VT-45-G40, Coulter-12. 18__. 1840s–1850s.

Rarity: *None known*

$10 • W-VT-160-010-G150a

CC

Overprint: Red TEN. *Engraver:* Danforth & Hufty. *Comments:* H-Unlisted. Similar to W-VT-160-010-G150. 18__. 1840s–1850s.

Rarity: URS-1
VF $1,600

$10 • W-VT-160-010-G150b

CC

Overprint: Green X, X. **Back:** Red outlining white TEN. **Engraver:** American Bank Note Co. **Comments:** H-VT-45-G40b. Similar to W-VT-160-010-G150 but with different date and engraver imprint. Feb. 1st, 1864.

Rarity: URS-2
EF $1,900

$20 • W-VT-160-020-G160

CC

Engraver: Durand, Perkins & Co. **Comments:** H-VT-45-G44, Coulter-15. 18__. Circa 1830–1860s.

Rarity: URS-3
Proof $1,000

$50 • W-VT-160-050-G170

CC

Engraver: Durand, Perkins & Co. **Comments:** H-VT-45-G48, Coulter-16. 18__. Circa 1830–1860s.

Rarity: URS-2
Proof $2,300

$100 • W-VT-160-100-G180

CC

Engraver: Durand, Perkins & Co. **Comments:** H-VT-45-G52, Coulter-17. 18__. Circa 1830–1860s.

Rarity: URS-2
Proof $3,200

Non-Valid Issues

$2 • W-VT-160-002-C050

Engraver: Durand & Wright. **Comments:** H-VT-45-C12, Coulter-5. Counterfeit of W-VT-160-002-G050. 18__. 1840s.

Rarity: URS-8
VF $125

$2 • W-VT-160-002-C060

CC

Engraver: Durand & Wright. **Comments:** H-VT-45-C14. Counterfeit of W-VT-160-002-G060. 18__. 1840s.

Rarity: URS-8
F $110

$2 • W-VT-160-002-C070

CJF

Engraver: Danforth & Hufty. **Comments:** H-VT-45-C18. Counterfeit of W-VT-160-002-G070. 18__. 1840s–1850s.

Rarity: URS-5
VG $125; F $150

$2 • W-VT-160-002-N010

Engraver: Danforth & Hufty. **Comments:** H-Unlisted, Coulter-4. Imitation of W-VT-160-002-C070. 18__. 1840s–1850s.

Rarity: *None known*

$2 • W-VT-160-002-A010

Left: II / Male portrait / II. *Center:* 2 / Beehive, Two women flanking 2 / 2. *Right:* TWO / Male portrait / TWO. *Engraver:* Rawdon, Clark & Co. *Comments:* H-VT-45-A5. Altered from W-VT-025-002-G020. 18__. 1840s.

Rarity: URS-4

F $150

$3 • W-VT-160-003-N020

Center: Two women seated. *Comments:* H-Unlisted, Coulter-7. 1840s.

Rarity: *None known*

$5 • W-VT-160-005-C120

CJF

Engraver: Graphic Co. *Comments:* H-VT-45-C30. Counterfeit of W-VT-160-005-G120. 18__. 1830s.

Rarity: URS-5

F $125

$5 • W-VT-160-005-N030

Comments: H-Unlisted, Coulter-9. Imitation of W-VT-160-005-C120 but with different dies. 18__. 1830s.

Rarity: *None known*

$5 • W-VT-160-005-N040

Center: Herd of horses. *Right:* Woman shading her eyes. *Comments:* H-Unlisted, Coulter-10. 1830s.

Rarity: *None known*

$5 • W-VT-160-005-N050

Left: Woman and eagle. *Right:* Ship. *Comments:* H-Unlisted, Coulter-11. 1830s.

Rarity: *None known*

$10 • W-VT-160-010-R010

Engraver: Danforth & Hufty. *Comments:* H-VT-45-R5, Coulter-13. Raised from W-VT-160-001-G030. 18__. 1840s–1850s.

Rarity: *None known*

$10 • W-VT-160-010-R020

Engraver: Danforth & Hufty. *Comments:* H-VT-45-R10, Coulter-13. Raised from W-VT-160-005-G130. 18__. 1840s–1850s.

Rarity: *None known*

$10 • W-VT-160-010-N060

Center: Woman, cows, Train. *Comments:* H-Unlisted, Coulter-14. 1830s.

Rarity: *None known*

Bank of the United States {2nd} (branch)
1830–1835
W-VT-170

History: On January 29, 1830, William H. Crawford of the United States Treasury wrote to the cashier of the Bank of Burlington, A. Thompson, to approve the designation of the Bank of Burlington as an acting branch of the Bank of the United States. In 1832 President Andrew Jackson vetoed the 1836 renewal of the Bank of the United States which had been brought up before Congress and passed by both House and Senate. This instituted a period of great debate and political turmoil. In late 1833 and early 1834 there was a depression in some areas of business which only served to strengthen the bank, as it was backed by the government. The branches, however, began closing and selling their buildings. By March 1836, only the Boston, New York City, Savannah, Nashville, and main Philadelphia facilities remained unsold.

Numismatic Commentary: In addition to notes, "drafts" resembling bank notes were issued. Some financial capers may have been practiced with these drafts.

VALID ISSUES

$5 • W-VT-170-005-G010

Left: FIVE vertically. *Center:* 5 / Eagle perched on shield, Ships / V. *Right:* FIVE vertically. *Engraver:* Fairman, Draper, Underwood & Co. *Comments:* H-US2-G160. 1830s.

Rarity: *None known*

$10 • W-VT-170-010-G020

Left: TEN vertically. *Center:* 10 / Eagle perched on shield, Ships / X. *Right:* TEN vertically. *Engraver:* Fairman, Draper, Underwood & Co. *Comments:* H-US2-G164. 1830s.

Rarity: *None known*

$20 • W-VT-170-020-G030

Left: Eagle / Portrait of Martha Washington / Minerva. *Center:* 20 / Eagle perched on shield, Ship / 20. *Right:* Eagle / Portrait of Benjamin Franklin / Female portrait. *Engraver:* Fairman, Draper, Underwood & Co. *Comments:* H-US2-G168. 1830s.

Rarity: *None known*

$20 • W-VT-170-020-G040

Left: 20 vertically. *Center:* 20 / Eagle perched on shield, Ship / 20. *Right:* XX vertically. *Engraver:* Draper, Underwood, Bald & Spencer. *Comments:* H-US2-G170. 1830s.

Rarity: *None known*

$50 • W-VT-170-050-G050

Left: Eagle / Portrait of Martha Washington / Minerva. *Center:* 50 / Eagle perched on shield, Ship / 50. *Right:* Eagle / Portrait of Benjamin Franklin / Female portrait. *Engraver:* Fairman, Draper, Underwood & Co. *Comments:* H-US2-G174. 1830s.

Rarity: *None known*

$50 • W-VT-170-050-G060

Left: L / Male portrait / 50. *Center:* 50 / Eagle perched on shield / L. *Right:* 50 / Male portrait / L. *Engraver:* Draper, Underwood, Bald & Spencer. *Comments:* H-US2-G176. 1830s.

Rarity: *None known*

$100 • W-VT-170-100-G070

Left: Eagle / Portrait of George Washington / Minerva. *Center:* 100 / Eagle perched on shield, Ship / 100. *Right:* Eagle / Portrait of Benjamin Franklin / Female portrait. *Engraver:* Fairman, Draper, Underwood & Co. *Comments:* H-US2-G180. 1830s.

Rarity: *None known*

$100 • W-VT-170-100-G080

Left: 100 / Male portrait / C. *Center:* 100 / Eagle perched on shield / 100. *Right:* C / Male portrait / 100. *Engraver:* Draper, Underwood, Bald & Spencer. *Comments:* H-US2-G182. 1830s.

Rarity: *None known*

NON-VALID ISSUES

$50 • W-VT-170-050-C050

Left: Eagle / Portrait of Martha Washington / Minerva. *Center:* 50 / Eagle perched on shield, Ship / 50. *Right:* Eagle / Portrait of Benjamin Franklin / Female portrait. *Engraver:* Fairman, Draper, Underwood & Co. *Comments:* H-US2-C174. Counterfeit of W-VT-170-050-G050. 1830s.

Rarity: *None known*

$100 • W-VT-170-100-C070

Left: Eagle / Portrait of George Washington / Minerva. *Center:* 100 / Eagle perched on shield, Ship / 100. *Right:* Eagle / Portrait of Benjamin Franklin / Female portrait. *Engraver:* Fairman, Draper, Underwood & Co. *Comments:* H-US2-C180. Counterfeit of W-VT-170-100-G070. 1830s.

Rarity: *None known*

Commercial Bank
1847–1867
W-VT-180

History: The Commercial Bank was chartered in 1846 with $150,000 in authorized capital. The following bank figures were given for 1857: capital $150,000; bills in circulation $86,397; specie $3,200; real estate $3,000. In July 1859, circulation was $86,397.

The charter of the bank was extended on November 19, 1861, and the bank continued in business until December 31, 1867, when it closed. The following day it returned its capital to the stockholders. The remaining circulation as of August 1, 1867, was $7,362, the redemption of which was guaranteed by bonds which the directors had placed with the state treasurer.

Numismatic Commentary: Genuine notes are hard to find. The vignettes of a great deal of Vermont notes are generic in nature, without local landmarks or historic scenes. This bank is typical in that regard.

VALID ISSUES

$1 • W-VT-180-001-G010   CC

Engraver: Danforth & Hufty. *Comments:* H-VT-50-G2, Coulter-19. 18__. 1847–1850s.

Rarity: URS-2
Proof $3,100

$1 • W-VT-180-001-G010a   CJF

Overprint: Red ONE. *Comments:* H-VT-50-G2c, Coulter-20. Similar to W-VT-180-001-G010 but with engraved payee name. 18__. 1860s.

Rarity: URS-2
F $1,000

$2 • W-VT-180-002-G020   CJF

Engraver: Danforth & Hufty. *Comments:* H-VT-50-G4, Coulter-22. 18__. 1847–1850s.

Rarity: URS-3
VG $750

$2 • W-VT-180-002-G020a

CC

Overprint: Red TWO. *Comments:* H-VT-50-G4c. Similar to W-VT-180-002-G020 but with engraved payee name. 18__. 1860s.

Rarity: URS-2
VG $1,000

$3 • W-VT-180-003-G030

Left: THREE / Hebe watering eagle / THREE. *Center:* Indian with spear and horse, Train. *Right:* 3 / Two women, one kneeling with sickle and grain. *Engraver:* Danforth & Hufty. *Comments:* H-VT-50-G6, Coulter-26. 18__. 1847–1850s.

Rarity: *None known*

$3 • W-VT-180-003-G030a

Overprint: Red THREE. *Engraver:* Danforth & Hufty. *Comments:* H-VT-50-G6c. Similar to W-VT-180-003-G030 but with engraved payee name. 18__. 1860s.

Rarity: *None known*

$3 • W-VT-180-003-G030b

CC

Engraver: Danforth, Bald & Co. *Comments:* H-Unlisted. Similar to W-VT-180-003-G030 but with different date and engraver imprint. January 1st, 18__. 1860s.

Rarity: URS-2
Proof $1,000

$5 • W-VT-180-005-G040

CJF

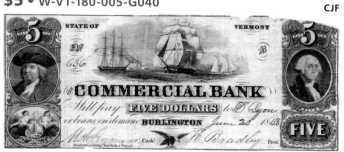

Engraver: Danforth & Hufty. *Comments:* H-VT-50-G8, Coulter-28. 18__. 1847–1850s.

Rarity: URS-4
F $750

$5 • W-VT-180-005-G040a

BH

Overprint: Red FIVE. *Comments:* H-VT-50-G8a. Similar to W-VT-180-005-G040 but with different date and engraved payee name. January 1st, 18__. 1850s–1860s.

Rarity: URS-2
F $750

$10 • W-VT-180-010-G050

CJF

Engraver: Danforth & Hufty. *Comments:* H-VT-50-G10, Coulter-37. Left corner torn. 18__. 1847–1850s.

Rarity: URS-3
F $500

$10 • W-VT-180-010-G050a

Left: Portrait of DeWitt Clinton / State arms / TEN. *Center:* TEN on medallion head / "Presentation of the Declaration of Independence". *Right:* X / TEN on medallion head / 10. *Overprint:* Red TEN. *Engraver:* Danforth & Hufty. *Comments:* H-VT-50-G10a. Similar to W-VT-180-010-G050 but with engraved payee name. 18__. 1850s–1860s.

Rarity: *None known*

$20 • W-VT-180-020-G060

Left: TWENTY / Two women seated, Sailor and mechanic standing. *Center:* Anchor, anvil, and barrels. *Right:* 20 / Two women, Man, dog, and oxen. *Engraver:* Danforth & Hufty. *Comments:* H-VT-50-G12, Coulter-44. 18__. 1847–1850s.

Rarity: URS-2
Selected auction price: Stack's Bowers Galleries, November 2008, Lot 5136, Unc $920

$20 • W-VT-180-020-G060a
TD

Engraver: Danforth, Bald & Co. **Comments:** H-Unlisted, Coulter-Unlisted. Similar to W-VT-180-020-G060 but with different date and engraver imprint. January 1st, 18__. 1860s.
Rarity: URS-3
Proof $1,500

$50 • W-VT-180-050-G070
Left: 50 / Male portrait / FIFTY. **Center:** State arms and two horses, Factory, train, and steamboat. **Right:** 50 / Female portrait / FIFTY. **Engraver:** Danforth & Hufty. **Comments:** H-VT-50-G14, Coulter-48. 18__. 1847–1850s.
Rarity: URS-3
Proof $1,000

$100 • W-VT-180-100-G080
Left: 100 / River, bridge, train. **Center:** Three women in clouds, one kneeling, two others seated / 100. **Bottom center:** 100. **Right:** Ship / 100. **Engraver:** Danforth & Hufty. **Comments:** H-VT-50-G16, Coulter-51. 18__. 1847–1850s.
Rarity: URS-3
Proof $1,500

Uncut Sheets
$1-$1-$2-$2 • W-VT-180-001.001.002.002-US010
Vignette(s): ($1) Portrait of George Washington / Train / Female portrait. **($1)** Portrait of George Washington / Train / Female portrait. **($2)** Portrait of Benjamin Franklin / Shield surmounted by eagle / Two women / Liberty and ship / Woman with rake. **($2)** Portrait of Benjamin Franklin / Shield surmounted by eagle / Two women / Liberty and ship / Woman with rake. **Engraver:** Danforth & Hufty. **Comments:** H-VT-50-G2, G2, G4, G4. 18__. 1847–1850s.
Rarity: URS-1
Proof $2,200

$3-$20 • W-VT-180-003.020-US020
Vignette(s): ($3) Woman watering eagle / Indian with spear and horse, Train / Two women, one kneeling with sickle and grain. **($20)** Two women seated, Sailor and mechanic standing / Anchor, anvil, and barrels / Two women, Man, dog, and oxen. **Engraver:** Danforth, Bald & Co. **Comments:** All unlisted in Haxby. January 1st, 18__. 1860s.
Rarity: URS-2
Proof $1,200

$5-$5-$5-$10 • W-VT-180-005.005.005.010-US030
Vignette(s): ($5) Portrait of William Penn / State arms / Harbor / Portrait of George Washington. **($5)** Portrait of William Penn / State arms / Harbor / Portrait of George Washington. **($5)** Portrait of William Penn / State arms / Harbor / Portrait of George Washington. **($10)** Portrait of DeWitt Clinton / State arms / TEN on medallion head / "Presentation of the Declaration of Independence" / TEN on medallion head. **Engraver:** Danforth & Hufty. **Comments:** H-VT-50-G8, G8, G8, G10. 18__. 1847–1850s.
Rarity: URS-2
Proof $2,200

$50-$100 • W-VT-180-050.100-US040
Vignette(s): ($50) Male portrait / State arms and two horses / Factory, train, and steamboat / Female portrait. **($100)** River, bridge, train / Three women in clouds, one kneeling, two others seated / Ship. **Engraver:** Danforth & Hufty. **Comments:** H-VT-50-G14, G16. 18__. 1847–1850s.
Rarity: URS-3
Proof $1,500

Non-Valid Issues
$1 • W-VT-180-001-A010
Left: Farmer with scythe. **Center:** Three horses drinking at trough. **Right:** Sailor holding spyglass. **Engraver:** Danforth, Wright & Co. **Comments:** H-VT-50-A5, Coulter-21. Altered from $1 Commercial Bank of New Jersey, Perth Amboy, New Jersey series. July 10, 1856.
Rarity: URS-5
F $100

$2 • W-VT-180-002-N010
Left: Woman. **Center:** Ceres seated with sheaf of wheat. **Bottom center:** Eagle. **Right:** Portrait of George Washington. **Comments:** H-VT-50-N5, Coulter-24. 18__. 1840s–1850s.
Rarity: *None known*

$2 • W-VT-180-002-A020
Left: TWO / Woman feeding chickens. **Center:** Ships. **Right:** 2 / Seated girl. **Engraver:** Danforth, Wright & Co. **Comments:** H-Unlisted, Coulter-23. Altered from $2 Commercial Bank of Perth Amboy, Perth Amboy, New Jersey. July 10, 1856.
Rarity: URS-3
F $90

$2 • W-VT-180-002-A030
Left: Woman. **Center:** Indian and dog. **Engraver:** Durand & Co. **Comments:** H-VT-50-A10, Coulter-25. Altered from W-VT-570-002-G020. 18__. 1840s–1850s.
Rarity: *None known*

$3 • W-VT-180-003-A040
Left: 3 / Portrait of George Washington / THREE. **Center:** Steamboat, Sailing vessel and city. **Right:** 3 / Woman / Eagle. **Engraver:** New England Bank Note Co. **Comments:** H-VT-50-A15, Coulter-27. Altered from $3 Commercial Bank, Gratiot, Michigan. 18__. 1840s.
Rarity: *None known*

$5 • W-VT-180-005-R010

Comments: H-Unlisted, Coulter-36. Raised from W-VT-180-001-G010. 1840s. **Rarity:** *None known*

$5 • W-VT-180-005-S010

CJF

Overprint: Red panel outlining white FIVE. *Engraver:* New England Bank Note Co. / ABNCo. monogram. *Comments:* H-VT-50-S5a, Coulter-29. Created using a rough verbal description of W-VT-180-005-G040. July 1st, 1863.

Rarity: URS-8
F $100

$5 • W-VT-180-005-S010a

CJF

Overprint: Red panels outlining white 5 / 5. *Engraver:* New England Bank Note Co. / ABNCo. monogram. *Comments:* H-Unlisted, Coulter-Unlisted. Similar to W-VT-180-005-S010 but printed in blue ink. July 1st, 1863.

Rarity: URS-6
Unc-Rem $400

$5 • W-VT-180-005-N020

Left: 5 / Allegorical figure / FIVE. *Center:* Steamship at sea. *Right:* 5 / FIVE on medallion head / FIVE. *Comments:* H-Unlisted, Coulter-30. 1840s.

Rarity: *None known*

$5 • W-VT-180-005-N030

Left: 5 / Female portrait / FIVE. *Center:* Steamer and sailing vessel / FIVE. *Right:* 5 / Female portrait / FIVE. *Engraver:* Rawdon, Wright & Hatch. *Comments:* H-Unlisted, Coulter-31. June 15, 1852.

Rarity: *None known*

$5 • W-VT-180-005-N040

Left: Sailor. *Center:* Sea view. *Comments:* H-Unlisted, Coulter-35. 1840s.

Rarity: *None known*

$5 • W-VT-180-005-A050

CJF

Engraver: Gavit & Co. *Comments:* H-VT-50-A20, Coulter-32. Altered from $5 Commercial Bank, Georgetown, D.C. Sept. 1st, 1852.

Rarity: URS-4
F $150

$5 • W-VT-180-005-A060

Left: 5 / Train / 5. *Center:* Three ships / FIVE. *Right:* Portrait of George Washington. *Engraver:* Gavit & Co. / J.E. Gavit & Co. *Comments:* H-VT-50-A25, Coulter-33. Altered from $5 Commercial Bank, Gratiot, Michigan. 18__. 1840s.

Rarity: *None known*

$5 • W-VT-180-005-A070

Left: 5 / Ship. *Center:* Whaling scene. *Right:* 5 / Sailor. *Engraver:* Danforth, Wright & Co. *Comments:* H-VT-50-A30, Coulter-34. Altered from $5 Commercial Bank of New Jersey, Perth Amboy, New Jersey series. September 1, 1856.

Rarity: *None known*

$10 • W-VT-180-010-R020

Engraver: Danforth & Hufty. *Comments:* H-VT-50-R5, Coulter-38. Raised from W-VT-180-001-G010 series. 18__. 1850s.

Rarity: *None known*

$10 • W-VT-180-010-R030

Comments: H-VT-50-R10, Coulter-39. Raised from W-VT-180-002-G020 series. 18__. 1847–1850s.

Rarity: *None known*

$10 • W-VT-180-010-N050

Center: Eagle / Three women. *Comments:* H-Unlisted, Coulter-42. 1840s. **Rarity:** *None known*

$10 • W-VT-180-010-N060

Center: Train. *Comments:* H-Unlisted, Coulter-43. 1840s.

Rarity: *None known*

$10 • W-VT-180-010-AR010

Left: X / Man seated. *Center:* Man watering horses at well, Sheep. *Right:* X, Sailor seated on ship with spyglass. *Engraver:* Danforth, Wright & Co. *Comments:* H-VT-50-AR40, Coulter-40. Altered and raised from $1 Commercial Bank of New Jersey, Perth Amboy, New Jersey series. July 10, 1856.

Rarity: *None known*

$10 • W-VT-180-010-A080
Left: TEN / Helmeted woman standing with lyre, Cornucopia *Center:* Ship. *Right:* 10 / Dock, vessels. *Engraver:* New England Bank Note Co. *Comments:* H-VT-50-A35, Coulter-41. Altered from $10 Commercial Bank, Gratiot, Michigan. 18__. 1840s.

Rarity: *None known*

$20 • W-VT-180-020-R040
Engraver: Danforth & Hufty. *Comments:* H-VT-50-R15, Coulter-45. Raised from W-VT-180-001-G010 series. 18__. 1850s.

Rarity: *None known*

$20 • W-VT-180-020-N070   BH

Engraver: Danforth & Hufty. *Comments:* H-VT-50-N10, Coulter-46. 18__. 1852.

Rarity: URS-4
F $150

$20 • W-VT-180-020-N080
Center: Train. *Comments:* H-Unlisted, Coulter-47. 1840s.

Rarity: *None known*

$50 • W-VT-180-050-R050
Engraver: Danforth & Hufty. *Comments:* H-VT-50-R20, Coulter-49. Raised from W-VT-180-001-G010 series. 18__. 1850s.

Rarity: *None known*

$50 • W-VT-180-050-N090
Left: FIFTY. *Center:* Train / Woman. *Right:* 50 / Portrait of Benjamin Franklin / 50. *Comments:* H-Unlisted, Coulter-50. 1840s.

Rarity: *None known*

Farmers and Mechanics Bank
1834–1867
W-VT-190

History: The Farmers and Mechanics Bank was chartered on November 4, 1834, with an authorized capital of $150,000, of which $105,000 was initially paid in. In 1845 the capital was $94,160, and circulation was $78,290.

On October 31, 1846, and November 20, 1861, the charter of the bank was extended. These figures were given for 1854: deposits in city banks $27,505; other resources $24,080; specie $4,870. 1857 saw capital at $100,000, circulation at $60,166, specie at $3,193, and real estate valued at $51,875. In July 1859, circulation was $60,166.

On September 10, 1866, the charter of the bank expired. Its outstanding circulation as of July 1, 1867, was reported to be $5,600. The redemption of outstanding bills was guaranteed by bonds which the directors had placed with the State Treasurer. The bank published a notice stating that it would not be liable to redeem its outstanding circulation after November 28, 1867.

Numismatic Commentary: The title of this bank is sometimes "Farmers and Mechanics Bank" as displayed on notes, and at other times it is "Farmers & Mechanics Bank." All genuine notes from this bank should be considered rare. However, non-valid issues populate the marketplace with frequency. A fraudulent enterprise, the Mechanics Exchange Bank said to have been based in New York City, produced notes with the Farmers and Mechanics Bank imprint. Even though the worthless nature of the notes was widely known at the time and appeared in various newspaper accounts, this did not deter merchants and banks from receiving them for goods and services and then passing the bills to others. The Bank of St. Albans, W-VT-640, also had notes fraudulently produced by this entity.

Remaining in the American Bank Note Co. archives as of 2003 was a $1-$1-$2-$3 face plate, a $1-$1-$2-$3 face plate, and a $50-$100 face plate.

VALID ISSUES

$1 • W-VT-190-001-G010   CC

Engraver: Draper, Toppan, Longacre & Co. *Comments:* H-VT-55-G2, Coulter-52. 18__. 1830s–1850s.

Rarity: URS-3
Proof $1,800

$1 • W-VT-190-001-G020   CJF

Overprint: Red ONE. *Engraver:* Toppan, Carpenter, Casilear & Co. *Comments:* H-VT-55-G4a, Coulter-53. Jan.y 1, 1853.

Rarity: URS-2
F $1,000

$2 • W-VT-190-002-G030

CC

Engraver: Draper, Toppan, Longacre & Co. **Comments:** H-VT-55-G6, Coulter-58. 18__. 1830s–1850s.
Rarity: URS-3
Proof $1,200

$2 • W-VT-190-002-G040

CC

Overprint: Red TWO. **Engraver:** Toppan, Carpenter, Casilear & Co. **Comments:** H-VT-55-G8a, Coulter-57. Jan.y 1st, 1853.
Rarity: URS-2
F $1,000

$3 • W-VT-190-003-G050

CC

Engraver: Draper, Toppan, Longacre & Co. **Comments:** H-VT-55-G10, Coulter-61. 18__. 1830s–1850s.
Rarity: URS-2
Proof $1,250

$3 • W-VT-190-003-G060

Left: 3 / THREE / 3. **Center:** Woman seated with fruit and grain. **Bottom center:** Eagle. **Right:** 3 / THREE / 3. **Engraver:** Toppan, Carpenter, Casilear & Co. **Comments:** H-VT-55-G12, Coulter-62. Jan. 1, 1853.
Rarity: *None known*

$3 • W-VT-190-003-G070

Left: 3 / THREE / 3. **Center:** Ceres seated, River, village. **Right:** 3 / THREE / 3. **Comments:** H-Unlisted, Coulter-63. 1830s–1850s.
Rarity: *None known*

$5 • W-VT-190-005-G080

CC

Engraver: Draper, Toppan, Longacre & Co. **Comments:** H-VT-55-G14, Coulter-72. 18__. 1830s–1850s.
Rarity: URS-3
Proof $1,000

$10 • W-VT-190-010-G090

CC

Engraver: Draper, Toppan, Longacre & Co. **Comments:** H-VT-55-G16, Coulter-80. Proof. 18__. 1830s–1860s.
Rarity: URS-3
Proof $1,000

$20 • W-VT-190-020-G100

CC

Engraver: Draper, Toppan, Longacre & Co. **Comments:** H-VT-55-G18, Coulter-84. 18__. 1830s–1850s.
Rarity: URS-3
Proof $1,200

$50 • W-VT-190-050-G110

Left: FIFTY / Woman with sickle and sheaf. **Center:** Spread eagle and shield. **Bottom center:** Train. **Right:** 50. **Engraver:** Draper, Toppan, Longacre & Co. **Comments:** H-VT-55-G20, Coulter-87. 18__. 1830s–1860s.
Rarity: *None known*

$100 • W-VT-190-100-G120

Left: 100 / Portrait of George Washington / 100. **Center:** Spread eagle and shield. **Bottom center:** Dog, key, and strongbox. **Right:** 100. **Engraver:** Draper, Toppan, Longacre & Co. **Comments:** H-VT-55-G22, Coulter-89. 18__. 1830s–1860s.
Rarity: *None known*

Uncut Sheets
$1-$1-$2-$3 • W-VT-190-001.001.002.003-US010
Vignette(s): ($1) Man shearing sheep / Tree and building / Farmer and horse, Cattle, Sheep / Pat Lyon at forge. *($1)* Man shearing sheep / Tree and building / Farmer and horse, Cattle, Sheep / Pat Lyon at forge. *($2)* Sheep / Harvest scene / Cattle. *($3)* Milkmaid / Blacksmith and train / Dog and strongbox / Reaper and dog. *Engraver:* Draper, Toppan & Longacre. *Comments:* H-VT-55-G2, G2, G6, G10. 18__. 1830s–1850s.

Rarity: URS-2
Proof $3,500

$5-$5-$10-$20 • W-VT-190-005.005.010.020-US020
Vignette(s): ($5) Eagle, shield, and arrows / Steamboat, sloop, and rowboat / Woman. *($5)* Eagle, shield, and arrows / Steamboat, sloop, and rowboat / Woman. *($10)* Ceres and cherub seated on plow, Reapers / Steamboat, sloop, rowboat. *($20)* Girl with pitcher and rake / Steamboats, sloops, and rowboat with four men / Blacksmith. *Engraver:* Draper, Toppan & Longacre. *Comments:* H-VT-55-G14, G14, G16, G18. 18__. 1830s–1850s.

Rarity: URS-2
Proof $3,500

Non-Valid Issues
$1 • W-VT-190-001-A010
Left: 1 on ONE / Man reaping. *Center:* Man striking bear with axe. *Right:* 1 on ONE / Man mowing. *Back:* Orange circles consisting of ONEs. *Engraver:* W.L. Ormsby. *Comments:* H-VT-55-A5, Coulter-54. Altered from $1 Farmers & Drovers Bank, Petersburg, Indiana. Oct. 1, 1858.

Rarity: *None known*

$2 • W-VT-190-002-A020
Left: Woman. *Center:* Farmer reaping. *Right:* Woman. *Back:* Orange circles consisting of 2s. *Engraver:* W.L. Ormsby. *Comments:* H-VT-55-A10, Coulter-59. Altered from $2 Farmers & Drovers Bank, Petersburg, Indiana. Oct. 1, 1858.

Rarity: *None known*

$3 • W-VT-190-003-C050
Engraver: Draper, Toppan, Longacre & Co. *Comments:* H-VT-55-C10, Coulter-61. Counterfeit of W-VT-190-003-G050. 18__. 1830s.

Rarity: *None known*

$3 • W-VT-190-003-S010
Left: 3 / Portrait of George Washington / 3. *Center:* Woman, barrels, ship, Neptune. *Right:* 3 / Portrait of George Washington / 3. *Engraver:* A.B. & C. Durand & Wright. *Comments:* H-VT-55-S5, Coulter-64. 18__. 1840.

Rarity: URS-4
F $150

$3 • W-VT-190-003-N010
Payee: Charles Adams. *Comments:* H-Unlisted, Coulter-66. 1830s–1850s.

Rarity: *None known*

$3 • W-VT-190-003-N020
Payee: D. Nash. *Comments:* H-Unlisted, Coulter-67. 1830s–1850s.

Rarity: *None known*

$3 • W-VT-190-003-N030
Payee: D. Cole. *Comments:* H-Unlisted, Coulter-68. 1830s–1850s.

Rarity: *None known*

$3 • W-VT-190-003-N040
Payee: H. Brown. *Engraver:* A.B. & C. Durand, Wright & Co. *Comments:* H-Unlisted, Coulter-69. 1830s–1850s.

Rarity: *None known*

$3 • W-VT-190-003-N050
Comments: H-Unlisted, Coulter-70. No description available. 1830s–1850s.

Rarity: *None known*

$3 • W-VT-190-003-A030
Left: Woman / Shield / 3. *Center:* Two women. *Right:* Indian girl / 3. *Comments:* H-VT-55-A15, Coulter-65. 1850s.

Rarity: *None known*

$5 • W-VT-190-005-N060
Payee: Samuel Blair. *Comments:* H-Unlisted, Coulter-71. 1830s–1850s.

Rarity: URS-5
F $90

$5 • W-VT-190-005-N070
Left: Portrait of George Washington. *Center:* Women, barrels, ship. *Right:* Portrait of George Washington. *Comments:* H-Unlisted, Coulter-73. 1830s–1850s.

Rarity: *None known*

$5 • W-VT-190-005-N080
Left: Dog. *Center:* Farming scene. *Right:* Female portrait. *Comments:* H-Unlisted, Coulter-74. 1830s–1850s.

Rarity: *None known*

$5 • W-VT-190-005-A040
Left: 5 / Dog's head. *Center:* Man binding sheaf, Woman standing with sheaf. *Right:* 5 / Portrait of girl with ringlets. *Back:* Five portraits of George Washington surrounded by 5s. *Engraver:* W.L. Ormsby. *Comments:* H-VT-55-A20, Coulter-75. Altered from $5 Farmers & Drovers Bank, Petersburg, Indiana. Oct. 1, 1858.

Rarity: *None known*

$5 • W-VT-190-005-A050
Left: Male portrait. *Center:* Train. *Right:* Justice. *Tint:* Red-orange outlining white FIVE. *Engraver:* American Bank Note Co. *Comments:* H-VT-55-A25, Coulter-77. Altered from $5 Clinton Bank, Westernport, Maryland series. 18__. Circa 1860.

Rarity: URS-4
F $90

$5 • W-VT-190-005-A060   cc

Engraver: Rawdon, Wright & Hatch. *Comments:* H-VT-55-A30, Coulter-78. Altered from $5 Farmers & Mechanics Bank at Pontiac, Pontiac, Michigan. 18__. 1840s.

Rarity: URS-4

F $150

$5 • W-VT-190-005-A070   cc

Overprint: Red FIVE. *Engraver:* Rawdon, Wright, Hatch & Edson. *Comments:* H-VT-55-A35, Coulter-76. Altered from $5 Farmers & Merchants Bank of Memphis, Memphis, Tennessee series. 1850s.

Rarity: URS-6

F $100

$5 • W-VT-190-005-A080

Center: Hebe watering eagle. *Engraver:* Burton & Gurley. *Comments:* H-VT-55-A40, Coulter-79. Altered from $5 Farmers & Mechanics Bank, Burlington, Wisconsin. 18__. 1830s–1840s.

Rarity: URS-4

F $125

$10 • W-VT-190-010-R010

Engraver: Draper, Toppan, Longacre & Co. *Comments:* H-VT-55-R5, Coulter-83. Raised from W-VT-190-002-G030. 18__. 1840s.

Rarity: *None known*

$10 • W-VT-190-010-N090

Left: Portrait of George Washington. *Center:* Woman, barrels, ship. *Right:* Portrait of George Washington. *Comments:* H-Unlisted, Coulter-81. 1830s–1850s.

Rarity: *None known*

$10 • W-VT-190-010-A090

Left: Woman with goblet. *Center:* Woman, sheaf of wheat, cattle. *Engraver:* Burton & Gurley. *Comments:* H-VT-55-A45, Coulter-82. Altered from $10 Farmers & Mechanics Bank, Burlington, Wisconsin. 18__. 1830s–1840s.

Rarity: URS-4

F $125

$20 • W-VT-190-020-N100

Left: Portrait of George Washington. *Center:* Woman, barrels, ship. *Right:* Portrait of George Washington. *Comments:* H-Unlisted, Coulter-85. 1830s–1850s.

Rarity: *None known*

$20 • W-VT-190-020-A100   cc

Engraver: Burton & Gurley. *Comments:* H-VT-55-A50, Coulter-86. Altered from $20 Farmers & Mechanics Bank, Burlington, Wisconsin. 18__. 1830s–1840s.

Rarity: URS-4

F $250

$50 • W-VT-190-050-A110   cc

Engraver: Burton & Gurley. *Comments:* H-VT-55-A55, Coulter-88. Altered from $50 Farmers & Mechanics Bank, Burlington, Wisconsin. 18__. 1830s–1840s.

Rarity: URS-3

F $350

$100 • W-VT-190-100-A120

Left: Portrait of George Washington. *Center:* Woman with left arm around eagle. *Right:* Medallion head of Marquis de Lafayette. *Engraver:* Burton & Gurley. *Comments:* H-VT-55-A60, Coulter-90. Altered from $100 Farmers & Mechanics Bank, Burlington, Wisconsin. 18__. 1830s–1840s.

Rarity: *None known*

Notes Payable at the Mechanics Exchange Company, New York

$1 • W-VT-190-001-S020

CJF

Engraver: S. Stiles, Sherman & Smith. **Comments:** H-Unlisted, Coulter-55. 183__. 1837.

Rarity: URS-7
F $100

$1 • W-VT-190-001-S030

CC

Engraver: S. Stiles, Sherman & Smith. **Comments:** H-Unlisted, Coulter-56. 183__. 1837.

Rarity: URS-2
G $200

$2 • W-VT-190-002-S040

CC

Engraver: S. Stiles, Sherman & Smith. **Comments:** H-Unlisted, Coulter-60. 183__. 1837.

Rarity: URS-6
F $125

$3 • W-VT-190-003-S050

CJF

Engraver: S. Stiles, Sherman & Smith. **Comments:** H-Unlisted, Coulter-Unlisted. 183__. 1837.

Rarity: URS-1
F $900

Merchants Bank
1848–1865
W-VT-200

History: The Merchants Bank was incorporated on November 10, 1848, with an authorized starting capital fixed at $150,000. $90,000 of this total was initially paid in.

In 1857 these figures were listed: capital $149,750; bills in circulation $30,774; specie $4,899; real estate $30,774. In July 1859, circulation was $99,484, and capital was $149,750. The charter was extended on November 20, 1861, and January 1863 saw the bank's capital reduced by $30,000.[3]

In May 1865, the business of the bank was succeeded by the Merchants National Bank of Burlington. The outstanding circulation as of July 1, 1867, was $7,254, redemption of which was guaranteed by the national bank.

Numismatic Commentary: Notes from this bank are somewhat scarce and enter the marketplace only occasionally. Some issues show a vignette of a railroad train of the period. Another, a $3 issue, bears the portrait of Commodore MacDonough, who defeated the British in a naval action barely 20 miles from Burlington at Plattsburg Bay during the War of 1812.

VALID ISSUES
$1 • W-VT-200-001-G010

CC

Engraver: Toppan, Carpenter, Casilear & Co. **Comments:** H-VT-60-G4, Coulter-94. May 1, 18__. 1850s.

Rarity: URS-2
Proof $3,000

$1 • W-VT-200-001-G010a

CJF

Overprint: Red ONE. *Engraver:* Toppan, Carpenter, Casilear & Co. *Comments:* H-VT-60-G4a, Coulter-95. Similar to W-VT-200-001-G010. May 1, 18__. 1850s–1860s.
Rarity: URS-2
F $1,000

$2 • W-VT-200-002-G020

BH

Engraver: Toppan, Carpenter, Casilear & Co. *Comments:* H-VT-60-G8, Coulter-97. May 1, 18__. 1850s.
Rarity: URS-2
Proof $1,000

$2 • W-VT-200-002-G020a

CC

Overprint: Red TWO. *Engraver:* Toppan, Carpenter, Casilear & Co. *Comments:* H-VT-60-G8a, Coulter-98. Similar to W-VT-200-002-G020. May 1, 18__. 1850s–1860s.
Rarity: URS-2
F $1,250

$2 • W-VT-200-002-G020b

CC

Overprint: Green TWO. *Engraver:* Toppan, Carpenter, Casilear & Co. *Comments:* H-Unlisted, Coulter-Unlisted. Similar to W-VT-200-002-G020. May 1, 18__. 1850s–1860s.
Rarity: URS-2
VF $600; **Proof** $1,000

$3 • W-VT-200-003-G030

Left: Portrait of Commodore Thomas MacDonough / 3. *Center:* Woman seated with basket of fruits and vegetables. *Bottom center:* State arms. *Right:* 3 / Female portrait. *Engraver:* Toppan, Carpenter, Casilear & Co. *Comments:* H-VT-60-G12, Coulter-100. May 1, 18__. 1850s.
Rarity: *None known*

$3 • W-VT-200-003-G030a

CJF

Overprint: Red THREE. *Engraver:* Toppan, Carpenter, Casilear & Co. *Comments:* H-VT-60-G12a, Coulter-101. Similar to W-VT-200-003-G030 but with different date. Sept. 1st, 185_. 1850s.
Rarity: URS-2
F $1,250

$3 • W-VT-200-003-G030b

TD

Overprint: Green THREE. *Engraver:* Toppan, Carpenter, Casilear & Co. *Comments:* H-Unlisted, Coulter-Unlisted. Similar to W-VT-200-003-G030 but with different date. Sept. 1st, 185_. 1850s.
Rarity: URS-2
F $1,000

$5 • **W-VT-200-005-G040**

Left: FIVE / Minerva / FIVE. *Center:* Woman with cornucopia, Bridge, canal, boat, and village. *Bottom center:* State arms. *Right:* 5 / Portrait of William Henry Harrison. *Comments:* H-VT-60-G14, Coulter-105. 18__. 1848–1850s.

Rarity: *None known*

$5 • **W-VT-200-005-G040a**   CJF

Overprint: Red FIVE. *Engraver:* Rawdon, Wright, Hatch & Edson. *Comments:* H-Unlisted, Coulter-Unlisted. Similar to W-VT-200-005-G040. May 1st, 1850. 1848–1850s.

Rarity: URS-3
F $800

$5 • **W-VT-200-005-G050**   CC

Engraver: Toppan, Carpenter, Casilear & Co. *Comments:* H-VT-60-G16, Coulter-104. May 1, 18__. 1850s.

Rarity: URS-3
Proof $800

$5 • **W-VT-200-005-G050a**   CC

Overprint: Red FIVE. *Engraver:* Toppan, Carpenter, Casilear & Co. *Comments:* H-VT-60-G16a. Similar to W-VT-200-005-G050. May 1, 18__. 1850s.

Rarity: URS-3
F $750

$10 • **W-VT-200-010-G060**   CJF

Engraver: Rawdon, Wright, Hatch & Edson. *Comments:* H-VT-60-G20, Coulter-112. May 1st, 1850. 1850s.

Rarity: URS-2
F $1,000

$10 • **W-VT-200-010-G060a**   CC

Overprint: Red TEN. *Engraver:* Rawdon, Wright, Hatch & Edson. *Comments:* H-VT-60-G20a, Coulter-113. Similar to W-VT-200-010-G060. Handwritten 63 over engraved 50 in date. May 1st, 1850.

Rarity: URS-2
F $1,250

$20 • **W-VT-200-020-G070**

Left: 20 / Minerva. *Center:* Woman holding rake seated between 2 and 0. *Right:* 20 / Woman with cornucopia / 20. *Engraver:* Rawdon, Wright, Hatch & Edson. *Comments:* H-VT-60-G22, Coulter-116. 18__. 1848–1855.

Rarity: *None known*

$20 • **W-VT-200-020-G070a**

Overprint: Red TWENTY. *Engraver:* Rawdon, Wright, Hatch & Edson. *Comments:* H-VT-60-G22a, Coulter-117. Similar to W-VT-200-020-G070. 18__. 1855–1860s.

Rarity: *None known*

$50 • **W-VT-200-050-G080**

Left: 50 / Minerva. *Center:* Ceres and Vulcan seated, Cornucopia. *Right:* 50 / Cherub steering sailboat / 50. *Engraver:* Rawdon, Wright, Hatch & Edson. *Comments:* H-VT-60-G24, Coulter-119. 18__. 1848–1855.

Rarity: *None known*

$50 • W-VT-200-050-G080a

Overprint: Red FIFTY. *Engraver:* Rawdon, Wright, Hatch & Edson. *Comments:* H-VT-60-G24a, Coulter-120. Similar to W-VT-200-050-G080. 18__. 1855–1860s.

Rarity: *None known*

$100 • W-VT-200-100-G090

Left: 100 / Vulcan. *Center:* Spread eagle on tree limb. *Bottom center:* 100. *Right:* 100 / Ceres with rake and cornucopia. *Engraver:* Rawdon, Wright, Hatch & Edson. *Comments:* H-VT-60-G26, Coulter-122. 18__. 1848–1855.

Rarity: *None known*

$100 • W-VT-200-100-G090a

Overprint: Red HUNDRED. *Engraver:* Rawdon, Wright, Hatch & Edson. *Comments:* H-VT-60-G26a, Coulter-123. Similar to W-VT-200-100-G090. 18__. 1855–1860s.

Rarity: *None known*

$100 • W-VT-200-100-G100

CC

Engraver: Rawdon, Wright, & Hatch. *Comments:* H-Unlisted, Coulter-Unlisted. 18__. 1848–1855.

Rarity: URS-2
F $2,000

NON-VALID ISSUES

$1 • W-VT-200-001-A010

Left: 1 / Male portrait. *Center:* Catching wild cattle / Medallion head of Mercury. *Bottom center:* Indian in canoe. *Right:* 1 / Indian. *Comments:* H-VT-60-A5, Coulter-96. Altered from $1 Merchants Bank, Mankato City, Minnesota. Sept. 1, 185_. 1850s.

Rarity: *None known*

$1 • W-VT-200-001-A020

Left: Woman with crown of leaves leaning on 1. *Center:* 1 / Buffalo with head lowered, Trees and horse. *Bottom center:* Road, trees, sign post. *Right:* 1 / Indian man / 1. *Comments:* H-VT-60-A10, Coulter-93. Altered from $1 Merchants Bank, Stillwater, Minnesota. Oct. 20, 1854.

Rarity: URS-9
VF $125

$2 • W-VT-200-002-A030

CC

Engraver: Doty & Bergen. *Comments:* H-VT-60-A15, Coulter-99. Altered from $2 Merchants bank, Mankato City, Minnesota. Sept. 1st, 185_. 1850s.

Rarity: URS-5
F $100

$3 • W-VT-200-003-N010

Center: Woman / Cows, sheep. *Comments:* H-Unlisted, Coulter-102. 1850s.

Rarity: *None known*

$3 • W-VT-200-003-A040

CJF

Engraver: Durand & Co. *Comments:* H-VT-60-A20, Coulter-103. Altered from $3 Pennsylvania Savings Bank, Philadelphia, Pennsylvania. 185_. 1850s.

Rarity: URS-8
VG $75

$5 • W-VT-200-005-A050

Left: 5 / Portrait of John Taylor / 5. *Center:* 5 / Two allegorical women and three cherubs surrounding 5 / 5. *Bottom center:* Train. *Right:* FIVE / Woman standing / FIVE. *Engraver:* Rawdon, Wright, Hatch & Edson. *Comments:* H-VT-60-A25, Coulter-111. Altered from $5 Merchants Bank, Washington, D.C. Dec. 1, 1852.

Rarity: *None known*

$5 • W-VT-200-005-R010

Engraver: Toppan, Carpenter, Casilear & Co. *Comments:* H-Unlisted. Raised from W-VT-200-001-G010. May 1, 18__. 1850s.

Rarity: *None known*

$5 • W-VT-200-005-S010

CJF

Engraver: New England Bank Note Co. *Comments:* H-VT-60-S10, Coulter-110. 18__. 1850s.

Rarity: URS-6
VG $75; F $150

$5 • W-VT-200-005-N020

Left: Milkmaid. *Center:* Two women and shield. *Comments:* H-VT-60-N5, Coulter-108. 18__. 1850s.

Rarity: *None known*

$5 • W-VT-200-005-N030

Left: Woman. *Center:* Train. *Right:* Woman. *Comments:* H-Unlisted, Coulter-109. 1850s.

Rarity: *None known*

$5 • W-VT-200-005-A060

Left: 5 / V / 5. *Center:* Farmer eating lunch, Boy and dog on ground, Girl and horses. *Bottom center:* Monument. *Right:* 5 / V / 5. *Overprint:* Red FIVE. *Engraver:* Bald, Cousland & Co. / Baldwin, Bald & Cousland. *Comments:* H-VT-60-A30, Coulter-107. Altered from $5 Southern Bank of Georgia, Bainbridge, Georgia. 18__. 1860s.

Rarity: *None known*

$5 • W-VT-200-005-A070

TD

Comments: H-VT-60-A35, Coulter-106. October 20th, 1854.

Rarity: URS-6
F $75

$10 • W-VT-200-010-C065

Center: Woman and globe. *Right:* Male portrait. *Comments:* H-Unlisted, Coulter-114. 1850s.

Rarity: *None known*

$10 • W-VT-200-010-R020

Engraver: Toppan, Carpenter, Casilear & Co. *Comments:* H-VT-60-R5, Coulter-115. Raised from W-VT-200-001-G010. May 1, 185_. 1850s.

Rarity: URS-4
F $90

$20 • W-VT-200-020-R030

Engraver: Toppan, Carpenter, Casilear & Co. *Comments:* H-VT-60-R10, Coulter-118. Raised from W-VT-200-001-G010. 18__. 1850s.

Rarity: URS-4
F $125

$50 • W-VT-200-050-A080

Center: L / Woman reclining on flowers. *Bottom center:* Clasped hands in wreath. *Right:* Woman with rake and plow. *Engraver:* Rawdon, Wright & Hatch. *Comments:* H-VT-60-A40, Coulter-121. Altered from W-VT-025-050-G100. 18__. 1830s–1841.

Rarity: URS-4
F $125

$100 • W-VT-200-100-A090

Left: ONE HUNDRED vertically. *Center:* 100 / Woman, strongbox, key / 100. *Bottom center:* Eagle. *Right:* ONE HUNDRED vertically. *Engraver:* Rawdon, Wright & Hatch. *Comments:* H-VT-60-A45, Coulter-124. Altered from W-VT-025-100-G110. 18__. 1830s–1841.

Rarity: *None known*

Vermont State Bank (branch)
1807–1812
W-VT-210

History: The Burlington branch of the Vermont State Bank issued paper money from 1807 until 1812. It was not managed by local people who might have furthered the interests of the city. In 1812 the records of the bank were moved to Woodstock, and the Burlington branch was closed. After 1812 many bills of the various branches remained in circulation. These were redeemed in later years until the affairs of the bank were wound up in 1845. See introductory text for general information.

See also listings under Middlebury, W-VT-450, Westminster, W-VT-830, and Woodstock, W-VT-900.

Numismatic Commentary: The Vermont State Bank issued identical notes for all four branches; there are plenty to satisfy collector demand. Even though many remainder sheets have been cut, there are still plenty of signed and dated examples in the marketplace. Most of the available stock are of the PSSP design.

VALID ISSUES

50¢ • W-VT-210-00.50-G010

Left: FIFTY CENTS vertically. *Center:* 50 / Woman seated. *Right:* 50/100. *Comments:* H-VT-4-G1, Coulter-127. 1806–1808.

Rarity: URS-9
VG $50

50¢ • W-VT-210-00.50-G020
Left: FIFTY CENTS vertically. *Center:* 50 / Woman seated / 50/100. *Comments:* H-VT-4-G2. 1806–1808.
Rarity: URS-9
F $75

50¢ • W-VT-210-00.50-G030　　　　　　　NJW

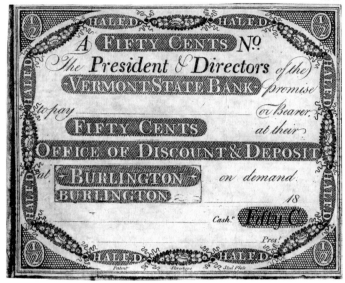

Engraver: PSSP. *Comments:* H-VT-4-G10, Coulter-128. 18__. 1808.
Rarity: URS-6
Unc-Rem $75

75¢ • W-VT-210-00.75-G040
Left: SEVENTY FIVE vertically. *Center:* Woman reclining / 75 in die. *Comments:* H-VT-4-G11, Coulter-129. 180_. 1806–1808.
Rarity: URS-5
VF $150

75¢ • W-VT-210-00.75-G050
Left: SEVENTY FIVE vertically. *Center:* Woman reclining / 75 in die. *Comments:* H-VT-4-G12. 180_. 1806–1808.
Rarity: *None known*

75¢ • W-VT-210-00.75-G060
Left: SEVENTY FIVE C vertically. *Center:* Woman seated / 75 Cents. *Comments:* H-VT-4-G13. 1806–1808.
Rarity: URS-8
F $50

75¢ • W-VT-210-00.75-G070
Left: SEVENTY FIVE vertically. *Center:* Woman reclining / 75 in die. *Comments:* H-VT-4-G14. 180_. 1806–1808.
Rarity: URS-4
VF $150

75¢ • W-VT-210-00.75-G080　　　　　　　CC

Engraver: PSSP. *Comments:* H-VT-4-G18. 18__. 1808.
Rarity: URS-6
VF $90

$1 • W-VT-210-001-G090
Left: Panel / ONE DOLLAR vertically. *Center:* ONE on three dies / Women flanking shield / Ribbon bearing FREEDOM & UNITY. *Bottom center:* 1 on die. *Right:* 1 on die. *Comments:* H-VT-4-G19, Coulter-131. 180_. 1806–1808.
Rarity: URS-5
VF $150

$1 • W-VT-210-001-G100
Left: Panel / ONE DOLLAR vertically. *Center:* ONE on three dies / Women flanking shield / Ribbon bearing FREEDOM & UNITY. *Bottom center:* 1 on die. *Right:* 1 on die. *Comments:* H-VT-4-G20. 180_. 1806–1808.
Rarity: URS-9
Unc-Rem $75

$1 • W-VT-210-001-G110　　　　　　　CC

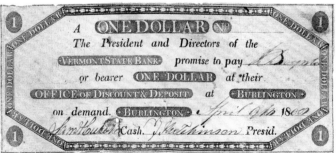

Engraver: PSSP. *Comments:* H-VT-4-G22, Coulter-132. 18__. 1808.
Rarity: URS-7
F $80

$1 • W-VT-210-001-G120

Center: ONE. *Engraver:* PSSP. *Comments:* H-VT-4-G23, Coulter-133. 18__. 1808.

Rarity: URS-5
VF $150

$1.25 • W-VT-210-001.25-G130

NJW

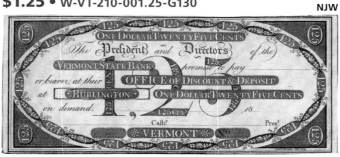

Engraver: PSSP. *Comments:* H-VT-4-G24, Coulter-134. 18__. 1808.

Rarity: URS-7
Unc-Rem $100

$1.50 • W-VT-210-001.50-G140

Left: 150 / 150 / 150 vertically. *Center:* 1.50. *Right:* 150 / 150 / 150 vertically. *Engraver:* PSSP. *Comments:* H-VT-4-G25, Coulter-135. 18__. 1808.

Rarity: URS-7
Unc-Rem $100

$1.75 • W-VT-210-001.75-G150

CC

Engraver: PSSP. *Comments:* H-VT-4-G26, Coulter-136. 18__. 1808.

Rarity: URS-7
Unc-Rem $125

$2 • W-VT-210-002-G160

Left: Panel / TWO DOLLARS vertically. *Center:* TWO / Women flanking shield / 2 on die. *Comments:* H-VT-4-G28, Coulter-137. 18__. 1806–1808.

Rarity: URS-5
VF $150

$2 • W-VT-210-002-G170

CC

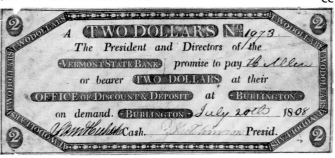

Engraver: PSSP. *Comments:* H-VT-4-G29, Coulter-Unlisted. 18__. 1808.

Rarity: URS-8
F $100

$2 • W-VT-210-002-G180

CJF

Engraver: PSSP. *Comments:* H-VT-4-G30, Coulter-138. 18__. 1808.

Rarity: URS-8
F $75; **VF** $150

$3 • W-VT-210-003-G190

Left: Panel / THREE vertically. *Center:* 3 on die / Women flanking shield. *Right:* 3 on die. *Comments:* H-VT-4-G31, Coulter-139. 18__. 1806–1808.

Rarity: URS-4
VF $150

How to Read the Whitman Numbering System

$1 • W-RI-010-001-G010a

Denomination: Value of the note shown.

W: Whitman number. This number is a sortable code unique to each bank and note.

RI: Abbreviation for the state under study.

010: Numerical designation specific to each bank.

001: The denomination in dollars.

G010a: G indicates a good or valid note. Other categories are indicated thus: C (counterfeit); R (raised); S (spurious); N (not-attributed); A (altered). Numbers are assigned starting with 010, 020, et seq. Terminal letters following the number indicate variations of a note: a series of different colored overprints, tints, payees, etc., all on the same design of note. For more information, see the "How to Use This Book" section at the front of the volume, page xiv.

$3 • W-VT-210-003-G200

CJF

Comments: H-VT-4-G32. 18__. 1806–1808.
Rarity: URS-7
F $100

$3 • W-VT-210-003-G210

Center: 3 / 3 / 3 / 3. **Engraver:** PSSP. **Comments:** H-VT-4-G33. 18__. 1806–1808.
Rarity: URS-5
VF $200

$3 • W-VT-210-003-G220

Center: THREE. **Engraver:** PSSP. **Comments:** H-VT-4-G34. 18__. 1806–1808.
Rarity: URS-5
VF $200

$5 • W-VT-210-005-G230

CC

Comments: H-VT-4-G35. 18__. 1806–1808.
Rarity: URS-8
F $100

$5 • W-VT-210-005-G240

Left: V V V V / VERMONT vertically. **Center:** 5 in die. **Right:** 5 in die. **Engraver:** PSSP. **Comments:** H-VT-4-G36. 18__. 1807 and 1808.
Rarity: *None known*

$5 • W-VT-210-005-G250

CC

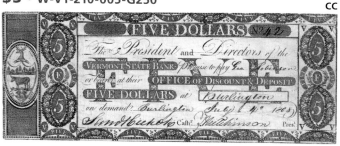

Engraver: PSSP. **Comments:** H-VT-4-G37. 18__. 1808.
Rarity: URS-8
F $150

$10 • W-VT-210-010-G260

Left: Panel / TEN vertically. **Center:** 10 on die / TEN on three dies / Women flanking shield. **Right:** 10 on die. **Comments:** H-VT-4-G38. 18__. 1806–1808.
Rarity: URS-9
F $75

$10 • W-VT-210-010-G270

Left: State arms / 10 / 10. **Right:** 10 / 10. **Engraver:** PSSP. **Comments:** H-VT-4-G40, Coulter-142. 18__. 1808.
Rarity: URS-4
VF $125

$20 • W-VT-210-020-G280

Left: State arms / 20 / 20. **Right:** 20 / 20. **Engraver:** PSSP. **Comments:** H-VT-4-G43. 18__. 1808.
Rarity: *None known*

Uncut Sheets
$1.75-$1.50-$1.25-50¢-75¢ •
W-VT-210-001.75.001.50.001.25.00.50.00.75-US010

Vignette(s): *($1.75)* 1.75. *($1.50)* 1.50. *($1.25)* 1.25. *(50¢)* 1/2 / 1/2 / 1/2 / 1/2. *(75¢)* 3/4 / 3/4 / 3/4 / 3/4. **Engraver:** PSSP. **Comments:** H-VT-4-G26, G25, G24, G10, G18. 18__. 1808.
Rarity: URS-6
Unc-Rem $300

NON-VALID ISSUES
50¢ • W-VT-210-00.50-C010

Comments: H-VT-4-C1. Counterfeit of W-VT-210-00.50-G010. 1808.
Rarity: URS-5
F $75

50¢ • W-VT-210-00.50-C020

PEM

Comments: H-VT-4-C2. Counterfeit of W-VT-210-00.50-G020. 1808.
Rarity: URS-5
VF $150

50¢ • W-VT-210-00.50-N010
Comments: H-Unlisted, Coulter-3. Imitation of PSSP. 1808.
Rarity: *None known*

75¢ • W-VT-210-00.75-C050
Comments: H-VT-4-C12. Counterfeit of W-VT-210-00.75-G050. 180_. 1808.
Rarity: URS-4
VF $125

75¢ • W-VT-210-00.75-C060   CC

Comments: H-VT-4-C13. Counterfeit of W-VT-210-00.75-G060. 180_. 1808.
Rarity: URS-5
F $100

75¢ • W-VT-210-00.75-N020
Comments: H-Unlisted, Coulter-5. Imitation of PSSP. 1808.
Rarity: *None known*

75¢ • W-VT-210-00.75-N030
Left: SEVENTY FIVE vertically. *Center:* Woman reclining / 75 in die. *Comments:* H-Unlisted, Coulter-15. 1808.
Rarity: *None known*

$1 • W-VT-210-001-C090
Comments: H-VT-4-C19. Counterfeit of W-VT-210-001-G090. 180_. 1808.
Rarity: URS-6
F $100

$2 • W-VT-210-002-C160
Comments: H-VT-4-C28, Coulter-Unlisted. Counterfeit of W-VT-210-002-G160. 180_. 1808.
Rarity: URS-6
F $100

$3 • W-VT-210-003-C190
Comments: H-VT-4-C31. Counterfeit of W-VT-210-003-G190. 18__. 1806–1808.
Rarity: URS-4
F $100

$3 • W-VT-210-003-C200
Comments: H-VT-4-C32. Counterfeit of W-VT-210-003-G200. 18__. 1808.
Rarity: URS-4
F $100

$3 • W-VT-210-003-C210   CJF

Engraver: PSSP. *Comments:* H-VT-4-C33. Counterfeit of W-VT-210-003-G210. 18__. 1806–1808.
Rarity: URS-7
Unc-Rem $100

$3 • W-VT-210-003-N040
Center: 3 / 3 / 3 / 3. *Right:* 100 / Woman with rake and cornucopia. *Comments:* H-Unlisted, Coulter-140. 1808.
Rarity: *None known*

$3 • W-VT-210-003-N050
Left: THREE vertically. *Center:* Women flanking shield / Ribbon bearing FREEDOM & UNITY. *Comments:* H-Unlisted, Coulter-26. 1808.
Rarity: *None known*

$5 • W-VT-210-005-C240
Engraver: PSSP. *Comments:* H-VT-4-C36. Counterfeit of W-VT-210-005-G240. 18__. 1807 and 1808.
Rarity: *None known*

$5 • W-VT-210-005-N060
Left: 5 / State arms / 5. *Center:* FIVE DOLLARS. *Right:* 5 / 5. *Engraver:* PSSP. *Comments:* H-Unlisted, Coulter-32. 1808.
Rarity: *None known*

$5 • W-VT-210-005-N070
Comments: H-Unlisted, Coulter-141. No description available. 1808.
Rarity: *None known*

$5 • W-VT-210-005-N080
Left: VERMONT vertically. *Engraver:* PSSP. *Comments:* H-Unlisted, Coulter-14. 1808.
Rarity: *None known*

$5 • W-VT-210-005-N090
Right: State arms. *Engraver:* PSSP. *Comments:* H-Unlisted, Coulter-15. 1808.
Rarity: *None known*

$5 • W-VT-210-005-N100
Left: VERMONT vertically. *Engraver:* PSSP. *Comments:* H-Unlisted, Coulter-28. 1808.
Rarity: *None known*

$10 • W-VT-210-010-C260
Comments: H-VT-4-C38. Counterfeit of W-VT-210-010-G260. 18__. 1807.
Rarity: URS-4
F $125

$10 • W-VT-210-010-N110

Center: 10 / 10 / State arms / 10 / 10. *Engraver:* PSSP. *Comments:* H-Unlisted, Coulter-34. 1808.

Rarity: *None known*

$10 • W-VT-210-010-N120

Engraver: PSSP. *Comments:* H-Unlisted, Coulter-35. 1808.

Rarity: *None known*

$10 • W-VT-210-010-N130

Left: VERMONT vertically. *Engraver:* PSSP. *Comments:* H-Unlisted, Coulter-16. 1808.

Rarity: *None known*

$20 • W-VT-210-020-N140

Center: 20 / 20 / TWENTY DOLLARS / 20 / 20. *Engraver:* PSSP. *Comments:* H-Unlisted, Coulter-143. 1808.

Rarity: *None known*

CABOT, VERMONT

Cabot was named by one of the original grantees, Lyman Hitchcock, after his intended bride, Miss Cabot of Connecticut. The first settler to arrive was Benjamin Webster: in 1783 he built a log cabin in Cabot and then brought his family back the following March. Others followed, and in 1787 the settlers requested to organize as a town.

Potatoes were raised primarily, but there was little market for crops. Profit was realized when distilleries were established to turn the potatoes into whiskey. These ardent spirits were distributed to Boston, Portland, and Canada during the late 18th century. In 1789 a sawmill was built on the Winooski River, and not long after, more businesses powered by water were set up. A wool-carding shop, a cloth-dressing shop, a starch factory, a carriage shop, a blacksmith shop, and a foundry were among some of the businesses. Sheep husbandry was also important for many years. When the wool market declined, the farmers switched to dairy products.

Bank of Cabot
1854
W-VT-220

History: In 1854 a charter application for the Bank of Cabot was rejected by the State Legislature.

Numismatic Commentary: It is possible that Proof notes were made, but no record has been found of such.

CASTLETON, VERMONT

Castleton was chartered in 1761 and included 36 square miles of land granted and divided into 70 shares. By 1767 the first settlers arrived in town, including Amos Bird and Noah Lee. In 1777 there were 17 families residing in Castleton.

Ethan Allen and the Green Mountain Boys met with Benedict Arnold in Castleton in May 1775 to plan their assault on Fort Ticonderoga. They were successful in capturing the fort and holding it for two years. Hessian mercenary soldiers fighting for the British who had been stationed at Castleton left when the fortunes of the war turned.

After the conflict, Castleton remained primarily agricultural in nature. Cattle and sheep were important. Sawmills and gristmills became established industries in town, and through the 19th century slate and marble were quarried. The railroad arrived in 1854, and a hotel helped attract tourists to the town.

Bank of Castleton
1852–1860
W-VT-230

History: The Bank of Castleton was established in 1852 with an authorized starting capital of $65,000. In 1854 figures included: notes discounted $66,147; deposits in city banks $40,564; other resources $81,580; specie $478. In May 1857, capital was $100,000, bills in circulation totaled $26,521, specie was $624, and real estate was valued at $1,610. In July 1859, capital was $100,500, and circulation was $26,521.

On July 6, 1859, the officers of the Bank of Castleton voted to cease business. The circulation at that time was $33,506. On July 28 of that year, the bank commissioner burned the bills remaining at the bank as well as all the sheets which had not yet been issued, a total of $20,004. The bank plates were also destroyed.

The outstanding circulation as of July 25, 1864, was $1,150, redemption of which was guaranteed by the Mutual Bank of Castleton, W-VT-250.

Numismatic Commentary: Genuine notes are not hard to locate and probably came from redeemed notes that survived, as the outstanding circulation reported above would have resulted in rarities. All issues have a state treasurer's seal that denotes that the bank operated under the Vermont Free Banking Law.

VALID ISSUES

$1 • W-VT-230-001-G010

CJF

Engraver: Danforth, Bald & Co. *Comments:* H-VT-65-G2, Coulter-1. 18___. 1850s.

Rarity: URS-3
F $750; **Proof** $1,200

$2 • W-VT-230-002-G020   CC

Engraver: Danforth, Bald & Co. *Comments:* H-VT-65-G4, Coulter-2. 18__. 1850s.

Rarity: URS-3
F $1,000; **Proof** $1,200

$5 • W-VT-230-005-G030   CJF

Engraver: Danforth, Bald & Co. *Comments:* H-VT-65-G6, Coulter-3. 18__. 1850s.

Rarity: URS-3
F $1,000; **Proof** $1,200

$10 • W-VT-230-010-G040   CC

Engraver: Danforth, Bald & Co. *Comments:* H-VT-65-G8, Coulter-5. 18__. 1850s.

Rarity: URS-4
Proof $1,000

$20 • W-VT-230-020-G050   CC

Engraver: Danforth, Bald & Co. *Comments:* H-VT-65-G10, Coulter-7. 18__. 1850s.

Rarity: URS-5
CU $200; **Proof** $1,500

Uncut Sheets

$1-$1-$2-$5 • W-VT-230-001.001.002.005-US010

Vignette(s): *($1)* State arms / Three men, Rocks and railroad. *($1)* State arms / Three men, Rocks and railroad. *($2)* State arms / Farmer's wife holding child, Sheaves and distant reapers. *($5)* State arms / Farmer on horseback, Dog, sheep, and mill. *Engraver:* Danforth, Bald & Co. *Comments:* H-VT-65-G2, G2, G4, G6. 18__. 1850s.

Rarity: URS-4
Unc-Rem $800

$10-$20 • W-VT-230-010.020-US020

Vignette(s): *($10)* State arms / Farmer, sailor, and mechanic / Building. *($20)* Train passing under bridge / State arms. *Engraver:* American Bank Note Co. *Comments:* H-VT-65-G8, G10. 18__. 1850s.

Rarity: URS-3
Proof $800

Non-Valid Issues

$5 • W-VT-230-005-C030

Engraver: Danforth, Bald & Co. *Comments:* H-VT-65-C6. Counterfeit of W-VT-230-005-G030. 18__. 1850s.

Rarity: *None known*

$5 • W-VT-230-005-R010

Engraver: Danforth, Bald & Co. *Comments:* H-VT-65-R5, Coulter-4. Raised from W-VT-230-001-G010. 18__. 1850s.

Rarity: *None known*

$10 • W-VT-230-010-R020

Engraver: Danforth, Bald & Co. *Comments:* H-VT-65-R6, Coulter-6. Raised from W-VT-230-001-G010. 18__. 1850s.

Rarity: *None known*

$20 • W-VT-230-020-R030   CC

Engraver: Danforth, Bald & Co. *Comments:* H-VT-65-R7, Coulter-8. Raised from W-VT-230-001-G010. 18__. 1850s.

Rarity: URS-2
Proof $2,000

Eagle Bank
1854
W-VT-240

History: In 1854 a charter application for the Eagle Bank was rejected by the State Legislature.

Numismatic Commentary: It is possible that Proofs were ordered in anticipation of the charter, but this seems unlikely.

Mutual Bank of Castleton
1859–1865
W-VT-250

History: The Mutual Bank succeeded the Bank of Castleton, W-VT-230. In July 1859, the authorized capital was $50,000; in 1861 it was $100,000. Capital in 1857 was still $50,000, but specie was listed at $2,631. In 1863 capital was the same.

In 1865 the business of the Mutual Bank of Castleton was succeeded by the Castleton National Bank, chartered October 21, 1865. It had an outstanding circulation of $3,020 as of July 1, 1867.

Numismatic Commentary: All genuine issues were engraved by the American Bank Note Co. and are quite colorful. Modern Proofs with a bright green tint are available.

Remaining in the American Bank Note Co. archives as of 2003 was a $10-$20 face plate, a $10-$20 tint plate, a $1-$2-$2-$5 face plate, and a $1-$2-$2-$5 tint plate.

VALID ISSUES

$1 • W-VT-250-001-G010

CJF

Tint: Red dies and panel of microletters outlining ONE / ONE. **Engraver:** American Bank Note Co. **Comments:** H-VT-70-G2, Coulter-9. July 1st, 1859.

Rarity: URS-3
F $1,000; **Proof** $1,500

$2 • W-VT-250-002-G020

Left: Two children / 2. **Center:** Two men, horse, and city. **Right:** 2 / Two farmers. **Tint:** Red with 2 / 2. **Engraver:** American Bank Note Co. **Comments:** H-VT-70-G4, Coulter-11. 1859–1865.

Rarity: *None known*

$5 • W-VT-250-005-G030

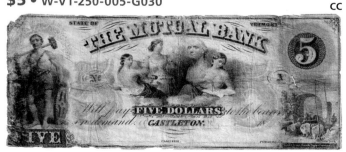

CC

Tint: Red with 5, FIVE, 5. **Engraver:** American Bank Note Co. **Comments:** H-VT-70-G6, Coulter-12. 18__. 1859–1865.

Rarity: URS-2
VG $750

$10 • W-VT-250-010-G040

CC

Tint: Red with die and TEN, X, TEN. **Engraver:** American Bank Note Co. **Comments:** H-VT-70-G8, Coulter-14. Proof. 18__. 1859–1865.

Rarity: URS-3
Proof $2,000

$10 • W-VT-250-010-G040a

CC

Tint: Green with die and TEN, X, TEN. **Engraver:** American Bank Note Co. **Comments:** H-Unlisted, Coulter-Unlisted. Similar to W-VT-250-010-G040. Modern Proof. 18__. 1859–1865.

Rarity: URS-3
Proof $1,000

$20 • W-VT-250-020-G050

CC

Tint: Red with die and TWENTY. **Engraver:** American Bank Note Co. **Comments:** H-VT-70-G10, Coulter-16. Proof. 18__. 1859–1865.

Rarity: URS-2
Proof $1,500

$20 • W-VT-250-020-G050a

CC

Tint: Green with die and TWENTY. **Engraver:** American Bank Note Co. **Comments:** H-Unlisted, Coulter-Unlisted. Similar to W-VT-250-020-G050. Modern Proof. 18___. 1859–1865.
Rarity: URS-3
Proof $1,500

Uncut Sheets

$1-$2-$2-$5 • W-VT-250-001.002.002.005-US010
Tint(s): Red. **Engraver:** American Bank Note Co. **Comments:** H-VT-70-G2, G4, G4, G6. July 1st, 1859.
Rarity: URS-1
Proof $6,500

$10-$20 • W-VT-250-010.020-US020

CC

Tint(s): Red. **Engraver:** American Bank Note Co. **Comments:** H-VT-70-G8, G10. Proof. 18___. 1859–1865.
Rarity: URS-1
Proof $3,000

NON-VALID ISSUES

$1 • W-VT-250-001-A010

CJF

Overprint: Red ONE. **Engraver:** Wellstood, Hay & Whiting. **Comments:** H-VT-70-A5, Coulter-10. Altered from $1 Thames Bank, Laurel, Indiana. August 12th, 18___. 1860.
Rarity: URS-7
F $100

$5 • W-VT-250-005-A020

CC

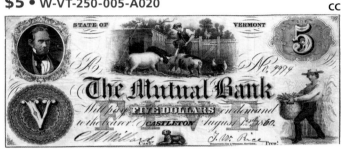

Overprint: Red FIVE. **Engraver:** Wellstood, Hay & Whiting. **Comments:** H-VT-70-A10, Coulter-13. Altered from $5 Thames Bank, Laurel, Indiana. August 12th, 18___. 1860.
Rarity: URS-5
VF $300

$10 • W-VT-250-010-N010
Center: Women, grain, and sheep. **Comments:** H-VT-70-N5, Coulter-15. 1850s–1860s.
Rarity: *None known*

CHELSEA, VERMONT

Settled in 1784, Chelsea was split into two commons in the early days: the North Common and the South Common. It was designated as the seat of county government in 1795. The first jail was built in the North Common in 1796, and in 1813 a church was built. In the early 19th century, the population was at its highest, with almost 2,000 citizens. The Court House in the South Common was built in 1847.

Bank of Orange County {1st}
1827–1842
W-VT-260

History: The Bank of Orange County was chartered on November 3, 1827, with $100,000 of authorized starting capital, $70,000 of which was soon paid in. The bank was the first and last of three succeeding state-chartered banks established in Chelsea, all with similar names: the Bank of Orange County, 1st, W-VT-260, the Orange County Bank, W-VT-280, and Bank of Orange County, 2nd, W-VT-270. The first Bank of Orange County issued notes of the PSSP type. It is highly likely that only one bank existed at a time, especially considering the small size of the town. There was also some transfer of personnel.[4]

In October 1841, the bank's capital was $70,000, circulation was $113,573, and real estate was valued at $2,000. Circulation was $114,573 as of November 6 that year. Two years later, the bank's charter expired. It was succeeded by the Orange County Bank, W-VT-280.

Numismatic Commentary: All genuine notes are of the PSSP design and are very hard to locate.

VALID ISSUES

$1 • W-VT-260-001-G010
Left: 1 / 1 vertically. *Center:* 1 / 1 / 1 / 1. *Right:* 1 / 1 vertically. *Engraver:* PSSP. *Comments:* H-VT-75-G4, Coulter-1. 18__. 1820s.
Rarity: *None known*

$1 • W-VT-260-001-G010a
Left: ONE / D / ONE vertically. *Right:* ONE / D / ONE vertically. *Engraver:* PSSP. *Comments:* H-VT-75-G8. Similar to W-VT-260-001-G010. 18__. 1830s–1840s.
Rarity: *None known*

$2 • W-VT-260-002-G020
Left: Five TWOs vertically. *Center:* 2 / 2 / 2 / 2. *Right:* Five TWOs vertically. *Engraver:* PSSP. *Comments:* H-VT-75-G16, Coulter-5. 18__. 1830s–1840s.
Rarity: *None known*

$2 • W-VT-260-002-G030
Left: 2 / TWO / Cupid. *Center:* Soldier, Bust of George Washington, Liberty, Two Indians, Spread eagle and shield. *Right:* Castleton Seminary and grounds. *Engraver:* Toppan, Carpenter & Co. *Comments:* H-VT-75-G18. 1830s–1840s.
Rarity: *None known*

$3 • W-VT-260-003-G040
Left: 3 / 3. *Center:* 3 / 3 / 3 / 3. *Right:* 3 / 3. *Engraver:* PSSP. *Comments:* H-VT-75-G20, Coulter-10. 18__. 1820s–1830s.
Rarity: *None known*

$3 • W-VT-260-003-G040a
Left: THREE vertically. *Right:* THREE vertically. *Engraver:* PSSP. *Comments:* H-VT-75-G24, Coulter-9. Similar to W-VT-260-003-G040. 18__. 1830s–1840s.
Rarity: *None known*

$5 • W-VT-260-005-G050
Left: VERMONT vertically. *Center:* Alternating flower garlands and gridwork segments bearing FIVE. *Right:* 5 / 5. *Engraver:* PSSP. *Comments:* H-VT-75-G28, Coulter-14. 18__. 1820s.
Rarity: *None known*

$5 • W-VT-260-005-G050a
Engraver: PSSP. *Comments:* H-VT-75-G32. Similar to W-VT-260-005-G050. 18__. 1820s–1830s.
Rarity: *None known*

$10 • W-VT-260-010-G060
Left: Panel bearing VERMONT / 10 / 10 vertically. *Center:* Alternating flower garlands and gridwork segments bearing TEN. *Right:* 10 / 10 vertically. *Engraver:* PSSP. *Comments:* H-VT-75-G36. 18__. 1820s.
Rarity: *None known*

$10 • W-VT-260-010-G060a
Engraver: PSSP. *Comments:* H-VT-75-G40. Similar to W-VT-260-010-G060. 18__. 1820s–1830s.
Rarity: *None known*

$20 • W-VT-260-020-G070
Left: Panel bearing VERMONT / 20 / 20 vertically. *Center:* Alternating flower garlands and gridwork segments bearing TWENTY. *Right:* 20 / 20 vertically. *Engraver:* PSSP. *Comments:* H-VT-75-G44. 18__. 1820s–1830s.
Rarity: *None known*

$50 • W-VT-260-050-G080
Left: Panel bearing VERMONT / 50 / 50 vertically. *Center:* Alternating flower garlands and gridwork segments bearing FIFTY. *Right:* 50 / 50 vertically. *Engraver:* PSSP. *Comments:* H-VT-75-G48. 18__. 1820s–1830s.
Rarity: *None known*

$50 • W-VT-260-050-G090
Left: 50 / Woman resting hand on column. *Center:* Man, Woman, horses at trough. *Right:* 50 / Woman, Man holding child on his shoulders. *Comments:* H-Unlisted, Coulter-20. 1820s–1830s.
Rarity: *None known*

$100 • W-VT-260-100-G100
Left: Panel bearing VERMONT / 100 / 100 vertically. *Center:* Alternating flower garlands and gridwork segments bearing 100. *Right:* 100 / 100 vertically. *Engraver:* PSSP. *Comments:* H-VT-75-G52. 18__. 1820s–1830s.
Rarity: *None known*

$100 • W-VT-260-100-G110
Left: C / 100. *Center:* Man and woman flanking shield, Girl, dog, oxen, and train. *Right:* 100 / Indian warrior on horseback. *Comments:* H-Unlisted, Coulter-21. 1820s–1830s.
Rarity: *None known*

Non-Valid Issues

$1 • W-VT-260-001-C010

Engraver: PSSP. *Comments:* H-VT-75-C4. Counterfeit of W-VT-260-001-G010. 18__. 1820s–1830s.

Rarity: *None known*

$1 • W-VT-260-001-C010a

CC

Engraver: PSSP. *Comments:* H-VT-75-C8. Counterfeit of W-VT-260-001-G010a. 18__. 1840s.

Rarity: URS-6

F $100

$1 • W-VT-260-001-C010b

Tint: Orange. *Engraver:* PSSP. *Comments:* H-Unlisted. Similar to W-VT-260-001-C010a. 18__. 1840s.

Rarity: —

F $175

$1 • W-VT-260-001-N010

Engraver: PSSP. *Comments:* H-Unlisted, Coulter-2. 1840s.

Rarity: *None known*

$1 • W-VT-260-001-N020

Center: Woman with rake, sickle, and sheaf of grain. *Comments:* H-Unlisted, Coulter-4. 1840s.

Rarity: *None known*

$2 • W-VT-260-002-C020

TD

Engraver: PSSP. *Comments:* H-VT-75-C16. Counterfeit of W-VT-260-002-G020. 18__. 1840s.

Rarity: URS-6

F $100

$2 • W-VT-260-002-N030

Left: 2 / Portrait of girl. *Center:* Wagon drawn by four horses / TWO. *Right:* 2 / Portrait of Thomas Jefferson. *Tint:* Red. *Engraver:* Bald, Cousland & Co. *Comments:* H-Unlisted, Coulter-8. 1840s.

Rarity: URS-4

F $125

$3 • W-VT-260-003-C040a

CJF

Engraver: PSSP. *Comments:* H-VT-75-C24. Counterfeit of W-VT-260-003-G040a. 18__. 1840s.

Rarity: URS-6

F $1,000

$3 • W-VT-260-003-N040

Engraver: PSSP. *Comments:* H-Unlisted, Coulter-12. 1840s.

Rarity: *None known*

$3 • W-VT-260-003-N050

Center: Woman, Agricultural implements. *Comments:* H-Unlisted, Coulter-13. 1840s.

Rarity: *None known*

$5 • W-VT-260-005-N060

Engraver: Toppan, Carpenter & Co. *Comments:* H-Unlisted, Coulter-16. Imitation of W-VT-260-003-N050. 1840s.

Rarity: *None known*

$10 • W-VT-260-010-R010

Comments: H-Unlisted, Coulter-18. Raised from W-VT-260-001-G010. 1840s.

Rarity: *None known*

Bank of Orange County {2nd}
1856–1865
W-VT-270

History: Chartered in January 1855 with an authorized capital of $75,000, the Bank of Orange County, 2nd, did not start business until 1859. It was a successor to the interests of the Orange County Bank, W-VT-280.

Figures for 1857 included: capital $45,000; bills in circulation $90,647; specie $9,249; real estate $1,700. In August 1859, capital was $45,000, and circulation was $99,647. From December 1860 to 1864, capital was $60,000. Circulation was listed at $119,345 in 1862.

In 1865 the business of the bank was succeeded by the Orange County National Bank, chartered on April 12, 1865. The outstanding circulation as of July 1, 1867, was $2,257. The redemption of these bills was guaranteed until December 31, 1867.

Numismatic Commentary: While not plentiful, genuine notes from this Bank of Orange County are a little easier to locate in the marketplace. All genuine issues were engraved by Toppan, Carpenter & Co.

VALID ISSUES

$1 • W-VT-270-001-G010

TD

Tint: Orange overall lathework. *Engraver:* Toppan, Carpenter & Co. *Comments:* H-VT-76-G2a. 18__. 1850s.

Rarity: URS-2

VF $1,000

$2 • W-VT-270-002-G020

CJF

Tint: Orange lathework outlining white 2. *Engraver:* Toppan, Carpenter & Co. *Comments:* H-VT-76-G4a. 18__. 1850s.

Rarity: URS-3

Proof $5,500

$3 • W-VT-270-003-G030

CC

Tint: Orange lathework outlining white THREE. *Engraver:* Toppan, Carpenter & Co. *Comments:* H-VT-76-G6a. 18__. 1850s.

Rarity: URS-2

Proof $3,700

$5 • W-VT-270-005-G040

Left: Scene at mill door, Horses / 5. *Center:* Portrait of boy. *Right:* 5 / Girl feeding chickens. *Tint:* Orange lathework outlining white FIVE. *Engraver:* Toppan, Carpenter & Co. *Comments:* H-VT-76-G8a. 18__. 1850s.

Rarity: *None known*

$10 • W-VT-270-010-G050

Left: 10 / Farmer and sheaf, Horse, dog. *Center:* "Dr. Kane's Arctic Expedition". *Right:* 10 / Blacksmith blowing fire. *Engraver:* Toppan, Carpenter & Co. *Comments:* H-VT-76-G10a. 18__. 1850s.

Rarity: URS-1

Proof $5,000

$20 • W-VT-270-020-G060

Left: 20 / Bull. *Center:* Portrait of George Washington, Cherubs seated in scrolls. *Right:* 20 / Milkmaid, Child and two cows. *Tint:* Orange. *Engraver:* Toppan, Carpenter & Co. *Comments:* H-VT-76-G12a. 18__. 1850s.

Rarity: *None known*

$50 • W-VT-270-050-G070

Left: 50 / Woman standing by column. *Center:* Two horses at trough, Woman standing, Man seated. *Right:* 50 / Woman and man with child on his back. *Tint:* Orange. *Engraver:* Toppan, Carpenter & Co. *Comments:* H-VT-76-G14a. 18__. 1850s.

Rarity: *None known*

$100 • W-VT-270-100-G080

Left: C / 100. *Center:* Woman and farmer flanking shield, Girl and dog, Train and oxen. *Right:* 100 / Indian man on horse. *Tint:* Orange. *Engraver:* Toppan, Carpenter & Co. *Comments:* H-VT-76-G16a. 18__. 1850s.

Rarity: *None known*

NON-VALID ISSUES

$2 • W-VT-270-002-A010

Left: 2 / Female portrait. *Center:* Wagon pulled by horses. *Right:* 2 / Portrait of Thomas Jefferson. *Tint:* Brown-orange overall lathework outlining white TWO. *Engraver:* Bald, Cousland & Co. *Comments:* H-VT-76-A5. Altered from $2 Pioneer Association, Lafayette, Indiana. 18__. 1850s–1860s.

Rarity: URS-6

F $125

$5 • W-VT-270-005-C040

ANS

Tint: Orange lathework outlining white FIVE. *Engraver:* Toppan, Carpenter & Co. *Comments:* H-VT-76-C8a. Counterfeit of W-VT-270-005-G040. 18__. 1850s–1860s.

Rarity: URS-7

F $125

$10 • W-VT-270-010-R010

Engraver: Toppan, Carpenter & Co. *Comments:* H-VT-76-R5. Raised from W-VT-270-001-G010. 18__. 1850s.

Rarity: *None known*

Orange County Bank
1842–1855
W-VT-280

History: The Orange County Bank succeeded the Bank of Orange County, 1st, W-VT-260, and commenced business in September 1842 with a starting authorized capital of $50,000.[5] Circulation in August 1845 was $79,870. By 1849 the capital had increased to $100,000. In that year counterfeit $5 notes of the bank were a problem.

The Orange County Bank's charter expired on January 1, 1859. However, the bank discontinued business in 1855, prior to that date.[6] In the meantime, in 1856 the interests of the bank were succeeded by the Bank of Orange County, 2nd, W-VT-270.[7] As of July 16, 1864, the outstanding circulation of the Orange County Bank was $1,700, the redemption of which was guaranteed by bonds which the directors had placed with the State Treasurer.

Numismatic Commentary: All genuine issues were engraved by New England Bank Note Co. and are very scarce.

VALID ISSUES

$1 • W-VT-280-001-G010

CJF

Engraver: New England Bank Note Co. **Comments:** H-VT-77-G2, Coulter-22. 18__. 1843–1850s.
Rarity: URS-3
F $750

$2 • W-VT-280-002-G020

Left: 2. **Center:** Man and boys driving sheep over river, Factories. **Right:** 2 on TWO / Woman holding wreath / 2 on TWO. **Engraver:** New England Bank Note Co. **Comments:** H-VT-77-G4, Coulter-24. 18__. 1843–1850s.
Rarity: URS-3
VF $400

$3 • W-VT-280-003-G030

CC

Engraver: New England Bank Note Co. **Comments:** H-VT-77-G6, Coulter-25. 18__. 1843–1850s.
Rarity: URS-2
VF $1,000

$5 • W-VT-280-005-G040

Left: FIVE / Eagle in 5. **Center:** Farmer and oxen / 5. **Right:** 5, Urn, Horse. **Engraver:** New England Bank Note Co. **Comments:** H-VT-77-G8, Coulter-27. 18__. 1843–1850s.
Rarity: URS-3
F $260

$10 • W-VT-280-010-G050

Left: 10 / Blacksmith / TEN. **Center:** X / Female portrait / Man on horseback, Man with dog. **Right:** 10 / Man and machinery. **Engraver:** New England Bank Note Co. **Comments:** H-VT-77-G10, Coulter-29. 18__. 1843–1850s.
Rarity: *None known*

$20 • W-VT-280-020-G060

Left: Steamboat / XX / Train. **Center:** Three women, eagle, ship. **Right:** XX / Woman standing. **Engraver:** New England Bank Note Co. **Comments:** H-VT-77-G12, Coulter-32. Beware of altered notes of the same design. 18__. 1843–1850s.
Rarity: *None known*

$50 • W-VT-280-050-G070

Left: FIFTY / Woman with wreath of flowers / FIFTY. **Center:** 50 / Man and horse / 50. **Right:** FIFTY / Woman with cornucopia / FIFTY. **Engraver:** New England Bank Note Co. **Comments:** H-VT-77-G14, Coulter-34. 18__. 1843–1850s.
Rarity: *None known*

$100 • W-VT-280-100-G080

Left: 100 / Vulcan. **Center:** Spread eagle, Railroad and canal. **Right:** 100 / Ceres. **Engraver:** Rawdon, Wright, Hatch & Edson. **Comments:** H-VT-77-G16, Coulter-36. 18__. 1850s.
Rarity: *None known*

$100 • W-VT-280-100-G090

Left: ONE HUNDRED and 100 / Portrait of William Henry Harrison. **Center:** Horses, Wagon and shipping. **Right:** ONE HUNDRED and 100 / **Engraver:** New England Bank Note Co. **Comments:** H-VT-77-G18, Coulter-37. 18__. 1843–1855.

Rarity: *None known*

Uncut Sheets

$2-$1-$3-$5 • W-VT-280-002.001.003.005-US010

Vignette(s): ($2) Man and boys driving sheep over river, Factories / Woman holding wreath. **($1)** Woman / Farmer mowing, Farmer with scythe / Two figures raking / Eagle with shield and arrows. **($3)** Officers on horseback / Blacksmith at forge / Indian girl with bow and arrow. **($5)** Eagle in 5 / Farmer and oxen / Urn / Horse. **Engraver:** New England Bank Note Co. **Comments:** H-VT-77-G4, G2, G6, G8. 18__. 1843–1850s.

Rarity: URS-1
Proof $3,000

Non-Valid Issues

$1 • W-VT-280-001-A010

Left: 1 / Woman wearing bonnet, standing by pail / ONE. **Center:** Woman holding rake and sickle. **Right:** 1 / Ship / ONE. **Engraver:** New England Bank Note Co. **Comments:** H-VT-77-A5, Coulter-23. Altered from $1 Washington County Bank, Calais, Maine, or from notes of other failed banks using the same plate. 18__. 1840s.

Rarity: *None known*

$3 • W-VT-280-003-A020

Left: THREE / Beehives / THREE. **Center:** Machinery and merchandise flanking Ceres holding sickle and rake, Factories and harbor. **Right:** 3 on THREE / Two reapers / 3 on THREE. **Engraver:** New England Bank Note Co. **Comments:** H-VT-77-A10, Coulter-26. Altered from $3 Washington County Bank, Calais, Maine, or from notes of other failed banks using the same plate. 18__. 1840s.

Rarity: *None known*

$5 • W-VT-280-005-C040

CJF

Engraver: New England Bank Note Co. **Comments:** H-VT-77-C8. Counterfeit of W-VT-280-005-G040. 18__. 1840s–1850s.

Rarity: URS-7
F $100

$5 • W-VT-280-005-N010

Left: FIVE / Eagle and 5. **Center:** Man with oxen / 5. **Right:** 5 / Pedestal with horse. **Comments:** H-Unlisted, Coulter-28. 1850s.

Rarity: *None known*

$10 • W-VT-280-010-A030

Left: 10 / Farmer sowing / TEN. **Center:** Mercury standing with 10, Merchandise, Factories and ship / Canal scene. **Right:** 10 / Ship / TEN. **Engraver:** New England Bank Note Co. **Comments:** H-VT-77-A15, Coulter-30. Altered from $10 Washington County Bank, Calais, Maine, or from notes of other failed banks using the same plate. 18__. 1840s.

Rarity: *None known*

$10 • W-VT-280-010-A040

Left: 10 / Sailor standing with U.S. flag / X. **Center:** 10 on medallion head / "Presentation of the Declaration of Independence" / 10 on medallion head. **Bottom center:** Eagle. **Right:** X / Pat Lyon standing by forge / 10. **Engraver:** Draper, Underwood & Co. / Underwood, Bald, Spencer & Hufty. **Comments:** H-VT-77-A20, Coulter-31. Altered from $10 Tenth Ward Bank, New York, New York. 18__. 1840s.

Rarity: *None known*

$20 • W-VT-280-020-A050

TD

Engraver: New England Bank Note Co. **Comments:** H-VT-77-A25, Coulter-33. Altered from $20 Hamilton Bank, Scituate, Rhode Island, or from notes of other failed banks using the same plate. Genuine notes of this design were issued, W-VT-280-020-G060. 18__. 1840s

Rarity: URS-6
F $190

$50 • W-VT-280-050-R010

Engraver: New England Bank Note Co. **Comments:** H-VT-77-R10, Coulter-35. Raised from W-VT-280-001-G010. 18__. 1840s–1850s.

Rarity: URS-1
F $300

Danby, Vermont

Situated in a very hilly area, Danby is flanked and intersected by Danby Mountain, Dorset Mountain, and the Green Mountains. Multiple streams and rivers flow through the town, including Otter Creek, Flower Brook, and Mill River.

Danby Bank
1850–1857
W-VT-290

History: The Danby Bank was incorporated in 1850 with $30,000 in authorized capital, $25,000 of which was required to be paid in before the bank could open. In June 1855, capital was $50,000. The bank failed in 1857.

The *Report of the Bank Commissioner* states: "This Bank passed into the hand of a Receiver, December 29, 1857. The time for presenting its bills to the Receiver expired December 20, 1858." The same report stated that $105,504 total in bills of the Danby Bank were counted and burned. 100 sheets were destroyed as well.

Numismatic Commentary: As is the case with many banks that failed, this bank left a legacy of bank notes for future collectors. These issues are not hard to locate and are quite attractive.

Remaining in the American Bank Note Co. archives as of 2003 was a $1-$1-$2-$3 face plate.

VALID ISSUES

$1 • W-VT-290-001-G010

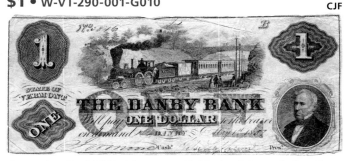

Overprint: Red ONE. **Engraver:** Baldwin, Adams & Co. **Comments:** H-VT-80-G2a, Coulter-1. May 1st, 18__. 1850s.

Rarity: URS-6
VG $75; **VF** $125

$1 • W-VT-290-001-G010a

Left: 1 / ONE. **Center:** Train under bridge. **Right:** 1 / Portrait of General Zachary Taylor. **Overprint:** Red ONE. **Engraver:** Baldwin, Bald & Cousland / Bald, Cousland & Co. **Comments:** H-VT-80-G4a, Coulter-2. Similar to W-VT-290-001-G010 but with different date and engraver imprint. April 1st, 1856.

Rarity: URS-6
VF $125

$2 • W-VT-290-002-G020

Left: 2 / 2. **Center:** Farmer and boy with horses and plow. **Right:** 2 / Milkmaid holding pail on head, Cattle. **Overprint:** Red TWO. **Engraver:** Baldwin, Adams & Co. **Comments:** H-VT-80-G6a, Coulter-3. May 1st, 18__. 1850s.

Rarity: URS-6
VF $125

$2 • W-VT-290-002-G020a

Overprint: Red TWO. **Engraver:** Baldwin, Bald & Cousland / Bald, Cousland & Co. **Comments:** H-VT-80-G8a, Coulter-4. Similar to W-VT-290-002-G020 but with different date and engraver imprint. April 1st, 1856.

Rarity: URS-6
VF $125

$3 • W-VT-290-003-G030

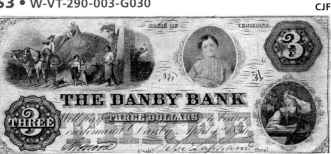

Overprint: Red THREE. **Engraver:** Baldwin, Bald & Cousland / Bald, Cousland & Co. **Comments:** H-VT-80-G12a, Coulter-5. April 1st, 1856.

Rarity: URS-8
VG $65; **F** $100

$5 • W-VT-290-005-G040

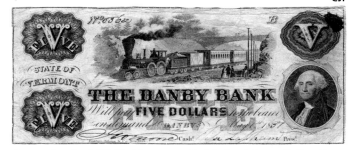

Overprint: Red FIVE. **Engraver:** Baldwin, Adams & Co. **Comments:** H-VT-80-G14a, Coulter-6. May 1st, 18__. 1850s.

Rarity: URS-9
VG $75

$5 • W-VT-290-005-G040a

Left: FIVE on V / FIVE on V. **Center:** Train. **Right:** V / Portrait of George Washington. **Overprint:** Red FIVE. **Engraver:** Baldwin, Adams & Co. **Comments:** H-Unlisted, Coulter-7. Similar to W-VT-290-005-G040 but with different date. April 1st, 1856.

Rarity: URS-5
VF $175

$10 • W-VT-290-010-G050

Overprint: Red TEN. **Engraver:** Baldwin, Adams & Co. **Comments:** H-VT-80-G16a, Coulter-9. May 1st, 18__. 1850s.

Rarity: URS-7
F $150; **VF** $275

$20 • W-VT-290-020-G060

Left: TWENTY / Agriculture. **Center:** Blacksmith, Train and factory. **Right:** XX / 20. **Overprint:** Red TWENTY. **Engraver:** Bald, Adams & Co. **Comments:** H-VT-80-G18a, Coulter-11. May 1st, 18__. 1850s.

Rarity: *None known*

$50 • **W-VT-290-050-G070**

Left: 50. *Center:* Two allegorical figures, Train and ship / 50. *Right:* Justice. *Overprint:* Red FIFTY. *Engraver:* Bald, Adams & Co. *Comments:* H-VT-80-G20a, Coulter-12. May 1st, 18__. 1850s.

Rarity: *None known*

NON-VALID ISSUES

$5 • **W-VT-290-005-S010**

Engraver: New England Bank Note Co. *Comments:* H-VT-80-S5, Coulter-8. 18__. 1850s.

Rarity: URS-5

F $150

$10 • **W-VT-290-010-A010**

Left: 10 on die and scrollwork panel. *Center:* X / Boar's head / X. *Bottom center:* Pledge. *Right:* Indian and man flanking shield surmounted by eagle. *Engraver:* New England Bank Note Co. *Comments:* H-VT-80-A5, Coulter-10. Altered from $10 Wayne County Bank, Plymouth, Michigan. 18__. 1850s.

Rarity: *None known*

DANVILLE, VERMONT

Danville was named after the French cartographer Jean-Baptiste Bourguignon d'Anville. It was chartered in 1786 and was settled first by Jesse Levenworth, who established a mill. A village rose up around the area, and the town quickly grew in commerce and industry. The pond and rivers made the town popular as a summer resort away from the cities.

Bank of Caledonia
1818–1865
W-VT-300

History: The Bank of Caledonia was organized in 1818. Its charter went into effect on November 1, 1825, with $75,000 in authorized capital.

In 1841 the bank had $100,000 in capital with $50,000 paid in. In August 1845, the same was $50,000, and circulation was $84,757. Figures for 1854 included: notes discounted $114,512; deposits in city banks $20,679; other resources $7,727; specie $2,091. The bank's charter expired on January 1, 1855, but it was re-chartered, and by May 1857, the capital was $75,000. In July 1859, circulation was $110,046, and in 1861 capital was $75,000.

In 1865 the business of the Bank of Caledonia was succeeded by the Caledonia National Bank of Danville. Circulation outstanding was reported to be $1,398 as of July 1, 1867. Notice was published that the bank would not be liable to redeem its bills after December 9, 1867.

Numismatic Commentary: Surviving examples of either Proof or circulation issues are few and far between. Very few genuine notes have come to the marketplace during the past decades.

VALID ISSUES

$1 • **W-VT-300-001-G010**

Comments: H-VT-85-G4. No description available. 18__. 1830s.

Rarity: *None known*

$1 • **W-VT-300-001-G020**

Left: ONE / Woman writing on desk / ONE. *Center:* Boy carrying sheaf and scythe, Farmhouse, trees, and sheep. *Right:* ONE vertically. *Engraver:* Draper, Toppan & Co. *Comments:* H-VT-85-G6, Coulter-1. 18__. 1840s–1850s.

Rarity: URS-3

VF $600; **Proof** $900

$1 • **W-VT-300-001-G020a**

Tint: Ochre. *Engraver:* Draper, Toppan & Co. / ABNCo. monogram. *Comments:* H-VT-85-G6a, Coulter-2. Similar to W-VT-300-001-G020 but with additional engraver imprint. 18__. 1850s–1860s.

Rarity: *None known*

$2 • **W-VT-300-002-G030**

Comments: H-VT-85-G10, Coulter-5. No description available. 1830s.

Rarity: *None known*

$2 • **W-VT-300-002-G040**

Left: TWO / Woman and cupid seated in 2 / TWO. *Center:* 2 / Farmer plowing, Two horses, boats, and farmhouse / 2. *Right:* TWO vertically. *Engraver:* Draper, Toppan & Co. *Comments:* H-VT-85-G12, Coulter-3. January 1st, 1856. 1850s–1860s.

Rarity: URS-3

Proof $900

$2 • **W-VT-300-002-G040a**

Overprint: Red TWO. *Engraver:* Draper, Toppan & Co. *Comments:* H-Unlisted, Coulter-Unlisted. Similar to W-VT-300-002-G040. January 1st, 1856. 1850s–1860s.

Rarity: URS-2

F $1,000

$2 • W-VT-300-002-G040b   CC

Tint: Ochre lathework and microletters outlining white TWO.
Engraver: Draper, Toppan & Co. *Comments:* H-VT-85-G12a,
Coulter-4. Similar to W-VT-300-002-G040. January 1st, 1856.
1850s–1860s.

Rarity: URS-2
F $1,000

$3 • W-VT-300-003-G050

Comments: H-VT-85-G16, Coulter-8. No description available.
18__. 1830s.

Rarity: *None known*

$3 • W-VT-300-003-G060

Left: THREE / Woman and two cupids in 3 / THREE. *Center:*
Two men on horseback, Cattle and sheep. *Right:* THREE verti-
cally. *Engraver:* Draper, Toppan & Co. *Comments:* H-VT-85-
G18, Coulter-6. 18__. 1840s–1860s.

Rarity: URS-3
VF $600; **Proof** $800

$3 • W-VT-300-003-G060a

Tint: Ochre. *Engraver:* Draper, Toppan & Co. / ABNCo.
monogram. *Comments:* H-VT-85-G18a, Coulter-7. Similar to
W-VT-300-003-G060 but with additional engraver imprint.
18__. 1850s–1860s.

Rarity: *None known*

$5 • W-VT-300-005-G070

Comments: H-VT-85-G22. 18__. 1830s.

Rarity: URS-1
G $400

$5 • W-VT-300-005-G080   CJF

Engraver: Draper, Toppan & Co. *Comments:* H-VT-85-G24,
Coulter-9. 18__. 1840s–1850s.

Rarity: URS-2
Proof $1,000

$5 • W-VT-300-005-G080a   CC

Overprint: Red FIVE. *Engraver:* Draper, Toppan & Co. *Comments:* H-Unlisted, Coulter-Unlisted. Similar to W-VT-300-005-
G080 but with different date. Jan.y 1st, 1856. 1850s–1860s.

Rarity: URS-2
F $1,000

$5 • W-VT-300-005-G080b

Left: FIVE / Woman seated in V / 5. *Center:* Five cherubs sport-
ing around 5 / 5. *Right:* FIVE vertically. *Tint:* Ochre. *Engraver:*
Draper, Toppan & Co. *Comments:* H-VT-85-G24a, Coulter-10.
Similar to W-VT-300-005-G080. 18__. 1850s–1860s.

Rarity: *None known*

$10 • W-VT-300-010-G090

Comments: H-VT-85-G28. No description available. 18__.
1830s.

Rarity: *None known*

$10 • W-VT-300-010-G100

Left: TEN / Girl with sheaf of grain on head, Boy and dog /
TEN. *Center:* X / Aurora dismounting from chariot, Goddesses,
chariot, and horses / X. *Right:* TEN DOLLARS vertically.
Engraver: Draper, Toppan & Co. *Comments:* H-VT-85-G30,
Coulter-12. 18__. 1840s–1850s.

Rarity: URS-1
Proof $1,000

$10 • W-VT-300-010-G100a   CJF

Tint: Ochre lathework and microletters outlining white TEN.
Engraver: Draper, Toppan & Co. *Comments:* H-VT-85-G30a,
Coulter-13. Similar to W-VT-300-010-G100 but with different
date. January 1st, 1856. 1850s–1860s.

Rarity: URS-1
VG $1,000

$20 • W-VT-300-020-G110

Comments: H-VT-85-G34. No description available. 18__.
1830s.

Rarity: *None known*

$20 • W-VT-300-020-G120
Left: 20 / Woman seated with book on lap, opening chest. *Center:* XX / Eagle on rock / XX. *Right:* 20 / Ship in harbor. *Engraver:* New England Bank Note Co. *Comments:* H-VT-85-G36. 18__. 1840s–1850s.
> **Rarity:** *None known*

$20 • W-VT-300-020-G130
Left: 20 / Farmer with bundle of grain, Dog and horse. *Center:* Drover bargaining for cow, Cattle and sheep. *Right:* 20 / Female portrait. *Engraver:* American Bank Note Co. *Comments:* H-VT-85-G38, Coulter-14. 1860s.
> **Rarity:** *None known*

$20 • W-VT-300-020-G130a
Tint: Ochre. *Comments:* H-Unlisted, Coulter-15. Similar to W-VT-300-020-G130. 1860s.
> **Rarity:** *None known*

$50 • W-VT-300-050-G140
Comments: H-VT-85-G42, Coulter-15. No description available. 18__. 1830s.
> **Rarity:** *None known*

$50 • W-VT-300-050-G150
Left: FIFTY / Woman standing with wreath and flowers / FIFTY. *Center:* 50 / Man restraining prancing horse / 50. *Right:* FIFTY / Woman standing with cornucopia / FIFTY. *Engraver:* New England Bank Note Co. *Comments:* H-VT-85-G44. 18__. 1840s–1850s.
> **Rarity:** *None known*

$50 • W-VT-300-050-G160
Left: 50 / Woman, Man with child on back / FIFTY. *Center:* "Landing of Roger Williams". *Right:* 50 / Male portrait. *Tint:* Yellow. *Engraver:* American Bank Note Co. *Comments:* H-VT-85-G46, Coulter-16. 1860s.
> **Rarity:** *None known*

$100 • W-VT-300-100-G170
Comments: H-VT-85-G50. No description available. 18__. 1830s.
> **Rarity:** *None known*

$100 • W-VT-300-100-G180
Left: ONE HUNDRED on 100 / Portrait of William Henry Harrison. *Center:* Wharf scene, Men loading wagon with barrels. *Right:* ONE HUNDRED on 100 / Portrait of Christopher Columbus. *Comments:* H-VT-85-G52. 18__. 1840s–1850s.
> **Rarity:** *None known*

$100 • W-VT-300-100-G190
Left: 100 / Farmer holding scythe, Woman holding child, Farmer standing. *Center:* Woman seated, Bales, Factories, mill, dam, and village. *Right:* 100 / Male portrait. *Tint:* Yellow. *Engraver:* American Bank Note Co. *Comments:* H-VT-85-G54, Coulter-17. 1860s.
> **Rarity:** *None known*

NON-VALID ISSUES

$2 • W-VT-300-002-C040
Engraver: Draper, Toppan & Co. *Comments:* H-VT-85-C12. Counterfeit of W-VT-300-002-G040. 18__. 1840s.
> **Rarity:** *None known*

$3 • W-VT-300-003-C050
Comments: H-VT-85-C16. Counterfeit of W-VT-300-003-G050. 18__. 1830s.
> **Rarity:** *None known*

$5 • W-VT-300-005-R010
Engraver: Draper, Toppan & Co. *Comments:* H-VT-85-R5. Raised from W-VT-300-003-G060. 18__. 1850s–1860s.
> **Rarity:** *None known*

$5 • W-VT-300-005-N010
Center: Cattle, Two men on horseback, Horse. *Comments:* H-VT-85-N5, Coulter-11. 18__. 1840s.
> **Rarity:** *None known*

$100 • W-VT-300-100-C170
Comments: H-VT-85-C50. Counterfeit of W-VT-300-100-G170. 18__. 1837.
> **Rarity:** *None known*

DERBY LINE, VERMONT

Incorporated in 1791, Derby Line was chartered on October 29, 1779. It was settled in 1795 and became known for its farming industry. It lies on the international line between the United States and Canada as a result of erratic surveys determining the border between the two countries during the 18th century. This division causes the interesting result that it is possible to prepare a meal in one part of a Derby Line home in Canada and eat it in another room in the United States.

Peoples Bank
1851–1865
W-VT-310

History: The Peoples Bank was organized in 1851 with an authorized capital of $50,000, $30,000 of which was required to be paid in before the bank could officially open for business.

In 1857 the figures for the bank were reported as: capital $75,000; bills in circulation $114,594; specie $3,458. In July 1859, circulation was $114,594.

The business of the Peoples Bank was succeeded by the National Bank of Derby Line, chartered on June 30, 1865. On July 1, 1867, it was reported to have $3,031 in outstanding circulation remaining, redemption of which was guaranteed by the national bank.

Numismatic Commentary: Genuine notes are very hard to locate. Beware of convincingly attractive spurious $1 and $2 issues with large red numerals placed in the center of the notes.

VALID ISSUES

$1 • W-VT-310-001-G010
Left: 1 / Portrait of George Washington. *Center:* Female portrait / Female portrait. *Right:* 1 / Portrait of Benjamin Franklin. *Engraver:* New England Bank Note Co. *Comments:* H-VT-90-G2, Coulter-8. 18__. 1850s.
> **Rarity:** *None known*

$1 • W-VT-310-001-G020

Left: Two horses, Farmhouse / ONE. *Center:* 1. *Right:* ONE / Boy gathering corn / ONE. *Engraver:* American Bank Note Co. *Comments:* H-VT-90-G4, Coulter-9. 1850s–1860s.
Rarity: *None known*

$1 • W-VT-310-001-G020a

CJF

Overprint: Red ONE. *Engraver:* Toppan, Carpenter & Co. *Comments:* H-Unlisted, Coulter-Unlisted. Similar to W-VT-310-001-G020 but with different engraver imprint. 1860s.
Rarity: URS-1
VG $750; **VF** $800

$2 • W-VT-310-002-G030

Left: 2 / Portrait of George Washington. *Center:* Portrait of Minerva / Female portrait. *Right:* 2 / Portrait of Benjamin Franklin. *Engraver:* New England Bank Note Co. *Comments:* H-VT-90-G6, Coulter-13. 18__. 1850s.
Rarity: *None known*

$2 • W-VT-310-002-G040

Left: 2 / Woman picking grapes. *Center:* Man seated on trough, Three horses drinking, Girl feeding swine, Farmhouse. *Right:* 2 / Farmer sharpening scythe. *Comments:* H-VT-90-G8, Coulter-11. 1850s–1860s.
Rarity: *None known*

$2 • W-VT-310-002-G040a

Overprint: Red TWO. *Comments:* H-Unlisted, Coulter-12. Similar to W-VT-310-002-G040. 1850s–1860s.
Rarity: *None known*

$3 • W-VT-310-003-G050

Left: 3 / Statue of George Washington on horseback. *Center:* Portrait of girl / 3 / Portrait of girl. *Right:* 3 / Blacksmith. *Engraver:* New England Bank Note Co. *Comments:* H-VT-90-G10, Coulter-15. 18__. 1850s.
Rarity: *None known*

$5 • W-VT-310-005-G060

Left: Spread eagle on shield, Village / FIVE. *Center:* Allegorical figure and cherub in V. *Right:* 5 / Girl with basket of flowers. *Overprint:* Red FIVE. *Engraver:* New England Bank Note Co. *Comments:* H-VT-90-G12, Coulter-17. 18__. 1850s.
Rarity: *None known*

$5 • W-VT-310-005-G070

Left: 5 / Portrait of George Washington. *Center:* Cattle and sheep. *Right:* 5 / Train. *Engraver:* New England Bank Note Co. *Comments:* H-VT-90-G14, Coulter-18. 1850s–1860s.
Rarity: *None known*

$10 • W-VT-310-010-G080

Left: Vulcan / TEN. *Center:* X. *Right:* 10 / Farmer, sickle, and sheaf. *Overprint:* Red TEN. *Engraver:* New England Bank Note Co. *Comments:* H-VT-90-G16, Coulter-21. 18__. 1850s.
Rarity: *None known*

$10 • W-VT-310-010-G090

Left: 10 / Portrait of George Washington, Portrait of John Adams, Portrait of Thomas Jefferson, Portrait of James Madison / 10. *Center:* Three farmers and woman at lunch under tree, Two horses. *Right:* X / Indian seated. *Comments:* H-VT-90-G18, Coulter-22. 1850s–1860s.
Rarity: *None known*

$20 • W-VT-310-020-G100

Left: 20 / Minerva. *Center:* Woman holding rake seated between 2 and 0. *Right:* 20 / Goddess of Plenty / 20. *Engraver:* Rawdon, Wright, Hatch & Edson. *Comments:* H-VT-90-G20, Coulter-24. 18__. 1850s–1860s.
Rarity: *None known*

$50 • W-VT-310-050-G110

Left: 50 / Minerva. *Center:* Ceres and Vulcan seated with rake, hammer, and cornucopia. *Right:* 50 / Cherub steering sailboat / 50. *Engraver:* Rawdon, Wright, Hatch & Edson. *Comments:* H-VT-90-G22, Coulter-25. 18__. 1850s–1860s.
Rarity: *None known*

$100 • W-VT-310-100-G120

Left: 100 / Vulcan holding scroll, Anchor. *Center:* Spread eagle on tree limb, Train and two canal boats. *Right:* Ceres holding rake. *Engraver:* Rawdon, Wright, Hatch & Edson. *Comments:* H-VT-90-G24, Coulter-26. 18__. 1850s–1860s.
Rarity: *None known*

Non-Valid Issues

$1 • W-VT-310-001-S010

CJF

Tint: Red 1. *Engraver:* New England Bank Note Co. *Comments:* H-VT-90-S5, Coulter-10. Similar to W-VT-310-001-G010. July 1st, 186_. 1860s.
Rarity: URS-8
VG $85; **F** $125

$2 • W-VT-310-002-S020

NJW

Tint: Red 2. *Engraver:* New England Bank Note Co. *Comments:* H-VT-90-S10, Coulter-14. Similar to W-VT-310-002-G030. July 1st, 186_. 1860s.

Rarity: URS-7
F $100

$3 • W-VT-310-003-A010

NJW

Overprint: Red THREE. *Engraver:* Rawdon, Wright, Hatch & Edson / New England Bank Note Co. *Comments:* H-VT-90-A5, Coulter-16. Altered from $3 Waubeek Bank, DeSoto, Nebraska. Handwritten 9 over engraved 7 in date. 1857.

Rarity: URS-6
F $150

$5 • W-VT-310-005-N010

Comments: H-Unlisted, Coulter-19. Similar to W-VT-310-005-G060. 1850s–1860s.

Rarity: *None known*

$5 • W-VT-310-005-A020

Left: Wild horses / V. *Center:* Liberty and Ceres flanking shield surmounted by horse's head. *Bottom center:* Sleeping dog. *Right:* 5 / Young girl shading eyes. *Engraver:* Bald, Cousland & Co. / Baldwin, Bald & Cousland. *Comments:* H-VT-90-A10, Coulter-20. Altered from $5 Bank of Morgan, Morgan, Georgia. 18__. 1850s.

Rarity: *None known*

$5 • W-VT-310-005-A030

Left: Medallion panel with FIVE / Medallion head / FIVE. *Center:* 5 / Liberty and Ceres seated flanking shield surmounted by horse's head / 5 / Medallion FIVE. *Bottom center:* Hay wagon. *Right:* Justice facing eagle with portrait of George Washington / Portrait of Benjamin Franklin. *Engraver:* Spencer, Hufty & Danforth / Danforth, Spencer & Hufty. *Comments:* H-VT-90-A15. Altered from $5 Peoples Bank of Paterson, Paterson, New Jersey. 18__. 1840s–1851.

Rarity: *None known*

$10 • W-VT-310-010-AR010

Left: 10 / Ship. *Center:* Three men forging iron / 1 on medallion shield. *Bottom center:* Woman swimming. *Right:* TEN / Ceres kneeling, Indian woman standing. *Engraver:* Danforth, Bald & Co. *Comments:* H-VT-90-AR20, Coulter-23. Altered and raised from $1 Peoples Bank, Georgetown, D.C. Dec. 1, 1852.

Rarity: *None known*

FAIR HAVEN, VERMONT

Fair Haven was chartered and settled in 1779 on land that originally included West Haven, which separated in 1792. By 1783 Colonel Matthew Lyon had come to Fair Haven, where he began building mills at the Castleon River falls. He erected a gristmill, a sawmill, a paper mill, an iron factory, and a forge. In 1785 Lyon built a dam to channel the river.

Slate was quarried beginning in 1839 and soon became a large industry. The marbleizing process was introduced in 1859. Green and variegated slate was quarried, as well as purple slate. Marble sawing arrived at the same time, and by 1859 there was a marble mill, a rolling mill, a nail factory, a paper mill, three sawmills, a wagon shop, a woolen factory, a machine shop, two blacksmith shops, and shoe shops. By 1860 the population was 1,378.

Western Vermont Bank
1854
W-VT-320

History: A charter application for the Western Vermont Bank was rejected during the 1854 session of the state legislature.

Numismatic Commentary: It is possible that Proof notes were made, but no record has been found of such.

FAIRFAX, VERMONT

Consisting of three parts, Fairfax was established in 1763. The first mill was built here in 1791 by Amos Fassett, and it was the first clothing works in the area. A woolen factory followed, accompanied by a flouring mill, a sawmill, and the rise of a lumbering industry. Other early enterprises included carding by machine, a casting furnace, and a blacksmith shop.

Fairfax Bank
1854
W-VT-330

History: In 1854 a charter application for the Fairfax Bank was rejected by the state legislature.

Numismatic Commentary: It is possible that Proof notes were made, but no record has been found of such.

GUILDHALL, VERMONT

Guildhall was chartered in 1761 to Elihu Hall. It is the seat of Essex County and is bordered by Maidstone, the Connecticut River, Lunenburge, and Branby. Many mills were built on the appropriately named Mill Stream that runs through the area.

Essex Bank
1833–1841
W-VT-340

History: The Essex Bank was chartered in 1832 with an authorized capital of $40,000. This bank is also sometimes reported as the Bank of Essex County. It was the only private bank in Vermont to issue bills in denominations greater than $100. This was mainly a sham operation operated from a desk, as noted in the introductory material.

On January 30, 1838, the Suffolk Bank, Boston, reported that bills of the Essex Bank would not be received. In 1839 its circulation was $66,202; deposits totaled $3,797. On November 21, 1839, the Legislature passed a bill to appoint a committee to inspect the concerns of the Essex Bank. However, for unexplained reasons the inspection did not take place, and on October 28, 1841, a new committee was appointed. Their report included these statements:

> It is worthy to remark, that during the years after the bank went into operation, it labored under embarrassments in the redemption of its bills, and was frequently obliged to obtain loans in Boston and elsewhere, sometimes at a high rate of interest, and that many of its loans were extravagantly large considering the amount of its capital.

The bank failed this same year. The bank commissioner reported that its assets and the amount of the safety fund then available were insufficient to pay the circulation, which amounted to $66,262. A committee of the General Assembly reported that the failure of the bank had been caused by fraudulent acts of the directors.[8]

Numismatic Commentary: This failed bank's misfortune has led to an ample supply of bank notes for today's collectors. One issue, a $10 bill of the PSSP design, also has a Congreve Patent Check Plate back, a security used on relatively few bank notes in America.

VALID ISSUES

$1 • W-VT-340-001-G010   CC

Engraver: Rawdon, Clark & Co. **Comments:** H-VT-95-G4. 18__. 1830s.

Rarity: URS-3
VG $600

$1 • W-VT-340-001-G020   CC

Engraver: Rawdon, Wright & Hatch. **Comments:** H-VT-95-G6, Coulter-1. 18__. 1830s.

Rarity: URS-5
F $350; **VF** $450

$2 • W-VT-340-002-G030   CC

Engraver: Rawdon, Clark & Co. **Comments:** H-VT-95-G10, Coulter-3. 18__. 1830s.

Rarity: URS-3
F $500

$2 • W-VT-340-002-G040   CC

Engraver: Rawdon, Wright & Hatch. **Comments:** H-VT-95-G12, Coulter-2. 18__. 1830s.

Rarity: URS-3
VF $600

$3 • W-VT-340-003-G050   CJF

Engraver: Rawdon, Clark & Co. **Comments:** H-VT-95-G16, Coulter-4. 18__. 1830s.

Rarity: URS-4
F $400

$5 • W-VT-340-005-G060

NJW

Engraver: Rawdon, Clark & Co. *Comments:* H-VT-95-G22. 18__. 1830s.

Rarity: URS-4
F $300; **VF** $550

$5 • W-VT-340-005-G070

NJW

Engraver: Rawdon, Wright & Hatch. *Comments:* H-VT-95-G24, Coulter-5. 18__. 1830s.

Rarity: URS-5
F $250

$10 • W-VT-340-010-G080

CJF

Back: Green and red Check Plate. *Engraver:* PSSP. *Comments:* H-VT-95-G28a, Coulter-6. 18__. 1830s.

Rarity: URS-2
VF $1,000

HINESBURG, VERMONT

Hinesburg was chartered on June 24, 1762. The town did not have an auspicious early period, and it suffered an epidemic in 1813 as well as an unnaturally cold year in 1816—every month experienced a freeze, essentially wiping out all crops for the entire year. This was true for all of New England, but not to the extent that crop-dependent Hinesburg experienced. There was not enough to eat nor enough seed to plant the following season. A pair of merchants, Jedediah Boynton and William Hurlburt, continually stayed on the road in an attempt to distribute rice from Troy to the hungry inhabitants.

In 1825 a sawmill, a gristmill, and a clothing works were erected on Lewis Creek. The town had a blacksmith shop and a goods shop for the sale of tobacco and other small articles. Chairs, turning wheels, and carding were also industries in the town. In 1856 the Hinesburg Woolen Mill was purchased by Andrew Dow, Nelson M. May, and Isaiah Dow.

Hinesburg Bank
1854
W-VT-350

History: In 1854 the charter application for the Hinesburg Bank was rejected by the state legislature.

Numismatic Commentary: It is possible that Proof notes were made, but no record has been found of such.

HYDE PARK, VERMONT

Hyde Park is a part of Lamoille County and was granted in 1780. Although the Continental Congress objected to the settling of the land, the Vermont Legislature granted 61 new townships that year, including Hyde Park. Captain Jedediah Hyde, William Dennison, and others were the proprietors, of which only two settled and lived there: Captain Hyde and Captain Jabez Fitch. At the time, the Republic of Vermont was a separate entity and not a colony. In 1791 Vermont joined the Union.

Lamoille County Bank
1854–1865
W-VT-360

History: The Lamoille County Bank was chartered in 1854 with $50,000 in authorized capital. It commenced business on May 11, 1855. Considerable opposition to the establishment of the bank was encountered at first, owing to the fact that some of the directors of the Waterbury Bank were residents of the county and did not want the competition. Resistance was short lived, however, and the bank was soon in operation and doing well.

In June 1855, the bank's capital was $75,000. The same was $50,000 in 1863. In July 1859, circulation was $68,277; in July 1862, it was $94,434.

The interests of the Lamoille County Bank were succeeded by Lamoille County National Bank in 1865. Its outstanding circulation was reported to be $1,321 on July 1, 1867. The redemption of these notes was guaranteed by the national bank, but the liability to do so expired on May 11, 1868.

Numismatic Commentary: While not plentiful, notes from this bank appear in the marketplace on occasion. Many collectors search for the $10 note with a titled vignette of Saint Nicholas in a sleigh being drawn by reindeer over rooftops.

All notes of the Lamoille County Bank bear the engraver imprint of Bald, Adams & Co. and Bald, Cousland & Co. Remaining in the American Bank Note Co. archives as of 2003 was a $1-$1-$2-$5 face plate and a $1-$2-$3-$5 face plate.

VALID ISSUES

$1 • W-VT-360-001-G010

CC

Comments: H-VT-100-G2, Coulter-1. Proof. May 21st, 1855. 1850s–1860s.

Rarity: URS-4
Proof $750

$2 • W-VT-360-002-G020

CC

Comments: H-VT-100-G4, Coulter-2. Proof. May 21st, 1855. 1850s–1860s.

Rarity: URS-3
Proof $750

$3 • W-VT-360-003-G030

CC

Comments: H-VT-100-G6, Coulter-3. May 21st, 1855. 1850s–1860s.

Rarity: URS-3
Proof $750

$3 • W-VT-360-003-G030a

CC

Overprint: Red 3 / 3. *Comments:* H-Unlisted, Coulter-Unlisted. Similar to W-VT-360-003-G030. May 21st, 1855. 1850s–1860s.

Rarity: URS-3
F $750

$5 • W-VT-360-005-G040

CC

Comments: H-VT-100-G8, Coulter-4. Proof. May 21st, 1855. 1850s–1860s.

Rarity: URS-3
Proof $750

$5 • W-VT-360-005-G040a

CC

Overprint: Red 5 / 5. *Comments:* H-Unlisted, Coulter-Unlisted. Similar to W-VT-360-005-G040. May 21st, 1855. 1850s–1860s.

Rarity: URS-3
VF $900

$10 • W-VT-360-010-G050

CC

Comments: H-VT-100-G10, Coulter-5. A coveted Santa Claus note. Proof. May 21st, 1855. 1850s–1860s.

Rarity: URS-4
Proof $5,000

$10 • W-VT-360-010-G050a

CC

Overprint: Red TEN. *Comments:* H-Unlisted, Coulter-Unlisted. Similar to W-VT-360-010-G050. A coveted Santa Claus note. Proof. May 21st, 1855. 1850s–1860s.

Rarity: URS-4
Proof $5,000

$20 • W-VT-360-020-G060

CC

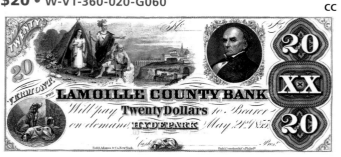

Comments: H-VT-100-G12, Coulter-6. Proof. May 21st, 1855. 1850s–1860s.

Rarity: URS-3
CU $500; **Proof** $900

$20 • W-VT-360-020-G060a

CC

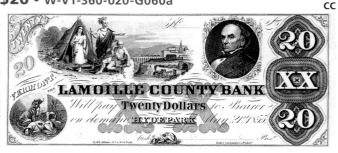

Overprint: Red XX. *Comments:* H-Unlisted, Coulter-Unlisted. Similar to W-VT-360-020-G060. Proof. May 21st, 1855. 1850s–1860s.

Rarity: URS-3
Proof $900

$50 • W-VT-360-050-G070

CC

Comments: H-VT-100-G14, Coulter-7. Proof. May 21st, 1855. 1850s–1860s.

Rarity: URS-3
Proof $1,200

$50 • W-VT-360-050-G070a

CC

Overprint: Red 50. *Comments:* H-Unlisted, Coulter-Unlisted. Similar to W-VT-360-050-G070. Proof. May 21st, 1855. 1850s–1860s.

Rarity: URS-3
Proof $1,300

$100 • W-VT-360-100-G080

CC

Comments: H-VT-100-G16, Coulter-8. Proof. May 21st, 1855. 1850s–1860s.

Rarity: URS-3
Proof $1,250

$100 • W-VT-360-100-G080a

cc

Overprint: Red 100. **Comments:** H-Unlisted, Coulter-Unlisted. Similar to W-VT-360-100-G080. Proof. May 21st, 1855. 1850s–1860s.

Rarity: URS-3
Proof $1,400

Uncut Sheets

$1-$2-$3-$5 • W-VT-360-001.002.003.005-US010

Vignette(s): ($1) Shed, Flowers on roof / Boy with pitchfork, Boy on cart load of hay drawn by two oxen / 1 on shield / Arm and hammer. **($2)** Woods, Stream and Indian creeping with gun / Justice in clouds / Geese / Two deer, one feeding. **($3)** Cattle and sheep lying down, Bull standing / Woman swimming / Female portrait with veil. **($5)** Woman with dinner horn, Three men with load of hay / Herd of horses running. **Comments:** H-VT-100-G2, G4, G6, G8. May 21st, 1855. 1850s–1860s.

Rarity: URS-2
Proof $5,000

$1-$2-$3-$5 • W-VT-360-001.002.003.005-US010a

Overprint(s): Red. **Comments:** All unlisted in Haxby. Similar to W-VT-360-001.002.003.005-US010. May 21st, 1855. 1850s–1860s.

Rarity: URS-2
Proof $5,000

$10-$20-$50-$100 •
W-VT-360-010.020.050.100-US020

cc

Comments: H-VT-100-G10, G12, G14, G16. A coveted Santa Claus note. Proof. May 21st, 1855. 1850s–1860s.

Rarity: URS-2
Proof $11,500

How to Read the Whitman Numbering System

$1 • W-RI-010-001-G010a

Denomination: Value of the note shown.

W: Whitman number. This number is a sortable code unique to each bank and note.

RI: Abbreviation for the state under study.

010: Numerical designation specific to each bank.

001: The denomination in dollars.

G010a: G indicates a good or valid note. Other categories are indicated thus: C (counterfeit); R (raised); S (spurious); N (not-attributed); A (altered). Numbers are assigned starting with 010, 020, et seq. Terminal letters following the number indicate variations of a note: a series of different colored overprints, tints, payees, etc., all on the same design of note. For more information, see the "How to Use This Book" section at the front of the volume, page xiv.

$10-$20-$50-$100 •
W-VT-360-010.020.050.100-US020a

CC

Overprint(s): Red. *Comments:* All unlisted in Haxby. Similar to W-VT-360-010.020.050.100-US020. A coveted Santa Claus note. May 21st, 1855. 1850s–1860s.

Rarity: URS-2
Proof $12,500

IRASBURG, VERMONT

Ira Allen was granted the land that became the town of Irasburg (also seen as Irasburgh on bank notes) on February 23, 1781, along with 69 other proprietors. Caleb Leach made the first settlement in 1798. The Black River flowed through the town, providing multiple water sources and small streams on which sawmills and a gristmill were built. There was also a carriage and blacksmith shop, a wagon manufactory, and shops for the building of sleighs.

Bank of Orleans
1832–1865
W-VT-370

History: The Bank of Orleans was incorporated on December 20, 1832, with an authorized capital of $60,000. The bank was originally housed in George Nye's Tavern in Irasburg, which was later converted into the Irasburg House, forming a wing of the hotel of the same name. Bills in circulation in 1833 totaled $49,168. By 1834 the same was $35,774. In 1847 the charter was extended, and in 1850 an act increased the capital of the bank to $80,000. During the financial crisis of September and October 1857, the bank was listed as having failed. However, it was reincorporated with $50,000 of capital in 1860. Bills in circulation were $69,472, specie was $2,687, and real estate was valued at $3,100. By July 1, 1862, the bank had $56,908 of bills in circulation.

On April 5, 1865, the Irasburgh National Bank of Orleans was chartered, succeeding the business of the state bank. It had an outstanding circulation of $805 as of July 1, 1867. The redemption of this circulation was guaranteed by the national bank until December 14, 1867.

Numismatic Commentary: Counterfeit or altered notes are seen most frequently. The New England Bank Note Co. $3 counterfeit is a fair representation of the genuine. Genuine issues are fairly scarce.

VALID ISSUES
$1 • W-VT-370-001-G010

TD

Engraver: New England Bank Note Co. *Comments:* H-VT-105-G2, Coulter-2. 18__. 1848–1850s.

Rarity: URS-3
F $750

$1 • W-VT-370-001-G020

Left: 1 / Allegorical woman / 1. *Center:* 1 / ONE. *Bottom center:* Dog and strongbox. *Right:* 1 / Ox / 1. *Engraver:* Rawdon, Wright, Hatch & Edson / New England Bank Note Co. *Comments:* H-VT-105-G4, Coulter-1. 18__. 1850s.

Rarity: *None known*

$1 • W-VT-370-001-G020a

Overprint: Red. *Engraver:* Rawdon, Wright, Hatch & Edson / New England Bank Note Co. *Comments:* H-VT-105-G4a. Similar to W-VT-370-001-G020. 18__. 1850s–1860s.

Rarity: URS-2
VF $600

$1.25 • W-VT-370-001.25-G030

Left: Train. *Center:* Ships at sea / $1.25 Cts. *Right:* 1 25/100 / Spread eagle. *Engraver:* New England Bank Note Co. *Comments:* H-Unlisted, Coulter-4. 1850s–1860s.

Rarity: *None known*

$2 • W-VT-370-002-G040

Left: TWO / Woman / 2. *Center:* Haymaking scene. *Right:* TWO / Ceres / 2. *Engraver:* New England Bank Note Co. *Comments:* H-VT-105-G6, Coulter-6. 18__. 1848–1850s.

Rarity: URS-3
VF $400

$2 • W-VT-370-002-G050

Left: 2 / Man with sledge on shoulder / 2. *Center:* 2. *Right:* 2 / Milkmaid and two cows / 2. *Engraver:* Rawdon, Wright, Hatch & Edson / New England Bank Note Co. *Comments:* H-VT-105-G8, Coulter-5. 18__. 1850s.

Rarity: *None known*

$2 • W-VT-370-002-G050a

Overprint: Red TWO. *Engraver:* Rawdon, Wright, Hatch & Edson / New England Bank Note Co. *Comments:* H-VT-105-G8a. Similar to W-VT-370-002-G050. 18__. 1850s–1860s.

Rarity: *None known*

$2 • W-VT-370-002-G060

Left: TWO / Allegorical woman / 2. *Center:* Family group. *Right:* TWO / 2. *Comments:* H-Unlisted, Coulter-7. 1850s–1860s.

Rarity: *None known*

$3 • W-VT-370-003-G070

Left: THREE / Farmer with scythe / 3 on THREE. *Center:* 3 / Hope, Eagle, Beehive, implements, and anchor / 3. *Right:* THREE / Sailor with hat / 3 on THREE. *Engraver:* New England Bank Note Co. *Comments:* H-VT-105-G10, Coulter-10. 18__. 1848–1850s.

Rarity: *None known*

$3 • W-VT-370-003-G080

Left: 3 / Man with axe, Oxen and cart / 3. *Center:* 3 / Man shearing sheep / 3. *Right:* 3 / Two men, Woman and three children. *Engraver:* Rawdon, Wright, Hatch & Edson / New England Bank Note Co. *Comments:* H-VT-105-G12, Coulter-9. 18__. 1850s.

Rarity: *None known*

$3 • W-VT-370-003-G080a

Overprint: Red. *Engraver:* Rawdon, Wright, Hatch & Edson / New England Bank Note Co. *Comments:* H-VT-105-G12a, Coulter-9. Similar to W-VT-370-003-G080. 18__. 1850s–1860s.

Rarity: *None known*

$5 • W-VT-370-005-G090

Left: FIVE vertically. *Center:* Allegorical woman unveiling shield bearing 5. *Right:* 5 / Ship. *Engraver:* New England Bank Note Co. *Comments:* H-VT-105-G14, Coulter-15. 18__. 1848–1850s.

Rarity: *None known*

$5 • W-VT-370-005-G100

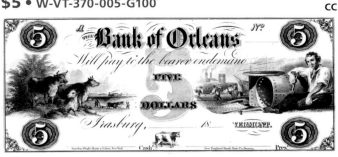

CC

Engraver: Rawdon, Wright, Hatch & Edson / New England Bank Note Co. *Comments:* H-VT-105-G16, Coulter-14. Proof. 18__. 1850s.

Rarity: URS-2
Proof $1,000

$5 • W-VT-370-005-G100a

Overprint: Red. *Engraver:* Rawdon, Wright, Hatch & Edson / New England Bank Note Co. *Comments:* H-VT-105-G16a. Similar to W-VT-370-005-G100. 18__. 1850s.

Rarity: *None known*

$10 • W-VT-370-010-G110

Left: "Presentation of the Declaration of Independence" / X. *Center:* X. *Right:* 10 / Train at station, Man with wheelbarrow. *Engraver:* New England Bank Note Co. *Comments:* H-VT-105-G18, Coulter-19. 18__. 1848–1850s.

Rarity: URS-4
VF $400

$10 • W-VT-370-010-G120

CC

Engraver: Rawdon, Wright, Hatch & Edson / New England Bank Note Co. *Comments:* H-VT-105-G20, Coulter-20. Proof. 18__. 1850s–1860s.

Rarity: URS-2
Proof $1,500

$20 • W-VT-370-020-G130

Left: 20 / Woman seated with book, opening chest. *Center:* XX / Eagle / XX. *Right:* 20 / Ship, Buildings. *Engraver:* New England Bank Note Co. *Comments:* H-VT-105-G24, Coulter-24. 18__. 1848–1850s.

Rarity: *None known*

$50 • W-VT-370-050-G140

Left: FIFTY / Woman with wreaths of flowers / FIFTY. *Center:* Man holding restive horse by mane. *Right:* FIFTY / Woman with cornucopia / FIFTY. *Engraver:* New England Bank Note Co. *Comments:* H-VT-105-G28, Coulter-25. 18__. 1848–1850s.

Rarity: *None known*

$100 • W-VT-370-100-G150

Left: ONE HUNDRED on 100 / Portrait of William Henry Harrison. *Center:* Wharf scene, Covered wagon. *Right:* ONE HUNDRED on 100 / Portrait of Christopher Columbus. *Engraver:* New England Bank Note Co. *Comments:* H-VT-105-G30, Coulter-27. 18__. 1848–1850s.

Rarity: None known

$100 • W-VT-370-100-G160

Left: 100 / Woman with cornucopia / 100. *Center:* 100 / 100. *Right:* 100 / Waterfall and eagle / 100. *Comments:* H-VT-105-G32, Coulter-26. 18__. 1850s–1860s.

Rarity: None known

NON-VALID ISSUES

$1 • W-VT-370-001-A010

CJF

Tint: Red-brown 1s and panel outlining white ONE DOLLAR. *Engraver:* Danforth, Wright & Co. *Comments:* H-VT-105-A5, Coulter-3. Altered from $1 Southern Bank of Georgia, Bainbridge, Georgia. March 1st, 1858.

Rarity: URS-7

F $125

$2 • W-VT-370-002-N010

Center: Girl feeding calf. *Comments:* H-Unlisted, Coulter-8. 1850s–1860s.

Rarity: None known

$3 • W-VT-370-003-C070

CJF

Engraver: New England Bank Note Co. *Comments:* H-VT-105-C10. Counterfeit of W-VT-370-003-G070. 18__. 1848–1850s.

Rarity: URS-9

F $90; VF $145

$3 • W-VT-370-003-N020

Left: THREE / Farmer with scythe / THREE with 3. *Center:* 3 / Hebe watering eagle / 3. *Right:* THREE / Sailor with hat, THREE with 3. *Engraver:* New England Bank Note Co. *Comments:* H-Unlisted, Coulter-11. 1850s–1860s.

Rarity: None known

$3 • W-VT-370-003-N030

Left: 5 in die / Justice and shipping. *Center:* Mercury and woman with dolphin. *Right:* FIVE / Two women, one holding caduceus, one with cornucopia / V. *Engraver:* Rawdon, Wright & Hatch. *Comments:* H-Unlisted, Coulter-12. 1850s–1860s.

Rarity: None known

$3 • W-VT-370-003-N040

Center: Wharf scene with houses, Shipping. *Right:* 3 / Portrait of Henry Clay. *Comments:* H-Unlisted, Coulter-13. 1850s–1860s.

Rarity: None known

$3 • W-VT-370-003-A020

Left: Helmeted man. *Center:* 3 / Buildings and ships. *Right:* 3. *Engraver:* Durand & Co. *Comments:* H-VT-105-A10. Altered from W-VT-570-003-G030. Jan. 15, 1850.

Rarity: URS-3

F $150

$5 • W-VT-370-005-S010

CJF

Engraver: New England Bank Note Co. *Comments:* H-VT-105-S5, Coulter-18. 18__. 1850s.

Rarity: URS-8

F $85

$5 • W-VT-370-005-N050

Center: Wharf scene. *Comments:* H-Unlisted, Coulter-16. 1850s–1860s.

Rarity: None known

$5 • W-VT-370-005-N060

Center: Spread eagle. *Comments:* H-VT-105-N5, Coulter-17. 1850s–1860s.

Rarity: None known

$10 • W-VT-370-010-R010

BH

Engraver: Rawdon, Wright, Hatch & Edson / New England Bank Note Co. *Comments:* H-VT-105-R5, Coulter-21. Raised from W-VT-370-001-G020. 18__. 1850s.

Rarity: URS-3

VG $350; F $300

$10 • **W-VT-370-010-R020**
Engraver: Rawdon, Wright, Hatch & Edson / New England Bank Note Co. *Comments:* H-VT-105-R10, Coulter-22. Raised from W-VT-370-002-G050. 18__. 1850s.
Rarity: None known

$10 • **W-VT-370-010-N070**
Left: Woman reclining. *Right:* Ox. *Comments:* H-Unlisted, Coulter-23. 1850s–1860s.
Rarity: None known

$10 • **W-VT-370-010-A030**
Left: 10 / Sailor standing with U.S. flag / X. *Center:* 10 on medallion head / "Presentation of the Declaration of Independence" / 10 on medallion head. *Bottom center:* Eagle. *Right:* X / Pat Lyon standing by forge / 10. *Engraver:* Draper, Underwood & Co. / Underwood, Bald, Spencer & Hufty. *Comments:* H-VT-105-A15. Altered from $10 Tenth Ward Bank, New York City, New York. 18__. 1840s.
Rarity: None known

Bank of Orleans County
1833–1848
W-VT-380

History: The Bank of Orleans County was chartered on November 8, 1832, with $60,000 in authorized capital, $30,000 of which was soon paid in, permitting the bank to go into operation. In August 1845, its capital was $30,000, and circulation was $32,868. Its charter expired on January 1, 1848.

Numismatic Commentary: All issues are very hard to locate. In addition to standard values, this bank issued three different bills with odd or fractional denominations such as $1.25, $1.50, and $1.75.

VALID ISSUES

$1 • **W-VT-380-001-G010**
Left: ONE / VERMONT / Woman seated. *Center:* ONE. *Right:* Lathework panel with 1 / ONE / 1. *Engraver:* PSSP. *Comments:* H-VT-110-G4. 18__. 1830s–1840s.
Rarity: None known

$1.25 • **W-VT-380-001.25-G020**
Left: 1 25/100 / Train / 1 25/100. *Center:* Sloop at sea, Vessels / $1.25 Cts. *Right:* 1 25/100 / Eagle. *Engraver:* New England Bank Note Co. *Comments:* H-VT-110-G8. 18__. 1830s.
Rarity: None known

$1.50 • **W-VT-380-001.50-G030**
Left: Panel with 1 DOLL.50 Cts. vertically. *Center:* Eagle on rock in ocean / $1 50/100. *Right:* 1 50/100 / Justice. *Engraver:* New England Bank Note Co. *Comments:* H-VT-110-G12. 18__. 1830s.
Rarity: None known

$1.75 • **W-VT-380-001.75-G040**
Left: $1.75 Cts. / Hebe watering eagle / 1 75/100. *Center:* Sailing ship and two sloops. *Right:* $1.75 Cts. / Woman standing / 1 75/100. *Engraver:* New England Bank Note Co. *Comments:* H-VT-110-G16. 18__. 1830s.
Rarity: None known

$2 • **W-VT-380-002-G050**
Left: TWO / VERMONT / Woman carrying hat and sheaf. *Center:* TWO. *Right:* Lathework panel with 2 / TWO / 2. *Engraver:* PSSP. *Comments:* H-VT-110-G20. 18__. 1830s–1840s.
Rarity: None known

$3 • **W-VT-380-003-G060**
Left: THREE / VERMONT / Woman. *Center:* THREE. *Right:* Lathework panel with 3 / THREE / 3. *Engraver:* PSSP. *Comments:* H-VT-110-G24. 18__. 1830s–1840s.
Rarity: None known

$5 • **W-VT-380-005-G070**
Left: Panel bearing VERMONT / 5 / 5 vertically. *Center:* Alternating flower garlands and gridwork segments bearing FIVE. *Right:* 5 / 5 vertically. *Engraver:* PSSP. *Comments:* H-VT-110-G28. 18__. 1830s–1840s.
Rarity: None known

$10 • **W-VT-380-010-G080**
Left: Panel bearing VERMONT / 10 / 10 vertically. *Center:* Alternating flower garlands and gridwork segments bearing TEN. *Right:* 10 / 10 vertically. *Engraver:* PSSP. *Comments:* H-VT-110-G32. 18__. 1830s–1840s.
Rarity: None known

$20 • **W-VT-380-020-G090**
Left: Panel bearing VERMONT / 20 / 20 vertically. *Center:* Alternating flower garlands and gridwork segments bearing TWENTY. *Right:* 20 / 20 vertically. *Engraver:* PSSP. *Comments:* H-VT-110-G36. 18__. 1830s–1840s.
Rarity: None known

$50 • **W-VT-380-050-G100**
Left: Panel bearing VERMONT / 50 / 50 vertically. *Center:* Alternating flower garlands and gridwork segments bearing FIFTY. *Right:* 50 / 50 vertically. *Engraver:* PSSP. *Comments:* H-VT-110-G40. 18__. 1830s–1840s.
Rarity: None known

$100 • **W-VT-380-100-G110**
Left: Panel bearing VERMONT / 100 / 100 vertically. *Center:* Alternating flower garlands and gridwork segments bearing 100. *Right:* 100 / 100 vertically. *Engraver:* PSSP. *Comments:* H-VT-110-G44. 18__. 1830s–1840s.
Rarity: None known

JAMAICA, VERMONT

William Hayward (also spelled Howard) and his sons Caleb and Silas were the first settlers of Jamaica. They arrived in 1775, two years before Vermont was established as a state. The town was named after the Natick word for beaver.

The West River and the Ball Mountain Brook join near Jamaica, offering the town a fine location for the placement of bridges, dams, and mills. In addition to mills, Merino sheep thrived on the graze lands, and for a while the town experienced a measure of prosperity. With the decline of the wool market following the Civil War, however, the economy took a downturn—this being after the note-issuing period.

West River Bank
1853–1865
W-VT-390

History: The West River Bank was chartered in 1853 with an authorized capital of $100,000. In 1857 its capital was $50,000, bills in circulation were $86,182, specie was $3,525, and real estate was valued at $2,500. Circulation in August 1859 was $80,812. In July 1862, the same was $97,877.

In 1865 the business of the West River Bank was succeeded by the West River National Bank at Jamaica. By July 1, 1867, the outstanding circulation for the bank was $1,820, redemption of which was guaranteed by the national bank.

Numismatic Commentary: Signed and circulated genuine notes from this bank are very hard to locate. Remainder notes and sheets without dates and signatures, however, are fairly easy to find and are very popular due to the coins pictured on the vignettes.

All of the notes listed bear the imprints of Rawdon, Wright, Hatch & Edson and the New England Bank Note Co. The $1, $2, $3, and $5 notes printed after the spring of 1858 bear the ABNCo. monogram. All notes have a red overprint except for the valid $10 note.

VALID ISSUES

$1 • W-VT-390-001-G010
Left: Justice and Minerva / 1. **Center:** Cherub rolling silver dollar, City / ONE. **Right:** 1 / Woman seated with arms around 1. **Overprint:** Red ONE. **Engraver:** Rawdon, Wright, Hatch & Edson / New England Bank Note Co. **Comments:** H-VT-115-G2a, Coulter-1. July 1st, 18__. 1850s.
Rarity: *None known*

$1 • W-VT-390-001-G010a
ANS

Overprint: Red ONE. **Engraver:** Rawdon, Wright, Hatch & Edson / New England Bank Note Co. / ABNCo. monogram. **Comments:** H-VT-115-G2b. Similar to W-VT-390-001-G010 but with additional engraver imprint. July 1st, 18__. 1860s.
Rarity: URS-8
Unc-Rem $175

$2 • W-VT-390-002-G020
Left: Two men carrying girl on shoulder / 2. **Center:** Two cherubs and two silver dollars, Train / TWO. **Right:** 2 / Woman churning. **Overprint:** Red TWO. **Engraver:** Rawdon, Wright, Hatch & Edson / New England Bank Note Co. **Comments:** H-VT-115-G4a, Coulter-2. July 1st, 18__. 1850s.
Rarity: *None known*

$2 • W-VT-390-002-G020a
CC

Overprint: Red TWO. **Engraver:** Rawdon, Wright, Hatch & Edson / New England Bank Note Co. / ABNCo. monogram. **Comments:** H-VT-115-G4b. Similar to W-VT-390-002-G020 but with additional engraver imprint. July 1st, 18__. 1860s.
Rarity: URS-8
Unc-Rem $175

$3 • W-VT-390-003-G030
Left: Justice / 3. **Center:** Three cherubs, Three silver dollars, Books, globe, palette. **Right:** 3 / State arms / THREE. **Overprint:** Red THREE. **Engraver:** Rawdon, Wright, Hatch & Edson / New England Bank Note Co. **Comments:** H-VT-115-G6a, Coulter-3. July 1st, 18__. 1850s.
Rarity: *None known*

$3 • W-VT-390-003-G030a
TD

Overprint: Red THREE. **Engraver:** Rawdon, Wright, Hatch & Edson / New England Bank Note Co. / ABNCo. monogram. **Comments:** H-VT-115-G6b. Similar to W-VT-390-003-G030 but with additional engraver imprint. July 1st, 18__. 1860s.
Rarity: URS-8
Unc-Rem $175

$5 • W-VT-390-005-G040
Left: Female portrait / V. **Center:** Five cherubs and five silver dollars / FIVE. **Right:** 5 / Sailor, Shield bearing FIVE, Indian. **Overprint:** Red FIVE. **Engraver:** Rawdon, Wright, Hatch & Edson / New England Bank Note Co. **Comments:** H-VT-115-G8a, Coulter-4. July 1st, 18__. 1850s.
Rarity: *None known*

$5 • W-VT-390-005-G040a   TD

Overprint: Red FIVE. *Engraver:* Rawdon, Wright, Hatch & Edson / New England Bank Note Co. / ABNCo. monogram. *Comments:* H-VT-115-G8b. Similar to W-VT-390-005-G040 but with additional engraver imprint. July 1st, 18__. 1860s.

Rarity: URS-8
Unc-Rem $100

$10 • W-VT-390-010-G050   CJF

Engraver: Rawdon, Wright, Hatch & Edson / New England Bank Note Co. *Comments:* H-VT-115-G10, Coulter-5. Proof. 18__. 1850s.

Rarity: URS-8
Unc-Rem $200

$20 • W-VT-390-020-G060   TD

Engraver: Rawdon, Wright, Hatch & Edson / New England Bank Note Co. *Comments:* H-VT-115-G12, Coulter-7. 185_. 1850s.

Rarity: URS-8
Unc-Rem $250
Selected auction price: Heritage,
September 2008, Lot 12749, Gem Unc $977

$20 • W-VT-390-020-G060a   CJF

Overprint: Red TWENTY. *Engraver:* Rawdon, Wright, Hatch & Edson / New England Bank Note Co. *Comments:* H-VT-115-G12a. Similar to W-VT-390-020-G060. 185_. 1850s.

Rarity: URS-8
Unc-Rem $400
Selected auction price: Stack's Bowers Galleries,
June 2008, Lot 2411, Gem Unc $834

$50 • W-VT-390-050-G070   CC

Engraver: Rawdon, Wright, Hatch & Edson / New England Bank Note Co. *Comments:* H-VT-115-G14. Proof. 185_. 1850s–1860s.

Rarity: URS-3
Proof $1,250

$50 • W-VT-390-050-G070a   CJF

Overprint: Red FIFTY. *Engraver:* Rawdon, Wright, Hatch & Edson / New England Bank Note Co. *Comments:* H-VT-115-G14a, Coulter-8. Similar to W-VT-390-050-G070. 185_. 1850s.

Rarity: URS-5
Unc-Rem $400

Uncut Sheets
$1-$2-$3-$5 • W-VT-390-001.002.003.005-US010   cc

Overprint(s): Red. **Engraver:** Rawdon, Wright, Hatch & Edson / New England Bank Note Co. / ABNCo. monogram. **Comments:** H-VT-115-G2b, G4b, G6b, G8b. July 1st, 18__. 1860s.

Rarity: URS-7
Unc-Rem $700
Selected auction price(s): Heritage,
April 2008, Lot 12555, AU $517;
Heritage, April–May 2010, Lot 12247, CU $632

$20-$50 • W-VT-390-020.050-US020

Vignette(s): ($20) Minerva / Commerce seated, Sheaf, Lighthouse and ship / Ceres seated. **($50)** Justice / Liberty draped in American flag, Eagle, clouds / Portrait of Andrew Jackson. **Overprint(s):** Red. **Engraver:** Rawdon, Wright, Hatch & Edson / New England Bank Note Co. **Comments:** H-VT-115-G12a, G14a. 18__. 1850s.

Rarity: URS-4
Unc-Rem $750

Non-Valid Issues
$10 • W-VT-390-010-R010

Overprint: Red. **Engraver:** Rawdon, Wright, Hatch & Edson / New England Bank Note Co. **Comments:** H-VT-115-R5, Coulter-6. Raised from W-VT-390-001-G010. 18__. 1850s.

Rarity: *None known*

JOHNSON, VERMONT

The town of Johnson, which includes an incorporated village of the same name, is located near Sterling Mountain and the Gihon and Lamoille rivers. It was granted in 1782. In 1792 William Johnson, Reverend Johnathan Edwards, and Charles Chauncey received the charter. The name is believed to have come from William Johnson, who was a statesman and educator and also the first president of Columbia College.

In 1842 the Johnson Woolen Mills were built, allowing local farmers to bring their wool to be woven into cloth. By 1855 the town had been annexed to the nearby town of Sterling, and the annexation was approved in 1856.

Bank of Lamoille
1854
W-VT-400

History: In 1854 the charter application for the Bank of Lamoille was rejected by the state legislature.

Numismatic Commentary: It is possible that Proof notes were made, but no record has been found of such.

LYNDON, VERMONT

Bordered by Sutton, Burke, Kirby, St. Johnsbury, and Wheelock, Lyndon was chartered in 1780 and settled in 1788 by Daniel Cahoon and Daniel Owen. The town was named after the son of Dr. Jonathan Arnold, Josiah Lyndon, to whom the land was initially chartered and who was a graduate of Dartmouth and studied law in Providence, Rhode Island. The population in 1800 was 542, rising to 1,092 in 1810, 1,926 in 1820, and 1,750 in 1830.

Lyndon had multiple mills including sawmills, gristmills, a pulp mill, stave mills, a butter factory, and a carriage company which produced steam carriages and lumber dressing.

Bank of Lyndon
1855–1865
W-VT-410

History: The Bank of Lyndon was chartered in 1854 with an authorized capital of $50,000. It commenced business on May 1, 1855. By 1857 the bank had a capital of $75,000. Circulation was $113,039, and specie was $3,278. In July 1859, circulation was $113,039. Capital stock was $100,000, and circulation was $89,693 by 1862.

After March 23, 1865, the business of the bank was succeeded by the National Bank of Lyndon. It had an outstanding circulation of $2,026 as of July 1, 1867, the redemption of which was guaranteed by the national bank. After December 15, 1867, the bank would no longer be liable to redeem the outstanding bills.

Numismatic Commentary: All genuine notes of this bank are scarce and require time to locate. A note with a standout vignette is the $1 issue showing Chief Pontiac at council with other Indians.

VALID ISSUES

$1 • W-VT-410-001-G010   TD

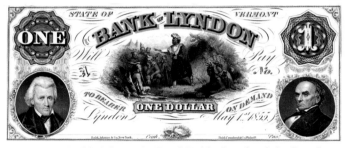

Engraver: Bald Adams & Co. / Bald, Cousland & Co. **Comments:** H-Unlisted, Coulter-Unlisted. Proof. May 1st, 1855.
Rarity: URS-4
Proof $750

$1 • W-VT-410-001-G010a   CC

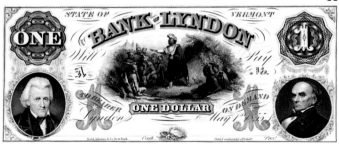

Overprint: Red 1 / 1. **Engraver:** Bald Adams & Co. / Bald, Cousland & Co. **Comments:** H-VT-125-G2a, Coulter-1. Similar to W-VT-410-001-G010. May 1st, 1855.
Rarity: URS-3
VG $795; **Proof** $1,000

$1 • W-VT-410-001-G020   CJF

Overprint: Red ONE. **Engraver:** Bald Adams & Co. / Bald, Cousland & Co. **Comments:** H-VT-125-G4a, Coulter-2. May 1st, 1855.
Rarity: URS-2
F $1,000

$1 • W-VT-410-001-G020a   CC

Overprint: Green 1 / 1 / ONE. **Engraver:** Bald Adams & Co. / Bald, Cousland & Co. / ABNCo. monogram. **Comments:** H-Unlisted, Coulter-Unlisted. Similar to W-VT-410-001-G020 but with additional engraver imprint. May 1st, 1855.
Rarity: URS-3
VF $900

$2 • W-VT-410-002-G030   CC

Engraver: Bald Adams & Co. / Bald, Cousland & Co. **Comments:** H-Unlisted, Coulter-Unlisted. Proof. May 1st, 1855.
Rarity: URS-4
Proof $500

$2 • W-VT-410-002-G030a   TD

Overprint: Red TWO. **Engraver:** Bald Adams & Co. / Bald, Cousland & Co. **Comments:** H-VT-125-G6a, Coulter-3. Similar to W-VT-410-002-G030. May 1st, 1855.
Rarity: URS-3
VF $900

$3 • W-VT-410-003-G040   TD

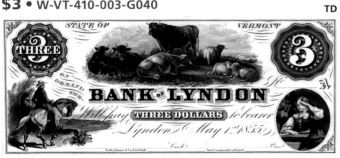

Engraver: Bald Adams & Co. / Bald, Cousland & Co. *Comments:* H-Unlisted, Coulter-Unlisted. Proof. May 1st, 1855.
Rarity: URS-4
Proof $600

$3 • W-VT-410-003-G040a   CC

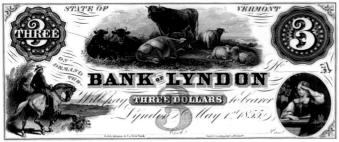

Overprint: Red 3. *Engraver:* Bald Adams & Co. / Bald, Cousland & Co. *Comments:* H-VT-125-G8a, Coulter-5. Similar to W-VT-410-003-G040. Proof. May 1st, 1855.
Rarity: URS-4
Proof $600

$5 • W-VT-410-005-G050   TD

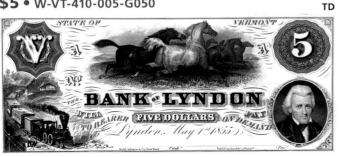

Engraver: Bald Adams & Co. / Bald, Cousland & Co. *Comments:* H-Unlisted, Coulter-Unlisted. Proof. May 1st, 1855.
Rarity: URS-5
Proof $400

$5 • W-VT-410-005-G050a   TD

Overprint: Red 5 / 5. *Engraver:* Bald Adams & Co. / Bald, Cousland & Co. *Comments:* H-VT-125-G10a, Coulter-6. Similar to W-VT-410-005-G050. May 1st, 1855.
Rarity: URS-3
F $750; **Proof** $1,000

$10 • W-VT-410-010-G060   CC

Engraver: Bald Adams & Co. / Bald, Cousland & Co. *Comments:* H-Unlisted, Coulter-Unlisted. Proof. May 1st, 1855.
Rarity: URS-2
Proof $1,250

$10 • W-VT-410-010-G060a   CC

Overprint: Red TEN. *Engraver:* Bald Adams & Co. / Bald, Cousland & Co. *Comments:* H-VT-125-G12a, Coulter-10. Similar to W-VT-410-010-G060. May 1st, 1855.
Rarity: URS-3
Proof $1,250

Collectors and Researchers:

If you have new information about any banks or notes
listed in this volume, contact Whitman Publishing,
Attn: Obsolete Paper Money,
3101 Clairmont Road, Suite G, Atlanta, GA 30329.

$20 • W-VT-410-020-G070   CC

Engraver: Bald, Adams & Co. / Bald, Cousland & Co. *Comments:* H-Unlisted, Coulter-Unlisted. Proof. May 1st, 1855.
Rarity: URS-3
Proof $1,500

$20 • W-VT-410-020-G070a   CC

Overprint: Red XX. *Engraver:* Bald, Adams & Co. / Bald, Cousland & Co. *Comments:* H-Unlisted, Coulter-Unlisted. Similar to W-VT-410-020-G070. Proof. May 1st, 1855.
Rarity: URS-3
Proof $1,500

$20 • W-VT-410-020-G070b

Left: XX / Indian drawing arrow from quiver. *Center:* Commerce, Shield, Indian. *Bottom center:* Man chopping tree. *Right:* 20 / Portrait of Samuel Houston. *Overprint:* Green TWENTY. *Engraver:* Bald, Adams & Co. / Bald, Cousland & Co. *Comments:* H-VT-125-G14a, Coulter-13. Similar to W-VT-410-020-G070. May 1st, 1855.
Rarity: URS-3
VF $850

$50 • W-VT-410-050-G080   TD

Engraver: Bald, Adams & Co. / Bald, Cousland & Co. *Comments:* H-Unlisted, Coulter-Unlisted. Proof. May 1st, 1855.
Rarity: URS-3
Proof $1,250

$50 • W-VT-410-050-G080a

Left: 50 / Eagle. *Center:* Three cows lying down, one standing, one drinking. *Right:* 50 / Portrait of Daniel Webster. *Overprint:* Red. *Engraver:* Bald, Adams & Co. / Bald, Cousland & Co. *Comments:* H-VT-125-G16a, Coulter-14. Similar to W-VT-410-050-G080. May 1st, 1855.
Rarity: URS-4
Proof $750

$100 • W-VT-410-100-G090   TD

Engraver: Bald, Adams & Co. / Bald, Cousland & Co. *Comments:* H-Unlisted, Coulter-Unlisted. Proof. May 1st, 1855.
Rarity: URS-3
Proof $1,500

$100 • W-VT-410-100-G090a

Left: C / Hunter warming hands by fire. *Center:* Two Indians and Indian woman on hill viewing train and city. *Bottom center:* Ducks. *Right:* 100 / Portrait of Henry Clay. *Overprint:* Red. *Engraver:* Bald, Adams & Co. / Bald, Cousland & Co. *Comments:* H-VT-125-G18a, Coulter-15. Similar to W-VT-410-100-G090. May 1st, 1855.
Rarity: URS-3
Proof $1,500

Uncut Sheets

$1-$2-$3-$5 • W-VT-410-001.002.003.005-US010

Vignette(s): *($1)* Portrait of Andrew Jackson / Indian council / Portrait of Andrew Jackson. *($2)* Two girls with sheaf / Indian paddling canoe, Three children / Dog / Portrait of Andrew Jackson. *($3)* Farmer on horseback / Cattle and sheep lying down / Bull and ram standing / Girl shading her eyes. *($5)* Train / Horses running / Portrait of Andrew Jackson. *Engraver:* Bald, Adams & Co. / Bald, Cousland & Co. *Comments:* All unlisted in Haxby. May 1st, 1855.
Rarity: URS-3
Proof $1,250

$1-$2-$3-$5 • W-VT-410-001.002.003.005-US010a

Overprint(s): Red. *Engraver:* Bald, Adams & Co. / Bald, Cousland & Co. *Comments:* H-VT-125-G2a, G6a, G8a, G10a. Similar to W-VT-410-001.002.003.005-US010. May 1st, 1855.
Rarity: URS-3
Proof $3,800

$10-$20 • W-VT-410-010.020-US020

Vignette(s): *($10)* Men driving cattle into river / Portrait of George Washington / Boy holding gate open, Boy on horseback driving cow and sheep. *($20)* Indian drawing arrow from quiver / Commerce / Shield / Indian / Man chopping tree / Portrait of S. Houston. *Engraver:* Bald, Adams & Co. / Bald, Cousland & Co. *Comments:* H-VT-125-G12a, G14a. May 1st, 1855.

Rarity: URS-3
Proof $1,800

$10-$20-$50-$100 •
W-VT-410-010.020.050.100-US030

Vignette(s): *($10)* Men driving cattle into river / Portrait of George Washington / Boy holding gate open, Boy on horseback driving cow and sheep. *($20)* Indian drawing arrow from quiver / Commerce / Shield / Indian / Man chopping tree / Portrait of S. Houston. *($50)* Eagle / Three cows lying down, one standing, one drinking / Portrait of Daniel Webster. *($100)* Hunter warming hands by fire / Three Indians on hill viewing train and city / Ducks / Portrait of Henry Clay. *Overprint(s):* None. *Engraver:* Bald, Adams & Co. / Bald, Cousland & Co. *Comments:* Similar to H-VT-125-G12a, G14a, G16a, G18a. May 1st, 1855.

Rarity: URS-3
Proof $3,600

$50-$100 • W-VT-410-050.100-US040

Vignette(s): *($50)* Eagle / Three cows lying down, one standing, one drinking / Portrait of Daniel Webster. *($100)* Hunter warming hands by fire / Three Indians on hill viewing train and city / Ducks / Portrait of Henry Clay. *Engraver:* Bald, Adams & Co. / Bald, Cousland & Co. *Comments:* H-VT-125-G16a, G18a. May 1st, 1855.

Rarity: URS-3
Proof $1,800

Non-Valid Issues

$2 • W-VT-410-002-A010

Left: 2 / Portrait of Benjamin Franklin / TWO. *Center:* Train. *Bottom center:* U.S. shield. *Right:* 2 / Minerva seated / 2 / TWO. *Overprint:* TWO. *Engraver:* Rawdon, Wright, Hatch & Edson. *Comments:* H-VT-125-A5, Coulter-4. Altered from $2 Farmers and Merchants Bank of Memphis, Tennessee series. 1850s.

Rarity: *None known*

$5 • W-VT-410-005-R010

Comments: H-Unlisted, Coulter-7. Raised from $1. 1850s.

Rarity: *None known*

$5 • W-VT-410-005-A020

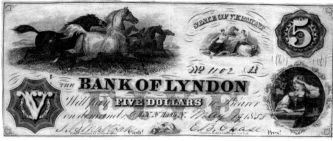

CC

Overprint: Red FIVE. *Engraver:* Bald, Cousland & Co. / Baldwin, Bald & Cousland. *Comments:* H-VT-125-A10, Coulter-8. Altered from $5 Bank of Morgan, Morgan, Georgia. 18__. 1850s.

Rarity: URS-5
F $150; **VF** $250

$5 • W-VT-410-005-A030

CJF

Engraver: Draper, Toppan, Longacre & Co. *Comments:* H-VT-125-A15, Coulter-9. Altered from $5 Bank of Saline, Saline, Michigan. 18__. 1850s.

Rarity: URS-3
VG $225

$10 • W-VT-410-010-R020

Engraver: Bald, Adams & Co. / Bald, Cousland & Co. *Comments:* H-VT-125-R5, Coulter-11. Raised from W-VT-410-001-G010a. 18__. 1850s.

Rarity: *None known*

$10 • W-VT-410-010-R030

Comments: H-Unlisted, Coulter-12. Raised from W-VT-410-001-G020a. 1850s.

Rarity: *None known*

MANCHESTER, VERMONT

Manchester was chartered in 1761 and named after Robert Montagu, 3rd Duke of Manchester, England. It was settled in 1764 and the town structured in 1784. The area was lush with good grazing land, and by 1839 there were 6,000 sheep pasturing in the fields. Iron mines and marble quarries were in operation, and mills and lumber companies added to industry. The Orvis Company, which was founded in 1856 for the making of fishing equipment, still exists today.

Bank of Manchester
1832–1848
W-VT-420

History: The Bank of Manchester was chartered on November 7, 1832, with $100,000 in authorized capital, $70,000 of which was soon paid in. The office was located in the home of its first cashier, Bernice Raymond.

The Suffolk Bank, Boston, reported in January 1838 that bills of this bank would not be received. In August 1845, the capital of the bank was $70,000, and circulation was $63,750. The bank was in precarious condition, and unfavorable reports were circulated as losses were sustained.

In 1847 it was voted to bring the affairs of the bank to an end, and it closed on January 1, 1848. Its affairs were finalized in January 1849 with an outstanding circulation of $81,933.

Numismatic Commentary: Years ago only the Proof issues by Durand & Co. were seen in the marketplace. Some notes engraved by Rawdon, Clark & Co appeared in later times. All issues are very scarce. No $100 bills were issued by this bank; existing examples are spurious.[9]

Remaining in the American Bank Note Co. archives as of 2003 was a $1-$1.50-$2-$3 face plate, a $1-$1-$2-$3 face plate, a $20-$50 face plate, a $5-$5-$5-$10 face plate, a $20 face plate, a $10-$5-$5-$5 face plate, a $1-$1-$2-$3 back plate, a $1-$1-$2-$3 face plate, and a $5-$5-$5-$10 tint plate.

VALID ISSUES

$1 • W-VT-420-001-G010
TD

Back: Plain. **Engraver:** Durand & Co. **Comments:** H-VT-135-G4, Coulter-1. 18___. 1830s–1840s.
Rarity: URS-3
Proof $1,500

$1 • W-VT-420-001-G010a
Left: Portrait of child. **Center:** 1 / Ceres with sickle / 1. **Right:** Portrait of child. **Back:** Red. **Engraver:** Durand & Co. **Comments:** H-VT-135-G4a. Similar to W-VT-420-001-G010. 18___. 1840s.
Rarity: *None known*

$1.50 • W-VT-420-001.50-G020
Engraver: Rawdon, Clark & Co. **Comments:** H-Unlisted. 18___. 1830s–1840s.
Rarity: *None known*

$2 • W-VT-420-002-G030
CC

Back: Plain. **Engraver:** Durand & Co. **Comments:** H-VT-135-G8, Coulter-2. 18___. 1830s–1840s.
Rarity: URS-3
VF $600

$2 • W-VT-420-002-G030a
Left: Woman talking to seated child. **Center:** 2 / Old man and two cherubs riding eagle / 2. **Bottom center:** Die. **Back:** Red. **Engraver:** Durand & Co. **Comments:** H-VT-135-G8a. Similar to W-VT-420-002-G030. 18___. 1840s.
Rarity: *None known*

$2 • W-VT-420-002-G040
CC

Engraver: Rawdon, Clark & Co. **Comments:** H-Unlisted. 18___. 1830s.
Rarity: URS-3
VF $1,400

$3 • W-VT-420-003-G050
CC

Back: Plain. **Engraver:** Durand & Co. **Comments:** H-VT-135-G12, Coulter-3. 18___. 1830s–1840s.
Rarity: URS-3
Proof $750

$3 • W-VT-420-003-G050a
Left: 3 on die. **Center:** 3 / Woman holding shield with eagle / 3. **Right:** 3 on die. **Back:** Red. **Engraver:** Durand & Co. **Comments:** H-VT-135-G12a. Similar to W-VT-420-003-G050. 18___. 1840s.
Rarity: *None known*

$5 • W-VT-420-005-G060

Comments: H-VT-135-G14, Coulter-5. No description available. 18__. 1830s–1840s.

Rarity: *None known*

$10 • W-VT-420-010-G070   SBG

Engraver: Rawdon, Clark & Co. *Comments:* H-VT-135-G16, Coulter-7. 18__. 1830s–1840s.

Rarity: URS-2
F $3,200

$20 • W-VT-420-020-G080

Comments: H-VT-135-G20, Coulter-9. No description available. 18__. 1830s–1840s.

Rarity: *None known*

$50 • W-VT-420-050-G090

Engraver: Rawdon, Clark & Hatch. *Comments:* H-VT-135-G24, Coulter-10. No description available. 18__. 1830s–1840s.

Rarity: *None known*

Uncut Sheets

$1-$1-$2-$3 • W-VT-420-001.001.002.003-US010

Vignette(s): ($1) Portrait of child / Woman with sickle / Portrait of child. *($1)* Portrait of child / Woman with sickle / Portrait of child. *($2)* Woman talking to seated child / Old man and two cherubs riding eagle. *($3)* Woman holding shield with eagle. *Engraver:* Durand & Co. *Comments:* H-VT-135-G4, G4, G8, G12. 18__. 1840s.

Rarity: URS-2
Proof $2,600

Non-Valid Issues

$3 • W-VT-420-003-C050

Engraver: Durand & Co. *Comments:* H-VT-135-C12. Counterfeit of W-VT-420-003-G050 series. 18__. 1840s.

Rarity: *None known*

$3 • W-VT-420-003-R010

Engraver: Durand & Co. *Comments:* H-VT-135-R5, Coulter-4. Raised from W-VT-420-001-G010 series. 18__. 1830s–1840s.

Rarity: *None known*

$5 • W-VT-420-005-R020

Engraver: Durand & Co. *Comments:* H-VT-135-R10, Coulter-6. Raised from W-VT-420-001-G010a. 18__. 1830s–1840s.

Rarity: *None known*

$5 • W-VT-420-005-N010

Center: Cattle. *Comments:* H-VT-135-N5. 18__. 1840s.

Rarity: *None known*

$10 • W-VT-420-010-R030

Engraver: Durand & Co. *Comments:* H-VT-135-R15, Coulter-8. Raised from W-VT-420-002-G030 series. 18__. 1830s–1840s.

Rarity: *None known*

$50 • W-VT-420-050-S010   CC

Engraver: Durand & Co. *Comments:* H-VT-135-S5, Coulter-11. 18__. 1840s.

Rarity: URS-3
VF $500

$100 • W-VT-420-100-S020

Center: Woman holding shield and flag / Eagle. *Engraver:* Durand & Co. *Comments:* H-VT-135-S10, Coulter-12. This bank issued no $100 bills. 18__. 1830s–1840s.

Rarity: URS-2

$1,000 • W-VT-420-1000-N020

Comments: H-VT-135-N10. No description available. 18__. 1830s–1840s.

Rarity: *None known*

Battenkill Bank
1848–1865
W-VT-430

History: The Battenkill Bank was organized in 1847 with an authorized capital of $50,000. It was the successor to the Bank of Manchester, W-VT-420. In May 1857, capital was $75,000. In August 1859, circulation was $56,549. Its circulation at that time was $56,549, specie was $2,719, and real estate was valued at $1,000. By 1860 its capital was $50,000 again, but by 1861 it was back up to $75,000. Circulation was $68,034 in 1862. The bank's charter was extended to January 1, 1885, by an act approved on November 26, 1862.

The business of the Battenkill Bank of Manchester was succeeded by the Battenkill National Bank on June 26, 1865. The bank then published a notice that it would not be liable to redeem its notes after December 13, 1867. The *Report of the Bank Commissioner* showed that this bank had no outstanding circulation as of July 1, 1867, an improbable situation.

Numismatic Commentary: Notes of this bank are only slightly less scarce than those of the previous bank and are probably redeemed bills that were not destroyed. The stone bank building still stands in Manchester next to the Equinox Hotel.

VALID ISSUES

$1 • W-VT-430-001-G010

CJF

Engraver: Danforth & Hufty. **Comments:** H-VT-130-G2, Coulter-13. January 1st, 1848.

Rarity: URS-3

F $900

$1 • W-VT-430-001-G010a

CJF

Overprint: Red ONE. **Engraver:** Danforth & Hufty. **Comments:** H-Unlisted. Similar to W-VT-430-001-G010. January 1st, 1848.

Rarity: URS-4

F $900

$1 • W-VT-430-001-G010b

Left: ONE / Portrait of George Washington / 1. **Center:** Seated milkmaid and cows / 1 bearing ONE. **Right:** 1 / Portrait of Martha Washington / ONE. **Overprint:** Green ONE. **Engraver:** Danforth & Hufty. **Comments:** H-VT-130-G2b. Similar to W-VT-430-001-G010. January 1st, 1848.

Rarity: None known

$1 • W-VT-430-001-G010c

CC

Overprint: Green ONE. **Engraver:** Danforth & Hufty / ABNCo. monogram. **Comments:** H-VT-130-G2c. Similar to W-VT-430-001-G010 but with additional engraver imprint. January 1st, 1848.

Rarity: URS-3

F $750

$2 • W-VT-430-002-G020

Left: 2 / State arms / TWO. **Center:** Two stonecutters at work / 2. **Right:** TWO / Portrait of Benjamin Franklin / TWO on medallion head. **Engraver:** Danforth & Hufty. **Comments:** H-VT-130-G4, Coulter-16. January 1st, 1848.

Rarity: URS-3

Proof $800

$2 • W-VT-430-002-G020a

Overprint: Green TWO. **Engraver:** Danforth & Hufty. **Comments:** H-VT-130-G4b. Similar to W-VT-430-002-G020. January 1st, 1848.

Rarity: None known

$2 • W-VT-430-002-G020b

CC

Overprint: Green TWO. **Engraver:** Danforth & Hufty / ABNCo. monogram. **Comments:** H-Unlisted. Similar to W-VT-430-002-G020 but with additional engraver imprint. January 1st, 1848.

Rarity: URS-2

F $1,250

$5 • W-VT-430-005-G030

Left: 5 / State arms / FIVE. **Center:** Portrait of DeWitt Clinton / 5 bearing FIVE / Portrait of Abby Hutchinson. **Right:** 5 / Medallion head / 5. **Engraver:** Danforth & Hufty. **Comments:** H-VT-130-G6, Coulter-20. January 1st, 1848.

Rarity: None known

$5 • W-VT-430-005-G030a

CC

Overprint: Red V / V. **Engraver:** Danforth & Hufty. **Comments:** H-VT-130-G6a. Similar to W-VT-430-005-G030. January 1st, 1848.

Rarity: URS-3

VF $800

$5 • W-VT-430-005-G030b

CJF

Overprint: Green FIVE. **Engraver:** Danforth & Hufty / ABNCo. monogram. **Comments:** H-VT-130-G6c. Similar to W-VT-430-005-G030 but with additional engraver imprint. January 1st, 1848.

Rarity: URS-3

F $1,250

$5 • W-VT-430-005-G040

Left: FIVE / State arms / FIVE. **Center:** Woman, Farmer seated in V, Woman. **Right:** 5 / Medallion head. **Comments:** H-VT-130-G8, Coulter-21. 18__. 1850s.

Rarity: *None known*

$10 • W-VT-430-010-G050

Left: 10 / State arms / TEN. **Center:** "Presentation of the Declaration of Independence" / X bearing portrait of George Washington. **Right:** X / Female portrait. **Engraver:** Danforth & Hufty. **Comments:** H-VT-130-G10, Coulter-24. January 1st, 1848.

Rarity: *None known*

$10 • W-VT-430-010-G050a

CC

Overprint: Red TEN. **Engraver:** Danforth & Hufty. **Comments:** H-Unlisted, Coulter-Unlisted. Similar to W-VT-430-010-G050. January 1st, 1848.

Rarity: URS-2

F $2,500

$20 • W-VT-430-020-G060

Left: TWENTY / State arms / TWENTY. **Center:** 20 / Two men loading hay on wagon drawn by oxen. **Right:** 20 / Liberty with eagle. **Engraver:** Unverified, but likely Danforth & Hufty. **Comments:** H-VT-130-G12, Coulter-26. January 1st, 1848.

Rarity: *None known*

$50 • W-VT-430-050-G070

Left: 50 / State arms / 50. **Center:** Man on horseback, Dog, sheep, and mill. **Bottom center:** Female portrait. **Right:** 50 / Liberty / FIFTY. **Engraver:** Unverified, but likely Danforth & Hufty. **Comments:** H-VT-130-G14, Coulter-27. January 1st, 1848.

Rarity: *None known*

Uncut Sheets

$5-$10 • W-VT-430-005.010-US010

Vignette(s): **($5)** State arms / Woman, Farmer seated in V, Woman / Medallion head. **($10)** State arms / "Presentation of the Declaration of Independence" / X bearing portrait of George Washington / Female portrait. **Engraver:** Danforth & Hufty. **Comments:** H-VT-130-G8, G10. January 1st, 1848.

Rarity: URS-2

Proof $2,500

$20-$50 • W-VT-430-020.050-US020

Vignette(s): **($20)** State arms / Two men loading hay on wagon drawn by oxen / Liberty with eagle. **($50)** State arms / Man on horseback, Dog, sheep, and mill / Female portrait / Liberty. **Engraver:** Danforth & Hufty. **Comments:** H-VT-130-G12, G14. January 1st, 1848.

Rarity: URS-2

Proof $4,000

Non-Valid Issues

$1 • W-VT-430-001-N010

Center: Farmers sitting, Woman / 1. **Comments:** H-Unlisted, Coulter-15. 1850s.

Rarity: *None known*

$1 • W-VT-430-001-A010

TD

Engraver: Danforth, Wright & Co. **Comments:** H-VT-130-A5, Coulter-14. Altered from $1 Commercial Bank of New Jersey, Perth Amboy, New Jersey series. July 10th, 1856.

Rarity: URS-7

F $100

$2 • W-VT-430-002-A020

Left: TWO / Woman feeding chickens. **Center:** Steamship and ship under full sail. **Right:** 2 / Indian woman. **Engraver:** Danforth, Wright & Co. **Comments:** H-VT-130-A10, Coulter-17. Altered from $2 Commercial Bank of New Jersey, Perth Amboy, New Jersey series. July 10, 1856.

Rarity: *None known*

$3 • **W-VT-430-003-S010**

CJF

Engraver: Danforth & Hufty. *Comments:* H-VT-130-S5, Coulter-19. The bank issued no $3 bills. March 1st, 1848.

Rarity: URS-8

VG $100

$3 • **W-VT-430-003-A030**

Left: Portrait of George Washington. *Center:* Woman, Bale of goods. *Right:* Three men. *Overprint:* THREE. *Engraver:* Rawdon, Wright, Hatch & Edson. *Comments:* H-VT-130-A15, Coulter-18. Altered from $3 Farmers and Merchants Bank of Memphis, Memphis, Tennessee series. 1850s.

Rarity: URS-7

F $100

$5 • **W-VT-430-005-A040**

Left: FIVE vertically. *Center:* 5 / Neptune and woman in shell / 5. *Right:* V / Canal scene / V. *Engraver:* Rawdon, Wright & Hatch. *Comments:* H-VT-130-A20, Coulter-22. Altered from $5 Commercial Bank of Millington, Millington, Maryland. 18__. 1850s.

Rarity: URS-5

VF $225

$5 • **W-VT-430-005-A050**

Left: 5 / FIVE / FIVE. *Center:* Hunter, Indian woman, cherubs, and five gold dollars. *Right:* 5 / Female portrait / FIVE. *Overprint:* FIVE. *Engraver:* Rawdon, Wright, Hatch & Edson. *Comments:* H-VT-130-A25, Coulter-23. Altered from $5 Farmers & Merchants Bank of Memphis, Memphis, Tennessee series. 1850s.

Rarity: *None known*

$10 • **W-VT-430-010-S020**

CJF

Engraver: Durand, Perkins & Co. *Comments:* H-VT-130-S10, Coulter-25. 18__. 1840s.

Rarity: URS-4

F $200

MIDDLEBURY, VERMONT

On November 2, 1761, Middlebury was chartered and named after its location, which lay between Salisbury and New Haven. The first settlers arrived in 1766. The Revolutionary War saw most of the town burned during Carleton's Raid in November 1778, but by 1783 the settlers had returned to build homes and establish farms on land cleared of forests. Grains and hay became principal crops, and industries including a cotton factory, a sawmill, a gristmill, a pail factory, a paper mill, a woolen factory, and an iron foundry were in operation. Lumber became a very important industry in Middlebury, and the opening of the canal to Whitehall developed this dramatically. Marble and limestone was manufactured into gravestones, tables, jambs, mantels, hearths, windows, door caps, sills, side boards, sinks, and other pieces of furniture. They were transported as far as Montreal, Quebec, and Georgia.

By 1830 Middlebury had become the second-largest town in Vermont, and one of the country's most esteemed liberal arts colleges, Middlebury College, was founded here.

Bank of Middlebury
1831–1865
W-VT-440

History: The Bank of Middlebury was chartered on November 9, 1831. It was authorized with $100,000 in capital, and $60,000 was soon paid in.

Circulation in 1834 was $120,653. 1843 saw the capital at $60,000, circulation at $54,633, and specie at $3,585.34. Figures for 1851 included: capital $75,000; circulation $112,202; other debts due $19,171. By 1857 the capital was $100,500, bills in circulation were $115,468, specie was $4,562, and real estate was valued at $3,000. In July 1859, circulation was $115,468; in July 1862, the same was $184,199. With some up and downs, the bank prospered over the years.

In 1865 the business of the Bank of Middlebury was succeeded by the National Bank of Middlebury. As of July 1, 1867, the outstanding circulation of the Bank of Middlebury was $1,769, redemption of which was guaranteed by the national bank.

Numismatic Commentary: Early issues of this bank were engraved by Rawdon, Clark & Co. This engraving company was able to service many of the Vermont banks expediently, as their plant was in Albany, New York, not far away. All issues are very scarce and probably hard to locate. Some bills of the Southern Bank of Georgia, Bainbridge, Georgia, were altered to the Bank of Middlebury.[10]

VALID ISSUES

$1 • **W-VT-440-001-G010**

CC

Engraver: Rawdon, Clark & Co. *Comments:* H-VT-140-G2, Coulter-1. 18__. 1830s–1860s.

Rarity: URS-3

F $750

$1 • W-VT-440-001-G010a

Left: 1 / Portrait of George Washington / 1. *Center:* 1 / Two men, Cattle and sheep / 1. *Right:* 1 / Horse's head / 1. *Engraver:* Rawdon, Clark & Co. / ABNCo. monogram. *Comments:* H-VT-140-G2a. Similar to W-VT-440-001-G010 but with additional engraver imprint. 18__. 1850s–1860s.

Rarity: *None known*

$2 • W-VT-440-002-G020   CJF

Engraver: Rawdon, Clark & Co. *Comments:* H-VT-140-G4, Coulter-2. 18__. 1830s–1860s.

Rarity: URS-2
F $1,250

$2 • W-VT-440-002-G020a

Left: 2 / Two men, Cattle and sheep / 2. *Center:* TWO / Six farmers reaping and binding / TWO. *Right:* 2 / Three cherubs / 2. *Engraver:* Rawdon, Clark & Co. / ABNCo. monogram. *Comments:* H-VT-140-G4a. Similar to W-VT-440-002-G020 but with additional engraver imprint. 18__. 1850s–1860s.

Rarity: *None known*

$3 • W-VT-440-003-G030

Left: 3 / Man and woman with hands clasped / 3. *Center:* Woman with arm resting on wheel. *Right:* 3 / Herd of cattle and sheep / 3. *Engraver:* Rawdon, Clark & Co. *Comments:* H-VT-140-G6, Coulter-5. 18__. 1830s–1850s.

Rarity: *None known*

$3 • W-VT-440-003-G030a

Engraver: Rawdon, Clark & Co. / ABNCo. monogram. *Comments:* H-VT-140-G6a. Similar to W-VT-440-003-G030 but with additional engraver imprint. 18__. 1850s–1860s.

Rarity: URS-4
VF $500

$5 • W-VT-440-005-G040

Left: 5 / Farmers and cattle / 5. *Center:* Liberty and shield. *Right:* Woman leaning on urn, Angel with trumpet / 5. *Engraver:* Rawdon, Clark & Co. *Comments:* H-VT-140-G8, Coulter-6. 18__. 1830s–1850s.

Rarity: *None known*

$5 • W-VT-440-005-G040a

Engraver: Rawdon, Clark & Co. / ABNCo. monogram. *Comments:* H-VT-140-G8a. Similar to W-VT-440-005-G040 but with additional engraver imprint. 18__. 1850s–1860s.

Rarity: *None known*

$10 • W-VT-440-010-G050

Left: TEN / Ten gold coins / TEN. *Center:* Blacksmith and two women. *Bottom center:* Portrait of George Washington. *Right:* Portrait of cherub / X / Portrait of cherub. *Engraver:* Rawdon, Clark & Co. *Comments:* H-VT-140-G10, Coulter-9. 18__. 1830s–1850s.

Rarity: *None known*

$10 • W-VT-440-010-G050a

Engraver: Rawdon, Clark & Co. / ABNCo. monogram. *Comments:* H-VT-140-G10a. Similar to W-VT-440-010-G050 but with additional engraver imprint. 18__. 1850s–1860s.

Rarity: *None known*

$20 • W-VT-440-020-G060

Left: 20 / Portrait of George Washington / 20. *Center:* Man and woman with hands clasped, Sheaf of wheat, Canal and reapers. *Bottom center:* Female portrait. *Right:* TWENTY vertically. *Comments:* H-VT-140-G12, Coulter-12. 18__. 1860s.

Rarity: *None known*

$50 • W-VT-440-050-G070

Left: 50 / Justice / 50. *Center:* 50 / Man on horseback / 50. *Right:* FIFTY vertically. *Comments:* H-VT-140-G14, Coulter-13. 18__. 1860s.

Rarity: *None known*

$100 • W-VT-440-100-G080   CC

Engraver: Toppan, Carpenter & Co. *Comments:* H-VT-140-G16, Coulter-14. 18__. 1840s–1860s.

Rarity: URS-2
Proof $2,500

Non-Valid Issues

$2 • W-VT-440-002-N010

Left: Medallion head. *Center:* Two men and horses plowing. *Right:* Medallion head. *Comments:* H-VT-140-N5, Coulter-4. 1840s–1860s.

Rarity: *None known*

$2 • W-VT-440-002-A010

Left: 2 / Man plowing with horses. *Center:* Farmers reaping, tying, loading grain. *Right:* 2 / Two cherubs. *Tint:* Red-brown 2s and TWO DOLLARS. *Engraver:* Danforth, Wright & Co. *Comments:* H-VT-140-A5, Coulter-3. Altered from $2 Southern Bank of Georgia, Bainbridge, Georgia. March 1, 1858.

Rarity: URS-7
F $125

$5 • W-VT-440-005-N020

Center: Train passing under bridge. *Right:* Portrait of George Washington. *Comments:* H-VT-140-N10, Coulter-7. 1840s–1860s.

Rarity: *None known*

$5 • W-VT-440-005-N030
Left: 5 / 5. *Center:* Men plowing. *Right:* 5 / 5 *Comments:*
H-Unlisted, Coulter-8. 1840s–1860s.
Rarity: *None known*

$10 • W-VT-440-010-N040
Comments: H-Unlisted, Coulter-10. Imitation of W-VT-440-
010-G050. 1840s–1860s.
Rarity: *None known*

$10 • W-VT-440-010-N050
Center: Ship, railroad, and Agriculture. *Comments:* H-VT-140-
N15, Coulter-11. 18__. 1840s.
Rarity: —
VF $495

Middlebury Bank
1840s
W-VT-445

History: A non-existent bank represented only by notes altered
from those of other banks. The notes were intended to pass for
those of the Bank of Middlebury, W-VT-440.

ISSUES
$10 • W-VT-445-010-A010

Comments: H-Unlisted. 18__. 1840s.
Rarity: URS-5
F $200

Vermont State Bank (branch)
1807–1812
W-VT-450

History: The Vermont State Bank branches began issuing
paper money in 1807. In 1812 the records of the Vermont State
Bank were moved to Woodstock. After 1812 many bills of the
various branches remained in circulation. These were redeemed
in later years until the affairs of the bank were wound up in
1845. See the introductory text for general information.

See also listings under Burlington, W-VT-210, Westminster,
W-VT-830, and Woodstock, W-VT-900.

Numismatic Commentary: The Vermont State Bank issued
identical notes for all four branches; there are plenty to satisfy
collector demand. Even though many remainder sheets have been
cut, there are still plenty of signed and dated examples in the marketplace. Most of the available stock are of the PSSP design.

VALID ISSUES
50¢ • W-VT-450-00.50-G010
Left: FIFTY CENTS vertically. *Center:* 50 / Woman. *Right:*
50/100. *Comments:* H-VT-4-G48, Coulter-10. 1806–1808.
Rarity: *None known*

50¢ • W-VT-450-00.50-G020

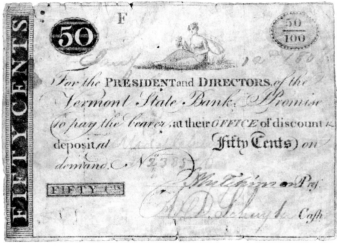

Comments: H-VT-4-G49. 1806–1808.
Rarity: URS-5
VF $150

How to Read the Whitman Numbering System
$1 • W-RI-010-001-G010a

Denomination: Value of the note shown.

W: Whitman number. This number is a sortable code unique
to each bank and note.

RI: Abbreviation for the state under study.

010: Numerical designation specific to each bank.

001: The denomination in dollars.

G010a: G indicates a good or valid note. Other categories are
indicated thus: C (counterfeit); R (raised); S (spurious); N (not-
attributed); A (altered). Numbers are assigned starting with
010, 020, et seq. Terminal letters following the number indicate
variations of a note: a series of different colored overprints,
tints, payees, etc., all on the same design of note. For more
information, see the "How to Use This Book" section at the
front of the volume, page xiv.

50¢ • W-VT-450-00.50-G030

CJF

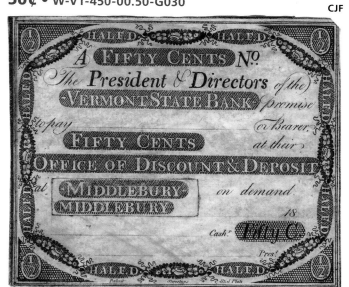

Engraver: PSSP. *Comments:* H-VT-4-G57, Coulter-20. 18__. 1808.

Rarity: URS-6
VF $150; **Unc-Rem** $75

75¢ • W-VT-450-00.75-G040

Left: SEVENTY FIVE vertically. *Center:* Woman reclining / 75 in die. *Comments:* H-VT-4-G58, Coulter-21. 180_. 1806–1808.

Rarity: URS-6
VF $150; **Unc-Rem** $75

75¢ • W-VT-450-00.75-G050

CJF

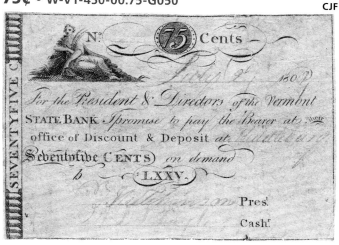

Comments: H-VT-4-G59. 180_. 1806–1808.

Rarity: URS-5
VF $150

75¢ • W-VT-450-00.75-G060

Left: SEVENTY FIVE vertically. *Center:* Woman reclining / 75 in die. *Comments:* H-VT-4-G60. 180_. 1806–1808.

Rarity: URS-6
VF $150

75¢ • W-VT-450-00.75-G070

Left: SEVENTY FIVE vertically. *Center:* Woman reclining / 75 in die. *Comments:* H-VT-4-G61. 180_. 1806–1808.

Rarity: URS-6
VF $150

75¢ • W-VT-450-00.75-G080

CJF

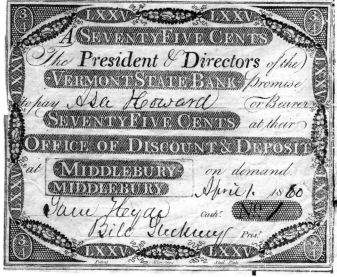

Engraver: PSSP. *Comments:* H-VT-4-G67, Coulter-22. 18__. 1808.

Rarity: URS-6
VF $150; **Unc-Rem** $75

$1 • W-VT-450-001-G090

CJF

Comments: H-VT-4-G68, Coulter-24. 180_. 1806–1808.

Rarity: URS-6
VF $200

$1 • W-VT-450-001-G100

Left: Panel / ONE DOLLAR vertically. *Center:* ONE on three dies / Women flanking shield, Ribbon bearing FREEDOM & UNITY. *Bottom center:* 1 on die. *Right:* 1 on die. *Comments:* H-VT-4-G69. 180_. 1806–1808.

Rarity: URS-6
VF $200

$1 • W-VT-450-001-G110

Center: 1 / 1 / 1 / 1. *Engraver:* PSSP. *Comments:* H-VT-4-G70, Coulter-25. 180_. 1808.

Rarity: *None known*

$1 • W-VT-450-001-G120

Center: ONE. *Engraver:* PSSP. *Comments:* H-VT-4-G71, Coulter-Unlisted. 18__. 1808.

Rarity: URS-6
VF $150; **Unc-Rem** $75

$1.25 • W-VT-450-001.25-G130   CC

Engraver: PSSP. *Comments:* H-VT-4-G72, Coulter-26. 18__.
1808.
Rarity: URS-6
VF $150; **Unc-Rem** $75

$1.50 • W-VT-450-001.50-G140   CJF

Engraver: PSSP. *Comments:* H-VT-4-G73, Coulter-27. 18__.
1808.
Rarity: URS-3
F $750

$1.75 • W-VT-450-001.75-G150   CC

Engraver: PSSP. *Comments:* H-VT-4-G74, Coulter-28. 18__.
1808.
Rarity: URS-8
EF $250; **Unc-Rem** $150

$2 • W-VT-450-002-G160   CC

Comments: H-VT-4-G76, Coulter-29. 180_. 1806–1808.
Rarity: URS-5
VF $200

$2 • W-VT-450-002-G170

Center: 2 / 2 / 2 / 2. *Engraver:* PSSP. *Comments:* H-VT-4-G77.
18__. 1808.
Rarity: *None known*

$2 • W-VT-450-002-G180

Left: TWO vertically. *Engraver:* PSSP. *Comments:* H-VT-4-
G78. 18__. 1808.
Rarity: URS-6
VF $150

$3 • W-VT-450-003-G190   CJF

Comments: H-VT-4-G79, Coulter-30. 18__. 1806–1808.
Rarity: URS-8
F $100

$3 • W-VT-450-003-G200

Left: Panel / THREE vertically. *Center:* 3 on die / Women flanking shield. *Right:* 3 on die. *Comments:* H-VT-4-G80. 18__.
1806–1808.
Rarity: URS-5
VF $200

$3 • W-VT-450-003-G210

Center: 3 / 3 / 3 / 3. *Engraver:* PSSP. *Comments:* H-VT-4-G81.
18__. 1808.
Rarity: *None known*

$3 • W-VT-450-003-G220

Center: THREE. *Engraver:* PSSP. *Comments:* H-VT-4-G82.
18__. 1808.
Rarity: URS-6
VF $150; **Unc-Rem** $75

$5 • W-VT-450-005-G230   CC

Comments: H-VT-4-G83, Coulter-31. 18__. 1806–1808.
Rarity: URS-5
VF $250

$5 • W-VT-450-005-G240

Left: V V V V / VERMONT vertically. *Center:* 5 in die. *Right:*
5 in die. *Engraver:* PSSP. *Comments:* H-VT-4-G84. 18__. 1807
and 1808.
Rarity: *None known*

$5 • W-VT-450-005-G250

CC

Engraver: PSSP. *Comments:* H-VT-4-G85. 18__. 1808.

Rarity: URS-6

VF $150

$10 • W-VT-450-010-G260

Left: TEN vertically. *Center:* 10 / TEN / State arms. *Right:* 10.
Comments: H-VT-4-G86, Coulter-33. 18__. 1806–1808.

Rarity: URS-7

VF $150

$10 • W-VT-450-010-G270

TD

Engraver: PSSP. *Comments:* H-VT-4-G88. 18__. 1808.

Rarity: URS-5

F $300

$20 • W-VT-450-020-G280

Engraver: PSSP. *Comments:* H-VT-4-G91. 18__. 1808.

Rarity: *None known*

Uncut Sheets
$1.75-$1.50-$1.25-50¢-75¢ •
W-VT-450-001.75.001.50.001.25.00.50.00.75-US010

Vignette(s): *($1.75)* 1.75. *($1.50)* 1.50. *($1.25)* 1.25. *(50¢)*
HALF D / 1/2 / 1/2 / 1/2 / 1/2 / HALF D. *(75¢)* 3/4 / 3/4 / 3/4 /
3/4. *Engraver:* PSSP. *Comments:* H-VT-4-G74, G73, G72, G57,
G67. 18__. 1808.

Rarity: URS-3

VF $500; **EF** $750

Non-Valid Issues

50¢ • W-VT-450-00.50-C010

Comments: H-VT-4-C48. Counterfeit of W-VT-450-00.50-
G010. 1808.

Rarity: URS-7

F $50

50¢ • W-VT-450-00.50-C020

Comments: H-VT-4-C49. Counterfeit of W-VT-450-00.50-
G020. 18__. 1808.

Rarity: URS-7

F $50

75¢ • W-VT-450-00.75-C050

Comments: H-VT-4-C59. Counterfeit of W-VT-450-00.75-
G050. 180_. 1808.

Rarity: *None known*

75¢ • W-VT-450-00.75-C060

Comments: H-VT-4-C60. Counterfeit of W-VT-450-00.75-
G060. 180_. 1808.

Rarity: *None known*

$1 • W-VT-450-001-C090

Comments: H-VT-4-C68. Counterfeit of W-VT-450-001-G090.
180_. 1808.

Rarity: URS-6

F $100

$2 • W-VT-450-002-C160

Comments: H-VT-4-C76. Counterfeit of W-VT-450-002-G160.
180_. 1808.

Rarity: URS-6

F $100

$3 • W-VT-450-003-C190

Comments: H-VT-4-C79. Counterfeit of W-VT-450-003-G190.
18__. 1808.

Rarity: URS-6

F $100

$3 • W-VT-450-003-C200

Comments: H-VT-4-C80. Counterfeit of W-VT-450-003-G200.
18__. 1806–1808.

Rarity: URS-6

F $100

$5 • W-VT-450-005-C240

Comments: H-VT-4-C84. Counterfeit of W-VT-450-005-G240.
18__. 1807 and 1808.

Rarity: *None known*

$10 • W-VT-450-010-C260

Comments: H-VT-4-C86. Counterfeit of W-VT-450-010-G260.
18__. 1807.

Rarity: URS-6

F $100

MONTPELIER, VERMONT

On August 14, 1781, the district that became Montpelier was
chartered and granted to Timothy Bigelow and 58 others. In
1787 the first settlement was established and the area was
named after the French city of Montpellier. By 1791 the population was 117. In 1805 the General Assembly voted to elect
Montpelier as the seat of government. It was incorporated as a
town in 1818 and became a local center for trade and govern-
mental processes. Manufacturing became important, particularly once a railroad connection was made in 1849. The same
year, East Montpelier was separated on its own.

The town's location on the Winooski River, which has several falls, allowed for the establishment of mills which produced lumber, flour, sashes, blinds, carriages, sleighs, hats, caps, furniture, and silver plates. There was also an iron foundry. In 1828 the Vermont Mutual Fire Insurance Company established a financial sector in the town. Two decades later the National Life Insurance Company was also established, followed shortly thereafter by the Union Mutual Fire Insurance Company.

Bank of Montpelier
1824–1865
W-VT-460

History: The Bank of Montpelier was chartered in 1824 with a modest authorized capital of $30,000. It went into operation in 1827. In 1830 the capital was the same amount.

On October 29, 1840, the charter was renewed with a capital of $75,000, of which $37,500 was paid in. In August 1845, circulation was $106,118. In 1857 the capital was $100,000. In July 1859, circulation was $72,938. In July 1862, it was $123,763.

The business of the Bank of Montpelier was succeeded by the Montpelier National Bank, chartered on March 3, 1865. It had an outstanding circulation of $3,196 as of July 1, 1867.

Numismatic Commentary: Some notes show an early vignette of the Vermont State House. Other notes have backs with a design in color. Many issues are collectible and can be found in a reasonable amount of time. Many different counterfeit and altered notes are in the marketplace.

VALID ISSUES

$1 • W-VT-460-001-G010   CC

Engraver: PSSP. **Comments:** H-VT-145-G4. 18__. 1820s–1830s.
Rarity: URS-4
F $150

$1 • W-VT-460-001-G010a
Left: ONE / D / ONE vertically. **Center:** Alternating flower garlands and gridwork segments bearing ONE. **Right:** ONE / D / ONE vertically. **Engraver:** PSSP. **Comments:** H-VT-145-G8. Similar to W-VT-460-001-G010. 18__. 1830s–1840s.
Rarity: None known

$1 • W-VT-460-001-G020
Left: ONE / Profile of George Washington, / ONE. **Center:** 1 / Two blacksmiths at anvil in front of forge / 1 / Panel outlining white ONE. **Right:** ONE / Woman / ONE. **Engraver:** New England Bank Note Co. **Comments:** H-VT-145-G10. 18__. 1840s–1850s.
Rarity: None known

$1 • W-VT-460-001-G030   CJF, CC

Engraver: Toppan, Carpenter, Casilear & Co. **Comments:** H-VT-145-G12, Coulter-1. July 1, 185_. 1850s.
Rarity: URS-3
F $750

$2 • W-VT-460-002-G040
Left: 2 / 2. **Center:** Alternating flower garlands and gridwork segments. **Right:** 2 / 2. **Engraver:** PSSP. **Comments:** H-VT-145-G16. 18__. 1820s–1830s.
Rarity: None known

$2 • W-VT-460-002-G040a
Left: Five TWOs vertically. **Right:** Five TWOs vertically. **Engraver:** PSSP. **Comments:** H-VT-145-G20. Similar to W-VT-460-002-G040. 18__. 1820s–1830s.
Rarity: None known

$2 • W-VT-460-002-G050
Left: TWO / Woman / 2. **Center:** 2 / Woman giving drink to one of two seated men / 2 / Panel outlining white TWO. **Right:** TWO / Reaper. **Engraver:** New England Bank Note Co. **Comments:** H-VT-145-G22. 18__. 1840s–1850s.
Rarity: None known

$2 • W-VT-460-002-G060
Left: 2 / Female portrait / Running horse. **Center:** 2. **Right:** Woman holding 2 / TWO. **Engraver:** Toppan, Carpenter, Casilear & Co. **Comments:** H-VT-145-G24, Coulter-3. July 1, 185_. 1850s.
Rarity: None known

$2 • W-VT-460-002-G060a

CC, CC

Engraver: Toppan, Carpenter, Casilear & Co. **Comments:** H-Unlisted, Coulter-Unlisted. Similar to W-VT-460-002-G060 but with different date. Oct.r 1, 1856.

Rarity: URS-3
VG $750

$3 • W-VT-460-003-G070

Left: 3 / 3. **Center:** Alternating flower garlands and gridwork segments. **Right:** 3 / 3. **Engraver:** PSSP. **Comments:** H-VT-145-G28. 18__. 1820s–1830s.

Rarity: *None known*

$3 • W-VT-460-003-G070a

Left: THREE vertically. **Right:** THREE vertically. **Engraver:** PSSP. **Comments:** H-VT-145-G32. Similar to W-VT-460-003-G070. 18__. 1830s–1840s.

Rarity: *None known*

$3 • W-VT-460-003-G080

CJF, CC

Engraver: New England Bank Note Co. **Comments:** H-VT-145-G34. 18__. 1840s–1850s.

Rarity: URS-8
F $100

$3 • W-VT-460-003-G090

Left: Woman seated holding 3 / THREE. **Center:** 3 / Female portrait. **Right:** 3 / Woman leaning against bale, Ship and factory. **Engraver:** Toppan, Carpenter, Casilear & Co. **Comments:** H-VT-145-G36, Coulter-6. July 1, 185_. 1850s.

Rarity: *None known*

$3 • W-VT-460-003-G090a

CC

Engraver: Toppan, Carpenter, Casilear & Co. **Comments:** H-Unlisted, Coulter-Unlisted. Similar to W-VT-460-003-G090 but with different date. Oct.r 1, 1856.

Rarity: URS-3
F $1,000

$5 • W-VT-460-005-G100

Left: Panel bearing VERMONT / 5 / 5 vertically. **Center:** Alternating flower garlands and gridwork segments bearing FIVE. **Right:** 5 / 5 vertically. **Engraver:** PSSP. **Comments:** H-VT-145-G40. 18__. 1820s–1830s.

Rarity: *None known*

$5 • W-VT-460-005-G110

Left: 5 / FIVE / 5. **Center:** V / Eagle on wharf with plow, Cannon and anchor, Ships / V / Panel outlining white FIVE. **Right:** 5 / FIVE / 5. **Engraver:** New England Bank Note Co. **Comments:** H-VT-145-G44. 18__. 1840s–1850s.

Rarity: *None known*

$5 • W-VT-460-005-G120

Left: State House at Montpelier / 5. **Center:** 5 bearing FIVE. **Right:** 5 / Portrait of George Washington. **Engraver:** Toppan, Carpenter, Casilear & Co. **Comments:** H-VT-145-G46, Coulter-9. July 1, 185_. 1850s.

Rarity: URS-2
Proof $1,900

$5 • **W-VT-460-005-G120a**

TD, TD

Engraver: Toppan, Carpenter, Casilear & Co. **Comments:** H-VT-145-G46a. Similar to W-VT-460-005-G120 but with different date. Oct.r 1, 1856.

Rarity: URS-3
F $1,250

$10 • **W-VT-460-010-G130**
Left: Panel bearing VERMONT / 10 / 10 vertically. **Center:** Alternating flower garlands and gridwork segments bearing TEN. **Right:** 10 / 10 vertically. **Engraver:** PSSP. **Comments:** H-VT-145-G50. 18__. 1820s–1830s.
Rarity: *None known*

$10 • **W-VT-460-010-G140**
Left: 10 / X / 10. **Center:** Allegorical man standing by oxen and plow / 10. **Right:** TEN / Woman standing with rudder, Cornucopia. **Engraver:** New England Bank Note Co. **Comments:** H-VT-145-G54. 18__. 1840s–1850s.
Rarity: *None known*

$10 • **W-VT-460-010-G150**
Left: State House at Montpelier / 10. **Center:** X. **Right:** TEN / Ceres. **Engraver:** Toppan, Carpenter, Casilear & Co. **Comments:** H-VT-145-G56, Coulter-12. July 1, 185_. 1850s.
Rarity: *None known*

$20 • **W-VT-460-020-G160**
Left: Panel bearing VERMONT / 20 / 20 vertically. **Center:** Alternating flower garlands and gridwork segments bearing TWENTY. **Right:** 20 / 20 vertically. **Engraver:** PSSP. **Comments:** H-VT-145-G60. 18__. 1820s–1840s.
Rarity: *None known*

$20 • **W-VT-460-020-G170**
Left: 20 / Woman seated with book on lap, opening chest. **Center:** XX / Eagle on rock / XX. **Right:** 20 / Ship in harbor. **Engraver:** New England Bank Note Co. **Comments:** H-VT-145-G64. 18__. 1840s–1850s.
Rarity: *None known*

$20 • **W-VT-460-020-G180**
Left: Female portrait / 20. **Center:** State House at Montpelier. **Bottom center:** Plow. **Right:** 20 / Portrait of Franklin Pierce. **Engraver:** Toppan, Carpenter, Casilear & Co. **Comments:** H-VT-145-G68, Coulter-15. July 1, 185_. 1850s.
Rarity: *None known*

$50 • **W-VT-460-050-G190**
Left: Panel bearing VERMONT / 50 / 50 vertically. **Center:** Alternating flower garlands and gridwork segments bearing FIFTY. **Right:** 50 / 50 vertically. **Engraver:** PSSP. **Comments:** H-VT-145-G72. 18__. 1820s–1840s.
Rarity: *None known*

$50 • **W-VT-460-050-G200**
Left: 50 / Woman with sickle / 50. **Center:** Two women, Train, Factories and ship. **Right:** 50 / Boy gathering corn. **Engraver:** Toppan, Carpenter, Casilear & Co. **Comments:** H-VT-145-G76, Coulter-16. 18__. 1850s.
Rarity: *None known*

$100 • **W-VT-460-100-G210**
Left: Panel bearing VERMONT / 100 / 100 vertically. **Center:** Alternating flower garlands and gridwork segments bearing 100. **Right:** 100 / 100 vertically. **Engraver:** PSSP. **Comments:** H-VT-145-G80. 18__. 1820s–1840s.
Rarity: *None known*

$100 • **W-VT-460-100-G220**
Left: 100 / Sailor seated with flag and hat. **Center:** Woman and cherubs in clouds over city, Vessels. **Right:** 100 / Female portrait / 100. **Engraver:** Toppan, Carpenter, Casilear & Co. **Comments:** H-VT-145-G84, Coulter-17. 18__. 1850s.
Rarity: *None known*

Non-Valid Issues

$1 • **W-VT-460-001-N010**
Comments: H-Unlisted, Coulter-2. Imitation of PSSP. 1820s–1840s.
Rarity: *None known*

$2 • **W-VT-460-002-C040a**
Engraver: PSSP. **Comments:** H-VT-145-C20. Counterfeit of W-VT-460-002-G040a. 18__. 1840s.
Rarity: *None known*

$2 • **W-VT-460-002-N020**

CJF

Comments: H-Unlisted, Coulter-4. Imitation of W-VT-460-002-C040a. Blank space under "Bank of Montpelier." 1840s.
Rarity: URS-7
VG $75

$2 • **W-VT-460-002-N030**

Comments: H-Unlisted, Coulter-5. Imitation of PSSP. 1820s–1840s.

Rarity: *None known*

$3 • **W-VT-460-003-C070a**　　　　　　　TD

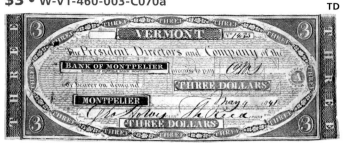

Engraver: PSSP. *Comments:* H-VT-145-C32. Counterfeit of W-VT-460-003-G070a. 18__. 1840s.

Rarity: URS-7
F $100

$3 • **W-VT-460-003-C080**

Engraver: New England Bank Note Co. *Comments:* H-VT-145-C34. Counterfeit of W-VT-460-003-G080. 18__. 1850s.

Rarity: URS-6
F $200

$3 • **W-VT-460-003-N040**

Left: THREE / Farmer with scythe / 3 on THREE. *Center:* 3 / Woman, eagle, beehive / 3. *Right:* THREE / Sailor / THREE on 3. *Comments:* H-Unlisted, Coulter-8. 1840s.

Rarity: *None known*

$3 • **W-VT-460-003-N050**

Comments: H-Unlisted, Coulter-7. Imitation of PSSP. 1820s–1840s.

Rarity: *None known*

$5 • **W-VT-460-005-C110**　　　　　　　CJF

Engraver: New England Bank Note Co. *Comments:* H-VT-145-C44. Counterfeit of W-VT-460-005-G110. 18__. 1850s.

Rarity: URS-7
F $75

$5 • **W-VT-460-005-R010**

Comments: H-Unlisted, Coulter-10. Raised from $1. 1850s.

Rarity: *None known*

$5 • **W-VT-460-005-N060**

Left: 5 / FIVE / 5. *Center:* V / Eagle, anchor, ship / V. *Right:* 5 / FIVE / 5. *Engraver:* New England Bank Note Co. *Comments:* H-Unlisted, Coulter-11. 1850s.

Rarity: *None known*

$10 • **W-VT-460-010-C150**　　　　　　　CC

Engraver: Toppan, Carpenter, Casilear & Co. *Comments:* H-VT-145-C56. Counterfeit of W-VT-460-010-G150. July 1, 185_. 1850s.

Rarity: URS-4
F $450

$10 • **W-VT-460-010-R020**

Comments: H-Unlisted, Coulter-14. Raised from W-VT-460-001-G030. 1850s.

Rarity: *None known*

$10 • **W-VT-460-010-R030**

Comments: H-Unlisted, Coulter-13. Raised from W-VT-460-010-G150. 1850s.

Rarity: *None known*

State Bank of Montpelier
1858–1860
W-VT-470

History: The State Bank of Montpelier was chartered in 1858 with $50,000 in authorized capital. It went into operation on May 5, 1858. In 1859 its circulation was $8,134.

The directors of the bank divided the capital among the stockholders on January 1, 1860. The bank ceased doing business shortly thereafter, having issued only $50,000 in circulation. In September 1861, the state treasurer, bank commissioner, and two officers of this bank burned $49,143 worth of the bank's bills. This left an outstanding circulation of $857.

Numismatic Commentary: Notes of this bank depict the Vermont State House. Some have the image of the renovated and enlarged State House. A quantity of Proof and remainder notes showing the new State House came to the market about 30 years ago and still show up in the marketplace.

Remaining in the American Bank Note Co. archives as of 2003 was a $1-$1-$2-$5 tint plate and a $1-$1-$2-$5 face plate.

Valid Issues

$1 • W-VT-470-001-G010

CJF

Overprint: Red-orange dies bearing white 1s, Bank title, and ONE, ONE. *Engraver:* Toppan, Carpenter & Co. *Comments:* H-VT-150-G2, Coulter-26. May 1st, 1858.

Rarity: URS-4; URS-3
CU $300
Proof $2,000

$2 • W-VT-470-002-G020

CC

Overprint: Red-orange dies bearing white 2s, Bank title, and TWO, 2, TWO. *Engraver:* Toppan, Carpenter & Co. *Comments:* H-VT-150-G4, Coulter-30. May 1st, 1858.

Rarity: URS-3
F $1,400

$5 • W-VT-470-005-G030

BH

Tint: Red-orange dies bearing white 5s, Bank title, and FIVE, FIVE, 5. *Engraver:* Toppan, Carpenter & Co. *Comments:* H-VT-150-G6, Coulter-35. May 1st, 1858.

Rarity: URS-4; URS-3
CU $400
Proof $2,500

Non-Valid Issues

$1 • W-VT-470-001-N010

Center: Woman with grain / Train / Reapers. *Right:* 1 / Portrait of George Washington. *Comments:* H-Unlisted, Coulter-28. 1850s.

Rarity: *None known*

$1 • W-VT-470-001-A010

Left: Two men picking and carrying cotton. *Center:* Volant bearing cornucopia / Dog. *Right:* Indian chief. *Engraver:* Bald, Cousland & Co. / Baldwin, Bald & Cousland. *Comments:* H-Unlisted, Coulter-27. Altered from $2 Bank of Morgan, Morgan, Georgia. 1850s.

Rarity: URS-6
F $125

$1 • W-VT-470-001-A020

CJF

Overprint: Red ONE. *Engraver:* Bald, Cousland & Co. / Baldwin, Bald & Cousland. *Comments:* H-VT-150-A5, Coulter-29. Altered from $1 Bank of Morgan, Morgan, Georgia. 18__. 1850s.

Rarity: URS-4
F $150

$2 • W-VT-470-002-A030

Left: 2 / Two men picking and carrying cotton. *Center:* Dog / Volant bearing cornucopia, Ship / TWO. *Right:* 2 / Indian chief. *Engraver:* Bald, Cousland & Co. / Baldwin, Bald & Cousland. *Comments:* H-Unlisted, Coulter-31. Altered from $2 Bank of Morgan, Morgan, Georgia. 18__. 1850s.

Rarity: URS-4
F $150

$2 • W-VT-470-002-A030a

Overprint: Red TWO. *Engraver:* Bald, Cousland & Co. / Baldwin, Bald & Cousland. *Comments:* H-VT-150-A10, Coulter-33. Similar to W-VT-470-002-A030. Altered from $2 Bank of Morgan, Morgan, Georgia. 18__. 1850s.

Rarity: URS-5
F $100

$2 • W-VT-470-002-A040

SI

Engraver: Danforth, Wright & Co. *Comments:* H-VT-150-A15, Coulter-32. Altered from $2 Bank of Washtenaw, Washtenaw, Michigan series. 185_. 1850s.

Rarity: URS-4
F $150

$3 • W-VT-470-003-N020

Left: Woman / 3. *Center:* Woman sitting on bank, Shield. *Right:* Woman / 3. *Comments:* H-VT-150-N5, Coulter-34. 1850s.

Rarity: *None known*

$5 • W-VT-470-005-A050
Left: Wild horses. *Right:* 5 / Girl seated. *Overprint:* Red FIVE.
Engraver: Bald, Cousland & Co. / Baldwin, Bald & Cousland.
Comments: H-VT-150-A20, Coulter-36. Altered from $5 Bank
of Morgan, Morgan, Georgia. 18__. 1850s.
Rarity: URS-4
F $150

$5 • W-VT-470-005-A060
Left: Portrait of Henry Clay / V. *Center:* Farmer feeding hogs.
Bottom center: Dog lying down. *Right:* 5 / Man with basket of
corn. *Overprint:* Red FIVE. *Engraver:* Wellstood, Hay & Whit-
ing. *Comments:* H-VT-150-A25, Coulter-37. Altered from $5
Thames Bank, Laurel, Indiana. 1850s.
Rarity: *None known*

$5 • W-VT-470-005-A070

CJF

Tint: Red panel. *Engraver:* Danforth, Wright & Co. *Com-
ments:* H-VT-150-A30, Coulter-38. Altered from $5 Bank of
Washtenaw, Washtenaw, Michigan. May 1st, 1858.
Rarity: URS-6
VG $75; **F** $100

$5 • W-VT-470-005-A080
Left: Medallion panel with FIVE / Medallion head / FIVE.
Center: 5 / Liberty and Ceres flanking shield surmounted by
horse's head / 5 / Medallion FIVE. *Bottom center:* Hay wagon.
Right: Justice facing eagle with portrait of George Washington
/ Portrait of Benjamin Franklin. *Engraver:* Danforth, Wright &
Co. *Comments:* H-VT-150-A35. Altered from $10 Brownville
Bank & Land Co., Omaha City, Nebraska series. Sept. 1, 1857.
Rarity: *None known*

$10 • W-VT-470-010-A090
Left: X / TEN. *Center:* Man on horseback overseeing harvest.
Right: Liberty / 10. *Engraver:* Danforth, Wright & Co. *Com-
ments:* H-VT-150-A40, Coulter-39. Altered from $10 Brownville
Bank & Land Co., Omaha City, Nebraska series. Sept. 1, 1857.
Rarity: *None known*

Vermont Bank
CIRCA 1849–1865
W-VT-480

History: The Vermont Bank was chartered in 1848 with an
authorized capital of $100,000. By 1851 the $100,000 capital
of the bank was all paid in. By 1857 it had dropped to $50,000,
bills in circulation were $99,149, and specie was $9,305. In
December 1860, the capital was back up to $100,000. Circula-
tion in 1862 was $188,030.

After December 22, 1864, the business of the Vermont Bank
was succeeded by the First National Bank of Montpelier. It had
an outstanding circulation of $2,852 as of July 1, 1867.

Numismatic Commentary: Pastoral scenes paint an idyllic
image of community farming on many of these notes. This
bank's notes are very scarce with usually only the lower denominations coming to market.

VALID ISSUES
$1 • W-VT-480-001-G010
Left: ONE / State arms / ONE. *Center:* Three cows, Man plow-
ing, Train. *Right:* 1 / Portrait of girl / ONE. *Engraver:* Rawdon,
Wright, Hatch & Edson / New England Bank Note Co. *Com-
ments:* H-VT-155-G2, Coulter-44. 18__. 1849–1850s.
Rarity: *None known*

$1 • W-VT-480-001-G010a

CC

Overprint: Red ONE. *Engraver:* Rawdon, Wright, Hatch &
Edson / New England Bank Note Co. / ABNCo. monogram.
Comments: H-Unlisted. Similar to W-VT-480-001-G010 but
with different date and additional engraver imprint. October 1st,
1859.
Rarity: URS-3
F $750

$1 • W-VT-480-001-G010b
Overprint: Green ONE. *Engraver:* Rawdon, Wright, Hatch &
Edson / New England Bank Note Co. / ABNCo. monogram.
Comments: H-VT-155-G2c. Similar to W-VT-480-001-G010
but with different date and additional engraver imprint. October
1st, 1859.
Rarity: URS-7
VG $425; **VF** $550

$2 • W-VT-480-002-G020

CC

Engraver: Rawdon, Wright, Hatch & Edson / New England
Bank Note Co. *Comments:* H-VT-155-G4, Coulter-45. 18__.
1849–1850s.
Rarity: URS-3
F $750

$2 • W-VT-480-002-G020a

CC

Overprint: Red TWO. *Engraver:* Rawdon, Wright, Hatch & Edson / New England Bank Note Co. / ABNCo. monogram. *Comments:* H-Unlisted. Similar to W-VT-480-002-G020 but with different date and additional engraver imprint. October 1st, 1859.

Rarity: URS-3
F $1,000

$2 • W-VT-480-002-G020b

Left: 2 / Portrait of Benjamin Franklin / TWO. *Center:* Ceres and Vulcan with rake and scroll, State arms surmounted by stag's head. *Right:* 2 / Portrait of George Washington / TWO. *Overprint:* Green TWO. *Engraver:* Rawdon, Wright, Hatch & Edson / New England Bank Note Co. / ABNCo. monogram. *Comments:* H-VT-155-G4c. Similar to W-VT-480-002-G020 but with different date and additional engraver imprint. October 1st, 1859.

Rarity: *None known*

$3 • W-VT-480-003-G030

CC

Engraver: Rawdon, Wright, Hatch & Edson / New England Bank Note Co. *Comments:* H-VT-155-G6 Coulter-46. 18__. 1849–1850s.

Rarity: URS-3
F $1,000

$3 • W-VT-480-003-G030a

Left: THREE / Train. *Center:* Plow and farmer with rake, State arms, Milkmaid and house. *Right:* 3 / Indian maid with bow and arrows. *Overprint:* Green THREE. *Engraver:* Rawdon, Wright, Hatch & Edson / New England Bank Note Co. / ABNCo. monogram. *Comments:* H-VT-155-G6c. Similar to W-VT-480-003-G030 but with different date and additional engraver imprint. October 1st, 1859.

Rarity: *None known*

$5 • W-VT-480-005-G040

SI

Engraver: Rawdon, Wright, Hatch & Edson / New England Bank Note Co. *Comments:* H-VT-155-G8, Coulter-48. 18__. 1849–1850s.

Rarity: URS-3
F $750

$5 • W-VT-480-005-G040a

Left: 5 / Ceres / FIVE. *Center:* Harvest scene, Men loading hay. *Right:* 5 / Woman, State arms, Woman / FIVE. *Overprint:* Green. *Engraver:* Rawdon, Wright, Hatch & Edson / New England Bank Note Co. / ABNCo. monogram. *Comments:* H-VT-155-G8c. Similar to W-VT-480-005-G040 but with different date and additional engraver imprint. October 1st, 1859.

Rarity: *None known*

$10 • W-VT-480-010-G050

BH

Engraver: Rawdon, Wright, Hatch & Edson / New England Bank Note Co. *Comments:* H-VT-155-G10, Coulter-51. 18__. 1849–1850s.

Rarity: URS-2
F $900

$10 • W-VT-480-010-G050a

Left: 10 / Female portrait / 10. *Center:* Farmer plowing, Village, Train. *Right:* 10 / Woman, State arms, Woman / TEN. *Overprint:* Green. *Engraver:* Rawdon, Wright, Hatch & Edson / New England Bank Note Co. / ABNCo. monogram. *Comments:* H-VT-155-G10c. Similar to W-VT-480-010-G050 but with different date and additional engraver imprint. October 1st, 1859.

Rarity: *None known*

$20 • W-VT-480-020-G060

Left: 20 / Minerva. *Center:* Ceres holding rake seated between 2 and 0. *Bottom center:* XX. *Right:* 20 / Plenty / 20. *Engraver:* Rawdon, Wright, Hatch & Edson. *Comments:* H-VT-155-G12, Coulter-52. 18__. 1850s.

Rarity: *None known*

$50 • W-VT-480-050-G070

Left: 50 / Minerva. *Center:* Ceres and Vulcan seated with rake, Cornucopia. *Bottom center:* 50. *Right:* 50 / Cherub steering sailboat / 50. *Engraver:* Rawdon, Wright, Hatch & Edson. *Comments:* H-VT-155-G14, Coulter-53. 18__. 1850s.

Rarity: *None known*

$100 • W-VT-480-100-G080

Left: 100 / Vulcan seated, Hammer, anvil. *Center:* Spread eagle on tree limb, Train and canal boats. *Bottom center:* 100. *Right:* 100 / Ceres with rake. *Engraver:* Rawdon, Wright, Hatch & Edson. *Comments:* H-VT-155-G16, Coulter-55. 18__. 1850s.

Rarity: *None known*

NON-VALID ISSUES

$3 • W-VT-480-003-A010

Left: 3 / Portrait of Daniel Webster. *Center:* Women flanking shield surmounted by eagle, Factory, steamboat. *Right:* THREE on 3 / Female portrait. *Overprint:* Red THREE. *Engraver:* Rawdon, Wright, Hatch & Edson / New England Bank Note Co. *Comments:* H-VT-155-A5, Coulter-47. Altered from $3 Waubeek Bank, De Soto, Nebraska. 1857.

Rarity: URS-6

F $150

$5 • W-VT-480-005-N010

Center: Train. *Right:* Portrait of George Washington. *Comments:* H-VT-155-N5, Coulter-50. 1850s.

Rarity: *None known*

$5 • W-VT-480-005-A020

Left: Bust of Henry Clay / V. *Center:* Man feeding pigs. *Right:* 5 / Man with basket of corn. *Overprint:* Red FIVE. *Engraver:* Wellstood, Hay & Whiting. *Comments:* H-VT-155-A10, Coulter-49. Altered from Thames Bank, Laurel, Indiana. Aug. 12, 1856.

Rarity: URS-7

F $100

$50 • W-VT-480-050-A030

Left: FIFTY vertically. *Center:* Woman reclining. *Bottom center:* Clasped hands. *Right:* Woman, Shield. *Engraver:* Rawdon, Wright & Hatch. *Comments:* H-VT-155-A15, Coulter-54. Altered from W-VT-025-050-G100. 18__. 1830s–1841.

Rarity: *None known*

$100 • W-VT-480-100-A040

Comments: H-Unlisted, Coulter-56. Altered note with bank location spelled "Montpieler." 1850s.

Rarity: *None known*

NEWBURY, VERMONT

Newbury was originally inhabited by the Pennacook tribe, who called the land Cowassuck. The area was settled by colonists in 1762 and chartered in 1763 to General Jacob Bayley and 74 others. The town lay at the mouth of the Bayley Hazen Military Road, which was started in 1760. Until it was completed, farmers were forced to transport their grain via canoe to Charlestown, New Hampshire, a distance of 60 miles, just to have it ground into flour.

In 1859 the town had a population of 2,984. Two gristmills, a paper mill, and a steam mill for the manufacturing of mackerel kits also existed. The primary industry resided in beef cattle and sheep, which also gave rise to the production of wool and dairy goods. In 1848 the Connecticut & Passumpsic Rivers Railroad opened to Newbury.

See also Wells River, Vermont.

Bank of Newbury
1832–1865
W-VT-490

History: The Bank of Newbury was chartered in 1832 with an authorized capital of $100,000. It began business on February 5, 1833, in the Spring Hotel. Business with the public did not start until May 22. In 1842 the bank voted to destroy its old and damaged bills, an amount totaling $48,287.50, as well as fractional currency that had never been used, an amount of $3,615.57. By August 1845, the bank's capital was $50,000, and its circulation was $114,227. In July of 1862, the same values were $75,000 and $140,781, respectively. On September 27, 1849, another $243,000 worth of bills were destroyed by burning. $228,700 was destroyed the same way in 1856, and in 1857 still another $14,300 followed suit.

On June 24, 1865, the National Bank of Newbury took over the assets of the Bank of Newbury. Redemption of the outstanding circulation was guaranteed by the national bank. As of July 1, 1867, the bank had an outstanding circulation of $5,008.

See also listing under Wells River, W-VT-790.

NEWFANE, VERMONT

Newfane is located west of the Connecticut River and bounded by Townshend, Dummerston, Putney, Brookline, Wardsboro, Dover, and Marlboro.

Newfane was chartered on June 19, 1753, to Abner Sawyer and 65 others. They named it Fane after the 7th Earl of Westmorland, John Fane. Hostilities during the French and Indian War put off settlement of the land, and the charter became void after five years. A new charter was issued in 1761 under the name of New Fane. In 1766 families settled there from Worcester County, Massachusetts. They built a village on a hilltop, but travel in winter proved difficult, and they relocated to the flatlands.

Newfane was originally chartered with 36 square miles. However, in 1820 the northeastern part of town across the West River was annexed to Brookline. Newfane contained good grazing land and streams for water power and mills. In 1859 the industries in town included the manufacturing of leather and linseed oil, flour mills, lumber mills, and a carriage factory.

Bank at Newfane
1854
W-VT-500

History: In 1854 a charter application for the Bank at Newfane was rejected by the state legislature.

Numismatic Commentary: It is possible that Proof notes were made, but no record has been found of such.

NORTHFIELD, VERMONT

Northfield was chartered in 1781. Around that time, a gristmill and sawmill were built there by Elijah Paine. The area was inhabited by 44 residents as early as 1790. Between 1785 and the 1820s, settlers from Connecticut, Massachusetts, and other Vermont towns came to Northfield. Irish immigrants came next, attracted by work on the railroad in the 1840s. Welsh settlers came for work in the slate quarries during the 1850s and 1860s. Stonework was also an attraction.

Four villages make up the whole of Northfield—South Village, home to the Red Mill; Center, which houses Norwich University; Northfield Village, known as the business center of the area; and Slab City, so called because of the saw mills that were established there. Grist mills and potash mills were also in existence.

Charles Paine led a time of prosperity in 1848 for the four villages, building the headquarters of the Vermont Central Railroad in Northfield. Engines and cars were built in the rail yard, providing work and industry for the entire area. However, in 1853 the Vermont Central Railroad went bankrupt on account of over-expansion and mismanagement. Hard times for Northfield followed, as the railroad was to be renamed the Central Vermont Railroad, received by new management, and moved to St. Albans. In 1855 the village of Northfield was incorporated as a town. During the 1870s the slate industry briefly eased Northfield's economic struggles.

Northfield Bank
1853–1865
W-VT-510

History: The Northfield Bank was chartered in 1853 with an authorized capital of $100,000. Figures for 1857 showed capital to be $99,550, bills in circulation were valued at $110,237, and specie totaled $2,974. In July 1859, circulation was $110,237.

In 1860 H.M. Bates, the cashier of the Northfield Bank and earlier the cashier of the State of Vermont, was discovered to have defaulted. He fled the state and was not seen again. He stood in high repute before that time. As such, his defalcation stunned those who knew him.[11]

In 1862 the capital of the bank was reduced by $25,000.[12] By July 1862, circulation was $54,008. The business of the Northfield Bank was succeeded by the Northfield National Bank in 1865. The bank's outstanding circulation as of July 1, 1867, was $2,140, redemption of which was guaranteed by the new national bank until December 20, 1867.

Numismatic Commentary: Some of the more attractive vignettes appear on notes from this bank. One series has a striking red tint covering most of the notes. Some show livestock, railroad trains, canal boats, and the historical vignette "John Eliot Preaching to the Indians." Collectors should be able to acquire an example or two within a few months of searching.

Remaining in the American Bank Note Co. archives as of 2003 was a $20 face plate, a $1-$1-$2-$3 face plate, a $1-$1-$2-$3 tint plate, a $50-$100 face plate, and a $5-$5-$5-$10 face plate.

VALID ISSUES

$1 • W-VT-510-001-G010
Left: 1 / Portrait of Franklin Pierce. *Center:* Drover and farmer looking at cattle. *Right:* 1 / Train. *Overprint:* Red. *Engraver:* Toppan, Carpenter, Casilear & Co. *Comments:* H-VT-160-G2a, Coulter-1. May 1st, 18__. 1850s.

Rarity: *None known*

$1 • W-VT-510-001-G010a
CJF

Tint: Red-orange microletters and lathework outlining white ONE and 1 / 1. *Engraver:* American Bank Note Co. *Comments:* H-VT-160-G2c. Similar to W-VT-510-001-G010 but with different engraver imprint. May 1st, 18__. 1860s.

Rarity: URS-4
VF $750; **Proof** $2,000

$1 • W-VT-510-001-G010b
CC

Tint: Green microletters and lathework outlining white ONE and 1 / 1. *Engraver:* American Bank Note Co. *Comments:* H-Unlisted. Similar to W-VT-510-001-G010 but with different engraver imprint. Proprietary Proof. May 1st, 18__. 1860s.

Rarity: URS-4
Proof $600

$1 • W-VT-510-001-G020
Left: ONE / State arms / Cherub and 1. *Center:* Farm scene, Four men, two women, child, dog, horse, hay. *Bottom center:* Merchandise. *Right:* 1 / Male portrait. *Engraver:* Unverified, but likely American Bank Note Co. *Comments:* H-VT-160-G4, Coulter-2. 1860s.

Rarity: *None known*

$2 • W-VT-510-002-G030
Left: 2 / Factory girl at work. *Center:* Blacksmith shop, Man shoeing horse. *Right:* 2 / Girl. *Overprint:* Red. *Engraver:* Toppan, Carpenter, Casilear & Co. *Comments:* H-VT-160-G6a, Coulter-4. May 1st, 18__. 1850s.

Rarity: *None known*

$2 • W-VT-510-002-G030a
Tint: Red-orange lathework. *Engraver:* American Bank Note Co. *Comments:* H-VT-160-G6c. Similar to W-VT-510-002-G030 but with different engraver imprint. May 1st, 18__. 1860s.

Rarity: URS-2
Proof $1,200

$2 • W-VT-510-002-G030b

CC

Tint: Green lathework outlining white TWO and 2 / 2. ***Engraver:*** American Bank Note Co. ***Comments:*** H-Unlisted. Similar to W-VT-510-002-G030 but with different engraver imprint. May 1st, 18__. 1860s.

Rarity: URS-2
Proof $5,200

$2 • W-VT-510-002-G040

CC

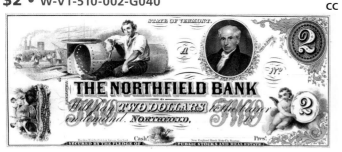

Engraver: Rawdon, Wright, Hatch & Edson / New England Bank Note Co. ***Comments:*** H-VT-160-G8, Coulter-3. 18__. 1860s.

Rarity: URS-2
Proof $1,000

$3 • W-VT-510-003-G050

Left: Horse market / 3. ***Center:*** Female portrait. ***Right:*** 3 / Milkmaid. ***Overprint:*** Red. ***Engraver:*** Toppan, Carpenter, Casilear & Co. ***Comments:*** H-VT-160-G10a, Coulter-5. May 1st, 18__. 1850s.

Rarity: *None known*

$3 • W-VT-510-003-G050a

CJF

Tint: Red-orange microletters and lathework outlining white THREE and 3 / THREE. ***Engraver:*** American Bank Note Co. ***Comments:*** H-VT-160-G10c. Similar to W-VT-510-003-G050 but with different engraver imprint. May 1st, 18__. 1860s.

Rarity: URS-3
VF $650; **Unc-Rem** $500; **Proof** $1,500

$3 • W-VT-510-003-G050b

CC

Tint: Green microletters and lathework outlining white THREE and 3 / THREE. ***Engraver:*** American Bank Note Co. ***Comments:*** H-Unlisted. Similar to W-VT-510-003-G050 but with different engraver imprint. Proprietary Proof. May 1st, 18__. 1860s.

Rarity: URS-3
Proof $900

$3 • W-VT-510-003-G060

Left: State arms / 3. ***Center:*** Milkmaid, Train. ***Right:*** 3 / Male portrait. ***Comments:*** H-Unlisted, Coulter-6. 1850s.

Rarity: *None known*

$5 • W-VT-510-005-G070

Left: State arms / 5. ***Center:*** Indian, Three cherubs with five gold dollars, Hunter. ***Right:*** 5 / Male portrait. ***Comments:*** H-Unlisted, Coulter-7. 1850s.

Rarity: *None known*

$5 • W-VT-510-005-G080

CJF

Overprint: Red lazy 5. ***Engraver:*** Toppan, Carpenter, Casilear & Co. ***Comments:*** H-VT-160-G14a, Coulter-8. May 1st, 185_. 1850s–1860s.

Rarity: URS-3
VF $650; **Unc-Rem** $500

$10 • W-VT-510-010-G090

CJF

Overprint: Red TEN. ***Engraver:*** Toppan, Carpenter, Casilear & Co. ***Comments:*** H-VT-160-G18a, Coulter-12. May 1st, 185_. 1850s.

Rarity: URS-3
VF $650; **Unc-Rem** $500

$10 • W-VT-510-010-G100

Left: TEN / State arms / 10. *Center:* Train, Steamboat. *Right:* 10 / Male portrait. *Comments:* H-Unlisted, Coulter-13. 1850s.
Rarity: *None known*

$20 • W-VT-510-020-G110   CC

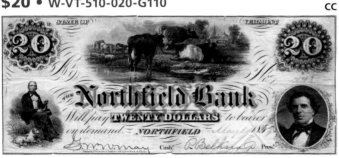

Overprint: Red XX. *Engraver:* Toppan, Carpenter, Casilear & Co. *Comments:* H-VT-160-G22a, Coulter-14. 185_. 1850s.
Rarity: URS-3
VF $650; **Unc-Rem** $500

$50 • W-VT-510-050-G120

Left: 50 / Blacksmith. *Center:* Man on horseback watering horse at trough. *Right:* 50 / Portrait of Governor Charles Paine. *Engraver:* Toppan, Carpenter, Casilear & Co. *Comments:* H-VT-160-G24, Coulter-15. 185_. 1850s.
Rarity: URS-2
Proof $700

$50 • W-VT-510-050-G120a   CJF

Overprint: Red 50. *Engraver:* Toppan, Carpenter, Casilear & Co. *Comments:* H-VT-160-G24a. Similar to W-VT-510-050-G120. 185_. 1850s.
Rarity: URS-4
VF $550; **Unc-Rem** $400

$100 • W-VT-510-100-G130   BH

Engraver: Toppan, Carpenter, Casilear & Co. *Comments:* H-VT-160-G26, Coulter-16. 185_. 1850s.
Rarity: URS-3
Proof $1,000

$100 • W-VT-510-100-G130a

Left: 100 / Blacksmith. *Center:* "John Eliot Preaching to the Indians". *Right:* 100 / Portrait of Governor Paine. *Overprint:* Red. *Engraver:* Toppan, Carpenter, Casilear & Co. *Comments:* H-VT-160-G26a. Similar to W-VT-510-100-G130. 185_. 1850s.
Rarity: *None known*

NON-VALID ISSUES

$5 • W-VT-510-005-R010

Engraver: Toppan, Carpenter, Casilear & Co. *Comments:* H-VT-160-R5, Coulter-9. Raised from W-VT-510-001-G010. May 1st, 18__. 1850s.
Rarity: *None known*

$5 • W-VT-510-005-S010   CC

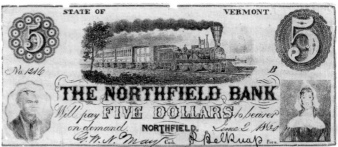

Comments: H-VT-160-S5, Coulter-11. Spurious design imitating a rough verbal description of W-VT-510-005-G080. 18__. Circa 1860.
Rarity: URS-6
F $100

$5 • W-VT-510-005-N010

Comments: H-Unlisted, Coulter-10. Design imitating a rough verbal description of W-VT-510-005-G070. 1850s.
Rarity: *None known*

ORWELL, VERMONT

Orwell was chartered in 1764, but it was not settled for eight years. A Scotsman, John Charter, finally made the first move to Orwell in 1771. During the 1770s, families slowly trickled into the land and began building farms. With the start of the Revolutionary War, many left for less perilous climates. Much of the area was later burnt by the British.

Early on, wheat was the main crop of Orwell. Later, cattle became important, and in Boston they were considered the finest cattle for sale. After 1825, when the wool market spiked, beef took a downturn and sheep became the major commerce of the day. Grist and sawmills were established, as well as a woolen factory and a carding-machine operation. In 1847 a small part of Benson was annexed to Orwell. A carriage and wagon factory opened, followed by the East Orwell Cheese Factory in 1867.

Farmers Bank
1833–1864
W-VT-525

History: The Farmers Bank was chartered on November 7, 1833, with $100,000 in authorized capital, of which $60,000 was soon paid in.

In August 1845, circulation was $58,335. The bank's charter expired on January 1, 1848, but it was renewed in a timely manner. In February 1848, the bank's capital was $92,190. Figures for 1857 were listed as: capital $75,000; bills in circulation $331,665; specie $3,231; real estate $2,500. In July 1859, circulation was $31,665.

In 1863 the business of the bank was succeeded by the First National Bank of Orwell. The bank commissioner burned a total of $693 in bills of the Farmers Bank on August 1, 1864. There was $8,500 worth of bills still in circulation at that time. All of the unsigned sheets and the plates were also destroyed. As of August 29, 1867, the remaining amount in circulation had dropped to $2,280. The First National Bank of Orwell guaranteed the redemption of this amount.

Numismatic Commentary: The small amount of bills remaining in circulation at the time of the bank's closure no doubt has dwindled to almost nothing. That in addition to the years of redemption of bills by the national bank accounts for the rarity of this bank's notes.

VALID ISSUES

$1 • W-VT-525-001-G010
Left: 1 / Three cherubs / ONE. *Center:* 1 / Cattle / 1. *Bottom center:* Arm and hammer. *Right:* 1 / Woman leaning on monument / ONE. *Engraver:* Unverified, but likely Rawdon, Wright & Hatch. *Comments:* H-VT-165-G2, Coulter-3. 18__. 1830s–1840s.
Rarity: *None known*

$1 • W-VT-525-001-G020
Left: 1 / Portrait of Benjamin Franklin / ONE. *Center:* Woman standing, woman seated / Harvest scene. *Bottom center:* Woman reclining with sheaf. *Right:* Agriculture / ONE. *Comments:* H-VT-165-G6, Coulter-2. 18__. 1850s.
Rarity: *None known*

$1 • W-VT-525-001-G030
CC

Engraver: Baldwin, Bald & Cousland / Bald, Cousland & Co. *Comments:* H-Unlisted. 18__. 1850s.
Rarity: URS-3
Proof $500

$1 • W-VT-525-001-G030a
CC

Tint: Brown-red lathework outlining white ONE, 1. *Engraver:* Baldwin, Bald & Cousland / Bald, Cousland & Co. *Comments:* H-VT-165-G10a. Similar to W-VT-525-001-G030. 18__. 1850s.
Rarity: URS-3
VG $350; **VF** $650; **Proof** $950
Selected auction price: Heritage, September 2008, Lot 12752, Choice Unc $920

$2 • W-VT-525-002-G040
Left: TWO / Indian, gun, dog / 2. *Center:* Cherub riding deer. *Right:* TWO / Man, sheaf / TWO. *Engraver:* Unverified, but likely Rawdon, Wright & Hatch. *Comments:* H-VT-165-G12, Coulter-6. 18__. 1830s–1840s.
Rarity: *None known*

$2 • W-VT-525-002-G050
Left: 2 / TWO / 2. *Center:* Woman and eagle / 2 / Three women. *Right:* TWO. *Comments:* H-VT-165-G16, Coulter-8. 184_. 1830s–1840s.
Rarity: *None known*

$2 • W-VT-525-002-G060
CC

Engraver: Baldwin, Bald & Cousland / Bald, Cousland & Co. *Comments:* H-Unlisted, Coulter-Unlisted. 18__. 1850s.
Rarity: URS-3
Proof $750

Collectors and Researchers:

If you have new information about any banks or notes listed in this volume, contact Whitman Publishing, Attn: Obsolete Paper Money, 3101 Clairmont Road, Suite G, Atlanta, GA 30329.

$2 • W-VT-525-002-G060a   CC

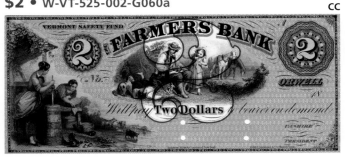

Tint: Brown-red lathework outlining white 2. *Engraver:* Baldwin, Bald & Cousland / Bald, Cousland & Co. *Comments:* H-VT-165-G18a, Coulter-7. Similar to W-VT-525-002-G060. 18__. 1850s.

Rarity: URS-3
VF $650; **Proof** $750

$3 • W-VT-525-003-G070

Left: 3 / Portrait / 3. *Center:* 3 on THREE / Allegorical figures, Sheep / 3. *Right:* VERMONT / 3 vertically. *Comments:* H-Unlisted, Coulter-11. 1850s.

Rarity: *None known*

$3 • W-VT-525-003-G080

Left: 3 / Cattle / 3. *Center:* Woman seated with agricultural tools / Woman churning / Woman seated with agricultural tools. *Bottom center:* Plow, rake, and sheaf. *Right:* 3 / Liberty / THREE. *Engraver:* Unverified, but likely Rawdon, Wright & Hatch. *Comments:* H-VT-165-G20. 18__. 1830s–1840s.

Rarity: *None known*

$3 • W-VT-525-003-G090   CC

Engraver: Baldwin, Bald & Cousland / Bald, Cousland & Co. *Comments:* H-Unlisted, Coulter-Unlisted. 18__. 1850s.

Rarity: URS-3
Proof $2,100

$3 • W-VT-525-003-G090a   CC

Tint: Brown-red outlining white 3. *Engraver:* Baldwin, Bald & Cousland / Bald, Cousland & Co. *Comments:* H-VT-165-G22a, Coulter-14. Similar to W-VT-525-003-G090. 18__. 1850s.

Rarity: URS-4
VF $650; **Proof** $900

$5 • W-VT-525-005-G100

Left: FIVE / Agriculture / V. *Center:* Neptune in chariot drawn by sea horses, Ship. *Bottom center:* Horse's head. *Right:* FIVE vertically. *Engraver:* Rawdon, Wright & Hatch. *Comments:* H-VT-165-G24, Coulter-16. 18__. 1830s–1840s.

Rarity: *None known*

$5 • W-VT-525-005-G110

Left: 5 / Eagle and serpent / 5. *Center:* V / Ceres, cattle, and plow / V. *Bottom center:* Male portrait. *Right:* 5 / Woman leaning against monument / V. *Comments:* H-VT-165-G26, Coulter-18. 18__. 1850s.

Rarity: *None known*

$5 • W-VT-525-005-G120   CJF

Comments: H-VT-165-G28, Coulter-17. 18__. 1850s.

Rarity: URS-3
VF $750

$10 • W-VT-525-010-G130   CC

Engraver: Rawdon, Clark & Co. *Comments:* H-VT-165-G32, Coulter-20. 18__. 1850s.

Rarity: URS-2
F $1,000

$20 • W-VT-525-020-G140

CC

Engraver: Draper, Toppan, Longacre & Co. *Comments:* H-VT-165-G36, Coulter-25. 18__. 1850s.

Rarity: URS-2

Proof $1,250

$50 • W-VT-525-050-G150

CC

Engraver: Draper, Toppan, Longacre & Co. *Comments:* H-VT-165-G40, Coulter-27. 18__. 1850s.

Rarity: URS-2

Proof $1,500

Uncut Sheets

$1-$1-$2-$3 • W-VT-525-001.001.002.003-US010

Vignette(s): ($1) Volant over city and river, Waterfall, Cattle and houses / Boy with armful of cornstalks, Child and horse. ($1) Volant over city and river, Waterfall, Cattle and houses / Boy with armful of cornstalks, Child and horse. ($2) Women churning and making cheese / Man and girl gazing at boy playing with dog / Farming scene. ($3) Woman blowing dinner horn, Three men on load of hay / Woman on load of hay drawn by two horses, Man, two children, dog, blacksmith, and shop / Girl. *Engraver:* Baldwin, Bald & Cousland / Bald, Cousland & Co. *Comments:* All unlisted in Haxby. 18__. 1850s.

Rarity: URS-3

Proof $2,000

$1-$1-$2-$3 • W-VT-525-001.001.002.003-US010a

Tint(s): Brown-red. *Engraver:* Baldwin, Bald & Cousland / Bald, Cousland & Co. *Comments:* H-VT-165-G10a, G10a, G18a, G22a. Similar to W-VT-525-001.001.002.003-US010. 18__. 1850s.

Rarity: URS-3

Proof $3,500

$20-$50 • W-VT-525-020.050-US020

CC

Engraver: Draper, Toppan, Longacre & Co. *Comments:* H-VT-165-G36, G40. 18__. 1850s.

Rarity: URS-2

Proof $3,500

NON-VALID ISSUES

$1 • W-VT-525-001-S010

Left: Panel. *Center:* 1 / Farmer, sheaf of grain, rake / ONE. *Bottom center:* Sheaf. *Right:* Woman leaning on 1. *Tint:* Blue. *Comments:* H-VT-165-S5, Coulter-5. June 6, 1856.

Rarity: URS-4

VG $250; F $300

$1 • W-VT-525-001-N010

Payee: R.P. Gould. *Comments:* H-Unlisted, Coulter-4. 1850s.

Rarity: *None known*

$2 • W-VT-525-002-C050

CC

Engraver: Rawdon, Wright & Hatch. *Comments:* H-VT-165-C16. Counterfeit of W-VT-525-002-G050. 18__. Circa 1846.

Rarity: URS-4

VF $400

$2 • W-VT-525-002-N020

Center: Men on horseback watering steeds. *Comments:* H-Unlisted, Coulter-9. 1850s.

Rarity: *None known*

$2 • W-VT-525-002-N030

Center: Farmer feeding hogs. *Comments:* H-Unlisted, Coulter-10. 1850s.

Rarity: *None known*

$2 • W-VT-525-002-A010

CC

Comments: H-Unlisted. Altered from W-VT-540-002-S020. 18__. 1850s.

Rarity: URS-4

F $150

$3 • W-VT-525-003-S020

CC

Comments: H-VT-165-S10, Coulter-12. 18__. 1830s.

Rarity: URS-5

VG $250

$3 • W-VT-525-003-N040

Payee: J. Kellogg. *Comments:* H-Unlisted, Coulter-15. 1850s.

Rarity: *None known*

$3 • W-VT-525-003-A020

Left: 3 / Wheelwrights at work. *Center:* Man on horseback watering steed. *Right:* 3 / Girl feeding chickens. *Overprint:* Red 3 / 3. *Engraver:* Toppan, Carpenter & Co. *Comments:* H-VT-165-A5, Coulter-13. Altered from $3 Farmers Bank, Wickford, Rhode Island. Aug. 6, 1855.

Rarity: URS-3

F $200

$5 • W-VT-525-005-N050

Left: X / Medallion head. *Center:* Man lying on ground, Sheaf of grain, Rake. *Right:* X / Girl / 10. *Comments:* H-Unlisted, Coulter-19. 1850s.

Rarity: *None known*

$10 • W-VT-525-010-S030

Left: X / Train / X. *Center:* Medallion head / Steamboat / Medallion head. *Bottom center:* Dog and strongbox. *Right:* TEN vertically. *Engraver:* Eastern Bank Note Co. *Comments:* H-VT-165-S15, Coulter-23. 18__. 1840s.

Rarity: URS-4

F $125

$10 • W-VT-525-010-N060

Left: X / Medallion head. *Center:* Man lying on ground, Sheaf of grain, Rake. *Right:* X / Girl / 10. *Comments:* H-Unlisted, Coulter-21. 1850s.

Rarity: *None known*

$10 • W-VT-525-010-N070

Left: Man, horse, dog. *Center:* Drovers and cattle. *Right:* Woman. *Comments:* H-Unlisted, Coulter-22. 1850s.

Rarity: *None known*

$10 • W-VT-525-010-A030

Left: 10 / Allegorical woman and Justice flanking shield bearing anchor. *Center:* Man standing over boy gathering corn, Horse-drawn wagon. *Right:* 10 / Portrait of girl with ringlets. *Overprint:* Red X / X. *Engraver:* Unverified, but likely Toppan, Carpenter & Co. *Comments:* H-VT-165-A10, Coulter-24. Altered from $10 Farmers Bank, Wickford, Rhode Island. 18__. 1855.

Rarity: *None known*

$20 • W-VT-525-020-S040

CC

Engraver: Eastern Bank Note Co. *Comments:* H-VT-165-S20, Coulter-26. 18__. Circa 1840.

Rarity: URS-3

F $300

PHILLIPSBURGH, VERMONT

There is no town of Phillipsburgh, Vermont. The name was used only by a non-existent bank intending to circulate notes fraudulently in the state. Phillipsburg, *New York*, possessed a silver mine and many other valuable mineral deposits. The Phenix Bank of the New England region was the basis on which the fraudulent bank was fabricated.

Phenix Bank
CIRCA 1840
W-VT-540

History: A non-existent bank represented by notes intended to circulate fraudulently in Vermont.

Numismatic Commentary: Examples of these spurious notes are available in the marketplace on occasion. Most notes found are in a mid-range state of preservation.

ISSUES

$1 • W-VT-540-001-S010

SBG

Comments: H-VT-170-S2, Coulter-Unlisted. 18__. 1840s.
Rarity: URS-4
F $750

$2 • W-VT-540-002-S020

CJF

Comments: H-VT-170-S4, Coulter-Unlisted. 18__. 1840s.
Rarity: URS-4
F $750

$3 • W-VT-540-003-S030

Comments: H-VT-170-S6, Coulter-Unlisted. 18__. 1840s.
Rarity: URS-3
VF $300

PITTSFIELD, VERMONT

Granted on November 8, 1780, Pittsfield was chartered on July 29, 1781. It was named after Pittsfield, Massachusetts, which was in turn named in honor of William Pitt. The first settlers arrived in 1786, and the area was found to be ideal for grazing livestock due to the hilly terrain.

Pittsfield Bank
1850s
W-VT-550

History: The Pittsfield bank was incorporated in 1850 with an authorized capital of $100,000 and commenced business in September. John L. Thorndike was the first president, and C.H. Carpenter was the cashier.

Numismatic Commentary: Confirmation of any genuine notes from this bank cannot be given at this time. Research has not yet turned up proof of existence of any of the listed issues.

VALID ISSUES

$1 • W-VT-550-001-G010

Left: Commerce seated with rudder leaning on barrel / 1. **Center:** 1 bearing "Presentation of the Declaration of Independence". **Right:** 1 / Woman standing with elbow on fence, Apron full of grain. **Engraver:** New England Bank Note Co. **Comments:** H-VT-175-G2. 18__. 1850s.
Rarity: *None known*

$2 • W-VT-550-002-G020

Left: Men driving sheep into stream / 2. **Center:** 2 bearing "Presentation of the Declaration of Independence". **Right:** TWO / Woman seated with wreath of flowers / TWO. **Engraver:** New England Bank Note Co. **Comments:** H-VT-175-G4. 18__. 1850s.
Rarity: *None known*

$3 • W-VT-550-003-G030

Left: Barnyard scene, Man on horse, boy and cattle / 3. **Center:** 3. **Right:** 3 on THREE / Woman with flowers / THREE. **Engraver:** New England Bank Note Co. **Comments:** H-VT-175-G6. 18__. 1850s.
Rarity: *None known*

$5 • W-VT-550-005-G040

Left: Eagle on shield and anchor, Factories and ships / FIVE. **Center:** V bearing woman with cornucopia and cherub. **Right:** 5 / Girl with ringlets holding basket. **Engraver:** New England Bank Note Co. **Comments:** H-VT-175-G8. 18__. 1850s.
Rarity: *None known*

$10 • W-VT-550-010-G050

Left: Mechanic seated with tools, Train and building / TEN. **Center:** X. **Right:** 10 / Reaper standing with sheaf on knee. **Engraver:** New England Bank Note Co. **Comments:** H-VT-175-G10. 18__. 1850s.
Rarity: *None known*

$20 • W-VT-550-020-G060

Left: 20 / Minerva standing with spear. **Center:** Woman seated between 2 and 0 / TWENTY. **Right:** 20 / Woman reclining on cornucopia / 20. **Engraver:** Rawdon, Wright, Hatch & Edson. **Comments:** H-VT-175-G12. 18__. 1850s.
Rarity: *None known*

$50 • W-VT-550-050-G070

Left: 50 / Minerva standing by column. **Center:** Ceres and Vulcan flanking cornucopia / FIFTY. **Right:** 50 / Cherub in sailboat / 50. **Engraver:** Rawdon, Wright, Hatch & Edson. **Comments:** H-VT-175-G14. 18__. 1850s.
Rarity: *None known*

$100 • W-VT-550-100-G080

Left: 100 / Vulcan seated with sledge and anchor. **Center:** Eagle on limb, Train on bridge, Canal locks / C C. **Bottom center:** 100. **Right:** 100 / Ceres seated, Cornucopia. **Engraver:** Rawdon, Wright, Hatch & Edson. **Comments:** H-VT-175-G15. 18__. 1850s.
Rarity: *None known*

POULTNEY, VERMONT

Poultney was chartered on September 21, 1761, and named after William Pulteney, 1st Earl of Bath. The town was settled by Thomas Ashley and Ebenezer Allen but grew slowly due to disputes between New York and New Hampshire over the land of Vermont. During the American Revolution, most of the families in residence left and returned to their former Massachusetts and Connecticut homes. They came back in the spring of 1778, once the unrest had settled.

Much of the village grew up around a gristmill that was built in 1777. During the 1820s, the founder of the *New York Tribune*, Horace Greeley, and the co-founder of the *New York Times*, George Jones, lived in East Poultney, the larger of the two villages until West Poultney grew dramatically in size in the late 19th century. Henry Stanley set up a foundry in West Poultney in 1828. The Union Academy was built in 1791 and the Melodeon Factory was built in 1840. The land remains the center for the world's slate belt, providing slate roofing, tiles, and building blocks.

See also West Poultney, Vermont.

Bank of Poultney
1841–1865
W-VT-560

History: The Bank of Poultney was chartered on October 29, 1840, with an authorized capital of $100,000. Business commenced on July 7, 1841. On November 7, 1842, the capital of the bank was reduced to $70,000. It was reduced again on November 2, 1843, to $50,000. There the value remained until the bank's charter expired.

In August 1845, circulation was $49,978. In 1851 circulation was $77,697, and other debts due were $15,486.

The Bank of Poultney was rechartered in 1859 with an authorized capital of $30,000. Circulation was $4,214. In December 1860, capital reached $90,000, and by July 1862, capital had risen further to $100,000. Circulation was as high as $178,988.

On July 1, 1865, the business of the Bank of Poultney was succeeded the National Bank of Poultney. The state bank had an outstanding circulation of $4,244, redemption of which was guaranteed by the national bank.

See also listing under West Poultney, W-VT-810.

Numismatic Commentary: Many of the notes from this bank are colorful and attractive. All issues are scarce.

Remaining in the American Bank Note Co. archives as of 2003 was a $10-$20 face plate, a $10-$20 tint plate, a $10-$20 tint plate, and a $1-$1-$2-$5 tint plate.

VALID ISSUES

$1 • W-VT-560-001-G010   CC

Tint: Green lathework and microletters outlining white ONE. *Engraver:* Draper, Toppan & Co. / ABNCo. monogram. *Comments:* H-VT-270-G14a, Coulter-1. 185_. 1850s.
Rarity: URS-3
Proof $3,900

$1 • W-VT-560-001-G010a   SBG

Tint: Brown-red lathework and microletters outlining white ONE. *Engraver:* Draper, Toppan & Co. / ABNCo. monogram. *Comments:* H-VT-270-G14b, Coulter-2. Similar to W-VT-560-001-G010 but with different date. 18__. 1860s.
Rarity: URS-3
VG $895; **F** $1,000

$1 • W-VT-560-001-G010b   CC

Tint: Green 1 / 1 and panel bearing white 1, 1. *Engraver:* American Bank Note Co. *Comments:* H-VT-270-G16, Coulter-Unlisted. Similar to W-VT-560-001-G010 but with different date and engraver imprint. Sept.r 4th, 1863.
Rarity: URS-2
F $1,250

$1 • W-VT-560-001-G010c
CC

Tint: Purple 1 / 1 and panel bearing white 1, 1. *Engraver:* American Bank Note Co. *Comments:* H-Unlisted, Coulter-Unlisted. Similar to W-VT-560-001-G010 but with different date and engraver imprint. Modern Proof. Sept.r 4th, 1863.
Rarity: URS-3
Proof $600

$2 • W-VT-560-002-G020
Left: TWO / Boy carrying sheaf and scythe / TWO. *Center:* 2 / Two milkmaids / 2. *Right:* TWO / Milkmaid, Fence and trees / TWO. *Tint:* Green lathework and microletters outlining white TWO. *Engraver:* Draper, Toppan & Co. / ABNCo. monogram. *Comments:* H-VT-270-G18a, Coulter-4. 185_. 1850s.
Rarity: *None known*

$2 • W-VT-560-002-G020a
CJF

Tint: Brown-red lathework and microletters outlining white TWO. *Engraver:* Draper, Toppan & Co. / American Bank Note Co. *Comments:* H-VT-270-G18b, Coulter-5. Similar to W-VT-560-002-G020 but with different engraver imprint. 185_. 1850s.
Rarity: URS-3
F $1,000

$2 • W-VT-560-002-G020b
Tint: Green 2 / 2 and panel. *Engraver:* American Bank Note Co. *Comments:* H-VT-270-G20, Coulter-Unlisted. Similar to W-VT-560-002-G020 but with different date and engraver imprint. Sept.r 4th, 1863.
Rarity: *None known*

$2 • W-VT-560-002-G020c
CC

Tint: Purple 2 / 2 and panel. *Engraver:* American Bank Note Co. *Comments:* H-VT-270-G20, Coulter-Unlisted. Similar to W-VT-560-002-G020 but with different date and engraver imprint. Modern Proof. Sept.r 4th, 1863.
Rarity: URS-3
Unc-Rem $200; **Proof** $600

$5 • W-VT-560-005-G030
Left: V / Woman seated in V / FIVE. *Center:* Girl with scroll, State arms, Justice. *Right:* V / Ceres seated in 5 / FIVE. *Tint:* Green lathework and microletters. *Engraver:* Draper, Toppan & Co. / ABNCo. monogram. *Comments:* H-VT-270-G22a, Coulter-7. 185_. 1850s.
Rarity: URS-3
VF $1,000

$5 • W-VT-560-005-G030a
Tint: Brown-red lathework and microletters. *Engraver:* Draper, Toppan & Co. / American Bank Note Co. *Comments:* H-VT-270-G22b, Coulter-8. Similar to W-VT-560-005-G030 but with different date and engraver imprint. 18__. 1860s.
Rarity: *None known*

$5 • W-VT-560-005-G030b
Tint: Green 5 / 5 and panel. *Engraver:* American Bank Note Co. *Comments:* H-VT-270-G24, Coulter-6. Similar to W-VT-560-005-G030 but with different date and engraver imprint. Sept.r 4th, 1863.
Rarity: URS-3
VF $1,000

$5 • W-VT-560-005-G030c
CC

Tint: Purple 5 / 5 and panel. *Engraver:* American Bank Note Co. *Comments:* H-Unlisted, Coulter-Unlisted. Similar to W-VT-560-005-G030 but with different date and engraver imprint. Modern Proof. Sept.r 4th, 1863.
Rarity: URS-3
Proof $600

$10 • W-VT-560-010-G040

Left: Portrait of Benjamin Franklin. *Center:* Train / Female portrait. *Right:* 10 / Indian maid. *Tint:* Brown-red lathework and microletters. *Engraver:* Toppan, Carpenter, Casilear & Co. / ABNCo. monogram. *Comments:* H-VT-270-G26a, Coulter-9. 185_. 1850s.

Rarity: *None known*

$10 • W-VT-560-010-G040a   CC

Tint: Green die bearing white 10 and panel. *Engraver:* Toppan, Carpenter, Casilear & Co. / ABNCo. monogram. *Comments:* H-VT-270-G26b, Coulter-Unlisted. Similar to W-VT-560-010-G040 but with different date. Sept.r 4th, 18__. 1860s.

Rarity: URS-2
F $1,250

$10 • W-VT-560-010-G050

Left: TEN / Woman holding scroll bearing 10 / TEN. *Center:* Spread eagle, Shield and agricultural implements. *Right:* 10 / Portrait of George Washington / TEN. *Comments:* H-Unlisted, Coulter-10. 1860s.

Rarity: *None known*

$20 • W-VT-560-020-G060   CC

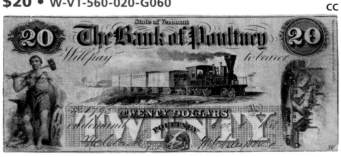

Tint: Brown-red lathework and microletters outlining white TWENTY. *Engraver:* Toppan, Carpenter, Casilear & Co. / ABNCo. monogram. *Comments:* H-VT-270-G28a, Coulter-11. 185_. 1850s.

Rarity: URS-2
F $2,000

$20 • W-VT-560-020-G060a   CC

Tint: Green die bearing white 20 and panel bearing white 20, TWENTY, 20. *Engraver:* Toppan, Carpenter, Casilear & Co. / ABNCo. monogram. *Comments:* H-VT-270-G28b, Coulter-12. Similar to W-VT-560-020-G060 but with different date. Sept.r 4th, 18__. 1860s.

Rarity: URS-2
F $2,000

NON-VALID ISSUES

$1 • W-VT-560-001-A010

Left: 1 in die / Cows, bridge. *Center:* Woman feeding calves. *Right:* 1 in die / Woman with hand on shoulder. *Engraver:* Danforth, Wright & Co. *Comments:* H-Unlisted, Coulter-3. Altered from $1 Southern Bank of Bainbridge, Bainbridge, Georgia. 1858.

Rarity: URS-4
F $100

Commercial Bank of Vermont
CIRCA 1840
W-VT-570

History: A non-existent bank represented by notes meant to circulate fraudulently in Vermont.

Numismatic Commentary: All issues seen are either fantasies or altered notes of other banks.

How to Read the Whitman Numbering System
$1 • W-RI-010-001-G010a

Denomination: Value of the note shown.

W: Whitman number. This number is a sortable code unique to each bank and note.

RI: Abbreviation for the state under study.

010: Numerical designation specific to each bank.

001: The denomination in dollars.

G010a: G indicates a good or valid note. Other categories are indicated thus: C (counterfeit); R (raised); S (spurious); N (not-attributed); A (altered). Numbers are assigned starting with 010, 020, et seq. Terminal letters following the number indicate variations of a note: a series of different colored overprints, tints, payees, etc., all on the same design of note. For more information, see the "How to Use This Book" section at the front of the volume, page xiv.

ISSUES

$1 • W-VT-570-001-N010

CJF

Engraver: Durand & Co. *Comments:* H-VT-180-G2, Coulter-1. 18__. Circa 1840.

Rarity: URS-2
F $1,000

$2 • W-VT-570-002-N020

Left: Woman. *Center:* Indian and dogs. *Right:* Man. *Engraver:* Durand & Co. *Comments:* H-VT-180-G4, Coulter-2. 18__. Circa 1840.

Rarity: *None known*

$3 • W-VT-570-003-N030

Left: Indian man seated on rock with bow, Dog. *Center:* 3 / Ships in harbor, Warehouse. *Bottom center:* Farm implements and sheaf. *Right:* 3. *Engraver:* Durand & Co. *Comments:* H-VT-180-G6, Coulter-3. 18__. Circa 1840.

Rarity: *None known*

$5 • W-VT-570-005-N040

Left: Panel of flowers and fruit with FIVE on die. *Bottom center:* Sailing ships. *Right:* 5 / Woman seated on anchor, Ship / 5. *Engraver:* Durand & Co. *Comments:* H-VT-180-G8, Coulter-4. 18__. Circa 1840.

Rarity: *None known*

PROCTORSVILLE, VERMONT

A village in the town of Cavendish, Proctorsville was named after the family who also inspired the name for the town of Proctor. Captain John Coffeen arrived with his family to first settle the land in 1769. They remained the only family there for two years. Finally, in the 1780s Leonard Proctor arrived to give his name to the settlement on the Black River, accompanied by Salmon Dutton, who also inspired a namesake in the settlement of Duttonsville. In 1784 Dutton helped lay the town's road, which later became part of the Green Mountain Turnpike. Boston coaches would come up to the village from the Duttonsville Gulf and proceed through Proctorsville. The stagecoach driver would blow his horn for as many passengers as he carried, allowing Dutton, the tavern keeper, to hear and know how many plates to set for dinner.

Between 1811 and 1813, epidemics of spotted fever and lung fever erupted in Cavendish, followed by summer snow and freezing weather all throughout the year of 1816. The crops failed and hunting was poor, and the locals went hungry. Gristmills were in operation in town, as well as a potash works. Potatoes, corn, and hops were sold, and by 1824 Cavendish had sawmills, gristmills, tanneries, distilleries, and factories that produced hats, nails, stoves, and tinware. Woolen mills built between 1832 and 1835 provided a market for the Merino sheep, producing 14,279 pounds of wool from 7,124 sheep a year. Broadcloth and cashmere were produced here, employing more than 100 workers. When a tariff on wool was established, many farmers shifted to raising dairy cows instead of sheep.

Bank of Black River
1845–1865
W-VT-580

History: The Bank of Black River was chartered in 1845 with an authorized capital of $40,000. Business began in early 1846. In 1857 these figures for the bank were reported: capital $50,000; bills in circulation $72,029; specie $3,631; real estate $1,687. 1862 saw the capital at $50,000 and circulation at $89,140.

On May 16, 1865, the business of the Bank of Black River was succeeded by the National Black River Bank of Proctorsville. The outstanding circulation of the bank as of July 1, 1867, was $6,037. Redemption of this amount was guaranteed by the national bank.

Numismatic Commentary: All genuine issues bear the imprints of Danforth, Spencer & Hufty and Spencer, Hufty & Danforth. These notes are considered scarce, as one or two appear at public auction only occasionally.

Remaining in the American Bank Note Co. archives as of 2003 was a $1-$1-$2-$3 face plate, a $5-$5-$5-$10 face plate, and a $20-$50 face plate.

VALID ISSUES

$1 • W-VT-580-001-G010

CC

Engraver: Danforth, Spencer & Hufty / Spencer, Hufty & Danforth. *Comments:* H-VT-185-G2, Coulter-1. 18__. 1845–1850s.

Rarity: URS-3
Proof $750

$1 • W-VT-580-001-G010a CJF

Overprint: Red ONE. *Engraver:* Danforth, Spencer & Hufty / Spencer, Hufty & Danforth. *Comments:* H-VT-185-G2a, Coulter-Unlisted. Similar to W-VT-580-001-G010 but with different date. January 1st, 18__. 1850s–1860s.
Rarity: URS-3
VG $600; **F** $750

$2 • W-VT-580-002-G020 CJF

Engraver: Danforth, Spencer & Hufty / Spencer, Hufty & Danforth. *Comments:* H-VT-185-G4, Coulter-2. 18__. 1845–1850s.
Rarity: URS-2
EF $1,500; **Proof** $2,100

$2 • W-VT-580-002-G020a CJF

Overprint: Red TWO. *Engraver:* Danforth, Spencer & Hufty / Spencer, Hufty & Danforth. *Comments:* H-VT-185-G4a. Similar to W-VT-580-002-G020 but with different date. January 1st, 18__. 1850s–1860s.
Rarity: URS-3
F $1,000

$3 • W-VT-580-003-G030

Left: THREE / Ceres seated on plow / THREE. *Center:* Shield, Two Indians, Woman kneeling. *Right:* 3 / Female portrait / 3. *Engraver:* Danforth, Spencer & Hufty / Spencer, Hufty & Danforth. *Comments:* H-VT-185-G6, Coulter-4. 18__. 1845–1850s.
Rarity: URS-2
Proof $650

$3 • W-VT-580-003-G030a

Overprint: Red. *Engraver:* Danforth, Spencer & Hufty / Spencer, Hufty & Danforth. *Comments:* H-VT-185-G6a. Similar to W-VT-580-003-G030 but with different date. January 1st, 18__. 1850s–1860s.
Rarity: *None known*

$5 • W-VT-580-005-G040 CC

Engraver: Danforth, Spencer & Hufty / Spencer, Hufty & Danforth. *Comments:* H-VT-185-G8, Coulter-6. 18__. 1845–1850s.
Rarity: URS-3
Proof $850

$5 • W-VT-580-005-G040a CC

Overprint: Red FIVE. *Engraver:* Danforth, Spencer & Hufty / Spencer, Hufty & Danforth. *Comments:* H-VT-185-G8a. Similar to W-VT-580-005-G040 but with different date. May 4th, 18__. 1850s–1860s.
Rarity: URS-2
F $1,000

$10 • W-VT-580-010-G050 CC

Engraver: Danforth, Spencer & Hufty / Spencer, Hufty & Danforth. *Comments:* H-VT-185-G10, Coulter-9. 18__. 1845–1850s.
Rarity: URS-3
Proof $2,300

$10 • W-VT-580-010-G050a

Left: 10 / Indian family on cliff overlooking river and city. *Center:* Female portrait. *Bottom center:* Train. *Right:* 10 / State arms / TEN. *Overprint:* Red. *Engraver:* Danforth, Spencer & Hufty / Spencer, Hufty & Danforth. *Comments:* H–VT-185-G10a. Similar to W-VT-580-010-G050. 18__. 1850s–1860s.

Rarity: URS-2
Proof $650

$20 • W-VT-580-020-G060

Engraver: Danforth, Spencer & Hufty / Spencer, Hufty & Danforth. *Comments:* H–VT-185-G12, Coulter-13. 18__. 1845–1850s.

Rarity: URS-2
Proof $2,000

$20 • W-VT-580-020-G060a

Overprint: Red TWENTY. *Engraver:* Danforth, Spencer & Hufty / Spencer, Hufty & Danforth. *Comments:* H–VT-185-G12a, Coulter-14. Similar to W-VT-580-020-G060. 18__. 1850s–1860s.

Rarity: URS-2
VG $1,000

$50 • W-VT-580-050-G070

Engraver: Danforth, Spencer & Hufty / Spencer, Hufty & Danforth. *Comments:* H–VT-185-G14, Coulter-16. 18__. 1845–1850s.

Rarity: URS-2
Proof $3,000

$50 • W-VT-580-050-G070a

Left: Liberty and eagle. *Center:* Allegorical woman, Angel offering apple to woman. *Right:* 50. *Overprint:* Red. *Engraver:* Danforth, Spencer & Hufty / Spencer, Hufty & Danforth. *Comments:* H–VT-185-G14a. Similar to W-VT-580-050-G070. 18__. 1850s–1860s.

Rarity: *None known*

Uncut Sheets

$1-$1-$2-$3 • W-VT-580-001.001.002.003-US010

Vignette(s): *($1)* Portrait of George Washington / Two horses / Train / Portrait of Martha Washington. *($1)* Portrait of George Washington / Two horses / Train / Portrait of Martha Washington. *($2)* Justice / Men loading hay, Oxen and wagon / Agriculture. *($3)* Ceres seated on plow / Shield, Two Indians, Woman kneeling / Female portrait. *Engraver:* Danforth, Spencer & Hufty / Spencer, Hufty & Danforth. *Comments:* H–VT-185-G2, G2, G4, G6. 18__. 1845–1850s.

Rarity: URS-2
Proof $2,700

$5-$5-$5-$10 • W-VT-580-005.005.005.010-US020

Vignette(s): *($5)* Portrait of Benjamin Franklin / Farmer plowing with yoke of oxen and horses / Portrait of Kate Sevier. *($5)* Portrait of Benjamin Franklin / Farmer plowing with yoke of oxen and horses / Portrait of Kate Sevier. *($5)* Portrait of Benjamin Franklin / Farmer plowing with yoke of oxen and horses / Portrait of Kate Sevier. *($10)* Indian family on cliff overlooking river and city / Female portrait / State arms. *Engraver:* Danforth, Spencer & Hufty / Spencer, Hufty & Danforth. *Comments:* H–VT-185-G8, G8, G8, G10. 18__. 1845–1850s.

Rarity: URS-2
Proof $2,600

$20-$50 • W-VT-580-020.050-US030

Vignette(s): *($20)* Male portrait / Two women, one supporting cornucopia and grain, one carrying XX. *($50)* Liberty and eagle / Allegorical figure / Angel offering apple to woman. *Engraver:* Danforth, Spencer & Hufty / Spencer, Hufty & Danforth. *Comments:* H–VT-185-G12, G14. 18__. 1845–1850s.

Rarity: URS-2
Proof $1,400

Non-Valid Issues

$2 • W-VT-580-002-A010

Center: Deer. *Right:* State arms. *Comments:* H-Unlisted, Coulter-3. Altered from $2 Southern Bank of Bainbridge, Bainbridge, Georgia. 1830s–1850s.

Rarity: URS-6
F $90

$3 • W-VT-580-003-A020

Center: Deer. *Right:* State arms. *Comments:* H-Unlisted, Coulter-5. Altered from $3 Southern Bank of Bainbridge, Bainbridge, Georgia. 1830s–1850s.

Rarity: *None known*

$5 • W-VT-580-005-A030

Center: Deer. *Right:* State arms. *Comments:* H-Unlisted, Coulter-7. Altered from $5 Southern Bank of Bainbridge, Bainbridge, Georgia. 1830s–1850s.

Rarity: *None known*

$5 • W-VT-580-005-A040

Left: Die bearing 5. *Center:* 5 / Ceres with grain / 5. *Right:* Justice and Liberty flanking shield surmounted by eagle. *Engraver:* Rawdon, Wright & Hatch. *Comments:* H-VT-185-A5, Coulter-8. 18__. 1830s–1850s.

Rarity: *None known*

$10 • W-VT-580-010-R010

Engraver: Danforth, Spencer & Hufty / Spencer, Hufty & Danforth. *Comments:* H-VT-185-R5. Raised from W-VT-580-001-G010. 18__. 1850s.

Rarity: *None known*

$10 • W-VT-580-010-A050

Center: Deer. *Right:* State arms. *Comments:* H-Unlisted, Coulter-10. Altered from $10 Southern Bank of Bainbridge, Bainbridge, Georgia. 1830s–1850s.

Rarity: *None known*

$10 • W-VT-580-010-A060

Left: 10 on die and scrollwork panel. *Center:* X / Wild boar / X. *Bottom center:* Pledge. *Right:* Indian, Eagle and man. *Engraver:* Rawdon, Wright & Hatch. *Comments:* H-VT-185-A10, Coulter-11. Altered from $10 Wayne County Bank, Plymouth, Michigan. 18__. 1830s–1850s.

Rarity: *None known*

$10 • W-VT-580-010-A070

Comments: H-Unlisted, Coulter-12. Altered from W-VT-580-001-G010 series. 1830s–1850s.

Rarity: *None known*

$20 • W-VT-580-020-A080

Left: XX on die and scrollwork panel. *Center:* 20 / Deer / 20. *Bottom center:* Pledge. *Right:* State arms. *Engraver:* Rawdon, Wright & Hatch. *Comments:* H-VT-185-A15, Coulter-15. Altered from $20 Wayne County Bank, Plymouth, Michigan. 18__. 1830s–1850s.

Rarity: *None known*

RICHMOND, VERMONT

In 1775 Amos Brownson and John Chamberlain settled with their families in the area known as Richmond. They abandoned the settlement during the Revolutionary War, returning in the spring of 1784 with more families. Richmond was incorporated on October 27, 1794, and was officially organized in 1795.

Water mills and other industries used power from the Winooski River and the Huntington River, allowing for the manufacturing of wagons, harnesses, tinware, brass, cabinet work, and wooden goods. In 1859 the population was 1,453. One of the notable features of Richmond is its Round Church, a meetinghouse built in 1812 and 1813 that has 16 sides.

Bank of Richmond
1854
W-VT-590

History: In 1854 a charter application for the Bank of Richmond was rejected by the state legislature.

Numismatic Commentary: It is possible that Proof notes were made, but no record has been found of such.

ROCKINGHAM, VERMONT

The town of Rockingham is located in the southeastern portion of Vermont. It was named after the Marquess of Rockingham. Through 1825 Rockingham was a primary commercial area. The only bank was located in the village of Bellows Falls.

See also Bellows Falls, Vermont.

Bank of Bellows Falls
1831–1866
W-VT-600

History: The Bank of Bellows Falls (also sometimes seen as the Bellows Falls Bank) was chartered on November 9, 1831. It was authorized with a capital stock of $50,000.

The bank's charter expired on January 1, 1847, but was renewed with a new capital stock of $100,000. After that time, bills bore the address of Bellows Falls instead of Rockingham. The business of the Bank of Bellows Falls was succeeded by the National Bank of Bellows Falls, chartered June 12, 1866.

See also listing under Bellows Falls, W-VT-010.

Numismatic Commentary: The title printed on the first notes issued, "Bellows Falls Bank," is a variant name. The bank was chartered by the Vermont General Assembly on November 9, 1831, by "An act to incorporate the president, directors and company of the Bank of Bellows Falls," which is the title that is most commonly found on notes.

VALID ISSUES

$1 • W-VT-600-001-G010   CC

Engraver: New England Bank Note Co. *Comments:* H-Unlisted, Coulter-Unlisted. 18__. 1830s–1850s.

Rarity: URS-2

VF $600; **Proof** $1,250

$1 • W-VT-600-001-G020

CC

Engraver: Rawdon, Clark & Co. **Comments:** H-Unlisted, Coulter-Unlisted. 18__. 1830s–1850s.

Rarity: URS-2

F $1,200; **VF** $1,500; **EF** $1,800

$2 • W-VT-600-002-G030

CC

Engraver: New England Bank Note Co. **Comments:** H-Unlisted, Coulter-Unlisted. 18__. 1830s–1850s.

Rarity: URS-1

Proof $2,000

$5 • W-VT-600-005-G040

CC

Engraver: New England Bank Note Co. **Comments:** H-VT-190-G8, Coulter-Unlisted. 18__. 1830s–1850s.

Rarity: URS-1

Proof $2,000

Uncut Sheets

$1-$1-$2-$5 • W-VT-600-001.001.002.005-US010 CC

Engraver: New England Bank Note Co. **Comments:** H-Unlisted, H-Unlisted, H-Unlisted, H-VT-190-G8. 18__. 1830s–1850s.

Rarity: URS-1

Proof $6,000

Non-Valid Issues

$5 • W-VT-600-005-C040

Comments: H-VT-190-C8, Coulter-Unlisted. Counterfeit of W-VT-600-005-G040. 18__. 1830s–1850s.

Rarity: *None known*

Collectors and Researchers:

If you have new information about any banks or notes listed in this volume, contact Whitman Publishing, Attn: Obsolete Paper Money, 3101 Clairmont Road, Suite G, Atlanta, GA 30329.

ROYALTON, VERMONT

Royalton was chartered on November 23, 1769, and was settled by Robert Havens and his family in 1771. The town was re-chartered in 1781 to settle land disputes and reapportion sections of acreage.

Sawmills and gristmills were built in 1776 and encouraged further settlement, but Royalton was considered wild land for some time. In 1780 it was destroyed by a massive Canadian-Indian attack. Only four of the settlers were killed, but the homes, barns, mills, and land were burned, captives were taken, and animals were slaughtered. Eventually almost all of the captives returned to Vermont during prisoner exchanges at the conclusion of the war.

At the turn of the century there was a blacksmith shop, a brickyard, a tannery, a shoemaker, and a tailor in town. There was also a post office. The Royalton Academy was founded in 1803. Several factories for wool processing and the making of woolen clothing were established, and soon the textile industry developed along with the production of butter tubs, knives, shoes, and croquet sets. Stagecoaches rotated out of Royalton on their way to Boston. The population of the town was as high as 1,917 in 1840.

See also South Royalton, Vermont.

Bank of Royalton
1853–1867
W-VT-610

History: The Bank of Royalton was chartered on November 30, 1853, with an authorized capital of $100,000. The stock was completely subscribed for by February 1854, and the bank went into business on March 10 of that year. Its first bills were issued on June 7, 1854.

In 1857 circulation was $45,987. During that autumn, the bank suffered large losses due to insolvent debtors. By the end of October it had suspended the redemption of its circulating bills in Boston and at its counter.

On January 12, 1858, a new board of directors was elected, and without delay they made great efforts to collect enough money in order to enable the bank to resume its business. Failing at this attempt, they borrowed funds on their private notes, and the bank was thus enabled to resume business and the redemption of its circulation on February 24, 1858. Because of the losses that the bank had sustained in 1857, its capital was reduced by an act of the Legislature on November 18, 1859, to $50,000.

By August 2, 1862, the Bank of Royalton had recovered to the point that its outstanding circulation stood at $86,702. In 1859 it was $45,987. The bank had also regained its attraction among the counterfeiters. In 1862 the Association for the Prevention of Counterfeiting in Boston paid four $25 rewards to persons who caught others passing counterfeit Bank of Royalton notes.

On September 16, 1867, the business of the Bank of Royalton was succeeded by the National Bank of Royalton. The outstanding circulation of the Bank of Royalton on July 1, 1867, was $2,276, redemption of which was guaranteed by the national bank.

Numismatic Commentary: All genuine issues bear the imprints of the New England Bank Note Co. and Rawdon, Wright, Hatch & Edson. These issues are still fairly plentiful in the marketplace.

VALID ISSUES

$1 • W-VT-610-001-G010

CJF

Engraver: Rawdon, Wright, Hatch & Edson / New England Bank Note Co. **Comments:** H-Unlisted, Coulter-Unlisted. 18__. 1850s–1860s.

Rarity: URS-3

F $750; **Unc-Rem** $400

$1 • W-VT-610-001-G010a

CC

Overprint: Red ONE. **Engraver:** Rawdon, Wright, Hatch & Edson / New England Bank Note Co. **Comments:** H-VT-195-G2a, Coulter-1. Similar to W-VT-610-001-G010. 18__. 1850s–1860s.

Rarity: URS-3

F $750

$2 • W-VT-610-002-G020

CC

Overprint: Red TWO. **Engraver:** Rawdon, Wright, Hatch & Edson / New England Bank Note Co. **Comments:** H-VT-195-G4a, Coulter-2. 18__. 1850s–1860s.

Rarity: URS-3

F $750

$3 • W-VT-610-003-G030

CC

Engraver: Rawdon, Wright, Hatch & Edson / New England Bank Note Co. **Comments:** H-Unlisted, Coulter-Unlisted. 18__. 1850s–1860s.

Rarity: URS-2
Unc-Rem $400; **Unc-S&D** $500; **Proof** $1,000

$3 • W-VT-610-003-G030a

CC

Overprint: Red THREE. **Engraver:** Rawdon, Wright, Hatch & Edson / New England Bank Note Co. **Comments:** H-VT-195-G6a, Coulter-3. Similar to W-VT-610-003-G030. 18__. 1850s–1860s.

Rarity: URS-3
F $1,000

$5 • W-VT-610-005-G040

CC

Overprint: Red FIVE. **Engraver:** Rawdon, Wright, Hatch & Edson / New England Bank Note Co. **Comments:** H-VT-195-G8a, Coulter-4. 18__. 1850s–1860s.

Rarity: URS-3
F $750

$10 • W-VT-610-010-G050

Left: 10 / Ceres seated with sheaf of wheat. **Center:** Man on bank, Boy and dog driving sheep. **Right:** 10 / Indian maid holding ear of corn and X. **Engraver:** Rawdon, Wright, Hatch & Edson / New England Bank Note Co. **Comments:** H-Unlisted, Coulter-5. 18__. 1850s–1860s.

Rarity: *None known*

$10 • W-VT-610-010-G050a

CC

Overprint: Red TEN. **Engraver:** Rawdon, Wright, Hatch & Edson / New England Bank Note Co. **Comments:** H-VT-195-G10a, Coulter-6. Similar to W-VT-610-010-G050. 18__. 1850s–1860s.

Rarity: URS-4
F $500

$20 • W-VT-610-020-G060

Left: Mercury seated between 2 and 0 / XX. **Center:** Herd of cattle and sheep, Drover on horseback. **Right:** 20 / Woman churning. **Engraver:** Rawdon, Wright, Hatch & Edson / New England Bank Note Co. **Comments:** H-VT-195-G12, Coulter-10. 18__. 1850s–1860s.

Rarity: *None known*

$50 • W-VT-610-050-G070

Left: Woman feeding horse / 50. **Center:** Farmers reclining at lunch in hayfield. **Right:** 50 / Portrait of Daniel Webster. **Engraver:** Rawdon, Wright, Hatch & Edson / New England Bank Note Co. **Comments:** H-VT-195-G14, Coulter-11. 18__. 1850s–1860s.

Rarity: *None known*

$100 • W-VT-610-100-G080

Left: 100 / Portrait of Millard Fillmore / 100. **Center:** Liberty crowning eagle with wreath / Portrait of George Washington. **Right:** 100 / Man on horseback, Oxen and load of hay. **Engraver:** Rawdon, Wright, Hatch & Edson / New England Bank Note Co. **Comments:** H-VT-195-G16, Coulter-12. 18__. 1850s–1860s.

Rarity: *None known*

NON-VALID ISSUES

$10 • W-VT-610-010-C050b

Engraver: Rawdon, Wright, Hatch & Edson / New England Bank Note Co. **Comments:** H-VT-195-C10b. Counterfeit of W-VT-610-010-G050a but with different style of overprint. 18__. 1859.

Rarity: URS-5
F $250

$10 • W-VT-610-010-C050c

Engraver: Rawdon, Wright, Hatch & Edson / New England Bank Note Co. **Comments:** H-VT-195-C10c. Counterfeit of W-VT-610-010-G050a but with different style of overprint. 18__. 1860.

Rarity: URS-5
F $250

$10 • W-VT-610-010-R010

Engraver: Rawdon, Wright, Hatch & Edson / New England Bank Note Co. **Comments:** H-VT-195-R5, Coulter-9. Raised from W-VT-610-002-G020. 18__. 1850s.

Rarity: *None known*

$10 • W-VT-610-010-R010a

Engraver: Rawdon, Wright, Hatch & Edson / New England Bank Note Co. *Comments:* H-Unlisted, Coulter-7. Similar to W-VT-610-010-R010 but with different style of overprint. 1850s–1860s.

Rarity: *None known*

$10 • W-VT-610-010-N010

Center: Woman seated, Cattle. *Comments:* H-Unlisted, Coulter-8. 1850s–1860s.

Rarity: *None known*

RUTLAND, VERMONT

Rutland was chartered in 1761 and was mostly likely named by John Murray of Rutland, Massachusetts. His was the first name given on the proprietor list. James Mead was the first permanent settler, building a house in 1769 and bringing his family in 1770.

Marble deposits were discovered in Rutland, and by the 1830s an almost solid deposit of marble was found in the western side of the land. The quarries became extremely profitable when the railroad came to Rutland in 1851, causing Rutland to become the railroad center for the state.

Bank of Rutland
1824–1865
W-VT-620

History: The Bank of Rutland was chartered on November 1, 1824. In 1826 a Mr. Dixon absconded with a large sum of money belonging to the bank. R.C. Royce, Esquire, of Rutland was hired to track him down. He recovered a portion of the funds. On July 24, 1833, a thief stole from the cashier an amount of $7,000, which was not recovered.

In 1841 the Bank of Rutland had $100,000 in capital. In August 1845, circulation was $103,628. The charter was renewed with $300,000 authorized capital in 1853. By June 1855, the bank had $150,000 capital. Figures for 1857 were listed as: capital $300,000; bills in circulation $181,914; specie $11,249; real estate $10,000. In July 1859, capital was $300,000, and circulation was $181,914.

The business of the Bank of Rutland was succeeded by the National Bank of Rutland in 1865.

Numismatic Commentary: Some issues have vignettes of the marble quarry with workman hoisting out a block of stone and others working at the wall inside the quarry. Other vignettes show a farmer with his scythe and an eagle with wings reaching almost to the borders of the note.

Remaining in the American Bank Note Co. archives as of 2003 was a $1-$1-$2-$3 face plate, a $1-$1-$2-$3 tint plate, a $5-$5-$5-$10 face plate, and a $5-$5-$5-$10 tint plate.

VALID ISSUES

$1 • W-VT-620-001-G010

Left: 1 / VERMONT / 1. *Center:* 1 / Steer, Woman / 1. *Right:* 1 / 1. *Engraver:* Graphic Co. *Comments:* H-VT-200-G2, Coulter-1. 18__. 1820s.

Rarity: *None known*

$1 • W-VT-620-001-G020   CC

Engraver: Rawdon, Wright, Hatch & Edson. *Comments:* H-VT-200-G8, Coulter-3. 18__. 1850s.

Rarity: URS-2

Unc-Rem $300; **AU** $900

$1 • W-VT-620-001-G030   CJF

Engraver: Danforth, Wright & Co. *Comments:* H-Unlisted, Coulter-Unlisted. January 1st, 18__. 1850s.

Rarity: URS-2

Proof $2,000

$1 • W-VT-620-001-G030a   CJF

Overprint: Red ONE. *Engraver:* Danforth, Wright & Co. *Comments:* H-VT-200-G10a, Coulter-4. Similar to W-VT-620-001-G030. January 1st, 18__. 1850s.

Rarity: URS-2

VG $1,500

$1 • W-VT-620-001-G040

CJF

Overprint: Green panel outlining white 1s and DOLLAR. **Engraver:** American Bank Note Co. **Comments:** H-Unlisted, Coulter-Unlisted. Similar to W-VT-620-001-G030 but with different date, engraver imprint, and right male portrait. July 1st, 1862. 1850s.

Rarity: URS-3
F $2,500

$1 • W-VT-620-001-G050

Left: Male portrait / 1 on ONE. **Center:** Marble quarry. **Right:** 1 / Army officer. **Engraver:** American Bank Note Co. **Comments:** H-Unlisted, Coulter-5. 1850s.

Rarity: *None known*

$2 • W-VT-620-002-G060

Left: 2 / VERMONT vertically / 2. **Center:** 2 / Justice overlooking town / 2. **Bottom center:** 2. **Right:** 2 / 2 vertically. **Engraver:** Graphic Co. **Comments:** H-VT-200-G12. 18__. 1820s.

Rarity: *None known*

$2 • W-VT-620-002-G070

Left: Woman churning / 2. **Center:** Portrait of Alexander Hamilton / Farmer sowing grain / Portrait of George Washington. **Bottom center:** Sheaf. **Right:** 2 / Farmer picking corn. **Engraver:** Unverified, but likely Rawdon, Wright, Hatch & Edson. **Comments:** H-VT-200-G18, Coulter-10. 18__. 1850s.

Rarity: *None known*

$2 • W-VT-620-002-G080

CC

Engraver: Danforth, Wright & Co. **Comments:** H-Unlisted, Coulter-Unlisted. January 1st, 18__. 1850s.

Rarity: URS-2
Proof $2,500

$2 • W-VT-620-002-G080a

Left: Portrait of George Washington / 2 bearing IIs and TWOs. **Center:** Herd of cattle drinking in stream, Man on horseback. **Right:** 2 / Portrait of Martha Washington. **Overprint:** Red TWO. **Engraver:** Danforth, Wright & Co. **Comments:** H-VT-200-G20a, Coulter-7. Similar to W-VT-620-002-G080. January 1st, 18__. 1850s.

Rarity: URS-3
VF $750; **Proof** $2,200

$2 • W-VT-620-002-G090

Left: Portrait of George Washington / 2. **Center:** Herd of cattle with farmer on horseback. **Right:** Male portrait / 2. **Tint:** Green. **Engraver:** American Bank Note Co. **Comments:** H-Unlisted, Coulter-8. July 4, 1862.

Rarity: *None known*

$3 • W-VT-620-003-G100

CC

Engraver: Danforth, Wright & Co. **Comments:** H-Unlisted, Coulter-11. January 1st, 18__. 1850s.

Rarity: URS-2
Proof $2,500

$3 • W-VT-620-003-G100a

CC

Overprint: Red 3 / 3. **Engraver:** Danforth, Wright & Co. **Comments:** H-VT-200-G24, Coulter-12. Similar to W-VT-620-003-G100. January 1st, 18__. 1850s.

Rarity: URS-1
F $2,000

$5 • W-VT-620-005-G110

CJF

Engraver: Graphic Co. **Comments:** H-VT-200-G28, Coulter-14. 18__. 1820s.

Rarity: URS-3
F $750

$5 • W-VT-620-005-G120

Left: Portrait of Marquis de Lafayette / Yorktown monument / V. **Center:** Liberty and eagle. **Bottom center:** Arm and hammer. **Right:** V / Men shearing sheep / V. **Comments:** H-VT-200-G34, Coulter-18. 18__. 1850s.

Rarity: *None known*

$5 • W-VT-620-005-G130   CC

Overprint: Red 5 / 5. *Engraver:* Rawdon, Wright, Hatch & Edson. *Comments:* H-VT-200-G36a, Coulter-19. Jan.y 1st, 18__. 1850s–1860s.

Rarity: URS-3
F $750; **VF** $850

$5 • W-VT-620-005-G130a   CJF

Tint: Green dies outlining white 5s. *Engraver:* Rawdon, Wright, Hatch & Edson / ABNCo. monogram. *Comments:* H-VT-200-G36c. Similar to W-VT-620-005-G130 but with different date and additional engraver imprint. Jan.y 1st, 1862.

Rarity: URS-2
F $1,250

$10 • W-VT-620-010-G140
Engraver: Graphic Co. *Comments:* H-VT-200-G38. No description available. 18__. 1820s.

Rarity: *None known*

$10 • W-VT-620-010-G150
Left: 10 / Cattle / 10. *Center:* Portrait of George Washington / Ceres / Portrait of Benjamin Franklin. *Bottom center:* Ceres. *Right:* 10 / Sheaf of corn and plow / 10. *Comments:* H-VT-200-G44, Coulter-23. 18__. 1850s.

Rarity: *None known*

$10 • W-VT-620-010-G160
Left: 10 / Portrait of General Winfield Scott. *Center:* Spread eagle. *Bottom center:* Cow and tree. *Right:* 10 / Portrait of George Washington. *Engraver:* Rawdon, Wright, Hatch & Edson. *Comments:* H-VT-200-G46, Coulter-22. 18__. 1850s.

Rarity: *None known*

$10 • W-VT-620-010-G160a   TD

Overprint: Red TEN. *Engraver:* Rawdon, Wright, Hatch & Edson. *Comments:* H-Unlisted, Coulter-Unlisted. Similar to W-VT-620-010-G160 but with different date. Jan.y 1st, 18__. 1850s.

Rarity: URS-3
F $1,500

$20 • W-VT-620-020-G170
Left: Portrait of George Washington. *Center:* Three allegorical figures / Portrait of George Washington. *Bottom center:* Portrait of George Washington. *Right:* 20 / VERMONT / 20. *Comments:* H-VT-200-G50, Coulter-30. 18__. 1850s.

Rarity: *None known*

$20 • W-VT-620-020-G180
Left: 20 / Farmer seated holding scythe, Basket and keg. *Center:* Block of stone on wagon drawn by four oxen, Two men leading oxen, Five men at work in stone quarry, Train. *Right:* 20 / Ceres sitting on plow. *Overprint:* Red TWENTY. *Engraver:* Rawdon, Wright, Hatch & Edson. *Comments:* H-VT-200-G52a, Coulter-29. 18__. 1850s.

Rarity: URS-2
Proof $800

$50 • W-VT-620-050-G190
Left: 50 / VERMONT / 50. *Center:* State arms and two women / Portrait of George Washington. *Right:* 50 / Justice / 50. *Comments:* H-VT-200-G56, Coulter-32. 18__. 1850s.

Rarity: URS-2
Proof $800

$50 • W-VT-620-050-G200
Left: 50 / Female portrait. *Center:* Train / Dog. *Right:* 50 / Female portrait. *Overprint:* Red L / L. *Engraver:* Rawdon, Wright, Hatch & Edson. *Comments:* H-VT-200-G58a, Coulter-31. 18__. 1850s.

Rarity: URS-2
Proof $800

$100 • W-VT-620-100-G210   CC

Overprint: Red C. *Engraver:* Rawdon, Wright, Hatch & Edson. *Comments:* H-VT-200-G62, Coulter-33. January 1st, 18__. 1850s.

Rarity: URS-1
Proof $5,000

Uncut Sheets

$1-$1-$2-$3 • W-VT-620-001.001.002.003-US010

Vignette(s): ($1) Portrait / View of marble quarry / Male portrait. *($1)* Portrait / View of marble quarry / Male portrait. *($2)* Portrait of George Washington / Herd of cattle drinking in stream, Man on horseback / Portrait of Martha Washington. *($3)* Girl with grain / Blacksmith beside anvil / Girl with cornucopia. *Engraver:* Danforth, Wright & Co. *Comments:* All unlisted in Haxby. January 1st, 18__. 1850s.

Rarity: URS-1

Proof $4,800

Non-Valid Issues

$1 • W-VT-620-001-N010

Center: Country scene, City. *Comments:* H-Unlisted, Coulter-6. 1850s.

Rarity: *None known*

$1 • W-VT-620-001-A010

SBG

Overprint: Red ONE. *Engraver:* Wellstood, Hay & Whiting. *Comments:* H-VT-200-A5, Coulter-2. Altered from $1 Thames Bank, Laurel, Indiana. August 12th, 1856.

Rarity: URS-7

F $150

$2 • W-VT-620-002-S010

CJF

Engraver: American Bank Note Co. *Comments:* H-VT-200-S5, Coulter-9. From a modified, fraudulent plate originally for a counterfeit $2 of the Bank of Belleville, Bellville, Illinois. 18__. 1860s.

Rarity: URS-6

VF $175

$3 • W-VT-620-003-N020

Center: Drover, cattle, boy. *Comments:* H-Unlisted, Coulter-13. 1850s.

Rarity: *None known*

$5 • W-VT-620-005-C020

CC

Engraver: Graphic Co. *Comments:* H-VT-200-C12. Counterfeit of W-VT-620-005-G020. 18__. 1830s.

Rarity: URS-7

F $75

$5 • W-VT-620-005-C110

Engraver: Graphic Co. *Comments:* H-VT-200-C28. Counterfeit of W-VT-620-005-G110. 18__. 1820s.

Rarity: *None known*

$5 • W-VT-620-005-R010

Comments: H-Unlisted, Coulter-16. Raised from W-VT-620-001-G010. 1850s.

Rarity: *None known*

$5 • W-VT-620-005-R020

Comments: H-Unlisted, Coulter-20. Raised from W-VT-620-002-G080a. 1850s.

Rarity: *None known*

$5 • W-VT-620-005-N030

Center: Woman. *Comments:* H-Unlisted, Coulter-15. 1850s.

Rarity: *None known*

$5 • W-VT-620-005-N040

Center: Drover, cattle, boy. *Comments:* H-Unlisted, Coulter-21. 1850s.

Rarity: *None known*

$10 • W-VT-620-010-R030

Comments: H-Unlisted, Coulter-25. Raised from W-VT-620-001-G030a. 1850s.

Rarity: *None known*

$10 • W-VT-620-010-R040

Comments: H-Unlisted, Coulter-26. Raised from W-VT-620-002-G080a. 1850s.

Rarity: *None known*

$10 • W-VT-620-010-N050

Left: 10 / Portrait of Benjamin Franklin / Agricultural scene / 10. *Center:* Woman, globe, and eagle. *Right:* 10 / Portrait of George Washington / Cattle / 10. *Comments:* H-VT-200-N5, Coulter-24. 18__. 1840s–1850s.

Rarity: *None known*

$10 • W-VT-620-010-N060

Center: Drover, cattle, boy. *Comments:* H-Unlisted, Coulter-27. 1850s.

Rarity: *None known*

$10 • W-VT-620-010-N070

Center: Portrait of George Washington / Woman with book and torch / Portrait of Benjamin Franklin. *Comments:* H-Unlisted, Coulter-28. 1850s.

Rarity: *None known*

Green Mountain Bank
1846 AND 1847
W-VT-625

History: The Green Mountain Bank was chartered on November 2, 1846. On October 25, 1847, its name was amended by an act of the Legislature to the Stark Bank, W-VT-060.

See also listing under Bennington, W-VT-050.

ISSUES
$1 • W-VT-625-001-N010

CC

Engraver: Rawdon & Balch. **Comments:** H-Unlisted, Coulter-Unlisted. 18__. 1820s–1840s.

Rarity: URS-3

F $750

Rutland County Bank
1862–1865
W-VT-630

History: The Rutland County Bank was chartered in 1861 and opened in 1862. In July of that year its circulation was $77,068. $50,000 of its capital stock was paid in by September. In 1864 the capital had risen to $100,000.

The business of the bank was succeeded by the Rutland County National Bank in 1865. Outstanding circulation of the Rutland County Bank as of July 1, 1867, was $2,670, redemption of which was guaranteed by the national bank.

Numismatic Commentary: All issues are very rare. Modern Proofs with vivid green tints exist. Some issues show workmen in various scenes with marble.

All issues of the Rutland County Bank bear the engraver's imprint of the American Bank Note Co.

VALID ISSUES
$1 • W-VT-630-001-G010

Left: 1 / Cattle. **Center:** Train moving blocks of marble / ONE 1 ONE. **Right:** 1 / Portrait. **Tint:** Green panel. **Comments:** H-VT-205-G2a, Coulter-38. July 15th, 1862.

Rarity: *None known*

$2 • W-VT-630-002-G020

Left: 2 / 2 / Man cutting marble / TWO DOLLARS. **Center:** 2 / Male portrait / 2. **Tint:** Green dies bearing white 2 and TWO DOLLARS. **Comments:** H-VT-205-G4a, Coulter-39. July 15th, 1862.

Rarity: *None known*

$2 • W-VT-630-002-G020a

CC

Tint: Green panels. **Comments:** H-Unlisted, Coulter-Unlisted. Similar to W-VT-630-002-G020. Modern Proof. July 15th, 1862.

Rarity: URS-1

Proof $3,500

$5 • W-VT-630-005-G030

Left: 5 / Two children and cattle under tree. **Right:** 5 / Male portrait. **Tint:** Green V and FIVE DOLLARS on die. **Comments:** H-VT-205-G6a, Coulter-40. July 15th, 1862.

Rarity: *None known*

$5 • W-VT-630-005-G030a

CC

Tint: Green die bearing white V. **Comments:** H-Unlisted, Coulter-Unlisted. Similar to W-VT-630-005-G030. Modern Proof. July 15th, 1862.

Rarity: URS-2

Proof $2,500

$10 • W-VT-630-010-G040

CC

Tint: Green X / X and frame. **Comments:** H-VT-205-G8a, Coulter-42. Modern Proof. July 15th, 1862.

Rarity: URS-2

Proof $3,000

$20 • W-VT-630-020-G050

Left: Portrait of General Winfield Scott / XX. **Center:** 20 / Sheaf and agricultural implements. **Right:** 20 / Portrait of General George McClellan. **Tint:** Green dies bearing white XX, 20, 20, TWENTY. **Comments:** H-VT-205-G10a, Coulter-43. July 15th, 1862.

Rarity: URS-1

Proof $1,200

$20 • W-VT-630-020-G050a

CC

Tint: Green dies and panel bearing white TWENTY. *Comments:* H-Unlisted, Coulter-Unlisted. Similar to W-VT-630-020-G050. Modern Proof. July 15th, 1862.

Rarity: URS-2
Proof $3,500

NON-VALID ISSUES

$5 • W-VT-630-005-R010

Comments: H-VT-205-R5, Coulter-41. Raised from W-VT-630-001-G010. 1850s.

Rarity: *None known*

SAINT ALBANS, VERMONT

Chartered on August 17, 1763, St. Albans was granted to Stephen Pomeroy and 63 others. It received its name from St. Albans, Hertfordshire, England. Jesse Welden settled the land during the Revolutionary War, but the conflict postponed additional arrivals until peace was restored. The soil was perfect for planting crops, as well as for the raising of cattle, horses, and sheep. Butter and cheese were also important products. The town was incorporated in 1859 and was soon called the "Railroad City," being home to a major depot and the central home of the Vermont & Canada Railroad. An iron foundry, a freight-car manufacturer, and mechanics shops were part of that industry.

The Civil War reached its farthest northern limits in the skirmish known as the St. Albans Raid, which took place on October 18, 1864. Confederate troops arrived in small numbers until they developed into a force large enough to take over St. Albans. They gathered the townsfolk together, robbed the three local banks, and escaped with more than $200,000. They attempted to burn the town but only accomplished the destruction of a woodshed.

Bank of St. Albans
1825–1855
W-VT-640

History: The Bank of St. Albans was chartered on October 28, 1825, with $100,000 in authorized capital. In October 1830, many counterfeit $2 bills of the Bank of St. Albans were in circulation.

On January 30, 1838, the Suffolk Bank reported that bills of this bank would not be received, but this was resolved after the affects of the Panic of 1837 were ameliorated. In 1841 its capital was $100,000 with $50,000 paid in. In August 1845, circulation was $66,680. In February 1854, the bank was rechartered and given an additional capital of $100,000. This charter expired on July 1, 1855. At this time the capital was divided among the stockholders and the bank closed. The outstanding circulation as of July 21, 1859, was reported to be $6,803.

Numismatic Commentary: Genuine bank notes from at least three different engravers are available in the marketplace. One Proof sheet that was engraved by Fairman, Draper & Underwood has an interesting notation in the lower margin. It states that after 6,000 impressions, the plate for the $3 denomination should be altered to a $5 denomination.

A fraudulent enterprise, the Mechanics Exchange Bank said to have been based in New York City, produced notes with the Bank of St. Albans imprint, even though the worthless nature of the notes was widely known at the time and appeared in various newspaper accounts. This did not deter merchants and banks from receiving them for goods and services and then passing the bills to others. The Farmers and Mechanics Bank, W-VT-190, also had notes fraudulently produced by this entity.

VALID ISSUES

$1 • W-VT-640-001-G010

Left: ONE / ONE / ONE. *Center:* Allegorical figure / 1 on shield surmounted by eagle / ONE. *Right:* ONE / VERMONT / ONE. *Engraver:* Rawdon, Clark & Co. *Comments:* H-VT-210-G2, Coulter-3. 18__. 1820s–1840s.

Rarity: *None known*

$1 • W-VT-640-001-G010a

Overprint: ONE. *Engraver:* Rawdon, Clark & Co. *Comments:* H-VT-210-G2a. Similar to W-VT-640-001-G010. 18__. 1840s.

Rarity: URS-3
VF $300

$1 • W-VT-640-001-G020

CC

Engraver: Rawdon, Wright, Hatch & Edson. *Comments:* H-VT-210-G6, Coulter-4. 18__. 1840s–1850s.

Rarity: URS-3
VF $450; **Proof** $2,800

$1 • W-VT-640-001-G030

CC

Engraver: Fairman, Draper, Underwood & Co. *Comments:* H-Unlisted, Coulter-Unlisted. 18__. 1820s–1840s.

Rarity: URS-3
Proof $750

$2 • **W-VT-640-002-G040**

Engraver: Rawdon, Clark & Co. *Comments:* H-VT-210-G8. No description available. 18__. 1820s.

Rarity: *None known*

$2 • **W-VT-640-002-G050**

Left: 2 in die / Two women. *Center:* 2. *Right:* TWO / Woman and cherub holding 2. *Engraver:* Rawdon, Wright, Hatch & Edson. *Comments:* H-VT-210-G12, Coulter-8. 18__. 1840s–1850s.

Rarity: URS-3

Proof $600

$2 • **W-VT-640-002-G060**   CJF

Engraver: Fairman, Draper, Underwood & Co. *Comments:* H-Unlisted. 18__. 1820s.

Rarity: URS-3

F $1,000

$3 • **W-VT-640-003-G070**   TD

Engraver: Rawdon, Wright, Hatch & Edson. *Comments:* H-VT-210-G18, Coulter-13. 18__. 1840s–1850s.

Rarity: URS-3

VF $350; **Proof** $1,000

$3 • **W-VT-640-003-G080**

Payee: L. Sandford. *Comments:* H-Unlisted, Coulter-14. 1840s–1850s.

Rarity: *None known*

$3 • **W-VT-640-003-G090**   CC

Engraver: Fairman, Draper, Underwood & Co. *Comments:* H-Unlisted. 18__. 1820s.

Rarity: URS-2

VF $400; **Proof** $1,000

$5 • **W-VT-640-005-G100**

Left: FIVE / VERMONT / FIVE. *Center:* 5 / Two cherubs playing with dolphins / 5 / FIVE. *Right:* FIVE / FIVE / FIVE. *Engraver:* Rawdon, Clark & Co. *Comments:* H-VT-210-G20. 18__. 1820s–1840s.

Rarity: *None known*

$5 • **W-VT-640-005-G100a**

Overprint: FIVE. *Engraver:* Rawdon, Clark & Co. *Comments:* H-VT-210-G20a, Coulter-16. Similar to W-VT-640-005-G100. 18__. 1850s.

Rarity: URS-2

VF $450; **Unc-Rem** $400

$5 • **W-VT-640-005-G100b**

Overprint: Ornate FIVE. *Engraver:* Rawdon, Clark & Co. *Comments:* H-VT-210-G20b. Similar to W-VT-640-005-G100. 18__. 1850s.

Rarity: URS-2

VF $450; **Unc-Rem** $400

$10 • **W-VT-640-010-G110**

Left: TEN / VERMONT vertically / TEN. *Center:* TEN, 10, TEN in die / Cherub, Sheaf of wheat on TEN, Cherub / TEN, 10, TEN in die. *Bottom center:* Ceres. *Right:* TEN / TEN vertically / TEN. *Engraver:* Rawdon, Clark & Co. *Comments:* H-VT-210-G26, Coulter-17. 18__. 1820s–1840s.

Rarity: *None known*

$10 • **W-VT-640-010-G110a**

Overprint: TEN. *Engraver:* Rawdon, Clark & Co. *Comments:* H-VT-210-G26a. Similar to W-VT-640-010-G110. 18__. 1850s.

Rarity: URS-2

VF $450; **Unc-Rem** $400

$20 • **W-VT-640-020-G120**   CC

Engraver: Rawdon, Wright, Hatch & Edson. *Comments:* H-VT-210-G32, Coulter-19. 18__. 1840s–1850s.

Rarity: URS-2

F $1,500

$50 • **W-VT-640-050-G130**

Comments: H-Unlisted, Coulter-20. No description available. 1840s–1850s.

Rarity: *None known*

$100 • **W-VT-640-100-G140**

Comments: H-Unlisted, Coulter-21. No description available. 1840s–1850s.

Rarity: *None known*

Uncut Sheets

$1-$2-$3 • W-VT-640-001.002.003-US010

Vignette(s): ($1) Minerva in alcove / Medallion head / Ceres and child with plow, cattle, anvil / Medallion head / Woman seated with 1 bearing ONE in alcove. *($2)* Portrait of Benjamin Franklin / Woman seated / Portrait of George Washington. *($3)* Portrait of George Washington / Man on horseback with cattle and sheep at stream / Portrait of Marquis de Lafayette. *Engraver:* Fairman, Draper & Underwood. *Comments:* All unlisted in Haxby. Only 6,000 of the $3 were printed, as seen by a notation at the bottom of the sheet. 18__. 1820s.
> **Rarity:** URS-1
> **Proof** $1,200

$1-$1-$2-$3 • W-VT-640-001.001.002.003-US020

Vignette(s): ($1) Minerva in alcove / Medallion head / Ceres and child with plow, cattle, anvil / Medallion head / Woman seated with 1 bearing ONE in alcove. *($1)* Minerva in alcove / Medallion head / Ceres and child with plow, cattle, anvil / Medallion head / Woman seated with 1 bearing ONE in alcove. *($2)* Portrait of Benjamin Franklin / Woman seated / Portrait of George Washington. *($3)* Portrait of George Washington / Man on horseback with cattle and sheep at stream / Portrait of Marquis de Lafayette. *Engraver:* Fairman, Draper & Underwood. *Comments:* All unlisted in Haxby. 18__. 1820s.
> **Rarity:** URS-1
> **Proof** $1,400

$1-$5-$5-$10 • W-VT-640-001.005.005.010-US030

Vignette(s): ($1) Allegorical figure / 1 on shield surmounted by eagle. *($5)* Two cherubs playing with dolphins. *($5)* Two cherubs playing with dolphins. *($10)* Cherub / Sheaf of wheat / Cherub / Ceres. *Engraver:* Rawdon, Clark & Co. *Comments:* H-VT-210-G2a, G20a, G20b, G26a. 18__. 1850s.
> **Rarity:** URS-1
> **Proof** $1,400

NON-VALID ISSUES

$2 • W-VT-640-002-C040

Engraver: Rawdon, Clark & Co. *Comments:* H-VT-210-C8. Counterfeit of W-VT-640-002-G040. 18__. 1820s.
> **Rarity:** *None known*

$2 • W-VT-640-002-N010

Payee: A. Jones. *Comments:* H-Unlisted, Coulter-11. 1820s.
> **Rarity:** *None known*

$2 • W-VT-640-002-N020

CC

Engraver: Fairman, Draper, Underwood & Co. *Comments:* H-VT-210-N5. 18__. 1820s.
> **Rarity:** URS-5
> **VG** $100; **F** $175

$10 • W-VT-640-010-C110

CC

Engraver: Rawdon, Clark & Co. *Comments:* H-VT-210-C26. Counterfeit of W-VT-640-010-G110. 18__. 1840s–1850s.
> **Rarity:** URS-3
> **VG** $170; **VF** $200

$10 • W-VT-640-010-N030

Comments: H-Unlisted, Coulter-18. Imitation of W-VT-640-010-G110 series. 1840s–1850s.
> **Rarity:** *None known*

Notes Payable at the Mechanics Exchange Company, New York

$1 • W-VT-640-001-S010

CJF

Engraver: S. Stiles, Sherman & Smith. *Comments:* H-Unlisted, Coulter-5. 183_. 1837.
> **Rarity:** URS-7
> **F** $100; **EF** $150

$1 • W-VT-640-001-S020

CC

Engraver: S. Stiles, Sherman & Smith. *Comments:* H-Unlisted, Coulter-6. 183_. 1837.
> **Rarity:** URS-7
> **F** $150

$1 • W-VT-640-001-S030   CC

Engraver: S. Stiles, Sherman & Smith. *Comments:* H-Unlisted, Coulter-7. 183_. 1837.

Rarity: URS-7
F $150

$2 • W-VT-640-002-S040   CC

Engraver: S. Stiles, Sherman & Smith. *Comments:* H-Unlisted, Coulter-9. 183_. 1837.

Rarity: URS-7
F $150

$2 • W-VT-640-002-S050

Left: Ship / 2. *Center:* Cattle under tree. *Right:* Blacksmith / 2. *Engraver:* S. Stiles, Sherman & Smith. *Comments:* H-Unlisted, Coulter-10. 183_. 1837.

Rarity: *None known*

$3 • W-VT-640-003-S055   CC

Engraver: S. Stiles, Sherman & Smith. *Comments:* H-Unlisted, Coulter-12. 183_. 1837.

Rarity: URS-7
EF $200

$3 • W-VT-640-003-S060   CC

Engraver: S. Stiles, Sherman & Smith. *Comments:* H-Unlisted, Coulter-15. 183_. 1837.

Rarity: URS-6
EF $250

Franklin County Bank
1849–1867
W-VT-650

History: The Franklin County Bank was chartered in 1849 with an authorized capital of $100,000, of which $70,000 was soon paid in. An act passed in 1852 amended the act incorporating the Franklin County Bank to have an address at St. Albans Bay, a lakeside district of the town.

In 1857 the figures for the bank included: capital $100,000; bills in circulation $79,520; specie $2,118; real estate $5,000. In 1859 circulation was the same, but by 1862 it had dropped to $74,184. By July of the same year it was $92,841. After the Confederate raid on the town in 1864, the bank went into liquidation, paying all debts, but it refused to redeem its bills where a satisfactory account of proper possession could not be proven, due to the repercussions of the Confederate raid.

See also listing under St. Albans Bay, W-VT-680.

Numismatic Commentary: Genuine notes of this bank are found in significant quantities. They can be found with both addresses.

Remaining in the American Bank Note Co. archives as of 2003 was a $10-$20 cancelled face plate and a $1-$1-$2-$5 cancelled face plate.

VALID ISSUES
$1 • W-VT-650-001-G010   CC

Overprint: Red ONE. *Engraver:* Rawdon, Wright, Hatch & Edson. *Comments:* H-VT-215-G12a. Feb.y 1st, 185_. 1850s–1860s.

Rarity: URS-8
VF $125

$2 • W-VT-650-002-G020

Left: TWO / Minerva. *Center:* Woman reclining on bale, Ships. *Right:* 2 / Seated woman holding distaff / TWO. *Overprint:* Red TWO. *Engraver:* Rawdon, Wright, Hatch & Edson. *Comments:* H-VT-215-G14a. Feb.y 1st, 185_. 1850s.

Rarity: URS-8

VG $95; VF $100

$5 • W-VT-650-005-G030

CJF

Overprint: Red FIVE. *Engraver:* Rawdon, Wright, Hatch & Edson. *Comments:* H-VT-215-G16a. Feb.y 1st, 185_. 1850s.

Rarity: URS-8

F $75; VF $125

$10 • W-VT-650-010-G040

CC

Overprint: Red panel outlining white TEN. *Engraver:* American Bank Note Co. *Comments:* H-Unlisted, Coulter-Unlisted. 18__. 1860s.

Rarity: URS-4

F $100; VF $450

$20 • W-VT-650-020-G050

CJF

Overprint: Red panel outlining white TWENTY. *Engraver:* American Bank Note Co. *Comments:* H-VT-215-G20a. 18__. 1860s.

Rarity: URS-4

F $200; VF $550

NON-VALID ISSUES

$3 • W-VT-650-003-N010

Center: Wharf scene, Warehouses and vessels. *Comments:* H-VT-215-N5. 1850s.

Rarity: *None known*

$5 • W-VT-650-005-N020

Left: Girl raking hay. *Center:* Woman with sheaf of grain. *Right:* FIVE. *Comments:* H-VT-215-N10, Coulter-29. 1850s.

Rarity: *None known*

$10 • W-VT-650-010-A010

Center: Amphitrite and Neptune in shell drawn by sea horses. *Comments:* H-VT-215-A10, Coulter-33. 18__. 1850s.

Rarity: URS-5

F $75

Northern Bank of Vermont
1854
W-VT-660

History: In 1854 a charter application for the Northern Bank of Vermont to be based in St. Albans was rejected by the state legislature.

Numismatic Commentary: It is possible that Proof notes were made, but no record has been found of such.

St. Albans Bank
1854–1866
W-VT-670

History: The St. Albans Bank was chartered in 1853 with an authorized capital of $150,000, of which $105,000 was paid in by December 1, 1854. Between 1857 and 1864 the capital was listed at $150,000. Selected figures for 1857 included: bills in circulation $197,226; specie $7,140; real estate $2,000. Circulation in July 1859 was $197,226, and in July 1862 it was $262,897.

The St. Albans Bank closed in 1866. Its outstanding and unredeemed circulation was valued at $28,867 as of July 1, 1867.

Numismatic Commentary: Most issues were engraved by Toppan, Carpenter, Casilear & Co. and are fairly plentiful. The issues engraved by the American Bank Note Co. are much harder to locate. It is interesting that on the notes the bank chose to spell St. Alban's (with an apostrophe) for the name of its location, but its charter had the regular St. Albans style.

Remaining in the American Bank Note Co. archives as of 2003 was a $1-$1-$2-$3 face plate, a $50-$100 face plate, and a $5-$5-$5-$10 face plate.

VALID ISSUES

$1 • W-VT-670-001-G010

CC

Engraver: Toppan, Carpenter, Casilear & Co. **Comments:** H-VT-211-G2, Coulter-36. 185_. 1850s.

Rarity: URS-2
Proof $1,100

$1 • W-VT-670-001-G010a

CC

Overprint: Red ONE. **Engraver:** Toppan, Carpenter, Casilear & Co. **Comments:** H-VT-211-G2b, Coulter-37. Similar to W-VT-670-001-G010 but with different date. August 15th, 18__. 1860s.

Rarity: URS-4
F $500

$2 • W-VT-670-002-G020

Left: 2 / Sailor, capstan, bale, and barrel. **Center:** Boys trying to catch wild horse. **Right:** 2 / Blacksmith, sledge, anvil, forge. **Engraver:** Toppan, Carpenter, Casilear & Co. **Comments:** H-VT-211-G4, Coulter-39. 185_. 1850s.

Rarity: URS-2
Proof $800

$2 • W-VT-670-002-G020a

CC

Overprint: Red 2 / 2. **Engraver:** Toppan, Carpenter, Casilear & Co. **Comments:** H-VT-211-G4b. Similar to W-VT-670-002-G020 but with different date. August 15th, 18__. 1860s.

Rarity: URS-4
F $750

$3 • W-VT-670-003-G030

Left: 3 / Blacksmith shop, Smith shoeing horse, Two men looking on. **Center:** Female portrait. **Right:** 3 / Woman carrying grain. **Engraver:** Toppan, Carpenter, Casilear & Co. **Comments:** H-VT-211-G6, Coulter-40. 185_. 1850s.

Rarity: URS-2
Proof $800

$3 • W-VT-670-003-G030a

CC

Overprint: Red THREE. **Engraver:** Toppan, Carpenter, Casilear & Co. **Comments:** H-VT-211-G6c. Similar to W-VT-670-003-G030 but with different date. August 15th, 18__. 1860s.

Rarity: URS-4
VF $800

$5 • W-VT-670-005-G040

Left: Three allegorical figures on cliff / FIVE. **Center:** Three water nymphs supporting cherub. **Bottom center:** Spread eagle. **Right:** 5 / Female portrait. **Engraver:** Toppan, Carpenter, Casilear & Co. **Comments:** H-VT-211-G8a, Coulter-41. August 15th, 18__. 1850s.

Rarity: URS-2
Proof $800

$5 • W-VT-670-005-G040a

CC

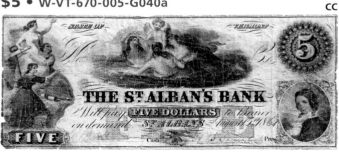

Overprint: Red FIVE. **Engraver:** Toppan, Carpenter, Casilear & Co. **Comments:** H-VT-211-G8b. Similar to W-VT-670-005-G040. August 15th, 18__. 1860s.

Rarity: URS-3
F $750; **VF** $900

$5 • W-VT-670-005-G040b

CC

Overprint: Red ornate FIVE. **Engraver:** Toppan, Carpenter, Casilear & Co. / ABNCo. monogram. **Comments:** H-Unlisted. Similar to W-VT-670-005-G040 but with different date and additional engraver imprint. Jan.y 1st, 1863.

Rarity: URS-3

F $750

$10 • W-VT-670-010-G050

Left: 10 / Portrait of Andrew Jackson. **Center:** Train, Train crossing bridge over river. **Bottom center:** Sheaf and plow. **Right:** 10 / Farmer carrying corn. **Engraver:** Toppan, Carpenter, Casilear & Co. **Comments:** H-VT-211-G10a, Coulter-42. August 15th, 18__. 1850s.

Rarity: URS-2

Proof $800

$10 • W-VT-670-010-G050a

CJF

Overprint: Red TEN. **Engraver:** Toppan, Carpenter, Casilear & Co. **Comments:** H-VT-211-G10b. Similar to W-VT-670-010-G050. August 15th, 18__. 1860s.

Rarity: URS-3

F $1,000

$20 • W-VT-670-020-G060

Left: 20 / Female portrait. **Center:** Three allegorical figures with wand, cornucopia, sword, and scales, Ships. **Right:** 20 / Woman standing and holding tablet on pedestal. **Engraver:** Toppan, Carpenter, Casilear & Co. **Comments:** H-VT-211-G12, Coulter-44. 18__. 1850s.

Rarity: *None known*

$20 • W-VT-670-020-G060a

CC

Overprint: Red TWENTY. **Engraver:** American Bank Note Co. **Comments:** H-Unlisted, Coulter-Unlisted. Similar to W-VT-670-020-G060 but with different date and engraver imprint. January 1st, 1863.

Rarity: URS-2

F $1,500

$50 • W-VT-670-050-G070

Left: 50 / Female portrait. **Center:** Woman, man, and child. **Right:** 50 / Train. **Comments:** H-Unlisted, Coulter-45. 1850s.

Rarity: *None known*

$50 • W-VT-670-050-G080

Left: 50 / Female portrait. **Center:** Portrait of George Washington. **Right:** 50 / Train, Village. **Engraver:** Toppan, Carpenter, Casilear & Co. **Comments:** H-VT-211-G14, Coulter-46. 18__. 1850s.

Rarity: *None known*

$100 • W-VT-670-100-G090

Left: 100 / Soldiers and drummer boy. **Center:** Liberty, eagle, and shield. **Right:** 100 / Portrait of child. **Comments:** H-Unlisted, Coulter-47. 1850s.

Rarity: *None known*

$100 • W-VT-670-100-G100

Left: 100 / Soldiers. **Center:** U.S. Capitol. **Right:** 100 / Portrait of Daniel Webster. **Engraver:** Toppan, Carpenter, Casilear & Co. **Comments:** H-VT-211-G16, Coulter-48. 18__. 1850s.

Rarity: *None known*

NON-VALID ISSUES

$1 • W-VT-670-001-N010

Center: Blacksmith. **Comments:** H-Unlisted, Coulter-38. 1850s.

Rarity: *None known*

$10 • W-VT-670-010-N020

Center: Blacksmith at forge. **Comments:** H-Unlisted, Coulter-43. 1850s.

Rarity: *None known*

How to Read the Whitman Numbering System

$1 • W-RI-010-001-G010a

Denomination: Value of the note shown.

W: Whitman number. This number is a sortable code unique to each bank and note.

RI: Abbreviation for the state under study.

010: Numerical designation specific to each bank.

001: The denomination in dollars.

G010a: G indicates a good or valid note. Other categories are indicated thus: C (counterfeit); R (raised); S (spurious); N (not-attributed); A (altered). Numbers are assigned starting with 010, 020, et seq. Terminal letters following the number indicate variations of a note: a series of different colored overprints, tints, payees, etc., all on the same design of note. For more information, see the "How to Use This Book" section at the front of the volume, page xiv.

Saint Albans Bay, Vermont

St. Albans Bay was a popular camping ground for local natives before the land was settled by colonists. The area includes the unincorporated land contiguous to but beyond the limits of St. Albans.

St. Albans Bay was a port city most notable for its construction of steamships, including the *Franklin*, which was built in 1827. The port was inconvenient to reach overland, and so it became well-known to smugglers along the Canadian border. Notable citizen Dr. John Stoddard even engaged the smuggling ship of notoriety, the *Black Snake*, for smuggling ashes into Canada.

Franklin County Bank
1849–1867
W-VT-680

History: The Franklin County Bank was chartered in 1849 with an authorized capital of $100,000, of which $70,000 was soon paid in. An act passed in 1852 amended the act incorporating the Franklin County Bank with an address at St. Albans Bay.

In 1857 the figures for the bank included: capital $100,000; bills in circulation $79,520; specie $2,118; real estate $5,000. In 1859 circulation was the same, but by 1862 it had dropped to $74,184. By July of the same year it was $92,841.

In 1867 the bank went into liquidation, paying all debts, but it refused to redeem its bills where a satisfactory account of proper possession could not be proven, due to the repercussions of the 1864 Confederate raid.

See also listing under St. Albans, W-VT-650.

Numismatic Commentary: Genuine notes of this bank can still be found in significant quantities with both addresses.

Remaining in the American Bank Note Co. archives as of 2003 was a $10-$20 cancelled face plate and a $1-$1-$2-$5 cancelled face plate.

Valid Issues

$1 • W-VT-680-001-G010   CJF

Engraver: Rawdon, Wright, Hatch & Edson. **Comments:** H-VT-215-G2, Coulter-22. Feb.y 1st, 1850.
Rarity: URS-3
Proof $750

$1 • W-VT-680-001-G010a

Left: ONE / Portrait of girl. **Center:** Blacksmith seated, Train / 1. **Right:** ONE / Minerva standing beside 1 / ONE. **Overprint:** Red ONE. **Engraver:** Rawdon, Wright, Hatch & Edson. **Comments:** H-VT-215-G2a, Coulter-23. Similar to W-VT-680-001-G010. Feb.y 1st, 1850.
Rarity: URS-6
F $75; **VF** $175

$2 • W-VT-680-002-G020

Left: TWO / Minerva. **Center:** Woman reclining on bale, Ships. **Right:** 2 / Seated woman holding distaff / TWO. **Engraver:** Rawdon, Wright, Hatch & Edson. **Comments:** H-VT-215-G4, Coulter-24. Feb.y 1st, 1850.
Rarity: URS-3
Proof $600

$2 • W-VT-680-002-G020a   CC

Overprint: Red TWO. **Engraver:** Rawdon, Wright, Hatch & Edson. **Comments:** H-VT-215-G4a, Coulter-25. Similar to W-VT-680-002-G020. Feb.y 1st, 1850.
Rarity: URS-6
F $75

$5 • W-VT-680-005-G030   CC

Engraver: Rawdon, Wright, Hatch & Edson. **Comments:** H-VT-215-G6, Coulter-27. Feb.y 1st, 1850.
Rarity: URS-3
Proof $750

$5 • W-VT-680-005-G030a   ANS

Overprint: Red FIVE. **Engraver:** Rawdon, Wright, Hatch & Edson. **Comments:** H-VT-215-G6a, Coulter-28. Similar to W-VT-680-005-G030. Feb.y 1st, 1850.
Rarity: URS-7
F $75; **VF** $175

$10 • W-VT-680-010-G040

Left: 10 / Portrait of Benjamin Franklin / 10. **Center:** Steamboat leaving dock. **Right:** 10 / Train / 10. **Engraver:** Wellstood, Benson & Hanks. **Comments:** H-VT-215-G8, Coulter-30. 18__. 1850s.
Rarity: *None known*

$10 • W-VT-680-010-G040a

CJF

Overprint: Red TEN. *Engraver:* Wellstood, Benson & Hanks. *Comments:* H-VT-215-G8a, Coulter-31. Similar to W-VT-680-010-G040. 18__. 1860s.

Rarity: URS-4
VG $150; **VF** $200

$20 • W-VT-680-020-G050

Left: 20 / Train / 20. *Center:* Woman seated with hand on shield bearing state arms, Sheaves. *Right:* 20 / Steamship / 20. *Engraver:* Wellstood, Benson & Hanks. *Comments:* H-VT-215-G10, Coulter-34. 18__. 1850s–1860s.

Rarity: *None known*

$20 • W-VT-680-020-G050a

CJF

Overprint: Red TWENTY. *Engraver:* Wellstood, Benson & Hanks. *Comments:* H-VT-215-G10a, Coulter-35. Similar to W-VT-680-020-G050. 18__. 1850s.

Rarity: URS-6
F $150

NON-VALID ISSUES

$3 • W-VT-680-003-A010

CC

Overprint: Red THREE. *Engraver:* Spencer, Hufty & Danforth. *Comments:* H-VT-215-A5, Coulter-26. Altered from W-VT-570-003-G030. January 15th, 1850.

Rarity: URS-5
F $175

$10 • W-VT-680-010-S010

CC

Overprint: Red TEN. *Engraver:* Durand, Perkins & Co. *Comments:* H-VT-215-S10, Coulter-32. 18__. 1850s.

Rarity: URS-5
F $100

SAINT JOHNSBURY, VERMONT

Originally called Bessborough, the area later known as St. Johnsbury was granted by New Hampshire governor Benning Wentworth in 1760. It was re-granted by Vermont in 1786 as Dunmore and settled that year. One of the early settlers was Jonathan Arnold, who left Rhode Island in 1787 with six families and built homes in what became the center of town.

By 1790 the population was 143. It is said that Ethan Allen suggested naming the town St. John in honor of a friend, who instead proposed the name St. Johnsbury to differentiate it from St. John, New Brunswick.

During the 19th century, the Fairbanks family developed a platform scale, the first widely successful commercial scale of its kind. Soon the business expanded and employed 1,000 workers in shops, forges, and foundries. Maple-sugar candy was also a major industry, and another was the making of bowling pins. In the 1850s the railroad arrived, and the Fairbanks family constructed locomotives. St. Johnsbury was designated the county seat in 1856, taking the place of Danville for the position.

Passumpsic Bank
1849–1864
W-VT-690

History: The Passumpsic Bank was chartered in 1849 but did not begin business until May 1, 1850. The authorized starting capital was $100,000. Figures of the bank for 1857 included: capital $100,000; bills in circulation $134,182; specie $8,966; real estate $4,000. In July 1859, circulation was $134,182. In 1862 it was $133,935.

In 1864 the interests of the bank were succeeded by the First National Bank. The outstanding circulation of the Passumpsic Bank was $3,375 as of July 1, 1867. The bank published a notice stating that it would not be liable to redeem its outstanding circulation after December 1, 1867.

Numismatic Commentary: Genuine notes are scarce and somewhat hard to find. The lower denominations appear more often.

VALID ISSUES

$1 • W-VT-690-001-G010

Left: Cattle and sheep / ONE. *Center:* 1. *Right:* 1 / Blacksmith and anvil. *Engraver:* Rawdon, Wright, Hatch & Edson / New England Bank Note Co. *Comments:* H-VT-220-G2a, Coulter-4. May 1st, 185_. 1850s.

Rarity: *None known*

$1 • W-VT-690-001-G010a

Overprint: Red ONE. *Engraver:* Rawdon, Wright, Hatch & Edson / New England Bank Note Co. *Comments:* H-VT-220-G2b. Similar to W-VT-690-001-G010. May 1st, 185_. 1850s

Rarity: *None known*

$1 • W-VT-690-001-G010b   CJF

Overprint: Red ONE. *Engraver:* Rawdon, Wright, Hatch & Edson / New England Bank Note Co. / ABNCo. monogram. *Comments:* H-VT-220-G2c. Similar to W-VT-690-001-G010 but with additional engraver imprint. May 1st, 185_. 1859.

Rarity: URS-4
F $750

$2 • W-VT-690-002-G020   CJF

Engraver: Rawdon, Wright, Hatch & Edson / New England Bank Note Co. *Comments:* H-VT-220-G4a, Coulter-5. May 1st, 185_. 1850s.

Rarity: URS-3
F $750

$2 • W-VT-690-002-G020a

Left: Mechanic seated / TWO. *Center:* 2. *Bottom center:* State arms. *Right:* 2 / Two women. *Overprint:* Red TWO. *Engraver:* Rawdon, Wright, Hatch & Edson / New England Bank Note Co. *Comments:* H-VT-220-G4b. Similar to W-VT-690-002-G020. May 1st, 185_. 1850s.

Rarity: *None known*

$2 • W-VT-690-002-G020b   CJF

Overprint: Red TWO. *Engraver:* Rawdon, Wright, Hatch & Edson / New England Bank Note Co. / ABNCo. monogram. *Comments:* H-VT-220-G4c. Similar to W-VT-690-002-G020 but with additional engraver imprint. May 1st, 185_. 1859.

Rarity: URS-3
F $750

$3 • W-VT-690-003-G030

Left: Woman seated with cornucopia / THREE. *Center:* 3. *Right:* 3 / Portrait of Daniel Webster. *Engraver:* Rawdon, Wright, Hatch & Edson / New England Bank Note Co. *Comments:* H-VT-220-G6a, Coulter-6. May 1st, 185_. 1850s.

Rarity: *None known*

$3 • W-VT-690-003-G030a

Overprint: Red THREE. *Engraver:* Rawdon, Wright, Hatch & Edson / New England Bank Note Co. *Comments:* H-VT-220-G6b. Similar to W-VT-690-003-G030. May 1st, 185_. 1850s.

Rarity: *None known*

$3 • W-VT-690-003-G030b

Overprint: Red THREE. *Engraver:* Rawdon, Wright, Hatch & Edson / New England Bank Note Co. / ABNCo. monogram. *Comments:* H-VT-220-G6c. Similar to W-VT-690-003-G030 but with additional engraver imprint. May 1st, 185_. 1859.

Rarity: *None known*

$5 • W-VT-690-005-G040

Left: Herd of cattle and sheep with man on horseback / 5. *Center:* 5. *Right:* FIVE / Indian maid with bow and spear. *Engraver:* Rawdon, Wright, Hatch & Edson / New England Bank Note Co. *Comments:* H-VT-220-G8a, Coulter-7. May 1st, 185_. 1850s.

Rarity: *None known*

$5 • W-VT-690-005-G040a

Overprint: Red FIVE. *Engraver:* Rawdon, Wright, Hatch & Edson / New England Bank Note Co. *Comments:* H-VT-220-G8b. Similar to W-VT-690-005-G040. May 1st, 185_. 1850s.

Rarity: *None known*

$5 • W-VT-690-005-G040b

Overprint: Red FIVE. *Engraver:* Rawdon, Wright, Hatch & Edson / New England Bank Note Co. / ABNCo. monogram. *Comments:* H-VT-220-G8c. Similar to W-VT-690-005-G040 but with additional engraver imprint. May 1st, 185_. 1859.

Rarity: *None known*

$10 • W-VT-690-010-G050

Left: Train / TEN. *Center:* Portrait of boy / X bearing TEN. *Right:* 10 / Minerva. *Engraver:* Rawdon, Wright, Hatch & Edson / New England Bank Note Co. *Comments:* H-VT-220-G10a, Coulter-9. May 1st, 185_. 1850s.

Rarity: *None known*

$10 • W-VT-690-010-G050a

TD

Overprint: Red TEN. *Engraver:* Rawdon, Wright, Hatch & Edson / New England Bank Note Co. *Comments:* H-VT-220-G10b. Similar to W-VT-690-010-G050. May 1st, 185_. 1850s.

Rarity: URS-2
F $1,000

$10 • W-VT-690-010-G050b

Overprint: Red TEN. *Engraver:* Rawdon, Wright, Hatch & Edson / New England Bank Note Co. / ABNCo. monogram. *Comments:* H-VT-220-G10c. Similar to W-VT-690-010-G050 but with additional engraver imprint. May 1st, 185_. 1859.

Rarity: *None known*

$20 • W-VT-690-020-G060

Left: Farm scene, Woman seated, Men loading grain / 20. *Right:* 20 / Justice. *Engraver:* Rawdon, Wright, Hatch & Edson / New England Bank Note Co. *Comments:* H-VT-220-G12, Coulter-11. May 1st, 185_. 1850s.

Rarity: *None known*

$20 • W-VT-690-020-G060a

CJF

Overprint: Red XX. *Engraver:* Rawdon, Wright, Hatch & Edson / New England Bank Note Co. *Comments:* H-VT-220-G12a. Similar to W-VT-690-020-G060. May 1st, 185_. 1850s.

Rarity: URS-1
F $1,250

$20 • W-VT-690-020-G060b

CC

Overprint: Red XX. *Engraver:* Rawdon, Wright, Hatch & Edson / New England Bank Note Co. / ABNCo. monogram. *Comments:* H-Unlisted. Similar to W-VT-690-020-G060 but with additional engraver imprint. May 1st, 185_. 1859.

Rarity: URS-1
F $1,250

$50 • W-VT-690-050-G070

Left: Eagle on shield, Bale, barrel, sheaf, and anchor, Falls and factory / 50. *Bottom center:* Farm products and implements. *Right:* 50 / Ceres seated with sickle and sheaf. *Engraver:* Rawdon, Wright, Hatch & Edson / New England Bank Note Co. *Comments:* H-VT-220-G14. 18__. 1850s.

Rarity: *None known*

$50 • W-VT-690-050-G070a

CJF

Overprint: Red L. *Engraver:* Rawdon, Wright, Hatch & Edson / New England Bank Note Co. *Comments:* H-VT-220-G14a, Coulter-12. Similar to W-VT-690-050-G070. 18__. 1850s.

Rarity: URS-1
F $2,000

$100 • W-VT-690-100-G080

Left: Liberty, shield, and eagle / 100. *Center:* C. *Bottom center:* Dog with key and strongbox. *Right:* Girl with basket of flowers / 100. *Engraver:* Rawdon, Wright, Hatch & Edson / New England Bank Note Co. *Comments:* H-VT-220-G16, Coulter-13. 18__. 1850s.

Rarity: *None known*

$100 • W-VT-690-100-G080a

Overprint: Red C. *Engraver:* Rawdon, Wright, Hatch & Edson / New England Bank Note Co. *Comments:* H-VT-220-G16a. Similar to W-VT-690-100-G080. 18__. 1850s.

Rarity: *None known*

Non-Valid Issues

$5 • W-VT-690-005-R010
Engraver: Rawdon, Wright, Hatch & Edson / New England Bank Note Co. *Comments:* H-VT-220-R4. Raised from W-VT-690-001-G010 series. May 1st, 185_. 1850s.
Rarity: *None known*

$5 • W-VT-690-005-N010
Center: Cattle and sheep. *Engraver:* Murray, Draper, Fairman & Co. *Comments:* H-VT-220-N5, Coulter-8. 18__. 1850s.
Rarity: *None known*

$10 • W-VT-690-010-R020
Engraver: Rawdon, Wright, Hatch & Edson / New England Bank Note Co. *Comments:* H-VT-220-R5, Coulter-10. Raised from W-VT-690-001-G010 series. May 1, 185_. 1850s.
Rarity: *None known*

SHELDON, VERMONT

Organized in 1791, Sheldon was originally known as Hungerford after Samuel Hungerford, to whom it was granted along with 64 other settlers. The name was changed on November 8, 1792. The village of Sheldon Springs resides within Sheldon, and the town is bordered by Highgate, Franklin, Enosburgh, Fairfield, and Swanton.

Three streams run through Sheldon, but there are no standing waters within the area's boundaries. Mineral springs were also located in Sheldon, including the Missisquoi, the Sheldon, the Central, and the Vermont. Dairying became a primary industry for the town, introduced by James Mason. Cheese production rose to the fore among dairy products. A blast-furnace was built in 1798 by Israel and Alfred Keith from Pittsford. Ore was turned to iron and the resulting castware received high demand, especially for potash kettles. Some travelers came from distant places to purchase these.

Missisquoi Bank
1849–1866
W-VT-700

History: The Missisquoi Bank was incorporated in November 1849. As of June 1855, capital was $100,000. Figures for 1857 included: capital $100,000; bills in circulation $59,729; specie $2,393; real estate $5,000. By 1862 circulation was $48,285. In October 1865, by which time the bank was not issuing new currency, cashier H.G. Hubbell disappeared, after which a shortage of $77,777 was discovered. The circulation at this time was $120,777, whereas it appeared, by the bank books left by Mr. Hubbell, to be only $43,000. The bank went into liquidation, and the receiver took control on January 17, 1866. Notes were able to be redeemed at a fifty percent discount.

As of July 17, 1866, $92,048 had been redeemed by the receiver, leaving an amount of $28,728 outstanding.

Numismatic Commentary: Genuine notes are plentiful and should be found with relative ease. Some of the more interesting vignettes from Vermont obsolete notes are found on these issues, including that of the eagle with wings that almost touch the left and right margins of the note.

Valid Issues

$1 • W-VT-700-001-G010

CJF

Engraver: New England Bank Note Co. *Comments:* H-VT-225-G2, Coulter-4. 18__. 1849–1850s.
Rarity: URS-3
F $500

$1 • W-VT-700-001-G020

CC

Engraver: Rawdon, Wright, Hatch & Edson / New England Bank Note Co. *Comments:* H-VT-225-G4, Coulter-5. Jan.y 1st, 185_. 1850s.
Rarity: URS-2
Proof $1,250

$1 • W-VT-700-001-G020a

NJW

Overprint: Red ONE. *Engraver:* Rawdon, Wright, Hatch & Edson / New England Bank Note Co. *Comments:* H-VT-225-G4a, Coulter-6. Similar to W-VT-700-001-G020. Jan.y 1st, 185_. 1850s.
Rarity: URS-6
F $200

$2 • W-VT-700-002-G030
Left: Man, Boy and dog driving sheep across river / 2. *Center:* Men in 2. *Right:* 2 on TWO / Woman seated / 2 on TWO. *Engraver:* New England Bank Note Co. *Comments:* H-VT-225-G6, Coulter-8. 18__. 1849–1850s.
Rarity: *None known*

$2 • W-VT-700-002-G040

Left: Female portrait / 2. *Center:* Woman and eagle reclining in clouds. *Right:* 2 / Female portrait. *Engraver:* Rawdon, Wright, Hatch & Edson / New England Bank Note Co. *Comments:* H-Unlisted, Coulter-9. Jan.y 1st, 185_. 1850s.

Rarity: *None known*

$2 • W-VT-700-002-G040a

CJF

Overprint: Red TWO. *Engraver:* Rawdon, Wright, Hatch & Edson / New England Bank Note Co. *Comments:* H-VT-225-G8a, Coulter-10. Similar to W-VT-700-002-G040. Jan.y 1st, 185_. 1850s.

Rarity: URS-5
F $250; **VF** $400

$3 • W-VT-700-003-G050

CC

Engraver: New England Bank Note Co. *Comments:* H-VT-225-G10, Coulter-11. 18__. 1849–1850s.

Rarity: URS-3
F $750

$3 • W-VT-700-003-G060

Left: Portrait of Indian / 3. *Center:* Goddess of Plenty beside money chest, Two milkmaids and cows, Train and ship. *Right:* 3 / Portrait of Indian. *Engraver:* Rawdon, Wright, Hatch & Edson / New England Bank Note Co. *Comments:* H-Unlisted, Coulter-12. Jan.y 1st, 185_. 1850s.

Rarity: *None known*

$3 • W-VT-700-003-G060a

CJF

Overprint: Red THREE. *Engraver:* Rawdon, Wright, Hatch & Edson / New England Bank Note Co. *Comments:* H-VT-225-G12a, Coulter-13. Similar to W-VT-700-003-G060. Jan.y 1st, 185_. 1850s.

Rarity: URS-7
F $250; **VF** $400

$5 • W-VT-700-005-G070

Left: Spread eagle on shield / FIVE. *Center:* Allegorical figure and cherub / V. *Right:* 5 / Girl with basket of flowers. *Engraver:* New England Bank Note Co. *Comments:* H-VT-225-G14, Coulter-15. 18__. 1849–1850s.

Rarity: *None known*

$5 • W-VT-700-005-G080

Left: FIVE / Farmer and dog. *Center:* 5 / Train / 5. *Right:* FIVE / Woman feeding chickens. *Overprint:* Red FIVE. *Engraver:* Rawdon, Wright, Hatch & Edson / New England Bank Note Co. *Comments:* H-VT-225-G16a. Oct. 1st, 18__. 1850s.

Rarity: *None known*

$5 • W-VT-700-005-G080a

CJF

Overprint: Red FIVE. *Engraver:* Rawdon, Wright, Hatch & Edson / New England Bank Note Co. / ABNCo. monogram. *Comments:* H-VT-225-G16b, Coulter-16. Similar to W-VT-700-005-G080 but with additional engraver imprint. Oct. 1st, 18__. 1860s.

Rarity: URS-5
F $150; **VF** $350

$10 • W-VT-700-010-G090

CC

Engraver: New England Bank Note Co. *Comments:* H-VT-225-G18, Coulter-18. 18__. 1849–1850s.
Rarity: URS-2
F $1,200

$10 • W-VT-700-010-G100

Left: TEN / Woman feeding chickens. *Center:* 10 / Indian maid seated on cliff overlooking river / 10. *Right:* TEN / Farmer feeding swine. *Overprint:* Red TEN. *Engraver:* Rawdon, Wright, Hatch & Edson / New England Bank Note Co. *Comments:* H-VT-225-G20a, Coulter-19. Oct. 1st, 18__. 1850s.
Rarity: *None known*

$10 • W-VT-700-010-G100a

CJF

Overprint: Red TEN. *Engraver:* Rawdon, Wright, Hatch & Edson / New England Bank Note Co. / ABNCo. monogram. *Comments:* H-VT-225-G20b. Similar to W-VT-700-010-G100 but with additional engraver imprint. Oct. 1st, 18__. 1850s–1860s.
Rarity: URS-6
F $250

$20 • W-VT-700-020-G110

CJF

Engraver: New England Bank Note Co. *Comments:* H-VT-225-G22, Coulter-21. 18__. 1840s–1850s.
Rarity: URS-5
VF $350; **Unc-Rem** $175

$20 • W-VT-700-020-G110a

CJF

Overprint: Red TWENTY. *Engraver:* New England Bank Note Co. *Comments:* H-VT-225-G22a, Coulter-22. Similar to W-VT-700-020-G110. 18__. 1850s–1860s.
Rarity: URS-6
EF $300; **Unc-Rem** $300

$20 • W-VT-700-020-G110b

Left: 20 / Woman with book. *Center:* XX / Eagle / XX. *Right:* 20 / Ship. *Overprint:* Red TWENTY. *Engraver:* New England Bank Note Co. / ABNCo. monogram. *Comments:* H-VT-225-G22b. Similar to W-VT-700-020-G110 but with additional engraver imprint. 18__. 1860s.
Rarity: URS-4
VF $400

$50 • W-VT-700-050-G120

CC

Engraver: New England Bank Note Co. *Comments:* H-VT-225-G26, Coulter-24. 18__. 1849–1850s.
Rarity: URS-5
VF $350; **Unc-Rem** $250
Selected auction price: Heritage, September 2008, Lot 12753, Gem Unc $546

$50 • W-VT-700-050-G120a

Left: FIFTY / Woman with wreath / FIFTY. *Center:* 50 / Man holding restive horse by mane / 50. *Right:* FIFTY / Woman with globe / FIFTY. *Overprint:* Red. *Engraver:* New England Bank Note Co. / ABNCo. monogram. *Comments:* H-VT-225-G26b. Similar to W-VT-700-050-G120 but with additional engraver imprint. 18__. 1860s.
Rarity: *None known*

$100 • W-VT-700-100-G130

Left: 100 / Eagle / 100. *Center:* "Phoebus in Chariot of the Sun". *Right:* C / Portrait of George Washington / C. *Engraver:* New England Bank Note Co. *Comments:* H-VT-225-G30, Coulter-25. 18__. 1849–1850s.
Rarity: *None known*

$100 • W-VT-700-100-G130a

Overprint: Red. *Engraver:* New England Bank Note Co. / ABNCo. monogram. *Comments:* H-VT-225-G30b. Similar to W-VT-700-100-G130 but with additional engraver imprint. 18__. 1860s.

Rarity: *None known*

$100 • W-VT-700-100-G140

Left: ONE HUNDRED over 100 / Male portrait. *Center:* Covered wagon. *Right:* ONE HUNDRED over 100 / Portrait of Christopher Columbus. *Engraver:* New England Bank Note Co. *Comments:* H-Unlisted. 18__. 1849–1850s.

Rarity: *None known*

$100 • W-VT-700-100-G140a   CC

Overprint: Red HUNDRED. *Engraver:* New England Bank Note Co. *Comments:* H-Unlisted. Similar to W-VT-700-100-G140. 18__. 1849–1850s.

Rarity: URS-4
VF $350; **EF** $750; **Unc-Rem** $1,700

Uncut Sheets

$20-$100 • W-VT-700-020.100-US010

Vignette(s): ($20) Woman seated / Eagle / Ship. *($100)* Male portrait / Covered wagon / Portrait of Christopher Columbus. *Overprint(s):* Red. *Engraver:* New England Bank Note Co. *Comments:* H-VT-225-G22a, H-Unlisted. 18__. 1849–1860s.

Rarity: URS-4
Unc-Rem $1,200

Non-Valid Issues

$1 • W-VT-700-001-A010

Center: Commerce seated on barrel, Vessels / 1 with "Presentation of the Declaration of Independence". *Right:* Woman resting on stile. *Overprint:* Red ONE. *Engraver:* New England Bank Note Co. *Comments:* H-VT-225-A5, Coulter-7. Altered from a note of some other bank using the same plate as W-VT-700-001-G010. 18__. 1850s.

Rarity: *None known*

$3 • W-VT-700-003-R010

Engraver: Rawdon, Wright, Hatch & Edson / New England Bank Note Co. *Comments:* H-VT-225-R5, Coulter-14. Raised from W-VT-700-001-G020a. 18__. 1850s–1860s.

Rarity: *None known*

$5 • W-VT-700-005-R020

Engraver: Rawdon, Wright, Hatch & Edson / New England Bank Note Co. *Comments:* H-VT-225-R6, Coulter-17. Raised from W-VT-700-001-G020a. 18__. 1850s–1860s.

Rarity: *None known*

$10 • W-VT-700-010-R030

Engraver: Rawdon, Wright, Hatch & Edson / New England Bank Note Co. *Comments:* H-VT-225-R7, Coulter-20. Raised from W-VT-700-001-G020a. 18__. 1850s–1860s.

Rarity: *None known*

$20 • W-VT-700-020-R040

Engraver: Rawdon, Wright, Hatch & Edson / New England Bank Note Co. *Comments:* H-VT-225-R8, Coulter-23. Raised from W-VT-700-001-G020 series. 18__. 1850s–1860s.

Rarity: *None known*

SOUTH HARDWICK, VERMONT

Likely named after Hardwick, Massachusetts, which was the hometown of a number of grantees of the land, the town of South Hardwick was granted on November 7, 1780. It was chartered on August 19 of the next year. In 1793 the first permanent settlement took place, led by families from New Hampshire. The town's main village changed names several times, including Hardwick, East Hardwick, Stevensville, Stevens Mills, Stevens Village, Stephens, North Hardwick, Lamoilleville, and South Hardwick. During all these changes, the area became the leading granite center in the state. Between 1790 and 1860 the town expanded dramatically, with agriculture as the main trade until the quarries opened. By 1859 the population was 1,402, and there were sawmills, gristmills, tanneries, a woolen mill, a tinware shop, and a carriage factory in operation.

Bank of South Hardwick
1854
W-VT-710

History: In 1854 a charter application for the Bank of South Hardwick was rejected by the state legislature.

Numismatic Commentary: It is possible that Proof notes were made, but no record has been found of such.

SOUTH ROYALTON, VERMONT

South Royalton, separated from Royalton by the White River, was primarily formed by Daniel Tarbell Jr., who arrived in 1848 from Tunbridge. He constructed roads and a bridge down the White River from Royalton, and soon the Vermont Central Railroad built passenger and freight stations at South Royalton.

Tarbell opened a general store in 1848, the same year the first train connected to the location. The store doubled as a depot until the railroad built its own. Tarbell continued to build structures that he sold or leased to settlers and businesses. In 1851 the post office was established, and Tarbell established the bank after that. A steam mill arrived in 1852, followed by a boot factory and a stage line.

See also Royalton, Vermont.

South Royalton Bank
1851–1857
W-VT-720

History: The South Royalton Bank was organized on December 8, 1851, under the General Banking Act, with $250,000 in authorized capital. It commenced business in 1852 under the slightly different Free Banking Act. Very little cash was ever paid in.

Daniel Tarbell Jr., president of the bank, owned more real estate in the town than did anyone else. The bank was at odds with the Suffolk Bank clearing house and refused to post a deposit and use its services. In 1853 an agent of the bank came to South Royalton with $45,000 in notes, demanding they be redeemed. Tarbell had the agent arrested for maliciously trying to harm the bank, and the bills were impounded. Three days later the Suffolk Bank president and his attorney arrived, posted a bond, and retrieved their bills. The cashier at the bank began with redeeming the $1 bills, counting and then re-counting them, and slowly counting the coins in payment. At two in the afternoon the cashier closed the process and told the Suffolk people to return the next day. They did, and after some discussion with prominent regional and state officials, the bank agreed to exchange their South Royalton Bank notes for those of the Chelsea Bank and the White River Bank, after which they went back to Boston.

The bank ran up debts, and on February 7, 1855, the Orange County Bank at Chelsea, W-VT-280, which was a major creditor, obtained a decree to foreclose on the bank. In that year the bank claimed a capital of $100,600. It limped along in business and finally closed in 1857. At the time David W. Cowdery was president. In the autumn of that year the bank's bills traded at a fifty percent discount.

Numismatic Commentary: The imprint of the American Bank Note Co. was used from 1854 to 1858 in conjunction with a separate entity—Jocelyn, Draper, Welsh & Co. Later notes were more ornate and were made by Toppan, Carpenter, Casilear & Co. Tarbell's South Royalton House is pictured on certain denominations and the portrait of Tarbell on others. The portrait of director Solomon Downer appeared on notes as well.

Remaining in the American Bank Note Co. archives as of 2003 was a $1-$2-$5-$10 face plate and a $50-$100 face plate.

VALID ISSUES

$1 • W-VT-720-001-G010 CJF

Engraver: Toppan, Carpenter, Casilear & Co. *Comments:* H-VT-230-G2, Coulter-1. 185_. 1850s.
Rarity: URS-6
F $150; **Unc-Rem** $400

$1 • W-VT-720-001-G020 CC

Engraver: American Bank Note Co. / Jocelyn, Draper, Welsh & Co. *Comments:* H-VT-230-G4, Coulter-2. 18__. 1850s.
Rarity: URS-9
F $75; **VF** $150

$2 • W-VT-720-002-G030 CC

Engraver: Toppan, Carpenter, Casilear & Co. *Comments:* H-VT-230-G6, Coulter-4. 185_. 1850s.
Rarity: URS-4
F $200; **Proof** $1,000

$2 • W-VT-720-002-G040 CC

Engraver: American Bank Note Co. / Jocelyn, Draper, Welsh & Co. *Comments:* H-VT-230-G8, Coulter-3. 18__. 1850s.
Rarity: URS-7
F $125; **Proof** $600

$3 • W-VT-720-003-G050 CC

Engraver: American Bank Note Co. / Jocelyn, Draper, Welsh & Co. *Comments:* H-VT-230-G10, Coulter-5. 18__. 1850s.
Rarity: URS-4
F $250; **Proof** $1,700

$5 • W-VT-720-005-G060

CC

Engraver: Toppan, Carpenter, Casilear & Co. **Comments:** H-VT-230-G12, Coulter-6. 185_. 1850s.
Rarity: URS-5
F $150; **VF** $300; **Unc-Rem** $175; **Proof** $1,200

$10 • W-VT-720-010-G070

CC

Engraver: Toppan, Carpenter, Casilear & Co. **Comments:** H-VT-230-G14, Coulter-8. 185_. 1850s.
Rarity: URS-5
F $200; **VF** $350; **Unc-Rem** $350; **Proof** $1,000

$50 • W-VT-720-050-G080

CC

Engraver: Toppan, Carpenter, Casilear & Co. **Comments:** H-VT-230-G18. 185_. 1850s.
Rarity: URS-3
EF $500; **Unc-Rem** $400; **Proof** $2,000

$100 • W-VT-720-100-G090

CC

Engraver: Toppan, Carpenter, Casilear & Co. **Comments:** H-VT-230-G20. 18__. 1850s.
Rarity: URS-4
VF $500; **EF** $900; **Unc-Rem** $400

Uncut Sheets
$50-$100 • W-VT-720-050.100-US010
Vignette(s): ($50) Two women / Woman reclining, Plow / Building / Portrait of D. Tarbell Jr. **($100)** Portrait of Solomon Downer / Two men driving cattle / Two women. **Engraver:** Toppan, Carpenter, Casilear & Co. **Comments:** H-VT-230-G18, G20. 18__. 1850s.
Rarity: URS-5
Unc-Rem $650

Non-Valid Issues
$5 • W-VT-720-005-R010
Engraver: Toppan, Carpenter, Casilear & Co. **Comments:** H-VT-230-R5, Coulter-7. Raised from W-VT-720-001-G010. 185_. 1850s.
Rarity: *None known*

$5 • W-VT-720-005-R020
Engraver: Toppan, Carpenter, Casilear & Co. **Comments:** H-VT-230-R10. Raised from W-VT-720-002-G030. 18__. 1850s.
Rarity: *None known*

Springfield, Vermont
The charter for Springfield was granted on August 20, 1761, and the land was awarded to Gideon Lyman. It was rechartered on March 16, 1772.

Springfield is bordered by Weathersfield, the Connecticut River, Rockingham, and Chester. The flat lands of Springfield made it one of the best agricultural towns in the state, but the Black River falls also spurred it on to become a mill town. It was located in the middle of what became known as the Precision Valley area, which was the birthplace for the Vermont machine-tool industry.

By 1880 Springfield claimed as many as 3,154 inhabitants, making it the largest town in the county in terms of population.

Exchange Bank of Springfield
1854–1864
W-VT-730

History: The Exchange Bank of Springfield was chartered in 1853 with an authorized capital of $50,000. Figures for 1857 included: circulation $84,239; specie $2,591.

The business of the bank was succeeded by the First National Bank of Springfield, chartered on November 11, 1863, but which did not open for business until January 12, 1864. The outstanding circulation of the Exchange Bank was reported to be $1,626 on July 1, 1867.

Numismatic Commentary: Genuine notes from this bank are rare. Many issues bear large, ornate engravings of presidents and other notable people of the era. One issue shows a vignette of two masons on scaffolding building a wall, while a third fellow brings material to the site.

VALID ISSUES

$1 • **W-VT-730-001-G010**   CJF

Engraver: Danforth, Wright & Co. **Comments:** H-Unlisted, Coulter-Unlisted. June 1st, 1854.

Rarity: URS-3

F $750; **Proof** $1,200

$1 • **W-VT-730-001-G010a**

Left: 1 / Milkmaid. **Center:** Male portrait, ONE DOLLAR on die. **Right:** 1 / Mechanic seated. **Overprint:** Red ONE. **Engraver:** Danforth, Wright & Co. **Comments:** H-VT-235-G2a, Coulter-1. Similar to W-VT-730-001-G010. June 1st, 1854.

Rarity: *None known*

$1 • **W-VT-730-001-G010b**   CC

Overprint: Red ONE / ONE vertically. **Engraver:** Danforth, Wright & Co. **Comments:** H-Unlisted. Similar to W-VT-730-001-G010. June 1st, 1854.

Rarity: URS-2

F $1,000

$1 • **W-VT-730-001-G010c**

Overprint: Red ONE. **Engraver:** Danforth, Wright & Co. / ABNCo. monogram. **Comments:** H-VT-235-G2b. Similar to W-VT-730-001-G010 but with additional engraver imprint. June 1st, 1854.

Rarity: *None known*

$2 • **W-VT-730-002-G020**

Left: TWO, 2, TWO on die, Portrait of Marquis de Lafayette. **Center:** Three bricklayers at work. **Right:** TWO, 2, TWO on die, Portrait of Andrew Jackson. **Overprint:** Red TWO. **Engraver:** Danforth, Wright & Co. **Comments:** H-VT-235-G4a, Coulter-4. June 1st, 1854.

Rarity: URS-1

Proof $1,500

$2 • **W-VT-730-002-G020a**   CJF

Overprint: Red TWO. **Engraver:** Danforth, Wright & Co. / ABNCo. monogram. **Comments:** H-VT-235-G4b. Similar to W-VT-730-002-G020 but with additional engraver imprint. June 1st, 1854.

Rarity: URS-3

VG $600; **F** $1,250

$3 • **W-VT-730-003-G030**   CC

Engraver: Danforth, Wright & Co. **Comments:** H-VT-235-G6a, Coulter-7. June 1st, 1854.

Rarity: URS-1

Proof $2,000

$3 • **W-VT-730-003-G030a**

Overprint: Red THREE. **Engraver:** Danforth, Wright & Co. / ABNCo. monogram. **Comments:** H-VT-235-G6b. Similar to W-VT-730-003-G030 but with additional engraver imprint. June 1st, 1854.

Rarity: *None known*

$5 • **W-VT-730-005-G040**   CC

Engraver: Danforth, Wright & Co. **Comments:** H-VT-235-G8, Coulter-9. June 1st, 1854.

Rarity: URS-3

Proof $1,500

$10 • W-VT-730-010-G050

Left: Medallion head / Portrait of Benjamin Franklin / Medallion head. *Center:* Indian family, X on shield, Settler family. *Right:* Two medallion heads, one bearing 10 / Portrait of Henry Clay / Two medallion heads, one bearing X. *Engraver:* Danforth, Wright & Co. *Comments:* H-VT-235-G10, Coulter-16. June 1st, 1854.

Rarity: URS-1
Proof $2,000

$10 • W-VT-730-010-G060

Center: Wheat field. *Right:* Dog's head. *Comments:* H-Unlisted, Coulter-18. 1850s.

Rarity: *None known*

$20 • W-VT-730-020-G070

CC

Engraver: Danforth, Wright & Co. *Comments:* H-VT-235-G12, Coulter-19. 18__. 1850s.

Rarity: URS-1
Proof $3,000

$50 • W-VT-730-050-G080

CC

Engraver: Danforth, Wright & Co. *Comments:* H-VT-235-G14, Coulter-21. 18__. 1850s.

Rarity: URS-1
Proof $3,500

Uncut Sheets

$20-$50 • W-VT-730-020.050-US010

Vignette(s): *($20)* White horse, Shield surmounted by eagle, Black horse. *($50)* Eagle on tree limb. *Engraver:* Danforth, Wright & Co. *Comments:* H-VT-235-G12, G14. June 1st, 1854.

Rarity: *None known*

NON-VALID ISSUES

$1 • W-VT-730-001-N010

Left: Woman. *Center:* Male portrait in die. *Right:* Mechanic. *Comments:* H-Unlisted, Coulter-2. 1850s.

Rarity: *None known*

$1 • W-VT-730-001-N020

Center: Agricultural scene. *Comments:* H-Unlisted, Coulter-3. 1850s.

Rarity: *None known*

$1 • W-VT-730-001-A010

Left: ONE across 1 / Dog's head, key. *Center:* Man kneeling binding sheaf, Woman standing holding sheaf. *Right:* ONE across 1 / Female portrait. *Engraver:* W.L. Ormsby. *Comments:* H-VT-235-A5. Altered from a spurious issue of the Exchange Bank, Hartford, Connecticut. Dec. 1, 1856.

Rarity: *None known*

$2 • W-VT-730-002-S010

CJF

Engraver: Baldwin, Adams & Co. *Comments:* H-VT-235-S5, Coulter-6. Jan.y 2nd, 185_. 1850s.

Rarity: URS-5
F $150

$2 • W-VT-730-002-N030

Center: Agricultural scene. *Comments:* H-Unlisted, Coulter-5. 1850s.

Rarity: *None known*

$2 • W-VT-730-002-A020

Left: TWO across 2 / Ceres. *Center:* Train, Two men, Hill and tree. *Right:* TWO across 2 / Woman seated, Shield. *Engraver:* W.L. Ormsby. *Comments:* H-VT-235-A10. Altered from a spurious issue of the Exchange Bank, Hartford, Connecticut. Dec. 1, 1856.

Rarity: *None known*

$3 • W-VT-730-003-N040

Center: Agricultural scene. *Comments:* H-Unlisted, Coulter-8. 1850s.

Rarity: *None known*

$5 • W-VT-730-005-N050

Center: Agricultural scene. *Comments:* H-Unlisted, Coulter-10. 1850s.

Rarity: *None known*

$5 • W-VT-730-005-N060

Left: Indian woman / FIVE. *Center:* Indian, Train, Eagle, Tree. *Right:* 5 / Woman, Ship. *Comments:* H-Unlisted, Coulter-11. 1850s.

Rarity: *None known*

$5 • W-VT-730-005-N070

Center: Portrait of George Washington surrounded by five women. *Comments:* H-Unlisted, Coulter-12. 1850s.

Rarity: *None known*

$5 • W-VT-730-005-N080

Center: 5 / Three women / 5. *Comments:* H-VT-235-N5, Coulter-13. 1850s.

Rarity: *None known*

$5 • W-VT-730-005-N090

Center: Cattle under tree. *Comments:* H-Unlisted, Coulter-14. 1850s.

> **Rarity:** *None known*

$5 • W-VT-730-005-N100

Center: Wheat field. *Right:* Dog's head. *Comments:* H-Unlisted, Coulter-15. 1850s.

> **Rarity:** *None known*

$5 • W-VT-730-005-A030

Left: 5 / 5. *Center:* Two allegorical women in clouds, U.S. shield and eagle. *Right:* 5 / 5. *Engraver:* W.L. Ormsby. *Comments:* H-VT-235-A15. Altered from a spurious issue of the Exchange Bank, Hartford, Connecticut. Dec. 1, 1856.

> **Rarity:** *None known*

$5 • W-VT-730-005-A040

Left: Indian man standing with bow / FIVE. *Center:* Eagle / Indian man standing on cliff with bow, watching train. *Bottom center:* Indian in canoe. *Right:* 5 / Man seated on anchor, Ship. *Comments:* H-VT-235-A20. Altered from $5, Merchants Bank, Mankato City, Minnesota. Sept. 1, 185_. 1850s.

> **Rarity:** *None known*

$10 • W-VT-730-010-N110

Center: Cattle under tree. *Comments:* H-Unlisted, Coulter-17. 1850s.

> **Rarity:** *None known*

$10 • W-VT-730-010-A050

Left: 10 / 10. *Center:* Indian man on horseback spearing bison, Bison and trees. *Right:* 10 / 10. *Engraver:* W.L. Ormsby. *Comments:* H-VT-235-A25. Altered from a spurious issue of the Exchange Bank, Hartford, Connecticut. Dec. 1, 1856.

> **Rarity:** *None known*

$20 • W-VT-730-020-N120

Center: Agricultural scene. *Comments:* H-Unlisted, Coulter-20. 1850s.

> **Rarity:** *None known*

$50 • W-VT-730-050-N130

Center: Agriculture scene. *Comments:* H-Unlisted, Coulter-22. 1850s.

> **Rarity:** *None known*

SWANTON FALLS, VERMONT

On July 20, 1734, Swanton Falls was granted and given to Phillipe-Rene le Gardeur de Beauvais Jr. Until 1740, when the first English settlement was made, the French occupied the land. A trading post and sawmill were established there in the early days. In 1762 the town was surveyed by William Brasier, and a grant of 23,040 acres to be called Swanton was affirmed in 1763. The town government was organized in 1790. A ferry was established in 1794 on the Missisquoi River south of the falls. Later it was replaced by John's Bridge.

By 1800 iron factories had been established, and the manufacturing of lime was also an industry. A woolen mill was built in 1806, and a plant to tan leather was erected in 1814. In 1812 a bridge was built across the falls, after which a marble mill was set up by Joseph Atkinson. Swanton was also a trading center where maple products could be bartered for fish. A cotton mill was constructed in 1820, and the Champlain Canal opened in 1823, providing access to New York City. During 1836 the northern section of Hog Island was annexed to Swanton. Black marble tile, the first of its kind in America, was made at Swanton in 1848.

Union Bank
1850–1865
W-VT-740

History: The Union Bank was chartered in 1850 with an authorized capital of $75,000, $50,000 of which was paid in. In 1857 these figures were reported: capital $75,000; bills in circulation $85,661; specie $2,405; real estate $2,800. In July 1859, circulation had dropped to $83,661.

In 1865 the business of the Union Bank was succeeded by the Union National Bank of Swanton. Outstanding circulation as of July 1, 1867, was reported to be $8,243, redemption of which was guaranteed by the national bank. The Union Bank published notices stating that it would not be liable to redeem its outstanding bills after January 12, 1868.

Numismatic Commentary: Genuine signed and dated notes are very rare. A few Proofs have entered the marketplace over the past decade. A common spurious note is the $5 denomination showing five presidents in "V" formation at the center. The plate for this spurious note has been altered and reused for various "Union" banks of many states.

VALID ISSUES

$1 • W-VT-740-001-G010

Left: 1 / Portrait of George Washington. *Center:* 1 / Female portrait / 1. *Right:* 1 / Portrait of Benjamin Franklin. *Engraver:* New England Bank Note Co. *Comments:* H-VT-240-G2, Coulter-1. 18__. 1850s.

> **Rarity:** *None known*

$1 • W-VT-740-001-G020

CJF

Overprint: Red 1. *Engraver:* Wellstood, Hanks, Hay & Whiting. *Comments:* H-VT-240-G4a, Coulter-2. January 2nd, 185_. 1850s.

> **Rarity:** URS-4
>
> F $750

$2 • W-VT-740-002-G030

Left: 2 / Portrait of Christopher Columbus. *Center:* Woman with cornucopia / 2 / Justice. *Right:* 2 / Male portrait. *Engraver:* New England Bank Note Co. *Comments:* H-VT-240-G6, Coulter-3. 18__. 1850s.

Rarity: *None known*

$2 • W-VT-740-002-G040

Left: 2 on shield / Justice. *Center:* Portrait of Benjamin Franklin between two cherubs. *Right:* 2 on shield / Liberty. *Engraver:* Wellstood, Hanks, Hay & Whiting. *Comments:* H-VT-240-G8, Coulter-4. January 2nd, 185_. 1850s.

Rarity: *None known*

$2 • W-VT-740-002-G040a   CC

Overprint: Red 2. *Engraver:* Wellstood, Hanks, Hay & Whiting. *Comments:* H-Unlisted, Coulter-Unlisted. Similar to W-VT-740-002-G040. January 2nd, 185_. 1850s.

Rarity: URS-4
F $750; **Proof** $2,500

$3 • W-VT-740-003-G050

Left: 3 / Portrait of George Washington with horse. *Center:* 3 / Two female portraits / 3. *Right:* 3 / Blacksmith and anvil. *Engraver:* New England Bank Note Co. *Comments:* H-VT-240-G10, Coulter-7. 18__. 1850s.

Rarity: URS-2
Proof $850

$3 • W-VT-740-003-G060   CJF

Overprint: Red 3. *Engraver:* Wellstood, Hanks, Hay & Whiting. *Comments:* H-VT-240-G12a, Coulter-8. Jan.y 2nd, 185_. 1850s.

Rarity: URS-2
VG $1,000

$5 • W-VT-740-005-G070

Left: FIVE on lathework vertically. *Center:* Woman unveiling shield bearing 5. *Right:* 5 / Ship. *Engraver:* New England Bank Note Co. *Comments:* H-VT-240-G14, Coulter-12. 18__. 1850s.

Rarity: *None known*

$5 • W-VT-740-005-G080   CJF

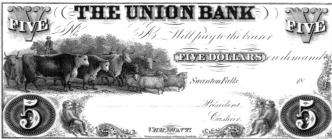

Engraver: Wellstood, Hanks, Hay & Whiting. *Comments:* H-VT-240-G16, Coulter-13. 18__. 1850s.

Rarity: URS-2
Proof $2,000

$5 • W-VT-740-005-G080a   CJF

Overprint: Red 5. *Engraver:* Wellstood, Hanks, Hay & Whiting. *Comments:* H-Unlisted, Coulter-Unlisted. Similar to W-VT-740-005-G080 but with different date. January 2nd, 185_. 1850s.

Rarity: URS-3
VG $500; **F** $1,000

$5 • W-VT-740-005-G080b

Left: FIVE over V / 5. *Center:* Cattle, sheep, and man on horseback. *Right:* FIVE over V / 5. *Overprint:* Red FIVE. *Engraver:* Wellstood, Hanks, Hay & Whiting. *Comments:* H-VT-240-G16a, Coulter-10. Similar to W-VT-740-005-G080. January 2nd, 185_. 1850s.

Rarity: URS-8
VF $350

$10 • W-VT-740-010-G095

Left: X / Indian with bow kneeling. *Center:* Steamboat, schooner, boats, and city. *Right:* 10 / Girl, Sheaf. *Engraver:* New England Bank Note Co. *Comments:* H-VT-240-G18, Coulter-17. 18__. 1850s.

Rarity: *None known*

$10 • W-VT-740-010-G110

CC

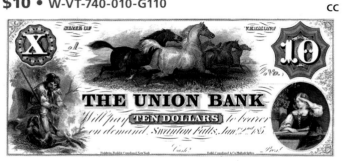

Engraver: Baldwin, Bald & Cousland / Bald, Cousland & Co.
Comments: H-VT-240-G20, Coulter-18. Jan.y 2nd, 185_. 1850s.
Rarity: URS-4
Proof $1,100

$10 • W-VT-740-010-G110a

CC

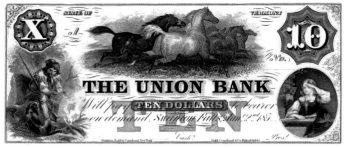

Overprint: Red TEN. **Engraver:** Baldwin, Bald & Cousland / Bald, Cousland & Co. **Comments:** H-Unlisted, Coulter-Unlisted. Similar to W-VT-740-010-G110. Jan.y 2nd, 185_. 1850s.
Rarity: URS-4
Proof $1,200

$20 • W-VT-740-020-G120

Left: 20 / Woman with book. **Center:** XX / Eagle / XX. **Right:** 20 / Ship. **Engraver:** New England Bank Note Co. **Comments:** H-VT-240-G22, Coulter-22. 18__. 1850s.
Rarity: *None known*

$20 • W-VT-740-020-G130

CC

Engraver: Baldwin, Bald & Cousland / Bald, Cousland & Co.
Comments: H-VT-240-G24, Coulter-21. Jan. 2nd, 185_. 1850s–1860s.
Rarity: URS-4
Proof $1,200

$20 • W-VT-740-020-G130a

CC

Overprint: Red XX. **Engraver:** Baldwin, Bald & Cousland / Bald, Cousland & Co. **Comments:** H-Unlisted, Coulter-Unlisted. Similar to W-VT-740-020-G130. Jan. 2nd, 185_. 1850s–1860s.
Rarity: URS-4
Proof $1,200

$50 • W-VT-740-050-G140

Left: FIFTY / Woman with wreath of flowers on head / FIFTY. **Center:** Man holding restive horse by mane. **Right:** FIFTY / Woman with flowers / FIFTY. **Engraver:** New England Bank Note Co. **Comments:** H-VT-240-G26, Coulter-23. 18__. 1850s.
Rarity: *None known*

$100 • W-VT-740-100-G150

Left: ONE HUNDRED on 100 / Portrait of William Henry Harrison. **Center:** Wharf scene. **Right:** ONE HUNDRED on 100 / Portrait of Christopher Columbus. **Engraver:** New England Bank Note Co. **Comments:** H-VT-240-G28, Coulter-24. 18__. 1850s.
Rarity: *None known*

Uncut Sheets

$10-$20 • W-VT-740-010.020-US010

Vignette(s): ($10) Hunter warming hands by fire / Herd of horses running / Girl shading eyes. ($20) Cattle and sheep / Portrait of girl / Hunter drinking from stream. **Engraver:** Baldwin, Bald & Cousland / Bald, Cousland & Co. **Comments:** All unlisted in Haxby. Jan. 2nd, 185_. 1850s.
Rarity: URS-3
Proof $1,700

$10-$20 • W-VT-740-010.020-US010a

Overprint(s): Red. **Engraver:** Baldwin, Bald & Cousland / Bald, Cousland & Co. **Comments:** All unlisted in Haxby. Similar to W-VT-740-010.020-US010. Jan. 2nd, 185_. 1850s.
Rarity: URS-2
Proof $1,800

Non-Valid Issues

$2 • W-VT-740-002-S010

Left: 2 / Male bust. **Center:** Female bust / 2 / Female bust. **Right:** 2 / Portrait of Benjamin Franklin. **Tint:** Brown. **Engraver:** Rawdon, Wright, Hatch & Edson. **Comments:** H-VT-240-S5, Coulter-5. March 10, 185_. 1850s.
Rarity: URS-6
F $125

$2 • W-VT-740-002-N010

Left: Farmer plowing. **Center:** Farm scene. **Comments:** H-VT-240-N5. 1850s.
Rarity: *None known*

$2 • W-VT-740-002-N020

Center: Man with sledge / Train. *Comments:* H-Unlisted, Coulter-6. 1850s.

Rarity: *None known*

$3 • W-VT-740-003-N030

Center: Man with sledge / Train. *Comments:* H-Unlisted, Coulter-9. 1850s.

Rarity: *None known*

$5 • W-VT-740-005-S020

cc

Engraver: Toppan, Carpenter & Co. *Comments:* H-VT-240-S10, Coulter-11. From a modified, fraudulent plate originally for a counterfeit $5 of the National Bank, Providence, Rhode Island. 185_. 1850s.

Rarity: URS-7
F $100; **Proof** $250

$5 • W-VT-740-005-N040

Center: Man with sledge / Train. *Comments:* H-Unlisted, Coulter-14. 1850s.

Rarity: *None known*

$5 • W-VT-740-005-N050

Left: Woman. *Center:* Steamship. *Right:* Portrait of George Washington. *Comments:* H-VT-240-N10, Coulter-15. 1850s.

Rarity: *None known*

$5 • W-VT-740-005-N060

Center: Woman seated by shield. *Comments:* H-Unlisted, Coulter-16. 1850s.

Rarity: *None known*

$10 • W-VT-740-010-N070

Center: Portrait of George Washington flanked by two cherubs. *Comments:* H-VT-240-N15, Coulter-19. 1850s.

Rarity: *None known*

$10 • W-VT-740-010-N080

Center: Man with sledge / Train. *Comments:* H-Unlisted, Coulter-20. 1850s.

Rarity: *None known*

TROY, VERMONT

Chartered on October 28, 1801, Troy was once known as Missisquoi (also Missiskouie). Its name was changed on October 26, 1803. The town of Troy was made up of two areas: Troy and North Troy, a village that was incorporated on the upper end of town. Potash and pearlash were primary businesses during the early years. There was also an iron-smelting furnace for processing iron ore.

Agricultural Bank
CIRCA 1839
W-VT-750

History: A non-existent bank represented by notes intended to circulate fraudulently in the West: "The Agricultural Bank of Troy, Vermont, is said to have some paper circulating West. Quite too fast—no such bank has yet been created."[13]

ISSUES

$3 • W-VT-750-003-S010

cc

Comments: H-VT-245-S6, Coulter-Unlisted. 18__. 1830s.
Rarity: URS-3
F $500

$5 • W-VT-750-005-S020

cc

Comments: H-VT-245-S8, Coulter-Unlisted. 18__. 1839.
Rarity: URS-3
F $600

VERGENNES, VERMONT

Vergennes was settled by Donald MacIntosh in 1766. It was incorporated in 1788 when portions of New Haven, Panton, and Ferrisburg were set off to create Vergennes, which was named for Charles Gravier, the Comte de Vergennes. In terms of population, it was the smallest city in Vermont and the only one to come into existence without having first been chartered as a town or village.

The Monkton Iron Works was established in 1807 and used water power to operate certain of the equipment. The War of 1812 brought orders for cannon shot to the extent of 300 tons. Because of the convenient location of the Iron Works and a shipbuilding yard, Commodore MacDonough selected Vergennes to provide housing for his Lake Champlain fleet. Soon after the War, though, the Iron Works shut down, and the city fell into economic depression. In 1828 John D. Ward revived industry in the city by building a canal which employed many people.

Bank of Vergennes
1826–1865
W-VT-760

History: The Bank of Vergennes was chartered on October 27, 1826, and commenced business on May 2, 1827. The authorized capital was $100,000, and $80,000 was soon paid in. In August 1845, circulation was $88,566.

The bank was rechartered in February 1854 and given an additional capital of $50,000. These figures were given for 1857: capital $150,000; bills in circulation $150,284; specie $3,944; real estate $7,000. Circulation was $150,284 in July 1859, and by 1862 it was as high as $219,327.

On May 14, 1865, the business of the bank was succeeded by the National Bank of Vergennes. The outstanding circulation of the Bank of Vergennes was reported to be $2,105 as of July 1, 1867, redemption of which was guaranteed by the national bank.

Numismatic Commentary: Genuine notes are very scarce. With this bank, collectors could be able to obtain a $1.50 odd denomination note engraved by Rawdon, Clark & Co. of Albany.

VALID ISSUES

$1 • W-VT-760-001-G010
Left: 1 / Portrait of Thomas MacDonough. *Center:* Herd of cattle. *Right:* 1 / ONE. *Engraver:* Danforth, Wright & Co. *Comments:* H-VT-250-G12, Coulter-1. 185_. 1850s.
Rarity: *None known*

$1 • W-VT-760-001-G010a
Overprint: Red 1. *Engraver:* Danforth, Wright & Co. *Comments:* H-VT-250-G12a. Similar to W-VT-760-001-G010. 185_. 1850s–1860s.
Rarity: *None known*

$1 • W-VT-760-001-G010b   CC

Overprint: Red die outlining white 1. *Engraver:* Danforth, Wright & Co. *Comments:* H-Unlisted. Similar to W-VT-760-001-G010. 185_. 1850s–1860s.
Rarity: URS-3
F $1,250

$1 • W-VT-760-001-G020   BH

Engraver: Rawdon, Clark & Co. *Comments:* H-Unlisted, Coulter-Unlisted. 18__. 1820s–1830s.
Rarity: URS-3
Proof $750

$1.50 • W-VT-760-001.50-G030   CC

Engraver: Rawdon, Clark & Co. *Comments:* H-Unlisted, Coulter-3. 18__. 1830s.
Rarity: URS-2
F $1,500

$2 • W-VT-760-002-G040   CC

Engraver: Rawdon, Clark & Co. *Comments:* H-VT-250-G16. 18__. 1820s–1830s.
Rarity: URS-2
Proof $1,000

$2 • W-VT-760-002-G050
Comments: H-VT-250-G20. No description available. 18__. 1840s.
Rarity: *None known*

$2 • W-VT-760-002-G060
Left: 2 / Cattle drinking, Man on horseback, two boys. *Bottom center:* Eagle. *Right:* 2 / 2. *Engraver:* Danforth, Wright & Co. *Comments:* H-VT-250-G24, Coulter-4. 185_. 1850s.
Rarity: *None known*

$2 • W-VT-760-002-G060a
Overprint: Red 2. *Engraver:* Danforth, Wright & Co. *Comments:* H-VT-250-G24a. Similar to W-VT-760-002-G060. 185_. 1850s–1860s.
Rarity: *None known*

$3 • W-VT-760-003-G070 CC

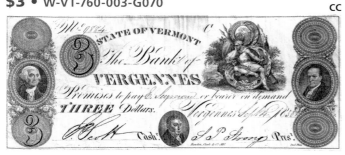

Engraver: Rawdon, Clark & Co. **Comments:** H-Unlisted, Coulter-Unlisted. 18__. 1820s–1830s.
Rarity: URS-3
F $750; **VF** $1,200

$3 • W-VT-760-003-G080

Left: 3 / Dogs scaring birds. **Center:** Two horses and train. **Right:** 3 on shield / 3. **Engraver:** Danforth, Wright & Co. **Comments:** H-VT-250-G32, Coulter-6. 185_. 1850s.
Rarity: *None known*

$3 • W-VT-760-003-G080a CJF

Overprint: Red 3. **Engraver:** Danforth, Wright & Co. **Comments:** H-VT-250-G32a. Similar to W-VT-760-003-G080. Handwritten 6 over 5 in date. 185_. 1850s–1860s.
Rarity: URS-2
F $1,500

$5 • W-VT-760-005-G090

Comments: H-VT-250-G36. No description available. 18__. 1820s–1830s.
Rarity: *None known*

$5 • W-VT-760-005-G100

Comments: H-VT-250-G40. No description available. 185_. 1850s.
Rarity: *None known*

$5 • W-VT-760-005-G110

Left: 5 over V / Medallion head of William Shakespeare / FIVE. **Center:** Woman, boy, girl, dog, and man with rake. **Right:** V / 5. **Engraver:** Danforth, Wright & Co. **Comments:** H-VT-250-G44. 185_. 1850s.
Rarity: *None known*

$5 • W-VT-760-005-G110a

Overprint: Red 5. **Engraver:** Danforth, Wright & Co. **Comments:** H-VT-250-G44a. Similar to W-VT-760-005-G110. 185_. 1850s.
Rarity: *None known*

$5 • W-VT-760-005-G110b CJF

Overprint: Red 5. **Engraver:** Danforth, Wright & Co. / ABNCo. monogram. **Comments:** H-VT-250-G44b, Coulter-8. Similar to W-VT-760-005-G110 but with additional engraver imprint and different date. 18__. 1860s.
Rarity: URS-2
F $1,000

$10 • W-VT-760-010-G120

Comments: H-VT-250-G48. No description available. 18__. 1820s–1830s.
Rarity: *None known*

$10 • W-VT-760-010-G130 CC

Engraver: Rawdon, Clark & Co. **Comments:** H-VT-250-G52. 18__. 1840s.
Rarity: URS-2
Unc-Rem $600; **Proof** $1,000

$10 • W-VT-760-010-G140

Left: X / TEN. **Center:** Allegorical figure / Angel offering apple to woman. **Right:** 10. **Engraver:** Danforth, Wright & Co. **Comments:** H-VT-250-G56, Coulter-10. 185_. 1850s.
Rarity: *None known*

$10 • W-VT-760-010-G140a

Overprint: Red. **Engraver:** Danforth, Wright & Co. **Comments:** H-VT-250-G56a. Similar to W-VT-760-010-G140. 185_. 1850s.
Rarity: *None known*

$20 • W-VT-760-020-G150

Left: Portrait of George Washington / 20 / XX. **Center:** Propeller. **Bottom center:** Steamship. **Right:** XX / Herd of horses. **Engraver:** Danforth, Wright & Co. **Comments:** H-VT-250-G64, Coulter-12. 18__. 1850s.
Rarity: *None known*

$50 • W-VT-760-050-G160

Left: Three figures, Canal and boat, Factories / 50. **Center:** L / Farmer plowing / L. **Bottom center:** Clasped hands. **Right:** 50 / Justice, eagle, and shield / 50. **Comments:** H-VT-250-G72, Coulter-13. 18__. 1860s.
Rarity: *None known*

$100 • W-VT-760-100-G170

Left: 100 / Liberty with scroll and eagle / 100. *Center:* 100 / Woman with key / 100. *Bottom center:* Eagle. *Right:* Three figures, two seated / 100. *Comments:* H-VT-250-G80, Coulter-14. 18__. 1860s.

Rarity: *None known*

NON-VALID ISSUES

$1 • W-VT-760-001-N010

Comments: H-Unlisted, Coulter-2. No description available. 1850s.

Rarity: *None known*

$1 • W-VT-760-001-S010

CC

Comments: H-Unlisted, Coulter-Unlisted. 18__. 1840s.

Rarity: URS-3
F $500

$2 • W-VT-760-002-N020

Left: Woman. *Center:* Train. *Right:* Ship. *Comments:* H-Unlisted, Coulter-5. 1840s.

Rarity: *None known*

$3 • W-VT-760-003-S020

CJF

Comments: H-VT-250-S5, Coulter-7. 18__. 1840s.

Rarity: URS-6
F $100

WATERBURY, VERMONT

Settlers from Waterbury, Connecticut, received a charter for land located in the Winooski River Valley in 1763. They named the new township after their former home. In 1783 James Marsh made the first permanent settlement in Waterbury. Early industries primarily focused around diverse specialties including lumber, baskets, children's carriages, leather products, starch, alcohol, and scythe handles. Agriculture contributed as well, circling between the fluctuation of sheep husbandry and the wool industry from 1830 to 1870. Dairy followed afterwards, as was the case in many Vermont towns.

Mills and manufacturing companies drew power from two falls in Thatcher Brook. Industries using this energy included the production of bobbins, a lumber mill, a willow plant, a clothes wringer, tanneries, distilleries, and starch making.

Bank of Waterbury
1854–1865
W-VT-770

History: The Bank of Waterbury was chartered in February 1854 with $100,000 in authorized capital. These figures were given for 1857: capital $80,000; bills in circulation $94,625; specie $7,597; real estate $1,200. In 1862 circulation was $95,509.

After the Waterbury National Bank commenced business on September 1, 1865, it took over the interests of the state bank. The outstanding circulation of the Bank of Waterbury was reported to be $1,942 in 1867.

Numismatic Commentary: Notes from this bank are very hard to locate. Two of the bank's lower denominations show silver dollars within the vignettes.

All issues of the Bank of Waterbury bear the engraver's imprint of Rawdon, Wright, Hatch & Edson and the New England Bank Note Co.

VALID ISSUES

$1 • W-VT-770-001-G010

CJF

Overprint: Red ONE. *Comments:* H-VT-255-G2a, Coulter-1. 18__. 1850s.

Rarity: URS-3
F $750; **VF** $850

$1 • W-VT-770-001-G010a

Left: Cupid rolling silver dollar on railroad track, Train and city / 1. *Center:* Mechanical instruments. *Right:* 1 / Justice, Globe and shield. *Overprint:* Green ONE. *Comments:* H-VT-255-G2b. Similar to W-VT-770-001-G010. 18__. 1850s.

Rarity: *None known*

$2 • W-VT-770-002-G020

CC

Overprint: Red TWO. *Comments:* H-VT-255-G4a, Coulter-2. 18__. 1850s.

Rarity: URS-2
F $1,250

$2 • W-VT-770-002-G020a
Left: Liberty and eagle / 2. *Center:* Two cupids and two silver dollars, Train and village. *Right:* 2 / Lake, Indian woman. *Overprint:* Green TWO. *Comments:* H-VT-255-G4b. Similar to W-VT-770-002-G020. 18__. 1850s.
Rarity: URS-2
VF $850

$3 • W-VT-770-003-G030

 CC

Overprint: Red THREE. *Comments:* H-VT-255-G6a, Coulter-3. 18__. 1850s–1860s.
Rarity: URS-2
VG $750

$3 • W-VT-770-003-G030a
Left: THREE / Liberty. *Center:* Two men, one woman, Dog, pail, basket, grain. *Right:* 3 / Portrait of George Washington. *Overprint:* Green THREE. *Comments:* H-VT-255-G6b. Similar to W-VT-770-003-G030. 18__. 1850s.
Rarity: *None known*

$5 • W-VT-770-005-G040
Left: FIVE / Officer with sword. *Right:* 5 / Liberty, eagle, globe. *Overprint:* Red FIVE. *Comments:* H-VT-255-G8a, Coulter-4. 18__. 1850s.
Rarity: *None known*

$5 • W-VT-770-005-G040a
Overprint: Green FIVE. *Comments:* H-VT-255-G8b. Similar to W-VT-770-005-G040. 18__. 1850s.
Rarity: *None known*

$10 • W-VT-770-010-G050
Left: 10 / Steamboat / Spread eagle and shield, U.S. Capitol. *Right:* X / Agricultural implements. *Comments:* H-VT-255-G10, Coulter-5. 18__. 1850s.
Rarity: *None known*

$20 • W-VT-770-020-G060
Left: TWENTY / Liberty seated on cornucopia, shield, fruit. *Center:* Herd of cattle and sheep, Two men and dog. *Right:* 20 / Portrait of Thomas Jefferson. *Comments:* H-VT-255-G12, Coulter-6. 18__. 1850s.
Rarity: *None known*

$50 • W-VT-770-050-G070
Left: 50 / 50. *Center:* Man reclining with compass and chart. *Right:* 50 / Liberty. *Comments:* H-VT-255-G14, Coulter-8. 18__. 1850s.
Rarity: *None known*

$100 • W-VT-770-100-G080
Left: Liberty / 100. *Center:* U.S. Capitol. *Right:* 100 / Train. *Comments:* H-VT-255-G16, Coulter-9. 18__. 1850s.
Rarity: *None known*

NON-VALID ISSUES
$20 • W-VT-770-020-A010
Comments: H-Unlisted, Coulter-7. No description available. 1842.
Rarity: *None known*

WATERVILLE, VERMONT
The towns of Belvidere, Johnson, Cambridge, Bakersfield, and Fletcher were in the area that later was adjusted to form Waterville. The land was chartered to James Whitelaw, James Savage, and William Coit on October 26, 1788. It was originally called Coit's Gore. Later in 1799, part of the area was annexed to Bakersfield. Then, on November 15, 1824, another act split lands from Bakersfield, Belvidere, and Coit's Gore to form Waterville.

Sugar of the highest quality was made in Waterville from the maple trees, and apple orchards were an early agricultural pursuit. Orchards produced barrels of cider, but later the farming grew neglected and the trees were cut down. A freestone or talc quarry was opened in the 1820s and gave rise to the manufacture of fire bricks, foot stones, fire arches, and other materials that were fire-resistant. A feed and sawmill was built in 1842, and other businesses followed.

Bank of Waterville
1854
W-VT-780

History: In 1854 a charter application for the Bank of Waterville was rejected by the state legislature.

Numismatic Commentary: It is possible that Proof notes were made, but no record has been found of such.

How to Read the Whitman Numbering System
$1 • W-RI-010-001-G010a

Denomination: Value of the note shown.

W: Whitman number. This number is a sortable code unique to each bank and note.

RI: Abbreviation for the state under study.

010: Numerical designation specific to each bank.

001: The denomination in dollars.

G010a: G indicates a good or valid note. Other categories are indicated thus: C (counterfeit); R (raised); S (spurious); N (not-attributed); A (altered). Numbers are assigned starting with 010, 020, et seq. Terminal letters following the number indicate variations of a note: a series of different colored overprints, tints, payees, etc., all on the same design of note. For more information, see the "How to Use This Book" section at the front of the volume, page xiv.

WELLS RIVER, VERMONT

A village of the town of Newbury, the area of Wells River was first called Governor's Right due to the fact that the 500 acres were granted to Governor Benning Wentworth of New Hampshire. The area was purchased by a man named Chamberlin. He built a gristmill on the Wells River.

Due to its location on the Connecticut River, Wells River became a center for trade, allowing boats to travel downriver with lumber, clapboards, and shingles. The boats returned filled with iron, salt, rum, and molasses, among other goods.

The Connecticut & Passumpsic Rivers Railroad opened to Wells River on November 6, 1848, putting an end to the barge traffic on the river.

See also Newbury, Vermont.

Bank of Newbury
1832–1865
W-VT-790

History: The Bank of Newbury was chartered in 1832 with an authorized capital of $100,000. The bank opened on February 5, 1833, in the Spring Hotel. Business with the public did not start until May 22. In 1842 the bank voted to destroy its old and damaged bills, an amount totaling $48,287.50, as well as fractional currency that had never been used, an amount of $3,615.57. By August 1845, the bank's capital was $50,000, and its circulation was $114,227. In July of 1862, the same values were $75,000 and $140,781, respectively.

On September 27, 1849, another $243,000 worth of bills were destroyed by burning. $228,700 was destroyed the same way in 1856, and in 1857 still another $14,300 followed suit.

On June 24, 1865, the National Bank of Newbury took over the assets of the Bank of Newbury. Redemption of the outstanding circulation was guaranteed by the national bank. As of July 1, 1867, the bank had an outstanding circulation of $5,008.

See also listing under Newbury, W-VT-490.

Numismatic Commentary: Variations in plate design exist throughout the PSSP series and denominations of notes. The earliest notes (1830s) show a Congreve Check Plate back along with plain backs which were printed later (1840s–1850s). At least two variations of the $5 face plate exist. This is possible for other denominations. All may not yet have been recorded. The notes themselves are considered scarce to rare, especially the earlier issues. The Congreve Check Plate back was used up through the $50 denomination.

VALID ISSUES
$1 • W-VT-790-001-G010
Left: ONE / Indian girl with bow and arrow. *Right:* 1 / ONE / 1. *Engraver:* PSSP. *Comments:* H-VT-260-G2, Coulter-1. 18__. 1830s–1850s.
Rarity: *None known*

$1 • W-VT-790-001-G010a   CC

Overprint: Red ONE. *Engraver:* PSSP. *Comments:* H-VT-260-G2a. Similar to W-VT-790-001-G010 but with different date. January 1st, 18__. 1850s.
Rarity: URS-3
F $750

$1 • W-VT-790-001-G010b
Overprint: Green ONE. *Engraver:* PSSP. *Comments:* H-VT-260-G2b, Coulter-3. Similar to W-VT-790-001-G010 but with different date. January 1st, 18__. 1850s.
Rarity: *None known*

$1 • W-VT-790-001-G020   CC

Engraver: PSSP. *Comments:* H-Unlisted, Coulter-Unlisted. 18__. 1830s–1850s.
Rarity: URS-2
Proof $1,000

$1.25 • W-VT-790-001.25-G030
Left: 1 / 25/100 / Train / 1 25/100. *Center:* Sloop and other vessels at sea / $1.25 Cts. *Right:* 1 25/100 / Eagle. *Engraver:* New England Bank Note Co. *Comments:* H-VT-260-G4. 18__. 1830s.
Rarity: URS-2
VF $850

$1.50 • W-VT-790-001.50-G040   CC

Engraver: New England Bank Note Co. *Comments:* H-VT-260-G6. 18__. 1830s.
Rarity: URS-3
VF $1,450

$1.75 • W-VT-790-001.75-G050

Left: $1.75 Cts. / Hebe watering eagle / 1 75/100. *Center:* Three sloops at sea. *Right:* $1.75 Cts. / Woman seated with grain, Dog / 1 75/100. *Engraver:* New England Bank Note Co. *Comments:* H-VT-260-G8. 18__. 1830s.

Rarity: URS-2

VF $850

$2 • W-VT-790-002-G060

CC

Engraver: PSSP. *Comments:* H-VT-260-G10, Coulter-2. 18__. 1830s–1850s.

Rarity: URS-3

F $1,000

$2 • W-VT-790-002-G060a

CC

Overprint: Red TWO. *Engraver:* PSSP. *Comments:* H-VT-260-G10a. Similar to W-VT-790-002-G060 but with different date. January 1st, 18__. 1850s.

Rarity: URS-3

VF $900

$2 • W-VT-790-002-G060b

Left: VERMONT vertically / 2 / Girl with sheaf / 2. *Right:* 2 / State arms / 2 / TWO DOLLARS vertically. *Overprint:* Green TWO. *Engraver:* PSSP. *Comments:* H-VT-260-G10b. Similar to W-VT-790-002-G060 but with different date. January 1st, 18__. 1850s.

Rarity: URS-3

VF $600

$3 • W-VT-790-003-G070

Left: THREE / VERMONT / Minerva. *Right:* 3 / THREE / 3. *Engraver:* PSSP. *Comments:* H-VT-260-G12. 18__. 1830s–1850s.

Rarity: *None known*

$3 • W-VT-790-003-G070a

CC

Overprint: Red THREE. *Engraver:* PSSP. *Comments:* H-VT-260-G12a. Similar to W-VT-790-003-G070 but with different date. January 1st, 18__. 1850s.

Rarity: URS-3

VG $700; F $1,000

$3 • W-VT-790-003-G070b

Overprint: Green THREE. *Engraver:* PSSP. *Comments:* H-VT-260-G12b. Similar to W-VT-790-003-G070 but with different date. January 1st, 18__. 1850s.

Rarity: *None known*

$5 • W-VT-790-005-G080

CJF, CJF

Back: Check plate. *Engraver:* PSSP. *Comments:* H-Unlisted. 18__. 1830s.

Rarity: URS-3

F $1,250

$5 • W-VT-790-005-G090

Left: FIVE / VERMONT / George Washington and horse. *Right:* 5 / Woman knitting / FIVE DOLLARS. *Back:* Check plate. *Engraver:* PSSP. *Comments:* H-VT-260-G14. January 1st, 18__. 1830s.

Rarity: *None known*

$5 • W-VT-790-005-G090a

CJF

Back: Plain. *Engraver:* PSSP. *Comments:* H-VT-260-G14a, Coulter-4. Similar to W-VT-790-005-G090. January 1st, 18__. 1840s.

Rarity: URS-4
F $750

$5 • W-VT-790-005-G090b

CC

Overprint: Red FIVE. *Back:* Plain. *Engraver:* PSSP. *Comments:* H-VT-260-G14b. Similar to W-VT-790-005-G090. January 1st, 18__. 1850s.

Rarity: URS-4
F $750

$10 • W-VT-790-010-G100

Left: Two men mowing. *Center:* Panels of microlettering. *Right:* Bust of George Washington. *Back:* Check plate. *Engraver:* PSSP. *Comments:* H-VT-260-G16, Coulter-6. 18__. 1830s.

Rarity: *None known*

$10 • W-VT-790-010-G100a

Back: Plain. *Engraver:* PSSP. *Comments:* H-VT-260-G16a. Similar to W-VT-790-010-G100. 18__. 1840s.

Rarity: *None known*

$10 • W-VT-790-010-G100b

Overprint: Red TEN. *Back:* Plain. *Engraver:* PSSP. *Comments:* H-VT-260-G16b. Similar to W-VT-790-010-G100 but with different date. January 1st, 18__. 1850s.

Rarity: *None known*

$10 • W-VT-790-010-G100c

Overprint: Green TEN. *Engraver:* PSSP. *Comments:* H-VT-260-G16c. Similar to W-VT-790-010-G100 but with different date. January 1st, 18__. 1850s.

Rarity: *None known*

$20 • W-VT-790-020-G110

Center: Panels of microlettering. *Back:* Check plate. *Engraver:* PSSP. *Comments:* H-VT-260-G18. 18__. 1830s.

Rarity: *None known*

$20 • W-VT-790-020-G110a

Back: Plain. *Engraver:* PSSP. *Comments:* H-VT-260-G18a. Similar to W-VT-790-020-G110. 18__. 1840s.

Rarity: *None known*

$20 • W-VT-790-020-G120

Left: 20 / Woman standing with spear. *Center:* Woman holding rake seated between 2 and 0. *Right:* 20 / Woman seated with cornucopia / 20. *Engraver:* Rawdon, Wright, Hatch & Edson. *Comments:* H-VT-260-G20, Coulter-8. 18__. 1850s.

Rarity: *None known*

$50 • W-VT-790-050-G130

Center: Panels of microlettering. *Back:* Check plate. *Engraver:* PSSP. *Comments:* H-VT-260-G22. 18__. 1830s.

Rarity: *None known*

$50 • W-VT-790-050-G130a

Back: Plain. *Engraver:* PSSP. *Comments:* H-VT-260-G22a. Similar to W-VT-790-050-G130. 18__. 1840s.

Rarity: *None known*

$50 • W-VT-790-050-G140

Left: 50 / Minerva. *Center:* Ceres and Vulcan seated with rake, hammer, and cornucopia. *Right:* 50 / Cherub steering sailboat / 50. *Engraver:* Rawdon, Wright, Hatch & Edson. *Comments:* H-VT-260-G24, Coulter-9. 18__. 1850s.

Rarity: *None known*

$100 • W-VT-790-100-G150

Left: 100 / Vulcan seated. *Center:* Spread eagle on limb, Train and canal boats. *Bottom center:* 100. *Right:* 100 / Ceres seated with rake. *Engraver:* Rawdon, Wright, Hatch & Edson. *Comments:* H-VT-260-G28, Coulter-10. 18__. 1850s.

Rarity: *None known*

NON-VALID ISSUES

$5 • W-VT-790-005-N010

Center: Woman, Cornucopia. *Back:* Check plate. *Comments:* H-Unlisted, Coulter-5. 1850s.

Rarity: *None known*

$10 • W-VT-790-010-A010

CC

Engraver: Rawdon, Wright & Hatch. *Comments:* H-VT-260-A5, Coulter-7. 18__. 1830s.

Rarity: URS-4
F $150

Wells River Bank
1830s
W-VT-800

History: Although some mentions of the Wells River Bank are found in old accounts, this was a shortcut for the Bank of Newbury, W-VT-790.

Numismatic Commentary: Although descriptions of three denominations from this bank have been handed down from the Bank of Newbury, as noted above, no physical proof of genuine notes with such an imprint has been established.

ISSUES

$5 • W-VT-800-005-G010
Left: Panel of lathework chains bearing VERMONT / 5 / 5 vertically. *Center:* Alternating garlands and gridwork segments bearing FIVE. *Right:* 5 / 5 vertically. *Engraver:* PSSP. *Comments:* H-VT-265-G12. 18__. 1830s.
Rarity: *None known*

$10 • W-VT-800-010-G020
Left: Panel of lathework chains bearing VERMONT / 10 / 10 vertically. *Center:* Alternating garlands and gridwork segments bearing TEN. *Right:* 10 / 10 vertically. *Engraver:* PSSP. *Comments:* H-VT-265-G16. 18__. 1830s.
Rarity: *None known*

$20 • W-VT-800-020-G030
Left: Panel of lathework chains bearing VERMONT / 20 / 20 vertically. *Center:* Alternating garlands and gridwork segments bearing TWENTY. *Right:* 20 / 20 vertically. *Engraver:* PSSP. *Comments:* H-VT-265-G20. 18__. 1830s.
Rarity: *None known*

WEST POULTNEY, VERMONT

Poultney is divided into two villages: East Poultney and West Poultney. East Poultney was the larger of the two until the latter 19th century, when West Poultney added territory. Henry Stanley raised a foundry in West Poultney in 1828. The Rutland & Washington Railroad connected to the village later and resulted in West Poultney becoming the center of business for the area.

See also Poultney, Vermont.

Bank of Poultney
1841–1865
W-VT-810

History: The Bank of Poultney was chartered on October 29, 1840, with an authorized capital of $100,000. Business commenced on July 7, 1841. On November 7, 1842, the capital of the bank was reduced to $70,000. It was reduced again on November 2, 1843, to $50,000. There the value remained until the bank's first charter expired.

In August 1845, circulation was $49,978. In 1851 circulation was $77,697, and other debts due were $15,486.

The Bank of Poultney was rechartered in 1859 with an authorized capital of $30,000. Circulation was $4,214. In December 1860, capital reached $90,000, and by July 1862, capital had risen further to $100,000. Circulation was as high as $178,988.

On July 1, 1865, the business of the Bank of Poultney was succeeded by the National Bank of Poultney. The state bank had an outstanding circulation of $4,244, redemption of which was guaranteed by the national bank.

See also listing under Poultney, W-VT-560.

VALID ISSUES

$1 • W-VT-810-001-G010   CC

Overprint: Red ONE. **Engraver:** Draper, Toppan & Co. **Comments:** H-VT-270-G2. 18__. 1840s.
Rarity: URS-2
VG $600

$1 • W-VT-810-001-G010a
Center: 1 / Two women seated beside shield / ONE / 1. **Engraver:** Draper, Toppan & Co. **Comments:** H-VT-270-G2a. Similar to W-VT-810-001-G010. 18__. 1840s–1850s.
Rarity: *None known*

$2 • W-VT-810-002-G020   CC

Engraver: Draper, Toppan & Co. **Comments:** H-VT-270-G4. 18__. 1840s.
Rarity: URS-2
Proof $1,400

$2 • W-VT-810-002-G020a
Left: TWO / Farmer with sickle / TWO. **Center:** 2 / Two women, house / TWO / 2. **Right:** TWO / Woman holding hat / TWO. **Engraver:** Draper, Toppan & Co. **Comments:** H-VT-270-G4a. Similar to W-VT-810-002-G020. 18__. 1840s–1850s.
Rarity: URS-3
VF $600

$5 • W-VT-810-005-G030　　　　　　　　　　　　　CC

Engraver: Draper, Toppan & Co. **Comments:** H-VT-270-G6. 18__. 1840s.

Rarity: URS-2
Proof $1,000

$10 • W-VT-810-010-G040
Left: TEN / Woman holding scroll bearing 10 / TEN. **Center:** X / Spread eagle and shield. **Bottom center:** Female portrait. **Right:** 10 / Portrait of George Washington / TEN. **Engraver:** Draper, Toppan & Co. **Comments:** H-VT-270-G8. 18__. 1840s.

Rarity: *None known*

$10 • W-VT-810-010-G050
Left: Portrait of Benjamin Franklin. **Center:** Train / Female portrait. **Right:** 10 / Man with spear. **Engraver:** Toppan, Carpenter, Casilear & Co. **Comments:** H-VT-270-G10. 18__. 1850s.

Rarity: *None known*

$10 • W-VT-810-010-G050a
Tint: Brown-orange X and panel outlining white TEN. **Engraver:** Toppan, Carpenter, Casilear & Co. **Comments:** H-VT-270-G10b. Similar to W-VT-810-010-G050 but with different date. Jan. 1, 1858.

Rarity: URS-2
Unc-Rem $900

$20 • W-VT-810-020-G060
Left: 20 / Man carrying sledge. **Center:** Train / TWENTY. **Right:** 20 / Indian in canoe. **Engraver:** Toppan, Carpenter, Casilear & Co. **Comments:** H-VT-270-G12. 18__. 1850s.

Rarity: *None known*

$20 • W-VT-810-020-G060a
Tint: Brown-orange panel outlining white TWENTY. **Engraver:** Toppan, Carpenter, Casilear & Co. **Comments:** H-VT-270-G12b. Similar to W-VT-810-020-G060 but with different date. Jan. 1, 1858.

Rarity: URS-2
Unc-Rem $900

WEST RANDOLPH, VERMONT

Granted on November 2, 1780, West Randolph was chartered on June 29, 1781, to Aaron Storrs and 70 others. It was originally known as Middlesex. The town was settled in 1778 and was renamed after Edmund Randolph.

There were three original villages in the area—Randolph Center, East Randolph, and West Randolph. Rich soil allowed farming to become a principal industry, and by 1830 the population had reached 2,743. There were 13,000 sheep grazing in the fields, and Randolph became famous for its butter, cheese, and mutton. The White River gave water power for mills, and by 1859 there were three gristmills, an oil mill, and a carding mill.

West Randolph Bank
1854
W-VT-820

History: In 1854 a charter application for the West Randolph Bank was rejected by the state legislature.

Numismatic Commentary: It is possible that Proof notes were made, but no record has been found of such.

WESTMINSTER, VERMONT

Vermont's oldest existing town, Westminster was the site where settlers met to declare independence as the Republic of Vermont. On January 15, 1777, they named themselves the Republic of New Connecticut, though the name was later changed to Vermont. Westminster is south of Bellows Falls by only four miles.

The first resistance in the Revolutionary War occurred in Westminster, as did the first bloodshed. On March 13, 1775, Vermont men took possession of the King's Courthouse. They were attacked and one was killed, but they were successful, for the court did not hold and was never again held under the king's rule. Farming was the main industry for the area.

Vermont State Bank (branch)
1807–1812
W-VT-830

History: The Vermont State Bank branches began issuing paper money in 1807. In 1812 the records of the Vermont State Bank were moved to Woodstock. After 1812 many bills of the various branches remained in circulation. These were redeemed in later years until the affairs of the bank were wound up in 1845. See the introductory text for general information.

See also listings under Burlington, W-VT-210, Middlebury, W-VT-450, and Woodstock, W-VT-900.

Numismatic Commentary: The Vermont State Bank issued identical notes for all four branches; there are plenty to satisfy collector demand. Even though many remainder sheets have been cut, there are still plenty of signed and dated examples in the marketplace. Most of the available stock are of the PSSP design.

VALID ISSUES

50¢ • W-VT-830-00.50-G010
Left: FIFTY CENTS vertically. **Center:** Woman. **Right:** 50/100. **Comments:** H-VT-4-G96, Coulter-1. 1806–1808.

Rarity: URS-6
VF $150

50¢ • W-VT-830-00.50-G020
Left: FIFTY CENTS vertically. **Center:** Woman. **Right:** 50/100. **Comments:** H-VT-4-G97. 1806–1808.

Rarity: URS-5
VF $150

50¢ • W-VT-830-00.50-G030
Left: 1/2 / 1/2. **Center:** HALF D, Text. **Right:** 1/2 / 1/2. **Engraver:** PSSP. **Comments:** H-VT-4-G104, Coulter-2. 18__. 1808.

Rarity: URS-7
VG $50; **VF** $150; **Unc-Rem** $75

50¢ • W-VT-830-00.50-G040

CC

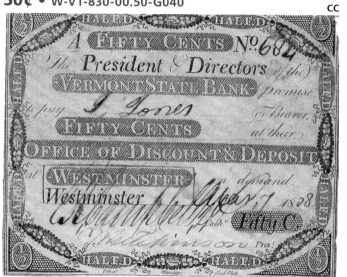

Engraver: PSSP. *Comments:* H-VT-4-G105. 18__. 1806–1808.
Rarity: *None known*

75¢ • W-VT-830-00.75-G050
Left: 3/4 / 3/4. *Center:* LXXV, Text. *Right:* 3/4 / 3/4. *Comments:* H-Unlisted, Coulter-23. 1806–1808.
Rarity: *None known*

75¢ • W-VT-830-00.75-G060
Left: SEVENTY FIVE vertically. *Center:* 75 in die. *Comments:* H-VT-4-G106, Coulter-4. 180_. 1806–1808.
Rarity: *None known*

75¢ • W-VT-830-00.75-G070
Left: SEVENTY FIVE vertically. *Center:* Woman reclining / 75 in die. *Comments:* H-VT-4-G107, Coulter-4. 180_. 1806–1808.
Rarity: *None known*

75¢ • W-VT-830-00.75-G080
Left: SEVENTY FIVE vertically. *Center:* Woman reclining / 75 in die. *Comments:* H-VT-4-G108, Coulter-4. 180_. 1806–1808.
Rarity: *None known*

75¢ • W-VT-830-00.75-G090
Left: SEVENTY FIVE vertically. *Center:* Woman reclining / 75 in die. *Comments:* H-VT-4-G109, Coulter-4. 180_. 1806–1808.
Rarity: URS-6
VF $150

75¢ • W-VT-830-00.75-G100
Left: 3/4 / 3/4. *Center:* LXXV, Text. *Right:* 3/4 / 3/4. *Engraver:* PSSP. *Comments:* H-VT-4-G114, Coulter-4. 18__. 1808.
Rarity: URS-6
VF $150; **Unc-Rem** $75

75¢ • W-VT-830-00.75-G110

SI

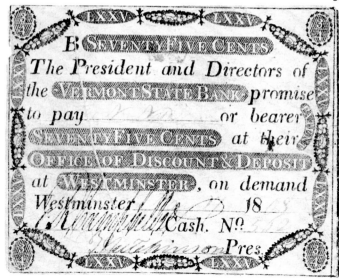

Engraver: PSSP. *Comments:* H-VT-4-G115, Coulter-4. 18__. 1808.
Rarity: URS-6
VG $75; **VF** $150; **Unc-Rem** $75

$1 • W-VT-830-001-G120
Left: Panel / ONE DOLLAR vertically. *Center:* ONE on three dies / Women flanking shield. *Bottom center:* 1 on die. *Right:* 1 on die. *Comments:* H-VT-4-G116. 180_. 1806–1808.
Rarity: URS-6
VF $150

$1 • W-VT-830-001-G120a
Center: ONE in square / Women flanking shield. *Comments:* H-VT-4-G117. Similar to W-VT-830-001-G120. 180_. 1806–1808.
Rarity: URS-6
VF $150

$1 • W-VT-830-001-G130

CC

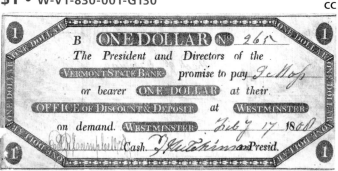

Comments: H-VT-4-G118, Coulter-6. 18__. 1808.
Rarity: URS-7
F $75; **VF** $150

$1 • W-VT-830-001-G140
CC

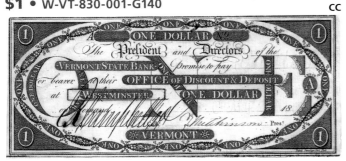

Engraver: PSSP. *Comments:* H-VT-4-G119, Coulter-7. 18__. 1808.
Rarity: URS-7
F $75; **VF** $150; **Unc-Rem** $100

$1.25 • W-VT-830-001.25-G150
CC

Engraver: PSSP. *Comments:* H-VT-4-G120, Coulter-8. 18__. 1808.
Rarity: URS-7
Unc-Rem $100

$1.50 • W-VT-830-001.50-G160
CC

Engraver: PSSP. *Comments:* H-VT-4-G121, Coulter-9. 18__. 1808.
Rarity: URS-7
Unc-Rem $100

$1.75 • W-VT-830-001.75-G170
CC

Engraver: PSSP. *Comments:* H-VT-4-G122, Coulter-10. 18__. 1808.
Rarity: URS-7
Unc-Rem $140

$2 • W-VT-830-002-G180
CC

Comments: H-VT-4-G124, Coulter-11. 180_. 1806–1808.
Rarity: URS-5
VF $200

$2 • W-VT-830-002-G190
Center: 2 / 2 / 2 / 2. *Engraver:* PSSP. *Comments:* H-VT-4-G125, Coulter-11. 18__. 1808.
Rarity: URS-5
VF $200

$2 • W-VT-830-002-G200
CC

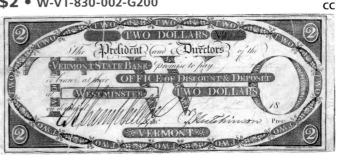

Engraver: PSSP. *Comments:* H-VT-4-G126, Coulter-12. 18__. 1808.
Rarity: URS-6
VF $150; **Unc-Rem** $75

$3 • W-VT-830-003-G210
Left: Panel / THREE vertically. *Center:* 3 on die / Women flanking shield. *Right:* 3 on die. *Comments:* H-VT-4-G127. 18__. 1808.
Rarity: URS-6
VF $150; **Unc-Rem** $75

$3 • W-VT-830-003-G220
Left: Panel / THREE vertically. *Center:* 3 on die / Women flanking shield. *Right:* 3 on die. *Comments:* H-VT-4-G128. 18__. 1806–1808.
Rarity: URS-6
VF $150; **Unc-Rem** $75

$3 • W-VT-830-003-G230
CC

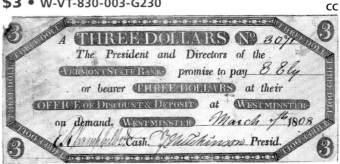

Engraver: PSSP. *Comments:* H-VT-4-G129, Coulter-13. 18__. 1808.
Rarity: URS-7
F $150

$3 • W-VT-830-003-G240

Center: THREE. *Engraver:* PSSP. *Comments:* H-VT-4-G130. 18__. 1808.

Rarity: URS-6

VF $150; **Unc-Rem** $75

$5 • W-VT-830-005-G250

Left: Panel / FIVE vertically. *Center:* 5 on die / Women flanking shield. *Right:* 5 on die. *Comments:* H-VT-4-G131. 18__. 1806–1808.

Rarity: URS-5

VF $150

$5 • W-VT-830-005-G260

Left: V V V V / VERMONT vertically. *Center:* 5 in die. *Right:* 5 in die. *Engraver:* PSSP. *Comments:* H-VT-4-G132. 18__. 1807 and 1808.

Rarity: *None known*

$5 • W-VT-830-005-G260a

Engraver: PSSP. *Comments:* H-VT-4-G132a. Similar to W-VT-830-005-G260. 18__. 1808.

Rarity: *None known*

$5 • W-VT-830-005-G270

Left: Stag and cow / 5 / 5. *Center:* FIVE bearing roses. *Right:* 5 / 5. *Engraver:* PSSP. *Comments:* H-VT-4-G133. 18__. 1808.

Rarity: *None known*

$5 • W-VT-830-005-G270a
cc

Engraver: PSSP. *Comments:* H-VT-4-G133a. Similar to W-VT-830-005-G270. 18__. 1808.

Rarity: URS-6

F $75; VF $500

$10 • W-VT-830-010-G280

Left: Panel / TEN vertically. *Center:* 10 on die / TEN on three dies / Women flanking shield. *Right:* 10 on die. *Comments:* H-VT-4-G134. 18__. 1806–1808.

Rarity: *None known*

$10 • W-VT-830-010-G290

Left: Stag and cow. *Center:* 10 vertically / 10 on panel / TEN DOLLARS / TEN. *Right:* 10 on die vertically / 10 on die vertically. *Engraver:* PSSP. *Comments:* H-VT-4-G136. 18__. 1808.

Rarity: URS-7

VF $150

$10 • W-VT-830-010-G290a

Engraver: PSSP. *Comments:* H-VT-4-G138. Similar to W-VT-830-010-G290. 18__. 1808.

Rarity: *None known*

Uncut Sheets

75¢-75¢-75¢-75¢-50¢-50¢-50¢-50¢ •
W-VT-830-00.75.00.75.00.75.00.75.00.50.00.50.00.50.00.50-US010

Vignette(s): (75¢) 3/4 / 3/4 / 3/4 / 3/4. *(50¢)* HALF D / 1/2 / 1/2 / 1/2 / 1/2 / HALF D. *Engraver:* PSSP. *Comments:* H-VT-4-G115, G115, G115, G115, G105, G105, G105, G105. 18__. 1806–1808.

Rarity: URS-4

F $400

NON-VALID ISSUES

50¢ • W-VT-830-00.50-C010

Comments: H-VT-4-C96. Counterfeit of W-VT-830-00.50-G010. 1808.

Rarity: URS-5

F $50

50¢ • W-VT-830-00.50-C020

Comments: H-VT-4-C97. Counterfeit of W-VT-830-00.50-G020. 1808.

Rarity: URS-5

F $50

75¢ • W-VT-830-00.75-C070

Comments: H-VT-4-C107, Coulter-4. Counterfeit of W-VT-830-00.75-G070. 180_. 1806–1808.

Rarity: URS-5

F $50

75¢ • W-VT-830-00.75-C080

Comments: H-VT-4-C108, Coulter-4. Counterfeit of W-VT-830-00.75-G080. 180_. 1806–1808.

Rarity: *None known*

$1 • W-VT-830-001-C120

Comments: H-VT-4-C116. Counterfeit of W-VT-830-001-G120. 180_. 1808.

Rarity: URS-5

F $100

$2 • W-VT-830-002-C180

Comments: H-VT-4-C124. Counterfeit of W-VT-830-002-G180. 180_. 1808.

Rarity: URS-5

F $100

$3 • W-VT-830-003-C210

Comments: H-VT-4-C127. Counterfeit of W-VT-830-003-G210. 18__. 1808.

Rarity: URS-5

F $100

$3 • W-VT-830-003-C220

Comments: H-VT-4-C128. Counterfeit of W-VT-830-003-G220. 18__. 1808.

Rarity: URS-5

F $100

$5 • W-VT-830-005-C260

Comments: H-VT-4-C132. Counterfeit of W-VT-830-005-G260. 18__. 1807 and 1808.

Rarity: *None known*

$5 • W-VT-830-005-C260a

Comments: H-VT-4-C132a. Counterfeit of W-VT-830-005-G260a. 18__. 1808.

Rarity: *None known*

$10 • **W-VT-830-010-C280**

Comments: H-VT-4-C134. Counterfeit of W-VT-830-010-G280. 1807.

Rarity: URS-5

F $100

WILMINGTON, VERMONT

Wilmington was chartered in 1751 and named in honor of Spencer Compton, 1st Earl of Wilmington. A second charter was granted in 1763 for the same area, but the land was granted to different people and was called Draper. The double charter caused land disputes and some strife. The town expanded in the 19th century with different aspects of agriculture and manufacturing.

Bank of Wilmington
1854
W-VT-840

History: In 1854 a charter application for the Bank of Wilmington was rejected by the state legislature.

Numismatic Commentary: It is possible that Proof notes were made, but no record has been found of such.

WINDSOR, VERMONT

Windsor, originally known to the Pennacook tribe as Cushankamaug, was settled by Captain Steele Smith. He erected the first buildings in 1759 and then returned with others the next year, returning again and again until he had finally brought his family back in 1764. Named after the town in Connecticut of the same title, Windsor was initially made up of 23,600 acres west of the Connecticut River. It was chartered in 1761 and granted to 59 settlers. Land disputes when the area was rechartered caused contention between New Hampshire and New York, but in 1777 the residents declared the lands to be independent. A public house in Windsor was the site of the constitutional convention, and thus Windsor is known as the Birthplace of Vermont.

A mountain range runs through the town from north to south. In 1793 the state legislature divided the east and west sections into their own parishes with a shared government. By 1814 they had been divided into two separate towns. A year later they rejoined, and then in 1848 they divided yet again.

A state prison was built in Windsor in 1808. By 1820 it was Vermont's largest town with a population of 2,956. A dam was built in 1835 on Mill Brook, providing water power for mills and factories, and a water company and a gas works were also organized here. The gun maker Robbins, Kendall & Lawrence was important in later years and provided 10,000 rifles for the war with Mexico. It also produced 50,000 rifles for federal troops during the Civil War.

Ascutney Bank
1847–1865
W-VT-850

History: The Ascutney Bank was chartered in 1847 with $50,000 in authorized capital. Figures for 1857 included: capital $50,000; bills in circulation $71,070; specie $6,247. Circulation was valued at $35,137 on July 1, 1862. In 1865 the Ascutney National Bank succeeded the business of the state bank. The outstanding circulation of the Ascutney Bank was reported as $1,275, redemption of which was guaranteed by the national bank.

Numismatic Commentary: Genuine notes are very rare and hard to locate. Some Proofs have appeared and two different uncut sheets are recorded.

VALID ISSUES

$1 • **W-VT-850-001-G010**   CC

Engraver: Danforth & Hufty. *Comments:* H-VT-275-G2, Coulter-1. May 1st, 1848.

Rarity: URS-2

Proof $1,700

$1 • **W-VT-850-001-G010a**   CC

Overprint: Red ONE. *Engraver:* Danforth & Hufty. *Comments:* H-Unlisted, Coulter-Unlisted. Similar to W-VT-850-001-G010. May 1st, 1848.

Rarity: URS-3

VG $750; **VF** $950

$2 • **W-VT-850-002-G020**   CC

Engraver: Danforth & Hufty. *Comments:* H-VT-275-G4, Coulter-2. May 1st, 1848.

Rarity: URS-2

Proof $2,000

$2 • W-VT-850-002-G020a

CC

Overprint: Red TWO. **Engraver:** Danforth & Hufty. **Comments:** H-Unlisted, Coulter-Unlisted. Similar to W-VT-850-002-G020. May 1st, 1848.

Rarity: URS-2
VG $750

$3 • W-VT-850-003-G030

CC

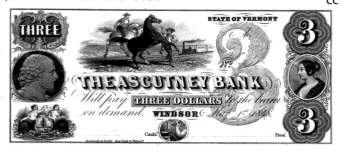

Engraver: Danforth & Hufty. **Comments:** H-VT-275-G6, Coulter-3. May 1st, 1848.

Rarity: URS-2
Proof $2,000

$3 • W-VT-850-003-G030a

CC

Overprint: Red THREE. **Engraver:** Danforth & Hufty. **Comments:** H-Unlisted, Coulter-Unlisted. Similar to W-VT-850-003-G030. May 1st, 1848.

Rarity: URS-2
F $1,000

$5 • W-VT-850-005-G040

CC

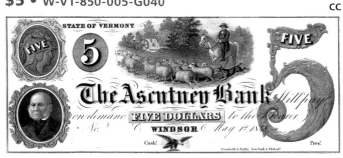

Engraver: Danforth & Hufty. **Comments:** H-VT-275-G8, Coulter-4. May 1st, 1848.

Rarity: URS-2
Proof $1,200

$10 • W-VT-850-010-G050

Left: X / Portrait of Benjamin Franklin / TEN. **Center:** "Presentation of the Declaration of Independence" / Portrait of Thomas Jefferson. **Right:** X / Portrait of John Adams / TEN. **Engraver:** Danforth & Hufty. **Comments:** H-VT-275-G10, Coulter-6. 18___. 1847–1860s.

Rarity: URS-2
Proof $1,500

$50 • W-VT-850-050-G060

CC

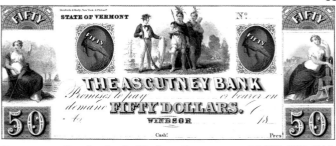

Engraver: Danforth & Hufty. **Comments:** H-VT-275-G12, Coulter-10. 18___. 1847–1860s.

Rarity: URS-1
Proof $2,000

Uncut Sheets

$1-$1-$2-$3 • W-VT-850-001.001.002.003-US010

Vignette(s): ($1) State arms / Farmer plowing with oxen, Girl / Steam engine / Portrait of George Washington. **($1)** State arms / Farmer plowing with oxen, Girl / Steam engine / Portrait of George Washington. **($2)** Portrait of Benjamin Franklin / Blacksmith shop / Wheelbarrow / State arms. **($3)** Medallion head / State arms / Two men and two horses crossing track, Train / Arm, hammer and anvil / Female portrait. **Engraver:** Danforth & Hufty. **Comments:** All unlisted in Haxby. May 1st, 1848.

Rarity: URS-1
Proof $4,500

$5-$5-$5-$10 • W-VT-850-005.005.005.010-US020
Vignette(s): ($5) Portrait of John Quincy Adams / Farmer on horseback driving sheep, Mill / Eagle. *($5)* Portrait of John Quincy Adams / Farmer on horseback driving sheep, Mill / Eagle. *($5)* Portrait of John Quincy Adams / Farmer on horseback driving sheep, Mill / Eagle. *($10)* Portrait of Benjamin Franklin / "Presentation of the Declaration of Independence" / Portrait of Thomas Jefferson / Portrait of John Adams. *Engraver:* Danforth & Hufty. *Comments:* All unlisted in Haxby. May 1st, 1848.

Rarity: URS-1
Proof $4,500

Non-Valid Issues

$5 • W-VT-850-005-S010
Left: FIVE / Woman in V / 5. *Center:* Drovers on horseback with flock of sheep. *Right:* FIVE vertically. *Engraver:* Draper, Toppan & Co. *Comments:* H-VT-275-S5, Coulter-5. May 1st, 1848.

Rarity: URS-5
F $125

$10 • W-VT-850-010-S020　　　　　　　　　　　**TD**

Engraver: Danforth & Hufty. *Comments:* H-VT-275-S10. 18__. 1848.

Rarity: URS-5
F $200

$10 • W-VT-850-010-N010
Left: Wharf, Train. *Center:* Reclining woman / Eagle and shield. *Comments:* H-Unlisted, Coulter-7. 1840s–1850s.

Rarity: *None known*

$10 • W-VT-850-010-N020
Center: Woman, bale, bridge, and train. *Comments:* H-Unlisted, Coulter-8. 1840s–1850s.

Rarity: *None known*

$10 • W-VT-850-010-A010
Center: Men gathering corn / Horse, cart. *Overprint:* Red X / X. *Engraver:* Unverified, but likely Toppan, Carpenter & Co. *Comments:* H-VT-275-A5, Coulter-9. Altered from $10 Farmers Bank, Wickford, Rhode Island. 18__. 1855.

Rarity: *None known*

Bank of Windsor
1818–1838
W-VT-860

History: The Bank of Windsor was incorporated on November 6, 1817, with an authorized capital of $150,000. The charter carried a provision making the stockholders personally liable for all demands against the bank. This was sufficient to discourage investors, and the bank never went into operation. A new act of incorporation, without the personal-liability clause, was passed by the legislature in 1818. This time the Bank of Windsor was capitalized at $100,000.

In November 1836, the capital of the bank was $80,000, and circulation was $52,272. By 1837 the bank was doing poorly. The Panic of 1837 saw the bank "failed, and failed heavily embarrassed." At the time, the Bank of Windsor was the largest bank in that part of Vermont. The bank lingered for a while and closed in 1838.

Numismatic Commentary: This bank left collectors a legacy of both signed and dated bank notes and a numerous amount of uncut sheets, all of the PSSP style. These notes are among the most common of all Vermont issues. There also exists a $5 specimen of an earlier Perkins product, the Perkins Patent Steel Plate (PPSP).

Valid Issues

$1 • W-VT-860-001-G010
Comments: H-VT-280-G2. No description available. 18__. 1810s.

Rarity: *None known*

$1 • W-VT-860-001-G020
Center: Alternating flower garlands and gridwork segments. *Engraver:* PSSP. *Comments:* H-VT-280-G4. 18__. 1820s–1830s.

Rarity: *None known*

$1 • W-VT-860-001-G020a　　　　　　　　　　**CC**

Engraver: PSSP. *Comments:* H-VT-280-G8, Coulter-11. Similar to W-VT-860-001-G020. 18__. 1830s.

Rarity: URS-8
Unc-Rem $50

$2 • W-VT-860-002-G030
Comments: H-VT-280-G10. No description available. 18__. 1810s.

Rarity: *None known*

$2 • W-VT-860-002-G040
Center: Alternating flower garlands and gridwork segments. *Engraver:* PSSP. *Comments:* H-VT-280-G12. 18__. 1820s–1830s.

Rarity: *None known*

$2 • W-VT-860-002-G040a

cc

Engraver: PSSP. *Comments:* H-VT-280-G16, Coulter-12. Similar to W-VT-860-002-G040. 18__. 1830s.
Rarity: URS-10
Unc-Rem $60

$3 • W-VT-860-003-G050

Comments: H-VT-280-G18. No description available. 18__. 1810s.
Rarity: *None known*

$3 • W-VT-860-003-G060

cc

Engraver: PSSP. *Comments:* H-VT-280-G20. 18__. 1820s–1830s.
Rarity: URS-8
F $75

$3 • W-VT-860-003-G060a

Left: THREE vertically. *Right:* THREE vertically. *Engraver:* PSSP. *Comments:* H-VT-280-G24, Coulter-13. Similar to W-VT-860-003-G060. 18__. 1830s.
Rarity: URS-8
Unc-Rem $50

$5 • W-VT-860-005-G070

cc

Engraver: PPSP. *Comments:* H-VT-280-G26. Proof. 18__. 1810s.
Rarity: URS-2
Proof $2,000

$5 • W-VT-860-005-G080

cc

Engraver: PSSP. *Comments:* H-VT-280-G32, Coulter-14. 18__. 1820s–1830s.
Rarity: URS-10
F $75

$10 • W-VT-860-010-G090

Comments: H-VT-280-G34. No description available. 18__. 1810s.
Rarity: *None known*

$10 • W-VT-860-010-G100

Left: VERMONT / 10 / 10 vertically. *Center:* Alternating flower garlands and gridwork segments. *Right:* 10 / 10 vertically. *Engraver:* PSSP. *Comments:* H-VT-280-G36, Coulter-15. 18__. 1820s.
Rarity: *None known*

$10 • W-VT-860-010-G100a

cc

Engraver: PSSP. *Comments:* H-VT-280-G40. Similar to W-VT-860-010-G100. 18__. 1820s–1830s.
Rarity: URS-8
VF $100; **Unc-Rem** $50

$20 • W-VT-860-020-G110

Left: VERMONT / 20 / 20 vertically. *Center:* Alternating flower garlands and gridwork segments. *Right:* 20 / 20 vertically. *Engraver:* PSSP. *Comments:* H-VT-280-G44. 18__. 1820s–1830s.
Rarity: *None known*

$50 • W-VT-860-050-G120

Left: VERMONT / 50 / 50 vertically. *Center:* Alternating flower garlands and gridwork segments. *Right:* 50 / 50 vertically. *Engraver:* PSSP. *Comments:* H-VT-280-G48. 18__. 1820s–1830s.
Rarity: *None known*

$100 • W-VT-860-100-G130

CJF

Engraver: PSSP. *Comments:* H-VT-280-G52, Coulter-16. 18__.
1820s–1830s.

Rarity: URS-3
F $750

Uncut Sheets

$1-$1-$2-$3 • W-VT-860-001.001.002.003-US010

CC

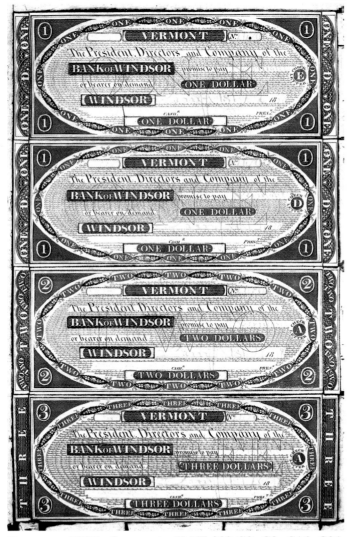

Engraver: PSSP. *Comments:* H-VT-280-G8, G8, G16, G24.
18__. 1830s.

Rarity: URS-7
Unc-Rem $300

$10-$5-$5-$5 • W-VT-860-010.005.005.005-US020

Vignette(s): ($10) Alternating flower garlands and gridwork segments. *($5)* Alternating flower garlands and gridwork segments. *($5)* Alternating flower garlands and gridwork segments. *($5)* Alternating flower garlands and gridwork segments. *Engraver:* PSSP. *Comments:* H-VT-280-G40, G32, G32, G32. 18__.
1820s–1830s.

Rarity: URS-7
Unc-Rem $300

Windsor Bank
CIRCA 1837
W-VT-870

History: A non-existent bank represented only by notes meant to represent the Bank of Windsor, W-VT-860.

ISSUES

$3 • W-VT-870-003-S010

CC

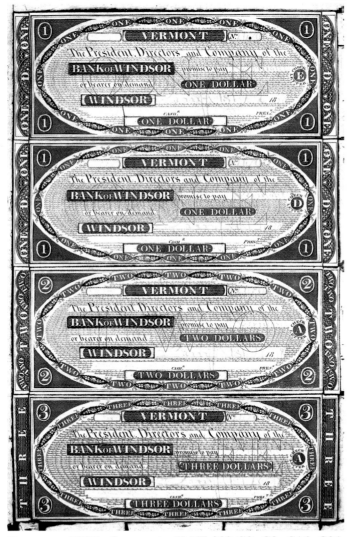

Comments: H-VT-281-S6, Coulter-13. 18__. 1830s.

Rarity: URS-5
F $275

WINOOSKI, VERMONT

"Winooski" is from the native language of the Abenaki people, meaning "where the wild onions grow." Ira Allen led settlers in the early 1770s through the wilderness to settle and construct a house on the Winooski River. The house served as both fort and general store for the Onion River Company. It was never used for defense, but its presence advanced local settlement.

Once the Revolutionary War had drawn to a close, Allen built a dam across the river and constructed a sawmill flanking both sides. Waterpower began to generate energy for the town, and mills rose up on both sides of the river. The Burlington Mill Company used the river to produce yarn and cloth, and textile mills rose up as well, worked by French Canadian immigrants who resided in a portion of town that came to be known as French Village.

Winooski Bank
1854
W-VT-880

History: In 1854 a charter application for the Winooski Bank was rejected by the state legislature.

WOODSTOCK, VERMONT

Woodstock was chartered on July 10, 1761, and granted to David Page and others. It took its name from Woodstock, Oxfordshire, England. By 1768 the town was settled by James Sanderson, along with his family. In 1776 a gristmill and a sawmill were built on a branch of the Ottauquechee River by Major Joab Hoisington.

Settlement slowed down due to the Revolutionary War, but after the hostilities had concluded, Woodstock grew strongly. Water power operated mills, and factories produced scythes, axes, carding machines, woolens, and flour. A machine shop, a gunsmith shop, furniture production, wooden wares, sashes, blinds, carriages, harnesses, saddles, trunks, and leather also contributed to industry here.

Bank of Woodstock
1831–1847
W-VT-890

History: The Bank of Woodstock was chartered on November 3, 1831, with an authorized capital of $100,000. The books for subscription to the capital stock of the Bank of Woodstock were opened on Wednesday, February 8, 1832. Applicants for the stock became as thick "as blackberries," and specie poured into the town in torrents, according to one account. The affairs of the bank went on very smoothly. The Panic of 1837 caused problems, but they were addressed and business continued. By August 1845, the circulation of the bank was $93,229.

On January 13, 1846, the directors held a meeting to discuss the proposition of Ammi Willard and Philo Hatch in regards to purchasing the banking house for a sum of $2,375, including the furniture. The bank would be allowed to settle up their affairs, and this was done in 1847.

Numismatic Commentary: The only engraver used by this bank was Rawdon, Clark & Co. of Albany. One issue shows a vignette of Archimedes with a lever raising the globe. Issues from this bank are very rare.

Remaining in the American Bank Note Co. archives as of 2003 was a $100 face plate and a $5-$5-$5-$10 face plate.

VALID ISSUES

$1 • W-VT-890-001-G010
Engraver: Rawdon, Clark & Co. **Comments:** H-VT-285-G2, Coulter-1. No description available. 18__. 1830s–1840s.
Rarity: *None known*

$2 • W-VT-890-002-G020
Engraver: Rawdon, Clark & Co. **Comments:** H-VT-285-G4, Coulter-2. No description available. 18__. 1830s–1840s.
Rarity: *None known*

$3 • W-VT-890-003-G030

CJF

Engraver: Rawdon, Clark & Co. **Comments:** H-VT-285-G6, Coulter-3. 18__. 1830s–1840s.
Rarity: URS-3
F $1,000

$5 • W-VT-890-005-G040

CC

Engraver: Rawdon, Clark & Co. **Comments:** H-VT-285-G8. 18__. 1830s–1840s.
Rarity: URS-3
F $1,000

$5 • W-VT-890-005-G050
Left: 5 / Portrait of George Washington. **Center:** State arms supported by two allegorical figures. **Right:** 5 / State arms. **Comments:** H-Unlisted, Coulter-5. 1830s–1840s.
Rarity: *None known*

$10 • W-VT-890-010-G060
Engraver: Rawdon, Clark & Co. **Comments:** H-VT-285-G10. No description available. 18__. 1830s–1840s.
Rarity: *None known*

NON-VALID ISSUES

$3 • W-VT-890-003-N010
Payee: H. Hall. **Comments:** H-VT-285-N5, Coulter-4. 18__. 1827.
Rarity: *None known*

$5 • W-VT-890-005-C040
Engraver: Rawdon, Clark & Co. **Comments:** H-VT-285-C8. Counterfeit of W-VT-890-005-G040. 18__. 1840.
Rarity: *None known*

$5 • W-VT-890-005-S010

CC

Engraver: Reed & Bissell. *Comments:* H-VT-285-S5, Coulter-6. 18__. 1840.

Rarity: URS-4
F $250

$5 • W-VT-890-005-N020
Comments: H-Unlisted, Coulter-7. Imitation of W-VT-890-005-S010. 1840.

Rarity: *None known*

$5 • W-VT-890-005-N030
Payee: A. Kent. *Comments:* H-Unlisted, Coulter-8. 1840.

Rarity: *None known*

$10 • W-VT-890-010-R010
Engraver: Rawdon, Clark & Co. *Comments:* H-VT-285-R5. Raised from W-VT-890-001-G010. 18__. 1830s–1840s.

Rarity: *None known*

$10 • W-VT-890-010-A010
Comments: H-Unlisted, Coulter-9. Altered from W-VT-890-001-G010. 1840.

Rarity: *None known*

Vermont State Bank (branch)
1807–1812
W-VT-900

History: The Vermont State Bank branches began issuing paper money in 1807. In 1812 the records of the Vermont State Bank were moved to Woodstock. After 1812 many bills of the various branches remained in circulation. These were redeemed in later years until the affairs of the bank were wound up in 1845. See the introductory text for general information.

See also listings under Burlington, W-VT-210, Middlebury, W-VT-450, and Westminster, W-VT-830.

Numismatic Commentary: The Vermont State Bank issued identical notes for all four branches; there are plenty to satisfy collector demand. Even though many remainder sheets have been cut, there are still plenty of signed and dated examples in the marketplace. Most of the available stock are of the PSSP design.

VALID ISSUES

50¢ • W-VT-900-00.50-G010
Left: FIFTY CENTS vertically. *Center:* 50 / Woman seated. *Right:* 50/100. *Comments:* H-VT-4-G143, Coulter-10. 1806–1808.

Rarity: *None known*

50¢ • W-VT-900-00.50-G020

CJF

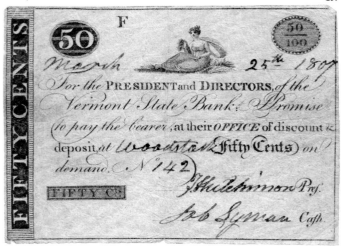

Comments: H-VT-4-G144. 1806–1808.
Rarity: URS-10
VG $50

50¢ • W-VT-900-00.50-G030
Left: FIFTY CENTS vertically / 50 over 100 over foliage. *Center:* Woman seated. *Right:* 50 Cts. *Comments:* H-VT-4-G148, Coulter-11. 18__. 1806–1808.
Rarity: URS-10
VF $75

50¢ • W-VT-900-00.50-G040

CJF

Comments: H-VT-4-G149, Coulter-12. 18__. 1806–1808.
Rarity: URS-10
VG $50

50¢ • W-VT-900-00.50-G050
Left: FIFTY CENTS vertically. *Center:* Woman / 50/100. *Right:* 50 Cts. *Comments:* H-VT-4-G150. 18__. 1806–1808.
Rarity: URS-10
VF $75

50¢ • **W-VT-900-00.50-G060**

CJF

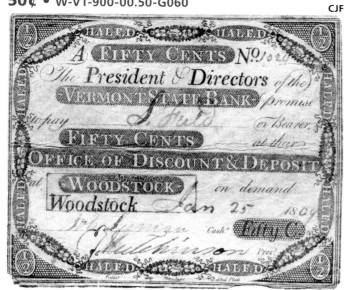

Engraver: PSSP. *Comments:* H-VT-4-G152, Coulter-13. 18__.
1808.
Rarity: URS-8
F $60

75¢ • **W-VT-900-00.75-G070**

Left: SEVENTY FIVE C vertically. *Center:* 75 cents in die /
Woman reclining. *Comments:* H-VT-4-G153. 180_. 1806–1808.
Rarity: URS-10
VF $75

75¢ • **W-VT-900-00.75-G080**

ANS

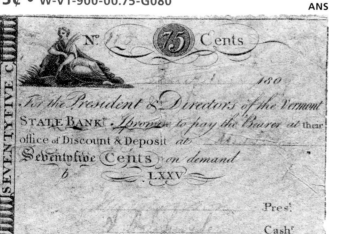

Comments: H-VT-4-G154. 180_. 1806–1808.
Rarity: URS-10
VG $75

75¢ • **W-VT-900-00.75-G090**

CJF

Comments: H-VT-4-G155. 180_. 1806–1808.
Rarity: URS-10
VG $75

75¢ • **W-VT-900-00.75-G100**

Left: SEVENTY FIVE C vertically. *Center:* 75 cents in die /
Woman reclining. *Comments:* H-VT-4-G156. 180_. 1806–1808.
Rarity: URS-10
VF $75

75¢ • **W-VT-900-00.75-G110**

Left: 3/4 / 3/4. *Center:* LXXV, Text. *Right:* 3/4 / 3/4. *Engraver:*
PSSP. *Comments:* H-VT-4-G162, Coulter-14. 18__. 1808.
Rarity: URS-10
VF $75

$1 • **W-VT-900-001-G120**

CJF

Comments: H-VT-4-G163, Coulter-16. 180_. 1806–1808.
Rarity: URS-9
F $75

$1 • **W-VT-900-001-G130**

Left: ONE DOLLAR vertically. *Center:* ONE / Women flanking
shield / 1. *Comments:* H-VT-4-G164, Coulter-16. 180_. 1806–
1808.
Rarity: URS-10
VF $100

$1 • W-VT-900-001-G140   CC

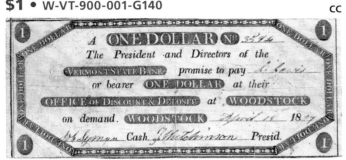

Engraver: PSSP. *Comments:* H-VT-4-G165, Coulter-17. 18__.
1808.

Rarity: URS-10

F $95

$1 • W-VT-900-001-G150   NJW

Engraver: PSSP. *Comments:* H-VT-4-G166, Coulter-18. 18__.
1808.

Rarity: URS-10

CU $75

$1.25 • W-VT-900-001.25-G160   CC

Engraver: PSSP. *Comments:* H-VT-4-G167, Coulter-19. 18__.
1808.

Rarity: URS-10

Unc-Rem $100

$1.50 • W-VT-900-001.50-G170   CC

Engraver: PSSP. *Comments:* H-VT-4-G168, Coulter-20. 18__.
1808.

Rarity: URS-10

F $150

$1.75 • W-VT-900-001.75-G180

Left: 175 / 175 vertically. *Center:* 1.75. *Right:* 175 / 175 vertically. *Engraver:* PSSP. *Comments:* H-VT-4-G169, Coulter-21.
18__. 1808.

Rarity: URS-10

Unc-Rem $150

$2 • W-VT-900-002-G190   CC

Comments: H-VT-4-G171, Coulter-22. 180_. 1806–1808.

Rarity: URS-9

F $75

$2 • W-VT-900-002-G200

Center: 2 / 2 / 2 / 2. *Engraver:* PSSP. *Comments:* H-VT-4-G172,
Coulter-23. 18__. 1806–1808.

Rarity: URS-10

VF $100

$2 • W-VT-900-002-G210   CC

Engraver: PSSP. *Comments:* H-VT-4-G173, Coulter-24. 18__.
1808.

Rarity: URS-10

Unc-Rem $75

$3 • W-VT-900-003-G220

Left: THREE vertically. *Center:* 3 / THREE DOLLARS.
Right: Women flanking shield / 3. *Comments:* H-VT-4-G174,
Coulter-25. 18__. 1806–1808.

Rarity: URS-10

VF $100

$3 • W-VT-900-003-G230   CJF

Comments: H-VT-4-G175, Coulter-25. 18__. 1806–1808.

Rarity: URS-9

F $75

$3 • W-VT-900-003-G240   CJF

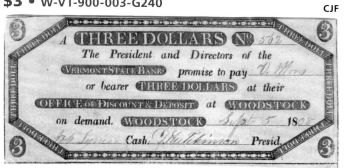

Engraver: PSSP. *Comments:* H-VT-4-G176, Coulter-27. 18__.
1808.

Rarity: URS-9
F $100

$3 • W-VT-900-003-G250   NJW

Engraver: PSSP. *Comments:* H-VT-4-G177, Coulter-27. 18__.
1808.

Rarity: URS-10
Unc-Rem $100

$5 • W-VT-900-005-G260   CJF

Comments: H-VT-4-G178, Coulter-29. 18__. 1806–1808.

Rarity: URS-9
F $75

$5 • W-VT-900-005-G270   CC

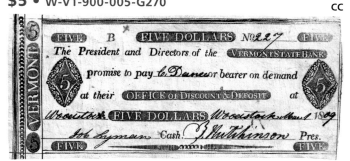

Engraver: PSSP. *Comments:* H-VT-4-G179, Coulter-28. 18__.
1807–1809.

Rarity: URS-8
F $125

$5 • W-VT-900-005-G280

Left: 5 / VERMONT / 5 vertically. *Engraver:* PSSP. *Comments:* H-VT-4-G180. 18__. 1808.

Rarity: *None known*

$10 • W-VT-900-010-G290

Left: 10 / VERMONT / 10 vertically. *Engraver:* PSSP. *Comments:* H-VT-4-G181. 18__. 1806–1808.

Rarity: URS-10
VF $100

$10 • W-VT-900-010-G300

Left: 10 / VERMONT / 10 vertically. *Engraver:* PSSP. *Comments:* H-VT-4-G183. 18__. 1808.

Rarity: *None known*

$20 • W-VT-900-020-G310

Left: 20 / VERMONT / 20 vertically. *Engraver:* PSSP. *Comments:* H-VT-4-G186. 18__. 1808.

Rarity: *None known*

Uncut Sheets

$1-$1-$2-$3 • W-VT-900-001.001.002.003-US010
Engraver: PSSP. *Comments:* H-Unlisted. No description available. 18__. 1806–1808.

Rarity: *None known*

$1.25-$1.25-$1.50-$1.75 •
W-VT-900-001.25.001.25.001.50.001.75-US020
Engraver: PSSP. *Comments:* H-Unlisted. No description available. 18__. 1806–1808.

Rarity: *None known*

Non-Valid Issues

50¢ • W-VT-900-00.50-C010
Comments: H-VT-4-C143. Counterfeit of W-VT-900-00.50-G010. 1808.

Rarity: URS-10
VF $75

How to Read the Whitman Numbering System
$1 • W-RI-010-001-G010a

Denomination: Value of the note shown.

W: Whitman number. This number is a sortable code unique to each bank and note.

RI: Abbreviation for the state under study.

010: Numerical designation specific to each bank.

001: The denomination in dollars.

G010a: G indicates a good or valid note. Other categories are indicated thus: C (counterfeit); R (raised); S (spurious); N (not-attributed); A (altered). Numbers are assigned starting with 010, 020, et seq. Terminal letters following the number indicate variations of a note: a series of different colored overprints, tints, payees, etc., all on the same design of note. For more information, see the "How to Use This Book" section at the front of the volume, page xiv.

50¢ • **W-VT-900-00.50-C020**
Comments: H-VT-4-C144. Counterfeit of W-VT-900-00.50-G020. 1808.
Rarity: URS-10
VF $75

50¢ • **W-VT-900-00.50-C030**

CJF

Comments: H-VT-4-C148. Counterfeit of W-VT-900-00.50-G030. 18__. 1808.
Rarity: URS-6
VG $100

75¢ • **W-VT-900-00.75-C080**
Comments: H-VT-4-C154. Counterfeit of W-VT-900-00.75-G080. 180_. 1808.
Rarity: URS-10
VF $75

75¢ • **W-VT-900-00.75-C090**

PEM

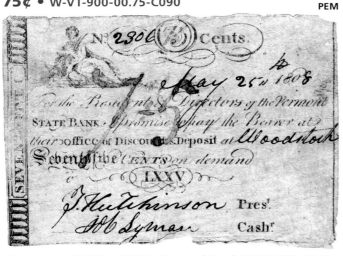

Comments: H-VT-4-C155. Counterfeit of W-VT-900-00.75-G090. 180_. 1808.
Rarity: URS-6
F $95

$1 • **W-VT-900-001-C120**
Comments: H-VT-4-C163. Counterfeit of W-VT-900-001-G120. 180_. 1808.
Rarity: URS-10
VF $100

$2 • **W-VT-900-002-C190**
Comments: H-VT-4-C171. Counterfeit of W-VT-900-002-G190. 180_. 1806–1808.
Rarity: URS-10
VF $100

$3 • **W-VT-900-003-C220**
Comments: H-VT-4-C174. Counterfeit of W-VT-900-003-G220. 18__. 1808.
Rarity: URS-10
VF $100

$3 • **W-VT-900-003-C230**

TD

Comments: H-VT-4-C175. Counterfeit of W-VT-900-003-G230. 18__. 1807 and 1808.
Rarity: URS-10
VF $100

$5 • **W-VT-900-005-C270**

CC

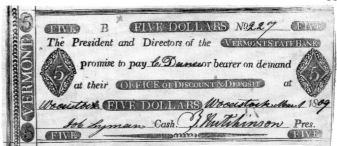

Comments: H-VT-4-C179. Counterfeit of W-VT-900-005-G270. 18__. 1807–1809.
Rarity: URS-8
F $150

$10 • **W-VT-900-010-C290**
Comments: H-VT-4-C181. Counterfeit of W-VT-900-010-G290. 1807.
Rarity: URS-10
VF $100

Windsor County Bank
1844
W-VT-905

History: The Windsor County Bank was chartered in 1844 with $60,000 in authorized capital. On October 22, 1845, the bank's name was changed to the Woodstock Bank, W-VT-910.

Woodstock Bank
1844–1865
W-VT-910

History: The Woodstock Bank was chartered in 1844 as the Windsor County Bank, W-VT-905, with $60,000 in authorized capital. On October 22, 1845, the bank's name was changed to the Woodstock Bank, and it went into operation in January 1847.

In 1854 these numbers were given: notes discounted $173,716; deposits in city banks $8,048; other resources $16,246; specie $6,289. Figures for 1857 included: capital $100,000; bills in circulation $139,089; specie $7,354; real estate $4,150. Circulation was $139,089 in July 1859 and $91,080 in 1862. That same year the capital reached $100,500.

On April 17, 1865, the Woodstock National Bank was chartered and succeeded the interests of the state bank. The outstanding circulation of the Woodstock Bank was $1,340 as of July 1, 1867, redemption of which was guaranteed by the national bank.

Numismatic Commentary: All issues are scarce. This is one of the scant few banks in New England that issued notes of a fraction of a dollar to give as change when specie was not available.

VALID ISSUES

5¢ • W-VT-910-00.05-G010

CJF

Overprint: Green 5. **Engraver:** American Bank Note Co. **Comments:** H-Unlisted, Coulter-32. January 1st, 1863.
Rarity: URS-8
F $35; **VF** $75

10¢ • W-VT-910-00.10-G020

CJF

Overprint: Green 10. **Engraver:** American Bank Note Co. **Comments:** H-Unlisted, Coulter-33. January 1st, 1863.
Rarity: URS-8
F $35; **VF** $75

25¢ • W-VT-910-00.25-G030
Left: 25. **Center:** State arms. **Right:** 25. **Overprint:** Green 25. **Engraver:** American Bank Note Co. **Comments:** H-Unlisted, Coulter-34. January 1st, 1863.
Rarity: URS-8
F $35; **VF** $75

50¢ • W-VT-910-00.50-G040

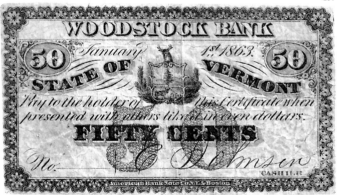

CJF

Overprint: Green 50. **Engraver:** American Bank Note Co. **Comments:** H-Unlisted, Coulter-35. January 1st, 1863.
Rarity: URS-8
F $35; **VF** $75

$1 • W-VT-910-001-G050   CJF

Engraver: Rawdon, Wright & Hatch. *Comments:* H-VT-286-G2, Coulter-36. 18__. 1844–1850s.

Rarity: URS-3

F $750

$1 • W-VT-910-001-G060

Left: ONE / Mechanic standing with hammer, Forge, Train. *Center:* ONE across 1 / Man on horse, Colt, cattle, sheep. *Right:* 1 / ONE. *Overprint:* Red ONE. *Engraver:* Rawdon, Wright, Hatch & Edson / New England Bank Note Co. *Comments:* H-VT-286-G4a. Jan.y 1st, 1857.

Rarity: *None known*

$1 • W-VT-910-001-G060a   CJF

Overprint: Red ONE. *Engraver:* Rawdon, Wright, Hatch & Edson / New England Bank Note Co. / ABNCo. monogram. *Comments:* H-VT-286-G4b, Coulter-37. Similar to W-VT-910-001-G060 but with additional engraver imprint. Jan.y 1st, 1857.

Rarity: URS-4

VF $500

$2 • W-VT-910-002-G070

Left: Farmer holding sheaf. *Center:* Ceres seated on plow / Train. *Bottom center:* Sheaf and plow. *Right:* Milkmaid standing. *Engraver:* Rawdon, Wright & Hatch. *Comments:* H-VT-286-G6, Coulter-39. 18__. 1844–1850s.

Rarity: *None known*

$2 • W-VT-910-002-G080   CC

Overprint: Red TWO. *Engraver:* Rawdon, Wright, Hatch & Edson / New England Bank Note Co. *Comments:* H-VT-286-G8a, Coulter-38. Jan.y 1st, 1857.

Rarity: URS-3

F $750

$2 • W-VT-910-002-G080a

Left: TWO / Two girls carrying grain. *Center:* Anvil, Woman holding cornucopia, Woman with hammer, Factory. *Right:* 2 / Female portrait. *Overprint:* Red TWO. *Engraver:* Rawdon, Wright, Hatch & Edson / New England Bank Note Co. / ABNCo. monogram. *Comments:* H-VT-286-G8b. Similar to W-VT-910-002-G080 but with additional engraver imprint. Jan.y 1st, 1857.

Rarity: *None known*

$3 • W-VT-910-003-G090

Left: Plenty / THREE. *Center:* Three deer in forest. *Bottom center:* Man plowing. *Right:* 3 / Indian maid. *Engraver:* Rawdon, Wright & Hatch. *Comments:* H-VT-286-G10, Coulter-41. 18__. 1844–1850s.

Rarity: *None known*

$3 • W-VT-910-003-G100   CJF

Overprint: Red THREE. *Engraver:* Rawdon, Wright, Hatch & Edson / New England Bank Note Co. *Comments:* H-VT-286-G12a, Coulter-40. Jan.y 1st, 1857.

Rarity: URS-3

F $750

$3 • W-VT-910-003-G100a

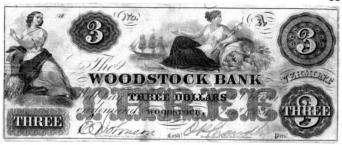

CC

Overprint: Red THREE. **Engraver:** Rawdon, Wright, Hatch & Edson / New England Bank Note Co. / ABNCo. monogram. **Comments:** H-VT-286-G12b. Similar to W-VT-910-003-G100 but with additional engraver imprint. Jan.y 1st, 1857.

Rarity: URS-3
VG $600; **VF** $750

$5 • W-VT-910-005-G110

Left: 5 / Portrait of George Washington. **Center:** Woman and cherub, State arms, Woman and cherub. **Right:** 5 / Portrait of Martha Washington. **Engraver:** Rawdon, Wright & Hatch. **Comments:** H-VT-286-G16, Coulter-43. 18__. 1844–1850s.

Rarity: URS-2
Proof $800

$5 • W-VT-910-005-G110a

CC

Engraver: Rawdon, Wright & Hatch. **Comments:** H-Unlisted, Coulter-Unlisted. Similar to W-VT-910-005-G110 but with different date. Jan.y __, 18__. 1840s–1850s.

Rarity: URS-3
VG $750

$5 • W-VT-910-005-G110b

CC

Overprint: Red FIVE. **Engraver:** Rawdon, Wright & Hatch. **Comments:** H-Unlisted, Coulter-Unlisted. Similar to W-VT-910-005-G110 but with different date. Jan.y 1st, 1849.

Rarity: URS-3
F $700; **VF** $750

$10 • W-VT-910-010-G120

Left: 10 / TEN on medallion head. **Center:** Allegorical figure, Shield, Eagle. **Bottom center:** Bull. **Right:** 10 / Man shearing sheep, Woman. **Engraver:** Rawdon, Wright & Hatch. **Comments:** H-VT-286-G18, Coulter-47. 18__. 1844–1850s.

Rarity: None known

$20 • W-VT-910-020-G130

Left: 20 / Portrait of girl / 20. **Center:** Cherub seated holding $20 gold coin / Barrel, cornucopia, box. **Bottom center:** Bull. **Right:** Two men carrying woman on shoulders / 20. **Engraver:** Rawdon, Wright & Hatch. **Comments:** H-VT-286-G20, Coulter-48. 18__. 1844–1850s.

Rarity: None known

$50 • W-VT-910-050-G140

Left: 50 / Minerva. **Center:** Liberty, shield, and eagle in clouds. **Bottom center:** Man plowing. **Right:** 50 / Woman with hand on capstan. **Engraver:** Rawdon, Wright & Hatch. **Comments:** H-VT-286-G22, Coulter-49. 18__. 1844–1850s.

Rarity: None known

$100 • W-VT-910-100-G150

Left: Woman with hand on capstan / 100. **Center:** Portrait of George Washington surrounded by flags and drums. **Right:** 100 / Cherub seated in sailboat / 100. **Engraver:** Rawdon, Wright & Hatch. **Comments:** H-VT-286-G24, Coulter-50. 18__. 1844–1850s.

Rarity: None known

NON-VALID ISSUES

$2 • W-VT-910-002-A010

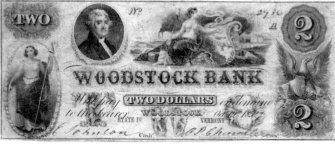

CC

Engraver: Rawdon, Wright, Hatch & Edson. **Comments:** H-VT-286-A5. Oct.r 19th, 1852.

Rarity: URS-3
F $125

$3 • W-VT-910-003-N010

Left: Female portrait. **Center:** Load of hay with man and woman, Children. **Comments:** H-VT-286-N5, Coulter-42. 1850s.

Rarity: None known

$5 • W-VT-910-005-R010

Comments: H-Unlisted, Coulter-44. Raised from W-VT-910-001-G050. 1850s.

Rarity: None known

$5 • W-VT-910-005-N020

Left: 5 / Portrait of George Washington / FIVE. **Center:** Atlas supporting world / 5. **Right:** FIVE DOLLARS vertically. **Engraver:** Rawdon, Clark & Co. **Comments:** H-Unlisted, Coulter-45. 1850s.

Rarity: None known

$5 • W-VT-910-005-N030

Center: Commerce. **Comments:** H-Unlisted, Coulter-46. 1850s.

Rarity: None known

ENDNOTES
Rhode Island

1. Roger H. Durand, *Obsolete Notes and Scrip of Rhode Island*, 1981.

2. Letter from the secretary of the Treasury relative to the condition of the banks in the United States, May 16, 1850, House of Representatives, Executive Document No. 68.

3. Letter from the secretary of the Treasury relative to the condition of the banks in the United States, May 16, 1850, House of Representatives, Executive Document No. 68; Roger H. Durand, *Obsolete Notes and Scrip of Rhode Island*.

4. *Banker's Magazine*, July 1853.

5. *Banker's Magazine,* December 1856 through May 1857.

6. *Congressional Serial Set*, Volume 509.

7. Roger H. Durand, *Obsolete Notes and Scrip of Rhode Island*, 1981.

8. *Banker's Magazine*, Volume 5, p. 341.

9. William M. Gouge, *The Curse of Paper-Money and Banking*, 1833, p. 116.

10. John Jay Knox, *The History of Banking*, New York, Bradford Rhodes & Company, 1900, p. 320.

11. *Annual Report, Secretary of the Treasury, Commencement of the Year 1863, State Auditor Statement.*

12. *At the General Assembly of the State of Rhode Island*, p. 166.

13. *A Brief History of the Town of Glocester, Rhode Island*, 1886, p. 51.

14. Roger H. Durand, *Obsolete Notes and Scrip of Rhode Island*, 1981.

15. Roger H. Durand, *Obsolete Notes and Scrip of Rhode Island*, 1981.

16. Roger H. Durand, *Obsolete Notes and Scrip of Rhode Island*, 1981.

17. *Rhode Island: Guide to the Smallest State.*

18. *Hunt's Merchants Magazine and Commercial Review*, Volume 22, p. 444.

19. Roger H. Durand, *Obsolete Notes and Scrip of Rhode Island*, 1981.

20. Roger H. Durand, *Obsolete Notes and Scrip of Rhode Island*, 1981.

21. Roger H. Durand, *Obsolete Notes and Scrip of Rhode Island*, 1981.

22. *Annual Report Showing the Condition of State Banks*, Volume 3, p. 262.

23. *House Documents, otherwise Published as Executive Documents: 13th…* p. 43.

24. *Banker's Magazine*, Volume 7, p. 333.

25. *A Brief History of the Town of Glocester, Rhode Island*, 1886, p. 51.

26. Roger H. Durand, *Obsolete Notes and Scrip of Rhode Island*, 1981.

27. *Congressional Serial Set*, Vol. 509.

28. *Hunt's Merchants Magazine and Commercial Review*, Volume 22, p. 444.

29. *Banker's Magazine.*

30. *New York Times*, February 12, 1914.

31. Davis R. Dewey, *State Banking Before the Civil War*, p. 203.

32. Roger H. Durand, *Obsolete Notes and Scrip of Rhode Island*, 1981.

33. *Annual Report.*

34. Roger H. Durand, *Obsolete Notes and Scrip of Rhode Island*, 1981.

35. Roger H. Durand, *Obsolete Notes and Scrip of Rhode Island*, 1981.

36. *Chartered Banking in Rhode Island, 1791–1900*, 1902, p. 3.

37. Roger H. Durand, *Obsolete Notes and Scrip of Rhode Island*, 1981.

38. John Jay Knox, *The History of Banking*, New York, Bradford Rhodes & Company, 1900, p. 320.

39. Roger H. Durand, *Obsolete Notes and Scrip of Rhode Island*, 1981.

40. *Annual Report, Secretary of the Treasury, Commencement of the Year 1863, State Auditor Statement.*

41. *At the General Assembly of the State of Rhode Island*, p. 166.

42. John J. Knox, *The History of Banking*, New York, Bradford Rhodes & Company, 1900, pp. 319, 320.

43. Roger H. Durand, *Obsolete Notes and Scrip of Rhode Island*, 1981.

44. Roger H. Durand, *Obsolete Notes and Scrip of Rhode Island*, 1981.

45. *Banker's Magazine and Statistical Register*, Volume 6, p. 769

46. Davis R. Dewey, *State Banking Before the Civil War*, p. 116.

47. *New England Families, Genealogical and Memorial*, 1915, Volume 4, p. 2146

48. Roger H. Durand, *Obsolete Notes and Scrip of Rhode Island*, 1981.

49. *New York Annual Register for the Year 1833, Fourth Year*, p. 400.

50. *American Annual Register*: Volume 1, p. 320.

51. *New York Annual Register for the Year 1833, Fourth Year*, p. 428.

52. Roger H. Durand, *Obsolete Notes and Scrip of Rhode Island*, 1981.

53. *Index to Printed Acts and Resolves*, 1856, p. 49.

54. *Banker's Magazine and Statistical Register*: Volume 6, p. 768.

55. Roger H. Durand, *Obsolete Notes and Scrip of Rhode Island*, 1981.

56. Roger H. Durand, *Obsolete Notes and Scrip of Rhode Island*, 1981.

57. *Banker's Magazine and Statistical Register*, Volume 6, p. 769.

58. *Congressional Edition.*

59. Roger H. Durand, *Obsolete Notes and Scrip of Rhode Island*, 1981.

60. Roger H. Durand, *Obsolete Notes and Scrip of Rhode Island*, 1981.

61. *Banker's Magazine and Statistical Register*, Volume 6, p. 768.

62. Roger H. Durand, *Obsolete Notes and Scrip of Rhode Island*, 1981.

63. *Banker's Magazine*, Volume 5, p. 429.

64. *Annual Report of the Secretary of the Treasury on the Condition of Banks*, 1850.

65. Roger H. Durand, *Obsolete Notes and Scrip of Rhode Island*, 1981.

66. *Banker's Magazine*, August 1856, p. 151.

67. *House Documents, otherwise Published as Executive Documents: 13th...* p. 43.

68. *Congressional Serial Set*, Volume 509.

69. Roger H. Durand, *Obsolete Notes and Scrip of Rhode Island*, 1981.

70. Roger H. Durand, *Obsolete Notes and Scrip of Rhode Island*, 1981.

71. Roger H. Durand, *Obsolete Notes and Scrip of Rhode Island*, 1981.

72. *Merchants' Magazine and Commercial Review*, Volume 22, p. 444.

73. Roger H. Durand, *Obsolete Notes and Scrip of Rhode Island*, 1981.

74. Roger H. Durand, *Obsolete Notes and Scrip of Rhode Island*, 1981.

75. *Congressional Serial Set*, Volume 509.

76. John Jay Knox, *The History of Banking*, New York, Bradford Rhodes & Company, 1900, p. 320.

77. Roger H. Durand, *Obsolete Notes and Scrip of Rhode Island*, 1981.

78. *Chartered Banking in Rhode Island, 1791–1900*, 1902, p. 44.

79. The *Financial Register*, Volume 1, p. 286.

80. James A. Haxby.

81. Roger H. Durand, *Obsolete Notes and Scrip of Rhode Island*, 1981.

82. *Plymouth Col. Laws*, p. 23.

83. *Fessenden's Hist.*, Warren, Rhode Island, p. 56.

84. Roger H. Durand, *Obsolete Notes and Scrip of Rhode Island*, 1981.

85. *At the General Assembly of the State of Rhode Island*, p. 152.

86. *New England Merchantile Union Business Directory for 1849*, p. 282.

87. Roger H. Durand, *Obsolete Notes and Scrip of Rhode Island*, 1981.

88. Roger H. Durand, *Obsolete Notes and Scrip of Rhode Island*, 1981.

89. *New England Merchantile Union Business Directory for 1849*, p. 282.

90. Roger H. Durand, *Obsolete Notes and Scrip of Rhode Island*, 1981.

91. Roger H. Durand, *Obsolete Notes and Scrip of Rhode Island*, 1981.

92. *Westerly (Rhode Island) and Its Successors*, p. 26.

93. Roger H. Durand, *Obsolete Notes and Scrip of Rhode Island*, 1981.

94. *Sound Currency*, Volumes 7–8, p. 227.

95. Roger H. Durand, *Obsolete Notes and Scrip of Rhode Island*, 1981.

96. *Annual Report Showing the Condition of State Banks*, Volume 3, p. 259.

97. Roger H. Durand, *Obsolete Notes and Scrip of Rhode Island*, 1981.

98. Roger H. Durand, *Obsolete Notes and Scrip of Rhode Island*, 1981.

Vermont

1. Terrence G. Hopper, "Vermont Paper Money," serially in the *Numismatic Scrapbook Magazine,* 1964.

2. Mayre Burns Coulter, *Vermont Obsolete Notes and Scrip*, 1972.

3. *Annual Report of the Secretary of the Treasury on the Condition of the Banks in the United States at the Commencement of the Year 1863*, p. 26.

4. Mayre Burns Coulter, *Vermont Obsolete Notes and Scrip*, 1972.

5. Mayre Burns Coulter, *Vermont Obsolete Notes and Scrip*, 1972.

6. Mayre Burns Coulter, *Vermont Obsolete Notes and Scrip*, 1972.

7. Mayre Burns Coulter, *Vermont Obsolete Notes and Scrip*, 1972.

8. John Jay Knox, *The History of Banking*, New York, Bradford Rhodes & Company, 1900.

9. Mayre Burns Coulter, *Vermont Obsolete Notes and Scrip*, 1972.

10. Mayre Burns Coulter, *Vermont Obsolete Notes and Scrip*, 1972.

11. *Springfield Republican*, Springfield, Massachusetts, November 6, 1860.

12. *Annual Report of the Bank Commissioner of Vermont.*

13. The *New Yorker*, 1838, Volume 5, p. 202.

GLOSSARY

back—the paper-money equivalent of "reverse" used for coins. The front side of a note is called the face.

bank—in the present context, a business set up under a state or federal (e.g. Bank of the United States) charter to engage in the business of receiving and disbursing funds, making loans, issuing paper money, and engaging in related activities.

bank note—a small, rectangular piece of paper money $1 face value or higher issued by a state-chartered bank. Imprinted with a denomination or value and the name/location of the issuing bank. Intended for use in commercial transactions. *Synonyms*: bill, note, bank bill.

bank-note reporter—commercial booklet or publication sold at a premium to bankers, merchants, etc., listing whether banks were solvent or not, descriptions of their notes, and the discounts at which their paper currency traded with exchange brokers and in commerce. *Synonym*: counterfeit detector.

bill—see *bank note*.

blue pup—nickname for a bank that later became insolvent or a circulating note issued by a bank that would not redeem their bills at par. *Synonyms*: owl, red dog.

burin—small, sharp, steel tool, often with a wooden handle, used to carefully engrave on a copper or steel plate.

Canada green—see *Patent green tint*.

capital of a bank—the amount of money authorized by a state charter to be paid in by shareholders and provide funds for a bank's operation.

cashier—in a small bank, the chief operating officer, sometimes the only employee, who opened and closed the bank, signed and supervised the issuance of currency, made loans (often subject to the approval of others), and conducted the business of the bank. The highest-salaried employee. In a large bank, the officer in charge of funds, receipts, and payments, the keeper of bank records.

certified note—a note graded and placed in a sealed holder by a commercial grading service.

charter—operating authorization given by a state legislature to permit a company to engage in banking.

charter expiration—charters were sometimes given to banks for a specific term, such as 20 years, after which a renewal could be applied for. In other instances, a corporation was dissolved and the same people obtained a new charter to continue in business.

circulation of a bank—the total face-value of a given bank's bills in commercial circulation (not including notes held in the bank's vault or not yet issued).

clearing house—a bank or organization that took in bills from various sources and sent them to member banks for exchange or redemption.

counter—technical name for the part of a note showing the denomination in a separate vignette, such as 5, 10, 20, etc., or as a Roman numeral, V, X, M, etc. Some counters are very ornate.

counterfeit—a bill in imitation of an original design but printed from false plates by someone not authorized to do so.

counterfeit detector—see *bank-note reporter*. Often spelled "detecter" in the mid-19th century.

country bank—a bank located in a town or village, not a city or metropolitan area. Sometimes bills of country banks traded at a discount in comparison to banks with large capital located in cities.

cycloidal configuration—latticework, usually printed in color, with arcs and inscriptions said to deter counterfeiting. Also referred to as the "cycloidal" or "kaleidograph counter." Term used by the National Bank Note Company, which utilized James McDonough's patent of March 23, 1860, in which an engraving combined the name of the issuer, the denomination, and geometric, cycloidal, rosette work into a product to prevent alteration or counterfeiting of bank notes.

cylinder die—see *transfer roll*.

date on a note—the time that a note or series of notes was issued. Sometimes a partial date such as 18__ was given, after which the year, month, and day would be added in ink. In other instances a full date was given, such as Jany. 1, 1853, representing the date of a certain series or design. Months were usually abbreviated. Notes with such a printed date could be used for a long time afterward.

denomination—the face or stated value printed on a bill, this being the amount for which the bill could be redeemed in specie or exchanged for other bills. Popular denominations of bills in use in commerce included $1, $2, $3, $5, $10, $20, $50, and $100. Other denominations were occasionally used.

deposit bank—a bank into which the Treasury Department placed federal funds. During the 1830s these were nicknamed "pet banks." Also spelled "deposite."

deuce—numismatic nickname for a $2 bill.

engraver—a skilled artist who, with a burin and other tools, hand-engraves lettering, motifs, and other elements into a printing plate or design element matrix. Various mechanical devices are sometimes used as well.

engraving—intaglio or recessed design elements and lettering engraved by hand or added by the siderographic process to a printing plate. A motif, print, or other reproduction on paper made from an engraved printing plate.

essay—an experimental impression of a partial or completed note printed to test the design or evaluate a concept. The paper-money equivalent of a pattern or trial-piece coin. French: *essai*.

exchange broker, broker—a person or business specializing in buying and selling current and obsolete paper money and gold and silver coins.

face—the paper-money equivalent of "obverse" used for coins. The reverse side of a note is called the back.

free bank—a bank set up under one or another of the state laws enacted from the late 1830s onward whereby any group of people could form a bank providing that assurances were made that sufficient capital would be raised.

geometric lathe—machine that uses gears and linkages to create rosettes, spirals, and other decorative elements on a soft metal plate, which is then hardened and reproduced through siderography for use in creating bank-note printing plates.

grade—designation assigned by numismatists to signify the amount of wear or circulation a note has experienced and its condition today (see chapter 1 for more information). Grading can be expressed by adjectives such as Good, Extremely Fine, and Uncirculated or by abbreviations in combination with numbers from 1 to 70, such as EF-40 or Unc-63 (adapted from the American Numismatic Association coin-grading system).

green tint—see *Patent green tint*.

imprint—printed information added to a bank note, especially the name of an engraver or printer.

ink ball—a porous ball of cloth or other absorbent substance that was charged with ink and then wiped across the face of a printing plate. Superseded by the ink roller.

ink roller—a rubber roller that is partly immersed in a pan or other supply of ink, then used to spread the ink across the face of a printing plate.

inked signature—the signature of a bank president or cashier on currency.

launder—often used in a derogatory sense, the cleaning of paper money to enhance its appearance. Careful cleaning, such as to remove grease or grime, can be beneficial but should be done only by experts. In the early 20th century the Treasury Department added several machines to launder soiled paper money, after which the reconditioned notes were again placed into circulation.

legal tender—a bank note that could be used to pay any and all debts except for custom duties. Most notes of state-chartered banks were accepted at par only within the region of issue.

margin—the blank area or white strip beyond the design or printed information at the border of a note. Wide margins are preferred to narrow ones. There are no general rules.

microprint, microprinting—nearly microscopic-size lettering added to a note, such as on Perkins Patent Stereotype Plate notes and related formats.

notaphily—originated by Kenneth R. Lake as a proposal to give a name to the study and appreciation of paper money. Originally found in Yasha Beresiner's "An Introduction to Paper Money," *The Numismatist*, March 1979.

note—see *bank note*.

obverse—see *face*.

overprint—color printing on a note; a design, grill, denomination, or other element intended to defer counterfeiting. Sometimes these were applied before the black section of the note was printed.

owl—nickname for a circulating note issued by a bank that would not redeem them at par or a bank that later became insolvent. Inspired by the worthless bills of the Owl Creek Bank of Mount Vernon, Ohio. *Synonyms*: blue pup, red dog.

panic—an excitement in financial circles caused by unfavorable economic or banking conditions in which holders of bank notes and securities became frightened and rushed to convert paper to gold and silver coins.

par—the value printed on a note.

Patent green tint, green tint, "Canada green"—green imprint, usually called "overprint," of lacy green said to be a deterrent against counterfeiting. Except for paper-money sheets that required bronzing, the adding of a green tint was the first printing operation on a blank sheet as reported by S.M. Clark, *Report to the Secretary of the Treasury*, November 26, 1864. As to whether this priority was always followed is not known. The patent was held by Rawdon, Wright, Hatch & Edson, later the American Bank Note Co., having been acquired from a Canadian inventor.

payee—the first person to receive the note when it was issued. This became a nuisance, and many cashiers simply added a short name and used it over and over again. In other instances a name such as Benjamin Franklin or Henry Clay was added to the printing plate.

pet bank—popular nickname for a bank into which the Treasury Department placed federal funds during the second Andrew Jackson administration.

pinhole—in the 19th century it was common practice to stitch several notes together for safekeeping, hiding within a coat's lining, or storing in a small pile. Today, when certain notes are held to the light, tiny holes can be seen.

plate—a rectangle of copper or hardened steel with engraved or otherwise recessed lettering, motifs, and other elements used to print bank notes. Currency of the period under study was often printed four notes to a plate or, if higher denominations, two notes to a plate.

plate letter—a printed letter, often from A to D, signifying the note's position on a four-subject printing plate. In other instances, single plates with various letters were locked into a frame and plate letters were not in any order. If a plate was slightly altered, the plate letter might be given another letter to accompany it, such as Aa, aA, Ab. If a sheet had more than one denomination, each would start anew with A. As examples, a $1-$1-$1-$2 sheet might use A, B, C, A. A four-subject sheet of $5 notes would use A, B, C, D.

plate position—the position of a note on a printing plate, sometimes determinable by the plate letter.

post note—a bill imprinted with a statement that it was redeemable at par only at a later specified date.

president—the chairman of the board of directors, presided over board meetings, signed currency. Often engaged in other activities, but visited a bank occasionally. Other times a local person who was on the premises often and made decisions beyond the duties of the cashier.

printer—an individual or firm that prints bank notes using a press, plates, paper, and ink. A printer may or may not have engraving skills. Most if not all printers of bank notes also produced other products such as book plates and decorative prints.

Progressive Proof note—a note printed from a plate which was not completely finished and was absent some lettering, ornaments, or other features. Used to inspect a design as it was being created.

Proof note—a Proof (capitalization optional) note is an impression from a complete or partially complete plate for testing or to illustrate its appearance such as showing to prospective bank clients. Proof notes are usually printed on only one side and show either the front or back. Such Proof notes are highly prized today. Specimen notes are related but were not issued for test purposes. Sometimes printed on ordinary bank-note paper, often on India paper, sometimes on light cardboard or mounted on a thin card. *Synonym*: Proof.

protector—a color overprint or underprint on a note; a design, grill, denomination, or other element intended to defer counterfeiting. *Synonym*: overprint.

rag—nickname for a circulating note that either had no value or was worn to the point of tattering.

ragpicker—nickname in the past for a collector of paper money.

red dog—nickname for a circulating note issued by a bank that would not redeem them at par or a bank that later became insolvent. *Synonyms*: blue pup, owl.

reenter, re-enter—engraving or transfer process whereby original information on a bank-note printing plate is removed and new information is entered in its place. This could permit an old plate to be used for a different bank.

reverse—see *back*.

roll, roller die—see *transfer roll*.

rose machine—a geometric lathe.

run on a bank—see *panic*. Sometimes engineered by profiteers who would encourage a run through rumors of insolvency (which would depreciate the value of a bank's bills), buy up discounted notes, and later redeem them at par as a form of speculation.

safety fund, safety fund bank—a bank chartered with the requirement that it deposit certain of its capital into approved bonds and other securities.

scrip, scrip note—a bill issued by an entity other than a chartered bank, such as a canal, railroad, factory, etc. A bill issued by a bank or other entity with a face value below $1.

security features—aspects of the design or printing of a note intended to deter copying and counterfeiting. In early times, this consisted of minute design elements expertly engraved, as well as printing on special paper. Chapter 7 of volume 1 in this series discusses various methods.

selvage—unused space on a sheet of paper money beyond the normal trim borders of the individual notes.

serial number—a number inked or printed by a numbering machine on a note prior to issuing it. Banks sometimes started serial numbers anew with each day or each month. Serial numbers were kept low by keying them to dates, making them faster to write. For this reason most serial numbers are in the hundreds or low thousands.

sheet of notes, uncut sheet—an uncut group of notes, as printed, usually four subjects with denominations from $1 to $20, usually with more than one denomination per sheet. $50, $100, and higher denominations were printed two to a sheet. Many notes were printed singly in earlier times.

shinplaster—derogatory nickname popular in the early 19th century to denote a scrip note or bank note that had no monetary value, such as an issue of the Hard Times era. Derived from the popular practice of mixing paper sheets and hardener to affix to a person's shins to relieve pain.

siderography, siderographic—the process of engraving a motif, lettering, or other elements on a soft steel plate, then hardening it, after which a cylinder die or transfer roll of soft steel is forcibly rolled into its surface under high pressure in a transfer press, picking up a relief image. The cylinder die is then hardened, placed into a transfer press, and rolled with pressure into a soft steel or copper plate. This transfers the design in recessed form. The plate is then hardened and used to print notes. Lettering, emblems, and other design elements can be added to plates in this manner.

signatures on notes—usually with the cashier's signature in ink at the lower left and the president's at the lower right. Legally a note had no value until signed by both officers.

specie—gold or silver coins.

specie payment—the payment of a gold or silver coin by a bank in exchange for a bank note presented for redemption.

specimen note—a Proof note for examination or display, a plate impression not intended for circulation.

spider press—a rectangular printing press used to make bank notes. The name derives from multiple thin arms extending from the press that are slowly turned by hand to press a sheet of dampened paper into the ink-filled recesses of a printing plate.

surcharge—extra printing or information added to a note after the main printing was finished. *Synonym*: overprint.

suspension, suspension of specie payments—when a bank refused to redeem its notes in silver or gold coins. This usually happened when a bank had problems or in times of general financial distress. See *run on a bank*.

transfer roll—a hard steel cylinder with a hole at the center for a shaft, on the outside face of which is a raised design, vignette, counter, or other element used in bank-note printing. Transfer rolls are used to imprint a design into a printing plate by the siderographic process. *Synonyms*: cylinder die, roll, roller die.

Unc-Rem—grade designator signifying that an Uncirculated note is an unsigned, undated remainder.

Unc-S&D—grade designator signifying that an Uncirculated note was signed and dated, but never issued.

vignette—an ornamental or illustrative element of a bank note, such as a portrait, allegorical scene, or motif from history. Pronounced "vinn-yet."

wildcat bank—a bank with or without charter that issued paper money with little or no backing. Such banks were often set up in remote locations.

BIBLIOGRAPHY

Baker, W.S. *American Engravers and Their Works*. Philadelphia: Gebbie & Barrie, 1875.

Ball, Douglas B. Historical information written for and included in the catalog of the *Abner Reed Sale of United States Paper Money*, NASCA, October 31 to November 2, 1983.

Bank Note Reporter. Iola, Wisconsin: 1990s to date.

Bathe, Greville and Dorothy. *Jacob Perkins: His Inventions, His Times & His Contemporaries*. The Historical Society of Philadelphia, Pennsylvania, 1943.

Berkey, William A. *The Money Question*. The Legal Tender Paper Monetary System of the United States. Grand Rapids, Michigan: Published by the author, 1876.

Blanchard, Julian. "Waterman Lily Ormsby, 1809–1883, Bank Note Engraver," commencing in the *Essay-Proof Journal*, January 1957.

Blanchard, Julian. "Cycloidal Configurations," *Essay-Proof Journal*, Vol. 20, No. 2 (1963) through Vol. 21, No. 2 (1964). Reprint of Ormsby's circa 1862 pamphlet, with new introductory remarks.

Bodenhorn, Howard. *State Banking in Early America: A New Economic History*. Oxford and New York: Oxford University Press, 2003.

Boggs, Winthrop S. *Ten Decades Ago 1840–1850: A Study of the Work of Rawdon, Wright, Hatch & Edson of New York City*. American Philatelic Society, 1949.

Bowers, Q. David. *Obsolete Paper Money Issued by Banks in the United States, 1782–1866*. Atlanta, Georgia: Whitman Publishing, LLC, 2006.

Bowers, Q. David and David M. Sundman. *100 Greatest American Currency Notes*. Atlanta, Georgia: Whitman Publishing, LLC, 2005.

Chaddock, Robert E. *The Safety Fund Banking System in New York 1829–1866*. Washington, D.C.: Government Printing Office, 1910, for the National Monetary Commission. 61st Congress, 2d Session, Senate, Document No. 581.

Cheap Money. New York City, New York: The Century Co., 1892.

Christie's. "Important Early American Bank Notes, 1810–1874" from the Archives of the American Bank Note Company, catalog of the auction sale held September 14 and 15, 1990.

Coulter, Mayre Burns. *Vermont Obsolete Notes and Scrip*. Published for the Society of Paper Money Collectors. Iola, Wisconsin: Krauss Publications, 1972.

Davis, Andrew McFarland (introduction by). *Colonial Currency Reprints*. 4 volumes. Boston, Massachusetts: The Prince Society, 1910 and 1911.

Dewey, Davis R. *State Banking Before the Civil War*. Washington, D.C.: Government Printing Office, 1910, for the National Monetary Commission. 61st Congress, 2d Session, Senate, Document No. 581.

Dewey, Davis R. *State Banking before the Civil War; and the Safety Fund Banking System in New York*. Published by the American Economic Association.

Dillistin, William H. *Bank Note Reporters and Counterfeit Detectors, 1826–1866*. Numismatic Notes and Monographs No. 114. New York City, New York: American Numismatic Society, 1949.

Doty, Richard. *Pictures from a Distant Country: Seeing America Through Old Paper Money*. Atlanta, Georgia: Whitman Publishing, LLC, 2013.

Dunbar, Charles F. *Chapters on the Theory and History of Banking*. New York and London: G.P. Putnam's Sons, 1892.

Dunbar, Seymour. *A History of Transportation in America*. 4 volumes. Indianapolis, Indiana: The Bobbs-Merrill Company, 1915.

Duncombe, Charles. *Duncombe's Free Banking: An Essay on Banking, Currency, Finance, Exchanges, and Political Economy*. Cleveland, Ohio: Sanford & Co., 1841.

Durand, Roger H. *Interesting Notes* series: *About Denominations* (1988), *About History* (1990), *About Indians* (1991), *About Territories* (1992), *About Christmas* (1993), *About Allegorical Representations* (1994), *About Vignettes* (1995), *About Portraits* (1996), *About Vignettes II* (1996), *About Portraits II* (1997), *About Vignettes III* (2001), *About Portraits III* (2004).

Durand, Roger H. *Obsolete Notes and Scrip of Rhode Island and the Providence Plantations*, 1981.

Essay-Proof Journal. New York, New York: The Essay-Proof Society, 1944.

Federal Writer's Project. *Rhode Island: A Guide to the Smallest State*. American guide series. Rhode Island: North American Book Dist LLC, 1937.

Financial Register of the United States, The. Vol. 1, July 1837 to July 1838. Philadelphia, Pennsylvania: Wirtz & Tatem, 1838.

Glaser, Lynn. *Counterfeiting in America*. New York City, New York: Clarkson N. Potter, Inc., 1968.

Golembe, Carter H. *State Banks and the Development of the West, 1830–1844*. New York City, New York: Arno Press, 1978. Originally presented as the author's thesis, Columbus University, 1952.

Gouge, William M. *The Curse of Paper-Money and Banking; or a Short History of Banking in the United States of America, with an Account of its Ruinous Effects on Landowners, Farmers, Trades, and on All the Illustrious Classes of the Community*. Philadelphia, Pennsylvania, 1833.

Griffiths, William H. *The Story of the American Bank Note Company*. New York City, New York: American Bank Note Company, 1959.

Harris, Elizabeth M. "Sir William Congreve and His Compound-Plate Printing," *United States National Museum Bulletin 252*, Paper 71 in *Contributions from The Museum of History and Technology*, Washington, D.C., Smithsonian Institution Press, 1967.

Haxby, James A. *Standard Catalog of United States Obsolete Bank Notes 1782–1866*. Krause Publications Inc., 1988.

Hessler, Gene. *The Engraver's Line*. Port Clinton, Ohio: BNR Press, 1993.

Hildreth, Richard. *The History of Banks, to Which is Added a Demonstration of the Advantages and Necessity of Free Competition in the World of Banking*. Boston, Massachusetts: Hilliard, Gray & Company, 1837.

Homans, Isaac Smith. *Hunt's Merchants' Magazine and Commercial Review*. Volume 22. Harvard University: Freeman Hunt, 1850.

Hunter, Dard. *Papermaking: The History and Technique of an Ancient Craft*. New York City, New York: Dover Publications, Inc., 1978. Reprint of 1943 edition by Alfred A. Knopf, Inc.

Kleeberg, John M. (editor). *Money of Pre-Federal America*. New York City, New York: American Numismatic Society, 1992 (programs presented at the Coinage of the Americas Conference, 1991).

Knapp, Samuel L. "Memoir of Jacob Perkins." Published in 1835 and 1836 in *Family Magazine*, New York. Reprinted with extensive added numismatic commentary in *The Colonial Newsletter*, Volume 27, No. 3, November 1987, Serial No. 77.

Knox, John Jay Knox. *History of Banking*. New York City, New York: Bradford Rhodes & Company, 1900. Anthology of Knox's articles and speeches published posthumously.

Lewis, Lawrence Jr. *A History of the Bank of North America, the First Bank Chartered in the United States*. Philadelphia, Pennsylvania: J.B. Lippincott & Co., 1882.

McCabe, Robert. "Waterman Lilly Ormsby and the Continental Bank Note Co.," *Paper Money*, March–April 2001. Includes much information found in the National Archives by Wayne DeCesar, fully credited by McCabe.

McCulloch, Hugh. *Men and Measures of Half a Century*. New York City, New York: Charles Scribner's Sons, 1889:

McKay, George L. *Early American Currency*. New York City, New York: The Typophiles, 1944.

Mossman, Philip L. *Money of the American Colonies and Confederation: A Numismatic, Economic & Historical Correlation*. New York City, New York: American Numismatic Society, 1993. Magisterial study of early money in America, emphasizing coins, but with a chapter on paper money.

Newman, Eric P. *Early Paper Money of America*. 4th edition. Iola, Wisconsin: Krause Publications, 1997.

Niles' Register. Various issues of *Niles' Weekly Register* 1811 to 1837, title change to *Niles' National Register*, September 2, 1837, continuing to 1849. Baltimore, Maryland, briefly Washington, D.C.

Numismatic Scrapbook Magazine. Hewitt Brothers and Sidney Printing and Publishing Co., 1935–1966.

Numismatist, The. Journal of the American Numismatic Association; established by Dr. George F. Heath in 1888.

O'Brien, Donald C. "Abner Reed: A Connecticut Engraver." *The Connecticut Historical Society Bulletin*, Volume 44, No. 1. Hartford, Connecticut, January 1979.

Ormsby, W.L. *Bank Note Engraving*. New York City, New York: Published by the author, 1852.

Ormsby, W.L. *Cycloidal Configurations, or the Harvest of Counterfeiters, Containing Matter of the Highest Importance concerning Paper Money, also Explaining the Unit System of Bank Note Engraving*. New York City, New York: Published by the author, 1862.

Paper Money. Journal of the Society of Paper Money Collectors: 1960s to date.

Peyton, George, *How to Detect Counterfeit Bank Notes; or, an Illustrated Treatise on the Detection of Counterfeit, Altered, and Spurious Bank Notes, with Original Bank Note Plates and designs, by Rawdon, Wright, Hatch & Edson, Bank Note Engravers, of New-York, the Whole Forming an Unerring Guide, by which Every Person Can, on Examination, Detect Spurious Bank Notes of Every Description, No Matter How Well Executed They May Appear*. New York City, New York: Published for the author, 1856.

Perry, Elizabeth A. *A Brief History of the Town of Glocester, Rhode Island: Preceded by a Sketch of the Territory While a Part of Providence*. Harvard University: Providence Press Company, 1886.

Raguet, Condy. *A Treatise on Currency & Banking*. 2nd edition. Philadelphia, Pennsylvania: Grigg & Elliot, 1840.

Reed, George B. *Sketch of the History of Early Banking in Vermont*. Boston, Massachusetts: Published by the author, 1879.

Remarks on the Manufacture of Bank Notes and Other Promises to Pay, Addressed to the Bankers of the Southern Confederacy. Columbia, South Carolina: Keatinge & Ball, 1864. Copy digitized by the UNC-CH digitization project, "Documenting the American South," from call number 2919 Conf. (Rare Book Collection, University of North Carolina at Chapel Hill) 31 p., [1] leaf of plates: ill. Columbia, S. C. Steam Power-press of F. G. DeFontaine & Co. 1864.

Rice, Foster Wild. "Antecedents of the American Bank Note Company of 1858," *The Essay-Proof Journal*, Fall 1961.

Scott, Kenneth. *Counterfeiting in Colonial America*. New York City, New York: Oxford University Press, 1957.

Sears, Louis Martin. *Jefferson and the Embargo*. Durham, North Carolina: Duke University Press, 1927.

Stauffer, David McNelly. *American Engravers Upon Copper and Steel*. New York, New York: The Grolier Club of the City of New York, 1907.

Stokes, Howard Kemble. *Chartered banking in Rhode Island, 1791–1900*. Providence, Rhode Island: Preston & Rounds Company, 1902.

Tomasko, Mark D. *The Feel of Steel: The Art and History of Bank-Note Engraving in the United States*. 2nd edition. New York, New York: American Numismatic Society, 2012.

White, Horace. *Money and Banking*. Boston and London: Ginn & Company, 1896.

ABOUT THE AUTHOR

Q. David Bowers became a professional numismatist as a teenager in 1953, later (1960) earning a B.A. in Finance from Pennsylvania State University, which in 1976 bestowed its Distinguished Alumnus Award on him. He served as president of the Professional Numismatists Guild from 1977 to 1979 and president of the American Numismatic Association from 1983 to 1985. He is a recipient of the Founders Award and Farran Zerbe Award, the highest honors of the PNG and the ANA. He is the author of more than 50 books, including many on paper money, and has received more honors from the Numismatic Literary Guild than has any other person. His column, "The Joys of Collecting," has been a feature of *Coin World* since 1961 and is the longest-running column by any author in the history of numismatics. He may be contacted at P.O. Box 539, Wolfeboro Falls, NH 03896 or by email at qdbarchive@metrocast.net.

ABOUT THE FOREWORD WRITER

One of the senior editors for *Coin World*, Michele Orzano is responsible for the vast majority of *Coin World*'s paper-money coverage and edits the periodical's section *Paper Money*. She joined the *Coin World* staff in 1985. In addition to paper money, she has written extensively on legislative and legal topics, as well as *Coin World*'s ambitious coverage of the 50 State quarters circulating commemorative coin program. Michele served as editor of *Coin World*'s *Paper Money Values* magazine from 2005 to 2010. She has won major state and national awards in graphic design, as well as feature and news writing.

ABOUT THE STATE EDITOR

C. John Ferreri is one of America's most accomplished collectors and researchers in the field of obsolete paper money, having specialized in the series for more than 40 years. In addition he has presented many programs on currency, especially for New England clubs and other organizations. His research has been important in the creation of several specialized texts on the subject.

GENERAL INDEX

INDEX TO BANKS, BY STATE
Rhode Island

Vermont

Lamoille County Bank (1854–
    1865; W-VT-360), 379–383

Merchants Bank (1848–1865;
    W-VT-200), 354–358

Middlebury Bank (1840s;
    W-VT-445), 400

Missisquoi Bank (1849–1866;
    W-VT-700), 446–449

Mutual Bank of Castleton
    (1859–1865; W-VT-250),
    365–366

Northern Bank of Vermont
    (1854; W-VT-660), 439

Northfield Bank (1853–1865;
    W-VT-510), 412–414

Orange County Bank (1842–
    1855; W-VT-280), 370–371

Passumpsic Bank (1849–1864;
    W-VT-690), 443–446

Peoples Bank (1821–1850s;
    W-VT-120), 334

Peoples Bank (1851–1865;
    W-VT-310), 375–377

Phenix Bank (Circa 1840;
    W-VT-540), 418–419

Pittsfield Bank (1850s;
    W-VT-550), 419

Rutland County Bank (1862–
    1865; W-VT-630), 434–435

South Royalton Bank (1851–
    1857; W-VT-720), 450–451

St. Albans Bank (1854–1866;
    W-VT-670), 439–441

Stark Bank (1847–1868;
    W-VT-060), 323–326

State Bank of Montpelier (1858–
    1860; W-VT-470), 407–409

Union Bank (1850–1865;
    W-VT-740), 454–457

Vermont Bank (Circa 1849–
    1865; W-VT-480), 409–411

Vermont State Bank (branch)
    (1807–1812; W-VT-210),
    358–363

Vermont State Bank (branch)
    (1807–1812; W-VT-450),
    400–403

Vermont State Bank (branch)
    (1807–1812; W-VT-830),
    466–470

Vermont State Bank (branch)
    (1807–1812; W-VT-900),
    476–480

Walloomsac Bank (1854–1858;
    W-VT-070), 326

Wells River Bank (1830s;
    W-VT-800), 465

West Randolph Bank (1854;
    W-VT-820), 466

West River Bank (1853–1865;
    W-VT-390), 387–389

Western Vermont Bank (1854;
    W-VT-320), 377

White River Bank (1851–1865;
    W-VT-080), 326–329

Windham County Bank (1857–
    1864; W-VT-150), 337–341

Windsor Bank (Circa 1837;
    W-VT-870), 474

Windsor County Bank (1844;
    W-VT-905), 480

Winooski Bank (1854; W-VT-
    880), 474

Woodstock Bank (1844–1865;
    W-VT-910), 481–483

HAXBY-TO-WHITMAN NUMBERS
CROSS-REFERENCE AND INDEX
Rhode Island

Haxby No.	Whitman No.	Pg.
H-RI-425-G2	W-RI-010-001-G010	3
H-RI-425-G2a	W-RI-010-001-G010a	3
H-RI-425-G4	W-RI-010-002-G020	4
H-RI-425-G4a	W-RI-010-002-G020a	4
H-RI-425-G6	W-RI-010-003-G030	4
H-RI-425-G6a	W-RI-010-003-G030a	4
H-RI-425-G8	W-RI-010-005-G040	4
H-RI-425-G8a	W-RI-010-005-G040a	4
H-RI-425-G10	W-RI-010-010-G050	4
H-RI-425-G10a	W-RI-010-010-G050a	4
H-RI-425-G2, G2, G4, G8	W-RI-010-001.001.002.005-US010	4
H-RI-425-G2a, G2a, G4a, G8a	W-RI-010-001.001.002.005-US010a	4
H-RI-425-G6a, G10a	W-RI-010-003.010-US020	5
H-RI-425-A5	W-RI-010-001-A010	5
H-RI-425-A10	W-RI-010-001-A020	5
H-RI-425-A15	W-RI-010-001-A030	5
	W-RI-010-001-A040	5
H-RI-425-N5	W-RI-010-002-N010	5
H-RI-425-A25	W-RI-010-002-A050	5
H-RI-425-A30	W-RI-010-002-A060	5
H-RI-425-A35	W-RI-010-002-A070	5
H-RI-425-A40	W-RI-010-003-A080	5
H-RI-425-A45	W-RI-010-005-A090	5
H-RI-10-G2	W-RI-020-001-G010	6
H-RI-10-G2b	W-RI-020-001-G010a	6
H-RI-10-G4	W-RI-020-002-G020	6
H-RI-10-G4b	W-RI-020-002-G020a	6
H-RI-10-G6	W-RI-020-005-G030	6
H-RI-10-G8	W-RI-020-005-G040	6
H-RI-10-G8a	W-RI-020-005-G040a	6
H-RI-10-G10	W-RI-020-010-G050	6
H-RI-10-G12	W-RI-020-020-G060	6
H-RI-10-G14	W-RI-020-050-G070	6
H-RI-10-G16	W-RI-020-100-G080	6
H-RI-10-R3	W-RI-020-003-R010	6
	W-RI-020-003-R020	6
H-RI-10-C6	W-RI-020-005-C030	6
	W-RI-020-005-R030	6
H-RI-10-R6	W-RI-020-005-R040	6
H-RI-10-R10	W-RI-020-010-R050	6
H-RI-10-R11	W-RI-020-010-R060	7
	W-RI-030-002-G010	7
H-RI-20-G4	W-RI-045-001-G010	7
H-RI-20-G8	W-RI-045-001-G020	7
H-RI-20-G8a	W-RI-045-001-G020a	7
H-RI-20-G12	W-RI-045-002-G030	8
H-RI-20-G16	W-RI-045-002-G040	8
H-RI-20-G16a	W-RI-045-002-G040a	8
H-RI-20-G20	W-RI-045-003-G050	8
H-RI-20-G24	W-RI-045-003-G060	8
H-RI-20-G24a	W-RI-045-003-G060a	8
H-RI-20-G28	W-RI-045-005-G070	8
H-RI-20-G32	W-RI-045-005-G080	8
H-RI-20-G32a	W-RI-045-005-G080a	8
H-RI-20-G36	W-RI-045-010-G090	8
H-RI-20-G40	W-RI-045-020-G100	8
H-RI-20-G44	W-RI-045-030-G110	9
H-RI-20-G48	W-RI-045-050-G120	9
H-RI-20-G4, G16, G24, G32	W-RI-045-001.002.003.005-US010	9
H-RI-20-C24a	W-RI-045-003-C060a	9
H-RI-20-C28	W-RI-045-005-C070	9
H-RI-20-R2	W-RI-045-005-R010	9
H-RI-20-R4	W-RI-045-010-R020	9
H-RI-20-N5	W-RI-045-010-N010	9
H-RI-20-R6	W-RI-045-020-R030	9
H-RI-20-R8	W-RI-045-050-R040	9
H-RI-25-G4	W-RI-060-001-G010	9
H-RI-25-G8	W-RI-060-002-G020	9
H-RI-25-G12	W-RI-060-003-G030	10
H-RI-25-G16	W-RI-060-005-G040	10
H-RI-25-R5	W-RI-060-010-R010	10
H-RI-30-G2	W-RI-070-001-G010	10
H-RI-30-G2a	W-RI-070-001-G010a	10
H-RI-30-G6	W-RI-070-001-G020	10
H-RI-30-G7	W-RI-070-001-G030	10
H-RI-30-G9a	W-RI-070-001-G040	10
H-RI-30-G13	W-RI-070-001.25-G050	10
H-RI-30-G14	W-RI-070-001.50-G060	10
H-RI-30-G15	W-RI-070-001.75-G070	10
H-RI-30-G18	W-RI-070-002-G080	10
H-RI-30-G18a	W-RI-070-002-G080a	11
H-RI-30-G21	W-RI-070-002-G090	11
H-RI-30-G22	W-RI-070-002-G100	11
H-RI-30-G26	W-RI-070-002-G110	11

Haxby No.	Whitman No.	Page
H-RI-150-G64	W-RI-530-020.050.100-US010	81
H-RI-150-A5	W-RI-530-001-A010	81
H-RI-150-A10	W-RI-530-001-A020	81
H-RI-150-C10	W-RI-530-001.50-C050	81
H-RI-150-C14	W-RI-530-002-C060	82
	W-RI-530-002-S010	82
H-RI-150-A15	W-RI-530-002-A030	82
H-RI-150-A20	W-RI-530-002-A040	82
H-RI-150-N15	W-RI-530-003-N010	82
H-RI-150-N20	W-RI-530-003-N020	82
H-RI-150-N25	W-RI-530-003-N030	82
H-RI-150-S5	W-RI-530-003-N040	82
H-RI-150-A25	W-RI-530-003-A050	82
	W-RI-530-003-A060	82
H-RI-150-R5	W-RI-530-005-R010	82
H-RI-150-S10	W-RI-530-005-S020	82
H-RI-150-S15	W-RI-530-005-N050	82
H-RI-150-N30	W-RI-530-005-N060	82
	W-RI-530-005-N070	82
H-RI-150-A30	W-RI-530-005-A070	82
H-RI-150-R10	W-RI-530-010-R020	82
H-RI-150-A35	W-RI-530-010-A080	82
	W-RI-530-020-R030	83
H-RI-150-S20	W-RI-530-020-N080	83
H-RI-150-R15	W-RI-530-050-R040	83
H-RI-150-S40	W-RI-530-050-N090	83
H-RI-155-G2	W-RI-540-001-G010	83
H-RI-155-G6	W-RI-540-001-G020	83
H-RI-155-G10	W-RI-540-001-G030	83
H-RI-155-G12	W-RI-540-001-G040	83
H-RI-155-G14	W-RI-540-001-G050	83
H-RI-155-G16a	W-RI-540-001-G060	83
H-RI-155-G18	W-RI-540-001.25-G070	84
H-RI-155-G20	W-RI-540-001.50-G080	84
H-RI-155-G22	W-RI-540-001.75-G090	84
H-RI-155-G26	W-RI-540-002-G100	84
H-RI-155-G32	W-RI-540-002-G110	84
H-RI-155-G36	W-RI-540-002-G120	84
H-RI-155-G38	W-RI-540-002-G130	84
H-RI-155-G40	W-RI-540-002-G140	84
H-RI-155-G44a	W-RI-540-002-G150	84
H-RI-155-G50	W-RI-540-003-G160	84
H-RI-155-G56	W-RI-540-003-G170	84
H-RI-155-G58	W-RI-540-003-G180	84
H-RI-155-G60a	W-RI-540-003-G190	85
H-RI-155-G64	W-RI-540-005-G200	85
H-RI-155-G66	W-RI-540-005-G210	85
H-RI-155-G70	W-RI-540-005-G220	85
H-RI-155-G76	W-RI-540-005-G230	85
H-RI-155-G76b	W-RI-540-005-G230a	85
H-RI-155-G80	W-RI-540-010-G240	85
H-RI-155-G82	W-RI-540-010-G250	85
H-RI-155-G86	W-RI-540-010-G260	86
H-RI-155-G86b	W-RI-540-010-G260a	86
H-RI-155-G92	W-RI-540-050-G270	86
H-RI-155-G94	W-RI-540-050-G280	86
H-RI-155-G96	W-RI-540-050-G290	86
H-RI-155-G98a	W-RI-540-050-G300	86
H-RI-155-G104	W-RI-540-100-G310	86
H-RI-155-G106	W-RI-540-100-G320	87
H-RI-155-G108	W-RI-540-100-G330	87
H-RI-155-G110a	W-RI-540-100-G340	87
	W-RI-540-001.001.002.003-US005	87
H-RI-155-G50, G32, G6, G6	W-RI-540-003.002.001.001-US010	87
H-RI-155-G70, G82	W-RI-540-005.010-US020	87
H-RI-155-G86b, G76b, G76b, G76b	W-RI-540-010.005.005.005-US030	87
H-RI-155-G92, G104	W-RI-540-050.100-US040	87
H-RI-155-G98a, G110a	W-RI-540-050.100-US050	87
H-RI-155-G106, G94	W-RI-540-100.050-US060	87
H-RI-155-C2	W-RI-540-001-C010	88
H-RI-160-G10	W-RI-550-001-G010	88
	W-RI-550-001-G020	88
H-RI-160-G14	W-RI-550-001-G030	88
H-RI-160-G14a	W-RI-550-001-G030a	88
	W-RI-550-002-G040	88

Haxby No.	Whitman No.	Page
H-RI-160-G20	W-RI-550-002-G050	88
H-RI-160-G24	W-RI-550-002-G060	89
H-RI-160-G24a	W-RI-550-002-G060a	89
	W-RI-550-005-G070	89
	W-RI-550-005-G080	89
H-RI-160-G30	W-RI-550-005-G090	89
H-RI-160-G30a	W-RI-550-005-G090a	89
	W-RI-550-010-G100	89
	W-RI-550-010-G110	89
H-RI-160-G36	W-RI-550-010-G120	89
H-RI-160-G36a	W-RI-550-010-G120a	89
H-RI-160-G40	W-RI-550-020-G130	89
H-RI-160-G44	W-RI-550-030-G140	89
	W-RI-550-050-G150	89
H-RI-160-G50	W-RI-550-050-G160	89
H-RI-160-G50a	W-RI-550-050-G160a	90
	W-RI-550-100-G170	90
H-RI-160-G56	W-RI-550-100-G180	90
H-RI-160-G56a	W-RI-550-100-G180a	90
H-RI-160-G10, G10, G20	W-RI-550-001.001.002.010-US010	90
	W-RI-550-050.005.005.005-US020	90
H-RI-160-C10	W-RI-550-001-C010	90
H-RI-160-S5	W-RI-550-001-S010	90
H-RI-160-S10	W-RI-550-002-S020	90
H-RI-160-S10a	W-RI-550-002-S020a	90
H-RI-160-R5	W-RI-550-005-R010	90
H-RI-160-A5	W-RI-550-005-A010	90
H-RI-160-R10	W-RI-550-010-R020	90
H-RI-160-S15	W-RI-550-010-S030	90
H-RI-160-S15a	W-RI-550-010-S030a	90
H-RI-160-A10	W-RI-550-010-A020	90
H-RI-165-G3	W-RI-560-001-G010	91
H-RI-165-G8	W-RI-560-002-G020	91
H-RI-165-G12	W-RI-560-003-G030	91
H-RI-165-G14	W-RI-560-005-G040	91
H-RI-165-G16	W-RI-560-010-G050	91
H-RI-165-G18	W-RI-560-020-G060	91
H-RI-165-G20	W-RI-560-050-G070	91
H-RI-165-G3, G3, G8, G12	W-RI-560-001.001.002.003-US010	91
H-RI-165-G14, G14, G16, G16	W-RI-560-005.005.010.010-US020	91
H-RI-165-S5	W-RI-560-002-N010	92
H-RI-165-S10	W-RI-560-005-S010	92
H-RI-165-A5	W-RI-560-005-A010	92
H-RI-165-S15	W-RI-560-010-S020	92
H-RI-165-A10	W-RI-560-010-A020	92
H-RI-175-G2	W-RI-570-001-G010	92
H-RI-175-G4	W-RI-570-001-G020	92
H-RI-175-G8	W-RI-570-001-G030	92
H-RI-175-G8a	W-RI-570-001-G030a	92
H-RI-175-G8b	W-RI-570-001-G030b	92
H-RI-175-G10a	W-RI-570-001-G040	93
H-RI-175-G14	W-RI-570-002-G050	93
H-RI-175-G16	W-RI-570-002-G060	93
H-RI-175-G20	W-RI-570-002-G070	93
H-RI-175-G20a	W-RI-570-002-G070a	93
H-RI-175-G20b	W-RI-570-002-G070b	93
H-RI-175-G22a	W-RI-570-002-G080	93
H-RI-175-G26	W-RI-570-003-G090	94
H-RI-175-G28	W-RI-570-003-G100	94
H-RI-175-G32	W-RI-570-005-G110	94
H-RI-175-G36	W-RI-570-005-G120	94
H-RI-175-G36a	W-RI-570-005-G120a	94
H-RI-175-G36b	W-RI-570-005-G120b	94
H-RI-175-G38a	W-RI-570-005-G130	94
H-RI-175-G42	W-RI-570-010-G145	94
H-RI-175-G44	W-RI-570-010-G160	94
H-RI-175-G46	W-RI-570-010-G170	95
H-RI-175-G48a	W-RI-570-010-G180	95
H-RI-175-G48b	W-RI-570-010-G180a	95
H-RI-175-G50a	W-RI-570-010-G190	95
H-RI-175-G56	W-RI-570-020-G200	95
H-RI-175-G56a	W-RI-570-020-G200a	95
H-RI-175-G56b	W-RI-570-020-G200b	95
H-RI-175-G58a	W-RI-570-020-G210	95
H-RI-175-G62	W-RI-570-050-G220	95
H-RI-175-G66	W-RI-570-100-G230	95

Haxby No.	Whitman No.	Page
H-RI-390-G6	W-RI-1200-003-G030	226
H-RI-390-G8	W-RI-1200-005-G040	227
H-RI-390-G10	W-RI-1200-010-G050	227
H-RI-390-G12	W-RI-1200-020-G060	227
H-RI-390-G14	W-RI-1200-050-G070	227
H-RI-390-G16	W-RI-1200-100-G080	227
H-RI-390-G18	W-RI-1200-500-G090	227
H-RI-390-G20	W-RI-1200-1000-G100	227
H-RI-390-G6, G12	W-RI-1200-003.020-US010	227
H-RI-390-S5	W-RI-1200-001-S010	227
H-RI-390-N5	W-RI-1200-001-A010	227
H-RI-390-N10	W-RI-1200-001-S020	227
H-RI-390-A5	W-RI-1200-002-A020	227
	W-RI-1200-003-S030	228
H-RI-390-R5	W-RI-1200-005-R010	228
H-RI-390-R10	W-RI-1200-005-R020	228
H-RI-390-S10	W-RI-1200-005-S040	228
	W-RI-1200-005-S050	228
H-RI-390-R15	W-RI-1200-010-R030	228
H-RI-390-A10	W-RI-1200-010-A030	228
H-RI-390-R20	W-RI-1200-020-R040	228
H-RI-390-R25	W-RI-1200-050-R050	228
H-RI-395-G2	W-RI-1210-001-G010	228
H-RI-395-G4	W-RI-1210-001-G020	228
H-RI-395-G4a	W-RI-1210-001-G020a	228
	W-RI-1210-001-G020b	229
H-RI-395-G6	W-RI-1210-001.25-G030	229
H-RI-395-G7	W-RI-1210-001.50-G040	229
H-RI-395-G8	W-RI-1210-001.75-G050	229
H-RI-395-G10	W-RI-1210-002-G060	229
H-RI-395-G12	W-RI-1210-002-G070	229
H-RI-395-G12a	W-RI-1210-002-G070a	229
H-RI-395-G14	W-RI-1210-003-G080	229
H-RI-395-G18a	W-RI-1210-003-G090	229
H-RI-395-G22	W-RI-1210-005-G100	229
H-RI-395-G26a	W-RI-1210-005-G110	229
H-RI-395-G30	W-RI-1210-010-G120	229
H-RI-395-G34	W-RI-1210-020-G130	229
H-RI-395-G38	W-RI-1210-050-G140	229
H-RI-395-G40	W-RI-1210-100-G150	229
	W-RI-1210-001-C020	230
H-RI-395-N5	W-RI-1210-002-N010	230
H-RI-395-A5	W-RI-1210-002-A010	230
H-RI-395-A10	W-RI-1210-002-A020	230
H-RI-395-A15	W-RI-1210-003-A030	230
H-RI-395-R5	W-RI-1210-005-R010	230
H-RI-395-N10	W-RI-1210-005-N020	230
H-RI-395-N15	W-RI-1210-005-N030	230
H-RI-395-N20	W-RI-1210-005-N040	230
	W-RI-1210-005-N050	230
H-RI-395-A20	W-RI-1210-005-A040	230
H-RI-395-A25	W-RI-1210-005-A050	230
H-RI-395-AR30	W-RI-1210-005-AR010	230
H-RI-395-A35	W-RI-1210-005-A060	230
H-RI-395-R6	W-RI-1210-010-R020	230
H-RI-395-N25	W-RI-1210-010-N060	230
H-RI-395-N30	W-RI-1210-010-N070	230
H-RI-395-N35	W-RI-1210-010-N080	231
	W-RI-1210-010-N090	231
H-RI-395-N45	W-RI-1210-020-N100	231
H-RI-395-N40	W-RI-1210-020-A070	231
H-RI-395-N50	W-RI-1210-050-N110	231
H-RI-395-A40	W-RI-1210-050-A080	231
H-RI-400-G2	W-RI-1220-001-G010	231
	W-RI-1220-001-G020	231
H-RI-400-G5	W-RI-1220-001-G030	231
H-RI-400-G6	W-RI-1220-001-G040	231
H-RI-400-G6b	W-RI-1220-001-G040a	231
H-RI-400-G6c	W-RI-1220-001-G040b	231
H-RI-400-G10	W-RI-1220-002-G050	232
H-RI-400-G13	W-RI-1220-002-G060	232
H-RI-400-G14	W-RI-1220-002-G070	232
H-RI-400-G14b	W-RI-1220-002-G070a	232
H-RI-400-G14c	W-RI-1220-002-G070b	232
H-RI-400-G18	W-RI-1220-003-G080	232
	W-RI-1220-003-G090	232

Haxby No.	Whitman No.	Page
H-RI-400-G21	W-RI-1220-003-G100	232
H-RI-400-G22	W-RI-1220-003-G110	232
H-RI-400-G22b	W-RI-1220-003-G110a	232
H-RI-400-G22c	W-RI-1220-003-G110b	232
H-RI-400-G26	W-RI-1220-005-G120	232
	W-RI-1220-005-G130	232
H-RI-400-G30	W-RI-1220-005-G140	233
H-RI-400-G30b	W-RI-1220-005-G140a	233
H-RI-400-G30c	W-RI-1220-005-G140b	233
H-RI-400-G34	W-RI-1220-010-G150	233
H-RI-400-G38	W-RI-1220-010-G160	233
H-RI-400-G38b	W-RI-1220-010-G160a	233
H-RI-400-G38c	W-RI-1220-010-G160b	233
H-RI-400-G42	W-RI-1220-050-G170	233
H-RI-400-G46	W-RI-1220-100-G180	233
H-RI-400-G50	W-RI-1220-500-G190	233
H-RI-400-G5, G5, G13, G21	W-RI-1220-001.001.002.003-US010	233
H-RI-400-C2	W-RI-1220-001-C010	233
H-RI-400-N5	W-RI-1220-002-N010	233
H-RI-400-N10	W-RI-1220-002-N020	233
H-RI-400-A5	W-RI-1220-002-A010	233
	W-RI-1220-003-S010	234
H-RI-400-N15	W-RI-1220-003-N030	234
H-RI-400-A10	W-RI-1220-003-A020	234
H-RI-400-C26	W-RI-1220-005-C120	234
H-RI-400-R5	W-RI-1220-005-R010	234
H-RI-400-S5	W-RI-1220-005-S020	234
H-RI-400-S10	W-RI-1220-005-S030	234
H-RI-400-N20	W-RI-1220-005-N040	234
H-RI-400-A15	W-RI-1220-005-A030	234
H-RI-400-A20	W-RI-1220-005-A040	234
H-RI-400-A22	W-RI-1220-005-A050	234
H-RI-400-C34	W-RI-1220-010-C150	234
H-RI-400-R6	W-RI-1220-010-R020	234
H-RI-400-N25	W-RI-1220-010-N050	234
H-RI-400-A25	W-RI-1220-010-AR010	235
H-RI-400-A30	W-RI-1220-010-A060	235
H-RI-400-R7	W-RI-1220-020-R030	235
H-RI-401-G4	W-RI-1230-003-A010	235
H-RI-405-G2a	W-RI-1240-001-G010	235
H-RI-405-G2c	W-RI-1240-001-G010a	235
H-RI-405-G4a	W-RI-1240-002-G020	235
H-RI-405-G4c	W-RI-1240-002-G020a	235
H-RI-405-G6a	W-RI-1240-005-G030	235
H-RI-405-G6c	W-RI-1240-005-G030a	236
	W-RI-1240-010-G045	236
H-RI-405-G8a	W-RI-1240-010-G045a	236
H-RI-405-G8c	W-RI-1240-010-G045b	236
	W-RI-1240-020-G060	236
H-RI-405-G10a	W-RI-1240-020-G060a	236
H-RI-405-G10c	W-RI-1240-020-G060b	236
H-RI-405-G12a	W-RI-1240-050-G070	236
H-RI-405-G12c	W-RI-1240-050-G070a	237
H-RI-405-G14a	W-RI-1240-100-G080	237
H-RI-405-G14c	W-RI-1240-100-G080a	237
H-RI-405-G16	W-RI-1240-500-G090	237
H-RI-405-G16b	W-RI-1240-500-G090a	237
H-RI-405-G6c, G6c, G8c, G10c	W-RI-1240-005.005.010.020-US010	237
H-RI-405-A5	W-RI-1240-001-A010	237
H-RI-405-R4	W-RI-1240-005-R010	237
	W-RI-1240-005-R020	238
H-RI-405-S5	W-RI-1240-005-S010	238
H-RI-405-R6	W-RI-1240-010-R030	238
H-RI-410-G2	W-RI-1250-001-G010	238
H-RI-410-G4	W-RI-1250-001-G020	238
H-RI-410-G6	W-RI-1250-001-G030	238
H-RI-410-G6b	W-RI-1250-001-G030a	238
H-RI-410-G6c	W-RI-1250-001-G030b	239
H-RI-410-G7	W-RI-1250-001.25-G040	239
H-RI-410-G8	W-RI-1250-001.50-G050	239
H-RI-410-G9	W-RI-1250-001.75-G060	239
H-RI-410-G10	W-RI-1250-002-G070	239
H-RI-410-G12	W-RI-1250-002-G080	239
H-RI-410-G14	W-RI-1250-002-G090	239
H-RI-410-G14b	W-RI-1250-002-G090a	239
H-RI-410-G14c	W-RI-1250-002-G090b	239

Haxby No.	Whitman No.	Page
H-RI-525-C12	W-RI-1540-002-C050	279
	W-RI-1540-002-S010	279
H-RI-525-A5	W-RI-1540-002-A010	279
H-RI-525-A10	W-RI-1540-003-A020	279
	W-RI-1550-001-G010	279
H-RI-530-G2a	W-RI-1550-001-G010a	280
	W-RI-1550-002-G020	280
H-RI-530-G4a	W-RI-1550-002-G020a	280
	W-RI-1550-003-G030	280
H-RI-530-G6a	W-RI-1550-003-G030a	280
	W-RI-1550-005-G040	280
H-RI-530-G8a	W-RI-1550-005-G040a	280
	W-RI-1550-010-G050	280
H-RI-530-G10a	W-RI-1550-010-G050a	280
H-RI-530-G12	W-RI-1550-050-G060	280
H-RI-530-G14	W-RI-1550-100-G070	280
	W-RI-1550-002-A010	280
H-RI-530-A5	W-RI-1550-003-A020	280
H-RI-530-R5	W-RI-1550-005-R010	280
H-RI-530-N5	W-RI-1550-005-S010	280
H-RI-530-R10	W-RI-1550-010-R020	280
H-RI-535-G2	W-RI-1560-001-G010	281
H-RI-535-G4	W-RI-1560-001-G020	281
H-RI-535-G8	W-RI-1560-001-G030	281
H-RI-535-G10	W-RI-1560-001-G040	281
H-RI-535-G12	W-RI-1560-001.25-G050	281
H-RI-535-G13	W-RI-1560-001.50-G060	281
H-RI-535-G14	W-RI-1560-001.75-G070	281
H-RI-535-G18	W-RI-1560-002-G080	281
H-RI-535-G22	W-RI-1560-002-G090	281
H-RI-535-G24	W-RI-1560-002-G100	281
H-RI-535-G28	W-RI-1560-003-G110	281
H-RI-535-G32	W-RI-1560-003-G120	281
H-RI-535-G34	W-RI-1560-003-G130	281
H-RI-535-G38	W-RI-1560-005-G140	281
H-RI-535-G42	W-RI-1560-005-G150	282
H-RI-535-G44	W-RI-1560-005-G160	282
	W-RI-1560-010-G170	282
H-RI-535-G48	W-RI-1560-010-G180	282
H-RI-535-G54	W-RI-1560-010-G190	282
H-RI-535-G56	W-RI-1560-010-G200	282
H-RI-535-G58	W-RI-1560-020-G210	282
H-RI-535-G60a	W-RI-1560-020-G220	282
H-RI-535-G64	W-RI-1560-050-G230	282
H-RI-535-G66a	W-RI-1560-050-G240	282
H-RI-535-G68	W-RI-1560-050-G250	282
H-RI-535-G72	W-RI-1560-100-G260	282
H-RI-535-G74a	W-RI-1560-100-G270	282
H-RI-535-G76	W-RI-1560-100-G280	282
H-RI-535-C2	W-RI-1560-001-C010	282
H-RI-535-C4	W-RI-1560-001-C020	282
H-RI-535-C24	W-RI-1560-002-C100	282
H-RI-535-S5a	W-RI-1560-002-S010	282
H-RI-535-N5	W-RI-1560-002-N010	283
H-RI-535-C28	W-RI-1560-003-C110	283
H-RI-535-S10	W-RI-1560-003-S020	283
H-RI-535-A5	W-RI-1560-005-A010	283
	W-RI-1560-010-C170	283
H-RI-535-C48	W-RI-1560-010-C180	283
H-RI-540-G2	W-RI-1570-001-G010	283
H-RI-540-G6	W-RI-1570-001-G020	283
H-RI-540-G8	W-RI-1570-001-G030	283
H-RI-540-G8a	W-RI-1570-001-G030a	284
H-RI-540-G12	W-RI-1570-002-G040	284
H-RI-540-G16	W-RI-1570-002-G050	284
H-RI-540-G18	W-RI-1570-002-G060	284
H-RI-540-G18a	W-RI-1570-002-G060a	284
H-RI-540-G22	W-RI-1570-003-G070	284
H-RI-540-G24	W-RI-1570-003-G080	284
H-RI-540-G26	W-RI-1570-003-G090	284
H-RI-540-G26a	W-RI-1570-003-G090a	284
H-RI-540-G30	W-RI-1570-005-G100	284
	W-RI-1570-005-G110	284
H-RI-540-G36	W-RI-1570-005-G120	284
H-RI-540-G36a	W-RI-1570-005-G120a	284
H-RI-540-G40	W-RI-1570-010-G130	285
H-RI-540-G46	W-RI-1570-010-G140	285
H-RI-540-G46a	W-RI-1570-010-G140a	285
H-RI-540-G50	W-RI-1570-020-G150	285
H-RI-540-G54	W-RI-1570-050-G160	285
H-RI-540-G58	W-RI-1570-050-G170	285
H-RI-540-G62	W-RI-1570-100-G180	285
H-RI-540-G66	W-RI-1570-100-G190	285
H-RI-540-N5	W-RI-1570-001-N010	285
H-RI-540-A5	W-RI-1570-001-A010	285
H-RI-540-A10	W-RI-1570-001-A020	285
H-RI-540-A15	W-RI-1570-002-A030	285
H-RI-540-A20	W-RI-1570-002-A040	285
H-RI-540-A25	W-RI-1570-002-A050	285
H-RI-540-N10a	W-RI-1570-003-N020	286
H-RI-540-N15	W-RI-1570-003-N030	286
H-RI-540-A30	W-RI-1570-003-A060	286
H-RI-540-A35	W-RI-1570-003-A070	286
H-RI-540-A40	W-RI-1570-003-A080	286
H-RI-540-A45	W-RI-1570-005-A090	286
H-RI-540-A50	W-RI-1570-005-A100	286
H-RI-540-A55	W-RI-1570-005-A110	286
	W-RI-1570-005-A120	286
H-RI-540-R6	W-RI-1570-010-R010	286
H-RI-540-A60	W-RI-1570-010-A130	286
H-RI-540-A65	W-RI-1570-050-A140	286
H-RI-545-G2	W-RI-1580-001-G010	287
H-RI-545-G8	W-RI-1580-001-G020	287
H-RI-545-G10	W-RI-1580-001-G030	287
H-RI-545-G12	W-RI-1580-001-G040	287
H-RI-545-G14a	W-RI-1580-001-G050	287
H-RI-545-G16a	W-RI-1580-001-G060	287
H-RI-545-G16b	W-RI-1580-001-G060a	287
H-RI-545-G20	W-RI-1580-002-G070	287
H-RI-545-G26	W-RI-1580-002-G080	287
H-RI-545-G28	W-RI-1580-002-G090	287
H-RI-545-G30	W-RI-1580-002-G100	288
H-RI-545-G32a	W-RI-1580-002-G110	288
H-RI-545-G34a	W-RI-1580-002-G120	288
H-RI-545-G34b	W-RI-1580-002-G120a	288
H-RI-545-G36	W-RI-1580-003-G130	288
H-RI-545-G42	W-RI-1580-003-G140	288
	W-RI-1580-003-G150	288
H-RI-545-G44	W-RI-1580-003-G160	288
H-RI-545-G46	W-RI-1580-003-G170	288
H-RI-545-G48a	W-RI-1580-003-G180	288
H-RI-545-G50a	W-RI-1580-003-G190	288
H-RI-545-G50b	W-RI-1580-003-G190a	288
H-RI-545-G52	W-RI-1580-005-G200	288
H-RI-545-G58	W-RI-1580-005-G210	289
	W-RI-1580-005-G220	289
H-RI-545-G60	W-RI-1580-005-G230	289
H-RI-545-G62a	W-RI-1580-005-G240	289
H-RI-545-G64	W-RI-1580-010-G250	289
H-RI-545-G70	W-RI-1580-010-G260	289
H-RI-545-G72	W-RI-1580-010-G270	289
H-RI-545-G74a	W-RI-1580-010-G280	289
H-RI-545-G82	W-RI-1580-020-G290	289
H-RI-545-G84a	W-RI-1580-020-G300	289
H-RI-545-G86	W-RI-1580-050-G310	289
H-RI-545-G86a	W-RI-1580-050-G310a	290
H-RI-545-G86b	W-RI-1580-050-G310b	290
H-RI-545-G62a, G62a, G74a, G84a	W-RI-1580-005.005.010.020-US010	290
H-RI-545-G86a	W-RI-1580-050-US020	290
H-RI-545-A5	W-RI-1580-005-A010	290
H-RI-545-A10	W-RI-1580-010-A020	290
H-RI-130-G12	W-RI-1590-001-G010	290
	W-RI-1590-001-G020	291
H-RI-130-G14a	W-RI-1590-001-G020a	291
H-RI-130-G16	W-RI-1590-002-G030	291
H-RI-130-G18a	W-RI-1590-002-G040	291
H-RI-130-G20	W-RI-1590-003-G050	291
	W-RI-1590-003-G060	291
H-RI-130-G22a	W-RI-1590-003-G060a	291
H-RI-130-G24	W-RI-1590-005-G070	291
	W-RI-1590-005-G080	292

Vermont

Haxby No.	Whitman No.	Page
H-VT-15-G6b	W-VT-060-005-G030a	324
H-VT-15-G8	W-VT-060-010-G040	324
H-VT-15-G8b	W-VT-060-010-G040a	324
H-VT-15-G10	W-VT-060-020-G050	324
H-VT-15-G12	W-VT-060-050-G060	324
H-VT-15-G12b	W-VT-060-050-G060a	324
H-VT-15-G2, G2, G4, G6	W-VT-060-001.001.002.005-US010	324
H-VT-15-G6, G8	W-VT-060-005.010-US020	325
H-VT-15-G10, G12	W-VT-060-020.050-US030	325
H-VT-15-C2	W-VT-060-001-C010	325
H-VT-15-S5	W-VT-060-002-S010	325
	W-VT-060-003-R010	325
	W-VT-060-003-N010	325
H-VT-15-R3	W-VT-060-005-R020	325
	W-VT-060-005-N020	325
	W-VT-060-005-N030	325
H-VT-15-A5	W-VT-060-005-A010	325
H-VT-15-R4	W-VT-060-010-R030	325
H-VT-15-S10	W-VT-060-010-S020	325
	W-VT-060-010-N040	325
H-VT-15-A10	W-VT-060-010-A020	325
H-VT-15-R5	W-VT-060-020-R040	326
H-VT-15-A15	W-VT-060-020-A030	326
H-VT-20-G2	W-VT-080-001-G010	326
H-VT-20-G4	W-VT-080-001-G020	326
H-VT-20-G4a	W-VT-080-001-G020a	326
	W-VT-080-001-G020b	327
H-VT-20-G6	W-VT-080-001-G030	327
H-VT-20-G8	W-VT-080-002-G040	327
H-VT-20-G10	W-VT-080-002-G050	327
	W-VT-080-002-G050a	327
H-VT-20-G10a	W-VT-080-002-G050b	327
H-VT-20-G12	W-VT-080-002-G060	327
H-VT-20-G14	W-VT-080-003-G070	327
H-VT-20-G16	W-VT-080-003-G080	327
H-VT-20-G16a	W-VT-080-003-G080a	327
H-VT-20-G18	W-VT-080-003-G090	328
H-VT-20-G20	W-VT-080-005-G100	328
H-VT-20-G20a	W-VT-080-005-G100a	328
H-VT-20-G22	W-VT-080-005-G110	328
H-VT-20-G24	W-VT-080-010-G120	328
H-VT-20-G24a	W-VT-080-010-G120a	328
H-VT-20-G26a	W-VT-080-010-G130	328
H-VT-20-G28	W-VT-080-020-G140	328
H-VT-20-G30a	W-VT-080-020-G150	328
H-VT-20-G32	W-VT-080-050-G160	328
H-VT-20-G34	W-VT-080-100-G170	328
H-VT-20-S5	W-VT-080-003-S010	328
H-VT-20-S5a	W-VT-080-003-S010a	328
H-VT-20-S10	W-VT-080-003-S020	329
	W-VT-080-003-N010	329
H-VT-20-S15	W-VT-080-005-S030	329
	W-VT-080-005-N020	329
H-VT-25-G2a	W-VT-090-001-G010	329
H-VT-25-G2b	W-VT-090-001-G010a	329
H-VT-25-G4a	W-VT-090-002-G020	329
H-VT-25-G4b	W-VT-090-002-G020a	329
H-VT-25-G6a	W-VT-090-003-G030	330
H-VT-25-G6b	W-VT-090-003-G030a	330
H-VT-25-G8a	W-VT-090-005-G040	330
H-VT-25-G8b	W-VT-090-005-G040a	330
H-VT-25-G10a	W-VT-090-010-G050	330
H-VT-25-G10b	W-VT-090-010-G050a	330
H-VT-25-G12a	W-VT-090-020-G060	330
H-VT-25-G12b	W-VT-090-020-G060a	330
H-VT-25-G14a	W-VT-090-050-G070	330
H-VT-25-G14b	W-VT-090-050-G070a	330
H-VT-25-G16a	W-VT-090-100-G080	330
H-VT-25-G16b	W-VT-090-100-G080a	330
	W-VT-090-001-A010	331
H-VT-25-C4a	W-VT-090-002-C020	331
	W-VT-090-002-N010	331
H-VT-25-S5	W-VT-090-003-S010	331
H-VT-25-A10	W-VT-090-005-A020	331
H-VT-25-C14b	W-VT-090-050-C070a	331
	W-VT-090-050-N020	331
H-VT-26-A5	W-VT-100-001-A010	331
H-VT-26-A10	W-VT-100-005-A020	331
	W-VT-110-00.05-G010	332
	W-VT-110-00.10-G020	332
	W-VT-110-00.25-G030	332
H-VT-30-G2	W-VT-110-001-G040	332
H-VT-30-G2a	W-VT-110-001-G040a	333
H-VT-30-G4	W-VT-110-002-G050	333
H-VT-30-G4a	W-VT-110-002-G050a	333
H-VT-30-G6	W-VT-110-003-G060	333
H-VT-30-G6a	W-VT-110-003-G060a	333
H-VT-30-G8	W-VT-110-005-G070	333
H-VT-30-G8a	W-VT-110-005-G070a	333
H-VT-30-G10	W-VT-110-010-G080	333
H-VT-30-G10a	W-VT-110-010-G080a	333
H-VT-30-G12	W-VT-110-020-G090	333
H-VT-30-G14	W-VT-110-050-G100	333
H-VT-30-G16	W-VT-110-100-G110	333
	W-VT-110-001-N010	334
H-VT-30-C4	W-VT-110-002-C050	334
	W-VT-110-002-N020	334
H-VT-30-C8a	W-VT-110-005-C070a	334
H-VT-30-R5	W-VT-110-005-R010	334
H-VT-30-R10	W-VT-110-005-R020	334
	W-VT-110-005-R030	334
	W-VT-110-005-N030	334
H-VT-30-N5	W-VT-110-005-N040	334
	W-VT-110-005-N050	334
H-VT-35-G2	W-VT-130-001-G010	335
H-VT-35-G6	W-VT-130-001-G020	335
H-VT-35-G10	W-VT-130-001-G030	335
H-VT-35-G12	W-VT-130-001-G040	335
	W-VT-130-001-G040a	335
H-VT-35-G14a	W-VT-130-001-G050	335
H-VT-35-G22	W-VT-130-002-G060	335
H-VT-35-G24	W-VT-130-002-G070	335
H-VT-35-G26a	W-VT-130-002-G080	335
	W-VT-130-002-G080a	335
H-VT-35-G34	W-VT-130-003-G090	336
H-VT-35-G36	W-VT-130-003-G100	336
H-VT-35-G38a	W-VT-130-003-G110	336
H-VT-35-G40	W-VT-130-005-G120	336
H-VT-35-G48	W-VT-130-005-G130	336
H-VT-35-G50	W-VT-130-005-G140	336
	W-VT-130-005-G140a	336
H-VT-35-G50b	W-VT-130-005-G140b	336
H-VT-35-G52a	W-VT-130-005-G150	336
H-VT-35-G54	W-VT-130-010-G160	336
H-VT-35-G62	W-VT-130-010-G170	336
H-VT-35-G64	W-VT-130-010-G180	336
	W-VT-130-010-G180a	336
H-VT-35-G66a	W-VT-130-010-G190	336
H-VT-35-G72	W-VT-130-020-G200	336
H-VT-35-G78	W-VT-130-050-G210	337
H-VT-35-G84	W-VT-130-100-G220	337
	W-VT-130-002-N010	337
H-VT-35-A5	W-VT-130-002-A010	337
	W-VT-130-003-N020	337
H-VT-35-S10	W-VT-130-003-S010	337
	W-VT-130-003-N030	337
H-VT-35-A10	W-VT-130-003-A020	337
	W-VT-130-005-N040	337
H-VT-35-A15	W-VT-130-005-A030	337
H-VT-35-R5	W-VT-130-010-R010	337
	W-VT-140-002-N010	337
	W-VT-140-002-N010a	337
H-VT-36-G4	W-VT-140-002-A010	337
H-VT-40-G2a	W-VT-150-001-G010	338
H-VT-40-G2b	W-VT-150-001-G010a	338
	W-VT-150-001-G020	338
	W-VT-150-001-G030	338
H-VT-40-G4a	W-VT-150-002-G040	338
H-VT-40-G4b	W-VT-150-002-G040a	338
	W-VT-150-002-G050	338
	W-VT-150-002-G060	338
H-VT-40-G6a	W-VT-150-003-G070	338

Haxby No.	Whitman No.	Page
H-VT-110-G28	W-VT-380-005-G070	386
H-VT-110-G32	W-VT-380-010-G080	386
H-VT-110-G36	W-VT-380-020-G090	386
H-VT-110-G40	W-VT-380-050-G100	386
H-VT-110-G44	W-VT-380-100-G110	386
H-VT-115-G2a	W-VT-390-001-G010	387
H-VT-115-G2b	W-VT-390-001-G010a	387
H-VT-115-G4a	W-VT-390-002-G020	387
H-VT-115-G4b	W-VT-390-002-G020a	387
H-VT-115-G6a	W-VT-390-003-G030	387
H-VT-115-G6b	W-VT-390-003-G030a	387
H-VT-115-G8a	W-VT-390-005-G040	387
H-VT-115-G8b	W-VT-390-005-G040a	388
H-VT-115-G10	W-VT-390-010-G050	388
H-VT-115-G12	W-VT-390-020-G060	388
H-VT-115-G12a	W-VT-390-020-G060a	388
H-VT-115-G14	W-VT-390-050-G070	388
H-VT-115-G14a	W-VT-390-050-G070a	388
H-VT-115-G2b, G4b, G6b, G8b	W-VT-390-001.002.003.005-US010	389
H-VT-115-G12a, G14a	W-VT-390-020.050-US020	389
H-VT-115-R5	W-VT-390-010-R010	389
	W-VT-410-001-G010	390
H-VT-125-G2a	W-VT-410-001-G010a	390
H-VT-125-G4a	W-VT-410-001-G020	390
	W-VT-410-001-G020a	390
	W-VT-410-002-G030	390
H-VT-125-G6a	W-VT-410-002-G030a	390
	W-VT-410-003-G040	391
H-VT-125-G8a	W-VT-410-003-G040a	391
	W-VT-410-005-G050	391
H-VT-125-G10a	W-VT-410-005-G050a	391
	W-VT-410-010-G060	391
H-VT-125-G12a	W-VT-410-010-G060a	391
	W-VT-410-020-G070	392
	W-VT-410-020-G070a	392
H-VT-125-G14a	W-VT-410-020-G070b	392
	W-VT-410-050-G080	392
H-VT-125-G16a	W-VT-410-050-G080a	392
	W-VT-410-100-G090	392
H-VT-125-G18a	W-VT-410-100-G090a	392
	W-VT-410-001.002.003.005-US010	392
H-VT-125-G2a, G6a, G8a, G10a	W-VT-410-001.002.003.005-US010a	392
H-VT-125-G12a, G14a	W-VT-410-010.020-US020	393
H-VT-125-G12a, G14a, G16a, G18a	W-VT-410-010.020.050.100-US030	393
H-VT-125-G16a, G18a	W-VT-410-050.100-US040	393
H-VT-125-A5	W-VT-410-002-A010	393
	W-VT-410-005-R010	393
H-VT-125-A10	W-VT-410-005-A020	393
H-VT-125-A15	W-VT-410-005-A030	393
H-VT-125-R5	W-VT-410-010-R020	393
	W-VT-410-010-R030	393
H-VT-135-G4	W-VT-420-001-G010	394
H-VT-135-G4a	W-VT-420-001-G010a	394
	W-VT-420-001.50-G020	394
H-VT-135-G8	W-VT-420-002-G030	394
H-VT-135-G8a	W-VT-420-002-G030a	394
	W-VT-420-002-G040	394
H-VT-135-G12	W-VT-420-003-G050	394
H-VT-135-G12a	W-VT-420-003-G050a	394
H-VT-135-G14	W-VT-420-005-G060	395
H-VT-135-G16	W-VT-420-010-G070	395
H-VT-135-G20	W-VT-420-020-G080	395
H-VT-135-G24	W-VT-420-050-G090	395
H-VT-135-G4, G4, G8, G12	W-VT-420-001.001.002.003-US010	395
H-VT-135-C12	W-VT-420-003-C050	395
H-VT-135-R5	W-VT-420-003-R010	395
H-VT-135-R10	W-VT-420-005-R020	395
H-VT-135-N5	W-VT-420-005-N010	395
H-VT-135-R15	W-VT-420-010-R030	395
H-VT-135-S5	W-VT-420-050-S010	395
H-VT-135-S10	W-VT-420-100-S020	395
H-VT-135-N10	W-VT-420-1000-N020	395
H-VT-130-G2	W-VT-430-001-G010	396
	W-VT-430-001-G010a	396
H-VT-130-G2b	W-VT-430-001-G010b	396

Haxby No.	Whitman No.	Page
H-VT-130-G2c	W-VT-430-001-G010c	396
H-VT-130-G4	W-VT-430-002-G020	396
H-VT-130-G4b	W-VT-430-002-G020a	396
	W-VT-430-002-G020b	396
H-VT-130-G6	W-VT-430-005-G030	396
H-VT-130-G6a	W-VT-430-005-G030a	396
H-VT-130-G6c	W-VT-430-005-G030b	397
H-VT-130-G8	W-VT-430-005-G040	397
H-VT-130-G10	W-VT-430-010-G050	397
	W-VT-430-010-G050a	397
H-VT-130-G12	W-VT-430-020-G060	397
H-VT-130-G14	W-VT-430-050-G070	397
H-VT-130-G8, G10	W-VT-430-005.010-US010	397
H-VT-130-G12, G14	W-VT-430-020.050-US020	397
	W-VT-430-001-N010	397
H-VT-130-A5	W-VT-430-001-A010	397
H-VT-130-A10	W-VT-430-002-A020	397
H-VT-130-S5	W-VT-430-003-S010	398
H-VT-130-A15	W-VT-430-003-A030	398
H-VT-130-A20	W-VT-430-005-A040	398
H-VT-130-A25	W-VT-430-005-A050	398
H-VT-130-S10	W-VT-430-010-S020	398
H-VT-140-G2	W-VT-440-001-G010	398
H-VT-140-G2a	W-VT-440-001-G010a	399
H-VT-140-G4	W-VT-440-002-G020	399
H-VT-140-G4a	W-VT-440-002-G020a	399
H-VT-140-G6	W-VT-440-003-G030	399
H-VT-140-G6a	W-VT-440-003-G030a	399
H-VT-140-G8	W-VT-440-005-G040	399
H-VT-140-G8a	W-VT-440-005-G040a	399
H-VT-140-G10	W-VT-440-010-G050	399
H-VT-140-G10a	W-VT-440-010-G050a	399
H-VT-140-G12	W-VT-440-020-G060	399
H-VT-140-G14	W-VT-440-050-G070	399
H-VT-140-G16	W-VT-440-100-G080	399
H-VT-140-N5	W-VT-440-002-N010	399
H-VT-140-A5	W-VT-440-002-A010	399
H-VT-140-N10	W-VT-440-005-N020	399
	W-VT-440-005-N030	400
	W-VT-440-010-N040	400
H-VT-140-N15	W-VT-440-010-N050	400
	W-VT-445-010-A010	400
H-VT-4-G48	W-VT-450-00.50-G010	400
H-VT-4-G49	W-VT-450-00.50-G020	400
H-VT-4-G57	W-VT-450-00.50-G030	401
H-VT-4-G58	W-VT-450-00.75-G040	401
H-VT-4-G59	W-VT-450-00.75-G050	401
H-VT-4-G60	W-VT-450-00.75-G060	401
H-VT-4-G61	W-VT-450-00.75-G070	401
H-VT-4-G67	W-VT-450-00.75-G080	401
H-VT-4-G68	W-VT-450-001-G090	401
H-VT-4-G69	W-VT-450-001-G100	401
H-VT-4-G70	W-VT-450-001-G110	401
H-VT-4-G71	W-VT-450-001-G120	401
H-VT-4-G72	W-VT-450-001.25-G130	402
H-VT-4-G73	W-VT-450-001.50-G140	402
H-VT-4-G74	W-VT-450-001.75-G150	402
H-VT-4-G76	W-VT-450-002-G160	402
H-VT-4-G77	W-VT-450-002-G170	402
H-VT-4-G78	W-VT-450-002-G180	402
H-VT-4-G79	W-VT-450-003-G190	402
H-VT-4-G80	W-VT-450-003-G200	402
H-VT-4-G81	W-VT-450-003-G210	402
H-VT-4-G82	W-VT-450-003-G220	402
H-VT-4-G83	W-VT-450-005-G230	402
H-VT-4-G84	W-VT-450-005-G240	402
H-VT-4-G85	W-VT-450-005-G250	403
H-VT-4-G86	W-VT-450-010-G260	403
H-VT-4-G88	W-VT-450-010-G270	403
H-VT-4-G91	W-VT-450-020-G280	403
H-VT-4-G74, G73, G72, G57, G67	W-VT-450-001.75.001.50.001.25.00.50.00.75-US010	403
H-VT-4-C48	W-VT-450-00.50-C010	403
H-VT-4-C49	W-VT-450-00.50-C020	403
H-VT-4-C59	W-VT-450-00.75-C050	403
H-VT-4-C60	W-VT-450-00.75-C060	403